GLEIM® | Aviation

2023 EDITION

INSTRUMENT PILOT
FAA Knowledge Test Prep

Instrument Rating - Airplane
Flight Instructor - Instrument - Airplane
Instrument Ground Instructor

Instrument Rating - Foreign Pilot
Flight Instructor - Instrument - Added Rating

by
Irvin N. Gleim, Ph.D., CFII
and
Garrett W. Gleim, CFII

Gleim Publications, Inc.

PO Box 12848
Gainesville, Florida 32604

(352) 375-0772
(800) 874-5346

www.GleimAviation.com
aviationteam@gleim.com

For updates to the first printing of the 2023 edition of

Instrument Pilot FAA Knowledge Test Prep

Go To: www.GleimAviation.com/updates

Or: Email update@gleim.com with **IPKT 2023-1** in the subject line. You will receive our current update as a reply.

Updates are available until the next edition is published.

ISSN 1553-6882
ISBN 978-1-61854-524-4

Let Us Know!

This 2023 edition is designed specifically for pilots who aspire to obtain the instrument rating. Feedback and suggestions for improvement will be received immediately through www.GleimAviation.com/questions.

A companion volume, ***Instrument Pilot Flight Maneuvers and Practical Test Prep***, focuses on the FAA practical test, just as this book focuses on the FAA knowledge test. Save time, money, and frustration--order online at www.GleimAviation.com today! Please bring these books to the attention of flight instructors, fixed-base operators, and others with a potential interest in acquiring their certificates and ratings. Wide distribution of these books and increased interest in flying depend on your assistance and good word. Thank you.

Returns of books purchased from bookstores and other resellers should be made to the respective bookstore or reseller. For more information regarding the Gleim Return Policy, please contact our offices at (800) 874-5346 or visit www.GleimAviation.com/returnpolicy.

Gleim offers free technical support to all users of the current versions. Fill out the technical support request form online (www.GleimAviation.com/contact), email support@gleim.com, or call (800) 874-5346.

ABOUT THE AUTHORS

Irvin N. Gleim, who began publishing pilot training books over 40 years ago and received both the Excellence in Pilot Training Award and the Wright Brothers Master Pilot Award, earned his private pilot certificate in 1965 from the Institute of Aviation at the University of Illinois, where he subsequently received his Ph.D. He then became a commercial pilot and flight instructor (instrument) with multi-engine and seaplane ratings and was a member of the Aircraft Owners and Pilots Association, American Bonanza Society, Civil Air Patrol, Experimental Aircraft Association, National Association of Flight Instructors, and Seaplane Pilots Association. He authored flight maneuvers and practical test prep books for the sport, private, instrument, commercial, and flight instructor certificates/ratings and developed study guides for the remote, sport, private/recreational, instrument, commercial, flight/ground instructor, fundamentals of instructing, airline transport pilot, and flight engineer FAA knowledge tests. Three additional Gleim pilot training books are *Pilot Handbook*, *Aviation Weather and Weather Services*, and *FAR/AIM*.

The late Dr. Gleim also wrote articles for professional accounting and business law journals and authored widely used review manuals for the CIA (Certified Internal Auditor) exam, the CMA (Certified Management Accountant) exam, the CPA (Certified Public Accountant) Exam, and the EA (IRS Enrolled Agent) exam. He was Professor Emeritus at the Fisher School of Accounting, University of Florida, and a CFM, CIA, CMA, and CPA.

Garrett W. Gleim leads production of Gleim pilot training and resources. He earned his private pilot certificate in 1997 in a Piper Super Cub. He is a commercial pilot (single- and multi-engine), ground instructor (advanced and instrument), and flight instructor (instrument and multi-engine) and a member of the Aircraft Owners and Pilots Association, the National Association of Flight Instructors, and the Society of Aviation and Flight Educators. He is the author of study guides for the remote, sport, private/recreational, instrument, commercial, flight/ground instructor, fundamentals of instructing, and airline transport pilot FAA knowledge tests. He received a Bachelor of Science in Economics from The Wharton School, University of Pennsylvania. Mr. Gleim is also a CPA, CIA, and CGMA.

REVIEWERS AND CONTRIBUTORS

Ryan Jeff, CFI, AGI, IGI, Remote Pilot, graduated summa cum laude from Embry-Riddle Aeronautical University with a degree in Aeronautics and a minor in Applied Meteorology. He is our Part 141 Chief Ground Instructor and Flight Simulation Specialist. He researched questions, wrote and edited answer explanations, and incorporated revisions into the text.

The CFIs who have worked with us throughout the years to develop and improve our pilot training materials.

The many FAA employees who helped, in person or remotely, primarily in Gainesville; Orlando; Oklahoma City; and Washington, DC.

The many pilots and learners who have provided comments and suggestions about *Instrument Pilot FAA Knowledge Test Prep* during the past several decades.

A PERSONAL THANKS

This manual would not have been possible without the extraordinary effort and dedication of Jedidiah Arnold, Jacob Bennett, Julie Cutlip, Fernanda Martinez, Bree Rodriguez, Veronica Rodriguez, Bobbie Stanley, Joanne Strong, Elmer Tucker, and Ryan Van Tress, who typed the entire manuscript and all revisions and drafted and laid out the diagrams, illustrations, and cover for this book.

The authors also appreciate the production and editorial assistance of Brianna Barnett, Michaela Giampaolo, Ethan Good, Doug Green, Jessica Hatker, Sonora Hospital-Medina, Bryce Owen, David Sox, and Alyssa Thomas.

The authors also appreciate the video production expertise of Gary Brook, Philip Brubaker, and Matthew Church, who helped produce and edit all Gleim Aviation videos.

Finally, we appreciate the encouragement, support, and tolerance of our families throughout this project.

TABLE OF CONTENTS

NOTE: The FAA does not release the complete database of test questions to the public. Instead, sample questions are released on the practice exam page of the PSI website. These questions are similar to the actual test questions, but they are not exact matches.

Gleim utilizes customer feedback and FAA publications to create additional sample questions that closely represent the topical coverage of each FAA knowledge test. In order to do well on the knowledge test, you must study the Gleim outlines in this book, answer all the questions under exam conditions (i.e., without looking at the answers first), and develop an understanding of the topics addressed. You should not simply memorize questions and answers. This will not prepare you for your FAA knowledge test, and it will not help you develop the knowledge you need to safely operate an aircraft.

If you see topics covered on your FAA knowledge test that are not contained in this book, please contact us at www.GleimAviation.com/questions to report your experience and help us fine-tune our test preparation materials.

Thank you!

PREFACE

The primary purpose of this book is to provide you with the easiest, fastest, and least expensive means of passing the instrument rating–airplane knowledge test. We have

1. Included all previously released knowledge test questions published by the FAA and developed similar questions to cover all knowledge test topics.
2. Reordered the questions into logical topics.
3. Organized these topics into 11 study units.
4. Explained the answer immediately to the right of each question.
5. Provided an easy-to-study outline of exactly what you need to know at the beginning of each study unit.

Accordingly, you can thoroughly prepare for the FAA pilot knowledge test by

1. Studying the brief outlines at the beginning of each study unit.
2. Answering the question on the left side of each page while covering up the answer explanations on the right side of each page.
3. Reading the answer explanation for each question that you answer incorrectly or have difficulty answering.
4. Reinforcing this Gleim process with our **FAA Test Prep Online**, which emulates the FAA testing experience.
5. Using our **Online Ground School**, which provides you with our outlines, practice problems, and sample tests. We give you a money-back guarantee with our **Online Ground School**. If you are unsuccessful, you get your money back!

The secondary purpose of this book is to introduce *Instrument Pilot Flight Maneuvers and Practical Test Prep* and *Pilot Handbook*.

Instrument Pilot Flight Maneuvers and Practical Test Prep is designed to help prepare pilots for their flight training and the FAA instrument rating practical test. Each task, objective, concept, and requirement is explained, analyzed, illustrated, and interpreted so pilots will be totally conversant with all aspects of the instrument pilot practical test.

Pilot Handbook is a textbook of aeronautical knowledge presented in easy-to-use outline format, with many charts, diagrams, and figures included. While this book contains only the material needed to pass the FAA knowledge test, *Pilot Handbook* contains the textbook knowledge required to be a safe and proficient pilot.

Also, this book is concerned with **airplane** flight training, not balloon, glider, or helicopter training. However, Appendix A contains additional consideration for ground instructor instrument certification related to rotorcraft. We are confident this book, **FAA Test Prep Online**, and/or **Online Ground School** will facilitate speedy completion of your knowledge test. We wish you the very best as you complete your instrument rating, in subsequent flying, and in obtaining additional ratings and certificates.

Enjoy Flying Safely!

Irvin N. Gleim
Garrett W. Gleim

INTRODUCTION: THE FAA PILOT KNOWLEDGE TEST

The beginning of this introduction explains how to obtain an instrument rating, and it explains the content and procedures of the Federal Aviation Administration (FAA) knowledge test, including how to take the test at a computer testing center.

Instrument Pilot FAA Knowledge Test Prep is one of five books contained in the Gleim **Instrument Pilot Kit**. The other four books are

1. **Instrument Pilot Flight Maneuvers and Practical Test Prep**
2. **Instrument Pilot Syllabus**
3. **Instrument Pilot ACS and Oral Exam Guide**
4. **Aviation Weather and Weather Services**

Instrument Pilot Flight Maneuvers and Practical Test Prep presents each flight maneuver you will perform in outline/illustration format so you will know what to expect and what to do before each flight lesson. This book will thoroughly prepare you to complete your FAA practical (flight) test confidently and successfully.

Instrument Pilot Syllabus is a step-by-step syllabus of ground and flight training lesson plans for your instrument rating training.

Instrument Pilot ACS and Oral Exam Guide contains the FAA Airman Certification Standards and hundreds of possible questions that applicants may face during the practical test.

The Gleim **Aviation Weather and Weather Services** book combines all of the information from the FAA's *Aviation Weather* (AC 00-6), *Aviation Weather Services* (AC 00-45), and numerous FAA resources into one easy-to-understand book.

While the following books are not included in the Instrument Pilot Kit, you may want to purchase them if you do not already have them:

Pilot Handbook is a complete pilot reference that combines over 100 FAA documents, including *AIM*, Federal Aviation Regulations, and ACs. Among the topics explained are aerodynamics, airplane systems, airspace, and navigation. This book, more than any other, will help make you a better pilot.

FAR/AIM is an essential part of every pilot's library. The Gleim **FAR/AIM** is an easy-to-read reference book containing all of the Federal Aviation Regulations applicable to general aviation flying, plus the full text of the FAA's *Aeronautical Information Manual (AIM)*.

WHAT IS AN INSTRUMENT RATING?

An instrument rating is added to your private or commercial pilot certificate. A new certificate will be issued to you by the FAA upon satisfactory completion of your training program, an FAA knowledge test, and a practical test. A sample private pilot certificate with an instrument rating is reproduced below.

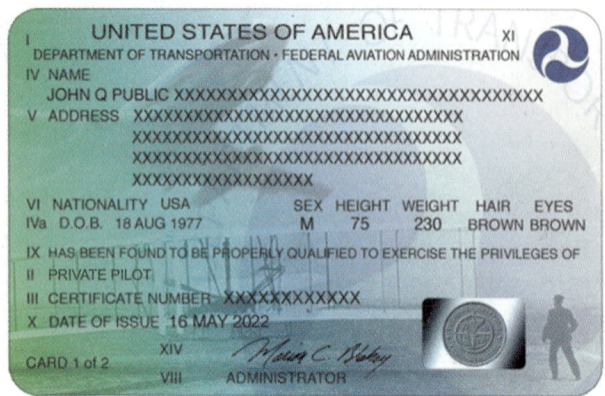
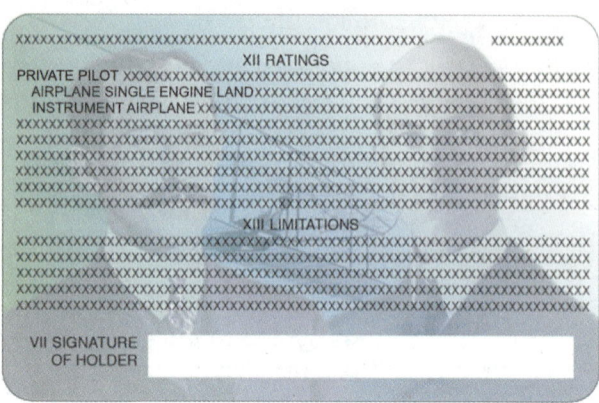

REQUIREMENTS TO OBTAIN AN INSTRUMENT RATING

1. Hold at least a private pilot certificate.

2. Be able to read, speak, write, and understand the English language (certificates with operating limitations may be available for medically related deficiencies).

3. Hold a current FAA medical certificate, or meet the requirements of BasicMed.

    a. You must undergo a routine medical examination, which may be administered only by FAA-designated doctors called aviation medical examiners (AME).

    b. Even if you have a physical disability, medical certificates can be issued in many cases. Operating limitations may be imposed depending upon the nature of the disability.

    c. Your certificated flight instructor-instrument (CFII) or fixed-base operator (FBO) will be able to recommend an AME.

        1) CFII is a flight instructor who has an instrument rating on his or her flight instructor certificate and is authorized to provide instruction for the instrument rating.

        2) An FBO is an airport business that gives flight lessons, sells aviation fuel, repairs airplanes, etc.

        3) Also, the FAA publishes an online directory that lists all authorized AMEs, searchable by name or location.

4. Receive and log ground training from an authorized instructor or complete a home-study course (such as studying this book, *Instrument Pilot Flight Maneuvers and Practical Test Prep*, and *Aviation Weather and Weather Services* or using the Gleim **Online Ground School**) to learn

    a. Federal Aviation Regulations that apply to flight operations under IFR

    b. Appropriate information that applies to flight operations under IFR in the *Aeronautical Information Manual*

    c. Air traffic control system and procedures for instrument flight operations

    d. IFR navigation and approaches by use of navigation systems

    e.   Use of IFR en route and instrument approach procedure charts

    f.   Procurement and use of aviation weather reports and forecasts and the elements of forecasting weather trends based on that information and personal observation of weather conditions

    g.   Safe and efficient operation of aircraft under instrument flight rules and conditions

    h.   Recognition of critical weather situations and wind shear avoidance

    i.   Aeronautical decision making and judgment

    j.   Crew resource management, including crew communication and coordination

5.   Pass a knowledge test with a score of 70% or better.

    a.   All FAA tests are administered at FAA-designated testing centers.

    b.   The instrument rating test consists of 60 multiple-choice questions selected from the airplane-related questions in the FAA's instrument rating test bank.

    c.   Questions similar to those you will see on your knowledge test are provided in this book with complete explanations.

6.   Accumulate flight experience (14 CFR 61.65).

    a.   50 hr. of cross-country flight time as pilot in command, of which at least 10 hr. must be in airplanes

        1)   The 50 hr. includes solo cross-country time as a student pilot, which is logged as pilot-in-command time.

        2)   Each cross-country must have a landing at an airport that was a straight-line distance of more than 50 NM from the original departure point.

    b.   A total of 40 hr. of actual or simulated instrument time in the areas of operations listed in item 7. below, including

        1)   15 hr. of instrument flight training from a CFII

        2)   3 hr. of instrument training from a CFII in preparation for the practical test within 2 calendar months preceding the practical test

        3)   Cross-country flight procedures that include at least one cross-country flight in an airplane that is performed under IFR and consists of

            a)   A distance of at least 250 NM along airways or ATC-directed routing
            b)   An instrument approach at each airport
            c)   Three different kinds of approaches with the use of navigation systems

    c.   If the instrument training was provided by an authorized instructor, a maximum of 20 hr. is permitted in an approved flight simulator or flight training device

7.   Demonstrate flight proficiency (14 CFR 61.65). You must receive and log training and obtain a logbook sign-off (endorsement) by your CFII on the following areas of operations:

    a.   Preflight preparation
    b.   Preflight procedures
    c.   Air traffic control clearances and procedures
    d.   Flight by reference to instruments
    e.   Navigation systems
    f.   Instrument approach procedures
    g.   Emergency operations
    h.   Postflight procedures

8. Alternatively, enroll in an FAA-certificated pilot school or training center that has an approved instrument rating course (airplane).

   a. These are known as Part 141 schools or Part 142 training centers because they are authorized by Part 141 or Part 142 of the Federal Aviation Regulations.

      1) All other regulations concerning the certification of pilots are found in Part 61 of the Federal Aviation Regulations.

9. Successfully complete a practical test that will be given as a final exam by an FAA inspector or designated pilot examiner. The practical test will be conducted as specified in the FAA's Instrument Rating Airman Certification Standards (FAA-S-ACS-8).

   a. FAA inspectors are FAA employees and do not charge for their services.

   b. FAA-designated pilot examiners are proficient, experienced flight instructors and pilots who are authorized by the FAA to conduct flight tests. They do charge a fee.

 The FAA's Instrument Rating Airman Certification Standards are outlined and reprinted in the Gleim *Instrument Pilot Flight Maneuvers and Practical Test Prep* book.

FAA PILOT KNOWLEDGE TEST AND TESTING SUPPLEMENT

1. This book is designed to help you prepare for and pass the following FAA knowledge tests:

   a. Instrument Rating - Airplane (IRA), which consists of 60 questions and has a time limit of 2 hr. 30 min.

   b. Flight Instructor Instrument - Airplane (FII), which consists of 50 questions and has a time limit of 2 hr. 30 min.

   c. Ground Instructor - Instrument (IGI), which consists of 50 questions and has a time limit of 2 hr. 30 min.

      1) This test may include some helicopter-related questions. Just read the question carefully and, if you do not know the answer, make your best guess. You need only 35 right out of 50 to pass the test.

   d. Instrument Rating - Foreign Pilot (IFP), which consists of 50 questions and has a time limit of 2 hr. 30 min.

      1) This test emphasizes Federal Aviation Regulations and weather more than the instrument rating (IRA) knowledge test.

   e. Flight Instructor Instrument - Airplane (Added Rating) (AIF), which consists of 20 questions and has a time limit of 1 hr.

      1) This test is for a CFII (helicopter) who wants to add an airplane rating to his or her CFII certificate.

2. The FAA legends and figures are contained in a book titled *Airman Knowledge Testing Supplement for Instrument Rating* (FAA-CT-8083-3), which you will be given to use at the time of your test.

   a. For the purpose of test preparation, the appropriate legends and figures are reproduced in this book.

3. In an effort to develop better questions, the FAA frequently **pretests** questions on knowledge tests by adding up to five "pretest" questions. The pretest questions will not be graded.

    a. You will **not** know which questions are real and which are pretest, so you must attempt to answer all questions correctly.

    b. When you notice a question **not** covered by Gleim, it might be a pretest question.

        1) We want to know about each pretest question you see.

        2) Please contact us at www.GleimAviation.com/questions or call 800-874-5346 with your recollection of any possible pretest questions so we may improve our efforts to prepare future instrument pilots.

KNOWLEDGE TESTS: CHEATING OR UNAUTHORIZED CONDUCT POLICY

The following is taken verbatim from an FAA knowledge test. It is reproduced here to remind all test takers about the FAA's policy against cheating and unauthorized conduct, a policy that Gleim consistently supports and upholds. Test takers must click "Yes" to proceed from this page into the actual knowledge test.

14 CFR part 61, section 61.37 Knowledge tests: Cheating or other unauthorized conduct

(a) An applicant for a knowledge test may not:
(1) Copy or intentionally remove any knowledge test;
(2) Give to another applicant or receive from another applicant any part or copy of a knowledge test;
(3) Give assistance on, or receive assistance on, a knowledge test during the period that test is being given;
(4) Take any part of a knowledge test on behalf of another person;
(5) Be represented by, or represent, another person for a knowledge test;
(6) Use any material or aid during the period that the test is being given, unless specifically authorized to do so by the Administrator; and
(7) Intentionally cause, assist, or participate in any act prohibited by this paragraph.

(b) An applicant who the Administrator finds has committed an act prohibited by paragraph (a) of this section is prohibited, for 1 year after the date of committing that act, from:
(1) Applying for any certificate, rating, or authorization issued under this chapter; and
(2) Applying for and taking any test under this chapter.

(c) Any certificate or rating held by an applicant may be suspended or revoked if the Administrator finds that person has committed an act prohibited by paragraph (a) of this section.

KNOWLEDGE TEST QUESTION BANK

In an effort to keep applicants from simply memorizing test questions, the FAA does not disclose all the questions you might see on your FAA knowledge test.

Using this book and other Gleim test preparation material to merely memorize the questions and answers is unwise and unproductive, and it will not ensure your success on your FAA knowledge test.

REORGANIZATION OF FAA QUESTIONS

1. Questions previously released by the FAA were **not** grouped together by topic; i.e., they appeared to be presented randomly.

   a. We have reorganized and renumbered the questions into study units and subunits.

2. Page 509 describes an online list of all of the questions in ACS code order, with cross-references to the study units and question numbers in this book.

3. Appendix A has sample questions relating to rotorcraft that may be encountered during the ground instructor instrument knowledge test.

HOW TO PREPARE FOR THE KNOWLEDGE TEST

1. Begin by carefully reading the rest of this introduction. You need to have a complete understanding of the examination process prior to initiating your study. This knowledge will make your studying more efficient.

2. After you have analyzed this introduction, set up a study schedule, including a target date for taking your knowledge test.

   a. Do not let the study process drag on and become discouraging; i.e., the quicker, the better.

   b. Consider enrolling in an organized ground school course, like the Gleim **Online Ground School**, or one held at your local FBO, community college, etc.

      1) Gleim Online Ground School is available 24/7. Demo Study Unit 1 for **free** at www.GleimAviation.com/free-demos.

   c. Determine where and when you are going to take your knowledge test.

3. Work through Study Units 1 through 11.

   a. All previously released questions in the FAA's instrument rating knowledge test question bank that are applicable to airplanes have been grouped into the following 11 categories, which are the titles of Study Units 1 through 11:

      Study Unit 1 -- Airplane Instruments
      Study Unit 2 -- Attitude Instrument Flying and Aerodynamics
      Study Unit 3 -- Navigation Systems
      Study Unit 4 -- Federal Aviation Regulations
      Study Unit 5 -- Airports, Air Traffic Control, and Airspace
      Study Unit 6 -- Holding and Instrument Approaches
      Study Unit 7 -- Aeromedical Factors
      Study Unit 8 -- Aviation Weather
      Study Unit 9 -- Aviation Weather Services
      Study Unit 10 -- IFR En Route
      Study Unit 11 -- IFR Flights

   b. Within each of the study units listed, questions relating to the same subtopic (e.g., thunderstorms, airplane stability, sectional charts, etc.) are grouped together to facilitate your study program. Each subtopic is called a subunit.

c. To the right of each question, we present

    1) The correct answer.

    2) The appropriate source document for the answer explanation. These publications can be obtained from the FAA (www.faa.gov) and aviation bookstores.

14 CFR	Federal Aviation Regulations
AC 00-6B	*Aviation Weather*
AC 00-45H	*Aviation Weather Services*
AC 91-74B	*Pilot Guide: Flight in Icing Conditions*
ACUG	Aeronautical Chart Users' Guide
AIM	*Aeronautical Information Manual*
Airport Diagram Legend	
Chart Supplement	
FAA-H-8083-2A	*Risk Management Handbook*
FAA-H-8083-3C	*Airplane Flying Handbook*
FAA-H-8083-6	*Advanced Avionics Handbook*
FAA-H-8083-15B	*Instrument Flying Handbook*
FAA-H-8083-16B	*Instrument Procedures Handbook*
FAA-H-8083-25B	*Pilot's Handbook of Aeronautical Knowledge*
FAA-P-8740-50	*On Landings, Part III*
IAP	Instrument approach procedures
NOAA	National Oceanic and Atmospheric Administration
NTSB	National Transportation Safety Board regulations
P/C Glossary	Pilot/Controller Glossary *(AIM)*

    a) The codes may refer to an entire document, such as an advisory circular, or to a particular chapter or subsection of a larger document.

        i) A complete list of abbreviations and acronyms used in this book begins on page 510.

    3) A comprehensive answer explanation, including

        a) A discussion of the correct answer or concept

        b) An explanation of why the other two answer choices are incorrect

4. Each study unit begins with a list of its subunit titles. The number after each title is the number of questions that cover the information in that subunit. The two numbers following the number of questions are the page numbers on which the outline and the questions for that particular subunit begin, respectively.

5. Begin by studying the outlines slowly and carefully. They are designed to help you pass the FAA knowledge test.

a. **CAUTION: The sole purpose** of this book is to expedite your passing the FAA knowledge test for the instrument rating. Accordingly, extraneous material (i.e., topics not directly tested on the FAA knowledge test) is omitted, even though much more knowledge is necessary to fly safely. This additional material is presented in four related Gleim books: ***Instrument Pilot Flight Maneuvers and Practical Test Prep***, ***FAR/AIM***, ***Aviation Weather and Weather Services***, and ***Pilot Handbook***.

6.   Answer the questions under exam conditions. Cover the answer explanations on the right side of each page with a piece of paper while you answer the questions.

Remember, it is very important to the learning (and understanding) process that you honestly commit to an answer. If you are wrong, your memory will be reinforced by having discovered your error. Therefore, it is crucial to make an honest attempt to answer the question before reading the answer.

   a.   Study the answer explanation for each question that you answer incorrectly, do not understand, or have difficulty with.

   b.   Use our **Online Ground School** or **FAA Test Prep Online** to ensure you do not refer to answers before committing to one **and** to simulate actual testing center exam conditions.

7.   Note that this test book contains questions grouped by topic. Thus, some questions may appear repetitive, while others may be duplicates or near-duplicates.

8.   As you move through study units, you may need further explanation or clarification of certain topics. You may wish to obtain and use the following Gleim books described on page 1:

   a.   *Instrument Pilot Flight Maneuvers and Practical Test Prep*
   b.   *Pilot Handbook*
   c.   *FAR/AIM*
   d.   *Aviation Weather and Weather Services*

9.   Keep track of your progress. As you complete a subunit, grade yourself with an A, B, C, or ? next to the subunit title at the front of the respective study unit.

   a.   The A, B, C, or ? is a self-evaluation of your comprehension of the material in that subunit and your ability to answer the questions.

      A   means a good understanding.
      B   means a fair understanding.
      C   means a shaky understanding.
      ?   means to ask your CFI or others about the material and/or questions, and read the pertinent sections in *Instrument Pilot Flight Maneuvers and Practical Test Prep* and/or *Pilot Handbook*.

   b.   This procedure will provide you with the ability to quickly see (by looking at the first page of each study unit) how much studying you have done (and how much remains) and how well you have done.

   c.   This procedure will also facilitate review. You can spend more time on the subunits that were more difficult for you.

   d.   **FAA Test Prep Online** provides you with your historical performance data.

GLEIM FAA TEST PREP ONLINE

Gleim **FAA Test Prep Online** is an all-in-one program designed to help anyone with a device and an interest in flying pass the FAA knowledge tests. Order today at www.GleimAviation.com or (800) 874-5346, or demo Study Unit 1 for **free** at www.GleimAviation.com/free-demos.

Recommended Study Program

1. Start with Study Unit 1 and proceed through study units in chronological order. Follow the three-step process below.

    a. First, carefully study the Gleim Outline.

    b. Second, create a Study Session of all questions in the study unit. Answer and study all questions in the Study Session.

    c. Third, create a Test Session of all questions in the study unit. Answer all questions in the Test Session.

2. After each Study Session and Test Session, create a new Study Session from questions answered incorrectly. This is of critical importance to allow you to learn from your mistakes.

Practice Test

Take an exam in the actual testing environment of an FAA testing center. **FAA Test Prep Online** simulates the testing formats of these testing centers, making it easy for you to study questions under actual exam conditions. After studying with **FAA Test Prep Online**, you will know exactly what to expect when you go in to take your pilot knowledge test.

On-Screen Charts and Figures

One of the most convenient features of **FAA Test Prep Online** is the easily accessible on-screen charts and figures. Many of the questions refer to drawings, maps, charts, and other pictures that provide information to help answer the question. In **FAA Test Prep Online**, you can pull up any of these figures with the click of a button. You can increase or decrease the size of the images, and you may also use our drawing feature to calculate the true course between two given points (required only on the private pilot knowledge test).

Instructor Sign-Off Sheets

FAA Test Prep Online can generate an instructor sign-off for FAA knowledge tests that require one. This sign-off has been approved by the FAA and can be presented at the testing center as authorization to take your test--you do **not** need an additional endorsement from your instructor.

In order to obtain the instructor sign-off sheet for your test, you must first answer all relevant questions in **FAA Test Prep Online** correctly. Then, select "Sign-Off Forms" under the "Tools" area on the Main page. If you have answered all of the required questions, the instructor sign-off sheet will appear for you to print. If you have not yet answered all required questions, a list of the unanswered questions, along with their location, will appear.

KNOWLEDGE TEST QUESTION-ANSWERING TECHNIQUE

Because the instrument pilot knowledge test has a set number of questions (60) and a set time limit (2.5 hours), you can plan your test-taking session to ensure that you leave yourself enough time to answer each question with relative certainty. The following steps will help you move through the knowledge test efficiently and produce better test results.

1. **Budget your time.** We make this point with emphasis.

    a. If you utilize the entire time limit for the test, you will have about 2.5 minutes per question.

    b. Time yourself when completing study sessions in this book to track your progress and adherence to the time limit and your own personal time allocation budget.

        1) Use any extra time you have to review questions that you are not sure about, cross-country planning questions with multiple steps and calculations, and similar questions in your exam that may help you answer other questions.

2. **Answer the questions in consecutive order.**

    a. Do **not** agonize over any one item. Stay within your time budget.

        1) We suggest that you skip cross-country planning questions and other similarly involved computational questions on your first pass through the exam. Come back to them after you have been through the entire test once.

    b. Mark any questions you are unsure of and return to them later as time allows.

        1) Once you initiate test grading, you can no longer review/change any answers.

    c. Never leave a multiple-choice question unanswered. Make your best educated guess in the time allowed. Remember, your score is based on the number of correct responses.

3. **For each multiple-choice question,**

    a. **Try to ignore the answer choices.** Do not allow the answer choices to affect your reading of the question.

        1) With three answer choices present, two of them are incorrect. These choices are called **distractors** for good reason and often are written to appear correct at first glance until further analysis.

        2) In computational items, the distractors are carefully calculated such that they are the result of making common mistakes. Be careful, and double-check your computations if time permits.

    b. **Read the question carefully** to determine the precise requirement.

        1) Focusing on what is required enables you to ignore extraneous information, to focus on the relevant facts, and to proceed directly to determining the correct answer.

            a) Be especially careful to note when the requirement is an **exception**; e.g., "Which of the following is **not** a type of hypoxia?"

    c.   **Determine the correct answer** before looking at the answer choices.

    d.   **Read the answer choices carefully.**

        1)   Even if the first answer appears to be the correct choice, do **not** skip the remaining answer choices. Questions often require the "best" answer of the choices provided. Thus, each choice requires your consideration.

        2)   Treat each answer choice as a true/false question as you analyze it.

    e.   **Click on the best answer.**

        1)   For many multiple-choice questions, at least one answer choice can be eliminated with minimal effort, thereby increasing your educated guess to a 50-50 proposition.

4.   After you have been through all the questions in the test, consult the question status list to determine which questions are unanswered and which are marked for review.

    a.   Go back to the marked questions and finalize your answer choices.

    b.   Verify that all questions have been answered.

EDUCATED GUESSING

> The FAA knowledge test sometimes includes questions that are poorly worded or confusing. Expect the unexpected and move forward. Do not let confusing questions affect your concentration or take up too much time; make your best guess and move on.

1.   If you don't know the answer, make an educated guess as follows:

    a.   Rule out answers that you think are incorrect.

    b.   Select the best answer or guess between equally appealing answers. Your first guess is usually the most intuitive. If you cannot make an educated guess, re-read the stem and each answer choice and pick the most intuitive answer.

SIMULATED FAA PRACTICE TEST

Appendix B, "Instrument Rating Practice Test," beginning on page 501, allows you to practice taking the FAA knowledge test without the answers next to the questions. This test has 60 questions with topical coverage similar to that of the FAA knowledge test.

It is important that you answer all 60 questions in one sitting. Do not consult the answers, especially when being referred to figures (charts, tables, etc.) where the questions are answered and explained. Analyze your performance based on the answer key that follows the practice test.

It is even better to practice with Test Sessions in the Gleim **FAA Test Prep Online**. These simulate actual computer testing conditions, including the screen layouts, instructions, etc.

AUTHORIZATION TO TAKE THE FAA PILOT KNOWLEDGE TEST

Before taking the instrument pilot knowledge test, you must receive an endorsement from an authorized instructor who conducted the ground training or reviewed your home-study in the areas listed in item 4. on pages 2 and 3, certifying that you are prepared to pass the knowledge test.

A standard authorization form for the instrument rating-airplane knowledge test is reproduced on page 519, which can be easily completed, signed by a flight or ground instructor, torn out, and taken to the test site.

Note that if you use the Gleim **FAA Test Prep Online** or **Online Ground School**, the program will generate an authorization signed in facsimile that is accepted at all PSI locations.

WHEN TO TAKE THE INSTRUMENT RATING KNOWLEDGE TEST

1.   You must be at least 15 years of age to take the instrument rating knowledge test.

2.   You must prepare for the test under the supervision of your CFII by successfully completing a ground instruction course or by using this book as your self-developed home study course.

    a.   See "Authorization to Take the FAA Pilot Knowledge Test" above.

3.   Take the FAA knowledge test within 30 days of beginning your study.

    a.   Complete the knowledge test early in your training so you can focus your effort toward building your skills through aeronautical experience.

4.   Your practical test must follow within 24 months.

    a.   Otherwise, you will have to retake your knowledge test.

KNOWLEDGE TESTING CENTERS AND PROCEDURES

PSI has testing centers throughout the country. More information can be found at www.GleimAviation.com/testingcenters.

You may take the following items to the test center:

1. An approved flight computer (ideally the one that you use to solve the test questions in this book, i.e., one you are familiar with and have used before)

2. A pocket calculator you are familiar with and have used before (no instructional material for the calculator is allowed)

3. Authorization to take the knowledge test (see the previous page and page 519)

4. Proper identification that contains your photograph, signature, date of birth, and actual residential address, if different from your mailing address.

NOTE: Paper and pencils are supplied at the examination site.

Positive proof of identification and documentary evidence of your age is required. The identification must include your photograph, signature, date of birth, and actual residential address if different from the mailing address. This information may be presented in more than one form of identification.

Next, you will sign in on the testing center's daily log. Your signature on the logsheet certifies that, if this is a retest, you meet the applicable requirements (discussed in "Retaking the FAA Pilot Knowledge Test" on page 14) and that you have not passed this test in the past 2 years.

A person from the testing center will assist you in logging onto the system, and you will be asked to confirm your personal data (e.g., name, Social Security number, etc.). Then you will be given an online introduction to the testing system, and you will take a sample test. If you have used our **FAA Test Prep Online**, you will be conversant with the testing methodology and environment.

YOUR FAA KNOWLEDGE TEST REPORT

1. You will receive your FAA Knowledge Test Report (FAAKTR) upon completion of the test. An example test report is reproduced on the next page.

    a. The expiration date is the date by which you must take your FAA practical test.

    b. The report lists the ACS codes of the questions you missed so you can review the topics you missed prior to your practical test.

2. Reach out to us at Gleim with your test report at FAAKTR@gleim.com.

    a. We can provide feedback, resources, and guidance toward review and improvement in preparation for your FAA practical test.

3. Refer to the Instrument Rating Airplane ACS to determine which topics you had difficulty with.

4. Keep your FAA Knowledge Test Report in a safe place. You must submit it to the FAA evaluator when you take your practical test.

RETAKING THE FAA PILOT KNOWLEDGE TEST

1. If you fail (score less than 70%) the knowledge test (which is virtually impossible if you follow the Gleim system), you may retake it after your instructor endorses the bottom of your FAA Knowledge Test Report certifying that you have received the necessary ground training to retake the test.

2. Upon retaking the test, you will find that the procedure is the same except that you must also submit your FAA Knowledge Test Report indicating the previous failure to the computer testing center.

3. Note that the pass rate on the instrument rating knowledge test is over 94%; i.e., fewer than 1 out of 10 fail the test initially. Reasons for failure include

    a. Failure to study the material tested and mere memorization of correct answers. (Relevant study material is contained in the outlines at the beginning of Study Units 1 through 11 of this book.)

    b. Failure to practice working through the questions under test conditions. (All of the previously released FAA questions appear in Study Units 1 through 11 of this book.)

    c. Poor examination technique, such as misreading questions and not understanding the requirements.

This Gleim Knowledge Test book will prepare you to pass the FAA knowledge test on your first attempt! In addition, the Gleim *Instrument Pilot Flight Maneuvers and Practical Test Prep* book will save you time and frustration as you prepare for the FAA practical test.

Just as this book organizes and explains the knowledge needed to pass your FAA knowledge test, *Instrument Pilot Flight Maneuvers and Practical Test Prep* will assist you in developing the competence and confidence to pass your FAA practical test.

Also, flight maneuvers are quickly perfected when you understand exactly what to expect before you get into an airplane to practice the flight maneuvers. You must be ahead of (not behind) your CFI and your airplane. Our flight maneuvers books explain and illustrate all flight maneuvers so the maneuvers and their execution are intuitively appealing to you. Visit www.GleimAviation.com or call (800) 874-5346 and order today!

U.S. DEPARTMENT OF TRANSPORTATION
Federal Aviation Administration
Airman Knowledge Test Report

NAME:

FAA TRACKING NUMBER (FTN):   **EXAM ID:**

EXAM: Instrument Rating Airplane

EXAM DATE: 10/08/22   **EXAM SITE:**

SCORE: 96   **GRADE:** Pass   **TAKE:** 1

The Airman Certification Standards (ACS) codes listed below represent incorrectly answered questions. These ACS codes and their associated Areas of Operation/Tasks/Elements may be found in the appropriate ACS document at http://www.faa.gov/training_testing/testing/acs.

A single code may represent more than one incorrect response.

IR.I.B.K1   IR.V.A.S2

EXPIRATION DATE: 10/31/2024

DO NOT LOSE THIS REPORT

AUTHORIZED INSTRUCTOR'S STATEMENT: (if applicable)

On _____ (date) I gave the above named applicant _____ hours of additional instruction, covering each subject area shown to be deficient, and consider the applicant competent to pass the knowledge test.

Name _____

Cert. No. _____ *(print clearly)*

Type of instructor certificate _____

Signature _____

FRAUDULENT ALTERATION OF THIS FORM BY ANY PERSON IS A BASIS FOR SUSPENSION OR REVOCATION OF ANY CERTIFICATES OR RATINGS HELD BY THAT PERSON.
ISSUED BY: PSI Services LLC
FEDERAL AVIATION ADMINISTRATION

THIS INFORMATION IS PROTECTED BY THE PRIVACY ACT. FOR OFFICIAL USE ONLY.

16

STUDY UNIT ONE

AIRPLANE INSTRUMENTS

(12 pages of outline)

This study unit contains outlines of major concepts tested, sample test questions and answers regarding airplane instruments, and an explanation of each answer.

Recall that the **sole purpose** of this book is to expedite your passing of the FAA pilot knowledge test for the instrument rating. Accordingly, all extraneous material (i.e., topics or regulations not directly tested on the FAA pilot knowledge test) is omitted, even though much more knowledge is necessary to fly safely. This additional material is presented in *Pilot Handbook*, *Aviation Weather and Weather Services*, *FAR/AIM*, and *Instrument Pilot Flight Maneuvers and Practical Test Prep*, available from Gleim Publications, Inc. Order online at www.GleimAviation.com.

1.1 COMPASS

1. During taxi, you should check your compass to see that it is swinging freely and indicating known headings.

2. The difference between direction indicated by a magnetic compass not installed in an airplane and one installed in an airplane is called **compass deviation**.

   a. Magnetic fields produced by metals and electrical accessories in an airplane disturb the compass needle.

3. Magnetic compasses can be considered accurate only during straight-and-level flight at constant airspeed.

   a. When turning and accelerating/decelerating, the fluid level and compass card do not remain level, and magnetic force pulls "down" as well as toward the pole.

   b. These are known as the magnetic dip characteristics.

4. In the Northern Hemisphere, **acceleration/deceleration error** occurs when an airplane is on an easterly or westerly heading. It does not occur on a northerly or southerly heading.

   a. A magnetic compass will indicate a turn toward the north during acceleration on an easterly or westerly heading.

   b. A magnetic compass will indicate a turn toward the south during deceleration on an easterly or westerly heading.

   c. Recall A-N-D-S: Accelerate North, Decelerate South.

5. In the Northern Hemisphere, **compass turning error** occurs when turning from a northerly or southerly heading.

   a. A magnetic compass will lag (and at the start of a turn indicate a turn in the opposite direction) when turning from a northerly heading.

      1) If turning to the east (right), the compass will initially indicate a turn to the west and then lag behind the actual heading until your airplane is headed east (at which point there is no error).

      2) If turning to the west (left), the compass will initially indicate a turn to the east and then lag behind the actual heading until your airplane is headed west (at which point there is no error).

   b. A magnetic compass will lead or precede the turn when turning from a southerly heading.

   c. A corrective factor will need to be applied for turns made to the north or to the south. Recall U-N-O-S: Undershoot North, Overshoot South.

      1) Typically, you should stop the northerly turn 15° plus half the latitude prior to the desired heading.

      2) Typically, you should stop the southerly turn 15° plus half the latitude after passing the desired heading.

   d. Turning errors do not occur when turning from or through an easterly or westerly heading; i.e., turning errors are minimized at 90° and 270° headings.

6. These magnetic dip errors diminish as acceleration/deceleration or turns are completed.

1.2 PITOT-STATIC SYSTEM

1. There are three kinds of airspeed useful for pilots.

    a. **Indicated airspeed (IAS)** is the direct instrument reading obtained from the airspeed indicator, uncorrected for variations in air density or installation and instrument errors.

    b. **Calibrated airspeed (CAS)** is IAS corrected for installation and instrument errors.

    c. **True airspeed (TAS)** is CAS corrected for density altitude. TAS is the true speed of an airplane through the air.

2. The CAS needed to maintain a certain TAS can be determined with a flight computer using the altitude and temperature.

    a. EXAMPLE: What CAS must be used to maintain a TAS of 180 kt. at an altitude of 12,000 ft. if the outside air temperature is +5°C?

        1) In the center of the slide rule side of your flight computer, on the right side, put the air temperature of +5°C over the altitude of 12,000 ft. On the outer scale, find the TAS of 180 kt., which is above the CAS on the inner scale of 147 KCAS.

3. When both the airspeed indicator pitot tube and the drain hole are blocked, the airspeed indicator acts as an altimeter.

    a. At a given altitude, airspeed changes would not change the indicated airspeed.

    b. During climbs, the indicated airspeed will increase.

    c. During descents, the indicated airspeed will decrease.

    d. These changes occur as a result of the differential between the pressure of the air locked in the pitot tube and the static air vent pressure.

4. If an alternate static source is vented inside an unpressurized airplane, the static pressure is usually lower than outside pressure due to the Venturi effect of the outside air flowing over the flight deck.

    a. The airspeed indicator will indicate a faster-than-actual airspeed.
    b. The vertical speed indicator (VSI) will momentarily show a climb.
    c. The altimeter will read higher-than-actual altitude.

5. If the pitot tube becomes clogged with ice during flight, only the airspeed indicator will be affected.

    a. The altimeter and vertical speed indicator depend upon the static air vents.

    b. If the static ports are iced over, the vertical speed indicator will not reflect climbs and descents because the change in air pressure cannot be detected by the VSI.

6. If the vertical speed indicator is not calibrated correctly (e.g., continually indicates a descent or climb), it can still be used for IFR flight by adjusting for the error when interpreting the indications.

    a. The VSI is not a required instrument for IFR flight. (Nonetheless, the FAA requires you to report the inability to climb/descend at least 500 fpm, and the FAA Instrument Rating ACS requires constant rate climbs/descents.)

7. If the outside air temperature increases during a flight at constant power and a constant indicated altitude, true airspeed (TAS) and true altitude will increase.

1.3 ALTIMETER

1. The altimeter indicates the true altitude at the field elevation if the local altimeter setting is used in an accurate altimeter.

    a. Thus, the altimeter indicates altitude in relation to the pressure level set in the barometric window.

2. Altimeters have three "hands" (like a clock's hour, minute, and second hands).

3. The three hands on the altimeter are generally arranged as follows:

    a. 10,000-ft. interval (thin needle with a flared triangular tip)
    b. 1,000-ft. interval (short, fat needle)
    c. 100-ft. interval (long, medium-thickness needle)

4. Altimeters are numbered 0 through 9.

5. To read an altimeter,

    a. First, determine whether the thin needle with the flared triangular tip rests between 0 and 1 (1-10,000 ft.), 1 and 2 (10,000-20,000 ft.), or 2 and 3 (20,000-30,000 ft.).

    b. Second, determine whether the shortest needle is between 0 and 1 (0-1,000 ft.), 1 and 2 (1,000-2,000 ft.), etc.

    c. Third, determine at which number the medium needle is pointing, e.g., 1 for 100 ft., 2 for 200 ft., etc.

6. Atmospheric pressure decreases about 1 in. Hg for every 1,000 ft. of altitude gained.

7. The altimeter setting dial allows adjustment for nonstandard pressure.

    a. A window in the face of the altimeter shows a barometric scale that can be adjusted.

    b. Rotating the altimeter setting dial changes the scale and the altimeter hands simultaneously in the same direction by 1,000 ft. per 1 in. Hg.

    c. For example, changing from 29.92 in. to 30.92 in. increases indicated altitude by 1,000 ft., or from 30.15 in. to 30.25 in. increases indicated altitude by 100 ft.

8. Prior to takeoff, the altimeter should be set to the current local altimeter setting.

    a. With the current altimeter setting, the indicated altitude of the airplane on the ground should be within 75 ft. of the actual elevation of the airport for acceptable accuracy.

    b. If the current local altimeter setting is not available, use the departure airport elevation.

    c. The local altimeter setting should be used by all pilots in a particular area, primarily to provide for better vertical separation of aircraft.

    d. During an IFR flight in Class E airspace below 18,000 ft. MSL, ATC will periodically provide the current altimeter setting.

9.   The standard temperature and pressure at sea level are 15°C (59°F) and 29.92 in. Hg (1,013.2 mb).

   a.   Pressure altitude is the indicated altitude when the altimeter setting is adjusted to 29.92 in. Hg, i.e., the height above the standard datum plane.

   b.   Pressure altitude is used in computations of density altitude, true altitude, and true airspeed.

   c.   Pressure altitude will equal true altitude when standard atmospheric conditions exist (as seen, for example, in aircraft A below).

   d.   Pressure altitude and density altitude are the same at standard temperature.

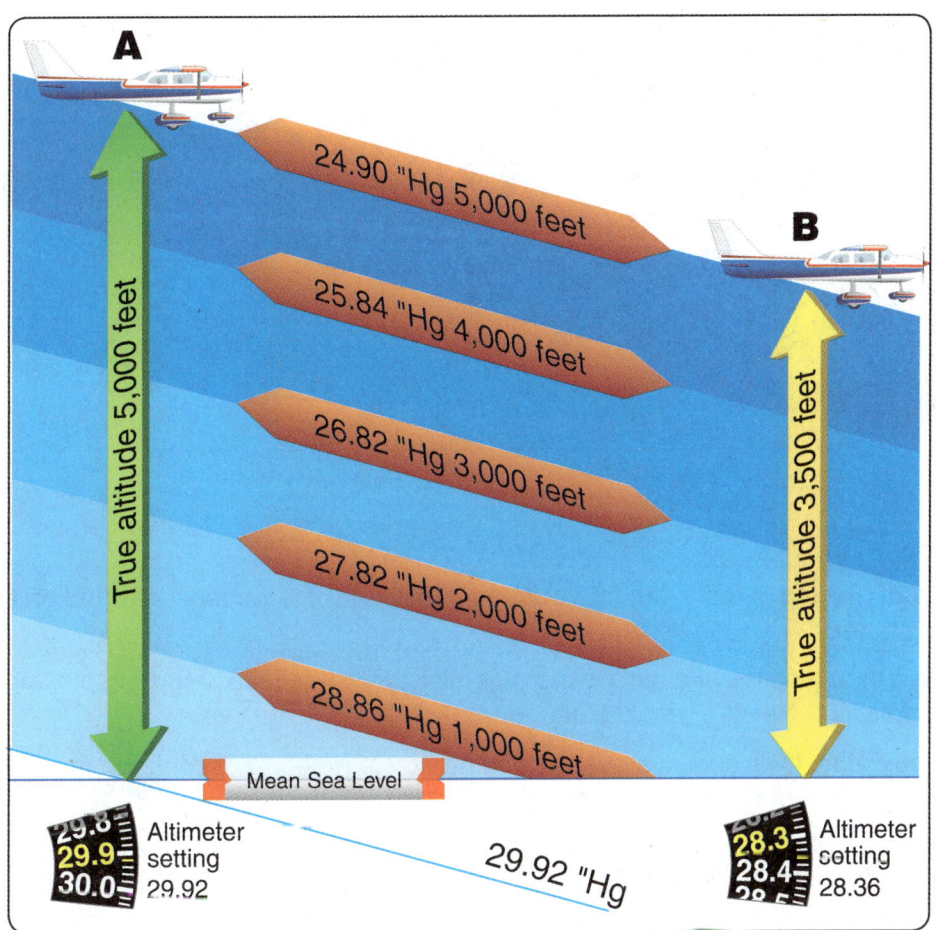

10.   The altimeter must be set to pressure altitude when flying at or above 18,000 ft. MSL.

   a.   This setting guarantees vertical separation of airplanes above 18,000 ft. MSL.

11.   When pressure lowers en route, your altimeter will register higher-than-actual altitude until you adjust the altimeter for the new altimeter setting (as seen, for example, in aircraft B above).

12. Since altimeter readings are adjusted for changes in barometric pressure but not for temperature changes, an airplane will be at lower-than-indicated altitude when flying in colder-than-standard air.

    a.   On warm days, you will be at a higher altitude (i.e., true altitude) than your altimeter indicates.

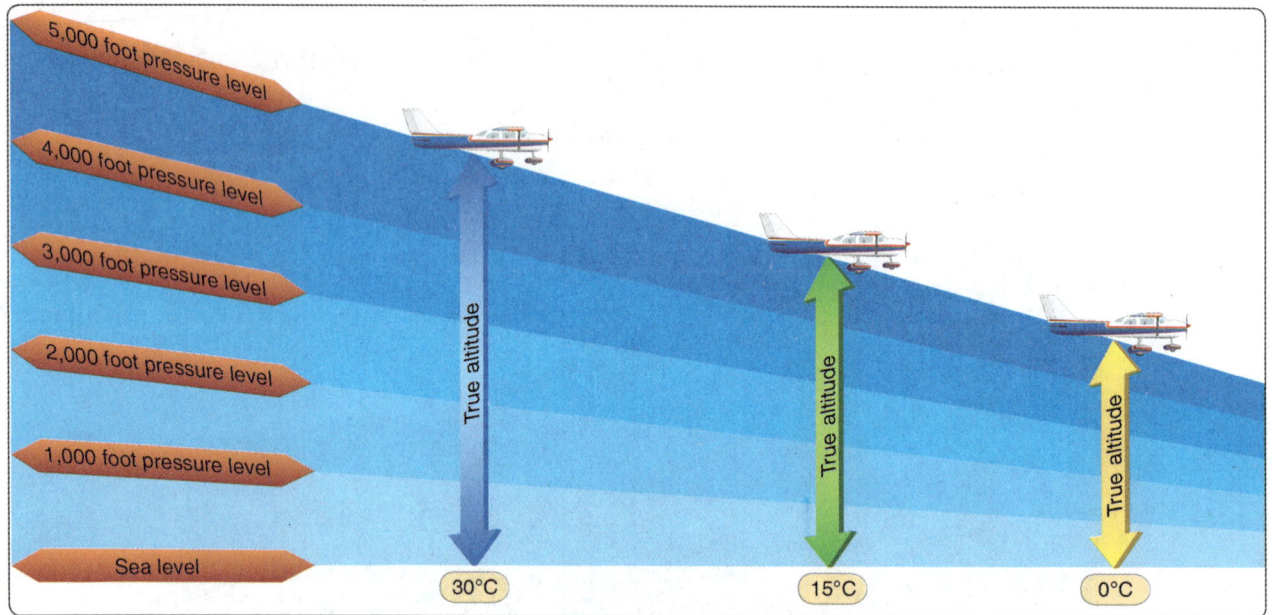

1.4 GYROSCOPES

1. Listen to your electric gyroscopes for unusual noises after the battery is turned on but before the engine is started.

2. One of the characteristics of a gyro is that it is resistant to deflection of the spinning wheel, which is based on two of Newton's laws of motion.

    a.   A body at rest will continue at rest, and a body in motion will continue in motion in a straight line, until acted upon by an outside force.

    b.   Deflection of a moving body is proportional to the deflective force applied and inversely proportional to the body's mass and speed.

1.5 HEADING INDICATOR

1. The heading indicator (HI) should be set to the correct magnetic heading 5 min. after the engine is started.

    a. Prior to takeoff, check the heading indicator to determine that it continues to maintain the correct heading after taxi turns.

2. The remote indicating compass (RIC) combines the functions of the magnetic compass and the heading indicator. One component of the RIC is the slaving control and compensator unit, as shown in the figure below.

Horizontal situation indicator (HSI)

Slaving control compensator unit   *Slaving meter*

    a. This unit contains a slaving meter needle that indicates the difference between the displayed heading and the actual magnetic heading.

        1) A right deflection (+) indicates a clockwise (right) error in the heading indicator compass card (i.e., the correct magnetic heading is to the right of the indicated heading).

            a) Depressing the right (counterclockwise) heading drive button will move the heading indicator compass card to the left, thus increasing (+) the indicated heading toward the correct value (i.e., from 180° to 190°).

        2) A left deflection (−) indicates a counterclockwise (left) error in the heading indicator compass card (i.e., the correct magnetic heading is to the left of the indicated heading).

            a) Depressing the left (clockwise) heading drive button will move the heading indicator compass card to the right, thus decreasing (−) the indicated heading toward the correct value (i.e., from 190° to 180°).

    b.   To make corrections to the RIC, the system must be placed in the free gyro mode.

        1)   After corrections are made, the system is returned to the slaved mode, which is the normal mode of operation.

3.   RICs were developed to compensate for the errors and limitations of the older type of heading indicators.

    a.   The two panel-mounted components of a typical system are the pictorial navigation indicator and the slaving control and compensator unit.

    b.   The slaving control and compensator unit has a push-button that provides a means of selecting either the "slaved gyro" or "free gyro" mode.

    c.   This unit also has a slaving meter and two manual heading-drive buttons.

    d.   The slaving meter indicates the difference between the displayed heading and the magnetic heading.

        1)   A right deflection indicates a clockwise error of the compass card; a left deflection indicates a counterclockwise error.

        2)   When the aircraft is in a turn and the card rotates, the slaving meter shows a full deflection to one side or the other.

        3)   When the system is in "free gyro" mode, the compass card may be adjusted by depressing the appropriate heading-drive button.

    e.   A magnetic slaving transmitter is a separate unit mounted remotely, usually in a wingtip to eliminate the possibility of magnetic interference.

        1)   It contains the flux valve, which is the direction-sensing device of the system.

            a)   A concentration of lines of magnetic force, after being amplified, becomes a signal relayed to the heading indicator unit, which is also remotely mounted.

            b)   This signal operates a torque motor in the heading indicator unit that precesses the gyro unit until it is aligned with the transmitter signal.

        2)   The magnetic slaving transmitter is connected electrically to the RIC or HSI.

1.6 ATTITUDE INDICATOR

1. Prior to IFR flight, you should check the horizon bar, which should be erect and stable within 5 min. of engine warm-up.

    a. The horizon bar should not tilt more than 5° when making taxi turns.

    b. Remember that you can adjust the position of the miniature airplane, but it is the horizon bar that moves to indicate attitude in flight.

        1) The horizon bar remains parallel to the horizon as the airplane's attitude changes.

        2) When using the attitude indicator for pitch attitude corrections, control pressures should be extremely light.

            a) Movements of the horizon bar above or below the miniature aircraft should not exceed one-half bar width.

            b) Additional inputs should not result in more than a one-half bar width correction.

2. **Precession errors** (both pitch and bank) on attitude indicators are greatest when rolling out of a 180° steep turn in either direction.

    a. As the airplane returns to straight-and-level coordinated flight, the miniature aircraft will show a slight climb and a turn in the direction opposite to the turn just made.

        1) If you indicate straight-and-level, you will be descending and turning in the direction of the turn just made.

    b. These precession errors during turns (including coordinated turns) are caused by centrifugal force acting on the pendulous vanes (erection mechanism in the attitude indicator). It results in the precession of the gyro toward the inside of the turn.

3. Attitude indicators also reflect an error during skidding turns, which precesses the gyro toward the inside of the turn.

    a. As the airplane returns to straight-and-level coordinated flight, the miniature aircraft shows a turn in the direction opposite to the skid. Pitch indication is not affected.

4. Deceleration precession makes some attitude indicators incorrectly indicate a descent.

    a. Conversely, acceleration through precession may result in attitude indicators incorrectly indicating a climb.

1.7 TURN-AND-SLIP INDICATOR

1. Prior to engine start, the turn-and-slip indicator should indicate the needle centered, the tube full of fluid, and the ball approximately centered.

2. During taxi turns, the needle should deflect in the direction of the turn, and the ball should move freely opposite the turn due to centrifugal force.

1.8 TURN COORDINATOR (TC)

1. The miniature aircraft in the turn coordinator indicates rate of roll and rate of turn.

   a. When the bank is changing, the rate of roll along the longitudinal axis is indicated.

   b. When the bank is constant, the rate of turn along the vertical axis is indicated.

   c. Thus, the angle of bank is only indirectly indicated.

2. On taxi turns, the miniature aircraft indicates a turn in the direction of the taxiing turn, and the ball moves to the outside of the turn due to centrifugal force.

3. The miniature airplane will show a turn in a wings-level yaw or during a turn while taxiing.

   a. The TC indicates direction of roll along the longitudinal axis or yaw along the vertical axis and rate of turn.

   b. The TC does not give a direct indication of the banked attitude of the airplane.

   c. The TC does not display bank angle and rate of turn indirectly simultaneously.

      1) During a turn, the TC first shows the rate of bank indirectly and, once stabilized, the rate of turn.

4. For any given airspeed, a specific angle of bank is necessary to maintain a coordinated turn at a given rate. The faster the airspeed, the greater the angle of bank required to obtain a desired rate of turn.

   a. Standard-rate turn

      1) When the turn needle points to one of the small side marks, it indicates that the airplane is turning at a rate of 3° per second.

5. The inclinometer of the TC consists of a sealed, curved glass tube containing kerosene and a ball which is free to move inside the tube. The fluid provides a dampening action which ensures smooth and easy movement of the ball.

   a. A rate of 3° per second is considered a standard-rate turn, and completing 360° of turn requires 2 minutes.

   b. The tube is curved so that the ball tends to seek the lowest point, which is the center of the tube during coordinated flight. Two reference markers aid in determining when the ball is in the center.

      1) During a coordinated turn, turning forces are balanced, causing the ball to remain centered in the tube.

      2) If turning forces are unbalanced, i.e., if improper rudder is used, the ball moves away from the center of the tube in the direction of the excessive force.

      3) In a skid, the rate of turn is too great for the angle of bank, and excessive centrifugal force moves the ball to the outside of the turn.

         a) To achieve coordinated flight from a skid, you should increase the bank angle, reduce the rate of turn by reducing the rudder force to center the ball, or use a combination of both.

4)   In a slip, the rate of turn is too slow for the angle of bank, and the lack of centrifugal force moves the ball to the inside of the turn.

   a)   To achieve coordinated flight from a slip, you should decrease the bank angle, increase the rate of turn by applying rudder pressure to center the ball, or use a combination of both.

5)   Remember: In slips, you have used too little rudder (or opposite rudder). In skids, you have used too much rudder.

6)   Apply rudder pressure on the side that the ball is exposed; i.e., step on the ball.

7)   The ball then is a visual aid to determine coordinated use of the aileron and rudder control. During a turn, it indicates the quality of the turn, i.e., whether the airplane has the correct rate of turn for the angle of bank.

1.9 GLASS PANEL DISPLAYS

1.   Glass panel displays on flight decks integrate many flight instruments with aircraft performance data on one or more screens to give flight status in a convenient, easy-to-read format.

   a.   Glass panel displays and advanced avionics were designed to increase safety by enhancing situational awareness, presenting data in an easy-to-understand format, and performing many necessary tasks automatically.

   b.   These systems are displayed in an electronic flight instrument system (EFIS).

2.   A **primary flight display (PFD)** combines many flight instruments into a single presentation.

   a.   These could include the altimeter, attitude indicator, vertical speed indicator, turn coordinator, HSI, and airspeed indicator.

   b.   Other flight status information that may be displayed on a PFD could include distance and bearing to the next waypoint, ground track, outside air temperature, navigation instruments, and communication frequencies.

   c.   Instrument sensor systems used to display information on a PFD are more sensitive and reliable than traditional gyroscopic instruments.

   d.   A **multi-function display (MFD)** is often used as a backup PFD and is usually used to monitor engine and powerplant performance, fuel status, traffic, route selection, moving maps, approach charts, weather, and terrain avoidance.

3.   EFDs utilize an air data computer (ADC) which receives the pitot and static inputs and computes the difference between the total pressure and the static pressure.

   a.   The ADC then generates the information necessary to display the airspeed, altitude, and vertical speed on the PFD.

4.   The attitude and heading reference system (AHRS) replaces free-spinning gyros with solid-state laser systems that are capable of flight at any attitude without tumbling.

   a.   The AHRS sends attitude information to the PFD in order to generate the pitch and bank information of the attitude indicator.

   b.   The heading information is derived from a magnetometer that senses the earth's lines of magnetic flux.

5. As with flying conventional instruments, care is needed to maintain a correct instrument scan to correctly interpret instrument indications and avoid fixation.

6. All human activity involving technical devices entails some element of risk. Knowledge, experience, and flight requirements tilt the odds in favor of safe and successful flights. The advanced avionics aircraft offers many new capabilities and simplifies the basic flying tasks, but only if the pilot is properly trained and all the equipment is working properly.

7. While they have many benefits, much more initial and recurrent training is needed to acquire and retain the knowledge and skills necessary to accomplish a flight safely by means of glass panel displays.

    a. Pilots flying with advanced avionics or glass panel displays must continually learn their system's functions, capabilities, and limitations.

    b. With failure a possibility of any given system or display, a pilot must be able to manually perform any task being accomplished automatically.

    c. All aircraft equipped with electric flight instruments must also contain a minimal set of backup conventional instruments, usually consisting of an attitude indicator, airspeed indicator, and altimeter.

    d. Safety can be hampered or compromised if a pilot is not aware of what data is being presented or if it is used as a substitute for required preflight planning.

8. Most of the aviation community believes automation has made flying safer, but there is a fear that pilots fail to see that automation is a double-edged sword.

    a. Pilots need to understand the advantages of automation while being aware of its limitations. Experience has shown that automated systems can make some errors more evident while sometimes hiding other errors or making them less obvious.

    b. Humans are characteristically poor monitors of automated systems. When passively monitoring an automated system for faults, abnormalities, or other infrequent events, humans perform poorly. The more reliable the system is, the worse the human performance becomes. Risk is increased when flightcrew members fail to monitor automated navigation systems.

    c. It is a paradox of automation that technologically advanced avionics can both increase and decrease pilot awareness.

9. Pilots should not become complacent or be lulled into a false sense of security simply because they have advanced avionics. Judgment and aeronautical decision-making serve as the bridge between technology and safety.

    a. Any flight you make involves almost infinite combinations of pilot skill, experience, condition, and proficiency; aircraft equipment and performance; environmental conditions; and external influences. Both individually and in combination, these factors can compress the safety buffer provided by your baseline personal minimums.

QUESTIONS AND ANSWER EXPLANATIONS: All of the instrument rating knowledge test questions chosen by the FAA for release as well as additional questions selected by Gleim relating to the material in the previous outlines are provided on the following pages. These questions have been organized into the same subunits as the outlines. To the immediate right of each question are the correct answer and answer explanations. You should cover these answers and answer explanations while responding to the questions. Refer to the general discussion in the Introduction on how to take the FAA knowledge test.

Remember that the questions from the FAA knowledge test bank have been reordered by topic and organized into a meaningful sequence. Also, the first line of the answer explanation gives the citation of the authoritative source for the answer.

QUESTIONS

1.1 Compass

1. On the taxi check, the magnetic compass should

    A. swing opposite to the direction of turn when turning from north.

    B. exhibit the same number of degrees of dip as the latitude.

    C. swing freely and indicate known headings.

Answer (C) is correct. (FAA-H-8083-15B Chap 5)
    DISCUSSION: When taxiing, the magnetic compass should be checked to make sure that the compass card is swinging freely and indicating known headings.
    Answer (A) is incorrect. The compass exhibits turning errors only when the airplane is airborne and in a bank.
Answer (B) is incorrect. Compass turning errors occur in flight as a result of magnetic dip.

2. What should be the indication on the magnetic compass as you roll into a standard-rate turn to the left from an east heading in the Northern Hemisphere?

    A. The compass will initially indicate a turn to the right.

    B. The compass will remain on east for a short time, then gradually catch up to the magnetic heading of the aircraft.

    C. The compass will indicate the approximate correct magnetic heading if the roll into the turn is smooth.

Answer (C) is correct. (FAA-H-8083-15B Chap 5)
    DISCUSSION: If you roll into a smooth, coordinated, standard-rate turn to the left or right from an east or west heading, the compass will indicate the approximate correct magnetic heading. There are no turning errors on turns from east or west headings.
    Answer (A) is incorrect. The compass will initially indicate a turn in the opposite direction of a bank only when the airplane is turning from a north heading. **Answer (B) is incorrect.** When the airplane is turning from an east heading, the compass will immediately indicate a turn if the roll into the turn is smooth.

3. What should be the indication on the magnetic compass as you roll into a standard rate turn to the right from an easterly heading In the Northern Hemisphere?

    A. The compass will initially indicate a turn to the left.

    B. The compass will remain on east for a short time, then gradually catch up to the magnetic heading of the aircraft.

    C. The compass will indicate the approximate correct magnetic heading if the roll into the turn is smooth.

Answer (C) is correct. (FAA-H-8083-15B Chap 5)
    DISCUSSION: If you roll into a smooth, coordinated, standard-rate turn to the left or right from an east or west heading, the compass will normally indicate the approximate correct magnetic heading. Acceleration, not turning, errors are found in east or west headings in the Northern Hemisphere.
    Answer (A) is incorrect. The compass will initially indicate a turn in the opposite direction of a bank only when turning from a north heading. **Answer (B) is incorrect.** When turning from an east heading, the compass will immediately indicate a turn if the roll into the turn is smooth.

4. On what headings will the magnetic compass read most accurately during a level 360° turn, with a bank of approximately 15°?

    A. 135° through 225°.

    B. 90° and 270°.

    C. 180° and 0°.

Answer (B) is correct. (FAA-H-8083-15B Chap 5)
    DISCUSSION: In a turn through north or south, the compass indication will usually be incorrect. But in a turn through east or west, the compass indication is usually accurate. Therefore, the compass should be indicating properly when passing through 90° and 270°. This holds true for only medium to shallow bank turns, e.g., 15-30°.
    Answer (A) is incorrect. The compass leads the heading in a turn through south. **Answer (C) is incorrect.** Compass turning errors are greatest at north and south headings.

5. What should be the indication on the magnetic compass as you roll into a standard rate turn to the right from a westerly heading in the Northern Hemisphere?

    A. The compass will initially show a turn in the opposite direction, then turn to a northerly indication but lagging behind the actual heading of the aircraft.

    B. The compass will remain on a westerly heading for a short time, then gradually catch up to the actual heading of the aircraft.

    C. The compass will indicate the approximate correct magnetic heading if the roll into the turn is smooth.

Answer (C) is correct. (FAA-H-8083-15B Chap 5)
    DISCUSSION: If you roll into a smooth, coordinated, standard-rate turn to the left or right from an east or west heading, the compass will indicate the approximate correct magnetic heading. There are no turning errors on turns from east or west headings.
    Answer (A) is incorrect. The compass will initially indicate a turn in the opposite direction of a bank only when turning from a north heading. **Answer (B) is incorrect.** When turning from a westerly heading, the compass will immediately indicate a turn if the roll into the turn is smooth.

6. What should be the indication on the magnetic compass as you roll into a standard rate turn to the right from a south heading in the Northern Hemisphere?

    A. The compass will indicate a turn to the right, but at a faster rate than is actually occurring.

    B. The compass will initially indicate a turn to the left.

    C. The compass will remain on south for a short time, then gradually catch up to the magnetic heading of the aircraft.

Answer (A) is correct. (FAA-H-8083-15B Chap 5)
    DISCUSSION: In turns from a southerly heading in the Northern Hemisphere, the compass leads the turn. That is, it indicates a turn in the proper direction but at a faster rate than is actually occurring.
    Answer (B) is incorrect. The compass will initially indicate a turn in the opposite direction if the turn is made from a north, not south, heading. **Answer (C) is incorrect.** It describes a shallower-than-standard turn from a north, not south, heading.

7. What should be the indication on the magnetic compass when you roll into a standard rate turn to the left from a south heading in the Northern Hemisphere?

    A. The compass will indicate a turn to the left, but at a faster rate than is actually occurring.

    B. The compass will initially indicate a turn to the right.

    C. The compass will remain on south for a short time, then gradually catch up to the magnetic heading of the aircraft.

Answer (A) is correct. (FAA-H-8083-15B Chap 5)
    DISCUSSION: In turns from a southerly heading in the Northern Hemisphere, the compass leads the turn. That is, it indicates a turn in the proper direction but at a rate faster than the actual rate.
    Answer (B) is incorrect. The compass will initially indicate a turn in the opposite direction if the turn is made from a north, not south, heading. **Answer (C) is incorrect.** It describes a shallower-than-standard turn from a north, not south, heading.

8. What should be the indication on the magnetic compass as you roll into a standard rate turn to the right from a northerly heading in the Northern Hemisphere?

    A. The compass will indicate a turn to the right, but at a faster rate than is actually occurring.

    B. The compass will initially indicate a turn to the left.

    C. The compass will remain on north for a short time, then gradually catch up to the magnetic heading of the aircraft.

Answer (B) is correct. (FAA-H-8083-15B Chap 5)
    DISCUSSION: In turns from a northerly heading in the Northern Hemisphere, the compass will initially indicate a turn to the opposite direction. Then the compass heading will lag behind the actual heading until the airplane approaches an east or west heading.
    Answer (A) is incorrect. It describes a turn to the right from a southerly heading. **Answer (C) is incorrect.** It describes a shallower-than-standard turn from north.

9. What causes the northerly turning error in a magnetic compass?

    A. Coriolis force at the mid-latitudes.

    B. Centrifugal force acting on the compass card.

    C. The magnetic dip characteristic.

Answer (C) is correct. (FAA-H-8083-15B Chap 5)
    DISCUSSION: Magnetic dip causes a compass needle to point both down toward the earth and to the magnetic pole. This characteristic causes turning errors.
    Answer (A) is incorrect. The Coriolis force of the spinning Earth affects winds rather than compass indications. **Answer (B) is incorrect.** Centrifugal force is not related to compass turning errors.

10. What should be the indication on the magnetic compass as you roll into a standard rate turn to the left from a west heading in the Northern Hemisphere?

    A. The compass will initially indicate a turn to the right.

    B. The compass will remain on west for a short time, then gradually catch up to the magnetic heading of the aircraft.

    C. The compass will indicate the approximate correct magnetic heading if the roll into the turn is smooth.

Answer (C) is correct. (FAA-H-8083-15B Chap 5)
    DISCUSSION: If you roll into a smooth, coordinated, standard-rate turn to the left or right from an east or west heading, the compass will indicate the approximate correct magnetic heading. Turning errors appear on turns from north or south headings, not east or west.
    Answer (A) is incorrect. The compass will initially indicate a turn in the opposite direction of a bank only in a turn from a north heading. **Answer (B) is incorrect.** In a turn from an east heading, the compass will immediately indicate a turn if the roll into the turn is smooth.

11. What should be the indication on the magnetic compass as you roll into a standard rate turn to the left from a north heading in the Northern Hemisphere?

    A. The compass will indicate a turn to the left, but at a faster rate than is actually occurring.

    B. The compass will initially indicate a turn to the right.

    C. The compass will remain on north for a short time, then gradually catch up to the magnetic heading of the aircraft.

Answer (B) is correct. (FAA-H-8083-15B Chap 5)
    DISCUSSION: In turns from a northerly heading in the Northern Hemisphere, the compass will initially indicate a turn to the opposite direction, and the compass heading will lag behind actual until the airplane approaches an east or west heading.
    Answer (A) is incorrect. It describes a turn to the left from a southerly heading. **Answer (C) is incorrect.** It describes a shallower-than-standard turn from north.

12. When initiating a left turn in the Northern Hemisphere from a heading of 270°. The magnetic compass will

    A. lag behind the actual rate of turn.

    B. initially indicate a turn in the opposite direction.

    C. initially indicate the actual rate of turn.

Answer (C) is correct. (FAA-H-8083-15B Chap 5)
    DISCUSSION: When making a coordinated entry into a standard-rate turn left or right from a heading of west, the magnetic compass will initially indicate the actual rate of turn. There are no turning errors on turns from east or west headings.
    Answer (A) is incorrect. In turns from a northerly heading in the Northern Hemisphere, the compass will initially indicate a turn to the opposite direction. Then the compass heading will lag behind the actual heading until the airplane approaches an east or west heading. **Answer (B) is incorrect.** In turns from a northerly heading in the Northern Hemisphere, the compass will initially indicate a turn to the opposite direction. Then the compass heading will lag behind the actual heading until the airplane approaches an east or west heading.

1.2 Pitot-Static System

13. While flying at an altitude of 8,000 ft., what CAS must be used to maintain a TAS of 155 kt. if the outside air temperature is –5°C?

    A.   134 KCAS.

    B.   139 KCAS.

    C.   142 KCAS.

Answer (B) is correct. (FAA-H-8083-25B Chap 16)
    DISCUSSION: In the center of the computer side of your flight computer, on the right side, put the air temperature of –5°C over the altitude of 8,000 ft. On the outer scale, find the true airspeed (TAS) of 155 kt., which is over the calibrated airspeed (CAS) on the inner scale of 139 KCAS.
    Answer (A) is incorrect. Maintaining 134 KCAS would result in a TAS of 150 kt., not 155 kt. **Answer (C) is incorrect.** Maintaining 142 KCAS would result in a TAS of 158 kt., not 155 kt.

14. What CAS must be used to maintain the filed TAS of 158 kt. at the flight planned altitude of 8,000 ft.? (Temperature 0°C.)

    A.   140 KCAS.

    B.   147 KCAS.

    C.   153 KCAS.

Answer (A) is correct. (FAA-H-8083-25B Chap 16)
    DISCUSSION: In the center of the slide rule side of your flight computer, on the right side, put the air temperature of 0°C over the altitude of 8,000 ft. On the outer scale, find the true airspeed (TAS) of 158 kt., which is over the calibrated airspeed (CAS) on the inner scale of 140 KCAS.
    Answer (B) is incorrect. Maintaining 147 KCAS would result in a TAS of 168 kt., not 158 kt. **Answer (C) is incorrect.** Maintaining 153 KCAS would result in a TAS of 173 kt., not 158 kt.

15. What CAS must be used to maintain 180 kt. TAS at the flight planned altitude of 8,000 ft. if the outside air temperature is +8°C?

    A.   154 KCAS.

    B.   157 KCAS.

    C.   163 KCAS.

Answer (B) is correct. (FAA-H-8083-25B Chap 16)
    DISCUSSION: In the center of the slide rule side of your flight computer, on the right side, put the air temperature of +8°C over the altitude of 8,000 ft. On the outer scale, find the true airspeed (TAS) of 180 kt., which is over the calibrated airspeed (CAS) on the inner scale of 157 KCAS.
    Answer (A) is incorrect. Maintaining 154 KCAS would result in a TAS of 176 kt., not 180 kt. **Answer (C) is incorrect.** Maintaining 163 KCAS would result in a TAS of 187 kt., not 180 kt.

16. If both the ram air input and the drain hole of the pitot system are blocked, what reaction should you observe on the airspeed indicator when power is applied and a climb is initiated out of severe icing conditions?

    A.   The indicated airspeed would show a continuous deceleration while climbing.

    B.   The airspeed would drop to, and remain at, zero.

    C.   No change until an actual climb rate is established, then indicated airspeed will increase.

Answer (C) is correct. (AC 91-43)
    DISCUSSION: When the airspeed indicator pitot tube and drain hole are blocked, the airspeed indicator will react as an altimeter. There will be a constant pressure within the pitot tube, and as the pressure from the static source decreases during a climb, the indicated airspeed on the airspeed indicator will increase.
    Answer (A) is incorrect. As there is an increase in altitude, the airspeed indicator will show an increase in airspeed as the air pressure within the pitot tube is relatively greater than that of the static air. **Answer (B) is incorrect.** This reaction would occur if the ram air input, but not the drain hole, were blocked.

17. If, while in level flight, it becomes necessary to use an alternate source of static pressure vented inside the airplane, which of the following variations in instrument indications should the pilot expect?

    A.   The altimeter will read lower than normal, airspeed lower than normal, and the VSI will momentarily show a descent.

    B.   The altimeter will read higher than normal, airspeed greater than normal, and the VSI will momentarily show a climb.

    C.   The altimeter will read lower than normal, airspeed greater than normal, and the VSI will momentarily show a climb and then a descent.

Answer (B) is correct. (FAA-H-8083-15B Chap 5)
    DISCUSSION: Most aircraft equipped with a pitot-static system are provided with an alternate source of static pressure for emergency use. This source is usually vented inside the cabin. The pressure within an unpressurized flight deck is slightly lower than the pressure outside the airplane because of the Venturi effect of the air moving past the outside of the flight deck. When the alternate static source is used, the altimeter and airspeed will read higher than actual and the vertical speed indicator will momentarily show a climb.
    Answer (A) is incorrect. The altimeter and airspeed indicators will read higher, not lower, than normal, and the vertical speed indicator will momentarily show a climb, not a descent. **Answer (C) is incorrect.** The altimeter and airspeed will read higher, not lower, than normal, and the vertical speed indicator will show level flight, not a descent, after the momentary climb.

18. If the outside air temperature increases during a flight at constant power and at a constant indicated altitude, the true airspeed will

    A. decrease and true altitude will increase.

    B. increase and true altitude will decrease.

    C. increase and true altitude will increase.

Answer (C) is correct. (FAA-H-8083-15B Chap 5)
    DISCUSSION: As temperature increases, pressure levels rise farther above sea level and true altitude increases given a constant indicated altitude. As altitude increases with constant power, true airspeed increases.
    Answer (A) is incorrect. True airspeed increases, not decreases. **Answer (B) is incorrect.** True altitude increases, not decreases.

19. During flight, if the pitot tube becomes clogged with ice, which of the following instruments would be affected?

    A. The airspeed indicator only.

    B. The airspeed indicator and the altimeter.

    C. The airspeed indicator, altimeter, and Vertical Speed Indicator.

Answer (A) is correct. (FAA-H-8083-15B Chap 5)
    DISCUSSION: The pitot-static system is a source of pressure for the altimeter, vertical speed indicator, and airspeed indicator. The pitot tube is connected directly to the airspeed indicator, and the static vents are connected directly to all three. The pressure of air coming into the pitot tube (impact air pressure) is compared with the air pressure at the static system vents to determine airspeed.
    Answer (B) is incorrect. The pitot tube is connected only to the airspeed indicator, not the altimeter. **Answer (C) is incorrect.** The pitot tube is connected only to the airspeed indicator, not the altimeter or vertical speed indicator.

20. If both the ram air input and drain hole of the pitot system become blocked, the indicated airspeed will

    A. increase during a climb.

    B. decrease during a climb.

    C. remain constant regardless of altitude change.

Answer (A) is correct. (FAA-H-8083-25B Chap 8)
    DISCUSSION: If both the pitot tube input and the drain hole on the pitot system are blocked, the airspeed indication will increase during a climb. This is due to the decrease in static pressure, allowing the instrument's diaphragm to expand showing an indication of greater airspeed.
    Answer (B) is incorrect. If both the pitot tube input and the drain hole on the pitot system are blocked, the airspeed indication will increase during a climb and decrease during a descent. **Answer (C) is incorrect.** If the pitot system and static port become blocked, the indicated airspeed will remain constant.

21. If the pitot tube ram air pressure hole and drain hole become obstructed, the airspeed indicator will operate

    A. like an altimeter as the aircraft climbs and descends.

    B. like a very sluggish airspeed indicator lagging all the changes by minutes.

    C. normally due to the static port pressure changes.

Answer (A) is correct. (FAA-H-8083-15B Chap 5)
    DISCUSSION: When the pitot tube and drain hole are blocked, the airspeed indicator will react as an altimeter. There will be a constant pressure within the pitot tube and, as the pressure from the static source decreases during a climb, the indicated airspeed will increase.
    Answer (B) is incorrect. The operation of the airspeed indicator has no association with time. **Answer (C) is incorrect.** When the pitot tube and drain hole are blocked, the airspeed indicator will react as an altimeter. There will be a constant pressure within the pitot tube and, as the pressure from the static source decreases during a climb, the indicated airspeed will increase.

22. If, while in level flight, it becomes necessary to use an alternate source of static pressure vented inside the airplane, which of the following should the pilot expect?

    A. The vertical speed to momentarily show a climb.

    B. The gyroscopic instruments to become inoperative.

    C. The altimeter and airspeed indicator to become inoperative.

Answer (A) is correct. (FAA-H-8083-15B Chap 5)
    DISCUSSION: Most aircraft equipped with a pitot-static system are provided with an alternate source of static pressure for emergency use. This source is usually vented inside the cabin. The pressure within an unpressurized flight deck is slightly lower than the pressure outside the airplane because of the Venturi effect of the air moving past the outside of the flight deck. When the alternate static source is used, the altimeter and airspeed indicator will read higher than actual and the vertical speed indicator will momentarily show a climb.
    Answer (B) is incorrect. The gyroscopic instruments are not affected by changes in the pitot-static system. **Answer (C) is incorrect.** The altimeter and airspeed indicator will read higher than actual, not become inoperative.

23. What would be the indication on the VSI during entry into a 500 FPM actual descent from level flight if the static ports were iced over?

A. The indication would be in reverse of the actual rate of descent (500 FPM climb).

B. The initial indication would be a climb, then descent at a rate in excess of 500 FPM.

C. The VSI pointer would remain at zero regardless of the actual rate of descent.

Answer (C) is correct. (FAA-H-8083-15B Chap 5)
DISCUSSION: The vertical speed indicator operates from the static pressure source and indicates change in pressure. Thus, if the static pressure ports became iced over, there would be no change in the static pressure, and there would be no indication of descent or climb.
Answer (A) is incorrect. With no change in pressure, the indication would be level flight, not a climb. **Answer (B) is incorrect.** With no change in pressure, the indication would be level flight, not a climb or descent.

24. If, while in level flight, it becomes necessary to use an alternate source of static pressure vented inside the airplane, which of the following should the pilot expect?

A. The vertical speed to show a climb.

B. The vertical speed to momentarily show a descent.

C. The altimeter to read higher than normal.

Answer (C) is correct. (FAA-H-8083-15B Chap 5)
DISCUSSION: Most aircraft equipped with a pitot-static system are provided with an alternate source of static pressure for emergency use. This source is usually vented inside the cabin. The pressure within an unpressurized flight deck is slightly lower than the pressure outside the airplane because of the Venturi effect of the air moving past the outside of the flight deck. When the alternate static source is used, the altimeter and airspeed indicator will read higher than actual, and the vertical speed indicator will momentarily show a climb.
Answer (A) is incorrect. The VSI will show only a momentary, not a steady-state, climb. **Answer (B) is incorrect.** The VSI indication will be a momentary climb, not a descent.

25. You check the flight instruments while taxiing and find the vertical speed indicator (VSI) indicates a descent of 100 feet per minute. In this case, you

A. may not proceed under IFR until the instrument is corrected by an authorized instrument repairman.

B. may take off under IFR and use 100 feet descent as the zero indication.

C. may take off and proceed under IFR but only in VFR weather conditions.

Answer (B) is correct. (FAA-H-8083-15B Chap 5)
DISCUSSION: The needle of the VSI should indicate zero when the aircraft is on the ground or is maintaining a constant pressure level in flight. If it does not indicate zero, you must allow for the error when interpreting the indications in flight. Since the VSI is not a required instrument, you may fly when it is out of adjustment.
Answer (A) is incorrect. The VSI can be used by making allowances in flight. **Answer (C) is incorrect.** The VSI is not a required instrument for IFR operations. You may proceed under IFR even if the VSI is out of adjustment, but you should allow for the adjustment of the error while in flight.

26. During a constant-rate climb in IMC above the freezing level, you notice that both the airspeed and altitude are increasing. This indicates the

A. aircraft is in an unusual attitude.

B. gyroscopic instruments have failed.

C. pitot static system has malfunctioned.

Answer (C) is correct. (FAA-H-8083-25B Chap 8)
DISCUSSION: If the pitot tube and its drain hole are blocked, then as the aircraft climbs, the trapped air in the pitot system will be compared against decreasing air pressure in the static system. The airspeed indication will rise, but it will not be accurate. If the aircraft descends, the airspeed indication will decrease. When this happens, the airspeed indicator behaves like an altimeter.
Answer (A) is incorrect. If the aircraft were in an unusual attitude, the altimeter and airspeed would not be simultaneously increasing. **Answer (B) is incorrect.** The gyroscopic instruments are not interconnected with the pitot and static instruments.

27. If you need to use an alternate static source during level flight, you can expect to see

A. a higher indication on the altimeter.

B. a momentary descent on the VSI.

C. a lower indicated airspeed.

Answer (A) is correct. (FAA-H-8083-15B Chap 5)
DISCUSSION: The pressure within an unpressurized flight deck is slightly lower than the pressure outside the airplane. This is where the alternate static source is vented to; when it is used, the altimeter and airspeed will read higher than actual and the vertical speed indicator will momentarily show a climb.
Answer (B) is incorrect. Since the alternate static source is vented within the airplane cabin, the VSI will momentarily show a climb as the static source that it senses against is changed. **Answer (C) is incorrect.** Since the alternate static source is vented within the airplane cabin, the ASI will read a higher than actual indicated airspeed as the static source that it senses against is changed.

1.3 Altimeter

28. Pressure altitude is the altitude read on your altimeter when the instrument is adjusted to indicate height above

   A. sea level.

   B. the standard datum plane.

   C. ground level.

Answer (B) is correct. (FAA-H-8083-15B Chap 5)
   DISCUSSION: Pressure altitude is the altitude read on your altimeter when the instrument is adjusted to indicate height above the standard datum plane, i.e., an altimeter setting of 29.92" Hg. The standard datum plane is a theoretical level where the weight of the atmosphere is 29.92" Hg.
   Answer (A) is incorrect. Indicated altitude, not pressure altitude, is the altitude read on your altimeter (when set to the correct altimeter setting) to indicate the approximate height above mean sea level. **Answer (C) is incorrect.** The height above ground (absolute altitude) may be indicated directly on a radar altimeter, not by adjusting a pressure altimeter to 29.92" Hg.

29. If you are departing from an airport where you cannot obtain an altimeter setting, you should set your altimeter

   A. on 29.92 inches Hg.

   B. on the current airport barometric pressure, if known.

   C. to the airport elevation.

Answer (C) is correct. (FAA-H-8083-15B Chap 5)
   DISCUSSION: If you cannot obtain an altimeter setting at an airport, adjust your altimeter so it reads the current airport elevation.
   Answer (A) is incorrect. Setting the altimeter to 29.92 in. Hg would provide only pressure altitude. **Answer (B) is incorrect.** The altimeter setting is the current barometric pressure adjusted to sea level.

30. How should you preflight check the altimeter prior to an IFR flight?

   A. Set the altimeter to 29.92" Hg. With current temperature and the altimeter indication, determine the true altitude to compare with the field elevation.

   B. Set the altimeter first with 29.92" Hg and then the current altimeter setting. The change in altitude should correspond to the change in setting.

   C. Set the altimeter to the current altimeter setting. The indication should be within 75 feet of the actual elevation for acceptable accuracy.

Answer (C) is correct. (FAA-H-8083-15B Chap 5)
   DISCUSSION: Set the altimeter to the local altimeter setting before taking off, and verify that the indication is within 75 ft. of the actual elevation. If the difference is greater than 75 ft., you should consult an instrument repair shop.
   Answer (A) is incorrect. Setting the altimeter to 29.92 in. Hg and adjusting for temperature gives density altitude, not true altitude. **Answer (B) is incorrect.** Only indicated altitude, not change in altitude, is checked.

31. How should you preflight check the altimeter prior to an IFR flight?

   A. Set the altimeter to the current temperature. With current temperature and the altimeter indication, determine the calibrated altitude to compare with the field elevation.

   B. Set the altimeter first with 29.92" Hg and then the current altimeter setting. The change in altitude should correspond to the change in setting.

   C. Set the altimeter to the current altimeter setting. The indication should be within 75 feet of the actual elevation for acceptable accuracy.

Answer (C) is correct. (FAA-H-8083-15B Chap 5)
   DISCUSSION: Set the altimeter to the local altimeter setting before taking off, and verify that the indication is within 75 ft. of the actual elevation. If the difference is greater than 75 ft., you should consult an instrument repair shop.
   Answer (A) is incorrect. An altimeter can be adjusted for nonstandard pressure, not temperature. **Answer (B) is incorrect.** Only indicated altitude, not change in altitude, is checked.

32. The local altimeter setting should be used by all pilots in a particular area, primarily to provide for

A. the cancellation of altimeter error due to nonstandard temperatures aloft.

B. better vertical separation of aircraft.

C. more accurate terrain clearance in mountainous areas.

Answer (B) is correct. (FAA-H-8083-15B Chap 5)
   DISCUSSION: Because the altimeter in each airplane is equally affected by temperature and pressure variation errors, use of the local altimeter setting in a given area provides for better vertical separation of aircraft.
   Answer (A) is incorrect. The altimeter setting does not compensate for nonstandard temperatures aloft. Rather, all altimeters in the area will reflect the same uncompensated amount. **Answer (C) is incorrect.** Temperatures aloft must also be considered to ensure terrain clearance.

33. Which altitude is indicated when the altimeter is set to 29.92" Hg?

A. Density.

B. Pressure.

C. Standard.

Answer (B) is correct. (FAA-H-8083-25B Chap 8)
   DISCUSSION: Pressure altitude is indicated when the altimeter is set to 29.92 in. Hg.
   Answer (A) is incorrect. Density altitude is pressure altitude corrected for nonstandard temperature. **Answer (C) is incorrect.** Standard altitude is a nonsense concept in this context.

34. Altimeter setting is the value to which the scale of the pressure altimeter is set so the altimeter indicates

A. pressure altitude at sea level.

B. true altitude at field elevation.

C. pressure altitude at field elevation.

Answer (B) is correct. (FAA-H-8083-25B Chap 8)
   DISCUSSION: The altimeter setting is the value that permits the altimeter to indicate the true altitude at field elevation. Within the vicinity of a particular airport, the altimeter setting provides an accurate means of separating traffic vertically and also provides obstruction clearance. Note that the use of the word "true" here is not completely accurate because the altimeter setting does not correct for nonstandard temperature.
   Answer (A) is incorrect. The altimeter setting causes the altimeter to indicate true altitude, not pressure altitude, at field elevation, not sea level. **Answer (C) is incorrect.** The altimeter setting causes the altimeter to indicate true altitude, not pressure altitude.

35. While you are flying at FL 250, you hear ATC give an altimeter setting of 28.92" Hg in your area. At what pressure altitude are you flying?

A. 24,000 feet.

B. 25,000 feet.

C. 26,000 feet.

Answer (B) is correct. (FAA-H-8083-15B Chap 5)
   DISCUSSION: The pressure altitude is 25,000 ft. in your area because at FL 250 your altimeter should be set at 29.92 in. Hg. A flight level (FL) by definition means a pressure altitude.
   Answer (A) is incorrect. FL 250 by definition means a pressure altitude of 25,000 ft., not 24,000 ft. **Answer (C) is incorrect.** FL 250 by definition means a pressure altitude of 25,000 ft., not 26,000 ft.

36. The pressure altitude at a given location is indicated on the altimeter after the altimeter is set to

A. the field elevation.

B. 29.92" Hg.

C. the current altimeter setting.

Answer (B) is correct. (FAA-H-8083-25B Chap 8)
   DISCUSSION: Pressure altitude, by definition, is indicated altitude when the altimeter setting is 29.92 in. Hg. This is true regardless of area or true altitude.
   Answer (A) is incorrect. You set the altimeter to a barometric pressure, not an elevation. **Answer (C) is incorrect.** The altitude indicated on the altimeter after it is set to the current altimeter setting is the indicated altitude, not pressure altitude.

37. Under which condition will pressure altitude be equal to true altitude?

A. When the atmospheric pressure is 29.92" Hg.

B. When standard atmospheric conditions exist.

C. When indicated altitude is equal to the pressure altitude.

Answer (B) is correct. (FAA-H-8083-15B Chap 5)
   DISCUSSION: Pressure altitude will equal true altitude when standard atmospheric conditions exist at the current altitude, i.e, 29.92" Hg and 15°C at sea level.
   Answer (A) is incorrect. To get true altitude from an altimeter, both temperature and pressure must be standard. **Answer (C) is incorrect.** Nonstandard temperatures will make indicated altitude deviate from true altitude.

38. How can you determine the pressure altitude on an airport without a tower or FSS?

A. Set the altimeter to 29.92" Hg and read the altitude indicated.

B. Set the altimeter to the current altimeter setting of a station within 100 miles and correct this indicated altitude with local temperature.

C. Use your computer and correct the field elevation for temperature.

Answer (A) is correct. (FAA-H-8083-25B Chap 8)
DISCUSSION: The pressure altitude is determined by setting your altimeter to 29.92" Hg and reading the altitude indicated. No matter what altitude or location, the altimeter reads pressure altitude when the barometric window is set to 29.92" Hg.
Answer (B) is incorrect. It describes true altitude.
Answer (C) is incorrect. Correcting field elevation for temperature is a nonsense concept.

39. How can you obtain the pressure altitude on flights below 18,000 feet?

A. Set your altimeter to 29.92" Hg and read the pressure altitude on the instrument face.

B. Set your altimeter to the field elevation and read the pressure altitude from the Kollsman window.

C. Contact an ATC facility FSS and request the current pressure altitude for the area.

Answer (A) is correct. (FAA-H-8083-25B Chap 8)
DISCUSSION: Pressure altitude can be determined anywhere by setting the altimeter to 29.92 in. Hg.
Answer (B) is incorrect. It is much easier to just change the altimeter to 29.92 in. Hg. Answer (C) is incorrect. Pressure altitude is determined by setting your altimeter to 29.92 in. Hg, not by contacting an FSS.

40. At an altitude of 6,500 feet MSL, the current altimeter setting is 30.42" Hg. The pressure altitude would be approximately

A. 7,500 feet.

B. 6,000 feet.

C. 6,500 feet.

Answer (B) is correct. (FAA-H-8083-15B Chap 5)
DISCUSSION: Rotating the altimeter's setting knob to a higher (or lower) barometric setting moves the hands to higher (or lower) indicated altitude at the rate of 1" Hg to 1,000 ft. of altitude. Given the current altimeter setting of 30.42" Hg and the indicated altitude of 6,500 ft., resetting the window to 29.92" Hg would lower indicated altitude by 500 ft. (30.42 − 29.92 = 0.5" Hg = 500 ft.). The new indicated altitude would be 6,000 ft. MSL, which would be pressure altitude.
Answer (A) is incorrect. A pressure change of 0.5" Hg results in an altitude change of 500 ft., not 1,000 ft. Answer (C) is incorrect. Pressure altitude is equal to actual altitude only when the current altimeter setting is 29.92" Hg.

41. How does a pilot normally obtain the current altimeter setting during an IFR flight in Class E airspace below 18,000 feet?

A. The pilot should contact ARTCC at least every 100 NM and request the altimeter setting.

B. FSS's along the route broadcast the weather information at 15 minutes past the hour.

C. ATC periodically advises the pilot of the proper altimeter setting.

Answer (C) is correct. (FAA-H-8083-15B Chap 5)
DISCUSSION: During IFR flight in Class E airspace below 18,000 ft. MSL, ATC periodically provides altimeter settings. Thus, you will continually hear the altimeter settings given to other pilots as you monitor ATC.
Answer (A) is incorrect. ATC provides the altimeter setting without being asked. Answer (B) is incorrect. FSSs do not broadcast the altimeter setting at 15 min. past the hour.

42. Which of the following defines the type of altitude used when maintaining FL 210?

A. Indicated.

B. Pressure.

C. Calibrated.

Answer (B) is correct. (FAA-H-8083-15B Chap 5)
DISCUSSION: Above 18,000 ft. MSL (FL 180), pressure altitude is used to separate traffic. Pressure altitude is the altitude indicated on an altimeter when it is set to 29.92 in. Hg.
Answer (A) is incorrect. Indicated altitude is the altitude shown on the altimeter after it is set to the current altimeter setting. Pressure altitude, not indicated altitude, is used at or above 18,000 ft. MSL. Answer (C) is incorrect. All altimeters are calibrated.

43. What is the procedure for setting the altimeter when assigned an IFR altitude of 18,000 feet or higher on a direct flight off airways?

A. Set the altimeter to 29.92" Hg before takeoff.

B. Set the altimeter to the current altimeter setting until reaching the assigned altitude, then set to 29.92" Hg.

C. Set the altimeter to the current reported setting for climb-out and 29.92" Hg upon reaching 18,000 feet.

Answer (C) is correct. (14 CFR 91.121)
    DISCUSSION: During climb-out below FL 180, it is important to adjust the altimeter to the nearest station pressure as provided by ATC for climb-out, and then 29.92" Hg upon reaching 18,000 feet.
    Answer (A) is incorrect. Indicated altitude (using local altimeter settings) should be used up to FL 180. **Answer (B) is incorrect.** This answer can be tricky and requires close attention to the details. You should set the altimeter to 29.92" Hg upon reaching FL 180, not upon reaching your assigned altitude. The question asks about "18,000 feet or higher." If the assigned altitude is higher than 18,000 feet, you would set 29.92" Hg when reaching 18,000 feet during your climb; not set the current reported setting for climb-out and then set 29.92" Hg when you reach your assigned altitude above 18,000 feet.

44. En route at FL 290, your altimeter is set correctly, but you fail to reset it to the local altimeter setting of 30.26 in. Hg during descent. If the field elevation is 134 feet and your altimeter is functioning properly, what will it indicate after landing?

A. 100 feet MSL.

B. 474 feet MSL.

C. 206 feet below MSL.

Answer (C) is correct. (FAA-H-8083-15B Chap 5)
    DISCUSSION: One inch of pressure equals approximately 1,000 ft. of altitude. If an altimeter should be set to 30.26 in. Hg but is set to 29.92 in. Hg, it is set 0.34 in. Hg too low and thus will indicate 340 ft. (1,000 ft. × 0.34 in.) less than actual altitude. Thus, if the airplane lands at an airport with a field elevation of 134 ft., the altimeter will indicate 206 ft. below sea level (134 ft. airport elevation − 340 ft. altimeter setting error).
    Answer (A) is incorrect. The amount of 100 ft. is obtained by subtracting 34 ft. rather than subtracting 340 ft. **Answer (B) is incorrect.** The amount of 474 ft. is obtained by adding 340 ft. rather than subtracting 340 ft.

45. En route at FL 290, the altimeter is set correctly, but not reset to the local altimeter setting of 30.57" Hg during descent. If the field elevation is 650 feet and the altimeter is functioning properly, what is the approximate indication upon landing?

A. 715 feet.

B. 1,300 feet.

C. Sea level.

Answer (C) is correct. (FAA-H-8083-15B Chap 5)
    DISCUSSION: One inch of pressure equals approximately 1,000 ft. of altitude. If an altimeter should be set to 30.57" Hg but is set to 29.92" Hg, it is set 0.65" Hg too low and thus will indicate 650 ft. (1,000 ft. × 0.65 in.) less than actual altitude. Thus, if the airplane lands at an airport with a field elevation of 650 ft., the altimeter will indicate sea level, i.e., 650 ft. elevation minus the 650 ft. altimeter setting error.
    Answer (A) is incorrect. This figure is obtained by adding 65 ft. rather than subtracting 650 ft. **Answer (B) is incorrect.** This figure is obtained by adding 650 ft. rather than subtracting 650 ft.

46. Under what condition is pressure altitude and density altitude the same value?

A. At standard temperature.

B. When the altimeter setting is 29.92" Hg.

C. When indicated, and pressure altitudes are the same value on the altimeter.

Answer (A) is correct. (FAA-H-8083-15B Chap 5)
    DISCUSSION: Density altitude, by definition, is pressure altitude adjusted for nonstandard temperature. Accordingly, pressure altitude will equal density altitude at standard temperature.
    Answer (B) is incorrect. Pressure altitude has not been adjusted for nonstandard temperature. **Answer (C) is incorrect.** Neither indicated nor pressure altitude is adjusted for nonstandard temperature.

47. Under what condition will true altitude be lower than indicated altitude with an altimeter setting of 29.92" Hg?

A. In warmer than standard air temperature.

B. In colder than standard air temperature.

C. When density altitude is higher than indicated altitude.

Answer (B) is correct. (FAA-H-8083-15B Chap 5)
    DISCUSSION: When temperature lowers en route, you are lower than your altimeter indicates. Similarly, when you are in colder-than-standard air temperatures, true altitude is lower than pressure altitude.
    Answer (A) is incorrect. When you are in warmer-than-standard air, the true altitude is above pressure altitude. **Answer (C) is incorrect.** Assuming an altimeter setting of 29.92" Hg, if density altitude is higher than indicated altitude, the air is thinner and thus warmer. When you are in warmer-than-standard air, the true altitude is above indicated altitude.

48. Which condition would cause the altimeter to indicate a lower altitude than actually flown (true altitude)?

A. Air temperature lower than standard.

B. Atmospheric pressure lower than standard.

C. Air temperature warmer than standard.

Answer (C) is correct. (FAA-H-8083-15B Chap 5)
DISCUSSION: When temperatures are warmer than standard, the pressure levels are raised. That is, the altimeter will indicate an altitude lower than that at which the aircraft is actually flying.
Answer (A) is incorrect. In colder-than-standard air, pressure levels drop. Thus, the altimeter reads higher, not lower, than true altitude. **Answer (B) is incorrect.** Using the correct altimeter setting adjusts for nonstandard pressure.

49. When an altimeter is changed from 30.11" Hg to 29.96" Hg, in which direction will the indicated altitude change and by what value?

A. Altimeter will indicate 15 feet lower.

B. Altimeter will indicate 150 feet lower.

C. Altimeter will indicate 150 feet higher.

Answer (B) is correct. (FAA-H-8083-15B Chap 5)
DISCUSSION: Altimeter settings vary approximately 1" Hg for each 1,000 ft. of altitude. When the altimeter setting is changed from 30.11" Hg to 29.96" Hg, it is lower by 0.15" Hg. Thus, the altimeter will indicate 150 ft. lower (1,000 ft. × 0.15). Remember that the indicated altitude and altimeter setting vary directly; i.e., when the altimeter setting is adjusted up, indicated altitude increases and vice versa.
Answer (A) is incorrect. A measure of 0.15" Hg is equal to 150 ft., not 15 ft. **Answer (C) is incorrect.** When the altimeter setting is lowered, indicated altitude decreases, not increases.

50. Below 18,000 feet pressure altitude may be obtained by

A. requesting the current pressure altitude for the area.

B. setting the altimeter to the local altimeter setting.

C. setting the altimeter to 29.92 inches Hg.

Answer (C) is correct. (FAA-H-8083-25B Chap 5)
DISCUSSION: Pressure altitude can be determined anywhere by setting the altimeter to 29.92 in. Hg.
Answer (A) is incorrect. Pressure altitude is determined by setting the altimeter to 29.92 in. Hg, not by contacting an FSS. **Answer (B) is incorrect.** Changing the altimeter to 29.92 in. Hg is much easier.

51. If you are not able to obtain the current altimeter setting prior to takeoff, you should set this instrument to

A. field elevation.

B. 29.92 inches Hg.

C. pressure altitude.

Answer (A) is correct. (FAA-H-8083-25B Chap 5)
DISCUSSION: In the absence of the current altimeter setting as per 14 CFR 91.121, the instrument shall be set to the field elevation of the departure airport or an appropriate altimeter setting available before departure.
Answer (B) is incorrect. The instrument will be set to 29.92 in. Hg when maintaining the cruising altitude or flight level at or above 18,000 ft. MSL. **Answer (C) is incorrect.** Prior to takeoff, it is vital to approximate altitude to the local field elevation if you are unable to obtain the current altimeter setting.

52. You are preflighting for an IFR flight and set in the current altimeter setting, it should be not more than

A. ±150 feet from your referenced level.

B. ±100 feet from your referenced level.

C. ±75 feet from your referenced level.

Answer (C) is correct. (FAA-H-8083-6 Chap 5)
DISCUSSION: The maximum tolerance for an altimeter in IFR flight will be ±75 ft. from the surveyed field elevation. If it exceeds that tolerance, the instrument may not be used for flight under IFR and should be referred to a certificated instrument repair station for recalibration.
Answer (A) is incorrect. The difference from the known field elevation and the altitude read from the altimeter should be no more than ±75 ft. for flight under IFR. **Answer (B) is incorrect.** The maximum tolerance between the known field elevation and the altitude read from the altimeter in order for the instrument to be used for IFR is ±75 ft.

1.4 Gyroscopes

53. Which practical test should be made on the electric gyro instruments prior to starting an engine?

- A. Check that the electrical connections are secure on the back of the instruments.
- B. Check that the attitude of the miniature aircraft is wings level before turning on electrical power.
- C. Turn on the electrical power and listen for any unusual or irregular mechanical noise.

Answer (C) is correct. (FAA-H-8083-15B Chap 5)
   DISCUSSION: Electric gyro instruments can be checked for irregular noises by listening to them after the battery is turned on but before the engine is started. You should notice any bearing clatters, clicks, or other unusual noises. Additionally, you can look at the instruments to see if they are in their expected positions. There are additional tests to pursue after the engine is started.
   Answer (A) is incorrect. Pilots should not be handling or touching electrical connections behind the instrument panel. **Answer (B) is incorrect.** Due to the construction of the turn coordinator, the miniature aircraft will be wings level before turning on the electrical power. Thus, this indication would not be a practical test for the electric gyro.

54. One characteristic that a properly functioning gyro depends upon for operation is the

- A. ability to resist precession 90° to any applied force.
- B. resistance to deflection of the spinning wheel or disc.
- C. deflecting force developed from the angular velocity of the spinning wheel.

Answer (B) is correct. (FAA-H-8083-15B Chap 5)
   DISCUSSION: Newton's second law of motion states that the deflection of a moving body is proportional to the deflective force applied and is inversely proportional to its mass and speed. For a gyro, the resistance to deflection is proportional to the deflective force. This property is used by the attitude indicator.
   Answer (A) is incorrect. Precession is the name for the reaction to deflection. The gyro uses precession rather than resisting it. **Answer (C) is incorrect.** The deflective force is applied to, not developed by, the gyro.

1.5 Heading Indicator

55. What pre-takeoff check should be made of a vacuum-driven heading indicator in preparation for an IFR flight?

- A. After 5 minutes, set the indicator to the magnetic heading of the aircraft and check for proper alignment after taxi turns.
- B. After 5 minutes, check that the heading indicator card aligns itself with the magnetic heading of the aircraft.
- C. Determine that the heading indicator does not precess more than 2° in 5 minutes of ground operation.

Answer (A) is correct. (FAA-H-8083-15B Chap 5)
   DISCUSSION: Vacuum-driven gyros take several minutes to get up to speed. After about 5 min., set the heading indicator to the correct magnetic heading. After taxiing to the runup area, verify that the heading indicator still indicates the correct magnetic heading.
   Answer (B) is incorrect. Non-slaved heading indicators must be manually set to the correct magnetic heading. **Answer (C) is incorrect.** A precession error of no more than 3° in 15 min., not 2° in 5 min., is acceptable for normal operations.

1.6 Attitude Indicator

56. What pre-takeoff check should be made of the attitude indicator in preparation for an IFR flight?

A. The horizon bar does not vibrate during warmup.

B. The miniature airplane should erect and become stable within 5 minutes.

C. The horizon bar should erect and become stable within 5 minutes.

Answer (C) is correct. (FAA-H-8083-15B Chap 5)
   DISCUSSION: The pre-takeoff check for attitude indicators is that, within the 5-min. warmup, the horizon bar should erect to the horizontal position and remain at the correct position. It should remain stable during straight taxiing and taxi turns.
   Answer (A) is incorrect. The horizon bar usually vibrates during warmup as the gyro gets up to speed. **Answer (B) is incorrect.** The miniature airplane can be adjusted manually but otherwise remains stationary. It is the horizon bar that moves within the instrument face.

57. Which condition during taxi is an indication that an attitude indicator is unreliable?

A. The horizon bar tilts more than 5° while making taxi turns.

B. The horizon bar vibrates during warmup.

C. The horizon bar does not align itself with the miniature airplane after warmup.

Answer (A) is correct. (FAA-H-8083-15B Chap 5)
   DISCUSSION: The horizon bar in an attitude indicator should not tilt more than 5° during a taxi turn. If it does, it is unreliable and should not be used for IFR flight.
   Answer (B) is incorrect. The horizon bar will vibrate as the gyros get up to speed during warmup. **Answer (C) is incorrect.** The horizon bar aligns itself with the center of the dial, indicating level flight. Then the miniature airplane must be adjusted to align with the horizon bar from the pilot's perspective.

58. During coordinated turns, which force moves the pendulous vanes of a vacuum-driven attitude indicator resulting in precession of the gyro toward the inside of the turn?

A. Acceleration.

B. Deceleration.

C. Centrifugal.

Answer (C) is correct. (FAA-H-8083-15B Chap 5)
   DISCUSSION: The attitude indicator normally erects itself by discharging air equally through four exhaust ports, each of which is partially covered by a pendulous vane. During coordinated (and skidding) turns, centrifugal force moves the vanes from their vertical position, precessing the gyro toward the inside of the turn.
   Answer (A) is incorrect. Acceleration is a force that induces climb/descent errors in the attitude indicator. **Answer (B) is incorrect.** Deceleration is a force that induces climb/descent errors in the attitude indicator.

59. If a 180° steep turn is made to the right and the aircraft is rolled out to straight-and-level flight by visual references, the attitude indicator

A. should immediately show straight-and-level flight.

B. may show a slight climb and turn.

C. show a slight skid and climb to the right.

Answer (B) is correct. (FAA-H-8083-15B Chap 5)
   DISCUSSION: In 180° coordinated steep turns, when the airplane is rolled out to straight-and-level flight, the attitude indicator will indicate a turn to the opposite direction along with a slight climb.
   Answer (A) is incorrect. When the airplane is rolled out of a coordinated 180° steep turn to straight-and-level flight, the attitude indicator will indicate a turn to the opposite direction with a slight climb; it will not immediately show straight-and-level flight. **Answer (C) is incorrect.** Evidence of a skid error cannot be read from the attitude indicator, and the turn error would be to the left, not to the right.

60. During normal coordinated turns, what error due to precession should you observe when rolling out to straight-and-level flight from a 180° steep turn to the right?

A. A straight-and-level coordinated flight indication.

B. The miniature aircraft would show a slight turn indication to the left.

C. The miniature aircraft would show a slight descent and wings-level attitude.

Answer (B) is correct. (FAA-H-8083-15B Chap 5)
   DISCUSSION: In 180° coordinated steep turns, when the airplane is rolled out to straight-and-level flight, the attitude indicator will indicate a turn to the opposite direction along with a slight climb. Thus, the indicated turn would be to the left if the steep turn were made to the right.
   Answer (A) is incorrect. The attitude indicator will show a slight climb to the left, not straight-and-level flight, and it does not indicate coordinated flight. **Answer (C) is incorrect.** It will indicate a slight climb, not a descent, and it will indicate a turning error.

61. During normal operation of a vacuum-driven attitude indicator, what attitude indication should you see when rolling out from a 180° skidding turn to straight-and-level coordinated flight?

- A. A straight-and-level coordinated flight indication.
- B. A nose-high indication relative to level flight.
- C. The miniature aircraft shows a turn in the direction opposite the skid.

Answer (C) is correct. (FAA-H-8083-15B Chap 5)
DISCUSSION: Similarly to coordinated turns, the attitude indicator will show a bank in the opposite direction when the aircraft is rolled out of a skidding turn. However, there will be no nose-up indication.
Answer (A) is incorrect. The attitude indicator will show a slight turn in the opposite direction, not straight-and-level flight, and it does not indicate coordinated flight. **Answer (B) is incorrect.** A nose-high indication will result only when the aircraft is rolling out of a coordinated turn.

62. Errors in both pitch and bank indication on an attitude indicator are usually at a maximum as the aircraft rolls out of a

- A. 180° turn.
- B. 270° turn.
- C. 360° turn.

Answer (A) is correct. (FAA-H-8083-15B Chap 5)
DISCUSSION: Errors for both pitch and bank indication on an attitude indicator are greatest when rolling out of a 180° turn. This precession error, normally between 3° and 5°, is self-correcting by the part of the attitude indicator called the erecting mechanism.
Answer (B) is incorrect. Pitch and bank errors are usually the greatest after 180°, not 270°, of turn. **Answer (C) is incorrect.** Pitch and bank errors are usually the greatest after 180°, not 360°, of turn.

63. When an aircraft is decelerated, some attitude indicators will precess and incorrectly indicate a

- A. left turn.
- B. climb.
- C. descent.

Answer (C) is correct. (FAA-H-8083-15B Chap 5)
DISCUSSION: Deceleration affects some attitude indicators through precession to incorrectly indicate a descent.
Answer (A) is incorrect. Acceleration and deceleration result in erroneous pitch readings, not turning errors.
Answer (B) is incorrect. Acceleration, not deceleration, may result in precession-related errors indicating a climb.

64. When an aircraft is accelerated, some attitude indicators will precess and incorrectly indicate a

- A. climb.
- B. descent.
- C. right turn.

Answer (A) is correct. (FAA-H-8083-15B Chap 5)
DISCUSSION: Acceleration affects some attitude indicators through precession to incorrectly indicate a climb.
Answer (B) is incorrect. Deceleration, not acceleration, may result in precession-related errors indicating a descent. **Answer (C) is incorrect.** Acceleration and deceleration result in erroneous pitch readings, not turning errors.

65. During normal flight with a vacuum driven attitude indicator, control pressures normally should not move the horizon bar more than

- A. One bar width, with not more than an additional one bar width for normal flight deviations.
- B. One-half bar width, with not more than an additional one bar width for normal flight deviations.
- C. One-half bar width, with not more than an additional one-half bar width for normal flight deviations.

Answer (C) is correct. (FAA-H-8083-15B Chap 4)
DISCUSSION: When using the attitude indicator for pitch attitude corrections, control pressures should be extremely light. Movements of the horizon bar above or below the miniature aircraft should not exceed one-half bar width. Additional inputs should not result in more than a one-half bar width correction.
Answer (A) is incorrect. The FAA recommends no more than a one-half bar width (not one bar width) indication when making pitch changes using the attitude indicator. **Answer (B) is incorrect.** The FAA recommends no more than a one-half bar width (not one bar width) indication when making pitch changes, either initially or as a follow up to the initial input.

1.7 Turn-and-Slip Indicator

66. Prior to starting an engine, you should check the turn-and-slip indicator to determine if the

    A. needle indication properly corresponds to the angle of the wings or rotors with the horizon.

    B. needle is approximately centered and the tube is full of fluid.

    C. ball will move freely from one end of the tube to the other when the aircraft is rocked.

Answer (B) is correct. (FAA-H-8083-15B Chap 5)
    DISCUSSION: Prior to starting an engine, you should determine that the needle of the turn-and-slip indicator is approximately centered and that the tube is full of fluid with the ball also approximately centered if the airplane is on a level surface.
    Answer (A) is incorrect. The needle corresponds to rate and direction of turn, not wing or rotor angle. **Answer (C) is incorrect.** Rocking the aircraft is not necessary. Freedom of movement of the ball is checked during taxi.

67. What indications should you observe on the turn-and-slip indicator during taxi?

    A. The ball moves freely opposite the turn, and the needle deflects in the direction of the turn.

    B. The needle deflects in the direction of the turn, but the ball remains centered.

    C. The ball deflects opposite the turn, but the needle remains centered.

Answer (A) is correct. (FAA-H-8083-15B Chap 5)
    DISCUSSION: During taxi, the turn-and-slip indicator ball should move freely opposite the direction of any turn since centrifugal force forces the ball to the outside. Also, the rate of turn indicator should indicate a turn in the proper direction.
    Answer (B) is incorrect. The ball will deflect opposite to the direction of the turn. **Answer (C) is incorrect.** The needle deflects in the direction of the turn.

1.8 Turn Coordinator (TC)

68. What indication should be observed on a turn coordinator during a right turn while taxiing?

    A. The miniature aircraft will show a turn to the left and the ball remains centered.

    B. The miniature aircraft will show a turn to the right and the ball moves to the left.

    C. Both the miniature aircraft and the ball will remain centered.

Answer (B) is correct. (FAA-H-8083-15B Chap 5)
    DISCUSSION: On a taxiing turn to the right, the turn coordinator shows a turn to the right, and the ball moves to the left. The centrifugal force of the turn, which is not offset by bank when taxiing, forces the ball opposite to the turn.
    Answer (A) is incorrect. The ball moves to the outside of the turn due to centrifugal force. **Answer (C) is incorrect.** The miniature aircraft reacts to yaw and shows a turn to the right, and the ball reacts to centrifugal force by moving left.

69. What indications are displayed by the miniature aircraft of a turn coordinator?

    A. Rate of roll and rate of turn.

    B. Direct indication of bank angle and pitch attitude.

    C. Indirect indication of bank angle and pitch attitude.

Answer (A) is correct. (FAA-H-8083-15B Chap 5)
    DISCUSSION: The turn coordinator indicates rate of roll and rate of turn. When the bank is constant, the rate of turn is indicated. When the bank is changing, the rate of roll is also indicated.
    Answer (B) is incorrect. The turn coordinator only indirectly indicates bank angle and has no relationship to pitch attitude. **Answer (C) is incorrect.** The turn coordinator has no relationship to pitch attitude.

70. What does the miniature aircraft of the turn coordinator directly display?

    A. Rate of roll and rate of turn.

    B. Angle of bank and rate of turn.

    C. Angle of bank.

Answer (A) is correct. (FAA-H-8083-15B Chap 5)
    DISCUSSION: The turn coordinator indicates rate of roll and rate of turn. When the bank is constant, the rate of turn is indicated. When the bank is changing, the rate of roll is also indicated.
    Answer (B) is incorrect. The angle of bank is not directly indicated by the turn coordinator. **Answer (C) is incorrect.** The angle of bank is not directly indicated by the turn coordinator.

71. To maintain a standard rate turn as the airspeed increases, the bank angle of the aircraft will need to

    A. remain constant.

    B. increase.

    C. decrease.

Answer (B) is correct. (FAA-H-8083-15B)
    DISCUSSION: A standard rate turn, although always 3° per sec., requires higher angles of bank as airspeed increases.
    Answer (A) is incorrect. A standard rate turn, although always 3° per sec., requires higher angles of bank as airspeed increases. **Answer (C) is incorrect.** To maintain a standard rate turn as the airspeed increases, the bank angle of the aircraft will need to increase, not decrease.

72. What indication is presented by the miniature aircraft of the turn coordinator?

A. Indirect indication of the bank attitude.

B. Direct indication of the bank attitude and the quality of the turn.

C. Quality of the turn.

Answer (A) is correct. (FAA-H-8083-15B Chap 5)
DISCUSSION: The miniature aircraft of the turn coordinator indicates the rate of roll when bank is changing. When the rotation around the longitudinal axis is zero, the instrument indicates the rate of turn. Thus, it provides only an indirect indication of the angle of bank.
Answer (B) is incorrect. The turn coordinator does not provide a direct indication of bank. **Answer (C) is incorrect.** The ball in the turn coordinator, not the miniature aircraft, provides information on the quality of the turn.

73. The displacement of a turn coordinator during a coordinated turn will

A. indicate the angle of bank.

B. remain constant for a given bank regardless of airspeed.

C. increase as angle of bank increases.

Answer (C) is correct. (FAA-H-8083-15B Chap 5)
DISCUSSION: The displacement of a turn coordinator increases as angle of bank (in coordinated flight) increases because the turn coordinator shows rate of turn, which increases as angle of bank increases.
Answer (A) is incorrect. The angle of bank is only indirectly indicated. **Answer (B) is incorrect.** When the rate of roll is zero, the turn coordinator provides information concerning the rate of turn, which in turn changes as airspeed changes given a constant bank.

74. What indication should be observed on a turn coordinator during a left turn while taxiing?

A. The miniature aircraft will show a turn to the left and the ball remains centered.

B. The miniature aircraft will show a turn to the left and the ball moves to the right.

C. Both the miniature aircraft and the ball will remain centered.

Answer (B) is correct. (FAA-H-8083-15B Chap 5)
DISCUSSION: On a taxiing turn to the left, the turn coordinator shows a turn to the left, and the ball moves to the right. The centrifugal force of the turn, which is not offset by bank when taxiing, forces the ball opposite to the turn.
Answer (A) is incorrect. The ball moves to the outside of the turn due to centrifugal force. **Answer (C) is incorrect.** The miniature aircraft reacts to yaw and shows a turn to the left, and the ball reacts to centrifugal force by moving right.

75. In a left turn, correct control coordination is indicated by

A. The ball of the turn coordinator in the center.

B. The ball of the turn coordinator to the left of center.

C. The ball of the turn coordinator to the right of center.

Answer (A) is correct. (FAA-H-8083-15B Chap 2)
DISCUSSION: When turning in either direction, a correctly coordinated turn will be indicated when the ball is centered in the inclinometer portion of the turn coordinator.
Answer (B) is incorrect. A left-of-center ball in a left turn indicates a slipping turn, which is caused by insufficient rudder input through the turn. To return to coordinated flight, decrease the angle of bank and apply left rudder pressure until the ball is centered. **Answer (C) is incorrect.** A right-of-center ball in a left turn indicates a skidding turn, which is the result of excessive rudder in the turn. To return to coordinated flight, increase bank angle and right rudder until the ball is centered.

76. What does the miniature aircraft of the turn coordinator display?

A. Initially rate of bank and then directly rate of turn.

B. Directly bank angle and then directly rate of turn.

C. Indirectly bank angle and indirectly rate of turn.

Answer (A) is correct. (FAA-H-8083-15B Chap 5)
DISCUSSION: During a turn, the miniature aircraft of the turn coordinator first shows the rate of bank and then, once stabilized, the rate of turn.
Answer (B) is incorrect. The turn coordinator initially shows the rate of bank and then, once stabilized, the rate of turn. The bank angle is shown indirectly, not directly.
Answer (C) is incorrect. The turn coordinator initially shows the rate of bank and then, once stabilized, the rate of turn. The rate of turn is shown directly, not indirectly, once the turn is stabilized.

77. To maintain a standard-rate turn as the airspeed decreases, the bank angle of the airplane will need to

A. decrease.

B. increase.

C. remain constant.

Answer (A) is correct. (FAA-H-8083-15B)
DISCUSSION: A standard rate turn, although always 3° per sec., requires lower angles of bank as airspeed decreases.
Answer (B) is incorrect. A standard rate turn, although always 3° per sec., requires lower angles of bank, not higher, as airspeed decreases. **Answer (C) is incorrect.** To maintain a standard rate turn as the airspeed decreases, the bank angle of the airplane will need to decrease.

1.9 Glass Panel Displays

78. Which is true of glass panel displays?

   A. They enhance situational awareness.

   B. They require less frequent training.

   C. They give less reliable information to the pilot than traditional instruments.

Answer (A) is correct. (FAA-H-8083-6 Chap 3)
   DISCUSSION: Glass panel displays integrate flight instruments, increase safety by enhancing situational awareness, present data in an easy-to-understand format, and perform many necessary tasks automatically.
   Answer (B) is incorrect. More initial and recurrent training is needed to acquire and retain the knowledge and skills necessary to accomplish a flight safely by means of glass panel displays. **Answer (C) is incorrect.** Instrument sensor systems, and thus glass panel displays themselves, are more sensitive and reliable than traditional gyroscopic instruments.

79. Primary flight displays

   A. primarily present terrain avoidance.

   B. provide traffic information.

   C. include instruments like the attitude indicator.

Answer (C) is correct. (FAA-H-8083-6 Chap 3)
   DISCUSSION: A primary flight display (PFD) combines many flight instruments into a single presentation, including the altimeter, attitude indicator, vertical speed indicator, turn coordinator, HSI, engine and powerplant information, and fuel status.
   Answer (A) is incorrect. Multi-function displays provide terrain avoidance information. **Answer (B) is incorrect.** Multi-function displays provide traffic avoidance information.

80. In a Technologically Advanced Aircraft, the pilot sees the flight instruments on what?

   A. PFD.

   B. AHRS.

   C. MFD.

Answer (A) is correct. (FAA-H-8083-6 Chap 3)
   DISCUSSION: The PFD, or primary flight display, is home to the basic flight instruments in a technologically advanced aircraft.
   Answer (B) is incorrect. The AHRS, or attitude and heading reference system, is one input source of flight information that feeds the primary flight display. It is not a viewing system. **Answer (C) is incorrect.** The MFD, or multi-function display, is home to engine instrumentation, navigation information, and other supplementary information.

81. When a pilot believes advanced avionics enable operations closer to personal or environmental limits,

   A. greater utilization of the aircraft is achieved.

   B. risk is increased.

   C. risk is decreased.

Answer (B) is correct. (FAA-H-8083-2A Chap 7)
   DISCUSSION: Pilots should not be lulled into a false sense of security simply because they have advanced avionics. Judgment and aeronautical decision making serve as the bridge between technology and safety. Any flight you make involves almost infinite combinations of pilot skill, experience, condition, and proficiency; aircraft equipment and performance; environmental conditions; and external influences. Both individually and in combination, these factors can compress the safety buffer provided by your baseline personal minimums. Consequently, you need a practical way to adjust your baseline personal minimums to accommodate specific conditions.
   Answer (A) is incorrect. While one may be able to use an aircraft in more challenging environments, the risks involved with such flights also increase. Therefore, the best answer choice is that risk is increased when a pilot believes advanced avionics enable operations closer to personal or environmental limits. **Answer (C) is incorrect.** Risk is increased, not decreased, when a pilot believes advanced avionics enable operations closer to personal or environmental limits.

82. The lighter workloads associated with glass panel flight deck instrumentation

    A. are instrumental in decreasing flightcrew fatigue.

    B. have proven to increase safety in operations.

    C. may lead to complacency by the flightcrew.

Answer (C) is correct. (FAA-H-8083-2 Chap 7)

    DISCUSSION: The enhanced situational awareness and automation capabilities offered by a glass flight deck vastly expand its safety and utility, especially for personal transportation use. At the same time, there is some risk that lighter workloads could lead to complacency. Humans are characteristically poor monitors of automated systems. When passively monitoring an automated system for faults, abnormalities, or other infrequent events, humans perform poorly. The more reliable the system is, the worse the human performance becomes. It is a paradox of automation that technically advanced avionics can both increase and decrease pilot awareness.

    Answer (A) is incorrect. The introduction of automation is often intended to reduce workload and augment performance; however, this is not always the result. Automation can lead to distraction from the primary task, increased workload, boredom, or complacency. **Answer (B) is incorrect.** It is helpful to note that all human activity involving technical devices entails some element of risk. Knowledge, experience, and flight requirements tilt the odds in favor of safe and successful flights. The advanced avionics aircraft offers many new capabilities and simplifies the basic flying tasks, but only if the pilot is properly trained and all the equipment is working properly.

83. The advancement of avionics in light general aviation airplanes has enhanced situational awareness for properly trained pilots. However, there is concern that this technology could lead to

    A. complacency.

    B. fatigue.

    C. resignation.

Answer (A) is correct. (FAA-H-8083-25B Chap 2)

    DISCUSSION: Pilots should not become complacent or be lulled into a false sense of security simply because they have advanced avionics. It takes initial and recurrent training to maintain proficiency using this equipment, but pilots should still maintain their skills and knowledge. Judgment and aeronautical decision making serve as the bridge between technology and safety.

    Answer (B) is incorrect. The reason for technologically advanced aircraft is to give the pilot more situational awareness. If the pilot knows his or her aircraft equipment and systems, fatigue should not be a factor while flying. **Answer (C) is incorrect.** For pilots that have the proper training and knowledge of the equipment and systems of their technologically advanced aircraft, the hazardous attitude of resignation would not be an issue. If a pilot has difficulty using the autopilot or other systems, all that needs to be done is to fall back on the basics of flying by hand, pilotage, and dead reckoning.

84. An aircraft which is equipped with an Electronic Flight Display (EFD) can

    A. compensate for a pilot's lack of skill or knowledge.

    B. offer new capabilities and simplify the basic flying task.

    C. improve flight awareness by allowing the pilot to simply watch for alerts.

Answer (B) is correct. (FAA-H-8083-25B Chap 8)

    DISCUSSION: EFDs offer new capabilities, such as enhanced situational awareness, and simplify basic flying tasks, such as traditional cross-country flight planning and fuel management.

    Answer (A) is incorrect. It is important to remember that EFDs do not replace basic flight knowledge and skills. An EFD is a tool for improving flight safety. Risk increases when the pilot believes gadgets will compensate for lack of skill and knowledge. It is especially important to recognize there are limits to what the electronic systems in any light GA aircraft can do. Being PIC requires sound ADM, which sometimes means saying "no" to a flight. **Answer (C) is incorrect.** An advanced avionics aircraft offers increased safety with enhanced situational awareness. Tools like the moving map, topography, terrain awareness, traffic, and weather datalink displays give the pilot unprecedented information for enhanced situational awareness, but, without a well-planned information management strategy, these tools also make it easy for an unwary pilot to slide into the complacent role of passenger in command.

85. Automation in aircraft has proven to

   A. present new hazards in its limitations.

   B. show that automation is basically flawless.

   C. prevent accidents.

Answer (A) is correct. (FAA-H-8083-2 Chap 7)
   DISCUSSION: Most of the aviation community believes automation has made flying safer, but there is a fear that pilots fail to see that automation is a double-edged sword. Pilots need to understand the advantages of automation while being aware of its limitations. Experience has shown that automated systems can make some errors more evident while sometimes hiding other errors or making them less obvious. When passively monitoring an automated system for faults, abnormalities, or other infrequent events, humans perform poorly. The more reliable the system is, the worse the human performance becomes. It is a paradox of automation that technically advanced avionics can both increase and decrease pilot awareness.
   Answer (B) is incorrect. Automation is not necessarily flawless. Proper use of checklists and systematic training should be used to control common error-prone tasks and notice errors from automation before they become a threat to safety of flight. **Answer (C) is incorrect.** While automation has prevented accidents, it can also cause accidents from complacency. Therefore, it is not the best answer choice. When passively monitoring an automated system for faults, abnormalities, or other infrequent events, humans perform poorly. The more reliable the system is, the worse the human performance becomes. It is a paradox of automation that technically advanced avionics can both increase and decrease pilot awareness.

86. You are flying an aircraft equipped with an electronic flight display and the air data computer fails. What instrument is affected?

   A. ADS-B in capability.

   B. Airspeed indicator.

   C. Attitude indicator.

Answer (B) is correct. (FAA-H-8083-25B Chap 8)
   DISCUSSION: Electronic flight displays (EFDs) utilize an air data computer (ADC) which receives the pitot and static inputs and computes the difference between the total pressure and the static pressure. It then generates the information necessary to display the airspeed, altitude, and vertical speed on the PFD.
   Answer (A) is incorrect. ADS-B in capability is not affected by the air data computer (ADC). **Answer (C) is incorrect.** The attitude indicator receives its information from the attitude and heading reference system (AHRS).

87. Risk is increased when flightcrew members

   A. fail to monitor automated navigation systems.

   B. allocate time to verify expected performance of automated systems.

   C. question the performance of each other's duties.

Answer (A) is correct. (FAA-H-8083-25B Chap 2)
   DISCUSSION: By failing to monitor systems and failing to check the results of the processes, the pilot becomes detached from the aircraft operations and slides into the complacent role of passenger in command.
   Answer (B) is incorrect. Monitoring and verifying the performance of automated systems enhances the crew's situational awareness of the progress of the flight and aircraft performance. **Answer (C) is incorrect.** Consciously or subconsciously cross-checking the performance of each other's duties reduces the risk of an error and enhances safety.

88. The primary flight display (PFD) receives attitude and heading data from the

   A. AHRS.

   B. vacuum system.

   C. pitot-static system.

Answer (A) is correct. (FAA-H-8083-6 Chap 3)
   DISCUSSION: The attitude and heading reference system (AHRS) is composed of three axis sensors providing heading, attitude, and yaw information. It sends attitude information to the PFD to generate the pitch and bank information of the attitude indicator.
   Answer (B) is incorrect. The vacuum system produces adequate suction to maintain the gyroscopic speed of traditional analog heading and attitude indicator instruments. **Answer (C) is incorrect.** The pitot-static system is a combined system utilizing the static and dynamic air pressure due to the motion of the aircraft through the air. The PFD obtains this data through the air data computer (ADC).

STUDY UNIT TWO

ATTITUDE INSTRUMENT FLYING AND AERODYNAMICS

(7 pages of outline)

This study unit contains outlines of major concepts tested, sample test questions and answers regarding attitude instrument flying and aerodynamics, and an explanation of each answer.

Recall that the **sole purpose** of this book is to expedite your passing of the FAA pilot knowledge test for the instrument rating. Accordingly, all extraneous material (i.e., topics or regulations not directly tested on the FAA pilot knowledge test) is omitted, even though much more knowledge is necessary to fly safely. This additional material is presented in *Pilot Handbook*, *Aviation Weather and Weather Services*, *FAR/AIM*, and *Instrument Pilot Flight Maneuvers and Practical Test Prep*, available from Gleim Publications, Inc. Order online at www.GleimAviation.com.

2.1 TURNS

1. An airplane requires a sideward force to make it turn.

   a. When the airplane is banked, lift (which acts perpendicular to the wingspan) acts not only upward but horizontally as well.

   b. The vertical component acts upward to oppose weight.

   c. The horizontal component acts sideward to turn the airplane, opposing centrifugal force.

   d. The rate of turn (at a given airspeed) depends on the magnitude of the horizontal lift component, which is determined by bank angle.

2. A turn is said to be coordinated when the horizontal lift component equals centrifugal force (the ball is centered).

   a. Centrifugal force is greater than horizontal lift in skidding turns (the ball is on the outside of the turn).

   b. Centrifugal force is less than horizontal lift in slipping turns (the ball is on the inside of the turn).

3. To coordinate a turn, center the ball on the turn-and-slip indicator or the turn coordinator.

   a. Center the ball by applying rudder pressure on the side where the ball is (e.g., if the ball is on the left, use left rudder).

4. A standard-rate turn is indicated when the needle is on the "doghouse" (i.e., standard rate) mark on the turn-and-slip indicator.

5. The angle of attack must be increased in turns to maintain altitude because additional lift is required to maintain a constant amount of vertical lift.

   a. Thus, load factor always increases in turns (assuming level flight).

6. If airspeed is increased in a turn, the angle of bank must be increased and/or the angle of attack decreased to maintain level flight.

   a. Conversely, if airspeed is decreased in a turn, the angle of bank must be decreased and/or the angle of attack must be increased to maintain level flight.

2.2 TURN RATES

1. The standard-rate turn is 360° in 2 min., i.e., 3°/sec.

   a. A half-standard-rate turn is 360° in 4 min., i.e., 1.5°/sec.

   b. EXAMPLE: A 150° heading change using a standard-rate turn would take 50 sec. (150° ÷ 3°/sec.).

2. A turn-and-slip indicator may be calibrated as 2-minute or 4-minute.

   a. On a 2-minute turn-and-slip indicator, a single width deflection of the needle indicates a turning rate of 3° per second, or a standard rate turn (i.e., 360° in 2 minutes).

   b. On a 4-minute turn-and-slip indicator, a single width deflection of the needle indicates a turning rate of 1.5° per second, or a half rate turn (i.e., 360° in 4 minutes). If the needle is on the doghouse, it is indicating a standard rate turn.

3. At a constant bank, an increase in airspeed decreases the rate of turn and increases the radius of the turn.

   a. The rate of turn can be increased and the radius of turn decreased by decreasing airspeed and/or increasing the bank.

2.3 CLIMBS AND DESCENTS

1. Conditions that determine the pitch attitude required to maintain level flight are

    a. Airspeed
    b. Air density
    c. Wing design
    d. Angle of attack

2. When leveling off from a climb or descent to a specific altitude, you must start the level-off before reaching the desired altitude.

    a. Throughout the transition to level flight, the aircraft will continue to climb or descend at a decreasing rate.

    b. An effective practice is to lead the altitude by 10% of the indicated vertical speed.

        1) Since the last 1,000 ft. of a climb or descent should be made at 500 fpm, you will generally use a lead of 50 ft.

    c. To level off from a descent at a higher airspeed than descent speed, begin adding power 100 to 150 ft. above the desired altitude, assuming a descent rate of 500 fpm.

3. The pitch instruments are the attitude indicator, the altimeter, the vertical speed indicator, and the airspeed indicator.

    a. The attitude indicator should be used to make a pitch correction when you have deviated from your altitude; then the altimeter and vertical speed indicator are used to monitor the result.

    b. Altitude corrections of less than 100 ft. should be corrected by using a half-bar-width (i.e., less than a full-bar-width) correction on the attitude indicator.

4. To enter a constant-airspeed descent from level cruise and maintain cruise airspeed, simultaneously reduce power and adjust the pitch using the attitude indicator as a reference to maintain cruise airspeed.

5. To enter a constant-airspeed climb from level cruise, increase the pitch such that the artificial horizon indicates an approximate nose-high attitude appropriate for the desired climb speed.

    a. Then apply the desired climb power setting.

2.4 FUNDAMENTAL INSTRUMENT SKILLS

1. The three fundamental skills for attitude instrument flying can be recalled with the letters C-I-A:

    a. **Cross-check** -- the continuous and logical observation of instruments for attitude and performance information

    b. **Interpretation** -- the understanding of each instrument's construction, operating principle, and relationship to the performance of the airplane

    c. **Airplane control** -- includes the following elements:

        1) Pitch control
        2) Bank control
        3) Power control

2. Instrument cross-check or scan errors can be recalled with the letters F-O-E:

    a. **Fixation**, or staring at a single instrument

    b. **Omission** of an instrument from cross-check

    c. **Emphasis** on a single instrument instead of on the combination of instruments necessary for attitude information

2.5 APPROPRIATE INSTRUMENTS FOR IFR

1. Flight instruments are divided into the following three categories:

    a. **Pitch** instruments

        1) Attitude indicator (AI)
        2) Altimeter (ALT)
        3) Airspeed indicator (ASI)
        4) Vertical speed indicator (VSI)

    b. **Bank** instruments

        1) Attitude indicator (AI)
        2) Heading indicator (HI)
        3) Turn coordinator (TC) or turn-and-slip indicator (T&SI)
        4) Magnetic compass

    c. **Power** instruments

        1) Manifold pressure gauge (MP)
        2) Tachometer (RPM)
        3) Airspeed indicator (ASI)

2. For any maneuver or condition of flight, the pitch, bank, and power control requirements are most clearly indicated by certain key instruments. Those instruments that provide the most pertinent and essential information are referred to as primary instruments. Supporting instruments back up and supplement the information shown on the primary instruments.

		PITCH	BANK	POWER
a.	Straight and level			
	Primary	ALT	HI	ASI
	Supporting	AI, VSI	AI, TC	MP and/or RPM
b.	Airspeed changes in straight and level			
	Primary	ALT	HI	MP and/or RPM initially
	Supporting	AI, VSI	AI, TC	ASI as desired airspeed is approached
c.	Establishing a level standard-rate turn			
	Primary	ALT	AI	ASI
	Supporting	AI, VSI	TC	MP and/or RPM
d.	Stabilized standard-rate turn			
	Primary	ALT	TC	ASI
	Supporting	AI, VSI	AI	MP and/or RPM
e.	Change of airspeed in level turn			
	Primary	ALT	TC	MP and/or RPM initially
	Supporting	AI, VSI	AI	ASI as desired airspeed is approached
f.	Transitioning from straight and level to constant airspeed climb			
	Primary	AI	HI	MP and/or RPM
	Supporting	ASI, VSI	AI, TC	ASI
g.	Straight constant airspeed climb			
	Primary	ASI	HI	MP and/or RPM
	Supporting	AI, VSI	AI, TC	ASI
h.	As power is increased to enter a straight, constant-rate climb			
	Primary	AI	HI	MP and/or RPM
	Supporting	ASI, VSI	AI, TC	--
i.	Straight, constant-rate, stabilized climb			
	Primary	VSI	HI	ASI
	Supporting	AI	AI, TC	MP and/or RPM

3. For straight-and-level flight, the magnetic compass replaces the HI as the primary bank instrument if the HI is inoperative.

4. The ball of the turn coordinator or turn-and-slip instrument indicates the quality of the turn.

2.6 UNUSUAL ATTITUDES

1. For recovery from nose-low unusual attitudes (negative VSI, increasing airspeed, decreasing altitude, airplane below horizon on attitude indicator),

    a. Reduce power to prevent excess airspeed and loss of altitude
    b. Level the wings with coordinated rudder and aileron
    c. Gently raise the nose to level flight attitude

2. For recovery from nose-high unusual attitudes (positive VSI, decreasing airspeed, increasing altitude, airplane above horizon on attitude indicator),

    a. Add power
    b. Lower the nose
    c. Level the wings
    d. Return to the original altitude and heading

3. When recovering without the aid of the attitude indicator, level flight attitude is reached when the altimeter and the airspeed indicator stop prior to reversing their direction of movement and the vertical speed indicator reverses trend.

4. If the attitude indicator has exceeded its limits in an unusual attitude, nose-low or nose-high attitude can be determined by the airspeed indicator and the altimeter.

    a. The vertical speed indicator is also useful but is not as reliable in turbulent air.

2.7 INOPERATIVE INSTRUMENTS

1. To determine which instrument is inoperative, analyze each instrument to determine what it is indicating, then cross-check and interpret to identify the instrument that is in conflict with the others.

2. Group the instruments by the systems that power them.

    a. The heading indicator and the attitude indicator are vacuum-driven.
    b. The turn coordinator is usually electric.
    c. The airspeed indicator, altimeter, and VSI rely on the static source.

        1) The airspeed indicator also relies on the pitot tube.

            a) Remember that if the pitot tube's ram air and drain hole are clogged, the airspeed indicator acts as an altimeter; i.e., lower altitudes result in lower airspeeds and vice versa.

            b) Also remember that if only the ram air hole is clogged, the pressure in the line will vent out the drain hole, causing the airspeed indication to drop to zero.

2.8 TURBULENCE AND WIND SHEAR

1. In severe turbulence, set power for the design maneuvering speed (V_A), and maintain a level flight attitude.

    a. Attempting to turn or maintain altitude or airspeed may impose excessive load on the wings.

2. Flight at or below V_A means the airplane will stall before excessive loads can be imposed on the wings.

3. When climbing or descending through an inversion or wind-shear zone, you should be alert for any sudden change in airspeed.

2.9 HYDROPLANING

1. Hydroplaning occurs when an aircraft's tires are separated from the runway by water.

    a. It usually occurs at high speeds when water is standing on a smooth runway.

2. **Viscous hydroplaning** occurs when a film of moisture covers the painted or rubber-coated portion of the runway.

    a. It occurs at a lower speed than dynamic hydroplaning.

3. **Dynamic hydroplaning** occurs when the groundspeed is at least 8.73 times the square root of the tire pressure of the main tires.

    a. EXAMPLE: The minimum speed for dynamic hydroplaning with a tire having an air pressure of 121 PSI is 96 kt.

$$8.73 \times \sqrt{121} = 8.73 \times 11 = 96 \text{ kt.}$$

4. When tires are hydroplaning, directional control and braking action are virtually impossible.

    a. Hydroplaning makes braking ineffective until a decrease of speed that can be determined by multiplying 8.73 times the square root of the tire pressure in PSI.

    b. When hydroplaning is experienced, aerodynamic braking (aerodynamic drag) should be used to its fullest advantage.

    c. Aerodynamic braking requires holding the nose up, which transfers more weight from the nose wheel to the main wheels.

    d. The use of aerodynamic drag is applicable only for deceleration to 60-70% of the touchdown speed. At speeds less than 60-70% of the touchdown speed, aerodynamic drag is so slight that it is of little use, so braking must be utilized to produce continued deceleration.

    e. Keep in mind that once hydroplaning starts, it can continue well below the minimum initial hydroplaning speed.

5. Reverted rubber hydroplaning occurs when an airplane's tires are effectively held off the smooth runway surface by steam generated by friction.

6. Landing at higher-than-recommended touchdown speeds increases hydroplaning potential.

QUESTIONS AND ANSWER EXPLANATIONS: All of the instrument rating knowledge test questions chosen by the FAA for release as well as additional questions selected by Gleim relating to the material in the previous outlines are provided on the following pages. These questions have been organized into the same subunits as the outlines. To the immediate right of each question are the correct answer and answer explanations. You should cover these answers and answer explanations while responding to the questions. Refer to the general discussion in the Introduction on how to take the FAA knowledge test.

Remember that the questions from the FAA knowledge test bank have been reordered by topic and organized into a meaningful sequence. Also, the first line of the answer explanation gives the citation of the authoritative source for the answer.

QUESTIONS

2.1 Turns

1. What force causes an airplane to turn?

A. Rudder pressure or force around the vertical axis.

B. Vertical lift component.

C. Horizontal lift component.

Answer (C) is correct. (FAA-H-8083-15B Chap 4)
DISCUSSION: An airplane, like any object, requires a sideward force to make it turn. This force is supplied by banking the airplane so that lift is separated into two components at right angles to each other. The lift acting upward and opposing weight is the vertical lift component, and the lift acting horizontally and opposing centrifugal force is the horizontal lift component. The horizontal lift component is the sideward force that causes an airplane to turn.
Answer (A) is incorrect. The rudder pressure coordinates flight only when the airplane is banked. **Answer (B) is incorrect.** The vertical component of lift counteracts weight and thus affects altitude.

2. The rate of turn at any airspeed is dependent upon

A. the horizontal lift component.

B. the vertical lift component.

C. centrifugal force.

Answer (A) is correct. (FAA-H-8083-15B Chap 4)
DISCUSSION: At a given airspeed, the rate at which an airplane turns depends upon the amount of the horizontal component of lift.
Answer (B) is incorrect. The vertical component of lift determines altitude and change in altitude. **Answer (C) is incorrect.** Centrifugal force acts against the horizontal lift component, thus acting against turning the airplane.

3. What is the relationship between centrifugal force and the horizontal lift component in a coordinated turn?

A. Horizontal lift exceeds centrifugal force.

B. Horizontal lift and centrifugal force are equal.

C. Centrifugal force exceeds horizontal lift.

Answer (B) is correct. (FAA-H-8083-15B Chap 4)
DISCUSSION: When a turn is coordinated, horizontal lift equals centrifugal force. This is indicated when the ball on the turn coordinator or turn-and-slip indicator is centered.
Answer (A) is incorrect. When horizontal lift exceeds centrifugal force, there is a slipping turn. **Answer (C) is incorrect.** When centrifugal force exceeds horizontal lift, there is a skidding turn.

4. When airspeed is increased in a turn, what must be done to maintain a constant altitude?

A. Decrease the angle of bank.

B. Increase the angle of bank and/or decrease the angle of attack.

C. Decrease the angle of attack.

Answer (B) is correct. (FAA-H-8083-15B Chap 4)
DISCUSSION: To compensate for added lift, which would result if airspeed were increased during a turn, the angle of attack must be decreased and the angle of bank increased if a constant altitude is to be maintained.
Answer (A) is incorrect. The angle of bank must be increased, not decreased. **Answer (C) is incorrect.** As an alternative, the angle of bank can be increased.

5. The primary reason the pitch attitude must be increased, to maintain a constant altitude during a coordinated turn, is because the

A. thrust is acting in a different direction, causing a reduction in airspeed and loss of lift.

B. vertical component of lift has decreased as the result of the bank.

C. use of pedals has increased the drag.

Answer (B) is correct. (FAA-H-8083-3C Chap 3)
DISCUSSION: In a constant altitude turn, as the turn is entered, some of the vertical component of lift is transferred to the horizontal component of lift, decreasing the vertical component, requiring the pitch attitude to be increased.
Answer (A) is incorrect. Relative to the wings, thrust is acting in the same direction. **Answer (C) is incorrect.** The effects of drag from the rudder are far outweighed by the redistribution of lift.

6. When airspeed is decreased in a turn, what must be done to maintain level flight?

    A. Decrease the angle of bank and/or increase the angle of attack.

    B. Increase the angle of bank and/or decrease the angle of attack.

    C. Increase the angle of attack.

Answer (A) is correct. *(FAA-H-8083-15B Chap 4)*
    DISCUSSION: To compensate for the decreased lift resulting from decreased airspeed during a turn, the angle of bank must be decreased and/or the angle of attack increased.
    Answer (B) is incorrect. The increased vertical lift required must be obtained by a decrease, not an increase, in angle of bank and/or an increase, not a decrease, in angle of attack.
    Answer (C) is incorrect. The angle of bank can be decreased as well as the angle of attack increased.

7. The primary reason the angle of attack must be increased, to maintain a constant altitude during a coordinated turn, is because the

    A. thrust is acting in a different direction, causing a reduction in airspeed and loss of lift.

    B. vertical component of lift has decreased as the result of the bank.

    C. use of ailerons has increased the drag.

Answer (B) is correct. *(FAA-H-8083-15B Chap 4)*
    DISCUSSION: In comparison to level flight, a bank results in the division of lift between vertical and horizontal components. To provide a vertical component of lift sufficient to maintain altitude in a level turn, an increase in the angle of attack is required.
    Answer (A) is incorrect. Thrust is always a forward-acting force. The reduction in airspeed (assuming constant power) is due to an increase in angle of attack to compensate for the loss of vertical lift in a turn, i.e., to maintain altitude. **Answer (C) is incorrect.** In a coordinated turn the ailerons are streamlined and no aileron drag exists. When entering or recovering from turns, you can counteract the adverse yaw caused by aileron drag by use of the rudder.

8. During a skidding turn to the right, what is the relationship between the component of lift, centrifugal force, and load factor?

    A. Centrifugal force is less than horizontal lift and the load factor is increased.

    B. Centrifugal force is greater than horizontal lift and the load factor is increased.

    C. Centrifugal force and horizontal lift are equal and the load factor is decreased.

Answer (B) is correct. *(FAA-H-8083-15B Chap 4)*
    DISCUSSION: In skidding turns, centrifugal force is greater than horizontal lift. The load factor increases in level turns.
    Answer (A) is incorrect. A slipping, not skidding, turn occurs when centrifugal force is less than horizontal lift. **Answer (C) is incorrect.** Centrifugal force and horizontal lift are equal in a coordinated, not skidding, turn and, in a level turn, the load factor is increased, not decreased.

9. When airspeed is decreased in a turn, what must be done to maintain level flight?

    A. Increase the pitch attitude and/or increase the angle of bank.

    B. Increase the angle of bank and/or decrease the pitch attitude.

    C. Decrease the angle of bank and/or increase the pitch attitude.

Answer (C) is correct. *(FAA-H-8083-15B Chap 4)*
    DISCUSSION: To compensate for the decreased lift resulting from decreased airspeed during a turn, the angle of bank must be decreased and/or the angle of attack increased by increasing the pitch attitude.
    Answer (A) is incorrect. The increased vertical lift required must be obtained by an increase in the pitch attitude and/or a decrease, not an increase, in the angle of bank. **Answer (B) is incorrect.** The increased vertical lift required must be obtained by a decrease, not an increase, in the angle of bank and/or an increase, not a decrease, in the pitch attitude.

10. (Refer to Figure 144 below.) Which illustration indicates a coordinated turn?

    A. 3

    B. 1

    C. 2

Answer (A) is correct. (FAA-H-8083-15B Chap 5)
    DISCUSSION: A coordinated turn is one in which the ball is centered as indicated in illustration 3. The horizontal component of lift equals centrifugal force.
    Answer (B) is incorrect. Illustration 1 shows a skidding turn, in which centrifugal force exceeds the horizontal component of lift. **Answer (C) is incorrect.** Illustration 2 shows a slipping turn, in which centrifugal force is less than the horizontal component of lift.

11. (Refer to Figure 144 below.) What changes in control displacement should be made so that "2" would result in a coordinated standard-rate turn?

    A. Increase left rudder and increase rate of turn.

    B. Increase left rudder and decrease rate of turn.

    C. Decrease left rudder and decrease angle of bank.

Answer (A) is correct. (FAA-H-8083-15B Chap 5)
    DISCUSSION: Illustration 2 is a 4-minute turn-and-slip indicator, indicating a slip in which the rate of turn is too slow for the angle of bank, and the lack of centrifugal force causes the ball to move to the inside of the turn. To return to a coordinated standard-rate turn, increase left rudder (i.e., step on the ball) and increase the rate of turn. For a 4-minute turn-and-slip indicator, a standard-rate turn is indicated when the needle is on the "doghouse" (i.e., standard rate) mark. It is presently showing a single width needle deflection, which indicates a half-standard-rate turn.
    Answer (B) is incorrect. The rate of turn must be increased, not decreased, to establish a standard-rate turn. **Answer (C) is incorrect.** Left rudder pressure must be increased, not decreased, in a slip to the left.

12. (Refer to Figure 144 below.) Which illustration indicates a skidding turn?

    A. 2

    B. 1

    C. 3

Answer (B) is correct. (FAA-H-8083-15B Chap 5)
    DISCUSSION: A skidding turn occurs when centrifugal force is greater than horizontal lift. As shown by illustration 1, the ball is outside the turn.
    Answer (A) is incorrect. Illustration 2 shows a slipping turn. **Answer (C) is incorrect.** Illustration 3 shows a coordinated turn.

13. (Refer to Figure 144 below.) Which illustration indicates a slipping turn?

    A. 1

    B. 3

    C. 2

Answer (C) is correct. (FAA-H-8083-15B Chap 5)
    DISCUSSION: A slipping turn is one in which the centrifugal force is less than horizontal lift. As shown by illustration 2, the ball is inside the turn.
    Answer (A) is incorrect. Illustration 1 shows a skidding turn. **Answer (B) is incorrect.** Illustration 3 shows a coordinated turn.

Figure 144. – Turn-and-Slip indicator.

14. (Refer to Figure 144 on page 58.) What changes in control displacement should be made so that "1" would result in a coordinated standard rate turn?

A. Increase right rudder and decrease rate of turn.

B. Increase right rudder and increase rate of turn.

C. Decrease right rudder and increase angle of bank.

Answer (B) is correct. (FAA-H-8083-15B Chap 5)
    DISCUSSION: Illustration 1 is a 4-minute turn-and-slip indicator, indicating a skid in which the rate of yaw is too great for the angle of bank, and excessive centrifugal force causes the ball to move to the outside of the turn. To return to coordinated flight, increase right rudder (i.e., step on the ball) to center the ball. On the 4-minute turn-and-slip indicator, a standard-rate turn is indicated when the needle is on the doghouse mark. Presently, it is showing a single needle width deflection, which indicates a half-standard-rate turn. Thus, the rate of turn must be increased to result in a standard-rate turn.
    Answer (A) is incorrect. The rate of turn must be increased, not decreased. **Answer (C) is incorrect.** Right rudder must be increased, not decreased.

2.2 Turn Rates

15. (Refer to Figure 144 on page 58.) What information is shown on turn coordinator #3?

A. A standard rate, skidding turn to the left.

B. A standard rate, slipping turn to the right.

C. A half standard rate, coordinated turn to the left.

Answer (C) is correct. (FAA-H-8083-15B Chap 4)
    DISCUSSION: The inclinometer of turn coordinator #3 is centered, indicating the quality of the turn as coordinated, while the needle is indicating a half-standard rate turn to the left.
    Answer (A) is incorrect. Turn coordinator #1 indicates a skidding turn to the left at half standard rate. **Answer (B) is incorrect.** None of these instruments depict a slipping turn to the right; however, turn coordinator #2 indicates a slipping turn to the left at half standard rate.

16. If a half-standard-rate turn is maintained, how long would it take to turn 360°?

A. 1 minute.

B. 2 minutes.

C. 4 minutes.

Answer (C) is correct. (FAA-H-8083-15B Chap 5)
    DISCUSSION: A standard-rate turn (3°/sec) takes 2 min. for 360°. A half-standard-rate turn (1.5°/sec.) would thus take 4 min. for 360°.
    Answer (A) is incorrect. A half-standard-rate turn would take 1 min. to turn 90°, not 360°. **Answer (B) is incorrect.** A standard-rate, not half-standard-rate, turn completes 360° in 2 min.

17. Rate of turn can be increased and radius of turn decreased by

A. decreasing airspeed and shallowing the bank.

B. decreasing airspeed and increasing the bank.

C. increasing airspeed and increasing the bank.

Answer (B) is correct. (FAA-H-8083-15B Chap 4)
    DISCUSSION: To increase the rate and decrease the radius of turn, you should decrease airspeed and increase the bank angle.
    Answer (A) is incorrect. Decreasing (shallowing) the bank decreases, not increases, the rate of turn. **Answer (C) is incorrect.** The airspeed should be decreased, not increased, to increase the rate of turn.

18. If a standard-rate turn is maintained, how much time would be required to turn to the left from a heading of 090° to a heading of 300°?

A. 30 seconds.

B. 40 seconds.

C. 50 seconds.

Answer (C) is correct. (FAA-H-8083-15B Chap 5)
    DISCUSSION: A standard-rate turn means an airplane is turning at a rate of 3°/sec. A left turn from 090° to 300° is a total of 150° (90° to north and another 60° to 300°). Thus, at standard rate, it would take 50 sec. (150° ÷ 3°/sec.).
    Answer (A) is incorrect. At a standard rate of turn, an airplane would turn left 90° to a heading of 360°, not 300°, in 30 sec. **Answer (B) is incorrect.** At a standard rate of turn, an airplane would turn left 120° to a heading of 330°, not 300°, in 40 sec.

19. If a half-standard-rate turn is maintained, how long would it take to turn 135°?

A. 1 minute.

B. 1 minute 20 seconds.

C. 1 minute 30 seconds.

Answer (C) is correct. (FAA-H-8083-15B Chap 5)
    DISCUSSION: A standard-rate turn means an airplane is turning at a rate of 3°/sec. Thus, a half-standard-rate turn is at the rate of 1.5°/sec. To turn 135° at half-standard rate would take 90 sec. (135° ÷ 1.5°/sec.) or 1 min. 30 sec.
    Answer (A) is incorrect. An airplane would turn 90°, not 135°, in 1 min. at half-standard rate. **Answer (B) is incorrect.** An airplane would turn 120°, not 135°, in 1 min. 20 sec. at half-standard rate.

20. If a standard-rate turn is maintained, how long would it take to turn 180°?

A. 1 minute.

B. 2 minutes.

C. 3 minutes.

Answer (A) is correct. (FAA-H-8083-15B Chap 5)
DISCUSSION: A standard-rate turn means an airplane is turning at a rate of 3°/sec. To turn 180° at a standard rate would take 60 sec. (180° ÷ 3°/sec.), or 1 min.
Answer (B) is incorrect. An airplane would turn 180° in 2 min. at a half-standard-rate, not standard-rate, turn. Answer (C) is incorrect. An airplane would turn 540° in 3 min. at a standard rate (3°/sec.).

21. If a half-standard-rate turn is maintained, how much time would be required to turn clockwise from a heading of 090° to a heading of 180°?

A. 30 seconds.

B. 1 minute.

C. 1 minute 30 seconds.

Answer (B) is correct. (FAA-H-8083-15B Chap 4)
DISCUSSION: A half-standard-rate turn means an airplane is turning at a rate of 1.5°/sec. A turn clockwise from 090° to 180° is a total of 90°. Thus, at a half-standard rate, it would take 60 sec. (90° ÷ 1.5°/sec.).
Answer (A) is incorrect. It would take 30 sec. to turn 90° at a standard, not half-standard, rate of turn. Answer (C) is incorrect. An airplane would turn 135°, not 90°, in 1 min. 30 sec. at a half-standard rate of turn.

22. During a constant-bank level turn, what effect would an increase in airspeed have on the rate and radius of turn?

A. Rate of turn would increase, and radius of turn would increase.

B. Rate of turn would decrease, and radius of turn would decrease.

C. Rate of turn would decrease, and radius of turn would increase.

Answer (C) is correct. (FAA-H-8083-15B Chap 4)
DISCUSSION: The radius of turn at a constant-bank level turn varies directly with the airspeed, while the rate of turn at a constant-bank level turn also varies with airspeed. If airspeed is increased during a constant-bank level turn, the radius of turn will increase, and rate of turn will decrease.
Answer (A) is incorrect. The rate of turn decreases, not increases. Answer (B) is incorrect. The radius of the turn increases, not decreases.

23. If a standard-rate turn is maintained, how much time would be required to turn to the right from a heading of 090° to a heading of 270°?

A. 1 minute.

B. 2 minutes.

C. 3 minutes.

Answer (A) is correct. (FAA-H-8083-15B Chap 5)
DISCUSSION: A standard-rate turn means an airplane is turning at the rate of 3°/sec. A turn to the right (or left) from 090° to 270° is a total of 180°. Thus, at standard rate, it would take 60 sec. (180° ÷ 3°/sec.), or 1 min.
Answer (B) is incorrect. It would take 2 min. to turn 180° at a half-standard, not standard, rate of turn. Answer (C) is incorrect. It would take 3 min. to turn 270°, not 180°, at a half-standard, not standard, rate of turn.

24. Displacement of the standard rate turn index during a coordinated turn will

A. indicate the angle of bank.

B. remain constant for a given bank regardless of airspeed.

C. increase as rate of turn increases.

Answer (C) is correct. (FAA-H-8083-15B Chap 4)
DISCUSSION: Changing the bank angle without changing speed causes the rate of turn to change. Increasing the bank angle without changing speed increases the rate of turn.
Answer (A) is incorrect. The standard rate turn coordinator will provide only an indirect indication of the bank attitude of the airplane. Answer (B) is incorrect. Rate of turn is measured in degrees per second and based on a set bank angle at a set speed. Should either one change, the rate of turn will change. Should the airplane increase speed without changing the bank angle, the rate of turn will decrease. Also, if the speed decreases without changing the bank angle, the rate of turn increases.

25. Your heading indicator has failed. To turn left from a heading of 090° to a heading of 360°, using a standard rate turn, how many seconds will it take?

A. 30 seconds.

B. 40 seconds.

C. 50 seconds.

Answer (A) is correct. (FAA-H-8083-15B Chap 4)
DISCUSSION: A left turn from 090° to 360° will take 90° to complete. Using a standard rate turn will complete the turn at a rate of 3° per second, which means it will take 30 sec. (90 ÷ 3) to complete this turn.
Answer (B) is incorrect. Completing this turn in 40 sec. would mean the turn is completed with a less than standard rate turn. Answer (C) is incorrect. Completing this turn in 50 sec. would mean the turn is completed at closer to a half-standard rate turn. This time would be 1.8° per second; whereas a half-standard rate turn would be 1.5° per second.

2.3 Climbs and Descents

26. Approximately what percent of the indicated vertical speed should be used to determine the number of feet to lead the level-off from a climb to a specific altitude?

A. 10 percent.

B. 20 percent.

C. 25 percent.

Answer (A) is correct. (FAA-H-8083-15B Chap 6)
DISCUSSION: To level off from a climb and maintain a specific altitude, start the level-off before reaching the desired altitude. If your airplane is climbing at 500 fpm, it will continue to climb at a decreasing rate throughout the transition to level flight. An effective practice is to lead the altitude by 10% of the indicated vertical speed (i.e., at 500 fpm, use a 50-ft. lead).
Answer (B) is incorrect. Begin to level off from a climb at approximately 10%, not 20%, of the indicated vertical speed.
Answer (C) is incorrect. Begin to level off from a climb at approximately 10%, not 25%, of the indicated vertical speed.

27. Conditions that determine pitch attitude required to maintain level flight are

A. flightpath, wind velocity, and angle of attack.

B. airspeed, air density, wing design, and angle of attack.

C. relative wind, pressure altitude, and vertical lift component.

Answer (B) is correct. (FAA-H-8083-15B Chap 4)
DISCUSSION: Conditions that determine the pitch attitude required to maintain level flight are airspeed, air density, wing design, and angle of attack. At a constant angle of attack, any change in airspeed will vary the lift. Lift varies directly with changes in air density. An airplane's wing has lift characteristics that are suited to its intended uses. Lift increases with any increase in the angle of attack (up to the critical angle).
Answer (A) is incorrect. Flight path is the direction of travel of the airplane, which in this case is level flight. Wind velocity is not considered in maintaining level flight. Angle of attack is the resultant pitch attitude to maintain level flight.
Answer (C) is incorrect. Relative wind is the direction of airflow produced by an airplane in flight, and the vertical lift component is an aerodynamic force that acts perpendicular to the relative wind. The density, not pressure, altitude is one condition that determines the pitch attitude required to maintain level flight.

28. To level off from a descent to a specific altitude, the pilot should lead the level-off by approximately

A. 10 percent of the vertical speed.

B. 30 percent of the vertical speed.

C. 50 percent of the vertical speed.

Answer (A) is correct. (FAA-H-8083-15B Chap 6)
DISCUSSION: To level off from a descent to a specific altitude, start the level-off before reaching the desired altitude. An airplane descending at 500 fpm will continue to descend at a decreasing rate throughout the transition to level flight. An effective practice is to lead the desired altitude by 10% of the indicated vertical speed (i.e., at 500 fpm, use a 50-ft. lead).
Answer (B) is incorrect. Begin to level off from a descent at approximately 10%, not 30%, of the indicated vertical speed.
Answer (C) is incorrect. Begin to level off from a descent at approximately 10%, not 50%, of the indicated vertical speed.

29. As a rule of thumb, altitude corrections of less than 100 feet should be corrected by using

A. two bar widths on the attitude indicator.

B. less than a full bar width on the attitude indicator.

C. less than a half bar width on the attitude indicator.

Answer (B) is correct. (FAA-H-8083-15B Chap 6)
DISCUSSION: As a general rule, altitude corrections of less than 100 ft. should be corrected by using a half-bar-width (i.e., less than a full-bar-width) correction on the attitude indicator.
Answer (A) is incorrect. Altitude corrections of less than 100 ft. should be corrected by using a half-bar-, not a two-bar-, width correction on the attitude indicator. **Answer (C) is incorrect.** Altitude corrections of less than 100 ft. should be corrected by using a half-bar-width correction on the attitude indicator, not less than a half-bar-width.

30. While cruising at 160 knots, you wish to establish a climb at 130 knots. When entering the climb (full panel), it is proper to make the initial pitch change by increasing back elevator pressure until the

A. attitude indicator, airspeed, and vertical speed indicate a climb.

B. vertical speed indication reaches the predetermined rate of climb.

C. attitude indicator shows the approximate pitch attitude appropriate for the 130-knot climb.

Answer (C) is correct. (FAA-H-8083-15B Chap 6)
DISCUSSION: To enter a constant-airspeed climb from cruising air-speed, raise the miniature aircraft in the attitude indicator to the approximate nose-high indication appropriate to the predetermined climb speed. The attitude will vary according to the type of airplane you are flying. Apply light elevator back pressure to initiate and maintain the climb attitude. The amount of back pressure will increase as the airplane decelerates.
Answer (A) is incorrect. For the predetermined climb speed, the adjustment should be to the climb attitude, not just a climb indication on the instruments. **Answer (B) is incorrect.** The airspeed is predetermined, i.e., constant climb speed, not constant climb rate.

31. To level off at an airspeed higher than the descent speed, the addition of power should be made, assuming a 500 FPM rate of descent, at approximately

A. 50 to 100 feet above the desired altitude.

B. 100 to 150 feet above the desired altitude.

C. 150 to 200 feet above the desired altitude.

Answer (B) is correct. (FAA-H-8083-15B Chap 6)
DISCUSSION: To level off from a descent at an airspeed higher than the descent speed, it is necessary to start the level-off before reaching the desired altitude. At 500 fpm, an effective practice is to lead the desired altitude by approximately 100 to 150 ft. above the desired altitude. At this point, add power to the appropriate level flight cruise setting.
Answer (A) is incorrect. Leading the desired altitude by 50 to 100 ft. would require the pilot to level off at descent airspeed, not a higher airspeed. Answer (C) is incorrect. When descending at 500 fpm, 150 to 200 ft. above the desired altitude is not a lead point.

32. Which instruments should be used to make a pitch correction when you have deviated from your assigned altitude?

A. Altimeter and VSI.

B. Manifold pressure gauge and VSI.

C. Attitude indicator, altimeter, and VSI.

Answer (C) is correct. (FAA-H-8083-15B Chap 6)
DISCUSSION: The pitch instruments are the attitude indicator, the altimeter, the vertical speed indicator, and the airspeed indicator. The attitude indicator gives you a direct indication of changes in pitch attitude when correcting for altitude variations. The rate and direction of the altimeter and vertical speed indicator confirm the correct pitch adjustment was made, and the altimeter is used to determine when you have reached your assigned altitude.
Answer (A) is incorrect. The question implies that you have all instruments available. Without an attitude indicator, you would use the altimeter and vertical speed indicator to make pitch corrections. Answer (B) is incorrect. The manifold pressure gauge is a power, not pitch, instrument.

33. As a rule of thumb, altitude corrections of less than 100 feet should be corrected by using a

A. full bar width on the attitude indicator.

B. half bar width on the attitude indicator.

C. two bar width on the attitude indicator.

Answer (B) is correct. (FAA-H-8083-15B Chap 6)
DISCUSSION: As a general rule, altitude corrections of less than 100 ft. should be corrected by using a half-bar-width correction on the attitude indicator.
Answer (A) is incorrect. As a general rule, altitude corrections in excess of, not less than, 100 ft. should be corrected by an initial full-bar-width correction on the attitude indicator. Answer (C) is incorrect. Altitude corrections of less than 100 ft. should be corrected by using a half-bar-, not a two-bar-, width correction on the attitude indicator.

34. To enter a constant-airspeed descent from level-cruising flight, and maintain cruising airspeed, the pilot should

A. first adjust the pitch attitude to a descent using the attitude indicator as a reference, then adjust the power to maintain the cruising airspeed.

B. first reduce power, then adjust the pitch using the attitude indicator as a reference to establish a specific rate on the VSI.

C. simultaneously reduce power and adjust the pitch using the attitude indicator as a reference to maintain the cruising airspeed.

Answer (C) is correct. (FAA-H-8083-15B Chap 6)
DISCUSSION: To enter a constant-airspeed descent from level cruising flight and maintain cruising airspeed, you should simultaneously reduce the power smoothly to the desired setting and reduce the pitch attitude slightly by using the attitude indicator as a reference to maintain the cruising airspeed.
Answer (A) is incorrect. Airspeed will increase if you adjust the pitch attitude first. Answer (B) is incorrect. Airspeed will decrease if you first reduce power. You use the airspeed, not vertical speed, indicator to maintain a constant airspeed.

35. To level off from a descent maintaining the descending airspeed, the pilot should lead the desired altitude by approximately

A. 20 feet.

B. 50 feet.

C. 60 feet.

Answer (B) is correct. (FAA-H-8083-15B Chap 6)
DISCUSSION: To level off from a descent at descent airspeed, lead the desired altitude by approximately 50 ft., simultaneously adjusting the pitch attitude to level flight and adding power to a setting that will hold airspeed constant. Trim off the control pressures and continue with the normal straight-and-level flight cross-check.
Answer (A) is incorrect. You should lead the desired altitude by approximately 50 ft., not 20 ft., when leveling off from a descent at descent airspeed. Answer (C) is incorrect. You should lead the desired altitude by approximately 50 ft., not 60 ft., when leveling off from a descent at descent airspeed.

36. While cruising at 190 knots, you wish to establish a climb at 160 knots. When entering the climb (full panel), it would be proper to make the initial pitch change by increasing back elevator pressure until the

    A. attitude indicator shows the approximate pitch attitude appropriate for the 160-knot climb.

    B. attitude indicator, airspeed, and vertical speed indicate a climb.

    C. airspeed indication reaches 160 knots.

Answer (A) is correct. (FAA-H-8083-15B Chap 6)
    DISCUSSION: To enter a constant-airspeed climb from cruising air speed, raise the miniature aircraft in the attitude indicator to the approximate nose-high indication appropriate to the predetermined climb speed. The attitude will vary according to the type of airplane you are flying. Apply light elevator back pressure to initiate and maintain the climb attitude. The required back pressure will increase as the airplane decelerates.
    Answer (B) is incorrect. For the predetermined climb speed, you make the adjustment to the climb attitude, not just a climb indication on the instruments. **Answer (C) is incorrect.** You make an initial pitch adjustment, not an increasing adjustment; i.e., airspeed will decrease gradually.

2.4 Fundamental Instrument Skills

37. What is the third fundamental skill in attitude instrument flying?

    A. Instrument cross-check.

    B. Power control.

    C. Aircraft control.

Answer (C) is correct. (FAA-H-8083-15B Chap 6)
    DISCUSSION: The third fundamental skill in instrument flying is aircraft control. It consists of pitch, bank, and power control.
    Answer (A) is incorrect. Instrument cross-check is the first, not third, fundamental skill in attitude instrument flying. Cross-checking is the continuous and logical observation of instruments for attitude and performance information. **Answer (B) is incorrect.** Power control is only one component of aircraft control.

38. What is the first fundamental skill in attitude instrument flying?

    A. Aircraft control.

    B. Instrument cross-check.

    C. Instrument interpretation.

Answer (B) is correct. (FAA-H-8083-15B Chap 6)
    DISCUSSION: The first fundamental skill in attitude instrument flying is instrument cross-check. Cross-checking is the continuous and logical observation of instruments for attitude and performance information.
    Answer (A) is incorrect. The third, not first, fundamental skill in attitude instrument flying is aircraft control, which is composed of three components: pitch, bank, and power control. **Answer (C) is incorrect.** The second, not first, fundamental skill in attitude instrument flying is instrument interpretation. For each maneuver, you must know the performance to expect and the combination of instruments that you must interpret in order to control airplane attitude during the maneuver.

39. What are the three fundamental skills involved in attitude instrument flying?

    A. Instrument interpretation, trim application, and aircraft control.

    B. Cross-check, instrument interpretation, and aircraft control.

    C. Cross-check, emphasis, and aircraft control.

Answer (B) is correct. (FAA-H-8083-15B Chap 6)
    DISCUSSION: The three fundamental skills involved in all instrument flight maneuvers are instrument cross-check, instrument interpretation, and aircraft control. Cross-checking is the continuous and logical observation of the instruments for attitude and performance information. Instrument interpretation requires you to understand each instrument's construction, operating principle, and relationship to the performance of your airplane. Aircraft control requires you to substitute instruments for outside references.
    Answer (A) is incorrect. Trim application is only one aspect of aircraft control. **Answer (C) is incorrect.** Emphasis (along with fixation and omission) are common errors in instrument cross checking.

40. What is the correct sequence in which to use the three skills used in instrument flying?

    A. Aircraft control, cross-check, and instrument interpretation.

    B. Instrument interpretation, cross-check, and aircraft control.

    C. Cross-check, instrument interpretation, and aircraft control.

Answer (C) is correct. (FAA-H-8083-15B Chap 6)
    DISCUSSION: The correct sequence in which to use the three fundamental skills of instrument flying is cross-check, instrument interpretation, and aircraft control. Although you learn these skills separately and in deliberate sequence, a measure of your proficiency in precision flying will be your ability to integrate these skills into unified, smooth, positive control responses to maintain any desired flight path.
    Answer (A) is incorrect. Aircraft control is the third, not first, skill used in instrument flying. **Answer (B) is incorrect.** Instrument interpretation is the second, not first, skill and cross-check is the first, not second, skill used in instrument flying.

2.5 Appropriate Instruments for IFR

41. Which instruments, in addition to the attitude indicator, are pitch instruments?

- A. Altimeter and airspeed only.
- B. Altimeter and VSI only.
- C. Altimeter, airspeed indicator, and vertical speed indicator.

Answer (C) is correct. *(FAA-H-8083-15B Chap 6)*
DISCUSSION: The pitch control instruments are the attitude indicator, altimeter, vertical speed indicator, and airspeed indicator.
Answer (A) is incorrect. The vertical speed indicator and the airspeed indicator also are pitch instruments. **Answer (B) is incorrect.** The airspeed indicator also is a pitch instrument.

42. For maintaining level flight at constant thrust, which instrument would be the least appropriate for determining the need for a pitch change?

- A. Altimeter.
- B. VSI.
- C. Attitude indicator.

Answer (C) is correct. *(FAA-H-8083-15B Chap 6)*
DISCUSSION: To maintain level flight at constant thrust, the attitude indicator is the least appropriate for determining the need for pitch change. Until you have established and identified the level flight attitude for that airspeed, you have no way of knowing whether level flight as indicated on the attitude indicator is resulting in level flight as shown on the altimeter, vertical speed indicator, and airspeed indicator.
Answer (A) is incorrect. Since level flight means a constant altitude, the altimeter is the primary pitch instrument in level flight. **Answer (B) is incorrect.** The vertical speed indicator (as a trend instrument) shows immediately the initial vertical movement of the airplane, which, disregarding turbulence, can be a reflection of pitch change at a constant thrust.

43. Which instrument indicates the quality of a turn?

- A. Attitude indicator.
- B. Heading indicator or magnetic compass.
- C. Ball of the turn coordinator.

Answer (C) is correct. *(FAA-H-8083-15B Chap 6)*
DISCUSSION: The quality (coordination) of a turn relates to whether the horizontal component of lift balances the centrifugal force. It is indicated by the ball of the turn coordinator or the ball in a turn-and-slip indicator. The airplane is neither slipping nor skidding when the ball is centered, indicating the desired quality of a turn.
Answer (A) is incorrect. The attitude indicator provides both pitch and bank information. **Answer (B) is incorrect.** The heading indicator and/or magnetic compass show current direction and changes in direction, not quality of a turn.

44. Which instrument provides the most pertinent information for pitch control in straight-and-level flight?

- A. Attitude indicator.
- B. Altimeter.
- C. Airspeed indicator.

Answer (B) is correct. *(FAA-H-8083-15B Chap 6)*
DISCUSSION: During straight-and-level flight, the primary instrument for pitch is the altimeter.
Answer (A) is incorrect. The altimeter is the primary instrument for pitch control, and the attitude indicator is the supporting instrument in straight-and-level flight. Once a deviation occurs, a pitch change should be made on the attitude indicator. **Answer (C) is incorrect.** The airspeed indicator is a primary instrument for power control in straight-and-level flight. The main focus of power is to maintain a desired airspeed during level flight.

2.6 Unusual Attitudes

45. While recovering from an unusual flight attitude without the aid of the attitude indicator, approximate level pitch attitude is reached when the

A. airspeed and altimeter stop their movement and the VSI reverses its trend.

B. airspeed arrives at cruising speed, the altimeter reverses its trend, and the vertical speed stops its movement.

C. altimeter and vertical speed reverse their trend and the airspeed stops its movement.

Answer (A) is correct. (FAA-H-8083-15B Chap 6)
DISCUSSION: As the rate of movement of the altimeter and airspeed indicator needles decreases, the attitude is approaching level flight. When the needles stop and reverse direction, the aircraft is passing through level flight.
Answer (B) is incorrect. The vertical speed indicator will be lagging, i.e., showing a decrease in vertical movement when vertical movement has stopped. **Answer (C) is incorrect.** The rate is only slowing and has not stabilized when the altimeter reverses its trend; i.e., it must stop to indicate level flight.

46. If an airplane is in an unusual flight attitude and the attitude indicator has exceeded its limits, which instruments should be relied on to determine pitch attitude before starting recovery?

A. Turn indicator and VSI.

B. Airspeed and altimeter.

C. VSI and airspeed to detect approaching VSI or VMO.

Answer (B) is correct. (FAA-H-8083-15B Chap 6)
DISCUSSION: If the attitude indicator is inoperative, a nose-low or nose-high attitude can be determined by the airspeed and altimeter. In a nose-high attitude, airspeed is decreasing and altimeter is increasing, and vice versa for nose-low attitudes.
Answer (A) is incorrect. The turn indicator indicates nothing about pitch attitude. **Answer (C) is incorrect.** The altimeter, not the VSI, is the primary pitch instrument. Note the FAA answer selection has VSI and VMO, which should be V_{S1} and V_{MO}, respectively.

47. Which is the correct sequence for recovery from a spiraling, nose-low, increasing airspeed, unusual flight attitude?

A. Increase pitch attitude, reduce power, and level wings.

B. Reduce power, correct the bank attitude, and raise the nose to a level attitude.

C. Correct the bank attitude, raise the nose to a level attitude, and reduce power.

Answer (B) is correct. (FAA-H-8083-15B Chap 6)
DISCUSSION: For nose-low unusual attitudes, one should reduce the power, level the wings, and then increase the pitch to raise the nose to a level attitude.
Answer (A) is incorrect. The power should be decreased first, then the wings leveled. **Answer (C) is incorrect.** The power should be reduced before the nose is raised to minimize the load factor.

48. During recoveries from unusual attitudes, level flight is attained the instant

A. the horizon bar on the attitude indicator is exactly overlapped with the miniature airplane.

B. a zero rate of climb is indicated on the VSI.

C. the altimeter and airspeed needles stop prior to reversing their direction of movement.

Answer (C) is correct. (FAA-H-8083-15B Chap 6)
DISCUSSION: In unusual attitudes, you can determine the attainment of level flight (not vertical movement) when the altimeter and airspeed needles stop prior to reversing their direction of movement.
Answer (A) is incorrect. The attitude indicator has a tendency to precess during an unusual attitude and may not be reliable. **Answer (B) is incorrect.** There is a lag or delay in the vertical speed indicator. It cannot be relied on for determining the instant level flight is attained.

49. (Refer to Figure 145 below.) What is the correct sequence for recovery from the unusual attitude indicated?

A. Reduce power, increase back elevator pressure, and level the wings.

B. Reduce power, level the wings, bring pitch attitude to level flight.

C. Level the wings, raise the nose of the aircraft to level flight attitude, and obtain desired airspeed.

Answer (B) is correct. *(FAA-H-8083-15B Chap 6)*
DISCUSSION: In Fig. 145, a nose-low attitude is indicated by a negative vertical speed indicator, high airspeed (i.e., near V_{NE}). For nose-low unusual attitudes, the correct sequence for recovery is to reduce power to prevent excessive airspeed and loss of altitude; level the wings with coordinated aileron and rudder pressure to straight flight by referring to the turn coordinator; and raise the nose to level flight attitude by smooth back elevator pressure. NOTE: The attitude indicator on the FAA figure does not correctly depict the nose-low attitude.

Answer (A) is incorrect. The wings should be level before you increase back pressure to decrease the load factor during leveling off. **Answer (C) is incorrect.** The power should be reduced first.

Figure 145. – Instrument Sequence (Unusual Attitude).

50. (Refer to Figure 147 below.) Which is the correct sequence for recovery from the unusual attitude indicated?

A. Level wings, add power, lower nose, descend to original attitude, and heading.

B. Add power, lower nose, level wings, return to original attitude and heading.

C. Stop turn by raising right wing and add power at the same time, lower the nose, and return to original attitude and heading.

Answer (B) is correct. (FAA-H-8083-15B Chap 6)
DISCUSSION: In Fig. 147, a nose-high attitude is indicated by the increasing altitude, the rate-of-climb indication on the vertical speed indicator, and the decreasing airspeed. The correct sequence for recovery is to add power, apply forward elevator pressure to lower the nose and prevent a stall, level the wings with coordinated aileron and rudder pressure to straight flight, and return to original altitude and heading.
Answer (A) is incorrect. You should both add power and lower the nose before you level the wings. **Answer (C) is incorrect.** You should both add power and lower the nose before you level the wings.

Figure 147. – Instrument Sequence (Unusual Attitude).

2.7 Inoperative Instruments

51. (Refer to Figure 146 below.) Identify the system that has failed and determine a corrective action to return the airplane to straight-and-level flight.

A. Static/pitot system is blocked; lower the nose and level the wings to level-flight attitude by use of attitude indicator.

B. Vacuum system has failed; reduce power, roll left to level wings, and pitchup to reduce airspeed.

C. Electrical system has failed; reduce power, roll left to level wings, and raise the nose to reduce airspeed.

Answer (A) is correct. *(FAA-H-8083-15B Chap 5)*
   DISCUSSION: In Fig. 146, the airplane is in a right turn as indicated by the attitude indicator, the heading indicator (HI) (the directional arrow of the HI reflects the instrument card direction of rotation), and the turn coordinator; thus, the vacuum and electrical instruments are consistent with each other. Since the attitude indicator indicates a climb, which is consistent with the altimeter and the VSI, the airspeed should not be increasing. Thus, the pitot tube ram air and drain holes are blocked, causing the airspeed indicator to react like an altimeter. To return the airplane to straight-and-level flight, you should lower the nose and level the wings to level-flight attitude by use of the attitude indicator.
   Answer (B) is incorrect. The attitude indicator and heading indicator are consistent with the turn coordinator.
   Answer (C) is incorrect. The turn coordinator, which is normally electric, is consistent with the attitude indicator, which is normally a vacuum system instrument.

Figure 146. – Instrument Sequence (System Failed).

52. (Refer to Figure 148 below.) What is the flight attitude? One system which transmits information to the instruments has malfunctioned.

A. Climbing turn to left.

B. Climbing turn to right.

C. Level turn to left.

Answer (B) is correct. (FAA-H-8083-15B Chap 5)
  DISCUSSION: Fig. 148 illustrates a climbing turn to the right. Note that the attitude indicator shows a turn to the right, the heading indicator (HI) (the directional arrow of the HI reflects the instrument card direction of rotation) shows a turn to the right, and both the altimeter and vertical speed indicator indicate a climb. The turn coordinator shows no turn and is malfunctioning.
  Answer (A) is incorrect. The turn is to the right, not the left. **Answer (C) is incorrect.** The altimeter and vertical speed indicator indicate a climb, and the turn is to the right, not left.

Figure 148. – Instrument Interpretation (System Malfunction).

53. (Refer to Figure 149 below.) What is the flight attitude? One system which transmits information to the instruments has malfunctioned.

   A.   Level turn to the right.

   B.   Level turn to the left.

   C.   Straight-and-level flight.

Answer (C) is correct. (FAA-H-8083-15B Chap 5)
   DISCUSSION: In Fig. 149, the vertical speed indicator, altimeter, and turn coordinator all indicate straight-and-level flight. The heading indicator (HI) (the directional arrow of the HI reflects the instrument card direction of rotation) indicates a turn to the south from west, which is a turn to the left. The attitude indicator indicates a turn to the right; i.e., the attitude indicator and heading indicator are in conflict. Thus, the vacuum system must be malfunctioning, and the airplane must be in straight-and-level flight.
   Answer (A) is incorrect. The vacuum system (i.e., the attitude and heading indicators) is inoperative, and the airplane is in straight flight, not a right turn. **Answer (B) is incorrect.** The vacuum system (i.e., the attitude and heading indicators) is inoperative, and the airplane is in straight flight, not a left turn.

Figure 149. – Instrument Interpretation (System Malfunction).

54. (Refer to Figure 150 below.) What is the flight attitude? One instrument has malfunctioned.

A. Climbing turn to the right.
B. Climbing turn to the left.
C. Descending turn to the right.

Answer (A) is correct. *(FAA-H-8083-15B Chap 5)*
    DISCUSSION: In Fig. 150, the airplane is in a climb as evidenced by the vertical speed indicator, altimeter, and airspeed indicator. The heading indicator (HI) (the directional arrow of the HI reflects the instrument card direction of rotation) indicates a turn from west to north, which is a turn to the right. The turn coordinator also indicates a turn to the right. Thus, the airplane is in a climbing turn to the right. The attitude indicator is the instrument that is malfunctioning since it indicates a level turn to the left.
    Answer (B) is incorrect. The attitude indicator is inoperative; thus, the airplane is turning to the right, not left.
    Answer (C) is incorrect. The airspeed indicator, altimeter, and vertical speed indicator all show that the airplane is climbing, not descending.

Figure 150. – Instrument Interpretation (Instrument Malfunction).

55. (Refer to Figure 151 below.) What is the flight attitude? One instrument has malfunctioned.

A. Climbing turn to the right.

B. Level turn to the right.

C. Level turn to the left.

Answer (B) is correct. (FAA-H-8083-15B Chap 5)
DISCUSSION: The vertical speed indicator, altimeter, and attitude indicator indicate level flight. The turn coordinator, attitude indicator, and heading indicator (HI) (the directional arrow of the HI reflects the instrument card direction of rotation) indicate a turn to the right. Accordingly, there is a level turn to the right, and the airspeed should not be near the stall speed. Thus, the ram air inlet and the drain hole of the pitot tube are clogged. The airspeed indicator will react the same way as an altimeter, if the static port is open, by showing a decrease in airspeed as altitude decreases and an increase in speed as altitude increases.

Answer (A) is incorrect. Flight is level, not climbing, according to the vertical speed indicator, altimeter, and attitude indicator. **Answer (C) is incorrect.** The turn is to the right, not left.

Figure 151. – Instrument Interpretation (Instrument Malfunction).

2.8 Turbulence and Wind Shear

56. If you fly into severe turbulence, which flight condition should you attempt to maintain?

    A. Constant airspeed (V_A).

    B. Level flight attitude.

    C. Constant altitude and constant airspeed.

Answer (B) is correct. (AC 00-6B Chap 11)
  DISCUSSION: In severe turbulence, you should attempt to maintain a level flight attitude. You will not be able to maintain a constant altitude and/or airspeed, but you should fly at or below design maneuvering speed (V_A) and attempt to maintain a level flight attitude.
  Answer (A) is incorrect. You want to maintain an airspeed at or below V_A, but in severe turbulence, there will be large variations in airspeed, and you will not be able to keep it constant. **Answer (C) is incorrect.** In severe turbulence, you will not be able to maintain a constant altitude and/or constant airspeed.

57. If severe turbulence is encountered during your IFR flight, the airplane should be slowed to the design maneuvering speed because the

    A. maneuverability of the airplane will be increased.

    B. amount of excess load that can be imposed on the wing will be decreased.

    C. airplane will stall at a lower angle of attack, giving an increased margin of safety.

Answer (B) is correct. (AC 00-6B Chap 11)
  DISCUSSION: Flight at or below the design maneuvering speed (V_A) means that the airplane will stall before excess loads can be imposed on the wings.
  Answer (A) is incorrect. You should slow the airspeed to reduce excessive loads, not because the airplane will be more maneuverable at a slow airspeed. **Answer (C) is incorrect.** An airplane will always stall when the critical angle of attack is exceeded.

58. When a climb or descent through an inversion or wind-shear zone is being performed, the pilot should be alert for which of the following change in airplane performance?

    A. A fast rate of climb and a slow rate of descent.

    B. A sudden change in airspeed.

    C. A sudden surge of thrust.

Answer (B) is correct. (AC 00-6B Chap 9)
  DISCUSSION: When climbing through an inversion or wind-shear zone, the danger is a sudden change in airspeed. If the airplane were to move abruptly from a headwind to a tailwind, the airspeed would slow dramatically, and a stall or rapid descent could be induced.
  Answer (A) is incorrect. A fast rate of climb and a slow rate of descent are usually not a safety problem, as the reverse could be. **Answer (C) is incorrect.** The amount of thrust does not change as a result of wind shears.

2.9 Hydroplaning

59. What is the best method of speed reduction if hydroplaning is experienced on landing?

    A. Step hard on the brakes.

    B. Hold nose up.

    C. Go around.

Answer (B) is correct. (AFM Chap 8)
  DISCUSSION: When confronted with the possibility of hydroplaning, it is best to land on a grooved runway (if available). Touchdown speed should be as slow as possible consistent with safety. After the nosewheel (or tailwheel) is lowered to the runway, apply moderate braking. If deceleration is not detected and hydroplaning is suspected, the nose should be raised (in tricycle-gear airplanes) and aerodynamic drag should be utilized to decelerate to a point where the brakes become effective.
  Answer (A) is incorrect. Applying full (hard) main wheel braking may increase or compound the problems associated with hydroplaning. If any brakes are used, a pumping or modulating motion like an antiskid system can be used. Aerodynamic braking by holding the nose up is recommended. **Answer (C) is incorrect.** A go around should be initiated if a stabilized approach has not been established. While hydroplaning could be caused by an unsafe condition on the runway, a go around would not usually be initiated after reaching the point after touchdown where hydroplaning occurs. Instead, apply aerodynamic braking by holding the nose up.

60. Which term describes the hydroplaning which occurs when an airplane's tire is effectively held off a smooth runway surface by steam generated by friction?

A. Reverted rubber hydroplaning.

B. Dynamic hydroplaning.

C. Viscous hydroplaning.

Answer (A) is correct. (FAA-H-8083-3C Chap 8)
    DISCUSSION: Reverted rubber hydroplaning is the result of a locked wheel skid in which reverted rubber becomes a barrier between the tire and the runway. Steam generated by the heat of friction will hold the wheel off a smooth runway surface.
    Answer (B) is incorrect. Dynamic hydroplaning occurs when there is standing water or slush on the runway that forms a wedge that lifts the tire away from contact with the runway surface. **Answer (C) is incorrect.** Viscous hydroplaning occurs on a thin film of water on a smooth (e.g., painted or rubber coated) runway surface.

61. What is the best method of speed reduction if hydroplaning is experienced on landing?

A. Apply full main wheel braking only.

B. Apply nosewheel and main wheel braking alternately and abruptly.

C. Apply aerodynamic braking to the fullest advantage.

Answer (C) is correct. (FAA-H-8083-3C Chap 8)
    DISCUSSION: During hydroplaning, the tire(s) is(are) not in contact with the runway surface, so there is no friction, and application of the brakes would do nothing. Aerodynamic braking must be used to its fullest advantage.
    Answer (A) is incorrect. Applying full main wheel braking may increase or compound the problems associated with hydroplaning. If any brakes are used, a pumping or modulating motion like an antiskid system can be used. Aerodynamic braking is recommended. **Answer (B) is incorrect.** Abrupt use of either the nosewheel or the mainwheel brakes will lock the wheels and compound the problem.

62. What effect, if any, will landing at a higher-than-recommended touchdown speed have on hydroplaning?

A. No effect on hydroplaning, but increases landing roll.

B. Reduces hydroplaning potential if heavy braking is applied.

C. Increases hydroplaning potential regardless of braking.

Answer (C) is correct. (FAA-H-8083-25B Chap 11)
    DISCUSSION: Landing at a higher-than-recommended touchdown speed increases the hydroplaning potential because the wings provide lift and reduce the contact between the tires and the runway, allowing a layer of water to form between the tire and the runway.
    Answer (A) is incorrect. Landing at a higher airspeed increases the hydroplaning potential. **Answer (B) is incorrect.** Landing at a higher airspeed increases, not reduces, the hydroplaning potential, regardless of braking.

63. Under which conditions is hydroplaning most likely to occur?

A. When rudder is used for directional control instead of allowing the nosewheel to contact the surface early in the landing roll on a wet runway.

B. During conditions of standing water, slush, high speed, and smooth runway texture.

C. During a landing on any wet runway when brake application is delayed until a wedge of water begins to build ahead of the tires.

Answer (B) is correct. (FAA-P-8740-50)
    DISCUSSION: In hydroplaning, the aircraft tire is separated from the runway by water. It is more apt to happen at higher speeds, with standing water or slush on the runway, and on a runway with a smooth texture.
    Answer (A) is incorrect. The nosewheel cannot hydroplane if it is not put down to the runway surface. **Answer (C) is incorrect.** Hydroplaning occurs regardless of brake timing.

64. Under what conditions might a pilot expect the possibility of hydroplaning?

A. When landing on a wet runway that is covered in rubber from previous landings.

B. When departing a grooved runway with less than a thousandth of an inch of water.

C. When the adiabatic lapse rate is high, and steam is rising from the landing surface.

Answer (A) is correct. (FAA-H-8083-25B Chap 11)
    DISCUSSION: Wet runways with standing water coupled with rubber deposits would present friction coefficients conducive to hydroplaning.
    Answer (B) is incorrect. Grooved runways offer higher friction capability, and the standing water present is less than that required to induce hydroplaning. **Answer (C) is incorrect.** Reverted rubber hydroplaning occurs when an airplane's tires are effectively held off the smooth runway surface by steam generated by friction, not by steam from a humid atmosphere.

STUDY UNIT THREE

NAVIGATION SYSTEMS

(10 pages of outline)

This study unit contains outlines of major concepts tested, sample test questions and answers regarding navigation systems, and an explanation of each answer.

Recall that the **sole purpose** of this book is to expedite your passing of the FAA pilot knowledge test for the instrument rating. Accordingly, all extraneous material (i.e., topics or regulations not directly tested on the FAA pilot knowledge test) is omitted, even though much more knowledge is necessary to fly safely. This additional material is presented in *Pilot Handbook, Aviation Weather and Weather Services, FAR/AIM,* and *Instrument Pilot Flight Maneuvers and Practical Test Prep,* available from Gleim Publications, Inc. Order online at www.GleimAviation.com.

3.1 DISTANCE MEASURING EQUIPMENT (DME)

1. DME displays slant range distance in nautical miles.

2. Ignore slant range error if the airplane is 1 NM or more from the ground facility for each 1,000 ft. AGL.

    a. The greatest slant range error comes at high altitudes very close to the VORTAC.
    b. EXAMPLE: If you are 6,000 ft. AGL directly above a VORTAC, your DME will read 1.0 NM.

3.2 VOR RECEIVER CHECK

1.   The Chart Supplement provides a listing of available VOR receiver ground checkpoints and VOTs (VOR receiver test facilities).

2.   Over airborne checkpoints designated by the FAA, the maximum permissible bearing error for the VOR receiver is plus or minus 6° of the designated radial.

   a.   An alternative to a certified airborne checkpoint is a prominent ground reference point that is more than 20 NM from a VOR station that is along an established VOR airway.

      1)   Once over this point with the CDI needle centered, the OBS should indicate plus or minus 6° of the published radial.

3.   The maximum difference between two indicators of a dual VOR system is 4° between the two indicated bearings to the VOR.

   a.   The CDI needles should be centered and the indicated bearings checked rather than setting to identical radials and looking at the CDI needles.

4.   VOTs are available at a specified frequency at certain airports. The facility permits you to check the accuracy of your VOR receiver while you are on the ground.

   a.   The VOT transmits only the 360° radial in all directions.

   b.   Tune the VOR receiver to the specified frequency, and turn the OBS (omnibearing selector) to select an omnibearing course of either 0° or 180°.

      1)   The CDI needle should be centered; if not, then center the needle.
      2)   If 0°, the TO/FROM indicator should indicate FROM.
      3)   If 180°, the TO/FROM indicator should indicate TO.
      4)   The maximum error is plus or minus 4°.

5.   When making a VOR receiver check with your airplane located on the designated ground checkpoint, the designated radial should be set on the OBS.

   a.   The CDI must center within plus or minus 4° of that radial with a FROM indication.

3.3 VERY HIGH FREQUENCY OMNIDIRECTIONAL RANGE (VOR) STATION

1.   When VORs are undergoing maintenance, the coded and/or voice identification is not broadcast from the VOR.

2.   DME/TACAN (Tactical Air Navigation) coded identification is transmitted one time for each three or four times the VOR identification is transmitted.

   a.   If the VOR is out of service, the DME identification will be transmitted about once every 30 seconds at 1350 Hz.

3.   A full-scale (from the center position to either side of the dial) deflection of a VOR CDI indicates a 10° deviation from the course centerline.

   a.   About 10° to 12° of change of the OBS setting should deflect the CDI from the center to the last dot.

4. An (H) Class VORTAC facility has a range of 40 NM from 1,000 ft. AGL to 14,500 ft. AGL, and a range of 100 NM from 14,500 ft. AGL to 18,000 ft.

     a. To use (H) Class VORTAC facilities to define a direct route of flight at 17,000 ft. MSL, the facilities should be no farther apart than 200 NM.

     b. Generally, for IFR operation off of established airways below 18,000 ft., VOR navigational aids should be no more than 80 NM apart.

     c. VOR/DME/TACAN Standard Service Volumes (SSV)

SSV Designator	Altitude above Transmitter Height (ATH) and Range Boundaries
T (Terminal)	• 1,000 ft. ATH up to 12,000 ft. with radial distance out to 25 NM
L (Low Altitude)	• 1,000 ft. ATH up to 18,000 ft. with radial distance out to 40 NM
H (High Altitude)	• 1,000 ft. ATH up to 14,500 ft. with radial distance out to 25 NM • 14,500 ft. ATH up to 60,000 ft. with radial distance out to 100 NM • 18,000 ft. ATH up to 45,000 ft. with radial distance out to 130 NM
VL (VOR Low)	• 1,000 ft. ATH up to < 5,000 ft. with radial distance out to 40 NM • 5,000 ft. ATH up to < 18,000 ft. with radial distance out to 70 NM
VH (VOR High)	• 1,000 ft. ATH up to < 5,000 ft. with radial distance out to 40 NM • 5,000 ft. ATH up to < 14,500 ft. with radial distance out to 70 NM • 14,500 ft. ATH up to 60,000 ft. with radial distance out to 100 NM • 18,000 ft. ATH up to 45,000 ft. with radial distance out to 130 NM
DL (DME Low)	• Line of site radial distance up to 12,900 ft. ATH • 12,900 ft. ATH up to < 18,000 ft. ATH with radial distance out to 130 NM
DH (DME High)	• Line of site radial distance up to 12,900 ft. ATH • 12,900 ft. ATH up to 60,000 ft. with radial distance out to 100 NM • 12,900 ft. ATH up to 45,000 ft. with radial distance out to 130 NM

5. VOR station passage is indicated by a complete reversal of the TO/FROM indicator.

     a. If after station passage the CDI shows a 1/2-scale deflection and remains constant for a period of time, you are flying away from the selected radial.

6. Airplane displacement from a course is approximately 200 ft. per dot per NM on VORs.

     a. At 30 NM out, one dot is 1 NM displacement; two dots, 2 NM.

     b. At 60 NM out, one dot is 2 NM displacement; two dots, 4 NM.

7. Time/distance to station formula. When tracking inbound, make a 90° turn and measure time and degrees of bearing change.

     a. $\text{Min. to station} = \dfrac{60 \times \text{Min. between bearings}}{\text{Degrees of bearing change}}$

     b. $\text{Distance to station} = \dfrac{\text{TAS} \times \text{Min. between bearings}}{\text{Degrees of bearing change}}$

         1) You may also use your flight computer to calculate the distance.

3.4 HORIZONTAL SITUATION INDICATOR (HSI)

1.   The **horizontal situation indicator (HSI)** is a combination of the heading indicator and the VOR/ILS indicator, as illustrated and explained below and on the following page.

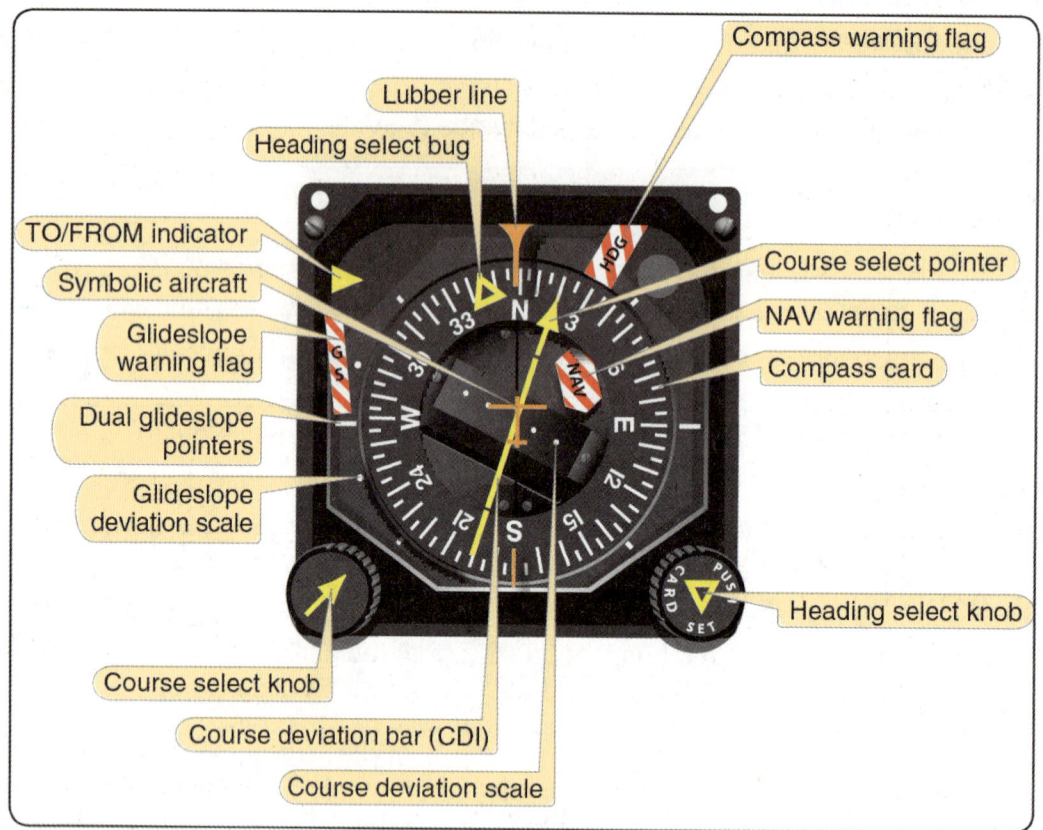

a.   The compass card -- rotates so that the heading is shown under the index at the top of the instrument

1)   The compass card may be part of a remote indicating compass (RIC), or

2)   The compass card must be checked against the magnetic compass and reset with a heading set knob.

b.   The course select pointer -- the VOR (OBS) indicator

c.   The TO/FROM indicator for the VOR

d.   Glide slope deviation pointer -- indicates above or below the glide slope, which is the longer center line

e.   Glide slope warning flag -- comes out when reliable signals are not received by the glide slope receiver

f.   Heading select knob -- used to coordinate the heading indicator (directional gyro, etc.) with the actual compass

1)   If the compass card is part of an RIC, this knob is normally a heading bug (pointer) set knob that moves a bug around the periphery of the azimuth card.

g.   Lubber line -- shows the current heading

    h.   Course deviation bar -- indicates the direction you would have to turn to intercept the desired radial if you were on the approximate heading of the OBS selection

    i.   The symbolic aircraft -- a fixed symbol that shows the airplane relative to the selected course as though you were above the airplane looking down

    j.   The course select knob -- used to adjust the OBS

    k.   Heading select bug -- indicates the heading selected with the heading select knob

    l.   NAV warning flag -- comes out when reliable signals are not received by the NAV indicator

    m.   Compass warning flag -- comes out when reliable signals are not received by the heading indicator

    n.   Glide slope deviation scale -- shows the deviation from the glide slope

    o.   Course deviation scale -- shows the deviation from the selected course

2.   Airplane displacement from a course is approximately 200 ft. per dot per NM on VORs.

    a.   At 30 NM out, one dot is 1 NM displacement; two dots, 2 NM.
    b.   At 60 NM out, one dot is 2 NM displacement; two dots, 4 NM.

3.   A full-scale deflection of a VOR CDI indicates a 10° deviation from the course centerline.

    a.   About 10° to 12° of change of the OBS setting should deflect the CDI from the center to the last dot.

    b.   With the CDI centered, rotate the OBS 180° to change the ambiguity (TO/FROM) indication.

4.   Solve all VOR problems by imagining yourself in an airplane heading in the general direction of the omnibearing setting.

    a.   If you are heading opposite your omnibearing course, the CDI needle will point away from the imaginary course line through the VOR determined by your omnibearing selector.

    b.   Remember that the VOR shows only your location (not your heading) with respect to the VOR.

5.   A few of the questions on the FAA instrument rating knowledge test require you to identify the position of your airplane relative to a VOR given an HSI presentation.

    a.   First, remember that the CDI needle does not point to the VOR. It indicates the position of the airplane relative to VOR radials.

        1)   Irrespective of your direction of flight, the CDI needle always points toward the imaginary course line through the VOR determined by your omnibearing selector.

    b.   The TO/FROM indicator operates independently of the direction (heading) of your airplane. It indicates which side of the VOR your airplane is on, based on the radial set on your omnibearing selector.

        1)   Irrespective of your direction of flight, the TO/FROM indicator shows you whether you are before, on, or past a line 90° (perpendicular) to the course line determined by your omnibearing setting.

6.   The following diagram explains the TO/FROM indicator and the CDI needle.

    a.   Remember that you must rotate the diagram so the omnibearing direction is pointed in the general direction in which your omnibearing selector is set.

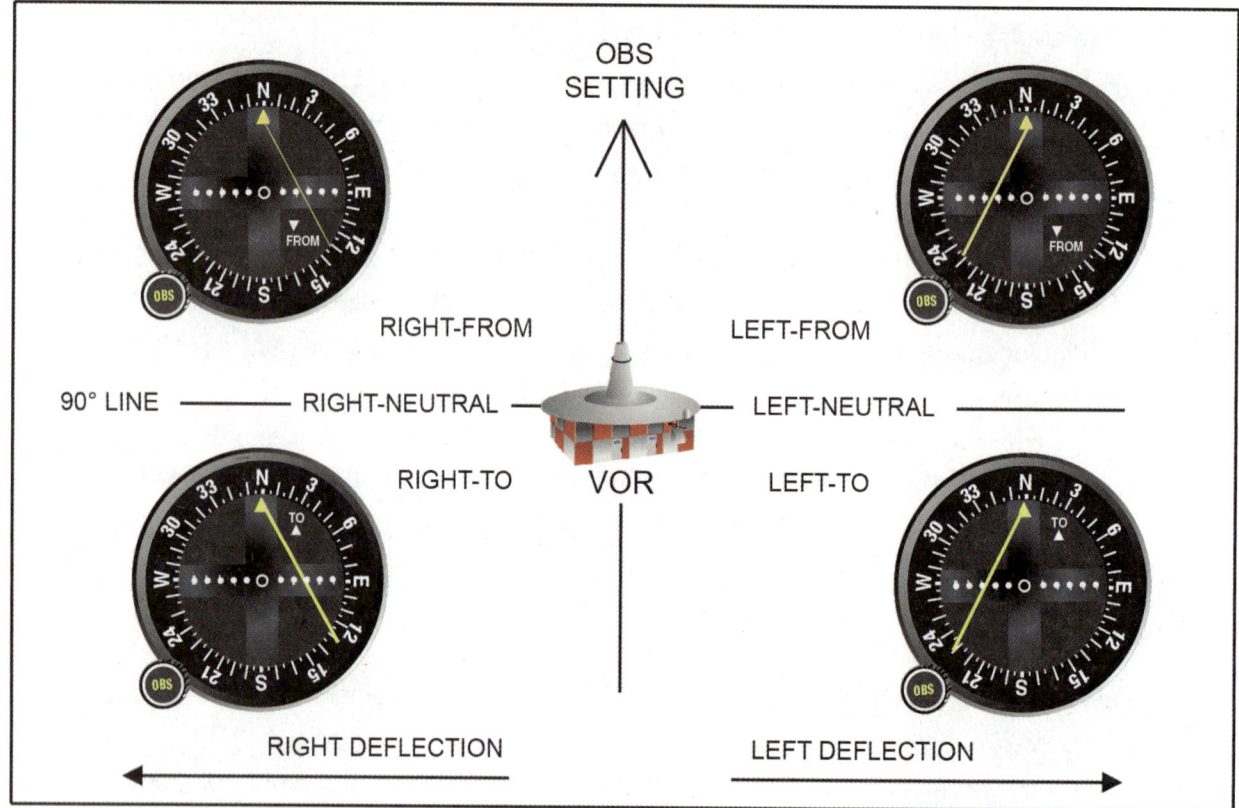

3.5 HSI/LOCALIZER

1.   When a VOR is tuned to a localizer frequency (108.10 to 111.95), the OBS (course selection) setting has no impact on the indications of the VOR.

2.   When an HSI is tuned to a localizer frequency (108.10 to 111.95), the setting of the front course heading with the head of the needle will eliminate reverse sensing on back courses. The front course can be identified as the side with the outer marker symbol.

    a.   Inbound on a back course, the tail of the needle will be at the top of the instrument, and you will have positive sensing.

    b.   If the HSI needle is set to the front course heading, you will have normal sensing on the HSI whether you are flying a front course or a back course approach.

    c.   If the HSI needle is set to the back course heading, you will have reverse sensing on the HSI whether you are flying a front course or a back course approach.

3.   The localizer information is reported on the face of the HSI instrument just as VOR signals are. That is, it is based upon position rather than heading.

4.   Similar to VORs, if you are going in the direction specified for an approach to a runway, a left deflection means you are to the right of course if you are facing in the approximate direction of the localizer.

NOTE: You will use Figure 97, "HSI Presentation," (below) to answer questions in this subunit. Be aware that presentations B, C, D, E, and I have backcourse settings of 90°, which means there is reverse sensing irrespective of the airplane's heading.

Figure 97. – HSI Presentation.

3.6 GLOBAL POSITIONING SYSTEM (GPS)

1. You should refer to the flight manual supplement to determine if an installed GPS is Technical Standard Order (TSO) TSO-C129 or TSO-C196 approved for IFR en route and IFR approaches.

   a. Handheld GPS systems and GPS systems certified for VFR operation may be used during IFR operations only as an aid to situational awareness.

   b. VFR waypoints are not recognized by the IFR systems and will be rejected for IFR routing.

2. During IFR en route and terminal operations using an approved TSO-C129 or TSO-C196 GPS system for navigation, the aircraft must be equipped with an approved and operational alternate navigation system that is appropriate to the route.

   a. Any ground-based navigational facilities required for use with the alternate navigation system (e.g., VORs, etc.) must be available and operational along the entire route of flight.

   b. It is not necessary to actively monitor an alternate means of navigation unless the GPS is not equipped with Receiver Autonomous Integrity Monitoring (RAIM), or RAIM becomes unavailable or predicts an outage.

3. To effectively navigate by means of GPS, pilots should

   a. Determine the GPS unit is approved for their planned flight

   b. Determine the status of the databases

      1) The current status of navigational databases, weather databases, NOTAMs, and signal availability should be ensured prior to takeoff.

      2) When in flight, compare the GPS database to the En Route Low Altitude chart. If they are the same, the GPS database is current. Comparing the two can verify the current status of the GPS database.

   c. Understand how to make and cancel all appropriate entries

      1) Stressful situations, heavy workloads, and turbulence make data entry errors real problems, and pilots should know how to recover basic aircraft controls quickly.

   d. Program and review the planned route

      1) Because each GPS layout can vary widely in type and function (knobs, switches, etc.), programming the units should be verified for accuracy.

      2) Name changes or spelling mistakes contribute to errors in flying appropriate routes.

   e. Ensure the track flown is approved by ATC

   f. Overriding an automatically selected sensitivity during an approach will cancel the approach mode annunciation.

4. One of the primary benefits of satellite-based area navigation (e.g., GPS or RNAV) is that it permits aircraft to fly optimum routes and altitudes.

5. Due to the use of, and reliance on, GPS systems for navigation, it is easy for pilots to lose proficiency in performing manual calculations on courses, times, distances, headings, etc.

    a. Emergency situations (i.e., electrical failures) make it important to maintain proficiency in these calculations.

6. Bear in mind that although handheld GPS units are an excellent aid to situational awareness, they are not an approved navigation source for any IFR operation, regardless of whether you are in visual or instrument meteorological conditions.

7. VFR waypoints have been created for VFR traffic only. These waypoints, identified with five letters and beginning with "VP," are for VFR pilots only. While VFR waypoints are specific to GPS users, they cannot be used in IFR flight plans. VFR waypoints are not recognized by the IFR systems and will be rejected for IFR routing.

8. There are limitations on and benefits to the operation of GPS units. These must be considered prior to flight.

    a. Aircraft using GPS TSO-C129 or TSO-C196 navigation equipment under IFR must be equipped with an approved and operational alternate means of navigation appropriate to the flight.

    b. GPS is not authorized as a substitute means of navigation guidance when conducting a conventional approach at an alternate airport.

        1) If the approach procedure requires distance measuring equipment (DME), the aircraft must be equipped with the appropriate DME avionics in order to use the approach as an alternate.

    c. GPS database updates are done on a 28-day cycle.

    d. WAAS improves the accuracy of GPS. If for some reason the WAAS service becomes unavailable, all GPS- or WAAS-equipped aircraft can revert to the LNAV MDA and land safely using GPS only, which is available nearly 100% of the time.

        1) A WAAS-enabled GPS unit provides advisory vertical guidance in association with LP or LNAV approaches using the notation of LNAV+V. The system will include an artificially created advisory glide path from the final approach fix to the touchdown point, which may aid the pilot in flying a constant descent to the MDA.

        2) LNAV+V is not the same as LNAV/VNAV or LPV. Pilots must use the barometric altimeter as the primary altitude reference to meet all altitude restrictions.

    e. Baro-VNAV is an RNAV system function that uses barometric altitude information from the aircraft's altimeter to compute and present a vertical guidance path to the pilot.

3.7 AUTOPILOTS

1. Autopilot systems are automatic flight control systems that keep an aircraft on a set course or in level flight during the en route or approach phase of flight.

    a. Autopilots contain servos, electromechanical devices that translate electrical commands into motion, moving the control surfaces.

2. Autopilot systems can be engaged so that an aircraft will fly a given

    a. Heading (set by turning the heading selection knob, tracking a VOR radial, or following the GPS track),

    b. Altitude (using the altitude hold function),

    c. Climb or descent (at a vertical speed chosen by the pilot), or

    d. Approach.

        1) The approach mode can be used to execute both precision or nonprecision approaches that rely on ground-based navigation facilities or GPS steering.

3. Benefits of using an autopilot system in flight include

    a. A reduction of the physical and mental demands of the pilot

        1) EXAMPLE: During stressful situations, such as flying in a busy terminal area or executing a missed approach in adverse weather conditions, the autopilot puts the pilot in a managerial role of monitoring an aircraft, thus reducing workload.

    b. Improved situational awareness

        1) After engaging the autopilot, it is important to verify that the aircraft is tracking the intended flight profile.

4. Because most autopilots are not capable of changing power settings, pilots must manage the throttle to control all airspeed when the autopilot is engaged.

    a. Care should be taken so aircraft speed limitations are not exceeded in a descent.

    b. Pitch attitude and throttle settings should be monitored in climbs so that the aircraft does not enter a stall.

5. Disadvantages of using an autopilot include

    a. Failing to maintain manual flying skills. Because all equipment will fail at some time, a pilot needs to remain proficient in the skills required for manual flying.

    b. Turbulence. Some autopilot systems will disengage or default to certain settings during moderate or severe turbulence.

    c. Malfunction. A pilot should immediately disengage an autopilot system if an unexpected or uncommanded behavior presents itself.

6. A good practice to clarify whether the autopilot is controlling the aircraft is to audibly announce that the autopilot is engaged, similar to the positive exchange of flight controls when flying with two pilots.

QUESTIONS

3.1 Distance Measuring Equipment (DME)

1. As a rule of thumb, to minimize DME slant range error, how far from the facility should you be to consider the reading as accurate?

A. Two miles or more for each 1,000 feet of altitude above the facility.

B. One or more miles for each 1,000 feet of altitude above the facility.

C. No specific distance is specified since the reception is line-of-sight.

Answer (B) is correct. (FAA-H-8083-15B Chap 9)
  DISCUSSION: You should consider the DME slant range error negligible if the airplane is 1 NM or more from the ground facility for each 1,000 ft. of altitude above the elevation of the facility.
  Answer (A) is incorrect. The accuracy is 1 NM, not 2 NM, for each 1,000 ft. AGL. **Answer (C) is incorrect.** A specific distance is required because the reception is line-of-sight.

2. Which distance is displayed by the DME indicator?

A. Slant range distance in NM.

B. Slant range distance in SM.

C. Line-of-sight direct distance from aircraft to VORTAC in SM.

Answer (A) is correct. (FAA-H-8083-15B Chap 9)
  DISCUSSION: DME (distance measuring equipment) displays line-of-sight direct distance, i.e., slant range, from the aircraft to the VORTAC in nautical miles.
  Answer (B) is incorrect. The measurement is in nautical miles, not statute miles. **Answer (C) is incorrect.** The measurement is in nautical miles, not statute miles.

3. Which DME indication should you receive when you are directly over a VORTAC site at approximately 6,000 feet AGL?

A. 0

B. 1

C. 1.3

Answer (B) is correct. (FAA-H-8083-15B Chap 9)
  DISCUSSION: Because the DME indicates slant range distance, it will indicate your altitude if you are directly above the VORTAC. One nautical mile equals approximately 6,000 ft., so the DME would read 1 NM.
  Answer (A) is incorrect. The DME would only indicate zero if you were at ground level next to the VORTAC.
  Answer (C) is incorrect. It would mean that your altitude was about 8,000 ft. AGL (6,000 × 1.3).

4. The greatest DME indication error between actual ground distance and displayed ground distance occurs at

A. high altitudes far from the VORTAC.

B. high altitudes close to the VORTAC.

C. low altitudes far from the VORTAC.

Answer (B) is correct. (FAA-H-8083-15B Chap 9)
  DISCUSSION: Because the DME reads slant range distance, its greatest error occurs at high altitudes very close to the VORTAC. For example, if one were at 12,000 ft. directly over the VOR, the DME would show a distance from the VOR of approximately 2 NM.
  Answer (A) is incorrect. As you get farther away from the station, the slant range error of the DME becomes minimal. **Answer (C) is incorrect.** The DME has the greatest error at high, not low, altitudes close to, not far from, the VORTAC.

3.2 VOR Receiver Check

5. To find the VOR receiver ground checkpoint(s) for an accuracy check, which publication should you consult?

    A. Airman's Information Manual.

    B. En Route Low Altitude Chart.

    C. Chart Supplement.

Answer (C) is correct. *(AIM Para 1-1-4)*
    DISCUSSION: The Chart Supplement provides a listing of available VOR receiver ground checkpoints.
    Answer (A) is incorrect. The *Aeronautical Information Manual* contains basic flight information and ATC procedures, not data concerning specific airports. **Answer (B) is incorrect.** En Route Low Altitude Charts do not indicate VOR receiver ground checkpoints.

6. When flying directly over a published airborne VOR checkpoint, what is the maximum error allowed for IFR flight?

    A. Plus or minus 6° of the designated radial.

    B. Plus 6° or minus 4° of the designated radial.

    C. Plus or minus 4° of the designated radial.

Answer (A) is correct. *(AIM Para 1-1-4)*
    DISCUSSION: Airborne checkpoints consist of certified radials that should be received over specific landmarks while airborne in the immediate vicinity of an airport. The maximum tolerance when the CDI is centered is ±6°.
    Answer (B) is incorrect. The tolerance for an airborne checkpoint is ±6°, not +6° or −4°. **Answer (C) is incorrect.** The tolerance for an airborne checkpoint is ±6°, not ±4°, which is the tolerance for a ground checkpoint or a VOT.

7. When using VOT to make a VOR receiver check, the CDI should be centered and the OBS should indicate that the aircraft is on the

    A. 090 radial.

    B. 180 radial.

    C. 360 radial.

Answer (C) is correct. *(AIM Para 1-1-4)*
    DISCUSSION: A VOT transmits only the 360° radial. Thus, with the CDI centered, the OBS should indicate 0° with a FROM indication and 180° with a TO indication.
    Answer (A) is incorrect. The VOT transmits only the 360°, not 090°, radial in all directions. **Answer (B) is incorrect.** The VOT transmits only the 360°, not 180°, radial in all directions.

8. When making an airborne VOR check, what is the maximum allowable tolerance between the two indicators of a dual VOR system (units independent of each other except the antenna)?

    A. 4° between the two indicated radials of a VOR.

    B. Plus or minus 4° when set to identical radials of a VOR.

    C. 6° between the two indicated radials of a VOR.

Answer (A) is correct. *(AIM Para 1-1-4)*
    DISCUSSION: If a dual system VOR (units independent of each other except for the antenna) is installed in the airplane, one system may be checked against the other in place of other VOR check procedures. The test consists of tuning both systems to the same VOR and centering the CDI needles, then noting the bearing variation between the two VOR units. It should be less than 4°.
    Answer (B) is incorrect. The CDIs are to be centered, not set to the same radials. **Answer (C) is incorrect.** It is a maximum tolerance of 4°, not 6°.

9. When the CDI needle is centered during an airborne VOR check, the omni-bearing selector and the TO/FROM indicator should read

    A. within 4° of the selected radial.

    B. within 6° of the selected radial.

    C. 0° TO, only if you are due south of the VOR.

Answer (B) is correct. *(AIM Para 1-1-4)*
    DISCUSSION: Airborne VOR checkpoints consist of certified radials that should be received over specific landmarks. If no checkpoint is available, a prominent ground point should be selected more than 20 NM from a VOR station that is along an established VOR airway. Once over this point with the CDI centered, the OBS should indicate within 6° of the published radial.
    Answer (A) is incorrect. The maximum error for a ground, not airborne, VOR check is ±4°. **Answer (C) is incorrect.** You should use a certified airborne checkpoint or select a ground reference that is under an established VOR airway, not a randomly selected radial.

10. (Refer to Figure 81 below.) When checking a dual VOR system by use of a VOT, which illustration indicates the VOR's are satisfactory?

    A. 1

    B. 2

    C. 4

Answer (A) is correct. *(AIM Para 1-1-4)*
    DISCUSSION: A VOT transmits a 360° radial in all directions. Thus, the tail of each indicator should point to 360°, ±4°.
    Answer (B) is incorrect. Illustration 2 shows the head, not the tail, of one indicator pointing to 360°. **Answer (C) is incorrect.** Illustration 4 shows the heads, not the tails, of both indicators pointing to 360°.

Figure 81. – Dual VOR System, VOT Check.

11. (Refer to Figure 82 below.) Which is an acceptable range of accuracy when performing an operational check of dual VOR's using one system against the other?

   A. 1

   B. 2

   C. 4

Answer (C) is correct. (AIM Para 1-1-4)
    DISCUSSION: When performing an operational check of dual VORs using one system against the other, the difference between the two indicated bearings must be 4° or less. On an RMI, which has two VOR indicators, the VORs should point in the same direction, as in illustration 4 of Fig. 82.
    Answer (A) is incorrect. In illustration 1, the needles have a 180° difference. **Answer (B) is incorrect.** In illustration 2, there is a 7° difference.

Figure 82. – Dual VOR System, Accuracy Check.

12. While airborne, what is the maximum permissible variation between the two indicated bearings when checking one VOR system against the other?

A. Plus or minus 4° when set to identical radials of a VOR.

B. 4° between the two indicated bearings to a VOR.

C. Plus or minus 6° when set to identical radials of a VOR.

Answer (B) is correct. (AIM Para 1-1-4)
    DISCUSSION: If a dual system VOR (units independent of each other except for the antenna) is installed in the airplane, one system may be checked against the other in place of other check procedures. The test consists of tuning both systems to the same VOR with the CDI centered and noting the bearing variation between the two VOR units. It should be less than 4°.
    Answer (A) is incorrect. The CDIs must be centered, not set to identical radials. **Answer (C) is incorrect.** It is a maximum permissible variation of 4°, not 6°, between the indicated bearings.

13. How should the pilot make a VOR receiver check when the aircraft is located on the designated checkpoint on the airport surface?

A. With the aircraft headed directly toward the VOR and the OBS set to 000°, the CDI should center within plus or minus 4° of that radial with a TO indication.

B. Set the OBS on the designated radial. The CDI must center within plus or minus 4° of that radial with a FROM indication.

C. Set the OBS on 180° plus or minus 4°; the CDI should center with a FROM indication.

Answer (B) is correct. (AIM Para 1-1-4)
    DISCUSSION: A VOR receiver check is a checkpoint on the airport surface near a VOR. When the aircraft is on the checkpoint, the designated radial should be set on the OBS. The CDI must then center within 4° of the radial. Also, there will be a FROM indication.
    Answer (A) is incorrect. VOR indications are given the same no matter which heading the aircraft is on. The VOR indication is based upon position, not heading. **Answer (C) is incorrect.** The specified radial, not 180°, should be set on the OBS.

14. Where can the VOT frequency for a particular airport be found?

A. On the IAP Chart and in the Chart Supplement.

B. Only in the Chart Supplement.

C. In the Chart Supplement and on the A/G Voice Communication Panel of the En Route Low Altitude Chart.

Answer (B) is correct. (AIM Para 1-1-4)
    DISCUSSION: The VOT frequency for a particular airport can be found only in the Chart Supplement.
    Answer (A) is incorrect. VOT frequencies are not listed on approach charts. **Answer (C) is incorrect.** There is no longer an A/G Voice Communication Panel included on the En Route Low Altitude Chart.

15. Which indications are acceptable tolerances when checking both VOR receivers by use of the VOT?

A. 360° TO and 003° TO, respectively.

B. 001° FROM and 005° FROM, respectively.

C. 176° TO and 003° FROM, respectively.

Answer (C) is correct. (AIM Para 1-1-4)
    DISCUSSION: A VOT transmits a 360° radial in all directions. Thus, with the course deviation indicator (CDI) centered, the omnibearing selector (OBS) should read 0° with the TO-FROM indicator showing FROM, or the OBS should read 180° with the TO-FROM indicator showing TO, with a maximum error of 4°.
    Answer (A) is incorrect. At 000°, FROM, not TO, should be indicated. **Answer (B) is incorrect.** The receiver reading 005° FROM exceeds the 4° maximum error limit.

3.3 Very High Frequency Omnidirectional Range (VOR) Station

16. What indication should a pilot receive when a VOR station is undergoing maintenance and may be considered unreliable?

- A. No coded identification, but possible navigation indications.
- B. Coded identification, but no navigation indications.
- C. A voice recording on the VOR frequency announcing that the VOR is out of service for maintenance.

Answer (A) is correct. (AIM Para 1-1-3)
DISCUSSION: The only positive method of identifying a VOR is by Morse Code identification and/or by the recorded voice identification, which is always indicated by use of the word "VOR" following the VOR name. During periods of maintenance, the facility identification is removed, although navigational signals may still be transmitted.
Answer (B) is incorrect. The coded identification is removed when the station is undergoing maintenance.
Answer (C) is incorrect. An out-of-service VOR is not announced by a voice recording.

17. A particular VOR station is undergoing routine maintenance. This is evidenced by

- A. removal of the navigational feature.
- B. broadcasting a maintenance alert signal on the voice channel.
- C. removal of the identification feature.

Answer (C) is correct. (AIM Para 1-1-3)
DISCUSSION: The only positive method of identifying a VOR is by Morse Code identification or by the recorded voice identification, which is always indicated by use of the word "VOR" following the VOR name. During periods of maintenance, the coded and/or voice facility identification is removed, although navigational signals may still be transmitted.
Answer (A) is incorrect. The navigational signals may continue even though they are not accurate. **Answer (B) is incorrect.** An out-of-service VOR is not announced by a voice recording.

18. When a VOR/DME is collocated under frequency pairings and the VOR portion is inoperative, the DME identifier will repeat at an interval of

- A. 20 second intervals at 1020 Hz.
- B. 30 second intervals at 1350 Hz.
- C. 60 second intervals at 1350 Hz.

Answer (B) is correct. (AIM Para 1-1-7)
DISCUSSION: The DME/TACAN coded identification is transmitted at 1350 Hz once for each three or four times the VOR or localizer coded identification is transmitted. When either the VOR or the DME is operative, but not both, it is important to recognize which identifier is retained for the operative facility. A single-coded identification repeated at intervals of approximately 30 sec. indicates that the DME is operative and the VOR is not.
Answer (A) is incorrect. The DME identifier repeats at 30-sec., not 20-sec., intervals at 1350 Hz, not 1020 Hz.
Answer (C) is incorrect. The DME identifier repeats at 30-sec., not 60-sec., intervals.

19. What is the meaning of a single coded identification received only once approximately every 30 seconds from a VORTAC?

- A. The VOR and DME components are operative.
- B. VOR and DME components are both operative, but voice identification is out of service.
- C. The DME component is operative and the VOR component is inoperative.

Answer (C) is correct. (AIM Para 1-1-7)
DISCUSSION: The DME/TACAN coded identification is transmitted at 1350 Hz once for each three or four times the VOR or localizer coded identification is transmitted. When either the VOR or the DME is operative, but not both, it is important to recognize which identifier is retained for the operative facility. A single-coded identification repeated at intervals of approximately 30 sec. indicates that the DME is operative and the VOR is not.
Answer (A) is incorrect. A constant series of identity codes indicates that both the VOR and DME are operative. **Answer (B) is incorrect.** Voice identification operates independently of the identity codes.

20. For operations off established airways at 17,000 feet MSL in the contiguous U.S., (H) Class VORTAC facilities used to define a direct route of flight should be no farther apart than

- A. 75 NM.
- B. 100 NM.
- C. 200 NM.

Answer (C) is correct. (AIM Para 1-1-8)
DISCUSSION: (H) Class VORTAC facilities have a range of 100 NM from 14,500 ft. AGL up to 18,000 ft. Thus, (H) Class VORTAC facilities should be no farther apart than 200 NM.
Answer (A) is incorrect. Seventy-five NM is not the range of an (H) Class VORTAC. **Answer (B) is incorrect.** One-hundred NM is the range of an (H) Class VORTAC at 17,000 ft. MSL; thus the distance between two (H) Class VORTAC facilities can be 200 NM.

21. You are planning an IFR flight off established airways below 18,000 feet MSL. If you use VOR navigation to define the route, the maximum distance between NAVAIDs should be

A. 80 NM.

B. 40 NM.

C. 70 NM.

Answer (A) is correct. (AIM Para 1-1-8)
DISCUSSION: (H) Class VOR facilities have a range of 40 NM from 1,000 ft. AGL up to 14,500 ft. AGL and a range of 100 NM from 14,500 ft. AGL up to 18,000 ft. Thus, in general, VOR navigational aids used to describe a route of flight off of established airways below 18,000 ft. (more specifically, below 14,500 ft. AGL) should be no more than 80 NM apart.
Answer (B) is incorrect. Forty NM is the range of an (H) Class VOR from 1,000 ft. AGL to 14,500 ft. AGL. VORs used to describe a route of flight off of established airways below 14,500 ft. AGL should be no more than 80 NM apart. **Answer (C) is incorrect.** VORs should be no more than 80 NM, not 70 NM, apart to define a route of flight off of established airways below 14,500 ft. AGL.

22. What angular deviation from a VOR course centerline is represented by a full-scale deflection of the CDI?

A. 4°.

B. 5°.

C. 10°.

Answer (C) is correct. (FAA-H-8083-15B Chap 9)
DISCUSSION: On VORs, full needle deflection from the center position to either side of the dial indicates that the aircraft is 10° or more off course, assuming normal needle sensitivity.
Answer (A) is incorrect. A deviation of 4° is indicated by a 2-dot deflection on a 5-dot VOR scale. **Answer (B) is incorrect.** A deviation of 5° is indicated by a 2-dot deflection on a 4-dot VOR scale.

23. Full scale deflection of a CDI occurs when the course deviation bar or needle

A. deflects from left side of the scale to right side of the scale.

B. deflects from the center of the scale to either far side of the scale.

C. deflects from half scale left to half scale right.

Answer (B) is correct. (FAA-H-8083-15B Chap 9)
DISCUSSION: Full-scale deflection of a CDI occurs when the needle deflects from the center of the scale to either far side of the scale. This indicates that the aircraft is 10° or more off course, assuming normal needle sensitivity.
Answer (A) is incorrect. It indicates moving from a left full deflection to a right full deflection, i.e., 10° left of course to 10° right of course. **Answer (C) is incorrect.** It indicates moving from a left half deflection to a right half deflection, i.e., 5° left of course to 5° right of course.

24. When using VOR for navigation, which of the following should be considered as station passage?

A. The first movement of the CDI as the airplane enters the zone of confusion.

B. The moment the TO-FROM indicator becomes blank.

C. The first positive, complete reversal of the TO-FROM indicator.

Answer (C) is correct. (FAA-H-8083-15B Chap 9)
DISCUSSION: When approaching a VOR, the TO-FROM indicator and the CDI flicker as the airplane flies into the zone of confusion (no signal area). Station passage is shown by complete reversal of the TO-FROM indicator.
Answer (A) is incorrect. It indicates flight into the zone of confusion over the VOR, not station passage. **Answer (B) is incorrect.** It is an indication that you are in the zone of confusion over the VOR, not an indication of station passage.

25. Which of the following should be considered as station passage when using VOR?

A. The first flickering of the TO-FROM indicator and CDI as the station is approached.

B. The first full-scale deflection of the CDI.

C. The first complete reversal of the TO-FROM indicator.

Answer (C) is correct. (FAA-H-8083-15B Chap 9)
DISCUSSION: When approaching a VOR, the TO-FROM indicator and the CDI flicker as the airplane flies into the zone of confusion (no signal area). Station passage is shown by complete reversal of the TO-FROM indicator.
Answer (A) is incorrect. It indicates flight into the zone of confusion over the VOR, not station passage. **Answer (B) is incorrect.** It is an indication that you are in the zone of confusion over the VOR, not an indication of station passage.

26. When checking the sensitivity of a VOR receiver, the number of degrees in course change as the OBS is rotated to move the CDI from center to the last dot on either side should be between

    A. 5° and 6°.

    B. 8° and 10°.

    C. 10° and 12°.

Answer (C) is correct. (FAA-H-8083-15B Chap 9)
    DISCUSSION: In addition to VOR receiver checks, course sensitivity may be checked by noting the number of degrees of change in the course selected as you rotate the OBS to move the CDI from center to the last dot on either side. This range should be between 10° and 12°.
    Answer (A) is incorrect. Course change of 5° to 6° should result in a 1/2-scale, not full-scale, needle deflection. **Answer (B) is incorrect.** Course change of 8° to 10° should result in a 3/4-scale, not full-scale, needle deflection.

27. A VOR receiver with normal five-dot course sensitivity shows a three-dot deflection at 30 NM from the station. The aircraft would be displaced approximately how far from the course centerline?

    A. 2 NM.

    B. 3 NM.

    C. 5 NM.

Answer (B) is correct. (FAA-H-8083-15B Chap 9)
    DISCUSSION: Airplane displacement from a course is approximately 200 ft. per dot per nautical mile for VORs. For example, at 30 NM from the station, a 1-dot deflection indicates approximately 1 NM displacement of the airplane from the course centerline. A full course deflection is 5 dots. With a 3-dot deflection, one would be about 3 NM from the course centerline.
    Answer (A) is incorrect. Two dots, not 3 dots, indicate 2 NM off course. **Answer (C) is incorrect.** Five dots, not 3 dots, indicate 5 NM off course.

28. An aircraft which is located 30 miles from a VOR station and shows a 1/2 scale deflection on the CDI would be how far from the selected course centerline?

    A. 1 1/2 miles.

    B. 2 1/2 miles.

    C. 3 1/2 miles.

Answer (B) is correct. (FAA-H-8083-15B Chap 9)
    DISCUSSION: Airplane displacement from a course is approximately 200 ft. per dot per nautical mile for VORs. For example, at 30 NM from the station, a 1-dot deflection indicates approximately 1 NM displacement of the airplane from the course centerline. A full course deflection is 5 dots. Since a 1/2-scale deflection on the CDI would be 2 1/2 dots, the airplane would be about 2 1/2 mi. from the course centerline.
    Answer (A) is incorrect. A distance of 1 1/2 mi. would be indicated by a 1 1/2-dot deflection. **Answer (C) is incorrect.** A distance of 3 1/2 mi. would be indicated by a 3 1/2-dot deflection.

29. What angular deviation from a VOR course centerline is represented by a 1/2 scale deflection of the CDI?

    A. 2°.

    B. 4°.

    C. 5°.

Answer (C) is correct. (FAA-H-8083-15B Chap 9)
    DISCUSSION: A full course deflection is 5 dots, which is approximately 10°. Since rotation of the OBS to move the CDI from the center to the last dot is approximately 10°, a 1/2-scale deflection would be approximately 5°.
    Answer (A) is incorrect. A full-scale deflection is 10°, not 4°. **Answer (B) is incorrect.** A full-scale deflection is 10°, not 8°.

30. Determine the approximate time and distance to a station if a 5° wingtip bearing change occurs in 1.5 minutes with a true airspeed of 95 knots.

    A. 16 minutes and 14.3 NM.

    B. 18 minutes and 28.5 NM.

    C. 18 minutes and 33.0 NM.

Answer (B) is correct. (FAA-H-8083-15B Chap 9)
    DISCUSSION: Use the following formulas:

Time-Distance Check

$$\text{Minutes to station} = \frac{\text{Time (sec.) between bearings}}{\text{Degrees (°) of bearing change}}$$

$$18 \text{ min. to station} = \frac{90 \text{ sec.}}{5° \text{ of bearing change}}$$

Distance from a Station

$$\text{TAS (NM/min.)} \times \text{Time (min.)} = \text{Distance to station (NM)}$$

$$95 \text{ kt.} \times 18 \text{ min.} = \text{Distance (NM)}$$

$$95 \text{ NM/hr.} \times 1 \text{ hr./60 min.} \times 18 \text{ min.} = 28.5 \text{ NM from station}$$

    Answer (A) is incorrect. The time is 18 min., not 16 min. **Answer (C) is incorrect.** Eighteen minutes is less than 1/3 hr., and 1/3 of 95 kt. is less than 33 NM.

31. (Refer to Figure 106 below.) The course selector of each aircraft is set on 360°. Which aircraft would have a FROM indication on the TO/FROM indicator and the CDI pointing right of center?

A. 1

B. 2

C. 3

Answer (A) is correct. (FAA-H-8083-15B Chap 9)
DISCUSSION: If airplane 1 set the OBS on 360°, the pilot would see a FROM indication and the CDI needle would displace to the right of center.
Answer (B) is incorrect. If airplane 2 set the OBS on 360°, the pilot would see a FROM indication and the CDI needle would displace to the left of center. **Answer (C) is incorrect.** If airplane 3 set the OBS on 360°, the pilot would see a TO indication and the CDI needle would displace to the right of center.

32. (Refer to Figure 106 below.) The course selector of each aircraft is set on 360°. Which aircraft would have a FROM indication on the TO/FROM indicator and the CDI pointing left of center?

A. 1

B. 2

C. 3

Answer (B) is correct. (FAA-H-8083-15B Chap 9)
DISCUSSION: If airplane 2 were heading 360°, the course would be to the left, and the airplane would fly away FROM the VOR. See discussion of VOR orientation presented at the end of the HSI outline.
Answer (A) is incorrect. If airplane 1 were heading 360°, the course would be to the right, not left. **Answer (C) is incorrect.** As airplane 3 is heading 360°, it is flying closer TO, not farther FROM, the station, and the CDI would be pointing right, not left, of center.

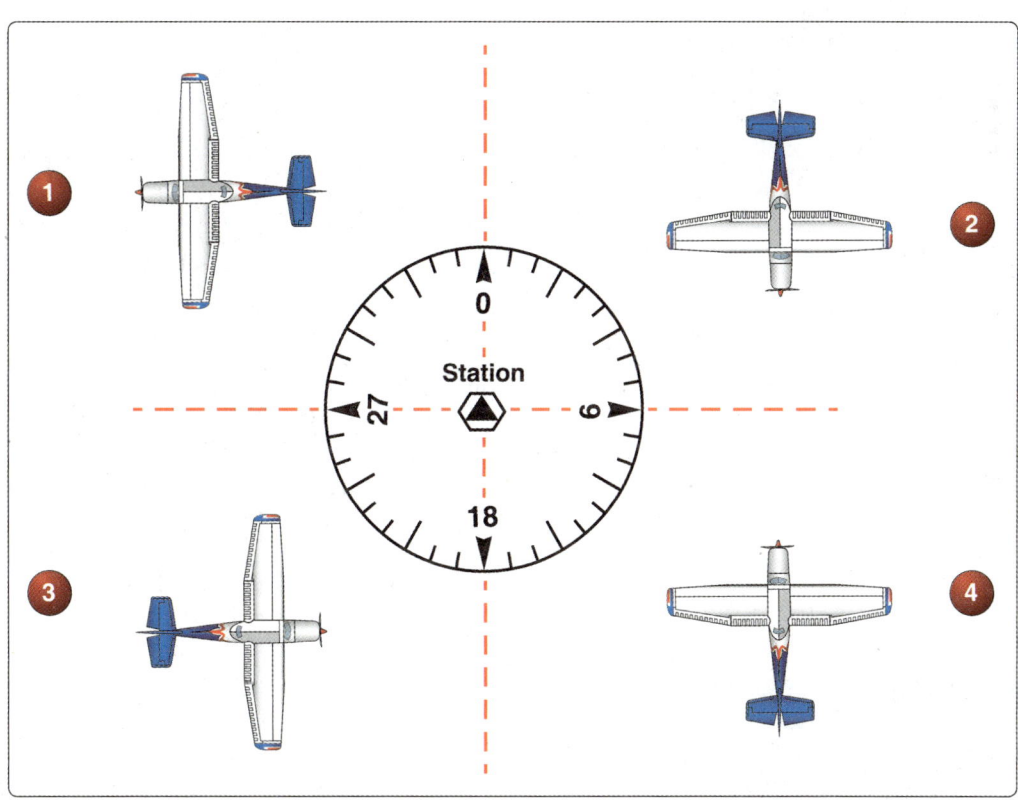

Figure 106. – Aircraft Location Relative to VOR.

33. After passing a VORTAC, the CDI shows 1/2-scale deflection to the right. What is indicated if the deflection remains constant for a period of time?

A. The airplane is getting closer to the radial.

B. The OBS is erroneously set on the reciprocal heading.

C. The airplane is flying away from the radial.

Answer (C) is correct. (FAA-H-8083-15B Chap 9)
DISCUSSION: If the CDI shows a 1/2-scale deflection to the right, the airplane is flying 5° to the left of course. If it is constant, it means the airplane is flying away from the radial because the 5° off course increases in actual distance as one gets farther away from the VORTAC.
Answer (A) is incorrect. A steady deflection would indicate the airplane is getting closer to the radial if it were flying TO, not FROM, the station. **Answer (B) is incorrect.** If you use the reciprocal heading, you get reverse indications from the CDI.

3.4   Horizontal Situation Indicator (HSI)

34. (Refer to Figure 109 below.) In which general direction from the VORTAC is the aircraft located?

A.   Northeast.

B.   Southeast.

C.   Southwest.

Answer (A) is correct. (FAA-H-8083-15B Chap 9)
  DISCUSSION: The course indicating arrow (OBS) is set to 180°, and the TO-FROM indicator indicates TO (triangle pointing TO arrowhead), which means the airplane is north of the VORTAC. Since the course deviation bar indicates that the airplane needs to be flown to the right, the airplane is to the east of the 360° radial of the VORTAC. Thus, the airplane is northeast of the VORTAC.
  Answer (B) is incorrect. If the airplane were southeast of the VORTAC, there would be a FROM, not TO, indication.
  Answer (C) is incorrect. If the airplane were southwest of the VORTAC, there would be a FROM, not TO, indication and a left, not right, bar deflection.

Figure 109. – CDI Direction from VORTAC.

35. (Refer to Figure 110 below.) In which general direction from the VORTAC is the aircraft located?

A.   Southwest.

B.   Northwest.

C.   Northeast.

Answer (C) is correct. (FAA-H-8083-15B Chap 9)
  DISCUSSION: The course indicator arrow (OBS) is set to 60°, and the TO-FROM indicates FROM (opposite the head of the arrow), which means the airplane is northeast of the VORTAC. Since the course deviation bar indicates a deflection of 3 dots to the right, the airplane is to the north of the 60° radial by 6°, which is in the northeast.
  Answer (A) is incorrect. Southwest would require a TO, not FROM, indication. **Answer (B) is incorrect.** Northwest would require a full right, not a 1/2-scale, deflection.

Figure 110. – CDI Direction from VORTAC.

36. (Refer to Figure 111 below.) In which general direction from the VORTAC is the aircraft located?

A. Northeast.

B. Southeast.

C. Northwest.

Answer (C) is correct. (FAA-H-8083-15B Chap 9)
   DISCUSSION: The course indicator arrow (OBS) is set to 360°, and the TO-FROM indicator is FROM, which means the airplane is north of the VORTAC. Since the course deviation bar is to the right, the airplane is to the west of the 360° radial of the VORTAC. Accordingly, the airplane is to the northwest of the VORTAC.
   Answer (A) is incorrect. A left, not right, deflection would indicate the airplane is in the northeast. **Answer (B) is incorrect.** An indication of TO, not FROM, would indicate the airplane is south of the VORTAC.

Figure 111. – CDI Direction from VORTAC.

37. (Refer to Figure 95 on page 97.) What is the lateral displacement of the aircraft in NM from the radial selected on the No. 1 NAV?

    A. 5.0 NM.

    B. 7.5 NM.

    C. 10.0 NM.

Answer (A) is correct. (FAA-H-8083-15B Chap 9)
    DISCUSSION: On VORs, the displacement from course is approximately 200 ft. per dot per nautical mile. At 30 NM from the station, one-dot deflection indicates approximately 1 NM displacement of the airplane from the course centerline. At 60 NM, it would be 2 NM for every dot of displacement. Since here, displacement is 2 1/2 dots, the airplane would be 5 NM from the centerline.
    Answer (B) is incorrect. A distance of 7.5 NM would be indicated by a 3/4 deflection. **Answer (C) is incorrect.** A distance of 10.0 NM would be indicated by a full deflection.

38. (Refer to Figure 95 on page 97.) On which radial is the aircraft as indicated by the No. 1 NAV?

    A. R-175.

    B. R-165.

    C. R-345.

Answer (C) is correct. (FAA-H-8083-15B Chap 9)
    DISCUSSION: The course selector in Fig. 95 is set on 350° with a FROM reading, indicating that, if the course deviation bar were centered, the airplane would be on R-350. Since a total deflection is approximately 10° to 12°, one-half deflection is 5° to 6°. Here, deflection is less than one-half, so it is about 5°. The course deviation bar indicates that this airplane is to the west of R-350, which would be R-345.
    Answer (A) is incorrect. R-175 would require a TO indicator and a left deflection. **Answer (B) is incorrect.** R-165 would require a TO indicator.

39. (Refer to Figure 95 on page 97.) Which OBS selection on the No. 1 NAV would center the CDI and change the ambiguity indication to a TO?

    A. 175°.

    B. 165°.

    C. 345°.

Answer (B) is correct. (FAA-H-8083-15B Chap 9)
    DISCUSSION: The course selector in Fig. 95 is set on 350°, resulting in a FROM reading and a 1/2-scale needle deflection. Thus, the airplane is 5° or 6° west of R-350, i.e., R-345. Setting the OBS to the reciprocal course of 165° would center the CDI with a TO indication.
    Answer (A) is incorrect. The airplane is currently on R-345, not R-355. **Answer (C) is incorrect.** The airplane is currently on R-345 with a FROM, not TO, indication.

40. (Refer to Figure 95 on page 97.) What is the lateral displacement in degrees from the desired radial on the No. 2 NAV?

    A. 1°.

    B. 2°.

    C. 4°.

Answer (C) is correct. (FAA-H-8083-15B Chap 9)
    DISCUSSION: Since, on a standard 5-dot VOR indicator, a full deflection of 5 dots is about 10°, 2 dots means a 4° deflection.
    Answer (A) is incorrect. Each dot is 2°, not 1/2°. **Answer (B) is incorrect.** Each dot is 2°, not 1°.

41. (Refer to Figure 95 on page 97.) Which OBS selection on the No. 2 NAV would center the CDI?

    A. 174°.

    B. 166°.

    C. 335°.

Answer (A) is correct. (FAA-H-8083-15B Chap 9)
    DISCUSSION: The course selector on NAV-2 in Fig. 95 is set to 170° (it is not an HSI, but a CDI), and the TO-FROM indicator indicates FROM, which means the airplane would be on R-170 if the course deviation bar were centered. Since the bar indicates a left 2-dot deflection, the airplane is 4° to the west of the radial, or on R-174.
    Answer (B) is incorrect. A right, not left, deflection would indicate R-166. **Answer (C) is incorrect.** On R-335 with an OBS setting of 170°, there would be a TO, not FROM, indication.

42. (Refer to Figure 95 below.) Which OBS selection on the No. 2 NAV would center the CDI and change the ambiguity indication to a TO?

    A. 166°.

    B. 346°.

    C. 354°.

Answer (C) is correct. (FAA-H-8083-15B Chap 9)
    DISCUSSION: The course selector in Fig. 95 is set to 170° (it is not an HSI; it is a VOR), and the TO-FROM indicator indicates FROM, which means the airplane would be on R-170 if the course deviation bar were centered. Since the bar indicates a 2-dot left deflection, the airplane is 4° to the west of the radial, or on R-174. To obtain a TO indication, one would have to change the OBS selection by 180° from 174° to 354°.
    Answer (A) is incorrect. The airplane is on R-174, not R-346. **Answer (B) is incorrect.** The airplane is on R-174, not R-166.

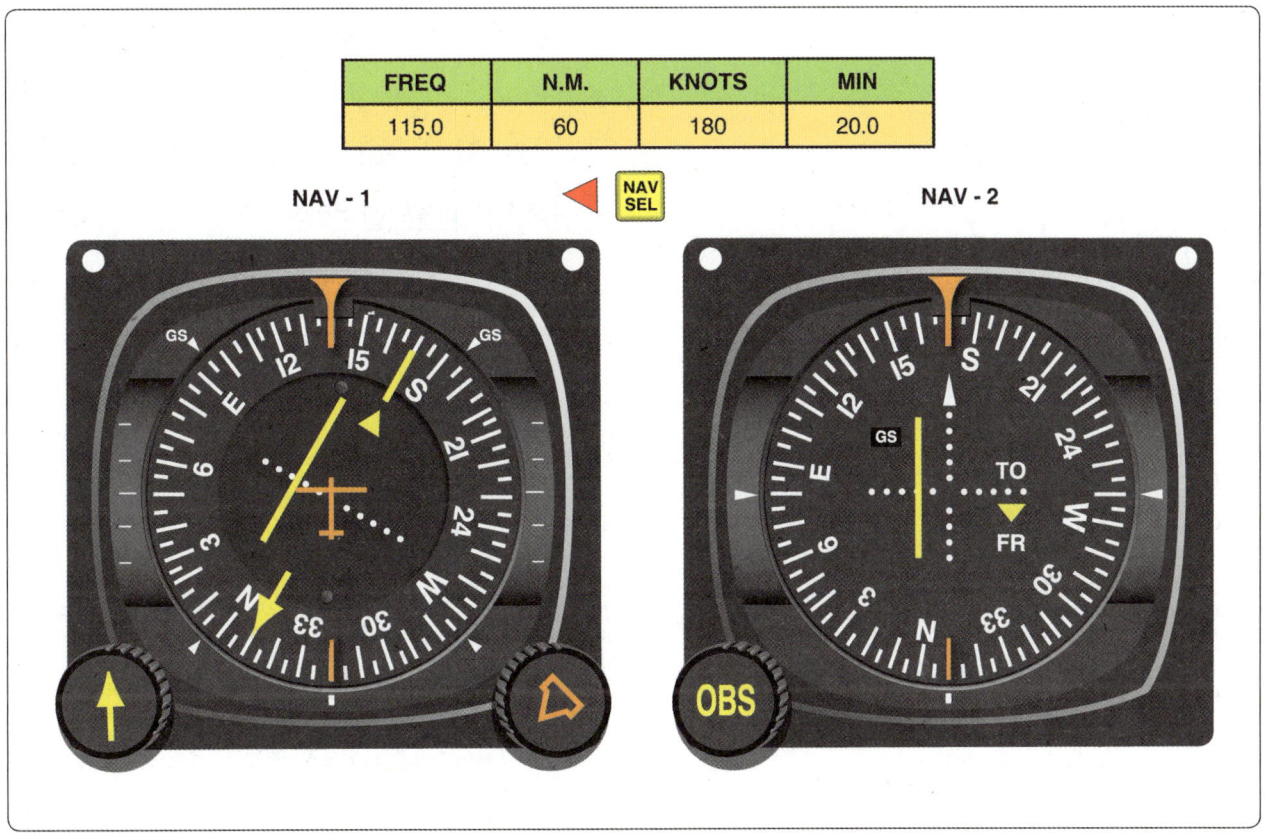

Figure 95. – No. 1 and No. 2 NAV Presentation.

43. (Refer to Figure 98 on page 99 and Figure 99 on page 99.) To which aircraft position does HSI presentation "A" correspond?

    A. 1

    B. 8

    C. 11

Answer (A) is correct. (FAA-H-8083-15B Chap 9)
    DISCUSSION: On Figs. 98 and 99, HSI "A" has a VOR course selection of 090°, with a TO indication, meaning the airplane is to the left of the 360/180 radials. It has a right deflection, which means it is north of the 270/90 radials. The airplane heading is 205°, which means airplane 1 is described.
    Answer (B) is incorrect. Airplane 8 is to the right of the 360/180 radials, which would require a FROM, not TO, indication. **Answer (C) is incorrect.** Airplane 11 is to the right of the 360/180 radials and is south of the 270/090 radials, which would require a FROM, not TO, indication and a left, not right, bar deflection.

44. (Refer to Figure 98 on page 99 and Figure 99 on page 99.) To which aircraft position does HSI presentation "B" correspond?

    A. 9

    B. 13

    C. 19

Answer (C) is correct. (FAA-H-8083-15B Chap 9)
    DISCUSSION: On Figs. 98 and 99, HSI "B" has a VOR course selection of 270° with a FROM indication, meaning that the airplane is to the left of the 360/180 radials. Since it has a right deflection, the airplane is south of R-270. Given a heading of 135°, airplane 19 is described.
    Answer (A) is incorrect. Airplane 9 would require a TO, not FROM, indication and a left, not right, bar deflection. **Answer (B) is incorrect.** Airplane 13 is to the right of the 360/180 radials, which would require a TO, not FROM, indication.

45. (Refer to Figure 98 on page 99 and Figure 99 on page 99.) To which aircraft position does HSI presentation "C" correspond?

    A. 6

    B. 7

    C. 12

Answer (C) is correct. (FAA-H-8083-15B Chap 9)
    DISCUSSION: On Figs. 98 and 99, HSI "C" has a VOR course selection of 360° with a TO indication, meaning the airplane is south of the 270/090 radials. Since the course deflection bar is to the left, the airplane is to the east of the 180° radial. Given a 310° heading, airplane 12 is described.
    Answer (A) is incorrect. Airplane 6 is north of the 270/090 radials, which would require a FROM, not TO, indication and has a north, not 310°, heading. **Answer (B) is incorrect.** Airplane 7 is north of the 270/090 radials, which would require a FROM, not TO, indication.

46. (Refer to Figure 98 on page 99 and Figure 99 on page 99.) To which aircraft position does HSI presentation "D" correspond?

    A. 4

    B. 15

    C. 17

Answer (C) is correct. (FAA-H-8083-15B Chap 9)
    DISCUSSION: On Figs. 98 and 99, HSI "D" has a VOR course selection (OBS) of 180°. Its FROM indication means the airplane is south of R-270/90. Since the course deflection bar is to the left, the airplane is west of R-180. Given the heading of 180°, the position describes airplane 17.
    Answer (A) is incorrect. Airplane 4 is north of the 270/090 radials, which would have a TO, not FROM, indication. **Answer (B) is incorrect.** Airplane 15 would have a centered deflection bar and a north, not 180°, heading.

47. (Refer to Figure 98 on page 99 and Figure 99 on page 99.) To which aircraft position does HSI presentation "E" correspond?

    A. 5

    B. 6

    C. 15

Answer (B) is correct. (FAA-H-8083-15B Chap 9)
    DISCUSSION: On Figs. 98 and 99, HSI "E" has a VOR course selection of 360°. Its FROM indication means the airplane is north of R-270/90. Given the course deflection bar to the left, the airplane is to the east of the 360° radial. Given the 360° heading, the position describes airplane 6.
    Answer (A) is incorrect. Airplane 5 would require a centered deflection bar, and has a south, not 360°, heading. **Answer (C) is incorrect.** Airplane 15 is south of the 270/090 radials, which would require a centered deflection bar and a TO, not FROM, indication.

48. (Refer to Figure 98 on page 99 and Figure 99 on page 99.) To which aircraft position does HSI presentation "F" correspond?

    A. 10

    B. 14

    C. 16

Answer (C) is correct. (FAA-H-8083-15B Chap 9)
    DISCUSSION: On Figs. 98 and 99, HSI "F" has a VOR course selection of 180° with a FROM indication, meaning that the airplane is south of the 270/90 radials. Since the course deflection bar is centered, the airplane is on R-180. Given a heading of 045° (at the top of the HSI), airplane 16 is described.
    Answer (A) is incorrect. Airplane 10 is east of the 360/180 radials and north of the 270/090 radials, which would require a bar deflection, not a centered bar, and a TO, not FROM, indication. **Answer (B) is incorrect.** Airplane 14 is east of the 360/180 radials, which would require a bar deflection, not a centered bar.

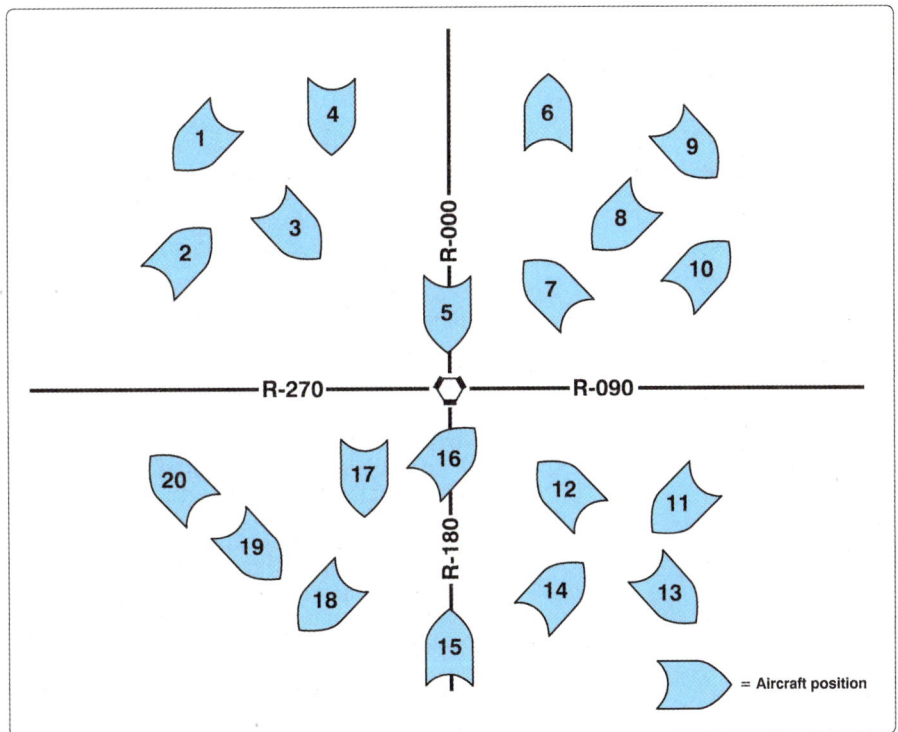

Figure 98. – Aircraft Position.

A   B   C

D   E   F

Figure 99. – HSI Presentation.

3.5   HSI/Localizer

NOTE: HSI presentations B, C, D, E, and I have backcourse settings of 090°, which means there is reverse sensing irrespective of the airplane's heading.

49. (Refer to Figure 96 below, and Figure 97 on page 101.) To which aircraft position(s) does HSI presentation "A" correspond?

    A. 9 and 6.

    B. 9 only.

    C. 6 only.

Answer (A) is correct. (FAA-H-8083-15B Chap 9)
    DISCUSSION: On Figs. 96 and 97, HSI "A" has a heading of 360° with no localizer deviation, which means the airplane is on the localizer. Airplanes 6 and 9 are on the localizer with a 360° heading.
    Answer (B) is incorrect. The indication will be the same on either localizer. **Answer (C) is incorrect.** The indication will be the same on either localizer.

50. (Refer to Figure 96 below, and Figure 97 on page 101.) To which aircraft position(s) does HSI presentation "B" correspond?

    A. 11.

    B. 5 and 13.

    C. 7 and 11.

Answer (B) is correct. (FAA-H-8083-15B Chap 9)
    DISCUSSION: On Figs. 96 and 97, HSI "B" has a heading of 090°. It has a right deflection with a backcourse HSI setting of 90°. This results in reverse sensing, meaning the airplane is south of the localizer. Thus, airplanes 5 and 13 are described. NOTE: The shading on the localizer in Fig. 96 is incorrect. However, the backcourse can still be identified because the front course is the side with the outer and middle marker symbols.
    Answer (A) is incorrect. Airplane 11 has a 270°, not 090°, heading. **Answer (C) is incorrect.** Airplanes 7 and 11 have 270°, not 090°, headings.

51. (Refer to Figure 96 below, and Figure 97 on page 101.) To which aircraft position does HSI presentation "C" correspond?

    A. 9

    B. 4

    C. 12

Answer (C) is correct. (FAA-H-8083-15B Chap 9)
    DISCUSSION: On Figs. 96 and 97, HSI "C" has a heading of 090° with a centered course deviation bar; thus, the airplane is on the localizer with a 090° heading, which describes airplane 12. The backcourse setting (090) has no effect because the deviation bar is centered.
    Answer (A) is incorrect. Airplane 9 has a 360°, not 090°, heading. **Answer (B) is incorrect.** Airplane 4 has a 270°, not 090°, heading.

52. (Refer to Figure 96 below, and Figure 97 on page 101.) To which aircraft position does HSI presentation "D" correspond?

    A. 1

    B. 10

    C. 2

Answer (C) is correct. (FAA-H-8083-15B Chap 9)
    DISCUSSION: On Figs. 96 and 97, HSI "D" has a heading of 315°. Airplane 2 is the only one with a northwest heading.
    Answer (A) is incorrect. Airplane 1 has a heading of 215°, not 315°. **Answer (B) is incorrect.** Airplane 10 has a heading of 135°, not 315°.

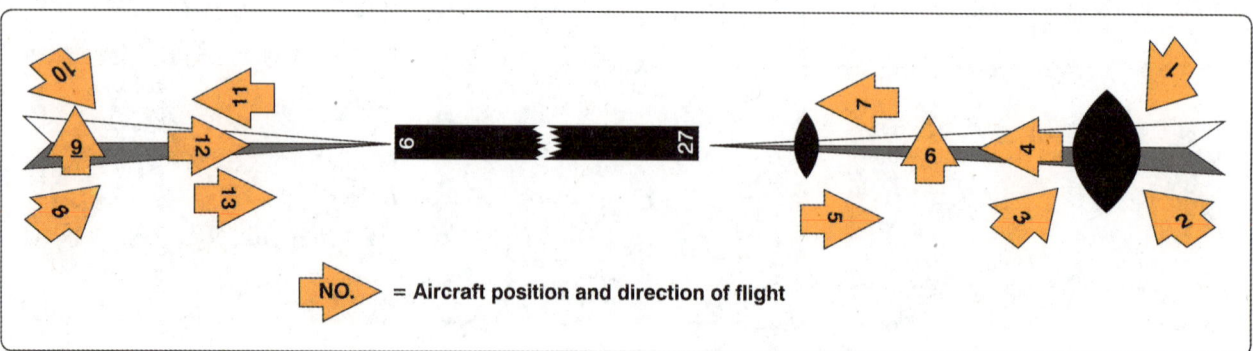

Figure 96. – Aircraft Position and Direction of Flight.

Figure 97. – HSI Presentation.

53. (Refer to Figure 96 on page 103 and Figure 97 on page 103.) To which aircraft position(s) does HSI presentation "G" correspond?

    A. 7 only.

    B. 7 and 11.

    C. 5 and 13.

Answer (B) is correct. (FAA-H-8083-15B Chap 9)
    DISCUSSION: On Figs. 96 and 97, HSI "G" has a localizer setting at 270° with a left deviation, meaning the airplane is north of the localizer. With a 270° heading, it corresponds to airplanes 7 and 11.
    Answer (A) is incorrect. Airplane 11 is also north of the localizer with a 270° heading. **Answer (C) is incorrect.** Airplanes 5 and 13 have a heading of 090°, not 270°, and are also south, not north, of the localizer.

54. (Refer to Figure 96 on page 103 and Figure 97 on page 103.) To which aircraft position does HSI presentation "F" correspond?

    A. 4

    B. 11

    C. 5

Answer (A) is correct. (FAA-H-8083-15B Chap 9)
    DISCUSSION: On Figs. 96 and 97, HSI "F" has a setting of 270° with a centered bar and a 270° heading, which corresponds to airplane 4.
    Answer (B) is incorrect. Airplane 11 would have a left, not centered, course deviation bar. **Answer (C) is incorrect.** Airplane 5 has a heading of 090°, not 270°.

55. (Refer to Figure 96 on page 103 and Figure 97 on page 103.) To which aircraft position(s) does HSI presentation "E" correspond?

    A. 8 only.

    B. 3 only.

    C. 8 and 3.

Answer (C) is correct. (FAA-H-8083-15B Chap 9)
    DISCUSSION: On Figs. 96 and 97, HSI "E" has a heading of 045°. It has a right deflection with a backcourse HSI setting of 090°. This results in reverse sensing, meaning the airplane is south of the localizer. Thus, airplanes 3 and 8 are described. NOTE: The shading on the localizer in Fig. 96 is incorrect. However, the backcourse can still be identified because the front course is the side with the outer and middle marker symbols.
    Answer (A) is incorrect. Airplane 3 is also south of the localizer with a 045° heading. **Answer (B) is incorrect.** Airplane 8 also has a 045° heading and is south of the localizer.

56. (Refer to Figure 96 on page 103 and Figure 97 on page 103.) To which aircraft position does HSI presentation "H" correspond?

    A. 8

    B. 1

    C. 2

Answer (B) is correct. (FAA-H-8083-15B Chap 9)
    DISCUSSION: On Figs. 96 and 97, HSI "H" has a heading of 215°. Airplane 1 is the only one with a southwest heading.
    Answer (A) is incorrect. Airplane 8 has a heading of 045°, not 215°. **Answer (C) is incorrect.** Airplane 2 has a heading of 315°, not 215°.

57. (Refer to Figure 96 on page 103 and Figure 97 on page 103.) To which aircraft position does HSI presentation "I" correspond?

    A. 4

    B. 12

    C. 11

Answer (C) is correct. (FAA-H-8083-15B Chap 9)
    DISCUSSION: On Figs. 96 and 97, HSI "I" has a heading of 270°. It has a left deviation with a backcourse HSI setting of 090°. This results in reverse sensing, meaning the airplane is north of the localizer. Thus, airplane 11 is described. NOTE: The shading on the localizer in Fig. 96 is incorrect. However, the backcourse can still be identified because the front course is the side with the outer and middle marker symbols.
    Answer (A) is incorrect. Airplane 4 would have a centered CDI, not a right deviation. **Answer (B) is incorrect.** Airplane 12 would have a centered CDI, not a right deviation, and has a heading of 090°, not 270°.

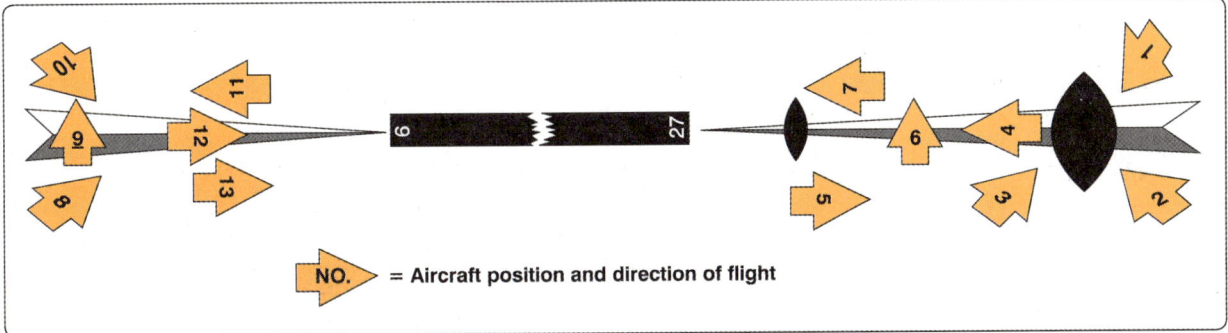

Figure 96. – Aircraft Position and Direction of Flight.

Figure 97. – HSI Presentation.

3.6 Global Positioning System (GPS)

58. How can a pilot determine if a Global Positioning System (GPS) installed in an aircraft is approved for IFR en route and IFR approaches?

    A. Flight manual supplement.

    B. GPS operator's manual.

    C. Aircraft owner's handbook.

Answer (A) is correct. (AC 20-138A)
    DISCUSSION: A supplement to the aircraft's POH (flight manual) is required for newly installed equipment. A supplement should state that the GPS is approved for IFR operations (en route and approaches).
    Answer (B) is incorrect. The GPS operator's manual will describe how to operate the GPS unit but will not provide approval for its use in a particular aircraft. **Answer (C) is incorrect.** The aircraft owner's handbook (i.e., information manual or POH) may not have any information on a GPS unit unless the unit was installed as a standard feature.

59. Hand-held GPS systems, and GPS systems certified for VFR operation, may be used during IFR operations as

    A. the principal reference to determine en route waypoints.

    B. an aid to situational awareness.

    C. the primary source of navigation.

Answer (B) is correct. (AIM Para 1-1-17)
    DISCUSSION: In order to use a GPS as the primary means of navigation under IFR or to perform instrument approaches, both the GPS receiver and the aircraft installation must be FAA-approved. Additionally, the receiver must have a current database of waypoints and instrument approach procedures. Hand-held GPS systems and VFR-only GPS systems are not FAA-approved for IFR operations, and may only be used during IFR operations as an aid to situational awareness.
    Answer (A) is incorrect. Hand-held and VFR-only GPS systems are not approved for IFR operations; they may only be used as an aid to situational awareness. Passage of en route reporting points and fixes (i.e., waypoints) must be verified by some other means (e.g., VOR, radar, etc.). **Answer (C) is incorrect.** Hand-held and VFR-only GPS systems are not approved as the primary source of navigation under IFR; they may only be used as an aid to situational awareness.

60. When may VFR waypoints be used in IFR flight plans?

    A. When GPS is used as the primary source of navigation.

    B. When the waypoints consist of 5 letter identifiers.

    C. VFR waypoints may not be used on IFR flight plans.

Answer (C) is correct. (FAA-H-8083-25B Chap 14)
    DISCUSSION: VFR waypoints are designed to ease radio congestion in populated areas for VFR traffic only. VFR waypoints are charted on terminal area and sectional aeronautical charts.
    Answer (A) is incorrect. VFR waypoints may not be used in IFR flight plans for instrument navigation. **Answer (B) is incorrect.** VFR waypoints may not be used in IFR flight plans for instrument navigation.

61. During IFR en route and terminal operations using an approved TSO-C129 or TSO-C196 GPS system for navigation, ground based navigational facilities

    A. are only required during the approach portion of the flight.

    B. must be operational along the entire route.

    C. must be operational only if RAIM predicts an outage.

Answer (B) is correct. (AIM Para 1-1-17)
    DISCUSSION: In order to conduct IFR en route and terminal operations using an approved TSO-C129 or TSO-C196 GPS system, the avionics necessary to receive all of the ground-based facilities that are appropriate for the route to the destination airport and to any alternate airport must be installed and operational, and the ground-based facilities necessary for these routes must be operational.
    Answer (A) is incorrect. Ground-based navigational facilities appropriate to the route must be available and operational along the entire route of flight, not just the approach portion. **Answer (C) is incorrect.** Ground-based navigational facilities appropriate to the route must be available and operational regardless of Receiver Autonomous Integrity Monitoring (RAIM) status. However, unless RAIM predicts an outage, active monitoring of these facilities is not necessary.

62. During IFR en route operations using an approved TSO-C129 or TSO-C196 GPS system for navigation,

    A. no other navigation system is required.

    B. active monitoring of an alternate navigation system is always required.

    C. the aircraft must have an approved TSO-C129 or TSO-C196 and operational alternate navigation system appropriate for the route.

Answer (C) is correct. (AIM Para 1-1-17)
    DISCUSSION: Aircraft using GPS under IFR must be equipped with an approved TSO-C129 or TSO-C196 and operational alternate means of navigation appropriate for the route. Active monitoring of alternative navigation equipment is not required if the GPS receiver uses Receiver Autonomous Integrity Monitoring (RAIM). However, active monitoring of an alternate means of navigation is required when the RAIM capability of the GPS equipment is lost or if RAIM predicts an outage.
    Answer (A) is incorrect. Aircraft using an approved GPS system for IFR operations must be equipped with an approved TSO-C129 or TSO-C196 and operational alternate means of navigation appropriate to the flight. **Answer (B) is incorrect.** Active monitoring of an alternate navigation system is only required when GPS RAIM capability is lost or when an outage is predicted, not at all times.

63. What are the primary benefits of satellite based area navigation (RNAV)?

    A. Provides optimal routing and altitudes.

    B. Radio tuning and controller communication is minimized.

    C. Standard Terminal Arrival Routes and Departure Procedures are not required.

Answer (A) is correct. (AIM Para 1-1-17)
    DISCUSSION: The primary benefits of satellite based area navigation (RNAV) are that it permits aircraft to fly optimum routes and altitudes, thereby increasing the efficiency of the entire National Airspace System.
    Answer (B) is incorrect. The primary benefits of satellite based area navigation (RNAV) are the ability to permit aircraft to fly optimum routes and altitudes, not the fact that radio tuning and controller communication is minimized. **Answer (C) is incorrect.** The primary benefits of satellite based area navigation (RNAV) are the ability to permit aircraft to fly optimum routes and altitudes, not that standard Terminal Arrival Routes and Departure Procedures are not required.

64. A handheld GPS is

    A. not authorized for IFR use.

    B. authorized for IFR use under VMC.

    C. authorized for IFR use under IMC until the runway is in sight.

Answer (A) is correct. (AIM Para 1-1-17)
    DISCUSSION: A handheld GPS may be used as an aid to situational awareness in any flight condition, but it is not authorized for any IFR operations.
    Answer (B) is incorrect. While a handheld GPS may be used as an aid to situational awareness in any flight condition, it is not authorized for any IFR operations, regardless of whether you are in instrument or visual conditions. **Answer (C) is incorrect.** While a handheld GPS may be used as an aid to situational awareness in any flight condition, it is not authorized for any IFR operations, regardless of whether you are in instrument or visual conditions.

65. Effective navigation by means of GPS includes

    A. determining the current status of all databases.

    B. ensuring that ATC approves your planned route.

    C. relying solely on the GPS for course information.

Answer (A) is correct. (FAA-H-8083-6 Chap 3)
    DISCUSSION: A pilot must determine the status of all appropriate databases. If a database is not current, the pilot must use an alternate means of navigation as the primary form.
    Answer (B) is incorrect. Pilots may be, and frequently are, given changes to their requested planned route by ATC. A pilot must ensure that the route flown is approved by ATC whether it was his or her requested plan or not. **Answer (C) is incorrect.** All systems have the possibility of failing at some point, and it would not be effective to rely solely on a GPS unit for navigation. It is wise to have another means (paper charts, approach plates, etc.) from which to navigate.

66. Why should pilots understand how to cancel entries made on a GPS?

    A. Because GPS units frequently provide wrong or false information.

    B. Because heavy workloads and turbulence can increase data entry errors.

    C. Because published route names commonly change.

Answer (B) is correct. (FAA-H-8083-6 Chap 3)
    DISCUSSION: Stressful situations, heavy workloads, and turbulence make data entry errors real problems, and pilots should know how to recover basic aircraft controls quickly.
    Answer (A) is incorrect. GPS units provide a high degree of accuracy and are unreliable very infrequently. **Answer (C) is incorrect.** It is not common for names of published routes to change.

67. Reliance on GPS units

    A. can cause pilots to lose proficiency in performing manual calculations of time, distance, and heading.

    B. will increase a pilot's skill in navigating by visual reference.

    C. does not decrease pilot workload.

Answer (A) is correct. (FAA-H-8083-6 Chap 3)
    DISCUSSION: Due to the reliance on GPS units for navigation, it is easy for pilots to lose proficiency in performing manual calculations on courses, times, distances, headings, etc.
    Answer (B) is incorrect. Reliance on GPS units for navigation does not increase skill in navigating by outside references, such as pilotage. **Answer (C) is incorrect.** Navigation by GPS does decrease pilot workload.

68. Before a pilot utilizes a GPS route or procedure, what would be an acceptable method of verifying the GPS database is current?

    A. Check to see if all waypoints on the GPS route match points on procedure charts.

    B. Call FSS and verify that the GPS database is current.

    C. Query the ATC facility issuing your IFR clearance as to database currency.

Answer (A) is the best answer. (FAA-H-8083-6 Chap 3)
    DISCUSSION: The way to determine database currency is by checking the database effective dates, presented when the GPS unit is powered on. Most units require the pilot to acknowledge this information before completing the start up cycle. Given the choices presented in this question, checking the GPS procedure against the approach chart is the best alternative to ensuring database currency.
    Answer (B) is incorrect. FSS has no way to determine if your GPS database information is accurate and/or current. **Answer (C) is incorrect.** ATC has no way to determine if your GPS database information is accurate and/or current.

69. When your aircraft is equipped with a TSO-C129 or TSO-C196 GPS, an airport may not be qualified for alternate use if

    A. the only standard approach procedure is GPS at the destination and alternate.

    B. the airport has only AWOS-3 weather reporting and no LAAS equipment operational.

    C. the airport is next to a restricted or prohibited area.

Answer (A) is correct. (AIM Para 1-2-3)
    DISCUSSION: Any required alternate airport must have an available instrument approach procedure that does not require the use of GPS.
    Answer (B) is incorrect. The AIM states, "any required alternate airport must have an available instrument approach procedure that does not require the use of GPS." **Answer (C) is incorrect.** It is irrelevant what type of airspace the airport is in or near, any required alternate airport must have an available instrument approach procedure that does not require the use of GPS.

70. When planning an IFR flight using GPS, the pilot should know that VFR waypoints

    A. are not recognized by the IFR system and will be rejected for IFR routing.

    B. can be used to aid in defining the route in the FAA flight plan if the waypoint name has a 5-letter identifier.

    C. can be used to define direct routing under IFR if they are retrieved from a current database and identified by a four-point star.

Answer (A) is correct. (AIM Para 1-1-17)
    DISCUSSION: VFR waypoints cannot be used for instrument flight planning.
    Answer (B) is incorrect. All GPS waypoints have 5-letter identifiers. VFR waypoints consist of five letters beginning with the letters "VP" and cannot be used in IFR flight planning. **Answer (C) is incorrect.** Although VFR waypoints also are the same four-point star as the IFR waypoint, they cannot be used for IFR flight planning.

71. Prior to using GPS waypoints for RNAV, what can you do to check the current status of the GPS database?

    A. Contact the local FSS and have them verify the current status of the database.

    B. Contact the ATC/ARTCC that issued the En Route Low Altitude chart to verify the current status of the GPS waypoints.

    C. Compare the GPS database to the En Route Low Altitude chart. If they are the same, the GPS database is current.

Answer (C) is correct. (AIM Para 1-1-17)
    DISCUSSION: GPS database updates are done on a 28-day cycle, which is the same as the schedule for updating En Route Low Altitude charts. You can compare the two to verify currency.
    Answer (A) is incorrect. It is not necessary to contact FSS to request verification of your GPS database currency. The FSS will not be able to assist you with determining database currency. They do not issue GPS databases. **Answer (B) is incorrect.** It is not necessary to contact ATC/ARTCC to request verification of your GPS database currency. ATC/ARTCC will not be able to assist you with determining currency. ATC/ARTCC do not issue GPS databases.

72. While conducting a GPS approach, if you disengage the auto sensitivity, what will occur?

    A. The approach mode annunciation will disengage.

    B. The altitude mode will disengage.

    C. The altitude and heading modes will disengage.

Answer (A) is correct. (AIM Para 1-1-17)
    DISCUSSION: Overriding an automatically selected sensitivity during an approach will cancel the approach mode annunciation.
    Answer (B) is incorrect. Altitude mode is an autopilot function, not a GPS function. **Answer (C) is incorrect.** Altitude and heading modes are autopilot functions, not GPS functions.

73. GPS systems certified for IFR operations cannot be used as a substitute for DME receivers

    A. to determine aircraft position or a DME fix at altitudes above 24,000 feet.

    B. to fly a DME arc.

    C. in selecting an alternate that requires use of DME.

Answer (C) is correct. (FAA-H-8083-16B Chap 1)
    DISCUSSION: GPS is not authorized as a substitute means of navigation guidance when conducting a conventional approach at an alternate airport if the approach procedure requires DME. The aircraft must be equipped with an appropriate DME in order to use the approach as an alternate.
    Answer (A) is incorrect. There is no rule barring a pilot from using GPS to determine aircraft position above 24,000 feet. **Answer (B) is incorrect.** There is no prohibition against using GPS to fly a DME arc.

74. When using a TSO-C129 or TSO-C196 GPS for navigation and instrument approaches, any required alternate airport must have

    A. a GPS approach with GBAS that is anticipated to be operational or available at the ETA.

    B. a GPS approach if no WAAS outage is expected.

    C. an approved operational instrument approach procedure other than GPS.

Answer (C) is correct. (AIM Para 1-1-17)
    DISCUSSION: Airports with only a global positioning system (GPS) approach procedure cannot be used as an alternate by TSO-129/129A users. Because GPS is not authorized as a substitute means of navigation guidance when conducting a conventional approach at an alternate airport, if the approach procedure requires distance measuring equipment (DME), the aircraft must be equipped with the appropriate DME avionics in order to use the approach as an alternate.
    Answer (A) is incorrect. GBAS is pertinent to a TSO-C161a/162a certified GPS unit, not the TSO-C129 or TSO-C196 specified by this question. **Answer (B) is incorrect.** WAAS certified GPS units comply with TSO-C145/146, not the TSO-C129 or TSO-C196 units specified by the question.

75. Your aircraft is equipped with a WAAS enabled GPS unit. While performing a GPS approach, you note an "LNAV+V available" indication on the moving map display. You know that

    A. you can use the LPV minimums line on the IAP chart with this indication.

    B. the indication reflects an artificially created advisory glidepath that you can use to descend to the LNAV MDA.

    C. you can descend to GBAS approach minimums indicated on the IAP.

Answer (B) is correct. (AIM Para 1-1-20)
    DISCUSSION: Even if WAAS becomes unavailable, you can follow the lateral and vertical guidance information as an aid to flying a constant descent to the MDA.
    Answer (A) is incorrect. Flying to LPV minimums requires an LPV annunciation on the GPS unit. **Answer (C) is incorrect.** Equipment requirements for a GBAS in the aircraft is a GBAS receiver. Current avionics conform either to GBAS or WAAS standards. No manufacturer has chosen to build a single avionics package integrating both GBAS and WAAS standards. This aircraft is equipped with a WAAS-enabled GPS unit.

76. Aircraft operating under IFR with TSO-C129 or TSO-C196 GPS for en route navigation must also have installed

    A. VOR/DME with RNAV capabilities.

    B. a backup GPS receiver.

    C. the avionics necessary to receive appropriate NAVAIDs along the route.

Answer (C) is correct. (AIM Para 1-1-17)
    DISCUSSION: Aircraft using GPS TSO-C129 or TSO-C196 navigation equipment under IFR must be equipped with an approved and operational alternate means of navigation appropriate to the flight.
    Answer (A) is incorrect. There is no specific requirement for VOR/DME with RNAV capabilities to be installed in the aircraft. **Answer (B) is incorrect.** There is no requirement for the aircraft to have a backup GPS installed.

3.7 Autopilots

77. Which of the following is a benefit of flying with an autopilot?

    A. Pilots will not need to worry about controlling airspeed or throttle settings.

    B. Airspace restrictions will automatically be avoided.

    C. Pilot workload is reduced.

Answer (C) is correct. (FAA-H-8083-6 Chap 4)
    DISCUSSION: Autopilots reduce the physical and mental demands of the pilot.
    Answer (A) is incorrect. Pilots must still manage the throttle to control airspeed when the autopilot is engaged because most autopilots are not capable of changing power settings on their own. **Answer (B) is incorrect.** It is a pilot's responsibility to avoid all airspace that is restricted or otherwise unavailable for use at a given time.

78. In an autopilot-controlled system, what device actually moves the control surfaces?

    A. Gyroscope.

    B. Servo.

    C. Vacuum pump.

Answer (B) is correct. (FAA-H-8083-6 Chap 4)
    DISCUSSION: Servos are electromechanical devices that translate electrical commands into motion, thus moving the control surfaces.
    Answer (A) is incorrect. Servos, not gyroscopes, translate electrical commands into motion, thus moving the control surfaces. **Answer (C) is incorrect.** Servos, not vacuum pumps, translate electrical commands into motion, thus moving the control surfaces.

79. To ensure situational awareness while using an autopilot system

    A. pilots must verify that the aircraft is tracking the intended flight profile.

    B. it is important to ensure that all navigational databases are current.

    C. current navigational charts are required.

Answer (A) is correct. (FAA-H-8083-6 Chap 4)
    DISCUSSION: After engaging the autopilot, it is important to verify that the aircraft is tracking the intended flight profile.
    Answer (B) is incorrect. Autopilot systems are not dependent on having current navigational databases. Pilots can use them to maintain a given heading or altitude. **Answer (C) is incorrect.** While a good practice, having physical paper charts in the aircraft is not a requirement.

STUDY UNIT FOUR

FEDERAL AVIATION REGULATIONS

(7 pages of outline)

This study unit contains outlines of major concepts tested, sample test questions and answers regarding Federal Aviation Regulations, and an explanation of each answer.

Recall that the **sole purpose** of this book is to expedite your passing of the FAA pilot knowledge test for the instrument rating. Accordingly, all extraneous material (i.e., topics or regulations not directly tested on the FAA pilot knowledge test) is omitted, even though much more knowledge is necessary to fly safely. This additional material is presented in *Pilot Handbook*, *Aviation Weather and Weather Services*, *FAR/AIM*, and *Instrument Pilot Flight Maneuvers and Practical Test Prep*, available from Gleim Publications, Inc. Order online at www.GleimAviation.com.

NOTE: The FAA refers to the Federal Aviation Regulations as "14 CFR" rather than "FAR." CFR stands for Code of Federal Regulations, and the Federal Aviation Regulations are in Title 14. For example, FAR Part 1 and FAR 61.109 are referred to as 14 CFR Part 1 and 14 CFR 61.109, respectively.

4.1   14 CFR PART 1

1.1 General Definitions

1. Airports are areas of land or water that are used or intended to be used for the landing and takeoff of aircraft, including any buildings and facilities.

2. A Glide Path Qualification Surface (GQS) is an imaginary surface extending from the runway threshold along the runway centerline to the Decision Altitude (DA) point.

4.2   14 CFR PART 61

61.3 Requirements for Certificates, Ratings, and Authorizations

1. The pilot in command must hold an instrument rating when operating under IFR or in weather conditions less than the minimums prescribed for VFR flight.

2. An IFR clearance is required when operating in Class A airspace.

61.23 Medical Certificates: Requirement and Duration

1. BasicMed allows a pilot to conduct certain VFR and IFR operations using a U.S. driver's license instead of a medical certificate as long as the pilot meets the following conditions:

    a. Has held an FAA medical certificate at any time after July 14, 2006, the most recent of which

        1) May have been a special issuance medical certificate

            a) A one-time special issuance medical certificate must be obtained for certain cardiovascular, neurological, and mental health conditions.

        2) May be expired

        3) Cannot have been suspended, revoked, withdrawn, or denied

    b. Completes an approved medical education course in the preceding 24 calendar months in accordance with 14 CFR Part 68

    c. Receives a comprehensive medical examination from a state-licensed physician in the previous 48 months in accordance with 14 CFR Part 68

        1) The exam is not required to be conducted by an aviation medical examiner (AME).

61.51 Pilot Logbooks

1. Instrument flight time may be logged when flight is solely by reference to instruments under actual or simulated flight conditions.

    a. The location and type of each instrument approach completed and the name of the safety pilot must be included in the logbook for each simulated instrument flight.

    b. During VMC, a view-limiting device must be used.

2. An instrument flight instructor (CFII) may log instrument time when acting as an instrument flight instructor in actual instrument weather conditions.

61.57 Recent Flight Experience: Pilot in Command

1. In order to act as pilot in command under IFR, one must have logged instrument time (actual or simulated) in either the same category of aircraft (airplane) to be used or an appropriate flight simulator or flight training device.

    a. Recall **6-6-H-I-T** for experience requirements:

        1) 6 - within the 6 calendar months preceding the month of the flight
        2) 6 - performed 6 instrument approaches
        3) H - holding procedures and tasks
        4) I - intercepting courses
        5) T - tracking courses through the use of navigational electronic systems

2. An instrument pilot who does not meet the experience requirements during the prescribed time or 6 calendar months thereafter must then pass an instrument proficiency check.

    a. This check may be conducted by an FAA inspector, an FAA-designated examiner, or a certificated instrument flight instructor.

61.113 Private Pilot Privileges and Limitations: Pilot in Command

1. A pilot in command of an aircraft operating under BasicMed must adhere to the following limitations:

    a. The aircraft may not

        1) Be certificated to carry more than six occupants
        2) Have a maximum certificated takeoff weight of more than 6,000 lb.

    b. No portion of the flight may be

        1) Carried out above 18,000 ft. MSL

        2) Conducted outside the United States unless authorized by the country in which the flight is conducted

        3) Carried out at an indicated airspeed greater than 250 kt.

    c. The pilot must have available in his or her logbook (in paper or electronic format) the

        1) Completed medical examination checklist
        2) Medical education course completion certificate

61.133 Commercial Pilot Privileges and Limitations

1. Commercial pilots without an instrument rating cannot carry passengers for hire on cross-country flights during the day beyond a radius of 50 NM.

    a. Carrying passengers at night is also prohibited without an instrument rating.

4.3 14 CFR PART 91

91.3 Responsibility and Authority of the Pilot in Command

1.   The pilot in command of an aircraft is directly responsible for, and is the final authority as to, determining the airworthiness and operation of that aircraft prior to each flight.

91.21 Portable Electronic Devices

1.   The use of certain portable electronic devices is prohibited on aircraft that are being operated under IFR.

91.103 Preflight Action

1.   Before beginning any IFR flight, the pilot must obtain and become familiar with information about weather reports and forecasts, fuel requirements, alternatives available if the planned flight cannot be completed, any known traffic delays, runway lengths at airports of intended use, and takeoff and landing distance information.

91.109 Flight Instruction; Simulated Instrument Flight and Certain Flight Tests

1.   To operate an airplane in simulated instrument flight, you must have at least a private pilot who is appropriately rated in your aircraft occupying the other control seat as a safety pilot.

91.123 Compliance with ATC Clearances and Instructions

1.   If you deviate from an ATC clearance in an emergency, you must notify ATC as soon as possible.

2.   If you are given priority by ATC in an emergency, ATC may request that you submit a detailed report within 48 hr. to the manager of that ATC facility.

     a.   The report may be required even though no rule has been violated.

3.   During an IFR flight in IMC, if a distress condition is encountered, the pilot should immediately declare an emergency and obtain an amended clearance.

     a.   Distress is a condition of being threatened by serious and/or imminent danger and of requiring immediate assistance.

91.167 Fuel Requirements for Flight in IFR Conditions

1.   When flying IFR, you must carry sufficient fuel to fly to the first airport of intended landing, fly to the alternate airport (if required), and then fly for 45 min. at normal cruising speed.

2.   An alternate airport is not required if the destination airport has at least one approved instrument approach procedure (IAP) and the conditions in a. below are met.

     a.   Recall **1-2-3** for forecast weather:

          1)   1 - For at least 1 hr. before and for 1 hr. after the ETA
          2)   2 - Ceiling will be at least 2,000 ft. above the airport elevation
          3)   3 - Visibility will be at least 3 SM

91.169 IFR Flight Plan: Information Required

1. Intended airports of landing on an IFR flight must have a forecast ceiling of at least 2,000 ft. and visibility of at least 3 SM for 1 hr. before and 1 hr. after the ETA. Otherwise, an alternate must be listed on your IFR flight plan.

2. When a pilot elects to proceed to the selected alternate airport, the landing minimums used should be the minimums specified for the approach procedure selected.

    a. To list an airport with a nonprecision approach as an alternate, the forecast weather must be for at least an 800-ft. ceiling and 2 SM visibility at your ETA.

    b. To list an airport with a precision approach as an alternate, the forecast weather must indicate at least a 600-ft. ceiling and 2 SM visibility at your ETA.

3. If no instrument approaches are prescribed, the minimums for listing an airport as an alternate on an IFR flight are forecast weather allowing descent from the MEA, approach, and landing under basic VFR.

91.171 VOR Equipment Check for IFR Operations

1. When making VOR operation checks, the date, place, bearing error, and pilot signature should be placed in the aircraft log or other record.

2. Operational checks of VORs must be made every 30 days.

3. The maximum allowable tolerance when performing an operational check of a dual VOR system is a 4° variation between the two indicated bearings.

    a. When performing an operational check using a ground-based VOT, the maximum tolerance is ±4°.

    b. When performing an operational check using an airborne checkpoint, the maximum tolerance is ±6°.

4. In addition to the VOR check that must be made at least every 30 days, the altimeter system and the transponder must have been inspected within 24 calendar months.

91.173 ATC Clearance and Flight Plan Required

1. No person may operate an aircraft in controlled airspace under IFR unless that person has

    a. Filed an IFR flight plan and
    b. Received an appropriate ATC clearance.

91.177 Minimum Altitudes for IFR Operations

1. Except when necessary for takeoff or landing, the minimum altitude for IFR flight (if none is prescribed in 14 CFR Parts 95 or 97) is one of the following:

    a. 2,000 ft. above the highest obstacle within a horizontal distance of 4 NM over designated mountainous terrain

    b. 1,000 ft. above the highest obstacle within a horizontal distance of 4 NM over nonmountainous terrain

91.205 Powered Civil Aircraft with Standard Category U.S. Airworthiness Certificates: Instrument and Equipment Requirements

1. For IFR flight, navigation equipment must be appropriate to the ground facilities to be used.

2. Above 24,000 ft. MSL, DME is required if VOR navigational equipment is required.

3. A gyroscopic directional indicator, a gyroscopic attitude indicator, and a gyroscopic rate-of-turn indicator are required for IFR flight.

4. Aircraft being operated under IFR are required to have a slip-skid indicator, a clock with a sweep second pointer or digital presentation, and a sensitive altimeter.

91.211 Supplemental Oxygen

1. At cabin pressure altitudes above 15,000 ft. MSL, each passenger of the aircraft must be provided with supplemental oxygen.

2. At cabin pressure altitudes above 14,000 ft. MSL, the required minimum flight crew must be provided and use supplemental oxygen during the entire flight time at those altitudes.

3. Pilots can fly at cabin pressure altitudes above 12,500 ft. MSL up to and including 14,000 ft. MSL for up to 30 min. without supplemental oxygen.

    a. If a flight is conducted at these altitudes for more than 30 min., oxygen must be provided to and used by the required minimum flight crew for the time in excess of 30 min.

91.215 ATC Transponder and Altitude Reporting Equipment and Use

1. All aircraft must have and use an altitude encoding transponder (Mode C) when operating

    a. Within Class B airspace
    b. Within 30 NM of the primary Class B airport
    c. Within and above Class C airspace
    d. At and above 10,000 ft. MSL except at and below 2,500 ft. AGL
    e. In Class A airspace

2. Request for deviations must be made to the controlling ATC facility.

    a. If the transponder fails during flight, ATC may authorize the aircraft to continue to the airport of ultimate destination.

        1) An aircraft with an operating transponder but without Mode C can request a deviation at any time.

    b. For operation of an aircraft that is not equipped with a transponder, the request for a deviation must be made at least 1 hr. before the proposed operation.

91.225 ADS-B Out Equipment and Use

1. No person may operate an aircraft in the following airspace unless the aircraft has the appropriate ADS-B Out equipment installed:

   a. Within Class A airspace
   b. Within and above Class B airspace
   c. Within 30 NM of the Class B airspace primary airport
   d. Within and above Class C airspace
   e. At and above 10,000 ft. MSL except at and below 2,500 ft. AGL
   f. At and above 3,000 ft. MSL over the Gulf of Mexico from the U.S. coastline out to 12 NM

2. These requirements do not apply to any aircraft not originally certificated with an electrical system or that has not subsequently been certified with such a system installed.

3. Requests for ATC-authorized deviations from these requirements must be made to the appropriate ATC facility

   a. At any time for an aircraft with an inoperative ADS-B Out

   b. At least 1 hr. before the proposed operation of an aircraft that is not equipped with ADS-B Out

4. Aircraft operating with ADS-B Out must operate this equipment in the transmit mode at all times unless

   a. Authorized by the Administrator in the interest of national defense, security, intelligence, or law enforcement purposes or

   b. Directed by ATC for safe air traffic control functions.

91.227 ADS-B Out Equipment Performance Requirements

1. ADS-B Out is a function of an aircraft's onboard avionics that periodically broadcasts the aircraft's state vector (3-dimensional position and 3-dimensional velocity).

2. Aircraft operating in Class A airspace are required to have ADS-B Out equipment installed that operates on the frequency of 1090 MHz.

3. Aircraft operating in airspace designated for ADS-B Out, but outside of Class A airspace, must have ADS-B Out equipment installed that either

   a. Operates on the frequency of 1090 MHz or
   b. Operates using a universal access transceiver (UAT) on the frequency of 978 MHz.

91.411 Altimeter System and Altitude Reporting Equipment Tests and Inspections

1. Each static pressure system and altimeter instrument must be tested and inspected by the end of the 24th calendar month following the current inspection.

4.4 NTSB PART 830

1. NTSB Part 830, "Notification and Reporting of Aircraft Accidents or Incidents and Overdue Aircraft, and Preservation of Aircraft Wreckage, Mail, Cargo, and Records," covers the procedures required for aircraft accident- and incident-reporting responsibilities for pilots.

QUESTIONS

4.1 14 CFR Part 1

1.1 General Definitions

1. Which of the following terms describes an airport?

A.   An area of land or water that is used or intended to be used for the landing and takeoff of aircraft, and includes its buildings and facilities, if any.

B.   An area of land that is used for the takeoff and landing of aircraft, but does not include buildings since not all airports have buildings.

C.   All runway, taxiway, and ramp areas created for use by aircraft.

Answer (A) is correct. (14 CFR 1.1)
  DISCUSSION: Section 1.1 of the Federal Aviation Regulations defines an airport as "an area of land or water that is used or intended to be used for the landing and takeoff of aircraft, and includes its buildings and facilities, if any."
  Answer (B) is incorrect. Section 1.1 of the Federal Aviation Regulations includes areas of water and any buildings and facilities in the definition of an airport. **Answer (C) is incorrect.** Section 1.1 of the Federal Aviation Regulations includes areas of land and water and any buildings and facilities in the definition of an airport.

2. The Glide Path Qualification Surface (GQS) limits the height of obstructions between

A.   The final approach fix and the missed approach point.

B.   Decision altitude and the runway threshold.

C.   Any initial approach fix(es) and the final approach fix.

Answer (B) is correct. (AC 150-5300-13A)
  DISCUSSION: The GQS is an imaginary surface extending from the runway threshold along the runway centerline to the Decision Altitude (DA) point.
  Answer (A) is incorrect. The GQS extends to the Decision Altitude (DA) point. **Answer (C) is incorrect.** The GQS extends to the Decision Altitude (DA) point.

3. The term "airport" means an area of land or water that is

A.   Scheduled for use as an airport.

B.   Used or intended to be used for the landing and takeoff of aircraft and includes taxiways and other ground movement areas.

C.   Used or intended to be used for the landing and takeoff of aircraft and includes its buildings and facilities, if any.

Answer (C) is correct. (14 CFR 1.1)
  DISCUSSION: The FAA defines an airport as an area of land or water that is used or intended to be used for the landing and takeoff of aircraft, including buildings or facilities.
  Answer (A) is incorrect. The FAA definition of an airport includes buildings and facilities. This answer option does not include the buildings and facilities stipulated by the FAA definition. **Answer (B) is incorrect.** This answer option does not include buildings or facilities, which are included in the FAA definition. The FAA definition does not include taxiways and ground movement areas.

4.2 14 CFR Part 61

61.3 Requirements for Certificates, Ratings, and Authorizations

4. Do regulations permit you to act as pilot in command of an airplane in IMC if you hold a private pilot certificate with ASEL, rotorcraft category, with helicopter class rating and instrument helicopter rating?

A. Yes, if you comply with the recent IFR experience requirements for a helicopter.

B. No. You must hold either an unrestricted airline transport pilot-airplane certificate or an airplane instrument rating.

C. No. However, you may do so if you hold an airline transport pilot-airplane certificate limited to VFR.

Answer (B) is correct. *(14 CFR 61.3)*
DISCUSSION: Instrument privileges are class-specific. To operate as pilot in command in an airplane in IMC, the pilot would need to have an instrument rating in the airplane class. An unrestricted airline transport pilot-airplane certificate would also meet this requirement.
Answer (A) is incorrect. Instrument operating privileges are class-specific. **Answer (C) is incorrect.** The airline transport pilot-airplane certificate would need to be unrestricted for this operation to meet the regulatory requirement.

5. Under which condition must the pilot in command of a civil aircraft have at least an instrument rating?

A. When operating in Class E airspace.

B. For a flight in VFR conditions while on an IFR flight plan.

C. For any flight above an altitude of 1,200 feet AGL, when the visibility is less than 3 miles.

Answer (B) is correct. *(14 CFR 61.3)*
DISCUSSION: No person may act as pilot in command of a civil aircraft under IFR or in weather conditions less than the minimums prescribed for VFR flight unless (s)he holds an instrument rating.
Answer (A) is incorrect. An instrument rating is required at all times when operating in Class A, not Class E, airspace. **Answer (C) is incorrect.** VFR is permitted in uncontrolled airspace during the day with visibilities of as little as 1 statute mile above 1,200 feet AGL but below 10,000 feet MSL.

6. The pilot in command of a civil aircraft must have an instrument rating only when operating

A. under IFR in positive control airspace.

B. under IFR, in weather conditions less than the minimum for VFR flight or in Class A airspace.

C. in weather conditions less than the minimum prescribed for VFR flight.

Answer (B) is correct. *(14 CFR 61.3 and 91.135)*
DISCUSSION: No person may act as pilot in command of a civil aircraft under IFR, in weather conditions less than the minimums prescribed for VFR flight, or in Class A airspace unless (s)he holds an instrument rating.
Answer (A) is incorrect. You must have an instrument rating when operating under IFR, in weather conditions less than the minimum for VFR flight, or in Class A airspace, not only under IFR in positive control airspace. Positive control airspace means that ATC will provide separation to all aircraft within that airspace. **Answer (C) is incorrect.** It omits flying in VFR conditions with an IFR clearance.

61.23 Medical Certificates: Requirement and Duration

7. In order to qualify for BasicMed, you must have received a comprehensive examination from:

A. An FAA-designated Aviation Medical Examiner within the previous 60 months.

B. A state-licensed physician within the previous 24 months.

C. A state-licensed physician within the previous 48 months.

Answer (C) is correct. *(14 CFR 61.23)*
DISCUSSION: In order to qualify for BasicMed, you must have received a comprehensive examination from a state-licensed physician within the previous 48 months.
Answer (A) is incorrect. You are required to have received the examination from a state-licensed physician, not an FAA-designated Aviation Medical Examiner, and you must have received the examination within the previous 48 months, not the previous 60 months. **Answer (B) is incorrect.** You must have received the examination from a state-licensed physician within the previous 48 months, not the previous 24 months.

61.51 Pilot Logbooks

8. What portion of dual instruction time may a certificated instrument flight instructor log as instrument flight time?

A. All time during which the instructor acts as instrument instructor, regardless of weather conditions.

B. All time during which the instructor acts as instrument instructor in actual instrument weather conditions.

C. Only the time during which the instructor flies the aircraft by reference to instruments.

Answer (B) is correct. (14 CFR 61.51)
DISCUSSION: An instrument flight instructor may log as instrument time that time during which (s)he acts as instrument flight instructor in actual instrument weather conditions.
Answer (A) is incorrect. The flight conditions must be IMC for the instructor to log flight instruction as instrument time. **Answer (C) is incorrect.** Instructing in (as well as flying in) actual IFR weather conditions can be logged as instrument time by the instructor.

9. To meet instrument experience requirements of CFR Part 61, section 61.57(c), a pilot enters the condition of flight in the pilot logbook as simulated instrument conditions, what other qualifying information must also be entered?

A. Location and type of each instrument approach completed and name of safety pilot.

B. Number and type of instrument approaches completed and route of flight.

C. Name and pilot certificate number of safety pilot and type of approaches completed.

Answer (A) is correct. (14 CFR 61.51)
DISCUSSION: A pilot may log as instrument flight time only that time during which (s)he operates the aircraft solely by reference to instruments, under actual or simulated instrument flight conditions. Each entry must include the location and type of each instrument approach completed and the name of the safety pilot for each simulated instrument flight.
Answer (B) is incorrect. The location and type of instrument approaches must be entered along with the safety pilot's name, not the route of flight. **Answer (C) is incorrect.** The location is required, but the safety pilot's certificate number is not.

10. Which flight time may be logged as instrument time when on an instrument flight plan?

A. All of the time the aircraft was not controlled by ground references.

B. Only the time you controlled the aircraft solely by reference to flight instruments.

C. Only the time you were flying in IFR weather conditions.

Answer (B) is correct. (14 CFR 61.51)
DISCUSSION: A pilot may log as instrument flight time only that time during which (s)he operates the aircraft solely by reference to instruments, under actual or simulated instrument flight conditions.
Answer (A) is incorrect. VFR flight can be conducted above a cloud layer without visual ground references, i.e., VFR-on-top. **Answer (C) is incorrect.** Time under the hood (i.e., simulated IFR) as well as actual IFR conditions counts as instrument time.

11. What are the requirements to log an ILS approach in VMC conditions for instrument currency?

A. The flight must remain on an IFR flight plan throughout the approach and landing.

B. The ILS approach can be credited only if you use a view-limiting device and log the name of the safety pilot.

C. The ILS approach can be credited regardless of actual weather if you are issued an IFR clearance.

Answer (B) is correct. (14 CFR 61.51, 61.57, 91.109)
DISCUSSION: To be credited for an ILS approach in VMC, the instrument rated pilot must use a view-limiting device and log the name of the safety pilot. If the instrument rated pilot is doing this for training, a view-limiting device is still required along with an authorized instructor instead of only a safety pilot. The instructor would then endorse the pilot's logbook for the training.
Answer (A) is incorrect. An IFR flight plan is not required in VMC conditions. However, it is required in IMC conditions. **Answer (C) is incorrect.** An IFR clearance is not required in VMC conditions. The approach can be credited in IMC conditions with a clearance and without a view-limiting device to remain instrument current.

61.57 Recent Flight Experience: Pilot in Command

12. How long does a pilot meet the recency of experience requirements for IFR flight after successfully completing an instrument proficiency check if no further IFR flights are made?

A. 90 days.

B. 6 calendar months.

C. 12 calendar months.

Answer (B) is correct. (14 CFR 61.57)
 DISCUSSION: No pilot may act as pilot in command when operating under IFR or in weather conditions less than the minimums prescribed for VFR unless (s)he has, within the 6 calendar months preceding the month of the flight, logged instrument time under actual or simulated IFR conditions in the category of aircraft involved or in an appropriate flight simulator or flight training device and has performed at least six instrument approaches, holding procedures, and intercepting and tracking courses through the use of navigation systems. Alternatively, the pilot may pass an instrument proficiency check in the category of aircraft involved.
 Answer (A) is incorrect. Ninety days refers to takeoff and landing currency to carry passengers. **Answer (C) is incorrect.** Twelve months is the time whereafter another instrument proficiency check is required.

13. No pilot may act as pilot-in-command of an aircraft, under IFR or in weather conditions less than the minimums prescribed for VFR unless that pilot has, within the preceding 6 calendar months, completed at least

A. six instrument approaches, holding procedures, intercepting and tracking courses using navigational systems, or passed an instrument proficiency check.

B. six instrument flights under actual IFR conditions.

C. three instrument approaches and logged 3 hours.

Answer (A) is correct. (14 CFR 61.57)
 DISCUSSION: No person may act as pilot in command under IFR or in weather conditions less than the minimums prescribed for VFR unless, within the 6 calendar months preceding the month of the flight, that person has performed and logged under actual or simulated instrument conditions, either in flight in the appropriate category of aircraft for the instrument privileges sought or in a flight simulator or flight training device that is representative of the aircraft category for the instrument privileges sought, at least six instrument approaches, holding procedures, and intercepting and tracking courses through the use of navigation systems. Alternatively, the pilot may pass an instrument proficiency check in the category of aircraft involved.
 Answer (B) is incorrect. A pilot must complete, under actual or simulated instrument conditions, at least six instrument approaches, holding procedures, and intercepting and tracking courses through the use of navigation systems, not six instrument flights under actual IFR conditions. **Answer (C) is incorrect.** A pilot must complete at least six, not three, instrument approaches, holding procedures, and intercepting and tracking courses through the use of navigation systems. There is no required minimum number of hours to be logged.

14. To meet the minimum required instrument flight experience to act as pilot in command of an aircraft under IFR, you must have logged within the 6 calendar months preceding the month of the flight, in the same category of aircraft:

A. holding procedures, intercepting and tracking courses through the use of navigation systems, and six instrument approaches.

B. six instrument approaches, three of which must be in the same category and class of aircraft to be flown, and 6 hours of instrument time in any aircraft.

C. 6 hours of instrument time in any aircraft, and six instrument approaches.

Answer (A) is correct. (14 CFR 61.57)
 DISCUSSION: No person may act as pilot in command under IFR or in weather conditions less than VFR minimums unless, within the 6 calendar months preceding the month of the flight, (s)he has performed and logged, under actual or simulated instrument conditions, at least six instrument approaches, holding procedures, and intercepting and tracking courses through the use of navigation systems, in the category of aircraft to be flown.
 Answer (B) is incorrect. All six, not three, approaches must be in the same category and aircraft. Additionally, you must have accomplished holding procedures and intercepting and tracking courses through the use of navigation systems, not accumulated 6 hr. of instrument time. **Answer (C) is incorrect.** You must have also accomplished holding procedures and intercepting and tracking courses through the use of navigation systems in the same category and class of aircraft, not accumulated 6 hr. of instrument time in any aircraft.

15. A pilot's recent IFR experience expires on July 1 of this year. What is the latest date the pilot can meet the IFR experience requirement without having to take an instrument proficiency check?

    A.   December 31, this year.

    B.   June 30, next year.

    C.   July 31, this year.

Answer (A) is correct. (14 CFR 61.57)
    DISCUSSION: A pilot who does not meet the recent instrument experience requirements during the prescribed time or 6 months thereafter may not serve as pilot in command under IFR or in weather conditions less than the minimums prescribed for VFR until (s)he passes an instrument proficiency check. If the 6 months' recency experience period expires on July 1, the 6 months thereafter would expire on December 31 this year.
    Answer (B) is incorrect. This date represents 12 months instead of 6 months. **Answer (C) is incorrect.** This date represents 1 month instead of 6 months.

16. After your recent IFR experience lapses, how much time do you have before you must pass an instrument proficiency check to act as pilot in command under IFR?

    A.   6 months.

    B.   90 days.

    C.   12 months.

Answer (A) is correct. (14 CFR 61.57)
    DISCUSSION: A pilot who does not meet the recent instrument experience requirements during the prescribed time or 6 months thereafter may not serve as pilot in command under IFR or in weather conditions less than the minimums prescribed for VFR until (s)he passes an instrument proficiency check.
    Answer (B) is incorrect. Ninety days refers to the takeoff and landing currency requirements to carry passengers. **Answer (C) is incorrect.** Twelve months is the time from when you gain IFR currency to when you are required to pass another instrument proficiency check (assuming you have not maintained currency since you gained proficiency).

17. To meet the minimum instrument experience requirements, within the last 6 calendar months you need

    A.   six instrument approaches, holding procedures, and intercepting and tracking courses in the appropriate category of aircraft.

    B.   six hours in the same category aircraft.

    C.   six hours in the same category aircraft, and at least 3 of the 6 hours in actual IFR conditions.

Answer (A) is correct. (14 CFR 61.57)
    DISCUSSION: No person may act as pilot in command under IFR or in weather conditions less than VFR minimums unless, within the 6 calendar months preceding the month of the flight, (s)he has performed and logged, under actual or simulated instrument conditions, at least six instrument approaches, holding procedures, and intercepting and tracking courses through the use of navigation systems, in the category of aircraft to be flown.
    Answer (B) is incorrect. To be current for IFR, you must have performed six instrument approaches, holding procedures, and intercepting and tracking courses in the same category of aircraft, not accumulated 6 hours in the same category of aircraft. **Answer (C) is incorrect.** To be current for IFR, you must have performed six instrument approaches, holding procedures, and intercepting and tracking courses in the same category of aircraft, not accumulated 6 hours in the same category aircraft with at least 3 hours in actual IFR conditions.

18. A pilot may satisfy the recent flight experience requirement necessary to act as pilot in command in IMC in powered aircraft by logging within the 6 calendar months preceding the month of the flight

    A.   six instrument approaches, holding procedures, and intercepting and tracking courses using navigational systems.

    B.   six instrument approaches and 3 hours under actual or 6 hours in simulated IFR conditions; three of the approaches must be in the category of aircraft involved.

    C.   6 hours of instrument time under actual or simulated IFR conditions, including at least six instrument approaches. Three of the 6 hours must be in flight in any category aircraft.

Answer (A) is the best answer. (14 CFR 61.57)
    DISCUSSION: Items required by 14 CFR 61.57 to remain current include six instrument approaches, holding procedures, and intercepting and tracking courses using navigational electronic systems.
    Answer (B) is incorrect. The answer does not include holding procedures or intercepting and tracking courses using navigational systems. **Answer (C) is incorrect.** The answer does not include holding procedures or intercepting and tracking courses using navigational systems.

19. What recent instrument flight experience requirements must be met before you may act as pilot in command of an airplane under IFR?

A. A minimum of six instrument approaches in an airplane, or an approved simulator (airplane) or ground trainer, within the preceding 6 calendar months.

B. A minimum of six instrument approaches, at least three of which must be in an aircraft within the preceding 6 calendar months.

C. A minimum of six instrument approaches in an aircraft, at least three of which must be in the same category within the preceding 6 calendar months.

Answer (A) is correct. (14 CFR 61.57)
DISCUSSION: No person may act as pilot in command under IFR or in weather conditions less than VFR minimums unless, within the 6 calendar months preceding the month of the flight, (s)he has performed and logged, under actual or simulated instrument conditions, at least six instrument approaches, holding procedures, and intercepting and tracking courses through the use of navigation systems, in the category of aircraft to be flown, in an approved simulator or flight training device, or in any combination of these.
Answer (B) is incorrect. All six approaches may be done in an approved flight simulator or flight training device; none are required to be done in an aircraft. **Answer (C) is incorrect.** All six approaches may be done in an approved flight simulator or flight training device; none are required to be done in an aircraft. In addition, all six approaches, not just three, must be done in the same category of aircraft or a simulator or flight training device representative of that aircraft category.

20. What minimum conditions are necessary for the instrument approaches required for IFR currency?

A. The approaches may be made in an aircraft, flight simulator, or flight training device.

B. At least three approaches must be made in the same category of aircraft to be flown.

C. At least three approaches must be made in the same category and class of aircraft to be flown.

Answer (A) is correct. (14 CFR 61.57)
DISCUSSION: For IFR currency, the six instrument approaches must be made either in the same category of aircraft to be flown or in a flight simulator or training device representative of the aircraft category to be flown, or in any combination of these.
Answer (B) is incorrect. All six approaches may be done in an approved flight simulator or training device, not necessarily in an airplane. **Answer (C) is incorrect.** All six approaches may be done in an approved flight simulator or training device, not necessarily in an airplane.

21. An instrument rated pilot who has not logged any instrument time in 1 year or more cannot serve as pilot in command under IFR, unless the pilot

A. completes the required 6 hours and six approaches, followed by an instrument proficiency check given by an FAA-designated examiner.

B. passes an instrument proficiency check in the category of aircraft involved, given by an approved FAA examiner, instrument instructor, or FAA inspector.

C. passes an instrument proficiency check in the category of aircraft involved, followed by 6 hours and six instrument approaches, 3 of those hours in the category of aircraft Involved.

Answer (B) is correct. (14 CFR 61.57)
DISCUSSION: A pilot who does not meet the recent instrument experience requirements during the prescribed time or 6 months thereafter may not serve as pilot in command under IFR or in weather conditions less than the minimums prescribed for VFR until (s)he passes an instrument proficiency check in the category of aircraft involved, given by an FAA inspector, a member of an armed force of the U.S. authorized to conduct flight tests, an FAA-approved check pilot, or a certificated instrument flight instructor. The proficiency check may be completed in an appropriate flight simulator or flight training device.
Answer (A) is incorrect. An instrument proficiency check by itself provides currency. Additional time and approaches are not required. **Answer (C) is incorrect.** An instrument proficiency check by itself provides currency. Additional time and approaches are not required.

22. How may a pilot satisfy the recent flight experience requirement necessary to act as pilot in command in IMC in powered aircraft? Within the previous 6 calendar months, logged

A. six instrument approaches, holding procedures, and intercepting and tracking courses using navigational systems.

B. six instrument approaches and 3 hours under actual or simulated IFR conditions within the last 6 months; three of the approaches must be in the category of aircraft involved.

C. 6 hours of instrument time under actual or simulated IFR conditions within the last 3 months, including at least six instrument approaches of any kind. Three of the 6 hours must be in flight in any category aircraft.

Answer (A) is correct. (14 CFR 61.57)
    DISCUSSION: No pilot may act as pilot in command of a powered aircraft under IFR or in weather conditions less than VFR minimums unless, within the 6 calendar months preceding the month of the flight, (s)he has performed and logged, under actual or simulated instrument conditions, at least six instrument approaches, holding procedures, and intercepting and tracking courses through the use of navigation systems, in the category of aircraft to be flown or in an airplane flight simulator or training device.
    Answer (B) is incorrect. There is no instrument flight time requirement. In addition to the six instrument approaches, you must also log holding procedures and intercepting and tracking courses using navigational systems. **Answer (C) is incorrect.** There is no instrument flight time requirement. You must log six instrument approaches, holding procedures, and intercepting and tracking courses using navigational systems within the past 6 months, not 3 months.

23. Which additional instrument experience, within the preceding 6 calendar months, is required to meet the requirements to act as pilot in command of an airplane under IFR if you already have 3 hours in an instrument simulator (including holding, intercepting, and tracking courses) and two instrument approaches in an airplane?

A. Another two instrument approaches in an airplane.

B. Another four instrument approaches in the same category.

C. Another 3 hours of actual or simulated instrument flight time in the same category.

Answer (B) is correct. (14 CFR 61.57)
    DISCUSSION: Regulations require a total of six instrument approaches in the category of aircraft for which instrument currency is sought.
    Answer (A) is incorrect. Regulations require a total of six, not four, instrument approaches to maintain instrument currency. **Answer (C) is incorrect.** While the additional 3 hours of simulator time would meet that particular requirement, you would still be four instrument approaches short of that requirement.

24. To act as pilot in command of an aircraft under IFR, what is the minimum instrument flight experience you must have logged during the preceding six months, in the same category of aircraft?

A. Holding procedures, intercepting and tracking courses through the use of navigation systems, and six instrument approaches.

B. Six hours of instrument time in any aircraft, and six instrument approaches.

C. Six instrument approaches, three of which must be in the same category and class of aircraft to be flown, and 6 hours of instrument time in any aircraft.

Answer (A) is correct. (14 CFR 61.57)
    DISCUSSION: Acting as PIC of an aircraft under IFR requires a minimum of six approaches logged in the 6 calendar months preceding the month of the flight, holding procedures, and intercepting and tracking courses through the use of navigation systems. This can be recalled with 66-HIT: 6 approaches, 6 months, holding, intercepting, and tracking.
    Answer (B) is incorrect. There are no minimum hourly requirements for maintaining instrument experience. **Answer (C) is incorrect.** All six of the minimum required six instrument approaches must be conducted in an airplane, powered-lift, helicopter, or airship, as appropriate, for the instrument rating privileges to be maintained in actual weather conditions or under simulated conditions using a view-limiting device.

25. Which additional IFR experience is required for you to meet the recent flight experience requirements to act as pilot in command of an airplane under IFR?

Your present instrument experience within the preceding 6 calendar months is

1. three hours with holding, intercepting and tracking courses in an approved airplane flight simulator.
2. two instrument approaches in an airplane.

    A. Three hours of simulated or actual instrument flight time in a helicopter and two instrument approaches in an airplane or helicopter.

    B. Four instrument approaches in an airplane, or an approved airplane flight simulator or training device.

    C. Three instrument approaches in an airplane.

Answer (B) is correct. (14 CFR 61.57)
    DISCUSSION: No person may act as pilot in command under IFR or in weather conditions less than the minimums prescribed for VFR, unless within the 6 calendar months preceding the month of the flight, that person has performed and logged under actual or simulated instrument conditions, either in flight in the appropriate category of aircraft for the instrument privileges being sought or in a flight simulator or flight training device that is representative of the aircraft category for the instrument privileges sought; at least six instrument approaches, holding procedures, and intercepting and tracking courses through the use of navigation systems. Having logged only two instrument approaches, the pilot must log four more.
    Answer (A) is incorrect. No minimum time is required; four, not two, more approaches are required; and all approaches must be in an airplane or flight simulator or flight training device representative of an airplane, not a helicopter. **Answer (C) is incorrect.** Four, not three, more approaches are required to have the required minimum of six.

26. A pilot plans an IFR flight on July 10 of this year. In order to meet IFR currency requirements the pilot must have

    A. performed his or her currency tasks between January 1 and July 10.

    B. performed his or her currency tasks between January 10 and July 10 with none of it before January 10.

    C. completed an IPC within the last year.

Answer (A) is correct. (14 CFR 61.57)
    DISCUSSION: For IFR currency, a pilot must meet the recent experience requirements within the 6 calendar months preceding the month of the flight to continue to fly as PIC in instrument conditions.
    Answer (B) is incorrect. A pilot has 6 full calendar months preceding the month of the flight to record for instrument currency and retain PIC privileges in instrument conditions. **Answer (C) is incorrect.** An IPC need only be completed if more than 12 calendar months have passed since the pilot was last qualified under the instrument recent experience requirements.

61.113 Private Pilot Privileges and Limitations: Pilot in Command

27. If you are operating under BasicMed, you may fly an aircraft with

    A. an actual takeoff weight of no more than 6,000 lb.

    B. a maximum certificated takeoff weight of no more than 6,000 lb.

    C. any weight, as long as you do not exceed the aircraft's maximum certificated takeoff weight.

Answer (B) is correct. (14 CFR 61.113)
    DISCUSSION: If you are operating under BasicMed, you may fly an aircraft with a maximum certificated takeoff weight of no more than 6,000 lb.
    Answer (A) is incorrect. To operate under BasicMed, you must fly aircraft with a maximum certificated takeoff weight, not an actual takeoff weight, of no more than 6,000 lb. **Answer (C) is incorrect.** To operate under BasicMed, you must fly aircraft with a maximum certificated takeoff weight of no more than 6,000 lb.

28. If you are operating under BasicMed, what is the maximum speed at which you may fly?

    A. 250 KIAS.

    B. 250 KIAS below 10,000 feet, and 230 KIAS above 10,000 feet.

    C. 200 KIAS below 10,000 feet, and 230 KIAS above 10,000 feet.

Answer (A) is correct. (14 CFR 61.113)
    DISCUSSION: If you are operating under BasicMed, you may fly an aircraft at a maximum speed of 250 KIAS.
    Answer (B) is incorrect. If you are operating under BasicMed, you may fly an aircraft at a maximum speed of 250 KIAS, whether you are above or below 10,000 ft. **Answer (C) is incorrect.** If you are operating under BasicMed, you may fly an aircraft at a maximum speed of 250 KIAS, whether you are above or below 10,000 ft.

29. You own an aircraft which is certificated to carry 8 occupants and has a total of 8 seats installed, including the pilot's seat. You have recently elected to fly under BasicMed. May you continue to fly the aircraft?

A. Yes, if you remove two of the seats.

B. Yes, as long as you carry no more than 5 passengers.

C. No.

Answer (C) is correct. (14 CFR 61.113)
DISCUSSION: If you are operating under BasicMed, you may only fly aircraft that are certificated to carry no more than 6 occupants.
Answer (A) is incorrect. If you are operating under BasicMed, you are limited to flying aircraft that are certificated to carry no more than 6 occupants. Removing 2 of the seats will not change the fact that the aircraft is certificated to carry more than 6 occupants. **Answer (B) is incorrect.** If you are operating under BasicMed, you are limited to carrying no more than 5 passengers and to flying aircraft that are certificated to carry no more than 6 occupants. However, carrying 5 passengers will not change the fact that the aircraft is certificated to carry more than 6 occupants.

30. You are a private pilot operating under BasicMed and recently earned your instrument rating. May you file an IFR flight plan and act as PIC while operating in weather that is less than VFR minimums?

A. Yes, BasicMed allows appropriately rated pilots to act as PIC under instrument flight rules.

B. No, pilots operating under BasicMed may file an IFR flight plan but cannot operate in IMC.

C. No, a pilot operating under BasicMed may only fly under VFR.

Answer (A) is correct. (14 CFR 61.113)
DISCUSSION: BasicMed does not restrict pilots from operating under IFR or in IMC, and an appropriately rated pilot is fully qualified to act as PIC in instrument conditions.
Answer (B) is incorrect. BasicMed does not restrict pilots from flying in IMC; it allows pilots to fully exercise the privileges of an instrument rating. **Answer (C) is incorrect.** Pilots operating with BasicMed may fly under VFR or IFR as long as they are appropriately rated.

31. What conditions allow a pilot who is exercising the privileges of BasicMed to act as a PIC under instrument flight rules (IFR)?

A. Flight in IMC is not permitted under BasicMed.

B. When the PIC is instrument rated and current.

C. When there is a safety pilot who shares the PIC responsibilities.

Answer (B) is correct. (14 CFR 61.113)
DISCUSSION: BasicMed does not restrict pilots from operating under IFR or in IMC, and an appropriately rated and current pilot is fully qualified to act as PIC in instrument conditions.
Answer (A) is incorrect. BasicMed does not restrict pilots from flying in IMC; it allows pilots to fully exercise the privileges of an instrument rating. **Answer (C) is incorrect.** Currently, a BasicMed pilot may only act as PIC and not as a required crewmember.

61.133 Commercial Pilot Privileges and Limitations

32. To carry passengers for hire in an airplane on cross-country flights of more than 50 NM from the departure airport, the pilot in command is required to hold at least

A. a Category II pilot authorization.

B. a First-Class Medical certificate.

C. a Commercial Pilot Certificate with an instrument rating.

Answer (C) is correct. (14 CFR 61.133)
DISCUSSION: To carry passengers for hire, the pilot in command is required to hold at least a commercial pilot certificate. Additionally, to carry those passengers for hire on cross-country flights of more than 50 NM (or at night), (s)he must hold an instrument rating on the commercial certificate.
Answer (A) is incorrect. Category II refers to an authorization for reduced ILS approach minimums. **Answer (B) is incorrect.** A first-class medical certificate is required for operations requiring an airline transport pilot certificate.

33. Which limitation is imposed on the holder of a Commercial Pilot Certificate if that person does not hold an instrument rating?

A. That person is limited to private pilot privileges at night.

B. The carrying of passengers or property for hire on cross-country flights at night is limited to a radius of 50 NM.

C. The carrying of passengers for hire on cross-country flights is limited to 50 NM and the carrying of passengers for hire at night is prohibited.

Answer (C) is correct. (14 CFR 61.133)
DISCUSSION: The applicant for a commercial pilot certificate must hold an instrument rating (airplane), or the commercial pilot certificate must be endorsed with a limitation prohibiting the carriage of passengers for hire in airplanes on cross-country flights of more than 50 NM or at night.
Answer (A) is incorrect. That person may exercise commercial pilot privileges at night, but with limitations.
Answer (B) is incorrect. No passengers may be carried at night without an instrument rating.

34. What limitation is imposed on a newly certificated commercial airplane pilot if that person does not hold an instrument pilot rating?

A. The carrying of passengers or property for hire on cross-country flights at night is limited to a radius of 50 nautical miles (NM).

B. The carrying of passengers for hire on cross-country flights is limited to 50 NM for night flights, but not limited for day flights.

C. The carrying of passengers for hire on cross-country flights is limited to 50 NM and the carrying of passengers for hire at night is prohibited.

Answer (C) is correct. (14 CFR 61.133)
DISCUSSION: The applicant for a commercial pilot certificate must hold an instrument rating (airplane), or the commercial pilot certificate must be endorsed with a limitation prohibiting the carriage of passengers for hire in airplanes on cross-country flights of more than 50 NM or at night.
Answer (A) is incorrect. The carriage of property (freight) is not limited at night. **Answer (B) is incorrect.** No passengers may be carried at night, and the flight is limited to 50 NM, not unlimited, for day flights without an instrument rating.

35. A certificated commercial pilot who carries passengers for hire at night or in excess of 50 NM is required to have at least

A. a type rating.

B. a first-class medical certificate.

C. an instrument rating in the same category and class of aircraft.

Answer (C) is correct. (14 CFR 61.133)
DISCUSSION: A certificated commercial pilot who carries passengers for hire at night or in excess of 50 NM is required to have an instrument rating.
Answer (A) is incorrect. Even if the airplane requires a type rating, the commercial pilot must have at least an instrument rating to carry passengers for hire at night or in excess of 50 NM. **Answer (B) is incorrect.** Only a second-class medical certificate is required of commercial pilots. First-class medical certificates are required of airline transport pilots.

36. You intend to carry passengers for hire on a night VFR flight in a single-engine airplane within a 25-mile radius of the departure airport. You are required to possess at least which rating(s)?

A. A Commercial Pilot Certificate with a single-engine land rating.

B. A Commercial Pilot Certificate with a single-engine and instrument (airplane) rating.

C. A Private Pilot Certificate with a single-engine land and instrument airplane rating.

Answer (B) is correct. (14 CFR 61.133)
DISCUSSION: A commercial pilot certificate with a single-engine airplane rating is required for a pilot to carry passengers for hire and to operate that class of aircraft. Also, an applicant for a commercial pilot certificate must hold an instrument rating (airplane), or the commercial pilot certificate will be endorsed with a limitation prohibiting carrying passengers for hire on cross-country flights of more than 50 nautical miles or at night.
Answer (A) is incorrect. To carry passengers for hire at night, one must have an instrument rating as well as a commercial pilot certificate. **Answer (C) is incorrect.** A commercial, not private, pilot certificate is required to carry passengers for hire.

4.3 14 CFR Part 91

91.3 Responsibility and Authority of the Pilot in Command

37. Who is responsible for determining that the altimeter system has been checked and found to meet 14 CFR Part 91 requirements for a particular instrument flight?

    A. Owner.

    B. Operator.

    C. Pilot-in-command.

Answer (C) is correct. (14 CFR 91.3)
    DISCUSSION: The pilot in command of an aircraft is directly responsible for, and is the final authority as to, the airworthiness and operation of that aircraft.
    Answer (A) is incorrect. The owner is primarily responsible for maintaining the aircraft, but the pilot in command is responsible for determining that the aircraft is airworthy.
    Answer (B) is incorrect. The operator is primarily responsible for maintaining the aircraft, but the pilot in command is responsible for determining that the aircraft is airworthy.

91.21 Portable Electronic Devices

38. The use of certain portable electronic devices is prohibited on aircraft that are being operated under

    A. IFR.

    B. VFR.

    C. DVFR.

Answer (A) is correct. (14 CFR 91.21)
    DISCUSSION: The use of portable electronic devices in carrier aircraft and other aircraft operated under IFR is prohibited. This prohibition does not apply to portable voice recorders, hearing aids, heart pacemakers, electric shavers, and other devices that do not interfere with the aircraft's navigation and communication systems.
    Answer (B) is incorrect. Portable electronic devices are not prohibited in aircraft operated under VFR. **Answer (C) is incorrect.** Portable electronic devices are not prohibited in aircraft operated under DVFR (defense VFR).

91.103 Preflight Action

39. Before beginning any flight under IFR, the pilot in command must become familiar with all available information concerning that flight. In addition, the pilot must

    A. list an alternate airport on the flight plan and become familiar with the instrument approaches to that airport.

    B. list an alternate airport on the flight plan and confirm adequate takeoff and landing performance at the destination airport.

    C. be familiar with the runway lengths at airports of intended use, and the alternatives available if the flight cannot be completed.

Answer (C) is correct. (14 CFR 91.103)
    DISCUSSION: Each pilot in command, before beginning a flight, shall become familiar with all available information concerning that flight. For a flight under IFR or a flight not in the vicinity of an airport, this information should include weather reports and forecasts, fuel requirements, alternatives available if the planned flight cannot be completed, and any known traffic delays of which (s)he has been advised by ATC. For any flight, the preflight information should include runway lengths at airports of intended use and takeoff and landing distance data.
    Answer (A) is incorrect. Listing an alternate airport is not required for all IFR flights, i.e., when the destination is forecast to have ceilings above 2,000 ft. and visibility of at least 3 SM. **Answer (B) is incorrect.** Listing an alternate airport is not required for all IFR flights, i.e., when the destination is forecast to have ceilings above 2,000 ft. and visibility of at least 3 SM.

40. Before beginning any flight under IFR, the pilot in command must become familiar with all available information concerning that flight including:

    A. all instrument approaches at the destination airport.

    B. an alternate airport and adequate takeoff and landing performance at the destination airport.

    C. the runway lengths at airports of intended use, and the aircraft's takeoff and landing data.

Answer (C) is correct. (14 CFR 91.103)
    DISCUSSION: Each pilot in command, before beginning a flight, shall become familiar with all available information concerning that flight. For a flight under IFR or a flight not in the vicinity of an airport, this information should include weather reports and forecasts, fuel requirements, alternatives available if the planned flight cannot be completed, and any known traffic delays of which (s)he has been advised by ATC. For any flight, the preflight information should include runway lengths at airports of intended use and takeoff and landing distance information.
    Answer (A) is incorrect. While knowing what approaches are available is a good operating procedure, it is not a required preflight action. **Answer (B) is incorrect.** A pilot must be familiar with the airplane's takeoff and landing performance at all airports of intended use, not just the destination airport.

91.109 Flight Instruction; Simulated Instrument Flight and Certain Flight Tests

41. What are the minimum qualifications for a person who occupies the other control seat as safety pilot during simulated instrument flight?

A. Private pilot certificate with appropriate category and class ratings for the aircraft.

B. Private pilot with instrument rating.

C. Private pilot with appropriate category, class, and instrument ratings.

Answer (A) is correct. (14 CFR 91.109)
DISCUSSION: No person may operate a civil aircraft in simulated instrument flight unless the other control seat is occupied by a safety pilot who possesses at least a private pilot certificate with category and class ratings appropriate to the aircraft being flown.
Answer (B) is incorrect. The safety pilot's certificate must carry an appropriate category and class (but not instrument) rating; e.g., a private pilot (helicopter) may not act as safety pilot in an airplane. **Answer (C) is incorrect.** The safety pilot does not need to be instrument rated.

91.123 Compliance with ATC Clearances and Instructions

42. When may ATC request a detailed report of an emergency even though a rule has not been violated?

A. When priority has been given.

B. Any time an emergency occurs.

C. When the emergency occurs in controlled airspace.

Answer (A) is correct. (14 CFR 91.123)
DISCUSSION: Each pilot in command who is given priority by ATC in an emergency (even though no Federal Aviation Regulations have been violated) shall, if requested by ATC, submit a detailed report of that emergency within 48 hr. to the manager of that ATC facility.
Answer (B) is incorrect. A written report may be requested when priority is given in an emergency, not any time an emergency occurs. **Answer (C) is incorrect.** A written report may be requested when priority is given in an emergency, regardless of where the emergency occurs.

43. While on an IFR flight, a pilot has an emergency which causes a deviation from an ATC clearance. What action must be taken?

A. Notify ATC of the deviation as soon as possible.

B. Squawk 7700 for the duration of the emergency.

C. Submit a detailed report to the chief of the ATC facility within 48 hours.

Answer (A) is correct. (14 CFR 91.123)
DISCUSSION: Each pilot in command who, in an emergency, deviates from an ATC clearance or instruction shall notify ATC of that deviation as soon as possible.
Answer (B) is incorrect. In an emergency, you must report a deviation from an ATC clearance as soon as possible, not just squawk 7700 during the emergency. **Answer (C) is incorrect.** A report in 48 hours is required only if you are given priority during the emergency and ATC requests such a report.

44. During an IFR flight in IMC, a distress condition is encountered, (fire, mechanical, or structural failure). The pilot should

A. not hesitate to declare an emergency and obtain an amended clearance.

B. wait until the situation is immediately perilous before declaring an emergency.

C. contact ATC and advise that an urgency condition exists and request priority consideration.

Answer (A) is correct. (14 CFR 91.123, P/C Glossary)
DISCUSSION: Distress is a condition of being threatened by serious and/or imminent danger and of requiring immediate assistance. Thus, during an IFR flight in IMC, if a distress condition is encountered, you should immediately declare an emergency and obtain an amended clearance.
Answer (B) is incorrect. A distress condition is perilous, and you should not hesitate to declare an emergency.
Answer (C) is incorrect. You should contact ATC and declare that an emergency, not urgency, condition exists and obtain an amended clearance, not a request for consideration.

45. While on an IFR flight, a pilot has an emergency that causes a deviation from an ATC clearance. What action must be taken?

A. Deviate as necessary and squawk 7700 for the duration of the emergency.

B. Do not deviate until an amended ATC clearance is received and separation from other aircraft is assured.

C. Notify ATC of the deviation as soon as possible and obtain an amended ATC clearance.

Answer (C) is correct. (14 CFR 91.123)
DISCUSSION: A pilot may deviate from an ATC clearance if required to do so by an emergency, but the pilot must notify ATC of the deviation as soon as possible and, if on an IFR flight, obtain an amended clearance.
Answer (A) is incorrect. It is not necessary to squawk 7700 when encountering an emergency. However, if the pilot deviates from a clearance as a result of an emergency, (s)he is required to notify ATC of the deviation as soon as possible and, if on an IFR flight, obtain an amended clearance. **Answer (B) is incorrect.** In an emergency, a pilot is permitted to deviate from a clearance as necessary. However, the pilot must notify ATC of the deviation as soon as possible and, if on an IFR flight, obtain a new clearance.

91.167 Fuel Requirements for Flight in IFR Conditions

46. What are the minimum fuel requirements in IFR conditions, if the first airport of intended landing is forecast to have a 1,500-foot ceiling and 3 miles visibility at flight-planned ETA? Fuel to fly to the first airport of intended landing,

    A. and fly thereafter for 45 minutes at normal cruising speed.

    B. fly to the alternate, and fly thereafter for 45 minutes at normal cruising speed.

    C. fly to the alternate, and fly thereafter for 30 minutes at normal cruising speed.

Answer (B) is correct. (14 CFR 91.167)
    DISCUSSION: In general, no person may operate a civil aircraft in IFR conditions unless it carries enough fuel (considering weather reports, forecasts, and conditions) to complete the flight to the first airport of intended landing, fly from that airport to the alternate airport, and fly after that for 45 min. at normal cruising speed.
    Answer (A) is incorrect. An alternate airport is required because the destination airport, from 1 hour before to 1 hour after ETA, has a forecast ceiling of less than 2,000 feet AGL. **Answer (C) is incorrect.** The fuel requirement after the alternate is 45 minutes, not 30 minutes.

47. During your preflight planning for an IFR flight, you determine that the first airport of intended landing has no instrument approach prescribed in 14 CFR part 97. The weather forecast for one hour before through one hour after your estimated time of arrival is 3,000 ft. scattered with 5 miles visibility. To meet the fuel requirements for this flight, you must be able to fly to the first airport of intended landing,

    A. and then fly for 45 minutes at normal cruising speed.

    B. then to the alternate airport, and then for 45 minutes at normal cruising speed.

    C. then to the alternate airport, and then for 30 minutes at normal cruising speed.

Answer (B) is correct. (14 CFR 91.167)
    DISCUSSION: Since your destination airport (first airport of intended landing) has no IAP, you must file an alternate airport and meet the applicable fuel requirements. You may not operate an aircraft (other than a helicopter) under IFR unless it carries sufficient fuel to fly to the first airport of intended landing, fly from that airport to the alternate airport, and fly thereafter for 45 minutes at normal cruising speed. An alternate airport is not required if the forecast weather conditions from one hour before to one hour after your estimated time of arrival call for a 2,000-ft. ceiling and 3 SM visibility, and your destination airport has at least one approved instrument approach procedure (IAP).
    Answer (A) is incorrect. You are required to file an alternate airport and meet the applicable fuel requirements because your destination airport has no IAP. **Answer (C) is incorrect.** You would be required to carry fuel sufficient for only 30 minutes at normal cruising speed after flying to the alternate airport if you were flying a helicopter, not an airplane. Airplanes must be able to fly for 45 minutes at normal cruising speed.

91.169 IFR Flight Plan: Information Required

48. For aircraft other than helicopters, is an alternate airport required for an IFR flight to ATL (Atlanta Hartsfield) if the proposed ETA is 1930Z?

TAF KATL 121720Z 121818 20012KT 5SM HZ BKN030
  FM2000 3SM TSRA OVC025CB
  FM2200 33015G20KT P6SM BKN015 OVC040
BECMG 0608 02008KT BKN040 BECMG 1012
00000KT
   P6SM CLR=

    A. Yes, because the ceiling could fall below 2,000 feet within 2 hours before to 2 hours after the ETA.

    B. No, because the ceiling and visibility are forecast to remain at or above 1,000 feet and 3 miles, respectively.

    C. No, because the ceiling and visibility are forecast to be at or above 2,000 feet and 3 miles within 1 hour before to 1 hour after the ETA.

Answer (C) is correct. (14 CFR 91.169)
    DISCUSSION: Since the ETA is 1930Z, you must check the forecast from 1830Z to 2030Z. In the TAF given, you will use the first forecast period (which is valid from 1800 to 2000Z) and the second forecast period (which is valid from 2000 to 2200Z). The lowest visibility and ceiling are forecast from 2000 to 2200Z. The visibility is 3 statute miles, and the ceiling is 2,500 feet. Thus, no alternate airport is required because the ceiling and visibility are forecast to be at or above 2,000 feet and 3 statute miles within 1 hour before to 1 hour after the ETA.
    Answer (A) is incorrect. The time frame of concern is 1 hour, not 2 hours, before and after the ETA. **Answer (B) is incorrect.** The ceiling must remain at least 2,000 feet, not 1,000 feet, for an alternate not to be required.

49. What are the alternate minimums for an airport with a precision approach procedure?

  A. 400-foot ceiling and 2 miles visibility.

  B. 600-foot ceiling and 2 miles visibility.

  C. 800-foot ceiling and 2 miles visibility.

Answer (B) is correct. (14 CFR 91.169)
  DISCUSSION: Unless otherwise authorized, no person may include an alternate airport that has a precision (ILS) approach in an IFR flight plan unless current weather forecasts indicate that at the ETA at the alternate airport the ceiling is at least 600 feet and visibility is 2 statute miles.
  Answer (A) is incorrect. A ceiling of 400 feet is not a standard minimum ceiling used as an alternative airport minimum. Answer (C) is incorrect. The alternate airport minimums for nonprecision approaches are 800 feet and 2 statute miles.

50. If a pilot elects to proceed to the selected alternate, the landing minimums used at that airport should be the

  A. minimums specified for the approach procedure selected.

  B. alternate minimums shown on the approach chart.

  C. minimums shown for that airport in a separate listing of "IFR Alternate Minimums."

Answer (A) is correct. (14 CFR 91.169)
  DISCUSSION: When one goes to an alternate airport to land, the landing minimums for the particular approach, not the minimums for listing the airport as an alternate, are the approach minimums to be used for the approach.
  Answer (B) is incorrect. Alternate minimums shown on the approach chart refer to the weather conditions required to list that airport as an alternate on your IFR flight plan, not to land there. Answer (C) is incorrect. Alternate minimums shown on the approach chart refer to the weather conditions required to list that airport as an alternate on your IFR flight plan, not to land there.

51. When a pilot elects to proceed to the selected alternate airport, which minimums apply for landing at the alternate?

  A. 600-1 if the airport has an ILS.

  B. Ceiling 200 feet above the published minimum; visibility 2 miles.

  C. The landing minimums for the approach to be used.

Answer (C) is correct. (14 CFR 91.169)
  DISCUSSION: When one goes to an alternate airport to land, the landing minimums for the particular approach, not the minimums for listing the airport as an alternate, are the minimums to be used for the approach.
  Answer (A) is incorrect. To be listed on the flight plan as an alternate airport, the weather conditions at the estimated time of arrival at the alternate must be a 600-foot ceiling and 2 statute miles, not 1 statute mile, visibility. Answer (B) is incorrect. The published approach minimums, not some adjustment thereof, should be used.

52. What minimum weather conditions must be forecast for your ETA at an alternate airport, that has only a VOR approach with standard alternate minimums, for the airport to be listed as an alternate on the IFR flight plan?

  A. 800-foot ceiling and 1 statute mile visibility.

  B. 800-foot ceiling and 2 statute miles visibility.

  C. 1,000-foot ceiling and visibility to allow descent from minimum en route altitude (MEA), approach, and landing under basic VFR.

Answer (B) is correct. (14 CFR 91.169)
  DISCUSSION: Unless otherwise authorized, no one may include an alternate airport with only a nonprecision approach in an IFR flight plan unless current weather forecasts indicate that, at the ETA at the alternate airport, the ceiling will be at least 800 feet and 2 statute miles visibility.
  Answer (A) is incorrect. The visibility requirement is 2 statute miles, not 1 statute mile. Answer (C) is incorrect. If no instrument approach procedure is available at an airport, the ceiling and visibility minimums are those allowing descent from the MEA, approach, and landing under basic VFR.

53. For aircraft other than helicopters, what minimum weather conditions must be forecast for your ETA at an alternate airport that has a precision approach procedure, with standard alternate minimums, in order to list it as an alternate for the IFR flight?

  A. 600-foot ceiling and 2 SM visibility at your ETA.

  B. 600-foot ceiling and 2 SM visibility from 2 hours before to 2 hours after your ETA.

  C. 800-foot ceiling and 2 SM visibility at your ETA.

Answer (A) is correct. (14 CFR 91.169)
  DISCUSSION: Unless otherwise authorized, no person may include an alternate airport that has a precision (ILS) approach in an IFR flight plan unless current weather forecasts indicate that at the ETA at the alternate airport the ceiling is at least 600 feet and visibility is 2 SM.
  Answer (B) is incorrect. The alternate airport weather minimums apply to the ETA, not 2 hours plus or minus. Answer (C) is incorrect. The alternate airport minimums for a nonprecision approach are 800 feet and 2 SM.

54. What standard minimums are required to list an airport as an alternate on an IFR flight plan if the airport has VOR approach only?

A. Ceiling and visibility at ETA, 800 feet and 2 miles, respectively.

B. Ceiling and visibility from 2 hours before until 2 hours after ETA, 800 feet and 2 miles, respectively.

C. Ceiling and visibility at ETA, 600 feet and 2 miles, respectively.

Answer (A) is correct. (14 CFR 91.169)
   DISCUSSION: Unless otherwise authorized, no person may include an alternate airport that has only a VOR (i.e., nonprecision) approach in an IFR flight plan unless current weather forecasts indicate that at the ETA at the alternate airport the ceiling is at least 800 feet and visibility is 2 statute miles.
   Answer (B) is incorrect. The alternate airport weather minimums apply to the ETA, not 2 hours plus or minus. **Answer (C) is incorrect.** The alternate airport weather minimums for a precision approach, i.e., ILS, are 600 feet and 2 statute miles.

55. An airport without an authorized IAP may be included on an IFR flight plan as an alternate, if the current weather forecast indicates that the ceiling and visibility at the ETA will

A. allow for descent from the IAF to landing under basic VFR conditions.

B. be at least 1,000 feet and 1 mile.

C. allow for a descent from the MEA, approach, and a landing under basic VFR conditions.

Answer (C) is correct. (14 CFR 91.169)
   DISCUSSION: Unless otherwise authorized, no person may include an alternate airport that does not have a standard instrument approach on an IFR flight plan unless current weather forecasts indicate that, at the ETA at the alternate airport, the ceiling and visibility will allow for a descent from the MEA, approach, and landing under basic VFR conditions.
   Answer (A) is incorrect. Descent must be possible from the MEA, not the IAF (initial approach fix), under basic VFR conditions. **Answer (B) is incorrect.** A ceiling of 800 feet, not 1,000 feet, and visibility of 2 statute miles, not 1 statute mile, are the standard alternate airport weather minimums at ETA for a nonprecision approach procedure.

56. For an airplane, determine the weather minimum conditions required at the destination airport to avoid listing an alternate on your IFR flight plan.

A. From 2 hours before to 2 hours after ETA, forecast ceiling 2,000, and visibility 2 and 1/2 miles.

B. From 2 hours before to 2 hours after ETA, forecast ceiling 3,000, and visibility 3 miles.

C. From 1 hour before to 1 hour after ETA, forecast ceiling 2,000, and visibility 3 miles.

Answer (C) is correct. (14 CFR 91.169)
   DISCUSSION: An alternate airport is not required to be listed on an IFR flight plan if the destination airport has a standard instrument approach procedure available and, for at least 1 hour before and 1 hour after the estimated time of arrival, the weather reports or forecasts, or any combination of them, indicate

1. The ceiling will be at least 2,000 ft. above the airport elevation; and
2. The visibility will be at least 3 statute miles.

   Answer (A) is incorrect. The destination weather condition forecast is from 1 hour, not 2 hours, before and after ETA, and the visibility must be at least 3 statute miles, not 2 1/2 statute miles. **Answer (B) is incorrect.** The destination weather condition forecast is from 1 hour, not 2 hours, before and after ETA, and the ceiling must be at least 2,000 feet AGL, not 3,000 feet AGL.

57. When an alternate airport is required, what are the weather minimums that must be forecast at the ETA for an alternate airport that has a precision approach procedure?

A. Ceiling 200 feet above the approach minimums and at least 1 statute mile visibility, but not less than the minimum visibility for the approach.

B. 600 foot ceiling and 2 statute miles visibility.

C. Ceiling 200 feet above field elevation and visibility 1 statute mile, but not less than the minimum visibility for the approach.

Answer (B) is correct. (14 CFR 91.169)
   DISCUSSION: Unless otherwise authorized, no person may include an alternate airport that has a precision (ILS) approach in an IFR flight plan unless current weather forecasts indicate that, at the ETA at the alternate airport, the ceiling is at least 600 feet and visibility is 2 statute miles.
   Answer (A) is incorrect. The minimum ceiling is 600 feet, not 200 feet above minimums, and 2 statute miles, not 1 statute mile, is the minimum visibility required to list an airport with a precision approach as an alternate. **Answer (C) is incorrect.** The alternate minimums for airports with precision approaches are 600 feet, not 200 feet, and 2 statute miles, not 1 statute mile.

58. What are the minimum weather conditions that must be forecast to list an airport as an alternate when the airport has no approved IAP?

    A. The ceiling and visibility at ETA, 2,000 feet and 3 miles, respectively.

    B. The ceiling and visibility from 2 hours before until 2 hours after ETA, 2,000 feet and 3 miles, respectively.

    C. The ceiling and visibility at ETA must allow descent from MEA, approach, and landing, under basic VFR.

Answer (C) is correct. (14 CFR 91.169)
    DISCUSSION: Unless otherwise authorized, no one may include an alternate airport that has no instrument approach in an IFR flight plan unless current weather forecasts indicate that, at the ETA at the alternate airport, the ceiling and visibility will allow descent from the MEA, approach, and landing under basic VFR.
    Answer (A) is incorrect. An alternate must be listed on your IFR flight plan unless the weather at your destination is forecast, from 1 hour before to 1 hour after ETA, to have a ceiling of 2,000 feet and visibility of 3 statute miles. **Answer (B) is incorrect.** An alternate must be listed on your IFR flight plan, unless the weather at your destination is forecast, from 1 hour, not 2 hours, before to 1 hour after ETA, to have at least a 2,000-foot ceiling and visibility of 3 statute miles.

91.171 VOR Equipment Check for IFR Operations

59. What is the maximum tolerance allowed for an operational VOR equipment check when using a VOT?

    A. Plus or minus 4°.

    B. Plus or minus 6°.

    C. Plus or minus 8°.

Answer (A) is correct. (14 CFR 91.171)
    DISCUSSION: When using a VOT for an operational VOR equipment check, the maximum permissible indicated bearing error is plus or minus 4°.
    Answer (B) is incorrect. Plus or minus 6° is the maximum error allowed when using an airborne checkpoint. **Answer (C) is incorrect.** Plus or minus 8° is not an acceptable error for any type of VOR equipment check.

60. What record shall be made in the aircraft log or other permanent record by the pilot making the VOR operational check?

    A. The date, place, bearing error, and signature.

    B. The date, frequency of VOR or VOT, number of flight hours since last check, and signature.

    C. The date, place, bearing error, aircraft total time, and signature.

Answer (A) is correct. (14 CFR 91.171)
    DISCUSSION: Each person making the VOR operational check shall enter the date, place, and bearing error and sign the aircraft log or other record.
    Answer (B) is incorrect. VOR frequency and number of flight hr. since last check are not required. **Answer (C) is incorrect.** The aircraft's total time is not required.

61. When must an operational check on the aircraft VOR equipment be accomplished when used to operate under IFR?

    A. Within the preceding 10 days or 10 hours of flight time.

    B. Within the preceding 30 days or 30 hours of flight time.

    C. Within the preceding 30 days.

Answer (C) is correct. (14 CFR 91.171)
    DISCUSSION: No person may operate a civil aircraft under IFR using the VOR system of radio navigation unless the VOR equipment of that aircraft is maintained, checked, and inspected under an approved procedure, or has been operationally checked within the preceding 30 days and was found to be within the limits of the permissible indicated bearing error.
    Answer (A) is incorrect. It must be checked every 30 days, not 10 days or 10 hours. **Answer (B) is incorrect.** There is no time requirement regarding hours of flight time.

62. Which data must be recorded in the aircraft log or other appropriate log by a pilot making a VOR operational check for IFR operations?

    A. VOR name or identification, date of check, amount of bearing error, and signature.

    B. Place of operational check, amount of bearing error, date of check, and signature.

    C. Date of check, VOR name or identification, place of operational check, and amount of bearing error.

Answer (B) is correct. (14 CFR 91.171)
    DISCUSSION: Each person making the VOR operational check shall enter the date, place, and bearing error and sign the aircraft log or other record.
    Answer (A) is incorrect. The place of operational check rather than the VOR name or identification is required. **Answer (C) is incorrect.** A signature is required, but the VOR name is not required.

63. Which checks and inspections of flight instruments or instrument systems must be accomplished before an aircraft can be flown under IFR?

A. VOR within 30 days, altimeter systems within 24 calendar months, and transponder within 24 calendar months.

B. ELT test within 30 days, altimeter systems within 12 calendar months, and transponder within 24 calendar months.

C. VOR within 24 calendar months, transponder within 24 calendar months, and altimeter system within 12 calendar months.

Answer (A) is correct. (14 CFR 91.171, 91.411, 91.413)
DISCUSSION: No person may operate a civil aircraft under IFR using the VOR system of radio navigation unless the VOR equipment of that aircraft is maintained, checked, and inspected under an approved procedure, or has been operationally checked within the preceding 30 days and was found to be within the limits of the permissible indicated bearing error. Also, within the preceding 24 calendar months, each altimeter system and transponder must be tested, inspected, and found to comply with the regulations.
Answer (B) is incorrect. Check and inspection of the altimeter system is required every 24 months, not 12 months, and ELTs must be inspected every 12 months, not tested within 30 days. **Answer (C) is incorrect.** VORs must be checked within 30 days, not 24 months, and altimeter systems must be inspected within 24 months, not 12 months.

64. A VOR equipment operational check must have been accomplished and found to be within the limits of permissible bearing error prior to use under IFR within the preceding

A. 60 days.

B. 24-calendar months.

C. 30 days.

Answer (C) is correct. (14 CFR 91.171)
DISCUSSION: No person may operate a civil aircraft under IFR using the VOR system of radio navigation unless the VOR equipment of that aircraft has been operationally checked within the preceding 30 days and was found to be within the limits of the permissible indicated bearing error.
Answer (A) is incorrect. VOR equipment must be operationally checked within the preceding 30-day period for IFR operations, not 60 days. **Answer (B) is incorrect.** The time frame for each static pressure system, altimeter instrument, and automatic pressure altitude reporting system to be tested, inspected, and found to comply with 14 CFR Part 43 is 24 calendar months.

91.173 ATC Clearance and Flight Plan Required

65. When departing from an airport located outside controlled airspace during IMC, you must file an IFR flight plan and receive a clearance before

A. takeoff.

B. entering IFR conditions.

C. entering Class E airspace.

Answer (C) is correct. (14 CFR 91.173)
DISCUSSION: No person may operate an aircraft in controlled airspace under IFR unless (s)he has filed an IFR flight plan and received an appropriate ATC clearance.
Answer (A) is incorrect. An IFR flight plan and clearance are not required until you enter controlled airspace. **Answer (B) is incorrect.** An IFR flight plan and clearance are not required until you enter controlled airspace.

66. To operate an aircraft under IFR, a flight plan must have been filed and an ATC clearance received prior to

A. controlling the aircraft solely by use of instruments.

B. entering weather conditions in any airspace.

C. entering controlled airspace.

Answer (C) is correct. (14 CFR 91.173)
DISCUSSION: No person may operate an aircraft in controlled airspace under IFR unless (s)he has filed an IFR flight plan and received an appropriate ATC clearance.
Answer (A) is incorrect. An IFR flight plan and clearance are not required until you enter controlled airspace. **Answer (B) is incorrect.** An IFR flight plan and clearance are not required until you enter controlled airspace.

67. To operate under IFR below 18,000 feet, a pilot must file an IFR flight plan and receive an appropriate ATC clearance prior to

A. entering controlled airspace.

B. entering weather conditions below VFR minimums.

C. takeoff.

Answer (A) is correct. (14 CFR 91.173)
DISCUSSION: No person may operate an aircraft in controlled airspace under IFR unless (s)he has filed an IFR flight plan and received an appropriate ATC clearance.
Answer (B) is incorrect. An IFR flight plan and clearance are not required until you enter controlled airspace. **Answer (C) is incorrect.** An IFR flight plan and clearance are not required until you enter controlled airspace.

68. Prior to which operation must an IFR flight plan be filed and an appropriate ATC clearance received?

A. Flying by reference to instruments in controlled airspace.

B. Entering controlled airspace when IMC exists.

C. Takeoff when IFR weather conditions exist.

Answer (B) is correct. (14 CFR 91.173)
DISCUSSION: No person may operate an aircraft in controlled airspace when instrument meteorological conditions (IMC) exist unless (s)he has filed an IFR flight plan and received an appropriate ATC clearance. **Answer (A) is incorrect.** You may fly by reference to instruments with a safety pilot in VFR weather conditions without an IFR flight plan or an IFR clearance. **Answer (C) is incorrect.** An IFR flight plan is not required until you enter controlled airspace.

69. No person may operate an aircraft in controlled airspace under IFR unless he or she files a flight plan

A. and receives a clearance by telephone prior to takeoff.

B. prior to takeoff and requests the clearance upon arrival on an airway.

C. and receives a clearance prior to entering controlled airspace.

Answer (C) is correct. (14 CFR 91.173)
DISCUSSION: No person may operate an aircraft in controlled airspace under IFR unless (s)he has filed an IFR flight plan and received an appropriate ATC clearance. **Answer (A) is incorrect.** It does not matter how the clearance is obtained. **Answer (B) is incorrect.** A person must file an IFR flight plan and receive clearance before operating in controlled airspace, e.g., a federal airway.

91.177 Minimum Altitudes for IFR Operations

70. Except when necessary for takeoff or landing or unless otherwise authorized by the Administrator, the minimum altitude for IFR flight is

A. 3,000 feet over all terrain.

B. 3,000 feet over designated mountainous terrain; 2,000 feet over terrain elsewhere.

C. 2,000 feet above the highest obstacle over designated mountainous terrain; 1,000 feet above the highest obstacle over terrain elsewhere.

Answer (C) is correct. (14 CFR 91.177)
DISCUSSION: Except when necessary for takeoff or landing, no person may operate an aircraft under IFR below 2,000 feet above the highest obstacle within a horizontal distance of 4 NM from the course to be flown over designated mountainous terrain, or 1,000 feet above the highest obstacle within a horizontal distance of 4 NM from the course to be flown over terrain elsewhere. **Answer (A) is incorrect.** The minimum IFR altitude is 2,000 feet above the highest obstacle over mountainous terrain or 1,000 feet over the highest obstacle over terrain elsewhere, not 3,000 feet over all terrain. **Answer (B) is incorrect.** The minimum IFR altitude is 2,000 feet, not 3,000 feet, above the highest obstacle over mountainous terrain, or 1,000 feet, not 2,000 feet, above the highest obstacle over terrain elsewhere.

71. Unless otherwise prescribed, what is the rule regarding altitude and course to be maintained during an IFR off airways flight over mountainous terrain?

A. 1,000 feet above the highest obstacle within a horizontal distance of 5 NM of course.

B. 2,000 feet above the highest obstacle within a horizontal distance of 4 NM of course.

C. 7,500 feet above the highest obstacle within a horizontal distance of 3 NM of course.

Answer (B) is correct. (14 CFR 91.177)
DISCUSSION: If no applicable minimum is prescribed, an altitude of 2,000 feet above the highest obstacle within a horizontal distance of 4 NM from the course to be flown is mandated. **Answer (A) is incorrect.** The mandated altitude minimum above obstacles in mountainous terrain is 2,000 feet, not 1,000 feet, and the horizontal distance requirement is 4 NM, not 5 NM. **Answer (C) is incorrect.** The mandated altitude minimum above obstacles in mountainous terrain is 2,000 feet, not 7,500 feet, and the horizontal distance requirement is 4 NM, not 3 NM.

91.205 Powered Civil Aircraft with Standard Category U.S. Airworthiness Certificates: Instrument and Equipment Requirements

72. What minimum navigation equipment is required for IFR flight?

A. VOR/LOC receiver, transponder, and DME.

B. VOR receiver and, if in ARTS III environment, a coded transponder equipped for altitude reporting.

C. Navigation equipment appropriate to the ground facilities to be used.

Answer (C) is correct. (14 CFR 91.205)
DISCUSSION: The minimum navigation equipment requirement for IFR flight is navigation equipment that is appropriate to the ground facilities to be used.
Answer (A) is incorrect. A VOR/LOC receiver and DME are required only if VORTAC stations will be used for navigation and DME fixes need to be identified. A transponder is not a navigation system. **Answer (B) is incorrect.** A VOR is required only if using VOR stations for navigation. A transponder is not a navigation system.

73. An aircraft operated during IFR under 14 CFR Part 91 is required to have which of the following?

A. Radar altimeter.

B. Dual VOR system.

C. Gyroscopic direction indicator.

Answer (C) is correct. (14 CFR 91.205)
DISCUSSION: An aircraft operated during IFR under 14 CFR Part 91 is required to have a gyroscopic direction indicator (directional gyro or equivalent).
Answer (A) is incorrect. Only a sensitive altimeter, not a radar altimeter, is required. **Answer (B) is incorrect.** If VOR navigation is to be used, only one, not two, VOR is required under 14 CFR Part 91.

74. Aircraft being operated under IFR are required to have, in addition to the equipment required for VFR and night, at least

A. a slip skid indicator.

B. dual VOR receivers.

C. distance measuring equipment.

Answer (A) is correct. (14 CFR 91.205)
DISCUSSION: An aircraft operated under 14 CFR Part 91 under IFR is required to have a slip-skid indicator (e.g., the ball of the turn coordinator).
Answer (B) is incorrect. The requirement is for navigational equipment appropriate to the ground facilities to be used, not necessarily dual VOR receivers. **Answer (C) is incorrect.** DME is required only above 24,000 ft. MSL when VOR navigational equipment is required.

75. Where is DME required under IFR?

A. At or above 24,000 feet MSL if VOR navigational equipment is required.

B. In positive control airspace.

C. Above 18,000 feet MSL.

Answer (A) is correct. (14 CFR 91.205)
DISCUSSION: If VOR navigational equipment is required, no person may operate a U.S.-registered civil aircraft within the 50 states and the District of Columbia, at or above 24,000 feet MSL (FL 240), unless that aircraft is equipped with approved distance measuring equipment (DME).
Answer (B) is incorrect. If VOR navigational equipment is required, DME is required at or above FL 240, not only in positive control airspace. Positive control airspace is that airspace in which ATC separates all aircraft, e.g., Class A, Class B, Class C. **Answer (C) is incorrect.** Class A airspace begins at 18,000 feet MSL, and DME is required at or above FL 240, if VOR navigational equipment is required.

76. To meet the requirements for flight under IFR, an aircraft must be equipped with certain operable instruments and equipment. One of those required is

A. a radar altimeter.

B. a transponder with altitude reporting capability.

C. a clock with sweep second pointer or digital presentation.

Answer (C) is correct. (14 CFR 91.205)
DISCUSSION: An aircraft operated under 14 CFR Part 91 under IFR is required to have a clock displaying hours, minutes, and seconds with a sweep-second pointer or digital presentation.
Answer (A) is incorrect. A radio (radar) altimeter is required under some circumstances for Category II operations with decision heights below 150 ft. AGL, not for all flights under IFR. **Answer (B) is incorrect.** A transponder with altitude encoding capability is required in certain airspace areas, not for all flights under IFR.

91.211 Supplemental Oxygen

77. What is the oxygen requirement for an unpressurized aircraft at 15,000 feet?

A. All occupants must use oxygen for the entire time at this altitude.

B. Crew must start using oxygen at 12,000 feet and passengers at 15,000 feet.

C. Crew must use oxygen for the entire time above 14,000 feet and passengers must be provided supplemental oxygen only above 15,000 feet.

Answer (C) is correct. (14 CFR 91.211)
　　DISCUSSION: No one may operate a U.S. civil aircraft at cabin pressure altitudes above 14,000 feet MSL unless the required minimum flight crew is provided with and uses supplemental oxygen during the entire flight time at those altitudes. At cabin pressure altitudes above 15,000 feet MSL, each passenger must be provided with supplemental oxygen.
　　Answer (A) is incorrect. The required minimum flight crew must use oxygen above 14,000 feet MSL, and others must be provided with oxygen above 15,000 feet MSL. **Answer (B) is incorrect.** The crew must start using oxygen above 14,000 feet MSL or after 30 minutes above 12,500 feet MSL.

78. What is the maximum IFR altitude you may fly in an unpressurized aircraft without providing passengers with supplemental oxygen?

A. 12,500 feet.

B. 14,000 feet.

C. 15,000 feet.

Answer (C) is correct. (14 CFR 91.211)
　　DISCUSSION: At cabin pressure altitudes above 15,000 feet MSL, each occupant must be provided with supplemental oxygen.
　　Answer (A) is incorrect. At cabin pressure altitudes above 12,500 feet MSL up to and including 14,000 feet MSL, only the minimum flight crew must use supplemental oxygen for that part of the flight at those altitudes that is more than 30 minutes duration. **Answer (B) is incorrect.** At cabin pressure altitudes above 14,000 feet MSL, only the required minimum flight crew must use supplemental oxygen.

79. If an unpressurized aircraft is operated above 12,500 feet MSL, but not more than 14,000 feet MSL, for a period of 2 hours 20 minutes, how long during that time is the minimum flightcrew required to use supplemental oxygen?

A. 2 hours 20 minutes.

B. 1 hour 20 minutes.

C. 1 hour 50 minutes.

Answer (C) is correct. (14 CFR 91.211)
　　DISCUSSION: No one may operate a U.S. civil aircraft at cabin pressure altitudes above 12,500 feet MSL up to and including 14,000 feet MSL unless the required minimum flight crew uses supplemental oxygen for that part of the flight at those altitudes that is of more than 30 minutes duration. If the flight lasts 2 hours and 20 minutes, the crew must use supplemental oxygen for all but 30 minutes, or 1 hour and 50 minutes.
　　Answer (A) is incorrect. One may fly for 30 minutes without supplemental oxygen between 12,500 feet MSL and 14,000 feet MSL. **Answer (B) is incorrect.** Thirty minutes of flight, not 1 hour, is permitted without supplemental oxygen between 12,500 feet MSL up to and including 14,000 feet MSL.

80. What is the maximum cabin pressure altitude at which a pilot can fly for longer than 30 minutes without using supplemental oxygen?

A. 10,500 feet.

B. 12,000 feet.

C. 12,500 feet.

Answer (C) is correct. (14 CFR 91.211)
　　DISCUSSION: No one may operate a U.S. civil aircraft at cabin pressure altitudes above 12,500 feet MSL up to and including 14,000 feet MSL unless the required minimum flight crew uses supplemental oxygen for that part of the flight at those altitudes that is of more than 30 minutes duration.
　　Answer (A) is incorrect. Supplemental oxygen is not required at any time at 10,500 feet. **Answer (B) is incorrect.** Supplemental oxygen is not required at any time at 12,000 feet.

91.215 ATC Transponder and Altitude Reporting Equipment and Use

81. In the 48 contiguous states, excluding the airspace at or below 2,500 feet AGL, an operable coded transponder equipped with Mode C capability is required in all controlled airspace at and above

A. 12,500 feet MSL.

B. 10,000 feet MSL.

C. Flight level (FL) 180.

Answer (B) is correct. (14 CFR 91.215)
　　DISCUSSION: Unless otherwise authorized or directed by ATC, no person may operate an aircraft in the 48 contiguous states at and above 10,000 feet MSL, excluding the airspace at or below 2,500 feet AGL, unless the aircraft is equipped with an operable Mode C transponder.
　　Answer (A) is incorrect. This figure pertains to supplemental oxygen, not Mode C, requirements. **Answer (C) is incorrect.** FL 180 is the floor of Class A airspace.

82. A coded transponder equipped with altitude reporting capability is required in all controlled airspace

- A. at and above 10,000 feet MSL, excluding at and below 2,500 feet AGL.
- B. at and above 2,500 feet above the surface.
- C. below 10,000 feet MSL, excluding at and below 2,500 feet AGL.

Answer (A) is correct. (14 CFR 91.215)
DISCUSSION: Unless otherwise authorized or directed by ATC, no person may operate an aircraft in the 48 contiguous states at and above 10,000 feet MSL, excluding the airspace at or below 2,500 feet AGL, unless the aircraft is equipped with an operable Mode C transponder.
Answer (B) is incorrect. The airspace above 2,500 feet AGL must also be at or above 10,000 feet MSL.
Answer (C) is incorrect. The limit is at and above, not below, 10,000 feet MSL.

83. Prior to operating an aircraft not equipped with a transponder in Class B airspace, a request for a deviation must be submitted to the

- A. FAA Administrator at least 24 hours before the proposed operation.
- B. nearest FAA General Aviation District Office 24 hours before the proposed operation.
- C. controlling ATC facility at least 1 hour before the proposed flight.

Answer (C) is correct. (14 CFR 91.215)
DISCUSSION: ATC may authorize deviations on a continuing basis, or for individual flights, for operations of aircraft without a transponder. The request for a deviation must be submitted to the ATC facility having jurisdiction over the airspace concerned at least 1 hr. before the proposed operation.
Answer (A) is incorrect. A request for a deviation to operate in Class B airspace in an airplane not equipped with a transponder must be submitted to the controlling ATC facility at least 1 hour before the proposed flight, not to the FAA Administrator at least 24 hours before the operation.
Answer (B) is incorrect. A request for a deviation to operate in Class B airspace in an airplane not equipped with a transponder must be submitted to the controlling ATC facility at least 1 hour before the proposed flight, not to the nearest Flight Standards office 24 hours before the proposed operation.

84. If the aircraft's transponder fails during flight within Class B airspace,

- A. the pilot should immediately request clearance to depart the Class B airspace.
- B. ATC may authorize deviation from the transponder requirement to allow aircraft to continue to the airport of ultimate destination.
- C. aircraft must immediately descend below 1,200 feet AGL and proceed to destination.

Answer (B) is correct. (14 CFR 91.215)
DISCUSSION: If an aircraft's transponder fails during flight within Class B airspace, ATC may authorize deviation from the transponder requirement to allow the aircraft to continue to the airport of ultimate destination, including any intermediate stops, or to proceed to a place where suitable repairs can be made, or both.
Answer (A) is incorrect. ATC can immediately authorize a deviation from the transponder requirement without requiring the pilot to request clearance to depart the Class B airspace area.
Answer (C) is incorrect. A pilot may descend only if clearance from ATC is obtained.

85. When an aircraft is not equipped with a transponder, what requirement must be met before ATC will authorize a flight within Class B airspace?

- A. A request for the proposed flight must be made to ATC at least 1 hour before the flight.
- B. The proposed flight must be conducted when operating under instrument flight rules.
- C. The proposed flight must be conducted in visual meteorological conditions (VMC).

Answer (A) is correct. (14 CFR 91.215)
DISCUSSION: Requests for ATC authorized deviations must be made to the ATC facility having jurisdiction over the concerned airspace. A request for a deviation from the transponder equipment requirement in Class B airspace must be made to the controlling ATC facility at least 1 hr. before the flight.
Answer (B) is incorrect. You must request a deviation from the transponder equipment requirement from ATC. The requirement is not that the proposed flight be conducted under IFR. **Answer (C) is incorrect.** You must request a deviation from the transponder equipment requirement from ATC. The requirement is not that the proposed flight be conducted in VMC.

91.225 ADS-B Out Equipment and Use

86. Automatic Dependent Surveillance-Broadcast (ADS-B) Out is mandated for aircraft operations in

- A. Class A, B, and C airspace.
- B. Class A, B, and C airspace above 2,500 ft. AGL.
- C. all airspace within the 48 contiguous states above 2,000 ft. AGL.

Answer (A) is correct. (14 CFR 91.225)
DISCUSSION: ADS-B Out equipment must be installed for all operations (1) in Class A, B, and C airspace; (2) above the ceiling and within the lateral boundaries of Class B and C airspace; and (3) in Class E airspace within the 48 contiguous states and the District of Columbia at and above 10,000 ft. MSL, excluding the airspace at and below 2,500 ft. above the surface.
Answer (B) is incorrect. ADS-B Out equipment is required in all Class A, B, and C airspace, not only the airspace above 2,500 ft. AGL. **Answer (C) is incorrect.** ADS-B Out equipment is required only in certain airspace areas as specified in 14 CFR 91.225.

87. Which of the following flights may be made without ADS-B Out equipment installed?

    A. An IFR flight that departs a Class E airport and cruises at 12,000 ft. MSL to a Class G destination airport.

    B. An IFR flight that overflies, but does not enter, a Class C airspace while en route at 6,000 ft. MSL.

    C. An IFR flight that departs a Class D airport, cruises in Class E airspace at 7,000 ft. MSL, and arrives at another Class D airport.

Answer (C) is correct. (14 CFR 91.225)
    DISCUSSION: An IFR flight that departs a Class D airport, cruises in Class E airspace at 7,000 ft. MSL, and arrives at another Class D airport may be made without ADS-B Out equipment installed because ADS-B Out is not required in Class D airspace or Class E airspace below 10,000 ft. MSL. ADS-B Out equipment must be installed for all operations (1) in Class A, B, and C airspace; (2) above the ceiling and within the lateral boundaries of Class B and C airspace; and (3) in Class E airspace within the 48 contiguous states and the District of Columbia at and above 10,000 ft. MSL, excluding the airspace at and below 2,500 ft. above the surface.
    Answer (A) is incorrect. ADS-B Out equipment is required for flights at and above 10,000 ft. MSL. **Answer (B) is incorrect.** ADS-B Out equipment is required for flights within and above Class C airspace.

88. Each person operating an aircraft equipped with ADS-B Out must operate it in the transmit mode

    A. at all times unless otherwise authorized by the FAA or directed by ATC.

    B. when operating in Class B and C airspace, excluding operations conducted under day VFR.

    C. all classes of airspace when the flight is operated for compensation or hire but not otherwise.

Answer (A) is correct. (14 CFR 91.225)
    DISCUSSION: As per 14 CFR 91.225, each person operating an aircraft equipped with ADS-B Out must operate this equipment in the transmit mode at all times unless otherwise authorized by the FAA or directed by ATC.
    Answer (B) is incorrect. ADS-B Out equipment is required to be operated in transmit mode at all times unless otherwise authorized by the FAA or directed by ATC. **Answer (C) is incorrect.** ADS-B Out equipment is not a requirement for operation within Class D airspace or above the Class D ceiling.

89. When is Automatic Dependent Surveillance-Broadcast (ADS-B) Out equipment required?

    A. Under the shelf of Class C airspace.

    B. In Class E airspace above 10,000 ft. MSL, except at and below 2,500 ft. AGL.

    C. In all controlled airspace.

Answer (B) is correct. (14 CFR 91.225)
    DISCUSSION: ADS-B Out equipment must be installed for all operations (1) in Class A airspace; (2) above the ceiling and within the lateral boundaries of Class B and C airspace (within the Mode C veil where applicable); and (3) in Class E airspace within the 48 contiguous states and the District of Columbia at and above 10,000 ft. MSL, excluding the airspace at and below 2,500 ft. above the surface. It is also required over the Gulf of Mexico at and above 3,000 ft. MSL within 12 NM of the United States coastline.
    Answer (A) is incorrect. ADS-B Out equipment is required within and above Class C airspace, not underneath Class C airspace. **Answer (C) is incorrect.** ADS-B Out equipment is not required in all controlled airspace, only the airspace designated by 14 CFR 91.225. It is not required in Class D airspace and some Class E airspace.

91.227 ADS-B Out Equipment Performance Requirements

90. What type of ADS-B equipment is required in Class A airspace?

    A. ADS-B Out that operates on the frequency 1090 MHz

    B. ADS-B Out that operates with UAT on the frequency 978 MHz.

    C. Any type of certified ADS-B In.

Answer (A) is correct. (14 CFR 91.227)
    DISCUSSION: Aircraft operating in Class A airspace are required to have ADS-B Out equipment installed that operates on the frequency of 1090 MHz.
    Answer (B) is incorrect. ADS-B Out that operates with a universal access transceiver (UAT) on the frequency 978 MHz may be used in airspace below 18,000 ft., but not in Class A airspace. **Answer (C) is incorrect.** ADS-B Out, not ADS-B In, is required in Class A airspace.

91.411 Altimeter System and Altitude Reporting Equipment Tests and Inspections

91. Your aircraft had the static pressure system and altimeter tested and inspected on January 5, of this year, and was found to comply with FAA standards. These systems must be reinspected and approved for use in controlled airspace under IFR by

    A. January 5, next year.

    B. January 5, 2 years hence.

    C. January 31, 2 years hence.

Answer (C) is correct. (14 CFR 91.411)
    DISCUSSION: Within the preceding 24 calendar months, each static pressure system, each altimeter instrument, and each automatic pressure altitude reporting system must be tested, inspected, and found to comply with the regulations. The 24-calendar-month period following January of this year begins February 1, this year, and ends on January 31, 2 years hence.
    Answer (A) is incorrect. These tests must be completed every 24 calendar months, not 1 year from the date of the last inspection. **Answer (B) is incorrect.** These tests must be completed within the preceding 24 calendar months, not 2 years from the date of the last inspection.

92. An aircraft altimeter system test and inspection must be accomplished within

    A. 12 calendar months.

    B. 18 calendar months.

    C. 24 calendar months.

Answer (C) is correct. (14 CFR 91.411)
    DISCUSSION: Within the preceding 24 calendar months, each static pressure system, each altimeter instrument, and each automatic pressure altitude reporting system must be tested, inspected, and found to comply with the regulations.
    Answer (A) is incorrect. An annual inspection, not the altimeter system, must be accomplished within the preceding 12 calendar months. **Answer (B) is incorrect.** The aircraft's altimeter system must be tested and inspected within 24, not 18, calendar months.

93. An aircraft altimeter system test and inspection are required to be accomplished within

    A. 18 calendar months of operating in IMC conditions.

    B. 24 calendar months of operating in IMC conditions.

    C. 24 calendar months of operating under IFR in controlled airspace.

Answer (C) is correct. (14 CFR 91.411)
    DISCUSSION: To operate under IFR in controlled airspace, each static pressure system, altimeter instrument, and automatic pressure altitude reporting system must be tested, inspected, and found to comply with the regulations every 24 calendar months.
    Answer (A) is incorrect. Regulation requires an altimeter inspection every 24 calendar months, not every 18 calendar months. Furthermore, the requirement limits operations under IFR in controlled airspace, not just in IMC conditions. **Answer (B) is incorrect.** The regulation limits operations under IFR in controlled airspace, not just in IMC conditions.

4.4 NTSB Part 830

94. Which publication covers the procedures required for aircraft accident and incident reporting responsibilities for pilots?

    A. 14 CFR Part 61.

    B. 14 CFR Part 91.

    C. NTSB Part 830.

Answer (C) is correct. (NTSB 830.1)
    DISCUSSION: NTSB Part 830 contains rules pertaining to the following:

1. Notification and reporting aircraft accidents and incidents and certain other occurrences in the operation of aircraft when they involve civil aircraft of the U.S. wherever they occur, or foreign civil aircraft when such events occur in the U.S., its territories, or possessions
2. Reporting aircraft accidents and listed incidents in the operation of aircraft when they involve certain public aircraft
3. Preservation of aircraft wreckage, mail, cargo, and records involving all civil aircraft in the U.S., its territories, or possessions

    Answer (A) is incorrect. 14 CFR Part 61 concerns certification of pilots, flight instructors, and ground instructors. **Answer (B) is incorrect.** 14 CFR Part 91 concerns general operating and flight rules.

STUDY UNIT FIVE

AIRPORTS, AIR TRAFFIC CONTROL, AND AIRSPACE

(17 pages of outline)

This study unit contains outlines of major concepts tested; sample test questions and answers regarding airports, air traffic control, and airspace; and an explanation of each answer.

Recall that the **sole purpose** of this book is to expedite your passing of the FAA pilot knowledge test for the instrument rating. Accordingly, all extraneous material (i.e., topics or regulations not directly tested on the FAA pilot knowledge test) is omitted, even though much more knowledge is necessary to fly safely. This additional material is presented in *Pilot Handbook*, *Aviation Weather and Weather Services*, *FAR/AIM*, and *Instrument Pilot Flight Maneuvers and Practical Test Prep*, available from Gleim Publications, Inc. Order online at www.GleimAviation.com.

5.1 PRECISION INSTRUMENT RUNWAY MARKINGS

1. The figure below depicts a precision instrument runway.

    a. The distance (A) from the runway threshold to the fixed distance marker is 1,000 ft.

    b. The distance (B) from the runway threshold to the touchdown zone marker is 500 ft.

    c. The distance (C) from the beginning of the touchdown zone marker to the beginning of the fixed distance marker is 500 ft.

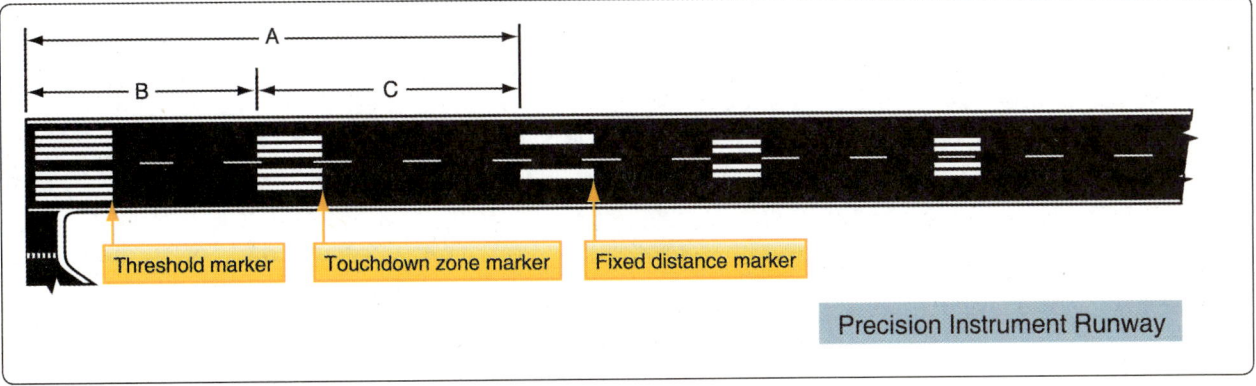

Figure 137. – Precision Instrument Runway.

2. A displaced threshold is a threshold that is not at the beginning of a runway. It is indicated by arrows in the middle of the runway pointing to a broad, solid line across the runway. The remainder of the runway, following the displaced threshold, is the landing portion of the runway.

    a. The paved area before the displaced threshold is available for taxiing, the landing rollout, and the takeoff of aircraft, but not for landing.

    b. In the runway diagram below, the approach end of the runway is on the right. Thus, taxiing and takeoff are permitted toward the green threshold lights (marked by the arrow).

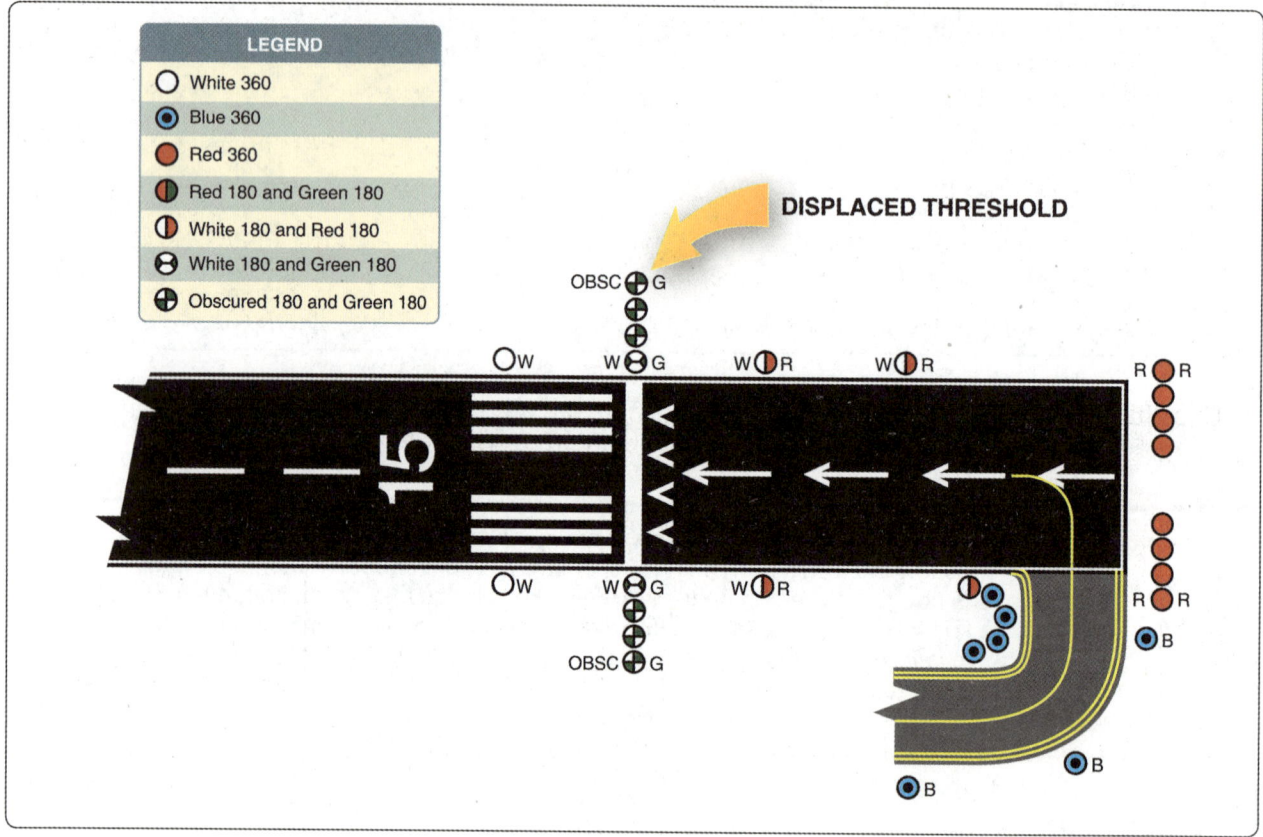

Figure 138. – Runway Legend.

5.2 AIRPORT SIGNS AND MARKINGS

1. Mandatory airport instruction signs have a red background with white lettering. Mandatory instruction signs include

   a. Runway approach area holding position signs and runway holding position signs, which denote an entrance to a runway from a taxiway or from an intersecting runway.

   b. No entry signs (example below), which denote paved areas where aircraft entry is prohibited.

2. Runway holding position markings (hold lines) at the intersection of taxiways and runways consist of four yellow lines, two solid and two dashed, that extend across the width of the taxiway with the dashed lines nearest the runway.

   a. These markings identify where an aircraft is to hold short of the runway.

3. The ILS critical area boundary sign identifies the edge of the ILS critical area.

   a. These signs indicate the area where, when an ILS is in use, aircraft must hold short to prevent blocking or interfering with the ILS glide slope antenna installed at the airport.

   b. These signs have a yellow background and black lines that look like a sideways ladder.

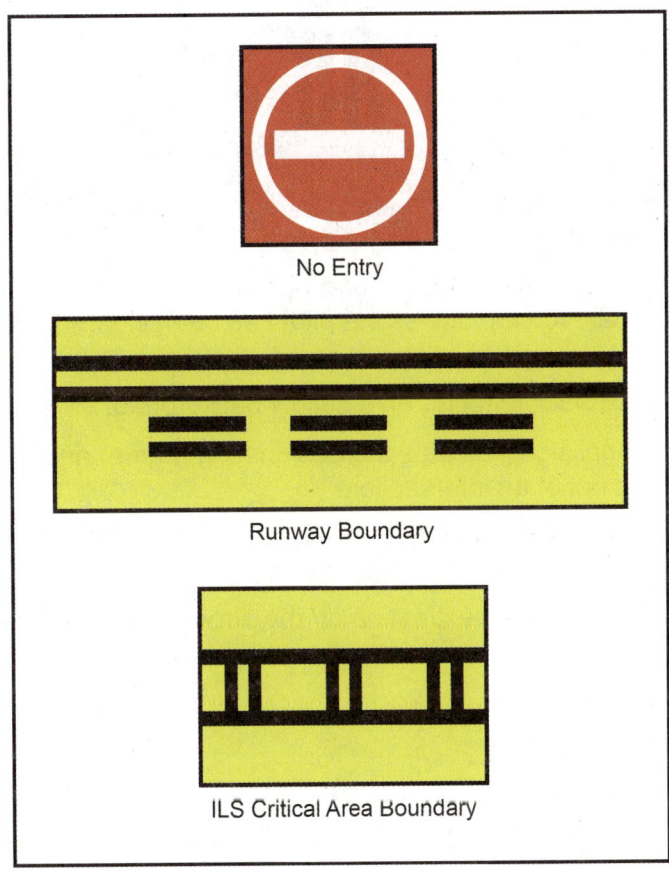

4.   Many airports use an enhanced taxiway centerline marking consisting of a parallel line of yellow dashes on either side of the normal taxiway centerline.

AIM Fig. 2-3-8. Enhanced Taxiway Centerline.

    a.   These taxiway centerlines are enhanced for a maximum of 150 ft. prior to a runway holding position marking.

    b.   They are used to warn the pilot of an approaching runway holding position marking. The pilot should prepare to stop unless the pilot has been cleared onto or across the runway by ATC.

5.   Direction signs consist of black lettering on a yellow background.

    a.   A taxiway directional sign indicates the designation (name) and direction (orientation) of taxiways leading out of an intersection.

    b.   A runway exit sign indicates the designation and direction of an exit taxiway from the runway.

6.   Destination signs direct pilots to a destination on the airport, such as runways, taxiways, aprons, terminals, FBOs, cargo areas, civil aviation areas, and military areas.

5.3 VISUAL APPROACH SLOPE INDICATOR (VASI)

1. Visual approach slope indicators (VASIs) are systems of lights that provide visual descent information during the approach to a runway.

2. The standard VASI consists of a two-barred tier of lights.

    a. If both light bars appear red, you are below the glide path. Remember this with the mnemonic, "red means dead."

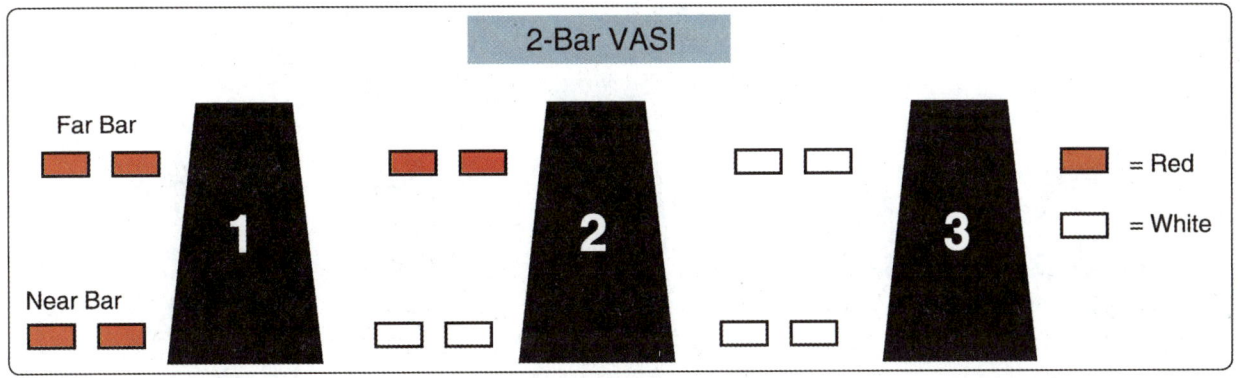

Figure 134. – 2-BAR VASI.

    b. If the far lights (on top visually) appear red and the near lights (on bottom visually) appear white, you are on the glide path.

        1) This glide path is normally set at 3°.

    c. If both light bars appear white, you are above the glide path.

3. Actually, each light bar marks a separate glide path. The far light bar marks a higher glide path than the glide path extended from the nearer light bar. You are between them when you are below the higher glide path and above the lower glide path.

    a. Remember that red over white (if it helps, R before W alphabetically) is the desired sequence.

        1) White over red is impossible.

4. VASIs also may have three light bars, which provide a lower glide path and a higher glide path. The higher glide path marked by the middle and far light bars is intended for use by high flight deck aircraft.

    a. If the nearest light bar is white and the two farther light bars are red, you are on the lower glide path, usually 3°.

    b. If the farthest light bar is red and the two nearer light bars are white, you are on the upper glide path, usually 3.25°.

    c. Above both glide paths, all lights are white. Below both glide paths, all lights are red.

5. If all VASI lights appear red as you reach the MDA, you should level off momentarily to intercept the proper glide path.

6. VASI provides only glide path guidance and safe obstruction clearance within ±10° of the extended runway centerline from as far as 4 NM from the runway threshold.

    a. It does not provide information on alignment with the runway.

5.4   PRECISION APPROACH PATH INDICATOR (PAPI)

1.   PAPI lights are similar to VASIs but are installed in a single row of either two or four lights.
2.   The glide path indications are depicted below.

    a.   The runway in illustration 8 depicts a high approach, more than 3.5°.
    b.   The runway in illustration 9 depicts a slightly high approach, 3.2°.
    c.   The runway in illustration 10 depicts an on glide path approach, 3.0°.
    d.   The runway in illustration 11 depicts a slightly low approach, 2.8°.
    e.   The runway in illustration 12 depicts a low approach, less than 2.5°.

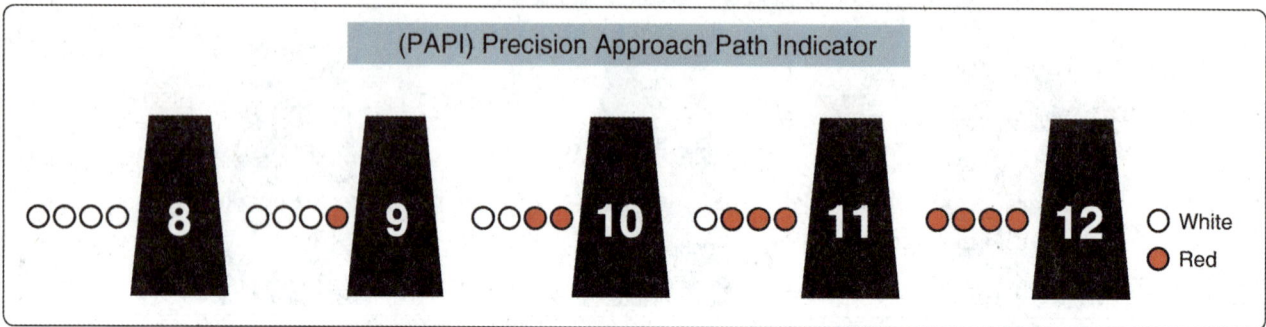

Figure 136. – Precision Approach Path Indicator (PAPI).

5.5   RUNWAY LIGHT SYSTEMS

1.   **Runway End Identifier Lights (REIL)**

    a.   The REIL system consists of a pair of synchronized flashing lights located laterally on each side of the runway threshold.

    b.   The lights are either omnidirectional or unidirectional facing the approach area.

    c.   The lights are effective for

        1)   Identification of a runway surrounded by a preponderance of other lighting,
        2)   Identification of a runway which lacks contrast with surrounding terrain, and
        3)   Identification of a runway during reduced visibility.

2.   **Runway Edge Lights Systems**

    a.   Runway edge lights are used to outline the edges of runways during periods of darkness or restricted visibility conditions.

    b.   The lights are classified according to the intensity they are capable of producing.

        1)   High Intensity Runway Lights (HIRL)
        2)   Medium Intensity Runway Lights (MIRL)
        3)   Low Intensity Runway Lights (LIRL)

    c.   HIRL and MIRL systems have variable intensity controls.

    d.   Runway edge lights are white, except on instrument runways where yellow replaces white on the last 2,000 feet or half of the runway length, whichever is less.

    e.   Light marking the ends of the runway emit

        1)   Red light toward the runway to indicate the end of the runway to a departing aircraft and

        2)   Green light outward from the runway end to indicate the threshold to landing aircraft.

3. **In-Runway Lighting**

   a. Runway Centerline Lighting System (RCLS)

      1) This system is installed on some instrument precision approach runways to facilitate landing under adverse visibility conditions.

      2) They are located along the runway centerline and are spaced at 50-foot intervals.

      3) They are white until the last 3,000 feet of the runway when viewed from the landing threshold.

      4) White lights begin to alternate with red for the next 2,000 feet, and for the last 1,000 feet of the runway, all centerline lights are red.

   b. Touchdown Zone Lights (TDZL)

      1) These lights are installed on some precision approach runways to indicate the touchdown zone when landing in adverse visibility conditions.

      2) They consist of two rows of transverse light bars disposed symmetrically about the runway centerline.

      3) The system consists of steady-burning white lights that start 100 feet beyond the landing threshold and extend to 3,000 feet beyond the landing threshold or to the midpoint of the runway, whichever is less.

   c. Taxiway Centerline Lead-Off Lights

      1) These lights provide visual guidance to persons exiting the runway.

      2) They are color-coded to warn pilots and vehicle drivers that they are within the runway environment or instrument landing system (ILS) critical area (whichever is more restrictive).

      3) They consist of alternate green and yellow lights, beginning with green from the runway centerline.

   d. Taxiway Centerline Lead-On Lights

      1) These lights provide visual guidance to persons entering the runway.

      2) "Lead-on" lights are color-coded in the same pattern as lead-off lights.

      3) They are color-coded to warn pilots and vehicle drivers that they are within the runway environment or instrument landing system (ILS) critical area (whichever is more restrictive).

      4) They are bidirectional, i.e., one side emits light for the lead-on function, while the other side emits light for the lead-off function.

   e. Land and Hold Short Lights

      1) These lights are used to indicate the hold short point on certain runways which are approved for Land and Hold Short Operations (LAHSO).

      2) They consist of a row of pulsing white lights installed across the runway at the hold short point.

      3) Where installed, the lights will be on any time LAHSO is in effect and off when it is not.

5.6 WAKE TURBULENCE

1. The greatest vortex strength occurs behind heavy, clean, and slow aircraft (e.g., during the takeoff of a jet transport because it has a high gross weight and a high angle of attack).

2. Light quartering tailwinds prolong the hazards of wake turbulence the longest because they move the vortices of preceding aircraft forward to the touchdown zone and hold the upwind vortex on the runway.

    a. A light crosswind of 1 to 5 kt. would result in an upwind vortex tending to remain over the runway.

3. When landing behind a large aircraft on the same runway, stay at or above the other aircraft's final approach flight path and land beyond that airplane's touchdown point.

5.7 COLLISION AVOIDANCE

1. When climbing to an assigned altitude on an airway, use the centerline except to avoid other aircraft when in VFR conditions.

2. During climbs and descents in VFR conditions, execute gentle banks left and right to permit continual scanning of surrounding airspace.

3. When weather conditions permit, i.e., in VFR conditions, you must assume the responsibility to see and avoid other aircraft, regardless of whether operating under IFR or VFR.

4. ADS-B (Automatic Dependent Surveillance-Broadcast) is technology that allows air traffic controllers (and ADS-B equipped aircraft) to see traffic with more precision. Instead of relying on old radar technology, ADS-B uses highly accurate GPS signals. Because of this, ADS-B works where radar often will not.

    a. This system

        1) Works in remote areas such as mountainous terrain

        2) Functions at low altitudes and even on the ground

        3) Can be used to monitor traffic on the taxiways and runways

        4) Allows air traffic controllers as well as aircraft with certain equipment to receive ADS-B traffic

        5) Provides subscription-free weather information to all aircraft flying over the U.S.

5.8 IFR FLIGHT PLANNING INFORMATION

1. Every pilot should receive a preflight briefing from a Flight Service Station (FSS), whether by telephone, radio, or personal visit, in addition to briefings obtained online.

    a. The briefing should contain weather advisories and notices about en route airports and other navigational aids.

2. The **Notice to Air Missions (NOTAM) System** disseminates time-critical aeronautical information that is temporary in nature or not known in time to publish on charts or in procedural publications.

    a. NOTAMs include airport or primary runway closures, changes in the status of navigational aids, instrument landing systems, radar service availability, and other information that could affect a pilot's decision to make a flight.

3. NOTAMs are progressing toward ICAO compliance. The following are some examples of types of NOTAMs:

    a. **NOTAMs (D)** include information such as airport or primary runway closures; changes in the status of navigational aids, ILSs, and radar service availability; and other information essential to planned en route, terminal, or landing operations. They also include information on airport taxiways, aprons, ramp areas, and associated lighting.

    b. **FDC NOTAMs** are issued by the Flight Data Center and contain regulatory information such as amendments to instrument flight procedures, service routes, airspace usage, and other flight restrictions.

    c. **Pointer NOTAMs** reduce total NOTAM volume by pointing to other NOTAMs (D) and FDC NOTAMs rather than duplicating potentially unnecessary information for an airport or NAVAID. They allow pilots to reference NOTAMs that might not be listed under a given airport or NAVAID identifier. These NOTAMs are issued by an FSS.

    d. **SAA NOTAMs** are issued when Special Activity Airspace (SAA) will be active outside the published schedule times and when required by the published schedule, although pilots must still check published schedule times for SAA as well as any other NOTAMs for that airspace.

    e. **Military NOTAMs** reference military airports and NAVAIDs and are rarely of any interest to civilian pilots.

    f. **TFR NOTAMs** define areas where air travel is restricted due to special events or hazardous conditions. IFR pilots must still be aware of temporary flight restrictions and should not attempt to file a flight plan through a TFR area.

4. NOTAMs are disseminated via telecommunications. They are included as part of a routine pilot weather briefing given by an FSS specialist.

5. The best source of airport conditions would be to combine data available from the Chart Supplement and NOTAMs (D).

6. **Automatic Terminal Information Service (ATIS)** broadcasts are updated whenever any official weather data are received, regardless of content change or reported values, or when there is a change in other pertinent data, such as active runway, instrument approach in use, etc.

    a. Absence of the sky condition and visibility from the ATIS broadcast specifically implies that the ceiling is more than 5,000 ft. and visibility is more than 5 SM.

7. In Class B, C, D, and E surface areas, operation of an airport beacon during daylight hours usually indicates IFR weather conditions (ground visibility less than 3 SM and/or ceiling less than 1,000 ft.).

5.9 IFR FLIGHT PLAN

Authors' Note: As of the publication date, the FAA's current instrument rating testing supplement does not include a figure of a flight plan. However, the FAA has announced its intention to include the ICAO flight plan form in the knowledge test in the future. We recommend that you familiarize yourself with the ICAO flight plan prior to its inclusion on the knowledge test. Check www.GleimAviation.com/updates for the latest information.

1. To operate under instrument flight rules in controlled airspace, you are required to file an IFR flight plan.

    a. The ICAO flight plan form appears in Figure 1A on the next page.

    b. The ICAO international flight plan form is used for domestic and international operations under VFR or IFR.

    c. "Stopover" flight plans with a stopover of more than 1 hr. must have a separate flight plan filed for each leg. Stopovers of 1 hr. or less should be mentioned in item 18, Other Information.

    d. The aircraft wake turbulence category should be specified in item 9 with one of the following abbreviations:

        1) L for light aircraft with a maximum certificated takeoff weight of 15,500 lb. or less

        2) M for medium aircraft with a maximum certificated takeoff weight between 15,500 lb. and 300,000 lb.

        3) H for heavy aircraft with a maximum certificated takeoff weight of 300,000 lb. or more

    e. A separate equipment code must be used for each type of equipment on board the aircraft instead of a single letter for an entire avionics package. Refer to *AIM* Appendix 4 and your equipment user's guide to determine the correct code. Common codes include

        1) S for a standard VHF radio, VOR receiver, and ILS receiver
        2) G for an IFR approved GPS
        3) R for performance based navigation (PBN) capability

    f. For complete guidance on filling out the ICAO flight plan form, refer to the *Aeronautical Information Manual (AIM)*, Paragraph 5-1-6 and Appendix 4.

2. When transitioning from VFR to IFR, you should contact the nearest FSS to close the VFR portion and request an ATC IFR clearance.

    a. You must obtain an IFR clearance before entering IFR conditions.

3. IFR flight plans can be canceled only if you are flying in VFR conditions outside Class A airspace.

    a. When landing at an airport with a control tower, IFR flight plans will be closed automatically by the tower; no action is required by the pilot.

4. When landing at an airport without a control tower or FSS on the field, the pilot must initiate IFR flight plan cancellation. The pilot may cancel

    a. By radio while airborne if conditions are VFR
    b. By radio or telephone as soon as (s)he is on the ground

5. A waypoint on an IFR flight is a predetermined geographical position used for an RNAV route or RNAV instrument approach identification or progress reporting. It is defined relative to a VORTAC position **or** by longitude and latitude; i.e., it does not have to be relative to a VORTAC.

Approved OMB No. 2120-0026
Exp. 5/31/2017

International Flight Plan

U S Department of Transportation
Federal Aviation Administration

PRIORITY   ADDRESSEE(S)

<=FF

<=

FILING TIME   ORIGINATOR   **<=**

SPECIFIC IDENTIFICATION OF ADDRESSEE(S) AND / OR ORIGINATOR

3 MESSAGE TYPE   7 AIRCRAFT IDENTIFICATION   8 FLIGHT RULES   TYPE OF FLIGHT

<=(FPL   —   —   ☐   —   ☐   **<=**

9 NUMBER   TYPE OF AIRCRAFT   WAKE TURBULENCE CAT.   10 EQUIPMENT

—   ☐   / ☐   — ☐   /   **<=**

13 DEPARTURE AERODROME   TIME

—   ☐   ☐   **<=**

15 CRUISING SPEED   LEVEL   ROUTE

—   ☐   ☐

<=

TOTAL EET

16 DESTINATION AERODROME   HR   MIN   ALTN AERODROME   2ND ALTN AERODROME

☐   ☐   ☐   ☐   **<=**

18 OTHER INFORMATION

—

<=

SUPPLEMENTARY INFORMATION (NOT TO BE TRANSMITTED IN FPL MESSAGES)

19   ENDURANCE   EMERGENCY RADIO
      HR   MIN   UHF   VHF   ELT

—E/ ☐   **P/** PERSONS ON BOARD ☐   **R/** U   V   E

SURVIVAL EQUIPMENT   JACKETS

      POLAR DESERT MARITIME JUNGLE   LIGHT FLUORES UHF   VHF

☐ / P   D   M   J   ☐ / L   F   U   V

DINGHIES

NUMBER CAPACITY COVER   COLOR

D / ☐   ☐   C   ☐   **<=**

AIRCRAFT COLOR AND MARKINGS

A/

REMARKS

N /   **<=**

PILOT-IN-COMMAND

C/   **)<=**

FILED BY   ACCEPTED BY   ADDITIONAL INFORMATION

FAA Form 7233-4 (7/15)

Figure 1A. – Flight Plan Form (not in supplement).

5.10 ATC CLEARANCES

1. Pilots of airborne aircraft should read back ATC clearances concerning altitude assignments and/or vectors and any part requiring verification.

2. An abbreviated IFR clearance includes

    a. Destination airport
    b. The route of flight, given fix-by-fix or "as filed"
    c. Initial altitude
    d. DP (instrument departure procedure) name, number, and/or transition, if appropriate

3. When a departure clearance from an airport without an operating control tower contains a void time, the pilot must advise ATC as soon as possible (but no later than 30 min. after the void time) if a decision is made NOT to take off.

4. A cruise clearance assigns a pilot a block of airspace from the minimum IFR altitude up to and including the altitude specified in the cruise clearance.

    a. Climb and descent within the block are at the discretion of the pilot.

    b. However, once the pilot starts descent and verbally reports leaving an altitude in the block, the pilot may not return to that altitude without additional ATC clearance.

5.11 ATC COMMUNICATION PROCEDURES

1. You should state your position on the airport when calling the tower for takeoff from a runway intersection (i.e., an intersection other than at the end of the runway).

2. When flying IFR, the pilot must maintain continuous contact with assigned ATC frequencies.

    a. All radio frequency changes are made at the direction of ATC.

3. When climbing or descending per ATC clearance, the pilot should use the optimum rate consistent with the aircraft to 1,000 ft. above or below the assigned altitude and then climb or descend at the rate of between 500 and 1,500 fpm until attaining the assigned altitude.

    a. It is sufficient to use a cruise climb rather than a maximum angle of climb.
    b. If you cannot climb or descend at least 500 fpm, you should notify ATC.
    c. You should lead your turns so that you remain in the center of the airway.

4. The reports that a pilot must make to ATC without a specific ATC request include

    a. At all times:

        1) Inability to climb or descend at a rate of at least 500 fpm
        2) Change in the average true airspeed at cruising altitude when it varies by more than the greater of 5% or 10 kt. from that filed in your flight plan
        3) Change from assigned altitude
        4) Missed approach
        5) Departure from any assigned holding fix or point
        6) The time and altitude when reaching holding fix or clearance limit
        7) Loss of communication or navigation capability or anything else affecting the safety of flight

    b.   When not in radar contact:

        1)   Departure from final approach fix inbound on final approach
        2)   Correction of an estimate which appears to be more than 2 min. in error
        3)   Passage over certain reporting points:

            a)   Compulsory reporting points as marked by solid black triangles on en route
                 charts
            b)   Each fix used in the flight plan to define the route of flight on a direct flight not
                 flown on radials or courses of established airways or routes

5.   Your Mode C transponder should always be set to Mode C and turned to ON unless otherwise
     requested by ATC, while ADS-B Out equipment should be set in the transmit mode at all times.

6.   When receiving traffic advisories from ATC, remember that the controller sees only the airplane's
     direction of travel, not the airplane heading.

     a.   You must adjust traffic reports for any wind correction you are holding.

7.   **Radar contact** means your airplane has been identified on the radar screen and radar flight
     following will be provided until radar identification is terminated by the controller.

8.   **Resume own navigation** means that you continue to be under ATC radar surveillance but are
     responsible for your own navigation. No more vectors will be given.

     a.   You are still in radar contact with ATC. Thus, you do not need to make position reports.

9.   **Radar service terminated** means that you are no longer under ATC radar surveillance and must
     resume position reports at compulsory reporting points.

10. IFR flights receive separation from all IFR aircraft and participating VFR aircraft operating within
     the outer area of Class C airspace.

11. When flying VFR on practice instrument approaches, you must avoid IFR conditions. You do not
     have an IFR clearance.

12. While you should comply with all headings and altitudes assigned by ATC, you should feel free
     to question any assigned altitude or heading believed to be incorrect. The pilot has ultimate
     responsibility for safe flight.

13. When ATC requests a specified airspeed, you are expected to maintain the speed plus or minus
     10 kt. based upon indicated airspeed.

14. If you cancel your IFR flight plan 10 mi. from your destination airport (located in Class D
     airspace), you must establish communications with the tower prior to entering the Class D
     airspace.

15. Pilots never have to accept a controller's clearance, regardless of meteorological conditions.

     a.   A pilot should only accept a LAHSO clearance provided (s)he feels (s)he can land the
          plane within the available distance without compromising safety.

16. **Minimum fuel** is just an advisory to ATC that indicates an emergency situation is possible
     should any undue delay occur.

5.12 RADIO COMMUNICATION FAILURE

1. In the event of two-way communications failure, ATC will assume the pilot is operating in accordance with 14 CFR 91.185.

    a. As always, pilot judgment is the final determinant of safest flying.

2. According to 14 CFR 91.185, if you lose two-way communications

    a. When holding and you receive an expected further clearance (EFC) time, you should leave the holding pattern at the EFC time.

    b. When on an IFR flight in VFR weather conditions, you should continue your flight under VFR and land as soon as practicable.

    c. When in IFR conditions, route selection is determined by A-V-E-F. Fly the route that is

        1) **A**ssigned -- the last routing assigned in ATC clearance

        2) **V**ectored -- the last routing provided via vector clearance

        3) **E**xpected -- in the absence of any assigned routing, the route provided by ATC in a further clearance

        4) **F**iled -- the route advised by ATC that may be expected in a further clearance by the initially filed route

    d. Continue on the route specified in your clearance (for each leg of your flight) at the highest of M-E-A:

        1) **M**EA (minimum en route altitude)

        2) **E**xpected altitude per ATC

        3) **A**ssigned -- the last assigned altitude

3. When losing radio communications, alert ATC by setting your transponder code to 7600.

    a. If you are in an emergency situation, set and leave the transponder at 7700.

5.13 NAVIGATION RADIO FAILURE

1. If your DME fails above FL 240, you should notify ATC of the failure and continue to the next airport of intended landing at which repairs or replacement of the equipment can be made.

2. When operating under IFR, you must immediately report to ATC the loss of VOR, TACAN, or LF navigation receiver capability; complete or partial loss of ILS receiver; and/or any impairment of radio communications capability.

5.14 AIRSPACE

1. En Route Low-Altitude Charts show the limits of controlled airspace, military training routes, and special-use airspace.

    a. However, they do not show Class A airspace. Class A airspace is shown on En Route High-Altitude Charts.

2. Class A Airspace

    a. Class A airspace is from 18,000 ft. MSL to FL 600.

    b. An IFR flight plan is required when flying in IFR conditions in controlled airspace and at all times in Class A airspace.

    c. Operations in Class A airspace require

        1) Two-way radio communications with ATC

        2) A Mode C transponder

        3) ADS-B Out equipment that operates on the frequency of 1090 MHz

3. Class B Airspace

    a.   Generally, the maximum altitude for Class B airspace is 10,000 ft. MSL.

    b.   Operations in Class B airspace require

        1)   Two-way radio communications with ATC

        2)   A Mode C transponder

        3)   ADS-B Out equipment that operates

            a)   On the frequency of 1090 MHz or

            b)   Using a universal access transceiver (UAT) on the frequency of 978 MHz

        4)   A VOR receiver if operating under IFR

    c.   If it is necessary to conduct training operations within Class B airspace, procedures established by ATC for such flights will be followed.

4. Class C Airspace

    a.   Class C airspace consists of controlled airspace within which all aircraft are subject to the operating rules and equipment requirements specified in 14 CFR Part 91.

    b.   Operations in Class C airspace require

        1)   Two-way radio communications with ATC

        2)   A Mode C transponder

        3)   ADS-B Out equipment that operates

            a)   On the frequency of 1090 MHz or

            b)   Using a UAT on the frequency of 978 MHz

5. Class D Airspace

    a.   The normal lateral limit for Class D airspace is 4 NM.

    b.   The normal upper limit of Class D airspace is 2,500 ft. AGL.

    c.   Operations in Class D airspace only require two-way radio communications with ATC.

        1)   If an aircraft's transponder fails during flight within Class D airspace, no deviation is required because a transponder is not required in Class D airspace.

6. Class E Airspace

    a.   Class E airspace provides sufficient airspace for the safe control and separation of aircraft during IFR operations.

        1)   Transition areas are Class E airspace and are used to transition between the terminal area and en route flight.

        2)   When designated in conjunction with an airport with a prescribed instrument approach, Class E airspace extends upward from 700 ft. AGL.

        3)   When designated in conjunction with airway route structures, etc., Class E airspace extends upward from 1,200 ft. AGL.

        4)   Both types of transition areas terminate at the base of overlying controlled airspace, i.e., Class A airspace.

    b.   ADS-B Out equipment that either operates on the frequency of 1090 MHz or operates using a UAT on the frequency of 978 MHz is required in Class E airspace

        1)   Above 10,000 ft. MSL over the 48 states and D.C., excluding airspace at and below 2,500 ft. AGL, and

        2)   Over the Gulf of Mexico at and above 3,000 ft. MSL within 12 NM of the coastline of the United States.

7. Class G Airspace

    a. Class G (uncontrolled) airspace is airspace where ATC does not control air traffic.

    b. The maximum altitude at which Class G airspace will exist is 14,500 ft. MSL (excluding the airspace less than 1,500 ft. AGL).

8. Military Operations Areas (MOAs)

    a. MOAs consist of airspace established for the purpose of separating certain military training activities from IFR traffic.

9. Basic VFR Weather Minimums

Cloud Clearance and Visibility Required for VFR

Airspace	Flight Visibility	Distance from Clouds
Class A	Not Applicable	Not applicable
Class B	3 SM	Clear of Clouds
Class C	3 SM	500 ft. below 1,000 ft. above 2,000 ft. horiz.
Class D	3 SM	500 ft. below 1,000 ft. above 2,000 ft. horiz.
Class E		
Less than 10,000 ft. MSL	3 SM	500 ft. below 1,000 ft. above 2,000 ft. horiz.
At or above 10,000 ft. MSL	5 SM	1,000 ft. below 1,000 ft. above 1 SM horiz.

Airspace	Flight Visibility	Distance from Clouds
Class G:		
1,200 ft. or less above the surface (regardless of MSL altitude)		
Day	1 SM	Clear of clouds
Night	3 SM	500 ft. below 1,000 ft. above 2,000 ft. horiz.
More than 1,200 ft. above the surface but less than 10,000 ft. MSL		
Day	1 SM	500 ft. below 1,000 ft. above 2,000 ft. horiz.
Night	3 SM	500 ft. below 1,000 ft. above 2,000 ft. horiz.
More than 1,200 ft. above the surface and at or above 10,000 ft. MSL	5 SM	1,000 ft. below 1,000 ft. above 1 SM horiz.

    a. An airplane may be operated clear of clouds in Class G airspace at night below 1,200 ft. AGL when the visibility is less than 3 SM but more than 1 SM in an airport traffic pattern and within 1/2 NM of the runway.

    b. When flying under a "VFR-on-top" clearance on IFR flights, you must fly at VFR altitudes and comply with VFR visibility and distance-from-clouds criteria.

10. Special VFR Weather Minimums

    a. With some exceptions, special VFR clearances can be requested in Class B, C, D, or E airspace areas.

    b. The flight requirements are to remain clear of clouds and have visibility of at least 1 SM.

    c. Flight under special VFR clearance at night is permitted only if the pilot is instrument rated and the airplane is IFR equipped.

5.15 AIRPORT DIAGRAM – CHART SUPPLEMENT

1. Airport Diagrams, published in regional booklets, provide information about airports, both VFR and IFR. The Chart Supplement Airport Diagram includes information such as runway slope (e.g., 0.3% DOWN) and runway heading (e.g., 003.6°). Review the Chart Supplement Airport Diagram on the next page for more information.

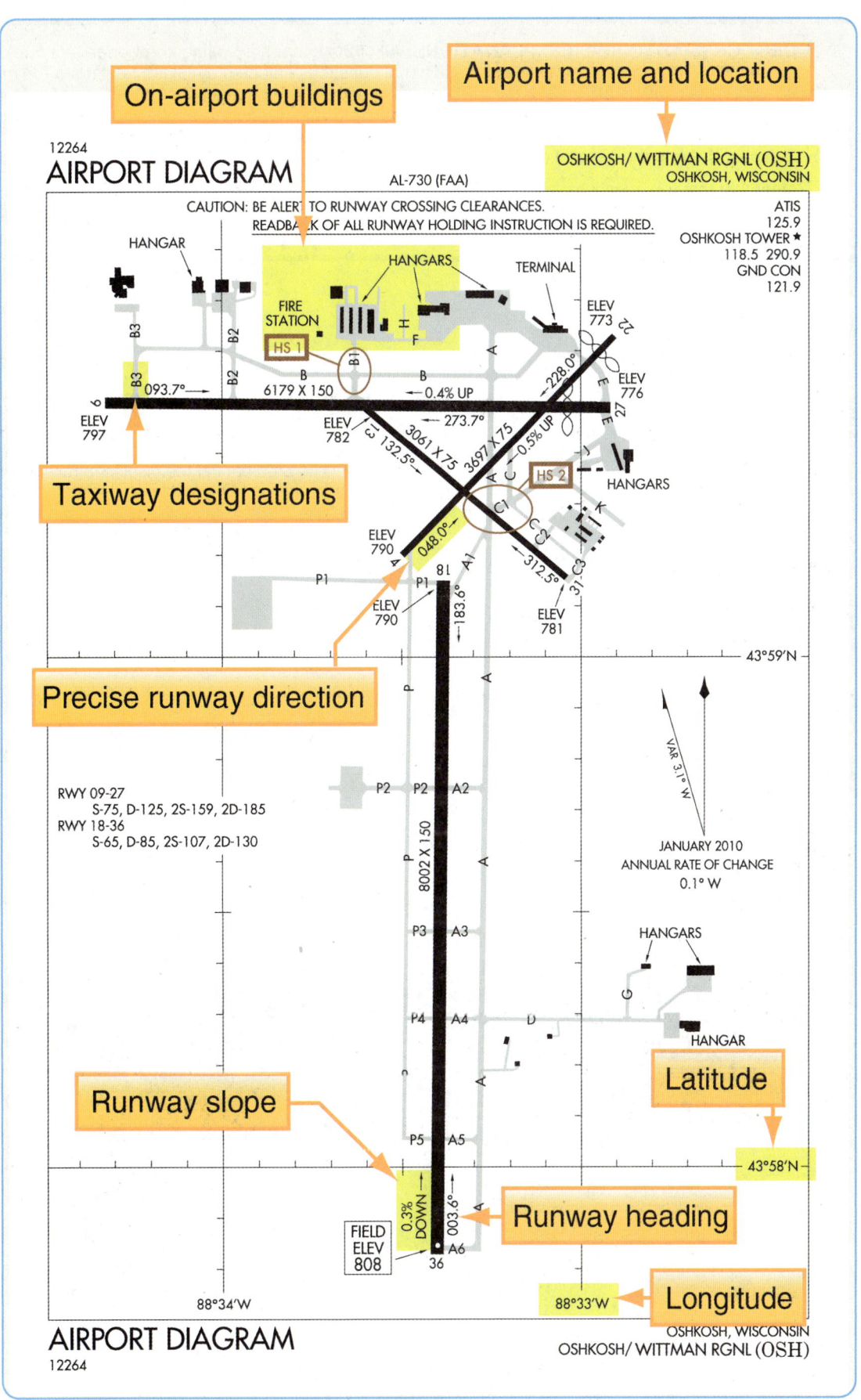

Airport Diagram: Osh Kosh/Wittman Regional (OSH).

QUESTIONS AND ANSWER EXPLANATIONS: All of the instrument rating knowledge test questions chosen by the FAA for release as well as additional questions selected by Gleim relating to the material in the previous outlines are provided on the following pages. These questions have been organized into the same subunits as the outlines. To the immediate right of each question are the correct answer and answer explanations. You should cover these answers and answer explanations while responding to the questions. Refer to the general discussion in the Introduction on how to take the FAA knowledge test.

Remember that the questions from the FAA knowledge test bank have been reordered by topic and organized into a meaningful sequence. Also, the first line of the answer explanation gives the citation of the authoritative source for the answer.

QUESTIONS

5.1 Precision Instrument Runway Markings

1. (Refer to Figure 138 below.) What night operations, if any, are authorized between the approach end of the runway and the threshold lights?

    A. No aircraft operations are permitted short of the threshold lights.

    B. Only taxi operations are permitted in the area short of the threshold lights.

    C. Taxi and takeoff operations are permitted, providing the takeoff operations are toward the visible green threshold lights.

Answer (C) is correct. (AIM Para 2-3-3)
    DISCUSSION: On displaced thresholds, runway edge lights appear red when taxiing toward the green threshold lights and white when taxiing away from the threshold to the departure end of the runway. The area behind the displaced runway threshold is available for taxiing, landing rollout, and takeoff of aircraft.
    Answer (A) is incorrect. Overrun areas are areas where only emergency operations are permitted. Overrun areas do not have any runway edge lights. **Answer (B) is incorrect.** Landing rollout and takeoff operations are also permitted behind displaced thresholds.

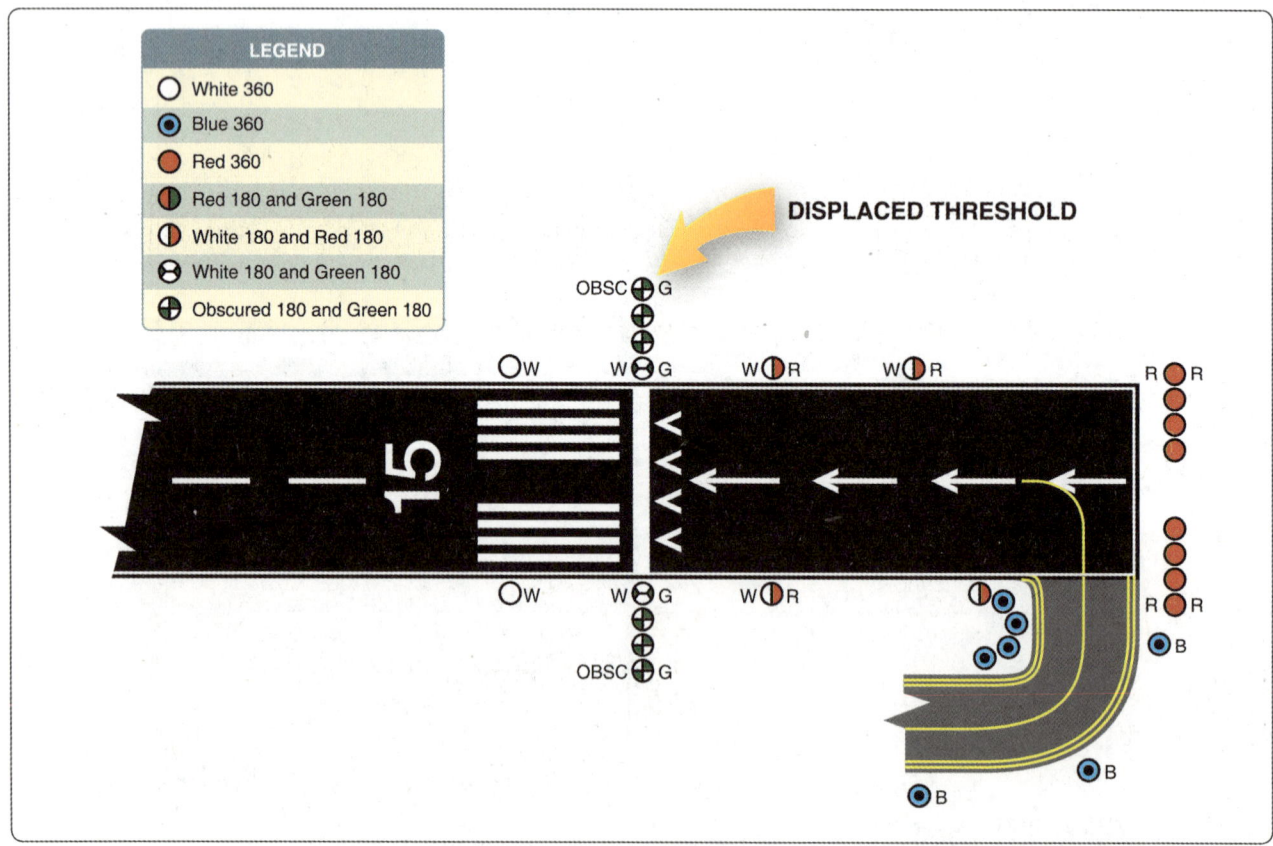

Figure 138. – Runway Legend.

2. Which runway marking indicates a displaced threshold on an instrument runway?

A. Arrows leading to the threshold mark.

B. Centerline dashes starting at the threshold.

C. Red chevron marks in the nonlanding portion of the runway.

Answer (A) is correct. (AIM Para 2-3-3)
DISCUSSION: On any runway, a displaced threshold is marked with a series of arrows in the middle of the runway pointing to the threshold mark, which is a solid line across the runway. A displaced threshold is available for taxiing, landing rollout, and takeoff, but not landing.
Answer (B) is incorrect. It describes the centerline marking of a runway. Answer (C) is incorrect. Chevron marks are usually yellow. They indicate a nonusable portion of the runway that is only available for emergency use (overrun and stopway areas).

3. (Refer to Figure 137 below.) What is the distance (A) from the beginning of the runway to the fixed distance marker?

A. 500 feet.

B. 1,000 feet.

C. 1,500 feet.

Answer (B) is correct. (AIM Para 2-3-3)
DISCUSSION: The fixed distance marker on precision instrument runways consists of two heavy lines parallel to the direction of the runway, 1,000 ft. from the runway threshold.
Answer (A) is incorrect. The six parallel lines (somewhat lighter and narrower than the fixed distance marker) 500 ft. from the threshold of the runway are the touchdown zone marker. Answer (C) is incorrect. The marker at roughly 1,500 ft. from the threshold is the next marker beyond the fixed distance marker, not the fixed distance marker.

4. (Refer to Figure 137 below.) What is the distance (B) from the beginning of the runway to the touchdown zone marker?

A. 250 feet.

B. 500 feet.

C. 750 feet.

Answer (B) is correct. (AIM Para 2-3-3)
DISCUSSION: The distance from the runway threshold to the touchdown zone marker is 500 ft. The touchdown zone marker consists of six lines parallel to the runway.
Answer (A) is incorrect. There is no standardized marking 250 ft. from the beginning of the runway. Answer (C) is incorrect. There is no standardized marking 750 ft. from the beginning of the runway.

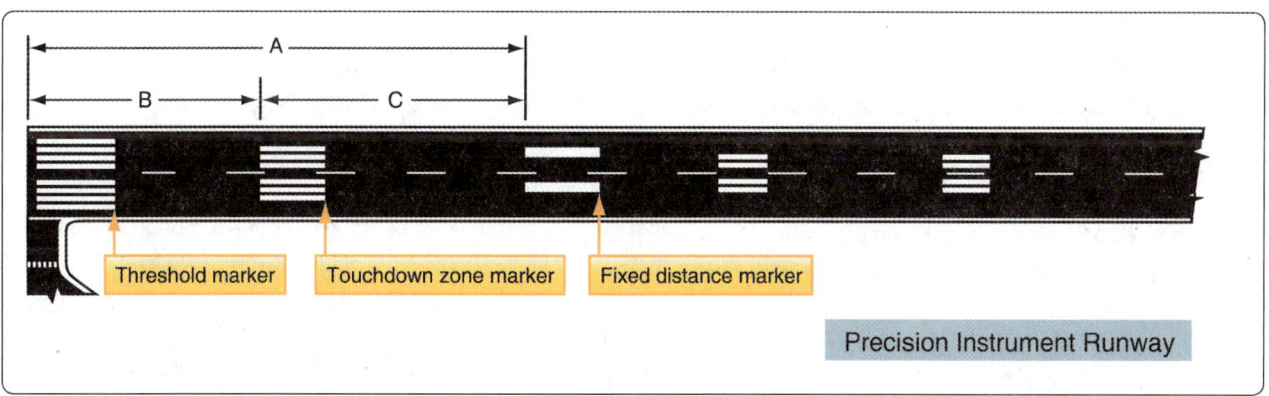

Figure 137. – Precision Instrument Runway.

5. (Refer to Figure 137 above.) What is the distance (C) from the beginning of the touchdown zone marker to the beginning of the fixed distance marker?

A. 1,000 feet.

B. 500 feet.

C. 250 feet.

Answer (B) is correct. (AIM Para 2-3-3)
DISCUSSION: Since the touchdown zone marker is 500 ft. from the runway threshold and the fixed distance marker is 1,000 ft. from the runway threshold, the distance from the beginning of the touchdown zone marker to the beginning of the fixed distance marker is 500 ft. (1,000 – 500).
Answer (A) is incorrect. The distance from the beginning of the runway to the fixed distance marker is 1,000 ft. Answer (C) is incorrect. A standard distance between runway markings is not 250 ft.

5.2 Airport Signs and Markings

6. The "ILS critical area boundary" sign identifies the

   A. Area where an aircraft is prohibited from entering.

   B. Edge of the ILS critical area.

   C. Exit boundary for the runway protected area.

Answer (B) is correct. (FAA-H-8083-25B Chap 13)
DISCUSSION: The ILS critical area boundary sign has a yellow background with two horizontal, parallel black lines and four sets of two vertical, parallel lines connecting the two horizontal lines. This sign is the same as the painted marking representing the ILS critical area boundary. When an ILS is in operation, aircraft must hold at this line and not pass it unless so authorized by ATC so as not to block or interfere with the signal from the ILS glide slope antenna installed at the airport. If taxiing off of a runway, the aircraft is not clear of the ILS critical area until all parts of the aircraft are past this sign and associated painted marking.
   Answer (A) is incorrect. This answer choice describes the purpose of a no entry sign. **Answer (C) is incorrect.** This answer choice describes the purpose of a runway hold position sign.

7. The "runway hold position" sign denotes

   A. an entrance to a taxiway from runway.

   B. an entrance to a runway from a taxiway.

   C. an area protected for an aircraft approaching a runway.

Answer (B) is correct. (AIM Para 2-3-8)
DISCUSSION: Runway holding position signs, consisting of white numbering on a red background, are found adjacent to runway holding position markings that are painted on a taxiway or a runway. These signs and markings indicate the point at which aircraft are expected to hold short of a runway if an ATC clearance to proceed onto that runway has not been received at an airport with an operating control tower or without making sure of adequate separation at an airport without an operating control tower. Runway holding position signs therefore denote the entrance to a runway from a taxiway or from an intersecting runway.
   Answer (A) is incorrect. A direction sign, not a runway holding position sign, denotes the entrance to a taxiway from a runway. **Answer (C) is incorrect.** A runway approach area holding position sign, not a runway holding position sign, denotes an area protected for aircraft approaching or departing a runway.

8. "Runway hold position" markings on the taxiway

   A. identifies where aircraft hold short of the runway.

   B. identifies area where aircraft are prohibited.

   C. allows an aircraft permission onto the runway.

Answer (A) is correct. (AIM Para 2-3-5)
DISCUSSION: Runway holding position markings on taxiways identify the location where you are supposed to stop when you do not have an ATC clearance to proceed at an airport with an operating control tower or without making sure of adequate separation at an airport without an operating control tower. These markings consist of four yellow lines, two solid and two dashed, spaced 6 in. apart and extending across the width of the taxiway, with the dashed lines nearest the runway. The solid lines are always on the side where the aircraft is to hold.
   Answer (B) is incorrect. A no entry sign, not a runway hold position marking, identifies an area where aircraft are prohibited. **Answer (C) is incorrect.** Runway holding position markings indicate that aircraft should hold short of the runway, not taxi onto it, until a clearance to proceed onto the runway is received.

9. (Refer to Figure 254 on page 159.) Which of the signs in the figure is a mandatory instruction sign?

   A. Top red.

   B. Middle yellow.

   C. Bottom yellow.

Answer (A) is correct. (AIM Para 2-3-8)
DISCUSSION: Mandatory signs have a red background with a white inscription and are used to denote an entrance to a runway or critical area and areas where an aircraft is prohibited from entering. The top red is a "No Entry" sign.
   Answer (B) is incorrect. The middle yellow sign is a runway boundary sign. It is located on taxiways on the back side of certain runway/taxiway holding position signs or runway approach area signs. **Answer (C) is incorrect.** The ILS critical area sign has a yellow background and black lines drawn that look like a sideways ladder. This sign identifies the ILS critical area exit boundary. If an aircraft is on this line and instrument approaches are in progress, the ILS signal may be blocked. Do not cross or block this during IMC unless clearance is given.

10. (Refer to Figure 254 below.) While clearing an active runway, you are clear of the ILS critical area when you pass which sign?

   A. Top red.

   B. Middle yellow.

   C. Bottom yellow.

Answer (C) is correct. (AIM Para 2-3-1)
   DISCUSSION: The ILS critical area sign has a yellow background and black lines drawn that looks like a sideways ladder. This sign identifies the ILS critical area exit boundary. If an aircraft is on this line and instrument approaches are in progress, the ILS signal may be blocked. Do not cross or block this during IMC unless clearance is given.
   Answer (A) is incorrect. The top red sign is a mandatory "No Entry" sign. It means "do not go beyond this sign."
Answer (B) is incorrect. The middle yellow sign is a runway boundary sign. It is located on taxiways on the back side of certain runway/taxiway holding position signs or runway approach area signs.

11. (Refer to Figure 254 below.) Which sign indicates you're holding short of the ILS critical area?

   A. Top red.

   B. Middle yellow.

   C. Bottom yellow.

Answer (C) is correct. (AIM Para 2-3-1)
   DISCUSSION: The ILS critical area sign has a yellow background and black lines drawn that look like a sideways ladder. This sign identifies the ILS critical area exit boundary. If an aircraft is on this line and instrument approaches are in progress, the ILS signal may be blocked. Do not cross or block this during IMC unless clearance is given.
   Answer (A) is incorrect. The top red sign is a mandatory "No Entry" sign. It means "do not go beyond this sign."
Answer (B) is incorrect. The middle yellow sign is a runway boundary sign. It is located on taxiways on the back side of certain runway/taxiway holding position signs or runway approach area signs.

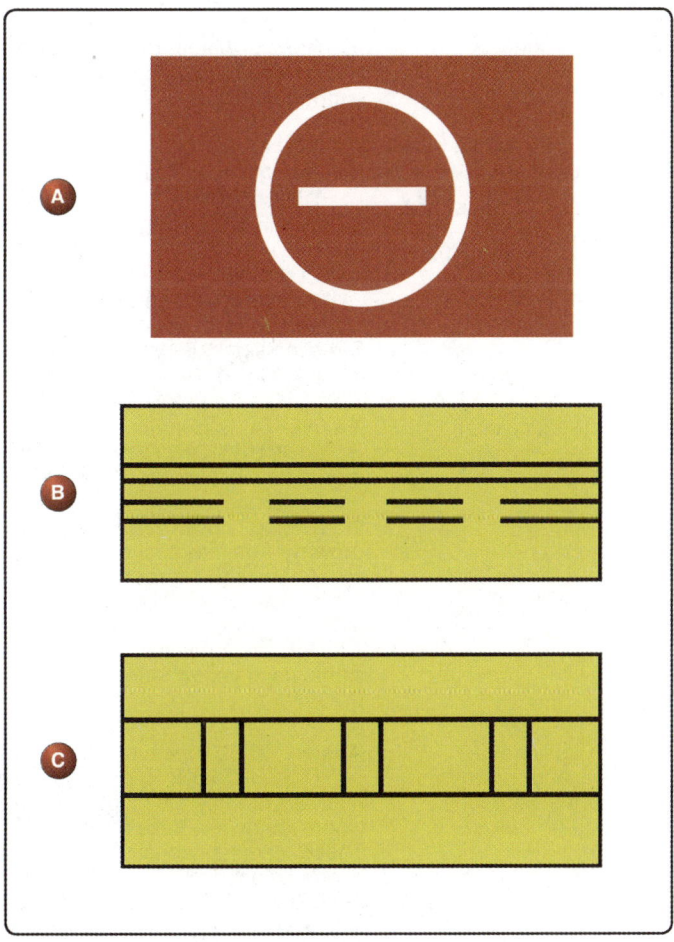

Figure 254. – Airport Sign.

12. Destination signs indicate

    A. The taxiway a pilot is on.

    B. The runway a pilot is on.

    C. The direction to takeoff runways.

Answer (C) is correct. (AIM Para 2-3-11)
    DISCUSSION: Destination signs direct pilots to a destination on the airport. These signs can direct pilots to runways, taxiways, aprons, terminals, FBOs, cargo areas, civil aviation areas, and military areas.
    Answer (A) is incorrect. Destination signs indicate the direction to a point, not the specific point where the pilot is currently located. **Answer (B) is incorrect.** Destination signs indicate the direction to a point, not the specific point where the pilot is currently located.

13. What is the purpose of the runway exit sign?

    A. Defines direction and designation of runway when exiting a taxiway.

    B. Defines direction and designation of exit taxiway from runway.

    C. Defines a mandatory exit point from the runway during Land and Hold Short Operations (LAHSO).

Answer (B) is correct. (AIM Para 2-3-10)
    DISCUSSION: A runway exit sign defines the direction and designation of an exit taxiway from the runway.
    Answer (A) is incorrect. A runway exit sign is positioned on the runway, not on a taxiway. This answer choice describes a runway destination sign. **Answer (C) is incorrect.** Runway exit signs are not mandatory exit points during LAHSO. This answer choice partially describes runway holding position markings.

14. (Refer to Figure 94 on page 161.) Mandatory airport instruction signs are designated by having

    A. yellow lettering with a black background.

    B. white lettering with a red background.

    C. black lettering with a yellow background.

Answer (B) is correct. (AIM Para 2-3-8)
    DISCUSSION: Mandatory airport instruction signs have a red background with white lettering and are used to denote an entrance to a runway or critical area and areas where an aircraft is prohibited from entering.
    Answer (A) is incorrect. Yellow lettering on a black background denotes taxiway or runway location signs (where the aircraft is located). **Answer (C) is incorrect.** Black lettering on a yellow background denotes direction, destination, and information signs.

15. (Refer to Figure 94 on page 161.) What sign is designated by illustration 7?

    A. Location sign.

    B. Mandatory instruction sign.

    C. Direction sign.

Answer (B) is correct. (AIM Para 2-3-8)
    DISCUSSION: Mandatory instruction signs have a red background with white lettering. The sign designated by illustration 7 (15-APCH) protects the approach to RWY 15 and/or the departure for RWY 33.
    Answer (A) is incorrect. Location signs use yellow lettering on a black background. **Answer (C) is incorrect.** Direction signs use black lettering on a yellow background.

16. (Refer to Figure 94 on page 161.) What colors are runway holding position signs?

    A. White with a red background.

    B. Red with a white background.

    C. Yellow with a black background.

Answer (A) is correct. (AIM Para 2-3-8)
    DISCUSSION: Runway holding position signs, like other mandatory instruction signs, have white lettering on a red background. Runway holding position signs are located at the holding position on taxiways that intersect a runway or on runways that intersect other runways.
    Answer (B) is incorrect. Red lettering on a white background is used on the landing area of a hospital heliport but is not used on any airport signs. **Answer (C) is incorrect.** Taxiway and runway location signs, not runway holding position signs, have yellow lettering on a black background.

17. (Refer to Figure 94 on page 161.) Hold line markings at the intersection of taxiways and runways consist of four lines that extend across the width of the taxiway. These lines are

    A. white, and the dashed lines are nearest the runway.

    B. yellow, and the dashed lines are nearest the runway.

    C. yellow, and the solid lines are nearest the runway.

Answer (B) is correct. (AIM Para 2-3-5)
    DISCUSSION: Runway holding position markings on taxiways identify the location where you are supposed to stop when you do not have a clearance to proceed onto the runway. These markings consist of four yellow lines, two solid and two dashed, spaced 6 in. apart and extending across the width of the taxiway, with the dashed lines nearest the runway. The solid lines are always on the side where the aircraft is to hold.
    Answer (A) is incorrect. The lines are yellow, not white. **Answer (C) is incorrect.** Solid lines are always on the holding side, not the runway side.

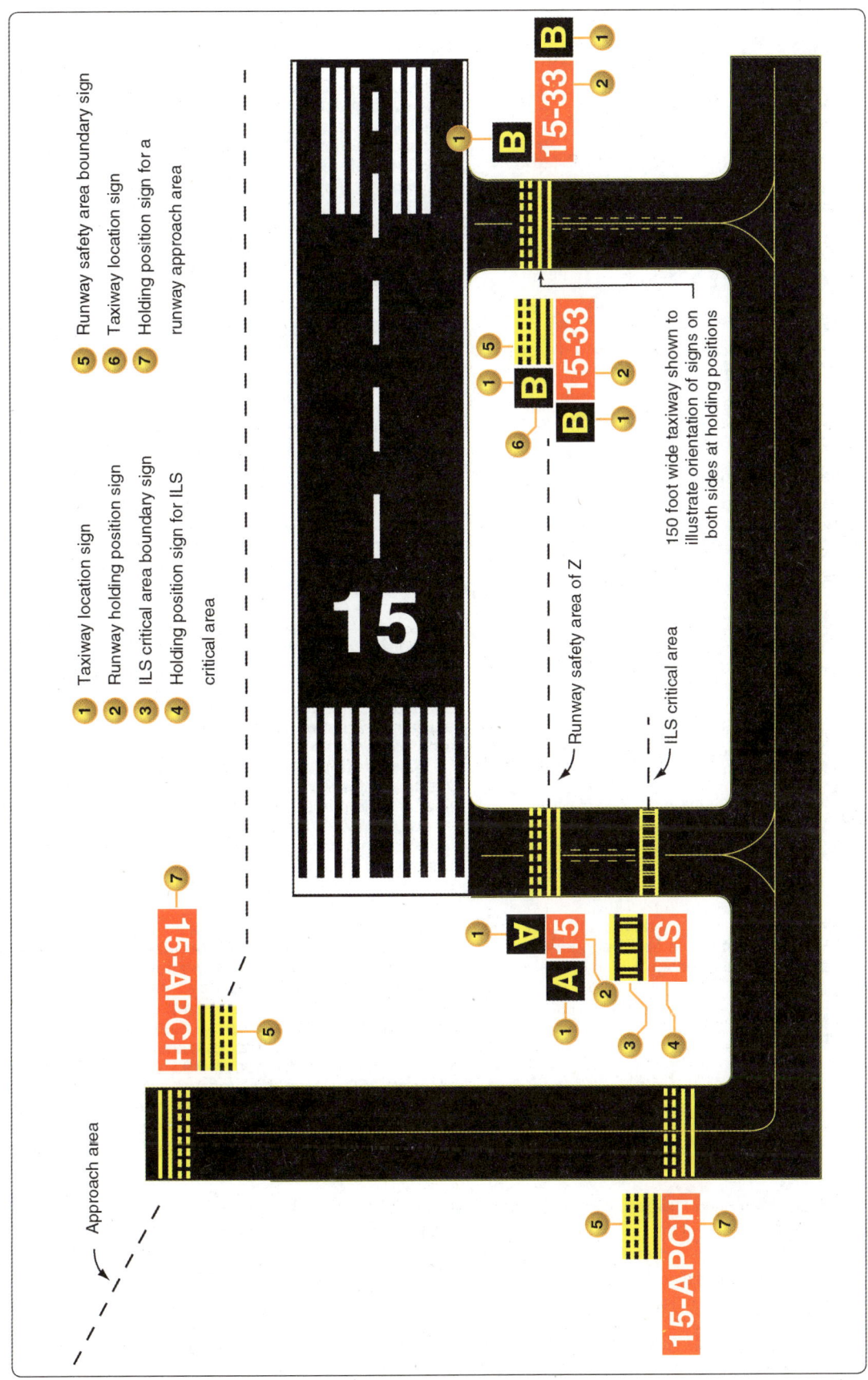

Figure 94. – Application Examples for Holding Positions.

18. The "No Entry" sign identifies

    A. the exit boundary for the runway protected area.

    B. an area that does not continue beyond intersection.

    C. paved area where aircraft entry is prohibited.

Answer (C) is correct. (AIM Para 2-3-8)
    DISCUSSION: No entry signs consist of a white horizontal line surrounded by a white circle on a red background. These signs are posted at points where aircraft entry is prohibited. These signs are typically found on taxiways that are intended to be used in only one direction and at the intersection of vehicle roadways with runways, taxiways, or ramp areas where the roadway may be mistaken for a taxiway or other aircraft movement area.
    Answer (A) is incorrect. A runway boundary sign, not a no entry sign, identifies the boundary of the runway protected area for aircraft leaving the runway. Runway boundary signs consist of a black depiction of a runway holding position marking on a yellow background. **Answer (B) is incorrect.** A taxiway ending marker sign, not a no entry sign, indicates that a taxiway does not continue beyond the next intersection. Taxiway ending marker signs consist of alternating yellow and black diagonal stripes.

19. When exiting the runway, what is the purpose of the runway exit sign?

    A. Indicates designation and direction of exit taxiway from runway.

    B. Indicates designation and direction of taxiway leading out of an intersection.

    C. Indicates direction to take-off runway.

Answer (A) is correct. (FAA-H-8083-25B Chap 14)
    DISCUSSION: This direction sign has a yellow background with black text, and it defines the direction and designation of an exit taxiway from the runway.
    Answer (B) is incorrect. A taxiway intersection sign is located on a taxiway and denotes proper taxi routes. It does not provide runway exit information. **Answer (C) is incorrect.** A direction sign indicates the necessary taxi route to get to the end of a specific runway. It does not provide guidance on exiting a runway.

20. When turning onto a taxiway from another taxiway, the "taxiway directional sign" indicates

    A. direction to the take-off runway.

    B. designation and direction of taxiway leading out of an intersection.

    C. designation and direction of exit taxiway from runway.

Answer (B) is correct. (AIM Para 2-3-10)
    DISCUSSION: Direction signs consist of black lettering on a yellow background. These signs identify the designations of taxiways leading out of an intersection. An arrow next to each taxiway designation indicates the direction that an aircraft must turn in order to taxi onto that taxiway.
    Answer (A) is incorrect. Outbound destination signs, not direction signs, indicate the direction that must be taken out of an intersection in order to follow the preferred taxi route to a runway. **Answer (C) is incorrect.** The question specifies that you are turning onto a taxiway from another taxiway, not from a runway.

21. Enhanced taxiway centerline markings are enhanced for a maximum of how many feet prior to the runway holding position markings?

    A. 50

    B. 100

    C. 150

Answer (C) is correct. (AIM Para 2-3-4)
    DISCUSSION: Enhanced taxiway centerlines will begin 150 ft. prior to the runway holding position markings to draw attention to the approaching runway entrance and holding position and to advise pilots to prepare to stop unless they have been cleared onto or across the runway by ATC.
    Answer (A) is incorrect. Although the enhanced markings may be 50 ft., the maximum enhanced taxiway centerlines will begin 150 ft. from the runway holding position markings. **Answer (B) is incorrect.** Although enhanced markings can often be 100 ft., the maximum enhanced taxiway centerlines will begin 150 ft. from the runway holding position markings.

22. The purpose of an enhanced taxiway centerline is to

    A. identify the location of taxiing aircraft during low visibility operations.

    B. highlight an approaching runway holding position marking.

    C. supplement location signs in confirming the designation of the taxiway.

Answer (B) is correct. (AIM Para 2-3-4)
    DISCUSSION: The enhanced taxiway centerline warns pilots that they are approaching a runway holding position marking and should prepare to stop unless they have been cleared onto or across the runway by ATC.
    Answer (A) is incorrect. Geographic position markings provide location information at points along low visibility taxi routes to help identify locations and are found left of the taxiway centerline. **Answer (C) is incorrect.** Surface painted location signs are used to supplement location signs to assist pilots in confirming the designation of the taxiway on which the aircraft is located.

23. A runway exit sign

   A. points toward a named taxiway that leads off the runway.

   B. designates an intersection of two or more runways.

   C. shows the direction to exit from a named taxiway onto a runway.

Answer (A) is correct. (FAA-H-8083-25B Chap 14)
   DISCUSSION: This direction sign has a yellow background with black text, and it defines the direction and designation of an exit taxiway from the runway.
   Answer (B) is incorrect. A runway intersection sign is a mandatory sign that indicates an area where an airplane must hold. It does not provide guidance on exiting the runway. **Answer (C) is incorrect.** The runway exit sign indicates the direction to exit from a runway onto a taxiway, not from a taxiway onto a runway.

24. Within aircraft movement areas, "destination signs" identify the

   A. runway on which an aircraft is located.

   B. direction to the takeoff runway.

   C. entrance to the runway from a taxiway.

Answer (B) is correct. (AIM Para 2-3-11)
   DISCUSSION: Destination signs help direct you toward other areas of the airport. These signs have a yellow background with black text.
   Answer (A) is incorrect. This answer choice describes a runway location sign. **Answer (C) is incorrect.** This answer choice describes a holding position sign.

5.3 Visual Approach Slope Indicator (VASI)

25. (Refer to Figure 135 below.) Which illustration would a pilot observe if the aircraft is above both glidepaths?

   A. 5

   B. 6

   C. 7

Answer (C) is correct. (AIM Para 2-1-2)
   DISCUSSION: If you are above both glide paths on a 3-bar VASI, you will observe that all three rows of lights appear white, which is illustration 7.
   Answer (A) is incorrect. Illustration 5 indicates that you are on the lower glide path. **Answer (B) is incorrect.** Illustration 6 indicates that you are on the upper glide path.

26. (Refer to Figure 135 below.) Which illustration would a pilot observe if the aircraft is below both glidepaths?

   A. 4

   B. 5

   C. 6

Answer (A) is correct. (AIM Para 2-1-2)
   DISCUSSION: If you are below both glide paths on a 3-bar VASI, you will observe that all three rows of lights appear red, which is illustration 4.
   Answer (B) is incorrect. Illustration 5 indicates that you are on the lower glide path. **Answer (C) is incorrect.** Illustration 6 indicates that you are on the upper glide path.

27. (Refer to Figure 135 below.) Which illustration would a pilot observe when on the lower glidepath?

   A. 4

   B. 5

   C. 6

Answer (B) is correct. (AIM Para 2-1-2)
   DISCUSSION: On the lower glide path of a 3-bar VASI, the near lights should be white and the middle and far bars should be red, which is illustration 5.
   Answer (A) is incorrect. Illustration 4 indicates that you are below both glide paths. **Answer (C) is incorrect.** Illustration 6 indicates that you are on the upper glide path.

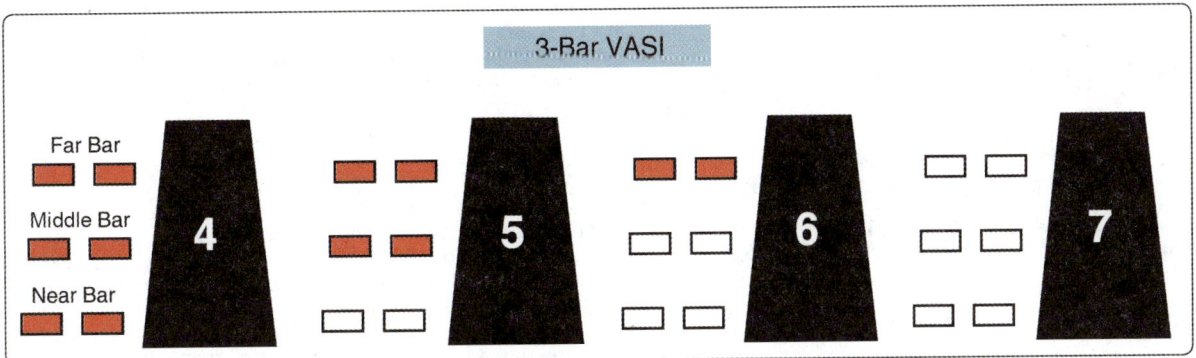

Figure 135. – 3-BAR VASI.

28. Which approach and landing objective is assured when the pilot remains on the proper glidepath of the VASI?

A. Continuation of course guidance after transition to VFR.

B. Safe obstruction clearance in the approach area.

C. Course guidance from the visual descent point to touchdown.

Answer (B) is correct. (AIM Para 2-1-2)
DISCUSSION: The VASI system provides visual descent guidance and provides safe obstruction clearance within plus or minus 10° of the extended runway centerline from as far as 4 NM from the runway threshold.
Answer (A) is incorrect. VASI does not provide course guidance. Answer (C) is incorrect. VASI does not provide course guidance.

29. When on the proper glidepath of a 2-bar VASI, the pilot will see the near bar as

A. white and the far bar as red.

B. red and the far bar as white.

C. white and the far bar as white.

Answer (A) is correct. (AIM Para 2-1-2)
DISCUSSION: When you are on the proper glide path of a 2-bar VASI, the near lights will be white and the far lights red.
Answer (B) is incorrect. White over red is impossible. Answer (C) is incorrect. White over white means you are above, not on, the glide path.

30. Which of the following indications would a pilot see while approaching to land on a runway served by a 2-bar VASI?

A. If on the glidepath, the near bars will appear red, and the far bars will appear white.

B. If departing to the high side of the glidepath, the far bars will change from red to white.

C. If on the glidepath, both near bars and far bars will appear white.

Answer (B) is correct. (AIM Para 2-1-2)
DISCUSSION: As you move to the high side of a VASI glide slope, the far bar will change from red to white. When you are on the glide slope, the far bar is red. When you are above the glide slope, the far bar is white.
Answer (A) is incorrect. If you are on the glide slope, the near bars are white, not red, and the far bars are red, not white (the opposite is impossible). Answer (C) is incorrect. If both near and far bars are white, you are above, not on, the glide slope.

31. If an approach is being made to a runway that has an operating 3-bar VASI and all the VASI lights appear red as the airplane reaches the MDA, the pilot should

A. start a climb to reach the proper glidepath.

B. continue at the same rate of descent if the runway is in sight.

C. level off momentarily to intercept the proper approach path.

Answer (C) is correct. (AIM Para 2-1-2)
DISCUSSION: If all three VASI bars are red, you are beneath both glide paths and should level off momentarily to intercept the proper approach path.
Answer (A) is incorrect. A climb is not necessary. If you level off you will soon be back on the glide path. Answer (B) is incorrect. You should briefly stop, not continue, your rate of descent to get back on the desired glide path.

32. The middle and far bars of a 3-bar VASI will

A. both appear white to the pilot when on the upper glidepath.

B. constitute a 2-bar VASI for using the lower glidepath.

C. constitute a 2-bar VASI for using the upper glidepath.

Answer (C) is correct. (AIM Para 2-1-2)
DISCUSSION: On 3-bar VASIs, the lower glide path is provided by the near and middle bars at a 3° glide slope. The middle and far bars normally have a 1/4° greater glide slope and are used for the upper glide path.
Answer (A) is incorrect. When both the middle and far bars are white, the airplane is above both glide paths. Answer (B) is incorrect. The near and middle bars are used for the lower glide path.

5.4 Precision Approach Path Indicator (PAPI)

33. (Refer to Figure 136 on page 165.) Which illustration depicts a "slightly low" (2.8°) indication?

A. 9

B. 10

C. 11

Answer (C) is correct. (AIM Para 2-1-2)
DISCUSSION: On PAPI, you are slightly (2.8°) below the glide path when three of the four lights indicate red as in illustration 11.
Answer (A) is incorrect. Illustration 9 indicates that you are slightly (3.2°) above the glide path. Answer (B) is incorrect. Illustration 10 indicates that you are on (3.0°) the glide path.

34. (Refer to Figure 136 below.) As you emerge from the clouds during an instrument approach and make visual contact with the runway environment, you see PAPI lights corresponding to those depicted in illustration 12. You are

    A. on the glidepath.

    B. above the glidepath.

    C. below the glidepath.

Answer (C) is correct. (AIM Para 2-1-2)
    DISCUSSION: Illustration 12 shows four red lights, indicating that the aircraft is far below the glide path. The following is an easy way to remember the meaning of the lights:

    "Red over red, you're dead!" (too low)
    "White over white, you're out of sight!" (too high)
    "Red over white, you're alright!" (on the glide path)

    Answer (A) is incorrect. Illustration 10 shows a balanced light display that shows two white lights and two red lights, indicating the aircraft is on the glide path. **Answer (B) is incorrect.** An imbalanced light display with more white lights on display than red lights indicates that the aircraft is above the glide path.

35. (Refer to Figure 136 below.) An "on glidepath" indication is

    A. 8

    B. 10

    C. 11

Answer (B) is correct. (AIM Para 2-1-2)
    DISCUSSION: The precision approach path indicator (PAPI) uses light units similar to the VASI, but they are installed in a single row of either two or four units, rather than bars. If all the light units indicate white, you are above the glide slope. If all indicate red, you are below the glide slope. If two lights indicate red and two lights indicate white, you are on the glide slope, as shown in illustration 10.
    Answer (A) is incorrect. Illustration 8 indicates that you are above the glide slope. **Answer (C) is incorrect.** Illustration 11 indicates that you are slightly below (2.8°) the glide slope.

36. (Refer to Figure 136 below.) Which illustration would a pilot observe if the aircraft is less than 2.5°?

    A. 10

    B. 11

    C. 12

Answer (C) is correct. (AIM Para 2-1-2)
    DISCUSSION: On PAPI systems, low is indicated by all red lights as in illustration 12. Low means the aircraft is on a glide slope of less than 2.5°.
    Answer (A) is incorrect. Illustration 10 indicates that you are on the glide path (3.0°). **Answer (B) is incorrect.** Illustration 11 indicates that you are slightly low (2.8°).

37. (Refer to Figure 136 below.) Which illustration would a pilot observe if the aircraft is far below the glidepath?

    A. 10

    B. 11

    C. 12

Answer (C) is correct. (AIM Para 2-1-2)
    DISCUSSION: Illustration 12 shows four red lights, indicating that the aircraft is far below the glidepath. An easy way to remember this is:

    "Red over red, you're dead!" (too low)
    "White over white, you're out of sight!" (too high)
    "Red over white, you're alright!" (on glidepath)

    Answer (A) is incorrect. Illustration 10 shows two white lights and two red lights, indicating the aircraft is on the glidepath, not below it. **Answer (B) is incorrect.** Illustration 11 shows one white light and three red lights, indicating the aircraft is slightly below the glidepath, not far below it.

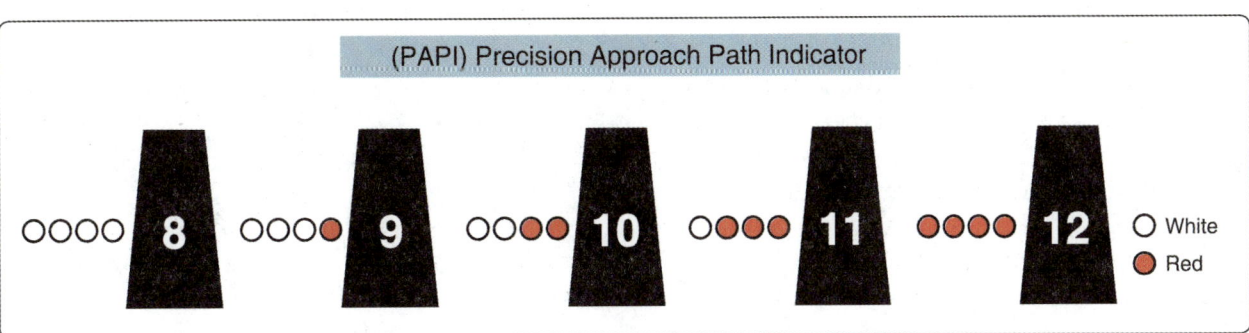

Figure 136. – Precision Approach Path Indicator (PAPI).

5.5 Runway Light Systems

OREGON   119

EUGENE

MAHLON SWEET FLD (EUG) 7 NW UTC–8(–7DT) N44°07.48′ W123°12.72′   KLAMATH FALLS
374   B S4 **FUEL** 100LL, JET A   OX 1, 2, 3, 4   TPA—1174(800) Class I, ARFF Index B   H–1B, L–1B
NOTAM FILE EUG   IAP, AD

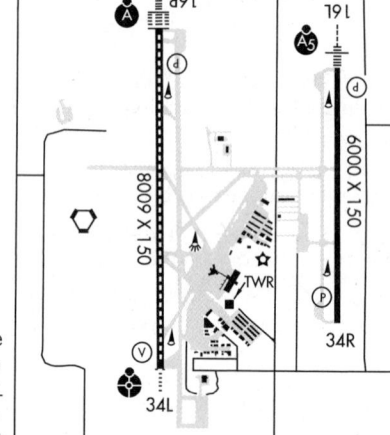

RWY 16R–34L: H8009X150 (ASPH–GRVD) S–75, D–200, 2D–400
HIRL CL
  RWY 16R: ALSF2. TDZL. PAPI(P4L)—GA 3.0° TCH 50′.
  RWY 34L: ODALS. VASI(V4L)—GA 3.0° TCH 53′.
RWY 16L–34R: H6000X150 (ASPH–GRVD) S–105, D–175, 2D–240
HIRL
  RWY 16L: MALSR. PAPI(P4L)—GA 3.0° TCH 52′.
  RWY 34R: REIL. PAPI(P4L)—GA 3.0° TCH 50′.
RUNWAY DECLARED DISTANCE INFORMATION
  RWY 16L:TORA–6000 TODA–6000 ASDA–6000 LDA–6000
  RWY 16R:TORA–8009 TODA–8009 ASDA–8009 LDA–8009
  RWY 34L:TORA–8009 TODA–8009 ASDA–8009 LDA–8009
  RWY 34R:TORA–6000 TODA–6000 ASDA–6000 LDA–6000
AIRPORT REMARKS: Attended continuously. Migratory waterfowl and other
  birds on and invof arpt. PPR for unscheduled air carrier ops with more
  than 30 passenger seats call 541–682–5430. ARFF svcs unavailable
  0000–0500 local except PPR 541–682–5430. No access to Rwy 34L
  byd Twy A9. Helicopters ldg and departing avoid overflying the airline
  passenger terminal and ramp located E of Rwy 16R–34L. Helipad west
  of Rwy 16R restricted, PPR phone 541–682–5430. Twys H and K unavailable to acft 21,000 pounds single weight and
  40,000 pounds dual gross weight. Terminal apron closed to acft except scheduled air carriers and flights with prior
  permission. PAPI Rwy 16R and Rwy 16L and 34R and VASI Rwy 34L opr 24 hrs. When twr clsd HIRL Rwy 16L–34R
  and Rwy 16R–34L preset medium ints. When twr clsd ACTIVATE ALSF2 Rwy 16R, ODALS Rwy 34L MALSR Rwy 16L
  and REIL Rwy 34R—CTAF.
WEATHER DATA SOURCES: ASOS (541) 461–3114 **HIWAS** 112.9 EUG.
COMMUNICATIONS: **CTAF** 118.9 **ATIS** 125.225 541–607–4699 **UNICOM** 122.95
  EUGENE RCO 122.3 (MC MINNVILLE RADIO)
Ⓡ **CASCADE APP/DEP CON** 119.6 (340°–159°) 120.25 (160°–339°) (1400–0730Z‡)
Ⓡ **SEATTLE CENTER APP/DEP CON** 125.8 (0730–1400Z‡)
  EUGENE TOWER 118.9 (Rwy 16R– 34L) 124.15 (Rwy 16L– 34R) (1400–0730Z‡) **GND CON** 121.7 **CLNC DEL** 121.7
AIRSPACE: **CLASS D** svc 1400–0730Z‡ other times CLASS E.
RADIO AIDS TO NAVIGATION: NOTAM FILE EUG.
  EUGENE (H) VORTACW 112.9   EUG Chan 76 N44°07.25′ W123°13.37′   at fld. 364/20E. **HIWAS.**
  ILS/DME 111.75 I–ADE Chan 54(Y) Rwy 16L. Class IE.
  ILS/DME 110.1 I–EUG Chan 38 Rwy 16R. Class IIIE. Unmonitored when ATCT clsd.

FLORENCE

FLORENCE MUNI (6S2) 1 N UTC–8(–7DT) N43°58.97′ W124°06.68′   KLAMATH FALLS
51   B **FUEL** 100LL, JET A TPA—1051(1000) NOTAM FILE MMV   L–1A
RWY 15–33: H3000X60 (ASPH) S–12.5 MIRL 0.4% up NW
  RWY 15: Hill. Rgt tfc.
  RWY 33: PAPI(P2L)—GA 3.0° TCH 40′. Trees.
AIRPORT REMARKS: Attended 1630–0030Z‡. Birds, deer and wildlife on and
  invof arpt. ACTIVATE MIRL Rwy 15–33—CTAF. PAPI Rwy 33 opr 24
  hrs.
WEATHER DATA SOURCES: AWOS–3 118.225 (541) 997–8664.
COMMUNICATIONS: **CTAF/UNICOM** 122.8
RADIO AIDS TO NAVIGATION: NOTAM FILE OTH.
  NORTH BEND (L) VORTACW 112.1   OTH Chan 58 N43°24.93′
    W124°10.11′ 346° 34.1 NM to fld. 707/18E. **HIWAS.**
  VORTAC unusable:
    012°–087° byd 30 NM blo 5,000′

Figure 162. – Excerpt from Chart Supplement.

38. (Refer to Figure 162 on page 166.) You have accepted a visual approach to RWY 16L at EUG at night. As you approach the runway, you notice runway centerline lights. This indicates

A. you are on the centerline for your assigned runway.

B. you are too low on the approach.

C. you have lined up with the wrong runway.

Answer (C) is correct. (AIM Para 2-1-5)
   DISCUSSION: RWY 16L does not have a runway centerline lighting system installed, so you have lined up with RWY 16R, which does have this lighting system. Runway centerline lights are installed on some precision approach runways to facilitate landing under adverse visibility conditions. They are located along the runway centerline and are spaced at 50-ft. intervals.
   Answer (A) is incorrect. RWY 16R has runway centerline lights, not RWY 16L, so you are not on the centerline for your assigned runway. **Answer (B) is incorrect.** Runway centerline lights do not indicate if you are low on an approach.

39. The primary purpose of runway end identifier lights, installed at many airfields, is to provide

A. rapid identification of the approach end of the runway during reduced visibility.

B. a warning of the final 3,000 feet of runway remaining as viewed from the takeoff or approach position.

C. rapid identification of the primary runway during reduced visibility.

Answer (A) is correct. (AIM Para 2-1-3)
   DISCUSSION: Runway end identifier lights (REIL) are effective for rapid and positive identification of the approach end of a runway that is surrounded by a preponderance of other lighting, lacks contrast with surrounding terrain, and/or has reduced visibility. They are white strobe lights, one on each side of the runway threshold.
   Answer (B) is incorrect. This answer choice describes runway remaining lights in the center of the runway, not REIL. **Answer (C) is incorrect.** REIL of other than the primary runway may be used to help identify the airport. In other words, REIL may be flashing at the end of a runway that is not the primary runway.

40. Which type of runway lighting consists of a pair of synchronized flashing lights, one on each side of the runway threshold?

A. MALSR.

B. HIRL.

C. REIL.

Answer (C) is correct. (AIM Para 2-1-3)
   DISCUSSION: Runway end identifier lights (REIL) consist of a pair of synchronized flashing lights, one on each side of the runway threshold.
   Answer (A) is incorrect. MALSR refers to runway alignment indicator lights, which are sequenced flashing lights that are used in combination with other approach lighting systems. **Answer (B) is incorrect.** HIRL refers to high-intensity runway lights, which are a runway edge light system.

5.6 Wake Turbulence

41. Wake turbulence is near maximum behind a jet transport just after takeoff because

    A. the engines are at maximum thrust output at slow airspeed.

    B. the gear and flap configuration increases the turbulence to maximum.

    C. of the high angle of attack and high gross weight.

Answer (C) is correct. (AIM Para 7-4-3)
    DISCUSSION: The greatest vortex strength occurs when the generating aircraft is heavy, clean, and slow, such as in takeoff climbout. At this time, there is a high gross weight and also a high angle of attack.
    Answer (A) is incorrect. Vortices have to do with airflows about the wingtips, not the engines. **Answer (B) is incorrect.** The gear and flap configuration will change the characteristics of the vortex.

42. What effect would a light crosswind of approximately 5 knots have on vortex behavior?

    A. The light crosswind would rapidly dissipate vortex strength.

    B. The upwind vortex would tend to remain over the runway.

    C. The downwind vortex would tend to remain over the runway.

Answer (B) is correct. (AIM Para 7-4-4)
    DISCUSSION: A light crosswind of 1 to 5 kt. could result in the upwind vortex of a preceding aircraft remaining in the touchdown zone for a period of time. Also, it could hasten the drift of the downwind vortex toward another runway.
    Answer (A) is incorrect. Strong, not light, winds would help rapidly dissipate vortex strength. **Answer (C) is incorrect.** The upwind, not downwind, vortex would tend to remain over the runway in a light crosswind.

43. What wind condition prolongs the hazards of wake turbulence on a landing runway for the longest period of time?

    A. Direct headwind.

    B. Direct tailwind.

    C. Light quartering tailwind.

Answer (C) is correct. (AIM Para 7-4-4)
    DISCUSSION: Light quartering tailwinds require maximum caution because they can move the vortices of preceding aircraft forward into the touchdown zone and hold the upwind vortex on the runway.
    Answer (A) is incorrect. A direct headwind will permit the vortices to move away from each side of the runway. **Answer (B) is incorrect.** A direct tailwind will permit the vortices to move away from each side of the runway.

44. When landing behind a large jet aircraft, at which point on the runway should you plan to land?

    A. If any crosswind, land on the windward side of the runway and prior to the jet's touchdown point.

    B. At least 1,000 feet beyond the jet's touchdown point.

    C. Beyond the jet's touchdown point.

Answer (C) is correct. (AIM Para 7-4-6)
    DISCUSSION: When landing behind a large aircraft on the same runway, stay at or above the large aircraft's final approach flight path, and land beyond its touchdown point.
    Answer (A) is incorrect. You must land beyond, not prior to, the touchdown point. **Answer (B) is incorrect.** There is no minimum distance (i.e., 1,000 ft.) that you should land beyond the jet's touchdown point.

45. (Refer to Figure 158 on page 169.) With winds reported as from 330° at 4 knots, you are given instructions to taxi to runway 4 for departure and to expect takeoff after an airliner departs from runway 29. What effect would you expect from that airliner's vortices?

    A. The winds will push the vortices southeast of your takeoff path.

    B. The upwind vortex would tend to remain over the runway.

    C. The downwind vortex will rapidly dissipate.

Answer (B) is correct. (AIM Para 7-4-4)
    DISCUSSION: A crosswind will decrease the lateral movement of the upwind vortex and increase the movement of the downwind vortex. Thus, with a light crosswind of 4 kt., you can expect the airliner's upwind vortex to tend to remain over runway 29 and the downwind vortex to hasten in drift toward your runway of intended departure.
    Answer (A) is incorrect. A light crosswind between 1 to 5 kt. could result in the upwind vortex remaining over the runway and hasten the drift of the downwind vortex toward your runway of intended departure. **Answer (C) is incorrect.** A light crosswind of 4 kt. will hasten the drift of the downwind vortex toward your runway of intended departure.

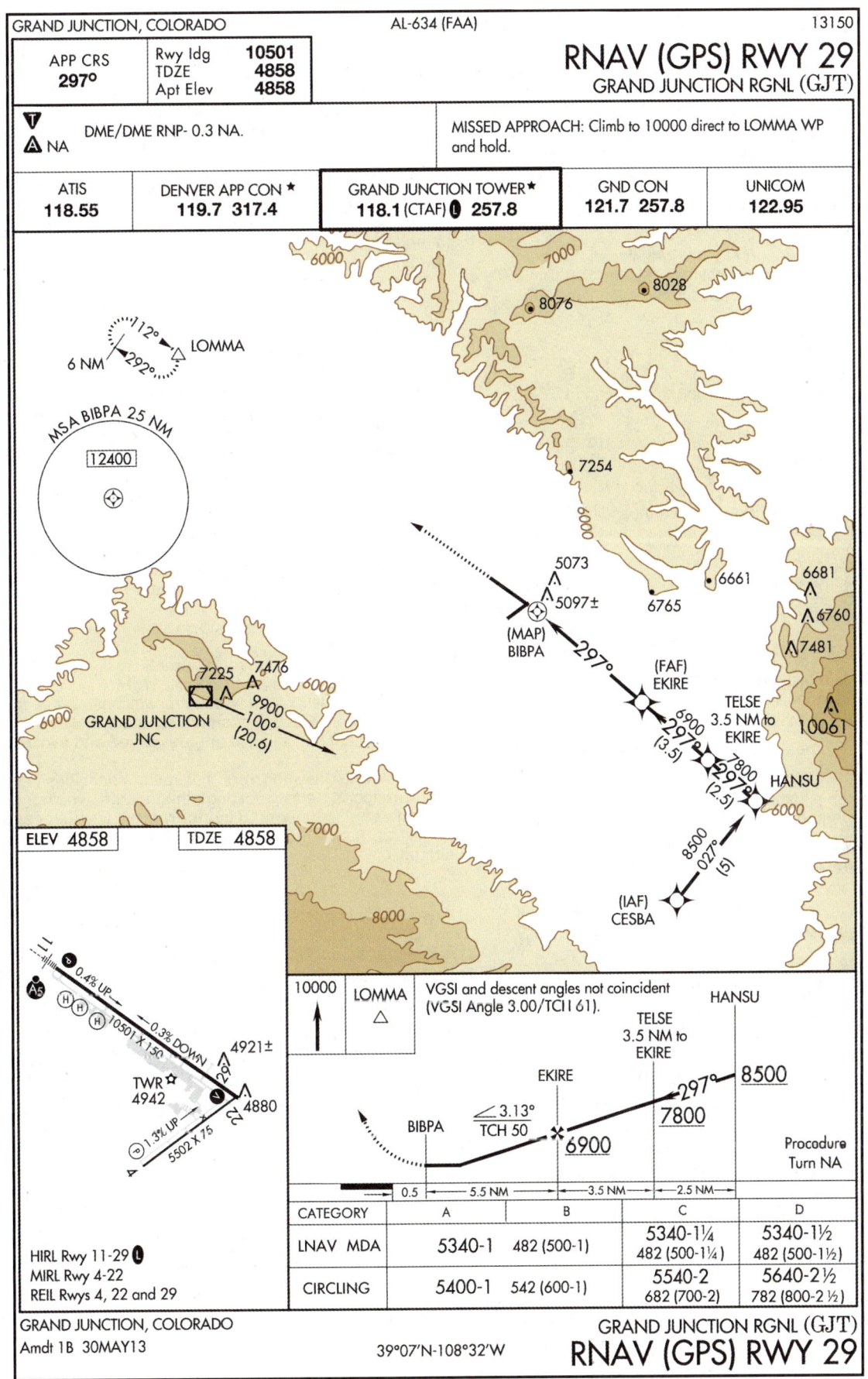

Figure 158. – ILS RWY 11 (GJT).

5.7 Collision Avoidance

46. Which procedure is recommended while climbing to an assigned altitude on the airway?

    A. Climb on the centerline of the airway except when maneuvering to avoid other air traffic in VFR conditions.

    B. Climb slightly on the right side of the airway when in VFR conditions.

    C. Climb far enough to the right side of the airway to avoid climbing or descending traffic coming from the opposite direction if in VFR conditions.

Answer (A) is correct. (14 CFR 91.181)
    DISCUSSION: When climbing to an assigned altitude on an airway, one should use the centerline except to avoid other aircraft when in VFR conditions. This procedure is specified in 14 CFR 91.181, which requires aircraft to operate along the centerline of federal airways.
    Answer (B) is incorrect. You are required to maintain the centerline, not remain on the right side, while operating on a federal airway. **Answer (C) is incorrect.** You are required to maintain the centerline, not remain on the right side, while operating on a federal airway.

47. What is expected of you as pilot on an IFR flight plan if you are descending or climbing in VFR conditions?

    A. If on an airway, climb or descend to the right of the centerline.

    B. Advise ATC you are in visual conditions and will remain a short distance to the right of the centerline while climbing.

    C. Execute gentle banks, left and right, at a frequency which permits continuous visual scanning of the airspace about you.

Answer (C) is correct. (AIM Para 4-4-15)
    DISCUSSION: During climbs and descents in VFR conditions, pilots should execute gentle banks left and right to permit continual scanning of surrounding airspace.
    Answer (A) is incorrect. You are required to maintain, not remain to the right of, the centerline while operating on a federal airway, except when maneuvering to avoid other traffic in VFR conditions. **Answer (B) is incorrect.** You are not required to advise ATC that you are in visual conditions, but you are required to maintain, not remain to the right of, the centerline while operating on a federal airway, except when maneuvering to avoid other traffic in VFR conditions.

48. When is a pilot on an IFR flight plan responsible for avoiding other aircraft?

    A. At all times when not in radar contact with ATC.

    B. When weather conditions permit, regardless of whether operating under IFR or VFR.

    C. Only when advised by ATC.

Answer (B) is correct. (14 CFR 91.113)
    DISCUSSION: When weather conditions permit, regardless of whether an operation is conducted under IFR or VFR, each pilot shall maintain vigilance in order to see and avoid other aircraft.
    Answer (A) is incorrect. If weather conditions permit, each pilot is responsible for avoiding other aircraft, whether in radar contact or not. **Answer (C) is incorrect.** If weather conditions permit, each pilot, not ATC, is responsible for avoiding other aircraft.

49. What responsibility does the pilot in command of an IFR flight assume upon entering VFR conditions?

    A. Reporting VFR conditions to ARTCC.

    B. Obtaining an amended clearance authorizing VFR flight.

    C. Seeing and avoiding other aircraft.

Answer (C) is correct. (14 CFR 91.113)
    DISCUSSION: When weather conditions permit, regardless of whether an operation is conducted under IFR or VFR, each pilot shall maintain vigilance in order to see and avoid other aircraft.
    Answer (A) is incorrect. VFR conditions are not reported unless so requested by ATC. **Answer (B) is incorrect.** IFR operating procedures are to be followed on an IFR flight, even when given a clearance for VFR flight, such as a "VFR-on-top" clearance.

5.8 IFR Flight Planning Information

50. The most current en route and destination flight information for planning an instrument flight should be obtained from

    A. the ATIS broadcast.

    B. the FSS.

    C. Notices to Air Missions.

Answer (B) is correct. (AIM Para 5-1-1)
    DISCUSSION: The FAA urges every pilot to receive a preflight briefing, which may be obtained online or from a Flight Service Station (FSS) by telephone, radio, or personal visit. The preflight briefing should cover weather, airport, and en route navigation data.
    Answer (A) is incorrect. The ATIS (Automatic Terminal Information Service) broadcasts only information pertaining to landing and departing operations at one airport. ATIS does not provide any en route information. **Answer (C) is incorrect.** Notices to Air Missions (NOTAMs) are not transmitted with weather information. They are only one aspect of a complete flight briefing.

51. What is the purpose of FDC NOTAMs?

    A. To provide the latest information on the status of navigation facilities to all FSS facilities for scheduled broadcasts.

    B. To issue notices for all airports and navigation facilities in the shortest possible time.

    C. To advise of changes in flight data which affect instrument approach procedures (IAP), aeronautical charts, and flight restrictions prior to normal publication.

Answer (C) is correct. (AIM Para 5-1-3)
    DISCUSSION: FDC (Flight Data Center) NOTAMs are regulatory in nature and issued to establish restrictions to flight or amend charts or published instrument approach procedures. FDC NOTAMs are published as needed.
    Answer (A) is incorrect. NOTAMs (D), not FDC NOTAMs, provide information for the status of navigational facilities. These NOTAMs are appended to the hourly weather reports. **Answer (B) is incorrect.** The purpose of NOTAMs (D) is to issue notices for all public-use airports and navigation facilities in the shortest possible time.

52. From what source can you obtain the latest FDC NOTAMs?

    A. *Aeronautical Information Manual.*

    B. FAA FSS.

    C. Chart Supplement.

Answer (B) is correct. (AIM Para 5-1-3)
    DISCUSSION: The National Flight Data Center occasionally publishes regulatory changes (either permanent or temporary) in FDC (Flight Data Center) NOTAMs. They are also used to advertise temporary flight restrictions caused by such things as natural disasters, large public events, and other events that may generate congested air traffic. FSSs are required to keep a file of current FDC NOTAMs.
    Answer (A) is incorrect. The *Aeronautical Information Manual (AIM)* is a source of basic flight information and ATC procedures. It is not issued to establish restrictions to flight or amend charts or published instrument approach procedures. **Answer (C) is incorrect.** The Chart Supplement is only published every 56 days. The Chart Supplement includes only permanent changes that were known at the time of publication.

53. Which sources of aeronautical information, when used collectively, provide the latest status of airport conditions (e.g., runway closures, runway lighting, snow conditions)?

    A. *Aeronautical Information Manual*, aeronautical charts, and NOTAMs (D).

    B. Chart Supplement and FDC NOTAMs.

    C. Chart Supplement and NOTAMs (D).

Answer (C) is correct. (AIM Para 5-1-3)
    DISCUSSION: The latest status of airport conditions can be determined by using the Chart Supplement for items that have been known for some time and NOTAMs (D), which contain the most up-to-date data.
    Answer (A) is incorrect. The *Aeronautical Information Manual (AIM)* is a source of basic flight information and ATC procedures, not specific airport information, and aeronautical charts do not indicate the latest status of runway conditions. **Answer (B) is incorrect.** FDC NOTAMs deal with regulatory changes or unusual air traffic congestion, not local airport conditions.

54. Absence of the sky condition and visibility on an ATIS broadcast specifically implies that

A. the ceiling is more than 5,000 feet and visibility is 5 miles or more.

B. the sky condition is clear and visibility is unrestricted.

C. the ceiling is at least 3,000 feet and visibility is 5 miles or more.

Answer (A) is correct. (AIM Para 4-1-13)
   DISCUSSION: The ATIS broadcast generally includes the latest weather sequence, sky conditions, temperature, dew point, wind direction and velocity, altimeter, runways in use, etc. Absence of the sky condition and visibility on an ATIS broadcast specifically implies that the ceiling is more than 5,000 ft. and visibility is more than 5 SM.
   Answer (B) is incorrect. The absence of the sky condition and visibility on an ATIS broadcast implies that ceilings are more than 5,000 ft., not clear, and visibility is 5 SM or more, not unrestricted. **Answer (C) is incorrect.** The absence of the sky condition on an ATIS broadcast implies a ceiling of more than 5,000 ft., not at least 3,000 ft.

55. The operation of an airport rotating beacon during daylight hours may indicate that

A. the in-flight visibility is less than 3 miles and the ceiling is less than 1,500 feet within Class E airspace.

B. the ground visibility is less than 3 miles and/or the ceiling is less than 1,000 feet in Class B, C, D, or E airspace.

C. an IFR clearance is required to operate within the airport traffic area.

Answer (B) is correct. (AIM Para 2-1-9)
   DISCUSSION: In Class B, C, D, and E surface areas, operation of an airport beacon during daylight hours often indicates that the ground visibility is less than 3 SM and/or the ceiling is less than 1,000 ft. Pilots should not rely solely on the beacon to indicate weather conditions because there is no regulatory requirement for daylight operation of the airport's rotating beacon.
   Answer (A) is incorrect. The operation of an airport rotating beacon during daylight hours at an airport located in Class E airspace may indicate that in-flight visibility (if ground is not reported) is less than 3 SM, and/or the ceiling is less than 1,000 ft., not 1,500 ft. **Answer (C) is incorrect.** An IFR clearance is required only in controlled airspace when IMC exists, not at an airport that is operating a rotating beacon during the day.

56. When are ATIS broadcasts updated?

A. Every 30 minutes if weather conditions are below basic VFR; otherwise, hourly.

B. Upon receipt of any official weather, regardless of content change or reported values.

C. Only when the ceiling and/or visibility changes by a reportable value.

Answer (B) is correct. (AIM Para 4-1-13)
   DISCUSSION: ATIS broadcasts are updated upon the receipt of any official weather regardless of content change or reported values. A new recording will also be made when there is a change in other pertinent data such as runway change, instrument approach in use, etc.
   Answer (A) is incorrect. The frequency of ATIS updates does not differ under VFR or IFR conditions. **Answer (C) is incorrect.** The recording will be updated whenever official weather is received, even if there is no change.

5.9 IFR Flight Plan

57. What point at the destination should be used to compute estimated time en route on an IFR flight plan?

    A. The final approach fix on the expected instrument approach.

    B. The initial approach fix on the expected instrument approach.

    C. The point of first intended landing.

Answer (C) is correct. (14 CFR 91.169)
    DISCUSSION: Estimated time en route on an IFR flight plan should be the time from takeoff at the departure airport to touchdown at the point of first intended landing.
    Answer (A) is incorrect. Due to varying weather conditions, runways in use, traffic, etc., there is no way of accurately telling which approach will be used. **Answer (B) is incorrect.** Due to varying weather conditions, runways in use, traffic, etc., there is no way of accurately telling which approach will be used.

58. What is a waypoint when used for an IFR flight?

    A. A predetermined geographical position used for an RNAV route or an RNAV instrument approach.

    B. A reporting point defined by the intersection of two VOR radials.

    C. A location on a victor airway which can only be identified by VOR and DME signals.

Answer (A) is correct. (FAA-H-8083-15B Chap 9)
    DISCUSSION: A waypoint on an IFR flight is a predetermined geographical position used for an RNAV route or an RNAV instrument approach definition or progress-reporting purposes. It is defined relative to a VORTAC position or in terms of latitude/longitude coordinates.
    Answer (B) is incorrect. A point defined by the intersection of two VOR radials is called an intersection, not a waypoint. **Answer (C) is incorrect.** A location on a victor airway that can be identified only by VOR and DME signals is called a DME fix, not a way point.

59. You may cancel an IFR flight plan

    A. at any time as long as you advise ATC.

    B. only in an emergency.

    C. if in VMC outside Class A airspace.

Answer (C) is correct. (AIM Para 5-1-15)
    DISCUSSION: An IFR flight plan may be canceled at any time you are operating in VFR conditions when not in Class A airspace by stating, "Cancel my IFR flight plan," to ATC. Once accepted by ATC, you should change to the appropriate communications frequency, transponder code, and altitude.
    Answer (A) is incorrect. You cannot proceed under VFR when IFR conditions exist or when you are flying above FL 180 (i.e., in Class A airspace). **Answer (B) is incorrect.** ATC will provide needed assistance in emergencies while you are operating under an IFR flight plan.

60. How is your flight plan closed when your destination airport has IFR conditions and there is no control tower?

    A. The ARTCC controller will close your flight plan when you report the runway in sight.

    B. You may close your flight plan any time after starting the approach by contacting any FSS or ATC facility.

    C. Upon landing, you must close your flight plan by radio or by telephone to any FSS or ATC facility.

Answer (C) is correct. (AIM Para 5-1-15)
    DISCUSSION: IFR flight plans are automatically closed by ATC if you land at an airport with an operating control tower. However, if operating under an IFR flight plan to an airport with no functioning control tower, you must cancel the IFR flight plan. You may cancel your IFR flight plan while airborne only if weather permits. If your destination airport has IFR conditions and there is no tower, you should close your IFR flight plan upon landing by radio or telephone to any FSS or ATC facility.
    Answer (A) is incorrect. You, not ATC, must close your IFR flight plan at airports without an operating control tower. **Answer (B) is incorrect.** When an airport has IFR conditions, you must have IFR clearances until you have safely landed.

61. How should an IFR flight plan be closed at the completion of the flight at a controlled airport?

    A. The tower will automatically close the flight plan when the aircraft lands.

    B. The pilot must close the flight plan with the nearest FSS or other FAA facility upon landing.

    C. The pilot must request the tower to relay the instructions to the nearest FSS after landing.

Answer (A) is correct. (AIM Para 5-1-15)
    DISCUSSION: The tower will automatically close an IFR flight plan after landing, and no action is required from the pilot.
    Answer (B) is incorrect. A pilot is responsible for ensuring that the IFR flight plan is canceled only when landing at a non-towered airport. **Answer (C) is incorrect.** There is no need to ask the tower to relay instructions to the nearest FSS. The flight plan will be canceled automatically.

62. (Refer to Figure 1A on page 175.) If more than one cruising altitude is intended, what information should be entered in item 15, "Level," of the flight plan?

    A. Initial cruising altitude.

    B. Highest cruising altitude.

    C. Lowest cruising altitude.

Answer (A) is correct. (AIM Para 5-1-6)
    DISCUSSION: If more than one cruising altitude is intended, enter the planned cruising level for the first (initial) portion of the route to be flown.
    Answer (B) is incorrect. The initial, not highest, altitude should be filed on your IFR flight plan. **Answer (C) is incorrect.** The initial, not lowest, altitude should be filed on your IFR flight plan.

63. (Refer to Figure 1A on page 175.) What information should be entered in item 15, "Level," for an IFR flight?

    A. Initial cruising altitude.

    B. Highest cruising altitude.

    C. Lowest cruising altitude.

Answer (A) is correct. (AIM Para 5-1-6)
    DISCUSSION: Enter the planned cruising level for the first (initial) portion of the route to be flown if more than one cruising altitude is intended for an IFR flight.
    Answer (B) is incorrect. The initial, not highest, altitude should be filed on your IFR flight plan. **Answer (C) is incorrect.** The initial, not lowest, altitude should be filed on your IFR flight plan.

64. (Refer to Figure 1A on page 175.) What information should be entered into item 16, "Destination Aerodrome," for an IFR flight?

    A. The destination airport identifier code and name of the FBO where the airplane will be parked.

    B. The destination airport identifier code.

    C. The destination city and state.

Answer (B) is correct. (AIM Para 5-1-6)
    DISCUSSION: In item 16, "Destination Aerodrome," of the flight plan form (Fig. 1A), enter the ICAO four-letter location identifier.
    Answer (A) is incorrect. The name of the FBO is not required. **Answer (C) is incorrect.** The ICAO four-letter indicator should be entered, not the city and state.

65. (Refer to Figure 1A on page 175.) What information should be entered in item 19, "Endurance," for an IFR flight?

    A. The estimated time en route plus 30 minutes.

    B. The estimated time en route plus 45 minutes.

    C. The amount of usable fuel on board expressed in time.

Answer (C) is correct. (AIM Para 5-1-6)
    DISCUSSION: Item 19, "Endurance," of the flight plan requires the amount of usable fuel in the airplane at the time of departure. It should be expressed in hours and minutes of flying time.
    Answer (A) is incorrect. The VFR fuel requirement for day flight is the estimated time en route plus 30 min. **Answer (B) is incorrect.** The IFR fuel requirement is the estimated time en route plus 45 min.

66. (Refer to Figure 1A on page 175.) What information should be entered in item 19, "Endurance," for an IFR flight?

    A. The actual time en route expressed in hours and minutes.

    B. The estimated time en route expressed in hours and minutes.

    C. The total amount of usable fuel onboard expressed in hours and minutes.

Answer (C) is correct. (AIM Para 5-1-6)
    DISCUSSION: Item 19, "Endurance," of the flight plan requires the amount of usable fuel in the airplane at the time of departure. It should be expressed in hours and minutes of flying time.
    Answer (A) is incorrect. Item 19 requires the amount of fuel on board at the time of departure expressed in time. **Answer (B) is incorrect.** Item 19 requires the amount of fuel on board at the time of departure expressed in time.

67. (Refer to Figure 1A on page 175.) What information should be entered in item 16, "Destination Aerodrome," for an IFR flight with an intended stopover of 30 minutes?

    A. The ICAO four-letter indicator of the airport of first intended landing.

    B. The ICAO four-letter indicator of the destination airport.

    C. The ICAO four-letter indicator of the airport where the aircraft is based.

Answer (B) is correct. (AIM Para 5-1-6)
    DISCUSSION: Item 16 of the flight plan form (Fig. 1A) requires the ICAO four-letter indicator of the airport of last intended landing for that flight, as long as no stopover exceeds 1 hr.
    Answer (A) is incorrect. The first intended landing, i.e., the end of the first leg of the flight, is included in the route of flight (item 15). **Answer (C) is incorrect.** The ICAO four-letter indicator of the airport where the airplane is based is not entered on the ICAO flight plan form.

Approved OMB No. 2120-0026
Exp. 5/31/2017

U S Department of Transportation
Federal Aviation Administration

International Flight Plan

PRIORITY   ADDRESSEE(S)

<=FF

FILING TIME   ORIGINATOR   **<=**

SPECIFIC IDENTIFICATION OF ADDRESSEE(S) AND / OR ORIGINATOR

3 MESSAGE TYPE   7 AIRCRAFT IDENTIFICATION   8 FLIGHT RULES   TYPE OF FLIGHT

<=(FPL   **<=**

9 NUMBER   TYPE OF AIRCRAFT   WAKE TURBULENCE CAT.   10 EQUIPMENT   **<=**

13 DEPARTURE AERODROME   TIME   **<=**

15 CRUISING SPEED   LEVEL   ROUTE

<=

TOTAL EET

16 DESTINATION AERODROME   HR   MIN   ALTN AERODROME   2ND ALTN AERODROME   **<=**

18 OTHER INFORMATION

<=

SUPPLEMENTARY INFORMATION (NOT TO BE TRANSMITTED IN FPL MESSAGES)

19   ENDURANCE   EMERGENCY RADIO
       HR   MIN   PERSONS ON BOARD   UHF   VHF   ELT
E/   **P/**   **R/** U   V   E

       SURVIVAL EQUIPMENT   JACKETS
       POLAR DESERT MARITIME JUNGLE   LIGHT FLUORES UHF   VHF
       / P   D   M   J   / L   F   U   V

DINGHIES
NUMBER CAPACITY COVER   COLOR
D /   C   **<=**

AIRCRAFT COLOR AND MARKINGS
A/

REMARKS
N /   **<=**

PILOT-IN-COMMAND
C/   **)<=**

FILED BY   ACCEPTED BY   ADDITIONAL INFORMATION

FAA Form 7233-4 (7/15)

Figure 1A. – Flight Plan Form (not in supplement).

5.10 ATC Clearances

68. What response is expected when ATC issues an IFR clearance to pilots of airborne aircraft?

A. Read back the entire clearance as required by regulation.

B. Read back those parts containing altitude assignments or vectors and any part requiring verification.

C. Read-back should be unsolicited and spontaneous to confirm that the pilot understands all instructions.

Answer (B) is correct. (AIM Para 4-4-7)
DISCUSSION: Pilots of airborne aircraft should read back those parts of ATC clearances and instructions containing altitude assignments or vectors and any part requiring verification. The read-back serves as a double-check between pilots and ATC and reduces the kinds of communications errors that occur when a number is either misheard or incorrect.
Answer (A) is incorrect. The read-back is an expected procedure, but there is no regulatory requirement to read back an ATC clearance. Only those parts containing altitude assignments or vectors and any part requiring verification, not the entire clearance, should be read back. **Answer (C) is incorrect.** Only those parts containing altitude assignments or vectors and any part requiring verification, not all instructions, should be read back.

69. Which clearance items are always given in an abbreviated IFR departure clearance? (Assume radar environment.)

A. Altitude, destination airport, and one or more fixes which identify the initial route of flight.

B. Destination airport, altitude, DP Name, Number, and/or Transition, if appropriate.

C. Clearance limit, DP Name, Number, and/or Transition, if appropriate.

Answer (B) is correct. (AIM Para 5-2-6)
DISCUSSION: An abbreviated IFR departure clearance will include the destination airport. En route altitude will be stated in the clearance, and the pilot will be advised to expect an assigned or filed altitude within a given time or at a certain point after departure. Any DP (instrument departure procedure) will also be specified by ATC stating the DP name, the current number, and the DP transition name.
Answer (A) is incorrect. The fixes are already included in the flight plan and do not need to be repeated in an abbreviated IFR departure clearance. **Answer (C) is incorrect.** An en route altitude is always given in an abbreviated IFR departure clearance.

70. Which information is always given in an abbreviated departure clearance?

A. DP or transition name and altitude to maintain.

B. Name of destination airport or specific fix and altitude.

C. Altitude to maintain and code to squawk.

Answer (B) is correct. (AIM Para 5-2-6)
DISCUSSION: An abbreviated IFR departure clearance always contains the name of your destination airport or clearance limit; altitude; and, if a DP is to be flown, the DP name, the current number, and the DP transition name.
Answer (A) is incorrect. The destination airport or clearance limit is always given in an abbreviated clearance. **Answer (C) is incorrect.** The destination airport or clearance limit is always given in an abbreviated clearance.

71. An abbreviated departure clearance "...CLEARED AS FILED..." will always contain the name

A. and number of the STAR to be flown when filed in the flight plan.

B. of the destination airport filed in the flight plan.

C. of the first compulsory reporting point if not in a radar environment.

Answer (B) is correct. (AIM Para 5-2-6)
DISCUSSION: An abbreviated IFR departure clearance will include the destination airport. En route altitude will be stated, and the pilot will be advised to expect an assigned or filed altitude by a certain time or at a certain point after departure either separately or as part of a DP. The abbreviated clearance also includes the DP name-number-transition, if appropriate.
Answer (A) is incorrect. A STAR, when filed in a flight plan, is considered a part of the filed route of flight and will not normally be stated in an initial departure clearance. **Answer (C) is incorrect.** Compulsory reporting points are not given in an abbreviated clearance.

72. When departing from an airport not served by a control tower, the issuance of a clearance containing a void time indicates that

A. ATC will assume the pilot has not departed if no transmission is received before the void time.

B. The pilot must advise ATC as soon as possible, but no later than 30 minutes, of their intentions if not off by the void time.

C. ATC will protect the airspace only to the void time.

Answer (B) is correct. (AIM Para 5-2-7)
DISCUSSION: If operating from an airport not served by a control tower, the pilot may receive a clearance containing a provision that, if the flight has not departed by a specific time (void time), the clearance is void. In this situation, the pilot who does not depart prior to the void time must advise ATC of his or her intentions as soon as possible, but no later than 30 min. after the void time.
Answer (A) is incorrect. ATC will assume a departure unless it hears from the pilot. **Answer (C) is incorrect.** The airspace is protected until ATC hears from the pilot.

73. On the runup pad, you receive the following clearance from ground control:

CLEARED TO THE DALLAS-LOVE AIRPORT AS FILED – MAINTAIN SIX THOUSAND – SQUAWK ZERO SEVEN ZERO FOUR JUST BEFORE DEPARTURE – DEPARTURE CONTROL WILL BE ONE TWO FOUR POINT NINER.

An abbreviated clearance, such as this, will always contain the

A. departure control frequency.

B. transponder code.

C. destination airport and route.

Answer (C) is correct. (AIM Para 5-2-6)
DISCUSSION: An IFR departure clearance will always contain the destination airport and the route of flight. The route of flight will either be given fix-by-fix by the controller or "as filed," in which case the route on the IFR flight plan is the assigned route. The statement, "Cleared to the Dallas-Love airport as filed," contains the destination airport and the specific route to be taken (the filed route).
Answer (A) is incorrect. If the abbreviated clearance contains a DP, the departure control frequency may not be given if the frequency is published in the DP. **Answer (B) is incorrect.** An abbreviated IFR departure clearance will always contain the destination airport and the route of flight, but not the transponder code.

74. What is the significance of an ATC clearance which reads "...CRUISE SIX THOUSAND..."?

A. The pilot must maintain 6,000 until reaching the IAF serving the destination airport, then execute the published approach procedure.

B. It authorizes a pilot to conduct flight at any altitude from minimum IFR altitude up to and including 6,000.

C. The pilot is authorized to conduct flight at any altitude from minimum IFR altitude up to and including 6,000, but each change in altitude must be reported to ATC.

Answer (B) is correct. (AIM Para 4-4-3)
DISCUSSION: The term "cruise" in a clearance assigns a pilot a block of airspace from the minimum IFR altitude up to and including the specified altitude (e.g., 6,000 ft. MSL). The pilot may level off at any intermediate altitude within this block of airspace. Climb and descent within the block are to be made at the discretion of the pilot. However, once the pilot starts descent and verbally reports leaving an altitude in the block, (s)he may not return to that altitude without additional ATC clearance.
Answer (A) is incorrect. The pilot need not maintain 6,000 ft. **Answer (C) is incorrect.** The pilot may change altitude without reporting to ATC.

75. What is the significance of an ATC clearance which reads "...CRUISE SIX THOUSAND..."?

A. The pilot must maintain 6,000 feet until reaching the IAF serving the destination airport, then execute the published approach procedure.

B. Climbs may be made to, or descents made from, 6,000 feet at the pilot's discretion.

C. The pilot may utilize any altitude from the MEA/MOCA to 6,000 feet, but each change in altitude must be reported to ATC.

Answer (B) is correct. (AIM Para 4-4-3)
DISCUSSION: The term "cruise" in a clearance assigns a pilot a block of airspace from the minimum IFR altitude up to and including the specified altitude (e.g., 6,000 ft. MSL). The pilot may climb to, level off at, or descend from any intermediate altitude within this block of airspace. Once the pilot starts descent and verbally reports leaving an altitude in the block, however, (s)he may not return to that altitude without additional ATC clearance.
Answer (A) is incorrect. The pilot need not maintain 6,000 ft. **Answer (C) is incorrect.** The pilot is assigned all the airspace from the minimum IFR altitude to 6,000 ft. MSL and may change altitudes without reporting to ATC.

76. What is the rule for a pilot receiving a "Land and Hold Short Operation (LAHSO) clearance?"

A. The pilot is required to accept the controller's clearance in visual meteorological conditions.

B. The pilot must accept the clearance if the pavement is dry and the stopping distance is adequate.

C. The pilot has the option to accept or reject all LAHSO clearances regardless of the meteorological conditions.

Answer (C) is correct. (FAA-H-8083-16B Chap 1)
   DISCUSSION: It is always the pilot's option to accept or reject all LAHSO clearances regardless of the meteorological conditions. Pilots have the option to decline any LAHSO clearance. The pilot should only accept a LAHSO clearance provided the pilot feels (s)he can land the plane within the available distance without compromising safety.
   Answer (A) is incorrect. Pilots never have to accept a controller's clearance, regardless of the meteorological conditions. Pilots have the option to decline any LAHSO clearance. A pilot should only accept a LAHSO clearance provided the pilot feels (s)he can land the plan within the available distance, without compromising safety. **Answer (B) is incorrect.** Pilots never have to accept a controller's clearance, regardless of the runway conditions or stopping distance. Pilots have the option to decline any LAHSO clearance. A pilot should only accept a LAHSO clearance provided the pilot feels (s)he can land the plane within the available distance, without compromising safety.

77. A "CRUISE FOUR THOUSAND FEET" clearance would mean that the pilot is authorized to

A. vacate 4,000 feet without notifying ATC.

B. climb to, but not descend from 4,000 feet, without further ATC clearance.

C. use any altitude from minimum IFR to 4,000 feet, but must report leaving each altitude.

Answer (A) is correct. (AIM Para 4-4-3)
   DISCUSSION: The term "cruise" in a clearance assigns a pilot a block of airspace from the minimum IFR altitude up to and including the specified altitude (e.g., 4,000 ft. MSL). The pilot may level off at any intermediate altitude within this block of airspace. Climb and descent within the block are to be made at the discretion of the pilot. However, once the pilot starts descent and verbally reports leaving an altitude in the block, (s)he may not return to that altitude without additional ATC clearance.
   Answer (B) is incorrect. Any airspace between the minimum IFR altitude and 4,000 ft. MSL may be used without further ATC clearance. **Answer (C) is incorrect.** Cruise clearances do not require reporting a change in altitude to ATC.

5.11 ATC Communication Procedures

78. When should pilots state their position on the airport when calling the tower for takeoff?

A. When visibility is less than 1 mile.

B. When parallel runways are in use.

C. When departing from a runway intersection.

Answer (C) is correct. (AIM Para 4-3-10)
   DISCUSSION: You should state your position on the airport when calling the tower for takeoff from a runway intersection. Additionally, you are expected to request from ground control approval for the intersection departure (i.e., a departure from any runway intersection except the end of the runway) prior to taxi.
   Answer (A) is incorrect. A pilot is not expected to state his or her position on the airport when calling the tower for takeoff when visibility is less than 1 mile. **Answer (B) is incorrect.** A pilot is not expected to state his or her position on the airport when calling the tower for takeoff when parallel runways are in use.

79. During a takeoff into IMC at a controlled field with low ceilings, you should contact departure

A. before entering the clouds.

B. when the tower instructs the change.

C. upon reaching the traffic pattern altitude.

Answer (B) is correct. (AIM Para 5-2-7)
   DISCUSSION: A pilot should not change to the departure control frequency until advised by ATC. Because the pilot maintains continuous contact with assigned ATC frequencies, all frequency changes are at the direction of ATC.
   Answer (A) is incorrect. The tower will advise the pilot when to contact departure control, and such contact is not based on whether the aircraft has penetrated the clouds. **Answer (C) is incorrect.** The tower will advise the pilot when to contact departure control, which may or may not be upon reaching the traffic pattern altitude.

80. When should your transponder be on Mode C while on an IFR flight?

A. Only when ATC requests Mode C.

B. At all times if the equipment has been calibrated, unless requested otherwise by ATC.

C. When passing 12,500 feet MSL.

Answer (B) is correct. (AIM Para 4-1-19)
DISCUSSION: If your airplane's transponder is equipped to reply on Mode C, it should be on at all times unless deactivation is directed by ATC.
Answer (A) is incorrect. Mode C should be turned off, not on, only when directed by ATC. **Answer (C) is incorrect.** Mode C is a requirement any time you are flying above 10,000 ft. MSL, not 12,500 ft. MSL.

81. What is the recommended climb procedure when a nonradar departure control instructs a pilot to climb to the assigned altitude?

A. Maintain a continuous optimum climb until reaching assigned altitude and report passing each 1,000 foot level.

B. Climb at a maximum angle of climb to within 1,000 feet of the assigned altitude, then 500 feet per minute the last 1,000 feet.

C. Maintain an optimum climb on the centerline of the airway without intermediate level-offs until 1,000 feet below assigned altitude, then 500 to 1,500 feet per minute.

Answer (C) is correct. (AIM Para 4-4-10)
DISCUSSION: When ATC clearances are given to descend or climb to a certain altitude, the pilot should use the optimum rate consistent with the operating characteristics of the aircraft to 1,000 ft. above or below the assigned altitude and then attempt to descend or climb at a rate of between 500 and 1,500 fpm until reaching the assigned altitude. Also, on airways, you should climb and descend on the centerline of the airway with no intermediate level-offs.
Answer (A) is incorrect. The pilot is not required to report passing each 1,000 ft. of altitude. **Answer (B) is incorrect.** You should normally use a cruise climb rather than a maximum angle of climb.

82. To comply with ATC instructions for altitude changes of more than 1,000 feet, what rate of climb or descent should be used?

A. As rapidly as practicable to 500 feet above/below the assigned altitude, and then at 500 feet per minute until the assigned altitude is reached.

B. 1,000 feet per minute during climb and 500 feet per minute during descents until reaching the assigned altitude.

C. As rapidly as practicable to 1,000 feet above/below the assigned altitude, and then between 500 and 1,500 feet per minute until reaching the assigned altitude.

Answer (C) is correct. (AIM Para 4-4-10)
DISCUSSION: When ATC clearances are given to descend or climb to a certain altitude, the pilot should use the optimum rate consistent with the operating characteristics of the aircraft to 1,000 ft. above or below the assigned altitude and then attempt to descend or climb at a rate of between 500 and 1,500 fpm until reaching the assigned altitude. Also, one should climb and descend on the centerline of the airway with no intermediate level-offs.
Answer (A) is incorrect. The rate should be between 500 and 1,500 fpm after you are within 1,000 ft., not 500 ft., of the target altitude. **Answer (B) is incorrect.** The rate of climb and descent should be based upon aircraft capability. Also, when 1,000 ft. above or below the assigned altitude, the pilot should attempt to descend or climb at a rate of between 500 and 1,500 fpm until the assigned altitude is reached.

83. Which report should be made to ATC without a specific request when not in radar contact?

A. Entering instrument meteorological conditions.

B. When leaving final approach fix in bound on final approach.

C. Correcting an ETA any time a previous ETA is in error in excess of 4 minutes.

Answer (B) is correct. (AIM Para 5-3-3)
DISCUSSION: The following reports (in addition to those that are made at all times) should be made to ATC without a specific request when not in radar contact:

1. A report when leaving final approach fix in bound on final approach (nonprecision approach) or when leaving the outer marker or fix used in lieu of the outer marker in bound on final approach (precision approach)
2. Position reports over compulsory reporting points
3. A corrected ETA to a reporting point at any time it becomes apparent that an estimate as previously submitted is in error in excess of 2 min.

Answer (A) is incorrect. A report should be made to ATC whether or not in radar contact any time you encounter any type of weather conditions that have not been forecast. If IMC were forecast, no report is necessary. **Answer (C) is incorrect.** A report should be made to ATC when correcting an ETA any time a previous ETA is in error in excess of 2 min., not 4 min.

84. When ATC has not imposed any climb or descent restrictions and aircraft are within 1,000 feet of assigned altitude, pilots should attempt to both climb and descend at a rate of between

    A.   500 feet per minute and 1,000 feet per minute.

    B.   500 feet per minute and 1,500 feet per minute.

    C.   1,000 feet per minute and 2,000 feet per minute.

Answer (B) is correct. (AIM Para 4-4-10)
    DISCUSSION: When ATC clearances are given to descend or climb to a certain altitude, the pilot should use the optimum rate consistent with the operating characteristics of the aircraft to 1,000 ft. above or below the assigned altitude and then attempt to descend or climb at a rate of between 500 and 1,500 fpm until reaching the assigned altitude. Also, on airways, one should climb and descend on the centerline of the airway with no intermediate level-offs.
    Answer (A) is incorrect. Within 1,000 ft. of the assigned altitude, pilots should attempt to climb/descend at a rate of between 500 and 1,500 fpm, not 1,000 fpm. **Answer (C) is incorrect.** Within 1,000 ft. of the assigned altitude, pilots should attempt to climb/descend at a rate of between 500 and 1,500 fpm, not 1,000 and 2,000 fpm.

85. What does the ATC term "Radar Contact" signify?

    A.   Your aircraft has been identified and you will receive separation from all aircraft while in contact with this radar facility.

    B.   Your aircraft has been identified on the radar display and radar flight-following will be provided until radar identification is terminated.

    C.   You will be given traffic advisories until advised the service has been terminated or that radar contact has been lost.

Answer (B) is correct. (P/C Glossary)
    DISCUSSION: The term "radar contact" is used by ATC to inform an aircraft that it is identified on the radar display and that radar flight following will be provided until radar service is terminated. Reporting over compulsory reporting points is not required when an aircraft is in radar contact.
    Answer (A) is incorrect. Separation from all aircraft occurs only in Class A, B, and C airspace. **Answer (C) is incorrect.** Traffic advisory service is provided only to the extent possible. Higher-priority duties take precedence, such as controlling or other limitations, volume of traffic, frequency congestion, or controller workload.

86. For IFR planning purposes, what are the compulsory reporting points when using VOR/DME or VORTAC fixes to define a direct route not on established airways?

    A.   Fixes selected to define the route.

    B.   There are no compulsory reporting points unless advised by ATC.

    C.   At the changeover points.

Answer (A) is correct. (AIM Para 5-3-2)
    DISCUSSION: When using VOR/DME or VORTAC fixes to define a direct route not on an established airway, those fixes selected to define the route automatically become compulsory reporting points (when not in radar contact) for the flight.
    Answer (B) is incorrect. On a direct flight, the compulsory reporting points are those fixes used to define the route. **Answer (C) is incorrect.** Some navigation systems used on direct flights do not require COPs to prevent the loss of navigation guidance, e.g., GPS.

87. While performing a VFR practice instrument approach, Radar Approach Control assigns an altitude or heading that will cause you to enter the clouds. What action should you take?

    A.   Continue as directed.

    B.   Advise "unable" and remain clear of clouds.

    C.   Deviate as needed; then rejoin the approach.

Answer (B) is correct. (AIM Para 4-3-21)
    DISCUSSION: During VFR practice instrument approaches, you are responsible to comply with basic VFR weather minimums. Therefore, if Radar Approach Control assigns an altitude or heading that will cause you to enter the clouds, you should advise "unable" and remain clear of clouds.
    Answer (A) is incorrect. While performing VFR practice instrument approaches, you are required to maintain basic VFR weather minimums; therefore, you should not continue as directed. **Answer (C) is incorrect.** You should advise Radar Approach Control "unable" and remain clear of clouds.

88. You have not yet been cleared for the approach, but you are being vectored to the ILS approach course. It is clear that you will pass through the localizer course unless you take action. You should

    A.   turn outbound and complete the procedure turn.

    B.   continue as assigned and query ATC.

    C.   turn inbound and join the final approach course.

Answer (B) is correct. (AIM Para 5-4-3)
    DISCUSSION: Normally, you will be informed by ATC when it is necessary to vector across the final approach course for spacing or other reasons. If you have not been cleared for the approach and it becomes evident that you will cross the approach course, you must continue on your assigned heading and question ATC.
    Answer (A) is incorrect. While you are being radar vectored, you are not authorized to make a procedure turn unless cleared by ATC. **Answer (C) is incorrect.** You must maintain your assigned heading, not turn inbound on the final approach course.

89. During a flight, the controller advises "traffic 2 o'clock 5 miles southbound." The pilot is holding 20° correction for a crosswind from the right. Where should the pilot look for the traffic?

   A. 40° to the right of the aircraft's nose.

   B. 20° to the right of the aircraft's nose.

   C. Straight ahead.

Answer (A) is correct. (AIM Para 4-1-14)
   DISCUSSION: ATC issues traffic advisories in terms of the aircraft's course (i.e., ground track), not its heading. Allowance must be made for drift correction or course change made simultaneously with the radar traffic information. Two o'clock is approximately 60° to the right of the aircraft's course. Since the pilot is already holding a 20° right-wind correction, (s)he should look only 40° to the right of the aircraft's nose for the traffic.
   Answer (B) is incorrect. This direction is 40° to the right of the aircraft's track, which is between 1 and 2 o'clock. **Answer (C) is incorrect.** Straight ahead is 20° (wind correction) to the right of the aircraft's track, which is between 12 and 1 o'clock.

90. What is the pilot in command's responsibility when flying a propeller aircraft within 20 miles of the airport of intended landing and ATC requests the pilot to reduce speed to 160? (Pilot complies with speed adjustment.)

   A. Reduce TAS to 160 knots and maintain until advised by ATC.

   B. Reduce IAS to 160 MPH and maintain until advised by ATC.

   C. Reduce IAS to 160 knots and maintain that speed within 10 knots.

Answer (C) is correct. (AIM Para 4-4-12)
   DISCUSSION: ATC will express all speed adjustments in terms of knots based on indicated airspeed (IAS) in 10-kt. increments below FL 240. When complying with an ATC speed adjustment to reduce to 160, you should reduce IAS to 160 kt. and maintain that speed within 10 kt.
   Answer (A) is incorrect. ATC speed restrictions are based on indicated airspeed (IAS), not true airspeed (TAS). **Answer (B) is incorrect.** Airspeeds are given in knots, not MPH.

91. Upon intercepting the assigned radial, the controller advises you that you are on the airway and to "RESUME OWN NAVIGATION." This phrase means that

   A. You are still in radar contact, but must make position reports.

   B. Radar services are terminated and you will be responsible for position reports.

   C. You are to assume responsibility for your own navigation.

Answer (C) is correct. (P/C Glossary)
   DISCUSSION: Assuming you have been vectored to an airway on your intended route of flight, you should maintain your course along the airway by use of your navigation equipment when ATC advises you to resume your own navigation.
   Answer (A) is incorrect. Position reporting is not required when in radar contact. **Answer (B) is incorrect.** "Resume navigation" means only that the radar controller is going to stop vectoring you, not stop observing you.

92. During the en route phase of an IFR flight, the pilot is advised "Radar service terminated." What action is appropriate?

   A. Set transponder to code 1200.

   B. Resume normal position reporting.

   C. Activate the IDENT feature of the transponder to re-establish radar contact.

Answer (B) is correct. (AIM Para 5-3-2)
   DISCUSSION: During the en route phase of an IFR flight, if you are advised of "radar service terminated" or "radar contact lost," you should resume normal position reporting as required when not in radar contact.
   Answer (A) is incorrect. You should set the transponder to code 1200 (VFR) only when you cancel your IFR flight plan with ATC and you are instructed to squawk VFR. **Answer (C) is incorrect.** You should activate the IDENT feature of the transponder only upon the request of ATC.

93. What is meant when departure control instructs you to "resume own navigation" after you have been vectored to a Victor airway?

   A. You should maintain the airway by use of your navigation equipment.

   B. Radar service is terminated.

   C. You are still in radar contact, but must make position reports.

Answer (A) is correct. (P/C Glossary)
   DISCUSSION: Assuming you have been vectored to an airway on your intended route of flight, you should maintain your course along the airway by use of your navigation equipment when ATC advises you to resume your own navigation.
   Answer (B) is incorrect. "Resume navigation" means that the radar controller will stop vectoring you, not stop observing you. **Answer (C) is incorrect.** Position reporting is not required when you are in radar contact with ATC.

94. What service is provided by departure control to an IFR flight when operating from an airport within the outer area of Class C airspace?

    A. Separation from all aircraft.

    B. Position and altitude of all traffic within 2 miles of the IFR pilot's line of flight and altitude.

    C. Separation from all IFR aircraft and participating VFR aircraft.

Answer (C) is correct. *(14 CFR 91.130)*
    DISCUSSION: In the outer area of Class C airspace, ATC provides an IFR flight with separation from all IFR aircraft and participating VFR aircraft. VFR aircraft participation in the outer area is voluntary.
    Answer (A) is incorrect. An IFR flight is provided traffic advisories and conflict resolution with other IFR aircraft and with only participating VFR aircraft within the outer area of Class C airspace. **Answer (B) is incorrect.** ATC provides position and altitude of aircraft that may conflict, not position and altitude of all traffic within 2 NM of your line of flight.

95. While on an IFR flight plan, you should notify ATC of a variation in speed when

    A. ground speed changes more than 5 knots.

    B. average TAS changes 10 knots or 5 percent.

    C. ground speed changes 10 MPH or more.

Answer (B) is correct. *(AIM Para 5-3-3)*
    DISCUSSION: There are a number of things a pilot needs to report to ATC without being requested. One is a change in the average TAS at cruising altitude when it varies by 10 kt. or 5% (whichever is greater) from that filed in the flight plan.
    Answer (A) is incorrect. ATC should be notified if TAS, not ground speed, varies more than 10 kt., not 5 kt., or 5%, whichever is greater. **Answer (C) is incorrect.** ATC should be notified if TAS, not ground speed, varies more than 10 kt., not 10 MPH, or 5%, whichever is greater.

96. When are you required to establish communications with the tower (Class D airspace), if you cancel your IFR flight plan 10 miles from the destination?

    A. Immediately after canceling the flight plan.

    B. When advised by ARTCC.

    C. Before entering Class D airspace.

Answer (C) is correct. *(14 CFR 91.129)*
    DISCUSSION: You must establish two-way radio communication with the tower before entering Class D airspace. Thus, if you cancel your IFR flight plan, you must notify the tower of your position and intentions prior to entering Class D airspace.
    Answer (A) is incorrect. While it is a good operating practice to make an initial call to the tower up to 15 mi. from a Class D airport, it is required only before entering Class D airspace. **Answer (B) is incorrect.** While ARTCC may advise you to contact the tower when the controller accepts your IFR flight plan cancellation, you are required to contact the tower only prior to entering Class D airspace.

97. What does declaring "minimum fuel" to ATC imply?

    A. Traffic priority is needed to the destination airport.

    B. Emergency handling is required to the nearest usable airport.

    C. Merely an advisory that indicates an emergency situation is possible should any undue delay occur.

Answer (C) is correct. *(AIM Para 5-5-15)*
    DISCUSSION: You should advise ATC of your minimum fuel status when your fuel supply has reached a state in which, upon reaching your destination, you cannot accept any undue delay. Be aware that this is not an emergency situation, but merely an advisory that indicates an emergency situation is possible should any undue delay occur.
    Answer (A) is incorrect. Priority may be issued when declaring an emergency, not when declaring minimum fuel. **Answer (B) is incorrect.** Minimum fuel advisory is not an emergency situation.

98. Which of the following reports should always be reported to ATC?

    A. Preferred runway choice to limit taxi time.

    B. When true airspeed (TAS) varies by 10 percent or 5 knots, whichever is less.

    C. When leaving an assigned holding fix.

Answer (C) is correct. *(AIM Para 5-3-3)*
    DISCUSSION: A report should be made to ATC without a specific request when leaving any assigned holding fix or point.
    Answer (A) is incorrect. Reporting your preferred takeoff runway is not required, but you can make a request for a runway other than the one in use. **Answer (B) is incorrect.** Reporting is required for variations in average true airspeed exceeding 5% or 10 kt., not 10% or 5 kt.

5.12 Radio Communication Failure

99. Which procedure should you follow if you experience two-way communications failure while holding at a holding fix with an EFC time? (The holding fix is not the same as the approach fix.)

A. Depart the holding fix to arrive at the approach fix as close as possible to the EFC time.

B. Depart the holding fix at the EFC time.

C. Proceed immediately to the approach fix and hold until EFC.

Answer (B) is correct. *(14 CFR 91.185)*
DISCUSSION: If you experience two-way radio communication failure at a holding fix that is not the same as the approach fix, leave the holding fix at the EFC time and complete the approach.
Answer (A) is incorrect. You would leave for, not arrive at, the approach fix at the EFC time. **Answer (C) is incorrect.** You should not leave the holding fix to go to the approach fix until the EFC time.

100. You are in IMC and have two-way radio communications failure. If you do not exercise emergency authority, what procedure are you expected to follow?

A. Set transponder to code 7600, continue flight on assigned route and fly at the last assigned altitude or the MEA, whichever is higher.

B. Set transponder to code 7700 for 1 minute, then to 7600, and fly to an area with VFR weather conditions.

C. Set transponder to 7700 and fly to an area where you can let down in VFR conditions.

Answer (A) is correct. *(14 CFR 91.185, AIM Para 6-4-2)*
DISCUSSION: When you lose two-way radio capability, you should alert ATC by changing your transponder to code 7600. If you experience two-way radio communication failure while in IMC, continue your flight on the assigned route and maintain the last assigned altitude or the MEA, whichever is higher.
Answer (B) is incorrect. The transponder should be set on 7600 at all times, not 7700 for 1 min., and you must maintain your assigned route and altitude (or MEA). If VMC are encountered, continue the flight under VFR and land as soon as practicable. **Answer (C) is incorrect.** You should set the transponder to 7600. While in IMC, you must maintain your assigned route and altitude (or MEA).

101. You enter a holding pattern (at a fix that is not the same as the approach fix) with an EFC time of 1530. At 1520 you experience complete two-way communications failure. Which procedure should you follow to execute the approach to a landing?

A. Depart the holding fix to arrive at the approach fix as close as possible to the EFC time and complete the approach.

B. Depart the holding fix at the EFC time, and complete the approach.

C. Depart the holding fix at the earliest of the flight planned ETA or the EFC time, and complete the approach.

Answer (B) is correct. *(14 CFR 91.185)*
DISCUSSION: If you experience two-way radio communication failure at a holding fix that is not the same as the approach fix, leave the holding fix at the EFC time and complete the approach.
Answer (A) is incorrect. You leave for, not arrive at, the approach fix at the EFC time. **Answer (C) is incorrect.** The EFC time takes precedence over the flight plan ETA.

102. What is the appropriate transponder code in response to lost communications?

A. 7400

B. 7500

C. 7600

Answer (C) is correct. *(14 CFR 91.185, AIM Para 6-4-2)*
DISCUSSION: Code 7600 is used in the event of a radio failure or lost communications. Other emergency codes are 7500 for hijacking and 7700 for a general emergency. Additionally, code 7777 is reserved for military interceptors.
Answer (A) is incorrect. Code 7400 is reserved for an unmanned aircraft experiencing a lost link **Answer (B) is incorrect.** Code 7500 is used in the event of unlawful interference or hijacking.

103. In the event of unlawful interference or hijacking, which transponder code should you input immediately?

A. 7500

B. 7600

C. 7777

Answer (A) is correct. *(14 CFR 91.185, AIM Para 6-4-2)*
DISCUSSION: The nondiscrete transponder code 7500 is used in the event of unlawful interference or hijacking. Once input, this code triggers a special emergency indicator in all radar ATC facilities.
Answer (B) is incorrect. Code 7600 is used in the event of a radio failure or lost communications. **Answer (C) is incorrect.** Code 7777 is the highest value code that may be entered on a 4096 transponder and a discrete code reserved for military interceptor operations.

104. What altitude and route should be used if you are flying in IMC and have two-way radio communications failure?

    A. Continue on the route specified in your clearance, fly at an altitude that is the highest of last assigned altitude, altitude ATC has informed you to expect, or the MEA.

    B. Fly direct to an area that has been forecast to have VFR conditions, fly at an altitude that is at least 1,000 feet above the highest obstacles along the route.

    C. Descend to MEA and, if clear of clouds, proceed to the nearest appropriate airport. If not clear of clouds, maintain the highest of the MEA's along the clearance route.

Answer (A) is correct. (14 CFR 91.185)
    DISCUSSION: When you lose two-way radio communication in IMC, continue the flight by the route assigned by the last ATC clearance, by the route that ATC has advised may be expected to be assigned, or by the flight plan. Use the highest of the altitude assigned in the last ATC clearance, the MEA, or the flight level ATC may be expected to assign.
    Answer (B) is incorrect. You should continue the assigned route. **Answer (C) is incorrect.** You should use the highest of the altitude assigned, the altitude expected to be assigned, or MEA.

105. Which procedure should you follow if, during an IFR flight in VFR conditions, you have two-way radio communications failure?

    A. Continue the flight under VFR and land as soon as practicable.

    B. Continue the flight at assigned altitude and route, start approach at your ETA, or, if late, start approach upon arrival.

    C. Land at the nearest airport that has VFR conditions.

Answer (A) is correct. (14 CFR 91.185)
    DISCUSSION: If a radio failure occurs during an IFR flight in VFR conditions or if VFR conditions are encountered after the failure, the pilot should continue the flight under VFR and land as soon as practicable.
    Answer (B) is incorrect. This procedure applies only if you are in instrument meteorological conditions, not VFR. **Answer (C) is incorrect.** The pilot retains the prerogative of exercising good judgment and is not required to land at an unauthorized airport or an airport unsuitable for the type of aircraft flown, nor is the pilot required to land only minutes short of the destination.

106. While flying on an IFR flight plan, you experience two-way communications radio failure while in VFR conditions. In this situation, you should continue your flight under

    A. VFR and land as soon as practicable.

    B. IFR and maintain the last assigned route and altitude to your flight plan destination.

    C. VFR and proceed to your flight plan destination.

Answer (A) is correct. (14 CFR 91.185)
    DISCUSSION: If a radio failure occurs during an IFR flight in VFR conditions or if VFR conditions are encountered after the failure, the pilot should continue the flight under VFR and land as soon as practicable.
    Answer (B) is incorrect. This procedure applies only if you are in instrument meteorological conditions, not VFR. **Answer (C) is incorrect.** You should land as soon as practicable rather than proceeding to your flight plan destination.

107. The transponder should be cycled to 7700 in the event of

    A. a hijacking.

    B. an emergency.

    C. lost communications.

Answer (B) is correct. (AIM Para 6-4-2)
    DISCUSSION: The nondiscrete transponder code 7700 is used in the event of an emergency to "squawk MAYDAY." Although a special indicator will alarm all control positions, pilots should understand that they may not be within a radar coverage area and should therefore continue to squawk and establish radio contact as soon as possible.
    Answer (A) is incorrect. Code 7700 is reserved for an emergency, whereas a hijacking or unlawful interference is coded under 7500. **Answer (C) is incorrect.** Code 7700 is reserved for an emergency, whereas a radio failure or loss of two-way communications is coded under 7600.

108. What is the hijack code?

    A. 7200

    B. 7500

    C. 7777

Answer (B) is correct. (14 CFR 91.185, AIM Para 6-4-2)
    DISCUSSION: Transponder code 7500 means: "I am being hijacked/forced to a new destination." Code 7500 will never be assigned by ATC without prior notification from the pilot that his or her airplane is being subjected to unlawful interference. Code 7500 will trigger special emergency indicators in all radar ATC facilities.
    Answer (A) is incorrect. Code 7200 is used for normal operating procedures. **Answer (C) is incorrect.** Under no circumstances should a pilot of a civil airplane operate the transponder on Code 7777. This code is reserved for military interceptor operations.

5.13 Navigation Radio Failure

109. What action should you take if your DME fails at FL 240?

A. Advise ATC of the failure and land at the nearest available airport where repairs can be made.

B. Notify ATC that it will be necessary for you to go to a lower altitude, since your DME has failed.

C. Notify ATC of the failure and continue to the next airport of intended landing where repairs can be made.

Answer (C) is correct. (14 CFR 91.205)
   DISCUSSION: When required DME fails at or above FL 240, the pilot should notify ATC immediately and may continue operations at and above FL 240 to the next airport of intended landing at which repairs or replacement of the equipment can be made.
   Answer (A) is incorrect. You can continue to your destination, not the nearest airport, and have repairs made there. **Answer (B) is incorrect.** You need not descend to a lower altitude after you notify ATC. You may continue to operate at or above FL 240.

110. What action should you take if your No. 1 VOR receiver malfunctions while operating in controlled airspace under IFR? Your aircraft is equipped with two VOR receivers. The No. 1 receiver has Omni/Localizer/Glide Slope capability, and the No. 2 receiver has only VOR/Localizer capability.

A. Report the malfunction immediately to ATC.

B. Continue the flight as cleared; no report is required.

C. Continue the approach and request a VOR approach.

Answer (A) is correct. (14 CFR 91.187)
   DISCUSSION: When operating under IFR in controlled airspace, you must immediately report to ATC as soon as practical any malfunctions of navigational, approach, or communication equipment occurring in flight. Each report should include the following:

1. Aircraft identification,
2. Equipment affected,
3. Degree to which the capability of the pilot to operate under IFR in the ATC system is impaired, and
4. Nature and extent of assistance desired from ATC.

   Answer (B) is incorrect. A report to ATC is required. **Answer (C) is incorrect.** ATC will know that you need a VOR approach if you report the ILS receiver inoperative.

111. What is the procedure when the DME malfunctions at or above 24,000 feet MSL?

A. Notify ATC immediately and request an altitude below 24,000 feet.

B. Continue to your destination in VFR conditions and report the malfunction.

C. After immediately notifying ATC, you may continue to the next airport of intended landing where repairs can be made.

Answer (C) is correct. (14 CFR 91.205)
   DISCUSSION: When required DME fails at or above FL 240, the pilot should notify ATC immediately and may continue operations at and above FL 240 to the next airport of intended landing at which repairs or replacement of the equipment can be made.
   Answer (A) is incorrect. There is no need to descend to a lower altitude. You may continue to your destination and have repairs made there. **Answer (B) is incorrect.** You may continue your flight as normal, even under IFR, and make repairs at your destination.

5.14 Airspace

112. Which types of airspace are depicted on the En Route Low Altitude Chart?

A. Limits of controlled airspace, military training routes, and special use airspace.

B. Class A, special use airspace, Class D, and Class E.

C. Special use airspace, Class E, Class D, Class A, Class B, and Class C.

Answer (A) is correct. (ACUG)
   DISCUSSION: En Route Low-Altitude Charts limits of controlled airspace, military training routes, and special use airspace.
   Answer (B) is incorrect. Class A airspace is airspace above FL 180. It is not depicted on En Route Low-Altitude Charts. **Answer (C) is incorrect.** Class A airspace is not depicted on En Route Low-Altitude Charts.

113. The vertical extent of the Class A airspace extends from

A. 18,000 feet to and including FL 450.

B. 18,000 feet to and including FL 600.

C. 12,500 feet to and including FL 600.

Answer (B) is correct. (AIM Para 3-2-2)
   DISCUSSION: Class A airspace extends from 18,000 ft. MSL to and including FL 600.
   Answer (A) is incorrect. FL 450 is the top of the jet routes. **Answer (C) is incorrect.** The base of Class A airspace is 18,000 ft. MSL, not 12,500 ft. MSL.

114. Which airspace is defined as a transition area when designated in conjunction with an airport which has a prescribed IAP?

A. The Class E airspace extending upward from 700 feet or more above the surface and terminating at the base of the overlying controlled airspace.

B. That Class D airspace extending from the surface and terminating at the base of the continental control area.

C. The Class C airspace extending from the surface to 700 or 1,200 feet AGL, where designated.

Answer (A) is correct. (AIM Para 3-2-6)
   DISCUSSION: Transition areas are Class E airspace that extends upward from 700 ft. or more above the surface when designated in conjunction with an airport for which an instrument approach procedure (IAP) has been prescribed. Class E airspace extends up to but does not include 18,000 ft. MSL, i.e., the base of Class A airspace.
   Answer (B) is incorrect. A transition area is classified as Class E, not Class D, airspace. **Answer (C) is incorrect.** Transition areas are Class E, not Class C, airspace and extend upward from, not to, 700 ft.

115. Class G airspace is that airspace where

A. ATC does not control air traffic.

B. ATC controls only IFR flights.

C. the minimum visibility for VFR flight is 3 miles.

Answer (A) is correct. (AIM Para 3-3-1)
   DISCUSSION: Class G airspace is that portion of the airspace that has not been designated as Class A, B, C, D, or E. In Class G airspace, ATC has neither the authority nor the responsibility for exercising control over air traffic in any weather condition.
   Answer (B) is incorrect. ATC does not control IFR flight in Class G airspace. **Answer (C) is incorrect.** The minimum visibility for VFR flight is 1 SM, not 3 SM, in Class G airspace during the day when below 10,000 ft. MSL.

116. What are the vertical limits of a transition area that is designated in conjunction with an airport having a prescribed IAP?

A. Surface to 700 feet AGL.

B. 1,200 feet AGL to the base of the overlying controlled airspace.

C. 700 feet AGL or more to the base of the overlying controlled airspace.

Answer (C) is correct. (AIM Para 3-2-6)
   DISCUSSION: Transition areas are controlled airspace extending upward from 700 ft. or more above the surface when designated in conjunction with an airport for which an instrument approach procedure has been prescribed. Transition areas terminate at the base of overlying controlled airspace (i.e., Class A airspace).
   Answer (A) is incorrect. A transition area begins at 700 ft. AGL, not the surface, when it is designated in conjunction with an IAP. **Answer (B) is incorrect.** Transition areas begin at 1,200 ft. AGL when designated in conjunction with an airway route structure or segment, not with an airport with an instrument approach.

117. In addition to a VOR receiver and two-way communications capability, which additional equipment is required for IFR operation in Class B airspace?

A. DME, an operable coded transponder having Mode C capability, and ADS-B Out equipment.

B. Standby communications receiver, DME, and coded transponder.

C. An operable coded transponder having Mode C capability and ADS-B Out equipment.

Answer (C) is correct. (14 CFR 91.131)
DISCUSSION: Unless otherwise authorized by ATC, no person may operate an aircraft within Class B airspace unless that aircraft is equipped with

1. An operable two-way radio,
2. An operable 4096-code transponder having Mode C capability,
3. ADS-B Out equipment that either operates on the frequency of 1090 MHz or operates using a UAT on the frequency of 978 MHz,
4. For IFR operations, an operable VOR or TACAN receiver.

Answer (A) is incorrect. DME is not required. **Answer (B) is incorrect.** A standby radio receiver and DME are not required, and the transponder must have Mode C capability.

118. Which of the following is required equipment for operating an aircraft within Class B airspace?

A. A 4096 code transponder with automatic pressure altitude reporting equipment.

B. A VOR receiver with DME.

C. A 4096 code transponder.

Answer (A) is correct. (14 CFR 91.131)
DISCUSSION: Unless otherwise authorized by ATC, no person may operate an aircraft within Class B airspace unless that aircraft is equipped with

1. An operable two-way radio,
2. An operable 4096-code transponder having Mode C capability,
3. ADS-B Out equipment that either operates on the frequency of 1090 MHz or operates using a UAT on the frequency of 978 MHz, and
4. For IFR operations, an operable VOR or TACAN receiver.

Answer (B) is incorrect. DME is not required, and a VOR receiver is only required when operating IFR. **Answer (C) is incorrect.** The 4096-code transponder must also have Mode C capability.

119. MOAs are established to

A. prohibit all civil aircraft because of hazardous or secret activities.

B. separate certain military activities from IFR traffic.

C. restrict civil aircraft during periods of high-density training activities.

Answer (B) is correct. (AIM Para 3-4-5)
DISCUSSION: MOAs consist of airspace of defined vertical and lateral limits established for the purpose of separating certain military training activities from IFR traffic. When an MOA is in use, nonparticipating IFR traffic may be cleared to fly through if ATC can provide IFR separation. Otherwise, ATC will reroute or restrict nonparticipating IFR traffic.

Answer (A) is incorrect. A prohibited area, not an MOA, prohibits all aircraft for reasons of national security. **Answer (C) is incorrect.** A restricted area, not an MOA, is used to restrict aircraft during certain periods.

120. What minimum aircraft equipment is required for operation within Class C airspace?

A. Two-way communications, a Mode C transponder, and ADS B Out equipment.

B. Two-way communications.

C. Transponder, ADS-B Out equipment, and DME.

Answer (A) is correct. (AIM Para 3-2-4)
DISCUSSION: In Class C airspace, the equipment requirement is an operating two-way communications radio, a Mode C transponder, and ADS-B Out equipment that either operates on the frequency of 1090 MHz or operates using a UAT on the frequency of 978 MHz.

Answer (B) is incorrect. A Mode C transponder and ADS-B Out equipment are also required. **Answer (C) is incorrect.** Two-way communications and Mode C capability are also required, and DME is not required.

121. Your transponder is inoperative. What are the requirements for flying in Class D airspace?

A. The entry into Class D is prohibited.

B. Continue the flight as planned.

C. Pilot must immediately request priority handling to proceed to destination.

Answer (B) is correct. (14 CFR 91.129)
DISCUSSION: If an aircraft's transponder fails during flight within Class D airspace, no deviation is required because a transponder is not required in Class D airspace.

Answer (A) is incorrect. Since a transponder is not required in Class D airspace, the pilot does not need to depart the Class D airspace. **Answer (C) is incorrect.** Since a transponder is not required in Class D airspace, a pilot does not need priority handling to proceed to his or her destination.

122. When is an IFR clearance required during VFR weather conditions?

A. When operating in the Class E airspace.

B. When operating in a Class A airspace.

C. When operating in airspace above 14,500 feet.

Answer (B) is correct. (14 CFR 91.135, 91.173)
DISCUSSION: No person may operate an aircraft within Class A airspace unless the aircraft is operated under an IFR clearance, regardless of the weather conditions. Class A airspace includes the airspace from 18,000 feet MSL up to and including FL 600.
Answer (A) is incorrect. An IFR clearance is not required in VMC in Class E airspace. Answer (C) is incorrect. An IFR clearance is not required in VMC in Class E airspace from 14,500 feet MSL up to but not including 18,000 feet MSL.

123. When is an IFR flight plan required?

A. When less than VFR conditions exist in either Class E or Class G airspace and in Class A airspace.

B. In all Class E airspace when conditions are below VFR, in Class A airspace, and in defense zone airspace.

C. In Class E airspace when IMC exists or in Class A airspace.

Answer (C) is correct. (14 CFR 91.135, 91.173)
DISCUSSION: No person may operate an aircraft in Class E airspace in IMC unless (s)he has filed an IFR flight plan and received an appropriate ATC clearance. Furthermore, under 14 CFR 91.135, no one may operate in Class A airspace unless the aircraft is operated under IFR at a specific flight level assigned by ATC. This implies having filed an IFR flight plan for Class A airspace also.
Answer (A) is incorrect. While an instrument rating is required, an IFR flight plan is not required in Class G airspace. Answer (B) is incorrect. VFR flights are permitted when VFR weather conditions exist in air defense identification zones (ADIZ).

124. Operation in which airspace requires filing an IFR flight plan?

A. Any airspace when the visibility is less than 1 mile.

B. Class E airspace with IMC and Class A airspace.

C. Positive control area, Continental Control Area, and all other airspace, if the visibility is less than 1 mile.

Answer (B) is correct. (14 CFR 91.135, 91.173)
DISCUSSION: No person may operate an aircraft in Class E airspace in IMC unless (s)he has filed an IFR flight plan and received an appropriate ATC clearance. Furthermore, under 14 CFR 91.135, no one may operate in Class A airspace unless the aircraft is operated under IFR at a specific flight level assigned by ATC. This implies having filed an IFR flight plan for Class A airspace also.
Answer (A) is incorrect. An IFR flight plan is not required in Class G airspace. Answer (C) is incorrect. An IFR flight plan is not required in uncontrolled Class G airspace.

125. What is the required flight visibility and distance from clouds if you are operating in Class E airspace at 9,500 feet MSL with a VFR-on-Top clearance during daylight hours?

A. 3 SM, 1,000 feet above, 500 feet below, and 2,000 feet horizontal.

B. 5 SM, 500 feet above, 1,000 feet below, and 2,000 feet horizontal.

C. 3 SM, 500 feet above, 1,000 feet below, and 2,000 feet horizontal.

Answer (A) is correct. (14 CFR 91.155)
DISCUSSION: In Class E airspace below 10,000 feet MSL, the basic VFR weather minimums are flight visibility of 3 SM and a distance from clouds of 500 feet below, 1,000 feet above, and 2,000 feet horizontal.
Answer (B) is incorrect. The visibility requirement is 3, not 5, SM, and the distances from clouds above and below are reversed. It should be 1,000 feet above and 500 feet below. Answer (C) is incorrect. The distances from clouds above and below are reversed. It should be 1,000 feet above and 500 feet below.

126. What is the minimum flight visibility and distance from clouds for flight at 10,500 feet with a VFR-on-Top clearance during daylight hours? (Class E airspace.)

A. 3 SM, 1,000 feet above, 500 feet below, and 2,000 feet horizontal.

B. 5 SM, 1,000 feet above, 1,000 feet below, and 1 mile horizontal.

C. 5 SM, 1,000 feet above, 500 feet below, and 1 mile horizontal.

Answer (B) is correct. (14 CFR 91.155)
DISCUSSION: In Class E airspace at or above 10,000 feet MSL, the basic VFR weather minimums are flight visibility of 5 SM and a distance from clouds of 1,000 feet above or below and 1 SM horizontal.
Answer (A) is incorrect. The minimum flight visibility and distance from clouds in Class E airspace below, not at or above, 10,000 feet MSL are 3 SM, 1,000 feet above, 500 feet below, and 2,000 feet horizontal. Answer (C) is incorrect. The vertical separation from clouds is 1,000 feet both above and below.

127. A flight is to be conducted in VFR-on-Top conditions at 12,500 feet MSL (above 1,200 feet AGL). What is the in-flight visibility and distance from clouds required for operation in Class E airspace during daylight hours?

A. 5 miles; above 1,000 feet; horizontal 2,000 feet; below 500 feet.

B. 5 miles; above 1,000 feet; horizontal 1 mile; below 1,000 feet.

C. 3 miles; above 1,000 feet; horizontal 2,000 feet; below 1,000 feet.

Answer (B) is correct. (14 CFR 91.155)
   DISCUSSION: In Class E airspace at or above 10,000 feet MSL, the basic VFR weather minimums are in-flight visibility of 5 statute miles and a distance from clouds of 1,000 feet above or below and 1 statute mile horizontal.
   Answer (A) is incorrect. The distance-from-clouds requirements listed are for below, not at or above, 10,000 feet MSL. **Answer (C) is incorrect.** The visibility requirement is 5 statute miles, not 3 statute miles, and the horizontal separation requirement from clouds is 1 statute mile, not 2,000 feet.

128. What is the minimum in-flight visibility and distance from clouds required for an airplane operating less than 1,200 feet AGL during daylight hours in Class G airspace?

A. 3 miles; above 1,000 feet; horizontally 2,000 feet; below 500 feet.

B. 1 mile; above clear of clouds; horizontally clear of clouds; below clear of clouds.

C. 1 mile; above 500 feet; horizontally 1,000 feet; below 500 feet.

Answer (B) is correct. (14 CFR 91.155)
   DISCUSSION: In Class G airspace at or below 1,200 feet AGL, the basic VFR weather minimums during daylight hours are in-flight visibility of 1 statute mile and clear of clouds.
   Answer (A) is incorrect. The minimum visibility and distance from clouds in VFR flight at night, not in daylight, are 3 statute miles visibility, 1,000 feet above, 500 feet below, and 2,000 feet horizontal. **Answer (C) is incorrect.** No such combination of requirements exists in any airspace.

129. What is the minimum in-flight visibility and distance from clouds required in VFR conditions above clouds at 13,500 feet MSL (above 1,200 feet AGL) in Class G airspace during daylight hours?

A. 5 miles; above 1,000 feet; horizontal 2,000 feet; below 500 feet.

B. 3 miles; above 1,000 feet; horizontal 1 mile; below 1,000 feet.

C. 5 miles; above 1,000 feet; horizontal 1 mile; below 1,000 feet.

Answer (C) is correct. (14 CFR 91.155)
   DISCUSSION: In Class G airspace at more than 1,200 feet AGL and at or above 10,000 feet MSL, the basic VFR weather minimums are in-flight visibility of 5 statute miles and a distance from clouds of 1,000 feet above or below and 1 statute mile horizontal.
   Answer (A) is incorrect. Distances of 1,000 feet above, 2,000 feet horizontal, and 500 feet below are the minimum cloud distances for VFR in Class G airspace above 1,200 feet AGL and below, not at or above, 10,000 feet MSL. **Answer (B) is incorrect.** The visibility minimum is 5 statute miles, not 3 statute miles.

130. What is the minimum in-flight visibility and distance from clouds required for a VFR-on-Top flight at 9,500 feet MSL (above 1,200 feet AGL) during daylight hours?

A. 2,000 feet; above 1,000 feet; horizontal 2,000 feet; below 500 feet.

B. 5 miles; above 1,000 feet; horizontal 2,000 feet; below 500 feet.

C. 3 miles; above 1,000 feet; horizontal 2,000 feet; below 500 feet.

Answer (C) is correct. (14 CFR 91.155)
   DISCUSSION: In Class E airspace at less than 10,000 feet MSL, the basic VFR weather minimums are in-flight visibility of 3 statute miles and a distance from clouds of 500 feet below, 1,000 feet above, and 2,000 feet horizontal.
   Answer (A) is incorrect. The visibility required is 3 statute miles, not 2,000 feet. **Answer (B) is incorrect.** The visibility required is 3 statute miles, not 5 statute miles.

131. What in-flight visibility and distance from clouds is required for a flight at 8,500 feet MSL (above 1,200 feet AGL) in Class G airspace in VFR conditions during daylight hours?

A. 1 mile; above 1,000 feet; horizontal 2,000 feet; below 500 feet.

B. 3 miles; above 1,000 feet; horizontal 2,000 feet; below 500 feet.

C. 5 miles; above 1,000 feet; horizontal 1 mile; below 1,000 feet.

Answer (A) is correct. (14 CFR 91.155)
  DISCUSSION: In Class G airspace at more than 1,200 feet AGL but less than 10,000 feet MSL, the basic VFR weather minimums during daylight hours are in-flight visibility of 1 statute mile and a distance from clouds of 500 feet below, 1,000 feet above, and 2,000 feet horizontal.
  Answer (B) is incorrect. The in-flight visibility of 3 statute miles is required for a night, not day, flight. **Answer (C) is incorrect.** In-flight visibility of 5 statute miles and a distance from clouds of 1,000 feet above or below and 1 statute mile horizontal are the VFR weather minimums in Class G airspace above 1,200 feet AGL and at or above, not below, 10,000 feet MSL.

132. What is the minimum in-flight visibility and distance from clouds required for an airplane operating less than 1,200 feet AGL under special VFR during daylight hours?

A. 1 mile; above 2,000 feet; horizontal 2,000 feet; below 500 feet.

B. 3 miles; above clear of clouds; horizontal clear of clouds; below 500 feet.

C. 1 mile; above clear of clouds; horizontal clear of clouds; below clear of clouds.

Answer (C) is correct. (14 CFR 91.157)
  DISCUSSION: In Class E airspace when an airplane is operating under special VFR, the distance-from-clouds requirement is clear of clouds. No one may take off or land an airplane under special VFR unless ground visibility is at least 1 statute mile. If ground visibility is not reported, the in-flight visibility during takeoff or landing must be at least 1 statute mile.
  Answer (A) is incorrect. Special VFR permits operation just clear of clouds. **Answer (B) is incorrect.** Special VFR permits operation just clear of clouds and with a minimum visibility of 1 statute mile, not 3 statute miles.

133. When are you required to have an instrument rating for flight in VMC?

A. Flight through an MOA.

B. Flight into an ADIZ.

C. Flight into Class A airspace.

Answer (C) is correct. (14 CFR 91.135)
  DISCUSSION: No person may operate an aircraft within Class A airspace at any time unless (s)he is rated for instrument flight and is on an instrument flight plan.
  Answer (A) is incorrect. An instrument rating is not required for flight through an MOA in VMC. **Answer (B) is incorrect.** An instrument rating is not required for flight into an ADIZ (air defense identification zone) in VMC.

5.15 Airport Diagram – Chart Supplement

134. (Refer to Figure 162 on page 191.) You are cleared to land on RWY 16L at Eugene Mahlon Sweet Field. As you break out of the clouds, you are lined up with the white lights down the center of the runway, which lets you know that you

A. are on course and lined up correctly.

B. are off course.

C. should recheck the winds prior to landing.

Answer (B) is correct. (Airport Diagram Legend)
  DISCUSSION: The description of RWY 16R – 34L in the Chart Supplement shows an entry for "CL," which indicates centerline lighting. The description for RWY 16L – 34R has no such entry. Because you are cleared for RWY 16L, you can deduce that the lights you see are centerline lights for RWY 16R, which indicates that you are off course.
  Answer (A) is incorrect. RWY 16L does not have centerline lighting. However, RWY 16R does have centerline lighting. See the note labeled "CL" in the Chart Supplement page for Eugene Mahlon, which indicates centerline lighting for only RWY 16R. **Answer (C) is incorrect.** You are off course. RWY 16L does not have centerline lighting, and there is insufficient information to suggest you are off course due to winds and should recheck the winds prior to landing. It is more important at this point that you recognize that you are off course and correct accordingly.

OREGON 119

EUGENE

MAHLON SWEET FLD (EUG)   7 NW   UTC–8(–7DT)   N44°07.48′ W123°12.72′

KLAMATH FALLS
H–1B, L–1B
IAP, AD

374   B   S4   **FUEL** 100LL, JET A   OX 1, 2, 3, 4   TPA—1174(800)   Class I, ARFF Index B
NOTAM FILE EUG
RWY 16R–34L: H8009X150 (ASPH–GRVD)   S–75, D–200, 2D–400
   HIRL   CL
   RWY 16R: ALSF2. TDZL. PAPI(P4L)—GA 3.0° TCH 50′.
   RWY 34L: ODALS. VASI(V4L)—GA 3.0° TCH 53′.
RWY 16L–34R: H6000X150 (ASPH–GRVD)   S–105, D–175, 2D–240
   HIRL
   RWY 16L: MALSR. PAPI(P4L)—GA 3.0° TCH 52′.
   RWY 34R: REIL. PAPI(P4L)—GA 3.0° TCH 50′.
RUNWAY DECLARED DISTANCE INFORMATION
   RWY 16L: TORA–6000   TODA–6000   ASDA–6000   LDA–6000
   RWY 16R: TORA–8009   TODA–8009   ASDA–8009   LDA–8009
   RWY 34L: TORA–8009   TODA–8009   ASDA–8009   LDA–8009
   RWY 34R: TORA–6000   TODA–6000   ASDA–6000   LDA–6000

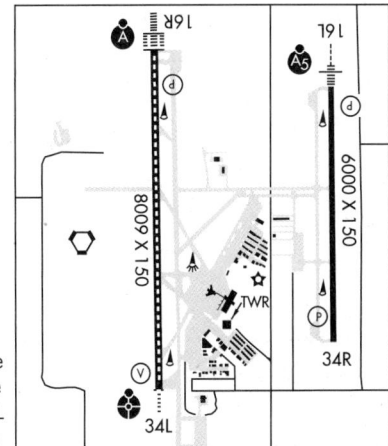

AIRPORT REMARKS: Attended continuously. Migratory waterfowl and other
   birds on and invof arpt. PPR for unscheduled air carrier ops with more
   than 30 passenger seats call 541–682–5430. ARFF svcs unavailable
   0000–0500 local except PPR 541–682–5430. No access to Rwy 34L
   byd Twy A9. Helicopters ldg and departing avoid overflying the airline
   passenger terminal and ramp located E of Rwy 16R–34L. Helipad west
of Rwy 16R restricted, PPR phone 541–682–5430. Twys H and K unavailable to acft 21,000 pounds single weight and
40,000 pounds dual gross weight. Terminal apron closed to acft except scheduled air carriers and flights with prior
permission. PAPI Rwy 16R and Rwy 16L and 34R and VASI Rwy 34L opr 24 hrs. When twr clsd HIRL Rwy 16L–34R
and Rwy 16R–34L preset medium ints. When twr clsd ACTIVATE ALSF2 Rwy 16R, ODALS Rwy 34L MALSR Rwy 16L
and REIL Rwy 34R—CTAF.
WEATHER DATA SOURCES: ASOS (541) 461–3114 **HIWAS** 112.9 EUG.
COMMUNICATIONS: CTAF 118.9 **ATIS** 125.225 541–607–4699 **UNICOM** 122.95
   EUGENE RCO 122.3 (MC MINNVILLE RADIO)
Ⓡ **CASCADE APP/DEP CON** 119.6 (340°–159°) 120.25 (160°–339°) (1400–0730Z‡)
Ⓡ **SEATTLE CENTER APP/DEP CON** 125.8 (0730–1400Z‡)
   EUGENE TOWER 118.9 (Rwy 16R– 34L) 124.15 (Rwy 16L– 34R) (1400–0730Z‡) **GND CON** 121.7 **CLNC DEL** 121.7
AIRSPACE: CLASS D svc 1400–0730Z‡ other times CLASS E.
RADIO AIDS TO NAVIGATION: NOTAM FILE EUG.
   EUGENE (H) VORTACW 112.9   EUG   Chan 76   N44°07.25′ W123°13.37′   at fld. 364/20E.   **HIWAS.**
   ILS/DME 111.75   I–ADE   Chan 54(Y)   Rwy 16L.   Class IE.
   ILS/DME 110.1   I–EUG   Chan 38   Rwy 16R.   Class IIIE.   Unmonitored when ATCT clsd.

FLORENCE

FLORENCE MUNI (6S2)   1 N   UTC–8(–7DT)   N43°58.97′ W124°06.68′

KLAMATH FALLS
L–1A

51   B   **FUEL** 100LL, JET A   TPA—1051(1000)   NOTAM FILE MMV
RWY 15–33: H3000X60 (ASPH)   S–12.5   MIRL   0.4% up NW
   RWY 15: Hill. Rgt tfc.
   RWY 33: PAPI(P2L)—GA 3.0° TCH 40′. Trees.
AIRPORT REMARKS: Attended 1630–0030Z‡. Birds, deer and wildlife on and
   invof arpt. ACTIVATE MIRL Rwy 15–33—CTAF. PAPI Rwy 33 opr 24
   hrs.
WEATHER DATA SOURCES: AWOS–3 118.225 (541) 997–8664.
COMMUNICATIONS: CTAF/UNICOM 122.8
RADIO AIDS TO NAVIGATION: NOTAM FILE OTH.
   NORTH BEND (L) VORTACW 112.1   OTH   Chan 58   N43°24.93′
      W124°10.11′   346° 34.1 NM to fld. 707/18E.   **HIWAS.**
   VORTAC unusable:
      012°–087° byd 30 NM blo 5,000′

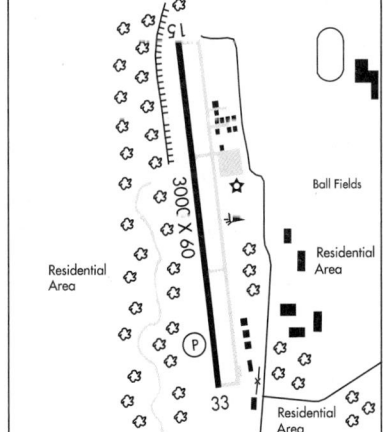

Figure 162. – Excerpt from Chart Supplement.

135. (Refer to Figure 251 on page 193.) What is the slope of RWY 9?

A. 0.4% up.

B. 0.4% down.

C. 0.3% down.

Answer (B) is correct. *(FAA-H-8083-16B Chap 1)*
   DISCUSSION: Fig. 251 shows an arrow pointing in the direction of RWY 27 labeled "0.4% UP." That indicates RWY 9, which is the reciprocal of RWY 27, is sloped 0.4% down.
   Answer (A) is incorrect. Fig. 251 shows an arrow pointing in the direction of RWY 27 labeled "0.4% UP." Therefore, RWY 27 has an upslope grade of 0.4%. **Answer (C) is incorrect.** Fig. 251 shows an arrow pointing in the direction of RWY 36 labeled "0.3% DOWN."

136. (Refer to Figure 251 on page 193.) When lined up for takeoff on runway 4, the compass and heading indicator should read a heading of about

A. 040°

B. 050°

C. 055°

Answer (B) is correct. *(Airport Diagram Legend)*
   DISCUSSION: Runway 4 includes a notation that reads "048.0°" with an arrow pointing in the direction of the runway alignment. This indicates that the actual alignment of runway 4 is 48°. Of the options offered, 050° is the closest to the correct heading.
   Answer (A) is incorrect. Although runway naming convention would suggest runway 4 is aligned with 040°, there is in fact a considerable amount of leeway in the actual heading. In this case, runway 4 includes a notation that reads "048.0°" with an arrow pointing in the direction of the runway alignment. This indicates that the actual alignment of runway 4 is 48°. **Answer (C) is incorrect.** Runway 4 includes a notation that reads "048.0°" with an arrow pointing in the direction of the runway alignment. This indicates that the actual alignment of runway 4 is 48°, not 55°.

137. (Refer to Figure 251 on page 193.) When lined up for takeoff on runway 18, the compass and heading indicator should display a heading of about

A. 180°

B. 185°

C. 175°

Answer (B) is correct. *(Airport Diagram Legend)*
   DISCUSSION: Runway 18 includes a notation that reads "183.6°" in conjunction with an arrow pointing in the direction of the runway alignment. This indicates that the actual heading can be rounded to 184° and could easily display on the compass and heading indicator as about 185°.
   Answer (A) is incorrect. Although runway naming convention would suggest runway 18 is aligned with 180°, there is in fact a considerable amount of leeway in the actual heading. Runway 18 includes a notation that reads "183.6°" in conjunction with an arrow pointing in the direction of the runway alignment. This indicates the actual heading can be rounded to 184° and could easily display on the compass and heading indicator as about 185°. **Answer (C) is incorrect.** This answer option would be more for a runway 17 with a notation such as "173.6°" with an arrow pointing in the direction of a runway 17.

138. (Refer to Figure 251 on page 193.) What is the actual heading of runway 36 at Oshkosh/Wittman Regional (OSH) airport?

A. 0.3%

B. 003.6°

C. 360°

Answer (B) is correct. *(AIM and Chart Supplement)*
   DISCUSSION: The actual heading of runway 36 is 003.6°, as shown on the right side of RWY 36 in the diagram.
   Answer (A) is incorrect. The indication of a DOWN slope on runway 36 is 0.3%. **Answer (C) is incorrect.** The runway number is the whole number nearest one-tenth the magnetic azimuth of the centerline of the runway, measured clockwise from the magnetic north. The runway number is 36, or 360, but the actual heading for this runway is 003.6°, not 360°.

139. (Refer to Figure 251 on page 193.) When lined up for takeoff on RWY 27, the compass and heading indicator should display a heading of about

A. 270°

B. 275°

C. 265°

Answer (B) is correct. *(Airport Diagram Legend)*
   DISCUSSION: Runway 27 includes a notation that reads "273.7°" in conjunction with an arrow pointing in the direction of the runway alignment. This indicates that the actual heading can be rounded to 274° and could easily display on the compass and heading indicator as about 275°.
   Answer (A) is incorrect. This would be correct if there was not an indication of "273.7°" with an arrow pointing in the direction of the runway. **Answer (C) is incorrect.** This answer would be more for a RWY 26 with a heading notation of about "263.7°" and an arrow pointing in the direction of the runway.

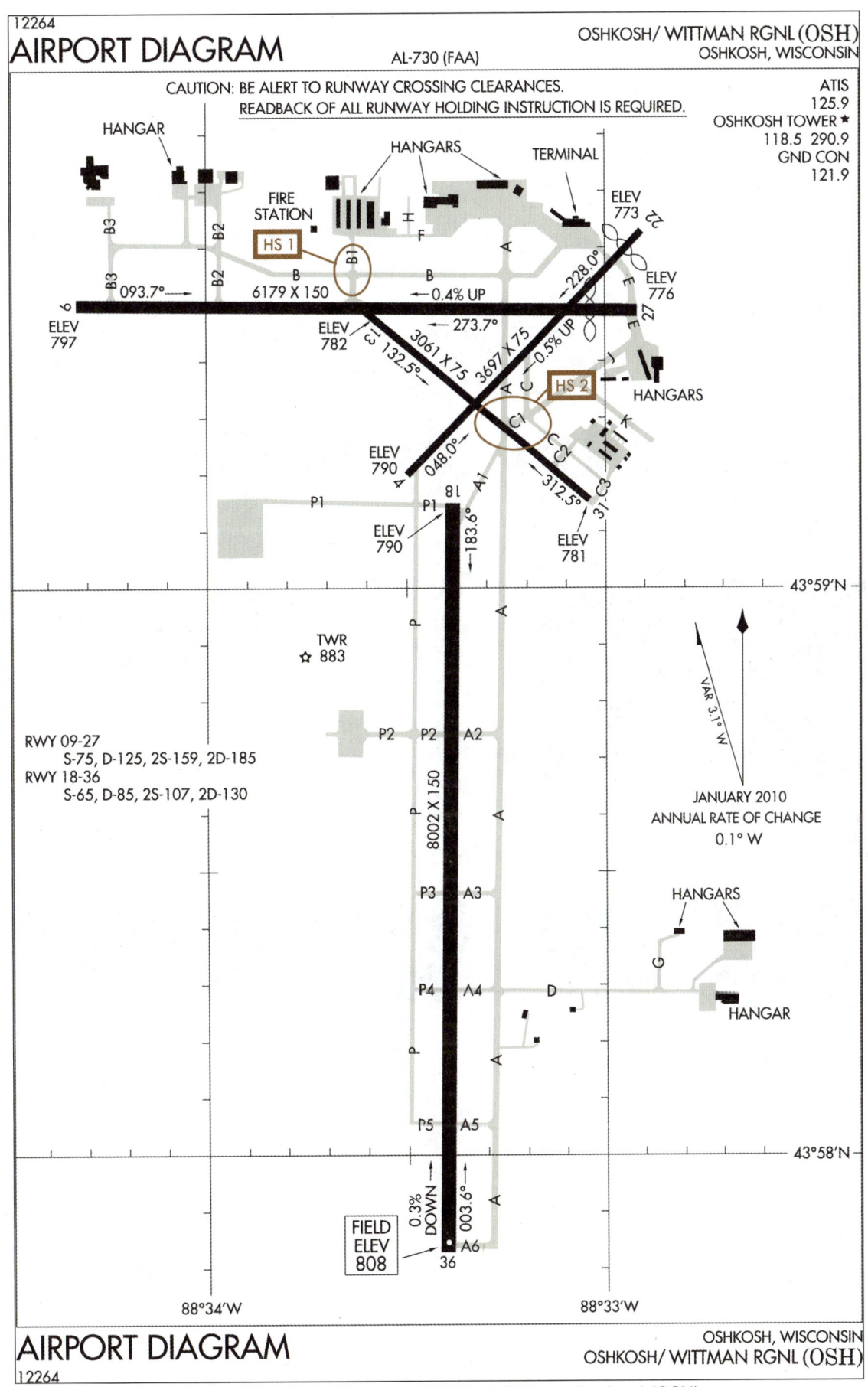

Figure 251. – Airport Diagram: Osh Kosh/Wittman Regional (OSH).

194

STUDY UNIT SIX

HOLDING AND INSTRUMENT APPROACHES

(34 pages of outline)

This study unit contains outlines of major concepts tested, sample test questions and answers regarding holding and instrument approaches, and an explanation of each answer.

Recall that the **sole purpose** of this book is to expedite your passing of the FAA pilot knowledge test for the instrument rating. Accordingly, all extraneous material (i.e., topics or regulations not directly tested on the FAA pilot knowledge test) is omitted, even though much more knowledge is necessary to fly safely. This additional material is presented in *Pilot Handbook, Aviation Weather and Weather Services, FAR/AIM,* and *Instrument Pilot Flight Maneuvers and Practical Test Prep*, available from Gleim Publications, Inc. Order online at www.GleimAviation.com.

6.1 CONTACT AND VISUAL APPROACHES

1. You may request a contact approach if there is 1 SM flight visibility and you can operate clear of clouds to the destination airport.

    a. A contact approach is an alternative to a standard instrument approach procedure (SIAP).

    b. ATC will assign a contact approach only upon request if the reported visibility is at least 1 mile.

2. ATC may assign a visual approach to an airport or authorize you to follow other airplanes for a landing if the approach can be accomplished in VFR.

    a. You must have the airport or the preceding aircraft in sight.

    b. Visual approaches can be assigned by ATC; contact approaches cannot.

    c. On visual approaches, radar service is automatically terminated when the aircraft is instructed to contact the tower.

6.2 LDA AND SDF APPROACHES

1.   An LDA (localizer-type directional aid) is as useful and accurate as a localizer (3° to 6° course width).

     a.   The LDA is very similar to an instrument landing system (ILS), but it usually does not have a glide slope (i.e., it has only a localizer) and is not aligned with the runway.

2.   An SDF (simplified directional facility) has a course width of either 6° or 12°.

     a.   SDF approaches may or may not be aligned with a runway (and their courses are wider). The SDF does not have a glide slope.

6.3 PRECISION RUNWAY MONITOR (PRM)

1.   Precision Runway Monitoring (PRM) is a RADAR system that has a high update rate and is able to monitor approaches to closely-spaced parallel runways.

2.   Simultaneous close parallel ILS Precision Runway Monitor (PRM) approaches are authorized for use at airports that have parallel runways separated by at least 3,400 ft. and no more than 4,300 ft. They are approved for airports with parallel runways separated by at least 3,000 ft. with an offset localizer (LOC) where the offset angle is at least 2.5° but no more than 3°. Two aircraft can make simultaneous ILS approaches next to each other.

     a.   Approval for ILS PRM approaches requires the airport to have a precision runway monitoring system and a final monitor controller who can only communicate with aircraft on the final approach course.

          1)   The controller is equipped with a monitoring system that tracks the aircraft performance on the final approach segment of the approach.

          2)   Additionally, two tower frequencies are required to be used, and the controller broadcasts over both frequencies to reduce the chance of instructions being missed.

     b.   Pilot training is required for pilots using the PRM system. This training is available for 14 CFR Parts 121 and 135 and general aviation pilots at www.faa.gov/training_testing/training/prm/.

6.4 RUNWAY VISUAL RANGE (RVR)

1.   RVR is an instrumentally derived value that represents the horizontal distance the pilot can see down the runway from the approach end.

     a.   It is based on the measurement of a transmissometer near the touchdown point of the instrument runway and is reported in hundreds of feet.

2.   If RVR is inoperative and cannot be reported, convert the RVR minimum to ground visibility, and use that as the visibility minimum for takeoffs and landings.

     a.   Legend 21 on the next page has a chart of RVR/visibility comparable values.

3.   The normal ILS visibility minimum is 1/2 SM, which is 2400 RVR.

13122
TERMS/LANDING MINIMA DATA

CIRCLING APPROACH OBSTACLE PROTECTED AIRSPACE

The circling MDA provides vertical clearance from obstacles when conducting a circle-to-land maneuver within the obstacle protected area. Circling approach obstacle protected areas extend laterally and longitudinally from the centerlines and ends of all runways at an airport by the distances shown in the following tables. The areas are technically defined by the tangential connection of arcs drawn at the radius distance shown from each runway end.

STANDARD CIRCLING APPROACH MANEUVERING RADIUS

Circling approach protected areas developed prior to late 2012 used the radius distances shown in the following table, expressed in nautical miles (NM), dependent on aircraft approach category. The approaches using standard circling approach areas can be identified by the absence of the **C** symbol on the circling line of minima.

Circling MDA in feet MSL	Approach Category and Circling Radius (NM)				
	CAT A	CAT B	CAT C	CAT D	CAT E
All Altitudes	1.3	1.5	1.7	2.3	4.5

C EXPANDED CIRCLING APPROACH MANEUVERING AIRSPACE RADIUS

Circling approach protected areas developed after late 2012 use the radius distance shown in the following table, expressed in nautical miles (NM), dependent on aircraft approach category, and the altitude of the circling MDA, which accounts for true airspeed increase with altitude. The approaches using expanded circling approach areas can be identified by the presence of the **C** symbol on the circling line of minima.

Circling MDA in feet MSL	Approach Category and Circling Radius (NM)				
	CAT A	CAT B	CAT C	CAT D	CAT E
1000 or less	1.3	1.7	2.7	3.6	4.5
1001-3000	1.3	1.8	2.8	3.7	4.6
3001-5000	1.3	1.8	2.9	3.8	4.8
5001-7000	1.3	1.9	3.0	4.0	5.0
7001-9000	1.4	2.0	3.2	4.2	5.3
9001 and above	1.4	2.1	3.3	4.4	5.5

Comparable Values of RVR and Visibility

The following table shall be used for converting RVR to ground or flight visibility. For converting RVR values that fall between listed values, use the next higher RVR value; do not interpolate. For example, when converting 1800 RVR, use 2400 RVR with the resultant visibility of ½ mile.

RVR (feet)	Visibility (statute miles)	RVR (feet)	Visibility (statute miles)
1600	¼	4500	⅞
2400	½	5000	1
3200	⅝	6000	1¼
4000	¾		

RADAR MINIMA

	RWY	GS/TCH/RPI	CAT	DA/ MDA-VIS	HAT/ HATh/ HAA	CEIL-VIS	CAT	DA/ MDA-VIS	HAT/ HATh/ HAA	CEIL-VIS
PAR	10	2.5°/42/1000	ABCDE	**195**/16	100	(100-¼)				
	28	2.5°/48/1068	ABCDE	**187**/16	100	(100-¼)				
ASR	10		ABC	**560**/40	463	(500-¾)	DE	**560**/50	463	(500-1)
	28		AB	**600**/50	513	(600-1)	CDE	**600**/60	513	(600-1¼)
CIR	10		AB	**560** 1¼	463	(500 1¼)	CDE	**560**-1½	463	(500-1½)
	28		AB	**600**-1¼	503	(600-1¼)	CDE	**600**-1½	503	(600-1½)

Visibility (RVR 100's of feet)

Visibility in Statute Miles

All minimums in parentheses not applicable to Civil Pilots. Military Pilots refer to appropriate regulations.

Radar Minima:

1. Minima shown are the lowest permitted by established criteria. Pilots should consult applicable directives for their category of aircraft.
2. The circling MDA and weather minima to be used are those for the runway to which the final approach is flown- not the landing runway. In the above RADAR MINIMA example, a category C aircraft flying a radar approach to runway 10, circling to land on runway 28, must use an MDA of 560 feet with weather minima of 500-1½.

NOTE: Military RADAR MINIMA may be shown with communications symbology that indicates emergency frequency monitoring capability by the radar facility as follows:

(E) VHF and UHF emergency frequencies monitored

(V) VHF emergency frequency (121.5) monitored

(U) UHF emergency frequency (243.0) monitored

Additionally, unmonitored frequencies which are available on request from the controlling agency may be annotated with an "x".

⚠ Alternate Minimums not standard. Civil users refer to tabulation. USA/USN/USAF pilots refer to appropriate regulations.

⚠ NA Alternate minimums are Not Authorized due to unmonitored facility or absence of weather reporting service.

▼ Takeoff Minimums not standard and/or Departure Procedures are published. Refer to tabulation.

TERMS/LANDING MINIMA DATA

Legend 21. – Instrument Approach Procedures Explanation of Terms.

6.5 MISSED APPROACHES

1.   When executing a missed approach prior to the missed approach point (MAP), continue the approach to the MAP at or above the minimum descent altitude (MDA) or decision height (DH) before executing any turns.

2.   If you lose visual reference in a circle to land from an instrument approach, you should make a climbing turn toward your landing runway to become established on the missed approach course.

6.6 ILS SPECIFICATIONS

1.   The ILS missed approach should be executed upon arrival at the DH on the glide slope if the visual reference requirements are not met.

2.   The normal decision height for a Category I ILS is 200 ft. AGL.

3.   The amount of deflection and distance from the localizer and the glide slope for an ILS is presented as Figure 139 on the following page.

   a.   A series of questions asks how far you are from the localizer or glide slope centerlines given certain types of deflection on your glide slope indicator. These questions require interpreting Figure 139.

4.   The direction of deflection of the localizer and glide slope bar shows where the actual course is located. You should "fly to the needles" or "fly the crosshair" to maintain a perfect course.

   a.   When the localizer bar is left of center and the glide slope bar is below center, you are right of the localizer course and above the glide slope course.

      1)   To correct your course, "fly to the needles." Make a left correction to intercept the localizer centerline and descend to intercept the glide slope centerline.

   b.   For each combination of localizer and glide slope deflection, use similar corrective actions.

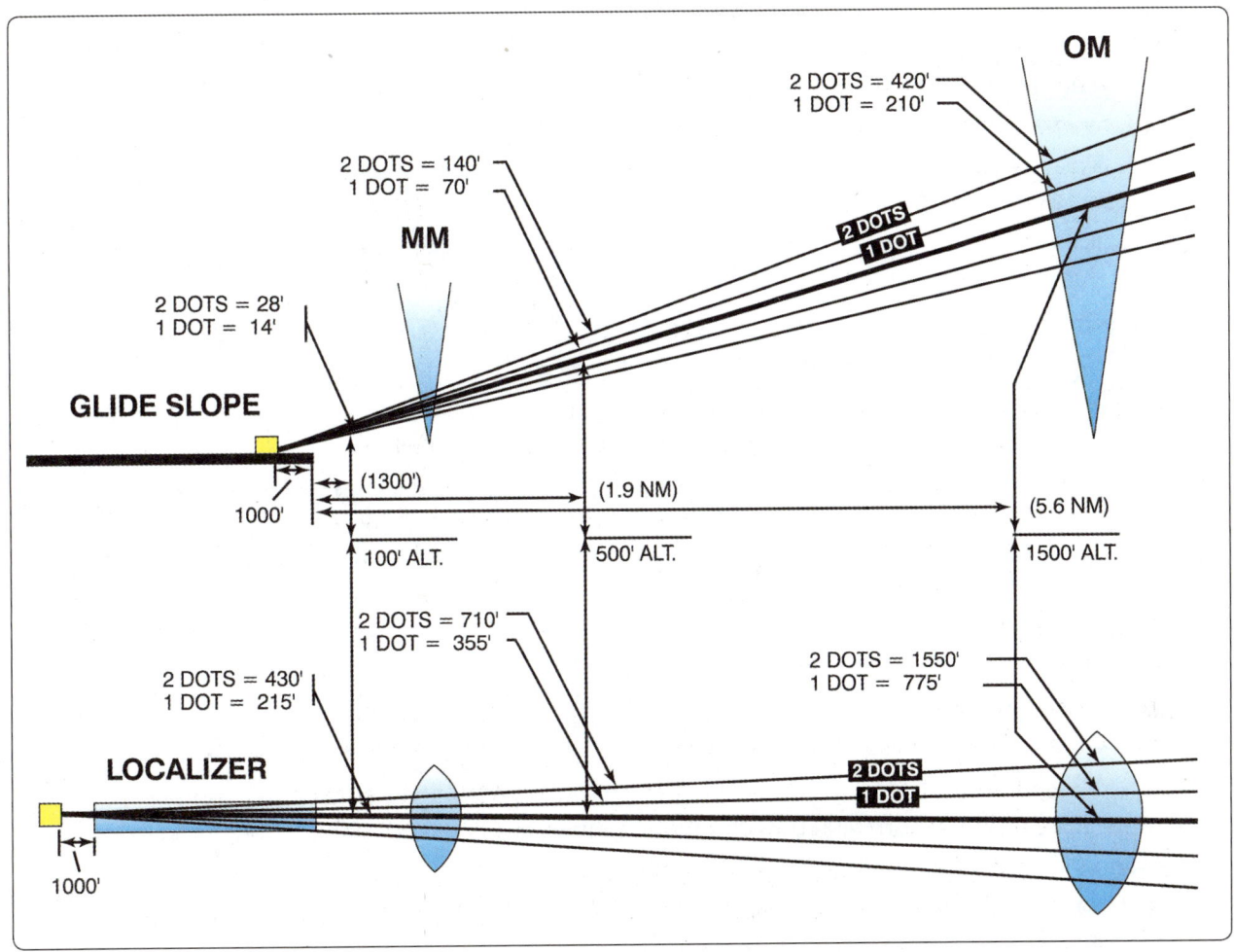

Figure 139. – Glide Slope and Localizer Illustration.

5. Compass locators, when used for the outer marker (OM) of an ILS, transmit two-letter identification groups.

    a. The outer compass locator (LOM) transmits the first two letters of the localizer identification group.

    b. The middle compass locator (LMM) transmits the last two letters of the localizer identification group.

    c. If the OM and/or MM are not compass locators, there is no two-letter identification transmission.

6. If DME is available on an ILS or localizer approach, the DME/TACAN channel will be indicated in the localizer frequency box on the instrument approach chart.

7. Parallel (dependent) ILS approaches provide aircraft a minimum of 1.5-mi. radar separation diagonally between successive aircraft on the adjacent localizer course.

8. Legend 38 on the following page contains the ILS standard characteristics and terminology.

6.7 UNUSABLE ILS COMPONENTS

1. ILS components include

    a. Localizer
    b. Glide slope
    c. Outer marker
    d. Approach lights

2. If more than one component is unusable, each minimum is raised to the highest minimum required by any single component that is inoperative.

3. A compass locator or precision approach radar (PAR) may be substituted for an inoperative OM or MM.

    a. An inoperative MM does not change the landing minimums; thus, no substitution is necessary.

4. When installed with the ILS and specified in the approach procedure, DME may be used in lieu of the OM.

5. When the glide slope fails, the ILS reverts to a nonprecision localizer (LOC) approach.

    a. The LOC MDA and visibility minimums will be used.

6. If you are on the glide slope when the ILS fails and a VASI is in sight, you should continue the approach using the VASI and report the malfunction to ATC.

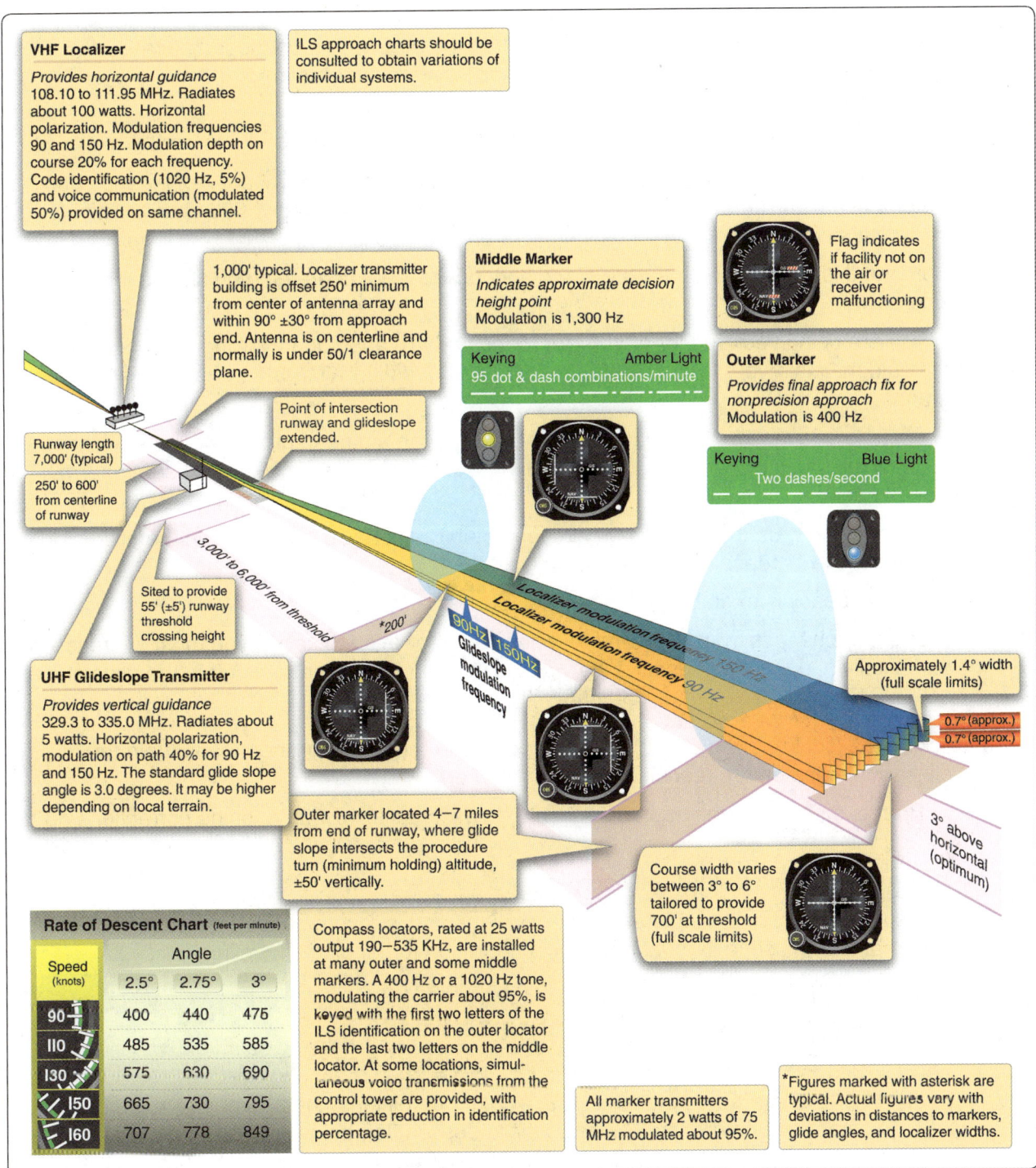

VHF Localizer

Provides horizontal guidance 108.10 to 111.95 MHz. Radiates about 100 watts. Horizontal polarization. Modulation frequencies 90 and 150 Hz. Modulation depth on course 20% for each frequency. Code identification (1020 Hz, 5%) and voice communication (modulated 50%) provided on same channel.

ILS approach charts should be consulted to obtain variations of individual systems.

1,000' typical. Localizer transmitter building is offset 250' minimum from center of antenna array and within 90° ±30° from approach end. Antenna is on centerline and normally is under 50/1 clearance plane.

Middle Marker

Indicates approximate decision height point Modulation is 1,300 Hz

Flag indicates if facility not on the air or receiver malfunctioning

Keying — Amber Light
95 dot & dash combinations/minute

Outer Marker

Provides final approach fix for nonprecision approach Modulation is 400 Hz

Keying — Blue Light
Two dashes/second

Point of intersection runway and glideslope extended.

Runway length 7,000' (typical)

250' to 600' from centerline of runway

3,000' to 6,000' from threshold

Sited to provide 55' (±5') runway threshold crossing height

*200'

90Hz 150Hz
Glideslope modulation frequency

Localizer modulation frequency 150 Hz
Localizer modulation frequency 90 Hz

Approximately 1.4° width (full scale limits)

0.7° (approx.)
0.7° (approx.)

UHF Glideslope Transmitter

Provides vertical guidance 329.3 to 335.0 MHz. Radiates about 5 watts. Horizontal polarization, modulation on path 40% for 90 Hz and 150 Hz. The standard glide slope angle is 3.0 degrees. It may be higher depending on local terrain.

Outer marker located 4–7 miles from end of runway, where glide slope intersects the procedure turn (minimum holding) altitude, ±50' vertically.

3° above horizontal (optimum)

Course width varies between 3° to 6° tailored to provide 700' at threshold (full scale limits)

Rate of Descent Chart (feet per minute)

Speed (knots)	Angle		
	2.5°	2.75°	3°
90	400	440	475
110	485	535	585
130	575	630	690
150	665	730	795
160	707	778	849

Compass locators, rated at 25 watts output 190–535 KHz, are installed at many outer and some middle markers. A 400 Hz or a 1020 Hz tone, modulating the carrier about 95%, is keyed with the first two letters of the ILS identification on the outer locator and the last two letters on the middle locator. At some locations, simultaneous voice transmissions from the control tower are provided, with appropriate reduction in identification percentage.

All marker transmitters approximately 2 watts of 75 MHz modulated about 95%.

*Figures marked with asterisk are typical. Actual figures vary with deviations in distances to markers, glide angles, and localizer widths.

Legend 38. – ILS Standard Characteristics and Terminology.

6.8 FLYING THE APPROACH

1. Rate of descent on the glide slope is dependent on the airplane groundspeed because the descent must be constant relative to the distance traveled over the ground.

   a. As groundspeed increases, the descent rate must increase.
   b. As groundspeed decreases, the descent rate must decrease.

2. The approach should be under the stabilized approach concept. Operational experience and research have shown that a descent rate of more than approximately 1,000 feet per minute (fpm) is unacceptable during the final stages of an approach.

3. If the airspeed is too fast and the glide slope and localizer are centered, you should initially reduce power.

4. When you are being vectored for an ILS approach and are about to fly through the localizer, you should maintain your last assigned heading and question ATC rather than deviate from a clearance.

5. If a wind shear changes from a headwind to a tailwind, the airspeed drops, the nose pitches down, and the vertical speed increases. You must initially increase power to resume normal approach speed.

   a. Then power must be reduced as airspeed stabilizes so you can maintain the glide slope due to the increased groundspeed.
   b. The tendency is to go below the glide slope.

6. If a wind shear changes from a tailwind to a headwind (or even to calm), you must decrease your power initially and then increase it once you are through the shear to maintain the glide slope.

   a. The tendency is to go above the glide slope.

7. In tracking the localizer, you should have your drift correction established to maintain the localizer centerline before reaching the outer marker.

   a. Then completion of the approach should be accomplished with heading corrections no greater than 2°.

8. The pilot must maintain a stabilized approach.

   a. A stabilized approach ensures safe operations and is recommended for all aircraft.
   b. The aircraft must be in an approved configuration for landing or circling.

      1) For turbojets, the engines should be spooled up.
      2) The airspeed should be correct for the approach.
      3) The flight path with a descent rate of less than 1,000 ft. above the airport or TDZE.
      4) For a straight-in approach in IFR weather conditions, the approach should be stabilized before the FAF and before descending below 1,000 ft. AGL.
      5) The descent rate should be less than 1,000 fpm before descending below the following minimum stabilized approach heights.

         a) For a visual approach or straight-in instrument approach in VFR weather conditions, the approach must be stabilized before descending below 500 ft. above the airport elevation.
         b) For the final segment of a circling approach maneuver, the approach must be stabilized 500 ft. above the airport elevation or at the MDA, whichever is lower.

      6) Once on a stabilized approach and below 500 ft. AGL, the bank angle should be less than 15°.

6.9 SIDE-STEP APPROACHES

1. A side-step approach is an instrument approach to one runway until you can see a parallel runway and "side step" to land on the parallel runway.

2. A side-step approach is used when a pilot (a) executes an approach procedure serving one of two or more parallel runways that are separated by 1,200 ft. or less and then (b) diverts to the other parallel runway using a straight-in approach.

3. Execute a side-step procedure as soon as possible after the runway environment is in sight.

6.10 HOLDING

1. A holding procedure is a predetermined maneuver that keeps aircraft within a specified airspace while awaiting further clearance from ATC.

2. Holding patterns are racetrack-shaped patterns based on a fix that is a radio navigation facility (VOR or other NAVAID); an intersection of NAVAID bearings, radials, or a DME fix; or a waypoint (GPS or other RNAV equipment).

3. Holding patterns consist of the following components (note that the fix is always at the end of the inbound leg):

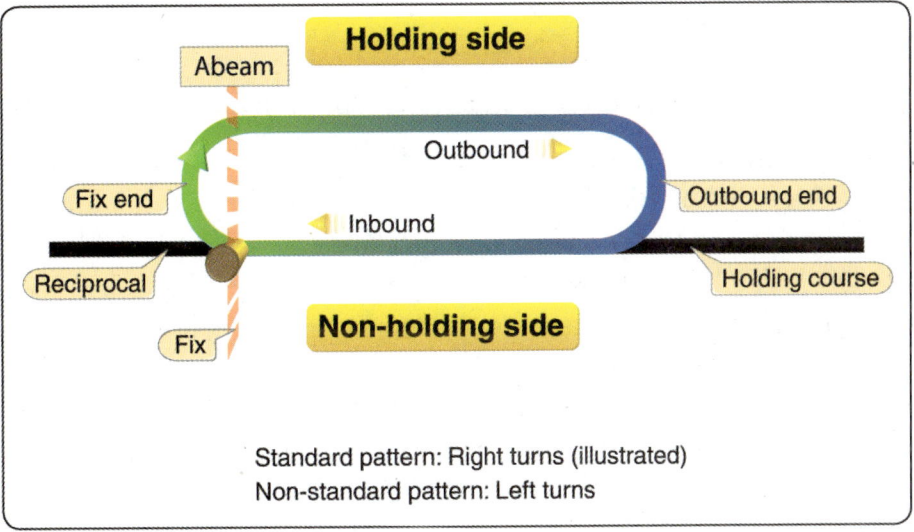

a. A **standard pattern** means the turns in the holding pattern are to the right.
b. A **nonstandard pattern** means the turns in the holding pattern are to the left.
   1) ATC will specify in the holding clearance if left turns are to be made.

4.   You enter a holding pattern using one of three procedures as illustrated in the figure below. This illustrates a standard pattern; the same concept is used in a nonstandard pattern.

   a.   Parallel procedure. Fly a parallel holding course, as in (a). Turn left and return to the holding fix or intercept the holding course.

   b.   Teardrop procedure. Proceed on an outbound track of 30° or less to the holding course; turn right to intercept the holding course, as in (b).

   c.   Direct entry procedure. Turn right and fly the pattern, as in (c).

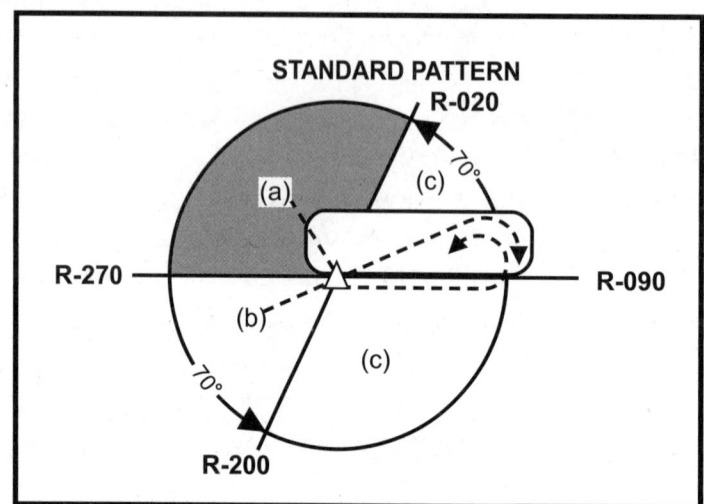

5.   The best way to determine the entry method on the FAA knowledge test is to draw a holding pattern complete with the fix and inbound leg.

   a.   Through the fix, draw the 70° angle such that it intersects the outbound leg at about 1/3 of the outbound leg length.

   b.   Then, slightly shade the (a) area, which is the 110° angle between the extension of the inbound leg and the 70° line.

   c.   The (b) area is the 70° angle between the 70° line and the extension of the inbound leg.

   d.   EXAMPLE: In the previous illustration, the inbound leg to the fix is 270°, and the outbound leg is 090°. If the fix is a VOR station, the following radials define which entry procedure to use:

        R-200 to R-270 -- teardrop procedure
        R-270 to R-020 -- parallel procedure
        R-020 to R-200 -- direct procedure

6.   The timing of the outbound leg begins over or abeam the fix, whichever occurs later.

   a.   If the abeam position cannot be determined, start timing when the turn to outbound is complete (i.e., wings level).

7. Maximum holding pattern airspeed (IAS) for all aircraft

    a. From the minimum holding altitude (MHA) through 6,000 ft. -- 200 kt.
    b. From 6,001 ft. through 14,000 ft. -- 230 kt.
    c. From 14,001 ft. and above -- 265 kt.

8. When a holding pattern is used in lieu of a procedure turn, the holding maneuver must still be executed within the time or leg length specified in the profile view on the instrument approach procedure (IAP) chart.

9. When more than one circuit of the holding pattern is needed to lose altitude or become better established on course, additional circuits can be made at the pilot's discretion only if the pilot advises ATC and ATC approves.

10. The descent gradient during a nonprecision approach is very important. Locate the approach ground speed and time table found in the lower left or right corner of an approach chart (plate) for the appropriate ground speed. Under the ground speed will be the required time to reach the MAP.

    a. Time (and altitude) establishes the MAP on most nonprecision approaches.

    b. The key elements one must know are

        1) Ground speed,
        2) Altitude descent distance, and
        3) Time required to reach a point (i.e., MAP).

    c. EXAMPLE:

        1) Ground speed is 90 kt.

        2) We are at the final approach fix (FAF) at 2,000 ft. MSL and must descend to the MAP at 600 ft. MSL, so we must descend 1,400 ft. (2,000 ft. – 600 ft.).

        3) We have to descend 1,400 ft. in 2 min., 44 sec.

        4) Convert seconds of time to a decimal number in minutes (44 sec. ÷ 60 = 0.73 min.).

        5) Add 2 min. to arrive at 2.73 min.

        6) Divide distance by time (1,400 ft. ÷ 2.73 min. = 513 fpm).

CLIMB/DESCENT TABLE 10042

INSTRUMENT TAKEOFF OR APPROACH PROCEDURE CHARTS
RATE OF CLIMB/DESCENT TABLE

(ft. per min)

A rate of climb/descent table is provided for use in planning and executing climbs or descents under known or approximate ground speed conditions. It will be especially useful for approaches when the localizer only is used for course guidance. A best speed, power, altitude combination can be programmed which will result in a stable glide rate and altitude favorable for executing a landing if minimums exist upon breakout. Care should always be exercised so that minimum descent altitude and missed approach point are not exceeded.

CLIMB/ DESCENT ANGLE (degrees and tenths)	ft/NM	GROUND SPEED (knots)										
		60	90	120	150	180	210	240	270	300	330	360
2.0	210	210	320	425	530	635	743	850	955	1060	1165	1275
2.5	265	265	400	530	665	795	930	1060	1195	1325	1460	1590
VERTICAL PATH ANGLE 2.7	287	287	430	574	717	860	1003	1147	1290	1433	1576	1720
2.8	297	297	446	595	743	892	1041	1189	1338	1486	1635	1783
2.9	308	308	462	616	770	924	1078	1232	1386	1539	1693	1847
3.0	318	318	478	637	797	956	1115	1274	1433	1593	1752	1911
3.1	329	329	494	659	823	988	1152	1317	1481	1646	1810	1975
3.2	340	340	510	680	850	1020	1189	1359	1529	1699	1869	2039
3.3	350	350	526	701	876	1052	1227	1402	1577	1752	1927	2103
3.4	361	361	542	722	903	1083	1264	1444	1625	1805	1986	2166
3.5	370	370	555	745	930	1115	1300	1485	1670	1860	2045	2230
4.0	425	425	640	850	1065	1275	1490	1700	1915	2125	2340	2550
4.5	480	480	715	955	1195	1435	1675	1915	2150	2390	2630	2870
5.0	530	530	795	1065	1330	1595	1860	2125	2390	2660	2925	3190
5.5	585	585	880	1170	1465	1755	2050	2340	2635	2925	3220	3510
6.0	640	640	960	1275	1595	1915	2235	2555	2875	3195	3510	3830
6.5	690	690	1040	1385	1730	2075	2425	2770	3115	3460	3805	4155
7.0	745	745	1120	1490	1865	2240	2610	2985	3355	3730	4105	4475
7.5	800	800	1200	1600	2000	2400	2800	3200	3600	4000	4400	4800
8.0	855	855	1280	1710	2135	2560	2990	3415	3845	4270	4695	5125
8.5	910	910	1360	1815	2270	2725	3180	3630	4085	4540	4995	5450
9.0	960	960	1445	1925	2405	2885	3370	3850	4330	4810	5295	5775
9.5	1015	1015	1525	2035	2540	3050	3560	4065	4575	5085	5590	6100
10.0	1070	1070	1605	2145	2680	3215	3750	4285	4820	5355	5890	6430

CLIMB/DESCENT TABLE 10042

Legend 27. – Instrument Takeoff or Approach Procedure Charts, Rate-of-Climb/Descent Table.

11. Some approach plates will have a glide path labeled in degrees near the bottom of the plate in the plan view area. Descent rates can be found on the Rate-of-Climb/Descent Table (Legend 27 on the previous page).

    a. Find the ground speed located across the top of the table.

    b. Find the angle of descent (or glide path) located from top to bottom on the left side of the table.

    c. Follow down and across, respectively, and where they meet is the descent rate for that ground speed and descent angle.

6.11 INSTRUMENT APPROACH CHARTS

1. The questions in this subunit are wide ranging. They are best prepared for by studying the approach chart legends on pages 215 through 228. The questions will not refer you to these legends, but the legends will be available to you in the FAA's *Airman Knowledge Testing Supplement for Instrument Rating* book. Use them when needed. Remember that approach charts consist of several parts:

    a. Top and bottom margin identification
    b. Planview
    c. Profile view
    d. Minimums section
    e. Airport diagram

2. Initial approach fixes (IAF) identify the beginning of an initial approach segment of an instrument approach procedure and are identified by the letters IAF on the planview of approach charts.

3. Aircraft approach categories are listed as A, B, C, D, and E based upon 1.3 times the stall speed of the aircraft in the landing configuration at maximum certified gross landing weight (1.3 V_{so}).

    a. The categories are as follows:

        1) Category A: Speed less than 91 kt.
        2) Category B: Speed 91 kt. or more but less than 121 kt.
        3) Category C: Speed 121 kt. or more but less than 141 kt.
        4) Category D: Speed 141 kt. or more but less than 166 kt.
        5) Category E: Speed 166 kt. or more.

4. The symbol "T" in a point-down black triangle indicates that takeoff minimums are not standard and/or departure minimums are published and you should consult alternative takeoff procedures.

    a The symbol "A" in a point-up black triangle indicates that nonstandard minimums exist to list the airport as an IFR alternate.

        1) Standard alternate minimums are 800-2 for a nonprecision approach and 600-2 for a precision approach.

5. An airport may not be qualified for alternate use if the NAVAIDs used for the final approach are unmonitored.

6. If there is penetration of the obstacle identification surfaces (OIS), the published visibility for the ILS approach can be no lower than 3/4 SM.

7. The absence of the procedure turn barb on the planview on an approach chart indicates that a procedure turn is not authorized for that approach.

    a. The term NoPT means that there is no procedure turn.

8. A course reversal (procedure turn) is not required (or authorized) when radar vectors are being provided.

9. Minimum safe-sector altitudes are depicted on approach charts. These provide at least 1,000 ft. of obstacle clearance within a 25-NM radius of the navigation facility upon which the procedure is predicated but do not necessarily ensure acceptable navigational signal coverage.

10. Published landing minimums apply when you are making an instrument approach to an airport.

11. If you adhere to the minimum altitudes depicted on the IAP, you can be assured of terrain and obstacle clearance.

12. When being radar-vectored to an instrument approach, you should comply with the last assigned altitude until the airplane is established on a segment of a published route or IAP and you have been cleared for the approach, after which you should continue descents to the listed minimum altitudes.

13. When simultaneous approaches are in progress, each pilot will be advised to monitor the tower frequency to receive advisories and instructions.

14. When straight-in minimums are not published, you can make a straight-in landing if the active runway is in sight, there is sufficient time to make a normal landing, and you have been cleared to land.

15. If you are doing an approach in a category B airplane but maintaining a speed faster than the maximum specified for that category, you should use category C minimums.

16. When an instrument approach procedure involves a procedure turn, the maximum allowable indicated airspeed is 200 kt.

17. When a DME is inoperative, there will be no code tone (identifier) broadcast.

18. On instrument approach segments, the minimum altitudes are indicated on the planview and profile view, which **you** are expected to be able to interpret and specify on the FAA instrument rating knowledge test.

19. When holding patterns exist in lieu of outbound procedure turns, the length of the outbound leg may be indicated as a distance rather than time. This information is given in both the planview and the profile view of the approach chart.

20. On RNAV approaches, the MAP is identified when the TO/FROM indicator changes, which indicates station passage at the MAP waypoint.

    a. On some RNAV approach charts, the distance from the MAP to another more prominent waypoint located along the extended final approach course may be shown in the profile and plan views.

21. RNAV waypoints, when used for an instrument approach, contain boxes in which the latitude and longitude are listed on the first line and the VOR direction and distance are listed on the second line.

22. RNAV approaches require an approved RNAV receiver; no other navigation equipment is specifically required.

23. On procedure turns, there may be a distance limitation from a NAVAID, and procedural turns should be made entirely on the side of the inbound radial or bearing to which the procedural turn arrow points.

    a. If a teardrop turn is depicted, only a teardrop course reversal can be executed.

24. The airport diagram at the top of the IAP chart contains the following important elevation figures in MSL:
    a. Airport elevation (ELEV)
    b. Touchdown elevation (TDZE)
    c. Threshold elevation (THRE)

25. If you are not able to identify a NAVAID marking a descent to a lower altitude on a nonprecision approach, you cannot descend to the next lower altitude.

26. The MAP of a precision approach is arrival at the DH on the glide slope.

27. The appropriate approach and tower frequencies are indicated at the top of the planview.

28. When a marker beacon receiver becomes inoperative and you cannot identify the MM during an ILS approach, you should use the published minimums.

29. A second VOR receiver may be needed when doing a localizer approach with a final step-down fix to be identified by a VOR radial.

30. Some nonprecision approaches will allow descents to lower altitudes at specified DME distances.
    a. The advantage of DME can be determined by comparing the two MDA values.

31. Use the recommended entry into holding patterns as discussed in the previous subunit.

32. The minimum navigation equipment required for a VOR/DME approach is one VOR receiver and DME.

33. Restrictions to circle-to-land procedures are found below the minimums section of the IAP chart.

34. The height above touchdown (HAT) is the height of the MDA or DH above the touchdown zone. It is the smaller numbers that appear after the MDA or DH.
    a. The numbers in parentheses are military minimums.

35. The minimums section of the approach chart provides the MDA or DH and the visibility (expressed as RVR or SM).

36. When making an LOC approach to the primary airport of the Class B airspace, the aircraft must be equipped with
    a. Two-way radio communication
    b. Mode C transponder
    c. VOR

37. When the glide slope becomes inoperative during an ILS approach, the approach becomes a nonprecision LOC approach.
    a. The LOC minimums then apply.

38. The final approach fix (FAF) for a precision approach is identified on the approach chart by a lightning bolt (✒).
    a. The intercept altitude is indicated next to the symbol.

39. On a nonprecision approach, the distance from the FAF to the MAP is indicated below the airport diagram.

40. If a runway has a displaced threshold, the distance available for landing will be shown by a notation in the airport diagram. For example, "Rwy 21 ldg 5957'" signifies that 5,957 ft. of the total length of runway 21 are available for landing.

41. A category C aircraft must use category C minimums, even if using category B approach speed.

42. Legends 20 through 32 concern instrument approaches and are presented on pages 215 through 228.

6.12 DPs AND STARs

1. DPs (instrument departure procedures), STARs (standard terminal arrival routes), and visual approaches are all routinely assigned by ATC as appropriate.

2. DPs and STARs are issued to simplify clearance delivery procedures when ATC deems it appropriate, unless you have requested "no DP" or "no STAR" in the remarks section of your flight plan.

    a. Less desirably, pilots may refuse DPs and STARs when they are part of a clearance.

3. Instrument procedures design criteria assume an initial climb of 200 ft./NM for obstacle clearance during a departure procedure.

4. When a DP requires a minimum climb rate of a specified number of ft. per NM, you may be asked to convert the climb rate into fpm.

    a. Use the Rate-of-Climb/Descent Table in Legend 27 on the following page.

    b. Another method is first to divide the groundspeed by 60 min. to get the NM per min. Then multiply NM per min. by the required climb rate per NM to determine climb rate in fpm.

        1) EXAMPLE: If 200 ft. per NM is required to a specified altitude and your groundspeed is 120 kt., you will be traveling 2 NM/min. (120 NM/60 min.), which will require a minimum climb rate of 400 fpm (200 required ft./NM × 2 NM/min.).

5. To accept a DP, you must have at least a textual description of it.

6. Preferred IFR routes are correlated with DPs and STARs and may be defined by airways, jet routes, and direct routes between NAVAIDs.

7. The departure route description of a DP explains the departure procedures. It also explains the route to be used if communication is lost.

CLIMB/DESCENT TABLE 10042

INSTRUMENT TAKEOFF OR APPROACH PROCEDURE CHARTS
RATE OF CLIMB/DESCENT TABLE

(ft. per min)

A rate of climb/descent table is provided for use in planning and executing climbs or descents under known or approximate ground speed conditions. It will be especially useful for approaches when the localizer only is used for course guidance. A best speed, power, altitude combination can be programmed which will result in a stable glide rate and altitude favorable for executing a landing if minimums exist upon breakout. Care should always be exercised so that minimum descent altitude and missed approach point are not exceeded.

CLIMB/ DESCENT ANGLE (degrees and tenths)	ft/NM	GROUND SPEED (knots)										
		60	90	120	150	180	210	240	270	300	330	360
2.0	210	210	320	425	530	635	743	850	955	1060	1165	1275
2.5	265	265	400	530	665	795	930	1060	1195	1325	1460	1590
VERTICAL PATH ANGLE 2.7	287	287	430	574	717	860	1003	1147	1290	1433	1576	1720
2.8	297	297	446	595	743	892	1041	1189	1338	1486	1635	1783
2.9	308	308	462	616	770	924	1078	1232	1386	1539	1693	1847
3.0	318	318	478	637	797	956	1115	1274	1433	1593	1752	1911
3.1	329	329	494	659	823	988	1152	1317	1481	1646	1810	1975
3.2	340	340	510	680	850	1020	1189	1359	1529	1699	1869	2039
3.3	350	350	526	701	876	1052	1227	1402	1577	1752	1927	2103
3.4	361	361	542	722	903	1083	1264	1444	1625	1805	1986	2166
3.5	370	370	555	745	930	1115	1300	1485	1670	1860	2045	2230
4.0	425	425	640	850	1065	1275	1490	1700	1915	2125	2340	2550
4.5	480	480	715	955	1195	1435	1675	1915	2150	2390	2630	2870
5.0	530	530	795	1065	1330	1595	1860	2125	2390	2660	2925	3190
5.5	585	585	880	1170	1465	1755	2050	2340	2635	2925	3220	3510
6.0	640	640	960	1275	1595	1915	2235	2555	2875	3195	3510	3830
6.5	690	690	1040	1385	1730	2075	2425	2770	3115	3460	3805	4155
7.0	745	745	1120	1490	1865	2240	2610	2985	3355	3730	4105	4475
7.5	800	800	1200	1600	2000	2400	2800	3200	3600	4000	4400	4800
8.0	855	855	1280	1710	2135	2560	2990	3415	3845	4270	4695	5125
8.5	910	910	1360	1815	2270	2725	3180	3630	4085	4540	4995	5450
9.0	960	960	1445	1925	2405	2885	3370	3850	4330	4810	5295	5775
9.5	1015	1015	1525	2035	2540	3050	3560	4065	4575	5085	5590	6100
10.0	1070	1070	1605	2145	2680	3215	3750	4285	4820	5355	5890	6430

CLIMB/DESCENT TABLE 10042

Legend 27. – Instrument Takeoff or Approach Procedure Charts, Rate-of-Climb/Descent Table.

8.   Legend 28 concerns DPs (formerly known as SIDs) and STARs.

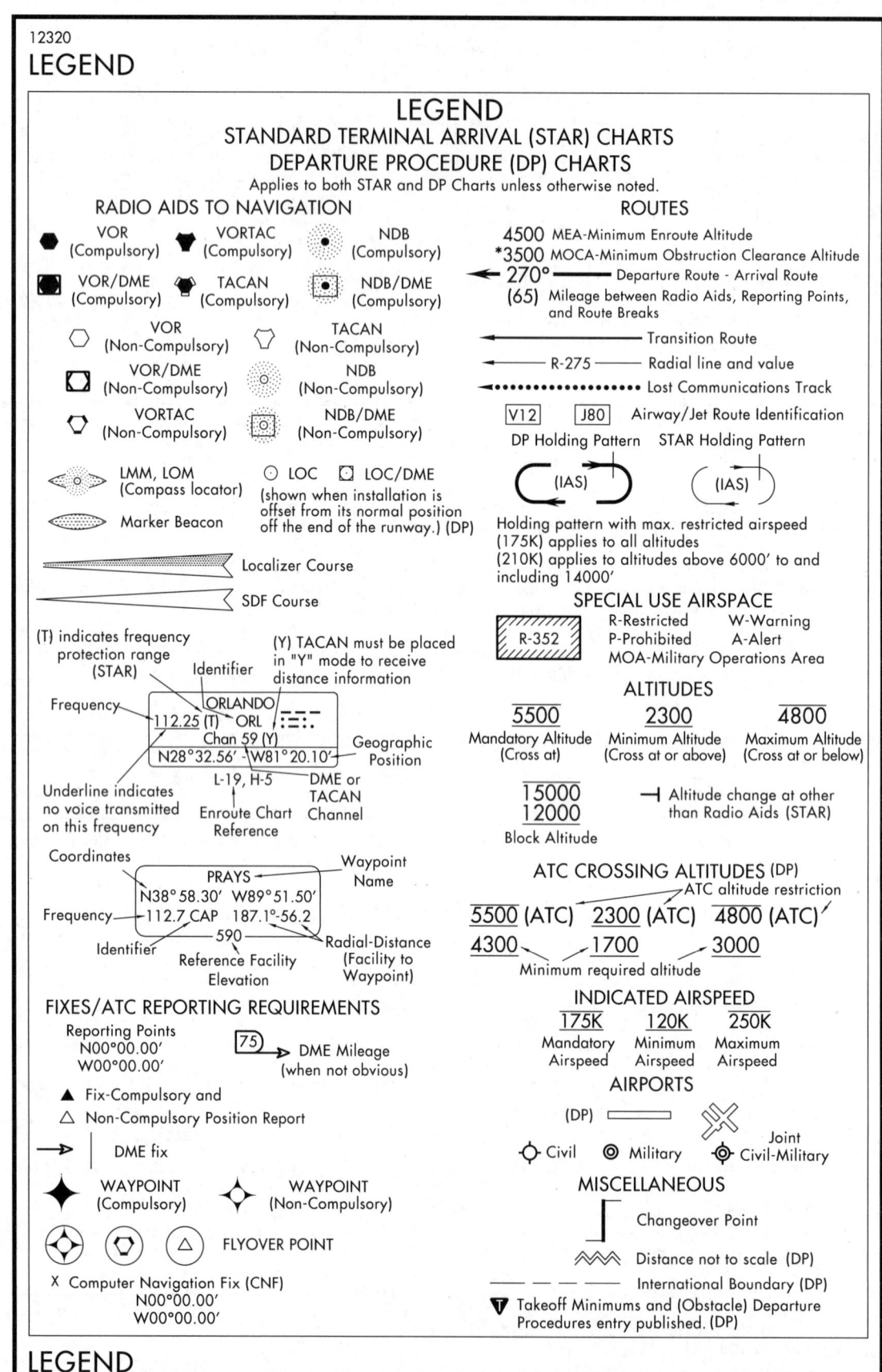

Legend 28. – Standard Arrival/Departure Charts.

6.13 GPS APPROACHES

1. Authorization to conduct any GPS approach requires that procedures be established for use in the event that the loss of RAIM capability occurs.

   a. In such an event, you must rely on other approved navigation equipment.

2. When you are using GPS for navigation and instrument approaches, any required alternate airport must have an approved instrument approach procedure, other than GPS, that is anticipated to be operational and available at the estimated time of arrival (ETA) and that the airplane is equipped to fly.

   a. Handheld GPS systems are not authorized for instrument approaches and are only considered an aid to situational awareness.

3. When shooting a GPS instrument approach, most systems require you to choose to load an approach or load and activate an approach.

   a. EXAMPLE: When ATC tells you to expect a certain approach, select that approach and load it into the flight plan. Once cleared for the approach, it can be activated.

4. There are two modes during an approach that pilots must be aware of:

   a. **Terminal mode** occurs within 30 NM of the destination airport and is used to increase sensitivity. Terminal mode increases the sensitivity on the course deviation indicator (CDI) from 5 NM to 1 NM.

   b. **Approach mode** further increases the sensitivity on the CDI within 2 NM of the final approach waypoint (FAWP) from 1 NM to 0.3 NM.

5. Pilots are commonly vectored by ATC to the final approach course, and many GPS units have a setting that guides a pilot using these vectors along the final approach course. It is commonly referred to as the "vectors-to-final" feature.

6. A fly-over waypoint is depicted on an approach plate's planview as a four-pointed star enclosed in a circle.

   a. A fly-over waypoint precludes any turn until the waypoint is overflown and is followed by either an intercept maneuver of the next flight segment or direct flight to the next waypoint.

   b. This type of waypoint is used to denote a missed approach point, a missed approach holding point, or other specific points in space that must be flown over.

7. If you examine the planview of the approach plate, you will see a box, usually in the lower left corner, that depicts the minimum safe altitude(s) (MSA) for a given segment of the approach coverage area.

   a. This notation gives you an obstacle clearance altitude while also telling you when you may begin descending to the indicated altitude when cleared to a specific waypoint.

8. The Wide Area Augmentation System (WAAS) is a ground-based enhancement component of the satellite-based GPS navigation system.

   a. This system improves GPS signal accuracy and allows pilots with WAAS-certified equipment to conduct various types of GPS instrument approaches to varying heights above the ground.

      1) This class of approach procedures provides vertical guidance but does not meet the more stringent requirements for precision approaches.

      2) These procedures are referred to in the general sense as approaches with vertical guidance (APV).

b.   The LNAV approach is a conventional, nonprecision, GPS (RNAV) approach. There is no vertical guidance offered with this approach type.

    1)   Some GPS receivers do offer advisory guidance for LNAV approaches. These approaches will appear as "LNAV+V" on your GPS receiver.

    2)   Note that the vertical guidance is only advisory. It will not offer lower approach minimums than what is published for the standard LNAV approach procedure.

    3)   The MAP for an LNAV-only approach is the runway threshold, marked as a waypoint on the instrument approach chart with the designation "RW" followed by the runway number.

    4)   In some cases, a visual descent point will appear on the profile view of an instrument approach chart, which allows the pilot to continue a descent below the published MDA as long as visual contact with the surface exists and is maintained throughout the descent.

        a)   Note that this allowance for a visual descent is only approved for the LNAV approach type.

c.   The LNAV/VNAV approach is a full WAAS-enabled approach that provides vertical guidance using an electronic glide slope indication.

    1)   This approach type will offer slightly lower minimums than a traditional LNAV (non-WAAS approach).

    2)   Similar to flying an ILS approach, you will see a decision altitude (DA) indicated on the instrument approach chart rather than the MDA seen in an LNAV-only approach procedure.

    3)   The missed approach point for an LNAV/VNAV approach is upon reaching the published decision altitude.

d.   When GPS accuracy allows, a localizer performance with vertical guidance (LPV) approach may be created for a given runway. This is a WAAS-enabled approach procedure that offers the lowest descent altitude for any GPS approach procedure, sometimes as low as 200 ft. AGL, the same as an ILS approach.

    1)   An LPV approach is commonly misinterpreted as a precision approach procedure. Instead, it is an approach with vertical guidance (APV) procedure, just like the other WAAS-enabled approach procedures.

    2)   It is flown almost identically to an LNAV/VNAV approach. However, the decision altitude for an LPV approach is usually much lower than the LNAV/VNAV approach.

    3)   Like the LNAV/VNAV approach, the missed approach point for an LPV approach is upon reaching the decision altitude (DA) published on the approach chart.

    4)   When GPS accuracy is sufficient in a given area but obstacles make vertical navigation unsafe, a localizer performance (LP) approach may be put in place instead of the LPV approach.

e.   Ultimately, the GPS receiver will determine what type of WAAS-enabled approach you can conduct. If the necessary accuracy does not exist for an LPV approach into a given runway, the receiver will default to the next most feature-rich approach procedure.

    1)   If your GPS receiver does not complete this function automatically, it will be up to you to determine the navigational accuracy available to you at the time of the approach.

    2)   Be sure that you understand the features and capabilities of your GPS before attempting these procedures on your own. We also recommend that you receive specialized instruction on completing WAAS-enabled approaches from a qualified certificated flight instructor.

12320
TERMS/LANDING MINIMA DATA

IFR LANDING MINIMA

The United States Standard for Terminal Instrument Procedures (TERPS) is the approved criteria for formulating instrument approach procedures. Landing minima are established for six aircraft approach categories (ABCDE and COPTER). In the absence of COPTER MINIMA, helicopters may use the CAT A minimums of other procedures.

LANDING MINIMA FORMAT

In this example airport elevation is 1179, and runway touchdown zone elevation is 1152.

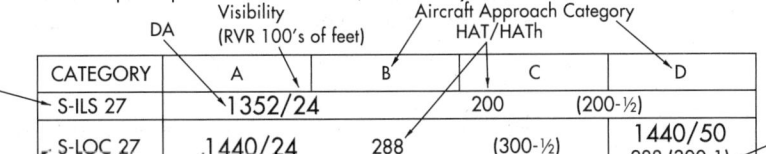

CATEGORY	A	B	C	D
S-ILS 27	1352/24		200 (200-½)	
S-LOC 27	1440/24	288 (300-½)		1440/50 288 (300-1)
CIRCLING	1540-1 361 (400-1)	1640-1 461 (500-1)	1640-1½ 461 (500-1½)	1740-2 561 (600-2)

Straight-in ILS to Runway 27

Straight-in with Glide Slope Inoperative or not used to Runway 27

DA

Visibility (RVR 100's of feet)

Aircraft Approach Category

HAT/HATh

MDA   HAA   Visibility in Statute Miles

All **weather** minimums in parentheses not applicable to Civil Pilots.

Military Pilots refer to appropriate regulations.

COPTER MINIMA ONLY

CATEGORY	COPTER
H-176°	680-½ 363 (400-½)

Copter Approach Direction

Height of MDA/DA Above Landing Area (HAL)

No circling minimums are provided

RNAV (GPS) MINIMA EXAMPLE

CATEGORY	A	B	C	D
LPV DA		1540/24 258 (300-½)		
LNAV/VNAV DA	1600/24	318 (400-½)		1600/40 318 (400-¾)
LNAV MDA	1840/24 558 (600-½)		1840/50 558 (600-1)	1840/60 558 (600-1 ¼)
CIRCLING	1840-1 545 (600-1)		1840-1½ 545 (600-1½)	1860-2 565 (600-2)

NOTE: The 🆆 symbol indicates outages of the WAAS vertical guidance may occur daily at this location due to initial system limitations. WAAS NOTAMS for vertical outages are not provided for this approach. Use LNAV minima for flight planning at these locations, whether as a destination or alternate. For flight operations at these locations, when the WAAS avionics indicate that LNAV/VNAV or LPV service is available, then vertical guidance may be used to complete the approach using the displayed level of service. Should an outage occur during the procedure, reversion to LNAV minima may be required. As the WAAS coverage is expanded, the 🆆 will be removed.

RNAV minimums are dependent on navigation equipment capability, as stated in the applicable AFM, AFMS, or other FAA approved document. See AIM paragraph 5-4-5, AC 90-105 and AC 90-107 for detailed requirements for each line of minima.

AIRCRAFT APPROACH CATEGORIES

Aircraft approach category indicates a grouping of aircraft based on a speed of VREF, if specified, or if VREF not specified, 1.3 VSO at the maximum certificated landing weight. VREF, VSO, and the maximum certificated landing weight are those values as established for the aircraft by the certification authority of the country of registry. Helicopters are Category A aircraft. An aircraft shall fit in only one category. However, if it is necessary to operate at a speed in excess of the upper limit of the speed range for an aircraft's category, the minimums for the category for that speed shall be used. For example, an airplane which fits into Category B, but is circling to land at a speed of 145 knots, shall use the approach Category D minimums. As an additional example, a Category A airplane (or helicopter) which is operating at 130 knots on a straight-in approach shall use the approach Category C minimums. See following category limits:

MANEUVERING TABLE

Approach Category	A	B	C	D	E
Speed (Knots)	0-90	91-120	121-140	141-165	Abv 165

TERMS/LANDING MINIMA DATA

Legend 20. – Instrument Approach Procedures Explanation of Terms.

13122
TERMS/LANDING MINIMA DATA

CIRCLING APPROACH OBSTACLE PROTECTED AIRSPACE

The circling MDA provides vertical clearance from obstacles when conducting a circle-to-land maneuver within the obstacle protected area. Circling approach obstacle protected areas extend laterally and longitudinally from the centerlines and ends of all runways at an airport by the distances shown in the following tables. The areas are technically defined by the tangential connection of arcs drawn at the radius distance shown from each runway end.

STANDARD CIRCLING APPROACH MANEUVERING RADIUS

Circling approach protected areas developed prior to late 2012 used the radius distances shown in the following table, expressed in nautical miles (NM), dependent on aircraft approach category. The approaches using standard circling approach areas can be identified by the absence of the **C** symbol on the circling line of minima.

Circling MDA in feet MSL	Approach Category and Circling Radius (NM)				
	CAT A	CAT B	CAT C	CAT D	CAT E
All Altitudes	1.3	1.5	1.7	2.3	4.5

C EXPANDED CIRCLING APPROACH MANEUVERING AIRSPACE RADIUS

Circling approach protected areas developed after late 2012 use the radius distance shown in the following table, expressed in nautical miles (NM), dependent on aircraft approach category, and the altitude of the circling MDA, which accounts for true airspeed increase with altitude. The approaches using expanded circling approach areas can be identified by the presence of the **C** symbol on the circling line of minima.

Circling MDA in feet MSL	Approach Category and Circling Radius (NM)				
	CAT A	CAT B	CAT C	CAT D	CAT E
1000 or less	1.3	1.7	2.7	3.6	4.5
1001-3000	1.3	1.8	2.8	3.7	4.6
3001-5000	1.3	1.8	2.9	3.8	4.8
5001-7000	1.3	1.9	3.0	4.0	5.0
7001-9000	1.4	2.0	3.2	4.2	5.3
9001 and above	1.4	2.1	3.3	4.4	5.5

Comparable Values of RVR and Visibility

The following table shall be used for converting RVR to ground or flight visibility. For converting RVR values that fall between listed values, use the next higher RVR value; do not interpolate. For example, when converting 1800 RVR, use 2400 RVR with the resultant visibility of ½ mile.

RVR (feet)	Visibility (statute miles)	RVR (feet)	Visibility (statute miles)
1600	¼	4500	⅞
2400	½	5000	1
3200	⅝	6000	1¼
4000	¾		

RADAR MINIMA

	RWY	GS/TCH/RPI	CAT	DA/ MDA-VIS	HAT/ HATh/ HAA	CEIL-VIS	CAT	DA/ MDA-VIS	HAT/ HATh/ HAA	CEIL-VIS
PAR	10	2.5°/42/1000	ABCDE	**195**/16	100	(100-¼)				
	28	2.5°/48/1068	ABCDE	**187**/16	100	(100-¼)			Visibility (RVR 100's of feet)	
ASR	10		ABC	**560**/40	463	(500-¾)	DE	**560**/50	463	(500-1)
	28		AB	**600**/50	513	(600-1)	CDE	**600**/60	513	(600-1¼)
CIR	10		AB	**560**-1¼	463	(500-1¼)	CDE	**560**-1½	463	(500-1½)
	28		AB	**600**-1¼	503	(600-1¼)	CDE	**600**-1½	503	(600-1½)

Visibility in Statute Miles / All minimums in parentheses not applicable to Civil Pilots. Military Pilots refer to appropriate regulations.

Radar Minima:

1. Minima shown are the lowest permitted by established criteria. Pilots should consult applicable directives for their category of aircraft.
2. The circling MDA and weather minima to be used are those for the runway to which the final approach is flown- not the landing runway. In the above RADAR MINIMA example, a category C aircraft flying a radar approach to runway 10, circling to land on runway 28, must use an MDA of 560 feet with weather minima of 500-1½.

NOTE: Military RADAR MINIMA may be shown with communications symbology that indicates emergency frequency monitoring capability by the radar facility as follows:

(E) VHF and UHF emergency frequencies monitored
(V) VHF emergency frequency (121.5) monitored
(U) UHF emergency frequency (243.0) monitored

Additionally, unmonitored frequencies which are available on request from the controlling agency may be annotated with an "x".

A Alternate Minimums not standard. Civil users refer to tabulation. USA/USN/USAF pilots refer to appropriate regulations.

A NA Alternate minimums are Not Authorized due to unmonitored facility or absence of weather reporting service.

▼ Takeoff Minimums not standard and/or Departure Procedures are published. Refer to tabulation.

TERMS/LANDING MINIMA DATA

Legend 21. – Instrument Approach Procedures Explanation of Terms.

13290
GENERAL INFO

GENERAL INFORMATION

This publication is issued every 56 days and includes Standard Instrument Approach Procedures (SIAPS), Standard Instrument Departures (SIDs), Standard Terminal Arrivals (STARs), IFR Takeoff Minimums and (Obstacle) Departure Procedures (ODPs), IFR Alternate Minimums, and Radar Instrument Approach Minimums for use by civil and military aviation. The organization responsible for SIAPs, Radar Minimums, SIDs, STARs and graphic ODPs is identified in parentheses in the top margin of the procedure; e.g., (FAA), (FAA-O), (USA), (USAF), (USN). SIAPS with the (FAA) and (FAA-O) designation are regulated under 14 CFR, Part 97. SIAPs with the (FAA-O) designation have been developed under Other Transaction Agreement (OTA) by private providers and have been certified by the FAA. See 14 CFR, Part 91.175 (a) and the AIM for further details. 14 CFR, Part 91.175 (g) and the Special Notices section of the Airport/Facility Directory contains information on civil operations at military airports.

STANDARD TERMINAL ARRIVALS AND DEPARTURE PROCEDURES

The use of the associated codified STAR/DP and transition identifiers are requested of users when filing flight plans via teletype and are required for users filing flight plans via computer interface. It must be noted that when filing a STAR/DP with a transition, the first three coded characters of the STAR and the last three coded characters of the DP are replaced by the transition code. Examples: ACTON SIX ARRIVAL, file (AQN.AQN6); ACTON SIX ARRIVAL, EDNAS TRANSITION, file (EDNAS.AQN6). FREEHOLD THREE DEPARTURE, file (FREH3.RBV), FREEHOLD THREE DEPARTURE, ELWOOD CITY TRANSITION, file (FREH3.EWC).

RNAV DP and STAR. Effective March 15,2007, these procedures, formerly identified as Type-A and Type-B, will be designated as RNAV 1 in accordance with amended Advisory Circular (AC) and ICAO terminology.

Refer to AC 90-100A U.S. TERMINAL AND EN ROUTE AREA NAVIGATION (RNAV) OPERATIONS and the Aeronautical Information Manual for additional guidance regarding these procedures.

Standard RNAV 1 Procedure Chart Notes

NOTE: RNAV 1
NOTE: DME/DME/IRU or GPS required

Some procedures may require use of GPS and will be identified by a "GPS required" note.

RNAV 1 Procedure Characteristics and Operations
1. Require use of an RNAV system with DME/DME/IRU, and/or GPS inputs.
2. Require use of a CDI, flight director, and/or autopilot, in lateral navigation mode, for flight guidance while operating on RNAV paths (track, course, or direct leg). Other methods providing an equivalent level of performance may be acceptable.
3. RNAV paths may start as low as 500 feet above airport elevation.

GENERAL INFO
13290

Legend 22. – General Information.

14149

GENERAL INFO   ABBREVIATIONS

AAUP	Attention All Users Page
ADF	Automatic Direction Finder
AFIS	Automatic Flight Information Service
ALS	Approach Light System
ALSF	Approach Light System with Sequenced Flashing Lights
AP	Autopilot System
APCH	Approach
APP CON	Approach Control
ARR	Arrival
ASOS	Automated Surface Observing System
ASR/PAR	Published Radar Minimums at this Airport
ATIS	Automatic Terminal Information Service
AUNICOM	Automated UNICOM
AWOS	Automated Weather Observing System
AZ	Azimuth
BC	Back Course
BND	Bound
C	Circling
CAT	Category
CCW	Counter Clockwise
CDI	Course Deviation Indicator
Chan	Channel
CIR	Circling
CLNC DEL	Clearance Delivery
CNF	Computer Navigation Fix
CTAF	Common Traffic Advisory Frequency
CW	Clockwise
DA	Decision Altitude
DER	Departure End of Runway
DH	Decision Height
DME	Distance Measuring Equipment
DTHR	Displaced Threshold
ELEV	Elevation
EMAS	Engineered Material Arresting System
FAF	Final Approach Fix
FD	Flight Director System
FM	Fan Marker
FMS	Flight Management System
GCO	Ground Communications Outlet
GLS	Ground Based Augmentation System Landing System
GPI	Ground Point of Interception
GPS	Global Positioning System
GS	Glide Slope

HAA	Height above Airport
HAL	Height above Landing
HAT	Height above Touchdown
HATh	Height Above Threshold
HGS	Head-up Guidance System
HIRL	High Intensity Runway Lights
HUD	Head-up Display
IAF	Initial Approach Fix
ICAO	International Civil Aviation Organization
IF	Intermediate Fix
IM	Inner Marker
INT	Intersection
LAAS	Local Area Augmentation System
LDA	Localizer Type Directional Aid
Ldg	Landing
LIRL	Low Intensity Runway Lights
LNAV	Lateral Navigation
LOC	Localizer
LP	Localizer Performance
LPV	Localizer Performance with Vertical Guidance
LR	Lead Radial. Provides at least 2 NM (Copter 1 NM) of lead to assist in turning onto the intermediate/final course.
MAA	Maximum Authorized Altitude
MALS	Medium Intensity Approach Light System
MALSR	Medium Intensity Approach Light System with RAIL
MAP	Missed Approach Point
MDA	Minimum Descent Altitude
MIRL	Medium Intensity Runway Lights
MLS	Microwave Landing System
MM	Middle Marker
MRA	Minimum Reception Altitude
N/A	Not Applicable
NA	Not Authorized
NDB	Non-directional Radio Beacon
NFD	National Flight Database
NM	Nautical Mile
NoPT	No Procedure Turn Required (Procedure Turn shall not be executed without ATC clearance)
ODALS	Omnidirectional Approach Light System
ODP	Obstacle Departure Procedure
OM	Outer Marker
PRM	Precision Runway Monitor

GENERAL INFO
14149

Legend 23. – Abbreviations.

14149
GENERAL INFO ABBREVIATIONS

R.	Radial
RA.	Radio Altimeter setting height
RAIL.	Runway Alignment Indicator Lights
RCLS.	Runway Centerline Light System
REIL.	Runway End Identifier Lights
RF.	Radius-to-Fix
RLLS.	Runway Lead-in Light System
RNAV.	Area Navigation
RNP.	Required Navigation Performance
RPI.	Runway Point of Intercept(ion)
RRL.	Runway Remaining Lights
Rwy.	Runway
RVR.	Runway Visual Range
S.	Straight-in
SALS.	Short Approach Light System
SSALR.	Simplified Short Approach Light System with RAIL
SDF.	Simplified Directional Facility
SM.	Statute Mile
SOIA.	Simultaneous Offset Instrument Approach
TAA.	Terminal Arrival Area
TAC.	TACAN
TCH.	Threshold Crossing Height (height in feet Above Ground level)
TDZ.	Touchdown Zone
TDZE.	Touchdown Zone Elevation
TDZ/CL.	Touchdown Zone and Runway Centerline Lighting
TDZL.	Touchdown Zone Lights
THR.	Threshold
THRE.	Threshold Elevation
TODA.	Takeoff Distance Available
TORA.	Takeoff Run Available
TR.	Track
VASI.	Visual Approach Slope Indicator
VCOA.	Visual Climb Over Airport
VDP.	Visual Descent Point
VGSI.	Visual Glide Slope Indicator
VNAV.	Vertical Navigation
WAAS.	Wide Area Augmentation System
WP/WPT.	Waypoint (RNAV)

GENERAL INFO
14149

Legend 23A. – Abbreviations.

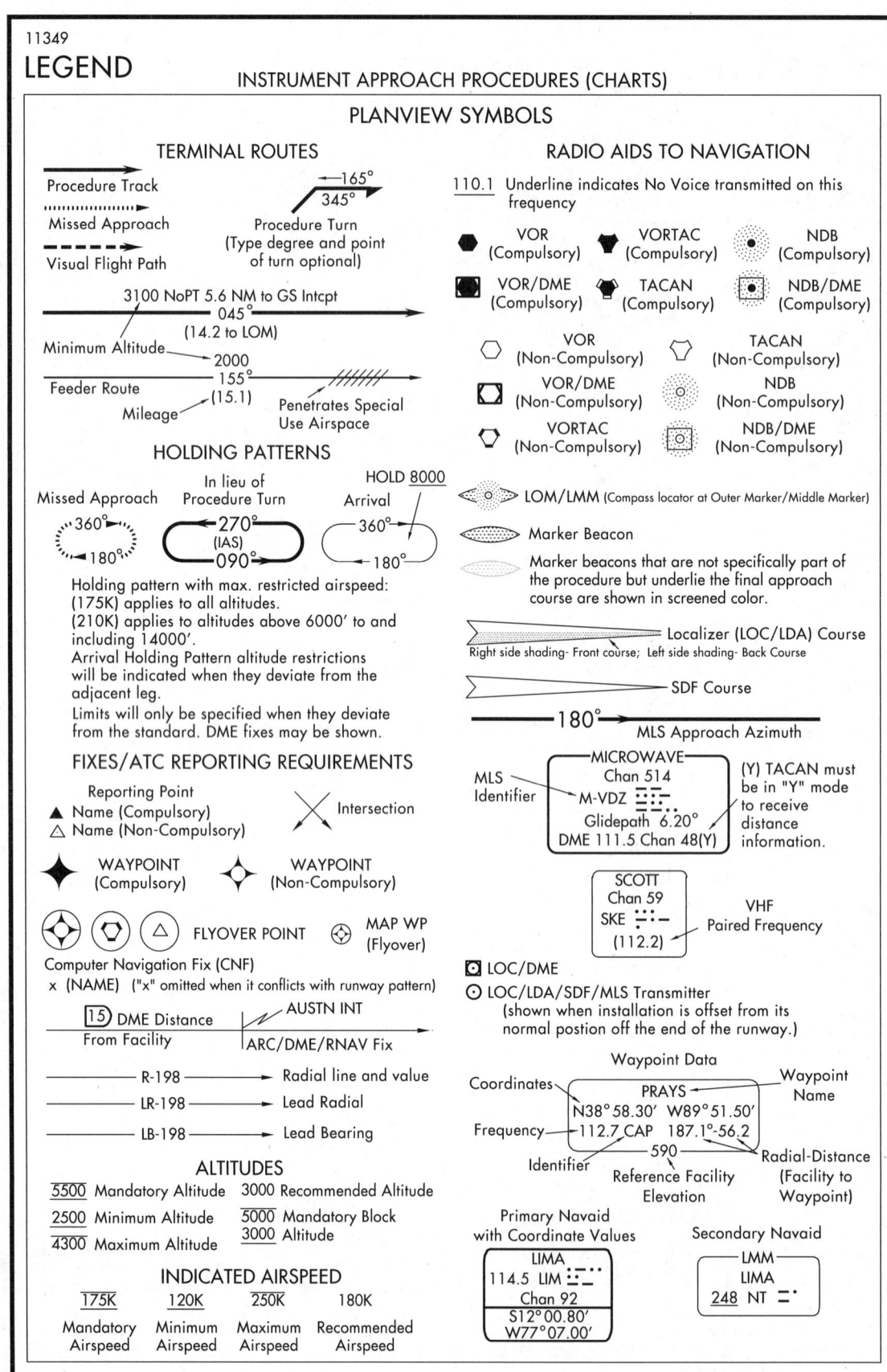

11349
LEGEND
INSTRUMENT APPROACH PROCEDURES (CHARTS)

PLANVIEW SYMBOLS

TERMINAL ROUTES

Procedure Track

Missed Approach

Visual Flight Path

Procedure Turn
(Type degree and point
of turn optional)
←165°
345°

3100 NoPT 5.6 NM to GS Intcpt
045°
(14.2 to LOM)
Minimum Altitude
2000
155°
(15.1)
Feeder Route
Mileage
Penetrates Special
Use Airspace

HOLDING PATTERNS

Missed Approach
360°
180°

In lieu of
Procedure Turn
270°
(IAS)
090°

HOLD 8000
Arrival
360°
180°

Holding pattern with max. restricted airspeed:
(175K) applies to all altitudes.
(210K) applies to altitudes above 6000' to and
including 14000'.
Arrival Holding Pattern altitude restrictions
will be indicated when they deviate from the
adjacent leg.
Limits will only be specified when they deviate
from the standard. DME fixes may be shown.

FIXES/ATC REPORTING REQUIREMENTS

Reporting Point
▲ Name (Compulsory)
△ Name (Non-Compulsory)

✕ Intersection

◆ WAYPOINT
(Compulsory)

◆ WAYPOINT
(Non-Compulsory)

FLYOVER POINT

MAP WP
(Flyover)

Computer Navigation Fix (CNF)
x (NAME) ("x" omitted when it conflicts with runway pattern)

15 DME Distance
From Facility

AUSTN INT
ARC/DME/RNAV Fix

———— R-198 ————→ Radial line and value

———— LR-198 ————→ Lead Radial

———— LB-198 ————→ Lead Bearing

ALTITUDES

5500 Mandatory Altitude   3000 Recommended Altitude

2500 Minimum Altitude   5000 Mandatory Block
                          3000 Altitude
4300 Maximum Altitude

INDICATED AIRSPEED

175K   120K   250K   180K

Mandatory   Minimum   Maximum   Recommended
Airspeed   Airspeed   Airspeed   Airspeed

RADIO AIDS TO NAVIGATION

110.1 Underline indicates No Voice transmitted on this
      frequency

VOR
(Compulsory)

VORTAC
(Compulsory)

NDB
(Compulsory)

VOR/DME
(Compulsory)

TACAN
(Compulsory)

NDB/DME
(Compulsory)

VOR
(Non-Compulsory)

TACAN
(Non-Compulsory)

VOR/DME
(Non-Compulsory)

NDB
(Non-Compulsory)

VORTAC
(Non-Compulsory)

NDB/DME
(Non-Compulsory)

LOM/LMM (Compass locator at Outer Marker/Middle Marker)

Marker Beacon

Marker beacons that are not specifically part of
the procedure but underlie the final approach
course are shown in screened color.

Localizer (LOC/LDA) Course
Right side shading- Front course; Left side shading- Back Course

SDF Course

———— 180° ————→
MLS Approach Azimuth

MICROWAVE
Chan 514
MLS
Identifier   M-VDZ
Glidepath 6.20°
DME 111.5 Chan 48(Y)

(Y) TACAN must
be in "Y" mode
to receive
distance
information.

SCOTT
Chan 59
SKE
(112.2)

VHF
Paired Frequency

◙ LOC/DME

⊙ LOC/LDA/SDF/MLS Transmitter
(shown when installation is offset from its
normal postion off the end of the runway.)

Waypoint Data
Coordinates
PRAYS
N38° 58.30' W89° 51.50'
Frequency   112.7 CAP   187.1°-56.2
590
Identifier
Reference Facility
Elevation

Waypoint
Name

Radial-Distance
(Facility to
Waypoint)

Primary Navaid
with Coordinate Values
LIMA
114.5 LIM
Chan 92
S12°00.80'
W77°07.00'

Secondary Navaid
LMM
LIMA
248 NT

LEGEND

Legend 24. – Instrument Approach Procedures (Symbols).

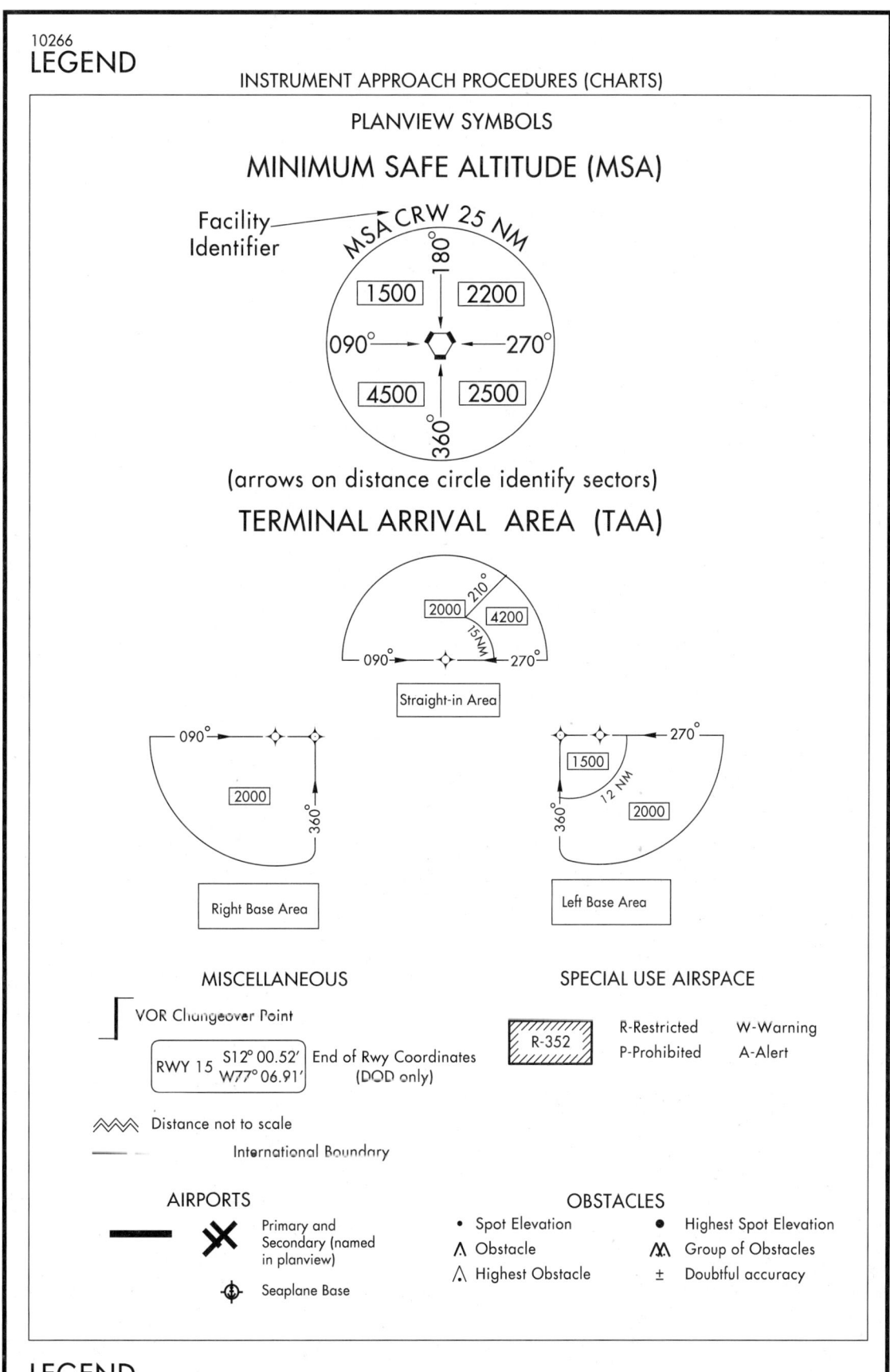

Legend 25. – Instrument Approach Procedures (Symbols).

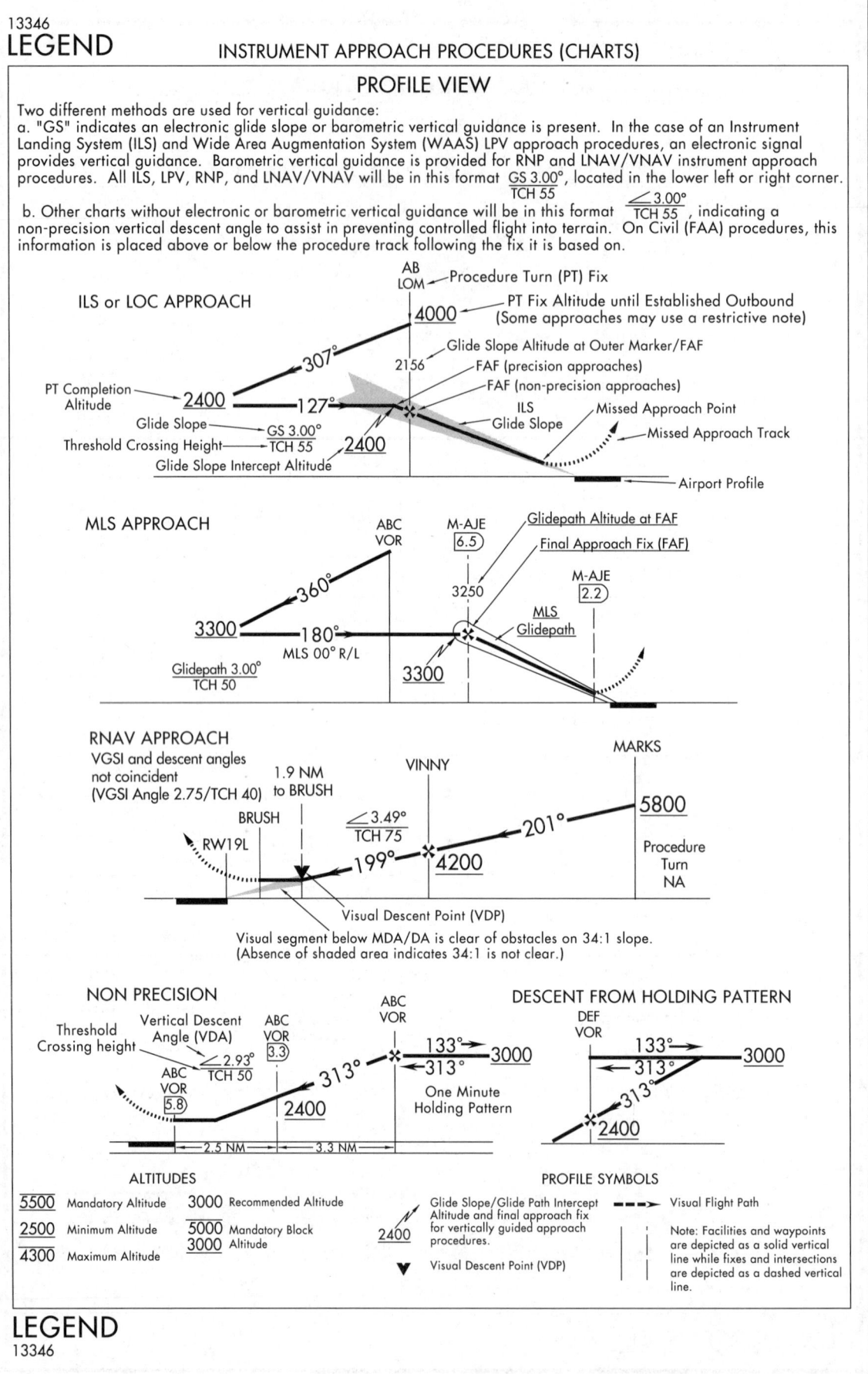

CLIMB/DESCENT TABLE 10042

INSTRUMENT TAKEOFF OR APPROACH PROCEDURE CHARTS RATE OF CLIMB/DESCENT TABLE

(ft. per min)

A rate of climb/descent table is provided for use in planning and executing climbs or descents under known or approximate ground speed conditions. It will be especially useful for approaches when the localizer only is used for course guidance. A best speed, power, altitude combination can be programmed which will result in a stable glide rate and altitude favorable for executing a landing if minimums exist upon breakout. Care should always be exercised so that minimum descent altitude and missed approach point are not exceeded.

	CLIMB/ DESCENT ANGLE (degrees and tenths)	ft/NM	GROUND SPEED (knots)										
			60	90	120	150	180	210	240	270	300	330	360
	2.0	210	210	320	425	530	635	743	850	955	1060	1165	1275
	2.5	265	265	400	530	665	795	930	1060	1195	1325	1460	1590
VERTICAL PATH ANGLE	2.7	287	287	430	574	717	860	1003	1147	1290	1433	1576	1720
	2.8	297	297	446	595	743	892	1041	1189	1338	1486	1635	1783
	2.9	308	308	462	616	770	924	1078	1232	1386	1539	1693	1847
	3.0	318	318	478	637	797	956	1115	1274	1433	1593	1752	1911
	3.1	329	329	494	659	823	988	1152	1317	1481	1646	1810	1975
	3.2	340	340	510	680	850	1020	1189	1359	1529	1699	1869	2039
	3.3	350	350	526	701	876	1052	1227	1402	1577	1752	1927	2103
	3.4	361	361	542	722	903	1083	1264	1444	1625	1805	1986	2166
	3.5	370	370	555	745	930	1115	1300	1485	1670	1860	2045	2230
	4.0	425	425	640	850	1065	1275	1490	1700	1915	2125	2340	2550
	4.5	480	480	715	955	1195	1435	1675	1915	2150	2390	2630	2870
	5.0	530	530	795	1065	1330	1595	1860	2125	2390	2660	2925	3190
	5.5	585	585	880	1170	1465	1755	2050	2340	2635	2925	3220	3510
	6.0	640	640	960	1275	1595	1915	2235	2555	2875	3195	3510	3830
	6.5	690	690	1040	1385	1730	2075	2425	2770	3115	3460	3805	4155
	7.0	745	745	1120	1490	1865	2240	2610	2985	3355	3730	4105	4475
	7.5	800	800	1200	1600	2000	2400	2800	3200	3600	4000	4400	4800
	8.0	855	855	1280	1710	2135	2560	2990	3415	3845	4270	4695	5125
	8.5	910	910	1360	1815	2270	2725	3180	3630	4085	4540	4995	5450
	9.0	960	960	1445	1925	2405	2885	3370	3850	4330	4810	5295	5775
	9.5	1015	1015	1525	2035	2540	3050	3560	4065	4575	5085	5590	6100
	10.0	1070	1070	1605	2145	2680	3215	3750	4285	4820	5355	5890	6430

CLIMB/DESCENT TABLE 10042

Legend 27. – Instrument Takeoff or Approach Procedure Charts, Rate-of-Climb/Descent Table.

12320
LEGEND

LEGEND
STANDARD TERMINAL ARRIVAL (STAR) CHARTS
DEPARTURE PROCEDURE (DP) CHARTS
Applies to both STAR and DP Charts unless otherwise noted.

RADIO AIDS TO NAVIGATION

VOR (Compulsory)

VORTAC (Compulsory)

NDB (Compulsory)

VOR/DME (Compulsory)

TACAN (Compulsory)

NDB/DME (Compulsory)

VOR (Non-Compulsory)

TACAN (Non-Compulsory)

VOR/DME (Non-Compulsory)

NDB (Non-Compulsory)

VORTAC (Non-Compulsory)

NDB/DME (Non-Compulsory)

LMM, LOM (Compass locator)

⊙ LOC   ▣ LOC/DME
(shown when installation is offset from its normal position off the end of the runway.) (DP)

Marker Beacon

Localizer Course

SDF Course

(T) indicates frequency protection range (STAR)

(Y) TACAN must be placed in "Y" mode to receive distance information

Frequency   Identifier

ORLANDO
112.25 (T) ORL ·—· · ·-··
Chan 59 (Y)
N28°32.56' - W81°20.10'
L-19, H-5

Geographic Position

DME or TACAN Channel

Underline indicates no voice transmitted on this frequency

Enroute Chart Reference

Coordinates   Waypoint Name

PRAYS
N38°58.30' W89°51.50'
112.7 CAP 187.1°-56.2
590

Frequency

Identifier

Reference Facility Elevation

Radial-Distance (Facility to Waypoint)

FIXES/ATC REPORTING REQUIREMENTS

Reporting Points
N00°00.00'
W00°00.00'

75 → DME Mileage (when not obvious)

▲ Fix-Compulsory and
△ Non-Compulsory Position Report

→| DME fix

◆ WAYPOINT (Compulsory)

◇ WAYPOINT (Non-Compulsory)

FLYOVER POINT

X Computer Navigation Fix (CNF)
N00°00.00'
W00°00.00'

ROUTES

4500 MEA-Minimum Enroute Altitude
*3500 MOCA-Minimum Obstruction Clearance Altitude
← 270° Departure Route - Arrival Route
(65) Mileage between Radio Aids, Reporting Points, and Route Breaks

Transition Route

R-275 Radial line and value

••••••••••• Lost Communications Track

V12 J80 Airway/Jet Route Identification

DP Holding Pattern   STAR Holding Pattern

(IAS)   (IAS)

Holding pattern with max. restricted airspeed (175K) applies to all altitudes
(210K) applies to altitudes above 6000' to and including 14000'

SPECIAL USE AIRSPACE

R-352   R-Restricted   W-Warning
P-Prohibited   A-Alert
MOA-Military Operations Area

ALTITUDES

5500   2300   4800
Mandatory Altitude (Cross at)   Minimum Altitude (Cross at or above)   Maximum Altitude (Cross at or below)

15000
12000
Block Altitude

⊣ Altitude change at other than Radio Aids (STAR)

ATC CROSSING ALTITUDES (DP)

ATC altitude restriction

5500 (ATC)   2300 (ATC)   4800 (ATC)
4300   1700   3000
Minimum required altitude

INDICATED AIRSPEED

175K   120K   250K
Mandatory Airspeed   Minimum Airspeed   Maximum Airspeed

AIRPORTS

(DP) ▭

◇ Civil   ◉ Military   ⊕ Joint Civil-Military

MISCELLANEOUS

Changeover Point

⋀⋀⋀ Distance not to scale (DP)

— — — International Boundary (DP)

▼ Takeoff Minimums and (Obstacle) Departure Procedures entry published. (DP)

LEGEND

Legend 28. — Standard Arrival/Departure Charts.

13010

LEGEND

INSTRUMENT APPROACH PROCEDURES (CHARTS)

AIRPORT DIAGRAM/AIRPORT SKETCH

Runways

Hard Surface

Other Than Hard Surface

Stopways, Taxiways, Parking Areas, Water Runways

Displaced Threshold

Closed Runway

Closed Taxiway

Under Construction

Metal Surface

ARRESTING GEAR: Specific arresting gear systems; e.g., BAK12, MA-1A etc., shown on airport diagrams, not applicable to Civil Pilots. Military Pilots refer to appropriate DOD publications.

uni-directional   bi-directional   Jet Barrier

ARRESTING SYSTEM

REFERENCE FEATURES

Buildings...■
24-Hour Self-Serve Fuel ##......................
Tanks..●
Obstructions...⋀
Airport Beacon #.....................................☆
Runway
Radar Reflectors.....................................
Hot Spot ....○
Control Tower #...................................TWR

When Control Tower and Rotating Beacon are co-located, Beacon symbol will be used and further identified as TWR.

A fuel symbol is shown to indicate 24-hour self-serve fuel available, see appropriate A/FD, Alaska or Pacific Supplement for information.

Runway length depicted is the physical length of the runway (end-to-end, including displaced thresholds if any) but excluding areas designated as stopways.

A **D** symbol is shown to indicate runway declared distance information available, see appropriate A/FD, Alaska or Pacific Supplement for distance information.

Runway Weight Bearing Capacity/or PCN Pavement Classification Number is shown as a codified expression. Refer to the appropriate Supplement/Directory for applicable codes e.g., RWY 14-32 PCN 80 F/D/X/U S-75, D-185, 2S-175, 2D-325

Helicopter Alighting Areas   (H)   ⊞   H   ⚠   ⊞

Negative Symbols used to identify Copter Procedures landing point...............................●   +   H   ⚠   +

Runway Threshold elevation............THRE 123
Runway TDZ elevation....................TDZE 123

←—0.3% DOWN
Runway Slope............................0.8% UP —→
   (shown when runway slope is greater than
      or equal to 0.3%)
NOTE:
Runway Slope measured to midpoint on runways 8000 feet or longer.

🔲 U.S. Navy Optical Landing System (OLS) "OLS" location is shown because of its height of approximately 7 feet and proximity to edge of runway may create an obstruction for some types of aircraft.

Approach light symbols are shown in the Flight Information Handbook.

Airport diagram scales are variable.

True/magnetic North orientation may vary from diagram to diagram

Coordinate values are shown in 1 or ½ minute increments. They are further broken down into 6 second ticks, within each 1 minute increments.

Positional accuracy within ±600 feet unless otherwise noted on the chart.

NOTE:
All new and revised airport diagrams are shown referenced to the World Geodetic System (WGS) (noted on appropriate diagram), and may not be compatible with local coordinates published in FLIP. (Foreign Only)

HS 1   BAK-12   Runway Slope   FIELD ELEV 174   Displaced Threshold   Runway Identification   EMAS

0.7% UP —→   023.2°   1000 X 200

20   ELEV 164   9000 X 200   2

Runway End Elevation   Runway Dimensions (in feet)   Runway Heading (Magnetic)   Movement Area Dimensions (in feet)

SCOPE

Airport diagrams are specifically designed to assist in the movement of ground traffic at locations with complex runway/taxiway configurations. Airport diagrams are not intended to be used for approach and landing or departure operations. For revisions to Airport Diagrams: Consult FAA Order 7910.4.

LEGEND

Legend 29. – Airport Diagram.

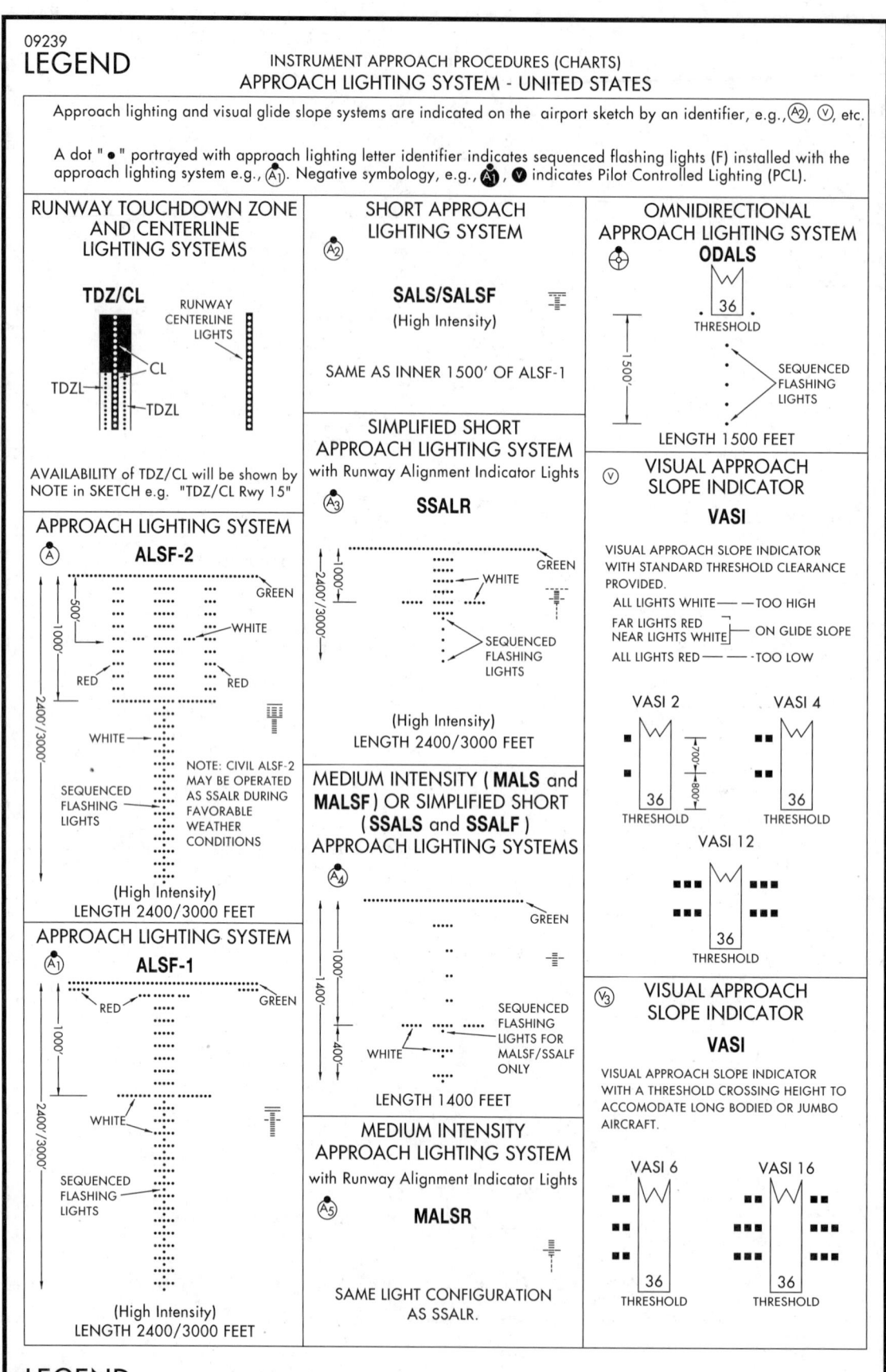

Legend 30. – Approach Lighting Systems.

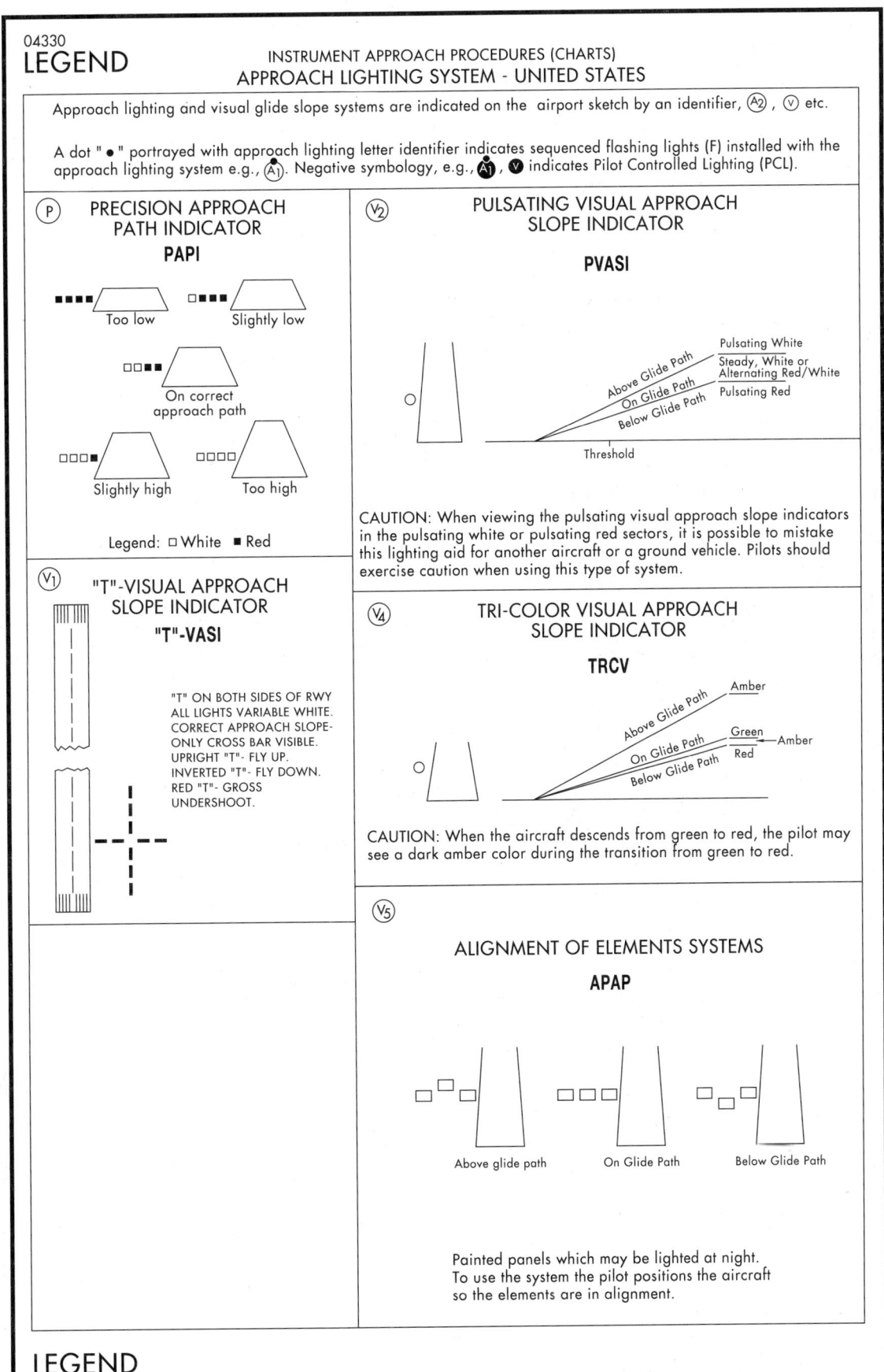

Legend 31. – Approach Lighting System.

13122
INOP COMPONENTS

INOPERATIVE COMPONENTS OR VISUAL AIDS TABLE

Landing minimums published on instrument approach procedure charts are based upon full operation of all components and visual aids associated with the particular instrument approach chart being used. Higher minimums are required with inoperative components or visual aids as indicated below. If more than one component is inoperative, each minimum is raised to the highest minimum required by any single component that is inoperative. ILS glide slope inoperative minimums are published on the instrument approach charts as localizer minimums. This table may be amended by notes on the approach chart. Such notes apply only to the particular approach category(ies) as stated. See legend page for description of components indicated below.

(1) ILS, MLS, PAR and RNAV (LPV line of minima)

Inoperative Component or Aid	Approach Category	Increase Visibility
ALSF 1 & 2, MALSR, & SSALR	ABCD	¼ mile

(2) ILS with visibility minimum of 1,800 RVR

ALSF 1 & 2, MALSR, & SSALR	ABCD	To 4000 RVR
TDZL RCLS	ABCD	To 2400 RVR*
RVR	ABCD	To ½ mile

*1800 RVR authorized with the use of FD or AP or HUD to DA.

(3) VOR, VOR/DME, TACAN, LOC, LOC/DME, LDA, LDA/DME, SDF, SDF/DME, GPS, ASR and RNAV (LNAV/VNAV, LP, LNAV lines of minima)

Inoperative Visual Aid	Approach Category	Increase Visibility
ALSF 1 & 2, MALSR, & SSALR	ABCD	½ mile
SSALS, MALS, & ODALS	ABC	¼ mile

(4) NDB

ALSF 1 & 2, MALSR, & SSALR	C	½ mile
	ABD	¼ mile
MALS, SSALS, ODALS	ABC	¼ mile

INOP COMPONENTS

Legend 32. – Inoperative Components or Visual Aids Table.

QUESTIONS AND ANSWER EXPLANATIONS: All of the instrument rating knowledge test questions chosen by the FAA for release as well as additional questions selected by Gleim relating to the material in the previous outlines are provided on the following pages. These questions have been organized into the same subunits as the outlines. To the immediate right of each question are the correct answer and answer explanations. You should cover these answers and answer explanations while responding to the questions. Refer to the general discussion in the Introduction on how to take the FAA knowledge test.

Remember that the questions from the FAA knowledge test bank have been reordered by topic and organized into a meaningful sequence. Also, the first line of the answer explanation gives the citation of the authoritative source for the answer.

QUESTIONS

6.1 Contact and Visual Approaches

1. What conditions are necessary before ATC can authorize a visual approach?

A. You must have the preceding aircraft in sight, and be able to remain in VFR weather conditions.

B. You must have the airport in sight or the preceding aircraft in sight, and be able to proceed to, and land in IFR conditions.

C. You must have the airport in sight or a preceding aircraft to be followed, and be able to proceed to the airport in VFR conditions.

Answer (C) is correct. (AIM Para 5-4-23)
 DISCUSSION: ATC may authorize airplanes to conduct visual approaches to an airport or to follow another airplane when flight to and landing at the airport can be accomplished in VFR weather. You must have the airport or preceding aircraft in sight before the clearance is issued.
 Answer (A) is incorrect. You can have the airport in sight instead of having the preceding aircraft in sight. **Answer (B) is incorrect.** You must be able to land in VFR, not IFR, conditions.

2. What are the main differences between a visual approach and a contact approach?

A. The pilot must request a contact approach; the pilot may be assigned a visual approach and higher weather minimums must exist.

B. The pilot must request a visual approach and report having the field in sight; ATC may assign a contact approach if VFR conditions exist.

C. Anytime the pilot reports the field in sight, ATC may clear the pilot for a contact approach; for a visual approach, the pilot must advise that the approach can be made under VFR conditions.

Answer (A) is correct. (AIM Para 5-4-23)
 DISCUSSION: Contact approaches can be issued only upon pilot request, but visual approaches may be assigned by ATC. Visual approaches require VFR conditions. Contact approaches require 1 SM flight visibility and the ability to remain clear of clouds.
 Answer (B) is incorrect. ATC may assign visual approaches without pilot request, and ATC cannot issue a contact approach clearance without the pilot's request. **Answer (C) is incorrect.** ATC cannot issue a contact approach clearance without the pilot's request.

3. A contact approach is an approach procedure that may be used

A. in lieu of conducting a SIAP.

B. if assigned by ATC and will facilitate the approach.

C. in lieu of a visual approach.

Answer (A) is correct. (AIM Para 5-4-25)
 DISCUSSION: A contact approach may be requested by the pilot if there is 1 SM flight visibility and the pilot can operate clear of clouds. It is an alternative to a standard instrument approach procedure (SIAP).
 Answer (B) is incorrect. ATC cannot assign a contact approach; pilots must request them. **Answer (C) is incorrect.** Using a contact approach is not necessary if a visual approach is possible.

4. You arrive at your destination airport on an IFR flight plan. Which is a prerequisite condition for the performance of a contact approach?

A. A ground visibility of at least 2 SM.

B. A flight visibility of at least 1/2 NM.

C. Clear of clouds and at least 1 SM flight visibility.

Answer (C) is correct. (AIM Para 5-4-25)
 DISCUSSION: A contact approach may be requested by the pilot if there is 1 SM flight visibility and the pilot can operate clear of clouds.
 Answer (A) is incorrect. The flight, not ground, visibility must be at least 1 SM, not 2 SM. **Answer (B) is incorrect.** The flight visibility must be at least 1 SM, not 1/2 NM.

5. Flying clear of clouds on an instrument flight plan, what are the requirements for a contact approach to an airport that has an approved IAP?

    A. The controller must determine that the pilot can see the airport at the altitude flown and can remain clear of clouds.

    B. The controller must have determined that the visibility was at least 1 mile and be reasonably sure the pilot can remain clear of clouds.

    C. The pilot must request the approach, have at least 1 mile visibility, and be reasonably sure of remaining clear of clouds.

Answer (C) is correct. *(AIM Para 5-4-24)*
    DISCUSSION: Pilots operating in accordance with an IFR flight plan, provided they are clear of clouds, who have at least 1 SM flight visibility, and who can reasonably expect to continue to the destination airport in those conditions may request ATC authorization for a contact approach.
    Answer (A) is incorrect. The pilot, not the controller, must determine whether (s)he can reasonably expect to continue to the airport in at least 1 SM flight visibility and clear of clouds. **Answer (B) is incorrect.** The pilot must request a contact approach; ATC does not solicit or assign contact approaches.

6. When is radar service terminated during a visual approach?

    A. Automatically when ATC instructs the pilot to contact the tower.

    B. Immediately upon acceptance of the approach by the pilot.

    C. When ATC advises, "Radar service terminated; resume own navigation."

Answer (A) is correct. *(AIM Para 5-4-23)*
    DISCUSSION: During a visual approach, radar service is automatically terminated without advising the pilot once the pilot has been instructed to contact the tower or change to advisory frequency.
    Answer (B) is incorrect. Approach clearance is given well before radar service is terminated. **Answer (C) is incorrect.** "Resume own navigation" is generally an en route instruction and is not applicable to approaches.

7. When may you obtain a contact approach?

    A. ATC may assign a contact approach if VFR conditions exist or you report the runway in sight and are clear of clouds.

    B. ATC may assign a contact approach if you are below the clouds and the visibility is at least 1 mile.

    C. ATC will assign a contact approach only upon request if the reported visibility is at least 1 mile.

Answer (C) is correct. *(AIM Para 5-4-25)*
    DISCUSSION: ATC will assign a contact approach only upon pilot request if the pilot is operating clear of clouds, has at least 1 SM flight visibility, and expects to reach the airport and land in those conditions.
    Answer (A) is incorrect. ATC may assign a visual, not a contact, approach if VFR weather conditions exist. ATC may not assign a contact approach. **Answer (B) is incorrect.** ATC may not assign a contact approach. The pilot must request one.

6.2 LDA and SDF Approaches

8. What are the main differences between the SDF and the localizer of an ILS?

    A. The usable off-course indications are limited to 35° for the localizer and up to 90° for the SDF.

    B. The SDF course may not be aligned with the runway and the course may be wider.

    C. The course width for the localizer will always be 5° while the SDF course will be between 6° and 12°.

Answer (B) is correct. *(AIM Para 1-1-10)*
    DISCUSSION: The approach techniques and procedures used in performance of an SDF instrument approach are essentially identical to those employed to execute a standard localizer approach, except that the SDF course may not be aligned with the runway and the course may be wider, resulting in less precision.
    Answer (A) is incorrect. The off-course indications are limited to 35° for both types of approach. **Answer (C) is incorrect.** The course width for the localizer is usually between 3° and 6°, and SDF is either 6° or 12° (not between).

9. How wide is an SDF course?

    A. Either 3° or 6°.

    B. Varies from 5° to 10°.

    C. Either 6° or 12°.

Answer (C) is correct. *(AIM Para 1-1-10)*
    DISCUSSION: The simplified directional facility (SDF) signal is fixed at either 6° or 12° as necessary to provide maximum flyability and optimum course quality.
    Answer (A) is incorrect. Either 3° or 6° is half the course width of an SDF. **Answer (B) is incorrect.** A course 5° to 10° wide does not relate to ILS, LDA, or SDF.

6.3 Precision Runway Monitor (PRM)

10. A Precision Runway Monitor (PRM) approach requires

A. simultaneously monitoring two frequencies.

B. special training to monitor two ILS receivers simultaneously.

C. tracking performance parameters at the decision point.

Answer (A) is correct. (AIM Para 5-4-16)
   DISCUSSION: Simultaneous monitoring of two frequencies is required for flying a PRM approach. To avoid blocked transmissions, each runway has two frequencies: primary and PRM. The tower controller transmits on both frequencies. The monitor controller's transmissions, if needed, override both frequencies. Pilots ONLY transmit on the tower controller's frequency, but listen to both frequencies. Select the PRM frequency audio only when instructed by ATC to contact the tower.
   Answer (B) is incorrect. Special training to monitor two ILS receivers simultaneously is not listed as a requirement of a PRM approach. Per the *AIM*, simultaneous PRM approaches must meet all of the following requirements: pilot training, PRM in the approach title, NTZ monitoring utilizing a final monitor aid, publication on an Attention All Users Page (AAUP), and use of a secondary PRM communication frequency. **Answer (C) is incorrect.** There is no tracking of a "decision point" in an ILS PRM approach. Tracking is done with high-update radar with 1-second or better update time. Tracking is done within the normal operating zones and non-transgression zones of the approach all the way down to the MAP.

11. Precision Runway Monitoring (PRM) is

A. an airborne RADAR system for monitoring approaches to two runways.

B. a RADAR system for monitoring approaches to closely spaced parallel runways.

C. a high update rate RADAR system for monitoring multiple aircraft ILS approaches to a single runway.

Answer (B) is correct. (FAA-H-8083-16B Chap 1)
   DISCUSSION: PRM is a RADAR system, which has a high update rate and is able to monitor approaches to closely spaced parallel runways.
   Answer (A) is incorrect. PRM is not an airborne RADAR system; it is a ground-based RADAR system, which has a high update rate and is able to monitor approaches to closely spaced parallel runways. **Answer (C) is incorrect.** PRM is not for monitoring multiple aircraft ILS approaches to a single runway. PRM is a RADAR system, which has a high update rate and is able to monitor approaches to two closely spaced parallel runways.

6.4 Runway Visual Range (RVR)

12. If the RVR equipment is inoperative for an IAP that requires a visibility of 2,400 RVR, how should the pilot expect the visibility requirement to be reported in lieu of the published RVR?

A. As a slant range visibility of 2,400 feet.

B. As an RVR of 2,400 feet.

C. As a ground visibility of 1/2 SM.

Answer (C) is correct. (14 CFR 91.175)
   DISCUSSION: Refer to Legend 21 on page 197 for a chart of RVR/visibility comparable values. An RVR of 2,400 ft. may be converted to 1/2 SM visibility when the RVR is not reported.
   Answer (A) is incorrect. RVR is a horizontal, not slant range, visibility. **Answer (B) is incorrect.** RVR cannot be reported if the RVR equipment is inoperative. It must be converted to ground visibility.

13. If the RVR is not reported, what meteorological value should you substitute for 2400 RVR?

A. A ground visibility of 1/2 NM.

B. A slant range visibility of 2,400 feet for the final approach segment of the published approach procedure.

C. A ground visibility of 1/2 SM.

Answer (C) is correct. (14 CFR 91.175)
   DISCUSSION: Refer to Legend 21 on page 197 for a chart of RVR/visibility comparable values. An RVR of 2,400 ft. may be converted to 1/2 SM visibility when the RVR is not reported.
   Answer (A) is incorrect. RVR is converted into statute, not nautical, miles. **Answer (B) is incorrect.** When RVR is not reported, ground visibility, not slant range visibility on approach, is substituted.

14. (Refer to Figure 178 on page 233 and Legend 21 below.) You have been cleared for the Straight-in Localizer approach for runway 13L at DAL. Prior to reaching the final approach fix, ATC advises you the RVR is not available and that the visibility is 1/2 SM. You may

A. convert the RVR to statute miles and continue the approach.

B. convert the RVR to statute miles and use the next higher minimums.

C. request the ILS approach and disregard the RVR value.

Answer (A) is correct. *(14 CFR 91.175)*

DISCUSSION: When the RVR is not available, RVR values may be derived by converting the reported visibility.

Answer (B) is incorrect. The next higher set of minimums should be used if the converted RVR values fall between listed values. Never interpolate; always select the next higher minimums in this scenario. **Answer (C) is incorrect.** You may continue with the original approved and briefed instrument approach with the RVR values replaced by the reported visibility.

13122

TERMS/LANDING MINIMA DATA

CIRCLING APPROACH OBSTACLE PROTECTED AIRSPACE

The circling MDA provides vertical clearance from obstacles when conducting a circle-to-land maneuver within the obstacle protected area. Circling approach obstacle protected areas extend laterally and longitudinally from the centerlines and ends of all runways at an airport by the distances shown in the following tables. The areas are technically defined by the tangential connection of arcs drawn at the radius distance shown from each runway end.

STANDARD CIRCLING APPROACH MANEUVERING RADIUS

Circling approach protected areas developed prior to late 2012 used the radius distances shown in the following table, expressed in nautical miles (NM), dependent on aircraft approach category. The approaches using standard circling approach areas can be identified by the absence of the C symbol on the circling line of minima.

Circling MDA in feet MSL	Approach Category and Circling Radius (NM)				
	CAT A	CAT B	CAT C	CAT D	CAT E
All Altitudes	1.3	1.5	1.7	2.3	4.5

C EXPANDED CIRCLING APPROACH MANEUVERING AIRSPACE RADIUS

Circling approach protected areas developed after late 2012 use the radius distance shown in the following table, expressed in nautical miles (NM), dependent on aircraft approach category, and the altitude of the circling MDA, which accounts for true airspeed increase with altitude. The approaches using expanded circling approach areas can be identified by the presence of the C symbol on the circling line of minima.

Circling MDA in feet MSL	Approach Category and Circling Radius (NM)				
	CAT A	CAT B	CAT C	CAT D	CAT E
1000 or less	1.3	1.7	2.7	3.6	4.5
1001-3000	1.3	1.8	2.8	3.7	4.6
3001-5000	1.3	1.8	2.9	3.8	4.8
5001-7000	1.3	1.9	3.0	4.0	5.0
7001-9000	1.4	2.0	3.2	4.2	5.3
9001 and above	1.4	2.1	3.3	4.4	5.5

Comparable Values of RVR and Visibility

The following table shall be used for converting RVR to ground or flight visibility. For converting RVR values that fall between listed values, use the next higher RVR value; do not interpolate. For example, when converting 1800 RVR, use 2400 RVR with the resultant visibility of ½ mile.

RVR (feet)	Visibility (statute miles)	RVR (feet)	Visibility (statute miles)
1600	¼	4500	⅞
2400	½	5000	1
3200	⅝	6000	1¼
4000	¾		

RADAR MINIMA

	RWY	GS/TCH/RPI	CAT	DA/ MDA-VIS	HAT/ HATh/ HAA	CEIL-VIS	CAT	DA/ MDA-VIS	HAT/ HATh/ HAA	CEIL-VIS
PAR	10	2.5°/42/1000	ABCDE	**195**/16	100	(100-¼)				
	28	2.5°/48/1068	ABCDE	**187**/16	100	(100-¼)				
ASR	10		ABC	**560**/40	463	(500-¾)	DE	**560**/50	463	(500-1)
	28		AB	**600**/50	513	(600-1)	CDE	**600**/60	513	(600-1¼)
CIR	10		AB	**560**-1¼	463	(500-1¼)	CDE	**560**-1½	463	(500-1½)
	28		AB	**600**-1¼	503	(600-1¼)	CDE	**600**-1½	503	(600-1½)

Visibility (RVR 100's of feet)

Visibility in Statute Miles

All minimums in parentheses not applicable to Civil Pilots. Military Pilots refer to appropriate regulations.

Radar Minima:

1. Minima shown are the lowest permitted by established criteria. Pilots should consult applicable directives for their category of aircraft.
2. The circling MDA and weather minima to be used are those for the runway to which the final approach is flown- not the landing runway. In the above RADAR MINIMA example, a category C aircraft flying a radar approach to runway 10, circling to land on runway 28, must use an MDA of 560 feet with weather minima of 500-1½.

NOTE: Military RADAR MINIMA may be shown with communications symbology that indicates emergency frequency monitoring capability by the radar facility as follows:

(E) VHF and UHF emergency frequencies monitored
(V) VHF emergency frequency (121.5) monitored
(U) UHF emergency frequency (243.0) monitored

Additionally, unmonitored frequencies which are available on request from the controlling agency may be annotated with an "x".

▲ Alternate Minimums not standard. Civil users refer to tabulation. USA/USN/USAF pilots refer to appropriate regulations.

▲ NA Alternate minimums are Not Authorized due to unmonitored facility or absence of weather reporting service.

▼ Takeoff Minimums not standard and/or Departure Procedures are published. Refer to tabulation.

TERMS/LANDING MINIMA DATA

Legend 21. – Instrument Approach Procedures Explanation of Terms.

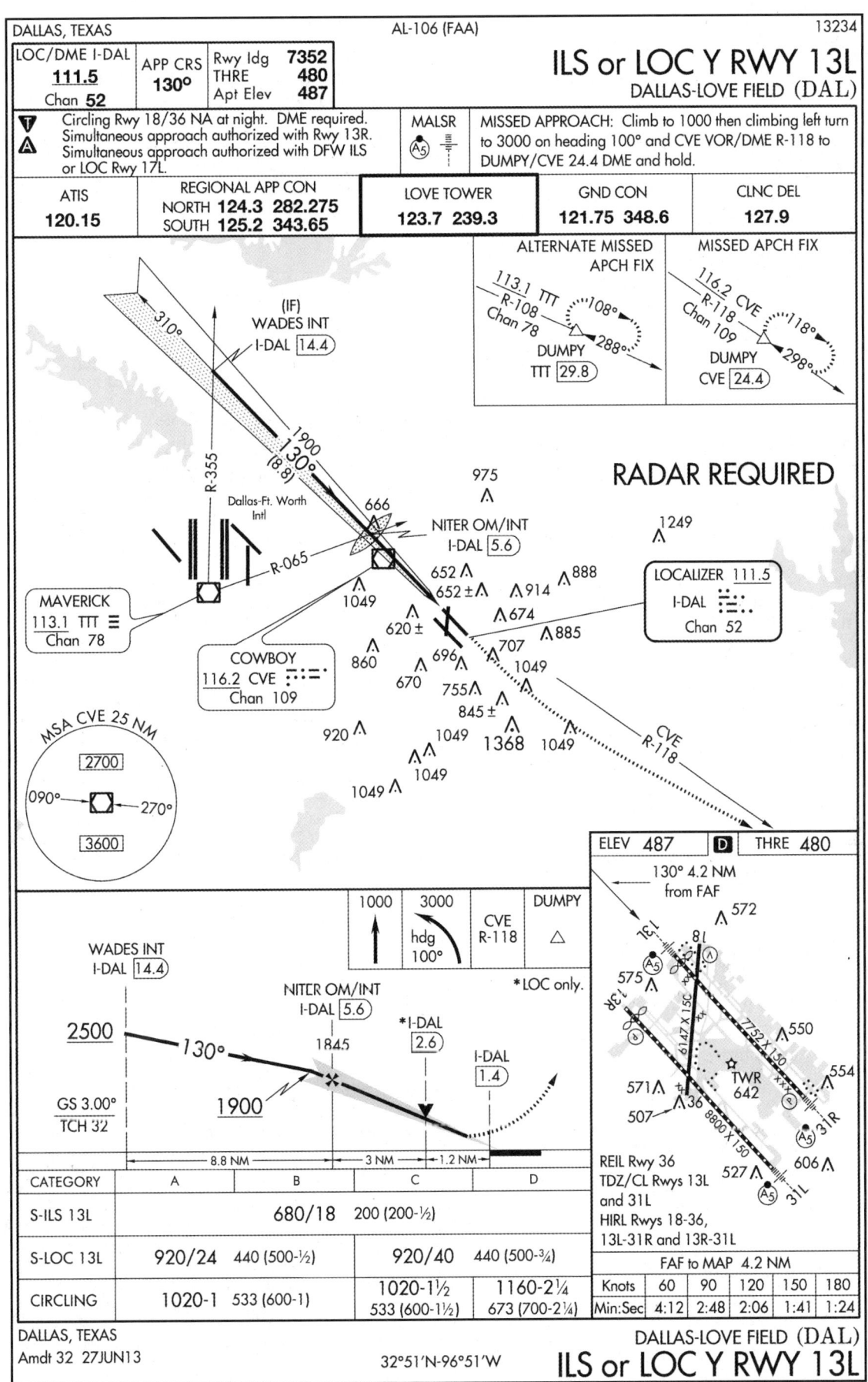

Figure 178. – ILS or LOC Y RWY 13L (DAL).

15. What does the Runway Visual Range (RVR) value, depicted on certain straight-in IAP Charts, represent?

A. The slant range distance the pilot can see down the runway while crossing the threshold on glide slope.

B. The horizontal distance a pilot should see when looking down the runway from a moving aircraft.

C. The slant visual range a pilot should see down the final approach and during landing.

Answer (B) is correct. (AC 00-45H Chap 2)
    DISCUSSION: RVR is an instrumentally derived value that represents the horizontal distance the pilot will see down the runway from the approach end. It is based on the measurement of a transmissometer near the touchdown point of the instrument runway and is reported in hundreds of feet.
    Answer (A) is incorrect. RVR is the horizontal, not slant range, distance the pilot will see down the runway. **Answer (C) is incorrect.** RVR is the horizontal, not slant range, distance the pilot will see down the runway, not the final approach.

16. The RVR minimums for takeoff or landing are published in an IAP, but RVR is inoperative and cannot be reported for the runway at the time. Which of the following would apply?

A. RVR minimums which are specified in the procedure should be converted and applied as ground visibility.

B. RVR minimums may be disregarded, providing the runway has an operative HIRL system.

C. RVR minimums may be disregarded, providing all other components of the ILS system are operative.

Answer (A) is correct. (14 CFR 91.175)
    DISCUSSION: If RVR minimums for takeoff or landing are prescribed in an instrument approach procedure, but RVR is inoperative and cannot be reported for the runway of intended operation, the RVR minimum shall be converted to ground visibility and shall be the visibility minimum for takeoff or landing on that runway.
    Answer (B) is incorrect. RVR minimums must be converted to ground visibility, not disregarded. **Answer (C) is incorrect.** RVR minimums must be converted to ground visibility, not disregarded.

17. RVR minimums for landing are prescribed in an IAP, but RVR is inoperative and cannot be reported for the intended runway at the time. Which of the following would be an operational consideration?

A. RVR minimums which are specified in the procedures should be converted and applied as ground visibility.

B. RVR minimums may be disregarded, providing the runway has an operative HIRL system.

C. RVR minimums may be disregarded, providing all other components of the ILS system are operative.

Answer (A) is correct. (14 CFR 91.175)
    DISCUSSION: If RVR minimums for takeoff or landing are prescribed in an instrument approach procedure, but RVR is inoperative and cannot be reported for the runway of intended operation, the RVR minimum shall be converted to ground visibility and shall be the visibility minimum for takeoff or landing on that runway.
    Answer (B) is incorrect. RVR minimums must be converted to ground visibility, not disregarded. **Answer (C) is incorrect.** RVR minimums must be converted to ground visibility, not disregarded.

6.5 Missed Approaches

18. (Refer to Figure 187 on page 235.) When conducting a missed approach from the RNAV (GPS) X RWY 28L approach at PDX, what is the Minimum Safe Altitude (MSA) while maneuvering?

A. 2,100 feet MSL.

B. 4,000 feet MSL.

C. 5,800 feet MSL.

Answer (C) is correct. (FAA-H-8083-16B Chap 4)
    DISCUSSION: The approach plate indicates that 5,800 feet MSL is the MSA. MSAs are published for emergency use on IAP charts. MSAs provide 1,000 feet of clearance over all obstacles but do not necessarily assure acceptable navigation signal coverage. The MSA depiction on the plan view of an approach chart contains the identifier of the center point of the MSA, the applicable radius of the MSA, a depiction of the sector(s), and the minimum altitudes above mean sea level that provide obstacle clearance.
    Answer (A) is incorrect. The initial altitude to climb to in the missed approach procedure, not the MSA, is 2,100 feet MSL. **Answer (B) is incorrect.** The final altitude specified in the missed approach procedure, not the MSA, is 4,000 feet MSL.

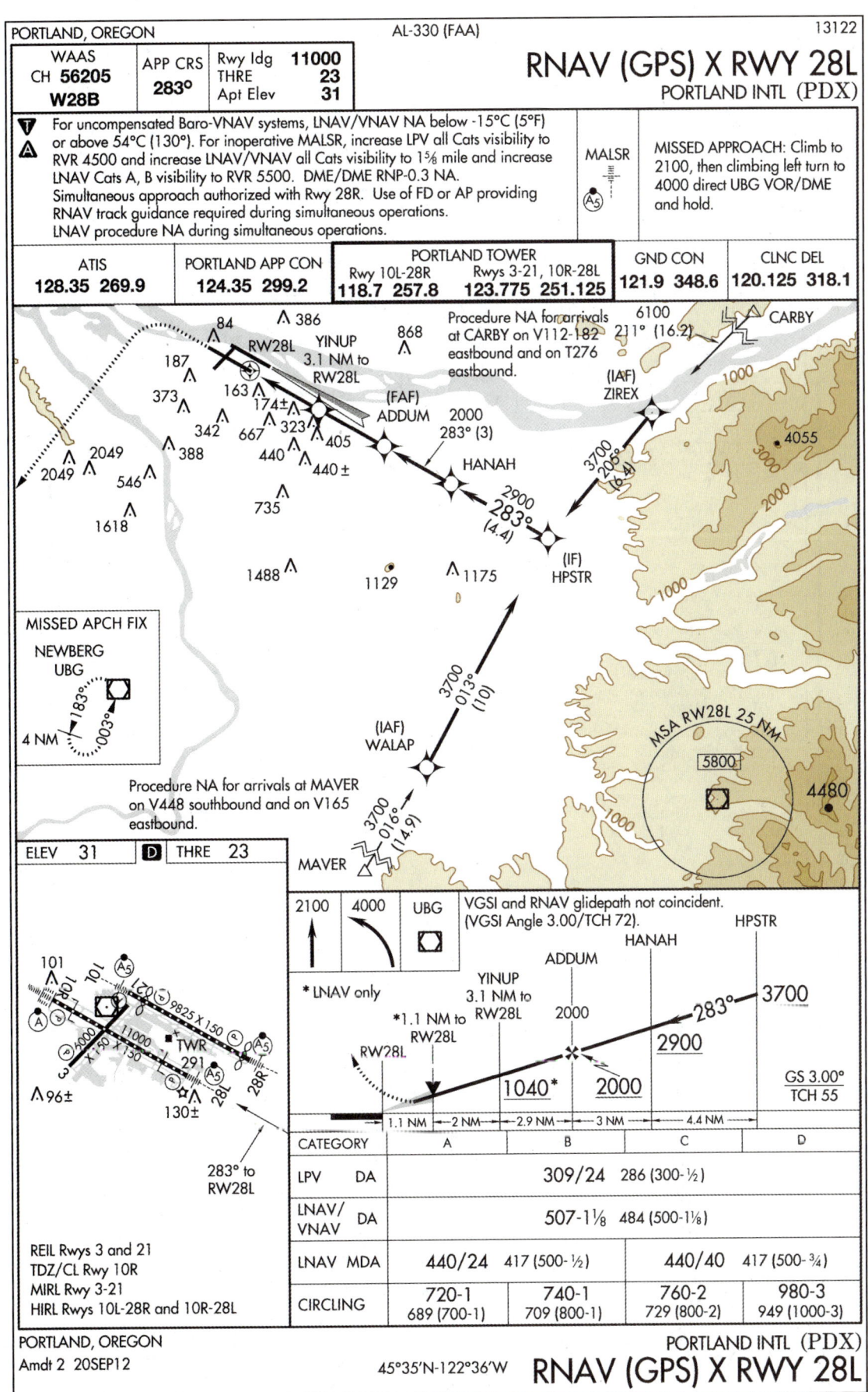

Figure 187. – RNAV (GPS) X RWY 28L (PDX).

19. (Refer to Figure 233 below.) The missed approach point for the DUC RNAV (GPS) RWY 17 (LNAV/VNAV) procedure is

A. 1,903 feet MSL.

B. 300 feet AGL.

C. 0.8 NM from runway threshold.

Answer (A) is correct. *(FAA-H-8083-16B Chap 4)*
DISCUSSION: The missed approach point is given as the LNAV/VNAV DA on the minimums section of Fig. 233. It is listed as 1,903 feet MSL.
Answer (B) is incorrect. The DA for the LNAV/VNAV approach is 789 feet AGL, not 300 AGL. **Answer (C) is incorrect.** The distance from TEPCO to a point 1.9 NM from the threshold is 0.8 NM. It is not the missed approach point.

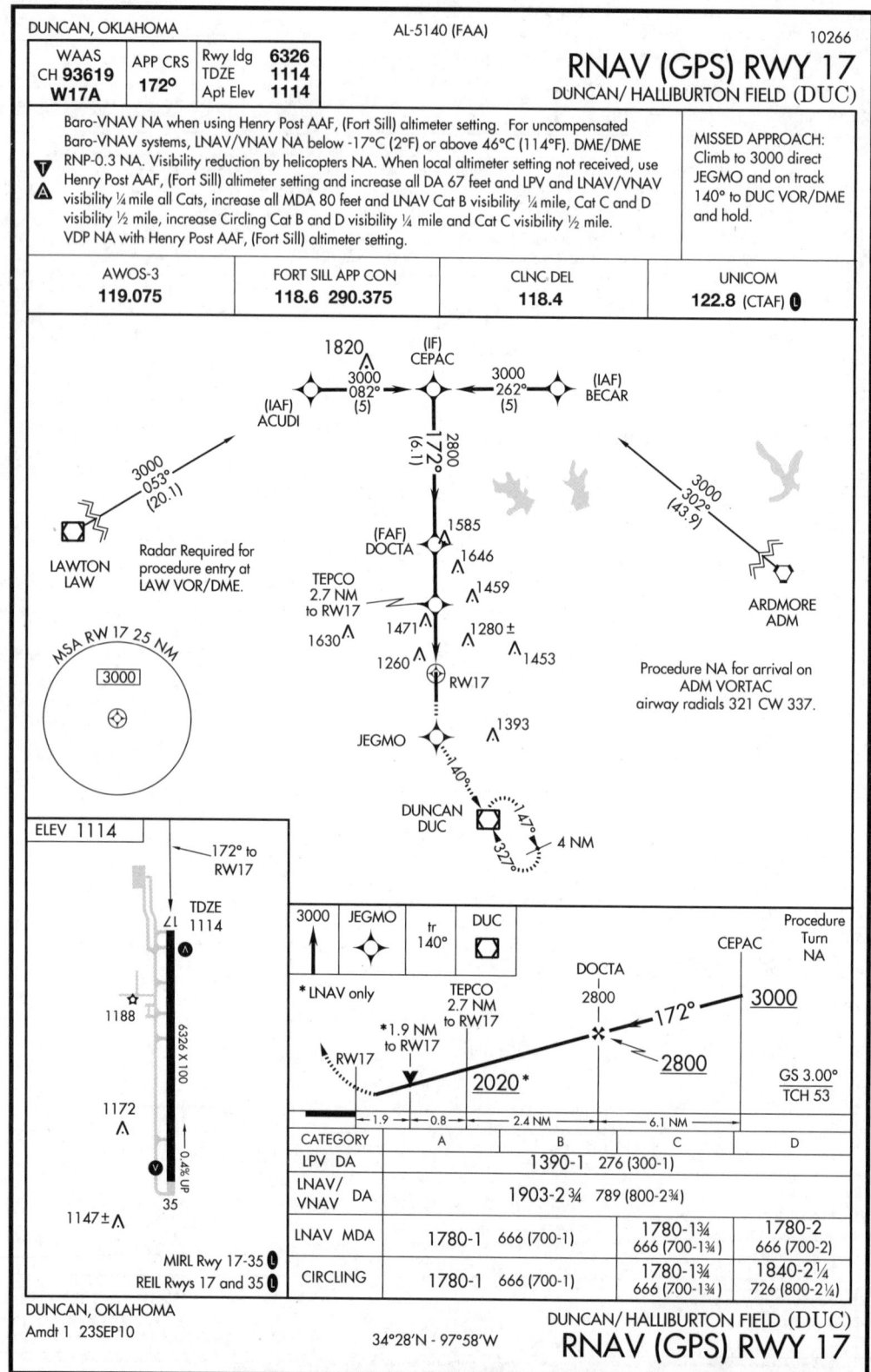

Figure 233. – RNAV (GPS) RWY 17 (DUC).

20. (Refer to Figure 249 below.) At what point would a pilot execute the missed approach for the LNAV approach at LBF?

A. 1.5 NM from the RW 30 waypoint for LNAV.

B. The BEMXI waypoint for the LNAV.

C. RW 30 waypoint for the LNAV.

Answer (C) is correct. *(FAA-H-8083-16B Chap 4)*
DISCUSSION: The missed approach point on an LNAV approach is the last waypoint shown in the profile view. This should not be confused with reaching the DA because this is an LNAV (non-precision) approach with an MDA. Fig. 249 shows the LNAV approach terminates at the RW 30 waypoint. It would be appropriate to execute a missed approach from this point.

Answer (A) is incorrect. The distance of 1.5 NM from the RW 30 waypoint is the VDP, not the missed approach point.
Answer (B) is incorrect. BEMXI is the FAF, not the missed approach point.

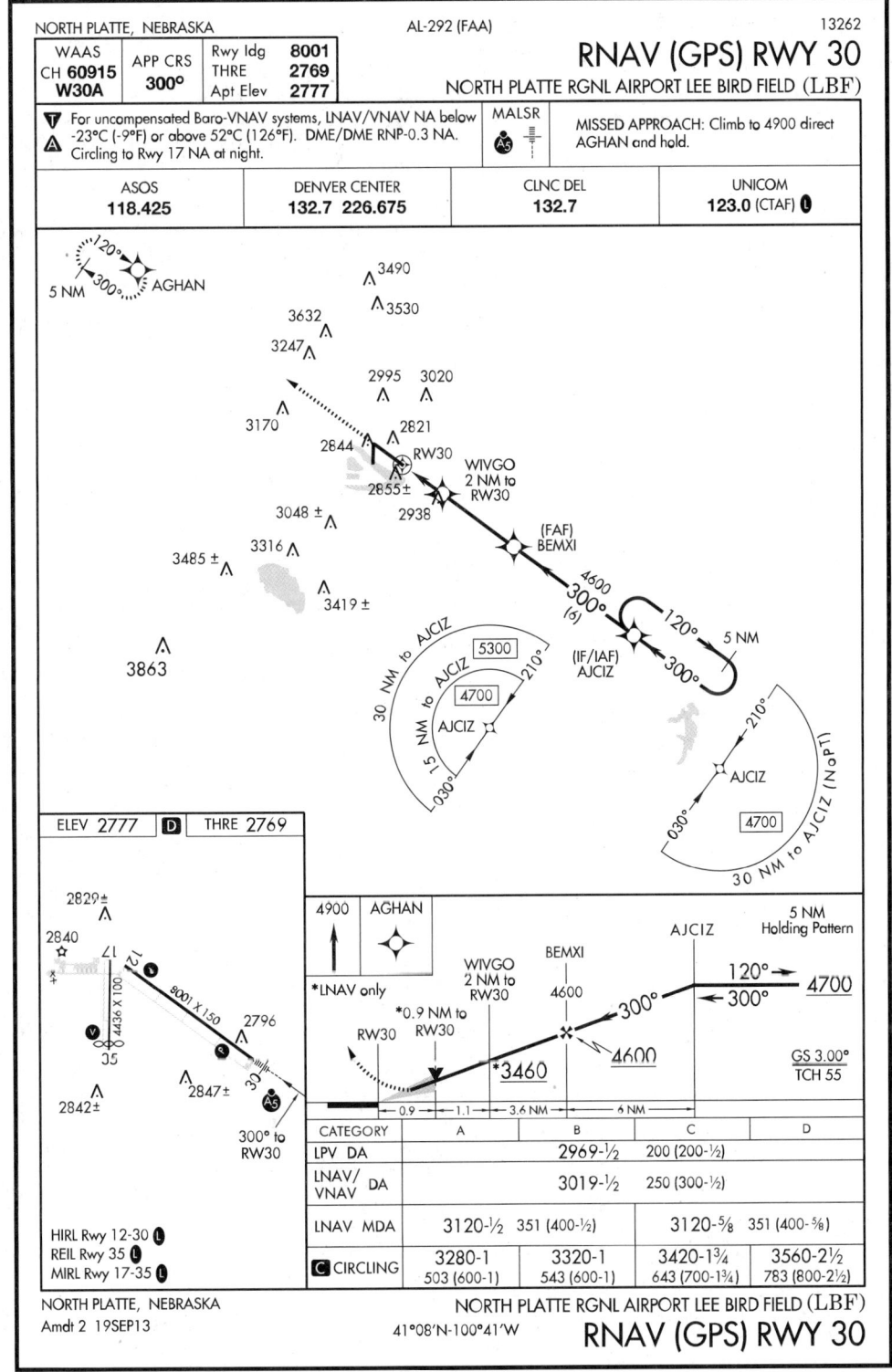

Figure 249. – RNAV (GPS) RWY 30 (LBF).

21. If an early missed approach is initiated before reaching the MAP, the following procedure should be used unless otherwise cleared by ATC.

    A. Proceed to the missed approach point at or above the MDA or DH before executing a turning maneuver.

    B. Begin a climbing turn immediately and follow missed approach procedures.

    C. Maintain altitude and continue past MAP for 1 minute or 1 mile whichever occurs first.

Answer (A) is correct. (AIM Para 5-4-21)
    DISCUSSION: When an early missed approach is executed, the pilot should, unless otherwise directed by ATC, fly the IAP as specified on the approach plate to the missed approach point at or above the MDA or DH before executing a turning maneuver.
    Answer (B) is incorrect. One should continue to the MAP before executing any turns. **Answer (C) is incorrect.** One need only continue to, not past, the MAP.

22. If the pilot loses visual reference while circling to land from an instrument approach and ATC radar service is not available, the missed approach action should be to

    A. execute a climbing turn to parallel the published final approach course and climb to the initial approach altitude.

    B. climb to the published circling minimums then proceed direct to the final approach fix.

    C. make a climbing turn toward the landing runway and continue the turn until established on the missed approach course.

Answer (C) is correct. (AIM Para 5-4-21)
    DISCUSSION: If visual reference is lost while circling to land, the missed approach specified for that particular procedure must be followed. To become established on the prescribed missed approach course, the pilot should make an initial climbing turn toward the landing runway and continue the turn until established on the missed approach course.
    Answer (A) is incorrect. The climbing turn should be toward the landing runway; then the pilot should execute the published missed approach procedures. **Answer (B) is incorrect.** There should be a climbing turn toward the landing runway.

6.6 ILS Specifications

23. Which of the following statements is true regarding Parallel ILS approaches?

    A. Parallel ILS approach runway centerlines are separated by at least 4,300 feet and standard IFR separation is provided on the adjacent runway.

    B. Parallel ILS approaches provide aircraft a minimum of 1 1/2 miles radar separation between successive aircraft on the adjacent localizer course.

    C. Landing minimums to the adjacent runway will be higher than the minimums to the primary runway, but will normally be lower than the published circling minimums.

Answer (B) is correct. (AIM Para 5-4-14)
    DISCUSSION: Aircraft are afforded a minimum of 1 1/2 miles radar separation diagonally between successive aircraft on the adjacent localizer course and a minimum 3 NM radar separation (reduced to 2.5 NM in certain circumstances) from aircraft on the same final approach during parallel ILS operations.
    Answer (A) is incorrect. Parallel approach runway centerlines are separated by at least 4,300 ft., a minimum of 2 NM diagonal radar separation is between successive aircraft, not standard IFR separation. **Answer (C) is incorrect.** A side-step maneuver, not a parallel ILS approach, will have landing minimums to the adjacent runway which are higher than the minimums to the primary runway, but these minimums will normally be lower than the published circling minimums.

24. If all ILS components are operating and the required visual references are not established, the missed approach should be initiated upon

    A. arrival at the DH on the glide slope.

    B. arrival at the MDA.

    C. expiration of the time listed on the approach chart for missed approach.

Answer (A) is correct. (14 CFR 91.175)
    DISCUSSION: The missed approach procedure should be executed upon arrival at the decision height (DH) on the glide slope if the visual reference requirements are not met. Thus, DH on an ILS is the MAP.
    Answer (B) is incorrect. The DH rather than the MDA is the MAP. **Answer (C) is incorrect.** The time listed on the approach chart for missed approaches is used in conjunction with the localizer for a timed approach if the glide slope fails during the ILS approach; i.e., it is not the primary indicator.

25. If during an ILS approach in IFR conditions, the approach lights are not visible upon arrival at the DH, the pilot is

A. required to immediately execute the missed approach procedure.

B. permitted to continue the approach and descend to the localizer MDA.

C. permitted to continue the approach to the approach threshold of the ILS runway.

Answer (A) is correct. (14 CFR 91.175)
DISCUSSION: The missed approach procedure should be executed upon arrival at the decision height (DH) on the glide slope if the visual reference requirements are not met. Thus, the DH on an ILS is the MAP.
Answer (B) is incorrect. The DH is the MAP on an ILS, which is lower than the localizer MDA. **Answer (C) is incorrect.** The pilot may continue the approach below the DH only if the required visual references (e.g., approach lights) are established.

26. How does a pilot determine if DME is available on an ILS/LOC?

A. IAP indicate DME/TACAN channel in LOC frequency box.

B. LOC/DME are indicated on en route low altitude frequency box.

C. LOC/DME frequencies available in the *Aeronautical Information Manual*.

Answer (A) is correct. (FAA-H-8083-15B Chap 10)
DISCUSSION: If DME is available on an ILS or localizer approach, the DME/TACAN channel will be indicated in the localizer frequency box on the approach plate.
Answer (B) is incorrect. LOC/DME frequencies are available on approach plates, not en route charts. **Answer (C) is incorrect.** The *AIM* gives general information on navigation systems, not specific frequencies.

27. (Refer to Figure 61 below.) Determine your position relative to the glide slope and localizer course.

A. Below the glide slope and right of the localizer course.

B. Above the glide slope and left of the localizer course.

C. Above the glide slope and right of the localizer course.

Answer (C) is correct. (FAA-H-8083-15B Chap 5)
DISCUSSION: The aircraft is represented in Fig. 61 by the central dot displayed at the center of the instrument face. This shows the aircraft to be displaced above the glide slope by one dot and to the right of the localizer course by one dot.
Answer (A) is incorrect. The lateral needle that represents the glide slope is below the aircraft glide path by one dot, and the aircraft is to the right of the localizer course deviation indicator needle by one dot. **Answer (B) is incorrect.** The lateral needle that represents the glide slope is below the aircraft glide path, while the localizer shows the aircraft to the right of the localizer course deviation indicator needle.

Figure 61. – CDI Indicator.

28. (Refer to Figure 140 below, and Figure 139 on page 241.) Which displacement from the localizer and glide slope at the 1.9 NM point is indicated?

A. 710 feet to the left of the localizer centerline and 140 feet below the glide slope.

B. 710 feet to the right of the localizer centerline and 140 feet above the glide slope.

C. 430 feet to the right of the localizer centerline and 28 feet above the glide slope.

Answer (B) is correct. (AIM Para 1-1-9)
    DISCUSSION: The airplane is to the right of the localizer and above the glide slope each by 2 dots at 1.9 NM out. Per Fig. 139, 2 dots at 1.9 NM are 140 ft. above the glide slope and 710 ft. to the right of the localizer.
    Answer (A) is incorrect. The airplane is to the right, not left, of the localizer and above, not below, the glide slope.
    Answer (C) is incorrect. The 430-ft. and 28-ft. deviations are at 1,300 ft., not 1.9 NM.

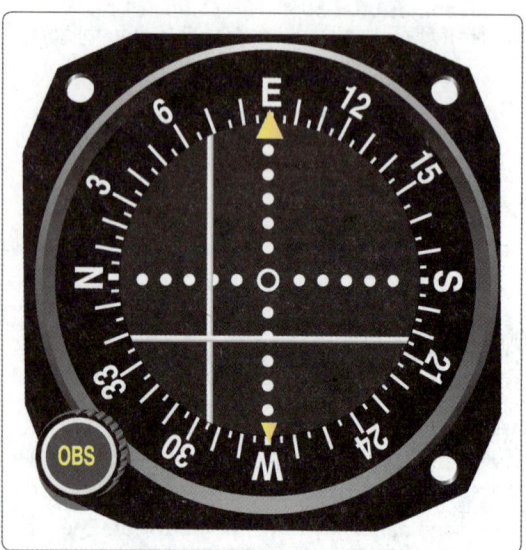

Figure 140. – OBS, ILS, and GS Displacement.

29. (Refer to Figure 139 on page 241 and Figure 141 on page 241.) Which displacement from the localizer centerline and glide slope at the 1,300-foot point from the runway is indicated?

A. 21 feet below the glide slope and approximately 320 feet to the right of the runway centerline.

B. 28 feet above the glide slope and approximately 250 feet to the left of the runway centerline.

C. 21 feet above the glide slope and approximately 320 feet to the left of the runway centerline.

Answer (C) is correct. (AIM Para 1-1-9)
    DISCUSSION: The airplane is above the glide slope and to the left of the localizer by 1 1/2 dots each at 1,300 ft. out. Per extrapolation and Fig. 139, this displacement is 21 ft. above the glide slope and about 320 ft. to the left of the localizer.
    Answer (A) is incorrect. The airplane is above, not below, the glide slope, and to the left, not right, of the localizer.
    Answer (B) is incorrect. A length of 28 ft. is 2 dots, and 250 ft. is less than 1 1/4 dots.

30. (Refer to Figure 139 on page 241 and Figure 142 on page 241.) Which displacement from the localizer and glide slope at the outer marker is indicated?

A. 1,550 feet to the left of the localizer centerline and 210 feet below the glide slope.

B. 1,550 feet to the right of the localizer centerline and 210 feet above the glide slope.

C. 775 feet to the left of the localizer centerline and 420 feet below the glide slope.

Answer (A) is correct. (AIM Para 1-1-9)
    DISCUSSION: The airplane is below the glide slope by 1 dot and to the left of the localizer by 2 dots at the outer marker. Per Fig. 139, 1 dot on the glide slope is 210 ft. at the outer marker (OM), and 2 dots on the localizer is 1,550 ft.
    Answer (B) is incorrect. The airplane is to the left, not right, of the localizer, and below, not above, the glide slope.
    Answer (C) is incorrect. At the OM, 775 ft. is 1 dot on the localizer, not the glide slope, and 420 ft. is 2 dots on the glide slope, not the localizer.

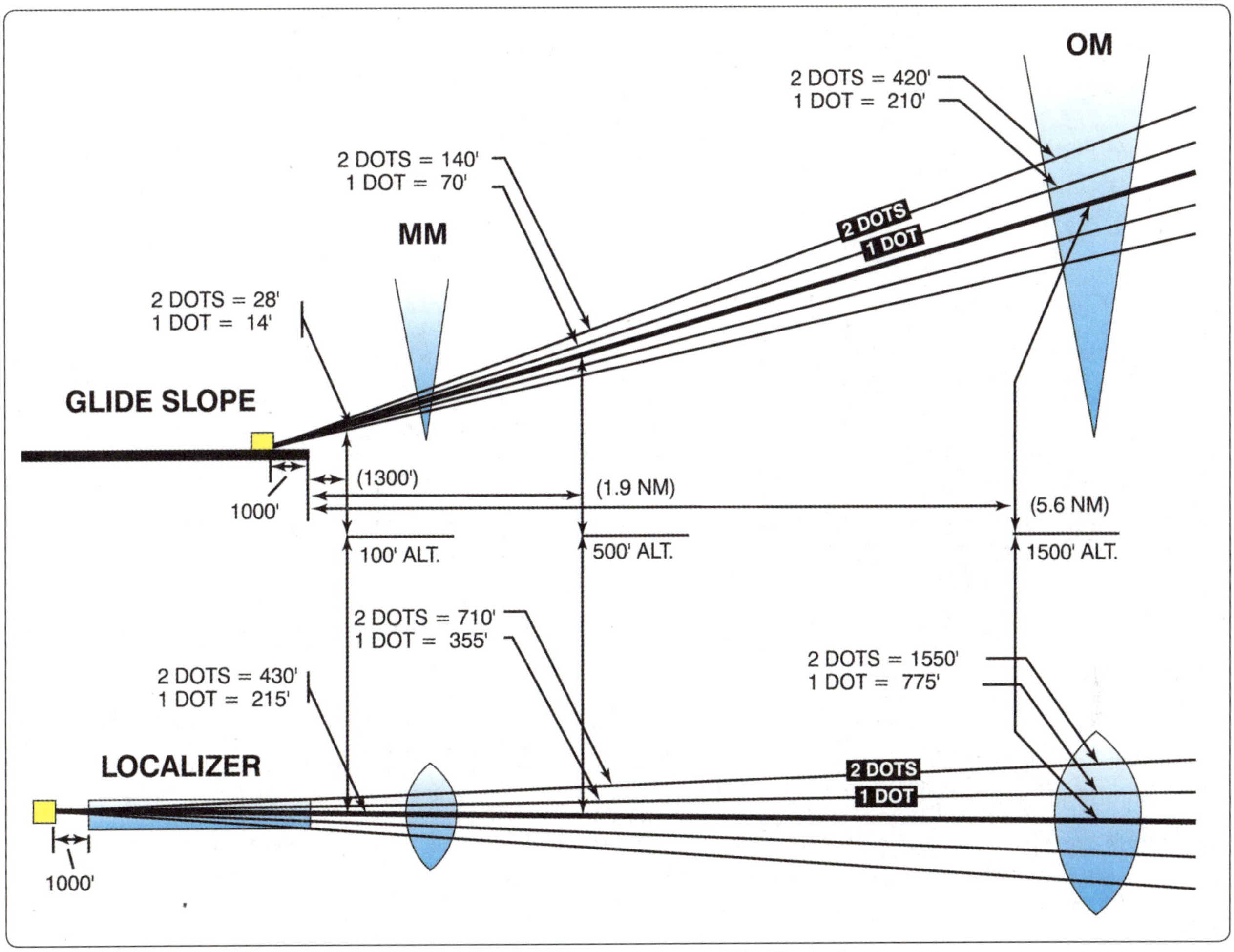

2 DOTS = 420'
1 DOT = 210'

OM

2 DOTS = 140'
1 DOT = 70'

MM

2 DOTS
1 DOT

2 DOTS = 28'
1 DOT = 14'

GLIDE SLOPE

1000'

(1300')   (1.9 NM)   (5.6 NM)

100' ALT.   500' ALT.   1500' ALT.

2 DOTS = 710'
1 DOT = 355'

2 DOTS = 1550'
1 DOT = 775'

2 DOTS = 430'
1 DOT = 215'

LOCALIZER

2 DOTS
1 DOT

1000'

Figure 139. – Glide Slope and Localizer Illustration.

Figure 141. – OBS, ILS, and GS Displacement.

Figure 142. – OBS, ILS, and GS Displacement.

31. (Refer to Figures 140, 141, and 142 below.) Which displacement from the localizer centerline and glide slope indicates you are high and to the left of the ILS course?

    A. Figure 140.

    B. Figure 141.

    C. Figure 142.

Answer (B) is correct. (AIM Para 1-1-9, FAA-H-8083-15B Chap 7)
    DISCUSSION: Fig. 141 shows an aircraft that is above the glideslope and to the left of the localizer. A correction downward and to the right would be appropriate.
    Answer (A) is incorrect. Fig. 140 shows an aircraft that is high and to the right of the localizer. **Answer (C) is incorrect.** Fig. 142 shows an aircraft that is low and to the left of the localizer.

32. (Refer to Figures 140, 141, and 142 below.) Which displacement from the localizer centerline and glide slope indicates you are low and to the left of the ILS course?

    A. Figure 140.

    B. Figure 141.

    C. Figure 142.

Answer (C) is correct. (FAA-H-8083-15B Chap 9)
    DISCUSSION: Fig. 142 shows an above-center glide slope indication and a right-from-center localizer indication. This deflection indicates that you are low and left of the ILS centerline because you are supposed to "fly to the needles" to maintain the proper course. Decrease your rate of descent and make a right correction to intercept the course centerline.
    Answer (A) is incorrect. Fig. 140 indicates that you are above and to the right of the course centerline. **Answer (B) is incorrect.** Fig. 141 indicates that you are above and to the left of the course centerline.

33. (Refer to Figures 140, 141, and 142 below.) Which displacement from the localizer centerline and glide slope indicates you are high and to the right of the ILS course?

    A. Figure 140.

    B. Figure 141.

    C. Figure 142.

Answer (A) is correct. (FAA-H-8083-15B Chap 9)
    DISCUSSION: Fig. 140 shows a below-center glide slope indication and a left-from-center localizer indication. This deflection indicates that your are above and right of the ILS centerline because you are supposed to "fly to the needles" to maintain the proper course. Increase your rate of descent and make a left correction to intercept the course centerline.
    Answer (B) is incorrect. Fig. 141 indicates that you are above and to the left of the course centerline. **Answer (C) is incorrect.** Fig. 142 indicates that you are below and to the left of the course centerline.

Figure 140. – OBS, ILS, and GS Displacement.

Figure 141. – OBS, ILS, and GS Displacement.

Figure 142. – OBS, ILS, and GS Displacement.

6.7 Unusable ILS Components

34. Which pilot action is appropriate if more than one component of an ILS is unusable?

A. Use the highest minimum required by any single component that is unusable.

B. Request another approach appropriate to the equipment that is usable.

C. Raise the minimums a total of that required by each component that is unusable.

Answer (A) is correct. (AIM Para 1-1-9)
DISCUSSION: Landing minimums published on instrument approach procedure charts are based upon full operation of all components and the use of visual aids associated with the particular instrument approach chart. Higher visibility minimums are required with inoperative components or visual aids as specified in FAA tables. If more than one component is inoperative, each minimum is raised to the highest minimum required by any single component that is inoperative.
Answer (B) is incorrect. An ILS can be used with some inoperative components, which increases the approach minimums, but you would not need to request another approach appropriate to the usable equipment. **Answer (C) is incorrect.** It is not cumulative; you need only use the highest minimum required as a result of any one component being unusable.

35. Which substitution is appropriate during an ILS approach?

A. A VOR radial crossing the outer marker site may be substituted for the outer marker.

B. LOC minimums should be substituted for ILS minimums whenever the glide slope becomes inoperative.

C. DME, when located at the localizer antenna site, should be substituted for either the outer or middle marker.

Answer (B) is correct. (AIM Para 1-1-9)
DISCUSSION: When the glide slope becomes inoperative during an ILS approach, the approach can be conducted as a localizer approach and the LOC minimums apply.
Answer (A) is incorrect. A VOR radial must be authorized in the standard approach procedure to be used as a substitute. **Answer (C) is incorrect.** DME can be substituted for the outer marker, but not the middle marker.

36. A pilot is making an ILS approach and is past the OM to a runway which has a VASI. What action is appropriate if an electronic glide slope malfunction occurs and the pilot has the VASI in sight?

A. The pilot should inform ATC of the malfunction and then descend immediately to the localizer DH and make a localizer approach.

B. The pilot may continue the approach and use the VASI glide slope in place of the electronic glide slope.

C. The pilot must request an LOC approach, and may descend below the VASI at the pilot's discretion.

Answer (B) is correct. (14 CFR 91.175)
DISCUSSION: Once the necessary specified visual requirements, e.g., the VASI, are attained for the intended runway, the pilot may continue the approach and use the VASI in place of the electronic glide slope.
Answer (A) is incorrect. Once the pilot has the necessary visual references, the approach may be continued visually. **Answer (C) is incorrect.** Once the pilot has the necessary visual references, the approach may be continued visually. Descent below the VASI glide path shall occur only when necessary for a safe landing.

37. Immediately after passing the final approach fix in bound during an ILS approach in IFR conditions, the glide slope warning flag appears. The pilot is

A. permitted to continue the approach and descend to the DH.

B. permitted to continue the approach and descend to the localizer MDA.

C. required to immediately begin the prescribed missed approach procedure.

Answer (B) is correct. (AIM Para 1-1-9)
DISCUSSION: When the glide slope fails, the approach can continue as a nonprecision localizer approach. Accordingly, if the glide slope fails on an ILS approach, the pilot may switch to the localizer approach and descend to the localizer MDA (minimum descent altitude).
Answer (A) is incorrect. Once the glide slope is inoperative, the localizer may be used only for a nonprecision approach, which uses MDA, not DH. **Answer (C) is incorrect.** The pilot should execute the missed approach procedure only after reaching the missed approach point.

38. When installed with the ILS and specified in the approach procedures, DME may be used

A. in lieu of the OM.

B. in lieu of visibility requirements.

C. to determine distance from TDZ.

Answer (A) is correct. (AIM Para 1-1-9)
DISCUSSION: When installed with the ILS and specified in the approach procedure, DME may be used in lieu of the outer marker (OM).
Answer (B) is incorrect. DME has no effect on visibility requirements. **Answer (C) is incorrect.** Touchdown zone (TDZ) is the first 3,000 ft. of the runway, not a specific point.

6.8 Flying the Approach

39. When passing through an abrupt wind shear which involves a shift from a tailwind to a headwind, what power management would normally be required to maintain a constant indicated airspeed and ILS glide slope?

A. Higher than normal power initially, followed by a further increase as the wind shear is encountered, then a decrease.

B. Lower than normal power initially, followed by a further decrease as the wind shear is encountered, then an increase.

C. Higher than normal power initially, followed by a decrease as the shear is encountered, then an increase.

Answer (B) is correct. (AC 00-54)
DISCUSSION: When an airplane is on the ILS glide slope and there is a change from a tailwind to a headwind, the groundspeed will decrease. During the tailwind, lower-than-normal power will be required. When the wind shear is encountered, even lower power will be required to decrease the spurt in airspeed. Once the wind shifts to a headwind, the airplane will require an increase in power to maintain the necessary groundspeed to stay on the ILS glide slope.
Answer (A) is incorrect. Initially there is lower-than-normal, not higher-than-normal, power with a tailwind, and when the headwind is encountered, a decrease, not an increase, in power is required. **Answer (C) is incorrect.** Initially there is lower-than-normal, not higher-than-normal, power with a tailwind.

40. The rate of descent on the glide slope depends on

A. true airspeed.

B. indicated airspeed.

C. ground speed.

Answer (C) is correct. (FAA-H-8083-15B Chap 10)
DISCUSSION: The rate of descent required to stay on the ILS glide slope depends on the ground speed because the descent must be constant relative to the distance traveled over the ground. Thus, the descent must be decreased if ground speed is decreased.
Answer (A) is incorrect. The rate of descent is based on ground speed, not true airspeed. **Answer (B) is incorrect.** The rate of descent is based on ground speed, not indicated airspeed.

41. The rate of descent required to stay on the ILS glide slope

A. must be increased if the ground speed is decreased.

B. will remain constant if the indicated airspeed remains constant.

C. must be decreased if the ground speed is decreased.

Answer (C) is correct. (FAA-H-8083-15B Chap 10)
DISCUSSION: The rate of descent required to stay on the ILS glide slope is dependent on the ground speed because the descent must be constant relative to the distance traveled over the ground. Thus, the descent must be decreased if ground speed is decreased.
Answer (A) is incorrect. If ground speed decreases and descent increases, the airplane will go below the glide slope. **Answer (B) is incorrect.** Ground speed rather than airspeed determines the rate of descent.

42. During a precision radar or ILS approach, the rate of descent required to remain on the glide slope will

A. remain the same regardless of groundspeed.

B. increase as the groundspeed increases.

C. decrease as the groundspeed increases.

Answer (B) is correct. (FAA-H-8083-15B Chap 10)
DISCUSSION: The rate of descent required to stay on the ILS glide slope is dependent on the groundspeed because the descent must be constant relative to the distance traveled over the ground. Thus, the descent must be increased if groundspeed is increased.
Answer (A) is incorrect. The descent rate varies with the groundspeed. **Answer (C) is incorrect.** The descent rate must increase, not decrease, as groundspeed increases.

43. (Refer to Figure 250 on page 245.) For a stabilized approach, the aircraft must be in an approved configuration for landing

A. with the engines spooled up, before descending below 1,768 feet MSL.

B. with the correct speed and on glide path before descending below 1,268 feet MSL.

C. with a descent rate of less than 1,000 fpm below 1,080 feet MSL and bank angles of less than 15° below 500 feet AGL.

Answer (B) is correct. (FAA-H-8083-16B Chap 4)
DISCUSSION: The stabilized approach concept includes maintaining a constant approach speed, descent rate, vertical flight path, and configuration during the final stages of an approach. In addition, a stabilized approach should be established at least 1,000 feet AGL or 1,268 feet MSL.
Answer (A) is incorrect. The aircraft should be spooled up before descending below 1,000 feet above the airport TDZE elevation of 268 feet, not 1,500 feet above that TDZE elevation. **Answer (C) is incorrect.** A stabilized approach should be established at least 1,000 feet AGL. The MDA is 1,080 feet MSL, which is only 812 feet above the TDZE.

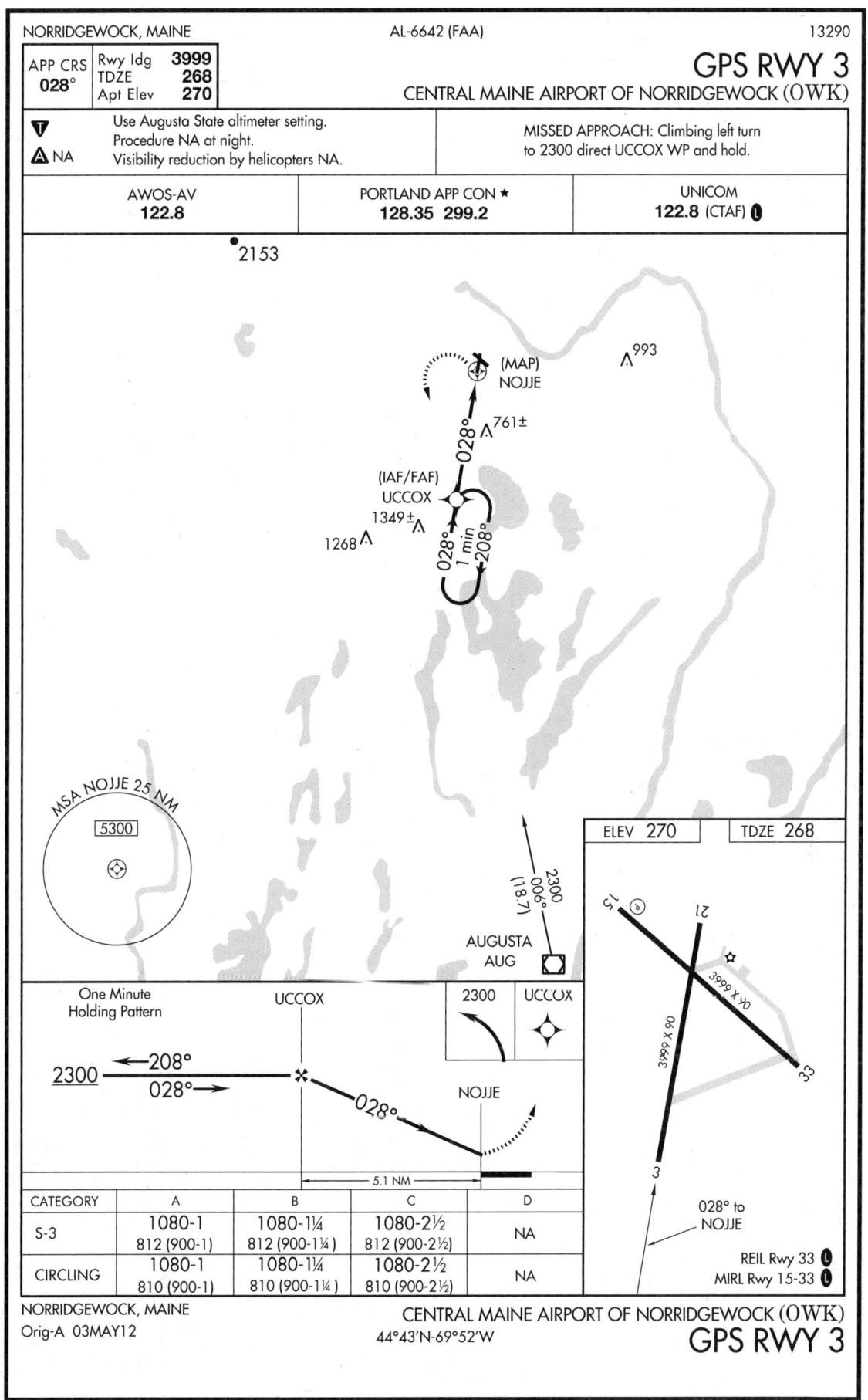

| NORRIDGEWOCK, MAINE | AL-6642 (FAA) | 13290 |

APP CRS **028°**

Rwy ldg **3999**
TDZE **268**
Apt Elev **270**

GPS RWY 3

CENTRAL MAINE AIRPORT OF NORRIDGEWOCK (OWK)

▼
▲ NA

Use Augusta State altimeter setting.
Procedure NA at night.
Visibility reduction by helicopters NA.

MISSED APPROACH: Climbing left turn
to 2300 direct UCCOX WP and hold.

| AWOS-AV **122.8** | PORTLAND APP CON ★ **128.35 299.2** | UNICOM **122.8** (CTAF) Ⓛ |

• 2153

(MAP) NOJJE

∧ 993

∧ 761±

028°

(IAF/FAF) UCCOX

1349± ∧

1268 ∧

028° 1 min 208°

MSA NOJJE 25 NM

5300

2300 006° (18.7)

AUGUSTA AUG

ELEV 270 | TDZE 268

15
21
☆
3999 X 90
OWK X 6666 (?)
33
3
028° to NOJJE

REIL Rwy 33 Ⓛ
MIRL Rwy 15-33 Ⓛ

One Minute Holding Pattern

UCCOX

2300 ←208°
028°→

UCCOX

2300

NOJJE

028°

5.1 NM

CATEGORY	A	B	C	D
S-3	1080-1 812 (900-1)	1080-1¼ 812 (900-1¼)	1080-2½ 812 (900-2½)	NA
CIRCLING	1080-1 810 (900-1)	1080-1¼ 810 (900-1¼)	1080-2½ 810 (900-2½)	NA

NORRIDGEWOCK, MAINE
Orig-A 03MAY12

CENTRAL MAINE AIRPORT OF NORRIDGEWOCK (OWK)
44°43'N-69°52'W
GPS RWY 3

Figure 250. – GPS RWY 3 (OWK).

44. When tracking in bound on the localizer, which of the following is the proper procedure regarding drift corrections?

    A. Drift corrections should be accurately established before reaching the outer marker and completion of the approach should be accomplished with heading corrections no greater than 2°.

    B. Drift corrections should be made in 5° increments after passing the outer marker.

    C. Drift corrections should be made in 10° increments after passing the outer marker.

Answer (A) is correct. (FAA-H-8083-15B Chap 10)
    DISCUSSION: When you are tracking in bound on the localizer, your drift correction should be small and reduced proportionately as the course narrows. By the time you reach the outer marker, your drift correction should be established accurately enough to permit completion of the approach with heading corrections no greater than 2°.
    Answer (B) is incorrect. After you pass the outer marker, your drift corrections should be no greater than 2°, not 5°. **Answer (C) is incorrect.** After you pass the outer marker, your drift corrections should be no greater than 2°, not 10°.

45. What effect will a change in wind direction have upon maintaining a 3° glide slope at a constant true airspeed?

    A. When ground speed decreases, rate of descent must increase.

    B. When ground speed increases, rate of descent must increase.

    C. Rate of descent must be constant to remain on the glide slope.

Answer (B) is correct. (FAA-H-8083-15B Chap 10)
    DISCUSSION: The rate of descent required to stay on the ILS glide slope is dependent on the ground speed because the descent must be constant relative to the distance traveled over the ground. Thus, the descent must be increased if ground speed is increased.
    Answer (A) is incorrect. If you increase the rate of descent when the ground speed decreases, you will fly below the glide slope. **Answer (C) is incorrect.** The rate of descent must change with changes in ground speed.

46. While being vectored, if crossing the ILS final approach course becomes imminent and an approach clearance has not been issued, what action should be taken by the pilot?

    A. Turn outbound on the final approach course, execute a procedure turn, and inform ATC.

    B. Turn inbound and execute the missed approach procedure at the outer marker if approach clearance has not been received.

    C. Maintain the last assigned heading and query ATC.

Answer (C) is correct. (AIM Para 5-4-3)
    DISCUSSION: While being vectored, if you determine that crossing the final approach course is imminent and you have not been informed that you will be vectored across it, you should question the controller. You should not turn inbound on the final approach course unless you have received an approach clearance.
    Answer (A) is incorrect. You should maintain the last assigned heading until you receive an amended clearance. When in doubt, query ATC. **Answer (B) is incorrect.** You should maintain the last assigned heading until you receive an amended clearance. When in doubt, query ATC.

47. Thrust is managed to maintain IAS, and glide slope is being flown. What characteristics should be observed when a headwind shears to be a constant tailwind?

    A. PITCH ATTITUDE: Increases; REQUIRED THRUST: Increased, then reduced; VERTICAL SPEED: Increases; IAS: Increases, then decreases to approach speed.

    B. PITCH ATTITUDE: Decreases; REQUIRED THRUST: Increased, then reduced; VERTICAL SPEED: Increases; IAS: Decreases, then increases to approach speed.

    C. PITCH ATTITUDE: Increases; REQUIRED THRUST: Reduced, then increased; VERTICAL SPEED: Decreases; IAS: Decreases, then increases to approach speed.

Answer (B) is correct. (AC 00-54)
    DISCUSSION: When a headwind shears to a tailwind, the airplane's airspeed drops, its nose pitches down, and its vertical speed increases. The power must be increased initially to resume normal approach speed, then reduced as airspeed stabilizes to maintain the glide slope due to the increased groundspeed.
    Answer (A) is incorrect. The airspeed decreases, not increases, initially as the headwind shears to a tailwind, causing the pitch to decrease, not increase. **Answer (C) is incorrect.** The pitch attitude decreases, not increases, due to the decreased airspeed, causing the vertical speed to increase, not decrease. Initially, the thrust must be increased, not decreased, to maintain approach airspeed.

48. The glide slope and localizer are centered, but the airspeed is too fast. Which should be adjusted initially?

A. Pitch and power.

B. Power only.

C. Pitch only.

Answer (B) is correct. (FAA-H-8083-15B Chap 10)
DISCUSSION: If the glide slope and localizer are centered but the airspeed is too fast, you should reduce power initially. Almost immediately, you will then have to make pitch adjustments to compensate for the power adjustment to maintain the glidepath.
Answer (A) is incorrect. Although the pitch and power adjustments must be closely coordinated, the power is actually adjusted first. **Answer (C) is incorrect.** Adjusting pitch initially would cause you to fly above the glide path.

49. While flying a 3° glide slope, a constant tailwind shears to a calm wind. Which conditions should the pilot expect?

A. Airspeed and pitch attitude decrease and there is a tendency to go below glide slope.

B. Airspeed and pitch attitude increase and there is a tendency to go below glide slope.

C. Airspeed and pitch attitude increase and there is a tendency to go above glide slope.

Answer (C) is correct. (AC 00-54)
DISCUSSION: When a constant tailwind shears to a calm wind, the airplane's airspeed increases, its nose pitches up, and it has a tendency to go above the glide slope. The nose pitches up due to the increased lift from the increased airspeed.
Answer (A) is incorrect. The airspeed and pitch increase, not decrease, and there is a tendency to go above, not below, the glide slope. **Answer (B) is incorrect.** The tendency is to go above, not below, the glide slope.

50. While flying a 3° glide slope, a headwind shears to a tailwind. Which conditions should the pilot expect on the glide slope?

A. Airspeed and pitch attitude decrease and there is a tendency to go below glide slope.

B. Airspeed and pitch attitude increase and there is a tendency to go above glide slope.

C. Airspeed and pitch attitude decrease and there is a tendency to remain on the glide slope.

Answer (A) is correct. (AC 00-54)
DISCUSSION: When a headwind shears to a tailwind, the airplane's airspeed drops, its nose pitches down, and it begins to drop below the glide slope. The airplane will be both slow and power deficient.
Answer (B) is incorrect. Airspeed and pitch decrease, not increase, and there is a tendency to go below, not above, the glide slope. **Answer (C) is incorrect.** There is a tendency to go below, not remain on, the glide slope.

6.9 Side-Step Approaches

51. When cleared to execute a published sidestep maneuver for a specific approach and landing on the parallel runway, at what point is the pilot expected to commence this maneuver?

A. At the published minimum altitude for a circling approach.

B. As soon as possible after the runway or runway environment is in sight.

C. At the localizer MDA minimum and when the runway is in sight.

Answer (B) is correct. (AIM Para 5-4-19)
DISCUSSION: Pilots are expected to commence the side-step maneuver as soon as possible after the runway or runway environment is in sight.
Answer (A) is incorrect. The side-step maneuver should be performed only when the runway environment is in sight. **Answer (C) is incorrect.** The side-step maneuver should be performed as soon as the runway environment is in sight, which may be before reaching the MDA.

52. Assume this clearance is received:

"CLEARED FOR ILS RUNWAY 07 LEFT APPROACH, SIDE-STEP TO RUNWAY 07 RIGHT."

When would the pilot be expected to commence the side-step maneuver?

A. As soon as possible after the runway environment is in sight.

B. Any time after becoming aligned with the final approach course of Runway 07 left, and after passing the final approach fix.

C. After reaching the circling minimums for Runway 07 right.

Answer (A) is correct. (AIM Para 5-4-19)
DISCUSSION: Pilots are expected to commence the side-step maneuver as soon as possible after the runway or runway environment is in sight.
Answer (B) is incorrect. The side-step maneuver should be performed as soon as possible but only after the runway or runway environment is in sight. **Answer (C) is incorrect.** The side-step maneuver should be performed as soon as possible but only after the runway or runway environment is in sight.

6.10 Holding

53. (Refer to Figure 112 below.) You arrive at the 15 DME fix on a heading of 350°. Which holding pattern correctly complies with the ATC clearance below, and what is the recommended entry procedure?

"...HOLD WEST OF THE ONE FIVE DME FIX ON THE ZERO NINE ZERO RADIAL OF THE ABC VORTAC, FIVE MILE LEGS, LEFT TURNS..."

    A. 1; teardrop entry.

    B. 1; direct entry.

    C. 2; direct entry.

Answer (B) is correct. *(AIM Para 5-3-8)*
    DISCUSSION: Holding pattern 1 is correct because the holding fix is always at the end of the inbound leg. Draw the 70° line through the fix such that it intersects the outbound leg 1/3 of the leg length from abeam the fix.

Airplane Heading to Fix	Entry
340° to 160°	Direct
160° to 270°	Parallel
270° to 340°	Teardrop

A 350° heading to the fix requires a direct entry, which requires a standard-rate left turn to 270° beginning over the holding fix.
    Answer (A) is incorrect. Approaching the fix on a heading of 350° requires a direct, not teardrop, entry. **Answer (C) is incorrect.** Holding pattern 2 does not show the holding fix at the end of the inbound leg.

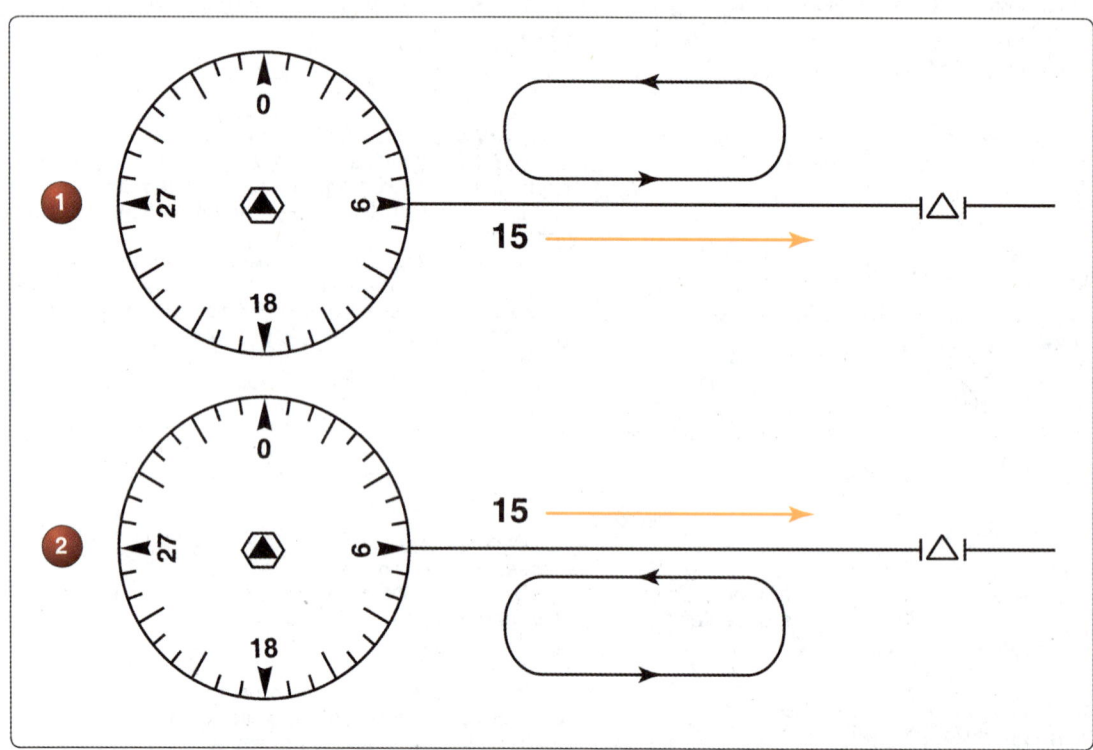

Figure 112. – Holding Entry Procedure.

54. (Refer to Figure 113 on page 249.) You receive this ATC clearance:

"...CLEARED TO THE ABC VORTAC. HOLD WEST ON THE TWO SEVEN ZERO RADIAL..."

What is the recommended procedure to enter the holding pattern?

    A. Parallel only.

    B. Direct only.

    C. Teardrop only.

Answer (B) is correct. *(AIM Para 5-3-8)*
    DISCUSSION: You are cleared to hold west on R-270 with right turns, so you will be south of R-270. Since you are coming in on R-240, you need to make a direct entry.

R-020 to R-090	Teardrop
R-090 to R-200	Parallel
R-200 to R-020	Direct

    Answer (A) is incorrect. A parallel entry is appropriate only on R-090 to R-200. **Answer (C) is incorrect.** A teardrop entry is appropriate only when coming in on R-020 to R-090.

55. (Refer to Figure 113 below.) You receive this ATC clearance:

"...HOLD EAST OF THE ABC VORTAC ON THE ZERO NINER ZERO RADIAL, LEFT TURNS..."

What is the recommended procedure to enter the holding pattern?

    A. Parallel only.

    B. Direct only.

    C. Teardrop only.

Answer (A) is correct. (AIM Para 5-3-8)
    DISCUSSION: You are cleared to hold east of the ABC VORTAC with left turns on R-090. The holding side will be south of R-090, with the holding fix being the VORTAC. Draw the 70° line through the VORTAC on R-340/R-160.

R-270 to R-340	Teardrop
R-340 to R-160	Direct
R-160 to R-270	Parallel

Since you are approaching the VORTAC from the southwest on R-240 (see Fig. 113), you will make a parallel entry.
    Answer (B) is incorrect. A direct entry would be appropriate if you were coming in on R-340 to R-160.
    Answer (C) is incorrect. A teardrop entry would be appropriate if you were coming in from R-270 to R-340.

56. (Refer to Figure 113 below.) You receive this ATC clearance:

"...CLEARED TO THE ABC VORTAC. HOLD SOUTH ON THE ONE EIGHT ZERO RADIAL..."

What is the recommended procedure to enter the holding pattern?

    A. Teardrop only.

    B. Direct only.

    C. Parallel only.

Answer (B) is correct. (AIM Para 5-3-8)
    DISCUSSION: You are cleared to hold south on the 180° radial with right turns, which means you will be to the east of R-180. Since you are coming in from the southwest (R-240), you can make a direct entry.

R-290 to R-360	Teardrop
R-360 to R-110	Parallel
R-110 to R-290	Direct

    Answer (A) is incorrect. A teardrop entry would be appropriate only from R-290 to R-360. **Answer (C) is incorrect.** A parallel entry would be appropriate only from R-360 to R-110.

57. (Refer to Figure 113 below.) You receive this ATC clearance:

"...CLEARED TO THE XYZ VORTAC. HOLD NORTH ON THE THREE SIX ZERO RADIAL, LEFT TURNS..."

What is the recommended procedure to enter the holding pattern?

    A. Parallel only.

    B. Direct only.

    C. Teardrop only.

Answer (C) is correct. (AIM Para 5-3-8)
    DISCUSSION: Holding north of the XYZ VORTAC with left turns on R-360 means you are on the east side of the radial. Since you are coming in from the southwest (R-240), you will be making a teardrop entry.

R-180 to R-250	Teardrop
R-250 to R-070	Direct
R-070 to R-180	Parallel

    Answer (A) is incorrect. A parallel approach would be appropriate only if you were coming in between R-070 and R-180. **Answer (B) is incorrect.** A direct entry is appropriate only between R-250 and R-070.

Figure 113. – Aircraft
Course and DME Indicator.

58. (Refer to Figure 114 below.) A pilot receives this ATC clearance:

"...CLEARED TO THE ABC VORTAC. HOLD WEST ON THE TWO SEVEN ZERO RADIAL..."

What is the recommended procedure to enter the holding pattern?

    A. Parallel or teardrop.

    B. Parallel only.

    C. Direct only.

Figure 114. – Aircraft
Course and DME Indicator.

Answer (C) is correct. (AIM Para 5-3-8)
    DISCUSSION: When holding west on the 270° radial, use right turns because left turns were not stated in the clearance. The holding pattern will be to the south of the 270° radial, so the VORTAC (the fix) is at the end of the inbound leg. To determine entry procedures, draw a 70° line through the holding fix such that it crosses through the outbound leg 1/3 of the leg length from abeam the fix.

R-020 to R-090	Teardrop
R-090 to R-200	Parallel
R-200 to R-020	Direct

Since you are approaching the holding fix from the northwest on R-330 of ABC VORTAC (Fig. 114), you will make a direct entry.
    Answer (A) is incorrect. The parallel or teardrop entries are alternatives only when approaching on R-090. **Answer (B) is incorrect.** The parallel entry is appropriate only when approaching on R-090 to R-200.

59. (Refer to Figure 114 above.) A pilot receives this ATC clearance:

"...CLEARED TO THE XYZ VORTAC. HOLD NORTH ON THE THREE SIX ZERO RADIAL, LEFT TURNS..."

What is the recommended procedure to enter the holding pattern?

    A. Teardrop only.

    B. Parallel only.

    C. Direct only.

Answer (C) is correct. (AIM Para 5-3-8)
    DISCUSSION: Visualize a 360° radial with left turns. The pattern will be to the east of the radial with the holding fix being the VORTAC. Since you are approaching from the northwest on R-330 of XYZ VORTAC (Fig. 114), you will be able to make a direct entry.

R-180 to R-250	Teardrop
R-250 to R-070	Direct
R-070 to R-180	Parallel

    Answer (A) is incorrect. If you were approaching on R-180 to R-250, you would make a teardrop entry. **Answer (B) is incorrect.** If you were approaching on R-070 to R-180, you would fly through the VOR, parallel the holding course, turn right to the holding course, and make an entry.

60. (Refer to Figure 114 above.) A pilot receives this ATC clearance:

"...CLEARED TO THE ABC VORTAC. HOLD SOUTH ON THE ONE EIGHT ZERO RADIAL..."

What is the recommended procedure to enter the holding pattern?

    A. Teardrop only.

    B. Parallel only.

    C. Direct only.

Answer (A) is correct. (AIM Para 5-3-8)
    DISCUSSION: If you are holding south on the 180° radial, you will have right turns because left turns are not specified, and you will be on the east side of the radial (to cross the VORTAC at the end of your inbound leg). Draw the 70° line through the VORTAC on R-110/R-290. Since you are inbound on R-330 (Fig. 114), you will make a teardrop entry.

R-290 to R-360	Teardrop
R-360 to R-110	Parallel
R-110 to R-290	Direct

    Answer (B) is incorrect. A parallel entry is appropriate from R-360 to R-110. **Answer (C) is incorrect.** A direct entry is appropriate from R-110 to R-290.

61. (Refer to Figure 115 below.) You receive this ATC clearance:

"...HOLD WEST OF THE ONE FIVE DME FIX ON THE ZERO NINE ZERO RADIAL OF ABC VORTAC, FIVE MILE LEGS, LEFT TURNS..."

You arrive at the 15 DME fix on a heading of 350°. Which holding pattern correctly complies with these instructions, and what is the recommended entry procedure?

    A. 1; teardrop.

    B. 2; direct.

    C. 1; direct.

Answer (C) is correct. (AIM Para 5-3-8)
    DISCUSSION: Holding pattern 1 is correct because the holding fix is always at the end of the inbound leg. Draw the 70° line through the fix such that it intersects the outbound leg 1/3 of the leg length from abeam the fix.

Airplane Heading to Fix	Entry
340° to 160°	Direct
160° to 270°	Parallel
270° to 340°	Teardrop

    A 350° heading to the fix requires a direct entry, which requires a standard-rate left turn to 270° beginning over the holding fix.
    Answer (A) is incorrect. Approaching the fix on a heading of 350° requires a direct, not teardrop, entry. **Answer (B) is incorrect.** Holding pattern 2 does not show the holding fix at the end of the inbound leg.

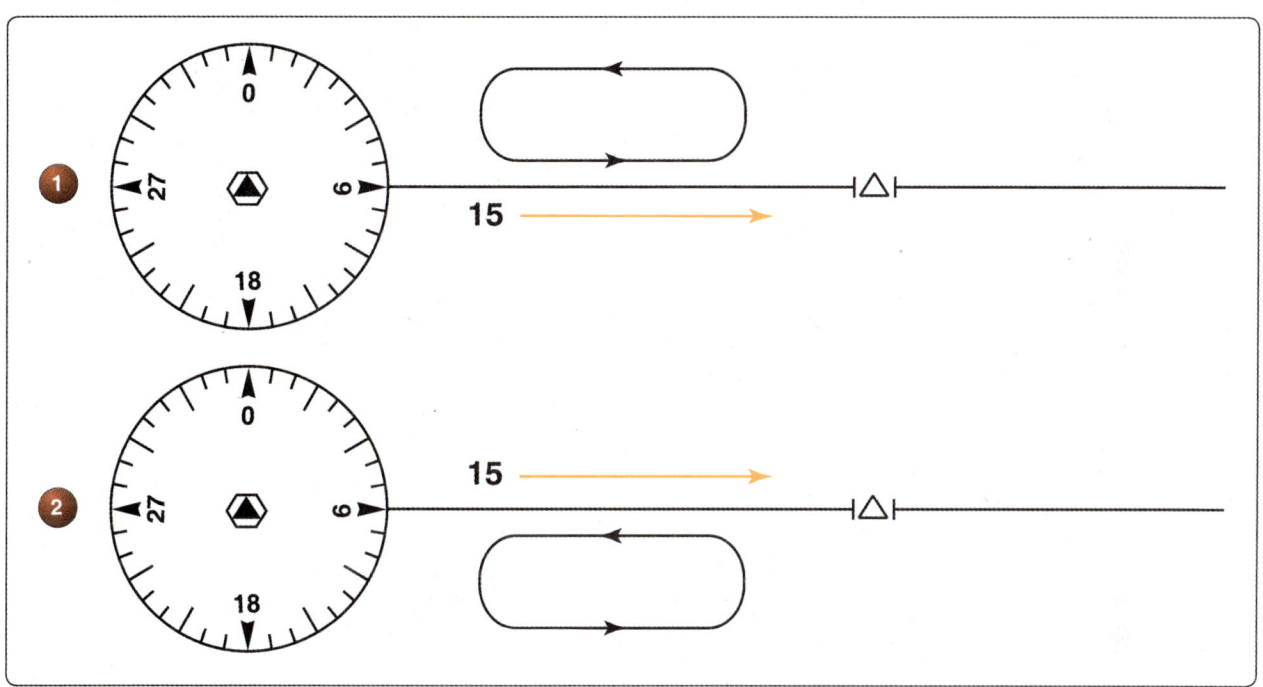

Figure 115. – DME Fix with Holding Pattern.

62. To ensure proper airspace protection while in a holding pattern above 14,000 feet in a propeller-driven airplane, what is the maximum indicated airspeed a pilot should use?

    A. 265 knots.

    B. 175 knots.

    C. 200 knots.

Answer (A) is correct. (AIM Para 5-3-8)
    DISCUSSION: The maximum indicated airspeed while in a holding pattern above 14,000 ft. in any airplane is 265 kt.
    Answer (B) is incorrect. This is a nonstandard maximum airspeed, which is depicted by an icon on the appropriate chart. **Answer (C) is incorrect.** This is the maximum holding airspeed for an airplane from the MHA through 6,000 ft., not above 14,000 ft.

63. To ensure proper airspace protection while in a holding pattern, what is the maximum airspeed above 14,000 feet for civil turbojet aircraft?

    A. 230 knots.

    B. 265 knots.

    C. 200 knots.

Answer (B) is correct. (AIM Para 5-3-8)
    DISCUSSION: For civil turbojets, the maximum indicated airspeed above 14,000 ft. MSL for holding patterns is 265 kt.
    Answer (A) is incorrect. This is the maximum holding airspeed for a civil turbojet from above 6,000 ft. through 14,000 ft., not above 14,000 ft. **Answer (C) is incorrect.** This is the maximum holding airspeed for a turbojet aircraft from the MHA through 6,000 ft., not above 14,000 ft.

64. (Refer to Figure 160 on page 253 and Legend 27 below.) What is the approximate rate of descent required (for planning purposes) to maintain the electronic glide slope at 105 knots ground speed?

A. 520 feet per minute.

B. 520 feet per NM.

C. 557 feet per minute.

Answer (C) is correct. (FAA-H-8083-16B Chap 5)
DISCUSSION: Fig. 160 confirms the glide slope is at 3°. On Legend 27, find "3.0" in the left-hand column labeled "Vertical Path Angle." Trace to the right until you find the columns for 90 and 120 kt. ground speed. Interpolate halfway between 478 and 637 fpm. The correct descent rate for planning purposes is 557 fpm. NOTE: The second column is the only one that lists values in feet per NM. All other columns are in fpm.

Answer (A) is incorrect. Planning to maintain a 3.0° glide slope at 105 kt. ground speed equates to a descent rate of 557, not 520, fpm. **Answer (B) is incorrect.** Planning to maintain a 3.0° glide slope at 105 kt. ground speed equates to a descent rate of 557 fpm, not 520 feet per NM. The second column in Legend 27 is the only one that lists values in feet per NM.

CLIMB/DESCENT TABLE 10042

INSTRUMENT TAKEOFF OR APPROACH PROCEDURE CHARTS
RATE OF CLIMB/DESCENT TABLE
(ft. per min)

A rate of climb/descent table is provided for use in planning and executing climbs or descents under known or approximate ground speed conditions. It will be especially useful for approaches when the localizer only is used for course guidance. A best speed, power, altitude combination can be programmed which will result in a stable glide rate and altitude favorable for executing a landing if minimums exist upon breakout. Care should always be exercised so that minimum descent altitude and missed approach point are not exceeded.

CLIMB/ DESCENT ANGLE (degrees and tenths)	ft/NM	GROUND SPEED (knots)										
		60	90	120	150	180	210	240	270	300	330	360
2.0	210	210	320	425	530	635	743	850	955	1060	1165	1275
2.5	265	265	400	530	665	795	930	1060	1195	1325	1460	1590
2.7	287	287	430	574	717	860	1003	1147	1290	1433	1576	1720
2.8	297	297	446	595	743	892	1041	1189	1338	1486	1635	1783
2.9	308	308	462	616	770	924	1078	1232	1386	1539	1693	1847
3.0	318	318	478	637	797	956	1115	1274	1433	1593	1752	1911
3.1	329	329	494	659	823	988	1152	1317	1481	1646	1810	1975
3.2	340	340	510	680	850	1020	1189	1359	1529	1699	1869	2039
3.3	350	350	526	701	876	1052	1227	1402	1577	1752	1927	2103
3.4	361	361	542	722	903	1083	1264	1444	1625	1805	1986	2166
3.5	370	370	555	745	930	1115	1300	1485	1670	1860	2045	2230
4.0	425	425	640	850	1065	1275	1490	1700	1915	2125	2340	2550
4.5	480	480	715	955	1195	1435	1675	1915	2150	2390	2630	2870
5.0	530	530	795	1065	1330	1595	1860	2125	2390	2660	2925	3190
5.5	585	585	880	1170	1465	1755	2050	2340	2635	2925	3220	3510
6.0	640	640	960	1275	1595	1915	2235	2555	2875	3195	3510	3830
6.5	690	690	1040	1385	1730	2075	2425	2770	3115	3460	3805	4155
7.0	745	745	1120	1490	1865	2240	2610	2985	3355	3730	4105	4475
7.5	800	800	1200	1600	2000	2400	2800	3200	3600	4000	4400	4800
8.0	855	855	1280	1710	2135	2560	2990	3415	3845	4270	4695	5125
8.5	910	910	1360	1815	2270	2725	3180	3630	4085	4540	4995	5450
9.0	960	960	1445	1925	2405	2885	3370	3850	4330	4810	5295	5775
9.5	1015	1015	1525	2035	2540	3050	3560	4065	4575	5085	5590	6100
10.0	1070	1070	1605	2145	2680	3215	3750	4285	4820	5355	5890	6430

CLIMB/DESCENT TABLE 10042

Legend 27. – Instrument Takeoff or Approach Procedure Charts, Rate-of-Climb/Descent Table.

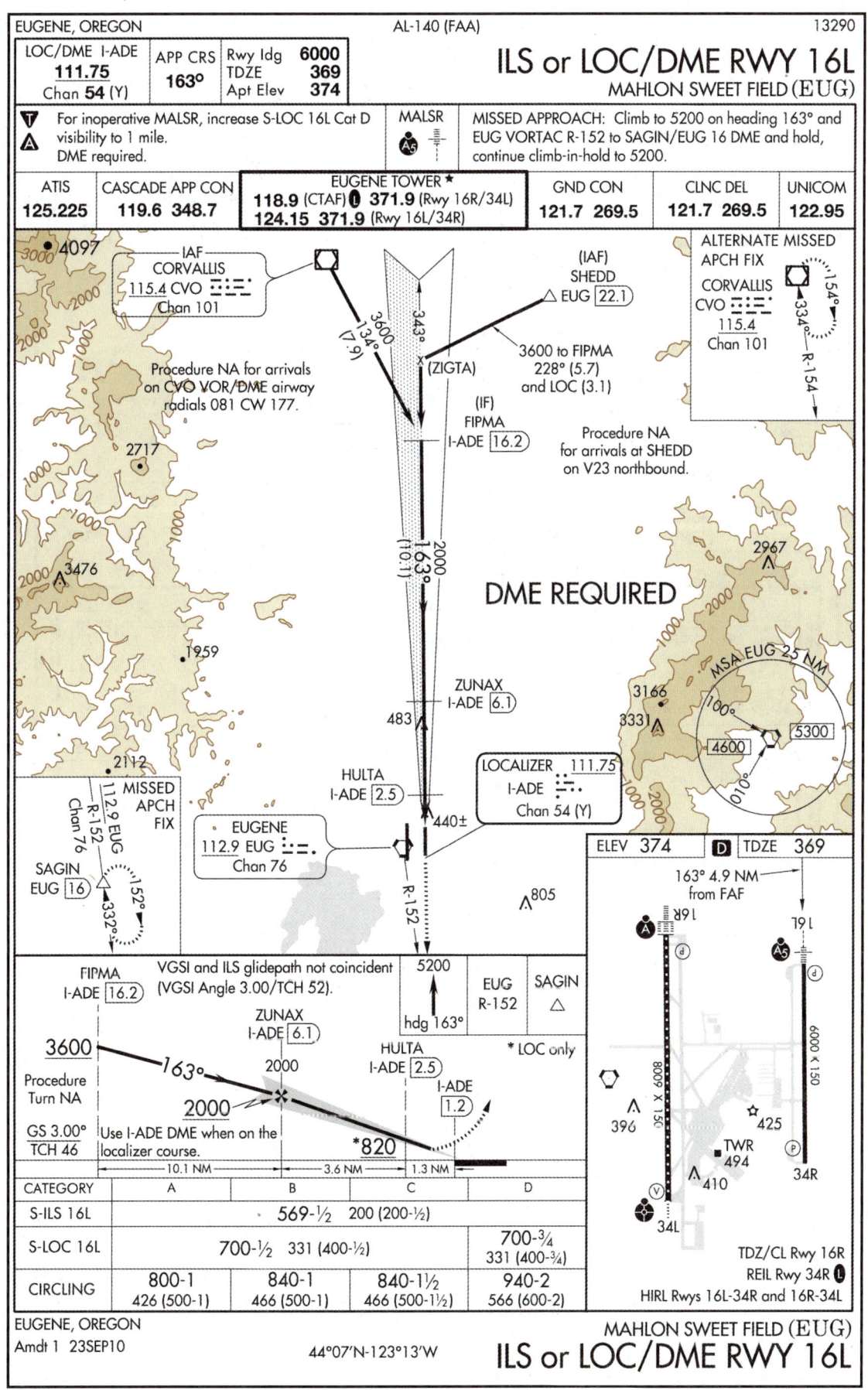

Figure 160. – ILS or LOC/DME RWY 16L (EUG).

65. (Refer to Figure 247 on page 255 and Legend 27 below.) With a 15 knot headwind while flying the ILS Rwy 9 at RAL with 90 knots, you expect to set power for a

A. 318 feet per minute rate of descent.

B. 398 feet per minute rate of descent.

C. 478 feet per minute rate of descent.

Answer (B) is correct. (FAA-H-8083-16B Chap 5)
DISCUSSION: Although flying at 90 kt., the 15-kt. headwind gives you a ground speed of 75 kt. Fig. 247 verifies the glide slope is 3.0°. Use Legend 27 to find the 3.0° vertical path angle, then move right until that row intersects with the 60- and 90-kt. ground speed columns. Interpolate halfway between 318 and 478 fpm. Expect to set power for a 398 fpm rate of descent.
Answer (A) is incorrect. Power set for a 318 fpm rate of descent would be appropriate for a 60-kt. ground speed.
Answer (C) is incorrect. Power set for a 478 fpm rate of descent would be appropriate for a 90-kt. ground speed.

CLIMB/DESCENT TABLE 10042

INSTRUMENT TAKEOFF OR APPROACH PROCEDURE CHARTS
RATE OF CLIMB/DESCENT TABLE
(ft. per min)

A rate of climb/descent table is provided for use in planning and executing climbs or descents under known or approximate ground speed conditions. It will be especially useful for approaches when the localizer only is used for course guidance. A best speed, power, altitude combination can be programmed which will result in a stable glide rate and altitude favorable for executing a landing if minimums exist upon breakout. Care should always be exercised so that minimum descent altitude and missed approach point are not exceeded.

CLIMB/DESCENT ANGLE (degrees and tenths)	ft/NM	GROUND SPEED (knots)										
		60	90	120	150	180	210	240	270	300	330	360
2.0	210	210	320	425	530	635	743	850	955	1060	1165	1275
2.5	265	265	400	530	665	795	930	1060	1195	1325	1460	1590
2.7	287	287	430	574	717	860	1003	1147	1290	1433	1576	1720
2.8	297	297	446	595	743	892	1041	1189	1338	1486	1635	1783
2.9	308	308	462	616	770	924	1078	1232	1386	1539	1693	1847
3.0	318	318	478	637	797	956	1115	1274	1433	1593	1752	1911
3.1	329	329	494	659	823	988	1152	1317	1481	1646	1810	1975
3.2	340	340	510	680	850	1020	1189	1359	1529	1699	1869	2039
3.3	350	350	526	701	876	1052	1227	1402	1577	1752	1927	2103
3.4	361	361	542	722	903	1083	1264	1444	1625	1805	1986	2166
3.5	370	370	555	745	930	1115	1300	1485	1670	1860	2045	2230
4.0	425	425	640	850	1065	1275	1490	1700	1915	2125	2340	2550
4.5	480	480	715	955	1195	1435	1675	1915	2150	2390	2630	2870
5.0	530	530	795	1065	1330	1595	1860	2125	2390	2660	2925	3190
5.5	585	585	880	1170	1465	1755	2050	2340	2635	2925	3220	3510
6.0	640	640	960	1275	1595	1915	2235	2555	2875	3195	3510	3830
6.5	690	690	1040	1385	1730	2075	2425	2770	3115	3460	3805	4155
7.0	745	745	1120	1490	1865	2240	2610	2985	3355	3730	4105	4475
7.5	800	800	1200	1600	2000	2400	2800	3200	3600	4000	4400	4800
8.0	855	855	1280	1710	2135	2560	2990	3415	3845	4270	4695	5125
8.5	910	910	1360	1815	2270	2725	3180	3630	4085	4540	4995	5450
9.0	960	960	1445	1925	2405	2885	3370	3850	4330	4810	5295	5775
9.5	1015	1015	1525	2035	2540	3050	3560	4065	4575	5085	5590	6100
10.0	1070	1070	1605	2145	2680	3215	3750	4285	4820	5355	5890	6430

CLIMB/DESCENT TABLE 10042

Legend 27. – Instrument Takeoff or Approach Procedure Charts, Rate-of-Climb/Descent Table.

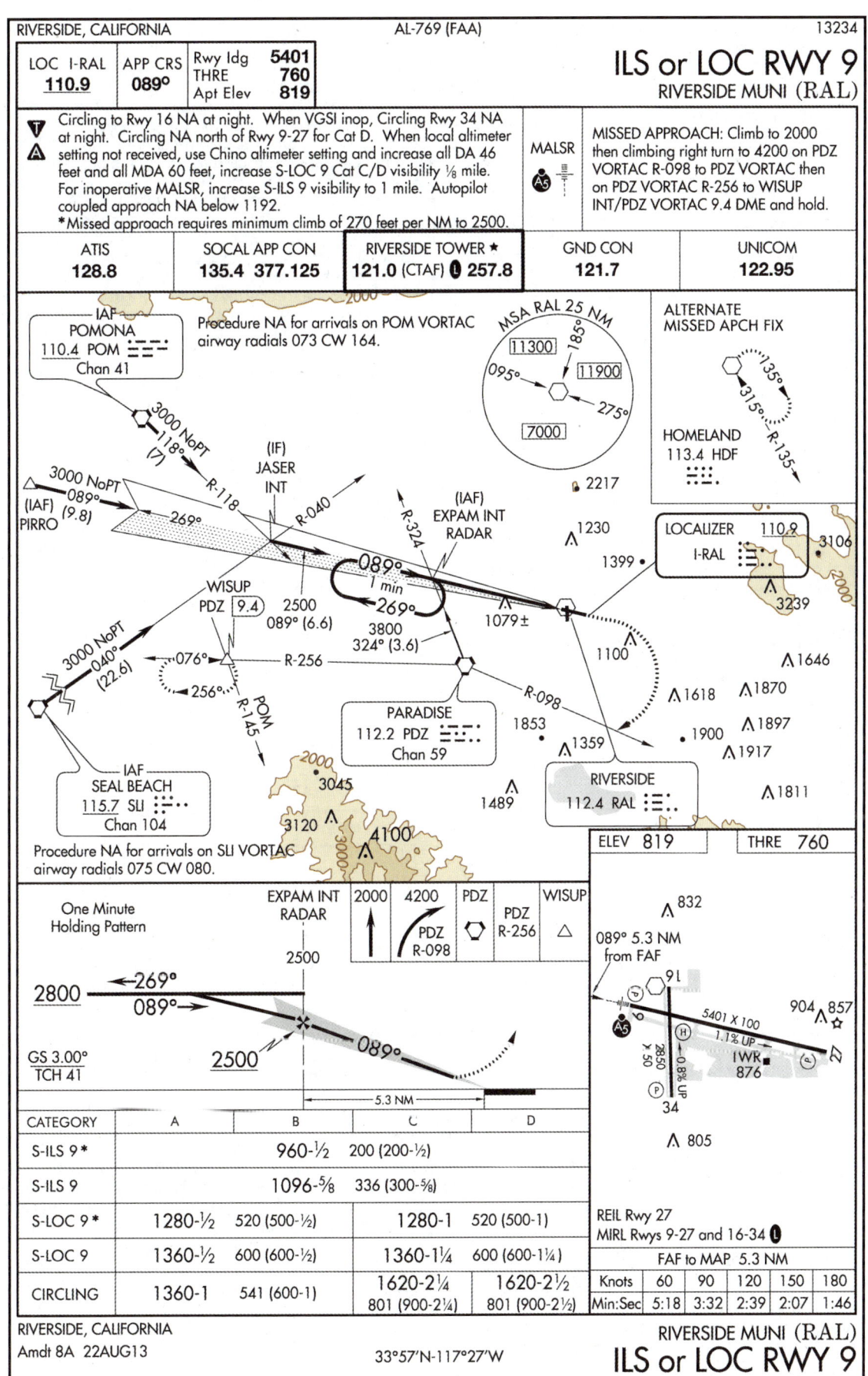

Figure 247. – ILS or RWY 9 (RAL).

66. (Refer to Figure 116 below.) You arrive over the 15 DME fix on a heading of 350°. Which holding pattern correctly complies with the ATC clearance below, and what is the recommended entry procedure?

"...HOLD WEST OF THE ONE FIVE DME FIX ON THE TWO SIX EIGHT RADIAL OF THE ABC VORTAC, FIVE MILE LEGS, LEFT TURNS..."

    A. 1; teardrop entry.

    B. 2; direct entry.

    C. 1; direct entry.

Answer (B) is correct. (AIM Para 5-3-8)
    DISCUSSION: Based on the drawing in image 2, you can cross the fix, then safely turn to the outbound heading (268°) and fly the outbound leg for 5 miles. A left turn inbound will bring you onto the appropriate radial, which you can track inbound to establish yourself in the hold. This procedure describes a direct entry with left turns. Draw the station, the radial, and your position out on paper to better visualize this procedure.
    Answer (A) is incorrect. The drawing in image 1 shows a track that leads away from the fix while established on the radial. That is opposite the norm, which has the pilot flying the inbound leg (flying toward the fix) while established on the radial. The entry type is immaterial, since the direction of the hold is incorrect. **Answer (C) is incorrect.** The drawing in image 1 shows a track that leads away from the fix while established on the radial. That is opposite the norm, which has the pilot flying the inbound leg (flying toward the fix) while established on the radial. The entry type is immaterial, since the direction of the hold is incorrect.

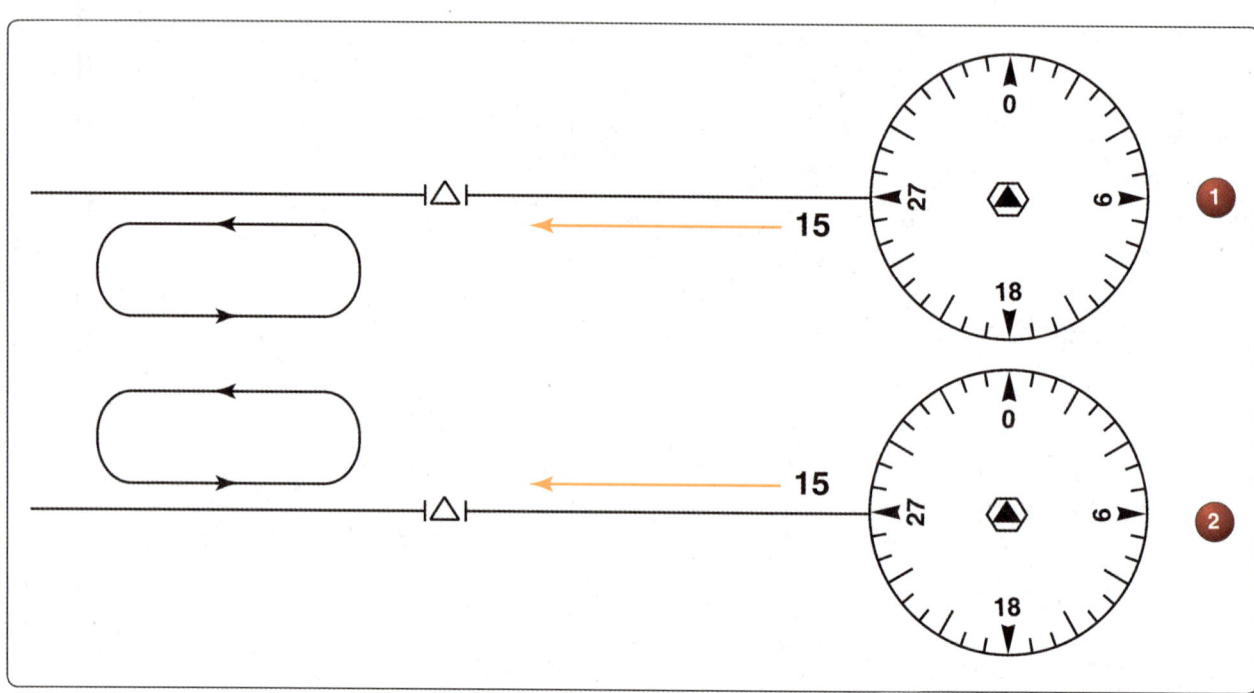

Figure 116. – Holding Entry Procedure.

67. (Refer to Figure 232 on page 257.) During the LOC RWY 35 missed approach at Duncan/Halliburton Field (DUC), what would be the appropriate entry for the holding?

    A. Direct.

    B. Teardrop.

    C. Parallel.

Answer (C) is correct. (FAA-H-8083-15B Chap 10)
    DISCUSSION: Because you will arrive at the fix aligned within approximately 25° of the reciprocal of the inbound hold, a parallel entry is appropriate.
    Answer (A) is incorrect. Upon arrival at the fix, you will be roughly aligned with the reciprocal of the inbound fix, not inbound on the fix itself. A direct entry would be impractical. **Answer (B) is incorrect.** You will arrive at the fix on a heading of approximately 170°, which nearly aligns with the outbound course of the hold. A teardrop entry would be for an aircraft arriving on a heading of somewhere between 77° and 147°.

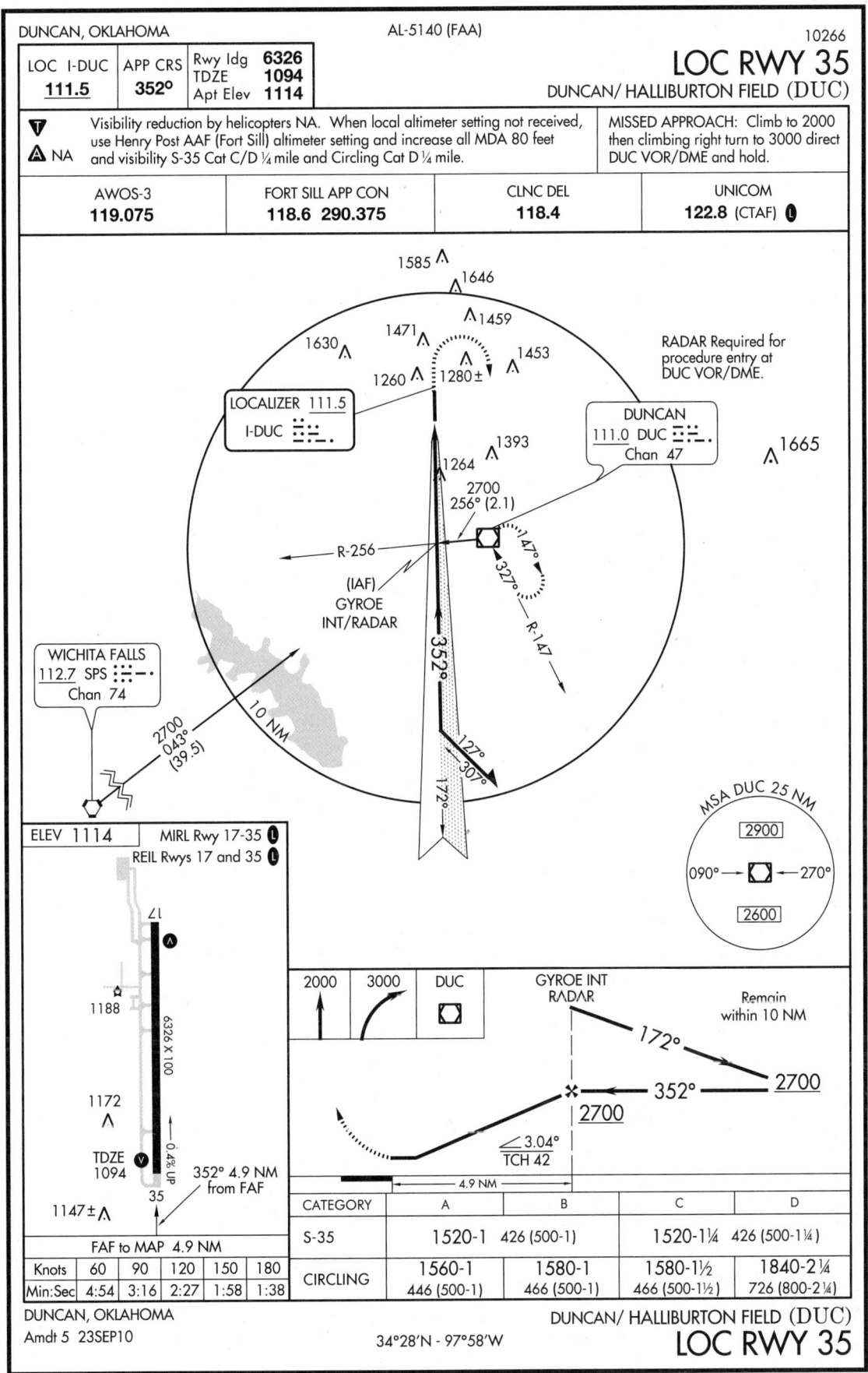

AL-5140 (FAA)

10266

LOC RWY 35
DUNCAN/ HALLIBURTON FIELD (DUC)

LOC I-DUC	APP CRS	Rwy ldg	6326
111.5	**352°**	TDZE	**1094**
		Apt Elev	**1114**

Visibility reduction by helicopters NA. When local altimeter setting not received, use Henry Post AAF (Fort Sill) altimeter setting and increase all MDA 80 feet and visibility S-35 Cat C/D ¼ mile and Circling Cat D ¼ mile.

NA

MISSED APPROACH: Climb to 2000 then climbing right turn to 3000 direct DUC VOR/DME and hold.

AWOS-3	FORT SILL APP CON	CLNC DEL	UNICOM
119.075	**118.6 290.375**	**118.4**	**122.8** (CTAF)

RADAR Required for procedure entry at DUC VOR/DME.

LOCALIZER 111.5
I-DUC

DUNCAN
111.0 DUC
Chan 47

2700
256° (2.1)

R-256

(IAF)
GYROE
INT/RADAR

147°
327°
R-147

352°

WICHITA FALLS
112.7 SPS
Chan 74

2700
043°
(39.5)

10 NM

127°
307°
172°

MSA DUC 25 NM

2900

090° — 270°

2600

ELEV 1114

MIRL Rwy 17-35
REIL Rwys 17 and 35

17

1188

6326 X 100

1172

0.4% UP

TDZE
1094

35

352° 4.9 NM
from FAF

1147±

FAF to MAP 4.9 NM

2000	3000	DUC		GYROE INT RADAR		Remain within 10 NM

172°
2700

352°
2700
2700

3.04°
TCH 42

4.9 NM

Knots	60	90	120	150	180
Min:Sec	4:54	3:16	2:27	1:58	1:38

CATEGORY	A	B	C	D
S-35	1520-1 426 (500-1)		1520-1¼ 426 (500-1¼)	
CIRCLING	1560-1 446 (500-1)	1580-1 466 (500-1)	1580-1½ 466 (500-1½)	1840-2¼ 726 (800-2¼)

DUNCAN/ HALLIBURTON FIELD (DUC)
LOC RWY 35

Figure 232. – LOC RWY 35 (DUC).

68. (Refer to Figure 223 on page 259 and Legend 27 below.) You have been cleared for the ILS RWY 31 approach to DSM. At a ground speed of 90 knots, what is the rate of descent on final approach?

A. 478 feet per minute.

B. 318 feet per minute.

C. 637 feet per nautical mile.

Answer (A) is correct. *(FAA-H-8083-16B Chap 5)*
DISCUSSION: Figure 223 confirms the glide slope is at 3°. On Legend 27, find "3.0" in the left-hand column labeled "Vertical Path Angle." Trace to the right until you find the column for 90 kt. groundspeed. The correct descent rate for planning purposes is 478 fpm. NOTE: The second column is the only one that lists values in feet per NM. All other columns are in fpm.
Answer (B) is incorrect. A 318 fpm descent rate corresponds to a vertical path angle of 3° at a 60 kt. groundspeed.
Answer (C) is incorrect. A 637 fpm descent rate corresponds to a vertical path angle of 3° at a 90 kt. groundspeed.

CLIMB/DESCENT TABLE 10042

INSTRUMENT TAKEOFF OR APPROACH PROCEDURE CHARTS
RATE OF CLIMB/DESCENT TABLE
(ft. per min)

A rate of climb/descent table is provided for use in planning and executing climbs or descents under known or approximate ground speed conditions. It will be especially useful for approaches when the localizer only is used for course guidance. A best speed, power, altitude combination can be programmed which will result in a stable glide rate and altitude favorable for executing a landing if minimums exist upon breakout. Care should always be exercised so that minimum descent altitude and missed approach point are not exceeded.

CLIMB/DESCENT ANGLE (degrees and tenths)	ft/NM	GROUND SPEED (knots)										
		60	90	120	150	180	210	240	270	300	330	360
2.0	210	210	320	425	530	635	743	850	955	1060	1165	1275
2.5	265	265	400	530	665	795	930	1060	1195	1325	1460	1590
2.7	287	287	430	574	717	860	1003	1147	1290	1433	1576	1720
2.8	297	297	446	595	743	892	1041	1189	1338	1486	1635	1783
2.9	308	308	462	616	770	924	1078	1232	1386	1539	1693	1847
3.0	318	318	478	637	797	956	1115	1274	1433	1593	1752	1911
3.1	329	329	494	659	823	988	1152	1317	1481	1646	1810	1975
3.2	340	340	510	680	850	1020	1189	1359	1529	1699	1869	2039
3.3	350	350	526	701	876	1052	1227	1402	1577	1752	1927	2103
3.4	361	361	542	722	903	1083	1264	1444	1625	1805	1986	2166
3.5	370	370	555	745	930	1115	1300	1485	1670	1860	2045	2230
4.0	425	425	640	850	1065	1275	1490	1700	1915	2125	2340	2550
4.5	480	480	715	955	1195	1435	1675	1915	2150	2390	2630	2870
5.0	530	530	795	1065	1330	1595	1860	2125	2390	2660	2925	3190
5.5	585	585	880	1170	1465	1755	2050	2340	2635	2925	3220	3510
6.0	640	640	960	1275	1595	1915	2235	2555	2875	3195	3510	3830
6.5	690	690	1040	1385	1730	2075	2425	2770	3115	3460	3805	4155
7.0	745	745	1120	1490	1865	2240	2610	2985	3355	3730	4105	4475
7.5	800	800	1200	1600	2000	2400	2800	3200	3600	4000	4400	4800
8.0	855	855	1280	1710	2135	2560	2990	3415	3845	4270	4695	5125
8.5	910	910	1360	1815	2270	2725	3180	3630	4085	4540	4995	5450
9.0	960	960	1445	1925	2405	2885	3370	3850	4330	4810	5295	5775
9.5	1015	1015	1525	2035	2540	3050	3560	4065	4575	5085	5590	6100
10.0	1070	1070	1605	2145	2680	3215	3750	4285	4820	5355	5890	6430

CLIMB/DESCENT TABLE 10042

Legend 27. – Instrument Takeoff or Approach Procedure Charts, Rate-of-Climb/Descent Table.

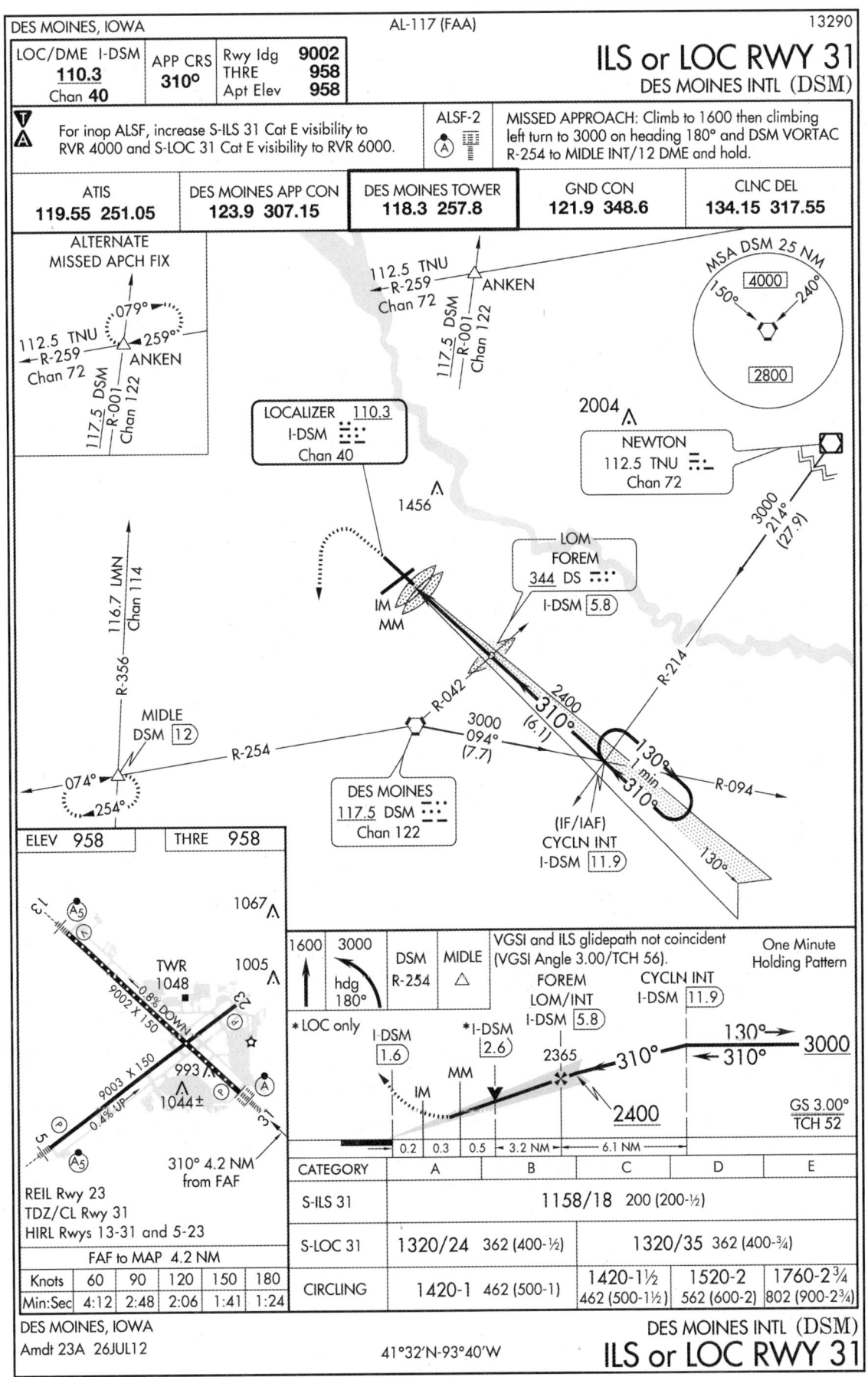

Figure 223. – ILS or LOC RWY 31 (DSM).

69. At what point should the timing begin for the first leg outbound in a nonstandard holding pattern?

A. Abeam the holding fix, or wings level, whichever occurs last.

B. When the wings are level at the completion of the 180° turn outbound.

C. When over or abeam the holding fix, whichever occurs later.

Answer (C) is correct. *(FAA-H-8083-15B Chap 10)*
DISCUSSION: Outbound leg timing begins when over or abeam the holding fix, whichever occurs later. If the abeam position cannot be determined, start timing when the turn to outbound is completed (i.e., wings return to level).
Answer (A) is incorrect. Timing begins on the outbound leg when the wings are level only if the abeam position cannot be determined. **Answer (B) is incorrect.** The wings may be level before you are abeam the fix.

70. What timing procedure should be used when performing a holding pattern at a VOR?

A. Timing for the outbound leg begins over or abeam the VOR, whichever occurs later.

B. Timing for the inbound leg begins when initiating the turn inbound.

C. Adjustments in timing of each pattern should be made on the inbound leg.

Answer (A) is correct. *(AIM Para 5-3-8)*
DISCUSSION: Outbound leg timing begins over or abeam the fix, whichever occurs later. If abeam the position cannot be determined, start timing when the turn to outbound is completed.
Answer (B) is incorrect. The timing for the inbound leg begins when the inbound turn is completed, not when it is initiated. **Answer (C) is incorrect.** The timing of the pattern is adjusted by varying the length of the outbound leg. Once inbound, you must fly to the holding fix and cannot adjust the length of the leg.

71. To ensure proper airspace protection while holding at 5,000 feet in a civil aircraft, what is the maximum indicated airspeed a pilot should use?

A. 230 knots.

B. 200 knots.

C. 210 knots.

Answer (B) is correct. *(AIM Para 5-3-8)*
DISCUSSION: The maximum airspeed in holding patterns for a civil aircraft is 200 kt. from the minimum holding altitude (MHA) through 6,000 ft.
Answer (A) is incorrect. This is the maximum holding speed from 6,001 ft. through 14,000 ft. **Answer (C) is incorrect.** This is the maximum holding airspeed from 6,001 ft. through 14,000 ft. where published.

72. Where a holding pattern is specified in lieu of a procedure turn, the holding maneuver must be executed within

A. the 1-minute time limitation or DME distance as specified in the profile view.

B. a radius of 5 miles from the holding fix.

C. 10 knots of the specified holding speed.

Answer (A) is correct. *(AIM Para 5-3-8)*
DISCUSSION: Holding patterns should always be executed within the time or leg length published in the profile view of the IAP.
Answer (B) is incorrect. A radius of 5 mi. for a procedure turn can be specified only for category A or helicopter aircraft. **Answer (C) is incorrect.** ATC does not specify a holding speed. You need only remain below the maximum allowable holding speed.

73. When more than one circuit of the holding pattern is needed to lose altitude or become better established on course, the additional circuits can be made

A. at pilot's discretion.

B. only in an emergency.

C. only if pilot advises ATC and ATC approves.

Answer (C) is correct. *(AIM Para 5-4-8)*
DISCUSSION: If you are cleared for the approach while in a holding pattern, ATC will not expect you to make any additional circuits in the hold. If you do elect to make additional circuits to lose altitude or become better established on course, it is your responsibility to so advise ATC when you receive your approach clearance.
Answer (A) is incorrect. While you may elect to make additional circuits in the holding pattern, you are required to advise ATC of your intentions. **Answer (B) is incorrect.** Additional circuits may be made at your discretion; declaring an emergency is not necessary.

6.11 Instrument Approach Charts

74. How can an initial approach fix be identified on a Standard Instrument Approach Procedure (SIAP) Chart?

    A. All fixes that are labeled "IAF" which are depicted on the plan view.

    B. Any fix depicted which is located on the final approach course.

    C. Any fix depicted which is located on the final approach course prior to the final approach fix.

Answer (A) is correct. (P/C Glossary)
    DISCUSSION: The fixes depicted on Instrument Approach Procedure Charts that identify the beginning of an initial approach segment are the initial approach fixes (IAF). Initial approach fixes are identified by the letters IAF on the plan view on instrument approach charts. There may be more than one for any given approach.
    Answer (B) is incorrect. IAFs are specifically identified with "IAF." **Answer (C) is incorrect.** IAFs are specifically identified with "IAF."

75. Which fixes on the IAP Charts are initial approach fixes?

    A. Any fix on the en route facilities ring, the feeder facilities ring, and those at the start of arc approaches.

    B. Only the fixes at the start of arc approaches and those on either the feeder facilities ring or en route facilities ring that have a transition course shown to the approach procedure.

    C. Any fix that is identified by the letters IAF.

Answer (C) is correct. (P/C Glossary)
    DISCUSSION: The fixes depicted on Instrument Approach Procedure Charts that identify the beginning of an initial approach segment are the initial approach fixes (IAF). Initial approach fixes are identified by the letters IAF on instrument approach charts. There may be more than one for any given approach.
    Answer (A) is incorrect. IAFs are specifically identified with "IAF." **Answer (B) is incorrect.** IAFs are specifically identified with "IAF."

76. Aircraft approach categories are based on

    A. certificated approach speed at maximum gross weight.

    B. 1.3 times the stall speed in landing configuration at maximum gross landing weight.

    C. 1.3 times the stall speed at maximum gross weight.

Answer (B) is correct. (FAA-H-8083-15B Chap 10)
    DISCUSSION: IFR approach minimums are specified for various aircraft speed/weight combinations. Speeds are based upon the value of 1.3 times the stall speed of the aircraft in the landing configuration at maximum certified gross landing weight.
    Answer (A) is incorrect. Aircraft do not have certificated approach speeds. **Answer (C) is incorrect.** Speeds are based on 1.3 times the stall speed in landing configuration at maximum gross landing weight, not just maximum gross weight.

77. How can the pilot determine, for an ILS runway equipped with MALSR, that there may be a penetration of the obstacle identification surfaces (OIS), and care should be taken in the visual segment to avoid any obstacles?

    A. The runway has a visual approach slope indicator (VASI).

    B. The published visibility for the ILS is no lower than 3/4 SM.

    C. The approach chart has a visual descent point (VDP) published.

Answer (B) is correct. (FAA-H-8083-16B Chap 5)
    DISCUSSION: If there is penetration of the obstacle identification surfaces (OIS), the published visibility for the ILS approach can be no lower than 3/4 SM.
    Answer (A) is incorrect. If there is penetration of the obstacle identification surfaces for a particular approach, the way to determine that is so is to refer to the visibility minimums for the approach. A VASI-equipped runway is not an indication of the penetration of obstacle identification surfaces. **Answer (C) is incorrect.** If there is penetration of the obstacle identification surfaces for a particular approach, the way to determine that is so is to refer to the visibility minimums for the approach. An approach chart that has a published visual descent point is not an indication of the penetration of obstacle identification surfaces.

78. (Refer to Figure 187 below.) When the MALSR are NOTAM'd out of service, what are the minimums for a category B airplane LPV approach?

A. 2400 RVR.

B. 5500 RVR.

C. 4500 RVR.

Answer (C) is correct. *(FAA-H-8083-15B Chap 8)*
DISCUSSION: See the note in the upper left-hand corner of the approach plate, which stipulates increased minimums for inoperative MALSR. It increases LPV minimums for all categories to 4500 RVR.

Answer (A) is incorrect. The note in the upper left-hand corner of the approach plate increases LPV minimums for all categories to 4500 RVR, not 2400 RVR. **Answer (B) is incorrect.** The note in the upper left-hand corner of the approach plate increases LPV minimums for all categories to 4500 RVR, not 5500 RVR. That higher value is established for LNAV category approaches, not LPV approaches.

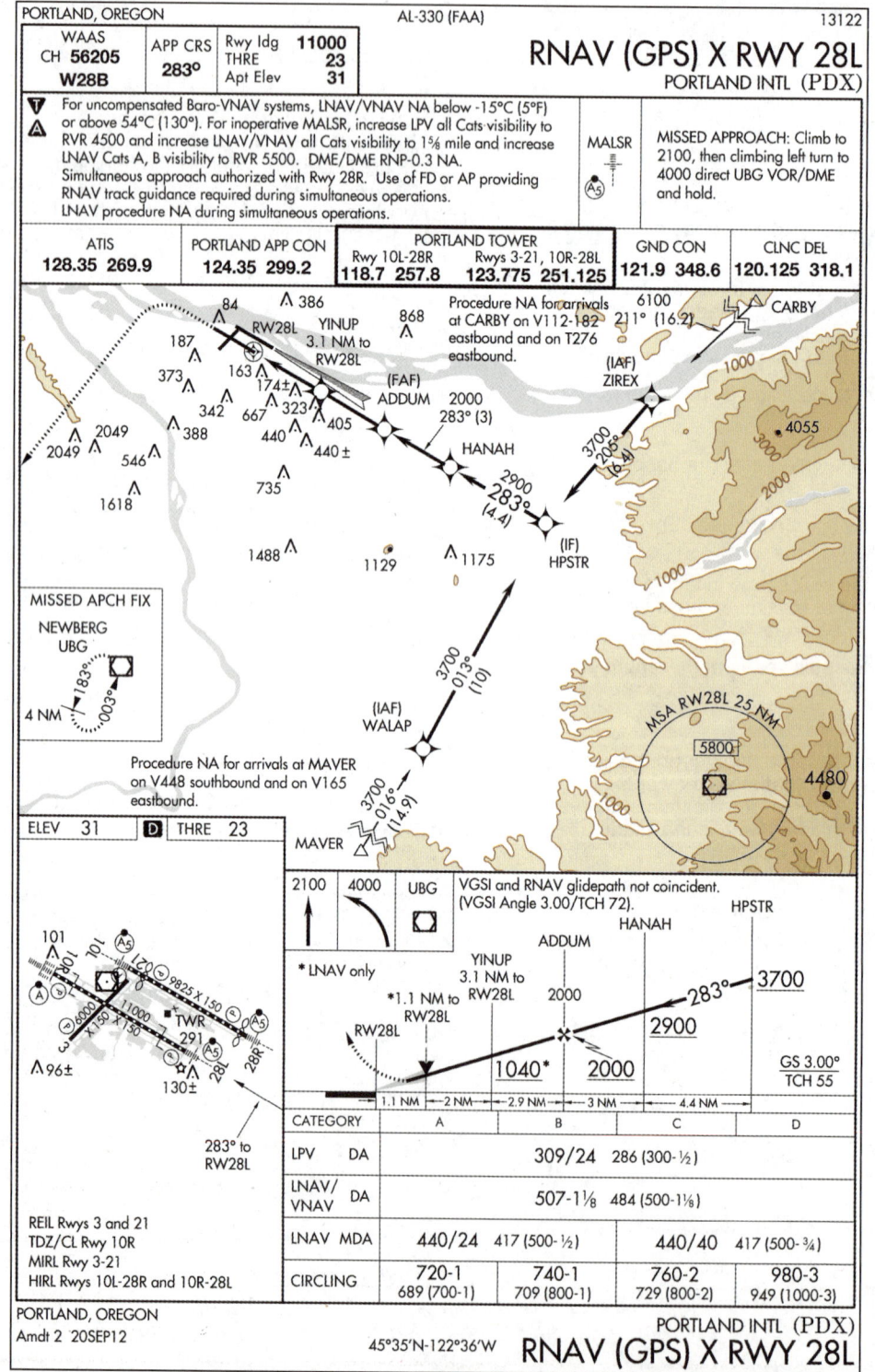

Figure 187. – RNAV (GPS) X RWY 28L (PDX).

79. (Refer to Figure 196 below.) What is the elevation of the TDZE for RWY 4?

A. 70 feet MSL.

B. 57 feet MSL.

C. 44 feet MSL.

Answer (C) is correct. *(FAA-H-8083-15B Chap 10)*
DISCUSSION: The TDZE (touchdown zone elevation) is the highest elevation in the first 3,000 ft. of the runway on a straight-in landing approach. It is marked at the top of the airport diagram block. Thus, the TDZE for RWY 4 is 44 ft. MSL.
Answer (A) is incorrect. This is the elevation of a tower near the approach end of RWY 4. **Answer (B) is incorrect.** This is the TCH (threshold crossing height) on the ILS RWY 4 approach, i.e., the height at which the airplane's glide slope antenna should cross the runway's threshold on the glide slope.

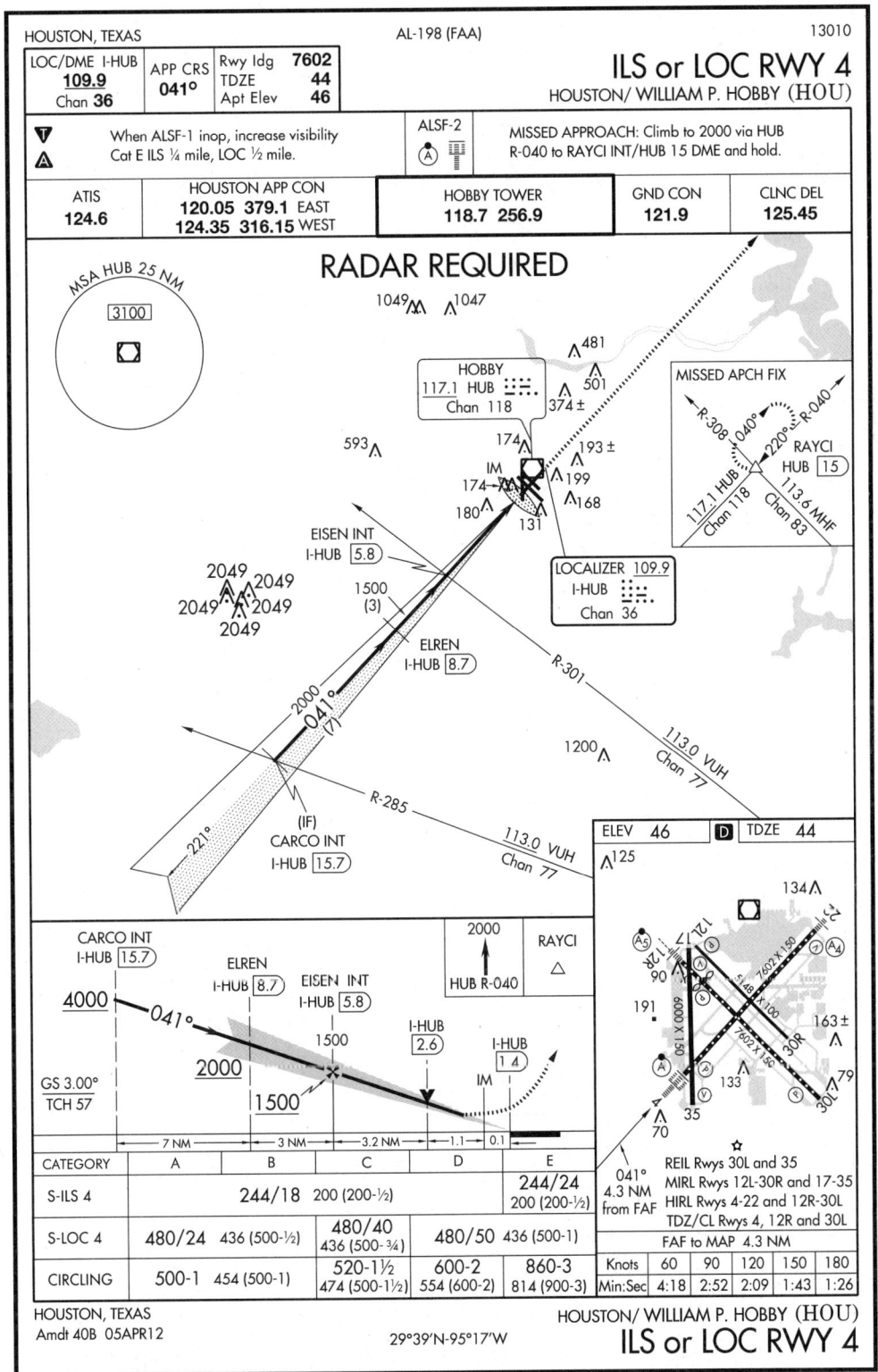

Figure 196. – ILS or LOC RWY 4 (HOU).

80. (Refer to Figure 210 below.) What is the TDZE elevation for RWY 6?

A. 173 feet MSL.

B. 200 feet AGL.

C. 270 feet MSL.

Answer (A) is correct. *(IAP Chart)*
  DISCUSSION: The instrument approach procedure (IAP) has the TDZE (touchdown zone elevation) located in the upper right corner of the airport diagram block. The TDZE is 173 ft. MSL.
  Answer (B) is incorrect. The altitude minimum for the ILS approach, not the TDZE, is 200 ft. AGL. **Answer (C) is incorrect.** The TDZE is labeled on the IAP chart as TDZE 173.

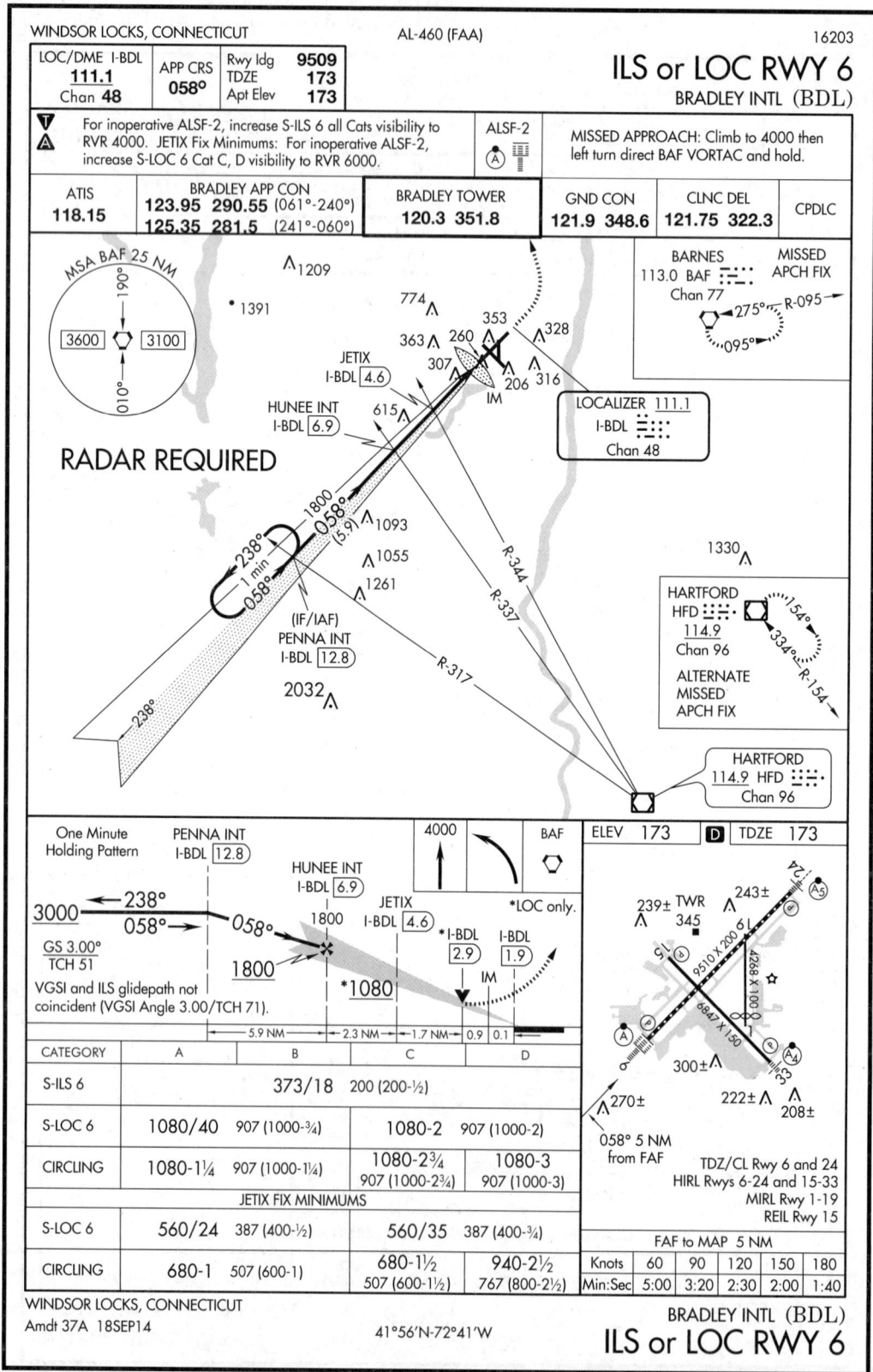

Figure 210. – ILS or LOC RWY 6 (CAT I) (BDL).

81. (Refer to Figure 213 below.) The threshold elevation for landing on RWY 28R is

A.   4,260 feet MSL.

B.   3,488 feet MSL.

C.   3,940 feet MSL.

Answer (B) is correct. *(AIM Para 5-4-6)*
   DISCUSSION: The threshold elevation for RWY 28R, visible in the briefing strip and airport diagram sections of the approach chart, is 3,488 ft. MSL. Touchdown zone elevation (TDZE) is commonly found on FAA approach charts.
   Answer (A) is incorrect. On Fig. 213, 4,260 ft. MSL is a minimum altitude, depicted as a number with a line below it on the profile view. **Answer (C) is incorrect.** On Fig. 213, 3,940 ft. MSL represents the straight-in landing minimum for RWY 28R, as seen in the landing minimums section.

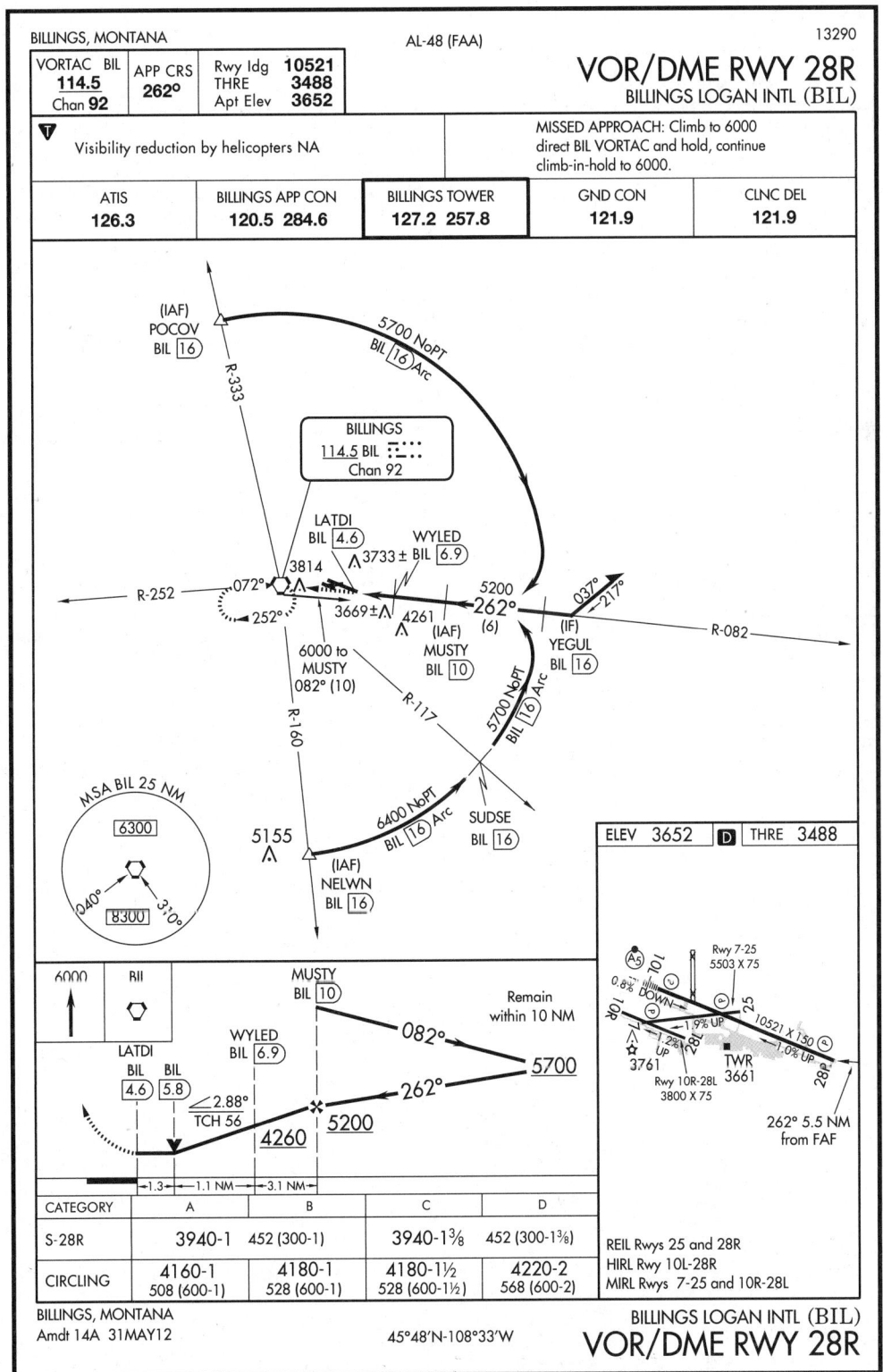

Figure 213. – VOR/DME RWY 28R (BIL).

82. (Refer to Figure 217 on page 267.) During the ILS RWY 13 procedure at DSM, what altitude minimum applies if the glide slope becomes inoperative?

A.   1,420 feet.

B.   1,380 feet.

C.   1,121 feet.

Answer (B) is correct. (AIM Para 1-1-9)
   DISCUSSION: If the glide slope fails during an ILS approach, the approach can be continued as a nonprecision localizer approach. The MDA for the LOC RWY 13 is 1,380 feet.
   Answer (A) is incorrect. This is the circling, not straight-in, MDA for Categories B and C. **Answer (C) is incorrect.** This is the DH for the ILS, not the MDA for the localizer.

83. (Refer to Figure 217 on page 267.) The symbol on the plan view of the ILS or LOC RWY 13 procedure at DSM represents a minimum safe sector altitude within 25 NM of

A.   Des Moines VORTAC.

B.   CLIVE outer marker.

C.   Des Moines International Airport.

Answer (A) is correct. (AIM Para 5-4-5)
   DISCUSSION: Minimum safe altitudes provide obstacle clearance within 25 NM of the specified navigational facility. In Fig. 217, the MSA circle specifies DSM VORTAC.
   Answer (B) is incorrect. An MSA for the ILS or LOC RWY 13 at DSM is based on Des Moines VORTAC, not the OM. **Answer (C) is incorrect.** An MSA will always be based on a navigation facility or a waypoint (GPS or RNAV approach), not an airport.

84. (Refer to Figure 217 on page 267.) During the ILS RWY 13 procedure at DSM, the minimum altitude for glide slope interception is

A.   2,548 feet MSL.

B.   2,600 feet MSL.

C.   3,500 feet MSL.

Answer (B) is correct. (P/C Glossary)
   DISCUSSION: The minimum glide slope interception altitude for an ILS is the FAF (marked by a lightning bolt). In Fig. 217, the FAF is 2,600 ft. MSL.
   Answer (A) is incorrect. This is the glide slope altitude over the LOM. **Answer (C) is incorrect.** This is the minimum procedure turn altitude.

85. (Refer to Figure 217 on page 267.) During the approach to DSM before you can begin the ILS RWY 13 procedure, the glide slope fails and you are cleared for the LOC RWY 13 at DSM. What altitude minimum applies?

A.   1,420 feet.

B.   1,380 feet.

C.   1,121 feet.

Answer (B) is correct. (AIM Para 1-1-9, IAP Chart)
   DISCUSSION: You are cleared for the LOC RWY 13 at DSM. At the bottom of the IAP chart under the heading "CATEGORY," you will see S-LOC 13 in the second line. To the right of that indicates the minimums for a straight-in, localizer approach to runway 13. The minimum altitude is indicated as 1,380 feet.
   Answer (A) is incorrect. The minimum altitude for a circling to land procedure for runway 13 is 1,420 feet. **Answer (C) is incorrect.** The minimum altitude for an ILS approach for runway 13 is 1,121 feet.

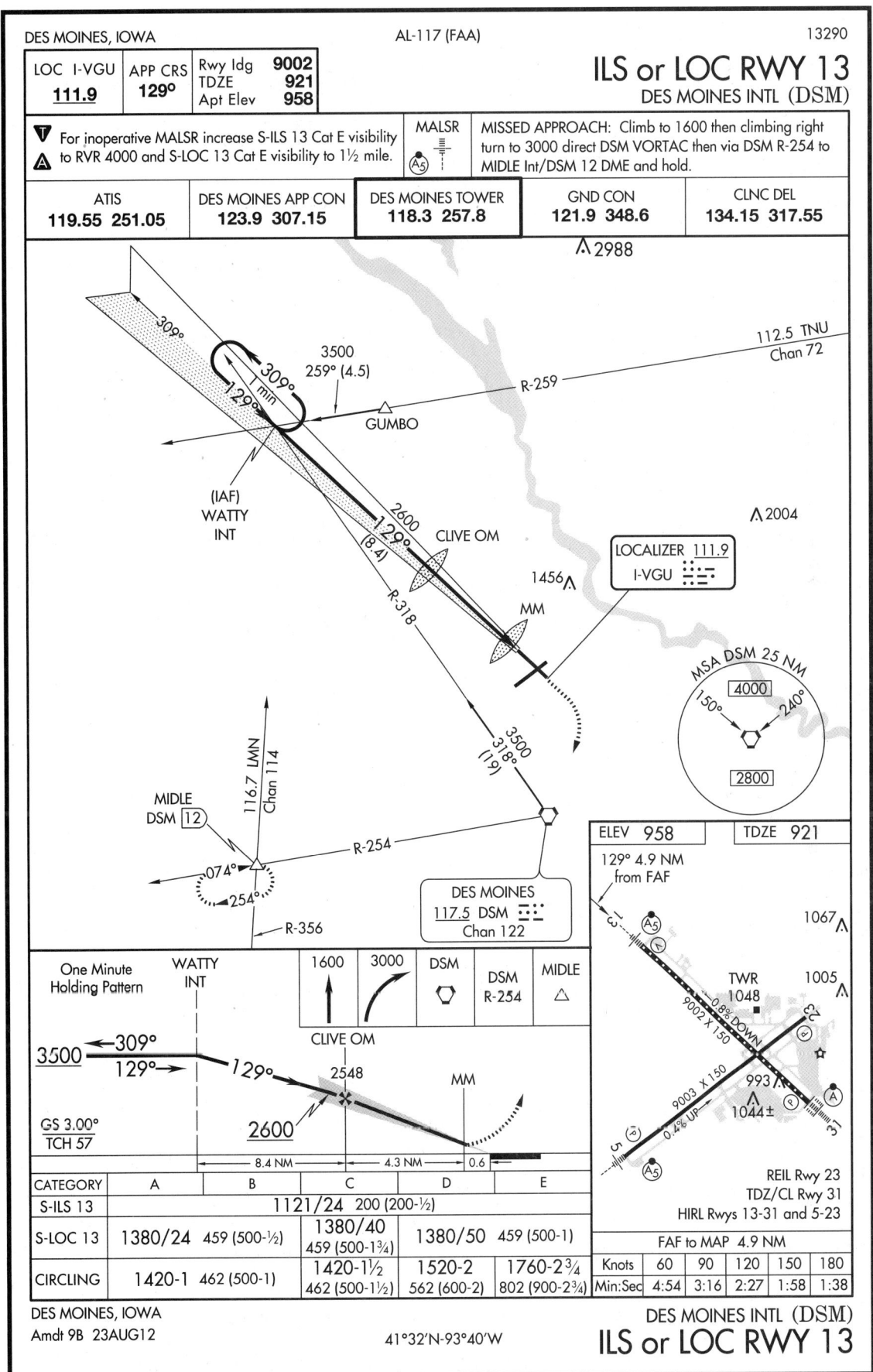

Figure 217. – ILS or LOC RWY 13 (DSM).

86. The primary reason single pilot operations in reduced visibility on an instrument approach procedure are made more difficult than multicrew operations is that the pilot must

A. continue to fly by instruments while attempting to acquire a visual reference for the runway.

B. multitask, coordinating the operation of the flight controls, avionics, and radio equipment.

C. manage a more complex aircraft than those commonly used in multicrew operations.

Answer (A) is correct. (FAA-H-8083-16B Chap 5)
DISCUSSION: Single pilot IFR operations are more complicated than multicrew operations because the pilot flying is responsible for both the instrument reference and visual reference tasks associated with an instrument approach.
Answer (B) is incorrect. A single pilot operating in instrument conditions must multitask the operation of the flight controls, avionics, and radio during all phases of flight, not just the instrument approach procedure. **Answer (C) is incorrect.** Multicrew operations generally involve more complex aircraft than those used in single pilot operations.

87. (Refer to Figure 221 on page 269.) The final approach fix for the precision approach is located at

A. RIIVR intersection.

B. Glide slope intercept (lightning bolt).

C. JETSA intersection/locator outer marker.

Answer (B) is correct. (P/C Glossary)
DISCUSSION: On a precision approach, the final approach fix is the glide slope intercept point at the published altitude. It is identified on an IAP chart by a lightning bolt.
Answer (A) is incorrect. RIIVR INT is an IAF, not the FAF. **Answer (C) is incorrect.** JETSA INT/LOM is the FAF on the LOC 24R, not the ILS 24R, approach.

88. (Refer to Figure 221 on page 269.) The final approach fix for the ILS RWY 24R is located at

A. MERCE intersection.

B. Glide Slope Intercept (lightning bolt).

C. JETSA intersection.

Answer (B) is correct. (FAA-H-8083-16B Chap 4)
DISCUSSION: The final approach fix for an ILS approach is indicated on an instrument approach procedure by a lightning bolt symbol. This is also the point of glide slope intercept.
Answer (A) is incorrect. The MERCE intersection is an initial fix (indicated by the "IF" notation), not the final approach fix. **Answer (C) is incorrect.** The Maltese cross symbol indicates that JETSA is the final approach fix for the nonprecision localizer approach, not for the precision ILS approach.

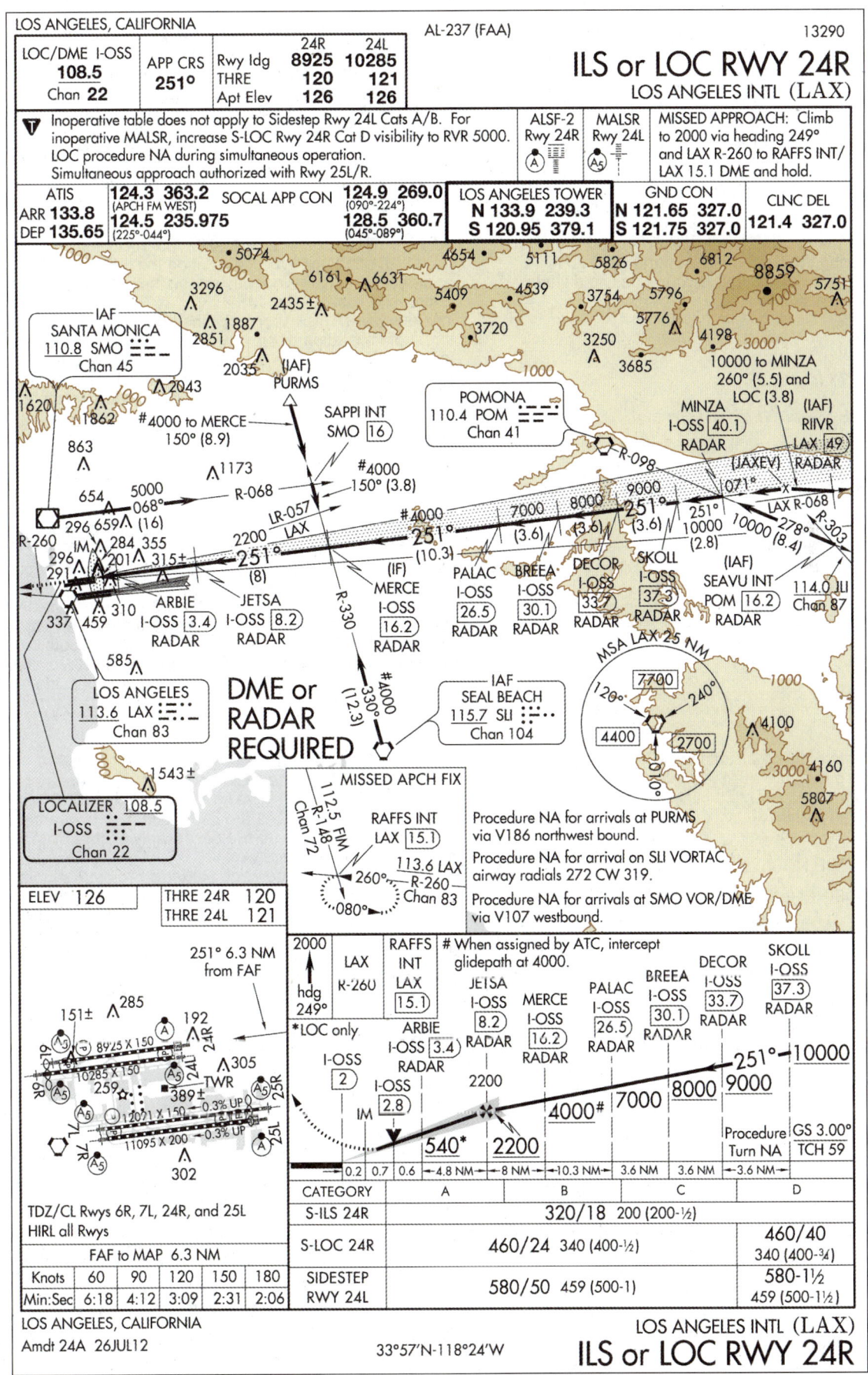

Figure 221. – ILS or LOC RWY 24R (LAX).

89. (Refer to Figure 227 on page 271.) Refer to the APA (Centennial) ILS RWY 35R procedure. The PFAF (Precision Final Approach Fix) intercept altitude is

A. 7,080 feet MSL.

B. 7,977 feet MSL.

C. 8,000 feet MSL.

Answer (C) is correct. (FAA-H-8083-16B Chap 5)
DISCUSSION: The glide slope intercept altitude at the PFAF (lightning bolt) is 8,000 feet MSL.
Answer (A) is incorrect. The minimum altitude for the nonprecision approaches, excluding the LECET-fix minimum altitude, is 7,080 feet MSL. **Answer (B) is incorrect.** The altitude at the LOM is 7,977 feet MSL.

90. (Refer to Figure 227 on page 271.) You are executing the Centennial Airport (APA) ILS RWY 35R approach. What is your crossing altitude at the outer marker?

A. 2,092 feet MSL.

B. 7,977 feet MSL.

C. 8,000 feet MSL.

Answer (B) is correct. (FAA-H-8083-16B Chap 5)
DISCUSSION: When executing the ILS RWY 35R approach, the glide slope altitude at the outer marker/final approach fix is 7,977 ft. MSL.
Answer (A) is incorrect. The height of the LOM above the threshold elevation of runway 35R is 2,092 ft. MSL. **Answer (C) is incorrect.** The glide slope intercept altitude is 8,000 ft. MSL, with the line beneath the altitude indicating that this is the minimum altitude for this segment until glide slope interception.

91. (Refer to Figure 227 on page 271.) What is the minimum safe altitude (MSA) when maneuvering northeast of APA?

A. 13,100 feet.

B. 8,100 feet.

C. 7,080 feet.

Answer (B) is correct. (FAA-H-8083-16B Chap 5)
DISCUSSION: When maneuvering northeast of APA, you will be located within the northeastern sector of the MSA that surrounds "AP" by 25 NM. This sector has an MSA of 8,100 ft. MSL. This will provide 1,000 ft. of clearance over all obstructions but does not necessarily ensure acceptable navigation signal coverage.
Answer (A) is incorrect. The MSA surrounding "AP" is divided in to two sectors. The sector that has an MSA of 13,100 ft. MSL covers the area to the west, south, and southeast of "AP." **Answer (C) is incorrect.** The minimum altitude when flying the localizer approach and inside I-APA is 7,080 ft.

92. (Refer to Figure 227 on page 271.) The ILS RWY 35R procedure at APA depicts a symbol on the plan view that represents a minimum safe altitude sector within 25 NM of

A. CASSE NDB/LOM.

B. the FIRPI intersection.

C. the I-APA Localizer.

Answer (A) is correct. (FAA-H-8083-16B Chap 5)
DISCUSSION: The radius of this MSA is centered around the CASSE NDB/LOM. The MSA is published for emergency use on IAP charts. MSAs provide 1,000 ft. of clearance over all obstacles, but they do not necessarily ensure acceptable navigation signal coverage.
Answer (B) is incorrect. Radar is required on this approach, and you will note the lack of an IAF. Therefore, the FIRPI intersection cannot be the focus of an MSA. The MSA is based on the primary NAVAID, waypoint, or airport reference point on which the IAP is predicated. **Answer (C) is incorrect.** The I-APA localizer is located 8.1 NM from the Localizer Outer Marker (LOM) around which the MSA is centered.

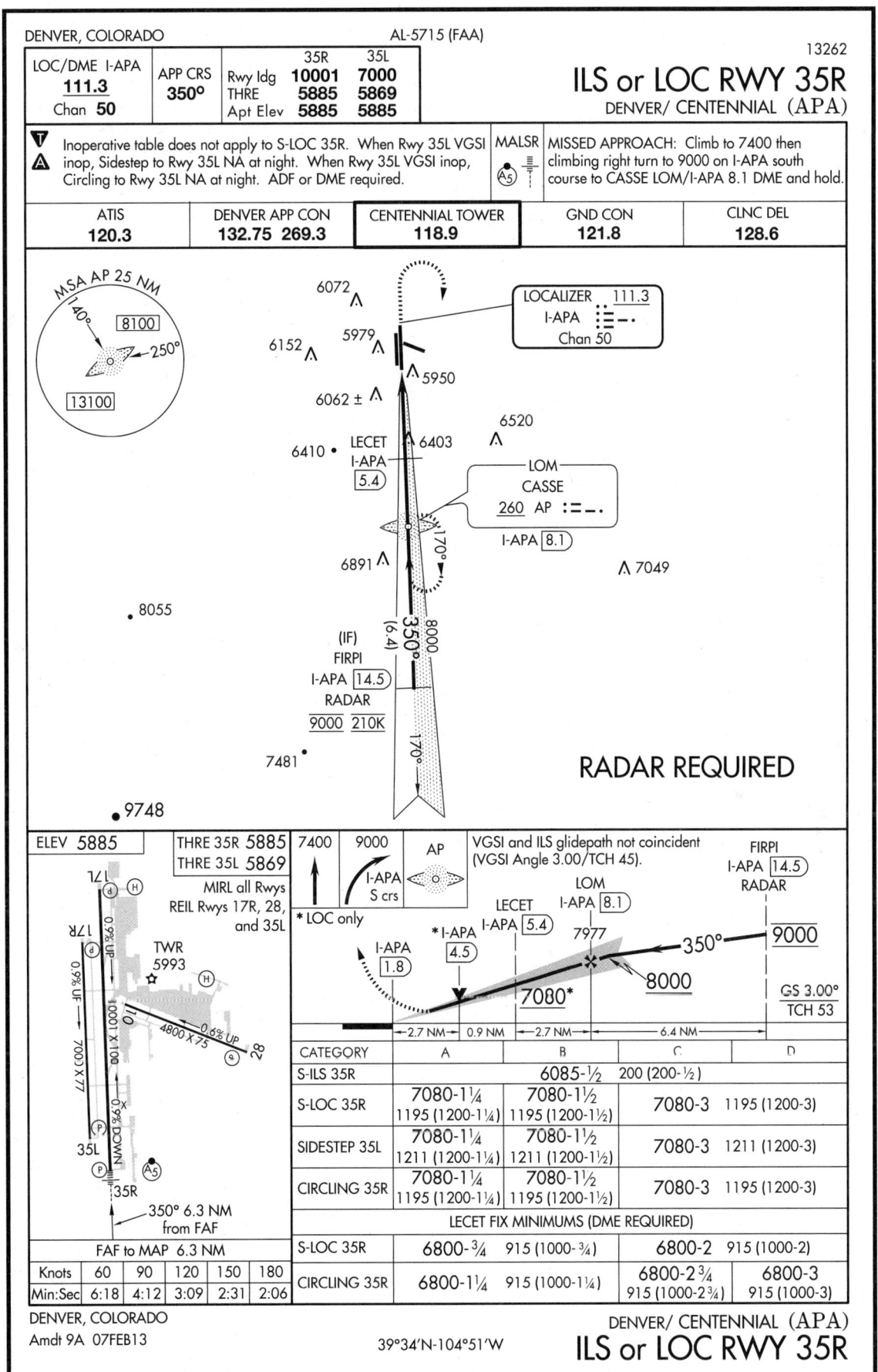

Figure 227. – ILS or LOC RWY 35R (APA).

93. When making an instrument approach at the selected alternate airport, what landing minimums apply?

   A. Standard alternate minimums (600-2 or 800-2).

   B. The IFR alternate minimums listed for that airport.

   C. The landing minimums published for the type of procedure selected.

Answer (C) is correct. (14 CFR 91.175)
   DISCUSSION: Published landing minimums always apply when making an instrument approach to an airport.
   Answer (A) is incorrect. Alternate minimums refer to the minimum forecast weather allowable to list an airport as an alternate on the flight plan. **Answer (B) is incorrect.** Alternate minimums refer to the minimum forecast weather allowable to list an airport as an alternate on the flight plan.

94. What obstacle clearance and navigation signal coverage is a pilot assured with the Minimum Sector Altitudes depicted on the IAP charts?

   A. 1,000 feet and acceptable navigation signal coverage within a 25 NM radius of the navigation facility.

   B. 1,000 feet within a 25 NM radius of the navigation facility but not acceptable navigation signal coverage.

   C. 500 feet and acceptable navigation signal coverage within a 10 NM radius of the navigation facility.

Answer (B) is correct. (AIM Para 5-4-5)
   DISCUSSION: Minimum sector altitudes are depicted on approach charts and provide at least 1,000 ft. of obstacle clearance within a 25-NM radius of the navigation facility upon which the procedure is predicated. These altitudes are for emergency use only and do not necessarily assure acceptable navigational signal coverage.
   Answer (A) is incorrect. Minimum sector altitudes do not guarantee acceptable signal coverage. **Answer (C) is incorrect.** Minimum sector altitudes do not guarantee acceptable signal coverage, and they provide 1,000 ft., not 500 ft., of obstacle clearance.

95. When being radar vectored for an ILS approach, at what point may you start a descent from your last assigned altitude to a lower minimum altitude if cleared for the approach?

   A. When established on a segment of a published route or IAP.

   B. You may descend immediately to published glide slope interception altitude.

   C. Only after you are established on the final approach unless informed otherwise by ATC.

Answer (A) is correct. (AIM Para 5-4-7)
   DISCUSSION: When you are cleared for the approach while being radar vectored, you must maintain your last assigned altitude until the airplane is established on a segment of a published route or IAP. Then use the published altitude to descend within each succeeding route or approach segment.
   Answer (B) is incorrect. You must wait to descend until you are on part of the published procedure. **Answer (C) is incorrect.** You should follow prescribed altitudes whenever you are on a segment of a published route or IAP.

96. (Refer to Figure 228 on page 273.) The missed approach point for the LOC RWY 31 procedure is

   A. 2:33 from PECAT.

   B. 200 feet AGL.

   C. 1,081 feet MSL.

Answer (A) is correct. (FAA-H-8083-16B Chap 4)
   DISCUSSION: On some nonprecision approaches, the missed approach point (MAP) is given as a fixed distance with an associated time from the final approach fix (FAF) to the MAP based on the groundspeed of the aircraft. A table (timing block) on the lower left-hand side of Fig. 228 shows the distance in NM from the FAF to the MAP and the time it takes at specific groundspeeds. Under the 120 knots speed is the time of 2:33 from PECAT to the MAP. Pilots must determine the approximate groundspeed and time based on the approach speed and true airspeed of their aircraft and the current winds along the final approach course. A clock or stopwatch should be started at the FAF of an approach requiring this method. Many nonprecision approaches designate a specific fix as the MAP. These can be identified by a course (LOC or VOR) and DME, a cross radial from a VOR, or a GPS waypoint.
   Answer (B) is incorrect. A MAP of 200 feet AGL is even lower than the DA for the ILS (274 feet AGL), which is a precision approach. The MAP for this nonprecision approach is 553 feet AGL (1,360 feet MSL). **Answer (C) is incorrect.** A height of 1,081 feet MSL is the DA for the ILS approach, not the MAP for the nonprecision localizer approach.

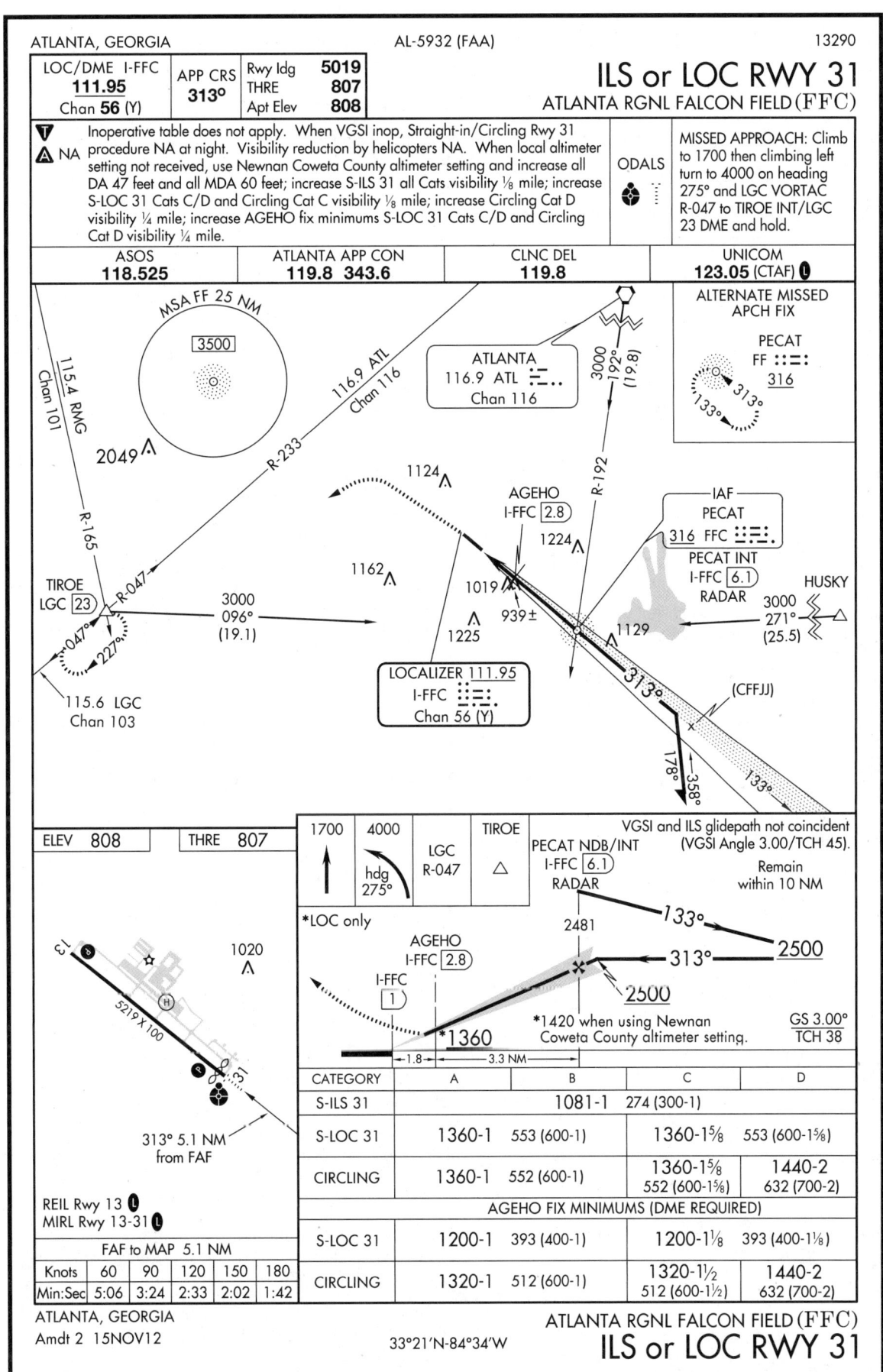

Figure 228. – ILS or LOC RWY 31 (FFC).

97. Which procedure should be followed by a pilot who is circling to land in a Category B airplane, but is maintaining a speed 5 knots faster than the maximum specified for that category?

A. Use the approach minimums appropriate for Category C.

B. Use Category B minimums.

C. Use Category D minimums since they apply to all circling approaches.

Answer (A) is correct. (FAA-H-8083-16B Chap 4)
   DISCUSSION: If it is necessary to maneuver at speeds in excess of the upper limit of the speed range for any category, the minimums for the next higher category should be used.
   Answer (B) is incorrect. A pilot should use minimums for the category appropriate to the approach speed being used. **Answer (C) is incorrect.** Category D minimums do not necessarily apply to all circling approaches.

98. When simultaneous approaches are in progress, how does each pilot receive radar advisories?

A. On tower frequency.

B. On approach control frequency.

C. One pilot on tower frequency and the other on approach control frequency.

Answer (A) is correct. (AIM Para 5-4-14)
   DISCUSSION: When simultaneous approaches are in progress, each pilot will be advised to monitor the tower frequency to receive advisories and instructions.
   Answer (B) is incorrect. Pilots will receive radar advisories on tower, not approach control, frequency. **Answer (C) is incorrect.** Both pilots will receive radar advisories on tower frequency.

99. When may a pilot make a straight-in landing, if using an IAP having only circling minimums?

A. A straight-in landing may not be made, but the pilot may continue to the runway at MDA and then circle to land on the runway.

B. The pilot may land straight-in if the runway is the active runway and (s)he has been cleared to land.

C. A straight-in landing may be made if the pilot has the runway in sight in sufficient time to make a normal approach for landing, and has been cleared to land.

Answer (C) is correct. (FAA-H-8083-15B Chap 10)
   DISCUSSION: When the normal rate of descent or the runway alignment factor of 30° is exceeded, a straight-in minimum is not published, and a circling minimum applies. Even without published straight-in minimums, the pilot may land straight-in if (s)he has the active runway in sight in sufficient time to make a normal landing and has been cleared to land.
   Answer (A) is incorrect. A straight-in landing may be made if it is the appropriate runway. **Answer (B) is incorrect.** The pilot must also have sufficient time to make a normal approach for a landing.

100. An airport may not be qualified for alternate use if

A. the airport has AWOS-3 weather reporting.

B. the airport is located next to a restricted or prohibited area.

C. the NAVAIDs used for the final approach are unmonitored.

Answer (C) is correct. (FAA-H-8083-16B Chap 2)
   DISCUSSION: Not all airports can be used as an alternate. An airport may not be qualified for alternate use if the NAVAIDs used for the final approach are unmonitored.
   Answer (A) is incorrect. An airport can qualify for alternate use if the airport has AWOS-3 weather reporting. An airport may not qualify for alternate use if the NAVAIDs used for final approach are unmonitored. **Answer (B) is incorrect.** An airport can qualify for alternate use if the airport is located next to a restricted or prohibited area. An airport may not qualify for alternate use if the NAVAIDs used for final approach are unmonitored.

101. (Refer to Figure 230 on page 275.) What minimum navigation equipment is required to complete the VOR/DME-A procedure?

A. One VOR receiver.

B. One VOR receiver and DME.

C. Two VOR receivers and DME.

Answer (B) is correct. (FAA-H-8083-15B Chap 10)
   DISCUSSION: Since all of the navigation for the VOR/DME-A approach (Fig. 230) is done from the White Cloud VORTAC, only one VOR receiver is required. DME is also required because it is a VOR/DME approach.
   Answer (A) is incorrect. DME is also required because this is a VOR/DME approach. **Answer (C) is incorrect.** Only one VOR receiver, not two receivers, is required.

102. (Refer to Figure 230 on page 275.) The minimum safe altitude (MSA) for the VOR/DME or GPS-A at 7D3 is geographically centered on what position?

A. DEANI intersection.

B. WHITE CLOUD VOR/DME.

C. MAJUB intersection.

Answer (B) is correct. (AIM Para 5-4-5)
   DISCUSSION: Minimum safe altitudes provide obstacle clearance within 25 NM of the specified navigational facility. In Fig. 230, the MSA circle specifies WHITE CLOUD VOR/DME.
   Answer (A) is incorrect. DEANI intersection is the point of descent to the final approach fix. **Answer (C) is incorrect.** MAJUB intersection is the MAP.

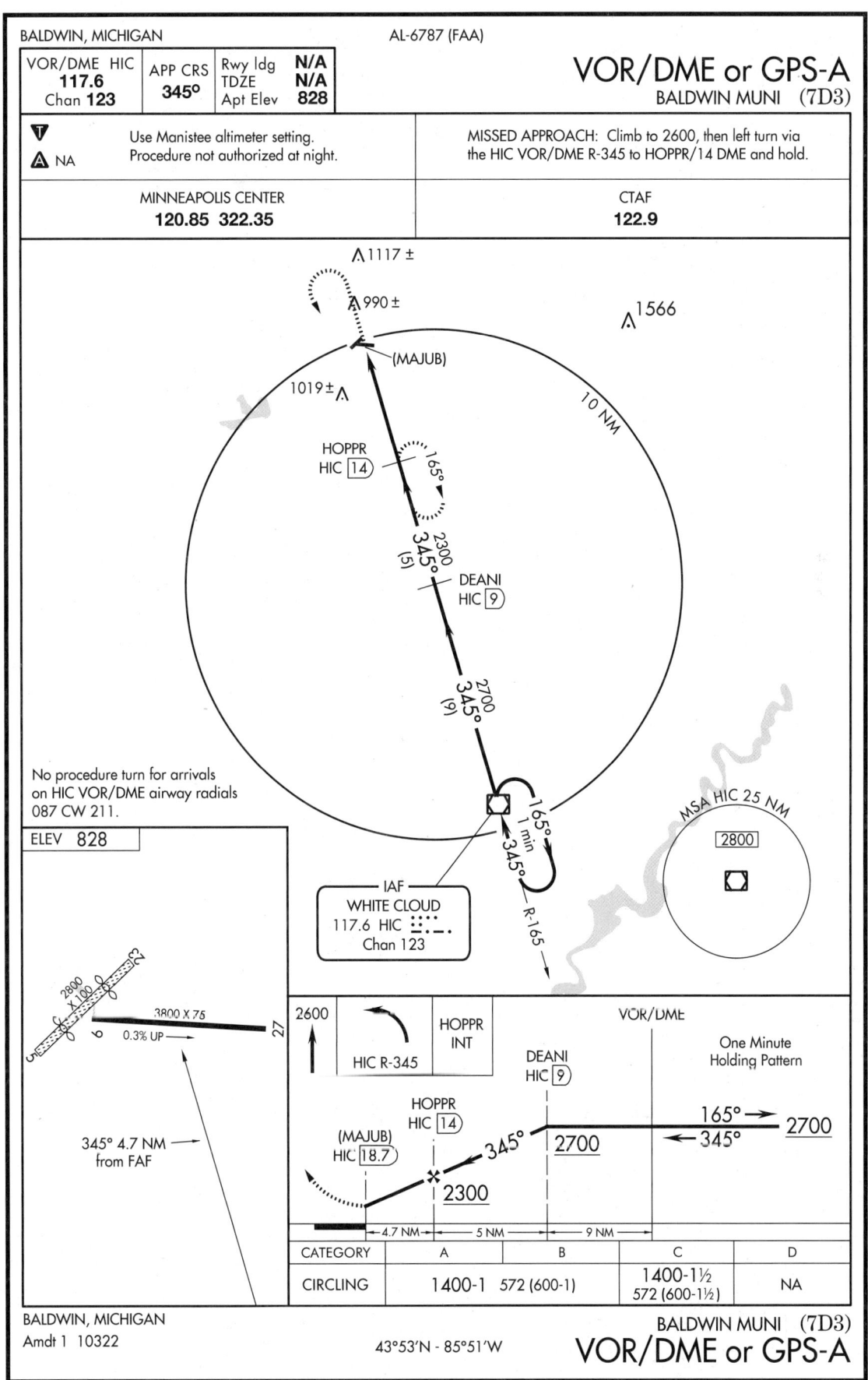

Figure 230. – VOR/DME or GPS-A (7D3).

103. (Refer to Figure 230 below, and Figure 231 on page 277.) You plan to fly to Baldwin for Christmas. What minimum equipment is required for the VOR/DME or GPS-A procedure, and can you complete the flight?

    A. One VOR receiver; yes, the trip will be fun.

    B. One VOR receiver and one DME receiver; no flight though, the airport is closed.

    C. Two VOR receivers; yes, but no fuel is available because the airport is unattended.

Answer (B) is correct. (FAA-H-8083-15B Chap 8)
    DISCUSSION: Note in the Airport Remarks section of the Chart Supplement page (Fig. 231) that the airport is closed November through April.
    Answer (A) is incorrect. The flight cannot be completed. The airport is closed November through April, as noted in the Airport Remarks in Fig. 231. **Answer (C) is incorrect.** Only one VOR receiver is required, not two, and the flight cannot take place as the Airport Remarks in Fig. 231 stipulate the airport is closed November through April.

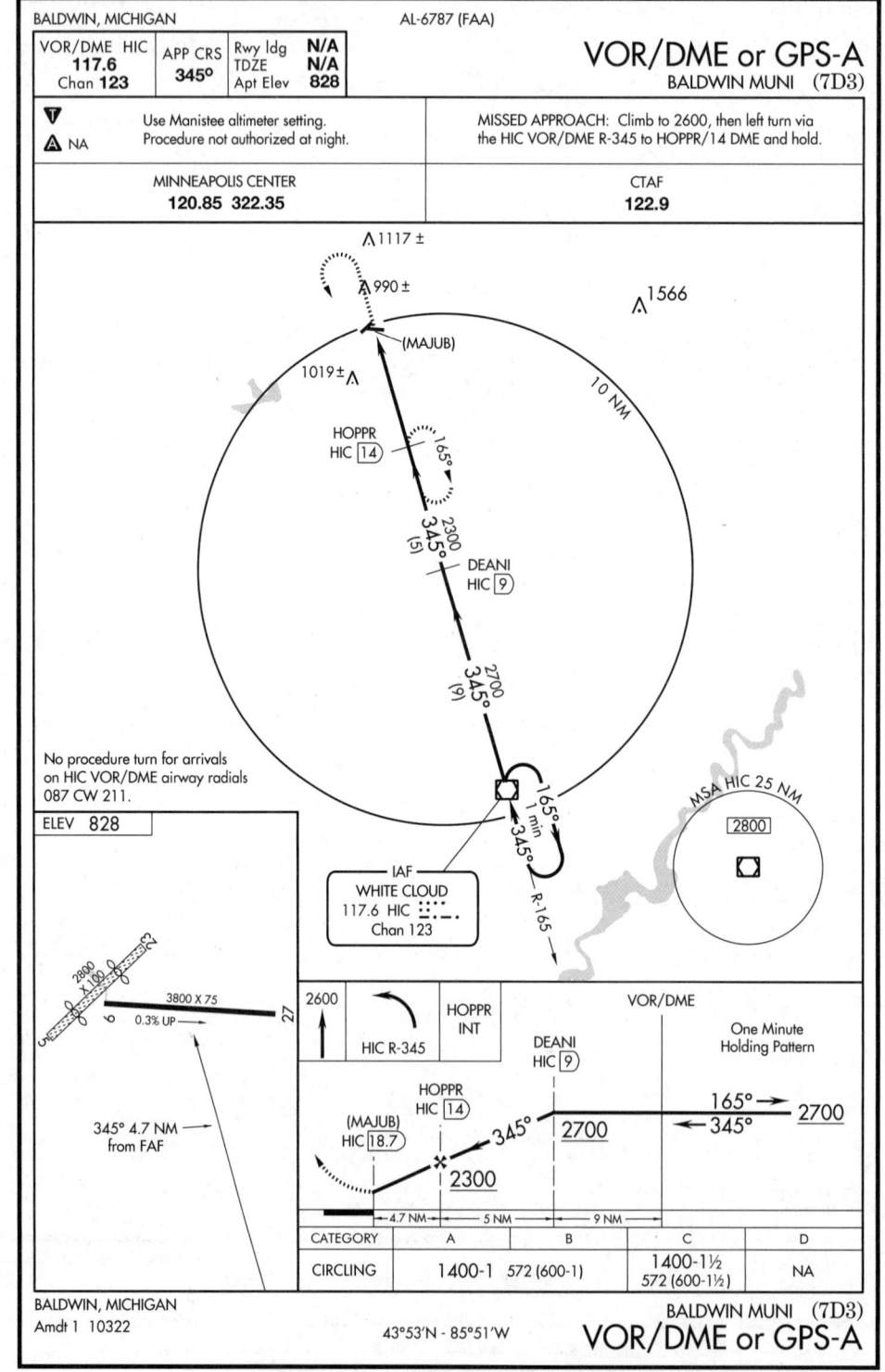

Figure 230. – VOR/DME or GPS-A (7D3).

130   **MICHIGAN**

BALDWIN MUNI (7D3)   2 S   UTC–5(–4DT)   N43°52.53´ W85°50.53´   CHICAGO
   828   TPA—1828(1000)   NOTAM FILE LAN   L–281
   RWY 09–27: H3800X75 (ASPH)   S–10   0.3% up E   IAP
      RWY 09: Trees.
      RWY 27: Trees.
   RWY 05–23: 2800X100 (TURF)
      RWY 05: Thld dsplcd 800´. Trees.
      RWY 23: Thld dsplcd 800´. Trees.
   AIRPORT REMARKS: Unattended. Deer on and invof arpt. Arpt CLOSED Nov
      thru Apr; no snow removal. Arpt manager cell 231–250–2551. Rwy
      09–27 sfc considerable pavement cracking with vegetation growing
      through cracks. Rwy 05–23 and dsplcd thlds marked with 3´ yellow
      cones.
   COMMUNICATIONS: CTAF 122.9
   Ⓡ **MINNEAPOLIS CENTER APP/DEP CON** 120.85
   RADIO AIDS TO NAVIGATION: NOTAM FILE LAN.
      WHITE CLOUD (L) VOR/DME 117.6   HIC   Chan 123   N43°34.49´
         W85°42.97´   344° 18.9 NM to fld. 920/1W.
      VOR/DME unusable:
         020°–090° byd 30 NM blo 3,000´
      DME portion unusable:
         270°–290° byd 35 NM blo 3,000´

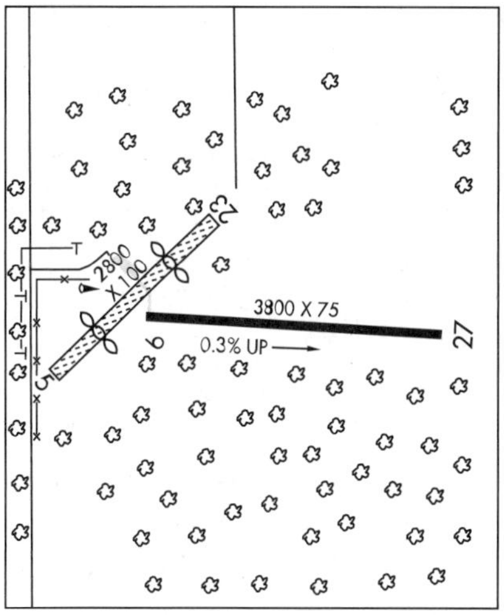

BANGU   N45°00.88´ W84°48.49´   NOTAM FILE GLR.   LAKE HURON
   NDB (LOM) 375   GL   097° 4.5 NM to Gaylord Rgnl. Unmonitored.

BANNISTER
   SHADY LAWN FLD (4M4)   2 E   UTC–5(–4DT)   N43°07.72´ W84°22.88´   CHICAGO
      680   TPA—1680(1000)   NOTAM FILE LAN
      RWY 09–27: 1850X50 (TURF)   LIRL
         RWY 09: Bldg.
         RWY 27: Trees.
      AIRPORT REMARKS: Attended irregularly. Ultralight and AG activity on and invof arpt. Deer and birds on and invof arpt. Crops
         adjacent to rwy during summer months. NSTD LIRL color and configuration, by prior arrangement. Rwy 09 and Rwy 27
         marked by 3´ yellow cones.
      COMMUNICATIONS: CTAF 122.9

BARAGA (2P4)   4 W   UTC–5(–4DT)   N46°47.10´ W88°34.67´   GREEN BAY
   845   TPA—1845(1000)   NOTAM FILE GRB
   RWY 09–27: 2200X100 (TURF)
      RWY 09: Trees.
      RWY 27: Trees.
   AIRPORT REMARKS: Unattended. Arpt CLOSED Nov–Apr except to ski equipped acft. 25´ p–line 850´ from thld Rwy 27. Deer
      and birds on and invof arpt.
   COMMUNICATIONS: CTAF 122.9

BATH
   UNIVERSITY AIRPARK (41G)   2 NW   UTC–5(–4DT)   N42°50.42´ W84°28.75´   DETROIT
      856   B   S2   NOTAM FILE LAN
      RWY 08–26: 1988X100 (TURF)   LIRL
         RWY 08: Trees.
         RWY 26: Tree.
      AIRPORT REMARKS: Attended irregularly. Rwy 08–26 occasionally soft/wet areas E end during spring thaw and after heavy rain.
         ACTIVATE LIRL Rwy 08–26 and NSTD rotating bcn—122.85. NSTD flashing strobe and alternating white/red bcn. Rwy
         08–26 marked with 3´ yellow cones.
      COMMUNICATIONS: CTAF 122.9

BATOL   N42°21.72´ W85°11.07´   NOTAM FILE BTL.   CHICAGO
   NDB (MHW/LOM) 272   BT   225° 4.4 NM to W K Kellogg.   L–281

Figure 231. – Excerpt from Chart Supplement.

104. During an instrument precision approach, terrain and obstacle clearance depends on adherence to

A. minimum altitude shown on the IAP.

B. terrain contour information.

C. natural and man-made reference point information.

Answer (A) is correct. (AIM Para 5-4-5)
DISCUSSION: A pilot adhering to the altitudes, flight paths, and weather minimums depicted on the IAP chart is assured of terrain and obstruction clearance.
Answer (B) is incorrect. The design of IAPs takes terrain and obstacle clearance into account. **Answer (C) is incorrect.** During instrument approaches, instrument, not visual, reference points are used to assure terrain and obstacle clearance.

105. During an instrument approach, under what conditions, if any, is the holding pattern course reversal not required?

A. When radar vectors are provided.

B. When cleared for the approach.

C. None, since it is always mandatory.

Answer (A) is correct. (AIM Para 5-4-9)
DISCUSSION: A course reversal (procedure turn) is not required when radar vectors are being provided.
Answer (B) is incorrect. A course reversal may be required when cleared for a full approach. **Answer (C) is incorrect.** A course reversal is not mandatory when radar vectors are provided.

106. On a nonprecision approach, what is the maximum acceptable descent rate during the final stages of the approach (below 1,000 ft. AGL)?

A. 1,000 fpm.

B. 1,000 fpm to 500 AGL, then 500 fpm.

C. 500 fpm.

Answer (A) is correct. (FAA-H-8083-16B Chap 5)
DISCUSSION: According to research, human perceptual limitations allow for a maximum rate of descent of 1,000 fpm in the final stages of the approach, regardless of the type of aircraft being flown. Descents greater than 1,000 fpm on the final stages of the approach are not permitted.
Answer (B) is incorrect. The maximum rate of descent below 1,000 ft. AGL is 1,000 fpm, but this descent rate does not change at 500 ft. AGL. **Answer (C) is incorrect.** The maximum rate of descent below 1,000 ft. AGL is 1,000 fpm, not 500 fpm.

107. (Refer to Figure 234 on page 279.) What options are available concerning the teardrop course reversal for LOC RWY 18 approach to Lincoln?

A. If a course reversal is required, only the teardrop can be executed.

B. The point where the turn is begun and the type and rate of turn are optional.

C. A normal procedure turn may be made if the 10 DME limit is not exceeded.

Answer (A) is correct. (AIM Para 5-4-9)
DISCUSSION: When a procedure turn track is specified for the LOC RWY 18 approach, the turn must be flown exactly as depicted. Thus, only the teardrop can be executed.
Answer (B) is incorrect. The turn must be begun at 12 DME of the VOR, and the procedure turn must be a teardrop. **Answer (C) is incorrect.** The procedure turn must be a teardrop.

108. (Refer to Figure 234 on page 279.) If your aircraft was cleared for the ILS RWY 18 at Lincoln Municipal and crossed the Lincoln VORTAC at 5,000 feet MSL, at what point in the teardrop could a descent to 3,200 feet commence?

A. As soon as intercepting LOC in bound.

B. Immediately.

C. Only at the point authorized by ATC.

Answer (B) is correct. (AIM Para 5-4-9)
DISCUSSION: The profile view of the IAP chart shows a descent to 3,200 ft. upon crossing LNK VORTAC outbound. Published altitudes apply when you are on a published route or procedure and have been cleared for the approach.
Answer (A) is incorrect. A descent to 3,200 ft. may begin when you are LNK VORTAC out bound, not LOC in bound. **Answer (C) is incorrect.** Published altitudes apply when you are on a published route or procedure and have been cleared for the approach.

109. (Refer to Figure 234 on page 279.) If cleared for an S-LOC 18 approach at Lincoln Municipal from over HUSKR, it means the flight should

A. land straight in on runway 18.

B. comply with straight-in landing minimums.

C. begin final approach without making a procedure turn.

Answer (C) is correct. (AIM Para 5-4-9)
DISCUSSION: When the symbol NoPT is shown, as in Fig. 234 on the transition from HUSKR, a procedure turn is not authorized.
Answer (A) is incorrect. The pilot may request clearance to land on another runway, if desired. **Answer (B) is incorrect.** Circling minimums should be used if landing on another runway is desired.

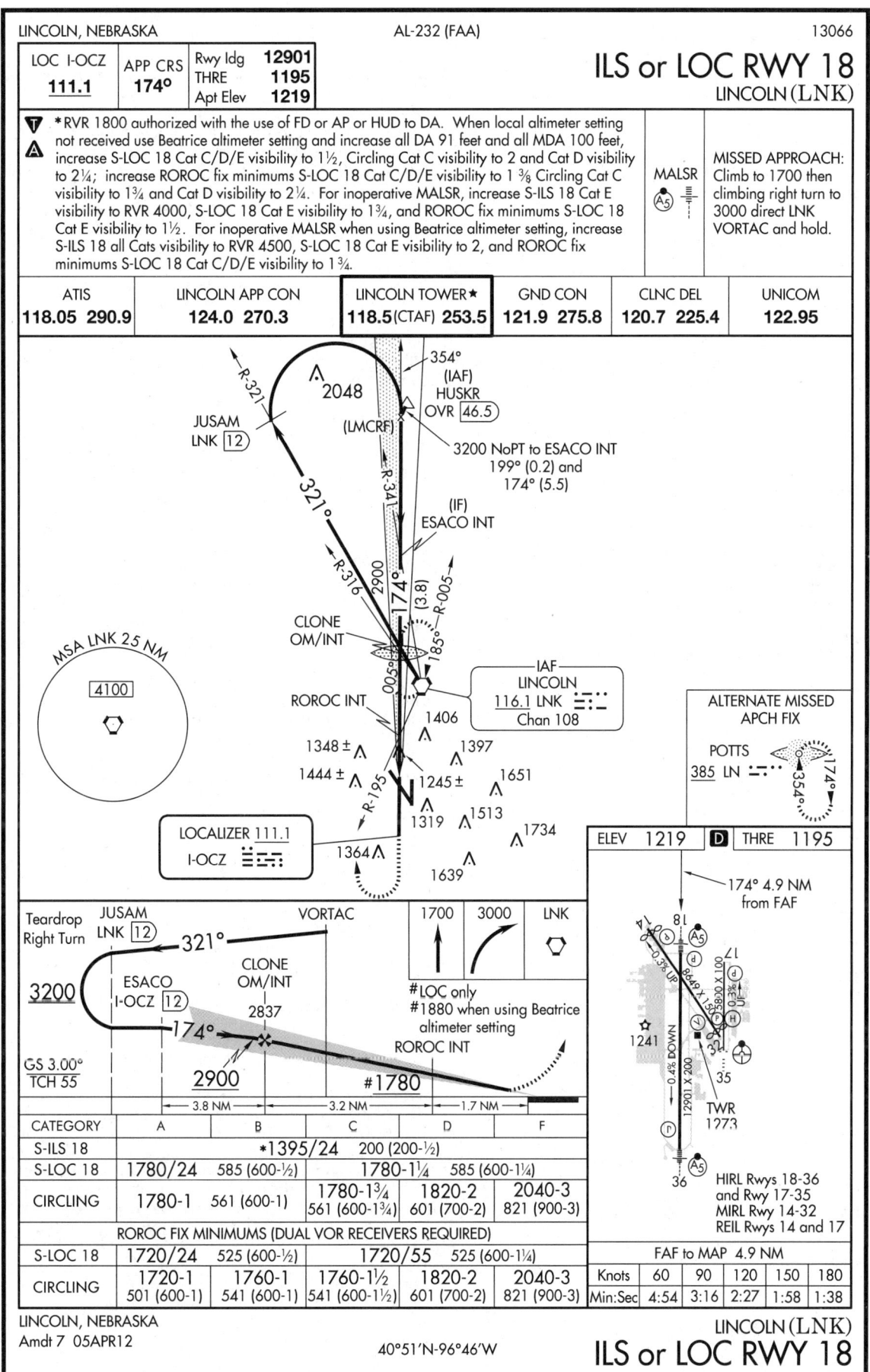

Figure 234. – ILS or LOC RWY 18 (LNK).

110. Under the stabilized approach concept, what is the maximum acceptable descent rate during the final stages of an approach?

A. 1,000 fpm for either precision or nonprecision approaches.

B. 1,200 fpm above 1,000 feet AGL and 500 fpm below 1,000 feet AGL for all approaches.

C. 1,000 fpm for precision and 1,200 fpm for nonprecision approaches.

Answer (A) is correct. (FAA-H-8083-16B Chap 4, AC 120-71A)
    DISCUSSION: Operational experience and research have shown that a descent rate of greater than approximately 1,000 fpm is unacceptable during the final stages of an approach.
    Answer (B) is incorrect. It has been found that a descent of 1,000 fpm in the final stages of an approach is the maximum allowable rate. This limitation is due to human perceptual limitations. There is no recommended limitation of 500 fpm below 1,000 feet AGL. **Answer (C) is incorrect.** The maximum acceptable descent rate for the final stages of precision and nonprecision approaches is identical. It has been established as 1,000 fpm, as a safety restriction due to the limitations of human perceptions.

111. When the approach procedure involves a procedure turn, the maximum speed should not be greater than

A. 180 knots IAS.

B. 200 knots IAS.

C. 250 knots IAS.

Answer (B) is correct. (AIM Para 5-4-9)
    DISCUSSION: When the approach procedure involves a procedure turn, a maximum speed of not greater than 200 kt. IAS should be observed, and the turn should be executed within the distance specified in the profile view.
    Answer (A) is incorrect. The maximum speed that should be used is 200 kt., not 180 kt. **Answer (C) is incorrect.** The maximum speed that should be used is 200 kt., not 250 kt.

112. What does the symbol T within a black triangle in the minimums section of the IAP for a particular airport indicate?

A. Takeoff minimums are 1 mile for aircraft having two engines or less and 1/2 mile for those with more than two engines.

B. Instrument takeoffs are not authorized.

C. Takeoff minimums are not standard and/or departure procedures are published.

Answer (C) is correct. (ACUG)
    DISCUSSION: The symbol in the question indicates that takeoff minimums are not standard and/or departure procedures are published, and one should consult the alternate takeoff procedures. Takeoff minimums apply to operations under Parts 121, 125, 127, 129, and 135, i.e., operations other than Part 91.
    Answer (A) is incorrect. It gives the standard minimums for takeoff when there is a published instrument approach. **Answer (B) is incorrect.** The alternate takeoff procedures will indicate if instrument takeoffs are not authorized.

113. (Refer to Figure 236 on page 281.) What landing minimums apply for a 14 CFR Part 91 operator at Dothan, AL using a category C aircraft during a circling LOC 32 approach at 120 knots? (Dual VORs available.)

A. MDA 860 feet MSL and visibility 1 SM.

B. MDA 860 feet MSL and visibility 1 and 1/2 SM.

C. MDA 1,220 feet MSL and visibility 2 and 1/2 SM.

Answer (B) is correct. (FAA-H-8083-15B Chap 10)
    DISCUSSION: Although the aircraft is circling at 120 knots (which is Category B), it is a Category C aircraft, and the higher category applies. Thus, the circling minimums (with dual VOR receivers) are 860 feet MSL and 1 and 1/2 SM.
    Answer (A) is incorrect. The minimum visibility for Category A or B, not C, is 1 SM. **Answer (C) is incorrect.** The Category C minimums when operating with a single VOR are 1,220 feet and 2 and 1/2 SM.

114. (Refer to Figure 236 on page 281.) If cleared for a straight-in LOC approach from over OALDY, it means the flight should

A. land straight in on runway 32.

B. comply with straight-in landing minimums.

C. begin final approach without making a procedure turn.

Answer (C) is correct. (AIM Para 5-4-9)
    DISCUSSION: A straight-in IFR approach is an instrument approach wherein final approach is begun without first having executed a procedure turn, not necessarily completed with a straight-in landing or made to straight-in landing minimums.
    Answer (A) is incorrect. The pilot may request clearance to land on another runway, if desired. **Answer (B) is incorrect.** Circling minimums should be used if landing on another runway is desired.

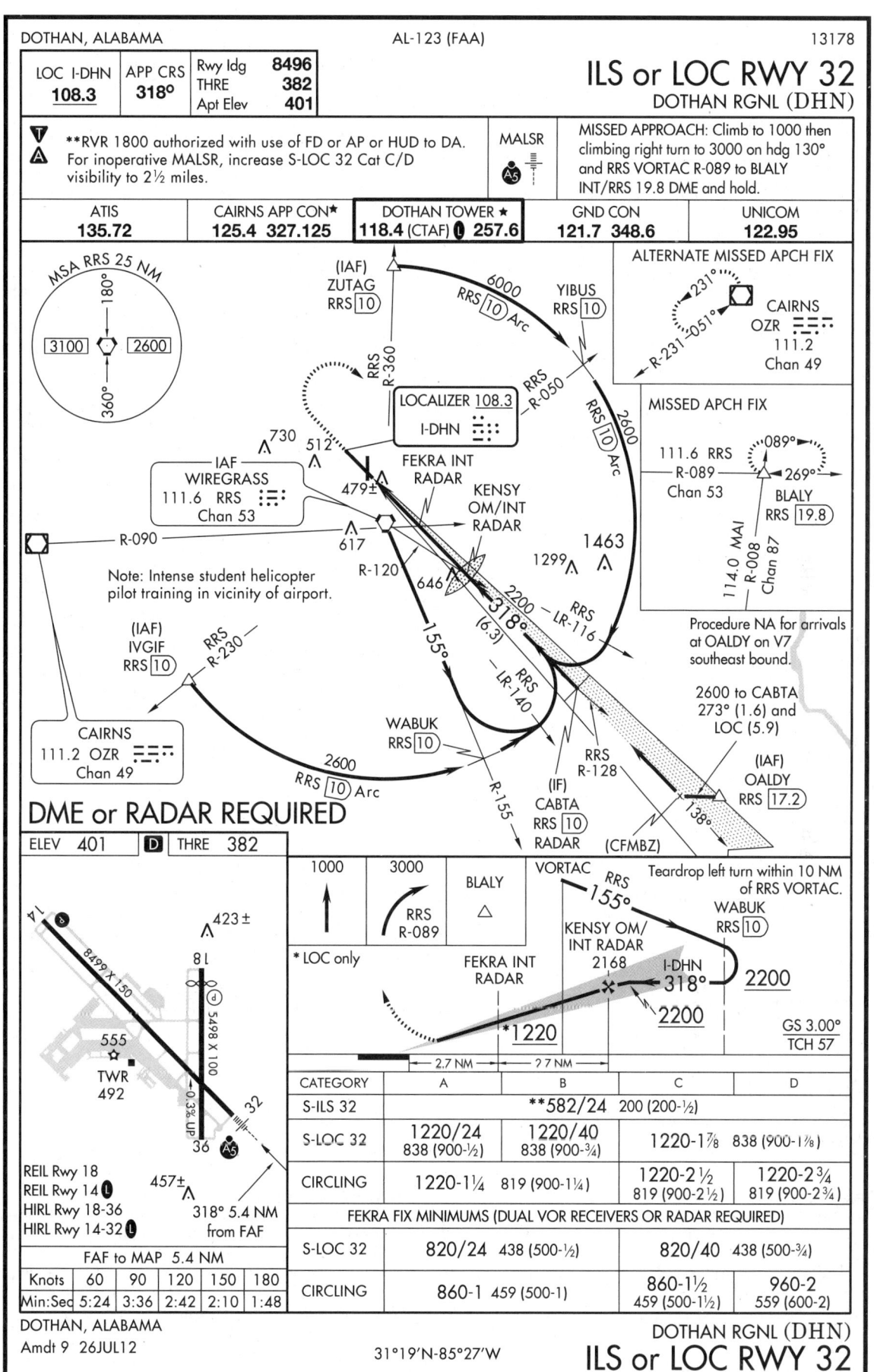

Figure 236. – ILS or RWY 32 (DHN).

115. While being radar vectored, an approach clearance is received. The last assigned altitude should be maintained until

    A. reaching the FAF.

    B. advised to begin descent.

    C. established on a segment of a published route or IAP.

Answer (C) is correct. (AIM Para 5-4-7)
    DISCUSSION: When an approach clearance is received, the last assigned altitude should be maintained until the aircraft is established on a segment of a published route or IAP. Then published altitudes apply.
    Answer (A) is incorrect. Published altitudes may be used as soon as the aircraft is on a published route, which should be before the FAF. **Answer (B) is incorrect.** When ATC issues an approach clearance, descent to published altitudes is left to the discretion of the pilot.

116. (Refer to Figure 240 on page 283.) What type entry is recommended for the missed approach holding pattern depicted on the VOR/DME RWY 36 approach chart for Price/Carbon County Airport?

    A. Direct only.

    B. Teardrop only.

    C. Parallel only.

Answer (C) is correct. (AIM Para 5-3-8)
    DISCUSSION: On the missed approach to VOR/DME RWY 36, the pilot makes a climbing right turn to 10,000 ft. via heading 200° and PUC VOR/DME R-164 to FOSOV/12 DME. Since the aircraft will be approaching FOSOV from the north, a parallel entry will be appropriate.
    Answer (A) is incorrect. A direct entry would only be appropriate if coming in from the south. **Answer (B) is incorrect.** A teardrop entry would be appropriate only if coming in from the northwest.

117. (Refer to Figure 240 on page 283.) At which points may you initiate a descent to the next lower minimum altitude when cleared for the VOR/DME RWY 36 approach, from the PUC R-095 IAF (DME operative)?

    A. Start descent from 8,900 when established on final, from 7,500 when at the 5.1 DME fix, and from 6,240 when landing requirements are met.

    B. Start descent from 8,900 when established on the PUC R-189, from 8,000 at the 8.3 DME fix, from 7,500 at the 5.1 DME fix, and from 6,240 when landing requirements are met.

    C. Start descent from 8,900 at the R-095, from 8,000 at the LR-164, from 7,500 at the 5.1 DME fix.

Answer (B) is correct. (FAA-H-8083-15B Chap 10)
    DISCUSSION: When cleared for the VOR/DME RWY 36 approach, maintain 8,900 ft. on the 12 DME arc until established on R-189, when you may begin descent to 8,000 ft. At the 8.3 DME fix, you may descend from 8,000 ft. to 7,500 ft. At the 5.1 DME you may descend to 6,240 ft., which is the MDA. With the runway environment in sight, at or before the MAP, you may descend below 6,240 ft.
    Answer (A) is incorrect. This approach does not consider the step down from 8,900 ft. to 8,000 ft. at the 8.3 DME fix. **Answer (C) is incorrect.** You may start your descent from 8,900 ft. when established on R-189, not R-095, from 8,000 ft. at the 8.3 DME fix, and from 6,240 ft. only with the runway environment in sight, at or before the MAP.

118. (Refer to Figure 240 on page 283.) What is the purpose of the 10,600 MSA on the Price/Carbon County Airport Approach Chart?

    A. It provides safe clearance above the highest obstacle in the defined sector out to 25 NM.

    B. It provides an altitude above which navigational course guidance is assured.

    C. It is the minimum vector altitude for radar vectors in the sector southeast of PUC between 023° and 293° magnetic bearing to PUC VOR.

Answer (A) is correct. (AIM Para 5-4-5)
    DISCUSSION: The MSA in PUC sector R-113 to R-203 at 10,600 ft. provides safe clearance above the highest obstacle plus 1,000 ft. in the defined sector out to 25 NM.
    Answer (B) is incorrect. Navigational course guidance is not assured by the MSA. **Answer (C) is incorrect.** MSA gives a safe clearance altitude, not a minimum vector altitude.

119. (Refer to Figure 240 on page 283.) If the DME at PUC airport is inoperative, the airborne DME will

    A. continuously indicate "99" as the mileage.

    B. enter "search" mode but fail to lock on.

    C. not transmit a coded identification audio tone.

Answer (C) is correct. (AIM Para 1-1-7)
    DISCUSSION: When a DME is inoperative, the code tone (identifier) will not be broadcast, although a signal may still be received.
    Answer (A) is incorrect. The airborne DME will give no indication if the DME is inoperative. **Answer (B) is incorrect.** The airborne DME may be inoperative.

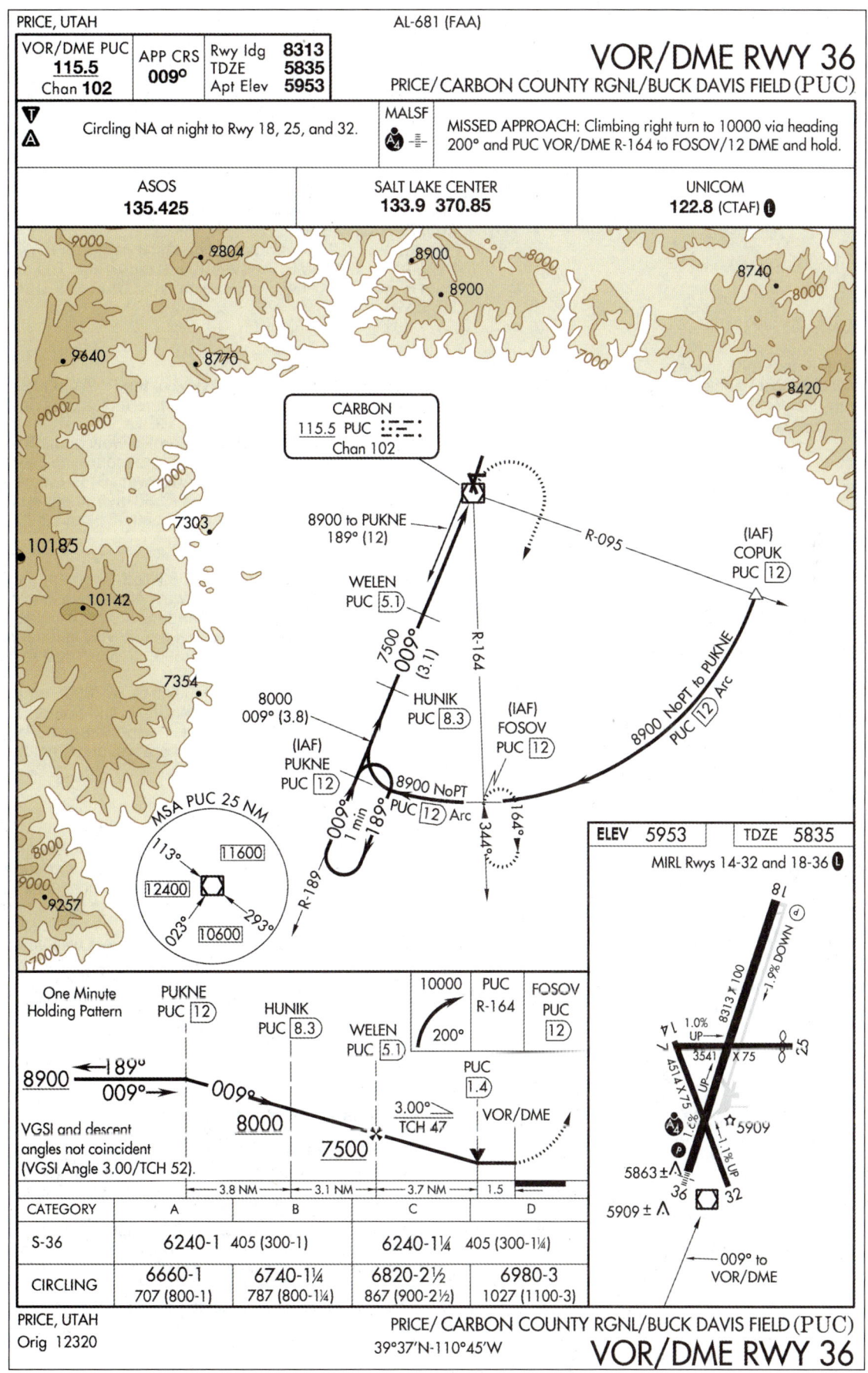

Figure 240. – VOR/DME RWY 36 (PUC).

120. (Refer to Figure 242 on page 285.) What indication should you get when it is time to turn in bound while in the procedure turn at FEHXE?

A.   4 DME miles from FEHXE.

B.   13.9 DME miles from the MAP.

C.   8.6 DME miles from KAGBE.

Answer (A) is correct. (AIM Para 5-3-8)
   DISCUSSION: DME/GPS holding is subject to the same entry and holding procedures except that distances (nautical miles) are used in lieu of time values. The outbound course of the DME/GPA (GPS Along Track Distance) holding pattern is called the outbound leg of the pattern. The instrument approach procedure chart specifies the length of the outbound leg. The end of the outbound leg is determined by the DME or ATD readout. The "4 NM" at the perpendicular line across the end of the outbound leg of the holding pattern southeast of FEHXE means the turn inbound should begin when 4 DME is indicated from FEHXE waypoint.
   Answer (B) is incorrect. The distance from FEHXE to the MAP is 13.9 DME. **Answer (C) is incorrect.** The distance from FEHXE to KAGBE, not the inbound DME to FEHXE, is 8.6 DME.

121. (Refer to Figure 242 on page 285.) What is the recommended descent angle for the RNAV (GPS) RWY 36 approach?

A.   2.12°.

B.   2.52°.

C.   3.00°.

Answer (C) is correct. (IAP)
   DISCUSSION: The profile view of the RNAV (GPS) RWY 36 instrument approach procedure indicates a descent angle of 3.00°.
   Answer (A) is incorrect. The profile view of the RNAV (GPS) RWY 36 instrument approach procedure indicates a descent angle of 3.00°, not 2.12°. **Answer (B) is incorrect.** The profile view of the RNAV (GPS) RWY 36 instrument approach procedure indicates a descent angle of 3.00°, not 2.52°.

122. (Refer to Figure 242 on page 285.) How should the missed approach point be identified when executing the RNAV (GPS) RWY 36 approach at Adams Field?

A.   When the TO-FROM indicator changes.

B.   Upon arrival at 760 feet on the glidepath.

C.   When time has expired for 5 NM past the FAF.

Answer (A) is correct. (FAA-H-8083-15B Chap 10)
   DISCUSSION: The MAP is a waypoint and is identified when the TO-FROM indicator changes, which indicates station passage at the waypoint; i.e., you have arrived at the MAP and the visual references are not there, so you must execute a missed approach.
   Answer (B) is incorrect. You will be at 760 ft. on a RWY 36 approach for approximately 1 1/2 NM before reaching the MAP. **Answer (C) is incorrect.** On the RNAV (GPS) RWY 36 approach, the MAP is identified by a waypoint, not by the time from the FAF.

123. (Refer to Figure 242 on page 285.) What minimum airborne equipment is required to be operative for RNAV (GPS) RWY 36 approach at Adams Field?

A.   An approved RNAV receiver that provides both horizontal and vertical guidance.

B.   A transponder and an approved RNAV receiver that provides both horizontal and vertical guidance.

C.   Any approved RNAV receiver.

Answer (C) is correct. (FAA-H-8083-15B Chap 10)
   DISCUSSION: An approved RNAV receiver is required for RNAV approaches. Area navigation, when approved by the FAA, is sufficient to conduct RNAV approaches. Area navigation simply moves the location of VORs based upon internal circuitry.
   Answer (A) is incorrect. RNAV receivers with vertical guidance are not required for RNAV approaches. **Answer (B) is incorrect.** RNAV receivers with vertical guidance are not required for RNAV approaches.

124. (Refer to Figure 242 on page 285.) When using the hold for course reversal for the RNAV (GPS) RWY 36, at what point will you turn inbound for the approach?

A.   4 DME miles from FEHXE.

B.   10 DME miles from the MAP.

C.   12 DME miles from LIT VORTAC.

Answer (A) is correct. (AIM Para 5-4-9)
   DISCUSSION: Given that "NO PT" is sanctioned, the holding pattern distance or time specified in the profile view must be observed. For a hold-in-lieu-of-PT, the holding pattern direction must be flown as depicted and the specified leg length/timing must not be exceeded.
   Answer (B) is incorrect. A VOR-A approach into LIT would require the course reversal to be conducted within 10 mi. of the MAP. **Answer (C) is incorrect.** This RNAV (GPS) RWY 36 into LIT requires following the instructions provided on the chart to fly the holding pattern as depicted, and the specified leg length of 4 NM must not be exceeded.

125. (Refer to Figure 242 below.) What type of entry is recommended to the missed approach holding pattern if the inbound heading is 050°?

A. Direct.

B. Parallel.

C. Teardrop.

Answer (C) is correct. *(AIM Para 5-3-8)*
    DISCUSSION: Extend the 222° radial from HIGHS. If you are coming in on a 050° heading, you are on R-230. The teardrop approach should be used because you are north of R-222.
    Answer (A) is incorrect. A direct entry would be from R-292 to R-112. **Answer (B) is incorrect.** The parallel entry would be from R-112 to R-222.

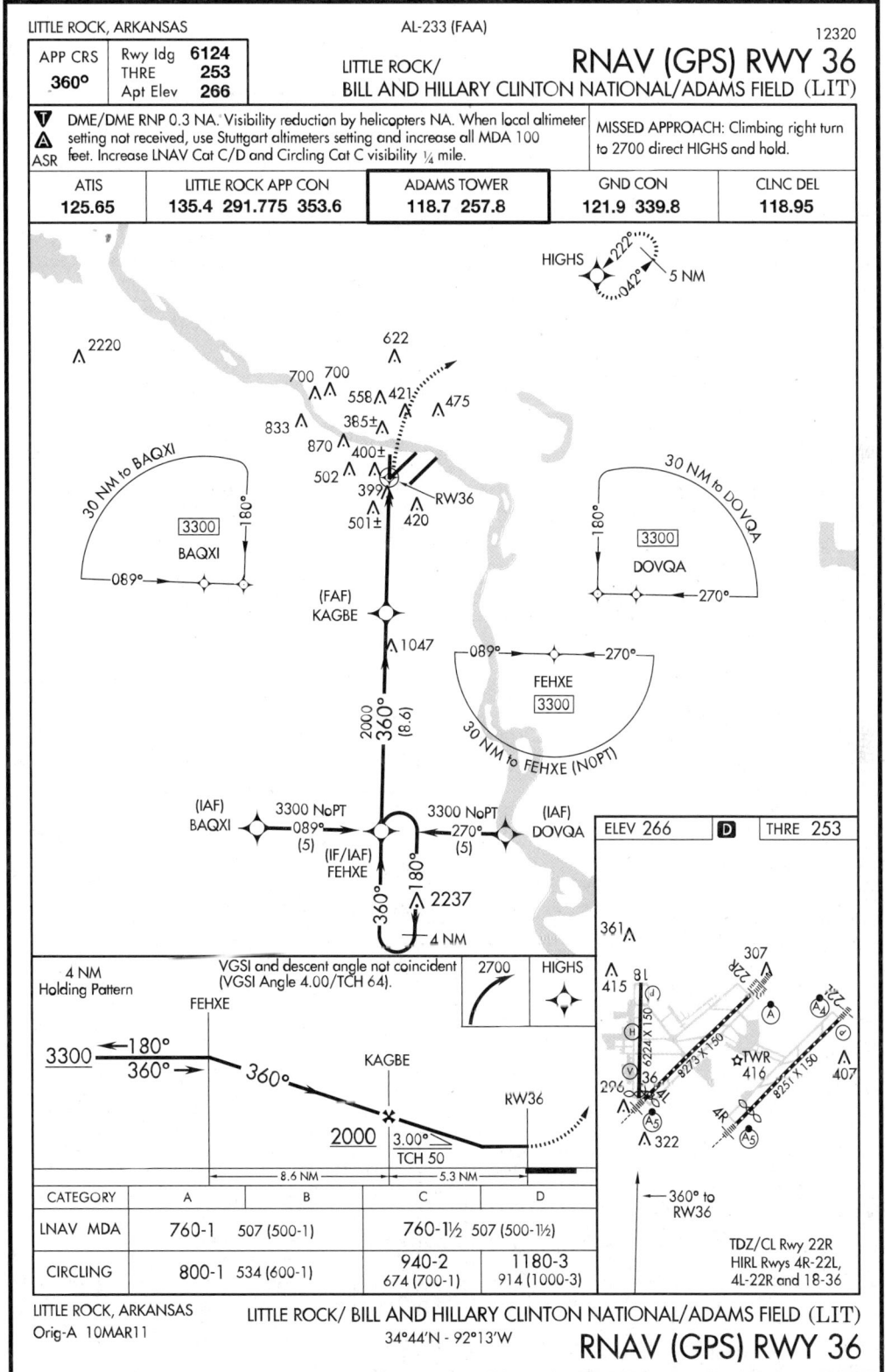

Figure 242. – RNAV RWY 36 (LIT).

126. (Refer to Figure 242 on page 287 and Legend 27 below.) You have been cleared for the RNAV (GPS) RWY 36 approach to LIT. At a groundspeed of 105 knots, what are the vertical descent angle and rate of descent on final approach?

A. 2.82 degrees and 524 feet per minute.

B. 3.00 degrees and 557 feet per minute.

C. 4.00 degrees and 550 feet per nautical mile.

Answer (B) is correct. *(FAA-H-8083-16B Chap 1)*

DISCUSSION: In Fig. 242, the notation in the profile view of the approach confirms the approach angle is 3.00°. To confirm the second portion of the answer, refer to Legend 27, the rate-of-descent table. On the left side of the chart, locate the angle of descent of 3.00°. Move to the right until under the columns for the airspeed of 90 and 120 kt., then interpolate halfway between 478 and 637. The rate of descent is 557 fpm.

Answer (A) is incorrect. The profile view in Fig. 242, under and to the right of KAGBE, shows 3.00° as the approach angle, not 2.82°. **Answer (C) is incorrect.** The profile view in Fig. 242, under and to the right of KAGBE, shows 3.00° as the approach angle, not 4.00°.

CLIMB/DESCENT TABLE 10042

INSTRUMENT TAKEOFF OR APPROACH PROCEDURE CHARTS
RATE OF CLIMB/DESCENT TABLE
(ft. per min)

A rate of climb/descent table is provided for use in planning and executing climbs or descents under known or approximate ground speed conditions. It will be especially useful for approaches when the localizer only is used for course guidance. A best speed, power, altitude combination can be programmed which will result in a stable glide rate and altitude favorable for executing a landing if minimums exist upon breakout. Care should always be exercised so that minimum descent altitude and missed approach point are not exceeded.

	CLIMB/ DESCENT ANGLE (degrees and tenths)	ft/NM	GROUND SPEED (knots)										
			60	90	120	150	180	210	240	270	300	330	360
	2.0	210	210	320	425	530	635	743	850	955	1060	1165	1275
	2.5	265	265	400	530	665	795	930	1060	1195	1325	1460	1590
VERTICAL PATH ANGLE	2.7	287	287	430	574	717	860	1003	1147	1290	1433	1576	1720
	2.8	297	297	446	595	743	892	1041	1189	1338	1486	1635	1783
	2.9	308	308	462	616	770	924	1078	1232	1386	1539	1693	1847
	3.0	318	318	478	637	797	956	1115	1274	1433	1593	1752	1911
	3.1	329	329	494	659	823	988	1152	1317	1481	1646	1810	1975
	3.2	340	340	510	680	850	1020	1189	1359	1529	1699	1869	2039
	3.3	350	350	526	701	876	1052	1227	1402	1577	1752	1927	2103
	3.4	361	361	542	722	903	1083	1264	1444	1625	1805	1986	2166
	3.5	370	370	555	745	930	1115	1300	1485	1670	1860	2045	2230
	4.0	425	425	640	850	1065	1275	1490	1700	1915	2125	2340	2550
	4.5	480	480	715	955	1195	1435	1675	1915	2150	2390	2630	2870
	5.0	530	530	795	1065	1330	1595	1860	2125	2390	2660	2925	3190
	5.5	585	585	880	1170	1465	1755	2050	2340	2635	2925	3220	3510
	6.0	640	640	960	1275	1595	1915	2235	2555	2875	3195	3510	3830
	6.5	690	690	1040	1385	1730	2075	2425	2770	3115	3460	3805	4155
	7.0	745	745	1120	1490	1865	2240	2610	2985	3355	3730	4105	4475
	7.5	800	800	1200	1600	2000	2400	2800	3200	3600	4000	4400	4800
	8.0	855	855	1280	1710	2135	2560	2990	3415	3845	4270	4695	5125
	8.5	910	910	1360	1815	2270	2725	3180	3630	4085	4540	4995	5450
	9.0	960	960	1445	1925	2405	2885	3370	3850	4330	4810	5295	5775
	9.5	1015	1015	1525	2035	2540	3050	3560	4065	4575	5085	5590	6100
	10.0	1070	1070	1605	2145	2680	3215	3750	4285	4820	5355	5890	6430

CLIMB/DESCENT TABLE 10042

Legend 27. – Instrument Takeoff or Approach Procedure Charts, Rate-of-Climb/Descent Table.

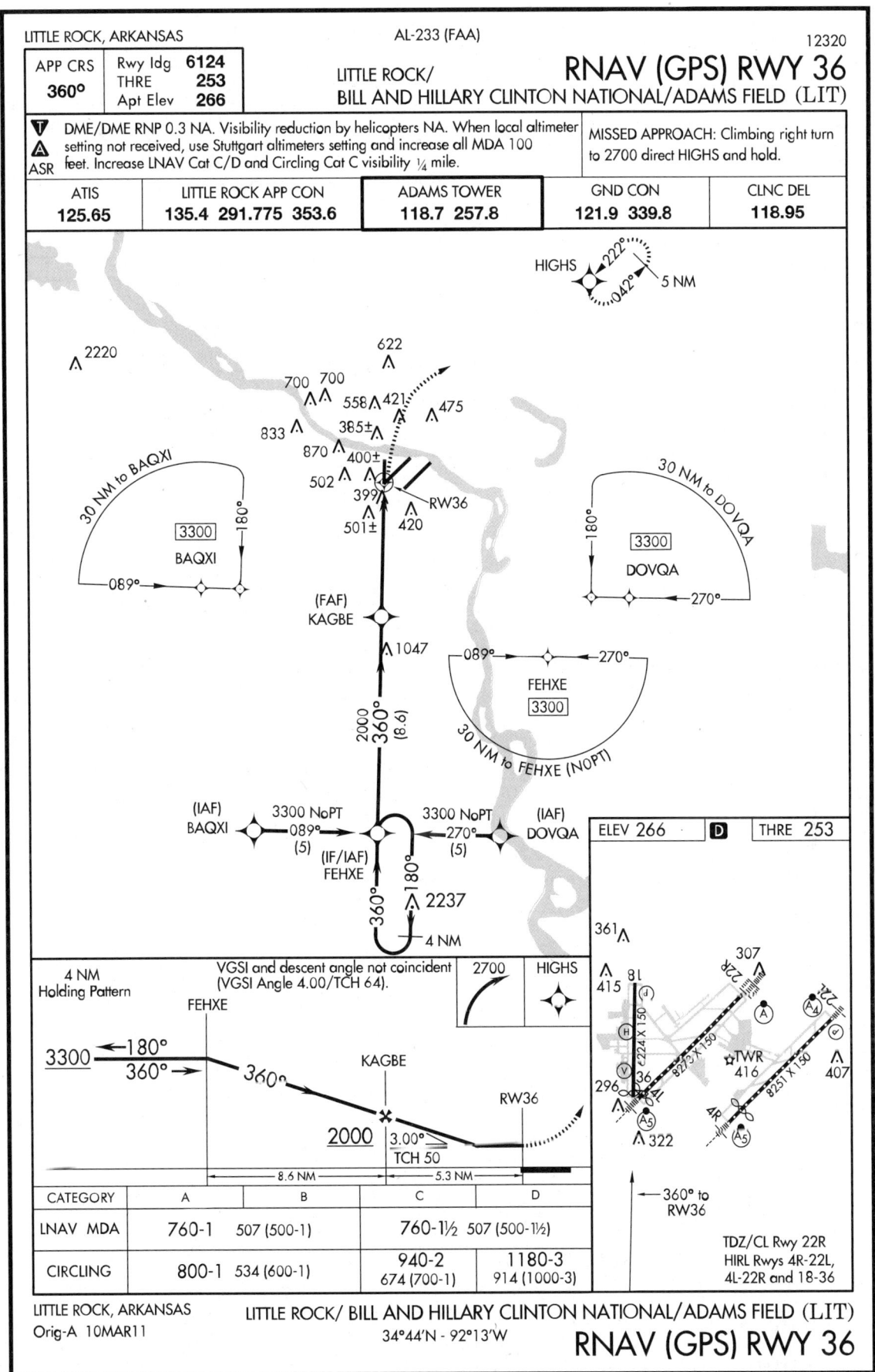

Figure 242. – RNAV RWY 36 (LIT).

127. If the plan view on an approach chart does not include a procedure turn barb, that means

   A. a procedure turn is not authorized.

   B. you should fly a teardrop entry.

   C. a racetrack-type turn is required.

Answer (A) is correct. (AIM Para 5-4-8)
   DISCUSSION: The absence of the procedure turn barb in the planview indicates that a procedure turn is not authorized for that approach.
   Answer (B) is incorrect. The absence of a procedure turn barb indicates that all, not just teardrop-type, procedure turns are not authorized. **Answer (C) is incorrect.** The absence of a procedure turn barb indicates that all, not just racetrack-type, procedure turns are not authorized.

128. The instrument approach criteria for a Category A airplane is based on a maximum airspeed of

   A. 100 knots.

   B. 90 knots.

   C. 80 knots.

Answer (B) is correct. (14 CFR 97.3)
   DISCUSSION: The instrument approach criteria for a Category A airplane is based on a maximum airspeed of 90 kt. An aircraft approach category is a grouping of aircraft based on a speed of V_{REF}, if specified, or if V_{REF} is not specified, 1.3 V_{SO} at the maximum certificated landing weight. V_{REF}, V_{SO}, and the maximum certificated landing weight are those values as established for the aircraft by the certification authority of the country of registry. The categories are as follows:

1. Category A: Speed less than 91 kt.
2. Category B: Speed 91 kt. or more but less than 121 kt.
3. Category C: Speed 121 kt. or more but less than 141 kt.
4. Category D: Speed 141 kt. or more but less than 166 kt.
5. Category E: Speed 166 kt. or more.

   Answer (A) is incorrect. The instrument approach criteria for a Category A airplane is based on a maximum airspeed of 90 kt., not 100 kt. **Answer (C) is incorrect.** The instrument approach criteria for a Category A airplane is based on a maximum airspeed of 90 kt., not 80 kt.

129. (Refer to Figure 244 on page 289.) At what minimum altitude should you cross RAMKE intersection during the S-LDA RWY 6 approach at ROA?

   A. 2,720 MSL.

   B. 4,300 MSL.

   C. 1,780 MSL.

Answer (B) is correct. (FAA-H-8083-16B Chaps 4, 8; IAP Legend)
   DISCUSSION: The profile view of the approach includes a Maltese cross at RAMKE and a notation of 4,300 feet MSL. That is the minimum altitude you should cross the intersection.
   Answer (A) is incorrect. The S-LDA 6 approach minimum is 2,720 feet MSL. **Answer (C) is incorrect.** The SKIRT minimum for the S-LDA 6 approach is 1,780 ft. MSL.

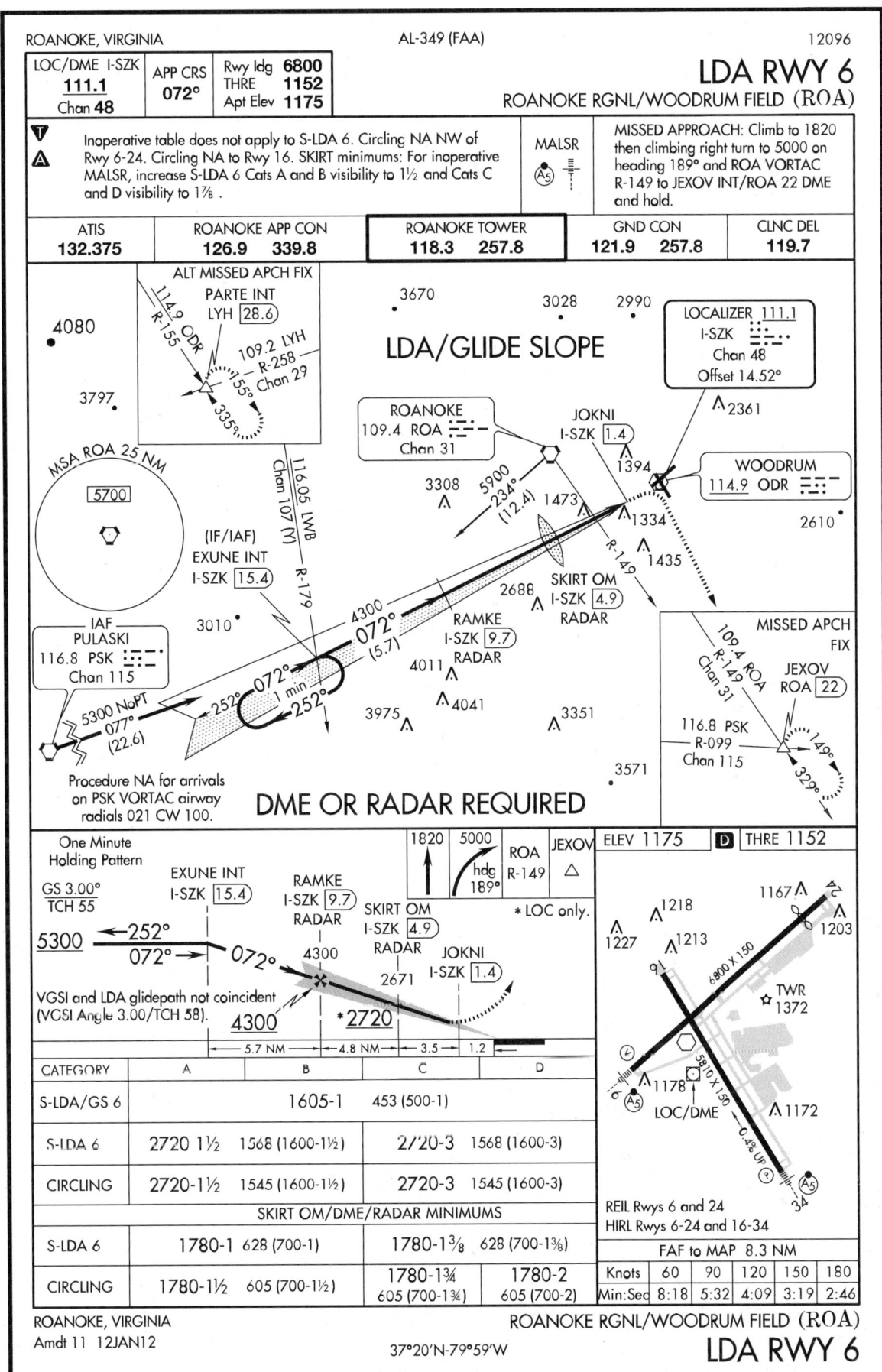

Figure 244. – LDA RWY 6 (ROA).

130. (Refer to Figure 245 on page 291.) While flying at an assigned altitude of 5,000 feet MSL, you are cleared to CEPUL for the RNAV (GPS)-B at CQX. At what point may you leave 5,000 feet MSL?

A. Upon crossing UMANE inbound for the approach.

B. Upon crossing UMANE for the procedure turn.

C. Upon crossing CEPUL.

Answer (C) is correct. (AIM Para 5-4-6)
DISCUSSION: Having been cleared to CEPUL for the approach, you must maintain the last altitude assigned by ATC until the aircraft is established on a published approach procedure segment for which a lower altitude is published on the chart.
Answer (A) is incorrect. Once cleared to commence the approach from the CEPUL IAF, you may begin a planned descent at CEPUL once you are established on the published approach procedure segment to whatever minimum altitude is listed for the segment. Answer (B) is incorrect. Upon crossing CEPUL, the aircraft has been cleared to descend on the published approach procedure segment, which is annotated to indicate a course reversal is not necessary in this Terminal Arrival Area (TAA).

131. (Refer to Figure 245 on page 291.) You are executing the missed approach at CQX from the RNAV (GPS)-B approach. How will you enter the holding pattern?

A. Direct.

B. Teardrop.

C. Parallel.

Answer (A) is correct. (AIM Para 5-3-8)
DISCUSSION: The missed approach procedure requires a climbing left turn from runway heading 240° to 3,000 ft. and direct to CEPUL. The inbound leg to hold at at CEPUL is 041° and will be achieved with a direct entry to the hold.
Answer (B) is incorrect. Given that the inbound leg of the hold at CEPUL is 041°, you would need to be approaching CEPUL from the northeast to enter on a teardrop entry.
Answer (C) is incorrect. Given that the inbound leg of the hold at CEPUL is 041°, you would need to be approaching CEPUL from the northwest to enter on a parallel entry.

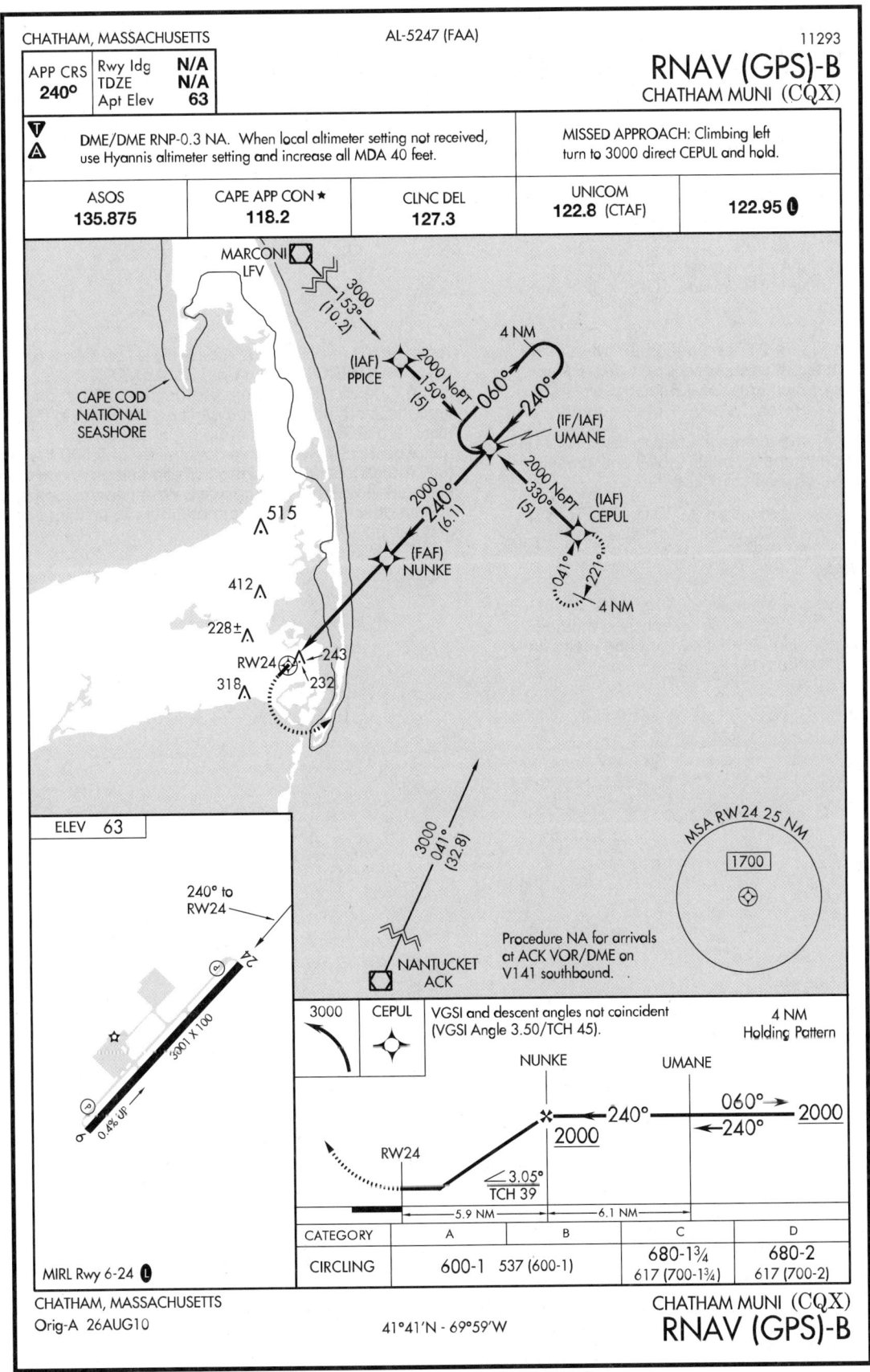

Figure 245. – RNAV (GPS)-B (CQX).

292   SU 6: Holding and Instrument Approaches

132. (Refer to Figure 247 on page 293.) How should a pilot reverse course to get established on the in bound course of the ILS RWY 9, if radar vectoring to EXPAM?

A. Execute a standard 45° procedure turn toward Seal Beach VORTAC or Pomona VORTAC.

B. Make an appropriate entry to the depicted holding pattern at EXPAM INT.

C. Use any type of procedure turn, but remain within 10 NM of Riverside VOR.

Answer (B) is correct. (AIM Para 5-4-9)
   DISCUSSION: If using radar vectoring for the ILS RWY 9 approach, you should make an appropriate entry into the depicted holding pattern at the EXPAM intersection.
   Answer (A) is incorrect. To execute a standard 45° procedure turn toward Seal Beach VORTAC or Pomona VORTAC is a nonsense statement. **Answer (C) is incorrect.** The depicted holding pattern is the only type of course reversal authorized for the ILS RWY 9 approach.

133. (Refer to Figure 247 on page 293.) What is the minimum altitude descent procedure if cleared for the S-ILS 9 approach from Seal Beach VORTAC?

A. Descend and maintain 3,000 to JASER INT, descend to and maintain 2,500 until crossing EXPAM, descend to 1,280 (DA).

B. Descend and maintain 3,000 to JASER INT, descend to 2,800 when established on the LOC course, intercept and maintain the GS to 960 (DA).

C. Descend and maintain 3,000 to JASER INT, descend to 2,500 while established on the LOC course inbound, intercept and maintain the GS to 960 (DA).

Answer (C) is correct. (FAA-H-8083-15B Chap 10)
   DISCUSSION: From Seal Beach VORTAC, descend to 3,000 ft. to Jaser INT, then descend to 2,500 ft. on the localizer inbound, and then descend on the glide slope to the decision altitude of 960 ft.
   Answer (A) is incorrect. A height of 2,500 ft. is maintained until the glide slope, and the ILS glide slope is flown down to 960 ft. **Answer (B) is incorrect.** When on the localizer, you should descend to 2,500 ft., not 2,800 ft., until intercepting the glide slope.

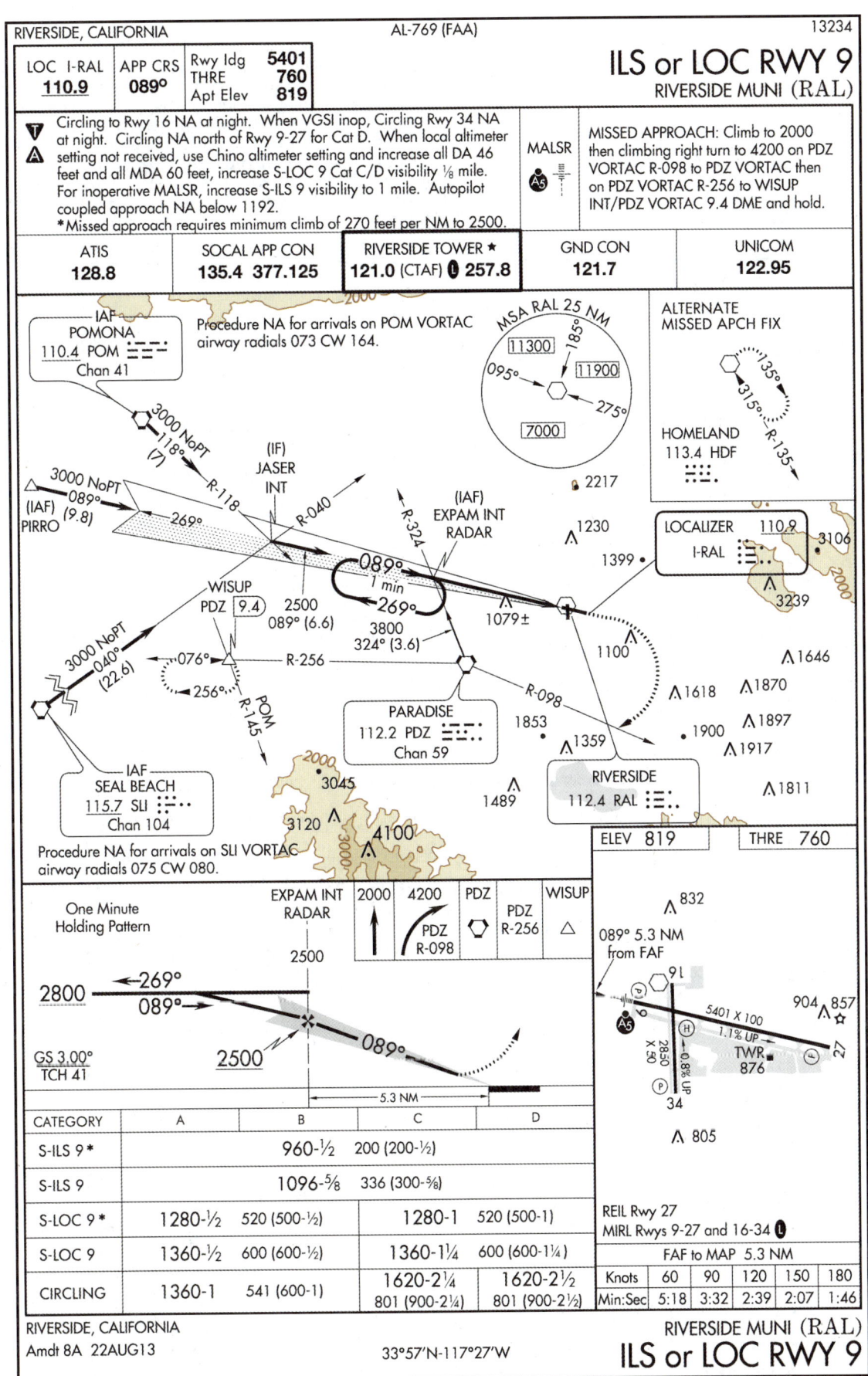

Figure 247. – ILS or RWY 9 (RAL).

6.12   DPs and STARs

134. (Refer to Figure 175 below, and Figure 174 on page 295.) At which point does the JEN.JEN9 arrival begin?

A. INK VOR.

B. GLEN ROSE VORTAC.

C. FEVER intersection.

Answer (B) is correct. (FAA-H-8083-16B Chap 4)
   DISCUSSION: Fig. 174 shows three feeder routes that converge at JEN, the identifier for the GLEN ROSE VORTAC. The arrival descriptions included in Fig. 175 all conclude at the JEN VORTAC, then proceed from there. The approach starts at that point, the GLEN ROSE VORTAC.
   Answer (A) is incorrect. INK VOR establishes the beginning of one of three feeder routes to the arrival; it is not the arrival itself. **Answer (C) is incorrect.** FEVER is the first intersection listed along the arrival; it is not the origination point of the arrival.

(JEN.JEN9)   09351

GLEN ROSE NINE ARRIVAL   ST-6039 (FAA)   DALLAS-FT. WORTH, TEXAS

ARRIVAL DESCRIPTION

<u>ABILENE TRANSITION (ABI.JEN9):</u> From over ABI VORTAC via R-099 to GEENI INT, then via JEN R-267 to JEN VORTAC. Thence. . . .

<u>CENTEX TRANSITION (CWK.JEN9):</u> From over CWK VORTAC via CWK R-321 and AGJ R-142 to AGJ VORTAC, then via AGJ R-350 to JUMBO INT, then via JEN R-197 to JEN VORTAC. Thence . . . .

<u>JUMBO TRANSITION (JUMBO.JEN9):</u> From over JUMBO INT via JEN R-197 to JEN VORTAC. Thence . . . .

<u>SAN ANTONIO TRANSITION (SAT.JEN9):</u> From over SAT VORTAC via SAT R-359 to JUMBO INT, then via JEN R-197 to JEN VORTAC. Thence . . . .

<u>WACO TRANSITION (ACT.JEN9):</u> From over ACT VORTAC via ACT R-305 and JEN R-128 to JEN VORTAC. Thence. . . .

<u>WINK TRANSITION (INK.JEN9):</u> From over INK VORTAC via INK R-071 and TQA R-254 to TQA VOR/DME, then via TQA R-082 to GEENI INT, then via JEN R-267 to JEN VORTAC. Thence. . . .

. . . . <u>ALL AIRCRAFT:</u> From over JEN VORTAC via JEN R-039, thence . . . .

<u>ALL AIRCRAFT LANDING NORTH:</u> To CURLE INT, expect vectors to final approach course.

<u>JETS LANDING SOUTH:</u> To DELMO, depart DELMO heading 355°.
<u>For /E, /F, /G and /R (RNP 2.0) EQUIPMENT SUFFIXED AIRCRAFT:</u> From over DELMO WP direct TEVON WP, expect vector to final approach course prior to TEVON WP. If not received by TEVON fly present heading.
<u>NON TURBOJETS LANDING SOUTH:</u> To CURLE INT, depart CURLE heading 010° for vectors to final approach course.

<u>AIRCRAFT LANDING DAL, ADS, TKI:</u> To DELMO INT, depart DELMO via FUZ R-171 to FUZ VORTAC then FUZ R-064 to HURBS INT, expect vectors to final approach course.

GLEN ROSE NINE ARRIVAL   DALLAS-FT. WORTH, TEXAS
(JEN.JEN9)   09351

Figure 175. – GLEN ROSE Nine Arrival (JEN.JEN9).

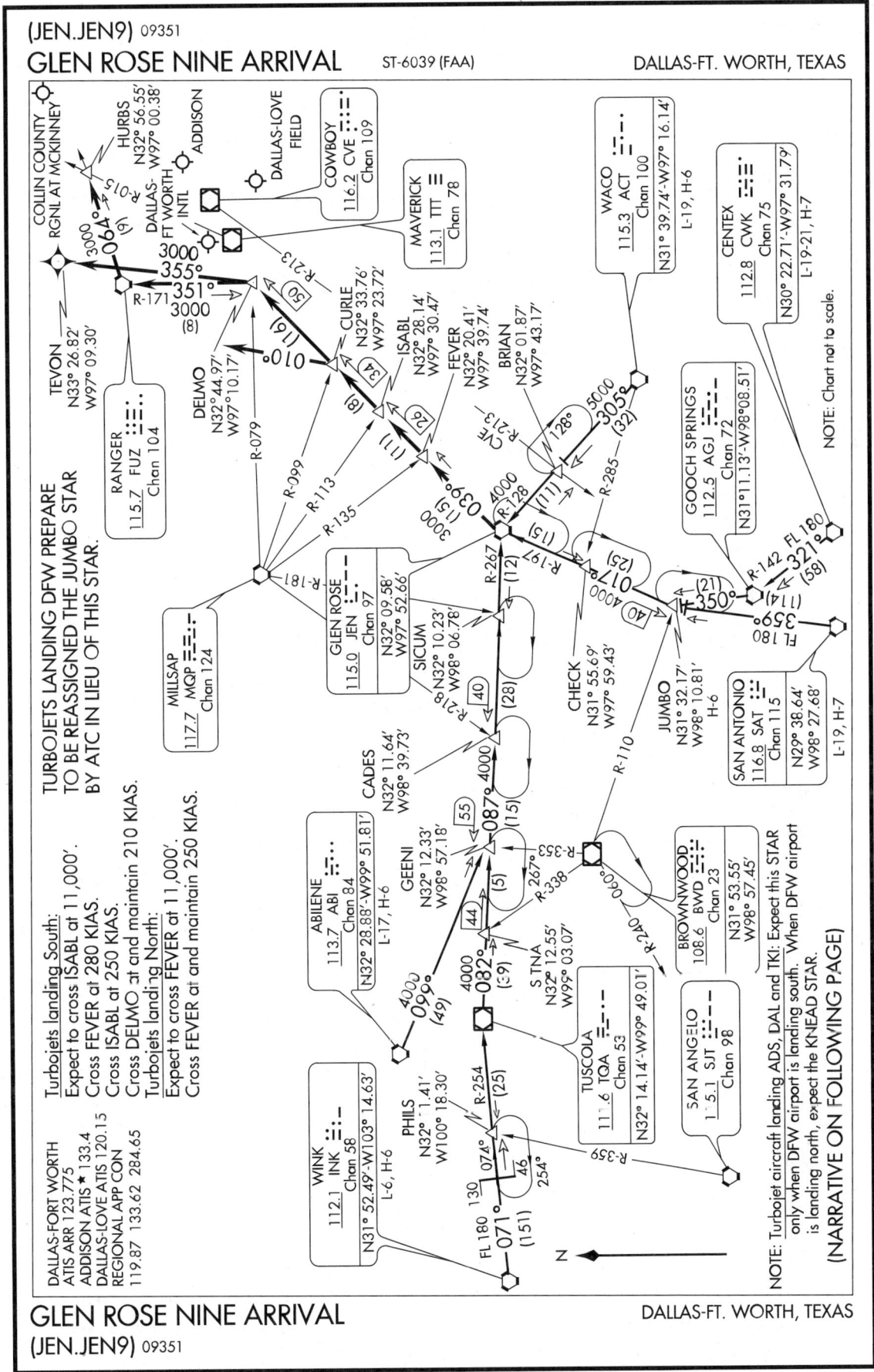

Figure 174. – GLEN ROSE Nine Arrival (JEN.JEN9).

135. (Refer to Figure 209 below, and Figure 208 on page 297.) At which location or condition does the STELA.STELA1 arrival begin?

A. ALB VORTAC.

B. CANAN intersection.

C. STELA intersection.

Answer (B) is correct. (FAA-H-8083-16B Chap 4)
   DISCUSSION: Fig. 208 shows three feeder routes that converge at CANAN intersection, with a single approach flowing from that point. Each of the arrival route descriptions included in Fig. 209 lead to CANAN before moving into the arrival itself. CANAN intersection is the starting point of the arrival procedure.
   Answer (A) is incorrect. Although the ALBANY VOR feeds into the STELA.STELA1 arrival, it does not include traffic from two additional feeder routes. **Answer (C) is incorrect.** STELA intersection establishes a holding fix along the route of the arrival procedure, but it is not the start of the arrival procedure.

(STELA.STELA1) 16259   ST-460 (FAA)
STELA ONE ARRIVAL
                                         WINDSOR LOCKS, CONNECTICUT

ARRIVAL ROUTE DESCRIPTION

ALBANY TRANSITION (ALB.STELA1): From over ALB VORTAC via ALB R-147 to CANAN INT. Thence. . . .
AUDIL TRANSITION (AUDIL.STELA1): From over AUDIL INT via RKA R-306 to RKA VOR/DME, then via RKA R-099 to CANAN INT. Thence. . . .
CAMBRIDGE TRANSITION (CAM.STELA1): From over CAM VOR/DME via CAM R-203 to CANAN INT. Thence. . . .
HANCOCK TRANSITION (HNK.STELA1): From over HNK VOR/DME via HNK R-060 to SWEDE INT, then via RKA R-099 to CANAN INT. Thence. . . .
WILET TRANSITION (WILET.STELA1): From over WILET INT via RKA R-292 to RKA VOR/DME, then via RKA R-099 TO CANAN INT. Thence. . . .

KBDL and KHFD ARRIVALS: From over CANAN INT via ALB R-147 to TOMES INT. Expect radar vectors to final approach course prior to TOMES INT.

KBAF, KCEF and KORH ARRIVALS: From over CANAN INT via ALB R-147 to MOLDS INT. Then via BAF R-295 to BAF VORTAC. Expect radar vectors to final approach course prior to BAF VORTAC.

STELA ONE ARRIVAL   WINDSOR LOCKS, CONNECTICUT
(STELA.STELA1) 31MAY12

Figure 209. – STELA One Arrival (STELA.STELA1).

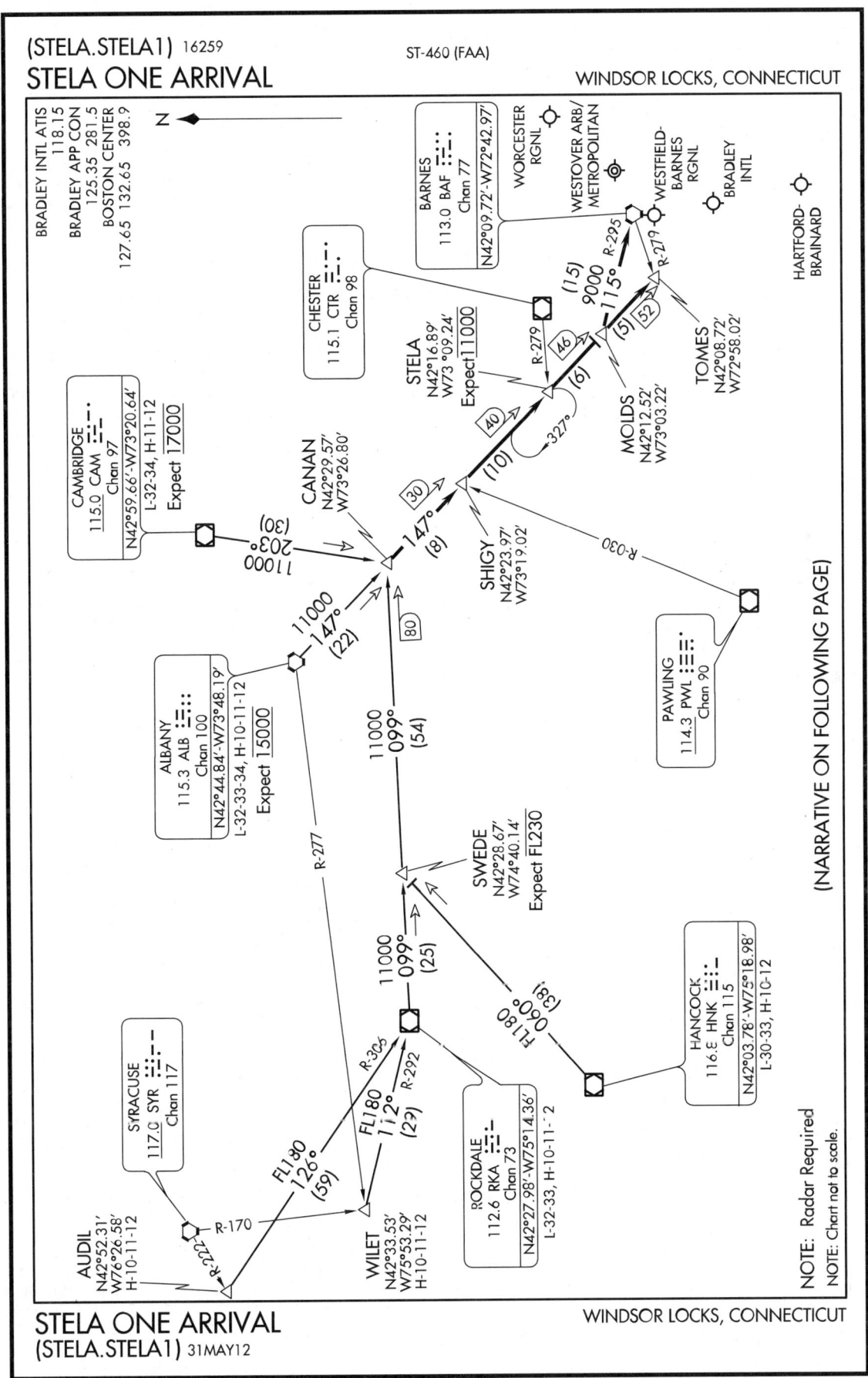

Figure 208. – STELA One Arrival (STELA.STELA1).

136. Preferred IFR routes beginning with a fix, indicate that departing aircraft will normally be routed to the fix by

    A. the established airway(s) between the departure airport and the fix.

    B. an instrument departure procedure (DP), or radar vectors.

    C. direct route only.

Answer (B) is correct. (P/C Glossary)
    DISCUSSION: Preferred IFR routes are correlated with DPs and STARs and may be defined by airways, jet routes, and direct routes between NAVAIDs. Thus, preferred routes beginning with a fix indicate that the departing traffic will normally be routed to the fix via a DP or radar vectors.
    Answer (A) is incorrect. Established airways may not exist between the airport and the fix, and other methods may be more efficient and effective. **Answer (C) is incorrect.** A direct route may not be appropriate due to obstructions or traffic flows.

137. Which procedure applies to instrument departure procedures?

    A. Instrument departure clearances will not be issued unless requested by the pilot.

    B. The pilot in command must accept an instrument departure procedure when issued by ATC.

    C. If an instrument departure procedure is accepted, the pilot must possess a textual or graphic description.

Answer (C) is correct. (AIM Para 5-2-6)
    DISCUSSION: Once an instrument departure procedure (DP) is accepted, the presumption by ATC is that the pilot possesses a textual description of the DP.
    Answer (A) is incorrect. Pilots operating from locations with DPs may expect ATC clearances containing a DP. **Answer (B) is incorrect.** You must reject a DP clearance if you do not have a text of the DP or if it is otherwise unacceptable.

138. Which is true regarding the use of an instrument departure procedure chart?

    A. The use of instrument departure procedures is mandatory.

    B. To use an instrument departure procedure, the pilot must possess at least the textual description of the approved procedure.

    C. To use an instrument departure procedure, the pilot must possess both the textual and graphic form of the approved procedure.

Answer (B) is correct. (AIM Para 5-2-6)
    DISCUSSION: Use of an instrument departure procedure (DP) requires that the pilot have at least the textual description of the procedure.
    Answer (A) is incorrect. Use of a DP is never mandatory. **Answer (C) is incorrect.** A pilot need only possess the textual form of the DP.

139. Which is true regarding STARs?

    A. STARs are used to separate IFR and VFR traffic.

    B. STARs are established to simplify clearance delivery procedures.

    C. STARs are used at certain airports to decrease traffic congestion.

Answer (B) is correct. (AIM Para 5-4-1)
    DISCUSSION: A STAR's purpose is to simplify clearance delivery procedures.
    Answer (A) is incorrect. STARs do not pertain to VFR traffic. **Answer (C) is incorrect.** STARs are used to decrease radio, not traffic, congestion.

140. (Refer to Figure 211 on page 299.) For takeoff on RWY 9 using an average groundspeed of 140 knots, what minimum rate of climb would meet the required minimum rate of climb as specified on the instrument departure procedure?

    A. 830 feet per minute.

    B. 415 feet per minute.

    C. 970 feet per minute.

Answer (C) is correct. (FAA-H-8083-16B Chap 1)
    DISCUSSION: Fig. 211 provides takeoff minimums for RWY 9 that stipulate a minimum climb of 415 feet per NM. Divide GS (140 knots) by time (60 minutes) to find the number of NM per minute (140 ÷ 60 = 2.33 NM per minute). Multiply the number of NM per minute (2.33) by the number of feet per NM (415) required to find the feet per minute (2.33 × 415 = 966.9, which can be rounded to 967). The best answer is 970 feet per minute.
    Answer (A) is incorrect. The rate of climb is 970, not 830, feet per minute. **Answer (B) is incorrect.** The number 415 is the feet per NM required for aircraft climbing out on this departure; it is not the number of feet per minute required.

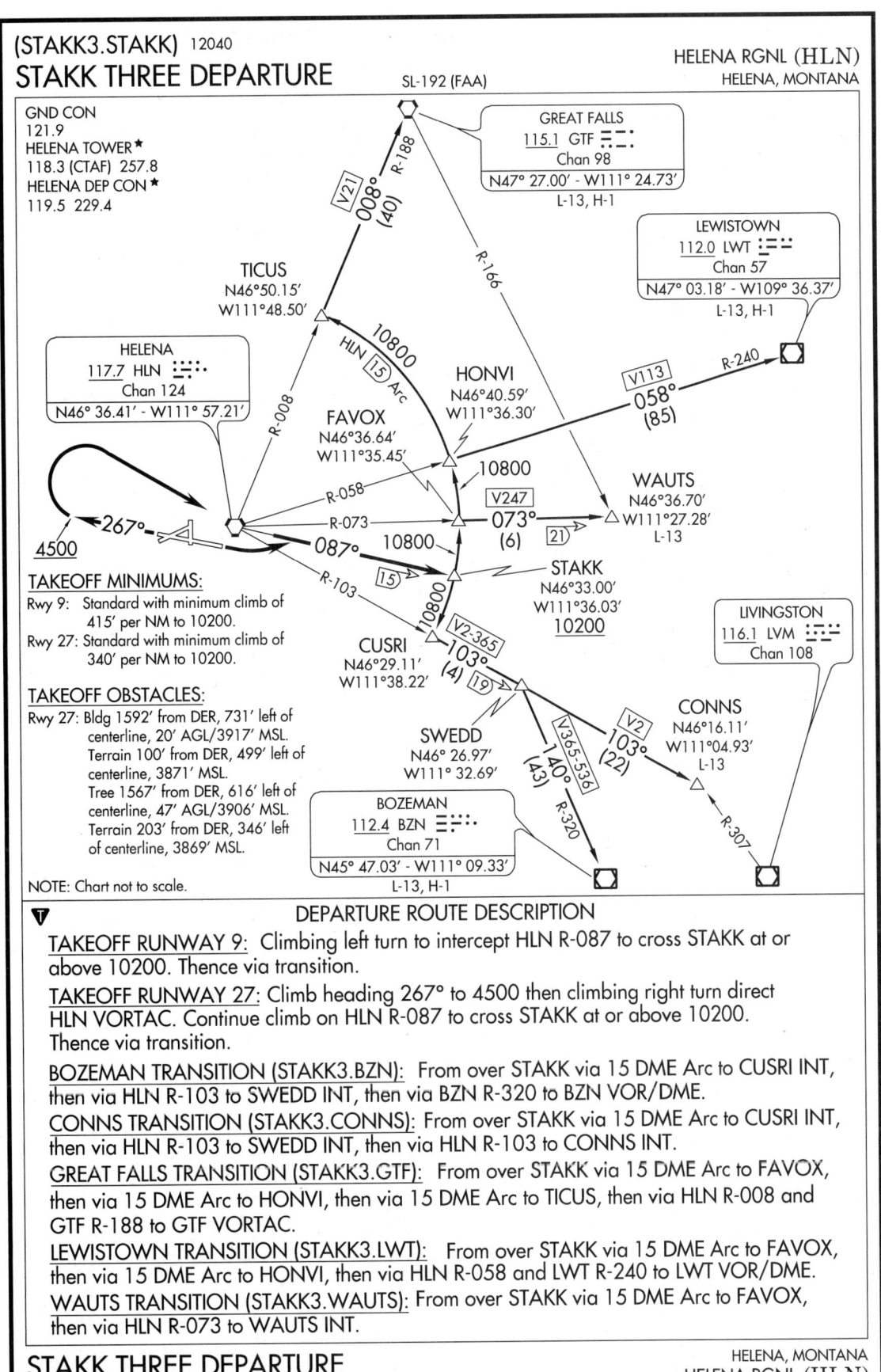

(STAKK3.STAKK) 12040

STAKK THREE DEPARTURE

SL-192 (FAA)

HELENA RGNL (HLN)
HELENA, MONTANA

GND CON
121.9
HELENA TOWER ★
118.3 (CTAF) 257.8
HELENA DEP CON ★
119.5 229.4

GREAT FALLS
115.1 GTF
Chan 98
N47° 27.00' - W111° 24.73'
L-13, H-1

LEWISTOWN
112.0 LWT
Chan 57
N47° 03.18' - W109° 36.37'
L-13, H-1

TICUS
N46°50.15'
W111°48.50'

HELENA
117.7 HLN
Chan 124
N46° 36.41' - W111° 57.21'

HONVI
N46°40.59'
W111°36.30'

FAVOX
N46°36.64'
W111°35.45'

V113
058°
(85)

R-240

WAUTS
N46°36.70'
W111°27.28'
L-13

V247
073°
(6)

STAKK
N46°33.00'
W111°36.03'
10200

LIVINGSTON
116.1 LVM
Chan 108

CUSRI
N46°29.11'
W111°38.22'

V2-365
103°
(4)

CONNS
N46°16.11'
W111°04.93'
L-13

4500

267°

087°

R-103

TAKEOFF MINIMUMS:
Rwy 9:   Standard with minimum climb of
         415' per NM to 10200.
Rwy 27: Standard with minimum climb of
         340' per NM to 10200.

TAKEOFF OBSTACLES:
Rwy 27: Bldg 1592' from DER, 731' left of
         centerline, 20' AGL/3917' MSL.
         Terrain 100' from DER, 499' left of
         centerline, 3871' MSL.
         Tree 1567' from DER, 616' left of
         centerline, 47' AGL/3906' MSL.
         Terrain 203' from DER, 346' left
         of centerline, 3869' MSL.

SWEDD
N46° 26.97'
W111° 32.69'

V365-536
140°
(43)

V2
103°
(22)

BOZEMAN
112.4 BZN
Chan 71
N45° 47.03' - W111° 09.33'
L-13, H-1

R-307

NOTE: Chart not to scale.

DEPARTURE ROUTE DESCRIPTION

TAKEOFF RUNWAY 9: Climbing left turn to intercept HLN R-087 to cross STAKK at or above 10200. Thence via transition.

TAKEOFF RUNWAY 27: Climb heading 267° to 4500 then climbing right turn direct HLN VORTAC. Continue climb on HLN R-087 to cross STAKK at or above 10200. Thence via transition.

BOZEMAN TRANSITION (STAKK3.BZN): From over STAKK via 15 DME Arc to CUSRI INT, then via HLN R-103 to SWEDD INT, then via BZN R-320 to BZN VOR/DME.

CONNS TRANSITION (STAKK3.CONNS): From over STAKK via 15 DME Arc to CUSRI INT, then via HLN R-103 to SWEDD INT, then via HLN R-103 to CONNS INT.

GREAT FALLS TRANSITION (STAKK3.GTF): From over STAKK via 15 DME Arc to FAVOX, then via 15 DME Arc to HONVI, then via 15 DME Arc to TICUS, then via HLN R-008 and GTF R-188 to GTF VORTAC.

LEWISTOWN TRANSITION (STAKK3.LWT): From over STAKK via 15 DME Arc to FAVOX, then via 15 DME Arc to HONVI, then via HLN R-058 and LWT R-240 to LWT VOR/DME.

WAUTS TRANSITION (STAKK3.WAUTS): From over STAKK via 15 DME Arc to FAVOX, then via HLN R-073 to WAUTS INT.

STAKK THREE DEPARTURE

HELENA, MONTANA
HELENA RGNL (HLN)

(STAKK3.STAKK) 12040

Figure 211. – STAKK Three Departure (STAKK3.STAKK) (HLN).

141. Which clearance procedures may be issued by ATC without prior pilot request?

    A. DP's, STAR's, and contact approaches.

    B. Contact and visual approaches.

    C. DP's, STAR's, and visual approaches.

Answer (C) is correct. (AIM Para 5-4-25)
    DISCUSSION: DPs, STARs, and visual approaches are all routinely assigned by ATC as appropriate. Contact approaches must be requested by the pilot and made in lieu of a standard or special instrument approach.
    Answer (A) is incorrect. Contact approaches must be requested by the pilot. **Answer (B) is incorrect.** Contact approaches must be requested by the pilot.

142. ATC can issue a STAR

    A. to all pilots wherever STARs are available.

    B. only if the pilot requests a STAR in the "Remarks" section of the flight plan.

    C. when ATC deems it appropriate, unless the pilot requests "No STAR."

Answer (C) is correct. (AIM Para 5-4-1)
    DISCUSSION: Pilots of IFR civil aircraft destined to locations for which STARs have been published may be issued a clearance containing a STAR whenever ATC deems it appropriate. The pilot should notify ATC if (s)he does not wish to use a STAR by placing "No STAR" in the remarks section of the flight plan or by the less desirable method of verbally stating the request to ATC.
    Answer (A) is incorrect. STARs are not mandatory to ATC or pilots. **Answer (B) is incorrect.** Pilot request is necessary to avoid, not obtain, STARs.

143. Which of the following statements regarding STARs is most accurate?

    A. STARs facilitate the transition between the departure procedure and en route portion of the flight.

    B. STARs facilitate the transition between the en route portion of the flight and the instrument approach procedure.

    C. STARs can be planned for use by aircraft with RNAV capability, subject to any limitations or requirements noted on en route charts in applicable Advisory Circulars, or by NOTAM.

Answer (B) is correct. (AIM Para 5-4-1)
    DISCUSSION: STARs facilitate the transition between the en route portion of the flight and the instrument approach procedure.
    Answer (A) is incorrect. STARs facilitate the transition between the en route portion of the flight and the instrument approach, not the departure procedure and en route portion of the flight. **Answer (C) is incorrect.** RNAV routes, not STARs, can be planned for use by aircraft with RNAV capability, subject to any limitations or requirements noted on en route charts or in applicable Advisory Circulars, or by NOTAM.

144. What action is recommended if a pilot does not wish to use an instrument departure procedure?

    A. Advise clearance delivery or ground control before departure.

    B. Advise departure control upon initial contact.

    C. Enter "No DP" in the REMARKS section of the IFR flight plan.

Answer (C) is correct. (AIM Para 5-2-6)
    DISCUSSION: A pilot who does not possess an instrument departure procedure (DP) chart or does not wish to use a DP should advise ATC by indicating "No DP" in the remarks section of the flight plan.
    Answer (A) is incorrect. Verbal requests are less desirable than entering "No DP" in the flight plan. **Answer (B) is incorrect.** Verbal requests are less desirable than entering "No DP" in the flight plan.

145. (Refer to Figure 216 on page 301.) If you take off from RWY 34L, or RWY 34R with minimum weather, which of the following is the minimum acceptable rate of climb (feet per minute) to 8,700 feet required for the RENO9.FMG departure at a GS of 150 knots?

    A. 960 feet per minute.

    B. 1,200 feet per minute.

    C. 430 feet per minute.

Answer (B) is correct. (FAA-H-8083-16B Chap 1, IAP Climb/ Descent Table)
    DISCUSSION: A note on Fig. 216 stipulates a 480 foot per NM climb for aircraft taking off from Runways 34L and 34R. Our GS is 150 knots. Divide GS by time to find NM per minute (150 knots ÷ 60 minutes = 2.5 NM per minute). Multiply feet per NM by number of NM per minute to find the answer (480 feet per NM × 2.5 NM per minute = 1,200 feet per minute). This can also be found on the climb/descent table found in any IAP booklet. Look under the column ft/NM. Follow it down to 480, then across to the right until under the column 150, and find 1,195 feet per minute.
    Answer (A) is incorrect. The actual requirement is 1,200, not 960, feet per minute. **Answer (C) is incorrect.** A 480 foot per NM climb for aircraft taking off from Runways 34L and 34R is required. At a ground speed of 150 knots, 430 feet per minute is far too low a value to meet the requirement.

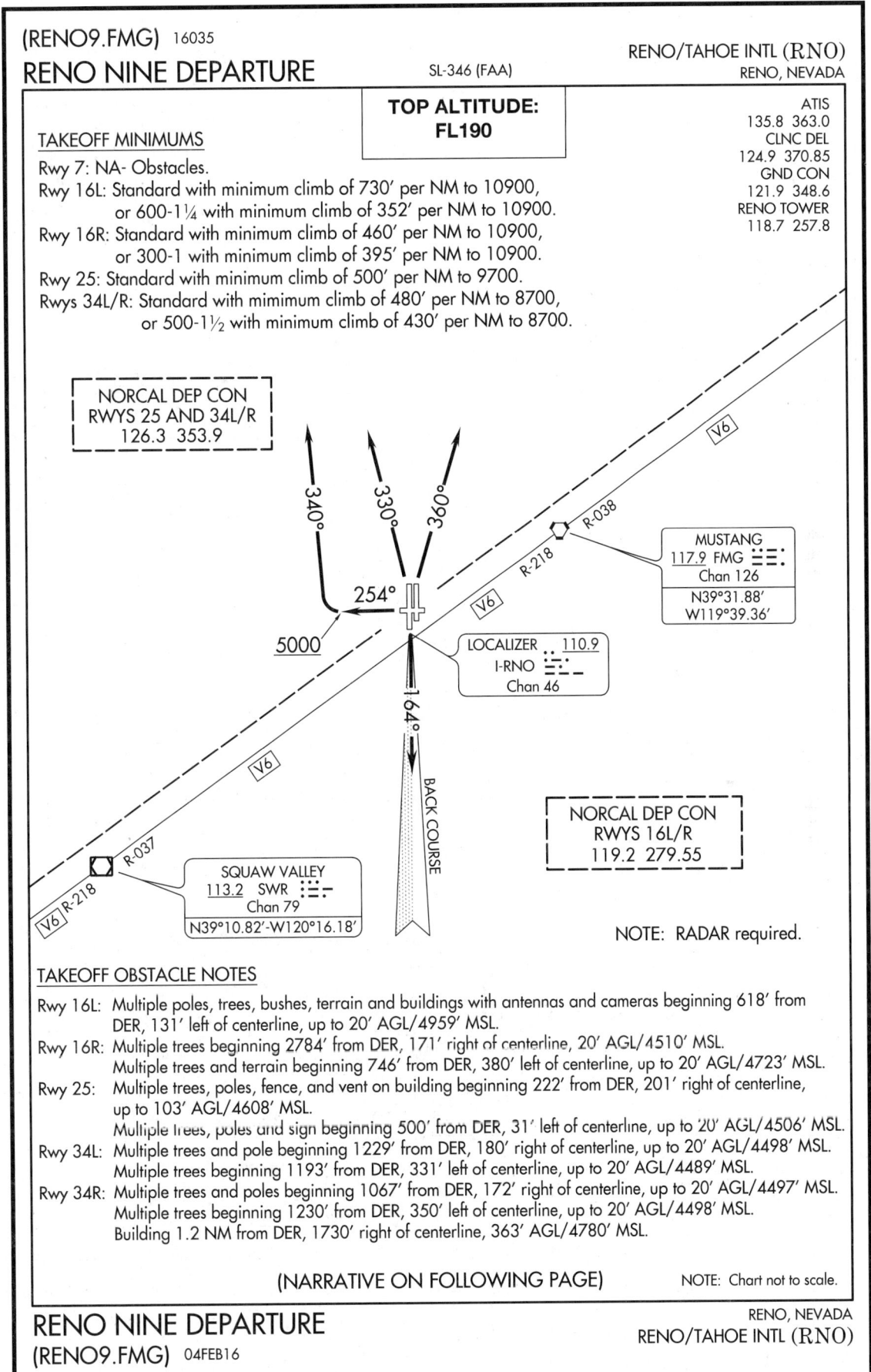

(RENO9.FMG) 16035

RENO NINE DEPARTURE
SL-346 (FAA)

RENO/TAHOE INTL (RNO)
RENO, NEVADA

TOP ALTITUDE:
FL190

ATIS
135.8 363.0
CLNC DEL
124.9 370.85
GND CON
121.9 348.6
RENO TOWER
118.7 257.8

TAKEOFF MINIMUMS

Rwy 7: NA- Obstacles.
Rwy 16L: Standard with minimum climb of 730' per NM to 10900,
　　　　or 600-1¼ with minimum climb of 352' per NM to 10900.
Rwy 16R: Standard with minimum climb of 460' per NM to 10900,
　　　　or 300-1 with minimum climb of 395' per NM to 10900.
Rwy 25: Standard with minimum climb of 500' per NM to 9700.
Rwys 34L/R: Standard with mimimum climb of 480' per NM to 8700,
　　　　or 500-1½ with minimum climb of 430' per NM to 8700.

NORCAL DEP CON
RWYS 25 AND 34L/R
126.3 353.9

340°   330°   360°

254°

5000

MUSTANG
117.9 FMG
Chan 126
N39°31.88'
W119°39.36'

R-038
R-218
V6

LOCALIZER   110.9
I-RNO
Chan 46

164°
BACK COURSE

NORCAL DEP CON
RWYS 16L/R
119.2 279.55

R-037
R-218
V6

SQUAW VALLEY
113.2 SWR
Chan 79
N39°10.82'-W120°16.18'

NOTE: RADAR required.

TAKEOFF OBSTACLE NOTES

Rwy 16L: Multiple poles, trees, bushes, terrain and buildings with antennas and cameras beginning 618' from
　　　　DER, 131' left of centerline, up to 20' AGL/4959' MSL.
Rwy 16R: Multiple trees beginning 2784' from DER, 171' right of centerline, 20' AGL/4510' MSL.
　　　　Multiple trees and terrain beginning 746' from DER, 380' left of centerline, up to 20' AGL/4723' MSL.
Rwy 25: Multiple trees, poles, fence, and vent on building beginning 222' from DER, 201' right of centerline,
　　　　up to 103' AGL/4608' MSL.
　　　　Multiple trees, poles and sign beginning 500' from DER, 31' left of centerline, up to 20' AGL/4506' MSL.
Rwy 34L: Multiple trees and pole beginning 1229' from DER, 180' right of centerline, up to 20' AGL/4498' MSL.
　　　　Multiple trees beginning 1193' from DER, 331' left of centerline, up to 20' AGL/4489' MSL.
Rwy 34R: Multiple trees and poles beginning 1067' from DER, 172' right of centerline, up to 20' AGL/4497' MSL.
　　　　Multiple trees beginning 1230' from DER, 350' left of centerline, up to 20' AGL/4498' MSL.
　　　　Building 1.2 NM from DER, 1730' right of centerline, 363' AGL/4780' MSL.

(NARRATIVE ON FOLLOWING PAGE)   NOTE: Chart not to scale.

RENO NINE DEPARTURE
(RENO9.FMG) 04FEB16

RENO, NEVADA
RENO/TAHOE INTL (RNO)

Figure 216. – RENO Nine Departure (RENO9.FMG) (RNO).

146. (Refer to Figure 247 on page 303 and Legend 27 below.) ATC assigns the RAL Runway 9 ILS. In the event that a missed approach is necessary, you determine you will climb with 120 knots ground speed. What would the missed approach rate of climb be?

A. 540 feet per minute minimum.

B. 200 feet per nautical mile.

C. 540 feet per nautical mile.

Answer (A) is correct. *(FAA-H-8083-16B Chap 1)*

DISCUSSION: The missed approach rate of climb will be as noted on the chart. It will provide a minimum climb rate of 270 ft./NM. Given the intended groundspeed of 120 kt., this would equal 2 NM/min., providing a 540 ft./min. minimum.

Answer (B) is incorrect. Missed approaches are developed based on standard approach speeds and a 200 ft./NM climb gradient in the missed approach, unless a higher climb gradient is published in the notes section of the approach procedure chart. **Answer (C) is incorrect.** At a predetermined groundspeed of 120 kt., a rate of 540 ft./NM for 2 min. would provide a climb rate in excess of 1,080 ft./min.

CLIMB/DESCENT TABLE 10042

INSTRUMENT TAKEOFF OR APPROACH PROCEDURE CHARTS
RATE OF CLIMB/DESCENT TABLE

(ft. per min)

A rate of climb/descent table is provided for use in planning and executing climbs or descents under known or approximate ground speed conditions. It will be especially useful for approaches when the localizer only is used for course guidance. A best speed, power, altitude combination can be programmed which will result in a stable glide rate and altitude favorable for executing a landing if minimums exist upon breakout. Care should always be exercised so that minimum descent altitude and missed approach point are not exceeded.

VERTICAL PATH ANGLE (2.7–3.4)

CLIMB/DESCENT ANGLE (degrees and tenths)	ft/NM	GROUND SPEED (knots) 60	90	120	150	180	210	240	270	300	330	360
2.0	210	210	320	425	530	635	743	850	955	1060	1165	1275
2.5	265	265	400	530	665	795	930	1060	1195	1325	1460	1590
2.7	287	287	430	574	717	860	1003	1147	1290	1433	1576	1720
2.8	297	297	446	595	743	892	1041	1189	1338	1486	1635	1783
2.9	308	308	462	616	770	924	1078	1232	1386	1539	1693	1847
3.0	318	318	478	637	797	956	1115	1274	1433	1593	1752	1911
3.1	329	329	494	659	823	988	1152	1317	1481	1646	1810	1975
3.2	340	340	510	680	850	1020	1189	1359	1529	1699	1869	2039
3.3	350	350	526	701	876	1052	1227	1402	1577	1752	1927	2103
3.4	361	361	542	722	903	1083	1264	1444	1625	1805	1986	2166
3.5	370	370	555	745	930	1115	1300	1485	1670	1860	2045	2230
4.0	425	425	640	850	1065	1275	1490	1700	1915	2125	2340	2550
4.5	480	480	715	955	1195	1435	1675	1915	2150	2390	2630	2870
5.0	530	530	795	1065	1330	1595	1860	2125	2390	2660	2925	3190
5.5	585	585	880	1170	1465	1755	2050	2340	2635	2925	3220	3510
6.0	640	640	960	1275	1595	1915	2235	2555	2875	3195	3510	3830
6.5	690	690	1040	1385	1730	2075	2425	2770	3115	3460	3805	4155
7.0	745	745	1120	1490	1865	2240	2610	2985	3355	3730	4105	4475
7.5	800	800	1200	1600	2000	2400	2800	3200	3600	4000	4400	4800
8.0	855	855	1280	1710	2135	2560	2990	3415	3845	4270	4695	5125
8.5	910	910	1360	1815	2270	2725	3180	3630	4085	4540	4995	5450
9.0	960	960	1445	1925	2405	2885	3370	3850	4330	4810	5295	5775
9.5	1015	1015	1525	2035	2540	3050	3560	4065	4575	5085	5590	6100
10.0	1070	1070	1605	2145	2680	3215	3750	4285	4820	5355	5890	6430

CLIMB/DESCENT TABLE 10042

Legend 27. – Instrument Takeoff or Approach Procedure Charts, Rate-of-Climb/Descent Table.

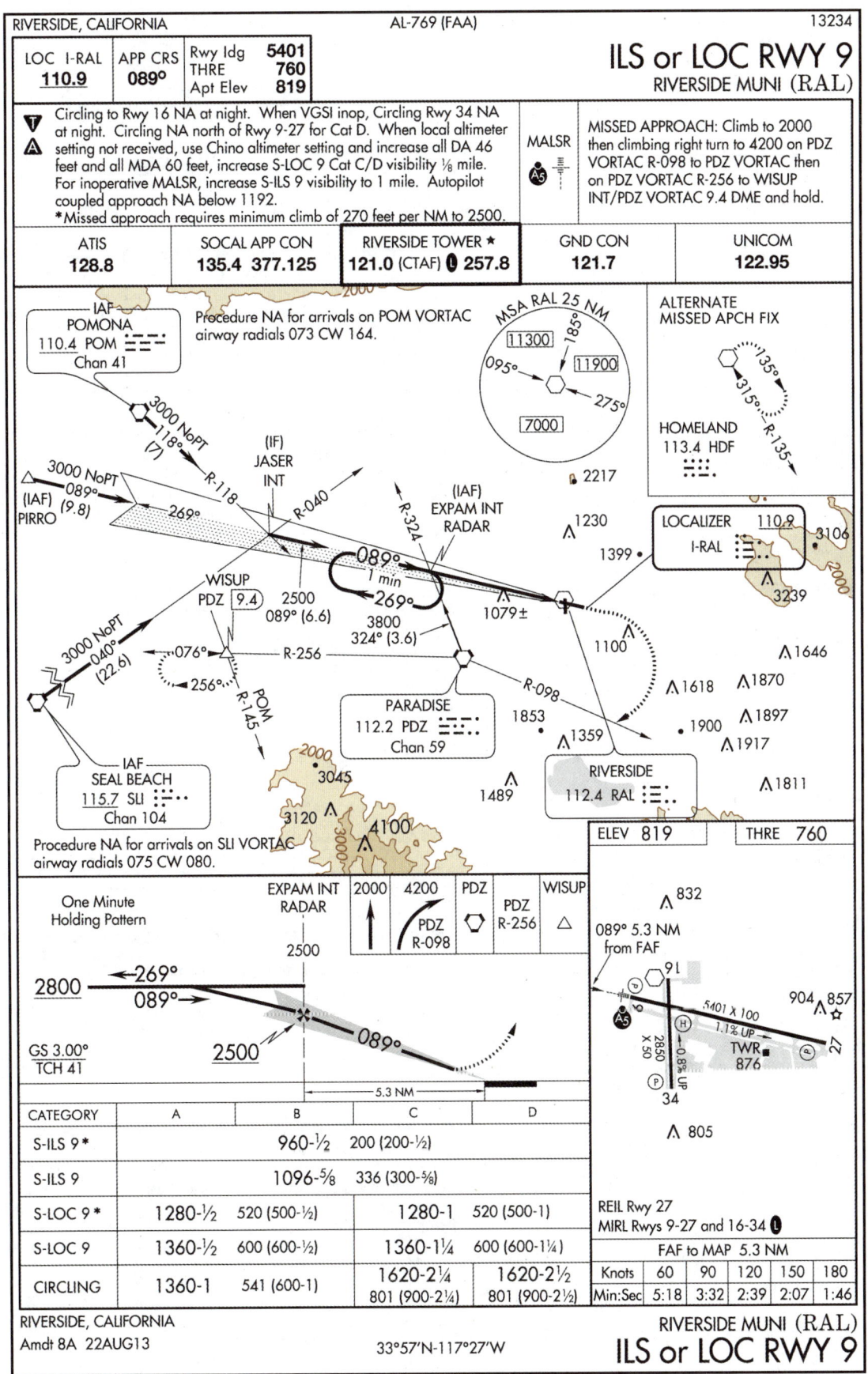

Figure 247. – ILS or RWY 9 (RAL).

147. A particular instrument departure procedure requires a minimum climb rate of 210 feet per NM to 8,000 feet. If you climb with a ground speed of 140 knots, what is the rate of climb required in feet per minute?

A. 210

B. 450

C. 490

Answer (C) is correct. (FAA-H-8083-16B Chap 1)
   DISCUSSION: First convert the ground speed to NM per minute.

$$140 \, \frac{NM}{hr.} \times \frac{1 \, hr.}{60 \, min.} = 2.33 \, \frac{NM}{min.}$$

Then find the rate of climb by multiplying the NM covered in a minute by the required minimum climb rate.

$$2.33 \, \frac{NM}{min.} \times 210 \, \frac{ft.}{NM} = 489.3 \, \frac{ft.}{min.}$$

   Answer (A) is incorrect. The number of feet we need to climb is 210 per nautical mile, not the number of feet per minute. **Answer (B) is incorrect.** Although close, 450 feet per minute is slightly short of the required 490 feet per minute we would need to climb for this departure procedure.

148. Unless otherwise stated, instrument procedures use the standard IFR climb gradient of

A. 500 feet per minute.

B. 400 feet per nautical mile.

C. 200 feet per nautical mile.

Answer (C) is correct. (FAA-H-8083-16B Chap 1)
   DISCUSSION: Instrument procedures design criteria assumes an initial climb of 200 feet per nautical mile for obstacle clearance during a departure procedure.
   Answer (A) is incorrect. Climb gradients are developed as a part of a departure procedure to ensure obstacle protection. The rate of climb is 200 feet per nautical mile. **Answer (B) is incorrect.** The rate of climb is 200 feet per nautical mile.

149. The standard IFR climb gradient is

A. 500 feet per NM.

B. 400 feet per NM.

C. 200 feet per NM.

Answer (C) is correct. (FAA-H-8083-16B Chap 1)
   DISCUSSION: The standard IFR climb gradient is 200 feet per NM.
   Answer (A) is incorrect. The standard IFR climb gradient is 200, not 500, feet per NM. **Answer (B) is incorrect.** The standard IFR climb gradient is 200, not 400, feet per NM.

6.13 GPS Approaches

150. On a GPS with WAAS capability, what is the significance of "LNAV+V" being displayed?

A. Approved vertical guidance to descend to the decision height is provided to the pilot.

B. Advisory vertical guidance is provided as an aid to the pilot during the descent to the runway.

C. Advisory vertical guidance is provided to the pilot that must be used in lieu of published step-down fixes on the instrument approach.

Answer (B) is correct. (AIM Para 1-1-20)
   DISCUSSION: LNAV+V is not an approach type; rather, it provides advisory vertical guidance that may be used in lieu of the published step-down fixes on the IAP.
   Answer (A) is incorrect. LNAV+V offers advisory, not approved, vertical guidance. **Answer (C) is incorrect.** LNAV+V offers advisory vertical guidance that may, not must, be used in lieu of the published step-down fixes on the IAP.

151. (Refer to Figure 235 on page 305.) What is the LPV decision altitude for the LNK RNAV (GPS) RWY 32?

A. 1,563 feet MSL.

B. 1,429 feet MSL.

C. 1,760 feet MSL.

Answer (B) is correct. (FAA-H-8083-16B Chap 4)
   DISCUSSION: The LPV decision altitude for the LNK RNAV (GPS) RWY 32 approach to LNK will be 1,429 ft. MSL. The height above touchdown elevation will then be 250 ft. The HAT is the difference between the touchdown zone elevation (rounded to the nearest foot) and the decision altitude.
   Answer (A) is incorrect. The LNAV/VNAV decision altitude is 1,563 ft. MSL. LNAV/VNAV approaches are different from LPV approaches because they do not involve any increase of angular guidance in proximity to the runway. **Answer (C) is incorrect.** The MDA for the LNAV approach is 1,760 ft. MSL; whereas the LNAV/VNAV approach is flown to the decision altitude.

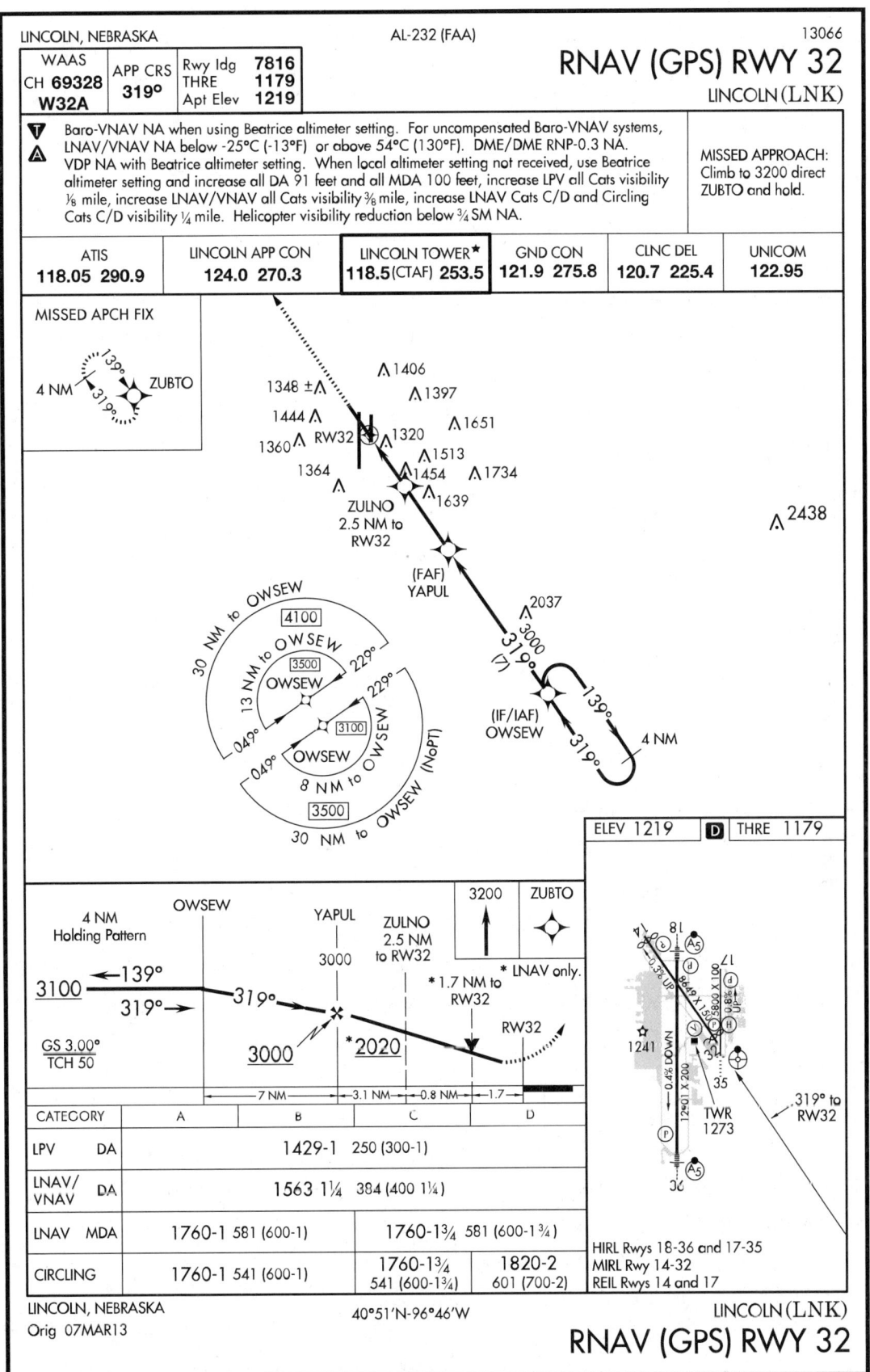

Figure 235. – RNAV (GPS) RWY 32 (LNK).

152. When proper RAIM sensitivity is not available, manually resetting sensitivity to 0.3 NM will

A. Not automatically change the RAIM sensitivity on some receivers.
B. Automatically change settings to approach mode.
C. Allow the approach to continue in terminal sensitivity.

Answer (A) is correct. (FAA-H-8083-15B Chap 9)
   DISCUSSION: When the proper RAIM sensitivity is not available and the CDI sensitivity does not automatically change to 0.3 NM, manually setting CDI sensitivity does not automatically change the RAIM sensitivity on some receivers.
   Answer (B) is incorrect. Manually resetting the sensitivity to 0.3 NM will not automatically initiate approach mode sensitivity. **Answer (C) is incorrect.** An instrument approach cannot continue with terminal sensitivity. However, manually setting CDI sensitivity does not automatically change the RAIM sensitivity on some receivers.

153. If Receiver Autonomous Integrity Monitoring (RAIM) is not available prior to beginning a GPS approach, the pilot should

A. use a navigation or approach system other than GPS for an approach.
B. continue to the MAP and hold until the satellites are recaptured.
C. continue the approach, expecting to recapture the satellites before reaching the FAF.

Answer (A) is correct. (AIM Para 1-1-19)
   DISCUSSION: RAIM outages may occur due to an insufficient number of satellites or due to unsuitable satellite geometry, which causes the error in the position solution to become too large. If RAIM is not available when setting up a GPS approach, you must select another type of navigation and approach system other than GPS.
   Answer (B) is incorrect. If RAIM is not available when setting up a GPS approach, you should select another type of navigation and approach system. You should not fly to the MAP and hold. Additionally, there is no holding pattern at the MAP. **Answer (C) is incorrect.** If RAIM is not available when setting up a GPS approach, you should select another type of navigation and approach system. If RAIM failure occurs while you are setting up the GPS approach or conducting a GPS approach, you must not continue the approach hoping that RAIM will become available before the FAF.

154. When flying a GPS approach procedure, what effect will overriding an automatically selected sensitivity have?

A. No effect.
B. Cancel the approach mode annunciation.
C. Initiate a descent to MDA.

Answer (B) is correct. (FAA-H-8083-15B Chap 9)
   DISCUSSION: Overriding an automatically selected sensitivity during an approach cancels the approach mode annunciation.
   Answer (A) is incorrect. Overriding an automatically selected sensitivity during an approach has the effect of canceling the approach mode annunciation. **Answer (C) is incorrect.** Overriding an automatically selected sensitivity during an approach cancels the approach mode annunciation. A missed approach will be required, not a descent to MDA.

155. Which of the following is true concerning GPS approaches?

A. Handheld GPS receivers are approved in emergency situations.
B. Terminal mode occurs within 20 NM of the destination airport.
C. In approach mode, the sensitivity on the CDI changes from 1 NM to 0.3 NM.

Answer (C) is correct. (FAA-H-8083-6 Chap 3)
   DISCUSSION: Approach mode increases the sensitivity on the CDI within 2 NM of the final approach waypoint from 1 NM to 0.3 NM.
   Answer (A) is incorrect. Handheld receivers are not approved for GPS approaches. They may be referenced in both normal and emergency situations as an aid to situational awareness. **Answer (B) is incorrect.** Terminal mode occurs within 30 NM of the destination airport, not 20 NM.

156. (Refer to Figure 238 on page 307.) If cleared for the RNAV (GPS) RWY 28 approach (Lancaster/Fairfield) over APE VORTAC, what will ATC expect of you?

A. Proceed to CASER, use the S-28 LOC 1620-1 minimums.
B. Proceed straight in from FAIRF, descend after FAIRF.
C. Proceed direct to FAIRF and execute the parallel entry depicted on the instrument approach procedure.

Answer (B) is correct. (FAA-H-8083-16B Chaps 4, 5)
   DISCUSSION: From APE, you would fly to NUMDE, which is an initial approach fix, then proceed to FAIRF and track inbound on the approach, descending as appropriate. Note the "NoPT" listed on the route from NUMDE to FAIRF. This means no procedure turn is necessary when flying the approach along this route.
   Answer (A) is incorrect. There is no CASER and there are no 1620 approach minimums for this RNAV (not an S-LOC) approach. **Answer (C) is incorrect.** You would not proceed direct to FAIRF; you would instead fly from APE to NUMDE, which is an initial approach fix, then proceed to FAIRF and track inbound on the approach, descending as appropriate.

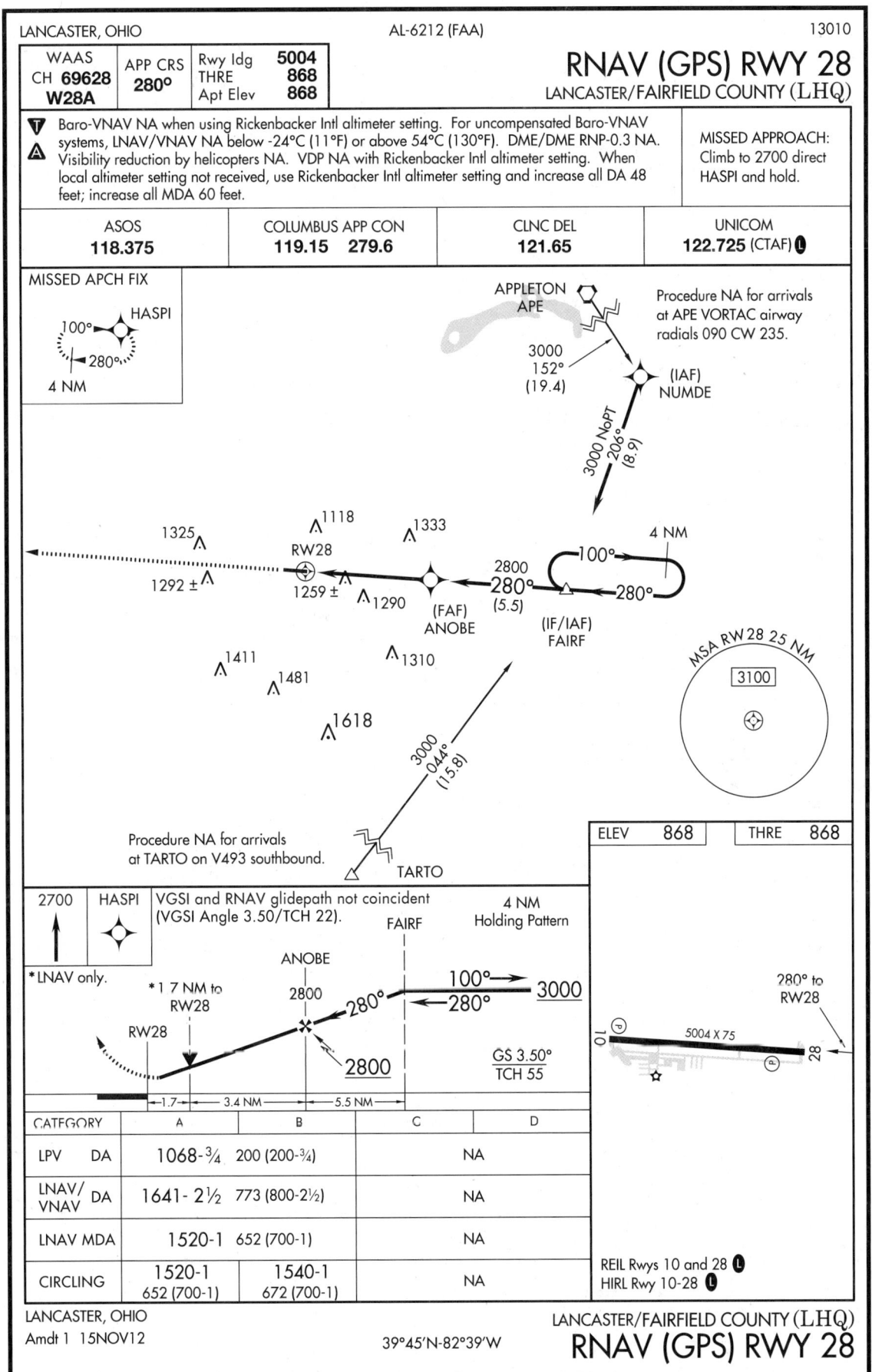

LANCASTER, OHIO

AL-6212 (FAA)

13010

RNAV (GPS) RWY 28
LANCASTER/FAIRFIELD COUNTY (LHQ)

WAAS CH 69628 W28A	APP CRS 280°	Rwy Idg 5004 THRE 868 Apt Elev 868

▼ Baro-VNAV NA when using Rickenbacker Intl altimeter setting. For uncompensated Baro-VNAV
△ systems, LNAV/VNAV NA below -24°C (11°F) or above 54°C (130°F). DME/DME RNP-0.3 NA.
Visibility reduction by helicopters NA. VDP NA with Rickenbacker Intl altimeter setting. When
local altimeter setting not received, use Rickenbacker Intl altimeter setting and increase all DA 48
feet; increase all MDA 60 feet.

MISSED APPROACH:
Climb to 2700 direct
HASPI and hold.

ASOS 118.375	COLUMBUS APP CON 119.15 279.6	CLNC DEL 121.65	UNICOM 122.725 (CTAF) ◐

CATEGORY	A	B	C	D
LPV DA	1068-¾ 200 (200-¾)		NA	
LNAV/ VNAV DA	1641- 2½ 773 (800-2½)		NA	
LNAV MDA	1520-1 652 (700-1)		NA	
CIRCLING	1520-1 652 (700-1)	1540-1 672 (700-1)	NA	

LANCASTER, OHIO
Amdt 1 15NOV12

39°45'N-82°39'W

LANCASTER/FAIRFIELD COUNTY (LHQ)
RNAV (GPS) RWY 28

Figure 238. — RNAV (GPS) RWY 28 (LHQ).

157. Your onboard GPS-based FMS/RNAV unit is IFR certified under TSO-C129() or TSO-C196(). Your destination is below minimums for the GPS RNAV approach and you proceed to your filed alternate. You know that

A. GPS units certified under TSO-C129() or TSO-C196() are not authorized for alternate approach requirements; subsequently, you must use an approach procedure based on ground-based NAVAIDs.

B. once diverted to the alternate airport, you may fly a GPS-based approach as long as there is an operational ground-based NAVAID and appropriate airborne receiver for use as a backup.

C. if your aircraft is equipped with a second TSO-C129() certified GPS as a backup in place of a ground-based NAVAID receiver, you may complete the approach even if the IAP is based on ground-based NAVAIDs.

Answer (B) is correct. (AIM Para 1-1-17)
DISCUSSION: Any required alternate airport must have an approved instrument approach procedure other than GPS, which is anticipated to be operational and available at the estimated time of arrival and which the aircraft is equipped to fly.
Answer (A) is incorrect. Before a GPS unit can be used for instrument approaches, it has to be authorized by TSO-C129 or TSO-C196. **Answer (C) is incorrect.** For flight planning purposes, any approved alternate airport must have an approved instrument approach procedure other than GPS.

158. During a WAAS GPS approach, you receive an LNAV+V annunciation on the GPS display. You should

A. descend to LNAV approach minimums using the barometric altimeter to comply with altitude restrictions, referencing advisory vertical guidance as an aid.

B. not descend any further, proceed to the missed approach point, and execute the missed approach.

C. descend to LNAV/VNAV approach minimums, while closely monitoring the vertical guidance for anomalies.

Answer (A) is correct. (AC 90-107)
DISCUSSION: The barometric altimeter remains the primary altitude reference instrument, even when the LNAV+V annunciation appears. This vertical guidance feature is advisory in nature and has not been approved for vertical guidance as those found on LNAV/VNAV or LPV approaches.
Answer (B) is incorrect. You may continue your descent using the barometric altimeter as your primary altitude reference instrument. **Answer (C) is incorrect.** You may only descend to the LNAV approach minimums, not to the lower LNAV/VNAV minimums.

159. (Refer to Figure 243 on page 309.) What is the minimum altitude to cross CLAMM intersection while conducting the RNAV (GPS) RWY 6 approach at ROA?

A. 4,300 MSL.

B. 5,200 MSL.

C. 2,700 MSL.

Answer (A) is correct. (FAA-H-8083-16B Chap 1)
DISCUSSION: The minimum altitude to cross the CLAMM intersection while conducting the RNAV (GPS) RWY 6 approach at ROA, as depicted with a line beneath the altitude, is 4,300 ft. MSL.
Answer (B) is incorrect. The minimum altitude between RIVRE and DIXXY, as depicted with a line beneath the altitude prior to crossing DIXXY, is 5,200 ft. MSL. **Answer (C) is incorrect.** The minimum altitude once inside the CLAMM intersection while conducting the RNAV (GPS) RWY 6 approach is 2,700 ft. MSL.

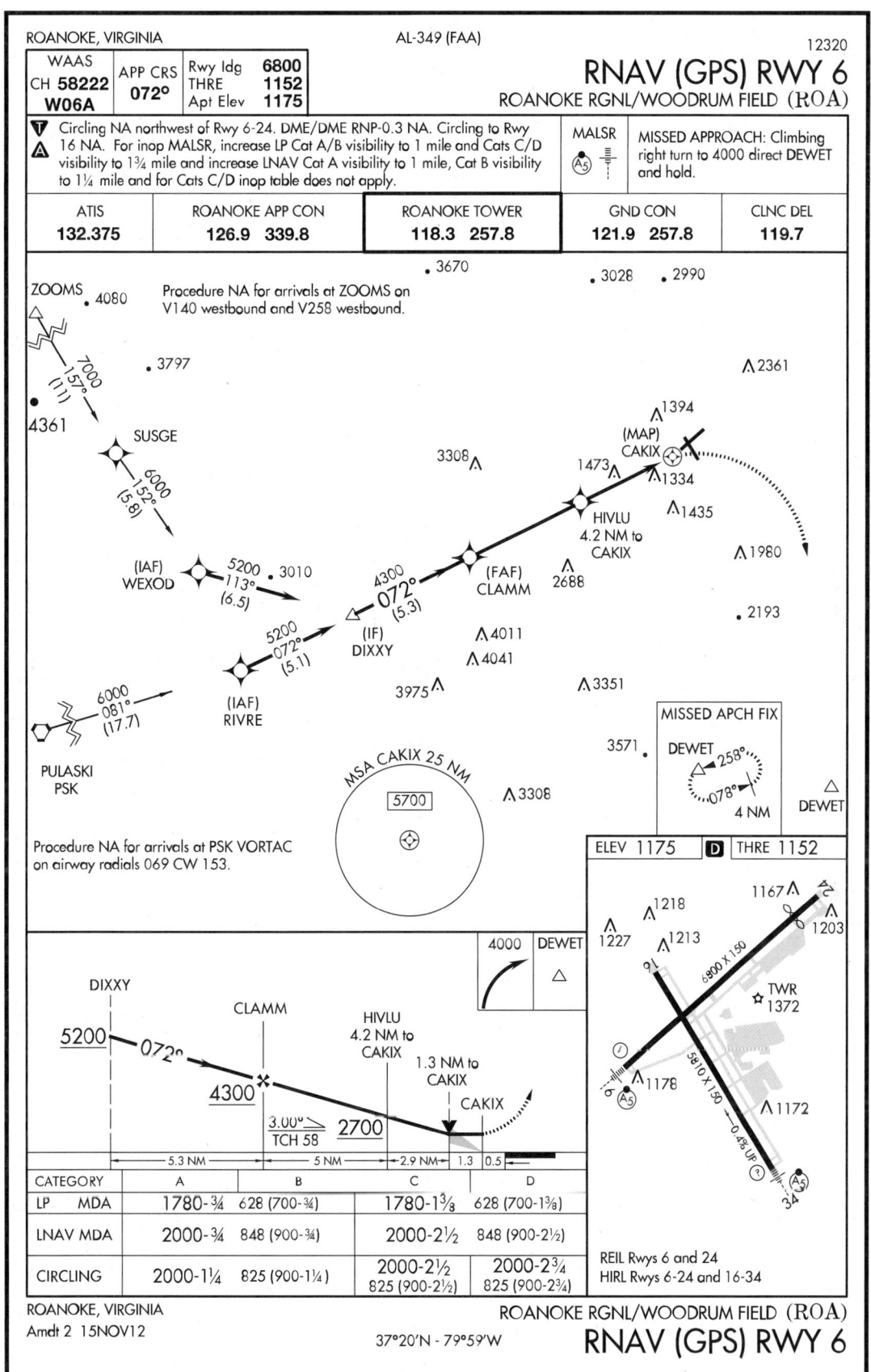

Figure 243. – RNAV (GPS) RWY 6 (ROA).

160. (Refer to Figure 249 on page 311.) Which of the following best describes BEMXI?

    A. The missed approach point (MAP).

    B. The initial approach fix (IAF).

    C. The final approach fix (FAF).

Answer (C) is correct. (FAA-H-8083-15B Chap 9)
    DISCUSSION: The Maltese cross in the profile view and the letters "FAF" above its designation on the plan view defines BEMXI as the FAF.
    Answer (A) is incorrect. The MAP on a GPS approach procedure is usually the runway threshold, indicated by "RW" and the runway number. This can be identified on both the plan and profile views of the approach chart. **Answer (B) is incorrect.** The IAFs on a GPS approach procedure are usually depicted in a straight line forming the cross of a "T" shape. They also have the letters "IAF," not "FAF," above their designations on the plan view of the instrument approach chart.

161. (Refer to Figure 249 on page 311.) When flying the LNAV approach, the missed approach point (MAP) would be indicated by reaching

    A. an altitude of 3,120 feet.

    B. a distance of 0.9 NM to RW30.

    C. the RW30 waypoint.

Answer (C) is correct. (FAA-H-8083-15B Chap 7)
    DISCUSSION: The missed approach point for LNAV approaches is the last waypoint depicted in the profile view and is usually designed to coincide with the runway threshold. In this example, the waypoint "RW30" represents the runway threshold for Runway 30.
    Answer (A) is incorrect. An altitude of 3,120 feet is the decision altitude, not the missed approach point, for the LNAV approach. **Answer (B) is incorrect.** The visual descent point (VDP) is 0.9 NM from the threshold for Runway 30. This is not the missed approach point.

162. (Refer to Figure 249 on page 311.) How do you recognize the missed approach point on the LNAV/VNAV approach?

    A. At the RW30 waypoint.

    B. At the Decision Altitude (DA) for the LPV portion of this approach.

    C. Arrival at the LNAV/VNAV Decision Altitude (DA).

Answer (C) is correct. (FAA-H-8083-16B Chap 4, FAA-H-8083-15B Chaps 7 and 8)
    DISCUSSION: The missed approach point for an LNAV/VNAV approach is the point at which the LNAV/VNAV DA is reached. In this case, a missed approach should be executed if the runway environment is not in sight upon reaching 3,019 ft. MSL.
    Answer (A) is incorrect. RW30 is the location of the runway threshold, not the missed approach point. **Answer (B) is incorrect.** This question is asking about LNAV/VNAV, not LPV.

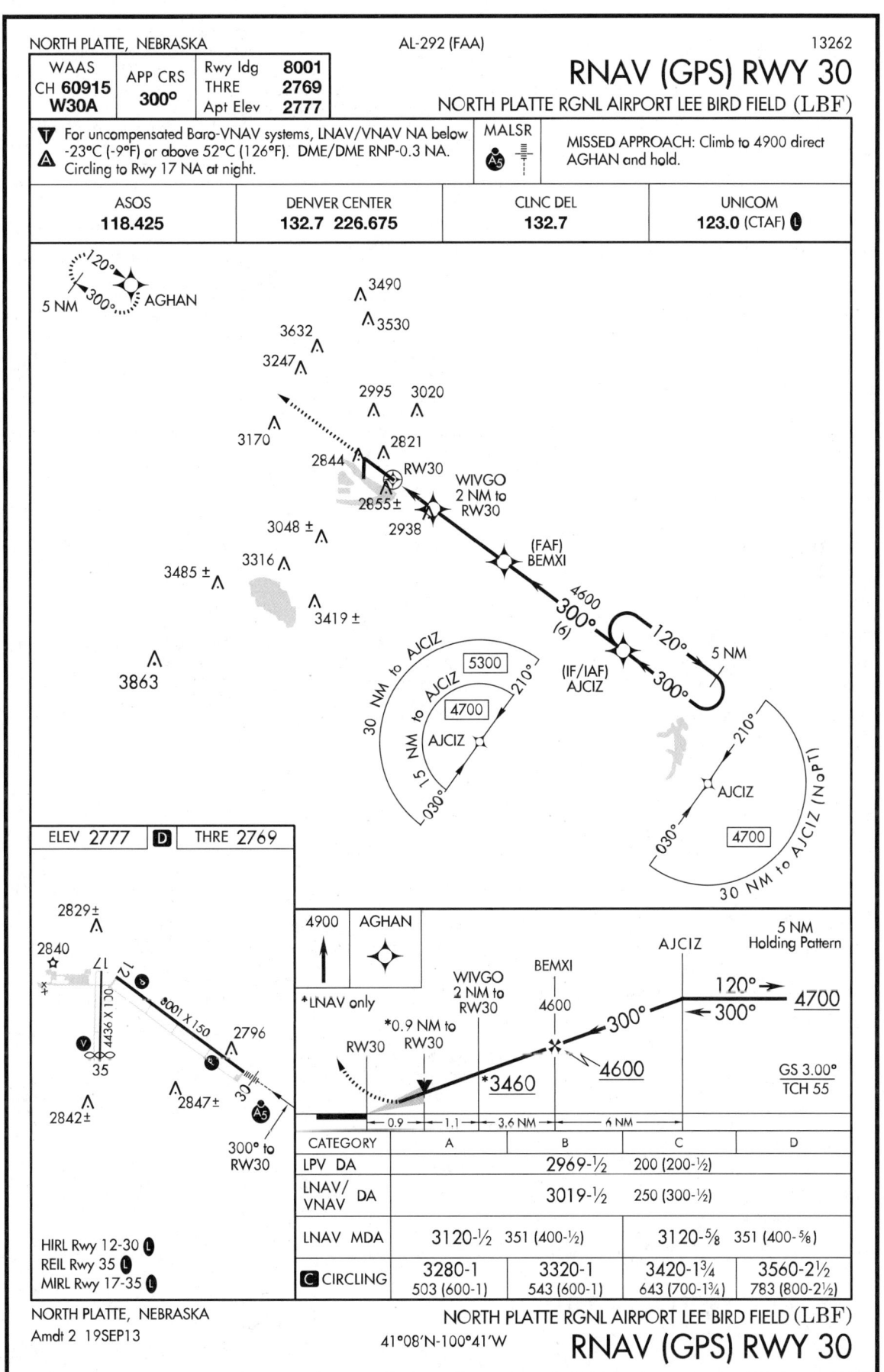

Figure 249. – RNAV (GPS) RWY 30 (LBF).

163. (Refer to Figure 249 on page 313.) The correct GPS entry when told by ATC to "expect the GPS approach to runway 30" is

A. load and activate the approach.

B. to select the vectors-to-final approach setting.

C. only load the approach.

Answer (C) is correct. (FAA-H-8083-6 Chap 3)
   DISCUSSION: When ATC tells you to expect a certain approach, select that approach and load it into the flight plan. Once cleared for the approach, it can be activated.
   Answer (A) is incorrect. A pilot should not activate an approach when only told to expect a certain approach. **Answer (B) is incorrect.** The vectors-to-final feature guides a pilot using vectors along the final approach course as directed by ATC.

164. (Refer to Figure 249 on page 313.) Which type of waypoint is the AGHAN fix?

A. Computer navigation fix (CNF).

B. Fly-over waypoint.

C. Fly-by waypoint.

Answer (C) is correct. (AIM Para 1-2-1)
   DISCUSSION: The AGHAN waypoint is not contained within a circle. This indicates a fly-by waypoint.
   Answer (A) is incorrect. CNFs are points used to define the navigational track for an airborne computer system. These include unnamed DME fixes, beginning and ending points of DME arcs, and sensor final approach fixes on some GPS overlay approaches. **Answer (B) is incorrect.** A fly-over waypoint is symbolized by a waypoint symbol contained within a circle. RW30 is a fly-over waypoint. AGHAN's symbology does not include that circle, so it is a fly-by waypoint.

165. (Refer to Figure 249 on page 313.) You are flying the RNAV(GPS) RWY 30 approach to LBF, over BEMXI, and you receive a RAIM failure/status annunciation. You should

A. Continue to the missed approach point while climbing to 4,900 feet, and then execute the missed approach instructions.

B. Continue the approach, but descend no lower than the circling minimums.

C. Continue the approach to published minimums, but complete the approach in 2 minutes or less.

Answer (A) is correct. (AIM Para 1-1-17)
   DISCUSSION: If a RAIM failure/status annunciation occurs after the final approach waypoint, the missed approach should be executed immediately. BEMXI is the FAWP on this approach. Climb to 4,900 feet as indicated in the missed approach procedure and fly direct to AGHAN where you will hold.
   Answer (B) is incorrect. Circling minimums do not apply in this situation as the correct response is to execute a missed approach due to a RAIM failure. **Answer (C) is incorrect.** In this situation, you may not continue to the published approach minimums. You must immediately perform a missed approach due to a RAIM failure.

166. (Refer to Figure 249 on page 313.) At what point is the pilot authorized to descend below 5,300 feet when cleared to the AJCIZ waypoint from the west?

A. 15 NM from the waypoint.

B. 6 NM past the waypoint.

C. 30 NM from the waypoint.

Answer (A) is correct. (FAA-H-8083-16B Chap 9, AIM Para 5-4-4)
   DISCUSSION: When arriving from the west, the IAP shows pilots must maintain at least 5,300 feet between 30 NM and 15 NM from AJCIZ. Within 15 NM from AJCIZ, they may descend to 4,700 feet. This is indicated on the IAP with 5,300 inside the box between the 30 NM line to the 15 NM line near AJCIZ. From the 15 NM line to AJCIZ is 4,700 feet, as indicated on the IAP with 4,700 inside the box.
   Answer (B) is incorrect. The profile view shows that pilots are expected to be at 4,700 feet, not 5,300 feet, when arriving at AJCIZ for an additional 6 NM. Pilots must maintain at least 5,300 feet between 30 NM and 15 NM from AJCIZ. Within 15 NM from AJCIZ, they may descend to 4,700 feet. **Answer (C) is incorrect.** Pilots must maintain at least 5,300 feet between 30 NM and 15 NM from AJCIZ. Only when they are within 15 NM from AJCIZ, may they descend to 4,700 feet.

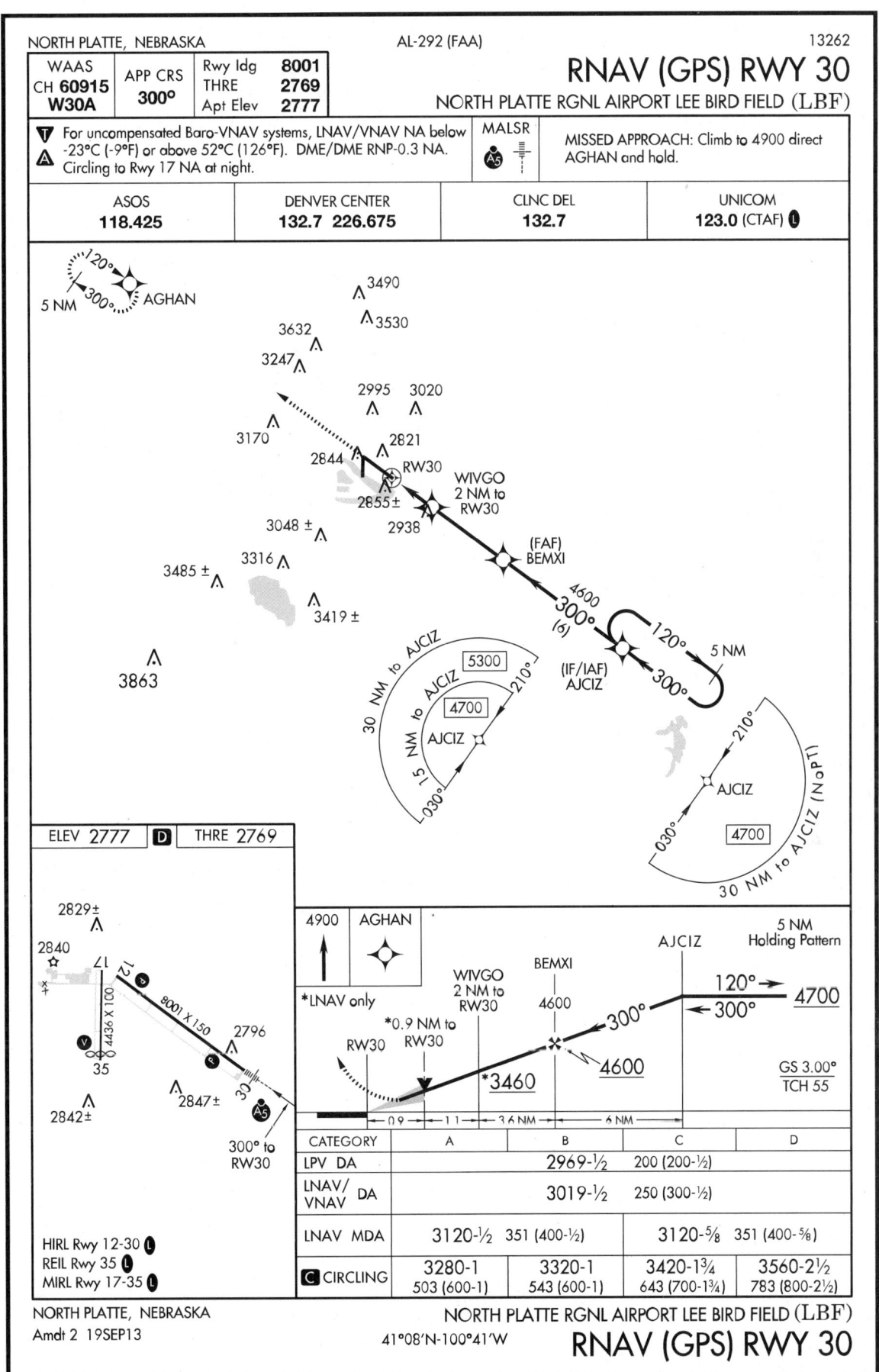

Figure 249. – RNAV (GPS) RWY 30 (LBF).

167. When using GPS for navigation and instrument approaches, any required alternate airport must have

    A. an approved operational instrument approach procedure other than GPS.

    B. authorization to fly approaches under IFR using GPS avionics systems.

    C. a GPS approach that is anticipated to be operational and available at the ETA.

Answer (A) is correct. (AIM Para 1-1-19)
    DISCUSSION: When you are using GPS for navigation and instrument approaches, any required alternate airport must have an approved instrument approach procedure, other than GPS, which is anticipated to be operational and available at the estimated time of arrival (ETA) and which the airplane is equipped to fly.
    Answer (B) is incorrect. Authorization to fly approaches under IFR using GPS avionics systems requires that the GPS unit and installation meet FAA standards and receive FAA approval. **Answer (C) is incorrect.** Any required alternate airport must have an approved instrument approach procedure other than GPS, not a GPS approach, that is anticipated to be operational and available at the ETA.

168. Your avionics system offers advisory VNAV functions, but does not use WAAS or baro-VNAV systems. Which statement is true?

    A. You could use your avionics system to execute approaches to LNAV/VNAV minimums.

    B. Your avionics system cannot be used to execute approaches to LNAV/VNAV minimums.

    C. You could use your avionics system to execute approaches to LNAV/VNAV and LPV minimums.

Answer (B) is correct. (AIM Para 1-1-17)
    DISCUSSION: A certified WAAS system or aircraft equipped with an FMS and certified baro-VNAV may utilize the LNAV/VNAV minimums.
    Answer (A) is incorrect. An avionics system-generated vertical path requires WAAS, except for those GPS units certified with baro-VNAV, which will allow descent to LNAV/VNAV minimums. **Answer (C) is incorrect.** Avionics systems certified with baro-VNAV will allow descent to LNAV/VNAV minimums.

169. (Refer to Figure 253 on page 315.) While executing the RNAV (GPS) RWY 18 LNAV approach at OSH, how would the missed approach point be identified?

    A. RW18 waypoint.

    B. 1.1 NM from RW18 waypoint.

    C. 1,040 feet MSL indicated.

Answer (A) is correct. (FAA-H-8083-16B Chap 7)
    DISCUSSION: The missed approach point for the LNAV approach at OSH is the RW18 waypoint. The missed approach is marked by a flyover waypoint symbol and is assigned an unpronounceable name when it is located at the runway threshold.
    Answer (B) is incorrect. The point located 1.1 NM from RW18 is the visual descent point (VDP). It is depicted as a bold letter "V" and is a defined point on the final approach course of a nonprecision straight-in approach procedure from which normal descent from the MDA to the runway touchdown point may be commenced. **Answer (C) is incorrect.** An answer of 1,040 ft. MSL would be based on attaining the local altimeter setting for the DA on the LPV approach to runway 18.

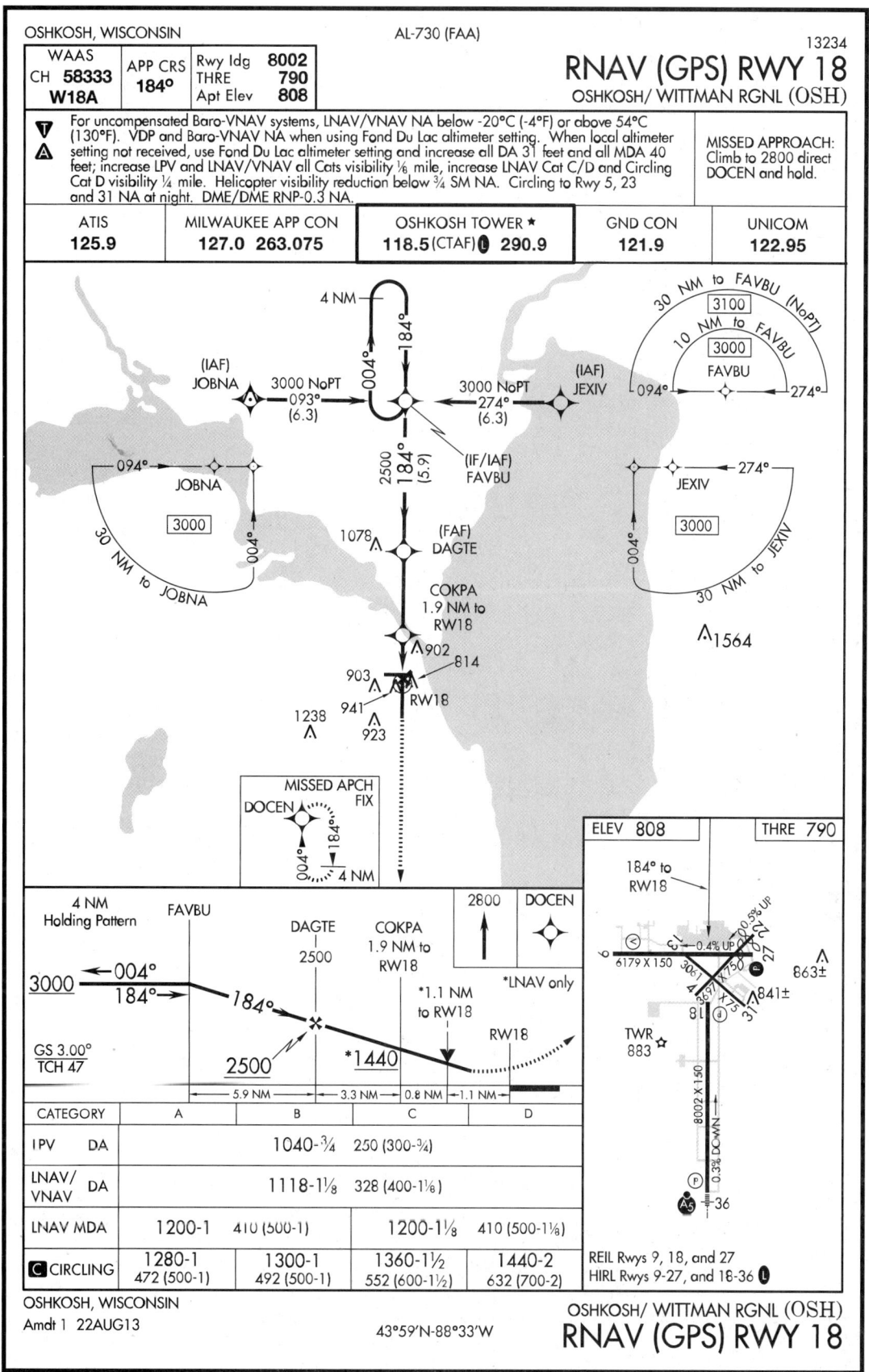

Figure 253. – RNAV (GPS) RWY 18 (OSH).

STUDY UNIT SEVEN

AEROMEDICAL FACTORS

(3 pages of outline)

This study unit contains outlines of major concepts tested, sample test questions and answers regarding aeromedical factors, and an explanation of each answer.

Recall that the **sole purpose** of this book is to expedite your passing of the FAA pilot knowledge test for the instrument rating. Accordingly, all extraneous material (i.e., topics or regulations not directly tested on the FAA pilot knowledge test) is omitted, even though much more knowledge is necessary to fly safely. This additional material is presented in *Pilot Handbook, Aviation Weather and Weather Services, FAR/AIM,* and *Instrument Pilot Flight Maneuvers and Practical Test Prep,* available from Gleim Publications, Inc. Order online at www.GleimAviation.com.

7.1 HYPOXIA AND HYPERVENTILATION

1. Hypoxia results from a lack of oxygen in the bloodstream and causes a lack of clear thinking, fatigue, euphoria, and, shortly thereafter, unconsciousness.

2. The following are four types of hypoxia based on their causes:

    a. **Hypoxic hypoxia** is a result of insufficient oxygen available to the body as a whole.

        1) EXAMPLE: Reduction of partial pressure at higher altitudes

    b. **Anemic (hypemic) hypoxia** occurs when the blood is not able to take up and transport a sufficient amount of oxygen to the cells in the body. The result is a deficiency in the oxygen-carrying capacity of blood rather than a lack of inhaled oxygen.

        1) EXAMPLE: Carbon monoxide poisoning or a reduced blood volume as a result of blood donation

    c. **Stagnant hypoxia** results when oxygen-rich blood in the lungs is not moving.

        1) EXAMPLE: Shock, reduced circulation due to extreme cold, or pulling excessive Gs in flight

    d. **Histotoxic hypoxia** is the inability of cells to effectively use oxygen.

        1) EXAMPLE: Impairment due to alcohol and drugs

3. Symptoms of hypoxia include an initial feeling of euphoria but lead to more serious concerns such as headache, delayed reaction time, visual impairment, tunnel vision, bluing of fingernails and lips (cyanosis), and eventual unconsciousness.

    a. Symptoms of hypoxia are difficult to detect before the pilot's reactions are affected.

4. To counteract feelings of hypoxia, lower altitude or use supplemental oxygen.

5. Hyperventilation occurs when an excessive amount of air is breathed into the lungs at an excessive rate.

    a. EXAMPLE: When one becomes excited as a result of stress, fear, or anxiety.
    b. Symptoms are dizziness, hot and cold sensations, nausea, tingling in the extremities, etc.
    c. Ways to overcome hyperventilation include

        1) Placing a paper bag over your nose and mouth and breathing into it,
        2) Talking aloud, and
        3) Slowing the breathing rate.

7.2 SPATIAL DISORIENTATION

1. Spatial disorientation (sometimes called vertigo) is a state of temporary confusion resulting from misleading information sent to the brain by various sensory organs.

2. The best way to overcome the effects of spatial disorientation is to rely on the airplane instruments and ignore body (kinesthetic) signals.

3. The nervous system often interprets centrifugal force as vertical movement, i.e., rising or falling.

4. The Coriolis illusion is caused by an abrupt head movement in a prolonged constant-rate turn.

    a. This can cause spatial disorientation.

5.   The three somatogravic illusions are caused by (a) an abrupt change from a climb to straight-and-level flight, which creates the illusion of tumbling backwards; (b) a rapid acceleration during flight (or on takeoff), which creates the illusion of the aircraft pitching up; and (c) a rapid deceleration during flight, which creates the illusion of the aircraft pitching down.

6.   False horizon is an illusion that is caused by a sloping cloud formation, an obscured horizon, or a dark scene spread with ground lights and stars.

7.   The vestibular system in the inner ear is responsible for most of the illusions leading to spatial disorientation. The vestibular sense (motion sensing) can confuse the pilot.

7.3 VISION AND VISUAL ILLUSION

1.   Pilots should adapt their eyes for night flying by avoiding bright white lights for 30 min. prior to flight.

   a.   Thereafter, white light must be avoided because it will cause temporary night blindness and impair night vision adaptation.

      1)   Because dark adaptation is lost within seconds of viewing a bright light, a pilot should close one eye when using a light to preserve some degree of night vision.

   b.   However, white flight deck lighting must be available when needed for map and instrument reading, especially under IFR conditions.

2.   The most effective way to scan for other aircraft in daylight is to use a series of short, regularly spaced eye movements that bring successive areas of the sky into your central vision field.

   a.   Each movement should not exceed 10°, and each area should be observed for at least 1 second to enable detection.

   b.   Only a very small center area of the eye has the ability to send clear, sharply focused messages to the brain. All other areas provide less detail.

   c.   At night, however, the eyes are most effective at seeing objects off center. Accordingly, pilots should scan slowly back and forth to facilitate off-center viewing.

3.   Haze can also create the illusion of being a greater distance from the runway, resulting in the pilot's flying a lower-than-normal approach.

4.   A narrower-than-usual runway may create the illusion that the airplane is higher than it actually is.

   a.   This illusion results in a lower-than-normal approach.
   b.   A wider-than-usual runway creates the opposite illusion and problem.

5.   An upward-sloping runway may create the illusion that the airplane is at a higher-than-actual altitude.

   a.   This illusion results in a lower-than-normal approach.
   b.   A downward-sloping runway creates the opposite illusion and problem.

7.4 FATIGUE

1.   Fatigue is one of the most treacherous hazards to flight safety.

2.   The nature of fatigue is such that pilots may not be aware they are feeling the effects of fatigue until after they have committed serious errors.

3.   Fatigue can be either acute (short-term) or chronic (long-term).

QUESTIONS AND ANSWER EXPLANATIONS: All of the instrument rating knowledge test questions chosen by the FAA for release as well as additional questions selected by Gleim relating to the material in the previous outlines are provided on the following pages. These questions have been organized into the same subunits as the outlines. To the immediate right of each question are the correct answer and answer explanations. You should cover these answers and answer explanations while responding to the questions. Refer to the general discussion in the Introduction on how to take the FAA knowledge test.

Remember that the questions from the FAA knowledge test bank have been reordered by topic and organized into a meaningful sequence. Also, the first line of the answer explanation gives the citation of the authoritative source for the answer.

QUESTIONS

7.1 Hypoxia and Hyperventilation

1. Why is hypoxia particularly dangerous during flights with one pilot?

A. Night vision may be so impaired that the pilot cannot see other aircraft.

B. Symptoms of hypoxia may be difficult to recognize before the pilot's reactions are affected.

C. The pilot may not be able to control the aircraft even if using oxygen.

Answer (B) is correct. (AIM Para 8-1-2)
   DISCUSSION: Hypoxia symptoms are gradual, and a pilot may not recognize the symptoms before his or her reactions are affected. Because the symptoms of hypoxia vary with the individual, having two pilots increases the chance of detection before pilot reactions are affected.
   Answer (A) is incorrect. Hypoxia, which is a lack of sufficient oxygen, affects all mental and physical activity, not just night vision. **Answer (C) is incorrect.** Hypoxia will not occur if supplemental oxygen is used properly.

2. What action should be taken if hyperventilation is suspected?

A. Breathe at a slower rate by taking very deep breaths.

B. Consciously breathe at a slower rate than normal.

C. Consciously force yourself to take deep breaths and breathe at a faster rate than normal.

Answer (B) is correct. (AIM Para 8-1-3)
   DISCUSSION: Hyperventilation occurs when abnormally large amounts of air are breathed in and out of the lungs. Early symptoms of hyperventilation and hypoxia are similar and include dizziness, drowsiness, tingling of the fingers and toes, and sensation of body heat. If hyperventilation is suspected, you should consciously breathe at a slower rate than normal.
   Answer (A) is incorrect. Taking deep breaths will only aggravate hyperventilation. **Answer (C) is incorrect.** Taking deep breaths and breathing at a faster rate than normal is the cause, not the cure, of hyperventilation.

3. Which is not a type of hypoxia?

A. Histotoxic.

B. Hypoxic.

C. Hypertoxic.

Answer (C) is correct. (FAA-H-8083-25B Chap 17)
   DISCUSSION: There is no such thing as hypertoxic hypoxia. The four types of hypoxia are histotoxic, hypoxic, anemic, and stagnant hypoxia.
   Answer (A) is incorrect. The four types of hypoxia are histotoxic, hypoxic, anemic, and stagnant hypoxia. **Answer (B) is incorrect.** The four types of hypoxia are histotoxic, hypoxic, anemic, and stagnant hypoxia.

4. If you experience tunnel vision and cyanosis, you may have symptoms of

A. hypoxia.

B. hyperventilation.

C. carbon monoxide poisoning.

Answer (A) is correct. (FAA-H-8083-25B Chap 17)
   DISCUSSION: The common symptoms of hypoxia include bluing of the fingernails and lips (cyanosis), headache, delayed reaction time, impaired judgment, euphoria, visual impairment, drowsiness, lightheadedness or dizziness, tingling in the fingers and toes, and numbness. If it becomes worse, tunnel vision begins.
   Answer (B) is incorrect. Hyperventilation is caused by breathing too rapidly. This leads to abnormal loss of carbon dioxide from the blood. **Answer (C) is incorrect.** The symptoms of carbon monoxide (CO) poisoning include blurred thinking and vision, uneasiness, dizziness, and tightness across the forehead, followed by headache and loss of muscle power. CO is a colorless, odorless gas produced by all combustion engines.

5. Which of the following is a correct response to counteract the feelings of hypoxia in flight?

   A. Promptly descend to a lower altitude.

   B. Increase cabin air flow.

   C. Avoid sudden inhalations.

Answer (A) is correct. (FAA-H-8083-25B Chap 17)
   DISCUSSION: The correct response to counteract feelings of hypoxia is to lower altitude or use supplemental oxygen if the aircraft is so equipped.
   Answer (B) is incorrect. Increasing the amount of air flowing inside an aircraft will not help counteract hypoxia. Because of the reduction of partial pressure at higher altitudes, there is less oxygen in the air to draw from. **Answer (C) is incorrect.** Breathing deeply or suddenly will not counteract feelings of hypoxia.

6. Anemic (hypemic) hypoxia has the same symptoms as hypoxic hypoxia, but it is most often a result of

   A. poor blood circulation.

   B. a leaking exhaust manifold.

   C. use of alcohol or drugs before flight.

Answer (B) is correct. (AIM Para 8-1-2)
   DISCUSSION: Anemic hypoxia refers to hypoxia resulting from a reduction in the oxygen-carrying capacity of the blood, rather than from a lack of atmospheric pressure. This can be the result of anemia, of carbon monoxide poisoning from a leaking exhaust manifold, or from smoking.
   Answer (A) is incorrect. Stagnant, not anemic, hypoxia is the result of poor blood circulation. **Answer (C) is incorrect.** Histotoxic, not anemic, hypoxia is caused by the use of alcohol or drugs before flight.

7. Altitude-induced hypoxia is caused by what atmospheric condition?

   A. Significantly less oxygen molecules at high altitude.

   B. Insufficient partial pressure of the inhaled oxygen.

   C. Incorrect balance of oxygen and carbon dioxide.

Answer (B) is correct. (AIM Para 8-1-2)
   DISCUSSION: As altitude is increased, the partial pressure of oxygen lowers, reducing the lungs' capacity to effectively transfer oxygen from the ambient air to the blood to be carried to the tissues of the body.
   Answer (A) is incorrect. The percentage of oxygen does not change at higher altitudes, though the molecules of oxygen in ambient air get further apart, exerting less pressure per square inch. **Answer (C) is incorrect.** An incorrect balance of oxygen and carbon dioxide is primarily associated with hyperventilation.

8. Carbon monoxide poisoning, common in flying as a result of an exhaust leak, is considered what type of hypoxia?

   A. Anemic.

   B. Histotoxic.

   C. Hypoxic.

Answer (A) is correct. (FAA-H-8083-25B Chap 17)
   DISCUSSION: Carbon monoxide poisoning is an example of anemic hypoxia in that it creates an oxygen deficiency in the blood.
   Answer (B) is incorrect. An example of histotoxic hypoxia, the inability of cells to effectively use oxygen, would be an impairment due to drugs or alcohol. **Answer (C) is incorrect.** An example of hypoxic hypoxia, a deficiency of oxygen to the body as a whole, would include drowning or a blocked airway.

9. Hyperventilation occurs when

   A. an insufficient amount of air is breathed into the lungs.

   B. there is a lack of oxygen in the bloodstream.

   C. an excessive amount of air is breathed into the lungs.

Answer (C) is correct. (FAA-H-8083-25B Chap 17)
   DISCUSSION: Hyperventilation occurs when an excessive amount of air is breathed into the lungs.
   Answer (A) is incorrect. An excessive, not insufficient, amount of air in the lungs is defined as hyperventilation. **Answer (B) is incorrect.** Hypoxia is a lack of oxygen in the bloodstream.

10. A corrective action to overcome symptoms of hyperventilation is to

   A. take quick, deep breaths.

   B. lower altitude immediately.

   C. slow the breathing rate.

Answer (C) is correct. (FAA-H-8083-25B Chap 17)
   DISCUSSION: Slowing the breathing rate, placing a paper bag over your mouth and nose and breathing into it, or talking aloud are all ways to overcome hyperventilation.
   Answer (A) is incorrect. Taking quick, deep breaths will further irritate and increase the feelings of hyperventilation. **Answer (B) is incorrect.** Lowering the altitude will not have an effect on hyperventilation or its causes.

11. A pilot making a blood donation in order to help a sick associate should be aware that for several weeks

A. sufficient oxygen may not reach the cells in the body.

B. fewer oxygen molecules will be available to the respiratory membranes.

C. the ability of the body tissues to effectively use oxygen is decreased.

Answer (A) is correct. (FAA-H-8083-25B Chap 17)
DISCUSSION: Blood donations can cause anemic hypoxia because not enough blood is available to carry a sufficient amount of oxygen to the cells.
Answer (B) is incorrect. The amount of oxygen available to the body does not change; however, there may not be enough blood to carry the oxygen to the cells. Answer (C) is incorrect. The body tissues have not lost the ability to use oxygen; however, the amount of blood available to deliver the oxygen has decreased.

12. Which is a common symptom of hyperventilation?

A. Tingling sensations.

B. Visual acuity.

C. Decreased breathing rate.

Answer (A) is correct. (AIM Para 8-1-3)
DISCUSSION: Hyperventilation results from an abnormal increase in the volume of air breathed in and out of the lungs. It can occur subconsciously when a stressful situation is encountered. The result is an excessive amount of carbon dioxide removed from the body. The symptoms are lightheadedness, suffocation, drowsiness, tingling of the extremities, and coolness.
Answer (B) is incorrect. Hyperventilation distorts one's abilities; it does not improve them. Answer (C) is incorrect. Decreasing the breathing rate is one way to overcome hyperventilation. It is not a symptom of it.

7.2 Spatial Disorientation

13. The sensations which lead to spatial disorientation during instrument flight conditions

A. are frequently encountered by beginning instrument pilots, but never by pilots with moderate instrument experience.

B. occur, in most instances, during the initial period of transition from visual to instrument flight.

C. must be suppressed and complete reliance placed on the indications of the flight instruments.

Answer (C) is correct. (AIM Para 8-1-5)
DISCUSSION: In instrument flight conditions, the only way to prevent spatial disorientation is by visual reference to and reliance on the flight instruments.
Answer (A) is incorrect. Pilots with moderate and even extensive instrument experience can experience spatial disorientation. Answer (B) is incorrect. Spatial disorientation can occur at any time outside visual references are lost. This can happen on a clear day flying in VMC or in IMC.

14. Which system is most likely responsible for a pilot suffering spatial disorientation?

A. Cardiopulmonary system.

B. Autokinesis system.

C. Vestibular system.

Answer (C) is correct. (FAA-H-8083-15B Chap 5)
DISCUSSION: Spatial disorientation is caused by conflicting signals sent to the brain by the vestibular system and the pilot's eyes.
Answer (A) is incorrect. The cardiopulmonary system is not responsible for spatial disorientation. Answer (B) is incorrect. Autokinesis is a form of visual illusion that leads to disorientation; it is not a system of the human body.

15. A pilot is more subject to spatial disorientation if

A. kinesthetic senses are ignored.

B. eyes are moved often in the process of cross-checking the flight instruments.

C. body signals are used to interpret flight attitude.

Answer (C) is correct. (AIM Para 8-1-5)
DISCUSSION: Spatial disorientation is a state of temporary confusion resulting from misleading information being sent to the brain by various sensory organs. Thus, the pilot should ignore sensations of muscles and inner ear and kinesthetic senses (those which sense motion).
Answer (A) is incorrect. Spatial disorientation is prevented or overcome by ignoring the kinesthetic senses. Answer (B) is incorrect. Spatial disorientation is prevented or overcome by using and trusting the flight instruments.

16. Which procedure is recommended to prevent or overcome spatial disorientation?

    A. Reduce head and eye movements to the extent possible.

    B. Rely on the kinesthetic sense.

    C. Rely on the indications of the flight instruments.

Answer (C) is correct. (AIM Para 8-1-5)
    DISCUSSION: To overcome the effect of spatial disorientation, pilots should rely entirely on the indications of the flight instruments.
    Answer (A) is incorrect. Although rapid head movements should be avoided, eye movement is necessary for proper scanning of the flight instruments. **Answer (B) is incorrect.** The kinesthetic sense is creating the problem; i.e., it should be ignored.

17. How can an instrument pilot best overcome spatial disorientation?

    A. Rely on kinesthetic sense.

    B. Use a very rapid cross-check.

    C. Read and interpret the flight instruments, and act accordingly.

Answer (C) is correct. (FAA-H-8083-15B Chap 3)
    DISCUSSION: To overcome spatial disorientation, the IFR pilot should read and interpret the flight instruments and ignore all the body senses.
    Answer (A) is incorrect. The kinesthetic sense is what causes the problem; i.e., it should be ignored. **Answer (B) is incorrect.** The flight instruments should be read and understood in a deliberate manner, not in haste or panic.

18. How can an instrument pilot best overcome spatial disorientation?

    A. Use a very rapid cross-check.

    B. Properly interpret the flight instruments and act accordingly.

    C. Avoid banking in excess of 30°.

Answer (B) is correct. (FAA-H-8083-15B Chap 3)
    DISCUSSION: To overcome spatial disorientation, the IFR pilot should read and interpret the flight instruments and ignore all the body senses.
    Answer (A) is incorrect. The flight instruments should be read and understood in a deliberate manner, not in haste or panic. **Answer (C) is incorrect.** Spatial disorientation can also occur in bank angles less than 30°.

19. Abrupt head movement during a prolonged constant rate turn in IMC or simulated instrument conditions can cause

    A. pilot disorientation.

    B. false horizon.

    C. elevator illusion.

Answer (A) is correct. (AIM Para 8-1-5)
    DISCUSSION: An abrupt head movement in a prolonged constant-rate turn that has ceased stimulating the motion sensing system can create the illusion of rotation or movement in an entirely different axis. This illusion is called the Coriolis illusion and can lead to spatial disorientation.
    Answer (B) is incorrect. A false horizon is an illusion caused by sloping cloud formations, an obscured horizon, a dark scene spread with ground lights and stars, or certain geometric patterns of ground light. This illusion creates the impression of not being aligned correctly with the actual horizon and can also lead to spatial disorientation. **Answer (C) is incorrect.** An elevator illusion is caused by an abrupt upward vertical acceleration, usually by an updraft. This illusion can also lead to spatial disorientation.

20. A rapid acceleration during takeoff can create the illusion of

    A. spinning in the opposite direction.

    B. being in a noseup attitude.

    C. diving into the ground.

Answer (B) is correct. (AIM Para 8-1-5)
    DISCUSSION: A rapid acceleration during takeoff can create the illusion of being in a nose-up attitude. The disoriented pilot will push the airplane into a nose-low, or dive, attitude. This is called a somatogravic illusion.
    Answer (A) is incorrect. A proper recovery from a spin that has ceased stimulating the motion sensing system (i.e., inner ear) can create the illusion of spinning in the opposite direction. This is known as a graveyard spin. **Answer (C) is incorrect.** A rapid deceleration or an abrupt downward vertical acceleration (usually caused by a downdraft) can cause the illusion of a nose-down, or dive, attitude.

21. An abrupt change from climb to straight-and-level flight can create the illusion of

    A. tumbling backwards.

    B. a noseup attitude.

    C. a descent with the wings level.

Answer (A) is correct. (AIM Para 8-1-5)
    DISCUSSION: An abrupt change from climb to straight-and-level flight can create the illusion of tumbling backwards. The disoriented pilot will push the airplane abruptly into a nose-low attitude, possibly intensifying this illusion, which is called an inversion illusion.
    Answer (B) is incorrect. A rapid acceleration during takeoff can create an illusion of being in a nose-up attitude. This is called a somatogravic illusion. **Answer (C) is incorrect.** An observed loss of altitude during a coordinated constant-rate turn that has ceased stimulating the motion sensing system (i.e., inner ear) can create the illusion of being in a descent with the wings level. This illusion is called a graveyard spiral.

22. A sloping cloud formation, an obscured horizon, and a dark scene spread with ground lights and stars can create an illusion known as .

    A. elevator illusions.

    B. autokinesis.

    C. false horizons.

Answer (C) is correct. (AIM Para 8-1-5)
    DISCUSSION: A sloping cloud formation, an obscured horizon, a dark scene spread with ground lights and stars, and certain geometric patterns of ground light can create an illusion known as false horizons. The disoriented pilot will place the airplane in a dangerous attitude.
    Answer (A) is incorrect. Elevator illusions are caused by abrupt upward or downward vertical accelerations, usually by updrafts and downdrafts. These lead to illusions of being in a climb or descent. **Answer (B) is incorrect.** At night, a static light will appear to move about when stared at for many seconds, creating an illusion known as autokinesis.

23. While making prolonged constant-rate turns under IFR conditions, an abrupt head movement can create the illusion of rotation on an entirely different axis. This is known as

    A. Coriolis illusion.

    B. autokinesis.

    C. the leans.

Answer (A) is correct. (AIM Para 8-1-5)
    DISCUSSION: An abrupt head movement in a prolonged constant-rate turn that has ceased stimulating the motion sensing system can create the illusion of rotation or movement in an entirely different axis. This illusion is called the Coriolis illusion and can lead to spatial disorientation.
    Answer (B) is incorrect. Autokinesis is a night-flying illusion. In the dark, a static light will appear to move about when stared at for many seconds. The disoriented pilot will lose control of the aircraft in attempting to align it with the light. **Answer (C) is incorrect.** The leans are caused by an abrupt correction of a banked attitude that has been entered too slowly.

24. Abrupt head movement during a prolonged constant rate turn in IMC or simulated instrument conditions can cause

    A. Coriolis illusion.

    B. elevator illusion.

    C. inversion illusion.

Answer (A) is correct. (AIM Para 8-1-5)
    DISCUSSION: An abrupt head movement in a prolonged constant-rate turn that has ceased stimulating the motion sensing system can create the illusion of rotation or movement in an entirely different axis. This illusion is called the Coriolis illusion and can lead to spatial disorientation.
    Answer (B) is incorrect. An elevator illusion is caused by an abrupt upward vertical acceleration, usually by an updraft. This illusion can also lead to spatial disorientation. **Answer (C) is incorrect.** An inversion illusion is caused by an abrupt change from climb to straight and level flight, which can create the illusion of tumbling backwards. The disoriented pilot will push the aircraft abruptly into a nose low attitude, possibly intensifying this illusion.

25. The sensory system responsible for most of the illusions leading to spatial disorientation is the

A. visual system.

B. vestibular system.

C. postural system.

Answer (B) is correct. (FAA-H-8083-15B Chap 3, AIM Para 8-1-5)
    DISCUSSION: The sensory system responsible for most of the illusions leading to spatial disorientation is the vestibular system. The vestibular sense (motion sensing by the inner ear) can confuse the pilot.
    Answer (A) is incorrect. Although visual illusions can cause spatial disorientation, the system responsible for most of the illusions leading to spatial disorientation is the vestibular system. Pilots use their visual system to monitor the flight instruments to help prevent spatial disorientation caused by the vestibular system. **Answer (C) is incorrect.** The postural system involves signals from the skin, muscles, and joints going to the brain. They are not responsible for the majority of illusions leading to spatial disorientation.

26. Without visual aid, a pilot often interprets centrifugal force as a sensation of

A. rising or falling.

B. turning.

C. motion reversal.

Answer (A) is correct. (FAA-H-8083-15B Chap 3)
    DISCUSSION: Nerves in tendons and muscles, including shifting of abdominal muscles, often incorrectly interpret centrifugal force as vertical movement, i.e., rising or falling.
    Answer (B) is incorrect. Centrifugal force is caused by turning but is often misinterpreted as rising or falling. **Answer (C) is incorrect.** Centrifugal force is caused by turning, not motion reversal.

27. Pilots should take care when retrieving charts or dropped objects on the flight deck to avoid

A. autokinesis.

B. false horizon.

C. Coriolis illusion.

Answer (C) is correct. (FAA-H-8083-15B Chap 5)
    DISCUSSION: The Coriolis illusion is created by rapid head movements. Pilots should take care when retrieving items like charts or dropped objects on the flight deck and ensure a proper instrument cross check is maintained.
    Answer (A) is incorrect. Autokinesis is the result of staring at an object, not rapid head movement. **Answer (B) is incorrect.** The false horizon illusion is the result of confusing a sloping cloud formation or shapes on the ground with the horizon.

28. You are most likely to experience somatogravic illusion during

A. a rapid descent.

B. deceleration upon landing.

C. rapid acceleration on takeoff.

Answer (C) is correct. (FAA-H-8083-25B)
    DISCUSSION: A rapid acceleration, such as experienced during takeoff, stimulates the otolith organs in the same way as tilting the head backwards. This action may create what is known as the "somatogravic illusion" of being in a nose-up attitude, especially in conditions with poor visual references.
    Answer (A) is incorrect. A rapid acceleration, not a rapid descent, stimulates the otolith organs in the same way as tilting the head backwards, which is a common experience of somatogravic illusion. **Answer (B) is incorrect.** During landing, a rapid deceleration may cause somatogravic illusion with the opposite effect of a rapid acceleration. However, a normal deceleration upon landing should not cause a somatogravic illusion.

29. The best way to counter the effects of spatial disorientation is to

A. trust your flight instruments and disregard your sensory perceptions.

B. disregard your flight instruments and rely on your senses.

C. breathe deeply and exhale slowly to increase your oxygen content.

Answer (A) is correct. (AIM Para 8-1-5)
    DISCUSSION: Once you have successfully checked all flight instruments prior to flight and continually evaluated their authenticity during flight, you should rely on them at all points in flight when a conflict arises between the instruments and the perceptions of your sensory system.
    Answer (B) is incorrect. You must override the urge to disregard flight instruments in favor of the sensory system. You must become proficient in the use of flight instruments and learn to rely on them. Trust the instruments and disregard your sensory perceptions. **Answer (C) is incorrect.** Breathing deeply and exhaling slowly is part of the mechanism to slow the breathing rate to overcome hyperventilation in flight.

7.3   Vision and Visual Illusion

30. To preserve night vision, the most appropriate flight deck lighting is

A. reducing the interior lighting intensity to a minimum level.

B. the use of regular white light, such as a flashlight, will not impair night adaptation.

C. increase the interior intensity to slightly above the outside level.

Answer (A) is correct. (AIM Para 8-1-6)
   DISCUSSION: In darkness, vision becomes more sensitive to light, making it possible for the pilot to see distant objects. A pilot can achieve a moderate degree of this dark adaptation within 20 min. under dim red flight deck lighting. White flight deck lighting is required for map and instrument reading, especially when operating under IFR. To maintain some night vision, the interior lighting intensity is to be kept at a minimum level.
   Answer (B) is incorrect. After a pilot's eyes have become adapted to darkness, the pilot must avoid exposing them to any bright white light, which would cause temporary night blindness and impair night adaptation. **Answer (C) is incorrect.** To maintain some night vision, the interior light intensity should be less than the outside level.

31. What effect does haze have on the ability to see traffic or terrain features during flight?

A. Haze causes the eyes to focus at infinity, making terrain features harder to see.

B. The eyes tend to overwork in haze and do not detect relative movement easily.

C. Haze creates the illusion of being a greater distance than actual from the runway, and causes pilots to fly a lower approach.

Answer (C) is correct. (AIM Para 8-1-5)
   DISCUSSION: Haze can create the illusion of being at a greater distance and height from an object. The pilot who does not recognize this illusion will fly a lower approach.
   Answer (A) is incorrect. Haze may cause the condition known as empty-field myopia. This condition results when the pilot has nothing specific to focus on outside the airplane and the eyes relax and focus at a range of about 10 to 30 ft., not infinity. **Answer (B) is incorrect.** In haze, the eyes tend to relax, not overwork, thus causing empty-field myopia, or looking without seeing.

32. Which statement is correct regarding the use of flight deck lighting for night flight?

A. Reducing the lighting intensity to a minimum level will eliminate blind spots.

B. The use of regular white light, such as a flashlight, will impair night adaptation.

C. Coloration shown on maps is least affected by the use of direct red lighting.

Answer (B) is correct. (AIM Para 8-1-6)
   DISCUSSION: After a pilot's eyes have become adapted to darkness, the pilot must avoid exposing them to any bright white light, which would cause temporary night blindness and impair night adaptation.
   Answer (A) is incorrect. The minimum level of flight deck lighting may be insufficient to read maps, gauges, etc. **Answer (C) is incorrect.** The colors on maps can be severely distorted when using a red light.

33. Which technique should a pilot use to scan for traffic to the right and left during straight-and-level flight?

A. Systematically focus on different segments of the sky for short intervals.

B. Concentrate on relative movement detected in the peripheral vision area.

C. Continuous sweeping of the windshield from right to left.

Answer (A) is correct. (AIM Para 8-1-6)
   DISCUSSION: The most effective way to scan for other aircraft during daylight is to use a series of short, regularly spaced eye movements that bring successive areas of the sky into your central vision field. Only a very small center area of the eye has the ability to send clear, sharply focused messages to the brain. All other areas provide less detail.
   Answer (B) is incorrect. The peripheral areas do not send sharply focused messages to the brain. Peripheral vision is more effective at night. **Answer (C) is incorrect.** Concentration for at least 1 second is needed for each 10° sector.

34. Due to visual illusion, when landing on a narrower-than-usual runway, the aircraft will appear to be

A. higher than actual, leading to a lower-than-normal approach.

B. lower than actual, leading to a higher-than-normal approach.

C. higher than actual, leading to a higher-than-normal approach.

Answer (A) is correct. (AIM Para 8-1-5)
   DISCUSSION: A narrower-than-usual runway may create the illusion that the aircraft is higher than actual, resulting in a lower-than-normal approach.
   Answer (B) is incorrect. Wider, not narrower, runways give a lower-than-actual altitude illusion. **Answer (C) is incorrect.** A higher-than-actual altitude illusion results in a lower-than-usual, not higher-than-usual, approach.

35. What visual illusion creates the same effect as a narrower-than-usual runway?

A. An upsloping runway.

B. A wider-than-usual runway.

C. A downsloping runway.

Answer (A) is correct. (AIM Para 8-1-5)
DISCUSSION: Both a narrower-than-usual runway and an upsloping runway may create the illusion that the airplane is at a higher altitude than it actually is. The pilot will fly a lower approach and risk striking obstructions or landing short.
Answer (B) is incorrect. A wider-than-usual runway may create the illusion that the aircraft is at a lower altitude than it actually is, and the unknowing pilot may land hard or overshoot the runway. Answer (C) is incorrect. A downsloping runway may create the illusion that the aircraft is at a lower altitude than it actually is, and the unknowing pilot may land hard or overshoot the runway.

36. The illusion associated with landing on a narrower than usual runway may result in the pilot flying a

A. lower approach with the risk of striking objects along the approach path or landing short.

B. slower approach with the risk of reducing airspeed below V_{SO} or landing hard.

C. higher approach with the risk of leveling out high and landing hard or overshooting the runway.

Answer (A) is correct. (FAA-H-8083-25B Chap 17)
DISCUSSION: A narrower-than-usual runway can create an illusion that the aircraft is at a higher altitude than it actually is, which could result in striking objects along the flight path or landing short.
Answer (B) is incorrect. Runway width has no effect on the perceived speed in an approach to landing. Answer (C) is incorrect. A wider-, not narrower-, than-usual runway can create the illusion that the aircraft is lower than actual altitude, creating the risk of the pilot leveling out the aircraft high and landing hard or overshooting the runway.

37. Flight deck lighting for night flight should include

A. reducing lighting intensity to a minimum level.

B. using a white light such as a flashlight.

C. using direct red lighting.

Answer (A) is correct. (AIM Para 8-1-6, FAA-H-8083-25B Chap 17)
DISCUSSION: Flight deck lighting for night flight should be kept as low as possible so that the light does not monopolize night vision.
Answer (B) is incorrect. The use of regular white light, such as a flashlight, will impair the dark adaptation process for the eyes at night. Answer (C) is incorrect. Red light will severely distort colors, especially on aeronautical charts, and can cause serious difficulty in focusing the eyes on objects inside the aircraft.

38. Having appropriate instrument lighting will

A. enable better recognition of outside references.

B. make a proper instrument scan difficult.

C. result in unnecessary eye strain.

Answer (A) is correct. (AIM Para 8-1-6)
DISCUSSION: Appropriate instrument lighting enables better recognition of outside references through dark adaptation.
Answer (B) is incorrect. Appropriate instrument lighting helps make a proper instrument scan more effective. Answer (C) is incorrect. Appropriate instrument lighting enhances flight deck vision and limits unnecessary eye strain.

7.4 Fatigue

39. Why is fatigue hazardous to flight safety?

A. The pilot hurries to get done in order to rest.

B. Fatigue may not be apparent to a pilot until serious errors are made (an impaired pilot is a dangerous pilot).

C. The pilot is lazy and rushes to get done quickly.

Answer (B) is correct. (FAA-H-8083-15B Chap 3, AIM Para 8-1-1)
DISCUSSION: Fatigue is one of the most treacherous hazards to flight safety because it may not become apparent to a pilot until serious errors are made.
Answer (A) is incorrect. The risk is not found in the pilot hurrying, but rather the risk is found in the diminished cognitive power that fatigue introduces to the situation, sometimes causing pilots to make serious errors before they realize how fatigued they are. Answer (C) is incorrect. The risk is not found in the pilot being lazy or rushing to complete a series of tasks, but rather the risk is found in the diminished cognitive power that fatigue introduces to the situation, sometimes causing pilots to make serious errors before they realize how fatigued they are.

STUDY UNIT EIGHT

AVIATION WEATHER

(11 pages of outline)

This study unit contains outlines of major concepts tested, sample test questions and answers regarding aviation weather, and an explanation of each answer.

Recall that the **sole purpose** of this book is to expedite your passing of the FAA pilot knowledge test for the instrument rating. Accordingly, all extraneous material (i.e., topics or regulations not directly tested on the FAA pilot knowledge test) is omitted, even though much more knowledge is necessary to fly safely. This additional material is presented in *Pilot Handbook*, *Aviation Weather and Weather Services*, *FAR/AIM*, and *Instrument Pilot Flight Maneuvers and Practical Test Prep*, available from Gleim Publications, Inc. Order online at www.GleimAviation.com.

8.1 CAUSES OF WEATHER

1. Every physical process of weather is accompanied by, or is the result of, heat exchanges.

2. Unequal heating of the Earth's surface causes differences in pressure and, thus, altimeter settings.

   a. On weather maps, the lines drawn to connect points of equal pressure show pressure contours called **isobars**.

3.   Three of the forces at work on winds are discussed below.

    a.   The pressure gradient force causes wind to flow from an area of high pressure to one of low pressure.

        1)   This flow is thus perpendicular to the isobars.

    b.   Coriolis force deflects winds to the right in the Northern Hemisphere. Coriolis force is a result of the Earth's rotation.

        1)   The Coriolis force is at a right angle to wind direction and directly proportional to wind speed. Its effect is more forceful at greater altitudes (above approximately 2,000 ft. AGL) because surface winds are slowed by friction.

        2)   It deflects winds so strongly that they flow parallel to isobars.

    c.   Friction with the Earth's surface weakens the wind.

        1)   Since these winds are slower, they are less affected by Coriolis force. The pressure gradient becomes stronger than Coriolis force, and the wind flows across, rather than parallel to, the isobars.

        2)   Friction is what causes winds to be greater at higher altitudes than at the surface.

4.   An **air mass** is an extensive body of air having uniform moisture and temperature properties.

5.   The average height of the layer of the Earth's atmosphere called the **troposphere** is about 37,000 ft. in mid-latitudes. It varies between approximately 25,000 ft. at the poles to 65,000 ft. at the equator.

6.   The boundary between the troposphere and the stratosphere is the thin layer called the **tropopause**.

    a.   Temperature and wind vary greatly in the vicinity of the tropopause.

    b.   It is associated with an abrupt change in the temperature lapse rate.

7.   The **stratosphere** is the layer of atmosphere above the tropopause.

    a.   It is characterized by low moisture content and absence of clouds.

    b.   It has relatively small changes in temperature with an increase in altitude.

8.   The **jet stream** is a narrow, disjointed, wandering "river" of maximum winds.

    a.   It moves with pressure ridges and troughs in the upper atmosphere near the tropopause.

    b.   It blows from a generally westerly direction and, by definition, has a speed of 50 kt. or more.

    c.   The jet stream is normally weaker and farther north in the summer.

    d.   The jet stream is normally stronger and farther south in the winter.

9.   A **front** is the zone of transition between two air masses of different temperature, humidity, and wind.

    a.   There is always a change in wind when you fly across a front.

    b.   The threat of low-level wind shear occurs just before the warm front passes the airport.

    c.   With a cold front, the most critical period for wind shear occurs just as or just after the cold front passes the airport.

10.   Frontal waves and cyclones (and areas of low pressure) usually form in slow-moving cold fronts or in stationary fronts.

11.   Squall lines usually develop ahead of a cold front.

8.2 STABILITY OF AIR MASSES

1. The **lapse rate** is a measure of how much temperature decreases (or possibly increases) with an increase in altitude. This is the actual temperature change associated with increases in altitude and sometimes is referred to as the **ambient lapse rate**.

   a. In contrast to the ambient or actual lapse rate is the **adiabatic lapse rate**. The adiabatic (or "expansional cooling") lapse rate is the temperature decrease due only to expansion of air as it rises. The adiabatic lapse rate means no heat gain or loss -- just a decrease in temperature because of expansion.

      1) The dry adiabatic lapse rate is 3°C per 1,000 ft.

      2) The adiabatic lapse rate varies from about 1.1°C to 2.8°C based on moisture content of the air.

      3) The average adiabatic lapse rate is 2°C per 1,000 ft.

2. The ambient lapse rate can thus be used by pilots to determine the stability of air masses.

   a. The greater the ambient lapse rate (more than 2°C per 1,000 ft.) and the higher the humidity, the more unstable the air -- and the more thunderstorms can be expected.

   b. Moist air is less stable than dry air because it cools adiabatically at a slower rate, which means that moist air must rise higher before its temperature cools to that of the air around it (i.e., cumulus build-up).

3. Cloud formation after lifting is determined by the stability of the air before lifting.

   a. Turbulence and clouds with vertical development (cumuliform) result when unstable air rises (due to convective currents).

   b. Moist, stable air moving up a mountain slope produces stratiform clouds as it cools.

      1) Unstable air moving up a mountain slope produces clouds with extensive vertical development.

4. When a cold air mass moves over a warm surface, heating from below provides unstable lifting action, giving rise to cumuliform clouds, turbulence, and good visibility.

5. The growth rate of precipitation is enhanced by upward air currents carrying water droplets upward where condensation increases droplet size.

6. The stability of an air mass can usually be determined by the cloud types and the type of precipitation.

7. Stable Air Characteristics

   a. Stratiform clouds and fog
   b. Smooth air
   c. Continuous (steady) precipitation
   d. Fair-to-poor visibility in haze and smoke
   e. Cool
   f. Dry

8. Unstable Air Characteristics

   a. Cumuliform clouds
   b. Turbulent air
   c. Showery precipitation
   d. Good visibility
   e. Warm
   f. Humid

8.3 TEMPERATURE INVERSIONS

1. Normally, temperature decreases as altitude increases. A temperature inversion occurs when temperature increases as altitude increases.

2. Temperature inversions usually result in a stable layer of warm air below the inversion.

3. A temperature inversion often develops near the ground on clear, cool nights when the wind is light.

    a. It is caused by terrestrial radiation.

4. Smooth air with restricted visibility (due to fog, haze, or low clouds) is usually found beneath a low-level temperature inversion.

5. Temperature and radiation variations over land with a clear sky typically lead to the minimum temperature occurring just after sunrise when the incoming solar radiation is not yet strong enough to offset the terrestrial radiation from the Earth.

8.4 TEMPERATURE, DEW POINT, AND FOG

1. When the temperature-dew point spread is 3°C (5°F) or less and decreasing, you should expect fog and/or low clouds.

2. Air temperature largely determines how much water vapor can be held by the air.

    a. **Dew point** is the temperature at which the air will be saturated with moisture, i.e., 100% humidity.

3. Frost forms when the temperature of the collecting surface (e.g., the airplane) is below the dew point of the surrounding air and the dew point is below freezing (0°C or 32°F).

4. Water vapor becomes visible as it condenses into clouds, fog, or dew.

    a. **Evaporation** is the conversion of liquid water to water vapor.
    b. **Sublimation** is the conversion of ice directly to water vapor.
    c. **Deposition** is the conversion of water vapor directly to ice.

5. **Radiation fog** is most likely to occur when there is a clear sky, little or no wind, and a small temperature-dew point spread over a land surface (especially low, flatland areas).

    a. As the ground cools rapidly due to radiation, the air close to the surface cools more quickly than slightly higher air.

        1) This is the most frequent type of surface-based temperature inversion.

    b. As the air reaches its dew point, radiation fog forms.

6. **Advection fog** forms as a result of moist air condensing as it moves over a colder surface (i.e., water or ground).

    a. It requires wind to force the movement.

    b. Advection fog is most likely to occur in coastal areas, when air moves inland from the coast in winter.

7. **Upslope fog** results from warm, moist air being cooled as it is forced up sloping terrain.

8. **Precipitation-induced fog** results from warm fronts (warmer air over cooler air), i.e., when warm rain or drizzle falls through the cooler air.

    a. Evaporation from the precipitation saturates the cooler air, causing fog.

9. Fog can also form easily in industrial areas where combustion pollution provides a high concentration of condensation nuclei (tiny particles on which moisture can condense as the air cools).

10. While flying at night, penetrating a fog layer can create the illusion of pitching up. Often, if the pilot does not recognize this illusion, (s)he will steepen the approach excessively, leading to increased speed at a steeper approach angle.

8.5 CLOUDS

1. Clouds are divided into four families based on their height:

    a. High clouds (consist of ice crystals and do not pose an icing threat)
    b. Middle clouds
    c. Low clouds
    d. Clouds with extensive vertical development

2. Lifting action, unstable air, and moisture are the ingredients for the formation of cumulonimbus clouds.

    a. Fair weather cumulus clouds form in convective currents and often indicate turbulence at and below the cloud level.

    b. Nimbus means rain cloud.

    c. Towering cumulus is an early stage of cumulonimbus.

    d. The greatest turbulence is in cumulonimbus clouds (thunderstorms).

3. Standing lenticular altocumulus clouds (ACSL) are almond or lens-shaped and form on the crests of waves created by barriers in the wind flow (e.g., on the leeward side of a mountain).

    a. The presence of these clouds indicates very strong turbulence.

8.6 THUNDERSTORMS

1. Thunderstorms have three phases in their life cycle:

    a. **Cumulus** -- the building stage of a thunderstorm when there are continuous updrafts

    b. **Mature** -- the time of greatest intensity when there are both updrafts and downdrafts (causing severe wind shear and turbulence)

        1) The commencing of rain on the Earth's surface indicates the beginning of the mature stage of a thunderstorm.

    c. **Dissipating** -- characterized predominantly by downdrafts; i.e., the phase of the storm raining itself out

2. A thunderstorm, by definition, always has lightning, because lightning causes thunder.

    a. Lightning strikes are most common when operating with an outside air temperature (OAT) of between −5°C and +5°C.

3. Thunderstorms are produced by cumulonimbus clouds. They form when there is

    a. Sufficient water vapor
    b. An unstable lapse rate
    c. An initial upward boost (i.e., a lifting action) to start the process

4. Thunderstorms produce wind shear turbulence, a hazardous and invisible phenomenon, particularly for airplanes landing and taking off.

    a. If a thunderstorm is penetrated, a pilot should fly straight ahead, set power for recommended turbulence penetration airspeed, and attempt to maintain a level attitude.

    b. Do not attempt to fly under the anvil of a thunderstorm because there is still potential for severe and extreme clear air turbulence in addition to hail.

    c. All thunderstorms, and especially those identified as severe or giving an intense radar echo, should be avoided by circumnavigating the cell by a minimum of 20 NM.

5. The most severe thunderstorm conditions (heavy hail, destructive winds, tornadoes, etc.) are generally associated with squall line thunderstorms.

    a. A **squall line** is a nonfrontal, narrow band of thunderstorms usually ahead of a cold front.

    b. Pilots should anticipate possible hail with any thunderstorm, especially beneath the anvil of a large cumulonimbus.

6. A **squall** (not squall line) is defined as a sudden increase in wind speed of at least 16 kt., the speed rising to 22 kt. or more and lasting at least 1 min.

7. Embedded thunderstorms are obscured because they occur in very cloudy conditions or thick haze layers.

8. Airborne weather-avoidance radar detects only precipitation drops. It does not detect minute cloud droplets (i.e., clouds and fog).

    a. Thus, airborne weather-avoidance radar provides no assurance of avoiding instrument weather conditions.

8.7 ICING

1. Structural icing requires two conditions:

    a. Flight through visible moisture
    b. The temperature at freezing or below

2. Ice pellets are caused when rain droplets freeze at a higher altitude; i.e., freezing rain exists above.

3. Heavy, wet snow indicates the temperature is above freezing at your altitude.

    a. Snow that is heavy and wet formed above you but is on the verge of melting.

4. Frost on wings disrupts the airflow over the wings, causing early airflow separation and resulting in a loss of lift. It should be removed before flight is attempted.

    a. Small patches of ice or frost can result in localized, asymmetrical stalls on the wing, which can then result in roll control problems during liftoff.

5. Test data indicate that ice, snow, or frost having a thickness and roughness similar to medium or coarse sandpaper on the leading edge and upper surface of a wing can reduce wing lift by as much as 30% and increase drag by 40%.

    a. When ice does accumulate, it is harder to remove from the upper surface of the wing than the leading edge. Generally speaking, smooth ice on top of the wing is more dangerous than heavy accumulated icing on the leading edge.

6. With a standard (average) temperature lapse rate of 2°C per 1,000 ft., the freezing level can be determined by knowing the current temperature and elevation.

    a. EXAMPLE: At a field elevation of 1,350 ft. MSL, the temperature is +8°C. To reach the freezing level, the temperature must drop 8°C. Thus the freezing level is 4,000 ft. (8°C ÷ 2°C/1,000 ft.) above field elevation, or 5,350 ft. MSL (1,350 + 4,000).

7. When conditions favoring the formation of ice are present, pilots should check for ice accumulation prior to flight by using a flashlight to scan the surface of the airframe and watch for light reflections.

    a. Ice on the surface of the wing is virtually undetectable and causes a reduction in lift over the wing.

    b. Narrow objects tend to pick up ice that is visually detectable. Ice accumulation on the air temperature probe or on a pitot tube (of a high-wing airplane) would be the first area that the pilot would observe ice buildup.

8. Ice tends to accumulate on small and narrow parts of the aircraft before others. The most susceptible surface of the airframe to accumulate icing is the tailplane due to its position being outside the visual range as well as its thin, simple shape.

    a. A tailplane stall as the result of ice accumulation is most likely to occur during the extension of the flaps to the landing position. Thus, tailplane stalls due to icing are mostly likely during the approach and landing phase of flight.

b. Any of the following symptoms, occurring singly or in combination, may be a warning of tailplane icing:

1) Elevator control pulsing, oscillations, or vibrations

2) Abnormal nose-down trim change

3) Any other unusual or abnormal pitch anomalies (possibly resulting in pilot induced oscillations)

4) Reduction or loss of elevator effectiveness

5) Sudden change in elevator force (control would move nose-down if unrestrained)

6) Sudden uncommanded nose-down pitch

c. To recover from a tailplane stall, you should retract the flaps to the last safe position and . increase power only to the extent that you compensate for the loss of lift created from retracting the flaps.

1) Over-increasing the power can aggravate and deepen a tailplane stall in some aircraft.

9. Another serious result of icing is uncommanded roll due to ice accumulation forward of the ailerons.

a. The following procedures apply if you experience roll upset while flying in icing conditions:

1) Reduce the angle of attack (AOA) by reducing the aircraft pitch. If in a turn, roll wings level.

2) Set appropriate power and monitor the airspeed/AOA. A controlled descent is a vastly better alternative than an uncontrolled descent.

3) If flaps are extended, do not retract them unless it can be determined that the upper surface of the airfoil is clear of ice, because retracting the flaps will increase the AOA at a given airspeed.

4) Verify that wing ice protection is functioning normally and symmetrically by visual observation of the left and right wing. If not, follow manufacturer's instructions.

10. If you detect icing accumulation in flight, especially if the aircraft is not equipped with a deicing system, you should leave the area of precipitation, if you are able, or fly to an altitude where the ambient temperature is above freezing.

a. Be aware that warmer temperatures are not always found at lower altitudes. In the case of a temperature inversion, for instance, warmer air will be above rather than below.

11. In an aircraft equipped with a pneumatic deicing system, the appropriate technique for removing ice is to operate the pneumatic deicing system several times.

a. This technique will clear accumulated ice as well as residual ice left behind between system cycles.

b. The FAA recommends that the deicing system be activated at the first indication of icing rather than after any significant amount of ice is allowed to accumulate.

1) Because some residual ice continues to adhere between pneumatic boot system cycles, the wing is never entirely "clean."

2) The amount of residual ice increases as airspeed and/or temperature decrease due to the more favorable conditions for ice accumulation associated with these conditions.

3) At airspeeds typical of small airplanes, it may take many boot cycles to effectively shed the ice.

12. Freezing rain usually causes the greatest accumulation of structural ice.

    a. Freezing rain indicates that temperatures are above freezing at some higher altitude.

    b. Supercooled Large Droplets (SLD) can accrue even if SLDs are not being observed at the surface.

13. SLDs are supercooled droplets with a diameter greater than 50 micrometers (0.05 mm). SLD conditions include freezing drizzle drops and freezing raindrops.

    a. When SLD conditions are encountered in temperatures below +5°C OAT, pilots should expect to see glossy, clear, or translucent ice.

    b. Ice may become visible on the upper or lower surface of the wing, aft of the active part of the deicing boots. Pilots should look for irregular or jagged lines of ice or for pieces of ice shedding off the airplane. During night operations, adequate illumination should be used to observe all areas. On most airplanes, the last inch of the deicing boot is inactive.

    c. Vigilance for SLD ice accretions should be exercised when flying into or over areas reporting precipitation at the surface, such as rain, freezing rain, sleet, ice pellets, drizzle, freezing drizzle, or snow, where temperatures are near freezing.

    d. Pilots should be aware that SLD could occur aloft without any SLD precipitation on the surface.

    e. Current weather information can miss SLD, so it is important to know and watch for cues on the airplane.

14. Pilots may consider periodically disengaging the autopilot and hand flying the airplane when operating in icing conditions.

    a. If this is not desirable due to flight deck workload levels, pilots should monitor the autopilot closely for abnormal trim, trim rate, or airplane attitude.

    b. As ice builds up on aircraft without auto-throttles, the autopilot will attempt to hold altitude without regard for airspeed, leading to a potential stall situation.

8.8 WIND SHEAR

1. **Wind shear** is any change in wind velocity (speed and/or direction).

    a. If the change is abrupt and of more than slight magnitude, it can be an extreme hazard to flight.

    b. A characteristic of low-level wind shear associated with a low-level temperature inversion is an increase in airspeed during climbout and while on approach.

        1) To reduce the risk of inadvertent stalls, pilots are advised to improve their awareness of normal climbout pitch attitude and to put less emphasis on strict airspeed control.

    c. Wind shear is any rapid change in wind direction or velocity, and severe wind shear is any rapid change in wind direction or velocity that causes airspeed changes greater than 15 kt. or vertical speed changes greater than 500 fpm.

2.   Wind shear can occur at any level in the atmosphere and be horizontal and/or vertical; i.e., it occurs wherever adjacent air flows in different directions and/or at different speeds.

3.   Wind shear is an atmospheric condition that may be associated with a low-level temperature inversion, a jet stream, or a frontal zone.

4.   **Light turbulence** momentarily causes slight, erratic changes in altitude and/or attitude.

5.   **Severe turbulence** and wind shear may be found on all sides of a thunderstorm, including directly beneath it and as much as 20 mi. laterally.

6.   Hazardous wind shear is commonly encountered near the ground during periods of strong temperature inversion and near thunderstorms.

     a.   Expect wind shear in a temperature inversion whenever wind speed at 2,000 to 4,000 ft. AGL is 25 kt. or more.

     b.   When going through the inversion, allow airspeed to go above normal climb and approach speed.

8.9 MICROBURSTS

1.   Microbursts are small-scale intense downdrafts that, on reaching the surface, spread outward in all directions from the downdraft center. This causes the presence of both vertical and horizontal wind shears that can be extremely hazardous to all types and categories of aircraft, especially at low altitudes.

2.   Parent clouds producing microburst activity can be any of the low or middle layer convective cloud types.

     a.   Microbursts commonly occur within the heavy rain portion of thunderstorms but also occur in much weaker, benign-appearing convective cells that have little or no precipitation reaching the ground.

3.   The life cycle of a microburst as it descends in a convective rain shaft is illustrated below.

     a.   "T" is the time the microburst strikes the ground.

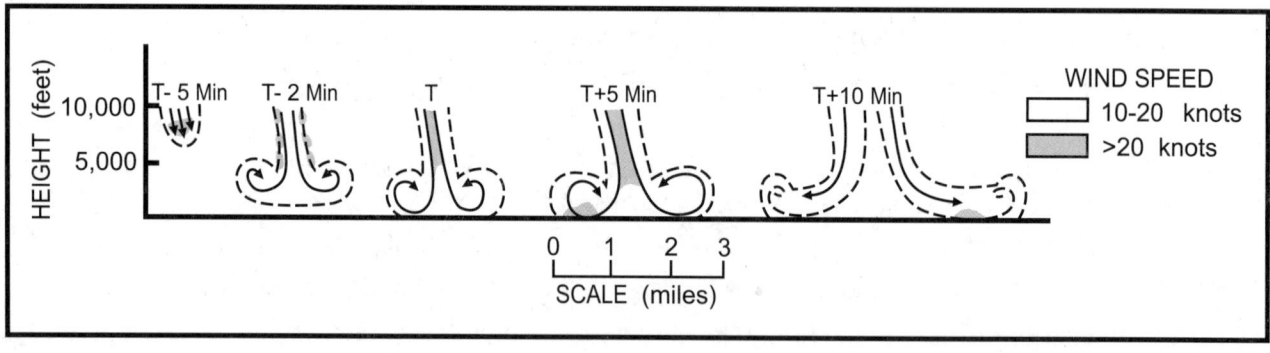

4. Characteristics of microbursts include

    a. Size. The microburst downdraft is typically less than 1 mi. in diameter as it descends from the cloud base to about 1,000-3,000 ft. above the ground.

        1) In the transition zone near the ground, the downdraft changes to a horizontal outflow that can extend to approximately 2 1/2 mi. in diameter.

    b. Intensity. The downdrafts can be as strong as 6,000 fpm.

        1) Horizontal winds near the surface can be as strong as 45 kt., resulting in a 90-kt. shear (headwind to tailwind change for a traversing aircraft) across the microburst.

        2) These strong horizontal winds occur within a few hundred feet of the ground.

    c. Visual signs. Microbursts can be found almost anywhere there is convective activity.

        1) They may be embedded in heavy rain associated with a thunderstorm or in light rain in benign-appearing virga.

        2) When there is little or no precipitation at the surface accompanying the microburst, a ring of blowing dust may be the only visual clue of its existence.

    d. Duration. An individual microburst will seldom last longer than 15 min. from the time it strikes the ground until dissipation.

        1) An important consideration for pilots is that the microburst intensifies for about 5 min. after it strikes the ground, with the maximum-intensity winds lasting approximately 2 to 4 min.

        2) Once microburst activity starts, multiple microbursts in the same general area are not uncommon and should be expected.

        3) Sometimes microbursts are concentrated into a line structure, and under these conditions, activity may continue for as long as an hour.

5. Microburst wind shear may create a severe hazard for aircraft within 1,000 ft. of the ground, particularly during the approach to landing and landing and takeoff phases.

    a. The aircraft may encounter a headwind (performance increasing) followed by a downdraft and tailwind (both performance decreasing), possibly resulting in terrain impact.

    b. Figure 13 below illustrates microburst wind shear.

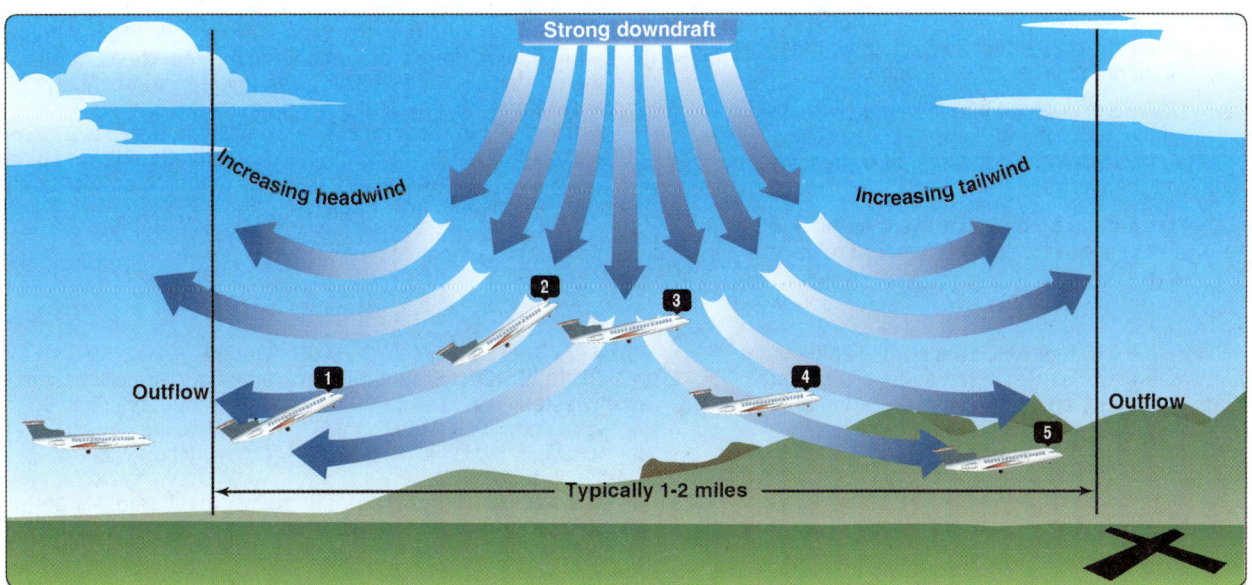

Figure 13. – Microburst Section Chart.

QUESTIONS AND ANSWER EXPLANATIONS: All of the instrument rating knowledge test questions chosen by the FAA for release as well as additional questions selected by Gleim relating to the material in the previous outlines are provided on the following pages. These questions have been organized into the same subunits as the outlines. To the immediate right of each question are the correct answer and answer explanations. You should cover these answers and answer explanations while responding to the questions. Refer to the general discussion in the Introduction on how to take the FAA knowledge test.

Remember that the questions from the FAA knowledge test bank have been reordered by topic and organized into a meaningful sequence. Also, the first line of the answer explanation gives the citation of the authoritative source for the answer.

QUESTIONS

8.1 Causes of Weather

1. The primary cause of all changes in the Earth's weather is

    A. variation of solar energy received by the Earth's regions.

    B. changes in air pressure over the Earth's surface.

    C. movement of the air masses.

Answer (A) is correct. (AC 00-6B Chap 2)
    DISCUSSION: Every physical process of weather is accompanied by, or is the result of, a heat exchange. Unequal solar heating of the Earth's surface causes differences in air pressure, which result in all changes in the Earth's weather.
    Answer (B) is incorrect. Changes in air pressure are a result of varying temperatures. **Answer (C) is incorrect.** Movement of air masses (wind) is a result of varying temperatures and pressures.

2. Which force, in the Northern Hemisphere, acts at a right angle to the wind and deflects it to the right until parallel to the isobars?

    A. Centrifugal.

    B. Pressure gradient.

    C. Coriolis.

Answer (C) is correct. (AC 00-6B Chap 7)
    DISCUSSION: Coriolis force is a result of the Earth's rotation. As the wind moves perpendicular to the isobars (from high to low pressure), it is apparently deflected to the right in the Northern Hemisphere, until it is moving parallel to the isobars. This effect is most pronounced above 2,000 ft. AGL.
    Answer (A) is incorrect. Centrifugal force is a force that acts outwardly on any object moving in a curved path. **Answer (B) is incorrect.** Pressure gradient causes the wind to move perpendicular to the isobars. The wind is then deflected by Coriolis force.

3. What relationship exists between the winds at 2,000 feet above the surface and the surface winds?

    A. The winds at 2,000 feet and the surface winds flow in the same direction, but the surface winds are weaker due to friction.

    B. The winds at 2,000 feet tend to parallel the isobars while the surface winds cross the isobars at an angle toward lower pressure and are weaker.

    C. The surface winds tend to veer to the right of the winds at 2,000 feet and are usually weaker.

Answer (B) is correct. (AC 00-6B Chap 7)
    DISCUSSION: Generally, winds near the surface are weaker than those aloft due to the friction between the Earth's surface and the wind. Also, because they are slower, winds near the surface are less affected by the Coriolis force. The pressure gradient forces are thus stronger near the surface, and the winds cross the isobars at an angle instead of flowing parallel to them.
    Answer (A) is incorrect. The Coriolis force is less at the surface, so surface winds flow in a direction different from those aloft. **Answer (C) is incorrect.** The winds aloft veer to the right of surface winds, not the opposite.

4. Winds at 5,000 feet AGL on a particular flight are southwesterly while most of the surface winds are southerly. This difference in direction is primarily due to

    A. a stronger pressure gradient at higher altitudes.

    B. friction between the wind and the surface.

    C. stronger Coriolis force at the surface.

Answer (B) is correct. (AC 00-6B Chap 7)
    DISCUSSION: Southerly winds at the surface will become southwesterly winds at 5,000 feet because the Coriolis force deflects winds aloft to the right. This force has less effect on surface winds which have been slowed by friction with the Earth's surface.
    Answer (A) is incorrect. The pressure differentials are approximately uniform through the altitudes. **Answer (C) is incorrect.** The Coriolis force at the surface is weaker with slower wind speed.

5. What causes surface winds to flow across the isobars at an angle rather than parallel to the isobars?

  A. Coriolis force.

  B. Surface friction.

  C. The greater density of the air at the surface.

Answer (B) is correct. (AC 00-6B Chap 7)
  DISCUSSION: Generally, winds near the surface are weaker than those aloft due to the friction between the Earth's surface and the wind. Also, because they are slower, winds near the surface are less affected by the Coriolis force. The pressure gradient forces are thus stronger near the surface, and the winds cross the isobars at an angle instead of flowing parallel to them.
  Answer (A) is incorrect. The Coriolis force is directly proportional to wind speed. At higher altitudes (above 2,000 to 3,000 ft. AGL), winds not slowed by surface friction are so deflected by the Coriolis force that they flow parallel to the isobars, not across them. **Answer (C) is incorrect.** The greater air density at the surface has little effect on the relationship of winds to the isobars.

6. An air mass is a body of air that

  A. has similar cloud formations associated with it.

  B. creates a wind shift as it moves across the Earth's surface.

  C. covers an extensive area and has fairly uniform properties of temperature and moisture.

Answer (C) is correct. (AC 00-6B Chap 10)
  DISCUSSION: An air mass is an extensive body of air within which the conditions of temperature and moisture in a horizontal plane are essentially uniformly distributed. Generally, an air mass takes on the properties of the large area it overlies.
  Answer (A) is incorrect. An air mass may have cloud formations or it may be clear and dry. **Answer (B) is incorrect.** Changes in wind, temperature, etc., indicate a frontal zone between two air masses.

7. A characteristic of the stratosphere is

  A. an overall decrease of temperature with an increase in altitude.

  B. a relatively even base altitude of approximately 35,000 feet.

  C. relatively small changes in temperature with an increase in altitude.

Answer (C) is correct. (AC 00-6B Chap 1)
  DISCUSSION: The stratosphere is the atmospheric layer above the tropopause. It is the band of altitude from about 7 to 22 mi. It is characterized by a slight average increase in temperature from base to top and thus is very stable. It also has a low moisture content and an absence of clouds.
  Answer (A) is incorrect. There is a slight increase, not decrease, in temperature with increase in altitude. **Answer (B) is incorrect.** The base of the stratosphere is considerably higher at the equator than at the poles.

8. The average height of the troposphere in the middle latitudes is

  A. 20,000 feet.

  B. 25,000 feet.

  C. 37,000 feet.

Answer (C) is correct. (AC 00-6B Chap 1)
  DISCUSSION: In the mid-latitudes, the average height of the troposphere is about 37,000 ft. It is 25,000 to 30,000 ft. at the poles and 55,000 to 65,000 ft. at the equator. It is generally higher in summer than in winter.
  Answer (A) is incorrect. The average height of the troposphere is 25,000 to 30,000 ft. at the poles, not the mid-latitudes. **Answer (B) is incorrect.** The average height of the troposphere is 25,000 to 30,000 ft. at the poles, not the mid-latitudes.

9. Where do squall lines most often develop?

  A. In an occluded front.

  B. In a cold air mass.

  C. Ahead of a cold front.

Answer (C) is correct. (AC 00-6B Chap 19)
  DISCUSSION: A squall line is a nonfrontal band of active thunderstorms that sometimes develops ahead of a cold front.
  Answer (A) is incorrect. Squall lines are usually associated with a fast-moving cold front. **Answer (B) is incorrect.** They occur ahead of the cold front, not behind the front in the cold air.

10. The strength and location of the jet stream is normally

  A. stronger and farther north in the winter.

  B. weaker and farther north in the summer.

  C. stronger and farther north in the summer.

Answer (B) is correct. (AC 00-6B Chap 8)
  DISCUSSION: In the mid-latitudes, the wind speed in the jet stream averages considerably less in the summer than in the winter. Also, the jet stream shifts farther north in summer than in winter.
  Answer (A) is incorrect. The jet stream is usually farther south, not north, in winter. **Answer (C) is incorrect.** The jet stream is usually weaker, not stronger, in summer.

11. A jet stream is defined as wind of

   A. 30 knots or greater.

   B. 40 knots or greater.

   C. 50 knots or greater.

Answer (C) is correct. (AC 00-6B Chap 8)
   DISCUSSION: The jet stream is a roughly horizontal stream of wind of 50 kt. or more (by definition) concentrated within a narrow band embedded in the westerly winds in the high troposphere. It occurs in an area of intensified pressure gradients. A second or even third jet stream may form at one time, and these may not be continuous.
   Answer (A) is incorrect. A jet stream, by definition, is a wind of 50 kt., not 30 kt., or greater. **Answer (B) is incorrect.** A jet stream, by definition, is a wind of 50 kt., not 40 kt., or greater.

12. Which feature is associated with the tropopause?

   A. Absence of wind and turbulent conditions.

   B. Absolute upper limit of cloud formation.

   C. Abrupt change in temperature lapse rate.

Answer (C) is correct. (AC 00-6B Chap 8)
   DISCUSSION: The tropopause is the transition layer of atmosphere between the troposphere (surface to about 7 to 22 mi.) and the stratosphere. A characteristic of the tropopause is that there is an abrupt change in the temperature lapse rate, i.e., the rate at which temperature decreases with height.
   Answer (A) is incorrect. There are usually very strong winds in the tropopause. These create narrow zones of wind shear, which may generate hazardous turbulence. **Answer (B) is incorrect.** Clouds may form above the tropopause even though there is little moisture in the stratosphere.

13. Which weather phenomenon is always associated with the passage of a frontal system?

   A. A wind change.

   B. An abrupt decrease in pressure.

   C. Clouds, either ahead or behind the front.

Answer (A) is correct. (AC 00-6B Chap 10)
   DISCUSSION: Whenever a front passes, a wind shift will always occur. This discontinuity may be in direction, speed, or both.
   Answer (B) is incorrect. The pressure and/or temperature may not change significantly as a weak front passes. **Answer (C) is incorrect.** Some fronts do not contain enough moisture to produce clouds. Therefore, clouds are not always associated with a frontal system.

14. Which is a characteristic of low-level wind shear as it relates to frontal activity?

   A. With a warm front, the most critical period is before the front passes the airport.

   B. With a cold front, the most critical period is just before the front passes the airport.

   C. Turbulence will always exist in wind-shear conditions.

Answer (A) is correct. (FAA-H-8083-25B Chap 12)
   DISCUSSION: Wind shear associated with a warm front occurs above an airport before the front passes the airport. A warm front is warmer air overtaking colder air.
   Answer (B) is incorrect. Cold front wind shear occurs just as or just after the front passes rather than before it passes. **Answer (C) is incorrect.** Wind shear can sometimes occur with no forewarning from turbulence.

15. Frontal waves normally form on

   A. slow moving cold fronts or stationary fronts.

   B. slow moving warm fronts and strong occluded fronts.

   C. rapidly moving cold fronts or warm fronts.

Answer (A) is correct. (AC 00-6B Chap 10)
   DISCUSSION: Frontal waves and cyclones (areas of low pressure) usually form in slow-moving cold fronts or in stationary fronts.
   Answer (B) is incorrect. Frontal waves are usually not associated with warm fronts or occluded fronts. **Answer (C) is incorrect.** Frontal waves usually form on slow-moving, not rapidly moving, cold fronts and not on warm fronts.

16. When compared to winds at the surface, winds at 2,000 feet are

   A. higher due to absence of friction.

   B. higher and go at right angles to the isobars due to friction.

   C. higher because they move from an area of higher pressure to lower pressure.

Answer (A) is correct. (AC 00-6B Chap 7)
   DISCUSSION: Friction between the wind and the terrain surface slows the wind. The rougher the terrain, the greater the frictional effect.
   Answer (B) is incorrect. Although the winds are higher at 2,000 ft. than they are at the surface, friction does not cause them to cross the isobars at right angles. It is the pressure gradient that forces the winds to cross the isobars in search of lower pressure. **Answer (C) is incorrect.** Although the winds at altitude are higher and do seek lower pressure, it is the action of friction at the surface that slows the winds at the surface. The rougher the terrain, the greater the frictional effect.

8.2 Stability of Air Masses

17. Which are characteristics of an unstable cold air mass moving over a warm surface?

    A. Cumuliform clouds, turbulence, and poor visibility.

    B. Cumuliform clouds, turbulence, and good visibility.

    C. Stratiform clouds, smooth air, and poor visibility.

Answer (B) is correct. *(FAA-H-8083-25B Chap 12)*
    DISCUSSION: When a cold air mass moves over a warm surface, the warm air near the surface rises and creates an unstable situation. These convective currents give rise to cumuliform clouds, turbulence, and good visibility.
    Answer (A) is incorrect. Unstable air lifts and blows haze away, resulting in good, not poor, visibility. **Answer (C) is incorrect.** Unstable conditions produce cumuliform rather than stratiform clouds. Also, the air is turbulent, and visibility is good.

18. What are the characteristics of stable air?

    A. Good visibility, steady precipitation, and stratus-type clouds.

    B. Poor visibility, intermittent precipitation, and cumulus-type clouds.

    C. Poor visibility, steady precipitation, and stratus-type clouds.

Answer (C) is correct. *(FAA-H-8083-25B Chap 12)*
    DISCUSSION: Stable air is air that is still or moving horizontally but not vertically. As a result, the pollutants hang in the air and visibility is poor. Also, stable air forms stratus-type clouds since the air is moving in layers. Relatedly, precipitation spreads out over a wide area and is relatively steady.
    Answer (A) is incorrect. The visibility is poor rather than good in stable air. **Answer (B) is incorrect.** The precipitation is steady, and the clouds are stratiform.

19. What type clouds can be expected when an unstable air mass is forced to ascend a mountain slope?

    A. Layered clouds with little vertical development.

    B. Stratified clouds with considerable associated turbulence.

    C. Clouds with extensive vertical development.

Answer (C) is correct. *(FAA-H-8083-25B Chap 12)*
    DISCUSSION: Unstable air has a greater lapse rate. Because the air above is much colder than the air below, the lower (warmer) air tends to rise very easily. When an unstable air mass is forced to ascend up a mountain slope, it will probably continue to ascend beyond the mountain slope. Once the air expands and cools to the dew point, cumulus clouds will form with considerable vertical development. Any unstable air mass movement will usually result in turbulence as well.
    Answer (A) is incorrect. Layered clouds are associated with stable air. **Answer (B) is incorrect.** Stratified clouds are associated with stable air and no turbulence.

20. Which is a characteristic of stable air?

    A. Fair weather cumulus clouds.

    B. Stratiform clouds.

    C. Unlimited visibility.

Answer (B) is correct. *(FAA-H-8083-25B Chap 12)*
    DISCUSSION: Stratiform clouds, i.e., layer-type clouds, characteristically form in stable air. A stable atmosphere resists any upward or downward displacement, so clouds tend to lie horizontally instead of developing vertically.
    Answer (A) is incorrect. Cumulus clouds indicate unstable conditions. **Answer (C) is incorrect.** Restricted, not unlimited, visibility near the ground is an indication of stable air.

21. The general characteristics of unstable air are

    A. good visibility, showery precipitation, and cumuliform-type clouds.

    B. good visibility, steady precipitation, and stratiform-type clouds.

    C. poor visibility, intermittent precipitation, and cumuliform-type clouds.

Answer (A) is correct. *(FAA-H-8083-25B Chap 12)*
    DISCUSSION: Unstable air is moving vertically and usually produces cumulus clouds. The precipitation from cumulus clouds is showery. The lifting associated with unstable air generally clears smoke and other pollution away; thus, visibility is relatively good.
    Answer (B) is incorrect. Unstable air generally has showery, not steady, precipitation and cumulus, not stratiform, clouds. **Answer (C) is incorrect.** Unstable air generally has good, not poor, visibility.

22. What type of clouds will be formed if very stable moist air is forced up slope?

    A. First stratified clouds and then vertical clouds.

    B. Vertical clouds with increasing height.

    C. Stratified clouds with little vertical development.

Answer (C) is correct. *(FAA-H-8083-25B Chap 12)*
    DISCUSSION: Even when being forced up slope, stable air forms stratus-type clouds. This is because the air resists any further upward movement.
    Answer (A) is incorrect. There would be vertical clouds if the air were unstable rather than stable. **Answer (B) is incorrect.** There would be vertical clouds if the air were unstable rather than stable.

23. Steady precipitation, in contrast to showers, preceding a front is an indication of

    A. stratiform clouds with moderate turbulence.

    B. cumuliform clouds with little or no turbulence.

    C. stratiform clouds with little or no turbulence.

Answer (C) is correct. (FAA-H-8083-25B Chap 12)
    DISCUSSION: Steady precipitation is a characteristic of stable air because of its lack of lifting action. Also characteristic are stratiform clouds with relatively little turbulence.
    Answer (A) is incorrect. Stable air has little or no turbulence. **Answer (B) is incorrect.** Stratiform rather than cumuliform clouds form in stable air.

24. What enhances the growth rate of precipitation?

    A. Advective action.

    B. Upward currents.

    C. Cyclonic movement.

Answer (B) is correct. (AC 00-6B Chap 14)
    DISCUSSION: The growth rate of precipitation is enhanced by upward currents, which carry moisture particles to cooler levels. The particles grow in size and weight (due to condensation) until the atmosphere can no longer hold them (saturation point) and they fall as precipitation.
    Answer (A) is incorrect. Advective action usually refers to the horizontal transport of atmospheric properties by wind, such as warm advection (warm land air moving out over colder water). **Answer (C) is incorrect.** Cyclonic movement refers to the counterclockwise movement around a low-pressure area.

25. Which of the following combinations of weather producing variables would likely result in cumuliform-type clouds, good visibility, rain showers, and possible clear-type icing in clouds?

    A. Unstable, moist air, and no lifting mechanism.

    B. Stable, dry air, and orographic lifting.

    C. Unstable, moist air, and orographic lifting.

Answer (C) is correct. (FAA-H-8083-25B Chap 12)
    DISCUSSION: Cumuliform clouds, good visibility, and showery rain are produced as unstable, moist air is lifted into higher, cooler regions. When the lifting is the result of movement over terrain (e.g., up a mountain slope), it is called orographic lifting. Clear icing is formed from large drops, such as those found in cumuliform clouds.
    Answer (A) is incorrect. Without a lifting mechanism, there would be no vertical development of clouds to result in showery rain and icing in clouds. **Answer (B) is incorrect.** Stable conditions result in stratiform rather than cumuliform clouds, and dry air does not result in showery rain or icing even when lifted.

26. What determines the structure or type of clouds which form as a result of air being forced to ascend?

    A. The method by which the air is lifted.

    B. The stability of the air before lifting occurs.

    C. The amount of condensation nuclei present after lifting occurs.

Answer (B) is correct. (FAA-H-8083-25B Chap 12)
    DISCUSSION: The structure of clouds is determined by the stability of the air before it is lifted. If unstable, the clouds will have vertical development. If stable, the clouds will be horizontal, i.e., stratiform.
    Answer (A) is incorrect. The stability of the air, not the lifting mechanism, determines the type of cloud formations. **Answer (C) is incorrect.** Condensation nuclei encourage the formation of rain droplets or ice but have no effect on the type of cloud formations.

27. Stability can be determined from which measurement of the atmosphere?

    A. Low-level winds.

    B. Ambient lapse rate.

    C. Atmospheric pressure.

Answer (B) is correct. (AC 00-6B Chap 12)
    DISCUSSION: The ambient lapse rate is the actual rate of decrease in temperature with height. A great decrease in temperature as altitude increases encourages warm air from below to rise and creates an unstable air mass. Lifting is inhibited by lesser or very small temperature decreases with altitude (i.e., a low lapse rate).
    Answer (A) is incorrect. Stability refers to vertical air movement, not horizontal air movement. **Answer (C) is incorrect.** Atmospheric pressure is a measure of the weight or downward force of air and does not affect air stability.

28. What are some characteristics of unstable air?

   A. Nimbostratus clouds and good surface visibility.

   B. Turbulence and poor surface visibility.

   C. Turbulence and good surface visibility.

Answer (C) is correct. (FAA-H-8083-25B Chap 12)
    DISCUSSION: The lifting tendency of unstable air creates turbulence and clears the surface air of clouds, dust, and other pollution.
    Answer (A) is incorrect. Stratus clouds are characteristic of stable, not unstable, air. **Answer (B) is incorrect.** Poor surface visibility is a characteristic of stable, not unstable, air.

29. Unsaturated air flowing up slope will cool at the rate of approximately (dry adiabatic lapse rate)

   A. 3°C per 1,000 feet.

   B. 2°C per 1,000 feet.

   C. 2.5°C per 1,000 feet.

Answer (A) is correct. (AC 00-6B Chap 6)
    DISCUSSION: The dry adiabatic lapse rate signifies a prescribed rate of expansional cooling or compressional heating. The dry adiabatic rate is 3°C for each 1,000 feet. Note that this rate differs from the average normal lapse rate of 2°C for each 1,000 feet of altitude. The average lapse rate does NOT occur in dry air, but rather in air with "average" humidity.
    Answer (B) is incorrect. This amount is the standard lapse rate in stable air. **Answer (C) is incorrect.** This amount is the rate at which the temperature and dew point converge in a convective current of unsaturated air.

30. What are the characteristics of an unstable atmosphere?

   A. A cool, dry air mass.

   B. A warm, humid air mass.

   C. Descending air in the northern hemisphere.

Answer (B) is correct. (FAA-H-8083-25B Chap 12)
    DISCUSSION: The stability of the atmosphere depends on its ability to resist vertical motion. As air temperature and air moisture increase, the density of the air decreases, causing it to rise. This creates an unstable atmosphere in which small vertical air movements tend to become larger, resulting in turbulent airflow and convective activity.
    Answer (A) is incorrect. When air is cool, it resists rising, resulting in stability. **Answer (C) is incorrect.** The characteristics of a stable atmosphere do not change whether you are in the northern or southern hemisphere.

31. Clouds with extensive vertical development over mountainous terrain are a sign of

   A. a dry adiabatic lapse rate.

   B. a stable air mass.

   C. an unstable air mass.

Answer (C) is correct. (AC 00-6B)
    DISCUSSION: Winds across mountains cause mountain waves that are associated with severe turbulence, strong vertical currents, and icing. The extent of the turbulence is relative to the height of the ground, speed of the wind, and instability of the atmosphere. With adequate moisture, lenticular clouds will form at the top of each wave.
    Answer (A) is incorrect. The dry adiabatic lapse rate is a measurement of air with no moisture available to form clouds. **Answer (B) is incorrect.** The vertical development of the clouds indicates the presence of multiple waves with adequate upward motion and moisture to cause cloud formation.

32. The stability of an air mass can usually be determined by

   A. the height of the tropopause.

   B. measuring the dry adiabatic lapse rate.

   C. cloud types and the type of precipitation.

Answer (C) is correct. (FAA-H-8083-25B Chap 12)
    DISCUSSION: Atmospheric stability influences weather by affecting the vertical motion of air. Stable air suppresses vertical motion, but unstable air enhances it. Clouds formed in stable air will be shallow and layered, e.g., stratus clouds. Clouds formed in unstable air will have more height and be of the cumulus or cumulonimbus type. Precipitation from stratus clouds tends to be over large areas and lasts for long periods. Precipitation from cumulus clouds tends to be more intense and lasts for short periods.
    Answer (A) is incorrect. The tropopause is a thin boundary area between the troposphere and the stratosphere. The height of the tropopause varies widely due to the location above the earth and the time of the year and is not necessarily indicative of air mass stability. **Answer (B) is incorrect.** Stability is determined by the change in the ambient lapse rate, not the dry lapse rate.

8.3   Temperature Inversions

33. What feature is associated with a temperature inversion?

    A. A stable layer of air.

    B. An unstable layer of air.

    C. Air mass thunderstorms.

Answer (A) is correct. (FAA-H-8083-25B Chap 12)
    DISCUSSION: A temperature inversion is defined as an increase in temperature with height; i.e., the lapse rate is less than standard. The cooler air stays near the surface, and there is little or no vertical movement.
    Answer (B) is incorrect. Instability occurs when the temperature decreases, not increases as in a temperature inversion, with an increase in height, and the warmer air continues to rise. **Answer (C) is incorrect.** Air mass thunderstorms result from instability. They do not occur when there is a temperature inversion.

34. Which weather conditions should be expected beneath a low-level temperature inversion layer when the relative humidity is high?

    A. Smooth air and poor visibility due to fog, haze, or low clouds.

    B. Light wind shear and poor visibility due to haze and light rain.

    C. Turbulent air and poor visibility due to fog, low stratus-type clouds, and showery precipitation.

Answer (A) is correct. (FAA-H-8083-25B Chap 12)
    DISCUSSION: A temperature inversion is an increase in temperature as altitude increases; normally temperature decreases with increases in altitude. In an inversion, warm air rises to its own temperature and forms a stable layer of air. A low-level inversion results in poor visibility by trapping fog, smoke, dust, etc., in low levels of the atmosphere.
    Answer (B) is incorrect. Wind shear may be expected within, not beneath, a low-level temperature inversion.
Answer (C) is incorrect. An inversion forms a stable layer of air, thus making it smooth, not turbulent, and causing steady, not showery, precipitation.

35. A common type of ground or surface based temperature inversion is that which is produced by

    A. warm air being lifted rapidly aloft in the vicinity of mountainous terrain.

    B. the movement of colder air over warm air, or the movement of warm air under cold air.

    C. ground radiation on clear, cool nights when the wind is light.

Answer (C) is correct. (AC 00-6B Chap 17)
    DISCUSSION: A temperature inversion means the temperature becomes warmer rather than cooler with increases in altitude. A ground- or surface-based temperature inversion is produced when the air near the surface is cooled faster than the overlying air as a result of radiation of heat on a clear, still night. The air very close to the surface is thus cooler than the air a few hundred feet above.
    Answer (A) is incorrect. When warm air is lifted, unstable, not stable, air is the result. **Answer (B) is incorrect.** A temperature inversion consists of warm air over colder air, not colder over warm.

36. A temperature inversion will normally form only

    A. in stable air.

    B. in unstable air.

    C. when a stratiform layer merges with a cumuliform mass.

Answer (A) is correct. (FAA-H-8083-25B Chap 12)
    DISCUSSION: In a temperature inversion, warm air overlies colder air; i.e., the lapse rate is inverted. By definition, this is a stable condition since there is no lifting action.
    Answer (B) is incorrect. Unstable air has colder air above warm air. **Answer (C) is incorrect.** A merger of stratus and cumulus clouds is associated with an occluded front, not necessarily a temperature inversion.

37. An increase in temperature with an altitude increase

    A. is indication of an inversion.

    B. denotes the beginning of the stratosphere.

    C. means a cold front passage.

Answer (A) is correct. (FAA-H-8083-25B Chap 12)
    DISCUSSION: Normally, as air rises and expands in the atmosphere, the temperature decreases. However, when the temperature of the air rises with altitude, this indicates that a temperature inversion exists.
    Answer (B) is incorrect. Although the temperature does begin to increase in the stratosphere, only specialized aircraft are likely to be able to operate high enough to see this change.
Answer (C) is incorrect. A cold front passage does not always cause the temperature to increase with altitude. If it did, this would be an indication of an inversion.

38. Temperature and radiation variations over land with a clear sky typically lead to

A. minimum temperature occurring after sunrise.

B. outgoing terrestrial radiation peaking at noon.

C. temperature reaching a maximum closer to noon than to sunset.

Answer (A) is correct. (AC 00-6B)
   DISCUSSION: At night, heating is absent, but terrestrial radiation continues cooling the earth's surface. Cooling continues until shortly after sunrise, when incoming solar radiation once again exceeds outgoing terrestrial radiation. Minimum surface air temperature usually occurs shortly after sunrise.
   Answer (B) is incorrect. Outgoing radiation peaks during the nighttime when no isolation occurs. **Answer (C) is incorrect.** Peak isolation occurs around noon, but maximum surface air temperature occurs during mid-afternoon.

8.4 Temperature, Dew Point, and Fog

39. Which conditions are favorable for the formation of radiation fog?

A. Moist air moving over colder ground or water.

B. Cloudy sky and a light wind moving saturated warm air over a cool surface.

C. Clear sky, little or no wind, small temperature/dew point spread, and over a land surface.

Answer (C) is correct. (AC 00-6B Chap 16)
   DISCUSSION: Conditions favorable for radiation fog are a clear sky, little or no wind, and a small temperature-dew point spread. The fog forms as terrestrial radiation cools the ground. The air near the ground is cooled to dew point, and fog forms.
   Answer (A) is incorrect. Advection fog, not radiation fog, forms when moist air moves over colder ground or water. The sky may be cloudy over advection fog. **Answer (B) is incorrect.** Advection fog, not radiation fog, forms when moist air moves over colder ground or water. The sky may be cloudy over advection fog.

40. What situation is most conducive to the formation of radiation fog?

A. Warm, moist air over low, flatland areas on clear, calm nights.

B. Moist, tropical air moving over cold, offshore water.

C. The movement of cold air over much warmer water.

Answer (A) is correct. (AC 00-6B Chap 16)
   DISCUSSION: Conditions favorable for radiation fog are a clear sky, little or no wind, and a small temperature-dew point spread. The fog forms as terrestrial radiation cools the ground. The air close to the surface cools more quickly than the slightly higher air. The air near the ground is cooled to dew point, and fog forms.
   Answer (B) is incorrect. Advection fog forms as a result of warm air moving over a colder surface. **Answer (C) is incorrect.** Steam fog forms when cold air moves over a warmer surface.

41. The most frequent type of ground- or surface-based temperature inversion is that produced by

A. radiation on a clear, relatively still night.

B. warm air being lifted rapidly aloft in the vicinity of mountainous terrain.

C. the movement of colder air under warm air, or the movement of warm air over cold air.

Answer (A) is correct. (FAA-H-8083-25B Chap 12)
   DISCUSSION: An inversion often develops near the ground on clear, cool nights when the wind is light. The ground radiates heat and cools much faster than the overlying air. Air in contact with the ground becomes cold, while the temperature a few hundred feet above changes very little. Thus, temperature increases with height.
   Answer (B) is incorrect. It describes orographic lifting. **Answer (C) is incorrect.** It describes a cold front and a warm front, respectively.

42. What types of fog depend upon a wind in order to exist?

A. Steam fog and down slope fog.

B. Precipitation-induced fog and ground fog.

C. Advection fog and up slope fog.

Answer (C) is correct. (AC 00-6B Chap 16)
   DISCUSSION: Up slope fog forms as a result of moist, stable air being cooled as it moves up a sloping terrain. Advection fog forms when moist air is blown over a cold surface, decreasing the moist air's temperature to its dew point. Thus, both up slope fog and advection fog depend on air moving from one area to another; i.e., they depend on wind.
   Answer (A) is incorrect. Down slope fog is a nonsense term. **Answer (B) is incorrect.** Precipitation fog forms when warm rain or drizzle falls through cool air, and ground fog requires little or no wind.

43. Which weather condition can be expected when moist air flows from a relatively warm surface to a colder surface?

    A. Increased visibility.

    B. Convective turbulence due to surface heating.

    C. Fog.

Answer (C) is correct. (FAA-H-8083-25B Chap 12)
    DISCUSSION: When moist air flows from a relatively warm surface to a colder surface, the warm, moist air is cooled to its dew point, and advection fog is produced.
    Answer (A) is incorrect. Fog forms, which decreases, not increases, visibility. **Answer (B) is incorrect.** The surface cools the air, resulting in stable air with little or no convective turbulence.

44. Fog is usually prevalent in industrial areas because of

    A. atmospheric stabilization around cities.

    B. an abundance of condensation nuclei from combustion products.

    C. increased temperatures due to industrial heating.

Answer (B) is correct. (FAA-H-8083-25B Chap 12)
    DISCUSSION: Fog often forms in industrial areas because the combustion products leave dust in the air on which water can condense. These particles are called condensation nuclei.
    Answer (A) is incorrect. Cities, per se, have no effect on air stability. **Answer (C) is incorrect.** The amount of heat that factories release into the air is not significant in the formation of fog.

45. In what localities is advection fog most likely to occur?

    A. Coastal areas.

    B. Mountain slopes.

    C. Level inland areas.

Answer (A) is correct. (AC 00-6B Chap 16)
    DISCUSSION: Advection fog forms when moist air moves over colder ground or water. This type of fog is thus most common along coastal areas. During the winter, advection fog over the central and eastern United States results when moist air from the Gulf of Mexico spreads northward over cold ground.
    Answer (B) is incorrect. Mountain slopes are required for up slope, not advection, fog. **Answer (C) is incorrect.** Level inland areas will most likely produce radiation, not advection, fog.

46. In which situation is advection fog most likely to form?

    A. An air mass moving inland from the coast in winter.

    B. A light breeze blowing colder air out to sea.

    C. Warm, moist air settling over a warmer surface under no-wind conditions.

Answer (A) is correct. (AC 00-6B Chap 16)
    DISCUSSION: Advection fog forms when moist air moves over colder ground or water. This type of fog is most likely to form when an air mass moves from the warmer water inland from the coast in winter. As the air moves over the cooler land, it cools to the dew point and forms advection fog.
    Answer (B) is incorrect. Colder air blowing out to sea results in steam, not advection, fog. **Answer (C) is incorrect.** Warm, moist air settling over a warmer surface would not cool, so fog would not form.

47. Under which condition does advection fog usually form?

    A. Moist air moving over colder ground or water.

    B. Warm, moist air settling over a cool surface under no-wind conditions.

    C. A land breeze blowing a cold air mass over a warm water current.

Answer (A) is correct. (AC 00-6B Chap 16)
    DISCUSSION: Advection fog forms when moist air moves over colder ground or water. The moist air is cooled to the dew point, and fog forms.
    Answer (B) is incorrect. Radiation fog, not advection fog, forms when warm, moist air settles over a cool surface under no-wind conditions. **Answer (C) is incorrect.** Steam fog, not advection fog, forms when a land breeze blows a cold air mass over a warm water current.

48. The amount of water vapor which air can hold largely depends on

A. relative humidity.

B. air temperature.

C. stability of air.

Answer (B) is correct. (AC 00-6B Chap 3)
   DISCUSSION: Air temperature largely determines how much water vapor can be held by the air. Warm air, which is less dense, can hold more water vapor than cold air.
   Answer (A) is incorrect. Relative humidity is the ratio of the existing amount of water vapor in the air at a given temperature to the maximum amount that could be held at that temperature. **Answer (C) is incorrect.** Air stability is related to the temperature lapse rate, not moisture.

49. To which meteorological condition does the term "dew point" refer?

A. The temperature to which air must be cooled to become saturated.

B. The temperature at which condensation and evaporation are equal.

C. The temperature at which dew will always form.

Answer (A) is correct. (AC 00-6B Chap 3)
   DISCUSSION: Dew point refers to the temperature to which air must be cooled to become saturated by the water vapor in the air. Dew point, when related to air temperature in aviation weather reports, reveals how close the air is to saturation and possible cloud, fog, or precipitation formation.
   Answer (B) is incorrect. Condensation (vapor to water) occurs at low temperatures, and evaporation (water to vapor) occurs at high temperatures. **Answer (C) is incorrect.** The formation of dew depends on relative humidity and the temperature of the collecting surface.

50. Clouds, fog, or dew will always form when

A. water vapor condenses.

B. water vapor is present.

C. the temperature and dew point are equal.

Answer (A) is correct. (AC 00-6B Chap 3)
   DISCUSSION: As water vapor condenses, it becomes visible as clouds, fog, or dew.
   Answer (B) is incorrect. Some water vapor is usually present, but it does not necessarily form clouds, fog, or dew. **Answer (C) is incorrect.** Even at 100% humidity (when the dew point equals actual temperature), water vapor may not condense if sufficient condensation nuclei are not present.

51. Which conditions result in the formation of frost?

A. The temperature of the collecting surface is at or below freezing and small droplets of moisture are falling.

B. When dew forms and the temperature is below freezing.

C. Temperature of the collecting surface is below the dew point of surrounding air and the dew point is colder than freezing.

Answer (C) is correct. (FAA-H-8083-25B Chap 12)
   DISCUSSION: If the air temperature drops below the dew point, the air becomes more dense and can no longer hold the water vapor. The water vapor will condense to form visible moisture. Frost will form only if the temperature of the collecting surfaces is below the dew point of the surrounding air AND the dew point is below freezing.
   Answer (A) is incorrect. The dew point must also be below freezing and droplets of moisture are not necessary. **Answer (B) is incorrect.** The formation of dew is not required. The dew point of surrounding air must be below freezing, and the temperature of the collecting surface must be less than the dew point.

52. Penetrating fog while flying an approach at night, you might experience the illusion of

A. pitching up.

B. flying at a lower altitude.

C. constant turning.

Answer (A) is correct. (AIM Para 8-1-5)
   DISCUSSION: Refractory effects can cause the perception of a nose high attitude.
   Answer (B) is incorrect. This results from the illusion of being farther away from the runway; thus, the pilot responds by flying a lower approach. **Answer (C) is incorrect.** This illusion is primarily perceived during and after motion disturbances leading to spatial disorientation.

8.5 Clouds

53. What are the four families of clouds?

A. Stratus, cumulus, nimbus, and cirrus.

B. Clouds formed by updrafts, fronts, cooling layers of air, and precipitation into warm air.

C. High, middle, low, and those with extensive vertical development.

Answer (C) is correct. (FAA-H-8083-25B Chap 12)
DISCUSSION: For identification purposes, clouds are divided into four "families" based on their height range. The families are high clouds, middle clouds, low clouds, and clouds with extensive vertical development.
Answer (A) is incorrect. It describes cloud formation and characteristic. **Answer (B) is incorrect.** It describes the way various clouds are formed.

54. Which family of clouds is least likely to contribute to structural icing on an aircraft?

A. Low clouds.

B. High clouds.

C. Clouds with extensive vertical development.

Answer (B) is correct. (AC 00-6B Chaps 13, 18)
DISCUSSION: High clouds are least likely to contribute to structural icing since they usually consist entirely of ice crystals. Since ice is already frozen, it will not freeze onto the structural surface of the airplane.
Answer (A) is incorrect. Low clouds can contain supercooled water, which freezes on contact with the airplane. **Answer (C) is incorrect.** Clouds with extensive vertical development can contain supercooled water, which freezes on contact with the airplane.

55. The presence of standing lenticular altocumulus clouds is a good indication of

A. a jetstream.

B. very strong turbulence.

C. heavy icing conditions.

Answer (B) is correct. (AC 00-6B Chaps 13, 17)
DISCUSSION: When stable air crosses a mountain barrier, it tends to flow in layers. The barrier may set up waves in these layers, which remain stationary while the wind blows rapidly through them. Wave crests extend well above the highest mountain tops. Under each wave crest is a rotary circulation, which can create very violent turbulence. Crests of the standing waves may be marked by stationary lens-shaped clouds known as standing lenticular clouds.
Answer (A) is incorrect. The jet stream flows around the world at high altitudes and at varying latitudes. **Answer (C) is incorrect.** Standing lenticular clouds occur at varying temperatures, not only below freezing.

56. Standing lenticular clouds, in mountainous areas, indicate

A. an inversion.

B. unstable air.

C. turbulence.

Answer (C) is correct. (AC 00-6B Chaps 13, 17)
DISCUSSION: The "waves" generated as wind flows across a mountain barrier may form standing lenticular clouds at the crest of each wave. Their presence indicates very strong turbulence, and they should be avoided.
Answer (A) is incorrect. Stratus, not standing lenticular, clouds indicate stable air which may be the result of a temperature inversion. **Answer (B) is incorrect.** Cumulus, not standing lenticular, clouds indicate unstable air.

57. The suffix "nimbus", used in naming clouds, means a

A. cloud with extensive vertical development.

B. rain cloud.

C. dark massive, towering cloud.

Answer (B) is correct. (AC 00-6B Chap 13)
DISCUSSION: The prefix "nimbo" or the suffix "nimbus" means raincloud. For example, stratified clouds from which rain is falling are called nimbostratus clouds. A heavy, swelling, cumulus-type cloud which produces precipitation is called a cumulonimbus cloud.
Answer (A) is incorrect. The prefix "cumulo," not the suffix "nimbus," denotes a cloud with extensive vertical development. **Answer (C) is incorrect.** It specifies a cumulonimbus cloud, not any nimbus cloud.

58. A high cloud is composed mostly of

A. ozone.

B. condensation nuclei.

C. ice crystals.

Answer (C) is correct. (FAA-H-8083-25B Chap 12)
DISCUSSION: The high cloud family is cirriform. It includes cirrus, cirrocumulus, and cirrostratus clouds. They are composed almost entirely of ice crystals. Their bases range from 16,500 ft. to 45,000 ft.
Answer (A) is incorrect. Ozone is an unstable form of oxygen. The heaviest concentrations are in the stratosphere, not in clouds. **Answer (B) is incorrect.** Condensation nuclei are the small particles in the air onto which water vapor condenses or deposits.

59. Which clouds have the greatest turbulence?

A. Towering cumulus.

B. Cumulonimbus.

C. Altocumulus castellanus.

Answer (B) is correct. (FAA-H-8083-25B Chap 12)
DISCUSSION: Cumulonimbus clouds are thunderstorms and the ultimate manifestation of instability. They are huge vertically developed clouds with dense, billowy tops often crowned with thick veils of dense cirrus, called the "anvil." Nearly the entire spectrum of flying hazards is contained in these clouds, including violent turbulence.
Answer (A) is incorrect. Towering cumulus clouds are only a preliminary stage of the cumulonimbus cloud. **Answer (C) is incorrect.** Altocumulus castellanus is a middle-level convective cloud which indicates rough turbulence with some icing, but thunderstorms are far more turbulent.

60. Fair weather cumulus clouds often indicate

A. turbulence at and below the cloud level.

B. poor visibility.

C. smooth flying conditions.

Answer (A) is correct. (FAA-H-8083-25B Chap 12)
DISCUSSION: Fair weather cumulus clouds form in convective currents and are characterized by relatively flat bases and dome-shaped tops. They indicate a shallow layer of instability, some turbulence, and no significant icing.
Answer (B) is incorrect. The instability producing the cumulus clouds provides good, not poor, visibility. **Answer (C) is incorrect.** The instability producing the cumulus clouds creates some turbulence, not smooth conditions.

8.6 Thunderstorms

61. When is an airplane most likely to be struck by lightning?

A. OAT greater than 0°C.

B. Independent of OAT.

C. OAT between −5°C and +5°C.

Answer (C) is correct. (AIM Para 7-1-25)
DISCUSSION: The greatest probability of a lightning strike occurs when flying with an outside air temperature (OAT) of between −5°C and +5°C. Lightning strikes with aircraft are extremely rare but can occur whenever you operate near a thunderstorm, even if you are in the clear.
Answer (A) is incorrect. The probability of a lightning strike is the greatest with an OAT of between −5°C and +5°C. **Answer (B) is incorrect.** The probability of a lightning strike does increase in a specific OAT range (−5°C and +5°C).

62. If squalls are reported at your destination, what wind conditions should you anticipate?

A. Sudden increases in wind speed of at least 16 knots rising to 22 knots or more, lasting for at least 1 minute.

B. Peak gusts of at least 35 knots for a sustained period of 1 minute or longer.

C. Rapid variation in wind direction of at least 20° and changes in speed of at least 10 knots between peaks and lulls.

Answer (A) is correct. (NOAA Glossary)
DISCUSSION: A squall is a sudden increase in wind speed by at least 16 knots, rising to 22 knots or more, and lasting for at least 1 minute. In contrast, a wind gust is a brief increase in wind with a variation between peaks and lulls of at least 10 knots. Note that these definitions involve variations in wind speed, not wind direction.
Answer (B) is incorrect. A squall is a sudden increase in wind speed of at least 16 knots, rising to a peak of 22 knots or more, not a peak gust of at least 35 knots lasting for at least 1 minute. **Answer (C) is incorrect.** Squalls refer to changes in wind speed, not direction. Additionally, the wind is reported as gusty when there are changes in speed of at least 10 knots between peaks and lulls.

63. What is an indication that downdrafts have developed and the thunderstorm cell has entered the mature stage?

    A. The anvil top has completed its development.

    B. Precipitation begins to fall from the cloud base.

    C. A gust front forms.

Answer (B) is correct. (AC 00-6B Chap 19)
    DISCUSSION: The mature stage of a thunderstorm is signaled when rain begins falling at the surface. This means that the downdrafts have developed sufficiently to carry water all the way through the thunderstorm.
    Answer (A) is incorrect. An anvil top does not necessarily develop over every thunderstorm. **Answer (C) is incorrect.** Gust front is a nonsense term.

64. Which procedure is recommended if a pilot should unintentionally penetrate embedded thunderstorm activity?

    A. Reverse aircraft heading or proceed toward an area of known VFR conditions.

    B. Reduce airspeed to maneuvering speed and maintain a constant altitude.

    C. Set power for recommended turbulence penetration airspeed and attempt to maintain a level flight attitude.

Answer (C) is correct. (FAA-H-8083-25B Chap 5)
    DISCUSSION: If a thunderstorm is penetrated, you should always attempt to maintain a constant attitude at or below the maneuvering or turbulence penetration speed recommended for the airplane. Note that the airspeed cannot always be kept constant, but the power can be set so that you will be operating generally at or below the maneuvering speed.
    Answer (A) is incorrect. A straight course will probably take you out of the storm most quickly. Also, turning maneuvers increase stresses on the aircraft. **Answer (B) is incorrect.** Maintaining a constant airspeed (V_A) in updrafts and downdrafts may be impossible. It is best to set power so you will operate at or below V_A. Also, attempting to maintain constant altitude, not attitude, increases the stress on the airplane.

65. Which thunderstorms generally produce the most severe conditions, such as heavy hail and destructive winds?

    A. Warm front.

    B. Squall line.

    C. Air mass.

Answer (B) is correct. (FAA-H-8083-25B Chap 12)
    DISCUSSION: A squall line is a nonfrontal narrow band of active thunderstorms. It often contains severe, steady-state thunderstorms and presents the single most intense weather hazard to airplanes.
    Answer (A) is incorrect. Warm fronts indicate stable air, which does not usually produce thunderstorms. **Answer (C) is incorrect.** An air mass thunderstorm is the least severe type of thunderstorm.

66. Which weather phenomenon is always associated with a thunderstorm?

    A. Lightning.

    B. Heavy rain showers.

    C. Supercooled raindrops.

Answer (A) is correct. (AC 00-6B Chap 19)
    DISCUSSION: A thunderstorm, by definition, has lightning, because lightning causes the thunder. Lightning is the discharge of electricity generated by thunderstorms.
    Answer (B) is incorrect. Hail may occur instead of heavy rain showers. **Answer (C) is incorrect.** Supercooled raindrops may not occur if the lifting process does not extend above the freezing level.

67. During the life cycle of a thunderstorm, which stage is characterized predominantly by downdrafts?

    A. Cumulus.

    B. Dissipating.

    C. Mature.

Answer (B) is correct. (AC 00-6B Chap 19)
    DISCUSSION: Thunderstorms have three stages in their life cycle: cumulus, mature, and dissipating. In the dissipating stage, the storm is characterized by downdrafts as the storm rains itself out.
    Answer (A) is incorrect. The cumulus stage is the building stage characterized by updrafts. **Answer (C) is incorrect.** The mature stage has both updrafts and downdrafts, which create strong wind shears.

68. Cumulus clouds often indicate

    A. possible turbulence.

    B. a temperature inversion.

    C. a dry adiabatic lapse rate.

Answer (A) is correct. (AC 00-6B)
    DISCUSSION: Cumulus clouds are formed in a convective updraft, build upward, and are associated with turbulence.
    Answer (B) is incorrect. A temperature inversion prevents updrafts from forming, which is needed for the formation of cumulus clouds. **Answer (C) is incorrect.** The dry adiabatic lapse rate is a measurement of air with no moisture available to form clouds.

69. What are the requirements for the formation of a thunderstorm?

A. A cumulus cloud with sufficient moisture.

B. A cumulus cloud with sufficient moisture and an inverted lapse rate.

C. Sufficient moisture, an unstable lapse rate, and a lifting action.

Answer (C) is correct. (AC 00-6B Chap 19)
DISCUSSION: For a thunderstorm to form, the air must have sufficient water vapor, an unstable lapse rate, and an initial upward lifting action to start the storm process in motion. Surface heating, converging winds, sloping terrain, a frontal surface, or any combination of these can provide the lift.
Answer (A) is incorrect. A lifting action is also required for formation of a thunderstorm. **Answer (B) is incorrect.** A lifting action and an unstable, not inverted, lapse rate are required for the formation of a thunderstorm.

70. What is indicated by the term "embedded thunderstorms"?

A. Severe thunderstorms are embedded within a squall line.

B. Thunderstorms are predicted to develop in a stable air mass.

C. Thunderstorms are obscured by massive cloud layers and cannot be seen.

Answer (C) is correct. (FAA-H-8083-25B Chap 12)
DISCUSSION: The term "embedded thunderstorms" means that the storms are embedded in clouds or thick haze layers and cannot be seen.
Answer (A) is incorrect. A squall line consists of severe thunderstorms, which can usually be seen. **Answer (B) is incorrect.** Thunderstorms do not usually occur in stable air masses.

71. Which weather phenomenon signals the beginning of the mature stage of a thunderstorm?

A. The start of rain at the surface.

B. Growth rate of cloud is maximum.

C. Strong turbulence in the cloud.

Answer (A) is correct. (AC 00-6B Chap 19)
DISCUSSION: The mature stage of a thunderstorm is indicated when rain begins falling at the surface. This means that downdrafts have developed sufficiently to carry water all the way through the thunderstorm.
Answer (B) is incorrect. Maximum growth rate occurs in the first or cumulus stage. **Answer (C) is incorrect.** Strong turbulence can occur in all stages.

72. The use of airborne weather-avoidance radar

A. provides no assurance of avoiding instrument weather conditions.

B. assures the avoidance of hail.

C. allows you to fly safely between echoes.

Answer (A) is correct. (AC 00-6B Chap 20)
DISCUSSION: Weather-avoidance radar provides information on precipitation based on echo returns. Avoiding the heaviest areas of precipitation will often (not always) keep you out of the greatest turbulence. Radar does not show water vapor. Thus, clouds and fog, i.e., instrument weather conditions, are not indicated.
Answer (B) is incorrect. Intense thunderstorms can often hurl hail for miles. **Answer (C) is incorrect.** Visual sighting of storms is not assured, because clouds and fog are not shown by radar. This could be detrimental to safety.

73. You are avoiding a thunderstorm that is in your flightpath. You are over 20 miles from the cell however, you are under the anvil of the cell. Is this a hazard?

A. No, you are at a safe distance from the cell.

B. Yes, hail can be discharged from the anvil.

C. Yes, this is still in the area of dissipation.

Answer (B) is correct. (AC 00-24C, AIM Para 7-1-12)
DISCUSSION: Pilots should anticipate possible hail with any thunderstorm, especially beneath the anvil of a large cumulonimbus.
Answer (A) is incorrect. Even if your flightpath is over 20 mi. from the cell, there is still potential to encounter hazards such as extreme clear air turbulence and hail when under the anvil. **Answer (C) is incorrect.** When underneath the anvil, the hazards you are most likely to encounter are clear air turbulence and hail.

74. When approaching a cumulonimbus cell that is on your route of flight, a pilot should

A. circumnavigate the cell by at least 20 nautical miles.

B. descend to an altitude that will allow the aircraft to fly under the cell.

C. fly under the anvil to protect the aircraft from violent parts of the cell.

Answer (A) is correct. (AC 00-24C, AIM Para 7-1-12)
DISCUSSION: You should avoid any thunderstorm identified as severe or giving an intense radar echo by at least 20 NM. This is especially true under the anvil of a large cumulonimbus.
Answer (B) is incorrect. Under no circumstances should you attempt to fly under a thunderstorm, even if you can see through to the other side. Turbulence and wind shear under the storm could be hazardous. **Answer (C) is incorrect.** You should never attempt to fly under the anvil of a thunderstorm. There is a potential for severe and extreme clear air turbulence. Hail can also be anticipated beneath the anvil of a large cumulonimbus.

8.7 Icing

75. In which meteorological environment is aircraft structural icing most likely to have the highest rate of accumulation?

    A. Cumulonimbus clouds.

    B. High humidity and freezing temperature.

    C. Freezing rain.

Answer (C) is correct. (AC 00-6B Chap 18)
    DISCUSSION: The condition most favorable for very hazardous icing is the presence of many large, supercooled water drops (i.e., freezing rain). The heaviest icing will usually be found at altitudes at or slightly above the freezing level where the temperature is never more than a few degrees below freezing.
    Answer (A) is incorrect. Icing does not necessarily occur in thunderstorms due to the large variation in temperature in thunderstorms. Answer (B) is incorrect. Visible moisture, not just high humidity, must be present for icing.

76. Test data indicate that ice, snow, or frost having a thickness and roughness similar to medium or coarse sandpaper on the leading edge and upper surface of an airfoil can

    A. reduce lift by as much as 50 percent and increase drag by as much as 50 percent.

    B. increase drag and reduce lift by as much as 25 percent.

    C. reduce lift by as much as 30 percent and increase drag by 40 percent.

Answer (C) is correct. (AC 120-58)
    DISCUSSION: Test data indicate that ice, snow, or frost formations having a thickness and surface roughness similar to medium or coarse sandpaper on the leading edge and upper surface of an airfoil can reduce lift by as much as 30% and increase drag by 40%. These changes in lift and drag significantly increase stall speed, reduce controllability, and alter aircraft flight characteristics.
    Answer (A) is incorrect. Ice, snow, or frost having a thickness or roughness similar to medium or coarse sandpaper on the leading edge and upper surface of an airfoil can reduce lift by as much as 30%, not 50%, and increase drag by 40%, not 50%. Answer (B) is incorrect. Ice, snow, or frost having a thickness or roughness similar to medium or coarse sandpaper on the leading edge and upper surface of an airfoil can reduce lift by as much as 30%, not 25%, and increase drag by 40%, not 25%.

77. Which precipitation type normally indicates freezing rain at higher altitudes?

    A. Snow.

    B. Hail.

    C. Ice pellets.

Answer (C) is correct. (FAA-H-8083-25B Chap 12)
    DISCUSSION: Ice pellets normally indicate that rain droplets are freezing at a higher altitude. Warmer air above exists from which rain is falling and freezing on the way down as it enters cooler air (i.e., freezing rain exists above).
    Answer (A) is incorrect. Snow indicates that the temperature of the air above you is well below freezing. Answer (B) is incorrect. Hail indicates instability of the air aloft where supercooled droplets above the freezing level begin to freeze. Once a drop has frozen, other drops latch onto it, and the hailstone grows.

78. What visual clue would alert a pilot to the presence of large supercooled water droplets?

    A. Formation of a glossy, transparent ice.

    B. Loss of RPM or manifold pressure due to induction icing.

    C. Entering an area of fog.

Answer (A) is correct. (AC 00-6B Chap 18)
    DISCUSSION: The formation of glossy, transparent ice slowly freezing on the surface of the aircraft is a visual clue to the presence of supercooled water droplets.
    Answer (B) is incorrect. Induction icing is the result of visible moisture not supercooled water. Answer (C) is incorrect. Fog does indicate the presence of visible moisture but not the presence of supercooled water droplets.

79. When large supercooled water droplets (SLD) are present in temperatures below +5°C, outside air temperature, what type of icing would be expected to form?

    A. Ice that is glossy, clear, or translucent.

    B. Thick, clumpy ice, that has a milky white color.

    C. Induction ice.

Answer (A) is correct. (AC 00-6B Chap 18)
    DISCUSSION: When large supercooled water droplets are encountered in temperatures below +5°C OAT, pilots should expect to see glossy, clear, or translucent ice. This ice accumulates quickly and is very dangerous if prompt action is not taken to leave the icing conditions and/or activate any deicing equipment that is present on the aircraft.
    Answer (B) is incorrect. Pilots should expect glossy, clear, or translucent ice, not ice that is clumpy with a milky white color. Answer (C) is incorrect. Supercooled water droplets are not required for induction icing, which may occur whenever the aircraft is operating in areas of visible moisture.

80. Which of the following would be an accurate description of supercooled large droplets (SLD)?

A. Subfreezing water drops greater than 40 microns located in or below clouds.

B. Subfreezing water drops greater than 50 micrometers located in or below clouds.

C. Subfreezing water drops greater than 50 microns at the surface.

Answer (B) is correct. (AC 91-74B)
DISCUSSION: SLDs are drops of subfreezing water that are 50 micrometers or greater in size. When present, these droplets will be found in or below clouds.
Answer (A) is incorrect. SLDs are 50, not 40, micrometers or greater. Answer (C) is incorrect. SLDs appear in or below clouds, not at the surface.

81. What is an operational consideration if you fly into rain which freezes on impact?

A. You have flown into an area of thunderstorms.

B. Temperatures are above freezing at some higher altitude.

C. You have flown through a cold front.

Answer (B) is correct. (FAA-H-8083-25B Chap 12)
DISCUSSION: Rain that freezes on impact is called freezing rain. If rain falls through freezing air, it will usually form supercooled water droplets, i.e., freezing rain. It indicates that temperatures somewhere above the airplane are above freezing.
Answer (A) is incorrect. Freezing rain does not necessarily indicate the presence of thunderstorms. Answer (C) is incorrect. Freezing rain does not necessarily indicate the presence of cold fronts.

82. What temperature condition is indicated if wet snow is encountered at your flight altitude?

A. The temperature is above freezing at your altitude.

B. The temperature is below freezing at your altitude.

C. You are flying from a warm air mass into a cold air mass.

Answer (A) is correct. (AC 00-6B Chap 14)
DISCUSSION: If snow is wet at your altitude, you are in above-freezing temperatures because the snow has started to melt.
Answer (B) is incorrect. The wet snow indicates the temperature is above freezing, not below freezing, at your altitude. Answer (C) is incorrect. The temperature is lower above you but not necessarily in front of you.

83. The presence of ice pellets at the surface is evidence that

A. there are thunderstorms in the area.

B. a cold front has passed.

C. there is freezing rain at a higher altitude.

Answer (C) is correct. (FAA-H-8083-25B Chap 12)
DISCUSSION: Ice pellets form as a result of rain freezing at a higher altitude. Rain droplets cool as they fall from a warmer layer through air with a temperature below freezing.
Answer (A) is incorrect. Thunderstorms do not necessarily cause ice pellets. Answer (B) is incorrect. Cold fronts do not necessarily cause ice pellets.

84. Why is frost considered hazardous to flight operation?

A. Frost changes the basic aerodynamic shape of the airfoil.

B. Frost decreases control effectiveness.

C. Frost causes early airflow separation resulting in a loss of lift.

Answer (C) is correct. (FAA-H-8083-25B Chap 5)
DISCUSSION: Frost spoils the smooth flow of air, thus causing a slowing of the airflow. This causes early airflow separation over the affected airfoil, resulting in a loss of lift. A heavy coat of hard frost will cause a 5 to 10% increase in stall speed. Even a small amount of frost on airfoils may prevent an aircraft from becoming airborne at normal takeoff speed.
Answer (A) is incorrect. Frost is very thin. It does not change the airfoil shape as structural icing does. Answer (B) is incorrect. Frost has no bearing on control effectiveness, only airfoil lift.

85. If the air temperature is +8°C at an elevation of 1,350 feet and a standard (average) temperature lapse rate exists, what will be the approximate freezing level?

A. 3,350 feet MSL.

B. 5,350 feet MSL.

C. 9,350 feet MSL.

Answer (B) is correct. (AC 00-6B Chap 11)
DISCUSSION: The decrease of temperature with altitude is defined as the lapse rate. The standard lapse rate is 2°C per 1,000 feet. To reach the freezing level, you must have a drop of 8°C. Thus the freezing level is 4,000 feet (8/2 × 1,000 ft.) up, or 5,350 feet MSL (1,350 + 4,000).
Answer (A) is incorrect. It represents a standard lapse rate of 4° per 1,000 feet. Answer (C) is incorrect. It represents a standard lapse rate of 1° per 1,000 feet.

86. A pilot who experiences tailplane icing on the approach should

A. notify ATC and request vectors to final.

B. disengage the autopilot and retract flaps.

C. add flaps and engage the autopilot.

Answer (B) is correct. (AC 91-74B)
    DISCUSSION: Since pilots using an autopilot are not feeling the subtle but constant changes in the flight controls, they are less likely to be aware of ice accumulation on the tail section of the aircraft. Any time tailplane icing is suspected, the autopilot should be deactivated and the flaps should be retracted to the last safe setting.
    Answer (A) is incorrect. While pilots should notify ATC upon encountering icing conditions, if the situation permits, the most correct answer to this question would be disconnecting the autopilot and retracting the flaps to the last safe setting. **Answer (C) is incorrect.** The autopilot should be disengaged, not engaged, and flaps should be retracted to the last safe position, not extended further.

87. When using inflight deicing systems in icing conditions, you should be aware that

A. there will be residual or some stage of intercycle ice on the wings.

B. residual or intercycle ice accumulation is unlikely if the deicing system is engaged prior to entering icing conditions.

C. ice accumulated during cruise flight can be expected to have little effect during approach or landing operations.

Answer (A) is correct. (AC 91-74B)
    DISCUSSION: Since deicing systems are activated after encountering icing conditions, ice is permitted to accrete between cycles. This is called intercycle or residual ice.
    Answer (B) is incorrect. Residual or intercycle ice accumulation is unlikely if the anti-icing system is engaged prior to entering icing conditions. **Answer (C) is incorrect.** Given the angle of attack typical of cruise flight, the ice accumulated here has little impact on lift. However, at the higher angles of attack typical of approach and landing, it will have a pronounced effect by increasing stall speed as the aircraft nears the C/L_{MAX}.

88. What happens to residual ice that remains after deice boots are inflated and shed ice?

A. Residual ice increases with a decrease in airspeed or temperature.

B. Residual ice remains the same until the aircraft exits icing conditions.

C. Residual ice decreases with a decrease in airspeed or temperature.

Answer (A) is correct. (AC 91-74B)
    DISCUSSION: The FAA recommends that the deicing system be activated at the first indication of icing. Because some residual ice continues to adhere between pneumatic boot system cycles, the wing is never entirely "clean." The amount of residual ice increases as airspeed and/or temperature decrease due to the more favorable conditions for ice accumulation associated with these conditions. At airspeeds typical of small airplanes, it may take many boot cycles to effectively shed the ice.
    Answer (B) is incorrect. Residual ice left behind between deicing system cycles will increase in magnitude if either airspeed or temperature decrease due to the more favorable conditions for ice accumulation associated with these conditions. **Answer (C) is incorrect.** The amount of residual ice increases, not decreases, as airspeed and/or temperature decrease due to the more favorable conditions for ice accumulation associated with these conditions.

89. On which surface of the aircraft could a pilot generally expect to see the first sign of ice accumulation?

A. Pitot tube.

B. Wing.

C. Propeller.

Answer (A) is correct. (AC 00-6B Chap 18)
    DISCUSSION: The smaller the surface, the more likely that surface is to pick up ice. Pitot tubes, being small protrusions into the airstream, are often the first parts of the aircraft to pick up ice.
    Answer (B) is incorrect. The pitot tube will show evidence of icing prior to the wings. **Answer (C) is incorrect.** The pitot tube will show evidence of icing prior to the propeller.

90. Tailplane icing can be detected by a(n)

A. increase in elevator effectiveness.

B. gradual uncommanded nose-up pitch.

C. sudden uncommanded nose-down pitch.

Answer (C) is correct. (AC 91-74B)
    DISCUSSION: A sudden uncommanded nose-down pitch is a symptom of tailplane icing that has caused a tailplane stall. The correct pilot reaction, unlike in a main wing stall, is to apply full aft-control pressure along with a reduction of the wing flaps to the last safe position.
    Answer (A) is incorrect. A decrease, not an increase, in rudder effectiveness is a symptom of tailplane icing. **Answer (B) is incorrect.** A sudden, not gradual, uncommanded nose-down, not nose-up, pitch is indicative of tailplane icing accumulation that has caused a tailplane stall.

91. What types of surfaces are most likely to see the first signs of ice accumulation?

A. Large wide areas.

B. Small narrow areas.

C. Areas made from metal.

Answer (B) is correct. (AC 00-6B Chap 18)
    DISCUSSION: Small narrow areas, like a pitot tube, are much more likely to accumulate ice.
    Answer (A) is incorrect. Large wide areas will accumulate ice after the accumulation has begun on small narrow areas.
    Answer (C) is incorrect. Metallic portions of the aircraft are no more likely to accumulate ice than nonmetal surfaces.

92. While flying a standard instrument departure procedure (DP) you encounter icing conditions and the autopilot is engaged, you should

A. continue the flight with the autopilot engaged.

B. increase the indicated airspeed setting for the autopilot.

C. disengage the autopilot.

Answer (C) is correct. (AC 91-74B)
    DISCUSSION: Since pilots using an autopilot are not feeling the subtle but constant changes in the flight controls, they are less likely to be aware of ice accumulation on the surface of the aircraft. When icing conditions are encountered, the autopilot should be disengaged.
    Answer (A) is incorrect. The autopilot should be disengaged whenever operating in real or forecast icing conditions. **Answer (B) is incorrect.** The autopilot should be disengaged whenever operating in real or forecast icing conditions. While airspeed should be increased, it should be accomplished using manual control, not the autopilot.

93. The most susceptible surface of the aircraft for ice accumulation is the

A. windshield.

B. main wing.

C. tailplane.

Answer (C) is correct. (AC 91-74B)
    DISCUSSION: On most aircraft the tailplane is not visible to the pilot, who therefore cannot observe how well it has been cleared of ice by any deicing system. Both the main wings and the windshield are in plain view of the pilot, making awareness of ice accumulation more obvious. As well, the thinness of the tailplane over the main wings and its simple shape compared to the windshield make it a more efficient ice collector.
    Answer (A) is incorrect. The windshield, while a good collector of ice, is directly in the pilot's line of sight making the pilot's awareness of windshield icing much greater. As well, the simple shape of the tailplane makes it a slightly more efficient collector of ice than the windshield. **Answer (B) is incorrect.** The main wings are visible by the pilot while the tailplane is not. This makes it much easier for the pilot to notice ice accumulation on the wings. As well, the thinness of the tailplane over the main wings make it a more efficient ice collector.

94. If you detect icing accumulation in flight, especially if the aircraft is not equipped with a deicing system, you should

A. move to a higher altitude.

B. leave the area of precipitation, if able, or fly to an altitude where the temperature is above freezing.

C. fly to an area with liquid precipitation.

Answer (B) is correct. (AC 91-74B)
    DISCUSSION: Regardless of the level of anti-ice or deice protection offered by the aircraft, the first course of action should be to leave the area of visible moisture. This might mean descending to an altitude below the cloud bases, climbing to an altitude that is above the cloud tops, or turning to a different course. If this is not possible, then the pilot must move to an altitude where the temperature is above freezing.
    Answer (A) is incorrect. The best action is to leave the area of precipitation, but, if that is not possible, the pilot should move to an altitude where the temperature is above freezing. Only during a temperature inversion would that be a higher altitude; usually it means descending to a lower altitude. **Answer (C) is incorrect.** Areas of liquid precipitation do not necessarily equate to areas where the temperature is above freezing. Freezing rain is an excellent example of liquid precipitation that is incredibly hazardous.

95. In an aircraft equipped with a pneumatic deicing system, the appropriate technique for removing ice is to

A. operate the pneumatic deicing system several times.

B. operate the pneumatic deicing system once.

C. confirm that ice has accumulated prior to engaging the pneumatic boots.

Answer (A) is correct. (AC 91-74B)
    DISCUSSION: To clear accumulated ice as well as residual ice that may be left between cycles, operate a pneumatic deicing system several times.
    Answer (B) is incorrect. To clear accumulated ice as well as residual ice that may be left between cycles, operate a pneumatic deicing system several times, not just once.
    Answer (C) is incorrect. This technique was formerly accepted as a rule of thumb, but current advisory guidance recommends activating deicing systems at the first indication of icing rather than after any significant amount has accumulated.

96. To recover from a tailplane stall brought on by ice accumulation, the pilot should

- A. retract the flaps and increase power, but only to compensate for the reduction in lift.
- B. decrease power and maintain a speed below V_A.
- C. extend the flaps and reduce power to slow the aircraft.

Answer (A) is correct. (AC 91-74B)
DISCUSSION: When a tailplane stall occurs, the pilot should immediately return the flaps to the previously selected position. Tailplane stalls are aggravated by an increase in flap extension. You will need to increase power to compensate for the reduction in lift caused by raising the flaps, but be careful to not increase power too drastically because an increase in airspeed can also aggravate a tailplane stall.
Answer (B) is incorrect. This procedure is appropriate for an encounter with moderate to severe turbulence, not a recovery from a tailplane stall. **Answer (C) is incorrect.** Extending the flaps during a tailplane stall with make the stall worse. Flaps should be retracted to their previous position and power should be increased, not reduced, to compensate for the loss in lift created by the retraction.

97. Tailplane icing can be detected by

- A. elevator control pulsing, oscillations, or vibrations.
- B. a gradual uncommanded reduction in engine power.
- C. an increase in elevator effectiveness.

Answer (A) is correct. (AC 91-74B)
DISCUSSION: Elevator control pulsing, oscillations, or vibrations as well as any other unusual or abnormal pitch anomalies (possibly resulting in pilot induced oscillations) are indicative of tailplane ice accumulation. If installed, anti-ice equipment should be activated. If no anti-ice system is installed or if the accumulation is not sufficiently combated by the anti-ice system, the pilot should exit icing conditions immediately.
Answer (B) is incorrect. A gradual uncommanded reduction in engine power is indicative of induction icing, not tailplane icing. **Answer (C) is incorrect.** A symptom of tailplane icing is a decrease, not an increase, in elevator effectiveness.

98. A tailplane stall as the result of ice accumulation is most likely to occur during

- A. cruise flight.
- B. approach and landing.
- C. an instrument holding pattern.

Answer (B) is correct. (AC 91-74B)
DISCUSSION: An ice-contaminated tailplane stall typically occurs either while extending the wing trailing edge flaps to the landing position or with the flaps already extended to that position when operating in, or departing from, icing conditions. Since flaps are normally only extended to the landing position during final approach to landing, tailplane stalls as the result of ice accumulation are most common in this phase of flight.
Answer (A) is incorrect. Ice-contaminated tailplane stalls are most common when the flaps are extended to the landing position, not during cruise flight. **Answer (C) is incorrect.** Ice-contaminated tailplane stalls are most common when the flaps are extended to the landing position, not during an instrument holding pattern.

99. With regards to icing, which is true?

- A. Heavy icing on the leading edge is not as bad as light icing on the upper surface.
- B. Smooth ice on the upper surface will not cause any problems.
- C. Light icing is more of a problem than heavy icing.

Answer (A) is correct. (AC 91-74B)
DISCUSSION: Ice on the leading edge, while seemingly more dangerous, can be removed using deicing systems. Ice on the upper surface is much more difficult to clear from the structure, thus making it more dangerous.
Answer (B) is incorrect. Smooth ice on the upper surface will disrupt laminar flow of the air across the upper wing surface, and it is much more difficult to remove than ice buildup on the leading edge. **Answer (C) is incorrect.** Light icing is generally less of a problem aerodynamically than heavy icing. Light icing is slightly more difficult to remove with most deicing systems, but it is considered less of an immediate threat than heavy icing.

100. When using deicing boots, the pilot should

- A. wait for a 1/4-inch to 1/2-inch layer of ice to form before cycling the boots to avoid ice bridging.
- B. deactivate the deicing system immediately after exiting the known icing conditions.
- C. activate the deicing system at the first indication of icing and do so in accordance with the manufacturer's guidance.

Answer (C) is correct. (AC 91-74B)
DISCUSSION: Due to the immediate and serious effects of ice accumulation, the FAA and manufacturer's guidance recommend that operators activate deicing boots at the first indication of ice accumulation.
Answer (A) is incorrect. While formerly accepted as correct procedure, modern research has shown that ice bridging is rare to non-existent in modern boot designs. **Answer (B) is incorrect.** Even though the aircraft has departed from icing conditions, there may still be residual ice accumulation on the aircraft. Boot operations should be continued after exiting icing conditions to ensure that accumulated ice is removed.

101. Should you experience buffeting or vibrations after extending the flaps upon exiting or during icing conditions, the most likely reason is

A. incipient tailplane stall.

B. aerodynamic stall due to increased angle of attack.

C. aerodynamic instability due to ice accumulation forward of the ailerons.

Answer (A) is correct. *(AC 91-74B)*
    DISCUSSION: Elevator control pulsing, oscillations, or vibrations as well as any other unusual or abnormal pitch anomalies (possibly resulting in pilot-induced oscillations) are indicative of tailplane ice accumulation and the potential for a tailplane stall. You should retract the flaps to the last safe setting in this situation.
    Answer (B) is incorrect. Buffeting after the extension of flaps, especially when in icing conditions, is characteristic of an incipient tailplane stall, not an aerodynamic stall. **Answer (C) is incorrect.** Uncommanded roll, not buffeting or vibrations, would accompany aerodynamic instability due to ice accumulation forward of the ailerons.

102. Which of the following is true about icing?

A. Small patches of ice sparsely distributed on the upper surface of the wing can cause asymmetrical stalls that result in roll control issues on takeoff.

B. Small areas of light snow or ice on the upper surface of the wing pose little or no threat to loss of lift.

C. Light ice on the surface of the wing is less of a concern than large accumulation on the leading edge of the wing.

Answer (A) is correct. *(AC 91-74B)*
    DISCUSSION: The disrupted airflow caused by icing accumulation on the upper wing surface can create isolated, asymmetrical stalls, which can cause roll upset in any phase of flight, but especially high-lift phases of flight such as the takeoff climb.
    Answer (B) is incorrect. Trace icing or frost on the upper surface of the wing can destroy as much as 30% of total lift, making it a significant danger in flight. **Answer (C) is incorrect.** Ice on the leading edge, while seemingly more dangerous, can be removed using deicing systems. Ice on the upper surface is much more difficult to clear from the structure, thus making it more dangerous.

103. Should you experience uncommanded roll due to icing forward of the ailerons, the most appropriate response is to

A. begin a climb.

B. retract the flaps in increments and employ available ice removal equipment.

C. reduce the angle of attack by reducing the aircraft pitch, and if in a turn, roll wings level.

Answer (C) is correct. *(AC 91-74B)*
    DISCUSSION: When encountering uncommanded roll due to ice accumulations forward of the ailerons, pilots can remedy roll up sets using the following guidelines:

1. Reduce the angle of attack by reducing the aircraft pitch. If in a turn, the pilot should roll the wings level.
2. Set the appropriate power and monitor the airspeed and angle of attack.
3. If flaps are extended, do not retract them unless it can be determined that the upper surface of the airfoil is clear of ice. Retracting the flaps will increase the angle of attack at a given airspeed.
4. Verify wing protection is functioning normally and systematically through visual observation of each wing.

    Answer (A) is incorrect. In the case of uncommanded roll, reduce the angle of attack by reducing the aircraft pitch, not increasing it to begin a climb. **Answer (B) is incorrect.** While you should employ any ice protection equipment available, you should not retract the flaps, regardless of their level of extension, during uncommanded roll as this will actually increase the angle of attack. However, if you can verify that the upper surface of the wing is clear of ice, you may retract the flaps if necessary. Bear in mind this is the exception to the rule.

104. Which is true concerning aircraft icing?

A. Small, almost imperceptible amounts of ice on the wing's upper surface cause the same aerodynamic penalties as much larger and more visible accumulations.

B. Ice accumulation on the wing's leading edge that conforms to the wing contour generally results in little performance degradation.

C. Small amounts of ice on the wing's surface usually result in correspondingly less performance degradation than larger amounts.

Answer (C) is the best answer. *(AC 91-74B)*
    DISCUSSION: Light icing is generally less of a problem aerodynamically than heavy icing. Light icing is slightly more difficult to remove with most deicing systems, but it is considered less of an immediate threat than heavy icing.
    Answer (A) is incorrect. While this statement can be true, it is not always true. **Answer (B) is incorrect.** Icing that follows the wing contour is generally clear ice, which is extremely hazardous to flight.

105. The best technique for using deicing boots is to

A. use them immediately upon visual detection of any ice.

B. allow ice to build first to reduce likelihood of "ice bridging."

C. cycle several times after exiting to obtain a completely clean wing.

Answer (A) is correct. (AC 91-74B)
DISCUSSION: The FAA recommends that the deicing system be activated at the first indication of icing.
Answer (B) is incorrect. In times past, the FAA did recommend delaying activation of deicing boots until a significant amount of ice built up on the surface. Due to the dangers associated with tailplane icing, however, the FAA now recommends that deicing boots be activated at the first indication of ice. Answer (C) is incorrect. Some residual ice continues to adhere between pneumatic boot system cycles, so the wing is never entirely "clean." The amount of residual ice increases as airspeed and/or temperature decrease due to the more favorable conditions for ice accumulation associated with these conditions.

106. The proper use of deicing boots should include

A. activation of the system at the first indication of icing and the continued cycling of the boots after leaving icing conditions to ensure any residual ice has been removed.

B. activation of the system at the first indication of icing and the one cycle of the boots after leaving icing conditions to ensure any residual ice has been removed.

C. discontinue the use of the boots upon exiting icing conditions.

Answer (A) is correct. (AC 91-74B)
DISCUSSION: The deicing boots should be activated at the first sign of ice accumulation and should be cycled multiple times upon leaving icing conditions to ensure any residual ice has been removed.
Answer (B) is incorrect. The deicing boots should be cycled multiple times upon leaving icing conditions, not just once, to ensure any residual ice has been removed. Answer (C) is incorrect. The deicing boots should be cycled multiple times upon leaving icing conditions to ensure any residual ice has been removed.

107. How should deicing boots be used after exiting flight in icing conditions?

A. It is no longer necessary to operate the boots after leaving icing conditions.

B. You should continue to cycle the boots several times to remove residual ice left behind after normal boot operation.

C. Only continue to cycle the boots if you are concerned you may still be accumulating ice.

Answer (B) is correct. (AC 91-74B)
DISCUSSION: Some residual ice continues to adhere between pneumatic boot system cycles. The amount of residual ice increases as airspeed and/or temperature decrease due to the more favorable conditions for ice accumulation associated with these conditions. At airspeeds typical of small airplanes, it may take many boot cycles to effectively shed the ice.
Answer (A) is incorrect. Residual ice lingers after normal boot system operation. You should continue to operate the boots until all possible residual ice is removed. Answer (C) is incorrect. Once you leave conditions favorable for icing conditions, you will not accumulate further ice. However, boots should still be operated after leaving icing conditions to remove residual ice left behind after normal boot system cycles.

108. Test data indicates that ice, snow, or frost having a thickness and roughness similar to medium or coarse sandpaper on the leading edge and upper surface of an airfoil can

A. increase drag and reduce lift by as much as 40 percent.

B. reduce lift by as much as 40 percent and increase drag by 30 percent.

C. reduce lift by as much as 30 percent and increase drag by 40 percent.

Answer (C) is correct. (AC 120-58, page 4)
DISCUSSION: Lift has been shown to be reduced by as much as 30%, while drag may be increased by up to 40% when ice, snow, or thick frost is present on the leading edge and upper surface of the wing.
Answer (A) is incorrect. Although the increase of drag can be as high as 40%, the reduction of lift has only been shown to be 30%, which is substantially less than this answer choice suggests. Answer (B) is incorrect. The values have been reduced in this answer choice. Actual lift reduction has been shown to be lower, at 30%, while the increase in drag is higher, at 40%.

109. Ice tends to accumulate first on parts of the plane that are

A. small and narrow.

B. outside the wind stream.

C. thick and big.

Answer (A) is correct. (AC 91-74B)
DISCUSSION: Small and narrow objects are the best collectors of droplets and ice up rapidly.
Answer (B) is incorrect. Although the type of ice that forms varies depending on the atmospheric and flight conditions, small and narrow parts tend to accumulate ice first, not parts that are outside the wind stream. Answer (C) is incorrect. Although the type of ice that forms varies depending on the atmospheric and flight conditions, small and narrow parts tend to accumulate ice first, not thick and big parts.

110. During or after flight in icing conditions, vibration or buffeting that follows, but was not evident prior to, flap deployment is

A. an aerodynamic instability due to ice buildup forward of the ailerons but aft of the deicer boots.

B. an incipient tailplane stall as a result of negative tailplane angle after flap deployment.

C. an aerodynamic wing stall due to increased angle of attack as a result of flap deployment.

Answer (B) is correct. (AC 91-74B)
DISCUSSION: Tailplane stall is most common when extending the flaps to the landing position, but it can occur with any extension of flaps. A vibration that occurs after flap extension is a warning signal of an impending tailplane stall.
Answer (A) is incorrect. This condition would likely result in uncommanded roll due to ice accumulation forward of the ailerons. It is not an indication of a tailplane stall. **Answer (C) is incorrect.** Pilots may assume that a normal wing stall is occurring, but attempting to recover from a potential wing stall by applying down-elevator pressure will only aggravate the likely tailplane stall condition.

111. Where would you see the first sign of ice buildup?

A. The pitot tube.

B. The leading edge of the wing.

C. The windshield.

Answer (A) is correct. (AC 91-74B)
DISCUSSION: Small extensions from the aircraft structure are generally the best visual indicators of ice accumulation. The pitot tube can be a good visually-identifiable structure in a high-wing airplane.
Answer (B) is incorrect. Ice accumulation on the leading edge of the wing can be difficult to determine, especially if the ice follows the general contour of the wing. Also, ice accumulation will begin to build on smaller aircraft structures before building on larger ones. **Answer (C) is incorrect.** While immediately in front of the pilot, ice accumulation on the windshield often begins after accumulation on smaller structures on the airplane.

112. Roll upsets caused by ice accumulation forward of the ailerons can be remedied by

A. retracting the flaps to decrease the angle of attack at a given airspeed and maintaining a level pitch attitude.

B. reducing the angle of attack by increasing airspeed or extending wing flaps to the first setting and rolling wings level.

C. decreasing engine power and maintaining a nose-low pitch attitude to dampen the rolling tendency of the wing tips.

Answer (B) is correct. (AC 91-74B)
DISCUSSION: Roll upsets are common during uneven ice accumulation on the wings. Because this ice accumulation builds forward of the ailerons and behind the deicing boots, it is often very difficult to remove. Reducing the angle of attack and increasing airspeed will assist you in maintaining positive control of the airplane.
Answer (A) is incorrect. You should increase airspeed to assist with roll control while also rolling the wings back to the level position. **Answer (C) is incorrect.** You should increase airspeed and maintain a level attitude, not begin a descent with a nose-low attitude.

113. Which is true regarding Supercooled Large Droplets (SLD) and their accumulation?

A. SLD can accrue aloft even if the droplets are not being observed at the surface.

B. SLD will not accrue even in visible moisture if the OAT is above 0°C.

C. SLD will not accrue even in freezing drizzle because of smaller size droplets.

Answer (A) is correct. (AC 91-74B)
DISCUSSION: Pilots should be aware that SLDs can occur aloft even if no SLD precipitation is evident at the surface.
Answer (B) is incorrect. Aircraft icing usually occurs in supercooled clouds where the outside air temperature is between +2° and -20°C. **Answer (C) is incorrect.** Water droplets larger than 50 micrometers (diameter), which includes freezing drizzle and freezing rain aloft, characterize SLD icing conditions.

114. What is true regarding ice accumulations on a wing surface?

A. A thin layer of ice on a wing's upper surface will result in little performance degradation if the ice is relatively smooth.

B. Small, visually imperceptible amounts of ice on a wing's surface during takeoff can result in significant performance degradation.

C. Frost, snow, and rime ice is easily detectable on a white upper wing surface, while clear ice is difficult to detect.

Answer (B) is correct. (AC 91-74B, NTSB Safety Alert SA-06)
DISCUSSION: Virtually imperceptible amounts of ice on a wing's upper surface can result in significant performance degradation.
Answer (A) is incorrect. Ice of any kind can cause significant performance issues. **Answer (C) is incorrect.** Fine particles of ice, even if they are the size of a grain of table salt and distributed as sparsely as one particle per square centimeter over a wing's upper surface, can destroy enough lift to prevent an airplane from taking off. The dangers of ice's imperceptibility is not limited to clear ice.

115. If you experience icing during an approach, you should

A. extend maximum flaps and keep the autopilot engaged.

B. retract the flaps as necessary and disengage the autopilot.

C. fly the airplane manually to the final approach fix and then engage the autopilot.

Answer (B) is correct. (AC 91-74B)
DISCUSSION: While the autopilot can help reduce pilot workload, it also disconnects the pilot from the control-loading effects of icing accumulation. In icing conditions, pilots should maintain manual control of the airplane. Also, flaps should be retracted, as necessary, to prevent a potential tailplane stall.
Answer (A) is incorrect. Pilots should avoid extending flaps in known icing conditions. If the autopilot is engaged, it should be disconnected to allow the pilot to maintain control of the airplane. **Answer (C) is incorrect.** If the autopilot is engaged, it should be disconnected to allow the pilot to maintain control of the airplane.

116. What type of icing should be expected when you encounter supercooled large droplets (SLD) that splash or splatter on impact at temperatures below +5°C OAT?

A. Ice that appears wet or visibly moist.

B. Ice that builds on the propeller spinner but forward of the blades.

C. Ice that forms on the wing aft of the active part of the deicing boots.

Answer (C) is correct. (AC 91-74B)
DISCUSSION: You can think of SLD-caused icing as "aft icing" in that it generally occurs aft of where normal icing forms. SLD icing is common aft of the active portion of deicing boots due to run-back caused after the SLDs impact the leading edge of the wing.
Answer (A) is incorrect. Due to the "fast-freeze" nature of SLD icing, you should expect this type of icing to be unusually extensive and solid. **Answer (B) is incorrect.** SLD icing forms aft of the impact site. SLD icing will not build forward from the point of impact, but aft.

117. Which of the following is true about icing characteristics?

A. Ice on the front and back of the airplane wing is easy to see from the pilot's position.

B. Ice is virtually undetectable when clear and may appear wet.

C. Ice on the surface of the wing is virtually undetectable and causes a reduction in lift over the wing.

Answer (C) is correct. (AC 91-74B, NTSB Safety Alert SA-06)
DISCUSSION: Virtually imperceptible amounts of ice on the aircraft wing's upper surface can result in significant performance degradation.
Answer (A) is incorrect. Ice is not always easy to see, and virtually imperceptible amounts of ice on the aircraft wing's upper surface can result in significant performance degradation. **Answer (B) is incorrect.** Clear ice can be difficult to spot due to its general conformity to the upper surface of the wing, but it is not virtually undetectable, especially when aided by a light source that can help identify the presence of icing.

118. After cycling of the deicing boots, residual ice will

A. increase as the airspeed or temperature decreases.

B. decrease as the airspeed decreases or the temperature increases.

C. remain constant until leaving the icing conditions.

Answer (A) is correct. (AC 91-74B)
DISCUSSION: The amount of residual ice increases as the airspeed or temperature decreases. Consequently, the FAA recommends that deicing systems be activated at the first indication of icing. Residual ice continues to adhere between pneumatic boot system cycles, meaning the wing is never entirely clean.
Answer (B) is incorrect. The amount of residual ice increases as airspeed or temperature decreases. It does not decrease as the airspeed decreases. **Answer (C) is incorrect.** Residual ice does not remain constant until the aircraft leaves the icing conditions. The amount of residual ice actually increases as airspeed or temperature decreases.

119. On initial climbout after takeoff and with the autopilot engaged, you encounter icing conditions. In this situation you can expect

A. ice to accumulate on the underside of the wings due to the higher AOA.

B. the autopilot to hold the vertical speed, if the anti-icing boots are working.

C. the increased airflow under the wings to prevent the accumulation of ice.

Answer (A) is correct. (AC 91-74B)
DISCUSSION: Airplanes are vulnerable to ice accumulation during the initial climbout in icing conditions because lower speeds often translate into a higher angle of attack (AOA). This exposes the underside of the airplane and its wings to the icing conditions and allows ice to accumulate further aft than it would in cruise flight.
Answer (B) is incorrect. The autopilot will hold the vertical speed whether the anti-icing boots are working or not. Therefore, extreme vigilance should be exercised while climbing with the autopilot engaged. Climbing in vertical speed (VS) mode in icing conditions is highly discouraged. **Answer (C) is incorrect.** Lower speeds and a higher AOA will expose the underside of the airplane and its wings to the icing conditions and allow, not prevent, the accumulation of ice.

120. Where will the pilot first notice an accumulation of ice?

- A. On the leading edge of the wing.
- B. On the propeller.
- C. On the air temperature probe.

Answer (C) is correct. (AC 91-74B)
  DISCUSSION: Small, narrow objects tend to pick up ice that is visually detectable. Strategically located protuberances may also serve as ice indicators. The air temperature probe is an excellent example of this.
  Answer (A) is incorrect. Small, narrow objects tend to pick up ice that is visually detectable. Strategically located protuberances may also serve as ice indicators. The leading edge of the wing is not small and narrow or a protuberance. Although ice may be visible there at some point, it is not the most likely place to see the first signs of ice accumulation.
  Answer (B) is incorrect. The propeller is spinning far too quickly for the pilot to visually identify early signs of ice on it.

121. Where is airplane icing most difficult to identify?

- A. On the wing's leading edge.
- B. On the flat upper wing surface.
- C. On the trailing edge of the wing.

Answer (B) is correct. (AC 91-74B)
  DISCUSSION: Ice accumulation on the wing's upper surface may be very difficult to detect from the flight deck, cabin, or front or back of the wing. Additionally, frost, snow, and rime ice may be very difficult to detect on a white upper wing surface.
  Answer (A) is incorrect. The leading edge is easily accessible while on the ground and is usually visible from the flight deck or cabin in flight. Conversely, ice accumulation on the wing's upper surface may be very difficult to detect from the flight deck, cabin, or front or back of the wing. Additionally, frost, snow, and rime ice may be very difficult to detect on a white upper wing surface. **Answer (C) is incorrect.** Well before ice appears on the trailing edge of the wing, it will have been evident elsewhere. However, ice accumulation on the wing's upper surface may be very difficult to detect from the flight deck, cabin, or front or back of the wing. Also, frost, snow, and rime ice may be very difficult to detect on a white upper wing surface.

122. A generally recommended practice for autopilot usage during cruise flight in icing conditions is

- A. keeping the autopilot engaged while monitoring the system.
- B. periodically disengaging the autopilot and hand flying the airplane.
- C. periodically disengaging and immediately reengaging the altitude hold function.

Answer (B) is correct. (AC 91-74B)
  DISCUSSION: The autopilot can mask changes in handling characteristics. The recommended procedure is, when possible, for pilots to periodically disengage the autopilot and hand fly the airplane to detect changes in handling characteristics due to aerodynamic effects of icing. But if this is not desirable because of flight deck workload levels, pilots should monitor the autopilot closely for abnormal trim, trim rate, or airplane attitude.
  Answer (A) is incorrect. The autopilot can mask changes in handling characteristics due to aerodynamic effects of icing that would be detected by the pilot when hand flying. The recommended procedure is to periodically disengage the autopilot and hand fly the airplane to detect any handling changes, not keep the autopilot engaged while monitoring the system. **Answer (C) is incorrect.** The pilot should disengage the autopilot and hand fly the airplane for the amount of time necessary to detect any changes in handling characteristics due to aerodynamic effects of icing, not periodically disengage and immediately reengage the altitude hold function.

123. On the initial climbout after takeoff with the autopilot engaged, you encounter icing conditions. In this situation, it is recommended that

- A. you trust that the autopilot will safely handle the icing situation.
- B. the vertical speed mode be disconnected.
- C. the vertical speed mode remain engaged.

Answer (B) is the best answer. (AC 91-74B)
  DISCUSSION: Extreme vigilance should be exercised while climbing with the autopilot engaged. Climbing in vertical speed (VS) mode in icing conditions is highly discouraged. When climbing with the autopilot engaged in the vertical speed mode, ice accretion will result in a loss of climb performance. If the vertical speed is not reduced, the autopilot will maintain the rate until stall. It is critical that the pilot monitor airspeed to assure that the aircraft maintains at least the minimum flight speed for the configuration and environmental conditions.
  Answer (A) is incorrect. Extreme vigilance should be exercised while climbing with the autopilot engaged. **Answer (C) is incorrect.** Climbing in vertical speed (VS) mode in icing conditions is highly discouraged. When climbing with the autopilot engaged in the vertical speed mode, ice accretion will result in a loss of climb performance. If the vertical speed is not reduced, the autopilot will maintain the rate until stall.

124. Which is true about ice formation on a wing surface?

    A. Ice or frost formation on a wing's upper surface will have no effect on takeoff performance as long as formations are distributed sparsely.

    B. Ice or frost formation on a wing surface can result in localized, asymmetrical stalls on the wing resulting in roll control problems during lift off.

    C. Small ice or frost formation on a wing's upper surface is not as serious as a large accumulation of ice on the wing's leading edge.

Answer (B) is correct. (AC 91-74B, NTSB Safety Alert SA-06)
    DISCUSSION: The NTSB has found that small patches of ice or frost can result in localized, asymmetrical stalls on the wing, which can result in roll control problems during lift off.
    Answer (A) is incorrect. Sparsely distributed ice formations can still pose a threat to the safety of flight.
    Answer (C) is incorrect. Any icing on an airfoil has the potential to be a factor in the safety of flight.

8.8 Wind Shear

125. When a climb or descent through an inversion or wind shear zone is being performed, the pilot should be alert for which of the following changes in airplane performance?

    A. A sudden change in airspeed.

    B. A sudden surge of thrust.

    C. A fast rate of climb and slow rate of descent.

Answer (A) is correct. (AC 00-54)
    DISCUSSION: Airspeed changes should be expected during flight through inversions due to the change in air pressure. In wind shear zones, airspeed changes are due to the change in direction and speed of the air flow aloft.
    Answer (B) is incorrect. A sudden surge of thrust would be consistent with a microburst encounter, but not necessarily with an encounter through a temperature inversion or a wind shear zone. **Answer (C) is incorrect.** A fast rate of climb and a slow rate of descent would be observed when flying in an updraft or thermal column, but not necessarily with an encounter through a temperature inversion or a wind shear zone.

126. What is an important characteristic of wind shear?

    A. It is an atmospheric condition that is associated exclusively with zones of convergence.

    B. The Coriolis phenomenon in both high- and low-level air masses is the principal generating force.

    C. It is an atmospheric condition that may be associated with a low-level temperature inversion, a jet stream, or a frontal zone.

Answer (C) is correct. (AC 00-54)
    DISCUSSION: Wind shear can occur at any level where winds are blowing in different directions or at different speeds. It is an atmospheric condition associated with low-level temperature inversions, the jet stream, or a frontal zone.
    Answer (A) is incorrect. Zones of convergence are low-pressure areas. Wind shear can occur in highs as well as lows. **Answer (B) is incorrect.** The Coriolis force is the deflective force of the Earth's rotation, which affects all wind flows, not just wind shear.

127. What is an important characteristic of wind shear?

    A. It is primarily associated with the lateral vortices generated by thunderstorms.

    B. It usually exists only in the vicinity of thunderstorms, but may be found near a strong temperature inversion.

    C. It may be associated with either a wind shift or a wind speed gradient at any level in the atmosphere.

Answer (C) is correct. (AC 00-54)
    DISCUSSION: Wind shear can occur at any level where winds are blowing in different directions or at different speeds.
    Answer (A) is incorrect. Wind shear is found in conditions other than thunderstorm turbulence, e.g., mountain waves, fronts, etc. **Answer (B) is incorrect.** Wind shear is found in conditions other than thunderstorm turbulence, e.g., mountain waves, fronts, etc.

128. Where does wind shear occur?

    A. Exclusively in thunderstorms.

    B. Wherever there is an abrupt decrease in pressure and/or temperature.

    C. With either a wind shift or a wind speed gradient at any level in the atmosphere.

Answer (C) is correct. (AC 00-54)
    DISCUSSION: Wind shear can occur at any level where winds are blowing in different directions (wind shift) or at different speeds (a wind speed gradient).
    Answer (A) is incorrect. Wind shear is also caused by barriers to wind flow, occurs behind and below airplanes generating lift, etc. **Answer (B) is incorrect.** Wind shear is the result of wind change, not a change in temperature or pressure, per se.

129. Where can wind shear associated with a thunderstorm be found? Choose the most complete answer.

    A. In front of the thunderstorm cell (anvil side) and on the right side of the cell.

    B. In front of the thunderstorm cell and directly under the cell.

    C. On all sides of the thunderstorm cell and directly under the cell.

Answer (C) is correct. (FAA-H-8083-25B Chap 12)
    DISCUSSION: Wind shear associated with thunderstorms may be found on all sides of the thunderstorm cell, including directly beneath it and as much as 20 mi. laterally.
    Answer (A) is incorrect. Wind shear may be found on all sides and beneath the thunderstorm cell. **Answer (B) is incorrect.** Wind shear may be found on all sides and beneath the thunderstorm cell.

130. Hazardous wind shear is commonly encountered near the ground

    A. during periods when the wind velocity is stronger than 35 knots.

    B. during periods when the wind velocity is stronger than 35 knots and near mountain valleys.

    C. during periods of strong temperature inversion and near thunderstorms.

Answer (C) is correct. (AC 00-54)
    DISCUSSION: Thunderstorms produce hazardous wind shear near the ground. Wind shear during temperature inversions is also hazardous when at low levels as it affects aircraft approaching and departing airports.
    Answer (A) is incorrect. Any wind, not only wind shear, is hazardous when in excess of 35 knots. **Answer (B) is incorrect.** Wind shear usually occurs on the leeward side of mountains, not in valleys.

131. When climbing or descending through an area of possible wind shear, the pilot should be aware of

    A. a fast rate of climb and a slow rate of descent.

    B. a rapid change of airspeed.

    C. airframe icing.

Answer (B) is correct. (AC 00-54)
    DISCUSSION: A rapid change in wind direction or velocity will be reflected in a rapid change of airspeed when climbing or descending through an area of potential wind shear.
    Answer (A) is incorrect. A fast rate of climb and a slow rate of descent would be observed when flying in an updraft or thermal column, not necessarily with an encounter through a temperature inversion or a wind shear zone. **Answer (C) is incorrect.** A pilot should remain vigilant of icing at all times and determine icing exit strategies during preflight. When transitioning through an area of possible wind shear, the pilot must be aware of rapid changes in airspeed.

132. Which is a characteristic of low-level wind shear as it relates to low-level temperature inversions?

    A. It allows airspeed to go above normal climb and approach speed.

    B. The pilot can ignore the possibilities of wind shear since all winds must always be light for this phenomenon to occur.

    C. The shear zone condition exists when upper-level winds are reported 5 to 10 knots.

Answer (A) is correct. (FAA-H-8083-25B Chap 12)
    DISCUSSION: Especially during takeoff and approach, be alert for airspeed fluctuations at the most critical period when passing through the temperature inversion. These fluctuations may be the first indications of wind shear. Pilots are advised to improve their awareness of normal climbout pitch attitude and to put less emphasis on strict airspeed control.
    Answer (B) is incorrect. Wind shear does not occur exclusively in low-wind conditions. In fact, wind variations can result from topographical conditions, temperature inversions, sea breezes, and frontal systems. **Answer (C) is incorrect.** There is no limitation that restricts wind shear to situations where upper-level winds are reported at 5 to 10 knots. Low-level wind shear is very dangerous and requires pilot awareness to deal with the issue safely. Especially during takeoff and approach, be alert for airspeed fluctuations. These fluctuations may be the first indications of wind shear. Pilots are advised to improve their awareness of normal climbout pitch attitude and to put less emphasis on strict airspeed control.

133. A pilot reporting turbulence that momentarily causes slight, erratic changes in altitude and/or attitude should report it as

    A. light turbulence.

    B. moderate turbulence.

    C. light chop.

Answer (A) is correct. (AIM Para 7-1-21)
    DISCUSSION: Light turbulence is defined as a disturbed air flow that momentarily causes slight erratic changes in altitude and/or attitude.
    Answer (B) is incorrect. Moderate turbulence is more intense. It is sufficient to cause changes in altitude, but the pilot maintains control throughout. **Answer (C) is incorrect.** Light chop means slight or moderate, rapid, and somewhat rhythmic bumpiness without appreciable changes in altitude or attitude.

8.9 Microbursts

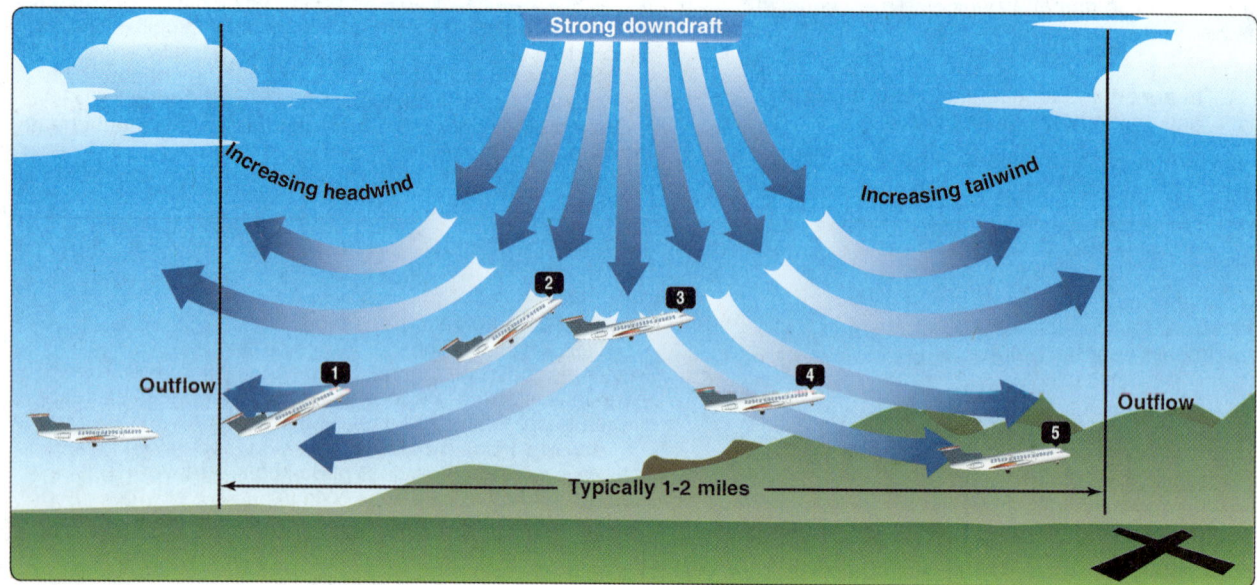

Figure 13. – Microburst Section Chart.

134. (Refer to Figure 13 above.) How will the aircraft in position 4 be affected by a microburst encounter?

    A. Performance increasing with a tailwind and updraft.

    B. Performance decreasing with a tailwind and downdraft.

    C. Performance decreasing with a headwind and downdraft.

Answer (B) is correct. (AIM Para 7-1-24)
    DISCUSSION: In Fig. 13, point 4 represents decreased performance as a result of both the wind shear shift from a headwind to a tailwind and a strong downdraft.
    Answer (A) is incorrect. Performance decreases at point 4 due to the tailwind and a downdraft, not an updraft. **Answer (C) is incorrect.** The performance decreases as a result of the tailwind, not headwind.

135. (Refer to Figure 13 above.) When penetrating a microburst, which aircraft will experience an increase in performance without a change in pitch or power?

    A. 3.

    B. 2.

    C. 1.

Answer (C) is correct. (AIM Para 7-1-24)
    DISCUSSION: Refer to Fig. 13 and note that, as the airplane at point 1 approaches the microburst, it will experience an increasing headwind and increasing performance.
    Answer (A) is incorrect. At point 3, the airplane is experiencing a strong downdraft. **Answer (B) is incorrect.** At point 2, the airplane is experiencing a decreasing headwind component.

136. (Refer to Figure 13 above.) The aircraft in position 3 will experience which effect in a microburst encounter?

    A. Decreasing headwind.

    B. Increasing tailwind.

    C. Strong downdraft.

Answer (C) is correct. (AIM Para 7-1-24)
    DISCUSSION: At point 3 in Fig. 13, the airplane is experiencing a strong downdraft as it is approaching the center of the microburst.
    Answer (A) is incorrect. At point 2, not 3, the airplane encounters decreasing headwind. **Answer (B) is incorrect.** At point 5, the airplane encounters an increasing tailwind that may result in an extreme situation as pictured, i.e., just before impact.

137. (Refer to Figure 13 above.) What effect will a microburst encounter have upon the aircraft in position 4?

    A. Strong tailwind.

    B. Strong updraft.

    C. Significant performance increase.

Answer (A) is correct. (AIM Para 7-1-24)
    DISCUSSION: At point 4 in Fig. 13, the airplane is encountering a strong tailwind in addition to a strong downdraft.
    Answer (B) is incorrect. There are no updrafts in microbursts, only downdrafts. **Answer (C) is incorrect.** The significance in performance increase occurs at point 1, not 4, where there is an increase in headwind.

138. (Refer to Figure 13 on page 366.) If involved in a microburst encounter, in which aircraft positions will the most severe downdraft occur?

A. 4 and 5.

B. 2 and 3.

C. 3 and 4.

Answer (C) is correct. (AIM Para 7-1-24)
DISCUSSION: The most severe downdrafts occur at the center of the microburst. Point 3 is the most severe, followed by point 4, where the downdraft occurs with a performance-decreasing tailwind.
Answer (A) is incorrect. Point 5 has significantly less downdraft even though it has considerably more tailwind.
Answer (B) is incorrect. The most severe downdrafts occur at the center of the microburst. Although point 2 is also near the center, the aircraft would still experience performance-increasing headwinds. The aircraft at point 4 would experience performance-decreasing tailwinds.

139. An aircraft that encounters a headwind of 45 knots, within a microburst, may expect a total shear across the microburst of

A. 40 knots.

B. 80 knots.

C. 90 knots.

Answer (C) is correct. (AIM Para 7-1-24, AC 00-54)
DISCUSSION: If a headwind in a microburst is 45 knots, the wind will be going in the opposite direction on the other side of the microburst at presumably the same 45 knots, resulting in a wind shear between the headwind and tailwind of 90 knots.
Answer (A) is incorrect. The total shear is the total headwind to tailwind change of a traversing aircraft; thus a 45-knot headwind would shear 90 knots, not 40 knots, to a 45-knot tailwind. **Answer (B) is incorrect.** The total shear is the total headwind to tailwind change of a traversing aircraft; thus a 45-knots headwind would shear 90 knots, not 80 knots, to a 45-knot tailwind.

140. Maximum downdrafts in a microburst encounter may be as strong as

A. 8,000 feet per minute.

B. 7,000 feet per minute.

C. 6,000 feet per minute.

Answer (C) is correct. (AIM Para 7-1-24)
DISCUSSION: Downdrafts in a microburst can be as strong as 6,000 feet per minute. Horizontal winds near the surface can be as strong as 45 knots, resulting in a 90-knot wind shear. The strong horizontal winds occur within a few hundred feet of the ground.
Answer (A) is incorrect. Maximum downdrafts are usually 6,000 feet per minute, not 8,000 feet per minute. **Answer (B) is incorrect.** Maximum downdrafts are usually 6,000 feet per minute, not 7,000 feet per minute.

141. What is the expected duration of an individual microburst?

A. Two minutes with maximum winds lasting approximately 1 minute.

B. One microburst may continue for as long as 2 to 4 hours.

C. Seldom longer than 15 minutes from the time the burst strikes the ground until dissipation.

Answer (C) is correct. (AIM Para 7-1-24)
DISCUSSION: An individual microburst will seldom last longer than 15 min. from the time it strikes ground until dissipation. The horizontal winds continue to increase during the first 5 min. with maximum-intensity winds lasting approximately 2 to 4 min.
Answer (A) is incorrect. Microbursts last 15, not 2 min., and maximum winds last 2 to 4 min., not 1 min. **Answer (B) is incorrect.** The maximum winds last 2 to 4 min., not 2 to 4 hr., and the microburst is usually limited to about 15 min.

142. As you approach an airport to land, you observe a convective cloud over the airport with virga below it. This could indicate

A. smooth air.

B. heavy rain showers.

C. the presence of a microburst.

Answer (C) is correct. (FAA-H-8083-25B Chap 12)
DISCUSSION: Rain that falls through the atmosphere but evaporates prior to striking the ground is known as virga. The process of evaporation cools the air around the virga and can create strong downdrafts and in some cases microbursts.
Answer (A) is incorrect. Virga are often associated with strong downdrafts due to the cooling effect of evaporation. Therefore, the air around virga would be very turbulent, not smooth. **Answer (B) is incorrect.** Virga occur when precipitation is not able to penetrate a layer of dry air and evaporates before it reaches the surface. Thus, heavy rain showers would not be indicated by virga.

STUDY UNIT NINE

AVIATION WEATHER SERVICES

(15 pages of outline)

This study unit contains outlines of major concepts tested, sample test questions and answers regarding aviation weather services, and an explanation of each answer.

Recall that the **sole purpose** of this book is to expedite your passing of the FAA pilot knowledge test for the instrument rating. Accordingly, all extraneous material (i.e., topics or regulations not directly tested on the FAA pilot knowledge test) is omitted, even though much more knowledge is necessary to fly safely. This additional material is presented in *Pilot Handbook, Aviation Weather and Weather Services, FAR/AIM,* and *Instrument Pilot Flight Maneuvers and Practical Test Prep*, available from Gleim Publications, Inc. Order online at www.GleimAviation.com.

Authors' note: The NWS continually evaluates and updates the products that it produces for aviation. In this fluid environment, it is difficult for the FAA to maintain current figures and questions. Since the sole purpose of this book is to expedite your passing the FAA knowledge test, the outline covers only what is on the test. The Gleim *Aviation Weather and Weather Services* book, Part II, "Aviation Weather Services," has supplemental information.

9.1 AIRMETS AND SIGMETS

1. AIRMETs are issued on a scheduled basis every 6 hr., with unscheduled amendments issued as required.

   a. An AIRMET is valid for 6 hr.

   b. An AIRMET may be issued when any of the following weather phenomena are occurring or are expected to occur over an area of at least 3,000 sq. mi.:

      1) Ceiling less than 1,000 ft. and/or visibility less than 3 SM (IFR)

      2) Widespread mountain obscuration (MTN OBSCN)

      3) Moderate turbulence (MOD TURB)

      4) Sustained surface wind greater than 30 kt. (STG SFC WND)

      5) Moderate icing (MOD ICE)

      6) Nonconvective low-level wind shear potential below 2,000 ft. AGL (LLWS POTENTIAL)

c.   There are three AIRMET series: SIERRA, TANGO, and ZULU.

   1)   AIRMET Sierra describes IFR (instrument flight rules) conditions and/or extensive mountain obscurations.

   2)   AIRMET Tango describes moderate turbulence, sustained surface winds of 30 kt. or greater, and nonconvective low-level wind shear.

   3)   AIRMET Zulu describes moderate icing and provides freezing-level heights.

d.   EXAMPLE:

KBOSS WA 211945 AIRMET SIERRA UPDT 3 FOR IFR AND MTN OBSCN VALID UNTIL 220200

AIRMET IFR. ME NH VT MA CT RI NY NJ AND CSTL WTRS FROM CAR TO YSJ TO 150 E ACL TO EWR TO YOW TO CAR CIG BLW 010/VIS BLW 3SM PCPN/BR. CONDS CONT BYD 02Z THRU 08Z.

   1)   **KBOS** AIRMET area identifier is for the Boston area.

   2)   **S** AIRMET series is SIERRA.

   3)   **WA** is the product type for an AIRMET.

   4)   **211945** is the issuance UTC date/time.

   5)   **AIRMET SIERRA UPDT 3** is the third updated issuance of this Boston AIRMET series.

   6)   **FOR IFR AND MTN OBSCN** is the product description.

   7)   **VALID UNTIL 220200** is the ending UTC date/time.

   8)   **AIRMET IFR. ME NH VT MA CT RI NY NJ AND CSTL WTRS** is the product type/ series and phenomenon location (states).

   9)   **FROM CAR TO YSJ TO 150 E ACL TO EWR TO YOW TO CAR** is the phenomenon location (VOR locations).

   10) **CIG BLW 010/VIS BLW 3SM PCPN/BR. CONDS CONT BYD 02Z THRU 08Z** is the phenomenon description.

2.   A SIGMET advises of nonconvective activity that is potentially hazardous to all aircraft.

   a.   SIGMETs are issued when the following phenomena occur or are expected to occur:

      1)   Severe icing not associated with thunderstorms

      2)   Severe or extreme turbulence or clear air turbulence (CAT) not associated with thunderstorms

      3)   Duststorms, sandstorms, or volcanic ash lowering surface or in-flight visibilities to below 3 SM

      4)   Volcanic eruption

9.2 AVIATION ROUTINE WEATHER REPORT (METAR)

1. Aviation routine weather reports (METARs) are actual weather observations at the time indicated on the report. There are two types of reports.

    a. METAR is an hourly routine observation (scheduled).
    b. SPECI is a special METAR observation (unscheduled).

2. Following the type of report are the elements listed below:

    a. The four-letter ICAO station identifier.
    b. Date and time of report. It is appended with a "Z" to denote Coordinated Universal Time (UTC).
    c. Modifier (as required).
    d. Wind.
    e. Visibility.
    f. Runway visual range (as required).
    g. Weather phenomena.
    h. Sky conditions.

        1) The ceiling is the lowest broken or overcast layer, or vertical visibility into an obscuration.
        2) Cloud bases are reported with three digits in hundreds of feet AGL.

            a) EXAMPLE: OVC007 means overcast cloud layer at 700 ft. AGL.

        3) Total obscurations are reported in the format "VVhhh" with "VV" meaning vertical visibility and "hhh" being the vertical visibility in hundreds of feet.

            a) EXAMPLE: VV008 means vertical visibility of 800 ft.

    i. Temperature-dew point.
    j. Altimeter.
    k. Remarks (RMK).

        1) RAE42SNB42 means rain ended at 42 min. past the hour and snow began at 42 min. past the hour.

3. EXAMPLE: METAR KAUS 301651Z 12008KT 4SM –RA HZ BKN010 BKN023 OVC160 21/17 A3005 RMK RAB25

    a. METAR is a routine weather observation.
    b. KAUS is Austin, TX.
    c. 301651Z means the observation was taken on the 30th day at 1651 UTC (or Zulu).
    d. 12008KT means the wind is from 120° true at 8 kt.
    e. 4SM means the visibility is 4 statute miles.
    f. –RA HZ means light rain and haze.
    g. BKN010 BKN023 OVC160 means broken cloud layers at 1,000 ft. and 2,300 ft. and an overcast cloud layer at 16,000 ft.
    h. 21/17 means the temperature is 21°C and the dew point is 17°C.
    i. A3005 means the altimeter setting is 30.05 in. of Hg.
    j. RMK RAB25 means remarks, rain began at 25 min. past the hour.

9.3 AIRCRAFT OBSERVATIONS AND REPORTS

1.   PIREPs are transmitted in the format illustrated below.

UUA/UA	Type of report: URGENT (UUA) - Any PIREP that contains any of the following weather phenomena: tornadoes, funnel clouds, or waterspouts; severe or extreme turbulence, including clear air turbulence (CAT); severe icing; hail; low-level wind shear (LLWS) (pilot reports air speed fluctuations of 10 knots or more within 2,000 feet of the surface); any other weather phenomena reported which are considered by the controller to be hazardous, or potentially hazardous, to flight operations. ROUTINE (UA) - Any PIREP that contains weather phenomena not listed above, including low-level wind shear reports with air speed fluctuations of less than 10 knots.
/OV	Location: Use VHF NAVAID(s) or an airport using the three- or four-letter location identifier. Position can be over a site, at some location relative to a site, or along a route. Ex: /OV KABC; /OV KABC090025; /OV KABC045020-DEF; /OV KABC-KDEF
/TM	Time: Four digits in UTC. Ex: /TM 0915
/FL	Altitude/Flight level: Three digits for hundreds of feet with no space between FL and altitude. If not known, use UNKN. Ex: /FL095; /FL310; /FLUNKN
/TP	Aircraft type: Four digits maximum; if not known, use UNKN. Ex: /TP L329; /TP B737; /TP UNKN
/SK	Sky cover: Describes cloud amount, height of cloud bases, and height of cloud tops. If unknown, use UNKN. Ex: /SK SCT040-TOP080; /SK BKNUNKN-TOP075; /SK BKN-OVC050-TOPUNKN; /SK OVCUNKN-TOP085
/WX	Flight visibility and weather: Flight visibility (FV) is reported first. Use standard METAR weather symbols. Intensity (– for light, no qualifier for moderate, and + for heavy) shall be coded for all precipitation types except ice crystals and hail. Ex: /WX FV05SM –RA; /WX FV01 SN BR; /WX RA
/TA	Temperature (Celsius): If below zero, prefix with an "M." Temperature should also be reported if icing is reported. Ex: /TA 15; /TA M06
/WV	Wind: Direction from which the wind is blowing coded in tens of degrees using three digits. Directions of less than 100 degrees shall be preceded by a zero. The wind speed shall be entered as a two- or three-digit group immediately following the direction, coded in whole knots using the hundreds, tens, and units digits. Ex: /WV 27045KT; /WV 280110KT
/TB	Turbulence: Use standard contractions for intensity and type (CAT or CHOP when appropriate). Include altitude only if different from FL. Ex: /TB EXTRM; /TB OCNL LGT-MDT BLO 090; /TB MOD-SEV CHOP 080-110
/IC	Icing: Describe using standard intensity and type contractions. Include altitude only if different from FL. Ex: /IC LGT-MDT RIME; /IC SEV CLR 028-045
/RM	Remarks: Use free form to clarify the report putting hazardous elements first. Ex: /RM LLWS – 15 KT SFC-030 DURGC RY 22 JFK

2. EXAMPLE: UA /OV OKC 063064/TM 1522/FL080/TP C172/TA –04/WV 245040/TB
              LGT/RM IN CLR.

   DECODED: Pilot report, 64 NM on the 063° radial from Oklahoma City VOR at
              1522 UTC (or Z), flight level 8,000 ft., type of aircraft is a Cessna 172, outside
              air temperature is –4°C, wind 245° at 40 kt., light turbulence, remarks are that
              the pilot is in clear skies.

3. AIREPs are also reported as routine or special and are reported by the pilot or generated
   automatically, with reports delivered to a ground station.

9.4 TERMINAL AERODROME FORECAST (TAF)

1. Terminal aerodrome forecasts (TAFs) are weather forecasts for selected airports throughout the
   country. They are a source of weather to expect at your destination airport at your ETA.

   a. The forecast is for a geographical area within a 5-SM radius of the airport's center.

      1) **VC** (vicinity) is used to refer to weather expected to occur between a 5- to 10-SM
         radius of the airport.

2. The elements of a TAF are listed below:

   a. Type of report

      1) TAF is a routine forecast.
      2) TAF AMD is an amended forecast.

   b. ICAO station identifier

   c. Date and time the forecast is actually prepared

   d. Valid period of the forecast

   e. Forecast meteorological conditions. This is the body of the forecast and includes the
      following:

      1) Wind

         a) **VRB** means that the wind direction is forecast to fluctuate due to convective
            activity or low wind speeds (1-6 kt. inclusive).

      2) Visibility

         a) **P6SM** means the forecast visibility is greater than 6 SM.

      3) Weather

      4) Sky condition

      5) Optional data (wind shear)

         a) Wind shear in a TAF is a forecast of nonconvective low-level wind shear (up to
            2,000 ft. AGL) and is forecast only when wind shear is expected.

         b) EXAMPLE: **WS005/27050KT** means low-level wind shear at 500 ft. AGL, wind
            270° true at 50 kt.

9.5   WINDS AND TEMPERATURES ALOFT FORECAST (FB)

1.   Forecast winds and temperatures, provided at specified altitudes for specific locations in the United States, are presented in table form.

2.   A four-digit group (used when temperatures are not forecast) shows wind direction with reference to **true** north and the wind speed in **knots**.

    a.   The first two digits indicate wind direction after a zero is added.
    b.   The next two digits indicate the wind speed.

3.   A six-digit group includes the forecast temperature aloft.

    a.   The last two digits indicate the temperature in degrees Celsius.

    b.   Plus or minus is indicated before the temperature, except at higher altitudes (above 24,000 ft. MSL) where it is always below freezing.

    c.   The ISA (International Standard Atmosphere) temperature is 15°C at the surface with a standard lapse rate of 2°C per 1,000 ft.

4.   When the wind speed is less than 5 kt., the forecast is coded **9900**, which means that the wind is light and variable.

5.   Note that at some of the lower levels the wind and temperature information is omitted.

    a.   Winds aloft are not forecast for levels within 1,500 ft. of the station elevation.

    b.   No temperatures are forecast for the 3,000-ft. level or for a level within 2,500 ft. of the station elevation.

6.   If the wind speed is forecast to be 100 to 199 kt., the forecaster adds 50 to the direction and subtracts 100 from the speed. To decode, you must do the reverse: subtract 50 from the direction and add 100 to the speed.

    a.   EXAMPLE: If the forecast for the 39,000-ft. level appears as **731960**, subtract 50 from 73 and add 100 to 19. The wind would be 230° at 119 kt. with a temperature of –60°C (above 24,000 ft.).

    b.   It is easy to know when the coded direction has been increased by 50. Coded direction (in tens of degrees) normally ranges from 01 (010°) to 36 (360°). Any coded direction with a numerical value greater than 36 indicates a wind of 100 kt. or greater. The coded direction for winds of 100 to 199 kt. thus ranges from 51 to 86.

7.   If the wind speed is forecast to be 199 kt. or more, the wind group is coded as 199 kt.; e.g., **7799** is decoded 270° at 199 kt. or more.

8.   EXAMPLES: Decode these FB winds and temperatures:

Coded	Decoded
9900+00	Winds light and variable, temperature 0°C
2707	270° at 7 kt.
850552	85 – 50 = 35; 05 + 100 = 105
	350° at 105 kt., temperature –52°C

9.6 LOW-LEVEL SIGNIFICANT WEATHER PROG

1. Low-level prognostic charts contain conditions forecast to exist at a valid time shown on the chart. Low-altitude significant weather charts are issued four times daily and are valid at fixed times: 0000, 0600, 1200, and 1800 UTC.

   a. The two panels forecast significant weather from the surface up to 24,000 ft.: one for 12 hr. and the other for 24 hr. from the time of issuance.

   b. Some service providers also include two lower panels with forecast surface conditions: one for 12 hr. and the other for 24 hr. from the time of issuance.

   c. The figures below are examples.

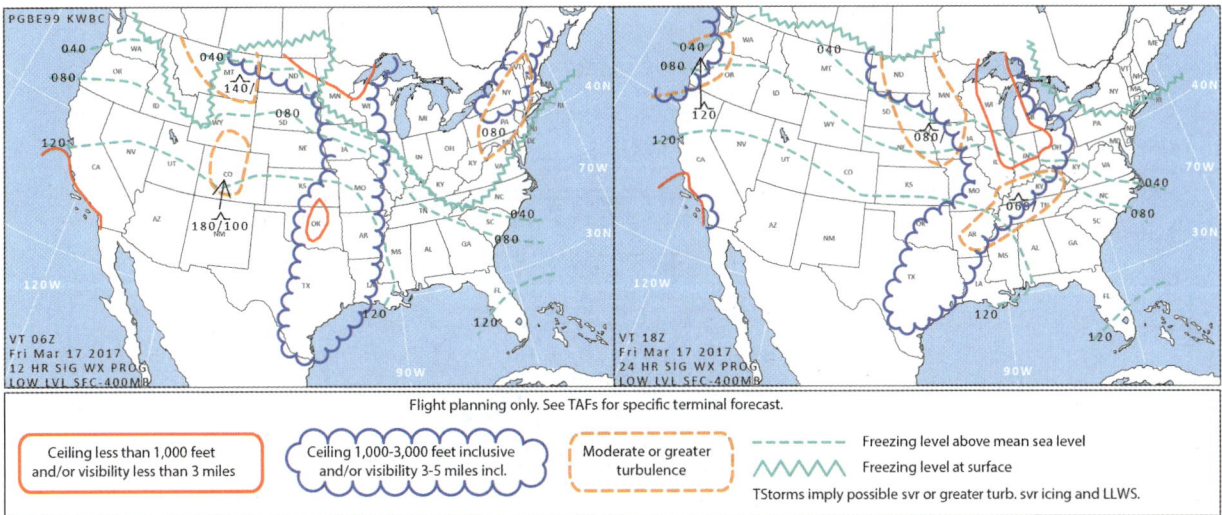

Figure 18. – U.S. Low-Level Significant Weather Prognostic Charts.

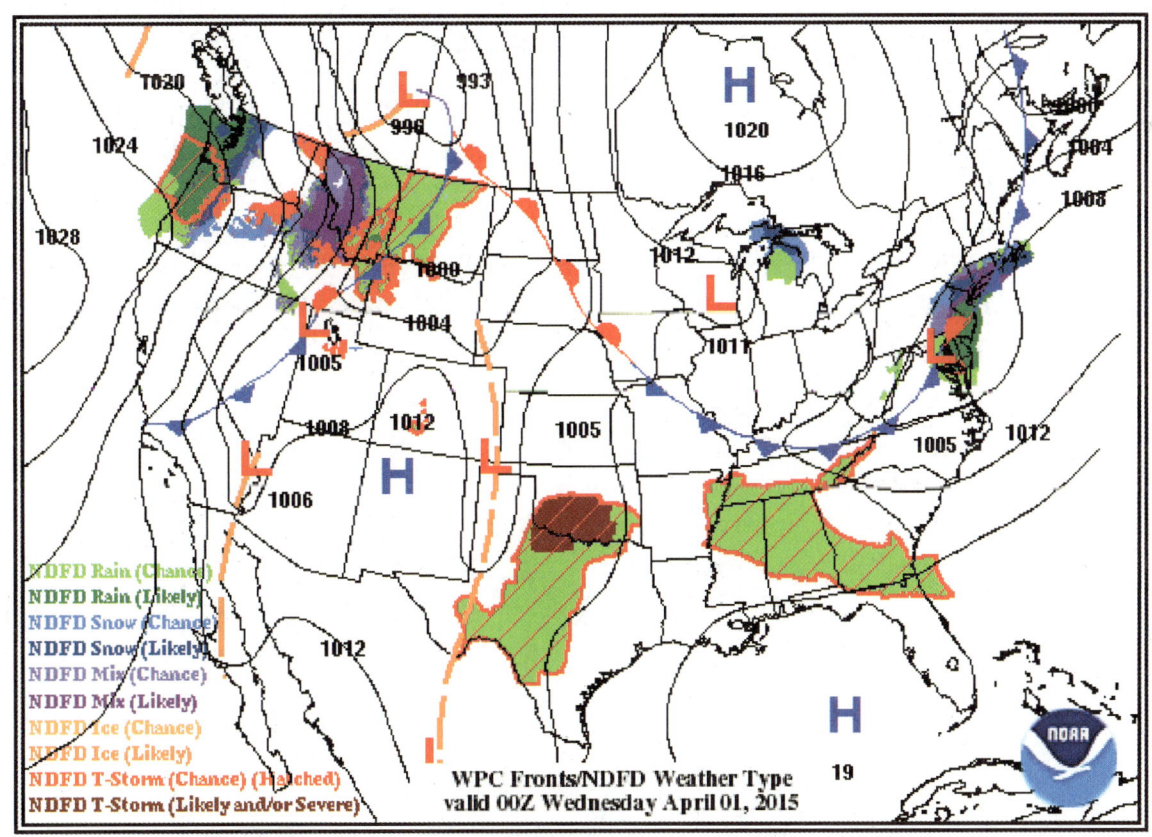

2.   The low-level significant weather prognostic charts depict

    a.   Ceilings less than 1,000 ft. and/or visibility less than 3 SM (IFR) indicated by a solid line around the area

    b.   Ceilings 1,000 to 3,000 ft. and/or visibility 3 to 5 SM (MVFR) indicated by a scalloped line around the area

    c.   Moderate or greater turbulence indicated by a broken line around the area

        1)   Altitudes "up to" are above a line; e.g., <u>120</u> is up to 12,000 ft.
        2)   Altitudes "down to" are below a line; $\overline{90}$ is down to 9,000 ft.

    d.   Freezing levels indicated by a dashed line corresponding to the height of the freezing level

3.   The bottom panels show location of

    a.   Highs, lows, fronts
    b.   Other areas of significant weather

4.   The following symbols are used on "prog" charts:

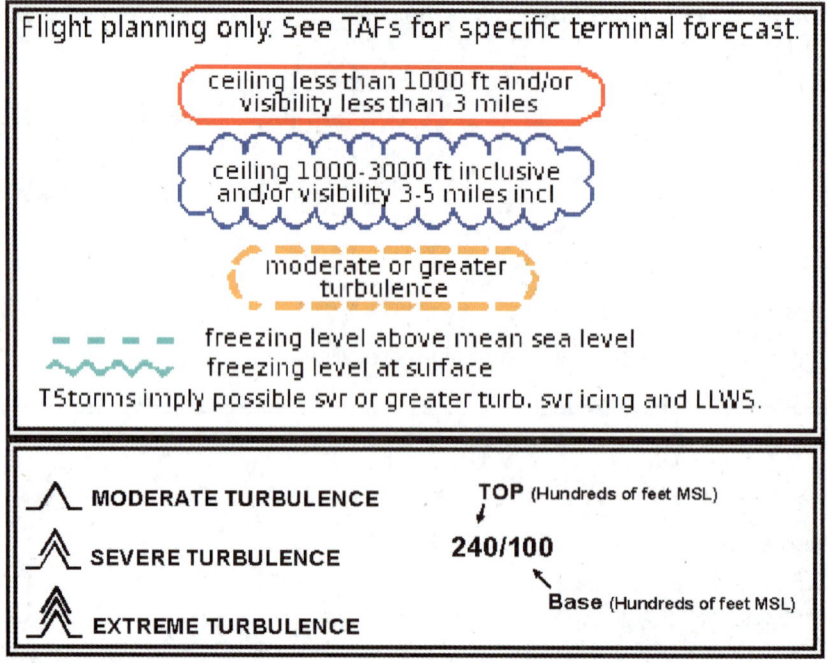

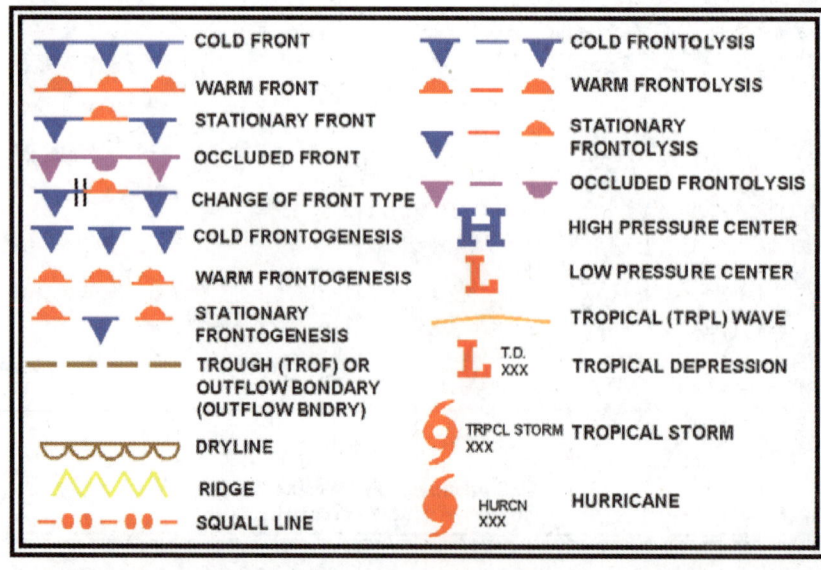

9.7 GRAPHICAL FORECASTS FOR AVIATION (GFAs)

1. GFAs are a continuously updated set of Internet-based displays that provide the necessary aviation weather information to give users a complete picture of weather that may affect flight in the continental United States.

    a. GFAs present forecasts, observational data, and warnings of weather phenomena that the user can view from 14 hr. in the past to 18 hr. in the future.

    b. GFA graphics depict chosen phenomena (e.g., clouds, turbulence, icing) from the surface up to 42,000 ft. MSL. The user may zoom in or out to view as large or small an area as desired.

    c. Users must first select either Forecasts or Observations/Warnings (Obs/Warn). The specific hour may then be set using the time slider.

        1) Forecasts. When using Forecasts, users may choose from TAF, CIG/VIS (ceiling/ visibility), Clouds, PCPN/WX (precipitation and weather type), TS (thunderstorm), Winds, Turb (turbulence), and Ice tabs.

        2) Observations/Warnings. This option allows the user to display data for the current time or up to 14 hr. in the past. The products available are METAR, PCPN/WX, CIG/VIS, PIREP, and RAD/SAT (radar/satellite imagery).

2. For users with limited Internet connectivity, Static Image GFAs give choices of

    a. Two types of plots

        1) Aviation Surface Forecast
        2) Aviation Clouds Forecast

    b. Ten regions

        1) CONUS (contiguous United States)
        2) Nine sub-sectors

    c. Forecast period

        1) 3-hr. increments out to 18 hr.

3. The product elements of Aviation Surface Forecast graphics include

    a. Graphics of surface visibility

        1) Low IFR: 0-1 SM
        2) IFR: 1-3 SM
        3) Marginal VFR: 3-5 SM

    b. Overlays of surface wind and gusts

        1) Depicted with standard wind barb
        2) Red coloring indicates wind gust speed

    c. Overlays of predominant precipitation type (i.e., rain, snow, mix, ice, or thunderstorm) coincident with any cloud

    d. Overlays of predominant weather type (i.e., haze, fog, smoke, blowing dust/sand)

    e. Overlays of Graphical AIRMETs

        1) Instrument Flight Rules (IFR)
        2) Strong Surface Wind

f.   Common symbols on GFAs include the following:

Symbol	Description	Symbol	Description
••	Light rain	☀☀	Moderate snow
•⋰•	Moderate rain	☀☀☀	Heavy snow
•⋱••	Heavy rain	▽̇	Light rain showers
∾	Light freezing rain	▽̇̇	Moderate to heavy rain showers
∾∾	Moderate to heavy freezing rain	☀▽	Light snow showers
✻	Light rain and snow	☀▽̇	Moderate to heavy snow showers
∾	Light freezing drizzle	✚	Blowing snow
∾∾	Moderate to heavy freezing drizzle	↰	Thunderstorm, rain
✳✳	Light snow	≡	Fog

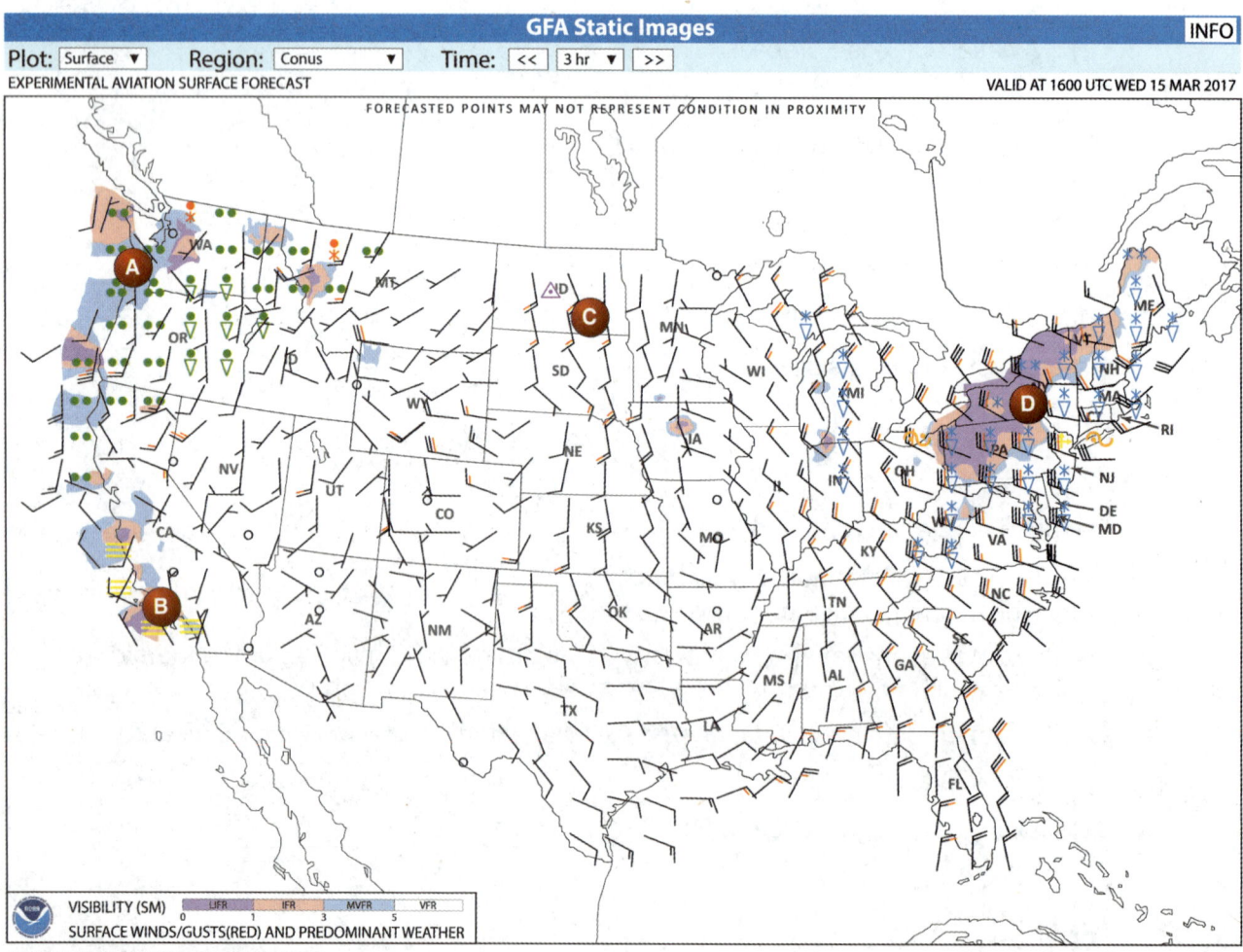

Figure 260. – Graphical Forecast for Aviation.

4. The product elements for Aviation Clouds Forecast graphics include

   a. Graphics of cloud coverage fraction (few/scattered, broken, overcast) for clouds with bases below Flight Level 180 (FL 180 - 18,000 ft. above MSL)

   b. Overlay of text indicating cloud coverage and height in feet above MSL

      1) Clouds above FL 180 are indicated as cirrus.

      2) The bases below FL 180 of FEW/SCT, BKN, and OVC clouds are labeled.

      3) The tops of the highest BKN or OVC layer with bases below FL 180 are labeled.

      4) When multiple layers of BKN or OVC clouds exist, the top of the highest layer will be given preceded by LYRD.

      5) Cirrus clouds above clouds with bases below FL 180 are labeled as CI ABV.

   c. Overlays of Graphical AIRMETs

      1) Mountain obscuration
      2) Icing

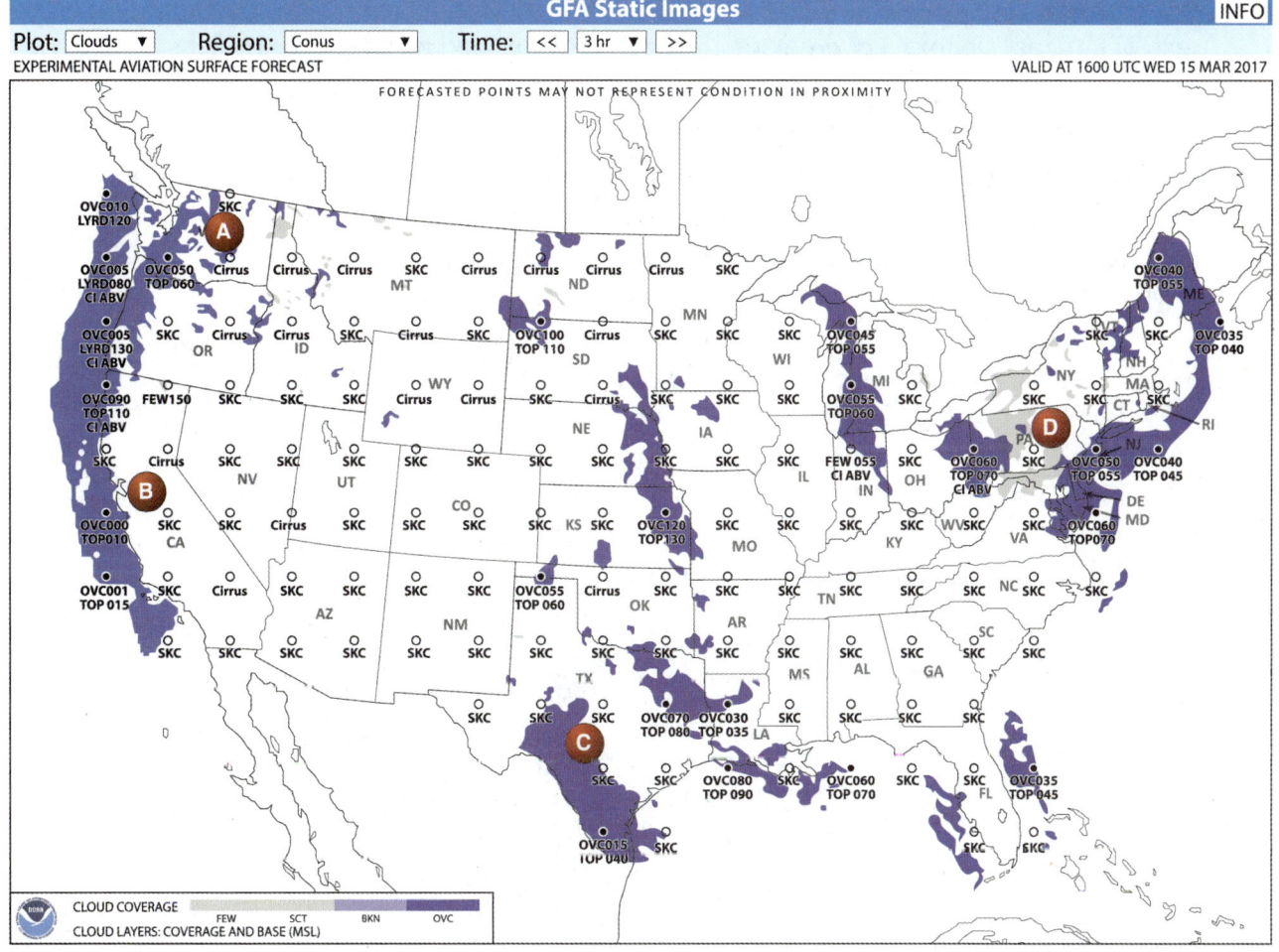

Figure 263. – Graphical Forecast for Aviation.

9.8 HIGH-LEVEL SIGNIFICANT WEATHER PROG

1. The U.S. High-Level Significant Weather Prognostic Chart encompasses airspace from 25,000 ft. to 63,000 ft. pressure altitude (FL 250 to FL 630).

2. Tropopause heights are depicted in hundreds of feet MSL, which may be presented by a five-sided polygon or a small rectangular block.

   a. The five-sided polygon indicates areas of high and low tropopause heights.

   b. The rectangular block indicates the tropopause height in areas that have a very flat tropopause slope.

3. The height and maximum wind speed of jet streams having a core speed of 80 kt. or greater are shown as a solid line with arrowheads indicating the flow direction.

   a. The height is given as a flight level (FL).

   b. The maximum core wind velocity is depicted by a shaft with a pennant equal to 50 kt. and a feather, or barb, equal to 10 kt.

   1) EXAMPLE: ▲▲⊩⊩ means a maximum core speed of 130 kt.

4. Areas of forecast moderate or greater turbulence are enclosed by bold, dashed lines.

   a. The enclosed area includes all turbulence not caused by thunderstorms or convective activity (thunderstorms imply turbulence).

   b. Areas are labeled with the appropriate turbulence symbol(s) and the vertical extent in hundreds of feet MSL.

5. Small scalloped lines enclose areas of expected cumulonimbus development. "CB" denotes cumulonimbus.

   a. CB refers to the occurrence or expected occurrence of an area of widespread cumulonimbus clouds or cumulonimbus clouds along a line with little or no space between the individual clouds, or cumulonimbus clouds embedded in cloud layers or concealed by haze or dust.

   b. CB bases below 25,000 ft. (FL 250), the lowest altitude limit of the chart, are shown as XXX.

   1) CB tops are expressed in hundreds of feet MSL.

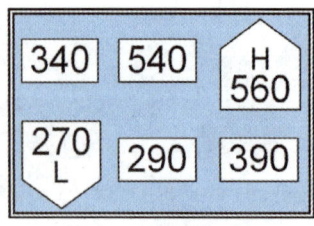

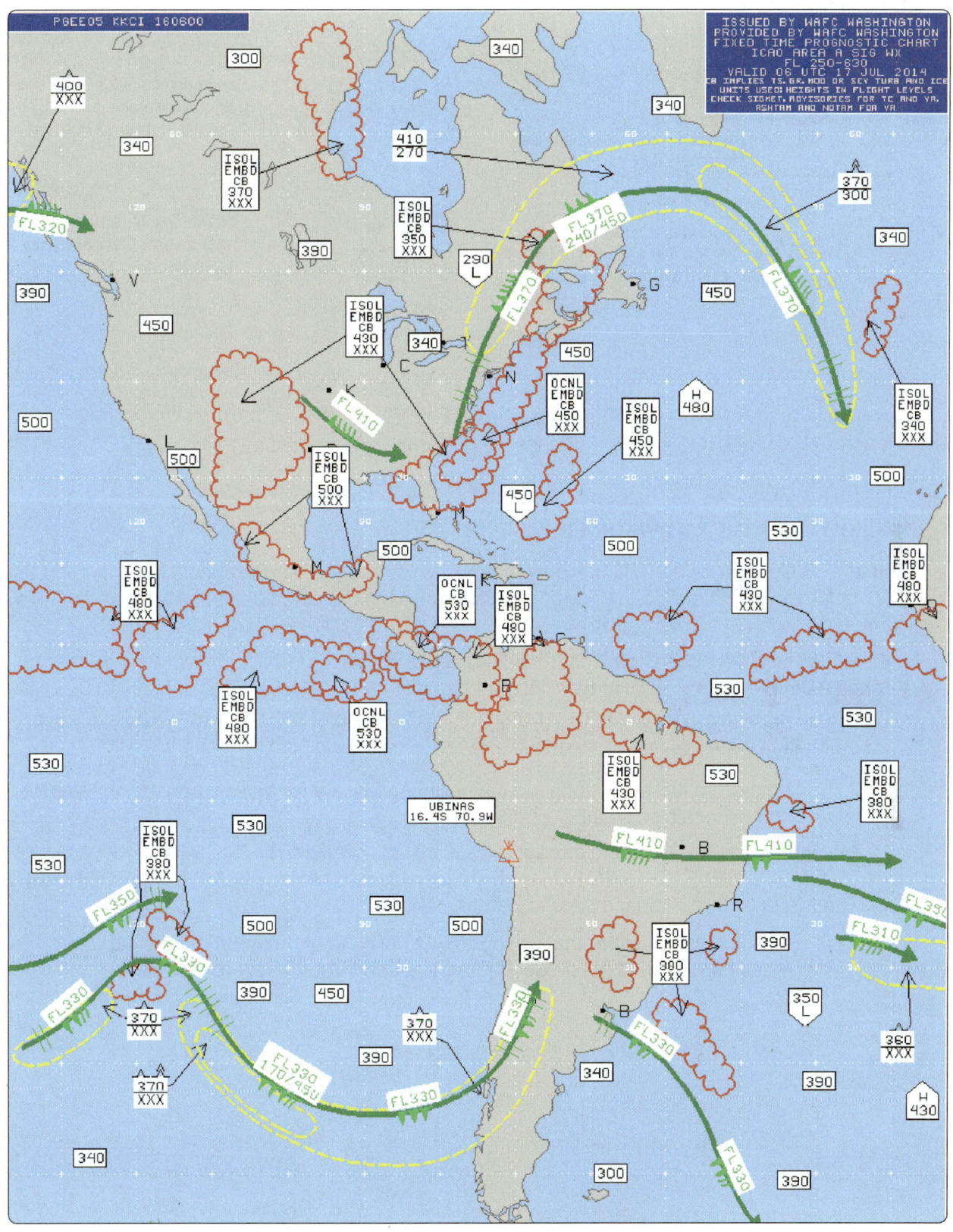

Figure 20. – High-Level Significant Weather Prognostic Chart.

6.   EXAMPLES:

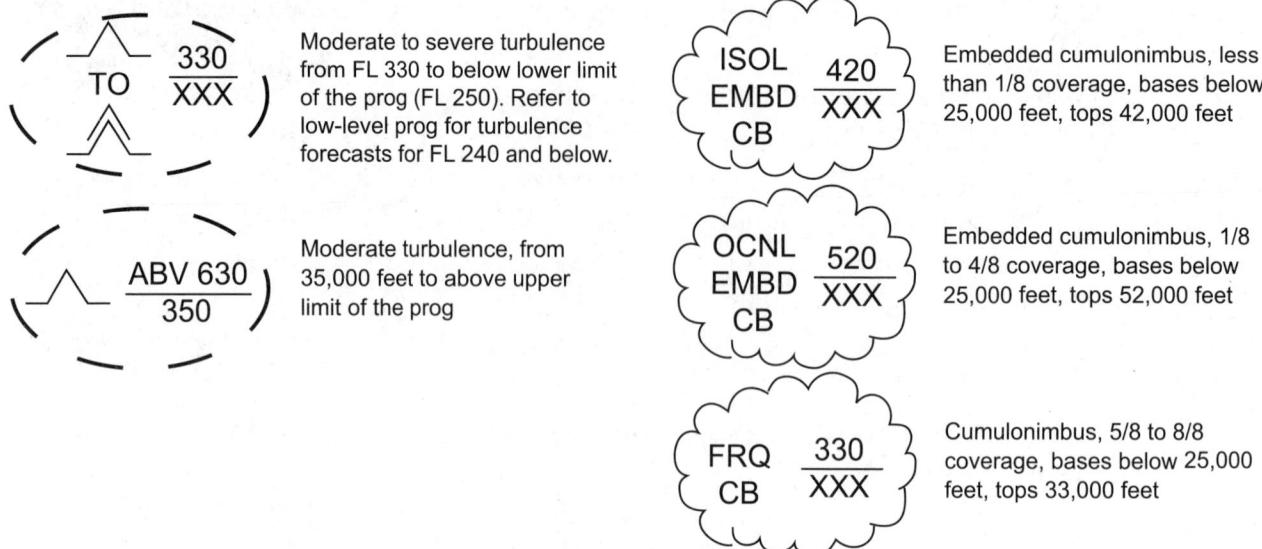

Moderate to severe turbulence from FL 330 to below lower limit of the prog (FL 250). Refer to low-level prog for turbulence forecasts for FL 240 and below.

Moderate turbulence, from 35,000 feet to above upper limit of the prog

Embedded cumulonimbus, less than 1/8 coverage, bases below 25,000 feet, tops 42,000 feet

Embedded cumulonimbus, 1/8 to 4/8 coverage, bases below 25,000 feet, tops 52,000 feet

Cumulonimbus, 5/8 to 8/8 coverage, bases below 25,000 feet, tops 33,000 feet

9.9 IN-FLIGHT WEATHER ADVISORIES

1.   Pilots of IFR flights seeking ATC in-flight weather avoidance assistance should keep in mind that ATC radar limitations and frequency congestion may limit the controller's ability to provide this service.

2.   Flight Information Services-Broadcast (FIS-B) is a ground-based broadcast system provided through ADS-B via the 978 MHz data link that can display in-flight weather data.

   a.   FIS-B information is intended for advisory use in assisting long- and near-term planning and decision making.

      1)   The system lacks the updating capability necessary for tactical aerial maneuvering around localized weather phenomena.

   b.   Many products are available through FIS-B, including AIRMETs, SIGMETs, convective SIGMETs, NEXRAD, D-NOTAMs, FDC-NOTAMs, METARs, TAFs, Winds Aloft, PIREPs, and Special Use Airspace status updates.

      1)   Pilots should be aware that the NEXRAD uplink may be up to 20 min. old upon receipt and should not be used for navigation through severe weather.

9.10 MISCELLANEOUS CHARTS AND FORECASTS

1. PIREPs, AIRMETs, and SIGMETs reflect the most accurate information on current and forecast icing conditions.

   a. The rate of icing accumulation (trace, light, moderate, severe) determines how icing is reported in a PIREP or to ATC when asked to report your icing conditions.

      1) The type of icing (rime, clear, mixed) may or may not be reported in the remarks section, but this does not impact the way icing is reported in the PIREP icing group.

2. From constant pressure charts, you can approximate the observed temperature, wind, and temperature-dew point spread along your proposed route.

3. A convective outlook (AC) describes the prospects for general thunderstorm activity during the following 24-hr. period.

   a. Areas in which there is a high, moderate, or slight risk of severe thunderstorms are included as well as areas where thunderstorms may approach severe limits.

4. The surface analysis chart depicts actual frontal positions, pressure patterns, temperature, dew point, wind, weather, and obstructions to vision at the valid time of the chart.

5. The Aviation Watch Notification Message product (SAW or AWW) is unscheduled and is issued as required.

   a. This product is an approximation of the area of a public severe thunderstorm watch or public tornado watch. It may be defined as a rectangle or parallelogram using VOR navigational aids as coordinates.

   b. Although the NWS uses the acronym SAW for an Aviation Watch Notification Message, AWW is used in the product header for processing by weather data systems.

QUESTIONS AND ANSWER EXPLANATIONS: All of the instrument rating knowledge test questions chosen by the FAA for release as well as additional questions selected by Gleim relating to the material in the previous outlines are provided on the following pages. These questions have been organized into the same subunits as the outlines. To the immediate right of each question are the correct answer and answer explanations. You should cover these answers and answer explanations while responding to the questions. Refer to the general discussion in the Introduction on how to take the FAA knowledge test.

Remember that the questions from the FAA knowledge test bank have been reordered by topic and organized into a meaningful sequence. Also, the first line of the answer explanation gives the citation of the authoritative source for the answer.

QUESTIONS

9.1 AIRMETs and SIGMETs

1. AIRMETs are issued on a scheduled basis every

- A. 15 minutes after the hour only.
- B. 15 minutes until the AIRMET is canceled.
- C. six hours.

Answer (C) is correct. (AC 00-45H Chap 5)
DISCUSSION: AIRMETs are issued on a scheduled basis every 6 hours, with unscheduled amendments issued as required.
Answer (A) is incorrect. AIRMETs are issued on a scheduled basis every 6 hours, not every 15 minutes past the hour. **Answer (B) is incorrect.** AIRMETs are issued on a scheduled basis every 6 hours, not every 15 minutes until the AIRMET is canceled.

2. SIGMETs are issued as a warning of weather conditions potentially hazardous

- A. particularly to light aircraft.
- B. to all aircraft.
- C. only to light aircraft operations.

Answer (B) is correct. (AC 00-45H Chap 5)
DISCUSSION: SIGMETs warn of weather considered potentially hazardous to all categories of aircraft. SIGMETs contain information on severe turbulence, severe icing, dust storms, sand storms, and volcanic ash.
Answer (A) is incorrect. SIGMETs apply to all aircraft. **Answer (C) is incorrect.** AIRMETs, not SIGMETs, apply to light aircraft.

3. Consider this AIRMET which includes your route of flight:

> DFWS WA 211445 AIRMET IFR . . . OK TX FROM END TO TXK TO HOU TO LBB TO END CIG BELOW 010. CONDS ENDG 15-18Z

This indicates

- A. there will be icing in clouds below 10,000 feet MSL.
- B. visibility will be less than 3 SM until 15Z.
- C. the area will have low ceilings before 15Z.

Answer (C) is correct. (AC 00-45H Chap 5)
DISCUSSION: CIG is the aviation weather code for ceiling, and 010 is the aviation weather code for 1,000 ft. Therefore, this AIRMET is referring to ceilings below 1,000 ft. within the defined area. CONDS ENDG 15-18Z means the forecast conditions will be ending between 1500 and 1800 Zulu time.
Answer (A) is incorrect. There is no mention of icing in clouds within this forecast. **Answer (B) is incorrect.** There is no mention of visibility within this forecast.

4. SIGMETs are issued as a warning of weather conditions potentially hazardous

- A. particularly to large commercial operators.
- B. to all aircraft regardless of size or operating environment.
- C. particularly to light aircraft.

Answer (B) is correct. (AC 00-45H Chap 5)
DISCUSSION: SIGMETs warn of weather considered potentially hazardous to all categories of aircraft.
Answer (A) is incorrect. SIGMETs are issued to warn of weather conditions that present a potential hazard to all aircraft, not just large commercial operators. SIGMETs can include potential hazards such as severe turbulence, severe icing, dust and/or sand storms, and volcanic ash. **Answer (C) is incorrect.** The potential hazards included in SIGMETs are of a severity that can affect the safety of flight for any aircraft, not only light aircraft. These can include potential hazards such as severe turbulence, severe icing, dust and/or sand storms, and volcanic ash.

9.2 Aviation Routine Weather Report (METAR)

5. The reporting station originating this Aviation Routine Weather Report has a field elevation of 620 feet. If the reported sky cover is one continuous layer, what is its thickness (tops of OVC are reported at 6,500 feet)?

> METAR KMDW 121856Z AUTO 32005KT 1 1/2SM +RA BR OVC007 17/16 A2980

- A. 5,180 feet.
- B. 5,800 feet.
- C. 5,880 feet.

Answer (A) is correct. (AC 00-45H Chap 3)
DISCUSSION: The sky cover for KMDW is reported as a ceiling of 700 feet AGL, overcast (OVC007). The field elevation is 620 feet MSL; thus, the base of the overcast layer is 1,320 feet MSL (700 + 620). The tops of the overcast layer are reported at 6,500 feet; thus, the thickness of the overcast layer is 5,180 feet (6,500 − 1,320).
Answer (B) is incorrect. This would be the thickness of the sky cover if the field elevation were 0 feet, not 620 feet. **Answer (C) is incorrect.** This is the height above ground of the tops of the overcast layer, not the thickness of the overcast layer.

6. The station originating the following weather report has a field elevation of 1,300 feet MSL. From the bottom of the overcast cloud layer, what is its thickness (tops of OVC are reported at 3,800 feet)?

SPECI KOKC 2228Z 28024G36KT 3/4SM BKN008 OVC020 28/23 A3000

   A. 500 feet.

   B. 1,700 feet.

   C. 2,500 feet.

Answer (A) is correct. *(AC 00-45H Chap 3)*
   DISCUSSION: The question is to determine the thickness of the overcast layer at KOKC. The SPECI reported the base of the overcast cloud layer at 2,000 feet AGL (OVC020). The field elevation is 1,300 feet MSL; thus, the base of the overcast layer is 3,300 feet MSL (2,000 + 1,300). The tops of the overcast layer are reported at 3,800 feet MSL; thus, the thickness of the overcast cloud layer is 500 feet (3,800 − 3,300).
   Answer (B) is incorrect. This is the distance from the base of the broken (BKN), not overcast (OVC), cloud layer to the top of the overcast. **Answer (C) is incorrect.** This is the height above the ground of the tops of the overcast, not the thickness of the overcast layer.

7. Interpret the remarks section of METAR surface report for KBNA.

METAR KBNA 211250Z 33018KT 290V260 1/2SM R31/2700FT +SN BLSNFG VV008 00/M03 A2991 RMK RAESNB42

   A. The wind is variable from 290° to 360°.

   B. Heavy blowing snow and fog on runway 31.

   C. Rain ended 42 minutes past the hour, snow began 42 minutes past the hour.

Answer (C) is correct. *(AC 00-45H Chap 3)*
   DISCUSSION: The contraction RMK follows the altimeter in the body and precedes remarks. RMK RAESNB42 means remarks follow, rain ended (RAE), and snow began (SNB) 42 min. past the hour.
   Answer (A) is incorrect. This METAR indicates that the wind is variable from 290° to 260°, not 290° to 360°. **Answer (B) is incorrect.** This METAR indicates that there is heavy snow, blowing snow, and fog at the airport, not heavy blowing snow and not just on Runway 31. The Runway 31 runway visual range (RVR) is 2,700 ft.

8. A ceiling is defined as the height of the

   A. highest layer of clouds or obscuring phenomena aloft that covers over 6/10 of the sky.

   B. lowest layer of clouds that contributed to the overall overcast.

   C. lowest layer of clouds or obscuring phenomena aloft that is reported as broken or overcast.

Answer (C) is correct. *(AC 00-45H Chap 3)*
   DISCUSSION: For aviation purposes, the ceiling is the lowest broken or overcast layer, or vertical visibility into an obscuration.
   Answer (A) is incorrect. The ceiling is the base of the lowest, not highest, broken or overcast layer. **Answer (B) is incorrect.** The lowest layer of clouds must be broken or overcast, not simply a contributor to the overall overcast.

9. What significant sky condition is reported in this METAR observation?

METAR KBNA 1250Z 33018KT 290V360 1/2SM R31/2700FT +SN BLSNFG VV008 00/M03 A2991 RMK RERAE42SNB42

   A. Runway 31 ceiling is 2,700 feet.

   B. Sky is obscured with vertical visibility of 800 feet.

   C. Measured ceiling is 300 feet overcast.

Answer (B) is correct. *(AC 00-45H Chap 3)*
   DISCUSSION: The sky condition follows the weather element. At KBNA, the sky cover is reported as VV008, which means the sky is obscured (indefinite ceiling) with a vertical visibility of 800 feet.
   Answer (A) is incorrect. Runway 31 RVR, not ceiling, is 2,700 feet. **Answer (C) is incorrect.** The observation 00/M03 means the temperature is 0°C and the dew point is −3°C, not that there is a measured ceiling of 300 feet overcast.

10. What is the thickness of the cloud layer given a field elevation of 1,500 feet MSL with tops of the overcast at 7,000 feet MSL?

METAR KHOB 151250Z 17006KT 4SM OVC010 13/11 A2998

   A. 4,500 feet.

   B. 6,500 feet.

   C. 5,500 feet.

Answer (A) is correct. *(FAA-H-8083-25B Chap 13)*
   DISCUSSION: To determine the thickness of the cloud layer, find the difference between the tops and the base. Find the base in MSL by adding the field elevation (1,500 ft. MSL) to the reported base (OVC010, or 1,000 ft. AGL). The overcast cloud layer tops are reported at 7,000 ft. MSL, so the thickness of the cloud layer is 4,500 ft. (7,000 ft. − 2,500 ft.).
   Answer (B) is incorrect. To determine the thickness of the cloud layer, you must first find the base in MSL by adding, not subtracting, the field elevation (1,500 ft. MSL) to the reported base (OVC010, or 1,000 ft. AGL). This is then subtracted from the tops (7,000 ft. − 2,500 ft.). **Answer (C) is incorrect.** To determine the thickness of the cloud layer, you must first find the base in MSL by adding the field elevation (1,500 ft. MSL) to the reported base (OVC010 or 1,000 ft. AGL). Then, subtract this total from the tops (7,000 ft. − 2,500 ft.).

9.3   Aircraft Observations and Reports

11. Interpret this PIREP.

MRB UA/OV MRB/TM 1430/FL 060/TP C182/SK BKN BL /WX RA/TB MDT.

    A.   Ceiling 6,000 feet intermittently below moderate thundershowers; turbulence increasing westward.

    B.   FL 60,000, intermittently below clouds; moderate rain, turbulence increasing with the wind.

    C.   At 6,000 feet; between layers; moderate turbulence; moderate rain.

Answer (C) is correct. (AC 00-45H Chap 3)
    DISCUSSION: The PIREP decodes as follows: pilot report, over Martinsburg, WV, at 1430 UTC, flight level is 6,000 feet, type of aircraft is a Cessna 182, and sky condition is broken with the pilot reporting between layers in moderate rain and moderate turbulence.
    Answer (A) is incorrect. The flight level, not the ceiling, is 6,000 feet, and TB MDT means moderate turbulence, not thundershowers. **Answer (B) is incorrect.** The flight level is 6,000 feet, not 60,000 feet, and BL means between layers, not below clouds.

12. Which response most closely interprets the following PIREP?

UA/OV OKC 063064/TM 1522/FL080/TP C172/TA – 04 /WV245040/TB LGT/RM IN CLR.

    A.   64 nautical miles on the 63 degree radial from Oklahoma City VOR at 1522 UTC, flight level 8,000 feet. Type of aircraft is a Cessna 172.

    B.   Reported by a Cessna 172, turbulence and light rime icing in climb to 8,000 ft.

    C.   63 nautical miles on the 64 degree radial from Oklahoma City, thunderstorm and light rain at 1522 UTC.

Answer (A) is correct. (AC 00-45H Chap 3)
    DISCUSSION: The PIREP decodes as follows: pilot report, 64 NM on the 063° radial from Oklahoma City VOR at 1522 UTC, flight level is 8,000 ft., type of aircraft is a Cessna 172, outside air temperature is –4°C, wind is from 245° at 40 knots with light turbulence, remarks are that the pilot is in clear skies.
    Answer (B) is incorrect. TB LGT RM IN CLR means light turbulence (remark) in clear, not turbulence and rime icing in climb. **Answer (C) is incorrect.** OKC 063064 means the aircraft was located 64 NM, not 63 NM, on the 063° radial, not the 064° radial. Additionally, there is no report of thunderstorm and rain.

13. What is the base of the ceiling in the following pilot report?

KMOB UA /OV APE230010/TM 1515/FL085/TP BE20/SK BKN065/WX FV03SM HZ FU/TA 20/TB LGT

    A.   There is not a defined ceiling in this report.

    B.   There is a layer reported at 8,500 feet.

    C.   There is a broken layer at 6,500 feet.

Answer (C) is correct. (FAA-H-8083-25B Chap 13, AIM Para 7-1-18)
    DISCUSSION: The PIREP is reporting a broken layer of 6,500 ft. (SK BKN065).
    Answer (A) is incorrect. The PIREP is reporting a broken layer of 6,500 ft. (SK BKN065), which constitutes a ceiling. **Answer (B) is incorrect.** The altitude of the reporting aircraft is at 8,500 ft. (FL085), not the lowest overcast layer.

14. What is indicated by the following report?

TYR UUA/OV TYR180015/TM 1757/FL310/TP B737/TB MOD-SEV CAT 350-390

    A.   An urgent pilot report for moderate to severe clear air turbulence.

    B.   A routine pilot report for overcast conditions from flight levels 350-390.

    C.   A special METAR issued on the 18th day of the month at 1757Z.

Answer (A) is correct. (AC 00-45H Sect 3.2)
    DISCUSSION: The UUA found in the first section of the report indicates an "Urgent Upper Air" report. The /TB MOD-SEV CAT 350-390 in the last section of the report indicates moderate to severe clear air turbulence for flight levels 350 to 390.
    Answer (B) is incorrect. If the report were a routine report, code UA would be used in the first section instead of UUA. **Answer (C) is incorrect.** The second section of the PIREP containing 1800 is the location section. In this example, /OV TYR 180015 indicates that the location of the weather-related phenomenon is on the 180° radial of the TYR VOR at 15 NM. A METAR is an aviation routine weather report; however, METAR coding is used to describe weather and visibility phenomena in the PIREP.

9.4 Terminal Aerodrome Forecast (TAF)

15. Use the TAF to determine the wind shear forecast.

TAF
KCVG 231051Z 231212 12012KT 4SM –RA BR
  OVC008 WS005/27050KT TEMPO 1719 1/2SM
  –RA FG
FM1930 09012KT 1SM –DZ BR VV003 =

  A. Wind shear from the surface to 500 feet AGL from 270° at 50 KT.

  B. Wind shear at 500 feet MSL from 270° at 50 KT.

  C. Wind shear at 500 feet AGL from 270° at 50 KT.

Answer (C) is correct. (AC 00-45H Chap 5)
    DISCUSSION: Wind shear in a TAF is a forecast of nonconvective low-level wind shear (up to 2,000 feet AGL) and is entered after the sky condition when wind shear is expected. The wind shear forecast for KCVG is coded as **WS005/27050KT**, which means low-level wind shear at 500 feet AGL, wind from 270° true at 50 KT.
    Answer (A) is incorrect. The height of the wind shear (WS005) is 500 feet AGL, not from the surface to 500 feet AGL. **Answer (B) is incorrect.** The height of the wind shear (WS005) is 500 feet AGL, not 500 feet MSL.

16. What is the forecast wind at 1800Z in the following TAF?

KMEM 091740Z 1818 00000KT 1/2SM RAFG
OVC005 =

  A. Calm.

  B. Unknown.

  C. Not recorded.

Answer (A) is correct. (AC 00-45H Chap 5)
    DISCUSSION: In the TAF for KMEM, the forecast wind at 1800Z is coded as 00000KT, which means a calm wind.
    Answer (B) is incorrect. The forecast wind at 1800Z is 00000KT, which means a calm, not unknown, wind. **Answer (C) is incorrect.** The forecast wind at 1800Z is 00000KT, which means a calm wind, not an unrecorded wind.

17. When the visibility is greater than 6 SM on a TAF, it is

  A. expressed as 6PSM.

  B. expressed as P6SM.

  C. omitted from the report.

Answer (B) is correct. (AC 00-45H Chap 5)
    DISCUSSION: When the forecast visibility is greater than 6 SM, it will be coded as P6SM.
    Answer (A) is incorrect. Forecast visibility greater than 6 SM will be coded as P6SM, not 6PSM. **Answer (C) is incorrect.** Forecast visibility greater than 6 SM will be coded as P6SM. It is not omitted from the report.

18. Which weather product is a concise statement of the expected weather for an airport's runway complex?

  A. Area Forecast (FA).

  B. Weather Depiction Charts.

  C. Terminal Aerodrome Forecast (TAF).

Answer (C) is correct. (AC 00-45H Chap 5)
    DISCUSSION: A TAF is a concise statement of the expected meteorological conditions at an airport during a specified period (usually 24 hours). Thus, a TAF contains information regarding the expected weather at the destination airport at the ETA.
    Answer (A) is incorrect. An FA was a forecast of general weather conditions over an area the size of several states. It has been discontinued by the FAA. **Answer (B) is incorrect.** Weather Depiction Charts are national weather maps of observed weather at a specific time. NOTE: This product is being phased out by the FAA.

19. A "VRB" wind entry in a Terminal Aerodrome Forecast (TAF) will be indicated when the wind is

  A. 3 knots or less.

  B. 6 knots or less.

  C. 9 knots or less.

Answer (B) is correct. (AC 00-45H Chap 5)
    DISCUSSION: A "VRB" wind entry in a TAF indicates that the wind direction is forecast to fluctuate due to convective activity or low wind speeds of 1 knot to 6 knots inclusive.
    Answer (A) is incorrect. A "VRB" wind entry in a TAF indicates that the wind direction is forecast to fluctuate due to convective activity or low wind speeds of 1 knot to 6 knots inclusive, not 3 knots or less. **Answer (C) is incorrect.** A "VRB" wind entry in a TAF indicates that the wind direction is forecast to fluctuate due to convective activity or low wind speeds of 1 knot to 6 knots inclusive, not 9 knots or less.

20. The body of a Terminal Aerodrome Forecast (TAF) covers a geographical proximity within a

    A.   5 nautical mile radius of the center of an airport.

    B.   5 statute mile radius from the center of an airport runway complex.

    C.   5 to 10 statute mile radius from the center of an airport runway complex.

Answer (B) is correct. (AC 00-45H Chap 5)
    DISCUSSION: The TAF is a concise statement of the expected meteorological conditions at an airport during a specified period (usually 24 hours). The TAF covers a geographic area within a 5-SM radius of the airport's center.
    Answer (A) is incorrect. The TAF covers a geographic area within a 5-SM radius of the airport's center, not a 5-NM radius. **Answer (C) is incorrect.** The TAF covers a geographic area within a 5-SM radius of the airport's center, not 5 to 10 SM. The letters VC in the TAF describe conditions that will occur within the vicinity of the airport (5 to 10 SM), not at the airport, and will be used only with FG (fog), SH (showers), or TS (thunderstorms).

21. Use the following TAF to determine the wind shear forecast.

KOKC 051130Z 051212 14008KT 5SM BR BKN030
TEMPO 1316 1 1/2SM BR
FM1600 16010KT P6SM SKC
FM2224 20013G20KT 4SM SHRA OVC020
PROB30 0006 2SM TSRA OVC008CB
  WS010/18040KT
FM0608 21015KT P6SM NSW SCT040 =

    A.   Wind shear is not in this forecast.

    B.   Wind shear at 200 feet MSL, 13kts gusting to 20kts.

    C.   Wind shear at 1,000 feet, wind from the south at 40kts.

Answer (C) is correct. (AC 00-45H Chap 5)
    DISCUSSION: The TAF indicates wind shear by the indicator WS. The wind shear indicator is followed by a three-digit number that is the top of the wind shear layer. LLWS is forecast to be present from the surface to 1,000 ft. (010). After the solidus (/), the five-digit wind group is the wind direction and speed at the top of the wind shear layer; wind is from the south at 40 kt.
    Answer (A) is incorrect. When low-level wind shear (LLWS) conditions are expected, the nonconvective LLWS code WS is included in the TAF as the last group (after cloud forecast); WS is included in this TAF. **Answer (B) is incorrect.** The code 20013G20KT is a prevailing wind group indicating a wind from 200° (relative to true north) and an average wind speed of 13 kt. with peak gusts up to 20 kt., not wind shear at 200 ft. MSL, 13 kt. gusting to 20 kt.

22. In the following METAR/TAF for HOU, what is the ceiling and visibility forecast on the 7th day of the month at 0600Z?

KHOU 061734Z 0618/0718 16014G22KT P6SM
  VCSH BKN018 BKN035
FM070100 17010KT P6SM BKN015 OVC025
FM070500 17008KT 4SM BR SCT008 OVC012
FM071000 18005KT 3SM BR OVC007
FM071500 23008KT 5SM BR VCSH SCT008
  OVC015

    A.   Visibility 6 miles with a broken ceiling at 15,000 feet MSL.

    B.   4 nautical miles of visibility and an overcast ceiling at 700 feet MSL.

    C.   4 statute miles visibility and an overcast ceiling at 1,200 feet AGL.

Answer (C) is correct. (AC 00-45H Chap 5)
    DISCUSSION: According to the TAF, there will be 4 statute miles visibility (4SM) and an overcast ceiling at 1,200 ft. AGL (OVC012) during the time period beginning on the 7th day of the month at 0500Z (FM070500) until the 7th day of the month at 1000Z (FM071000). The 7th day of the month at 0600Z is included within this period.
    Answer (A) is incorrect. The ceiling and visibility for the 7th day of the month at 0600Z is included within the forecast beginning on the 7th day of the month at 0500Z (FM070500). **Answer (B) is incorrect.** Prevailing visibility in the United States is in statute miles. The overcast layer is forecast to begin after 1000Z on the 7th day (FM071000). The ceiling and visibility for the 7th day of the month at 0600Z is included within the forecast beginning on the 7th day of the month at 0500Z (FM070500).

9.5 Winds and Temperatures Aloft Forecast (FB)

23. A station is forecasting wind and temperature aloft at FL 390 to be 300° at 200 knots; temperature –54°C. How would this data be encoded in the FB?

    A. 300054

    B. 809954

    C. 309954

Answer (B) is correct. (AC 00-45H Chap 5)
    DISCUSSION: At FL 390, a 300° wind at 200 knots is encoded as 809954. Note that the first two digits are the direction. The second two digits are velocity. Wind speeds of 200 knots or greater are coded as 99 for the speed, and 50 is added to the two-digit direction code. Here, the direction is 80 for 300°. The temperature is the last two digits, and minus signs are omitted above 24,000 feet MSL.
    Answer (A) is incorrect. This code indicates winds from 300° at 0 knots. However, when forecast speed is less than 5 knots, the code is 9900 for wind direction and speed. **Answer (C) is incorrect.** This code indicates a 99-knot wind speed from 300°.

24. What wind direction and speed is represented by the entry 9900+00 for 9,000 feet, on a Wind and Temperature Aloft Forecast (FB)?

    A. Light and variable; less than 5 knots.

    B. Vortex winds exceeding 200 knots.

    C. Light and variable; less than 10 knots.

Answer (A) is correct. (AC 00-45H Chap 5)
    DISCUSSION: The entry 9900 in a winds and temperatures aloft forecast indicates light and variable winds. The air temperature on the Celsius scale is +00.
    Answer (B) is incorrect. An example of the code for winds over 200 knots would be 7099, for 200° at 199 knots or greater. **Answer (C) is incorrect.** Light and variable means less than 5 knots, not 10 knots.

25. When is the temperature at one of the forecast altitudes omitted at a specific location or station in the Wind and Temperature Aloft Forecast (FB)?

    A. When the temperature is standard for that altitude.

    B. For the 3,000-foot altitude (level) or when the level is within 2,500 feet of station elevation.

    C. Only when the winds are omitted for that altitude (level).

Answer (B) is correct. (AC 00-45H Chap 5)
    DISCUSSION: No temperatures are forecast for the 3,000-foot level or for a level within 2,500 feet of station elevation. No winds are forecast within 1,500 feet of the station elevation.
    Answer (A) is incorrect. Temperatures are reported whether standard or not. **Answer (C) is incorrect.** The winds are omitted within 1,500 feet of the ground and temperatures are omitted within 2,500 feet of the ground.

26. How much colder than standard temperature is the forecast temperature at 9,000 feet, as indicated in the following excerpt from the Wind and Temperature Aloft Forecast?

FT	6000	9000
	0737-04	1043-10

    A. 3°C.

    B. 10°C.

    C. 7°C.

Answer (C) is correct. (AC 00-45H Chap 5)
    DISCUSSION: At 9,000 feet, the forecast temperature is –10°C. Standard temperature is 15°C at sea level with a lapse rate of 2°C per 1,000 feet, which would bring the standard temperature to –3°C at 9,000 feet (15° – 18°). Therefore, the forecast temperature of –10°C is 7° colder than the standard temperature of –3°C.
    Answer (A) is incorrect. Standard temperature at 9,000 feet is –3°C, not –7°C. **Answer (B) is incorrect.** Standard temperature at 9,000 feet is –3°C, not 0°C.

27. When is the wind group at one of the forecast altitudes omitted at a specific location or station in the Wind and Temperature Aloft Forecast (FB)? When the wind

    A. is less than 5 knots.

    B. is less than 10 knots.

    C. at the altitude is within 1,500 feet of the station elevation.

Answer (C) is correct. (AC 00-45H Chap 5)
    DISCUSSION: No winds are forecast within 1,500 feet of the station elevation. No temperatures are forecast for 3,000 feet MSL or for a level within 2,500 feet of station elevation.
    Answer (A) is incorrect. When forecast wind speed is less than 5 knots, the code 9900 is used for direction and velocity. **Answer (B) is incorrect.** When forecast wind speed is less than 5 knots, not 10 knots, the code 9900 is used for direction and velocity.

28. Which values are used for winds aloft forecasts?

    A. Magnetic direction and knots.

    B. Magnetic direction and MPH.

    C. True direction and knots.

Answer (C) is correct. (AC 00-45H Chap 5)
    DISCUSSION: Winds aloft are forecast in true direction and knots.
    Answer (A) is incorrect. True, not magnetic, direction is used. **Answer (B) is incorrect.** True, not magnetic, direction and knots, not MPH, are used.

29. Decode the excerpt from the Winds and Temperature Aloft Forecast (FB) for OKC at 39,000 feet.

FT	3000	9000	12000	24000	39000
OKC	9900	2018+00	2130-06	2361-30	830558

    A. Wind 130° at 50 knots, temperature –58°C.

    B. Wind 330° at 105 knots, temperature –58°C.

    C. Wind 330° at 205 knots, temperature –58°C.

Answer (B) is correct. (AC 00-45H Chap 5)
    DISCUSSION: At OKC at 39,000 feet, the 83 for wind direction means that 100 knots have been deducted from the wind speed and 50 added to the wind direction. Thus, the wind speed is 105 knots. Also, subtract 50 from the first two-digit code for direction to get 330°. Above 24,000 feet, the temperatures are always negative.
    Answer (A) is incorrect. Wind 130° at 50 knots and temperature –58°C would be 135058. **Answer (C) is incorrect.** Wind 330° at 205 knots and temperature –58°C would be 839958.

30. (Refer to Figure 2 on page 391.) What approximate wind direction, speed, and temperature (relative to ISA) should a pilot expect when planning for a flight over ALB at FL 270?

    A. 270° magnetic at 97 knots; ISA –4°C.

    B. 260° true at 110 knots; ISA +5°C.

    C. 275° true at 97 knots; ISA +4°C.

Answer (C) is correct. (AC 00-45H Chap 5)
    DISCUSSION: For conditions at FL 270 over ALB in Fig. 2, you must interpolate between values at FL 240 and FL 300. First, decode the two given flight levels:

FL 240	= 270°	at	77 kt. and	–28°C
FL 300	= 280°	at	118 kt. and	–42°C
Difference	= 10°		41 kt.	–14°C

Interpolation for each value gives

    FL 270 = 275° at 97 kt. and –35°C

Finally, note that the answer asks for ISA (standard temperature). At 2° per 1,000 ft., ISA would be 54°C (27 × 2) less than surface standard of 15°C. Thus, at FL 270, the standard temperature is 15° – 54° = –39°C. The –35°C forecast temperature is ISA + 4°C.
    Answer (A) is incorrect. Winds aloft are always given in true, not magnetic, direction. **Answer (B) is incorrect.** Interpolating between 270° and 280° results in 275°, not 260°.

31. (Refer to Figure 2 below.) What approximate wind direction, speed, and temperature (relative to ISA) should a pilot expect when planning for a flight over PSB at FL 270?

    A. 260° magnetic at 93 knots; ISA +7°C.

    B. 280° true at 113 knots; ISA +3°C.

    C. 255° true at 93 knots; ISA +6°C.

Answer (C) is correct. (AC 00-45H Chap 5)
    DISCUSSION: For conditions at FL 270 over PSB in Fig. 2, you must interpolate between values at FL 240 and FL 300. First, decode the two given flight levels:

FL 240	= 230° at	68 kt. and	−26.0°C
FL 300	= 280° at	119 kt. and	−39.0°C
Difference	= 50°	51 kt.	−13.0°C

Interpolation for each value gives

        FL 270 = 255° at 93 kt. and −33°C

Finally, to compare the temperature to standard, subtract the lapse rate at FL 270 [(27,000 ÷ 1,000) × 2° = 54°] from surface standard of 15°C to get FL 270 standard of −39°C. The forecast temperature of about −33°C at FL 270 is thus 6°C warmer than standard.
    Answer (A) is incorrect. Winds aloft are always given in true, not magnetic, direction. **Answer (B) is incorrect.** Interpolating between 230° and 280° results in 255°, not 280°.

32. (Refer to Figure 2 below.) What approximate wind direction, speed, and temperature (relative to ISA) should a pilot expect when planning for a flight over EMI at FL 270?

    A. 265° true; 100 knots; ISA +3°C.

    B. 270° true; 110 knots; ISA +5°C.

    C. 260° magnetic; 100 knots; ISA −5°C.

Answer (A) is correct. (AC 00-45H Chap 5)
    DISCUSSION: For conditions at FL 270 over EMI in Fig. 2, you must interpolate between values at FL 240 and FL 300. First, decode the two given flight levels:

FL 240	= 280° at	91 kt. and	−30.0°C
FL 300	= 250° at	110 kt. and	−41.0°C
Difference	= 30°	19 kt.	−11.0°C

Interpolation for each value gives approximately

        FL 270 = 265° at 100 kt. and −36°C

Finally, to compare the temperature to standard, subtract the lapse rate at FL 270 [(27,000 ÷ 1,000) × 2° = 54°] from surface standard of 15°C to get FL 270 standard of −39°C. The forecast temperature of about −36°C at FL 270 is thus 3°C warmer than standard.
    Answer (B) is incorrect. Interpolating between 250° and 280° results in 265°, not 270°. **Answer (C) is incorrect.** Winds aloft are given in true, not magnetic, direction.

VALID 1600Z FOR USE 0900-1500Z. TEMPS NEG ABV 24000									
FT	3000	6000	9000	12000	18000	24000	30000	34000	39000
EMI	2807	2715-07	2728-10	2842-13	2867-21	2891-30	751041	771150	780855
ALB	0210	9900-07	2714-09	2728-12	2656-19	2777-28	781842	760150	269658
PSB		1509+04	2119+01	2233-04	2262-14	2368-26	781939	760850	780456
STL	2308	2613+02	2422-03	2431-08	2446-19	2461-30	760142	782650	760559

Figure 2. – Wind and Temperatures Aloft Forecast.

9.6 Low-Level Significant Weather Prog

33. A prognostic chart depicts the conditions

    A. existing at the surface during the past 6 hours.

    B. which presently exist from the 1,000-millibar through the 700-millibar level.

    C. forecast to exist at a specific time in the future.

Answer (C) is correct. (AC 00-45H Chap 5)
    DISCUSSION: Prognostic charts show conditions as they are forecast to be at the valid time (UTC or Zulu) for the chart. The charts are issued four times daily.
    Answer (A) is incorrect. Prognostic charts relate to the future, not the past. **Answer (B) is incorrect.** Prognostic charts relate to the future, not the present.

34. The Low-Level Significant Weather Prognostic Chart depicts weather conditions

    A. that are forecast to exist at a valid time shown on the chart.

    B. as they existed at the time the chart was prepared.

    C. that existed at the time shown on the chart which is about 3 hours before the chart is received.

Answer (A) is correct. (AC 00-45H Chap 5)
    DISCUSSION: Prognostic charts show conditions as they are forecast to be at the valid time for the chart. The charts are issued four times daily.
    Answer (B) is incorrect. The low-level prog chart consists of 12- and 24-hour forecasts. **Answer (C) is incorrect.** Prognostic charts look to the future; they do not report the past.

35. Which meteorological conditions are depicted by a prognostic chart?

    A. Conditions existing at the time of the observation.

    B. Interpretation of weather conditions for geographical areas between reporting stations.

    C. Conditions forecast to exist at a specific time shown on the chart.

Answer (C) is correct. (AC 00-45H Chap 5)
    DISCUSSION: Prognostic charts show conditions as they are forecast to be at the valid time for the chart. The charts are issued four times daily.
    Answer (A) is incorrect. Prognostic charts relate to the future, not the present. **Answer (B) is incorrect.** Prognostic charts relate to the future, not the present.

36. (Refer to Figure 18 on page 393.) The U.S. Low-Level Significant Weather Prognostic Chart at 06Z indicates that central Colorado and southeastern Wyoming can expect

    A. moderate or greater turbulence from the FL 100 to FL 180.

    B. moderate or greater turbulence above FL 240.

    C. no turbulence is indicated.

Answer (A) is correct. (AC 00-45H Chap 5)
    DISCUSSION: The 12-hour significant weather prog (SFC-400MB) chart at 0600Z is on the left panel. Northwestern Colorado and southeastern Wyoming are enclosed by a long, dashed line, which indicates moderate or greater turbulence. The number 180/100 (shown in northern NM with an arrow) and the symbols above mean moderate-to-severe turbulence from FL 100 to FL 180 (10,000 feet to 18,000 feet MSL).
    Answer (B) is incorrect. Forecast turbulence from the surface to above FL 240 would be depicted as /SFC, not 180/100. **Answer (C) is incorrect.** Turbulence is forecast for central Colorado and southeastern Wyoming.

37. (Refer to Figure 19 on page 393.) The 24-Hour Low-Level Significant Weather Prognostic Chart at 06Z indicates that Ohio will likely experience

    A. ceilings less than 1,000 feet, visibility less than 3 miles.

    B. clear sky and visibility greater than 6 miles.

    C. ceilings 1,000 to 3,000 feet and visibility 3 to 5 miles.

Answer (A) is correct. (AC 00-45H Chap 5)
    DISCUSSION: The 24-hr. significant weather prognostic chart (SFC-400MB) is on the right panel. Ohio is enclosed by a solid line, which indicates a forecast of IFR with ceilings less than 1,000 feet and/or visibility less than 3 SM.
    Answer (B) is incorrect. The low-level significant weather prognostic chart does not show areas of clear skies, only areas of ceilings above 3,000 feet, by not being enclosed by solid or scalloped lines. **Answer (C) is incorrect.** Forecast ceilings of 1,000 to 3,000 feet inclusive and/or visibility 3 to 5 SM inclusive are indicated by an area enclosed by a scalloped, not solid, line.

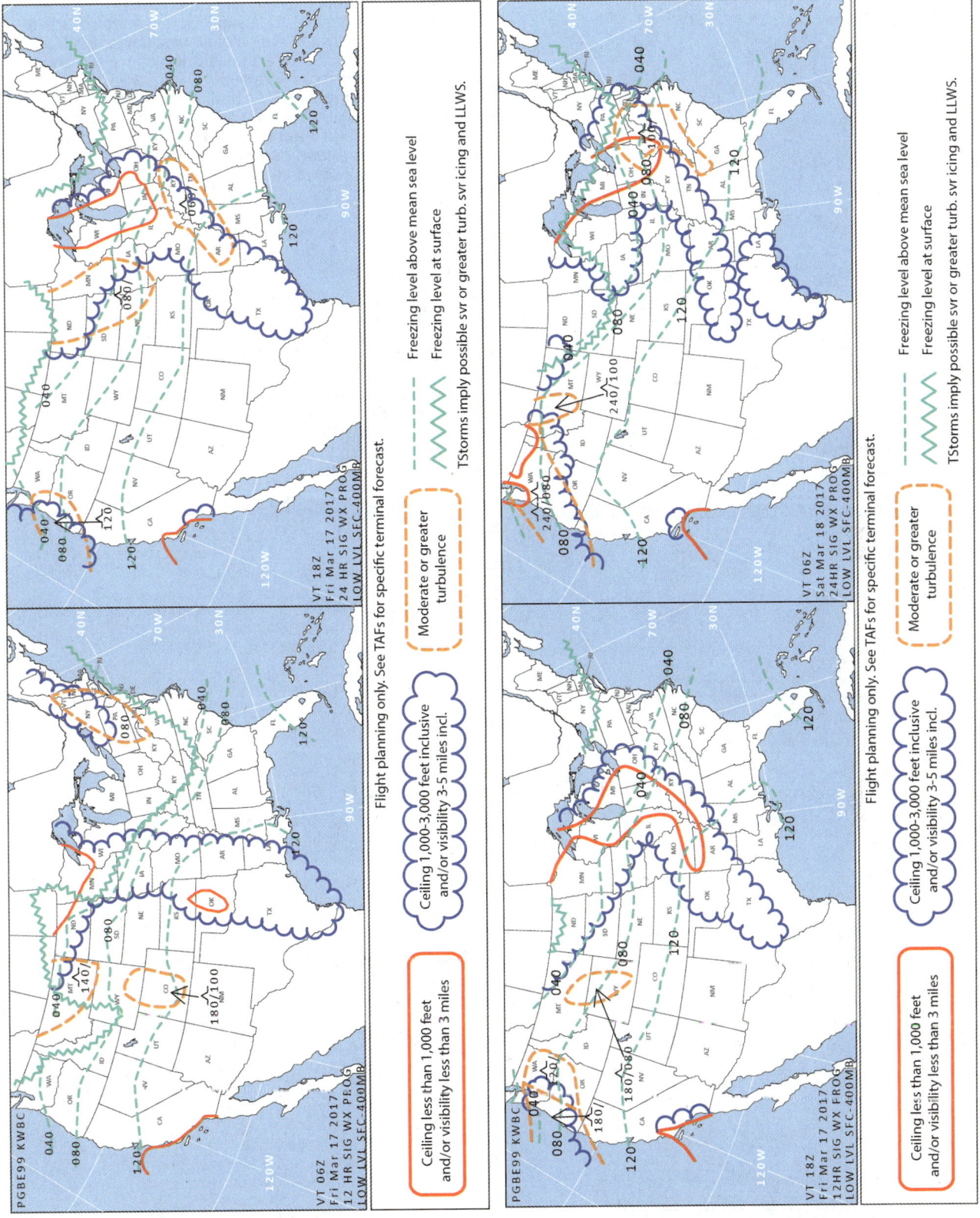

Figure 18. – U.S. Low-Level
Significant Weather Prognostic Charts.

Figure 19. – U.S. Low-Level
Significant Weather Prognostic Charts.

38. What is the time frame for the validity of Low-Level Significant Weather Prog Charts?

A. 12 to 24 hours in the future.

B. From 3 hours before to 3 hours after the time on the chart.

C. Up to 48 hours in the future.

Answer (A) is correct. (AC 00-45H Chap 5)
DISCUSSION: Low-altitude significant weather charts are issued four times daily and are valid at fixed times: 0000, 0600, 1200, and 1800 UTC. Each chart is divided on the left and right into 12- and 24-hr. forecast intervals.
Answer (B) is incorrect. Low-altitude significant weather charts are issued four times daily and are valid at fixed times: 0000, 0600, 1200, and 1800 UTC. **Answer (C) is incorrect.** A surface prognostic chart provides an analysis updated every 3 hr., plus 12- and 24-hr. forecasts updated four times daily and a 36- and 48-hr. forecast updated twice daily.

9.7 Graphical Forecasts for Aviation (GFAs)

39. (Refer to Figure 260 below.) What will the predominant weather be at 1600Z in area A?

A. Thunderstorms and moderate rain.

B. Light to moderate rain.

C. Heavy rain.

Answer (B) is correct. (AC 00-45H Chap 4)
DISCUSSION: The green dots indicate that light to moderate rain is forecast for area A at a valid time of 1600Z (UTC).
Answer (A) is incorrect. Thunderstorms are not forecast in area A. **Answer (C) is incorrect.** Light to moderate rain, not heavy rain, is forecast for area A. Heavy rain is indicated by four dots in a diamond shape.

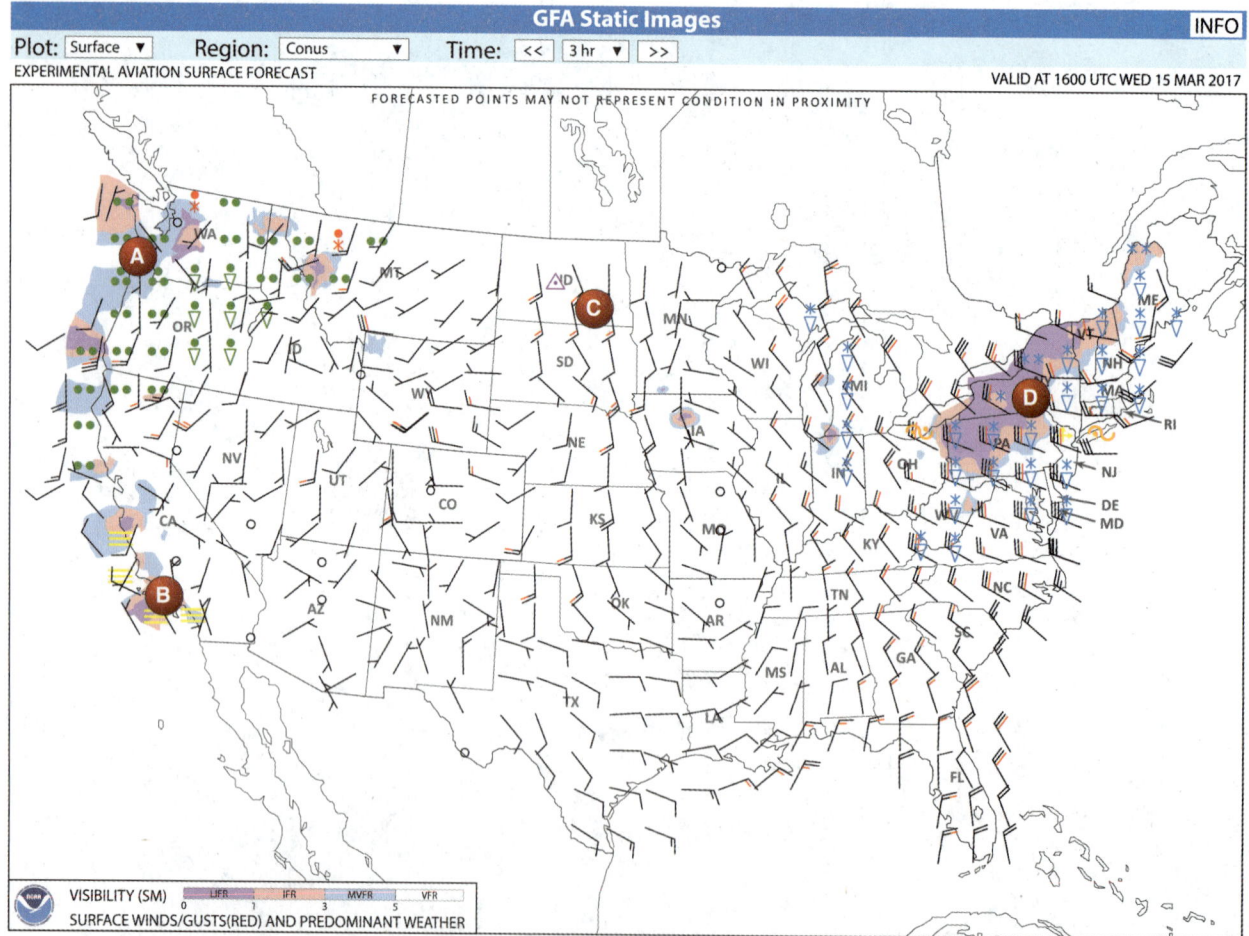

Figure 260. – Graphical Forecast for Aviation.

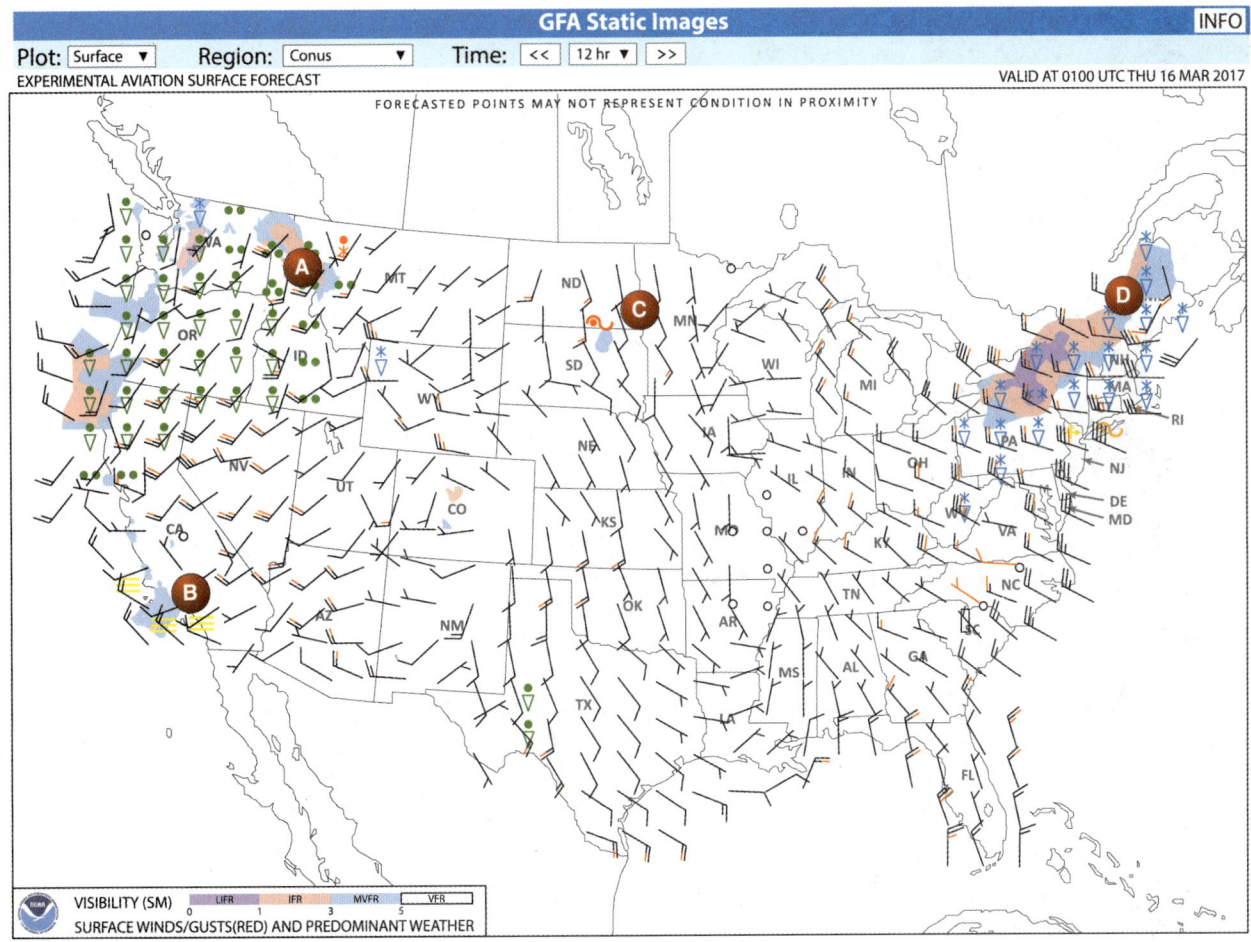

Figure 261. – Graphical Forecast for Aviation.

40. (Refer to Figure 261 above.) What weather condition is forecast to exist in area B?

A. Visibility less than 3 miles.

B. Low ceilings.

C. Fog.

Answer (C) is correct. (AC 00-45H Chap 4)

DISCUSSION: Fog is forecast to exist in area B as indicated by the three yellow bars.

Answer (A) is incorrect. The weather is forecast to be VFR or MVFR, with visibility greater than, not less than, 3 miles. **Answer (B) is incorrect.** Ceiling heights are not indicated on Aviation Surface Forecast graphics.

41. The best product to provide an overview of forecast weather conditions creating a complete picture of weather affecting regions across the United States is

A. Terminal Area Forecast (TAF).

B. satellite mapping.

C. Graphical Forecasts for Aviation (GFA).

Answer (C) is correct. (AC 00-45H Chap 4.1)

DISCUSSION: GFA are a continuously updated set of internet-based displays of the necessary aviation weather information to provide users a complete picture of weather that may affect flight in the continental U.S.

Answer (A) is incorrect. A TAF is a concise statement of the expected meteorological conditions at an airport during a specified period. **Answer (B) is incorrect.** Though satellite is perhaps the single most important source of weather data worldwide, visible, infrared, and water vapor imagery have limitations and this product is primarily an observational tool.

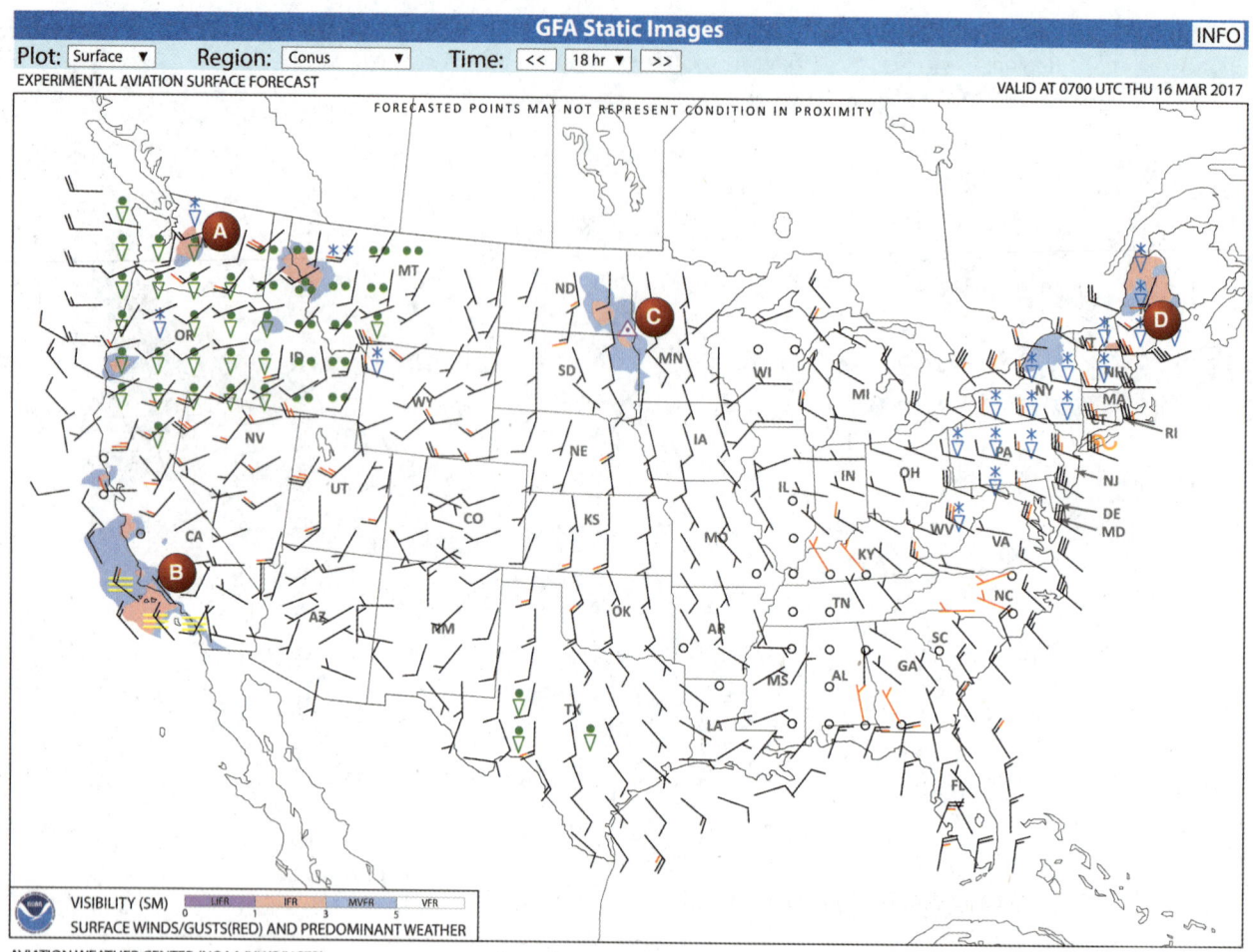

Figure 262. – Graphical Forecast for Aviation.

42. (Refer to Figure 262 above.) When was this forecast issued?

A. 1358Z.

B. 0700 UTC.

C. 1800Z.

Answer (A) is correct. (AC 00-45H Chap 3)
   DISCUSSION: The time of issuance, 1358Z (UTC), is listed in the bottom right-hand corner of the chart.
   Answer (B) is incorrect. The valid time of the chart, not the time of issuance, is 0700 UTC. **Answer (C) is incorrect.** This is an 18 hr. forecast; it was not issued at 1800Z.

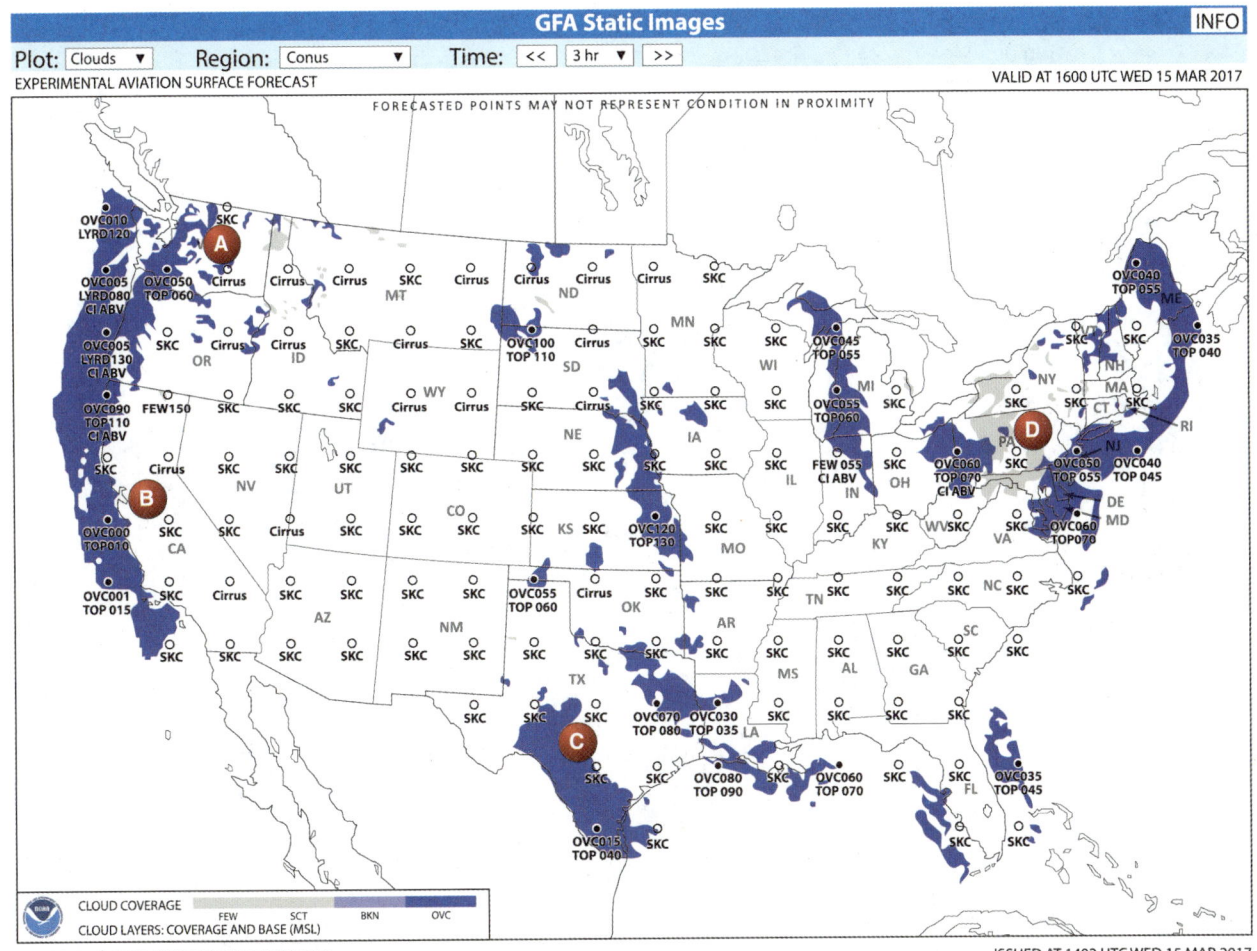

Figure 263. – Graphical Forecast for Aviation.

43. (Refer to Figure 263 above.) What cloud coverage is forecast to exist in area C?

A. Broken ceiling at 1,500 ft. AGL.

B. Overcast ceiling at 1,500 ft. MSL.

C. Overcast ceiling at 4,000 ft. MSL.

Answer (B) is correct. (AC 00-45H Chap 3)
   DISCUSSION: An overcast ceiling at 1,500 ft. MSL is forecast to exist as indicated by the purple shading and OCV015.
   Answer (A) is incorrect. A broken layer is not forecast, and cloud layers are reported in MSL. **Answer (C) is incorrect.** The tops of the overcast layer, not the base, are at 4,000 ft. MSL.

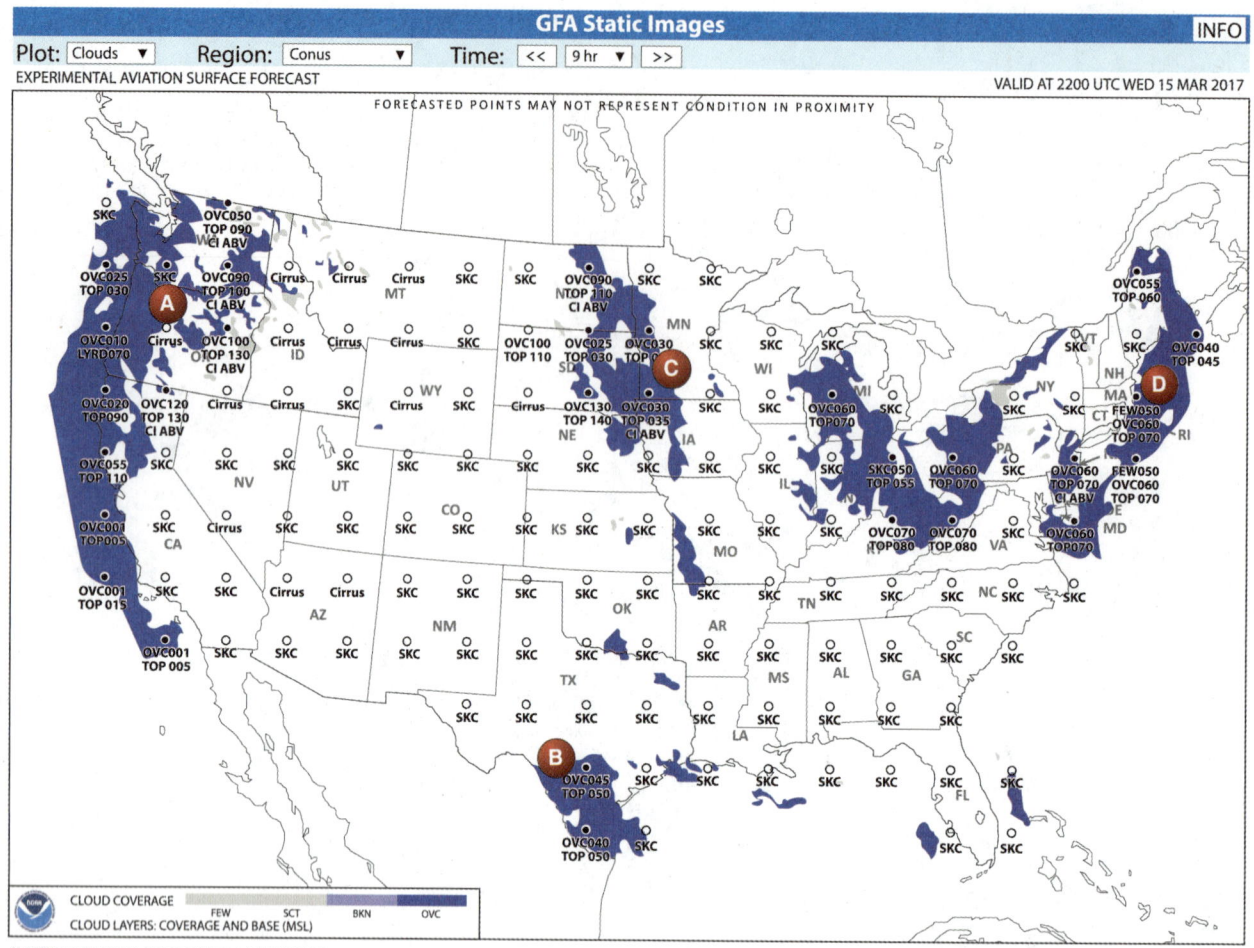

Figure 264. – Graphical Forecast for Aviation.

44. (Refer to Figure 264 above.) What does the term "cirrus" in area A indicate?

A. Clouds above FL180.

B. Clouds above 10,000 ft. MSL.

C. No clouds above 18,000 ft. MSL.

Answer (A) is correct. (AC 00-6B Chap 13)
DISCUSSION: The term "cirrus" indicates that clouds only exist above FL180.
Answer (B) is incorrect. The term "cirrus" indicates that clouds only exist above FL180, not 10,000 ft. MSL. **Answer (C) is incorrect.** The term "cirrus" indicates that clouds do exist above FL180.

9.8 High-Level Significant Weather Prog

45. (Refer to Figure 20 on page 399.) What is the maximum wind velocity forecast in the jet stream shown on the High Level Significant Weather Prognostic Chart over Eastern Canada?

A. 80 knots.

B. 140 knots.

C. 150 knots.

Answer (C) is correct. (AC 00-45H Chap 5)
DISCUSSION: The forecast jet streams having a core speed of 80 knots or greater are shown on the high-level significant weather prog as a solid line with arrowheads indicating the flow direction. The forecast maximum core wind velocity is depicted by a shaft with each pennant (solid triangle) equal to 50 knots and each feather (single line) equal to 10 knots. The maximum core speed forecast for the jet stream over eastern Canada is 150 knots (3 pennants = 150 knots).
Answer (A) is incorrect. The presence of the line depicting the jet stream indicates that the minimum core speed is 80 knots, but the maximum core speed is depicted by a shaft with pennants and/or feathers. Over eastern Canada, the maximum speed is forecast at 150 knots. **Answer (B) is incorrect.** The area with 2 pennants and 4 feathers indicates 140 knots; however, the maximum core speed of the jet stream over eastern Canada is 150 knots, not 140 knots.

46. (Refer to Figure 20 below.) What is the height of the center of the low tropopause height over eastern Canada?

A. FL 240 sloping to FL 450.

B. FL 290.

C. FL 340.

Answer (B) is correct. (AC 00-45H Chap 5)
DISCUSSION: Over eastern Canada is a five-sided polygon that has 290 over a letter "L." This indicates a low tropopause height of 29,000 feet.
Answer (A) is incorrect. The area enclosed by a dashed line centered over eastern Canada depicts minimum and maximum height of the 80-knot jet stream, not a sloping tropopause. **Answer (C) is incorrect.** FL 340 is the height of the tropopause surrounding the Great Lakes region (indicated by "FL 340" inside a rectangle).

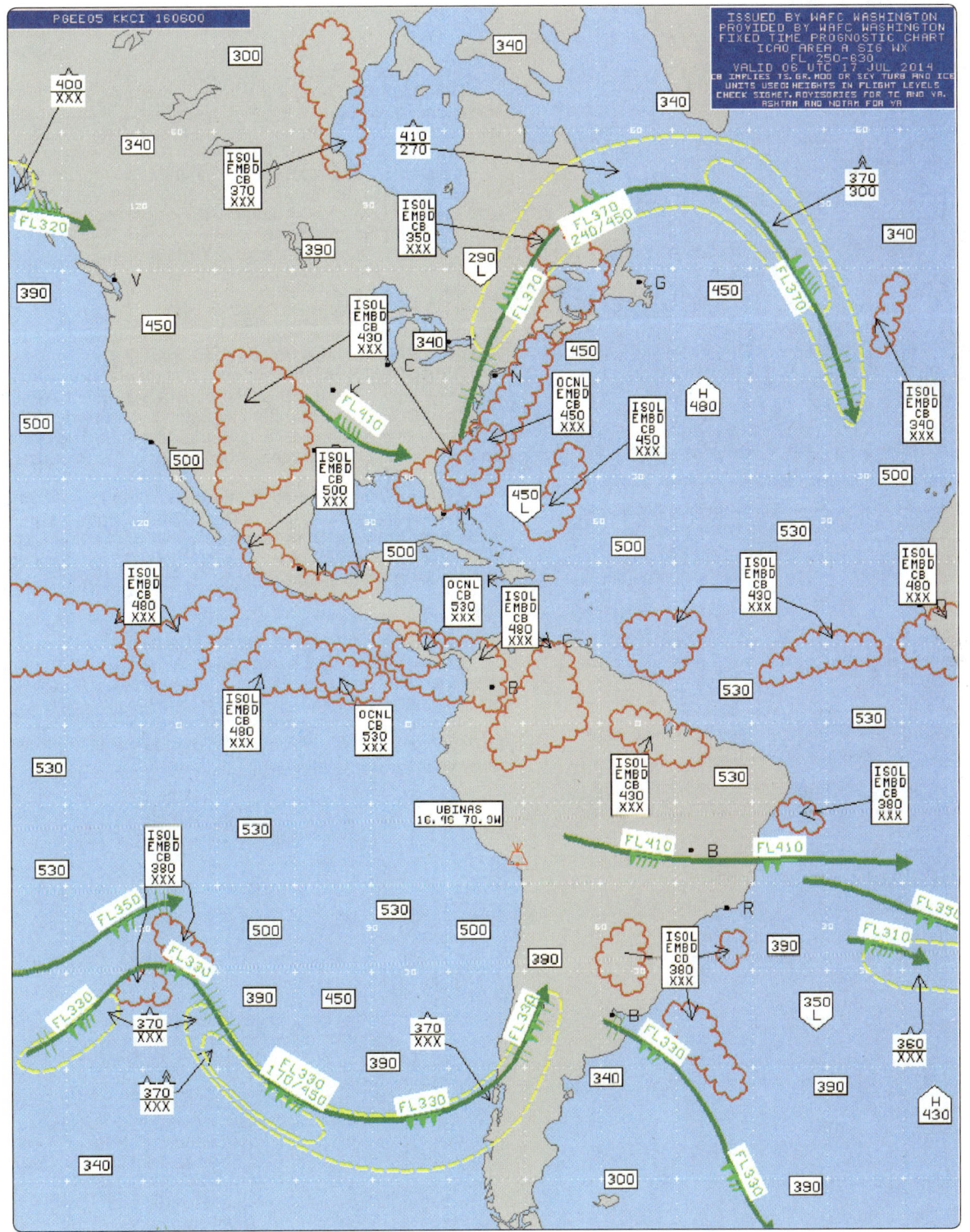

Figure 20. – High-Level Significant Weather Prognostic Chart.

47. (Refer to Figure 7 on page 401.) What weather conditions are predicted within area 3?

   A. Light turbulence at FL 370 within the area outlined by dashes.

   B. Severe turbulence from FL 300 to FL 370.

   C. Moderate to severe CAT has been reported at FL 320.

Answer (B) is correct. *(AC 00-45H Chap 5)*
   DISCUSSION: Area 3 is located in a banana-shaped oval area outlined by a heavy dashed line. About an inch east of the area 3 circle, there is a symbol composed of a double "mountain peak," or upside-down V, over the numbers 370 which is separated from 300 by a horizontal line. This symbol indicates that severe turbulence is forecast in the outlined area from FL 300 to FL 370.
   Answer (A) is incorrect. Severe, not light, turbulence is forecast within the area outlined by dashes. **Answer (C) is incorrect.** This chart does not specify whether turbulence is in cloud or is clear air turbulence (CAT).

48. (Refer to Figure 7 on page 401.) What weather conditions are depicted within area 7?

   A. Frequent embedded thunderstorms, less than 1/8 coverage, and tops at FL 370.

   B. Frequent lightning in thunderstorms at FL 370.

   C. Occasional cumulonimbus, bases below 25,000 feet MSL and tops at 53,000 feet MSL.

Answer (C) is correct. *(AC 00-45H Chap 5)*
   DISCUSSION: Area 7 is within a scalloped area indicating occasional (OCNL), i.e., 1/8 to 4/8, coverage of cumulonimbus clouds and thunderstorms. They are from below FL 250 to FL 530.
   Answer (A) is incorrect. The thunderstorms are not embedded. Also, there is 1/8 to 4/8 area coverage (OCNL), not less than 1/8 coverage. **Answer (B) is incorrect.** The high-level prog does not indicate lightning.

49. (Refer to Figure 7 on page 401.) The U.S. HIGH-LEVEL SIGNIFICANT WEATHER PROG, area 8, represents the

   A. height of the jet stream (53,000 feet).

   B. height of the tropopause.

   C. height of maximum wind shear (53,000 feet).

Answer (B) is correct. *(AC 00-45H Chap 5)*
   DISCUSSION: Area 8 shows a rectangular box with a number inside it. On the U.S. High-Level Significant Weather Prognostic Chart, the number inside this symbol indicates the height of the tropopause in hundreds of feet. The box at area 8 has "530," which means the height of the tropopause is 53,000 ft., or FL 530.
   Answer (A) is incorrect. The "530" is the height of the tropopause in hundreds of feet (53,000 ft.), not the height of the jet stream. **Answer (C) is incorrect.** The "530" is the height of the tropopause in hundreds of feet (53,000 ft.), not the height of the maximum wind shear.

50. (Refer to Figure 7 on page 401.) What type of weather can be expected in the red scalloped area near area 9?

   A. 2/8 to 6/8 coverage, occasional embedded thunderstorms, tops at FL 330.

   B. 1/8 to 4/8 coverage, occasional embedded thunderstorms, maximum tops at 51,000 feet MSL.

   C. Isolated embedded cumulonimbus with tops to FL 330.

Answer (C) is correct. *(AC 00-45H Chap 5)*
   DISCUSSION: The scalloped area on Fig. 7 near area 9 shows isolated embedded cumulonimbus clouds from below FL 250 (XXX) to FL 330.
   Answer (A) is incorrect. The coverage codes show ISOL (to 1/8), not 2/8 to 6/8. **Answer (B) is incorrect.** The tops are forecast to be at FL 330, not 51,000 feet MSL.

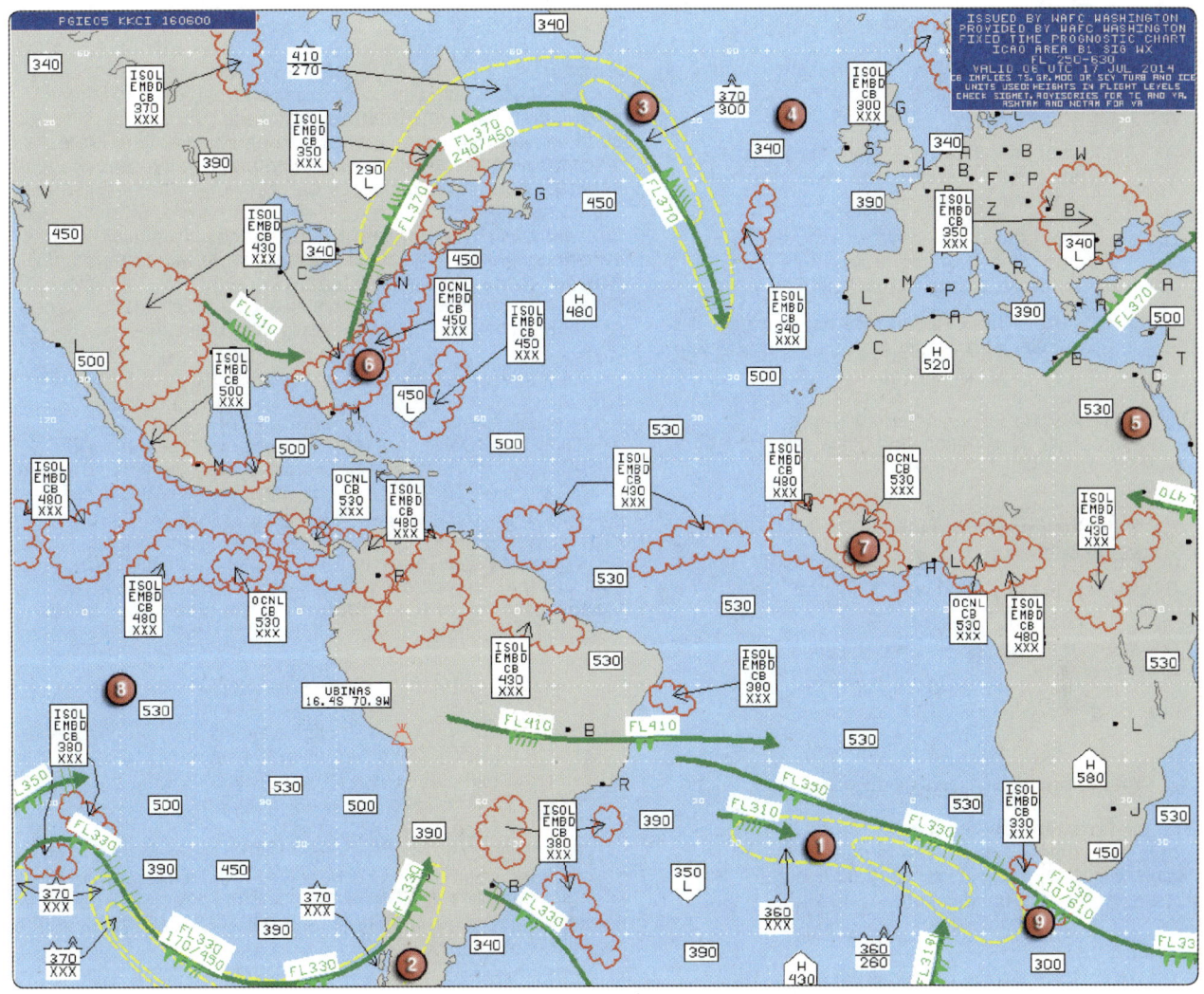

Figure 7. – High-Level Significant Weather Prognostic Chart.

9.9 In-Flight Weather Advisories

51. Pilots of IFR flights seeking ATC in-flight weather avoidance assistance should keep in mind that

    A. ATC radar limitations and, frequency congestion may limit the controllers capability to provide this service.

    B. circumnavigating severe weather can only be accommodated in the en route areas away from terminals because of congestion.

    C. ATC Narrow Band Radar does not provide the controller with weather intensity capability.

Answer (A) is correct. (AIM Para 7-1-12)
    DISCUSSION: The controllers' primary function is to provide safe separation between aircraft. Any additional service, such as weather avoidance, can be provided only to the extent it does not interfere with the primary function. Unfortunately, the separation workload is usually greater when weather disrupts the normal flow of traffic.
    Answer (B) is incorrect. Controllers can provide weather circumnavigation in terminal areas when workload permits. **Answer (C) is incorrect.** ATC narrowband radar is replacing digitized radar weather displays in ARTCC facilities to provide even better measurement of precipitation density.

52. How could you receive in-flight weather information about your destination while still 150 NM away?

    A. Tune the frequency and listen to the ATIS for your destination.

    B. Review the destination METAR and TAF through FIS-B.

    C. Contact Flight Service on the frequency 121.5 MHz.

Answer (B) is correct. (FAA-H-8083-25B Chap 13)
    DISCUSSION: Flight Information Services-Broadcast (FIS-B) is a ground-based broadcast system provided through ADS-B via the 978 MHz data link that can display in-flight weather data such as METARs, TAFs, Winds Aloft, and PIREPs.
    Answer (A) is incorrect. When you are 150 NM from your destination, you are too far away to receive the ATIS broadcast. **Answer (C) is incorrect.** The emergency frequency is 121.5 MHz. Flight Service can be contacted on 122.2 MHz.

9.10 Miscellaneous Charts and Forecasts

53. A pilot planning to depart at 1100Z on an IFR flight is particularly concerned about the hazard of icing. What sources reflect the most accurate information on icing conditions (current and forecast) at the time of departure?

    A. Low-Level Significant Weather Prognostic Chart, and the Area Forecast.

    B. The Area Forecast, and the Freezing Level Chart.

    C. Pilot weather reports (PIREPs), AIRMETs, and SIGMETs.

Answer (C) is correct. (AC 00-45H Chaps 3 and 5)
    DISCUSSION: Pilot reports (PIREPs) can reflect the most current icing conditions for a specific area, including type and intensity. AIRMET Zulu is for icing and freezing levels for a specified time and normally an outlook. A SIGMET is issued for areas of severe icing.
    Answer (A) is incorrect. Low-level significant weather prognostic charts do not forecast icing conditions but do forecast freezing levels, and an area forecast does not provide any information on icing conditions. **Answer (B) is incorrect.** A freezing-level chart cannot be used to determine current or forecast icing conditions, and an area forecast does not provide any information on icing conditions.

54. What determines how icing is reported on a PIREP?

    A. Type of ice.

    B. Thickness of ice.

    C. Rate of accumulation.

Answer (C) is correct. (AIM Para 7-1-19)
    DISCUSSION: Icing intensities are classified based on the rate of icing accumulation.
    Answer (A) is incorrect. The type of icing accumulation can be listed in the PIREP remarks, but not in the primary icing group. **Answer (B) is incorrect.** The thickness of ice would likely not be reported in a PIREP since that information does not provide direct information to pilots on what conditions to expect. Also, it is usually very difficult for a pilot to accurately estimate the thickness of the accumulated ice.

55. What flight planning information can a pilot derive from constant pressure charts?

    A. Clear air turbulence and icing conditions.

    B. Levels of widespread cloud coverage.

    C. Winds and temperatures aloft.

Answer (C) is correct. (AC 00-45H Chap 4)
    DISCUSSION: Constant pressure charts provide information about the observed temperature, wind, and temperature/dew point spread along your proposed route.
    Answer (A) is incorrect. Clear air turbulence is shown on the low-level prog chart. **Answer (B) is incorrect.** Areas and levels of widespread cloud coverage are shown on the weather depiction and surface analysis charts.

56. The Surface Analysis Chart depicts

   A. actual pressure systems, frontal locations, cloud tops, and precipitation at the time shown on the chart.

   B. frontal locations and expected movement, pressure centers, cloud coverage, and obstructions to vision at the time of chart transmission.

   C. actual frontal positions, pressure patterns, temperature, dew point, wind, weather, and obstructions to vision at the valid time of the chart.

Answer (C) is correct. (AC 00-45H Chap 4)
   DISCUSSION: The surface analysis chart provides the locations of pressure systems, dew points, wind, and obstructions to vision at the valid time of the chart.
   Answer (A) is incorrect. The surface analysis chart does not depict cloud tops. **Answer (B) is incorrect.** Expected movement of weather systems is not depicted. This chart depicts current conditions at the time of issuance.

57. What conclusion(s) can be drawn from a 500-millibar Constant Pressure Chart for a planned flight at FL 180?

   A. Winds aloft at FL 180 generally flow across the height contours.

   B. Observed temperature, wind, and temperature/dew point spread along the proposed route can be approximated.

   C. Upper highs, lows, troughs, and ridges will be depicted by the use of lines of equal pressure.

Answer (B) is correct. (AC 00-45H Chap 5)
   DISCUSSION: From a constant pressure analysis chart, you can approximate the observed temperature, wind, and temperature/dew point spread along a proposed route.
   Answer (A) is incorrect. The winds usually flow parallel to, not across, the height contours. **Answer (C) is incorrect.** Heights of the specified pressure for each station are depicted via solid lines called contours to give a height pattern. The contours depict high height centers and low height centers, not highs and lows.

58. Which weather forecast describes prospects for an area coverage of both severe and general thunderstorms during the following 24 hours?

   A. Terminal Aerodrome Forecast.

   B. Convective outlook.

   C. Radar Summary Chart.

Answer (B) is correct. (AC 00-45H Chap 5)
   DISCUSSION: The convective outlook (AC) describes the prospects for general thunderstorm activity during the following 24 hours. Areas with a high, moderate, or slight risk of severe thunderstorms are included, as well as areas where thunderstorms may approach severe limits.
   Answer (A) is incorrect. A terminal aerodrome forecast (TAF) is a statement of expected conditions around an airport, not a forecast of thunderstorms only. **Answer (C) is incorrect.** The radar summary chart is obsolete. It depicted observed radar returns, which showed precipitation intensity, at the time shown on the chart. It provided an indication of observed, not forecast, severe and general thunderstorms.

59. What information is provided by a Convective Outlook (AC)?

   A. It describes areas of probable severe icing and severe or extreme turbulence during the next 24 hours.

   B. It provides prospects of both general and severe thunderstorm activity during the following 24 hours.

   C. It indicates areas of probable convective turbulence and the extent of instability in the upper atmosphere (above 500 MB).

Answer (B) is correct. (AC 00-45H Chap 5)
   DISCUSSION: The AC describes the prospects for general thunderstorm activity during the following 24 hours. Areas with a high, moderate, or slight risk of severe thunderstorms are included, as well as areas where thunderstorms may approach severe limits.
   Answer (A) is incorrect. Areas of severe or extreme turbulence are forecast in the significant weather prog charts, not in an AC. Additionally, icing is not specifically forecast but is implied in clouds and precipitation above the freezing level. **Answer (C) is incorrect.** Areas of probable convective turbulence and with the extent of instability above 500 MB/hPa (18,000 feet MSL) are depicted by the contraction "CB" in a high-level significant weather prog, not an AC.

60. When are Aviation Watch Notification Messages (SAW) issued?

   A. Every 12 hours as required.

   B. Every 24 hours as required.

   C. Unscheduled and issued as required.

Answer (C) is correct. (AC 00-45H Chap 5)
   DISCUSSION: An SAW defines areas of possible severe thunderstorms or tornado warnings. SAWs are unscheduled and are issued as required by the National Weather Service with AWW in the product header.
   Answer (A) is incorrect. SAWs are unscheduled and are issued as required, not every 12 hr. as required. **Answer (B) is incorrect.** SAWs are unscheduled and are issued as required, not every 24 hr. as required.

61. What does a Convective Outlook (AC) describe for a following 24-hr. period?

A.   General thunderstorm activity.

B.   A severe weather watch bulletin.

C.   When forecast conditions are expected to continue beyond the valid period.

Answer (A) is correct. (AC 00-45H Chap 5)
   DISCUSSION: An AC describes the prospects for general thunderstorm activity during the following 24 hr.
   Answer (B) is incorrect. A severe weather watch bulletin is a separate product. An AC forecasts general thunderstorm activity for the following 24 hr., while a severe weather watch bulletin is issued as necessary to define areas of possible severe thunderstorms or tornado activity. **Answer (C) is incorrect.** An AC is a forecast of thunderstorm activity for the following 24-hr. period, not a statement of forecast conditions that are expected to continue beyond the valid period.

62. If you encounter in-flight icing and ATC asks you to report your conditions, what are the official reportable icing values that you are expected to use?

A.   Light, moderate, severe, extreme.

B.   Trace, light, moderate, severe.

C.   Few, light, moderate, severe.

Answer (B) is correct. (AC 00-45H Chap 3)
   DISCUSSION: These values classify icing intensities according to their operational effects on aircraft. When a pilot gives a PIREP, icing is reported as trace, light, moderate, or severe. These are the same icing values a pilot should give to ATC if asked to report icing conditions.
   Answer (A) is incorrect. The term "extreme" is a precipitation intensity level used with radar and satellite imagery such as Doppler radar, not a report term given to ATC. **Answer (C) is incorrect.** The term "few" is used in describing the level of cloud coverage and is not an icing value.

63. When does the National Weather Service release an Aviation Watch Notification Message (SAW)?

A.   At 0000 (UTC).

B.   0000 and 1200 (UTC).

C.   Unscheduled and issued as required.

Answer (C) is correct. (AC 00-45H Chap 5)
   DISCUSSION: Aviation Watch Notification Messages define areas of possible severe thunderstorms or tornado warnings. They are unscheduled and are issued as required by the National Weather Service. A watch means severe weather is possible during the next few hours.
   Answer (A) is incorrect. Aviation Watch Notification Messages are unscheduled and issued as required, not at 0000 (UTC). **Answer (B) is incorrect.** Aviation Watch Notification Messages are unscheduled and issued as required, not at 0000 and 1200 (UTC).

64. The distance measured in millibars separating isobars on surface analysis charts is typically

A.   2 mb.

B.   4 mb.

C.   6 mb.

Answer (B) is correct. (AC 00-45H Chap 4.1)
   DISCUSSION: An isobar connects areas of similar barometric pressure. On a surface analysis chart, isobars are used to depict the sea-level pressure pattern; they are depicted with a series of solid black lines surrounding the defined pressure area. The interval between isobars is typically 4 mb, based on a standard pressure gradient.
   Answer (A) is incorrect. A 2-mb distance between isobars indicates a greater rate of pressure change over a distance. **Answer (C) is incorrect.** A 6-mb distance between isobars indicates a more gradual pressure change over a distance.

65. The locations of fronts and pressure systems as of chart time are best determined by referring to a

A.   constant pressure analysis chart.

B.   CIP/FIP chart.

C.   surface analysis chart.

Answer (C) is correct. (AC 00-45H Chap 4.1)
   DISCUSSION: In addition to high-and-low pressure centers, a surface analysis chart depicts barometric pressures relative to sea level in MSL.
   Answer (A) is incorrect. Constant pressure charts can be used to determine the observed temperature, wind, and temperature/dewpoint spread at specified flight levels. **Answer (B) is incorrect.** The current icing potential (CIP) and forecast icing potential (FIP) plots aid flight planning and situational awareness through graphical depiction of current and forecast icing conditions across an area or along a route of flight.

STUDY UNIT TEN

IFR EN ROUTE

(4 pages of outline)

This study unit contains outlines of major concepts tested, sample test questions and answers regarding IFR en route, and an explanation of each answer.

Recall that the **sole purpose** of this book is to expedite your passing of the FAA pilot knowledge test for the instrument rating. Accordingly, all extraneous material (i.e., topics or regulations not directly tested on the FAA pilot knowledge test) is omitted, even though much more knowledge is necessary to fly safely. This additional material is presented in *Pilot Handbook*, *Aviation Weather and Weather Services*, *FAR/AIM*, and *Instrument Pilot Flight Maneuvers and Practical Test Prep*, available from Gleim Publications, Inc. Order online at www.GleimAviation.com.

10.1 MINIMUM IFR ALTITUDES

1. **Minimum reception altitude (MRA)** is the lowest altitude at which an intersection can be determined.

2. **Minimum obstruction clearance altitude (MOCA)** ensures acceptable navigational signal coverage only within 22 NM (25 SM) of a VOR.

   a. ATC may assign the MOCA as an assigned altitude when certain special conditions exist and when the airplane is within 22 NM of a VOR.

3. **Minimum en route altitude (MEA)** is the lowest published altitude between radio fixes that ensures acceptable navigational signal coverage and meets obstacle clearance requirements between those fixes.

4. **Minimum crossing altitude (MCA)** is the minimum altitude to cross a fix beyond which a higher minimum applies.

5. MOCA and all other minimum IFR altitudes guarantee obstruction clearance in nonmountainous areas by providing at least 1,000 ft. of vertical distance from the highest obstruction 4 NM either side of the center of the airway to be flown.

   a. In mountainous areas, 2,000 ft. of vertical distance is provided.

6. Routes designed to serve aircraft operating from 18,000 ft. MSL up to and including FL 450 are referred to as jet routes or "J" routes.

10.2 VFR-ON-TOP

1. VFR-on-top operations can be conducted only after a pilot has received a VFR-on-top clearance to operate in VFR conditions.

NOTE: The pilot must request a VFR-on-top clearance.

2. VFR-on-top must comply with the appropriate VFR cruising altitudes as prescribed in 14 CFR 91.159, which is based upon magnetic courses.

    a. 000° through 179° -- odd 1,000 ft. plus 500 ft.
    b. 180° through 359° -- even 1,000 ft. plus 500 ft.

3. VFR-on-top must be conducted at an altitude above the minimum IFR altitude.

4. VFR-on-top is conducted such that both VFR and IFR rules apply.

5. A clearance "to VFR-on-top" is authorization to fly through cloud layers to VFR conditions on top.

6. VFR-on-top operations are specifically prohibited in Class A airspace.

7. In VFR-on-top clearances, you must provide the same reports to ATC that are required for any other IFR flight, and you must adhere to any ATC clearances.

10.3 IFR EN ROUTE CHART INTERPRETATION

1. The sample knowledge test questions in this subunit are wide ranging. They are best prepared for by studying the legends for En Route Low-Altitude Charts.

    a. Legends 33, 34, and 35 are presented below and on the following pages.
    b. Some questions require application of previously covered topics, such as interpretation of VOR indicators.

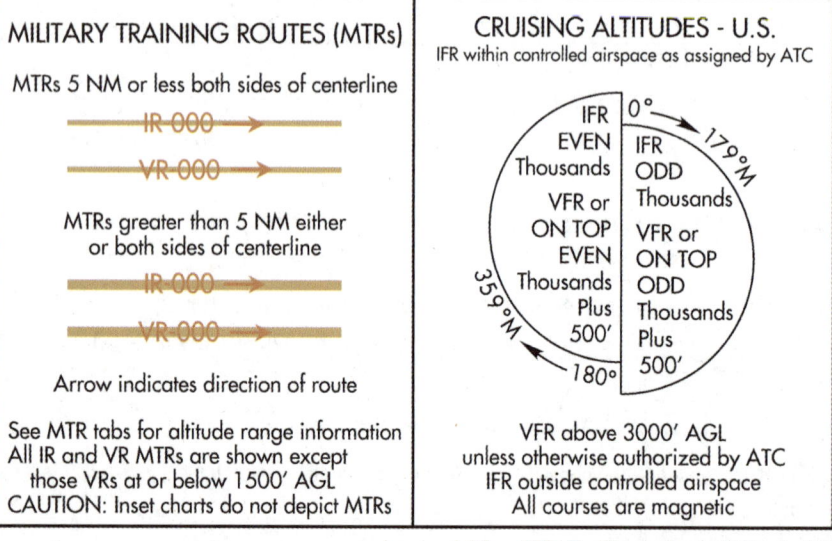

Legend 35. – IFR En Route Low Altitude (U.S.)

PANELS
ABCDE
1"=16 NM

PANELS
FGHIJ
1"=14 NM

UNITED STATES GOVERNMENT
FLIGHT INFORMATION PUBLICATION

IFR ENROUTE LOW ALTITUDE - U.S.

For use up to but not including 18,000' MSL
HORIZONTAL DATUM: NORTH AMERICAN DATUM OF 1983

L E G E N D

AIRPORTS

Facilities in BLUE or GREEN have an approved Instrument Approach Procedure and/or RADAR MINIMA published in either the FAA Terminal Procedures Publications or the DoD FLIPs. Those in BLUE have an Instrument Approach Procedure and/or RADAR MINIMA published at least in the High Altitude DoD FLIPs. Facilities in BROWN do not have a published Instrument Approach Procedure or RADAR MINIMA.

LAND
⊕ ⊙ ⊙ Civil
⊕ ⊙ ⊙ Civil - Military
◎ ◎ ◎ Military
Ⓗ Ⓗ Ⓗ Heliport

SEA
⊕ ⊙ ⊙ Civil

1. A solid line box enclosing the airport name indicates FAR 93 Special Requirements-see Directory/Supplement
2. "NO SVFR" above the airport name indicates FAR 91 fixed-wing special VFR flight is prohibited
3. C or D following the airport name indicates Class C or Class D Airspace

4. Pvt - Private use
5. Associated city names for public airports are shown above or preceding the airport name. If airport name and city name are the same, only the airport name is shown. City names for military and private airports are not shown. The airport identifier in parentheses follows the airport name.

Airport Ident
ICAO Location Indicator
shown outside contiguous U.S.

CITY
Airport Name
(APT) (ICAO) D ★
280 Ⓛ★ 43s
(A) ★109.8

Part-time or established by NOTAM. See Airport/Facility Directory for times of operation. In Alaska see Supplement Alaska

Airport Elevation

ATIS or AFIS (Alaska Only)

Part-time   Frequency

Longest runway length to nearest 100 feet with 70 feet as the dividing point (add 00) s indicates soft surface

Lighting Capability:
L Lighting available
Ⓛ Pilot Controlled Lighting
★ Part-time or on request

- No lighting available
   At private facilities - indicates no lighting information is available.

NAVAIDS

VHF/UHF Data is depicted in BLACK
LF/MF Data is depicted in BROWN

COMPASS ROSE and/or NORTH ARROW
Oriented to Magnetic North of NAVAID which may not be adjusted to the charted isogonic values.

Smaller sizes are used in congested areas.

⬡ ⬡ ⬠ ⬟   VOR VOR/DME TACAN VORTAC

⬢ ⬢ ⬟   LF/MF Non-directional Radiobeacon or Marine Radiobeacon

LF/MF Non-directional Radiobeacon /DME

Non Compulsory Reporting or Off Airway

Compulsory Reporting

Compass Locator Beacon

⊙ Flight Service Station (FSS), Remote Communications Outlet (RCO) or Automated Weather Observing Station (ASOS/AWOS) not associated with a charted NAVAID or airport

ILS Localizer Course with additional navigation function

COMMUNICATION BOXES

NAME (T)   Ⓗ
000.0 IDT 000(Y) ☰··

VOR with TACAN compatible DME

Underline indicates No Voice transmitted on this frequency. TACAN Channels are without voice but not underlined.

▨▨ Crosshatch indicates
▨▨ Shutdown status

(T) Frequency protection usable range at 12,000' AGL - 25NM

(Y) TACAN must be placed in "Y" mode to receive distance information

NAME
000 IDT ☰·· (000.0)
N00°00.00' W000°00.00'

TACAN Channel paired with VHF Frequency in parenthesis.

Automated Weather Broadcast Systems:

Ⓐ ASOS/AWOS   Ⓗ HIWAS

Automated weather, when available, is broadcast on the associated NAVAID frequency.

NAME ASOS 000.0   Stand Alone ASOS/AWOS

000.0
NAME
000.0 IDT 000 ☰··
N00°00.00' W000°00.00'
NAME ← FSS name

Freq(s) positioned above thin line NAVAID box is remoted to the NAVAID site. Other freq(s) at the named FSS radio are available, however, altitude and terrain may determine their reception.

Thin line NAVAID boxes without freq(s) and FSS radio name indicates no freq(s) available.

000.0 000.0
NAME
000.0 IDD 000 ☰::
N00°00.00' W000°00.00'

Shadow NAVAID box indicates NAVAID and Flight Service Station (FSS) have same name

000.0 000.0
NAME IDT   FSS name and identifier not associated with NAVAID

NAME 000.0   Remote Communications Outlet (RCO). FSS radio name and remoted freq(s) are shown.

Part-Time or On-Request   NAME
★ 000 IDT 00(000.0) ☰··

LF/MF Non-directional Radiobeacon/DME VHF Freq paired with TACAN Channel

SHADOW BOXES indicate Flight Service Stations (FSS). Frequencies 122.2, 255.4 and emergency 121.5 and 243.0 (Canada-121.5, 126.7 and 243.0) are available at many FSSs and are not shown. All other frequencies are shown. Certain FSSs provide Airport Advisory Service, see A/FD. Frequencies transmit and receive except those followed by R or T:
R - Receive only
T - Transmit only

In Canada, a "D" after the frequency indicates a Dial-up Remote Communications Outlet.

Legend 33. – IFR En Route Low Altitude (U.S.)

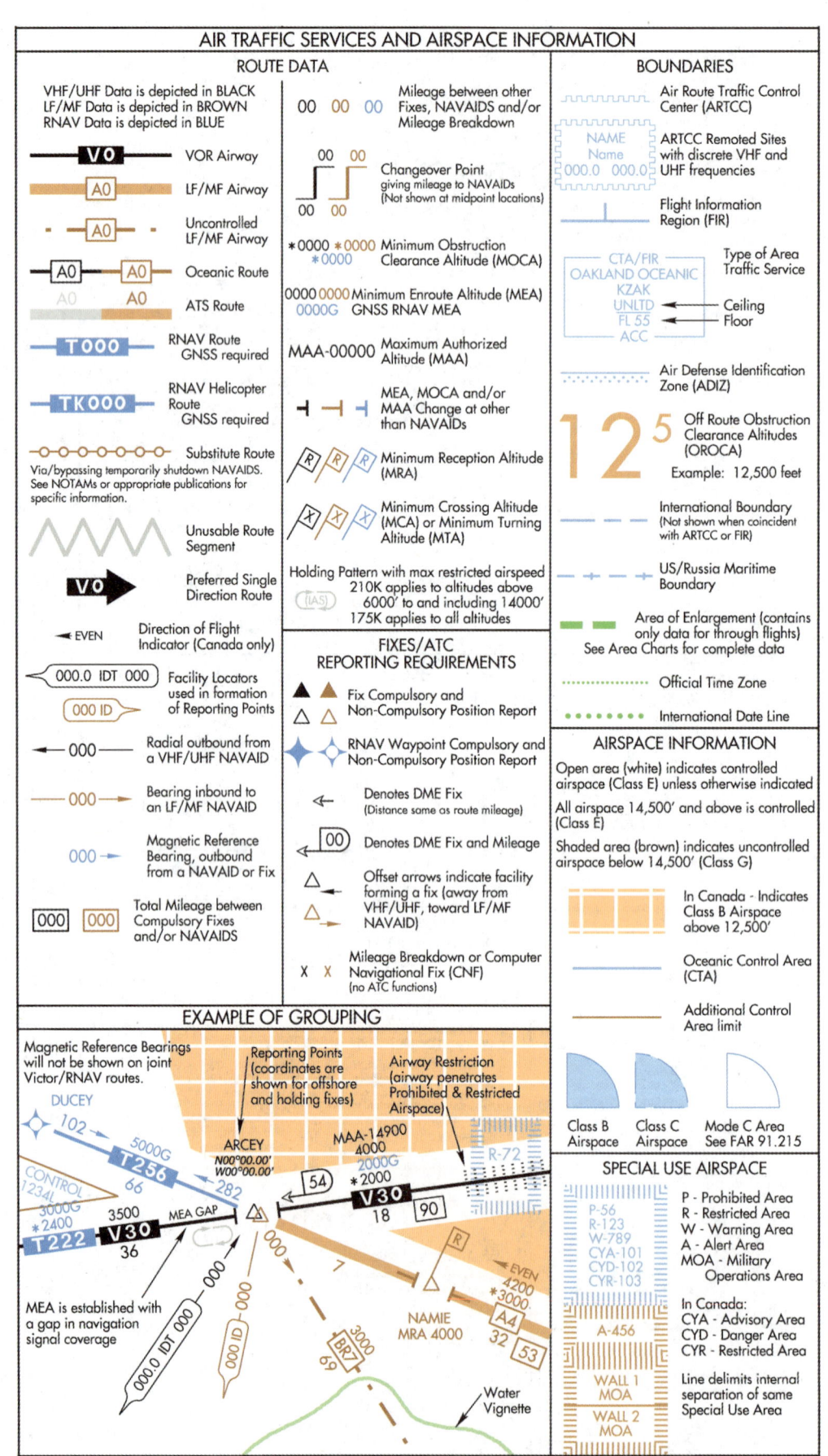

Legend 34. – IFR En Route Low Altitude (U.S.)

QUESTIONS AND ANSWER EXPLANATIONS: All of the instrument rating knowledge test questions chosen by the FAA for release as well as additional questions selected by Gleim relating to the material in the previous outlines are provided on the following pages. These questions have been organized into the same subunits as the outlines. To the immediate right of each question are the correct answer and answer explanations. You should cover these answers and answer explanations while responding to the questions. Refer to the general discussion in the Introduction on how to take the FAA knowledge test.

Remember that the questions from the FAA knowledge test bank have been reordered by topic and organized into a meaningful sequence. Also, the first line of the answer explanation gives the citation of the authoritative source for the answer.

QUESTIONS

10.1 Minimum IFR Altitudes

1. What is the definition of MEA?

A. The lowest published altitude which meets obstacle clearance requirements and assures acceptable navigational signal coverage.

B. The lowest published altitude which meets obstacle requirements, assures acceptable navigational signal coverage, two-way radio communications, and provides adequate radar coverage.

C. An altitude which meets obstacle clearance requirements, assures acceptable navigation signal coverage, two-way radio communications, adequate radar coverage, and accurate DME mileage.

Answer (A) is correct. (P/C Glossary)
DISCUSSION: The minimum en route altitude (MEA) is the lowest published altitude between radio fixes that ensures acceptable navigational signal coverage and meets the obstacle clearance requirements between those fixes.
Answer (B) is incorrect. By definition, the MEA does not ensure either two-way radio communications or adequate radar coverage. **Answer (C) is incorrect.** By definition, the MEA is the lowest published altitude that meets obstacle clearance requirements and ensures acceptable navigation signal coverage. It does not provide for either two-way radio communications or adequate radar coverage.

2. The lowest published altitude which meets obstacle clearance requirements and assures acceptable navigational signal coverage is the

A. MEA.

B. MRA.

C. MOCA.

Answer (A) is correct. (P/C Glossary)
DISCUSSION: The MEA (minimum en route altitude) is the lowest published altitude between radio fixes that ensures acceptable navigational signal coverage and meets obstacle clearance requirements between those fixes.
Answer (B) is incorrect. The MRA (minimum reception altitude) is the lowest altitude at which an intersection can be identified. It is usually higher than the MEA. **Answer (C) is incorrect.** The MOCA (minimum obstruction clearance altitude) only guarantees acceptable navigational signal coverage and meets obstacle clearance requirements when within 22 NM of a NAVAID, not along an entire route that takes the aircraft more than 22 NM from a NAVAID.

3. Reception of signals from an off-airway radio facility may be inadequate to identify the fix at the designated MEA. In this case, which altitude is designated for the fix?

A. MRA.

B. MCA.

C. MOCA.

Answer (A) is correct. (P/C Glossary)
DISCUSSION: MRA (minimum reception altitude) is the lowest altitude at which an intersection can be determined. It is the altitude assigned for a fix when the MEA will not provide adequate reception of an off-airway radio facility (NAVAID) identifying the fix.
Answer (B) is incorrect. MCA (minimum crossing altitude) is the lowest altitude at a fix at which an aircraft must cross when proceeding in the direction of a higher MEA. **Answer (C) is incorrect.** The MOCA (minimum obstruction clearance altitude) is the lowest published altitude in effect between radio fixes on VOR airways, off-airway routes, or route segments that meets obstacle clearance requirements for the entire route segment and that ensures acceptable navigation signal coverage only within 22 NM of a VOR.

4. Reception of signals from a radio facility, located off the airway being flown, may be inadequate at the designated MEA to identify the fix. In this case, which altitude is designated for the fix?

A. MOCA.

B. MRA.

C. MCA.

Answer (B) is correct. (P/C Glossary)
DISCUSSION: MRA (minimum reception altitude) is the lowest altitude at which an intersection can be determined. It is the altitude assigned for a fix when the MEA will not provide adequate reception of an off-airway radio facility (NAVAID) identifying the fix.
Answer (A) is incorrect. The MOCA (minimum obstruction clearance altitude) is the lowest published altitude in effect between radio fixes on VOR airways, off-airway routes, or route segments that meets obstacle clearance requirements for the entire route segment and that ensures acceptable navigation signal coverage only within 22 NM of a VOR. **Answer (C) is incorrect.** MCA (minimum crossing altitude) is the lowest altitude at a fix at which an aircraft must cross when proceeding in the direction of a higher MEA.

5. ATC may assign the MOCA when certain special conditions exist, and when within

A. 22 NM of a VOR.

B. 25 NM of a VOR.

C. 30 NM of a VOR.

Answer (A) is correct. (P/C Glossary)
DISCUSSION: MOCA (minimum obstruction clearance altitude) is the lowest published altitude in effect between radio fixes on VOR airways, off-airway routes, or route segments that meets obstacle clearance requirements for the entire route segment and that ensures acceptable navigational signal coverage only within 22 NM of a VOR. Thus, ATC may assign the MOCA as an assigned altitude, but only within 22 NM of a VOR.
Answer (B) is incorrect. The MOCA provides acceptable navigational signal coverage only within 25 SM, not 25 NM, of a VOR. **Answer (C) is incorrect.** ATC may assign the MOCA as an assigned altitude only within 22 NM, not 30 NM.

6. Acceptable navigational signal coverage at the MOCA is assured for a distance from the VOR of only

A. 12 NM.

B. 22 NM.

C. 25 NM.

Answer (B) is correct. (P/C Glossary)
DISCUSSION: MOCA (minimum obstruction clearance altitude) is the lowest published altitude in effect between radio fixes on VOR airways, off-airway routes, or route segments that meets obstacle clearance requirements for the entire route segment and that ensures acceptable navigational signal coverage only within 22 NM of a VOR. Thus, ATC may assign the MOCA as an assigned altitude, but only within 22 NM of a VOR.
Answer (A) is incorrect. Acceptable navigational signal coverage at the MOCA is ensured for a distance from the VOR of 22 NM, not 12 NM. **Answer (C) is incorrect.** Acceptable navigational signal coverage at the MOCA is ensured for a distance from the VOR of 22 NM, not 25 NM.

7. The altitude that provides acceptable navigational signal coverage for the route, and meets obstacle clearance requirements is the minimum:

A. obstacle clearance altitude.

B. reception altitude.

C. enroute altitude.

Answer (C) is correct. (P/C Glossary)
DISCUSSION: The MEA (minimum en route altitude) is the lowest published altitude between radio fixes that ensures acceptable navigational signal coverage and meets obstacle clearance requirements between those fixes.
Answer (A) is incorrect. The MOCA (minimum obstruction clearance altitude) only guarantees acceptable navigational signal coverage and meets obstacle clearance requirements when within 22 NM of a NAVAID, not along an entire route that takes the aircraft more than 22 NM from a NAVAID. **Answer (B) is incorrect.** The MRA (minimum reception altitude) is the lowest altitude at which an intersection can be identified. It is usually higher than the MEA.

8. Which condition is guaranteed for all of the following altitude limits: MAA, MCA, MRA, MOCA, and MEA? (Non-mountainous area.)

A. Adequate navigation signals.

B. Adequate communications.

C. 1,000-foot obstacle clearance.

Answer (C) is correct. (P/C Glossary)
DISCUSSION: The MAA, MCA, MRA, MOCA, and MEA meet the minimum obstacle clearance requirements. In non-mountainous areas, 1,000 feet above the highest obstacle is guaranteed within a horizontal distance of 4 NM from the course to be flown.
Answer (A) is incorrect. The MOCA ensures acceptable navigational signals only within 22 NM of a VOR. **Answer (B) is incorrect.** The minimum IFR altitudes do not guarantee adequate communications coverage.

9. If no MCA is specified, what is the lowest altitude for crossing a radio fix, beyond which a higher minimum applies?

    A. The MEA at which the fix is approached.

    B. The MRA at which the fix is approached.

    C. The MOCA for the route segment beyond the fix.

Answer (A) is correct. (14 CFR 91.177)
    DISCUSSION: If no MCA (minimum crossing altitude) is specified, the lowest altitude for crossing a radio fix beyond which a higher minimum IFR altitude exists is the MEA at which the fix is approached. A climb must be initiated to a higher minimum immediately after passing the point beyond which that minimum altitude applies.
    Answer (B) is incorrect. If a higher minimum altitude exists after the fix and a higher altitude is needed to identify a fix, usually an MCA, not an MRA, is established at that fix. **Answer (C) is incorrect.** If there is no MCA, the higher minimum altitude does not apply until immediately after passing the fix.

10. In the case of operations over an area designated as a mountainous area, no person may operate an aircraft under IFR below 2,000 feet above the highest obstacle within a horizontal distance of

    A. 3 SM from the course flown.

    B. 4 SM from the course flown.

    C. 4 NM from the course flown.

Answer (C) is correct. (14 CFR 91.177)
    DISCUSSION: In the case of operations over an area designated as a mountainous area where no other minimum altitude is prescribed, no person may operate an aircraft under IFR below 2,000 feet above the highest obstacle within a horizontal distance of 4 NM from the course to be flown.
    Answer (A) is incorrect. The horizontal distance is 4 NM, not 3 SM, from the course flown. **Answer (B) is incorrect.** The horizontal distance is 4 NM, not SM, from the course flown.

11. In the case of operations over an area designated as a mountainous area where no other minimum altitude is prescribed, no person may operate an aircraft under IFR below an altitude of

    A. 500 feet above the highest obstacle.

    B. 1,000 feet above the highest obstacle.

    C. 2,000 feet above the highest obstacle.

Answer (C) is correct. (14 CFR 91.177)
    DISCUSSION: In the case of operations over an area designated as a mountainous area where no other minimum altitude is prescribed, no person may operate an aircraft under IFR below 2,000 feet above the highest obstacle within a horizontal distance of 4 NM from the course to be flown.
    Answer (A) is incorrect. No person may operate an aircraft under IFR below an altitude of 2,000 feet, not 500 feet, above the highest obstacle in a mountainous area. **Answer (B) is incorrect.** No person may operate an aircraft under IFR below an altitude of 1,000 feet above the highest obstacle in a nonmountainous, not mountainous, area.

12. MEA is an altitude which assures

    A. obstacle clearance, accurate navigational signals from more than one VORTAC, and accurate DME mileage.

    B. a 1,000-foot obstacle clearance within 2 miles of an airway and assures accurate DME mileage.

    C. acceptable navigational signal coverage and meets obstruction clearance requirements.

Answer (C) is correct. (P/C Glossary)
    DISCUSSION: The minimum en route altitude (MEA) is the lowest published altitude between radio fixes that ensures acceptable navigational signal coverage and meets the obstacle clearance requirements between those fixes.
    Answer (A) is incorrect. Only one VORTAC is needed at a time to provide acceptable coverage, and DME is not a required navigational signal. **Answer (B) is incorrect.** The clearance is within 4 NM, not 2 mi., and there is no assurance of DME coverage.

13. Unless otherwise specified on the chart, the minimum en route altitude along a jet route is

    A. 18,000 feet MSL.

    B. 24,000 feet MSL.

    C. 10,000 feet MSL.

Answer (A) is correct. (14 CFR 71.33)
    DISCUSSION: Each designated jet route consists of a direct course for navigating from 18,000 feet MSL up to and including FL 450 between the navigational aids and intersections specified for that route. Thus, the MEA along a jet route is 18,000 feet MSL.
    Answer (B) is incorrect. This amount (FL 240) is the minimum altitude at which DME is required when navigating by VOR, not the MEA for a jet route. **Answer (C) is incorrect.** This amount is the minimum altitude at which aircraft are required to operate the transponder on Mode C, not the MEA for a jet route.

10.2 VFR-on-Top

14. Under which of the following circumstances will ATC issue a VFR restriction to an IFR flight?

    A. Whenever the pilot reports the loss of any navigational aid.

    B. When it is necessary to provide separation between IFR and special VFR traffic.

    C. When the pilot requests it.

Answer (C) is correct. (AIM Para 4-4-8)
    DISCUSSION: VFR-on-top is an ATC authorization for an IFR aircraft to operate in VFR conditions at any appropriate VFR altitude. ATC may not authorize VFR-on-top operations unless the pilot requests the clearance to operate in VFR conditions.
    Answer (A) is incorrect. A pilot would report only a malfunction of navigation equipment, not a loss of any navigational aid, to ATC. **Answer (B) is incorrect.** Special VFR traffic would be found near an airport in Class B, C, or D airspace or Class E airspace designated for an airport that is currently experiencing IMC. Thus, ATC would not issue a VFR restriction to an IFR flight.

15. What altitude may a pilot on an IFR flight plan select upon receiving a VFR-on-Top clearance?

    A. Any altitude at least 1,000 feet above or 1,000 feet below the meteorological condition.

    B. Any appropriate VFR altitude at or above the MEA in VFR weather conditions.

    C. Any VFR altitude appropriate for the direction of flight at least 500 feet above the meteorological condition.

Answer (B) is correct. (AIM Para 4-4-8)
    DISCUSSION: When operating in VMC with an ATC authorization to "maintain VFR-on-top/maintain VFR conditions," pilots on IFR flight plans are required to

1. Fly at the appropriate VFR altitude;
2. Comply with the VFR visibility and distance from clouds criteria; and
3. Comply with instrument flight rules that are applicable to the flight, i.e., minimum IFR altitudes, position reporting, course to be flown, adherence to ATC clearances, etc.

    Answer (A) is incorrect. After receiving a VFR-on-top clearance, the pilot may select any appropriate VFR altitude at or above the minimum IFR altitude in VMC, not only 1,000 ft. above or below the meteorological condition. This may be above, below, between layers, or in areas where there is no meteorological obscuration. **Answer (C) is incorrect.** After receiving a VFR-on-top clearance, the pilot may select any appropriate VFR altitude at or above the minimum IFR altitude in VMC, not only 500 ft. above the meteorological condition. This may be above, below, between layers, or in areas where there is no meteorological obscuration.

16. Which rules apply to the pilot in command when operating on a VFR-on-Top clearance?

    A. VFR only.

    B. VFR and IFR.

    C. VFR when "in the clear" and IFR when "in the clouds."

Answer (B) is correct. (AIM Para 4-4-8)
    DISCUSSION: When operating in VMC with an ATC authorization to "maintain VFR-on-top/maintain VFR conditions," pilots on IFR flight plans are required to

1. Fly at the appropriate VFR altitude;
2. Comply with the VFR visibility and distance from clouds criteria; and
3. Comply with instrument flight rules that are applicable to the flight, i.e., minimum IFR altitudes, position reporting, course to be flown, adherence to ATC clearances, etc.

    Answer (A) is incorrect. An ATC clearance to operate VFR-on-top does not imply cancellation of the IFR flight plan. **Answer (C) is incorrect.** A VFR-on-top clearance is issued when the pilot is in VMC and must remain in VMC unless the VFR-on-top clearance is canceled. It does not allow a pilot to fly in IMC.

17. Which ATC clearance should instrument-rated pilots request in order to climb through a cloud layer or an area of reduced visibility and then continue the flight VFR?

    A. To VFR on Top.

    B. Special VFR to VFR Over-the-Top.

    C. VFR Over-the-Top.

Answer (A) is correct. (AIM Para 4-4-8)
    DISCUSSION: Pilots desiring to climb through a cloud, haze, smoke, or other meteorological formation and then either cancel their IFR flight plan or operate VFR-on-top may request an ATC clearance to climb to VFR-on-top.
    Answer (B) is incorrect. A special VFR clearance is issued only in Class B, C, or D airspace or Class E airspace designated for an airport, and the pilot must remain clear of clouds, not climb through them. **Answer (C) is incorrect.** It is VFR-on-top, not VFR-over-the-top.

18. When can a VFR-on-Top clearance be assigned by ATC?

   A. Only upon request of the pilot when conditions are indicated to be suitable.

   B. Any time suitable conditions exist and ATC wishes to expedite traffic flow.

   C. When VFR conditions exist, but there is a layer of clouds below the MEA.

Answer (A) is correct. (AIM Para 4-4-8)
   DISCUSSION: ATC may assign a VFR-on-top clearance only when the pilot requests such a clearance, and the flight must be conducted in VFR weather conditions.
   Answer (B) is incorrect. ATC can issue a VFR-on-top clearance only upon a pilot's, not ATC's, request. **Answer (C) is incorrect.** ATC can issue a VFR-on-top clearance only upon a pilot's request; clearance is not based only on the meteorological conditions.

19. When must a pilot fly at a cardinal altitude plus 500 feet on an IFR flight plan?

   A. When flying above 18,000 feet in VFR conditions.

   B. When flying in VFR conditions above clouds.

   C. When assigned a VFR-on-Top clearance.

Answer (C) is correct. (AIM Para 4-4-8)
   DISCUSSION: VFR-on-top clearances are flown at VFR altitudes, which are even or odd thousand-foot intervals plus 500 feet. This is in contrast to IFR altitudes that are at even or odd thousand-foot intervals. Cardinal altitude means 1,000-foot intervals, e.g., 3,000, 4,000, etc.
   Answer (A) is incorrect. VFR-on-top is not permitted in Class A airspace, which is from 18,000 feet MSL to and including FL 600. **Answer (B) is incorrect.** A pilot on an IFR flight plan uses VFR altitudes only when assigned a VFR-on-top clearance.

20. Where are VFR-on-Top operations prohibited?

   A. In Class A airspace.

   B. During off-airways direct flights.

   C. When flying through Class B airspace.

Answer (A) is correct. (AIM Para 4-4-8)
   DISCUSSION: ATC will not authorize VFR or VFR-on-top operations in Class A airspace.
   Answer (B) is incorrect. VFR-on-top operations during off-airway direct flights are not prohibited. **Answer (C) is incorrect.** VFR-on-top operations within Class B airspace are permitted.

21. What minimums must be considered in selecting an altitude when operating with a VFR-on-Top clearance?

   A. At least 500 feet above the lowest MEA, or appropriate MOCA, and at least 1,000 feet above the existing meteorological condition.

   B. At least 1,000 feet above the lowest MEA, appropriate MOCA, or existing meteorological condition.

   C. Minimum IFR altitude, minimum distance from clouds, and visibility appropriate to altitude selected.

Answer (C) is correct. (AIM Para 4-4-8)
   DISCUSSION: When operating in VMC with an ATC authorization to "maintain VFR-on-top/maintain VFR conditions," pilots on IFR flight plans are required to

1. Fly at the appropriate VFR altitude;
2. Comply with the VFR visibility and distance from clouds criteria; and
3. Comply with instrument flight rules that are applicable to the flight, i.e., minimum IFR altitudes, position reporting, course to be flown, adherence to ATC clearances, etc.

   Answer (A) is incorrect. You must be at or above, not a specified distance from, the minimum IFR altitude, and while on a VFR-on-top clearance, you may operate above, below, or between layers of, not only above, the existing meteorological condition. **Answer (B) is incorrect.** You must be at or above, not a specified distance from, the minimum IFR altitude, and while on a VFR-on-top clearance, you may operate above, below, or between layers of, not only above, the existing meteorological condition.

22. When operating under IFR with a VFR-On-Top clearance, what altitude should be maintained?

    A. An IFR cruising altitude appropriate to the magnetic course being flown.

    B. A VFR cruising altitude appropriate to the magnetic course being flown and as restricted by ATC.

    C. The last IFR altitude assigned by ATC.

Answer (B) is correct. (AIM Para 4-4-8)
    DISCUSSION: When operating in VMC with an ATC authorization to maintain VFR-on-top/maintain VFR conditions, pilots on IFR flight plans are required to

1. Fly at the appropriate VFR altitude;
2. Comply with the VFR visibility and distance from clouds criteria; and
3. Comply with instrument flight rules that are applicable to the flight, i.e., minimum IFR altitudes, position reporting, course to be flown, adherence to ATC clearances, etc.

    Answer (A) is incorrect. Pilots operating with a VFR-on-top clearance should maintain a VFR, not an IFR, cruising altitude appropriate to the magnetic course being flown. **Answer (C) is incorrect.** Pilots operating with a VFR-on-top clearance should maintain a VFR, not an IFR, cruising altitude.

23. In which airspace is VFR-on-Top operation prohibited?

    A. Class B airspace.

    B. Class E airspace.

    C. Class A airspace.

Answer (C) is correct. (AIM Para 4-4-8)
    DISCUSSION: ATC will not authorize VFR or VFR-on-top operations in Class A airspace.
    Answer (A) is incorrect. VFR-on-top operations are permitted, not prohibited, in Class B airspace. **Answer (B) is incorrect.** VFR-on-top operations are permitted, not prohibited, in Class E airspace.

24. What reports are required of a flight operating on an IFR clearance specifying VFR on Top in a nonradar environment?

    A. The same reports that are required for any IFR flight.

    B. All normal IFR reports except vacating altitudes.

    C. Only the reporting of any unforecast weather.

Answer (A) is correct. (AIM Para 4-4-8)
    DISCUSSION: When on a VFR-on-top clearance, you must comply with instrument flight rules that are applicable to the flight, e.g., minimum flight altitudes, position reporting, radio communications, course to be flown, adherence to ATC communications, etc.
    Answer (B) is incorrect. All normal IFR reports are required when operating on a VFR-on-top clearance. You should advise ATC prior to any altitude change to ensure the exchange of accurate traffic information. **Answer (C) is incorrect.** All IFR reports, not only unforecast weather, must be made while operating on a VFR-on-top clearance.

25. When on a VFR-on-Top clearance, the cruising altitude is based on

    A. true course.

    B. magnetic course.

    C. magnetic heading.

Answer (B) is correct. (14 CFR 91.159)
    DISCUSSION: While operating under a VFR-on-top clearance, you must fly at the appropriate VFR altitude, which is based on magnetic course.
    Answer (A) is incorrect. VFR cruising altitudes are based on magnetic, not true, course. **Answer (C) is incorrect.** VFR cruising altitudes are based on magnetic course, not heading.

26. You have filed an IFR flight plan with a VFR-on-Top clearance in lieu of an assigned altitude. If you receive this clearance and fly a course of 180°, at what altitude should you fly? (Assume VFR conditions.)

    A. Any IFR altitude which will enable you to remain in VFR conditions.

    B. An odd thousand-foot MSL altitude plus 500 feet.

    C. An even thousand-foot MSL altitude plus 500 feet.

Answer (C) is correct. (14 CFR 91.159)
    DISCUSSION: When operating in VMC with a VFR-on-top clearance, you must fly at the appropriate VFR cruising altitude. On a magnetic course of 180° through 359°, an even thousand-foot MSL altitude plus 500 feet must be flown.
    Answer (A) is incorrect. On VFR-on-top, one uses VFR, not IFR, altitudes. **Answer (B) is incorrect.** Odd thousand-foot altitudes plus 500 feet are for a magnetic course of 0° through 179°, not 180°.

27. What cruising altitude is appropriate for VFR on Top on a westbound flight below 18,000 feet?

    A. Even thousand-foot levels.

    B. Even thousand-foot levels plus 500 feet, but not below MEA.

    C. Odd thousand-foot levels plus 500 feet, but not below MEA.

Answer (B) is correct. (14 CFR 91.159)
    DISCUSSION: When operating in VMC with a VFR-on-top clearance, you must fly at the appropriate VFR cruising altitude but not below the minimum IFR altitude (e.g., MEA). On a magnetic course of 180° through 359° (i.e., westbound), an even thousand-foot MSL altitude plus 500 feet must be flown.
    Answer (A) is incorrect. An even thousand-foot level is an IFR, not VFR, cruising altitude for a westbound flight. VFR-on-top clearances must maintain VFR altitudes. **Answer (C) is incorrect.** An odd thousand-foot level plus 500 feet is for eastbound, not westbound, flight or a magnetic course from 0° to 179°.

28. If, while in Class E airspace, a clearance is received to "maintain VFR conditions on top," the pilot should maintain a VFR cruising altitude based on the direction of the

    A. true course.

    B. magnetic heading.

    C. magnetic course.

Answer (C) is correct. (14 CFR 91.159)
    DISCUSSION: While operating under a VFR-on-top clearance, you must fly at the appropriate VFR cruising altitude, which is based on magnetic course.
    Answer (A) is incorrect. VFR cruising altitudes are based on magnetic, not true, course. **Answer (B) is incorrect.** VFR cruising altitudes are based on magnetic course, not heading.

29. You are flying on an IFR flight plan at 5,500 feet with a VFR-on-top clearance when you encounter icing. You know there is clear air above and you request 9,500 feet from ATC. They deny the request, but give you 7,500 feet. Are you still VFR-on-top?

    A. Yes, you are still IFR with a VFR-on-top clearance.

    B. No, you are now VFR.

    C. No, your VFR-on-top clearance has been canceled.

Answer (A) is correct. (AIM Para 5-5-13)
    DISCUSSION: While flying on an IFR flight plan and cleared for VFR-on-top, a pilot has latitude to change altitude as necessary to maintain VFR visibility and distance from clouds criteria. The pilot reports those altitude changes to ATC, or ATC assigns another altitude.
    Answer (B) is incorrect. VFR-on-top is not automatically canceled due to an altitude change. The pilot must maintain a VFR cruising altitude and inform ATC of altitude changes, but the VFR-on-top clearance remains valid until the pilot cancels it, provided that aircraft remains in VFR conditions. **Answer (C) is incorrect.** VFR-on-top is not automatically canceled due to an altitude change. The pilot must cancel VFR-on-top.

30. You encounter structural icing on an IFR flight plan at 7,000 feet. Your request for 9,000 feet is rejected by ATC. You request VFR-on-top at 7,500 feet, which is granted. What must you do with your IFR flight plan?

    A. Comply only with VFR rules.

    B. Cancel it.

    C. Continue as planned.

Answer (C) is correct. (AIM Para 5-5-13)
    DISCUSSION: A pilot may request VFR-on-top and, if granted, must comply with both visual and instrument flight rules. However, granting VFR-on-top does not cancel or invalidate an IFR flight plan, nor does it suggest the pilot can ignore instrument flight rules while flying VFR-on-top.
    Answer (A) is incorrect. A pilot may request VFR-on-top and, if granted, must comply with both visual and instrument flight rules while operating VFR-on-top. The pilot must cancel VFR-on-top when VFR rules can no longer be maintained. **Answer (B) is incorrect.** A pilot may request VFR-on-top and, if granted, must comply with both visual and instrument flight rules. However, granting VFR-on-top does not cancel or invalidate an IFR flight plan. The pilot can continue without canceling his or her IFR flight plan.

31. ATC has approved your request for VFR-on-top while on an IFR clearance. Therefore, you

    A. should set your transponder to code 1200.

    B. must fly appropriate IFR altitudes.

    C. must fly appropriate VFR altitudes.

Answer (C) is correct. (AIM Para 4-4-8)
    DISCUSSION: When operating in VFR conditions with an ATC authorization to "maintain VFR-on-top, maintain VFR conditions," pilots on IFR flight plans must fly at the appropriate VFR altitudes and are still on filed IFR flight plans.
    Answer (A) is incorrect. Transponder code 1200 is for VFR operations only and not for IFR flights. **Answer (B) is incorrect.** VFR-on-top is an IFR clearance to operate in VFR conditions; therefore, pilots must fly at the appropriate VFR altitudes. Aircraft that are on an IFR flight plans flying in VMC without a VFR-on-top clearance must maintain IFR altitudes.

10.3   IFR En Route Chart Interpretation

32. (Refer to Figure 65 on page 417.) Which point would be the appropriate VOR COP on V552 from the LFT to the TBD VORTACs?

A. CLYNT intersection.

B. HATCH intersection.

C. 34 DME from the LFT VORTAC.

Answer (C) is correct. (AIM Para 5-3-6)
  DISCUSSION: The changeover point (COP) is located midway between the navigation facilities for straight route segments, unless the COP symbol (⌐) is depicted on the route, in which case the indicated location is the COP. Since no COP symbol appears on V552 from LFT VORTAC (middle left) to TBD VORTAC (lower right), in Fig. 65, the COP is at the midway point. Since the leg is 68 NM, the COP would be at 34 DME from LFT VORTAC.
  Answer (A) is incorrect. CLYNT INT is only about 1/4, not 1/2, the distance from LFT to TBD VORTACs. **Answer (B) is incorrect.** HATCH INT is 5 NM before the COP at 34 NM (i.e., midway point between the LFT and TBD VORTACs).

33. (Refer to Figure 66 below, and Figure 65 on page 417.) What is your position relative to GRICE intersection?

A. Right of V552 and approaching GRICE intersection.

B. Right of V552 and past GRICE intersection.

C. Left of V552 and approaching GRICE intersection.

Answer (A) is correct. (FAA-H-8083-15B Chap 9)
  DISCUSSION: GRICE INT is located at the lower middle portion of Fig. 65 along V552; it is the intersection of V552 and the localizer course to Harry P. Williams Mem. Airport. Your No. 1 VOR (Fig. 66) is tuned to the TBD VORTAC with an OBS setting of 116E TO the station. If you are flying toward TBD VORTAC on V552 (R-296), a left CDI deflection indicates that you are to the right of V552. Your No. 2 VOR is tuned to the I-PTN localizer course. If you are flying inbound on the localizer, a left CDI needle deflection indicates that you are to the right of the localizer course. Thus, you are right of V552 and approaching GRICE INT.
  Answer (B) is incorrect. If you were past GRICE INT, you would be to the left of the localizer; thus, the CDI needle would have a right, not left, deflection. **Answer (C) is incorrect.** If you were to the left of V552, the CDI needle would have a right, not left, deflection.

Figure 66. – CDI and OBS Indicators.

34. (Refer to Figure 65 on page 417 and Figure 67 on page 417.) What is the significance of the symbol at GRICE intersection?

A. It signifies a localizer-only approach is available at Harry P. Williams Memorial.

B. The localizer has an additional navigation function.

C. GRICE intersection also serves as the FAF for the ILS approach procedure to Harry P. Williams Memorial.

Answer (B) is correct. (ACUG)
  DISCUSSION: The large localizer symbol from Harry P. Williams Memorial to GRICE INT (Fig. 65) indicates that the localizer has a navigation function in addition to course guidance. In this case, the localizer's navigational function is to identify GRICE INT.
  Answer (A) is incorrect. The localizer symbol indicates the availability of an ILS, not an LOC only, approach. **Answer (C) is incorrect.** GRICE INT is identified by the localizer course. The FAF on an ILS is the interception of the glide slope, not an intersection.

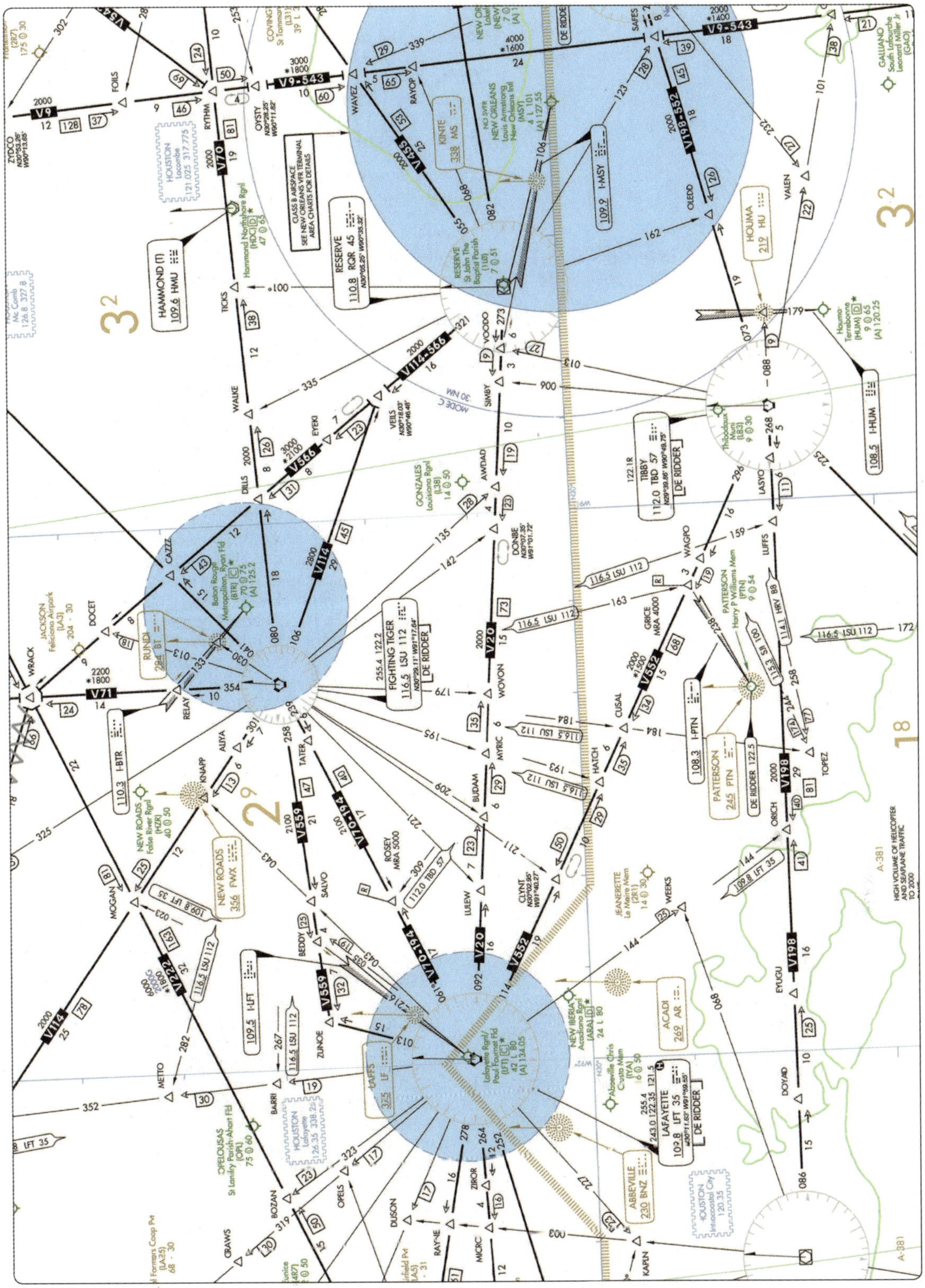

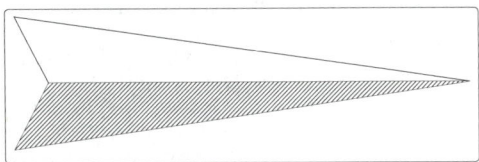

Figure 65. — En Route Low-Altitude Chart Segment.
NOTE: Chart is not to scale and should not be used for navigation. Chart is for testing purposes only.

Figure 67. — Localizer Symbol.

35. (Refer to Figure 87 on page 419.) Where is the VOR COP when flying east on V306 from Daisetta to Lake Charles?

    A. 50 NM east of DAS.

    B. 40 NM east of DAS.

    C. 30 NM east of DAS.

Answer (C) is correct. (AIM Para 5-3-6)
    DISCUSSION: On Fig. 87, when flying east on V306 from Daisetta to Lake Charles, the VOR changeover point (COP) is indicated by the symbol "⌐," and the mileages are given to each VORTAC station. The COP is 30 NM east of Daisetta and 50 NM west of Lake Charles.
    Answer (A) is incorrect. The COP is 50 NM west, not east, of Lake Charles, not DAS. **Answer (B) is incorrect.** The midway point, not the prescribed COP, is 40 NM.

36. (Refer to Figure 87 on page 419.) What is indicated by the localizer course symbol at Jack Brooks Regional Airport?

    A. A published LDA localizer course with voice capability.

    B. A published ILS localizer course, which has an additional navigation function.

    C. A published SDF localizer course with back course capabilities.

Answer (B) is correct. (ACUG)
    DISCUSSION: When a localizer course symbol is shown on an en route low-altitude chart, this indicates that the published ILS localizer has a navigation function in addition to course guidance. The localizer at Jack Brooks Regional Airport, which is located near the center of Fig. 87, is used to define the MARSA intersection.
    Answer (A) is incorrect. ILS course symbols, not LDA, are shown as depicted to indicate an additional navigation function. **Answer (C) is incorrect.** ILS course symbols, not SDF, are shown as depicted to indicate an additional navigation function.

37. (Refer to Figure 87 on page 419.) While holding at the 10 DME fix east of LCH for an ILS approach to RWY 15 at Lake Charles Muni Airport, ATC advises you to expect clearance for the approach at 1015. At 1000 you experience two-way radio communications failure. Which procedure should be followed?

    A. Squawk 7600 and listen on the LOM frequency for instructions from ATC. If no instructions are received, start your approach at 1015.

    B. Squawk 7700 for 1 minute, then 7600. After 1 minute, descend to the minimum final approach fix altitude. Start your approach at 1015.

    C. Squawk 7600; plan to begin your approach at 1015.

Answer (C) is correct. (AIM Para 6-4-1)
    DISCUSSION: Upon radio failure, the transponder should be set to 7600. Since the expected clearance for the approach was 1015, you should plan to begin your approach at 1015.
    Answer (A) is incorrect. There is no LOM shown on the chart at Lake Charles Muni. **Answer (B) is incorrect.** You should not squawk 7700 unless you are in an emergency situation, and you should hold at your altitude until the time necessary to begin your approach at 1015.

38. (Refer to Figure 87 on page 419.) Which VHF frequencies, other than 121.5, can be used to receive De Ridder FSS in the Lake Charles area?

    A. 122.1, 126.4.

    B. 123.6, 122.65.

    C. 122.2, 122.3.

Answer (C) is correct. (ACUG)
    DISCUSSION: The Lake Charles VORTAC communication box is located in the upper right of Fig. 87. The available frequencies are shown above the box, and the controlling FSS (De Ridder) is shown below the box. All FSSs normally use frequency 122.2 and emergency 121.5, which are not shown. Note the thin line box indicates that other frequencies at the controlling FSS are available; however, altitude and terrain may determine their reception. On top of the box is frequency 122.3. Thus, you can receive De Ridder FSS on the VHF frequencies (other than 121.5) of 122.2 and 122.3.
    Answer (A) is incorrect. Neither 122.1 nor 126.4 is an available frequency to receive De Ridder FSS. **Answer (B) is incorrect.** Neither 123.6 nor 122.65 is an available frequency to receive De Ridder FSS.

39. (Refer to Figure 87 on page 419.) At STRUT intersection headed eastbound, ATC instructs you to hold west on the 10 DME fix west of LCH on V306, standard turns. What entry procedure is recommended?

    A. Direct.

    B. Teardrop.

    C. Parallel.

Answer (A) is correct. (AIM Para 5-3-7)
    DISCUSSION: You are instructed to hold west at the 10 DME fix west of LCH VORTAC on V306. Since you are at STRUT int., flying eastbound on V306, you should make a direct entry to a heading of 265°. Since the direction of turn was not specified, you should make right turns, which is a standard holding pattern.
    Answer (B) is incorrect. A teardrop entry may be used if you are instructed to hold east, not west, of the 10 DME fix. **Answer (C) is incorrect.** A parallel entry may be used if you are instructed to hold east, not west, of the 10 DME fix.

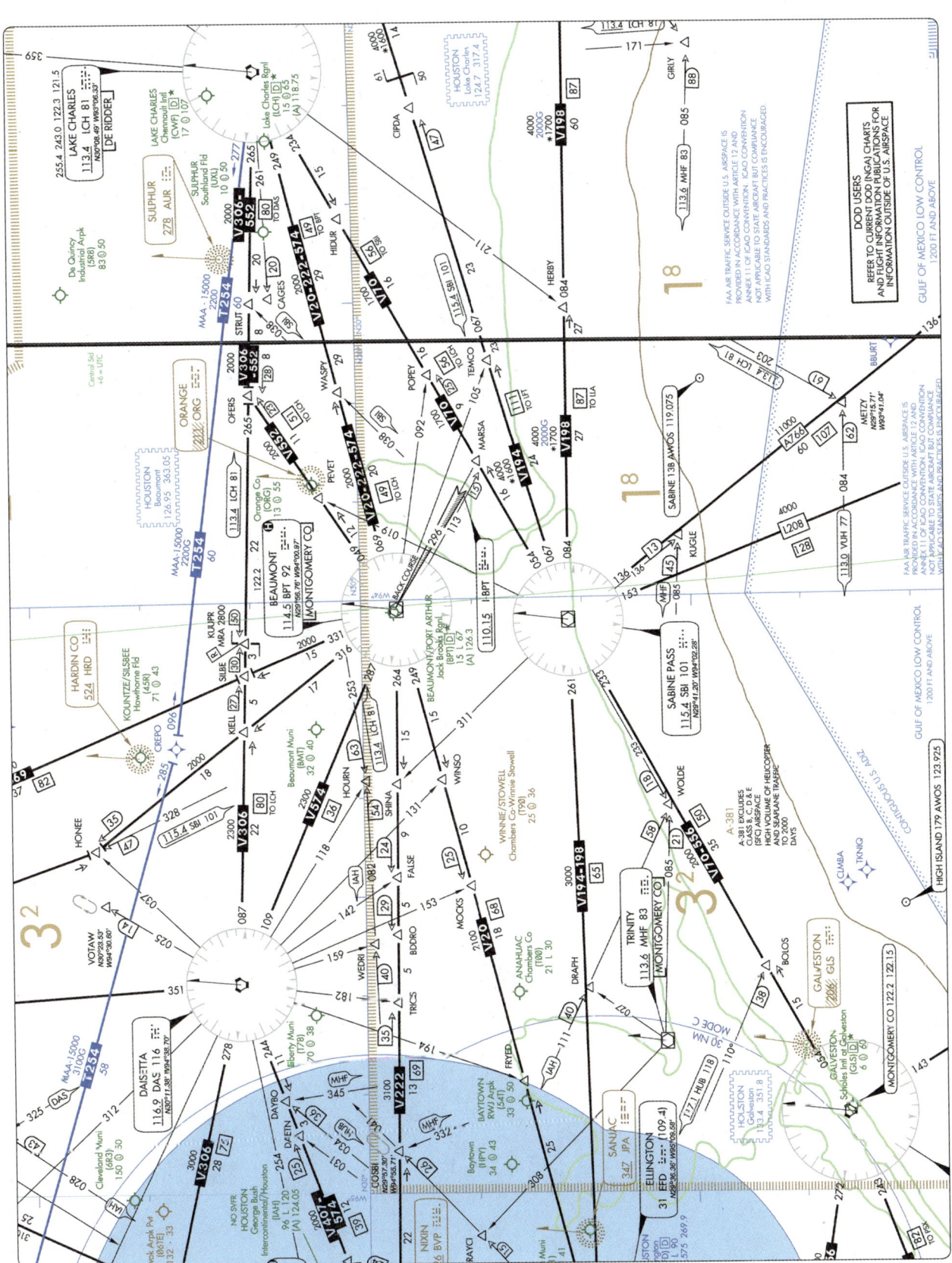

Figure 87. – En Route Low-Altitude Chart Segment.
NOTE: Chart is not to scale and should not be used for navigation. Chart is for testing purposes only.

40. (Refer to Figure 87 below, and Legend 34 on page 421.) Where is the VOR changeover point on V70 between Sabine Pass and Lake Charles?

A. Halfway point.

B. POPEY intersection.

C. 41 DME from the SBI VOR/DME.

Answer (A) is correct. (AIM Para 5-3-6)
DISCUSSION: In Fig. 87, V70 connects Sabine Pass (SBI) VOR/DME and Lake Charles (LCH) VORTAC. The changeover point (COP) is located midway between SBI and LCH, which is 28 DME. When the COP is not located at the midway point, the symbol "⌐" is used, and the mileage to each NAVAID is given.
Answer (B) is incorrect. POPEY INT is 25 DME from SBI, and the halfway point is 28 DME. The next VOR should be tuned at the halfway point when another changeover point (COP) is not designated. **Answer (C) is incorrect.** The changeover point (COP) is located midway between two VORs unless there is a changeover symbol at another location. Halfway between SBI and LCH is 28 DME, not 41 DME.

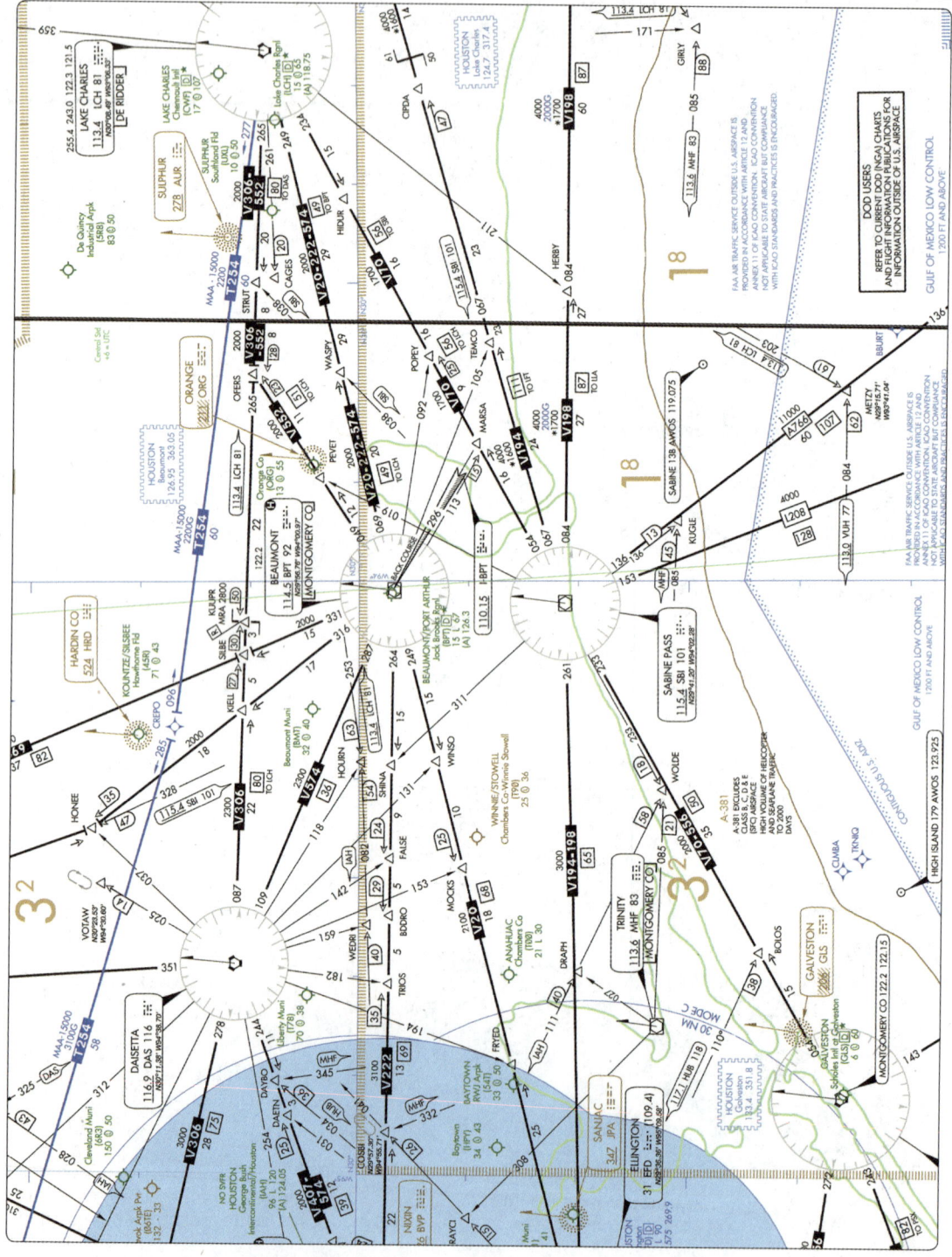

Figure 87. – En Route Low-Altitude Chart Segment.
NOTE: Chart is not to scale and should not be used for navigation. Chart is for testing purposes only.

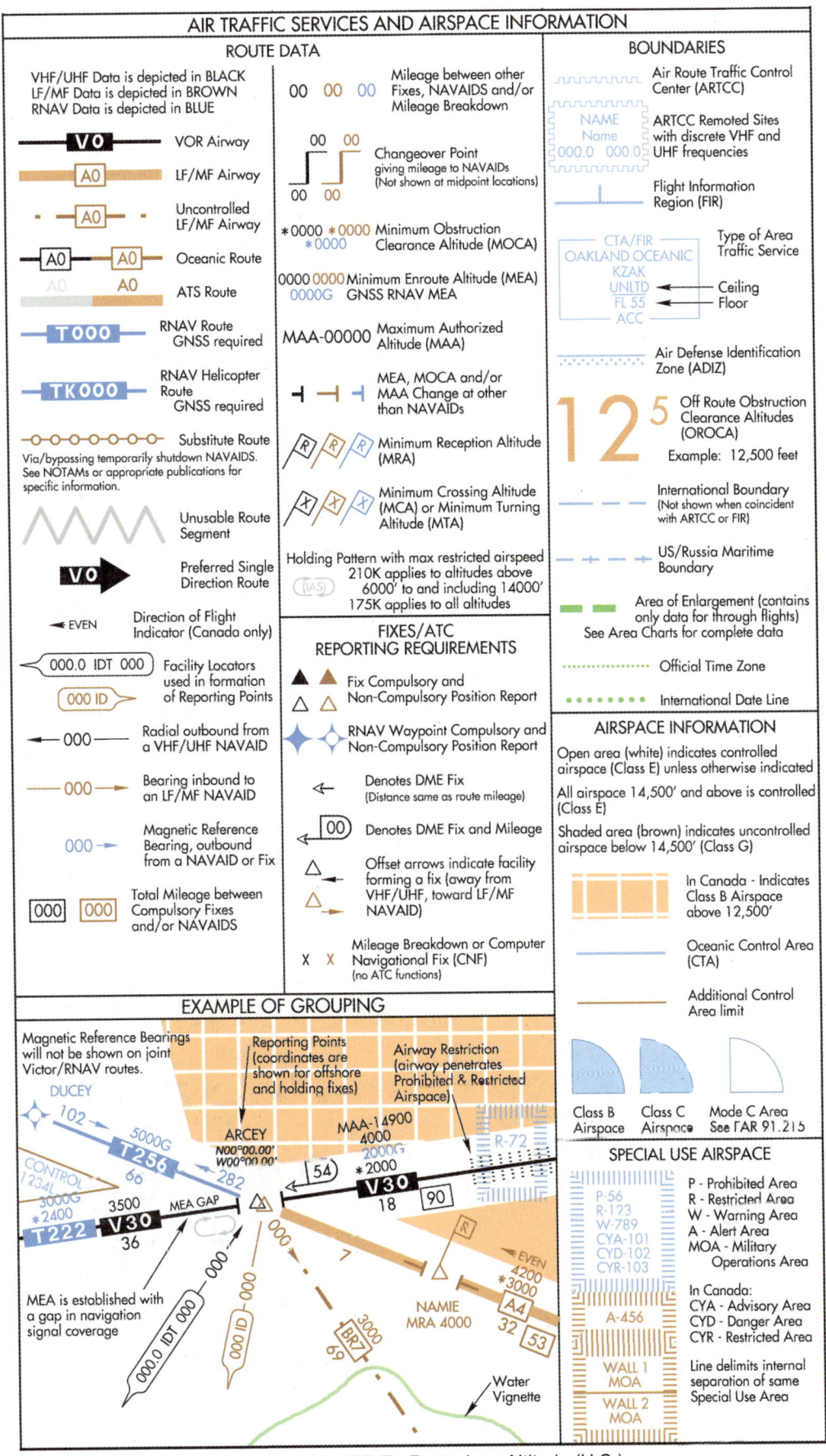

Legend 34. – IFR En Route Low Altitude (U.S.)

41. (Refer to Figure 87 on page 423.) You are flying on V306 from Lake Charles to Daisetta. Where is the VOR changeover point?

    A. 50 NM west of LCH.

    B. 50 NM east of DAS.

    C. 30 NM west of LCH.

Answer (A) is correct. *(AIM Para 5-3-6)*
    DISCUSSION: Follow west along V306 from LCH. At the end of the third route segment is the VOR changeover point symbol. Located above is 50 in the DME fix encircled mileage marker with directional arrow. This means the changeover point is located 50 NM west of LCH.
    Answer (B) is incorrect. A location of 50 NM east of DAS would be 2 NM west of OFERS intersection. **Answer (C) is incorrect.** A location of 30 NM west of LCH would be 2 NM west of OFERS intersection.

42. (Refer to Figure 87 on page 423.) When northeast bound on V70 between SBI and LCH and using the VORs to navigate, where is the changeover point (COP)?

    A. 28 NM from SBI.

    B. MARSA intersection.

    C. Anahuac Beacon.

Answer (A) is correct. *(AIM Para 5-3-6)*
    DISCUSSION: When the changeover point is not located at the midway point, it is depicted with the changeover point symbol. In this case, locate the total mileage for the route between SBI and LCH, depicted as 56 NM inside a box. This means the changeover point is 28 NM from SBI and will be the point to change the navigation receiver frequency from the station behind the aircraft to the station ahead.
    Answer (B) is incorrect. MARSA intersection is 16 NM from SBI and not located at the midpoint between the VORs of 28 NM. **Answer (C) is incorrect.** Anahuac Beacon is not a part of this route structure, and the changeover point is located equidistant between SBI and LCH.

43. (Refer to Figure 88 below, and Figure 87 on page 423.) What is your position with reference to FALSE intersection (V222) if your VOR receivers indicate as shown?

    A. South of V222 and east of FALSE intersection.

    B. North of V222 and east of FALSE intersection.

    C. South of V222 and west of FALSE intersection.

Answer (A) is correct. *(FAA-H-8083-15B Chap 9)*
    DISCUSSION: Note: In this edition of the test, Fig. 88 was not updated; thus VOR No. 2 incorrectly shows an OBS setting of 139 instead of 142.
    Your No. 1 VOR (Fig. 88) is tuned to the BPT VORTAC, Fig. 87, with an OBS setting of 264. If you are flying outbound (FROM) BPT on V222 (R-264), a right deflection indicates that V222 is to the right of your location. Thus, you are to the south of V222. Your No. 2 VOR is tuned to the DAS VORTAC with an OBS setting of 142. If you are flying outbound (FROM) DAS on R-142, a right deflection would mean that R-142 is to the right of your location. Thus, you are to the east of R-142. FALSE INT is the intersection of V222 (BPT R-264) and DAS R-142; you are presently to the south of V222 and east of FALSE INT.
    Answer (B) is incorrect. To be north of V222 would be indicated by a left, not right, CDI deflection in the No. 1 VOR. **Answer (C) is incorrect.** To be west of FALSE INT would be indicated by a left, not right, CDI deflection on the No. 2 VOR.

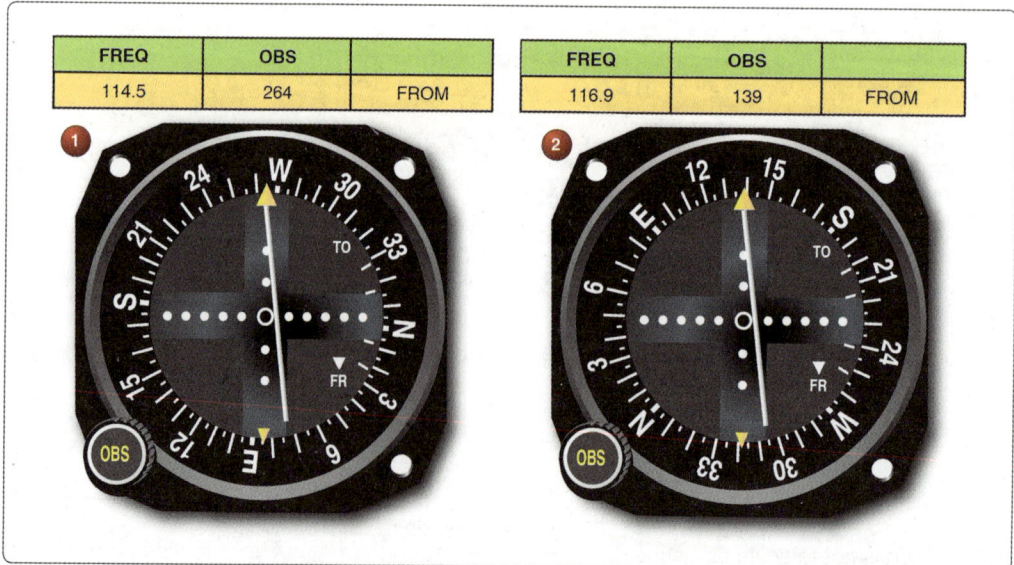

FREQ	OBS	
114.5	264	FROM

FREQ	OBS	
116.9	139	FROM

Figure 88. – CDI and OBS Indicators.

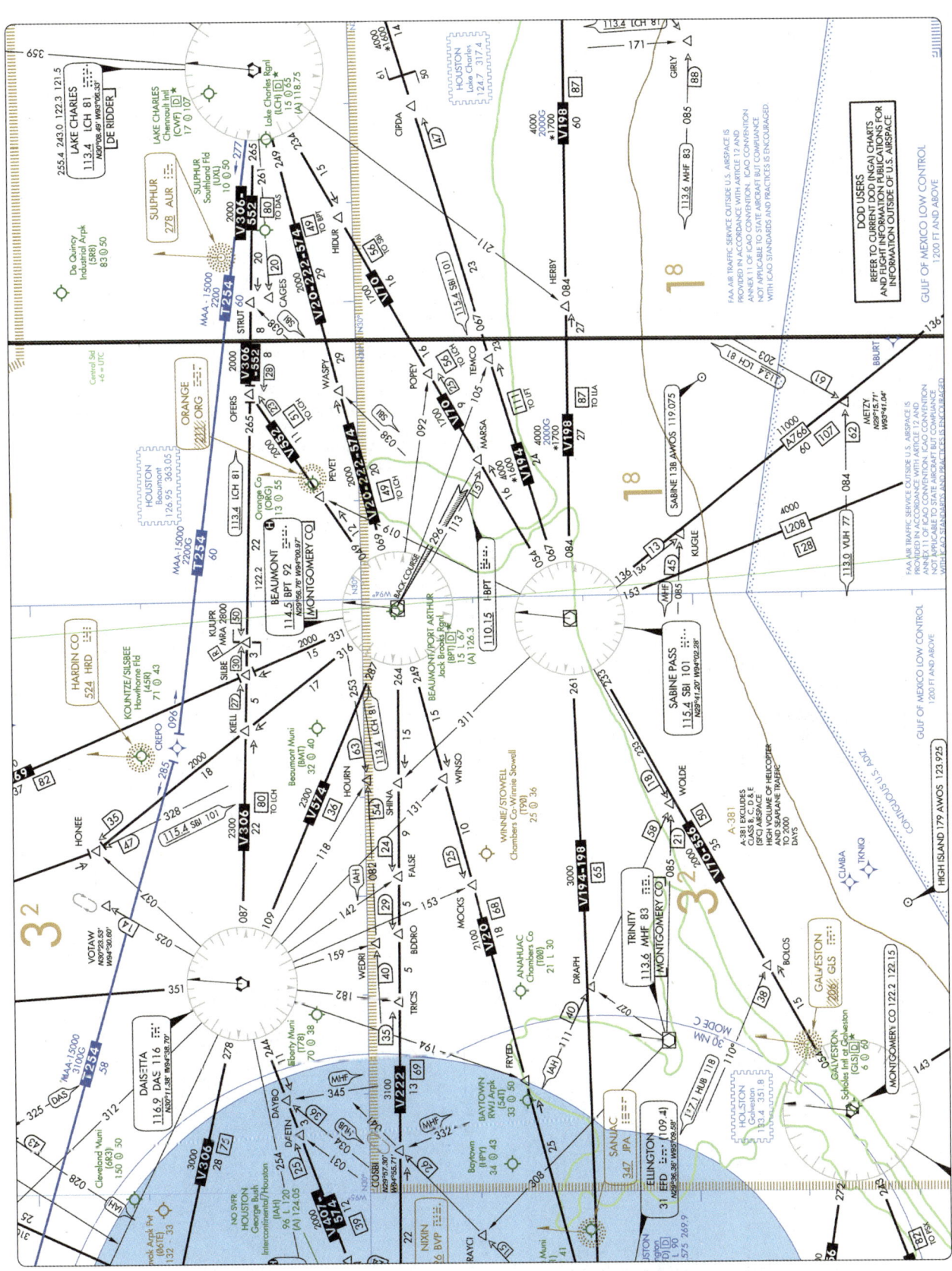

Figure 87. – En Route Low-Altitude Chart Segment.
NOTE: Chart is not to scale and should not be used for navigation. Chart is for testing purposes only.

44. (Refer to Figure 89 on page 425.) When flying from Milford Municipal to Bryce Canyon via V235 and V293, what minimum altitude should you be at when crossing Cedar City VOR?

    A. 11,400 feet.

    B. 12,000 feet.

    C. 13,000 feet.

Answer (B) is correct. (ACUG)
    DISCUSSION: In Fig. 89, CDC VOR has a flag with an "X" inside to indicate an MCA (minimum crossing altitude). The MCA is indicated below the CDC communication box. When flying east on V293 to Bryce Canyon, you must cross CDC at a minimum altitude of 12,000 feet (V293 12000E).
    Answer (A) is incorrect. This is the MCA when flying south on V235. **Answer (C) is incorrect.** This is the MEA for V293 east of CDC.

45. (Refer to Figure 89 on page 425.) What VHF frequencies are available for communications with Cedar City FSS?

    A. 123.6, 121.5, 108.6, and 112.8.

    B. 122.2, 121.5, 122.6, and 122.1.

    C. 122.2, 121.5, 122.0, and 123.6.

Answer (B) is correct. (ACUG)
    DISCUSSION: On top of the Cedar City (CDC) communication box is frequency 122.6. Additionally, VHF frequencies 122.2 and 121.5 are available at all FSSs. Frequency 122.1 is used by pilots to contact Cedar City FSS in the vicinity of Milford (MLF), and the FSS would transmit (pilots receive) on the MLF VORTAC frequency 112.1.
    Answer (A) is incorrect. The figure of 123.6 is not listed above any communication boxes controlled by Cedar City FSS and both CDC and BCE VORTACs are underlined, which means there is no voice on that frequency. **Answer (C) is incorrect.** The figures of 122.0 and 123.6 are not listed above any communication boxes controlled by Cedar City FSS.

46. (Refer to Figure 89 on page 425.) What are the oxygen requirements for an IFR flight east bound from Milford to Hanksville on V244 at the lowest appropriate altitude in an unpressurized aircraft?

    A. The required minimum crew must be provided and use supplemental oxygen for that part of the flight of more than 30 minutes.

    B. The required minimum crew must be provided and use supplemental oxygen for that part of the flight of more than 30 minutes, and the passengers must be provided supplemental oxygen.

    C. The required minimum crew must be provided and use supplemental oxygen, and all occupants must be provided supplemental oxygen for the entire flight above 15,000 feet.

Answer (C) is correct. (14 CFR 91.211)
    DISCUSSION: At cabin pressure altitudes above 14,000 feet MSL, the required minimum flight crew must be provided with and use supplemental oxygen during the entire flight time at those altitudes. Additionally, each occupant must be provided with supplemental oxygen at cabin pressure altitudes above 15,000 feet MSL. The MEA for V244 is 16,000 feet MSL.
    Answer (A) is incorrect. The requirement that the required minimum crew be provided with and use supplemental oxygen for that part of the flight of more than 30 minutes describes the oxygen requirements when at cabin pressure altitudes above 12,500 feet MSL up to and including 14,000 feet MSL, not at 16,000 feet MSL. **Answer (B) is incorrect.** The requirement that the required minimum crew be provided with and use supplemental oxygen for that part of the flight of more than 30 minutes describes the oxygen requirements when at cabin pressure altitudes above 12,500 feet MSL up to and including 14,000 feet MSL, not at 16,000 feet MSL.

47. (Refer to Figure 89 on page 425.) What is the ARTCC discrete frequency at the COP on V208 southwest bound from HVE to PGA VOR/DME?

    A. 122.65

    B. 122.4

    C. 127.55

Answer (C) is correct. (ACUG)
    DISCUSSION: The COP on V208 southwest bound to PGA VOR/DME from HVE VORTAC is indicated by the symbol "⌐", and the mileages are given to each VOR station. The COP is 61 NM northeast of PGA and 35 NM southwest of HVE. Notice the ragged line (see Legend 34 on page 408) south of HVE VORTAC, which is the symbol that divides Salt Lake City ARTCC to the north and Denver ARTCC to the south. Thus, the COP is in Salt Lake City ARTCC airspace. To the lower-right of HVE VORTAC is a box indicating that Salt Lake City ARTCC uses an RCO at Hanksville on a discrete frequency of 127.55.
    Answer (A) is incorrect. This frequency is shown above the communications boxes at HVE VORs and is used for communicating with FSSs, not the ARTCC. **Answer (B) is incorrect.** This frequency is shown in the remote communications outlet (RCO) boxes at Bullfrog Basin and Cal Black Memorial Airports and is used for communicating with Cedar City FSS, not the ARTCC.

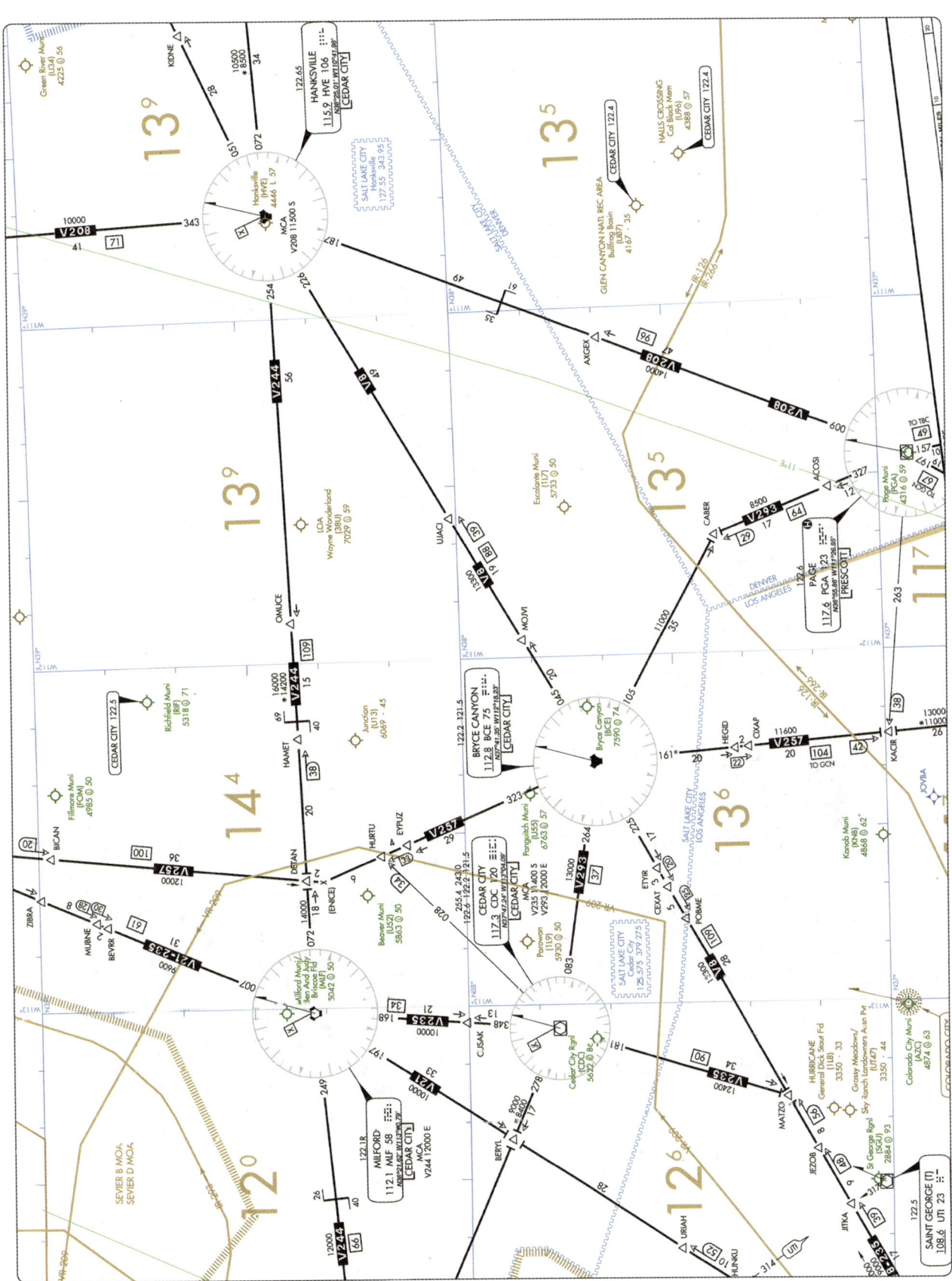

Figure 89. – En Route Low-Altitude Chart Segment.
NOTE: Chart is not to scale and should not be used for navigation. Chart is for testing purposes only.

48. (Refer to Figure 89 on page 427.) What type airspace exists above Wayne Wonderland Airport from the surface to 1,200 feet AGL?

A.   Class D.

B.   Class E.

C.   Class G.

Answer (C) is correct. (ACUG and AIM Para 3-3-1)
    DISCUSSION: Wayne Wonderland Airport symbol is brown in color, which means it does not have a published IAP. The airport is not indicated to be in Class B or C airspace but does lie below a federal airway (the white area to either side of and along V244). Federal airways are Class E airspace and, unless otherwise specified, extend upward from 1,200 feet AGL to, but not including, 18,000 feet MSL. Wayne Wonderland is not a Class D airport (indicated by ▣ following the airport name). Class E surface areas are not shown on En Route Low-Altitude Charts. However, since Wayne Wonderland has no IAP, we can assume that no Class E surface area is associated with the airport. Therefore, Class G airspace extends from the surface upward to 1,200 feet AGL, the floor of the federal airway.
    Answer (A) is incorrect. Class D airports are indicated by a ▣ following the airport name. **Answer (B) is incorrect.** Federal airways normally extend upward from 1,200 feet AGL, not from the surface.

49. (Refer to Figure 90 below, and Figure 89 on page 427.) What is your relationship to the airway while en route from BCE VORTAC to HVE VORTAC on V8?

A.   Left of course on V8.

B.   Left of course on V382.

C.   Right of course on V8.

Answer (A) is correct. (FAA-H-8083-15B Chap 9)
    DISCUSSION: Your No. 2 VOR is tuned to the HVE VORTAC with an OBS setting of 046° TO the station, which is the inbound course on V8. The CDI is deflected to the right, which means you are to the left of course on V8.
    Answer (B) is incorrect. V382 does not exist on this low en route chart. **Answer (C) is incorrect.** If you were right of V8, you would have a left, not right, CDI deflection on NAV No. 2.

Figure 90. – CDI/OBS Indicators.

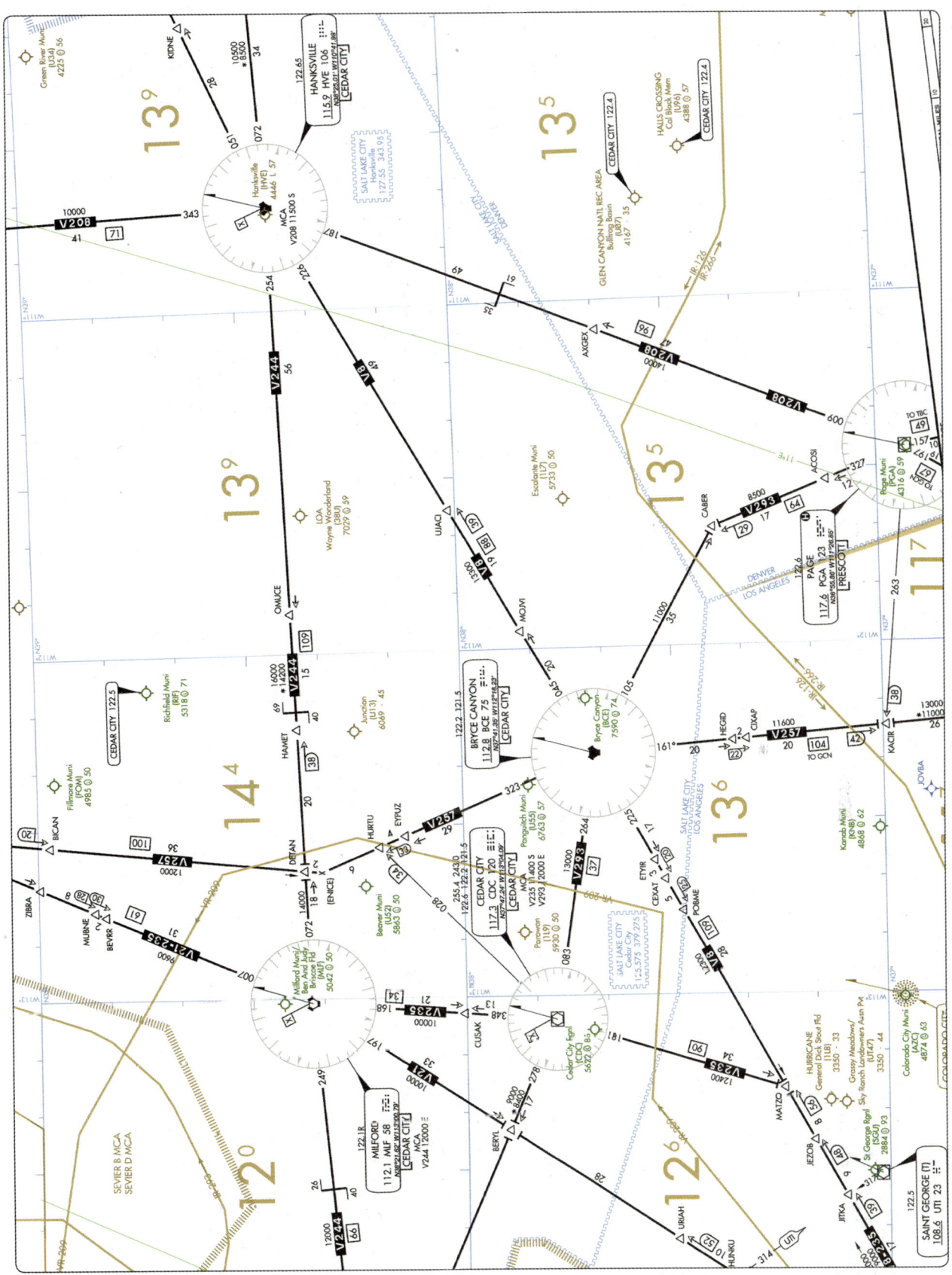

Figure 89. – En Route Low-Altitude Chart Segment.
NOTE: Chart is not to scale and should not be used for navigation. Chart is for testing purposes only.

50. (Refer to Figure 91 on page 429.) What are the two limiting cruising altitudes usable on V343 for a VFR-on-Top flight from DBS VORTAC to RANEY intersection?

    A.   14,500 and 16,500 feet.

    B.   15,000 and 17,000 feet.

    C.   15,500 and 17,500 feet.

Answer (C) is correct. (14 CFR 91.159)
    DISCUSSION: In Fig. 91, a flight from DBS VORTAC to RANEY intersection on V343 has an MEA of 15,000 feet. A flight with a clearance of VFR-on-top will operate at appropriate VFR cruising altitudes, at or above the minimum IFR altitude. On a magnetic course of 008°, you must be at an odd thousand-foot altitude plus 500 feet. Thus, a VFR-on-top flight is limited to only 15,500 feet and 17,500 feet. You cannot operate VFR in Class A airspace, i.e., 18,000 feet MSL to FL 600.
    Answer (A) is incorrect. The appropriate VFR-on-top altitudes for a magnetic course of 008° are odd, not even, thousand-foot altitudes plus 500 feet. Also, 14,500 feet is below the MEA. **Answer (B) is incorrect.** VFR-on-top altitudes are cardinal (1,000, 2,000, etc.) plus 500 feet.

51. (Refer to Figure 91 on page 429.) What should be the approximate elapsed time from BZN VOR to DBS VORTAC, if the wind is 24 knots from 260° and your intended TAS is 185 knots?

    A.   33 minutes.

    B.   37 minutes.

    C.   39 minutes.

Answer (C) is correct. (FAA-H-8083-25B Chap 16)
    DISCUSSION: First convert your wind from 260° true to 248° magnetic because of the 12°E variation. Then place the 248 below the true index on the wind side of your flight computer and mark the wind speed of 24 knots up from the grommet (center hole). Then place your magnetic course of 186° under the true index. Next, slide the scale so that the pencil mark is on the 185-knots TAS and note that the grommet is at 173 knots, which is the groundspeed.
    On the computer side, put 173 knots on the outer scale under the true index. Locate 111 NM on the outer scale and read the time below on the inner scale, which is approximately 39 minutes.
    Answer (A) is incorrect. This is the approximate time going north from DBS VORTAC to BZN VOR, not from BZN VOR to DBS VORTAC. **Answer (B) is incorrect.** This is the approximate time from BZN VOR to DBS VORTAC using the wind direction of 260°, not the magnetic wind direction of 248°.

52. (Refer to Figure 91 on page 429.) Southbound on V257, at what time should you arrive at DBS VORTAC if you crossed over CPN VORTAC at 0850 and over DIVID intersection at 0854?

    A.   0939

    B.   0943

    C.   0947

Answer (B) is correct. (FAA-H-8083-25B Chap 16)
    DISCUSSION: CPN VORTAC is on the left side of the chart about 1 1/2 in. down from the top. Going south on V257, DIVID INT is 9 NM from CPN VORTAC. Use your flight computer to determine the groundspeed. Locate 9 on the outer scale and place 4 on the minute scale under the 9. The groundspeed is read over the index, which is 135 kt.
    From DIVID to DLN VORTAC is 39 NM; then from DLN VORTAC to DBS VORTAC is 71 NM, or a total of 110 NM. To determine the time, place 135 knots over the index of your flight computer and locate 110 NM on the outer scale; the time is read below on the minute scale, which is 49 minutes from DIVID INT to DBS VORTAC. Thus, your ETA at DBS VORTAC is 0943 (0854 + 49).
    Answer (A) is incorrect. The 49 minutes is added to the time you crossed DIVID INT (0854), not the time you crossed CPN VORTAC (0850). **Answer (C) is incorrect.** The distance from CPN VORTAC to DIVID INT (9 NM) must be subtracted from the 48 NM between CPN VORTAC and DLN VORTAC.

53. (Refer to Figure 91 on page 429.) When flying a northbound IFR flight on V257, what is the minimum crossing altitude at DBS VORTAC?

    A.   7,500 feet.

    B.   8,600 feet.

    C.   11,100 feet.

Answer (B) is correct. (ACUG)
    DISCUSSION: DBS VORTAC is at the center of the large compass rose in the lower left of Fig. 91. At DBS VORTAC, there is a flag with an "X" inside that indicates an MCA. The MCA is indicated next to the VORTAC symbol. When flying north on V257, you must cross DBS VORTAC at a minimum altitude of 8,600 feet (V21-257 8600N).
    Answer (A) is incorrect. This is the MEA on V257 south of DBS VORTAC. **Answer (C) is incorrect.** This is the MOCA on V21-257 northwest of DBS VORTAC.

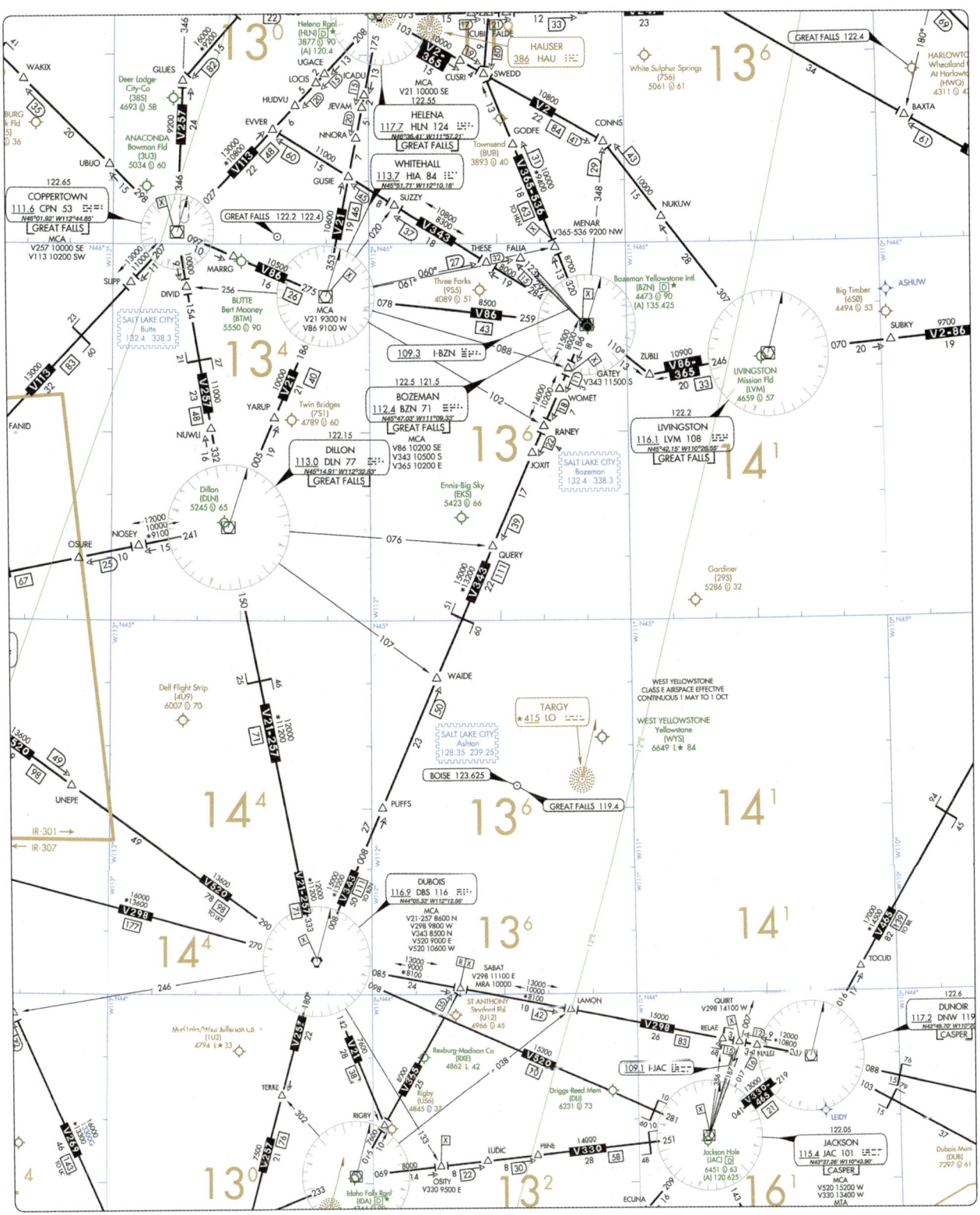

Figure 91. – En Route Low-Altitude Chart Segment.
NOTE: Chart is not to scale and should not be used for navigation. Chart is for testing purposes only.

54. (Refer to Figure 91 on page 431.) What are the oxygen requirements for an IFR flight eastbound on V520 from DBS VORTAC in an unpressurized aircraft at the MEA?

A. The required minimum crew must be provided and use supplemental oxygen for that part of the flight of more than 30 minutes.

B. The required minimum crew must be provided and use supplemental oxygen for that part of the flight of more than 30 minutes, and the passengers must be provided supplemental oxygen.

C. The required minimum crew must be provided and use supplemental oxygen, and the passengers must be provided supplemental oxygen.

Answer (C) is correct. (14 CFR 91.211)
 DISCUSSION: On Fig. 91, when going eastbound from DBS VORTAC on V520, the MEA is 15,300 feet MSL. At cabin pressure altitudes above 14,000 feet MSL, the flight crew must be provided and use supplemental oxygen for the entire flight. At cabin pressure altitudes above 15,000 feet MSL, the passengers must be provided with supplemental oxygen.
 Answer (A) is incorrect. The required minimum crew must be provided and use supplemental oxygen for that part of the flight of more than 30 minutes at cabin pressure altitudes above 12,500 feet MSL up to and including 14,000 feet MSL. **Answer (B) is incorrect.** The required minimum crew must be provided and use supplemental oxygen at all times, not only that part of the flight of more than 30 minutes, at cabin pressure altitudes above 14,000 feet MSL. Passengers must be provided supplemental oxygen at cabin pressure altitudes above, not at, 15,000 feet MSL.

55. (Refer to Figure 91 on page 431.) Where should you change VOR frequencies when en route from DBS VORTAC to JAC VOR/DME on V520?

A. 35 NM from DBS VORTAC.

B. 60 NM from DBS VORTAC.

C. 60 NM from JAC VOR/DME.

Answer (B) is correct. (AIM Para 5-3-6)
 DISCUSSION: When flying from DBS VORTAC to JAC VOR/DME on V520 (Fig. 91), notice that very close to the JAC VOR/DME is a VOR changeover point symbol (⌐), which is 60 NM from the DBS VORTAC.
 Answer (A) is incorrect. In this case, the changeover point (COP) is not located at the midway point; the COP is marked by the symbol "⌐", and mileage is given to the VORs. **Answer (C) is incorrect.** The COP is located 10 NM, not 60 NM, from JAC VOR/DME.

56. (Refer to Figure 91 on page 431.) What lighting is indicated on the chart for Jackson Hole Airport?

A. Lights on prior request.

B. No lighting available.

C. Pilot controlled lighting.

Answer (C) is correct. (ACUG)
 DISCUSSION: The Jackson Hole Airport is located at the lower right of Fig. 91. The "L" indicates that Jackson Hole Airport has night lighting. The circle indicates pilot-controlled lighting.
 Answer (A) is incorrect. An asterisk would indicate lighting on request or in operation for only part of the night. **Answer (B) is incorrect.** If no lighting were available, there would be a "–" after the airport elevation.

57. (Refer to Figure 91 on page 431.) What does "15000" on V343 between DBS and BZN guarantee?

A. The lowest altitude that ensures navigational signal coverage and obstacle clearance.

B. The highest altitude that ensures 120 nautical mile navigational signal coverage between VORs.

C. The lowest altitude that ATC may use to vector an aircraft from the en route structure to the approach segment.

Answer (A) is correct. (ACUG)
 DISCUSSION: The listed 15000 refers to the minimum en route altitude (MEA) and is the lowest published altitude between radio fixes, in this case DBS and BZN, that will ensure acceptable navigation signal coverage while meeting the obstacle clearance requirements between these radio fixes.
 Answer (B) is incorrect. The 15000 depiction is a minimum en route altitude (MEA). The only maximum altitude will be a maximum authorized altitude (MAA) depicted as MAA and in feet MSL. It is the highest altitude on an airway for which an MEA is designated at which adequate reception of navigation signals is assured. **Answer (C) is incorrect.** The published 15000 is a minimum en route altitude (MEA), as opposed to this description of a minimum vectoring altitude (MVA).

58. (Refer to Figure 91 on page 431.) What is the minimum crossing altitude at SABAT intersection when eastbound from DBS VORTAC on V298?

A. 8,300 feet.

B. 11,100 feet.

C. 13,000 feet.

Answer (B) is correct. (ACUG)
 DISCUSSION: SABAT INT is located east of DBS VORTAC on V298 at the lower middle area in Fig. 91. There is a flag with an "X" in it, which indicates an MCA at SABAT. Underneath the SABAT is the MCA, which is 11,100 feet when eastbound on V298 (V298 11100E).
 Answer (A) is incorrect. This is the MOCA between DBS VORTAC and SABAT INT (*8300). **Answer (C) is incorrect.** This is the MEA when eastbound on V298 between DBS VORTAC and SABAT INT.

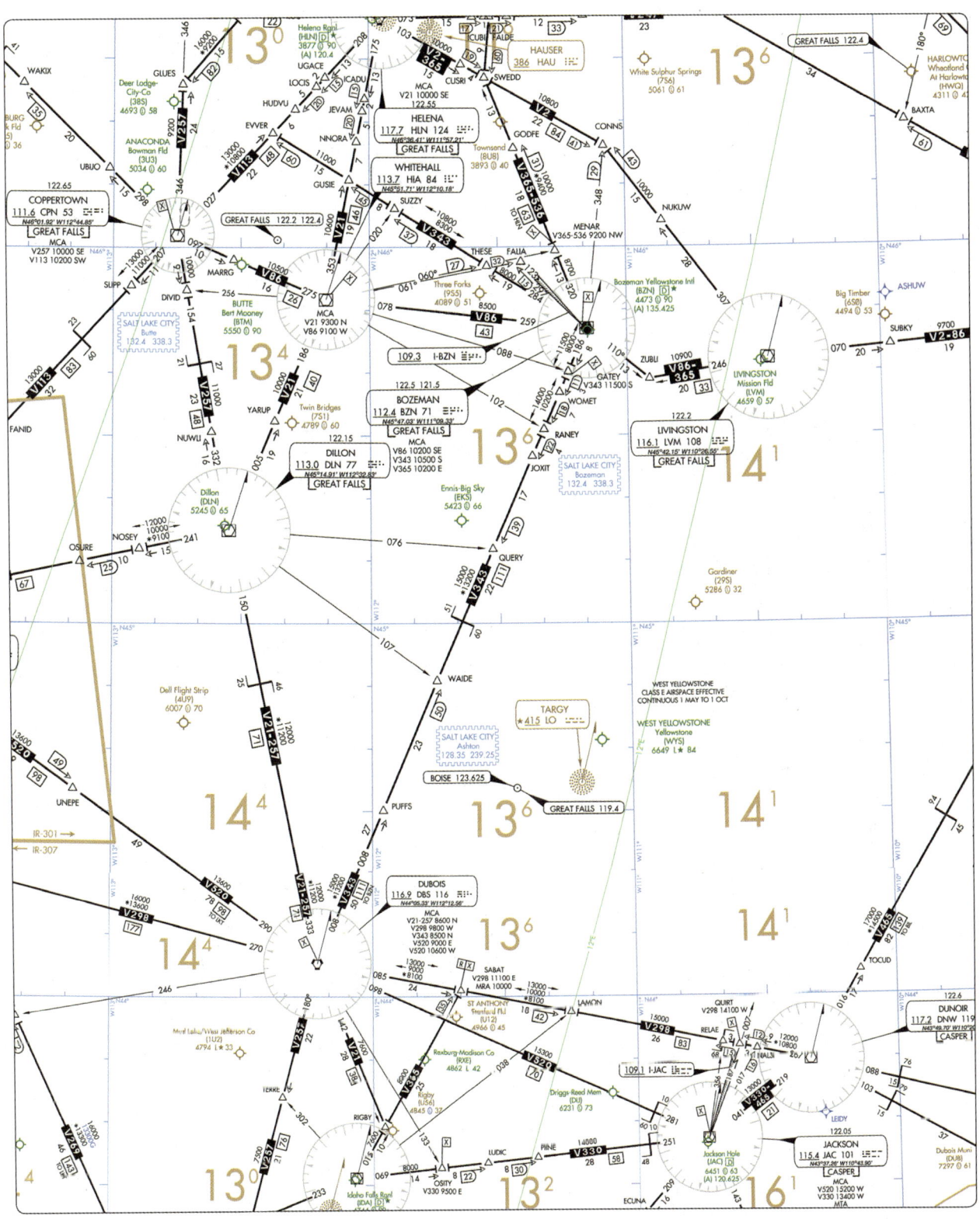

Figure 91. – En Route Low-Altitude Chart Segment.
NOTE: Chart is not to scale and should not be used for navigation. Chart is for testing purposes only.

59. (Refer to Figure 91 below, and Legend 33 on page 433.) What is the function of the Great Falls RCO (Yellowstone vicinity)?

A. Long range communications outlet for Great Falls Center.

B. Remote communications outlet for Great Falls FSS.

C. Satellite remote controlled by Salt Lake Center with limited service.

Answer (B) is correct. (ACUG)

DISCUSSION: The Great Falls RCO communication box is located in the center of the chart, in Fig. 91, just above the DBS VORTAC box. An arrow points to a symbol ⊙, which indicates an FSS remote communications outlet. Thus, Great Falls RCO is a remote communications outlet for Great Falls FSS on 119.4 MHz.

Answer (A) is incorrect. The center for that area is Salt Lake City, not Great Falls, as indicated by the ARTCC RCO box above the Great Falls RCO box. **Answer (C) is incorrect.** Great Falls RCO is just an antenna site for an FSS that extends the communication range for the controlling FSS (e.g., Great Falls FSS), not ARTCC (e.g., Salt Lake Center).

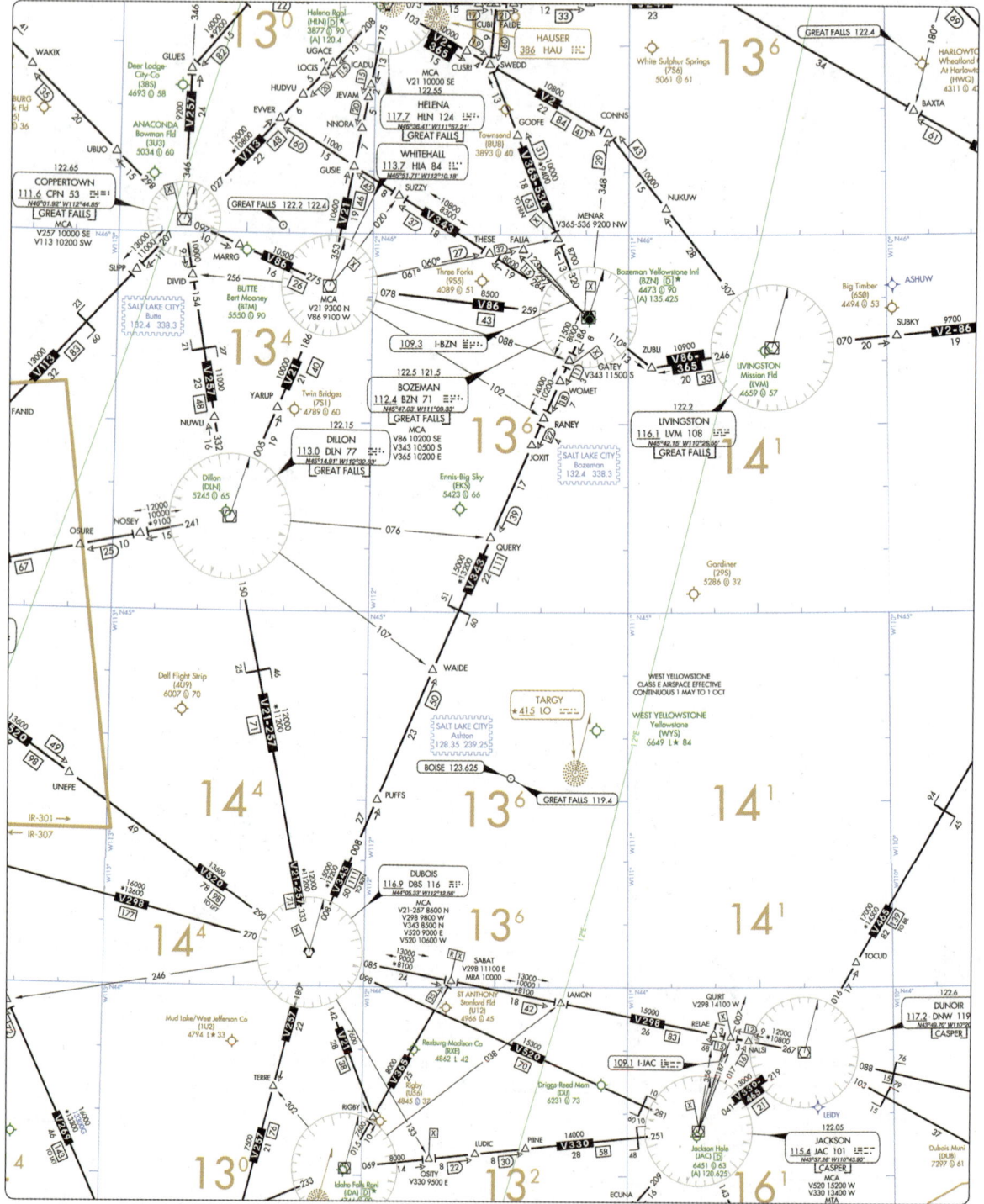

Figure 91. – En Route Low-Altitude Chart Segment.
NOTE: Chart is not to scale and should not be used for navigation. Chart is for testing purposes only.

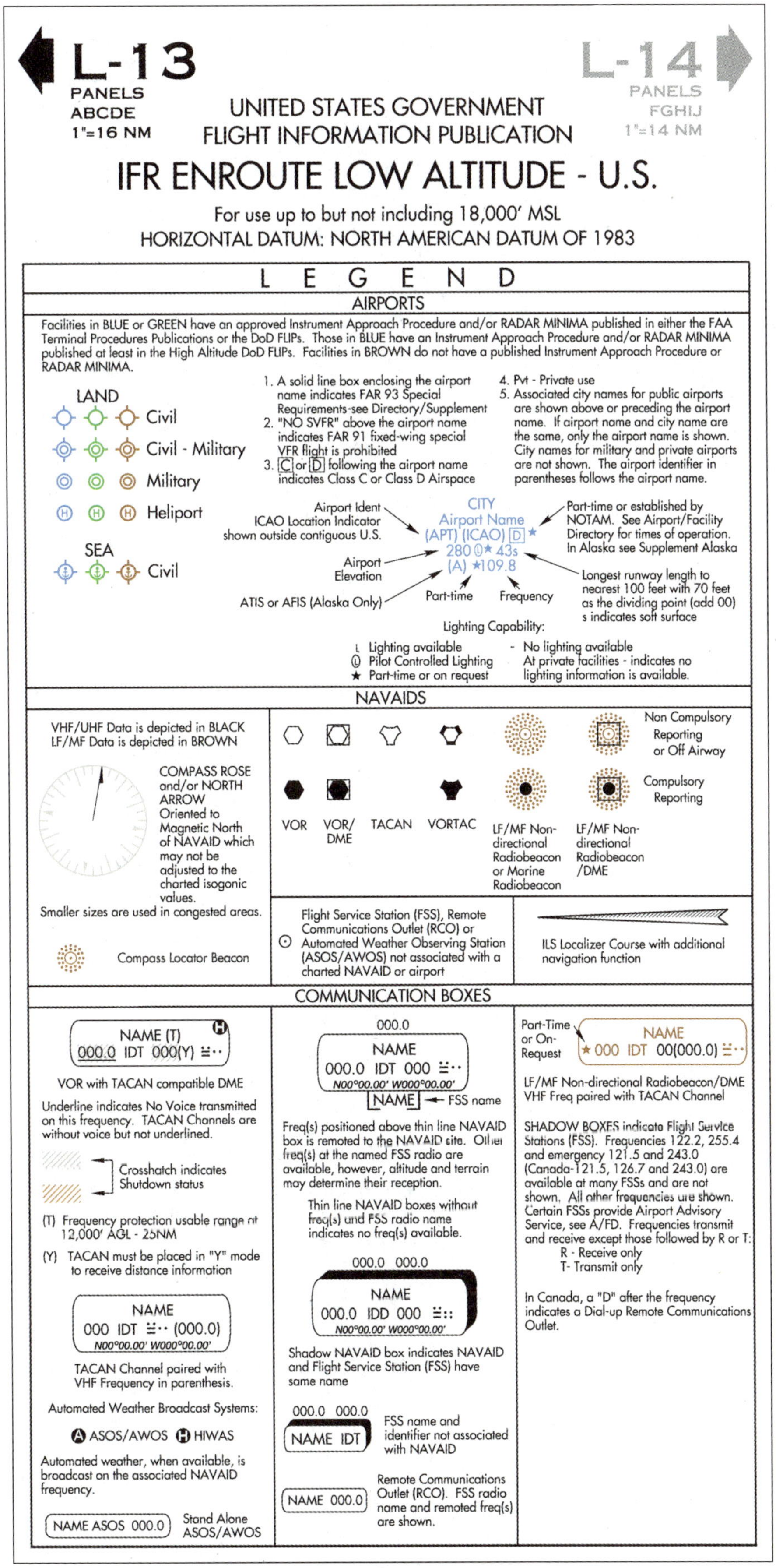
L-13
PANELS
ABCDE
1"=16 NM
UNITED STATES GOVERNMENT
FLIGHT INFORMATION PUBLICATION
L-14
PANELS
FGHIJ
1"=14 NM
IFR ENROUTE LOW ALTITUDE - U.S.
For use up to but not including 18,000' MSL
HORIZONTAL DATUM: NORTH AMERICAN DATUM OF 1983
L E G E N D
AIRPORTS
Facilities in BLUE or GREEN have an approved Instrument Approach Procedure and/or RADAR MINIMA published in either the FAA Terminal Procedures Publications or the DoD FLIPs. Those in BLUE have an Instrument Approach Procedure and/or RADAR MINIMA published at least in the High Altitude DoD FLIPs. Facilities in BROWN do not have a published Instrument Approach Procedure or RADAR MINIMA.
LAND
Civil
Civil - Military
Military
Heliport
SEA
Civil
1. A solid line box enclosing the airport name indicates FAR 93 Special Requirements-see Directory/Supplement
2. "NO SVFR" above the airport name indicates FAR 91 fixed-wing special VFR flight is prohibited
3. C or D following the airport name indicates Class C or Class D Airspace
4. Pvt - Private use
5. Associated city names for public airports are shown above or preceding the airport name. If airport name and city name are the same, only the airport name is shown. City names for military and private airports are not shown. The airport identifier in parentheses follows the airport name.
Airport Ident
ICAO Location Indicator shown outside contiguous U.S.
CITY
Airport Name
(APT) (ICAO) D ★
280 ★ 43s
(A) ★109.8
Part-time or established by NOTAM. See Airport/Facility Directory for times of operation. In Alaska see Supplement Alaska
Airport Elevation
Longest runway length to nearest 100 feet with 70 feet as the dividing point (add 00) s indicates soft surface
ATIS or AFIS (Alaska Only)
Part-time
Frequency
Lighting Capability:
L Lighting available
Pilot Controlled Lighting
★ Part-time or on request
- No lighting available
At private facilities - indicates no lighting information is available.
NAVAIDS
VHF/UHF Data is depicted in BLACK
LF/MF Data is depicted in BROWN
COMPASS ROSE and/or NORTH ARROW Oriented to Magnetic North of NAVAID which may not be adjusted to the charted isogonic values.
Smaller sizes are used in congested areas.
Compass Locator Beacon
Non Compulsory Reporting or Off Airway
Compulsory Reporting
VOR
VOR/DME
TACAN
VORTAC
LF/MF Non-directional Radiobeacon or Marine Radiobeacon
LF/MF Non-directional Radiobeacon /DME
Flight Service Station (FSS), Remote Communications Outlet (RCO) or Automated Weather Observing Station (ASOS/AWOS) not associated with a charted NAVAID or airport
ILS Localizer Course with additional navigation function
COMMUNICATION BOXES
NAME (T)
000.0 IDT 000(Y)
VOR with TACAN compatible DME
Underline indicates No Voice transmitted on this frequency. TACAN Channels are without voice but not underlined.
Crosshatch indicates Shutdown status
(T) Frequency protection usable range at 12,000' AGL - 25NM
(Y) TACAN must be placed in "Y" mode to receive distance information
NAME
000 IDT (000.0)
N00°00.00' W000°00.00'
TACAN Channel paired with VHF Frequency in parenthesis.
Automated Weather Broadcast Systems:
A ASOS/AWOS H HIWAS
Automated weather, when available, is broadcast on the associated NAVAID frequency.
NAME ASOS 000.0
Stand Alone ASOS/AWOS
000.0
NAME
000.0 IDT 000
N00°00.00' W000°00.00'
NAME ← FSS name
Freq(s) positioned above thin line NAVAID box is remoted to the NAVAID site. Other freq(s) at the named FSS radio are available, however, altitude and terrain may determine their reception.
Thin line NAVAID boxes without freq(s) and FSS radio name indicates no freq(s) available.
000.0 000.0
NAME
000.0 IDD 000
N00°00.00' W000°00.00'
Shadow NAVAID box indicates NAVAID and Flight Service Station (FSS) have same name
000.0 000.0
NAME IDT
FSS name and identifier not associated with NAVAID
NAME 000.0
Remote Communications Outlet (RCO). FSS radio name and remoted freq(s) are shown.
Part-Time or On-Request
NAME
★ 000 IDT 00(000.0)
LF/MF Non-directional Radiobeacon/DME VHF Freq paired with TACAN Channel
SHADOW BOXES indicate Flight Service Stations (FSS). Frequencies 122.2, 255.4 and emergency 121.5 and 243.0 (Canada-121.5, 126.7 and 243.0) are available at many FSSs and are not shown. All other frequencies are shown. Certain FSSs provide Airport Advisory Service, see A/FD. Frequencies transmit and receive except those followed by R or T:
R - Receive only
T- Transmit only
In Canada, a "D" after the frequency indicates a Dial-up Remote Communications Outlet.

Legend 33. – IFR En Route Low Altitude (U.S.)

60. In the event of two-way radio communications failure while operating on an IFR clearance in VFR conditions, the pilot should continue

- A. by the route assigned in the last ATC clearance received.
- B. the flight under VFR and land as soon as practical.
- C. the flight by the most direct route to the fix specified in the last clearance.

Answer (B) is correct. (14 CFR 91.185)
DISCUSSION: If two-way radio communications fail while operating in VFR conditions, or if VFR conditions are encountered after the failure, each pilot shall continue the flight under VFR and land as soon as practicable.
Answer (A) is incorrect. If the failure occurs in IFR, not VFR, conditions, and VFR conditions are not encountered after the failure, each pilot shall continue the flight by the route assigned in the last ATC clearance received. **Answer (C) is incorrect.** One continues the last route assigned by ATC if in IFR, not the most direct route to the next fix.

61. Military training routes (MTR) above 1,500 feet are depicted on

- A. IFR Planning Charts.
- B. IFR Low Altitude En Route Charts.
- C. IFR High Altitude En Route Charts.

Answer (B) is correct. (AIM Para 3-5-2)
DISCUSSION: IFR En Route Low-Altitude Charts depict all IFR and VFR MTRs (IR and VR routes) that accommodate operations above 1,500 feet AGL.
Answer (A) is incorrect. The U.S. IFR/VFR Planning Chart does not depict MTRs. The DOD Area Planning Chart depicts all MTRs, not only those above 1,500 feet AGL. **Answer (C) is incorrect.** IFR En Route High-Altitude Charts cover altitudes at and above 18,000 feet MSL; generally, MTRs are established below 10,000 feet MSL.

62. (Refer to Figure 193 on page 435.) On which frequencies could you communicate with the Montgomery County FSS while on the ground at College Station?

- A. 122.65, 122.2, 122.1, 113.3.
- B. 122.65, 122.2.
- C. 118.5, 122.65, 122.2.

Answer (B) is correct. (Chart Supplement)
DISCUSSION: Fig. 193 is an excerpt from the Chart Supplement for Easterwood Field located at College Station, TX. Locate the **Communications** heading for information on frequencies. There is a College Station RCO to communicate with the Montgomery County FSS on frequencies 122.65 and 122.2 only.
Answer (A) is incorrect. The frequencies 122.1 and 113.3 are not available at College Station to contact the Montgomery County FSS. **Answer (C) is incorrect.** The frequency 118.5 is the tower/CTAF, not FSS, frequency.

63. (Refer to Figure 193 on page 435.) Which indications on the VOR receivers and DME at the Easterwood Field VOR receiver checkpoint would meet the regulatory requirement for this flight?

	VOR No. 1	TO/FROM	VOR No. 2	TO/FROM	DME
A.	097°	FROM	101°	FROM	3.2
B.	097°	TO	096°	TO	3.2
C.	277°	FROM	280°	FROM	3.3

Answer (A) is correct. (14 CFR 91.171)
DISCUSSION: The bottom portion of Fig. 193 lists the VOR receiver checkpoints. Locate College Station (Easterwood Field) to determine that the checkpoint is on the ground (on west edge of parking ramp), the azimuth from the VORTAC is 097° (i.e., R-097), and the distance is 3.2 NM from the VORTAC. On the R-097, you want the CDI needle centered with an OBS setting of 097° FROM or 277° TO the station, with the acceptable error of ±4°. Thus, the acceptable VOR indications are 097° FROM and 101° FROM the station. Keep in mind that 14 CFR 91.171 makes reference to maximum degrees and does not reference DME indications.
Answer (B) is incorrect. The magnetic azimuth (i.e., radial) from the station at the ground checkpoint is 097°, which should result in a FROM, not TO, indication with the OBS set to 097°. **Answer (C) is incorrect.** The magnetic azimuth (i.e., radial) from the station at the ground checkpoint is 097°, which should result in a TO, not FROM, indication with the OBS set to 277°.

TEXAS — **231**

COLLEGE STATION

EASTERWOOD FLD (CLL) 3 SW UTC–6(–5DT) N30°35.32′ W96°21.83′

HOUSTON
H–7C, L–19D, 21A
IAP, AD

321 B S4 **FUEL** 100LL, JET A Class I, ARFF Index A NOTAM FILE CLL

RWY 16–34: H7000X146 (ASPH–CONC–GRVD) S–70, D–90, 2S–114, 2D–150 HIRL

　RWY 16: VASI(V4R)—GA 3.0° TCH 51′. Tree.

　RWY 34: MALSR.

RWY 10–28: H5158X150 (ASPH–GRVD) S–27, D–50, 2D–87 MIRL

　RWY 10: VASI(V4L)—GA 3.0° TCH 50′. Tree.

　RWY 28: REIL. VASI(V4L)—GA 3.0° TCH 54′. Tree.

RWY 04–22: H5150X150 (CONC) S–27, D–50, 2D–87

　RWY 04: Tree.

　RWY 22: Tree.

RUNWAY DECLARED DISTANCE INFORMATION

　RWY 04: TORA–5149 TODA–5149 ASDA–5149 LDA–5149

　RWY 10: TORA–5159 TODA–5159 ASDA–5159 LDA–5159

　RWY 16: TORA–7000 TODA–7000 ASDA–7000 LDA–7000

　RWY 22: TORA–5149 TODA–5149 ASDA–5149 LDA–5149

　RWY 28: TORA–5159 TODA–5159 ASDA–5159 LDA–5159

　RWY 34: TORA–7000 TODA–7000 ASDA–7000 LDA–7000

AIRPORT REMARKS: Attended 1200–0400Z‡. For fuel after hours PPR call 979–845–4811 or ctc Texas A and M University police 979–845–2345; late ngt fee. CLOSED to unscheduled air carrier ops with more than 30 passenger seats except 24 hours PPR call arpt manager 979–845–4811. Rwy 04–22 day VFR ops only. Rwy 10–28 mandatory hold short sign on Rwy 16–34 unlgtd. Itinerant acft park in front of twr, overnight parking fee. Ldg fee scheduled FAR 135 and all FAR 121 ops. Rwy 04–22 and Twy E S of Rwy 10–28 not avbl for air carrier acft with over 30 passenger seats. Rwy 16–34 first 1850′ Rwy 34 conc. PAEW adjacent all twys 1200–2200Z‡. When twr clsd ACTIVATE HIRL Rwy 16–34 and MALSR Rwy 34—CTAF. MIRL Rwy 10–28 and REIL Rwy 28 preset low ints only.

WEATHER DATA SOURCES: ASOS (979) 846–1708 **HIWAS** 113.3 CLL.

COMMUNICATIONS: CTAF 118.5 **ATIS** 126.85 **UNICOM** 122.95

　COLLEGE STATION RCO 122.65 122.2 (MONTGOMERY COUNTY RADIO).

Ⓡ **HOUSTON APP/DEP CON** 134.3

　TOWER 118.5 (1400–0300Z‡) **GND CON/CLNC DEL** 128.7 **CLNC DEL** 120.4 (when twr clsd)

AIRSPACE: CLASS D svc 1400–0300Z‡ other times **CLASS E.**

VOR RECEIVER CHECK

TEXAS

VOR RECEIVER CHECKPOINTS

Facility Name (Arpt Name)	Freq/Ident	Type Check Pt. Gnd. AB/ALT	Azimuth from Fac. Mag	Dist. from Fac. N.M.	Checkpoint Description
Abilene (Abilene Rgnl)	113.7/ABI	A/2800	047	10.1	Over silos in center of Ft Phantom Lake.
Alice (Alice International)	114.5/ALI	G	272	0.5	On twy near FBO.
Borger (Hutchinson Co)	108.6/BGD	G	173	6.7	On twy intersection at N end of ramp.
Brownsville (Brownsville/South Padre Island Intl)	116.3/BRO	G	247	3.2	3.2 NM on hold line Rwy 13R.
Brownwood (Brownwood Rgnl)	108.6/BWD	A/2600	169	6.2	Over rotating bcn.
Childress Muni	117.6/CDS	G	353	3.7	At the apron and the twy from Rwy 04–22.
College Station (Easterwood Fld)	113.3/CLL	G	97	3.2	On west edge of parking ramp.
Corpus Christi (Alfred C 'Bubba' Thomas)	115.5/CRP	A/1000	318	9.3	Over Rwy 32 thld.
Corpus Christi (Corpus Christi Intl)	115.5/CRP	A/1100	187	7.5	Over grain elevator.
Daisetta (Liberty Muni)	116.9/DAS	A/1200	195	7.5	Over hangar S of arpt.
Dalhart (Dalhart Muni)	112.0/DHT	A/5000	176	4.1	Over water tower on arpt.
Eagle Lake (Eagle Lake)	116.4/ELA	A/1200	180	4.1	Over water tank 0.4 NM SW of arpt.

Figure 193. – Excerpts from Chart Supplement.

64. (Refer to Figure 64 on page 437.) The course deviation indicator (CDI) is centered. Which indications on the No. 1 and No. 2 VOR receivers over the Lafayette Regional Airport would meet the requirements for the VOR receiver check?

	VOR No. 1	TO/FROM	VOR No. 2	TO/FROM
A.	162°	TO	346°	FROM
B.	160°	FROM	162°	FROM
C.	341°	FROM	330°	FROM

Answer (A) is correct. (14 CFR 91.171)
DISCUSSION: The top portion of Fig. 64 lists the VOR receiver checkpoints. Locate Lafayette (Lafayette Regional) to determine that the checkpoint is an airborne checkpoint at 1,000 feet over the rotating beacon and the azimuth from the VORTAC is 343° (i.e., R-343). On the R-343, you want the CDI needle centered with an OBS setting of 343° FROM or 163° TO the station, with an acceptable error of ±6°. Thus, acceptable VOR indications are 162° TO and 346° FROM the station.
Answer (B) is incorrect. The magnetic azimuth (radial) from the station at the checkpoint is 343°, resulting in a TO, not FROM, indication with the OBS set to 163° and 162°. **Answer (C) is incorrect.** The No. 2 VOR OBS of 330° is greater than 6° difference from the 343° azimuth from the VORTAC.

LOUISIANA
VOR RECEIVER CHECKPOINTS

Facility Name (Arpt Name)	Freq/Ident	Type Check Pt. Gnd. AB/ALT	Azimuth from Fac. Mag	Dist. from Fac. N.M.	Checkpoint Description
Alexandria (Alexandria Intl)	116.1/AEX	G	328	4.3	On runup Rwy 32.
Baton Rouge (Baton Rouge Metro, Ryan).	116.5/BTR	A/1500	063	7.2	Over water tank W side of arpt.
Lafayette (Lafayette Rgnl/Paul Fournet Fld)	109.8/LFT	A/1000	343	22.1	Over rotating beacon at St. Landry Parish–Ahart Fld. arpt.
	109.8/LFT	G	355	0.5	On Twy F run up area Rwy 04L.
	109.8/LFT	G	341	0.9	On Twy B run up area Rwy 11.
	109.8/LFT	G	025	1.4	On Twy J run up area Rwy 22L.
	109.8/LFT	G	039	0.8	On Twy B run up area Rwy 29.
Lake Charles (Lake Charles Rgnl)	113.4/LCH	A/1000	253	6.2	Over rotg bcn on twr.
Monroe (Monroe Rgnl)...........................	117.2/MLU	G	212	0.7	On Twy G South of twr.
Natchez (Concordia Parish)....................	110.0/HEZ	A/1000	247	10.5	Over hangar NW end of fld.
Reserve (St John The Baptist Parish).......	110.8 RQR	A/1500	270	16.8	Over center of bridge.
Tibby (Houma–Terrebonne)	112.0/TBD	A/1000	121	10.7	Over intersection of Rwys 18–36 and 12–30.
Tibby (Thibodaux Muni)........................	112.0/TBD	A/1000	356	5.0	Over microwave twr near arpt.

---

84 | **LOUISIANA**

LAFAYETTE RGNL (LFT)   2 SE   UTC–6(–5DT)   N30°12.30′ W91°59.27′   **HOUSTON**
  42   B S4 **FUEL** 100LL, JET A OX 1, 4 Class I, ARFF Index B   NOTAM FILE LFT   **H–7D, L–21B, 22E, GOMC**
RWY 04R–22L: H8001X150 (ASPH–GRVD) S–140, D–170, 2S–175,   **IAP, AD**
    2D–290 HIRL

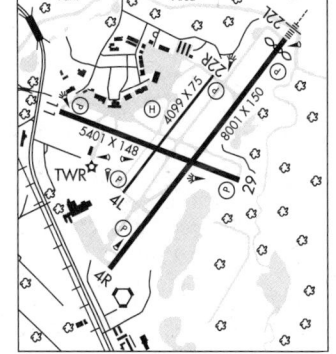

    RWY 04R: REIL. PAPI(P4L)—GA 3.0° TCH 53′. Pole. Rgt tfc.
    RWY 22L: MALSR. PAPI(P4L)—GA 3.0° TCH 52′. Thld dsplcd 342′. Trees.
RWY 11–29: H5401X148 (ASPH–GRVD) S–85, D–110, 2S–140, 2D–175 MIRL
    RWY 11: REIL. PAPI(P4L)—GA 3.0° TCH 35′. Trees. Rgt tfc.
    RWY 29: REIL. PAPI(P4L)—GA 3.0° TCH 35′. Tree.
RWY 04L–22R: H4099X75 (ASPH) S–25, D–32 MIRL
    RWY 04L: REIL. PAPI(P2L)—GA 3.0° TCH 26′. Tree.
    RWY 22R: REIL. PAPI(P2L)—GA 3.0° TCH 27′. Tree. Rgt tfc.
RUNWAY DECLARED DISTANCE INFORMATION
    RWY 04L:TORA–4099 TODA–4099 ASDA–4099 LDA–4099
    RWY 04R:TORA–8001 TODA–8001 ASDA–8001 LDA–8001
    RWY 11: TORA–5401 TODA–5401 ASDA–5401 LDA–5401
    RWY 22L:TORA–8001 TODA–8001 ASDA–8001 LDA–7659
    RWY 22R:TORA–4099 TODA–4099 ASDA–4099 LDA–4099
    RWY 29: TORA–5401 TODA–5401 ASDA–5401 LDA–5401
ARRESTING GEAR/SYSTEM
    RWY 04R: EMAS
    RWY 22L: EMAS
AIRPORT REMARKS: Attended continuously. Numerous birds on and invof arpt. PPR for unscheduled air carrier ops with more than 30 passenger seats call arpt manager 337–266–4400. Rwy 04L–22R not avbl for air carrier ops with more than 30 passenger seats. Ctc ground control prior to push back from terminal. 155′ oil rig 1 NM southeast of arpt. Rwy 22L runway visual range touchdown avbl. Twy B between Twy C and Twy D clsd to acft with wingspan over 80′. Twy F south of Twy B clsd to single wheel acft over 25,000 lbs and dual wheel acft over 32,000 lbs. Twy F south of Twy B reduces to 40′ wide. When twr clsd ACTIVATE MALSR Rwy 22L—CTAF, MIRL Rwy 04L–22R not avbl.
WEATHER DATA SOURCES: ASOS (337) 237–8153 HIWAS 109.8 LFT.
COMMUNICATIONS: CTAF 118.5 ATIS 134.05 UNICOM 122.95
    RCO 122.35 (DE RIDDER RADIO)
Ⓡ APP/DEP CON 121.1 (020°–210°) 128./ (211°–019°) (1130–0430Z‡)
Ⓡ HOUSTON CENTER APP/DEP CON 126.35 (0430–1130Z‡)
    TOWER 118.5 (1130–0430Z‡) GND CON 121.8 CLNC DEL 125.55
AIRSPACE: CLASS C svc ctc APP CON svc 1130–0430Z‡ other times CLASS E.
RADIO AIDS TO NAVIGATION: NOTAM FILE LFT.
    (L) VORTACW 109.8 LFT Chan 35 N30°11.63′ W91°59.55′ at fld. 36/3E. HIWAS.
    LAFFS NDB (LOM) 375 LF N30°17.36′ W91°54.48′ 216° 6.5 NM to fld. Unmonitored when ATCT clsd.
    ILS/DME 110.9 I–TYN Chan 46 Rwy 04R. Class IE.
    ILS/DME 109.5 I–LFT Chan 32 Rwy 22L. Class IE. LOM LAFFS NDB. ILS and LOM unmonitored when ATCT clsd.
    ASR (1130–0430Z‡)

Figure 64. – Excerpt from Chart Supplement (LFT).

438

STUDY UNIT ELEVEN

IFR FLIGHTS

(2 pages of outline)

This study unit contains sample test questions and answers regarding eight IFR flights and an explanation of each answer. The table of contents above lists the individual trips within this study unit, the number of questions pertaining to that particular trip, and the page on which the trip begins.

IFR FLIGHTS

The following provides you with a list of the eight IFR trips. The departure and destination airports are listed, followed by the question numbers that relate to that trip.

1. Grand Junction, CO to/from Durango, CO (Questions 1-5)
2. Medford, OR to/from Eugene, OR (Questions 6-12)
3. Yakima, WA to/from Portland, OR (Questions 13-25)
4. Santa Barbara, CA to/from Paso Robles, CA (Questions 26-31)
5. Hot Springs, AR to/from Dallas, TX (Questions 32-37)
6. Big Spring, TX to/from Fort Worth, TX (Questions 38-45)
7. W. Milford, NJ to/from Windsor Locks, CT (Questions 46-53)
8. Helena, MT to/from Billings, MT (Questions 54-62)

Each trip provides you with the following types of data:

1. DPs and STARs
2. Appropriate Chart Supplement excerpts
3. Instrument approach chart(s)
4. En route low-altitude chart

The questions cover the following topics:

1. Interpretation of VOR, HSI, and GS/LOC indicators to determine position relative to a position specified on a particular approach, DP, STAR, or en route chart

    a. These interpretations are covered in Study Unit 3, "Navigation Systems."

2. Interpretation of appropriate procedures, minimum altitude, and other restrictions on instrument approach charts

    a. Instrument approach chart legends are on pages 215 through 228 in Study Unit 6, "Holding and Instrument Approaches."

    b. The formula for converting feet per nautical mile to feet per minute is

$$\frac{GS \times FT/NM}{60} = FPM$$

3. Interpretation of appropriate procedures, minimum altitude, and other restrictions on low-altitude en route charts

    a. IFR en route chart Legends 33, 34, and 35 appear on pages 406-408 in Study Unit 10, "IFR En Route."

4. Interpretation of DPs and STARs

    a. A careful reading of the DP or STAR usually provides the correct answer, especially in conjunction with the DP/STAR Legend 28 reproduced on page 212 in Study Unit 6.

5. Calculating climbs and descents

    a. When calculating rates of climb or descent, specifically be aware of whether you are seeking feet per minute or feet per nautical mile.

    b. If a climb or descent is specified in feet per nautical miles, calculate the required feet per minute as follows:

        1) Find groundspeed.

        2) Find distance.

        3) 120 knot groundspeed equates to 2 NM per minute. A 90 knot groundspeed equates to 1.5 NM per minute.

        4) To achieve a climb or descent of 435 feet per NM at 120 knots groundspeed (2 NM per minute), 435 feet per NM × 2 NM per minute = 870 feet per minute.

        5) To achieve a climb or descent of 435 feet per NM at 90 knots groundspeed (1.5 NM per minute), 435 feet per NM × 1.5 NM per minute = 652.5 feet per minute.

    c. If the rate of descent is given in feet per NM but must be solved in feet per minute, calculate the required rate as follows:

        1) Find your groundspeed.

        2) Find the altitude to be lost or gained.

        3) Find the distance between two points where the climb or descent must occur.

        4) Divide altitude by distance to find feet per NM. For example, 750 feet ÷ 3NM = 250 feet per nautical mile.

        5) Divide groundspeed by 60 (minutes per hour) to find NM per minute. 120 knots ÷ 60 minutes = 2 NM per minute. 90 knots ÷ 60 minutes = 1.5 NM per minute.

        6) Multiply speed per minute × rate per NM to arrive at feet per minute. 1.5 NM per minute × 250 feet per NM = 375 feet per minute. 2 NM per minute × 250 feet per NM = 500 feet per minute.

6. Calculating a DME arc

    a. Find the degrees from the beginning waypoint or intersection to start the arc, then go to the radial to start the final approach course. For example, if we start on R-251 and go to R-333 (333 − 251 = 82), on a 15 DME arc, it would look like this:

$$\text{Distance of arc} = \frac{\text{\# of degrees} \times \text{DME arc}}{60}$$

$$\text{Distance of arc} = \frac{82 \times 15}{60} = 20.5 \text{ NM}$$

    b. Once established on the arc, maintain the path by turning 10° to 20° toward the arc for each 1/2 NM off the desired arc.

QUESTIONS AND ANSWER EXPLANATIONS: All of the instrument rating knowledge test questions chosen by the FAA for release as well as additional questions selected by Gleim relating to the material in the previous outlines are provided on the following pages. These questions have been organized into the same subunits as the outlines. To the immediate right of each question are the correct answer and answer explanations. You should cover these answers and answer explanations while responding to the questions. Refer to the general discussion in the Introduction on how to take the FAA knowledge test.

Remember that the questions from the FAA knowledge test bank have been reordered by topic and organized into a meaningful sequence. Also, the first line of the answer explanation gives the citation of the authoritative source for the answer.

QUESTIONS

11.1 GJT To/From DRO

Questions 1 through 5 pertain to an IFR flight from Grand Junction Rgnl, Grand Junction, Colorado, to Durango-La Plata County Airport, Durango, Colorado.

The figure provided for this flight is listed below and is presented within the sequence of questions.

Fig.	Page	
24	443	En Route Low-Altitude Chart Segment

1. (Refer to Figure 24 on page 443.) For planning purposes, what would be the highest MEA on V187 between Grand Junction, Walker Airport, and Durango, La Plata Co. Airport?

A. 12,000 feet.

B. 15,000 feet.

C. 16,000 feet.

Answer (B) is correct. (ACUG)
DISCUSSION: The highest MEA along the route is 15,000 ft. MSL along V187 between HERRM INT. and MANCA INT.
Answer (A) is incorrect. The MEA between JNC and HERRM INT. is 12,000 ft. MSL, but it is not the highest. **Answer (C) is incorrect.** There is no MEA of 16,000 ft. MSL along any part of this route.

2. (Refer to Figure 24 on page 443.) While passing near the CORTEZ VOR, southbound on V187, contact is lost with Denver Center. You should attempt to reestablish contact with Denver Center on

A. 118.575 MHz.

B. 108.4 MHz.

C. 122.3 MHz.

Answer (A) is correct. (ACUG)
DISCUSSION: To the southwest of the Cortez VOR and south of Dove Creek VORTAC is a box with serrated edges. This box shows the frequency for Denver Center in the Cortez VOR area as 118.575.
Answer (B) is incorrect. The frequency for the Cortez VOR, not Denver Center, is 108.4. Additionally, 108.4 is underlined, indicating that the VOR has no voice capability (i.e., that there would be nothing to receive on 108.4). **Answer (C) is incorrect.** This is the frequency you would use to contact Denver Flight Service when in the vicinity of the Cortez VOR, not Denver Center.

3. (Refer to Figure 24 on page 443.) What is the MOCA between JNC and MANCA intersection on V187?

A. 10,900 feet MSL.

B. 15,000 feet MSL.

C. 12,400 feet MSL.

Answer (C) is correct. (ACUG)
DISCUSSION: The MOCA (minimum obstruction clearance altitude) appears with an asterisk under the MEA on V187. It is 12,400 ft. MSL.
Answer (A) is incorrect. This is the MEA, not MOCA, between MANCA and RIZAL intersections. **Answer (B) is incorrect.** This is the MEA, not MOCA, between JNC and MANCA INT.

4. (Refer to Figure 24 on page 443.) At what point should a VOR changeover be made from JNC VOR to MANCA intersection southbound on V187?

    A.   36 NM south of JNC.

    B.   52 NM south of JNC.

    C.   74 NM south of JNC.

Answer (B) is correct. (AIM Para 5-3-6)
    DISCUSSION: The VOR changeover point is depicted on V187, south of HERRM INT. and depicts the mileage between the VORTAC stations. It shows the COP as being 52 NM south of JNC.
    Answer (A) is incorrect. The COP is depicted as 52 NM, not 36 NM, south of JNC. **Answer (C) is incorrect.** The COP is depicted as 52 NM, not 74 NM, south of JNC.

5. (Refer to Figure 24 on page 443.) Your original route of flight was CEZ V391 JNC. However, due to thunderstorms en route, ATC revises your route to CEZ V391 DVC V68 MTJ V26 JNC. Calculate how much additional fuel you will consume given the following:

Winds = 230@40kts
TAS = 130 kts
GPH = 17

    A.   13.2 gallons.

    B.   5.5 gallons.

    C.   9.1 gallons.

Answer (B) is correct. (FAA-H-8083-16B Chap 10)
    DISCUSSION: To solve this problem, you must determine the fuel required for each of the routes. Then subtract the fuel required for the original route from the alternate route to determine the additional fuel consumed.
    Create a flight log for each route. Calculate the groundspeed for the cruise portions of each trip using the wind side of the flight computer. Remember to convert wind direction to magnetic direction first; i.e., 230° − 10°E var. = 220° at 40 kt. Then compute ETE for each leg and fuel consumption for each trip using the slide rule side of the computer.

CEZ V391 JNC

	Distance	MC	Ground-speed	Time	Fuel (gal.)
CEZ-DVC	31	311	124	:14:57	4.2
DVC-JNC	75	351	153	:29:28	8.3
					12.5

CEZ V391 DVC V68 MTJ V26 JNC

	Distance	MC	Ground-speed	Time	Fuel (gal.)
CEZ-DVC	31	311	124	:14:57	4.2
DVC-ETL	35	52	169	:12:26	3.5
ETL-MTJ	33	19	167	:11:53	3.4
MTJ-JNC	53	297	115	:27:38	7.8
					18.9

    The difference in fuel consumed is 6.4 gal. (18.9 − 12.5). The closest answer given is 5.5 gal.
    Answer (A) is incorrect. The fuel consumed is 6.4 gal., not 13.2 gal. **Answer (C) is incorrect.** The fuel consumed is 6.4 gal., not 9.1 gal.

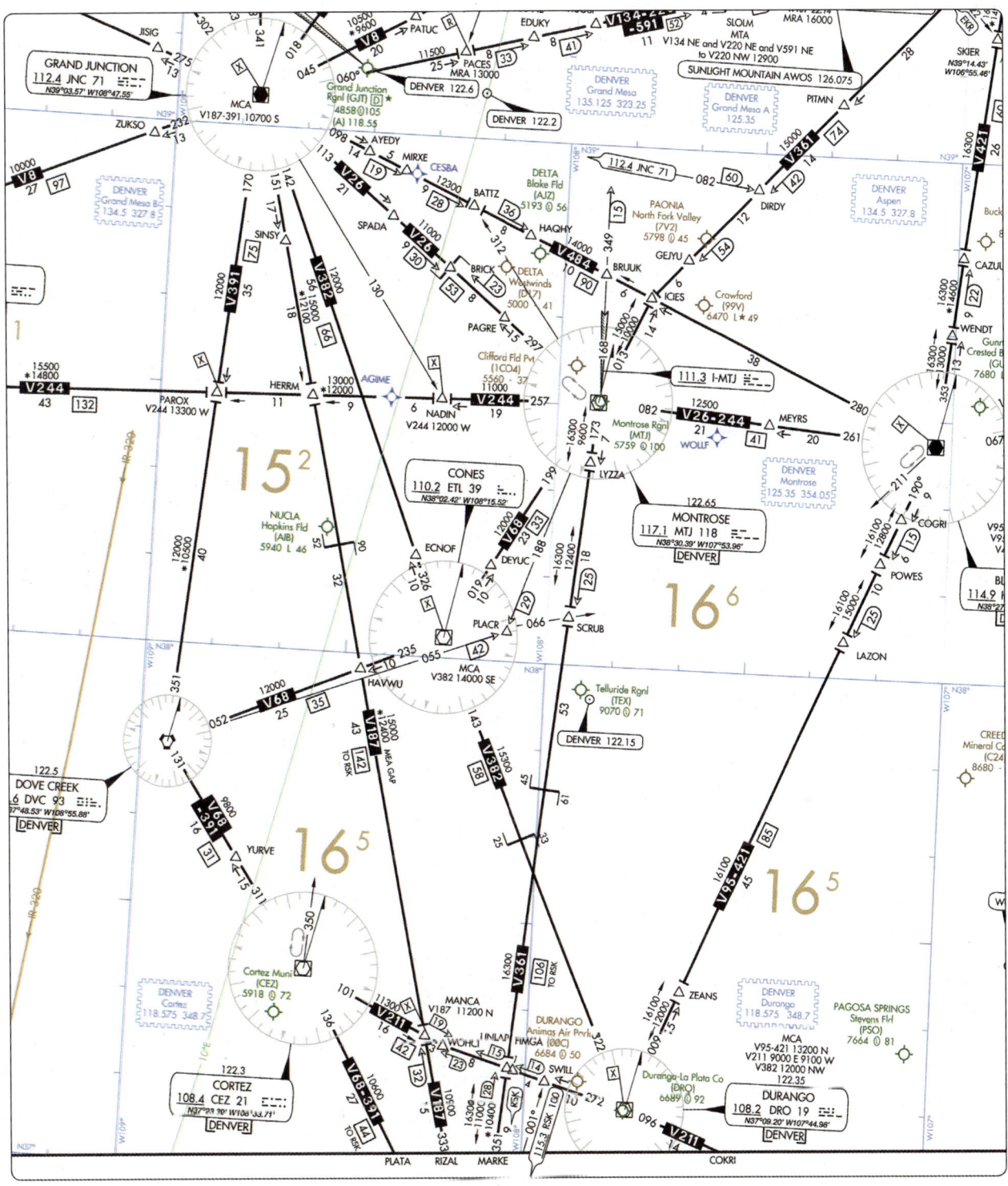

Figure 24. – En Route Low-Altitude Chart Segment.
NOTE: Chart is not to scale and should not be used for navigation. Chart is for testing purposes only.

11.2 MFR To/From EUG

Questions 6 through 12 pertain to an IFR flight from Medford-Rogue Valley Int'l, Medford, Oregon, to the Mahlon Sweet Field, Eugene, Oregon.

The figures provided for this flight are listed below and are presented at the end of the sequence of questions.

Fig.	Page	
31	446	En Route Low-Altitude Chart Segment
161	447	ILS or LOC/DME RWY 16R (EUG)
162	448	Excerpt from Chart Supplement
163	449	GNATS Six Departure (GNATS6.GNATS)
164	450	GNATS Six Departure (GNATS6.GNATS)
165	451	Excerpt from Chart Supplement
Legend 27	452	Instrument Takeoff or Approach Procedure Charts, Rate-of-Climb/ Descent Table

6. (Refer to Figure 31 on page 446.) What minimum navigation equipment is required en route on V448 to identify MOPIO?

A. One VOR receiver.

B. Two VOR receivers and DME.

C. One VOR receiver and DME.

Answer (C) is correct. (ACUG)
DISCUSSION: MOPIO is located on the OED 316° radial at 17 NM DME. An operational VOR receiver and DME would be required to identify MOPIO.
Answer (A) is incorrect. An operational DME would also be required, in addition to an operational VOR receiver, to identify MOPIO. **Answer (B) is incorrect.** Only one VOR receiver is required to identify MOPIO.

7. (Refer to Figure 161 on page 447.) What is the TDZ elevation for RWY 16R on Eugene/Mahlon Sweet Field?

A. 363 feet MSL.

B. 374 feet MSL.

C. 396 feet MSL.

Answer (A) is correct. (ACUG)
DISCUSSION: On the IAP chart, the TDZE is shown in the airport diagram. The TDZE for RWY 16R at EUG is 363 ft.
Answer (B) is incorrect. This is the airport elevation. **Answer (C) is incorrect.** This is the height of an obstacle to the right of RWY 16R.

8. (Refer to Figure 161 on page 447 and Legend 27 on page 452.) Using a groundspeed of 90 knots on the ILS final approach course, what rate of descent should be used as a reference to maintain the ILS glide slope?

A. 415 feet per minute.

B. 478 feet per minute.

C. 555 feet per minute.

Answer (B) is correct. (FAA-H-8083-15B Chap 1)
DISCUSSION: The profile view of the approach chart shows a glide slope (GS) angle of 3.00°. Legend 27 gives rates of descent based on various glide slope angles and groundspeeds. Find the 3.0° glide slope at the left margin and move right to the 90-kt. groundspeed column to determine a rate of descent of 478 feet per minute.
Answer (A) is incorrect. This is the rate of descent required for a 2.6° glide slope, not a 3.0° glide slope. **Answer (C) is incorrect.** This is the required rate of descent at 90 kt. on a 3.5°, not 3.0°, glide slope.

9. (Refer to Figure 162 on page 448.) What are the hours of operation (local standard time) of the control tower at Eugene/Mahlon Sweet Field?

A. 0800 - 2130
B. 0730 - 1400
C. 0600 - 2330

Answer (C) is correct. (AIM Para 4-2-12)
 DISCUSSION: The Chart Supplement entry for Eugene Mahlon Sweet Field reads, "UTC – 8 (-7DT)." This indicates the field is 8 hours behind Zulu Time during standard time and 7 hours behind during Daylight Savings Time. The Eugene Tower entry shows the tower is in operation between 1400 and 0730Z. 1400 – 0800 = 0600 local standard time. If we back up 8 hours from 0730Z, that equates to 2330 local standard. The tower at Eugene Mahlon Sweet Field operates from 0600 – 2330 local standard time.
 Answer (A) is incorrect. Local standard time of 0800 is 6 hours behind 1400 Zulu, not 8 hours as specified in the upper portion of the Mahlon Sweet Field entry. The correct opening time for the tower would be 1400Z – 0800 = 0600 local standard time. **Answer (B) is incorrect.** Local standard time of 0730 + 0800 variance from Zulu Time equals 1530 Zulu time, not 1400 Zulu as stipulated in the Eugene Tower entry. The correct opening time for Eugene Tower would be 1400Z – 0800 = 0600 local standard time.

10. (Refer to Figure 165 on page 451.) To which maximum service volume distance from the OED VORTAC should you expect to receive adequate signal coverage for navigation at 8,000 ft.?

A. 100 NM.
B. 80 NM.
C. 40 NM.

Answer (C) is correct. (AIM Para 1-1-8)
 DISCUSSION: OED VORTAC is an H-type (high altitude) as indicated in the Chart Supplement in Fig. 165 by (H) VORTAC in the first line of **Radio Aids to Navigation.** For such VORTACs, the altitude and range boundaries are from 1,000 ft. AGL up to and including 14,500 ft. AGL at distances out to 40 NM.
 Answer (A) is incorrect. This applies to 14,500 ft. AGL up to 18,000 ft. AGL and from 45,000 ft. AGL up to 60,000 ft. AGL. **Answer (B) is incorrect.** This is not given as a range for VORs.

11. (Refer to Figure 165 on page 451.) Which restriction to the use of the OED VORTAC would be applicable to the (GNATS6.MOURN) departure?

A. R-295 beyond 35 NM below 8,500 feet.
B. R-210 beyond 35 NM below 8,500 feet.
C. R-265 within 15 NM below 9,000 feet.

Answer (A) is correct. (ACUG)
 DISCUSSION: On Fig. 165, in the Chart Supplement under the **Radio Aids to Navigation** for the OED VORTAC, the VORTAC is listed as being unusable in certain segments. For example, it indicates that radials 290° to 300° are not usable below 8,500 ft. beyond 35 NM. This includes R-295.
 Answer (B) is incorrect. There is no restriction to R-210. **Answer (C) is incorrect.** The restriction to R-265 is beyond 35 NM, not within 15 NM.

12. (Refer to Figure 163 on page 449 and Figure 164 on page 450.) Using an average ground speed of 120 knots and taking off on Runway 14, what minimum rate of climb must be maintained to meet the required climb rate (in feet per NM) to 4,800 feet as specified on the instrument departure procedures?

A. 435 feet per minute.
B. 500 feet per minute.
C. 1,000 feet per minute.

Answer (C) is correct. (FAA-H-8083-16B Chap 2)
 DISCUSSION: The Takeoff Minimums note in the lower left corner of Fig. 163 stipulates "a minimum climb of 435' per NM to 4,800." Note this is feet per NM, not feet per minute. With a ground speed of 120 knots, you are covering 2 NM per minute. 2 × 435 = 870 feet per minute to achieve 435 feet per nautical mile. This leaves the answer option of 1,000 feet per minute as the best answer of those available, even though it is higher than the actual minimum rate of climb required.
 Answer (A) is incorrect. When traveling at a ground speed of 120 knots, 435 feet per minute equates to 218 feet per NM. That rate is well below the specified minimum requirement to 4,800 feet. **Answer (B) is incorrect.** When traveling at a ground speed of 120 knots, 500 feet per minute equates to only 250 feet per NM. The GNATS SIX departure stipulates a minimum of 435 feet per NM.

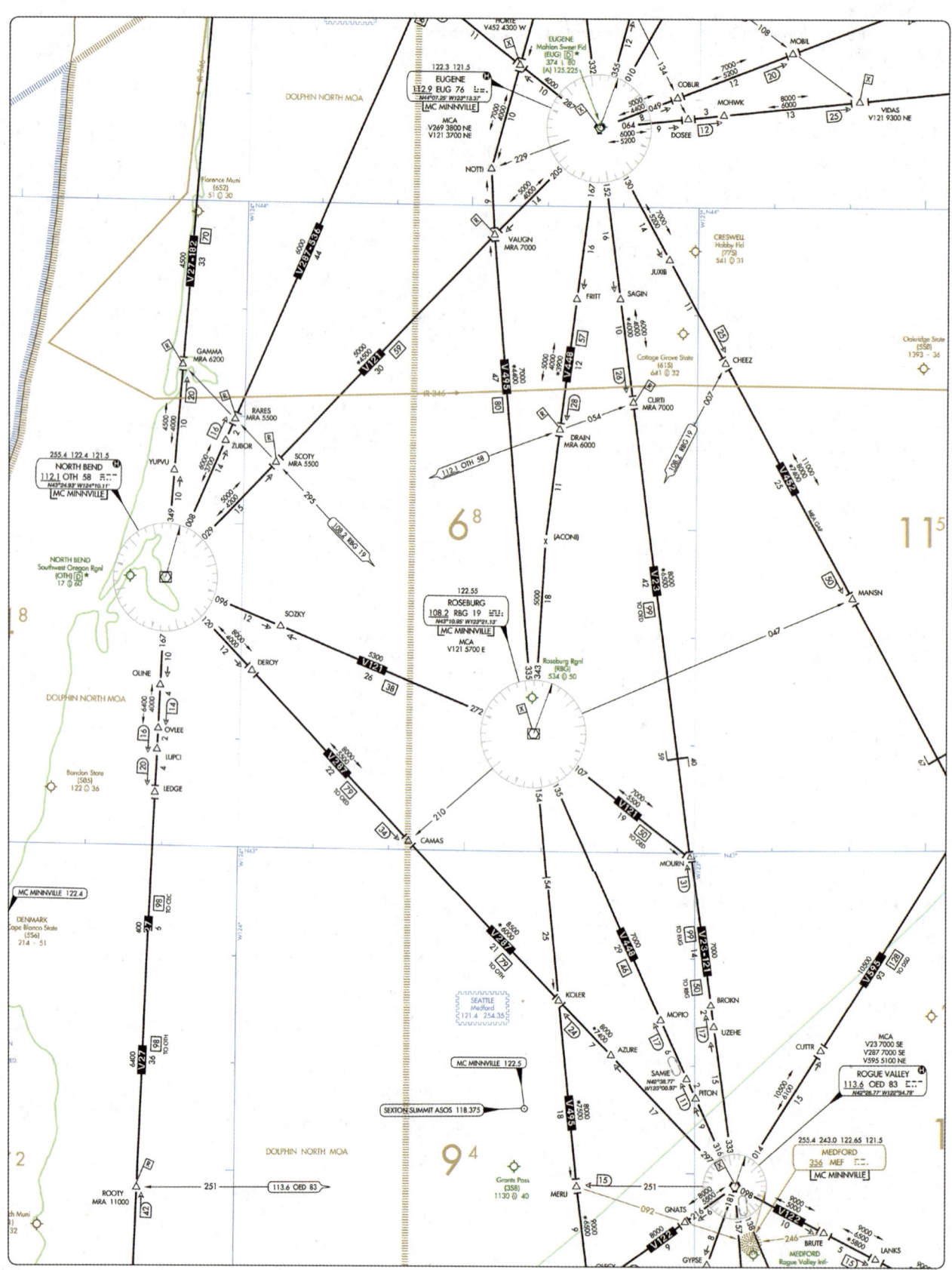

Figure 31. – En Route Low-Altitude Chart Segment.
NOTE: Chart is not to scale and should not be used for navigation. Chart is for testing purposes only.

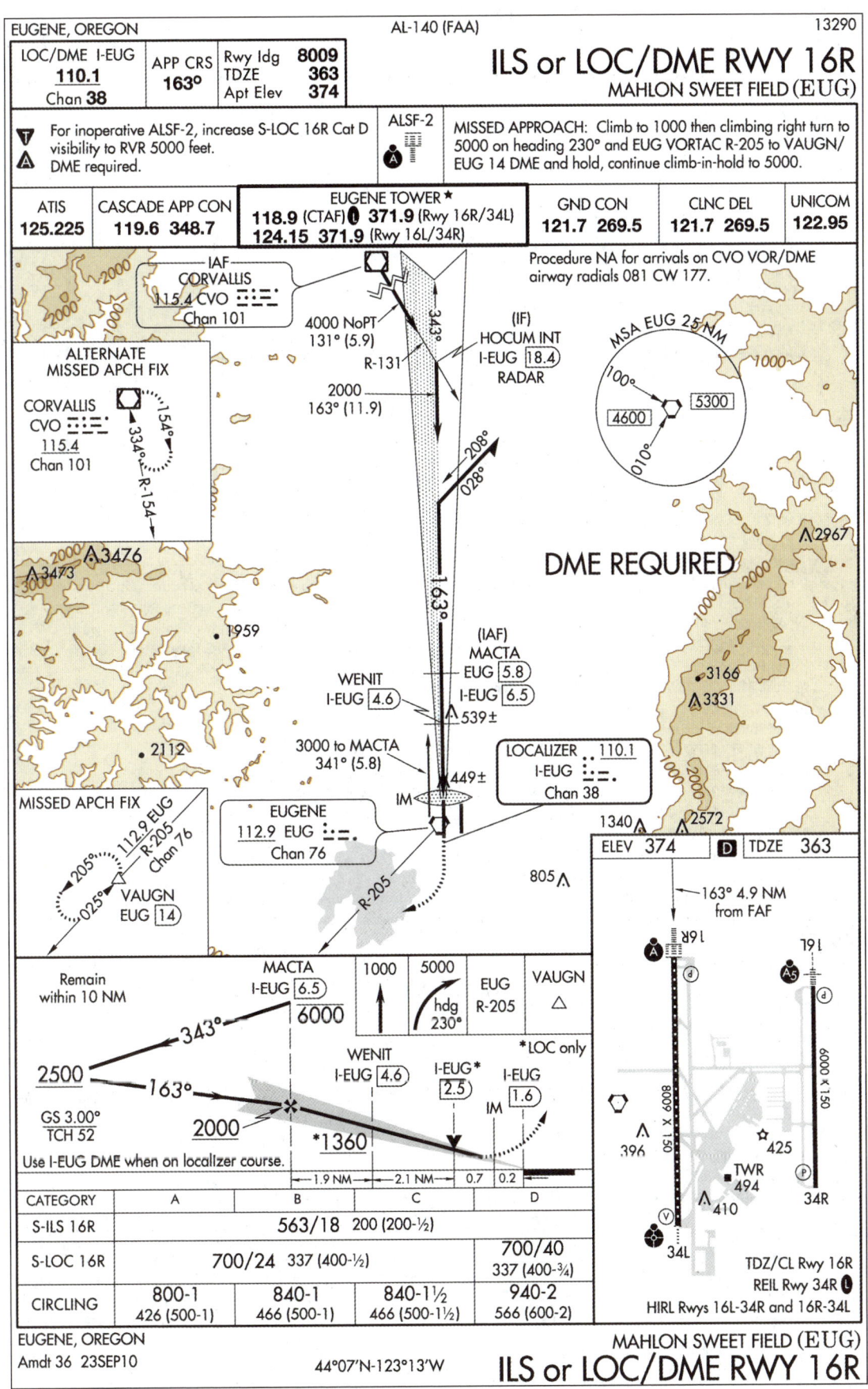

Figure 161. – ILS or LOC/DME RWY 16R (EUG).

OREGON   119

EUGENE

MAHLON SWEET FLD (EUG)   7 NW   UTC–8(–7DT)   N44°07.48′ W123°12.72′   **KLAMATH FALLS**
374   B   S4   **FUEL** 100LL, JET A   OX 1, 2, 3, 4   TPA—1174(800)   Class I, ARFF Index B   **H–1B, L–1B**
NOTAM FILE EUG   **IAP, AD**
RWY 16R–34L: H8009X150 (ASPH–GRVD)   S–75, D–200, 2D–400
  HIRL   CL
  RWY 16R: ALSF2. TDZL. PAPI(P4L)—GA 3.0° TCH 50′.
  RWY 34L: ODALS. VASI(V4L)—GA 3.0° TCH 53′.
RWY 16L–34R: H6000X150 (ASPH–GRVD)   S–105, D–175, 2D–240
  HIRL
  RWY 16L: MALSR. PAPI(P4L)—GA 3.0° TCH 52′.
  RWY 34R: REIL. PAPI(P4L)—GA 3.0° TCH 50′.
RUNWAY DECLARED DISTANCE INFORMATION
  RWY 16L:TORA–6000   TODA–6000   ASDA–6000   LDA–6000
  RWY 16R:TORA–8009   TODA–8009   ASDA–8009   LDA–8009
  RWY 34L:TORA–8009   TODA–8009   ASDA–8009   LDA–8009
  RWY 34R:TORA–6000   TODA–6000   ASDA–6000   LDA–6000

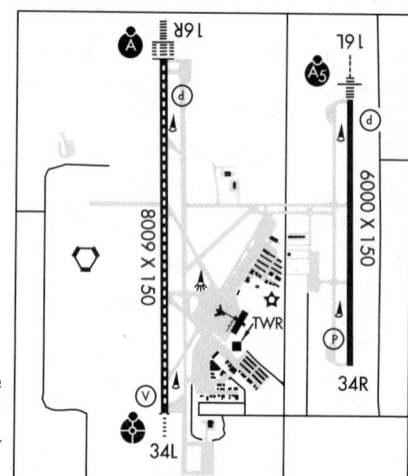

AIRPORT REMARKS: Attended continuously. Migratory waterfowl and other birds on and invof arpt. PPR for unscheduled air carrier ops with more than 30 passenger seats call 541–682–5430. ARFF svcs unavailable 0000–0500 local except PPR 541–682–5430. No access to Rwy 34L byd Twy A9. Helicopters ldg and departing avoid overflying the airline passenger terminal and ramp located E of Rwy 16R–34L. Helipad west of Rwy 16R restricted, PPR phone 541–682–5430. Twys H and K unavailable to acft 21,000 pounds single weight and 40,000 pounds dual gross weight. Terminal apron closed to acft except scheduled air carriers and flights with prior permission. PAPI Rwy 16R and Rwy 16L and 34R and VASI Rwy 34L opr 24 hrs. When twr clsd HIRL Rwy 16L–34R and Rwy 16R–34L preset medium ints. When twr clsd ACTIVATE ALSF2 Rwy 16R, ODALS Rwy 34L MALSR Rwy 16L and REIL Rwy 34R—CTAF.
WEATHER DATA SOURCES: ASOS (541) 461–3114 **HIWAS** 112.9 EUG.
COMMUNICATIONS: CTAF 118.9 **ATIS** 125.225 541–607–4699 **UNICOM** 122.95
  EUGENE RCO 122.3 (MC MINNVILLE RADIO)
Ⓡ CASCADE APP/DEP CON 119.6 (340°–159°) 120.25 (160°–339°) (1400–0730Z‡)
Ⓡ SEATTLE CENTER APP/DEP CON 125.8 (0730–1400Z‡)
  EUGENE TOWER 118.9 (Rwy 16R– 34L) 124.15 (Rwy 16L– 34R) (1400–0730Z‡) **GND CON** 121.7 **CLNC DEL** 121.7
AIRSPACE: CLASS D svc 1400–0730Z‡ other times CLASS E.
RADIO AIDS TO NAVIGATION: NOTAM FILE EUG.
  EUGENE (H) VORTACW 112.9   EUG   Chan 76   N44°07.25′ W123°13.37′   at fld. 364/20E.   **HIWAS.**
  ILS/DME 111.75   I–ADE   Chan 54(Y)   Rwy 16L.   Class IE.
  ILS/DME 110.1   I–EUG   Chan 38   Rwy 16R.   Class IIIE.   Unmonitored when ATCT clsd.

FLORENCE

FLORENCE MUNI (6S2)   1 N   UTC–8(–7DT)   N43°58.97′ W124°06.68′   **KLAMATH FALLS**
51   B   **FUEL** 100LL, JET A   TPA—1051(1000)   NOTAM FILE MMV   **L–1A**
RWY 15–33: H3000X60 (ASPH)   S–12.5   MIRL   0.4% up NW
  RWY 15: Hill. Rgt tfc.
  RWY 33: PAPI(P2L)—GA 3.0° TCH 40′. Trees.

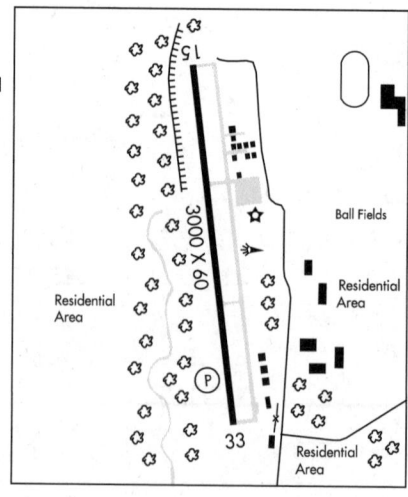

AIRPORT REMARKS: Attended 1630–0030Z‡. Birds, deer and wildlife on and invof arpt. ACTIVATE MIRL Rwy 15–33—CTAF. PAPI Rwy 33 opr 24 hrs.
WEATHER DATA SOURCES: AWOS–3 118.225 (541) 997–8664.
COMMUNICATIONS: CTAF/UNICOM 122.8
RADIO AIDS TO NAVIGATION: NOTAM FILE OTH.
  NORTH BEND (L) VORTACW 112.1   OTH   Chan 58   N43°24.93′
  W124°10.11′   346° 34.1 NM to fld. 707/18E.   **HIWAS.**
  VORTAC unusable:
    012°–087° byd 30 NM blo 5,000′

Figure 162. – Excerpt from Chart Supplement.

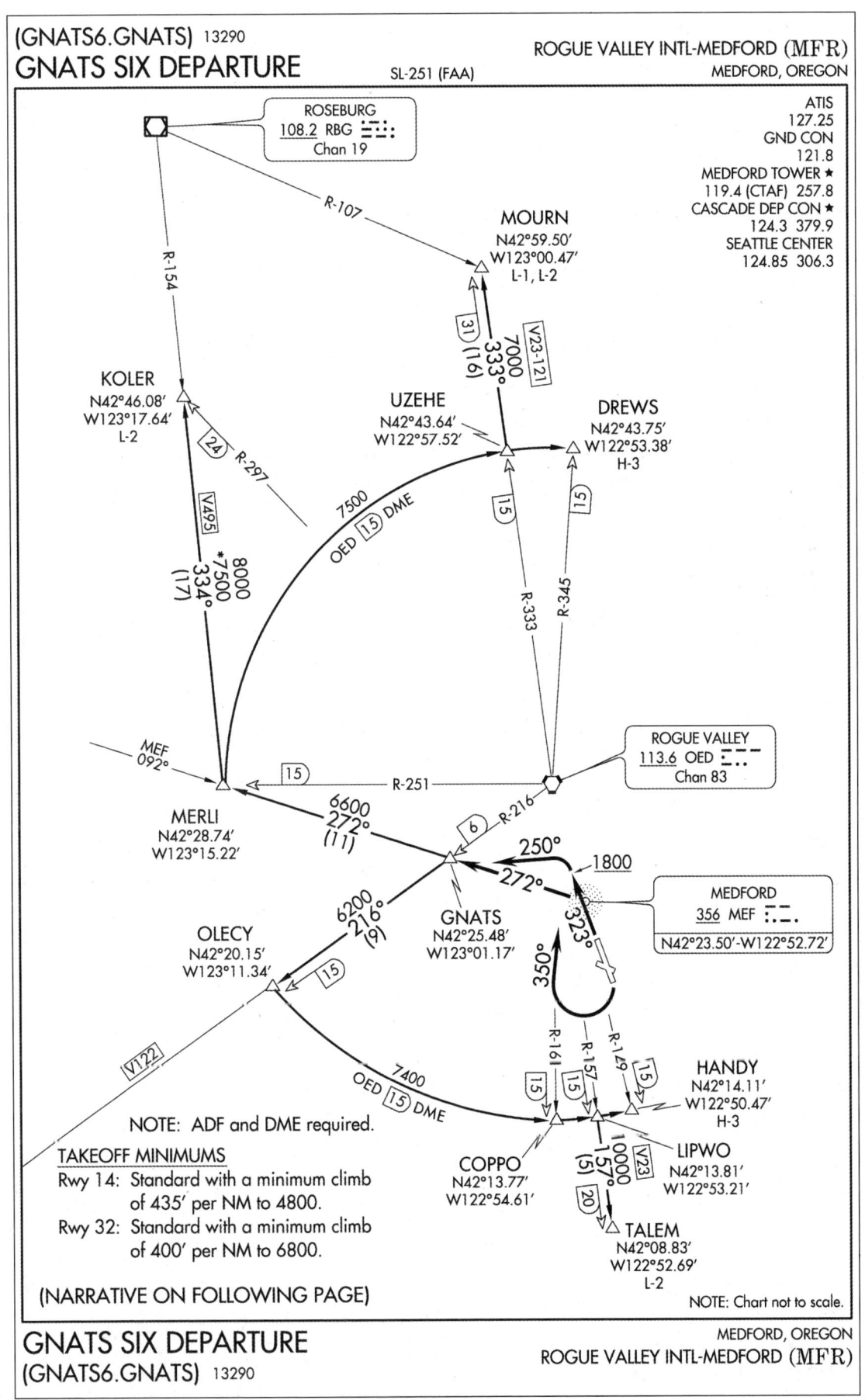

Figure 163. – GNATS Six Departure (GNATS6.GNATS).

(GNATS6.GNATS) 13290
GNATS SIX DEPARTURE
SL-251 (FAA)

ROGUE VALLEY INTL-MEDFORD (MFR)
MEDFORD, OREGON

DEPARTURE ROUTE DESCRIPTION

<u>TAKEOFF RUNWAY 14</u>: Climbing right turn on heading 350° to intercept bearing 272° from MEF NDB to GNATS INT. Thence . . . .

<u>TAKEOFF RUNWAY 32</u>: Climb on heading 323° to 1800 then climbing left turn on heading 250° to intercept bearing 272° from MEF NDB to GNATS INT. Thence . . . .

. . . . via (transition) or (assigned route). Maintain 11000 or assigned lower altitude.

<u>COPPO TRANSITION (GNATS6.COPPO)</u>: From over GNATS INT via OED VORTAC R-216 to OLECY DME, then via the OED VORTAC 15 DME Arc CCW to COPPO DME.

<u>DREWS TRANSITION (GNATS6.DREWS)</u>: From over GNATS INT via MEF NDB 272° to MERLI INT, then via the OED VORTAC 15 DME Arc CW to DREWS DME.

<u>HANDY TRANSITION (GNATS6.HANDY)</u>: From over GNATS INT via the OED VORTAC R-216 to OLECY DME, then via the OED VORTAC 15 DME Arc CCW to HANDY DME.

<u>KOLER TRANSITION (GNATS6.KOLER)</u>: From over GNATS INT via MEF NDB 272° to MERLI INT, then via RBG VOR/DME R-154 to KOLER INT.

<u>MOURN TRANSITION (GNATS6.MOURN)</u>: From over GNATS INT via MEF NDB 272° to MERLI INT, then via the OED VORTAC 15 DME Arc CW to UZEHE DME, then via OED VORTAC R-333 to MOURN INT.

<u>TALEM TRANSITION (GNATS6.TALEM)</u>: From over GNATS INT via OED VORTAC R-216 to OLECY DME, then via the OED VORTAC 15 DME Arc CCW to LIPWO DME, then via OED VORTAC R-157 to TALEM DME.

GNATS SIX DEPARTURE
(GNATS6.GNATS) 13290

MEDFORD, OREGON
ROGUE VALLEY INTL-MEDFORD (MFR)

Figure 164. – GNATS Six Departure (GNATS6.GNATS).

OREGON 129

MEDFORD

ROGUE VALLEY INTL – MEDFORD (MFR) 3 N UTC–8(–7DT) N42°22.45′ W122°52.41′ KLAMATH FALLS
1335 B S4 **FUEL** 100LL, JET A OX 1, 3 TPA—See Remarks Class I, ARFF Index B H–3B, L–2I
NOTAM FILE MFR IAP, AD
RWY 14–32: H8800X150 (ASPH–GRVD) S–200, D–200, 2S–175,
2D–400 HIRL CL
RWY 14: MALSR. TDZL. PAPI(P4L)—GA 3.0° TCH 73′. 0.4% up.
RWY 32: REIL. PAPI(P4R)—GA 3.0° TCH 50′. 0.5% down.
RUNWAY DECLARED DISTANCE INFORMATION
RWY 14: TORA–8800 TODA–8800 ASDA–8800 LDA–8800
RWY 32: TORA–8800 TODA–8800 ASDA–8800 LDA–8800
AIRPORT REMARKS: Attended 1300–0800Z‡. For fuel after hrs call
541–779–5451, or 541–842–2254. Bird haz large flocks of
migratory waterfowl in vicinity Nov–May. Terminal apron clsd to acft
exc scheduled air carrier and flts with prior permission. PPR for
unscheduled ops with more than 30 passenger seats, call arpt ops
541–776–7228. Tran tie–downs avbl thru FBOs only. Rwy 32
preferred for tkfs and ldgs when twr clsd. TPA—2304(969) for
propeller acft, 2804(1469) for turbo acft. PAPI Rwy 14 and VASI
Rwy 32 on continuously. ACTIVATE HIRL Rwy 14–32, MALSR Rwy
14, REIL Rwy 32, TDZL Rwy 14, centerline lgts Rwy 14 and Rwy
32, and twy lgts—CTAF. Ldg fee applies to all corporate acft and all
other acft with weight exceeding 12,500 lbs.

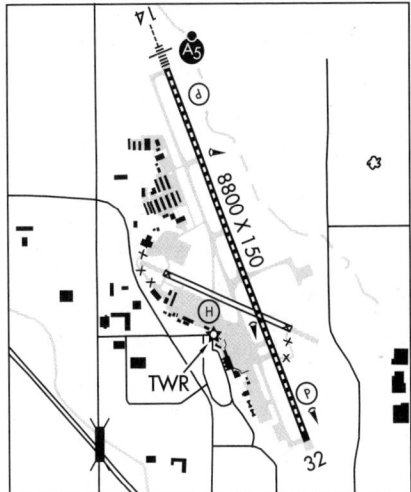

WEATHER DATA SOURCES: ASOS (541) 776–1238 SAWRS.
COMMUNICATIONS: CTAF 119.4 **ATIS** 127.25 **UNICOM** 122.95
MEDFORD RCO 122.65 (MC MINNVILLE RADIO)
®️ **CASCADE APP/DEP CON** 124.3 (1400–0730Z‡)
SEATTLE CENTER APP/DEP CON 124.85 (0730–1400Z‡)
TOWER 119.4 (1400–0500Z‡) **GND CON** 121.8
AIRSPACE: CLASS D svc 1400–0500Z‡ other times CLASS E.
VOR TEST FACILITY (VOT) 117.2
RADIO AIDS TO NAVIGATION: NOTAM FILE MFR.
(H) VORTACW 113.6 OED Chan 83 N42°28.77′ W122°54.78′ 145° 6.6 NM to fld. 2083/19E. **HIWAS.**
VOR portion unusable:
260°–270° byd 35 NM blo 9,000′
290°–300° byd 35 NM blo 8,500′
MEDFORD NDB (MHW) 356 MEF N42°23.50′ W122°52.73′ 151° 1.1 NM to fld.
NDB unusable:
220°–240° byd 15 NM
PUMIE NDB (LOM) 373 MF N42°27.06′ W122°54.80′ 143° 4.9 NM to fld. LOM unusable 260°–270° beyond 10 NM.
Unmonitored when ATCT closed.
ILS/DME 110.3 I–MFR Chan 40 Rwy 14. Class IA. LOM PUMIE NDB. LOM unusable 260°–270° beyond 10 NM.
Unmonitored when ATCT closed. Localizer backcourse unusable byd 11 NM blo 7,000′, byd 13 NM blo 8,300′, byd
17 NM blo 8,700′. Localizer backcourse unusable byd 20° left of course.

MEMALOOSE (See IMNAHA on page 122)

MILLER MEM AIRPARK (See VALE on page 145)

MONUMENT MUNI (12S) 1 NW UTC–8(–7DT) N44°49.89′ W119°25.78′ SEATTLE
2323 TPA—3323(1000) NOTAM FILE MMV
RWY 14–32: H2104X29 (ASPH)
RWY 14: Hill.
AIRPORT REMARKS: Unattended. Intermittently clsd winters due to snow. Wildlife on and invof arpt. Rwy ends marked at each
corner by a single white tire.
COMMUNICATIONS: CTAF 122.9

MULINO STATE (See PORTLAND–MULINO on page 137)

Figure 165. – Excerpt from Chart Supplement.

CLIMB/DESCENT TABLE 10042

INSTRUMENT TAKEOFF OR APPROACH PROCEDURE CHARTS
RATE OF CLIMB/DESCENT TABLE
(ft. per min)

A rate of climb/descent table is provided for use in planning and executing climbs or descents under known or approximate ground speed conditions. It will be especially useful for approaches when the localizer only is used for course guidance. A best speed, power, altitude combination can be programmed which will result in a stable glide rate and altitude favorable for executing a landing if minimums exist upon breakout. Care should always be exercised so that minimum descent altitude and missed approach point are not exceeded.

CLIMB/ DESCENT ANGLE (degrees and tenths)	ft/NM	GROUND SPEED (knots)										
		60	90	120	150	180	210	240	270	300	330	360
2.0	210	210	320	425	530	635	743	850	955	1060	1165	1275
2.5	265	265	400	530	665	795	930	1060	1195	1325	1460	1590
2.7	287	287	430	574	717	860	1003	1147	1290	1433	1576	1720
2.8	297	297	446	595	743	892	1041	1189	1338	1486	1635	1783
2.9	308	308	462	616	770	924	1078	1232	1386	1539	1693	1847
3.0	318	318	478	637	797	956	1115	1274	1433	1593	1752	1911
3.1	329	329	494	659	823	988	1152	1317	1481	1646	1810	1975
3.2	340	340	510	680	850	1020	1189	1359	1529	1699	1869	2039
3.3	350	350	526	701	876	1052	1227	1402	1577	1752	1927	2103
3.4	361	361	542	722	903	1083	1264	1444	1625	1805	1986	2166
3.5	370	370	555	745	930	1115	1300	1485	1670	1860	2045	2230
4.0	425	425	640	850	1065	1275	1490	1700	1915	2125	2340	2550
4.5	480	480	715	955	1195	1435	1675	1915	2150	2390	2630	2870
5.0	530	530	795	1065	1330	1595	1860	2125	2390	2660	2925	3190
5.5	585	585	880	1170	1465	1755	2050	2340	2635	2925	3220	3510
6.0	640	640	960	1275	1595	1915	2235	2555	2875	3195	3510	3830
6.5	690	690	1040	1385	1730	2075	2425	2770	3115	3460	3805	4155
7.0	745	745	1120	1490	1865	2240	2610	2985	3355	3730	4105	4475
7.5	800	800	1200	1600	2000	2400	2800	3200	3600	4000	4400	4800
8.0	855	855	1280	1710	2135	2560	2990	3415	3845	4270	4695	5125
8.5	910	910	1360	1815	2270	2725	3180	3630	4085	4540	4995	5450
9.0	960	960	1445	1925	2405	2885	3370	3850	4330	4810	5295	5775
9.5	1015	1015	1525	2035	2540	3050	3560	4065	4575	5085	5590	6100
10.0	1070	1070	1605	2145	2680	3215	3750	4285	4820	5355	5890	6430

(left vertical label spanning 2.7–3.4 rows: VERTICAL PATH ANGLE)

CLIMB/DESCENT TABLE 10042

Legend 27. – Instrument Takeoff or Approach Procedure Charts, Rate-of-Climb/Descent Table.

11.3 YKM To/From PDX

Questions 13 through 22 pertain to an IFR flight from Yakima Air Terminal (YKM), Yakima, Washington, to the Portland International Airport (PDX), Portland, Oregon, whereas questions 23 through 25 pertain to an IFR flight from PDX to YKM.

The figures provided for these flights are listed below and are presented throughout the sequence of questions.

Fig.	Page	
47	457	En Route Low-Altitude Chart Segment
48	454	CDI—NAV 1
182	458	GROMO Three Departure (GROMO3.GROMO)
188	459	LOC/DME RWY 21 (PDX)

13. (Refer to Figure 47 on page 457.) When en route on V448 from YKM VORTAC to BTG VORTAC, what minimum navigation equipment is required to identify ANGOO intersection?

A. One VOR receiver.

B. One VOR receiver and DME.

C. Two VOR receivers.

Answer (A) is correct. (FAA-H-8083-15B Chap 10)
DISCUSSION: To identify ANGOO INT., only one VOR receiver is required. It is important to establish yourself on V448 and maintain heading while you orient yourself to LTJ VORTAC R-330. Your position checks and tuning will need to be done quickly and accurately.
Answer (B) is incorrect. Since ANGOO INT. can be determined by cross radials, only one VOR receiver is required; a DME is not. Answer (C) is incorrect. Only one VOR receiver, not two, is required to identify ANGOO INT.

14. (Refer to Figure 188 on page 459.) What is the MDA and visibility criteria for a straight-in LOC/DME RWY 21 approach at Portland International in a Category B airplane?

A. 1,120 ft. MSL; visibility 1 SM.

B. 700 ft. MSL; visibility 1 SM.

C. 700 ft. MSL; visibility 1 NM.

Answer (B) is correct. (ACUG)
DISCUSSION: The minimums for the LOC/DME RWY 21 approach, Category B, are 700 ft. MSL and 1 SM visibility.
Answer (A) is incorrect. The minimum altitude after crossing HUDUT FAF, but before reaching the 4 DME fix on the localizer, is 1,120 ft. MSL. Answer (C) is incorrect. Visibility minimums are given in statute miles, not nautical miles.

15. (Refer to Figure 188 on page 459.) With a ground speed of 120 knots, approximately what minimum rate of descent will be required between I-GPO 11.3 DME fix (COVDU) and the I-GPO 7.3 DME fix?

A. 320 feet per minute.

B. 600 feet per minute.

C. 710 feet per minute.

Answer (B) is correct. (FAA-H-8083-16B Chap 5)
DISCUSSION: Fig. 188 shows an altitude loss of 1,200 feet between I-GPO 11.3 DME and 7.3 DME. The aircraft must lose 1,200 feet while traveling 4 miles. Divide distance by speed to find time. 4 NM ÷ 120 knots = 0.033 (hours) × 60 (minutes) = 2 minutes. Divide altitude to lose by time to arrive at fpm. 1,200 feet ÷ 2 minutes = 600 feet per minute.
Answer (A) is incorrect. The required descent rate would be 600, not 320, feet per minute. Answer (C) is incorrect. The required descent rate would be 600, not 710, feet per minute.

16. (Refer to Figure 182 on page 458.) Using an average ground speed of 140 knots, what minimum indicated rate of climb must be maintained to meet the required climb rate (feet per NM) to 6,300 feet as specified on the instrument departure procedure for RWY 22?

A. 380 feet per minute.

B. 583 feet per minute.

C. 887 feet per minute.

Answer (C) is correct. (ACUG)
DISCUSSION: The DP in Fig. 182 has a note that indicates a minimum climb of 380 feet per NM to 6,300 feet. To convert this to a rate of climb (feet per minute), use the following formula to determine a rate of climb of 887 feet per minute.

$$\frac{(GS \times FT/NM)}{60} = FPM$$

$$\frac{(140 \times 380)}{60} = 887 \ FPM$$

Answer (A) is incorrect. The feet per NM is 380.
Answer (B) is incorrect. A 583 feet per minute climb rate at an average groundspeed of 140 knots would result in a climb rate of 250 feet per NM, not 380 feet per NM.

17. (Refer to Figure 188 on page 459.) You have been cleared to the CREAK intersection via the BTG 054° radial at 7,000 ft. Approaching CREAK, you are cleared for the LOC/DME RWY 21 approach to PDX. Descent to procedure turn altitude should not begin prior to

A. completion of the procedure turn, and established on the localizer.

B. intercepting the glide slope.

C. CREAK outbound.

Answer (C) is correct. (ACUG)
   DISCUSSION: CREAK intersection is an initial approach fix, identified by the letters IAF. It is the fix at which the procedure turn should begin. Because you were cleared to CREAK intersection at an altitude of 7,000 ft., you should remain at that altitude until you reach the intersection. Since you have been cleared for the approach, you may then turn to the northeast and track the localizer outbound (the first portion of the procedure turn) while descending to the minimum procedure turn altitude of 5,700 ft. MSL.
   Answer (A) is incorrect. You should be at the procedure turn altitude (5,700 ft. MSL) at or before the completion of the procedure turn. Descent to the first step-down fix minimum altitude (not the procedure turn altitude) should begin after completion of the procedure turn and when established on the localizer (if you are past CREAK intersection). **Answer (B) is incorrect.** The LOC/DME RWY 21 approach has no glide slope. Additionally, descent to the procedure turn altitude may begin after crossing CREAK intersection.

18. (Refer to Figure 48 below, and Figure 182 on page 458.) What is your position relative to the 9 DME ARC and the 206° radial of the instrument departure procedure?

A. On the 9 DME arc and approaching R-206.

B. Outside the 9 DME arc and past R-206.

C. Inside the 9 DME arc and approaching R-206.

Answer (A) is correct. (FAA-H-8083-15B Chap 9)
   DISCUSSION: The HSI shows that you are currently on a 130° heading, thus flying in a southeasterly direction. The OBS selector is set on R-206, and a left deflection is indicated. This means you are west and north of R-206. (If you were flying out the R-206 with a left deflection, you would turn left to intercept.) You are approaching R-206 because you are flying in a southeasterly direction. The DME indicates 9 NM out, so you are on the 9 DME arc.
   Answer (B) is incorrect. You are on, not outside, the arc and approaching, not past, R-206. **Answer (C) is incorrect.** You are on, not inside, the arc.

Figure 48. – CDI—NAV 1.

19. (Refer to Figure 188 on page 459.) With a ground speed of 120 knots, approximately what minimum rate of descent will be required between I-GPO 7.3 DME fix (HUDUT) and the I-GPO 4.1 DME fix?

    A. 320 fpm.

    B. 740 fpm.

    C. 510 fpm.

Answer (B) is correct. (FAA-H-8083-16B Chap 3)
DISCUSSION:

$$\frac{\text{Altitude \# (ft.)}}{\text{Distance (NM)}} \times \text{GS (kt.)} \times \frac{1 \text{ hr.}}{60 \text{ min.}} = \frac{\text{Minimum rate of}}{\text{descent (fpm)}}$$

$$\frac{2{,}300 \text{ ft.} - 1{,}120 \text{ ft.}}{7.3 \text{ NM} - 4.1 \text{ NM}} \times 120 \frac{\text{NM}}{\text{hr.}} \times \frac{1 \text{ hr.}}{60 \text{ min.}} = \text{Min. ROD (fpm)}$$

$$\frac{1{,}180 \text{ ft.}}{3.2 \text{ NM}} \times 120 \frac{\text{NM}}{\text{hr.}} \times \frac{1 \text{ hr.}}{60 \text{ min.}} = \text{Min. ROD (fpm)}$$

$$368.75 \frac{\text{ft.}}{\text{NM}} \times 120 \frac{\text{NM}}{\text{hr.}} \times \frac{1 \text{ hr.}}{60 \text{ min.}} = \text{Min. ROD (fpm)}$$

$$737.5 \frac{\text{ft.}}{\text{min.}} = \text{Min. ROD (fpm)}$$

    Answer (A) is incorrect. The descent rate of 320 feet per minute is less than half of what you would need to reach the 4.1 DME fix at the correct altitude. **Answer (C) is incorrect.** A descent rate of 510 feet per minute is insufficient to reach the 4.1 DME fix at the correct altitude.

20. (Refer to Figure 188 on page 459.) What determines the MAP on the LOC/DME RWY 21 approach at Portland International Airport?

    A. I-GPO 1.2 DME.

    B. 6.2 NM from HUDUT FAF.

    C. 160° radial of BTG VORTAC.

Answer (A) is correct. (ACUG)
    DISCUSSION: The MAP on the LOC/DME RWY 21 approach is the 1.2 DME fix on the localizer (I-GPO).
    Answer (B) is incorrect. While the MAP is located 6.2 NM from HUDUT FAF, the MAP is the 1.2 DME fix on the localizer. **Answer (C) is incorrect.** The 160° radial of BTG VORTAC is part of the missed approach procedure, not the missed approach point (MAP).

21. (Refer to Figure 188 on page 459.) When conducting the LOC/DME RWY 21 approach at PDX, what is the Minimum Safe Altitude (MSA) while maneuvering between the BTG VORTAC and CREAK intersection?

    A. 3,500 feet MSL.

    B. 5,700 feet MSL.

    C. 6,200 feet MSL.

Answer (C) is correct. (ACUG)
    DISCUSSION: The circle in the northwest corner of the planview of the LOC/DME RWY 21 approach into PDX indicates that the minimum safe sector altitudes for this approach are based on the BTG VORTAC. The circle also indicates that the minimum safe sector altitude in the area between the 120° and 300° radials in a clockwise direction is 6,200 ft. MSL. Because CREAK intersection lies in this area, the minimum safe altitude for maneuvering between BTG VORTAC and CREAK intersection is 6,200 ft. MSL.
    Remember, MSA altitudes are for emergency use only and may differ from published minimum altitudes on the IAP chart.
    Answer (A) is incorrect. This is the minimum safe sector altitude in the area between the 120° and 300° radials in a counterclockwise direction. CREAK intersection, which is defined by the intersection of the 054° radial of the BTG VORTAC and the localizer, is not in this area. **Answer (B) is incorrect.** This is the minimum altitude for flying the charted feeder route, not maneuvering, between BTG VORTAC and CREAK intersection.

22. (Refer to Figure 188 on page 459.) When conducting a missed approach from the LOC/DME RWY 21 approach at PDX, what is the Minimum Safe Altitude (MSA) while maneuvering between the runway and BTG VORTAC?

A. 4,200 feet MSL.

B. 3,500 feet MSL.

C. 6,200 feet MSL.

Answer (B) is correct. (AIM Para 5-4-5)
DISCUSSION: The missed approach would place the aircraft in the MSA sector indicating 3,500 feet. This MSA sector is from the 120° radial clockwise through the 300° radial of the BTG VORTAC. MSAs are published for emergency use on IAP charts. They provide 1,000 feet of clearance over all obstacles but do not necessarily ensure acceptable navigation signal coverage. MSAs are depicted in feet above mean sea level. A single sector altitude is normally established; however, when necessary to obtain relief from obstacles, an MSA with up to four sectors may be established.
Answer (A) is incorrect. The missed approach altitude is 4,200 feet, not the MSA while maneuvering between the runway and BTG VORTAC while on the missed approach. **Answer (C) is incorrect.** An MSA of 6,200 feet would apply to flight between the 300° radial clockwise through the 120° radial of the BTG VORTAC, which is not the area maneuvering between the runway and BTG VORTAC while on the missed approach.

23. (Refer to Figure 47 on page 457.) En route on V112 from BTG VORTAC to LTJ VORTAC, the minimum altitude crossing Gymme intersection is

A. 6,400 feet.

B. 6,500 feet.

C. 7,000 feet.

Answer (C) is correct. (14 CFR 91.177)
DISCUSSION: When no minimum crossing altitude (MCA) is specified, e.g., at GYMME intersection, the intersection may be crossed at or above the preceding MEA. Since the MEA along V112 eastbound is 7,000 ft., GYMME may be crossed no lower than 7,000 ft.
Answer (A) is incorrect. This is the MOCA, not the MEA, along V112. **Answer (B) is incorrect.** This is the MEA west of GYMME when westbound, not eastbound.

24. (Refer to Figure 47 on page 457.) En route on V468 from BTG VORTAC to YKM VORTAC, the minimum altitude at TROTS intersection is

A. 7,100 feet.

B. 10,000 feet.

C. 11,500 feet.

Answer (C) is correct. (14 CFR 91.177)
DISCUSSION: TROTS intersection (45 NM northeast of BTG VORTAC on V468 in Fig. 47) shows a minimum crossing altitude (MCA) of 11,500 ft. when northeastbound on V468.
Answer (A) is incorrect. This is the MOCA along V468, not the MCA at TROTS. **Answer (B) is incorrect.** This is the MEA before TROTS, not the MCA at TROTS.

25. (Refer to Figure 47 on page 457.) Due to thunderstorms along your planned route, you decide to file Battle Ground (BTG) VORTAC, V520 to OGYAJ intersection, KLICKITAT (LTJ) VORTAC, V25 to YAKIMA (YKM) VORTAC. Calculate the time and fuel burn for the route with the following conditions:

TAS: 140 kts
Reported winds: 270@30 kts
Fuel burn rate: 17 GPH

A. 49 minutes, 13.7 gallons.

B. 53 minutes, 15.1 gallons.

C. 60 minutes, 17 gallons.

Answer (A) is correct. (FAA-H-8083-16B Chap 5)
DISCUSSION: This filed flight routing from BTG to YKM takes three legs, with a total distance of 124 NM. Use your E6B to calculate the route.

- BTG → OGYAJ = 32 NM at 168 kt. groundspeed for 12 min. using 3.4 gal.
- OGYAJ → LTJ = 34 NM at 169 kt. groundspeed for 13 min. using 3.5 gal.
- LTJ → YKM = 58 NM at 152 kt. groundspeed for 24 min. using 6.8 gal.

Set the E6B datum to the various speeds; then use the E6B outer disc for distance to read off the times required on the inner disc. Total time will be approximately 49 min. Account for a fuel consumption rate of 17 GPH to find approximately 13.7 gal.
Answer (B) is incorrect. The time and fuel consumption for a TAS of 135 kt. would be 53 min. and 15.1 gal. **Answer (C) is incorrect.** The time and fuel consumption for a TAS of 130 kt. would be 60 min. and 17 gal.

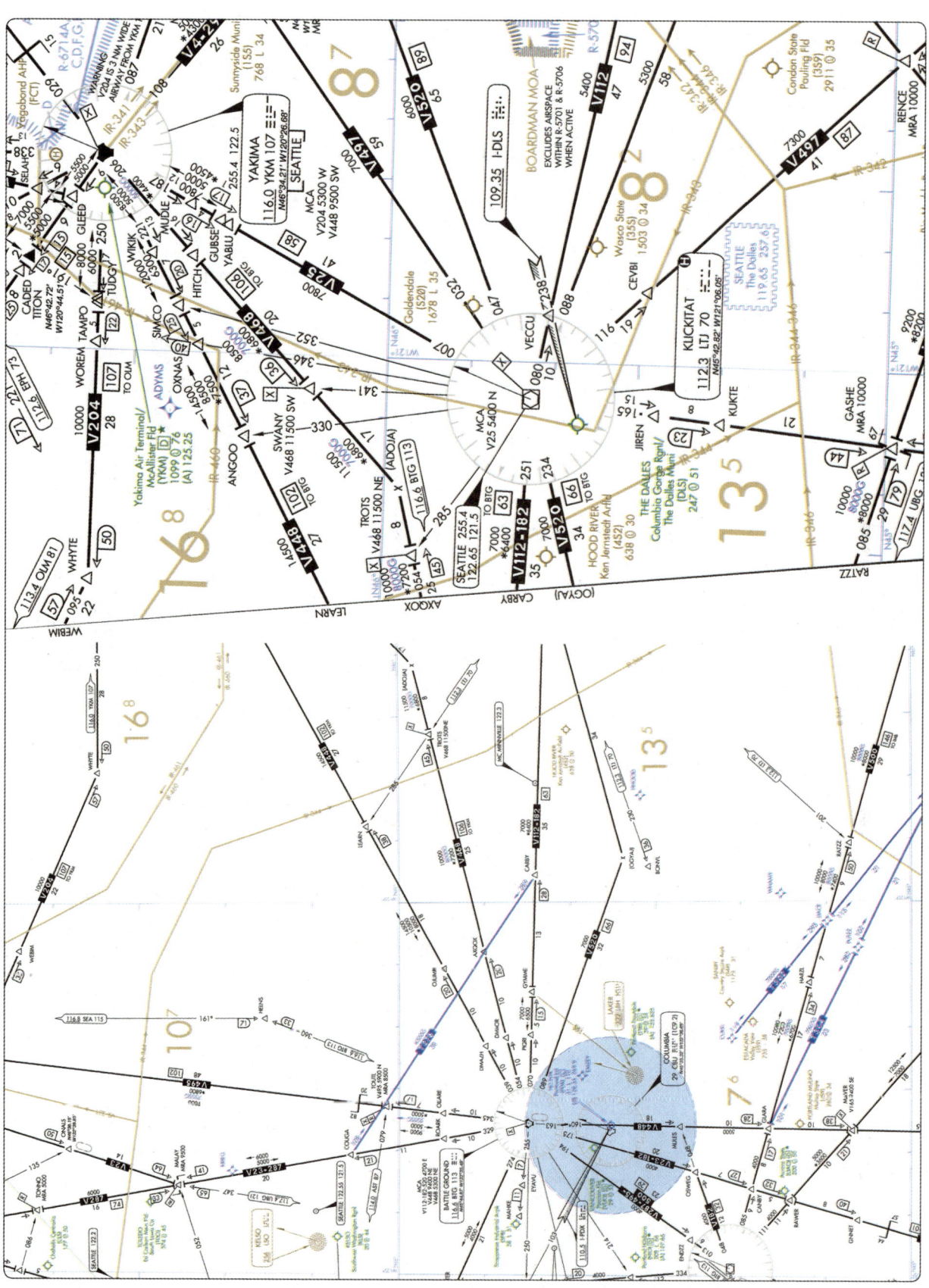

Figure 47. – En Route Low-Altitude Chart Segment.
NOTE: Chart is not to scale and should not be used for navigation. Chart is for testing purposes only.

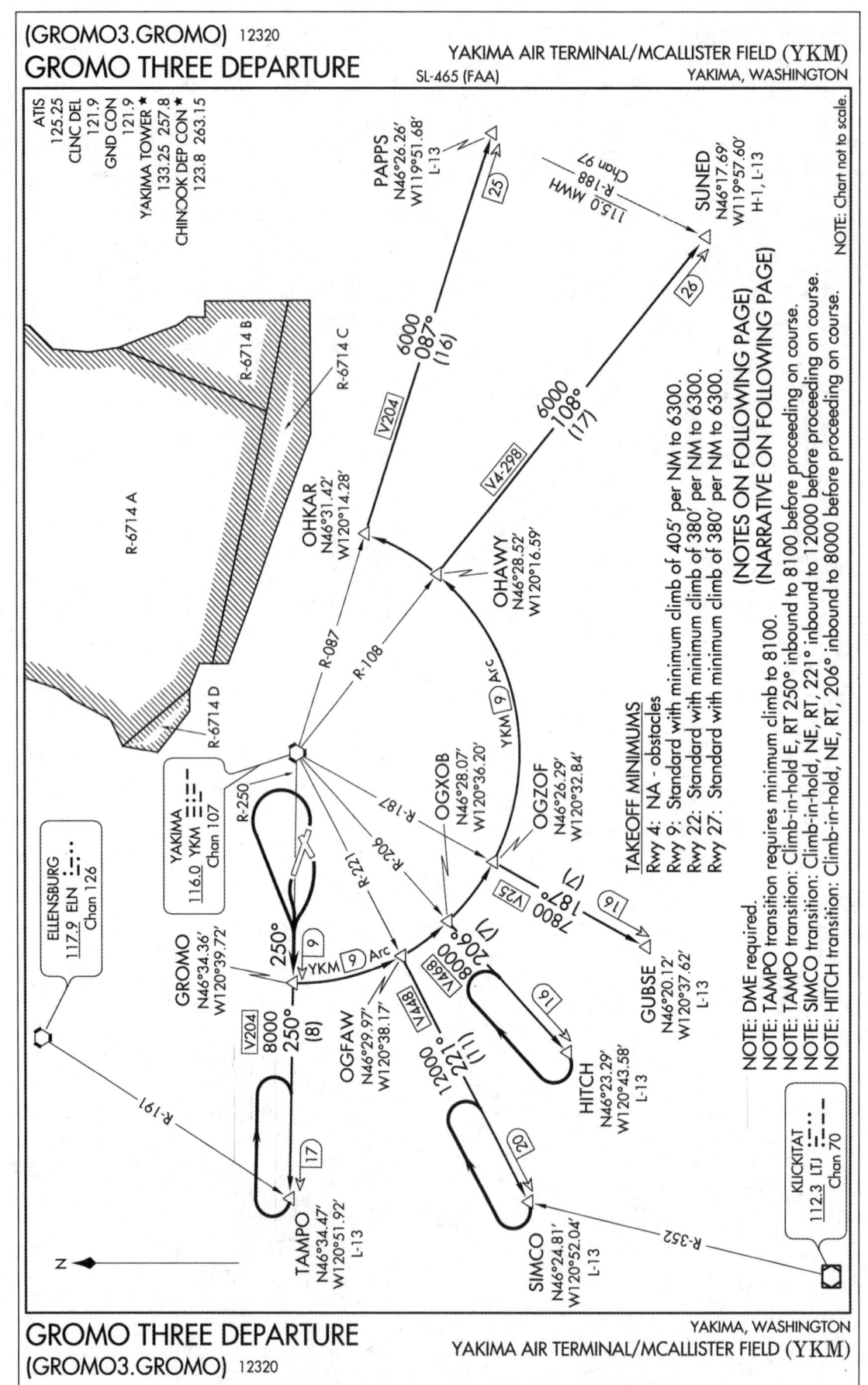

Figure 182. – GROMO Three Departure (GROMO3.GROMO).

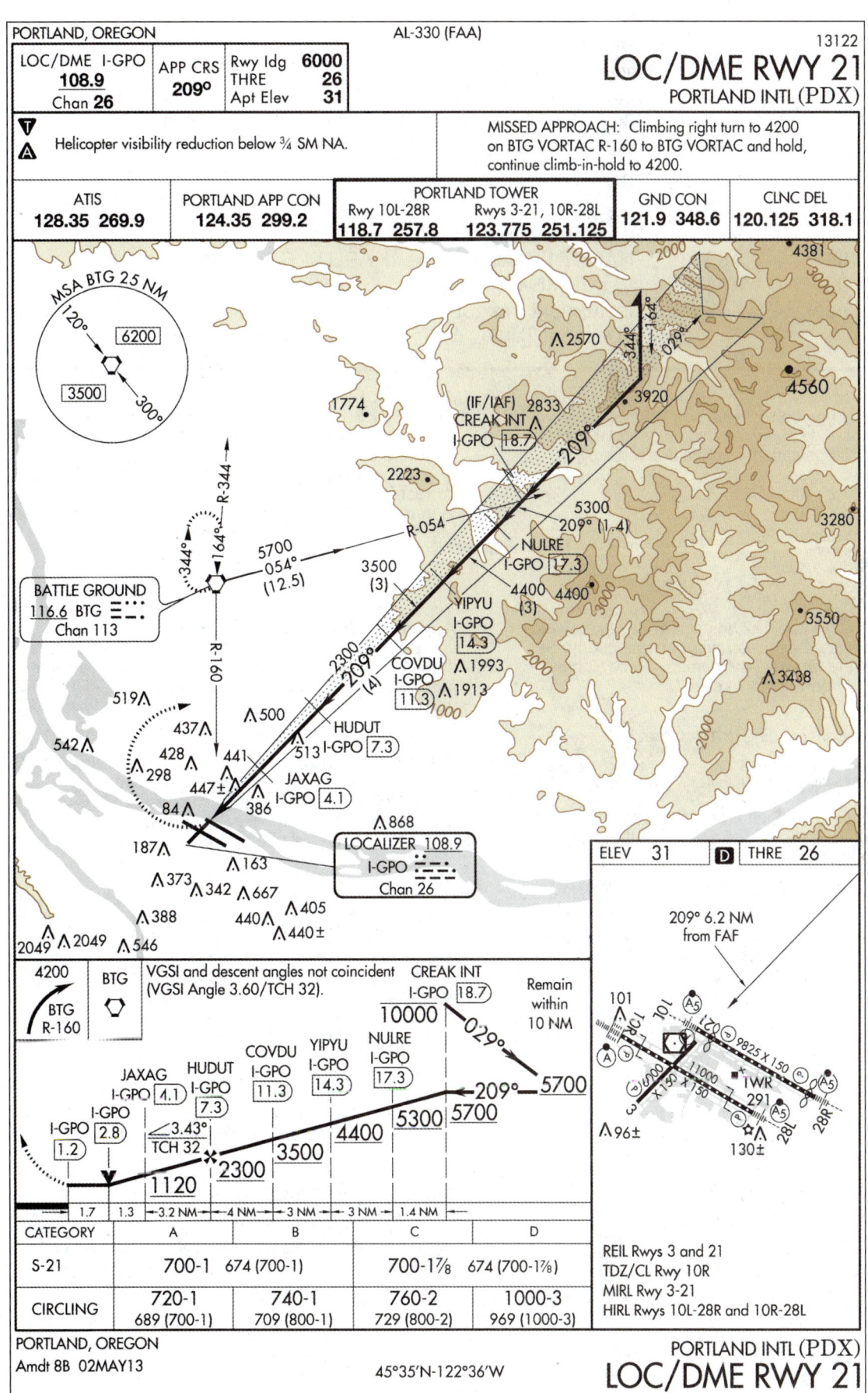

Figure 188. – LOC/DME RWY 21 (PDX).

11.4 SBA To/From PRB

Questions 26 through 31 pertain to an IFR flight from Santa Barbara Municipal Airport, Santa Barbara, California, to the Paso Robles Municipal Airport, Paso Robles, California.

The figures provided for this flight are listed below and are presented at the end of the sequence of questions.

26. (Refer to Figure 192 on page 464.) As a guide in making range corrections, how many degrees of relative bearing change should be used for each one-half-mile deviation from the desired arc?

A. 2° to 3°.

B. 5° maximum.

C. 10° to 20°.

Answer (C) is correct. (FAA-H-8083-15B Chap 9)
DISCUSSION: As a guide in making corrections when tracking DME arcs, turn 10° to 20° toward the arc for each 1/2 NM that you are off the desired arc.
Answer (A) is incorrect. You should make 10° to 20° corrections, not 2° to 3°, for each 1/2-NM deviation. **Answer (B) is incorrect.** There is no maximum; the amount of correction should be proportional to the amount of error.

27. (Refer to Figure 192 on page 464.) Under which condition should a missed approach procedure be initiated if the runway environment (Paso Robles Municipal Airport) is not in sight?

A. After descending to 1,440 feet MSL.

B. After descent to 1,440 feet or reaching the 1 NM DME, whichever occurs first.

C. When you reach the established missed approach point and determine the visibility is less than 1 mile.

Answer (C) is correct. (14 CFR 91.175)
DISCUSSION: The missed approach point is the point prescribed in each instrument approach procedure at which a missed approach procedure shall be executed if the required visual reference has not been sighted or the flight visibility is less than visibility prescribed in the IAP. The MAP for VOR/DME-B is the PRB VORTAC. Thus, when you reach the VORTAC and you determine the visibility is less than 1 SM, you must execute the missed approach procedure.
Answer (A) is incorrect. The MAP is PRB VORTAC, not arrival at the MDA. **Answer (B) is incorrect.** The MAP is PRB VORTAC, not arrival at the MDA or the 1 DME fix.

28. (Refer to Figure 189 on page 463.) Using an average ground speed of 100 knots, what minimum rate of climb would meet the required minimum climb rate per NM as specified by the instrument departure procedure?

A. 425 feet per minute.

B. 580 feet per minute.

C. 642 feet per minute.

Answer (C) is correct. (ACUG)
DISCUSSION: The DP on Fig. 189 has a note that indicates a minimum climb rate of 385 feet per NM to 6,000 feet. To convert this to a rate of climb (feet per minute), use the following formula:

$$\frac{(GS \times FT/NM)}{60} = FPM$$

$$\frac{100 \times 385}{60} = 642 \text{ FPM}$$

The minimum rate of climb required would be 642 feet per minute.
Answer (A) is incorrect. A 425-feet-per-minute climb rate at an average groundspeed of 100 knots would result in a climb rate of 255 feet per NM, not 385 feet per NM. **Answer (B) is incorrect.** A 580-feet-per-minute climb rate at an average groundspeed of 100 knots would result in a climb rate of approximately 350 feet per NM, not 385 feet per NM.

29. (Refer to Figure 53 on page 462.) Where is the VOR COP on V27 between the GVO and MQO VORTACs?

    A. 20 DME from GVO VORTAC.

    B. 20 DME from MQO VORTAC.

    C. 30 DME from SBA VORTAC.

Answer (A) is correct. (ACUG)
    DISCUSSION: When going north from GVO VORTAC to MQO VORTAC, there is a VOR changeover point (COP) 20 NM northwest of GVO VORTAC and 34 NM southeast of MQO VORTAC.
    Answer (B) is incorrect. The COP is 20 NM from GVO, not MQO. **Answer (C) is incorrect.** SBA is Santa Barbara localizer, which is not on V27.

30. (Refer to Figure 189 on page 463 and Legend 27 on page 465.) Using an average ground speed of 90 knots, what minimum rate of climb would meet the required minimum climb rate per NM as specified by the instrument departure procedure?

    A. 578 feet per minute.

    B. 543 feet per minute.

    C. 642 feet per minute.

Answer (A) is correct. (FAA-H-8083-16B Chap 2)
    DISCUSSION: A note included with the instrument departure procedure specifies a minimum climb of 385 feet per NM. With an average ground speed of 90 knots, your aircraft is covering 1.5 miles per minute. 385 feet per NM × 1.5 miles per minute = 577.5 feet per minute as your minimum rate of climb that will meet the minimum feet per NM value as specified in the procedure. This can also be interpolated by using the chart in Legend 27 on page 465.
    Answer (B) is incorrect. At an average ground speed of 90 knots, 543 feet per minute is less than 385 feet per NM. Your aircraft is covering 1.5 miles per minute. 385 feet per NM × 1.5 miles per minute = 577.5 feet per minute as your minimum rate of climb that will meet the minimum feet per NM value as specified in the procedure. **Answer (C) is incorrect.** Although 642 feet per minute exceeds the minimum of 385 feet per NM, it is not the minimum rate of climb necessary.

31. (Refer to Figure 192 on page 464.) Using an average ground speed of 90 knots, what constant rate of descent from 3,100 feet MSL at the 6 DME fix would enable the aircraft to arrive at 2,400 feet MSL at the FAF?

    A. 350 feet per minute.

    B. 400 feet per minute.

    C. 450 feet per minute.

Answer (A) is correct. (FAA-H-8083-16B Chap 3)
    DISCUSSION: The distance between the 6 DME fix and the FAF (ILSIC) is 3 NM. The altitude lost will be 700 feet (3,100 feet − 2,400 feet = 700 feet). Your aircraft must lose 700 feet in 3 NM. At 90 knots, your aircraft will cover 1.5 NM per minute or 3 NM in 2 minutes. 700 feet ÷ 2 minutes = 350 feet per minute.
    Answer (B) is incorrect. Losing 400 feet for 2 minutes would equate to an 800-foot altitude loss, putting you 100 feet below the glide slope. **Answer (C) is incorrect.** Losing 450 feet for 2 minutes would equate to a 900-foot altitude loss, putting you 200 feet below the glide slope.

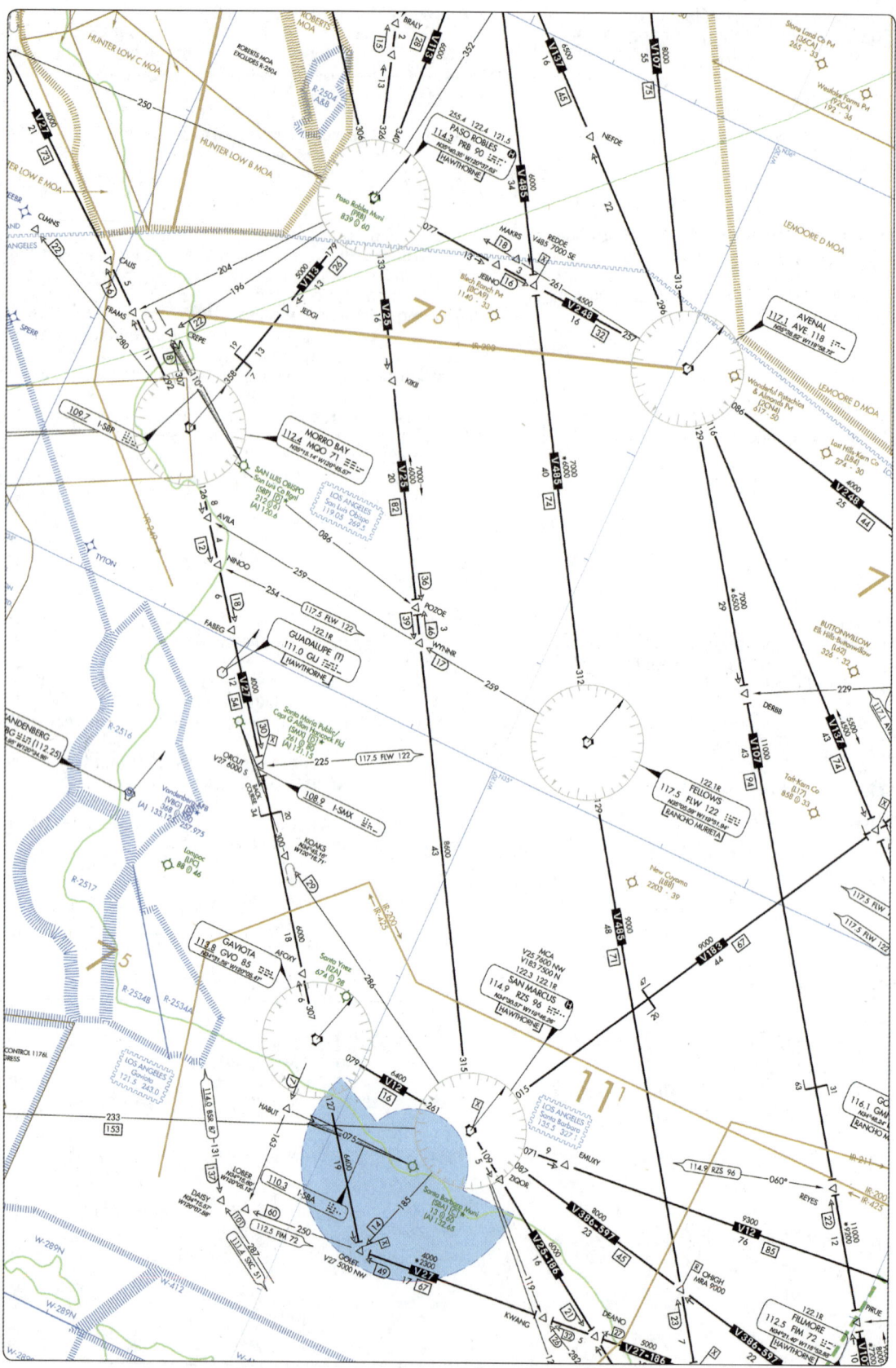

Figure 53. – En Route Low-Altitude Chart Segment.
NOTE: Chart is not to scale and should not be used for navigation. Chart is for testing purposes only.

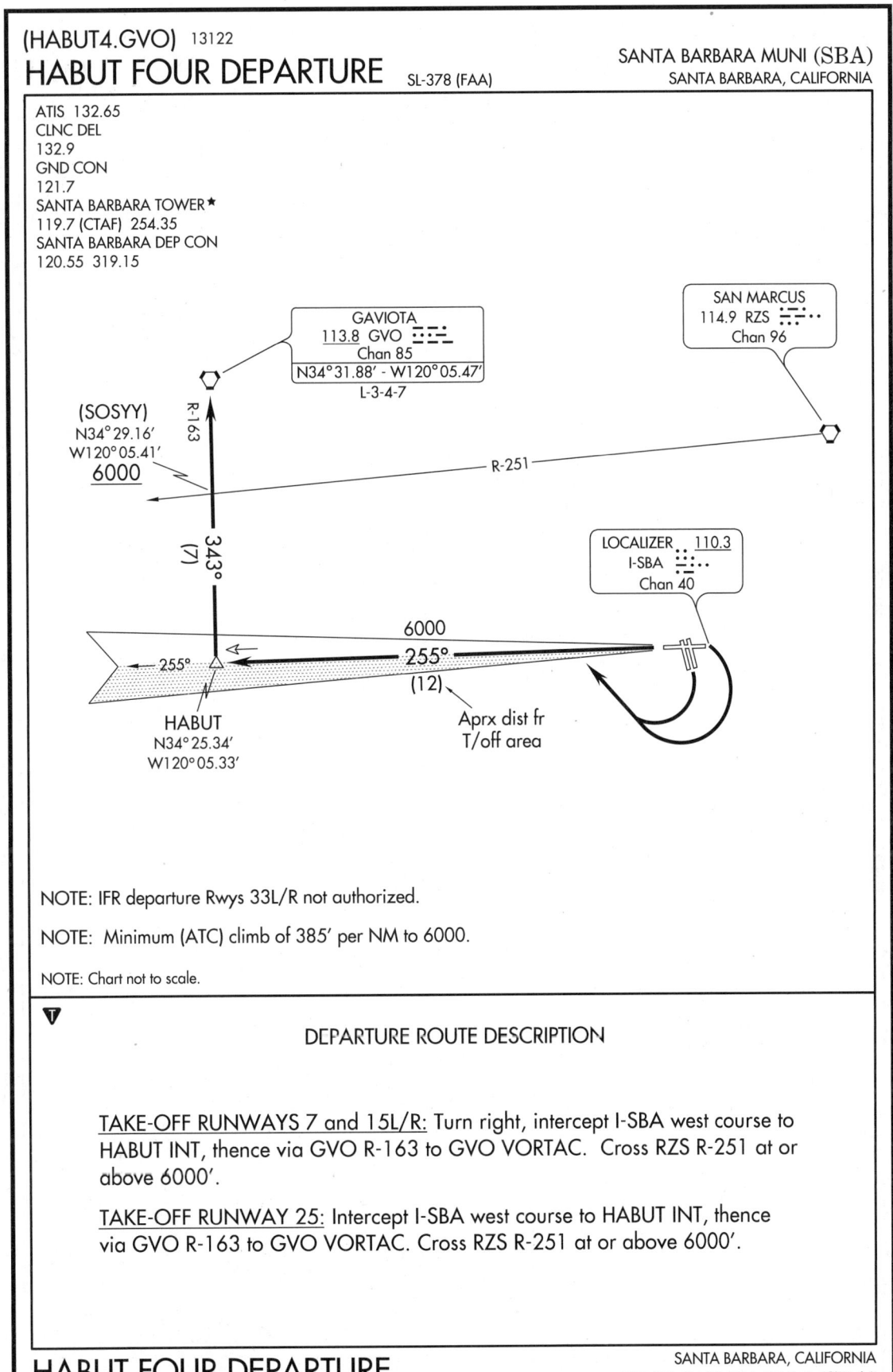

(HABUT4.GVO) 13122
HABUT FOUR DEPARTURE SL-378 (FAA)

SANTA BARBARA MUNI (SBA)
SANTA BARBARA, CALIFORNIA

ATIS 132.65
CLNC DEL
132.9
GND CON
121.7
SANTA BARBARA TOWER ★
119.7 (CTAF) 254.35
SANTA BARBARA DEP CON
120.55 319.15

SAN MARCUS
114.9 RZS
Chan 96

GAVIOTA
113.8 GVO
Chan 85
N34°31.88' - W120°05.47'
L-3-4-7

(SOSYY)
N34°29.16'
W120°05.41'
6000

R-163

R-251

343°
(7)

LOCALIZER 110.3
I-SBA
Chan 40

6000
255°
(12)

255°

255°

HABUT
N34°25.34'
W120°05.33'

Aprx dist fr
T/off area

NOTE: IFR departure Rwys 33L/R not authorized.

NOTE: Minimum (ATC) climb of 385' per NM to 6000.

NOTE: Chart not to scale.

DEPARTURE ROUTE DESCRIPTION

TAKE-OFF RUNWAYS 7 and 15L/R: Turn right, intercept I-SBA west course to
HABUT INT, thence via GVO R-163 to GVO VORTAC. Cross RZS R-251 at or
above 6000'.

TAKE-OFF RUNWAY 25: Intercept I-SBA west course to HABUT INT, thence
via GVO R-163 to GVO VORTAC. Cross RZS R-251 at or above 6000'.

HABUT FOUR DEPARTURE
(HABUT4.GVO) 13122

SANTA BARBARA, CALIFORNIA
SANTA BARBARA MUNI (SBA)

Figure 189. – HABUT Four Departure (HABUT4.GVO) (SBA).

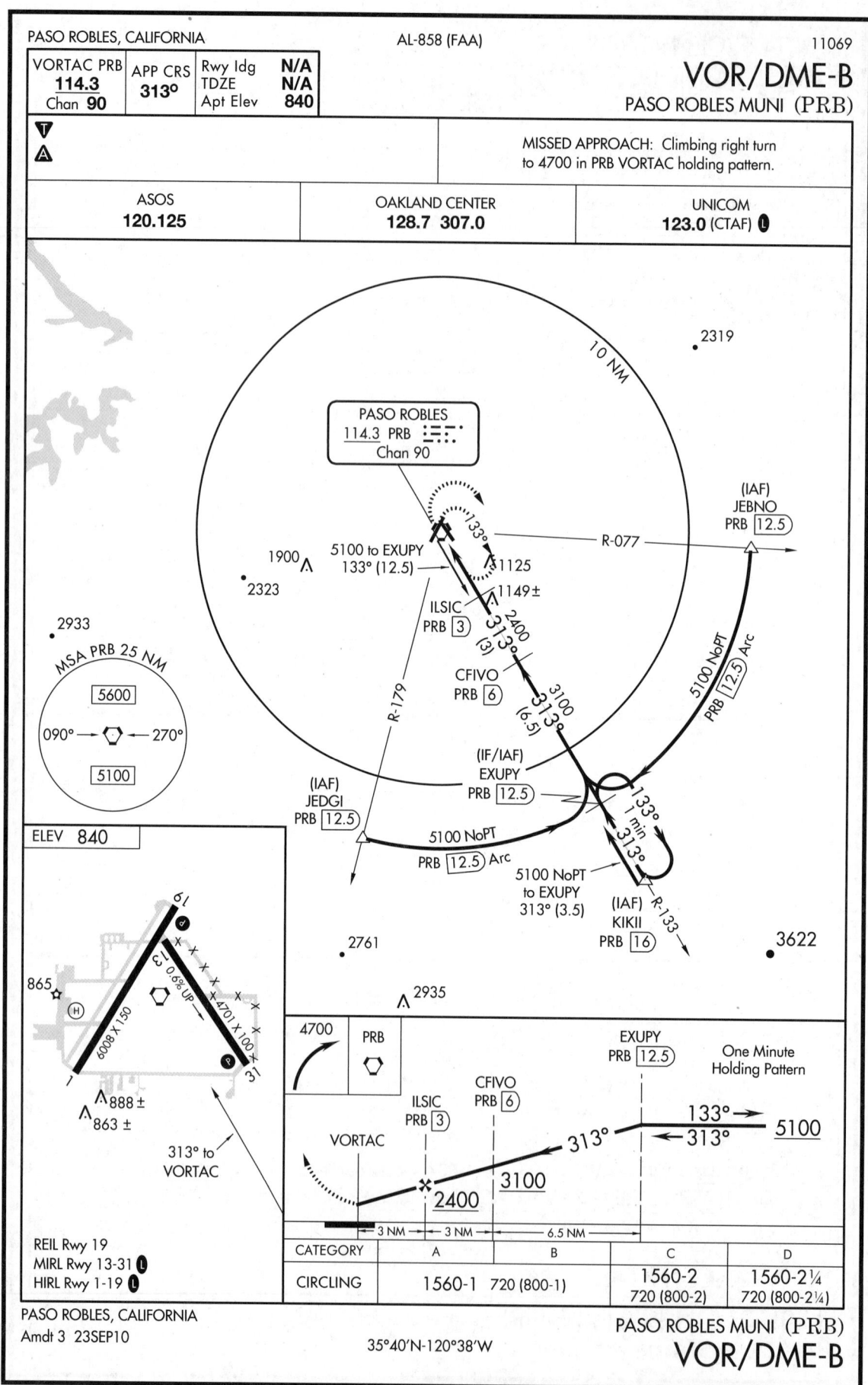

Figure 192. – VOR/DME-B (PRB).

CLIMB/DESCENT TABLE 10042

INSTRUMENT TAKEOFF OR APPROACH PROCEDURE CHARTS
RATE OF CLIMB/DESCENT TABLE

(ft. per min)

A rate of climb/descent table is provided for use in planning and executing climbs or descents under known or approximate ground speed conditions. It will be especially useful for approaches when the localizer only is used for course guidance. A best speed, power, altitude combination can be programmed which will result in a stable glide rate and altitude favorable for executing a landing if minimums exist upon breakout. Care should always be exercised so that minimum descent altitude and missed approach point are not exceeded.

	CLIMB/ DESCENT ANGLE (degrees and tenths)	ft/NM	GROUND SPEED (knots)										
			60	90	120	150	180	210	240	270	300	330	360
	2.0	210	210	320	425	530	635	743	850	955	1060	1165	1275
	2.5	265	265	400	530	665	795	930	1060	1195	1325	1460	1590
VERTICAL PATH ANGLE	2.7	287	287	430	574	717	860	1003	1147	1290	1433	1576	1720
	2.8	297	297	446	595	743	892	1041	1189	1338	1486	1635	1783
	2.9	308	308	462	616	770	924	1078	1232	1386	1539	1693	1847
	3.0	318	318	478	637	797	956	1115	1274	1433	1593	1752	1911
	3.1	329	329	494	659	823	988	1152	1317	1481	1646	1810	1975
	3.2	340	340	510	680	850	1020	1189	1359	1529	1699	1869	2039
	3.3	350	350	526	701	876	1052	1227	1402	1577	1752	1927	2103
	3.4	361	361	542	722	903	1083	1264	1444	1625	1805	1986	2166
	3.5	370	370	555	745	930	1115	1300	1485	1670	1860	2045	2230
	4.0	425	425	640	850	1065	1275	1490	1700	1915	2125	2340	2550
	4.5	480	480	715	955	1195	1435	1675	1915	2150	2390	2630	2870
	5.0	530	530	795	1065	1330	1595	1860	2125	2390	2660	2925	3190
	5.5	585	585	880	1170	1465	1755	2050	2340	2635	2925	3220	3510
	6.0	640	640	960	1275	1595	1915	2235	2555	2875	3195	3510	3830
	6.5	690	690	1040	1385	1730	2075	2425	2770	3115	3460	3805	4155
	7.0	745	745	1120	1490	1865	2240	2610	2985	3355	3730	4105	4475
	7.5	800	800	1200	1600	2000	2400	2800	3200	3600	4000	4400	4800
	8.0	855	855	1280	1710	2135	2560	2990	3415	3845	4270	4695	5125
	8.5	910	910	1360	1815	2270	2725	3180	3630	4085	4540	4995	5450
	9.0	960	960	1445	1925	2405	2885	3370	3850	4330	4810	5295	5775
	9.5	1015	1015	1525	2035	2540	3050	3560	4065	4575	5085	5590	6100
	10.0	1070	1070	1605	2145	2680	3215	3750	4285	4820	5355	5890	6430

CLIMB/DESCENT TABLE 10042

Legend 27. – Instrument Takeoff or Approach Procedure Charts, Rate-of-Climb/Descent Table.

11.5   HOT To/From ADS

Questions 32 through 37 pertain to an IFR flight from Hot Springs Memorial Field, Hot Springs, Arkansas, to the Dallas/Addison Airport, Dallas, Texas.

The figures provided for this flight are listed below and are presented at the end of the sequence of questions.

32. (Refer to Figure 34 on page 469.) For planning purposes, what is the highest usable altitude for an IFR flight on V573 from the HOT VORTAC to the TXK VORTAC?

A. 16,000 feet MSL.

B. 14,500 feet MSL.

C. 13,999 feet MSL.

Answer (A) is correct. (AIM Para 3-2-6)
   DISCUSSION: The VOR airway system consists of airways designated from 1,200 ft. AGL up to, but not including, 18,000 ft. MSL. Flying on V573 from HOT to TXK is a generally westerly course which requires an even-thousands altitude. Thus, 16,000 ft. MSL is the highest usable altitude.
   Answer (B) is incorrect. This is a VFR, not IFR, cruising altitude from 180° to 359°. **Answer (C) is incorrect.** IFR altitudes are even or odd thousands of feet.

33. (Refer to Figure 167 on page 470 and Figure 168 on page 471.) At which point does the BYP.BYP6 arrival begin?

A. At the LIT VORTAC.

B. At GLOVE intersection.

C. At the BYP VORTAC.

Answer (C) is correct. (ACUG)
   DISCUSSION: The arrival, in contrast to the transition, begins over the BYP VORTAC as explained in the written description in Fig. 168.
   Answer (A) is incorrect. The Little Rock transition, LIT.BYP6, begins over the LIT VORTAC. **Answer (B) is incorrect.** GLOVE INT. is an intersection along a feeder route within the LIT.BYP6 transition.

34. (Refer to Figure 171 on page 472.) Under which condition should the missed approach procedure for the RNAV(GPS) RWY 33 approach be initiated?

A. When passage of the MAP waypoint is shown on the ambiguity indicator.

B. After the MDA is reached and 1.8 DME fix from the MAP waypoint.

C. Immediately upon reaching 4.1 DME from the FAF.

Answer (A) is correct. (AIM Para 1-1-18)
   DISCUSSION: If a missed approach is necessary, the ambiguity indicator will show arrival and passage of the Missed Approach Waypoint (MAWP).
   Answer (B) is incorrect. There is no requirement to continue past the Missed Approach Waypoint (MAWP) by 1.8 DME before initiating the missed approach. The ambiguity indicator will show arrival and passage of the MAWP. It is at that point the missed approach can be initiated. **Answer (C) is incorrect.** Although the missed approach point is 4.1 DME from the FAF (PORTR), it is the ambiguity indicator's display of arrival and passage of the missed approach waypoint that establishes the position where the missed approach should be initiated.

35. (Refer to Figure 171 on page 472.) What is the MDA and visibility criteria respectively for the circling approach procedure?

    A. 1,240 feet MSL; 1/2 SM.

    B. 1,240 feet MSL; 1 SM.

    C. 1,280 feet MSL; 1 and 1/4 SM.

Answer (B) is correct. (ACUG)
    DISCUSSION: The MDA and visibility criteria are found in the minimums section of the RNAV (GPS) RWY 33 approach chart. The circling MDA and visibility criteria for Category A and B aircraft are 1,240 ft. MSL and 1 SM, respectively (note that the question does not specify the aircraft category).
    Answer (A) is incorrect. The minimum visibility is not shown to be 1/2 SM for any category of aircraft using the circling RNAV (GPS) RWY 33 approach into ADS. **Answer (C) is incorrect.** The minimum visibility is not shown to be 1 and 1/4 SM for any category of aircraft using the circling RNAV (GPS) RWY 33 approach into ADS.

36. (Refer to Figure 171 on page 472.) You are briefing the RNAV (GPS) RWY33 approach at ADS. Where would you plan to execute the missed approach?

    A. 4.1 DME from PORTR.

    B. RWY33 waypoint.

    C. 1,240 feet indicated on altimeter.

Answer (B) is correct. (FAA-H-8083-16B Chap 5)
    DISCUSSION: The RWY33 waypoint would be defined in the approach briefing as the beginning point for executing the missed approach procedure.
    Answer (A) is incorrect. The 4.1 DME from PORTR on a 335° course to RWY33 would be coincident with the point defined as the RWY33 waypoint. **Answer (C) is incorrect.** Depending on the altimeter setting used, 1,240 ft. would be the straight-in LNAV minimum descent altitude.

37. (Refer to Figure 175 on page 468 and Figure 174 on page 473.) When DFW is landing to the north, at CURLE, expect

    A. to be instructed to maintain 200 knots.

    B. to fly a course of 010°.

    C. radar vectors.

Answer (C) is correct. (FAA-H-8083-16B Chap 3)
    DISCUSSION: According to the arrival description in Fig. 175, "ALL AIRCRAFT LANDING NORTH; to CURLE INT, expect vectors to final approach course." Each aircraft landing north at CURLE intersection should expect vectors to final approach.
    Answer (A) is incorrect. There are no notes indicating that an airspeed of 200 knots is to be maintained upon arrival at CURLE. **Answer (B) is incorrect.** A heading of 010° is for nonturbojets landing south.

(JEN.JEN9) 09351

GLEN ROSE NINE ARRIVAL   ST-6039 (FAA)   DALLAS-FT. WORTH, TEXAS

ARRIVAL DESCRIPTION

<u>ABILENE TRANSITION (ABI.JEN9)</u>: From over ABI VORTAC via R-099 to GEENI INT, then via JEN R-267 to JEN VORTAC. Thence. . . .

<u>CENTEX TRANSITION (CWK.JEN9)</u>: From over CWK VORTAC via CWK R-321 and AGJ R-142 to AGJ VORTAC, then via AGJ R-350 to JUMBO INT, then via JEN R-197 to JEN VORTAC. Thence . . . .

<u>JUMBO TRANSITION (JUMBO.JEN9)</u>: From over JUMBO INT via JEN R-197 to JEN VORTAC. Thence . . . .

<u>SAN ANTONIO TRANSITION (SAT.JEN9)</u>: From over SAT VORTAC via SAT R-359 to JUMBO INT, then via JEN R-197 to JEN VORTAC. Thence . . . .

<u>WACO TRANSITION (ACT.JEN9)</u>: From over ACT VORTAC via ACT R-305 and JEN R-128 to JEN VORTAC. Thence. . . .

<u>WINK TRANSITION (INK.JEN9)</u>: From over INK VORTAC via INK R-071 and TQA R-254 to TQA VOR/DME, then via TQA R-082 to GEENI INT, then via JEN R-267 to JEN VORTAC. Thence. . . .

. . . . <u>ALL AIRCRAFT</u>: From over JEN VORTAC via JEN R-039, thence . . . .

<u>ALL AIRCRAFT LANDING NORTH</u>: To CURLE INT, expect vectors to final approach course.

<u>JETS LANDING SOUTH</u>: To DELMO, depart DELMO heading 355°.

For /E, /F, /G and /R (RNP 2.0) EQUIPMENT SUFFIXED AIRCRAFT: From over DELMO WP direct TEVON WP, expect vector to final approach course prior to TEVON WP. If not received by TEVON fly present heading.

<u>NON TURBOJETS LANDING SOUTH</u>: To CURLE INT, depart CURLE heading 010° for vectors to final approach course.

<u>AIRCRAFT LANDING DAL, ADS, TKI</u>: To DELMO INT, depart DELMO via FUZ R-171 to FUZ VORTAC then FUZ R-064 to HURBS INT, expect vectors to final approach course.

GLEN ROSE NINE ARRIVAL   DALLAS-FT. WORTH, TEXAS
(JEN.JEN9) 09351

Figure 175. – GLEN ROSE Nine Arrival (JEN.JEN9).

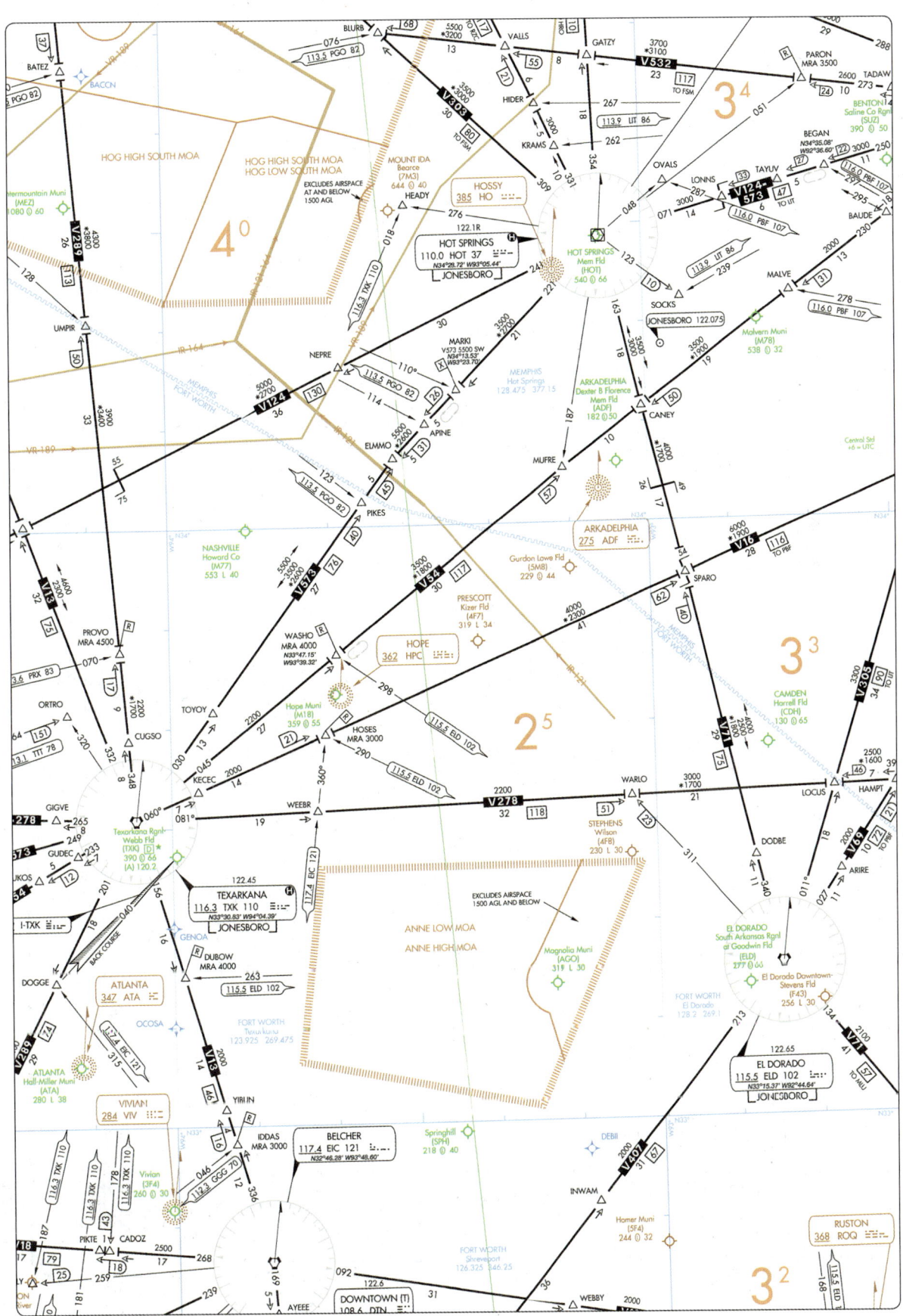

Figure 34. – En Route Low-Altitude Chart Segment.
NOTE: Chart is not to scale and should not be used for navigation. Chart is for testing purposes only.

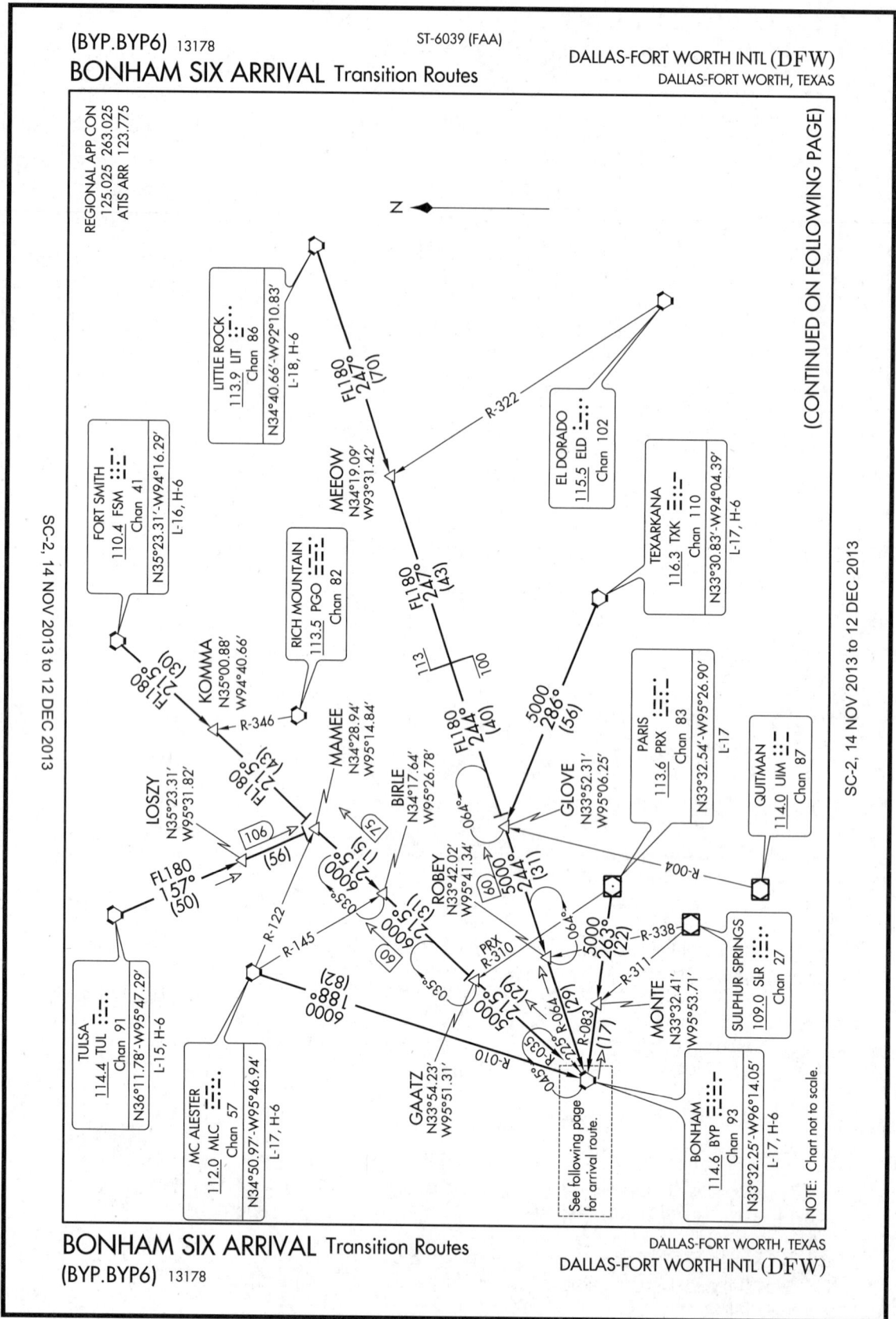

Figure 167. – BONHAM Six Arrival Transition Routes (BYP.BYP6) (DFW).

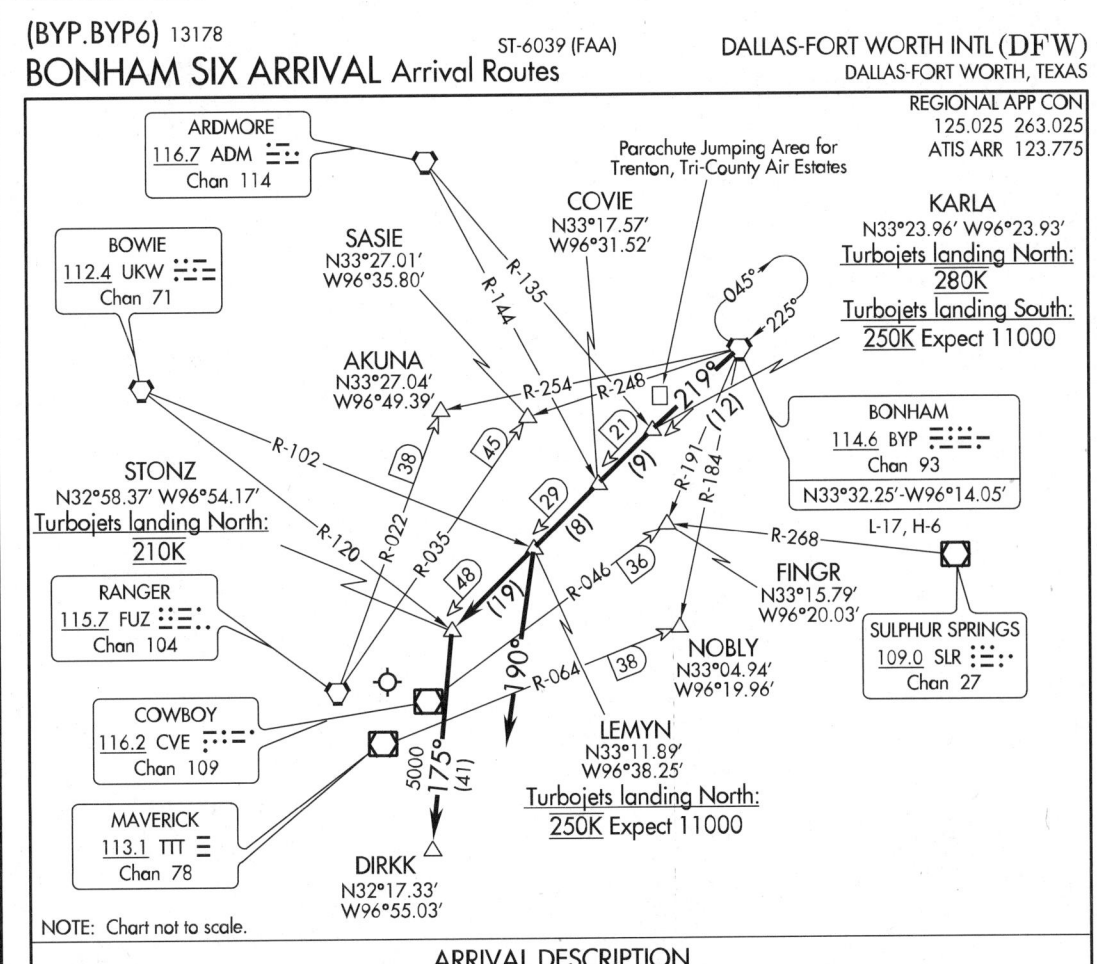

(BYP.BYP6) 13178
BONHAM SIX ARRIVAL Arrival Routes
ST-6039 (FAA)   DALLAS-FORT WORTH INTL (DFW)
DALLAS-FORT WORTH, TEXAS

REGIONAL APP CON
125.025 263.025
ATIS ARR 123.775

ARDMORE
116.7 ADM
Chan 114

Parachute Jumping Area for
Trenton, Tri-County Air Estates

COVIE
N33°17.57'
W96°31.52'

KARLA
N33°23.96' W96°23.93'
Turbojets landing North:
280K
Turbojets landing South:
250K Expect 11000

BOWIE
112.4 UKW
Chan 71

SASIE
N33°27.01'
W96°35.80'

AKUNA
N33°27.04'
W96°49.39'

BONHAM
114.6 BYP
Chan 93
N33°32.25'-W96°14.05'
L-17, H-6

STONZ
N32°58.37' W96°54.17'
Turbojets landing North:
210K

FINGR
N33°15.79'
W96°20.03'

RANGER
115.7 FUZ
Chan 104

SULPHUR SPRINGS
109.0 SLR
Chan 27

COWBOY
116.2 CVE
Chan 109

NOBLY
N33°04.94'
W96°19.96'

LEMYN
N33°11.89'
W96°38.25'
Turbojets landing North:
250K Expect 11000

MAVERICK
113.1 TTT
Chan 78

DIRKK
N32°17.33'
W96°55.03'

NOTE: Chart not to scale.

ARRIVAL DESCRIPTION

__FORT SMITH TRANSITION (FSM.BYP6):__ From over FSM VORTAC on FSM R-215 to
MAMEE INT, then on BYP R-035 to BYP VORTAC. Thence....
__LITTLE ROCK TRANSITION (LIT.BYP6):__ From over LIT VORTAC on LIT R-247 to MEEOW INT
then on LIT R-247 and BYP R-064 to GLOVE INT, then on BYP R-064 to BYP VORTAC. Thence...
__MC ALESTER TRANSITION (MLC.BYP6):__ From over MLC VORTAC on MLC R-188
and BYP R-010 to BYP VORTAC. Thence....
__PARIS TRANSITION (PRX.BYP6):__ From over PRX VOR/DME on PRX R-263 to MONTE INT
then on BYP R-083 to BYP VORTAC. Thence....
__TEXARKANA TRANSITION (TXK.BYP6):__ From over TXK VORTAC on TXK R-286 to GLOVE INT
then on BYP R-064 to BYP VORTAC. Thence....
__TULSA TRANSITION (TUL.BYP6):__ From over TUL VORTAC on TUL R-157 to MAMEE
INT, then on BYP R-035 to BYP VORTAC. Thence....

.... __ALL AIRCRAFT:__ From over BYP VORTAC on BYP R-219, thence....

__ALL AIRCRAFT LANDING SOUTH:__ To LEMYN INT, expect vectors to final approach course.
__JETS LANDING NORTH:__ FOR /E, /F, /G, and /R (RNP-2.0) EQUIPPED AIRCRAFT:
From over STONZ INT direct DIRKK, expect vector to final approach course prior to DIRKK, if
not received by DIRKK fly present heading.
__ALL OTHERS:__ To STONZ depart STONZ heading 175° for vector to final approach course.
__PROPS LANDING NORTH:__ Depart LEMYN INT heading 190°, expect vectors to final
approach course.

BONHAM SIX ARRIVAL Arrival Routes
(BYP.BYP6) 13178

DALLAS-FORT WORTH, TEXAS
DALLAS-FORT WORTH INTL (DFW)

Figure 168. – BONHAM Six Arrival Routes (BYP.BYP6) (DFW).

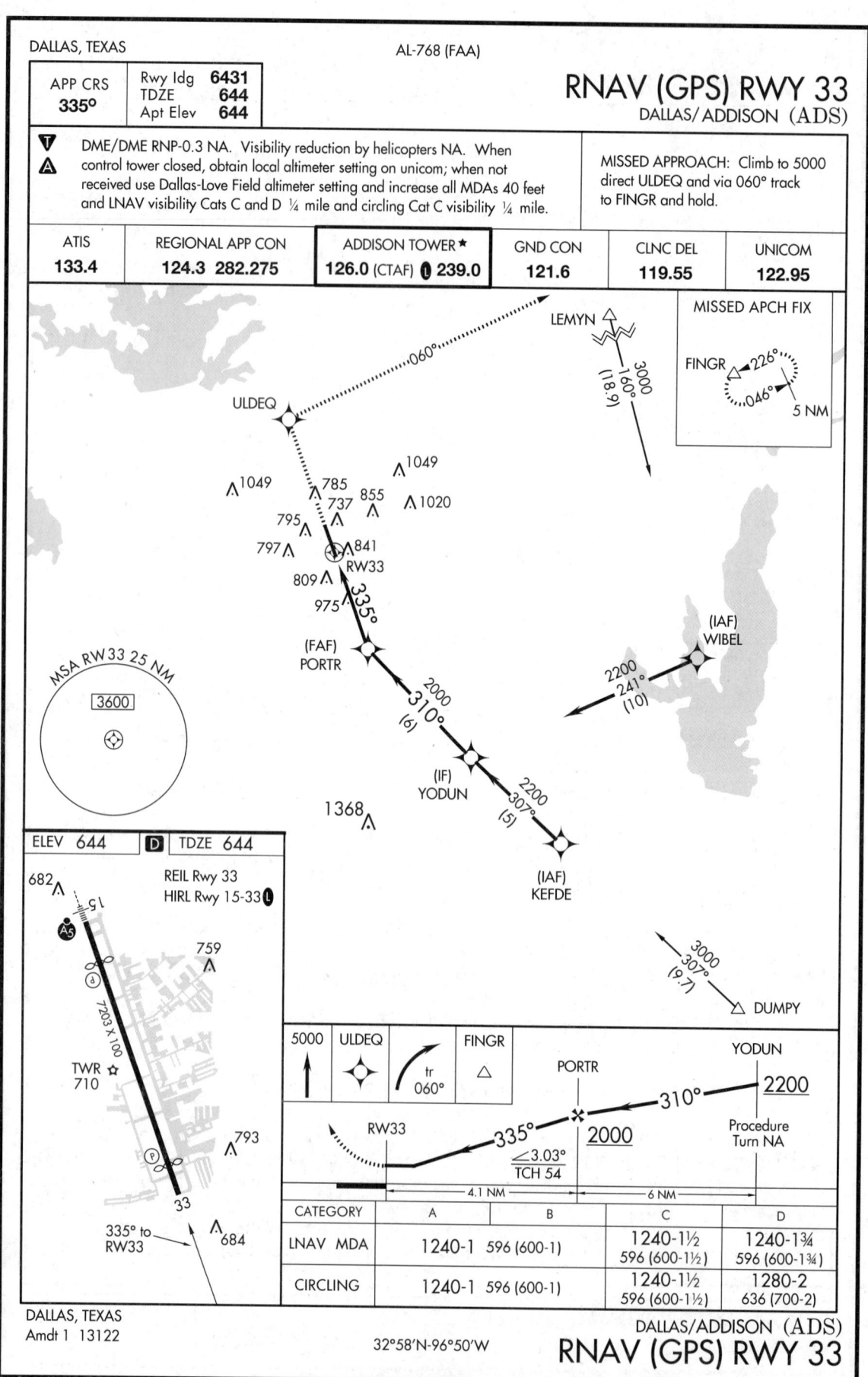

Figure 171. – RNAV (GPS) RWY 33 (ADS).

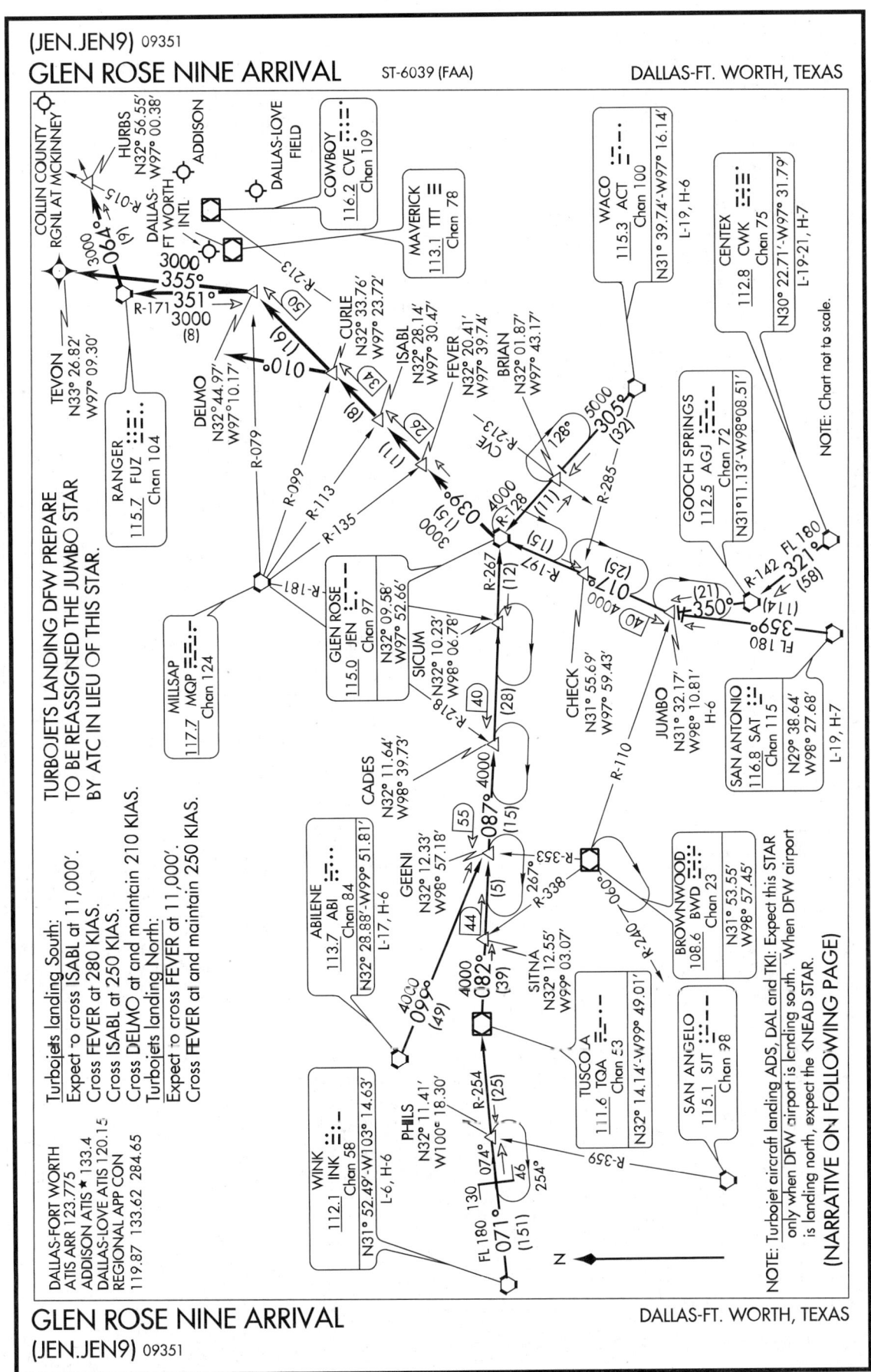

Figure 174. – GLEN ROSE Nine Arrival (JEN.JEN9).

11.6 21XS To/From DFW

Questions 38 through 45 pertain to an IFR flight from Big Spring McMahon-Wrinkle Airport, Big Spring, Texas, to the Dallas-Ft. Worth International Airport, Ft. Worth, Texas.

The figures provided for this flight are listed below and are presented at the end of the sequence of questions.

Fig.	Page	
40	476	En Route Low-Altitude Chart Segment
174	477	GLEN ROSE Nine Arrival (JEN.JEN9)
175	478	GLEN ROSE Nine Arrival (JEN.JEN9)
177	479	Converging ILS RWY 36L (DFW)
Legend 27	480	Instrument Takeoff or Approach Procedure Charts, Rate-of-Climb/ Descent Table

38. (Refer to Figure 40 on page 476.) For planning purposes, what is the highest usable altitude for an IFR flight on V16 from the BGS VORTAC to ABI VORTAC?

A. 17,000 feet MSL.

B. 18,000 feet MSL.

C. 6,500 feet MSL.

Answer (A) is correct. (AIM Para 3-2-6)
DISCUSSION: The VOR airway system consists of airways designated from 1,200 ft. AGL up to, but not including, 18,000 ft. MSL.
Answer (B) is incorrect. Victor airways go up through 17,999 ft. but do not include 18,000 ft. **Answer (C) is incorrect.** The altitude of 6,500 ft. is the MRA at LORAN intersection.

39. (Refer to Figure 174 on page 477 and Figure 175 on page 478.) At which point does the JEN.JEN9 arrival begin?

A. ABI VORTAC.

B. GLEN ROSE VORTAC.

C. DELMO intersection.

Answer (B) is correct. (ACUG)
DISCUSSION: The arrival, in contrast to the transition, begins over the JEN VORTAC, as explained in the written description in Fig. 175.
Answer (A) is incorrect. The ABI VORTAC is the beginning of the Abilene transition. **Answer (C) is incorrect.** DELMO intersection is part, not the beginning, of the JEN.JEN9 arrival.

40. (Refer to Figure 174 on page 477 and Figure 175 on page 478.) Which frequency would you anticipate using to contact Regional Approach Control? (GLEN ROSE NINE ARRIVAL).

A. 123.775

B. 115.0

C. 119.87

Answer (C) is correct. (ACUG)
DISCUSSION: The upper left-hand corner of the STAR chart (Fig. 174) shows the pertinent frequencies to be used. The appropriate approach frequency is 119.87 or 133.62. Only 119.87 is an answer choice.
Answer (A) is incorrect. This frequency is the ATIS. **Answer (B) is incorrect.** This frequency is the JEN VOR.

41. (Refer to Figure 174 on page 477 and Figure 175 on page 478.) On which heading should you plan to depart DELMO intersection?

A. 016°.

B. 039°.

C. 355°.

Answer (C) is correct. (ACUG)
DISCUSSION: The arrival indicates that you should maintain a heading of 355° after DELMO.
Answer (A) is incorrect. This heading is not an applicable heading in this STAR. **Answer (B) is incorrect.** This heading is the course from JEN to DELMO INT., not after DELMO INT.

42. (Refer to Figure 177 on page 479.) What is the difference in elevation (in feet MSL) between the airport elevation and the THRE for RWY 36L?

A. 25 feet.

B. 18 feet.

C. No difference.

Answer (A) is correct. (ACUG)
 DISCUSSION: The airport elevation (607 feet) and the THRE (582 feet) is shown in the top of the airport diagram. The difference between the two is 25 feet (607 – 582).
 Answer (B) is incorrect. The difference of 607 and 582 is 25 feet, not 18 feet. **Answer (C) is incorrect.** The difference is shown in the top of the airport diagram.

43. (Refer to Figure 177 on page 479.) Which navigational information and services would be available to the pilot when using the localizer frequency?

A. Localizer and glide slope, DME, TACAN with no voice capability.

B. Localizer information only, ATIS and DME are available.

C. Localizer and glide slope, DME, and no voice capability.

Answer (C) is correct. (ACUG)
 DISCUSSION: ILS RWY 36L is an ILS (localizer and glide slope). On the NOS chart, a channel number indicates DME. The line under the I-BXN frequency 111.9 means no voice capability.
 Answer (A) is incorrect. There is no TACAN indicated in the IAP chart. TACAN is the military version of VOR/DME. **Answer (B) is incorrect.** It is an ILS approach with glide slope.

44. (Refer to Figure 177 on page 479.) Approaching DFW from Abilene and preparing for arrival, which frequencies will you use for regional approach control, control tower, and ground control, respectively, when landing RWY 36?

A. 118.425; 127.5; 128.25.

B. 119.05; 126.55; 121.8.

C. 118.425; 124.15; 121.85.

Answer (C) is correct. (ACUG)
 DISCUSSION: The briefing strip of the instrument approach chart provides 118.425 as the regional approach control frequency. The corresponding tower and ground frequencies are then the west side frequencies of 124.15 and 121.85.
 Answer (A) is incorrect. Although the regional approach control frequency of 118.425 is accurate, the tower frequency available is the east frequency, and 128.25 is the clearance delivery frequency. **Answer (B) is incorrect.** The regional approach control frequency is 118.425, and the tower and ground control frequencies of 126.55 and 121.8 are east side frequencies.

45. (Refer to Figure 177 on page 479 and Legend 27 on page 480.) What rate of descent should you plan to use initially to establish the glidepath for the ILS RWY 36L approach? (Use 120 knots ground speed.)

A. 425 feet per minute.

B. 530 feet per minute.

C. 637 feet per minute.

Answer (C) is correct. (ACUG)
 DISCUSSION: The profile view of the IAP chart (Fig. 177) shows a glide slope angle of 3.00°. Legend 27 gives rates of descent based on various glide slope angles and ground speeds. Find the 3.0° on the left margin and move right to the 120-kt. groundspeed column to determine a rate of descent of 637 fpm.
 Answer (A) is incorrect. This is the required rate of descent at 120-kt. groundspeed on a 2.0°, not 3.0°, glide slope. **Answer (B) is incorrect.** This is the required rate of descent at 120-kt. groundspeed on a 2.5°, not 3.0°, glide slope.

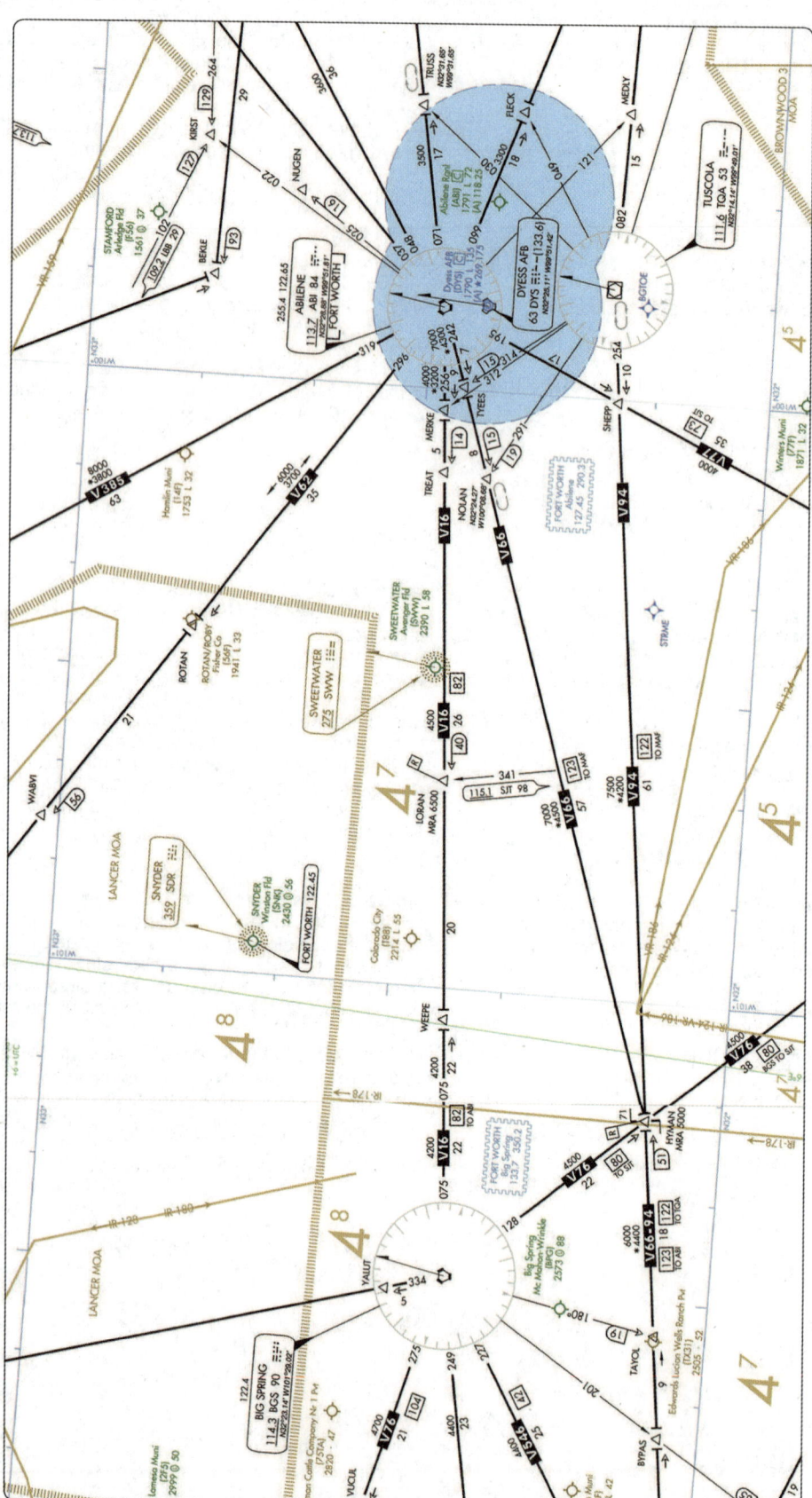

Figure 40. – En Route Low-Altitude Chart Segment.
NOTE: Chart is not to scale and should not be used for navigation. Chart is for testing purposes only.

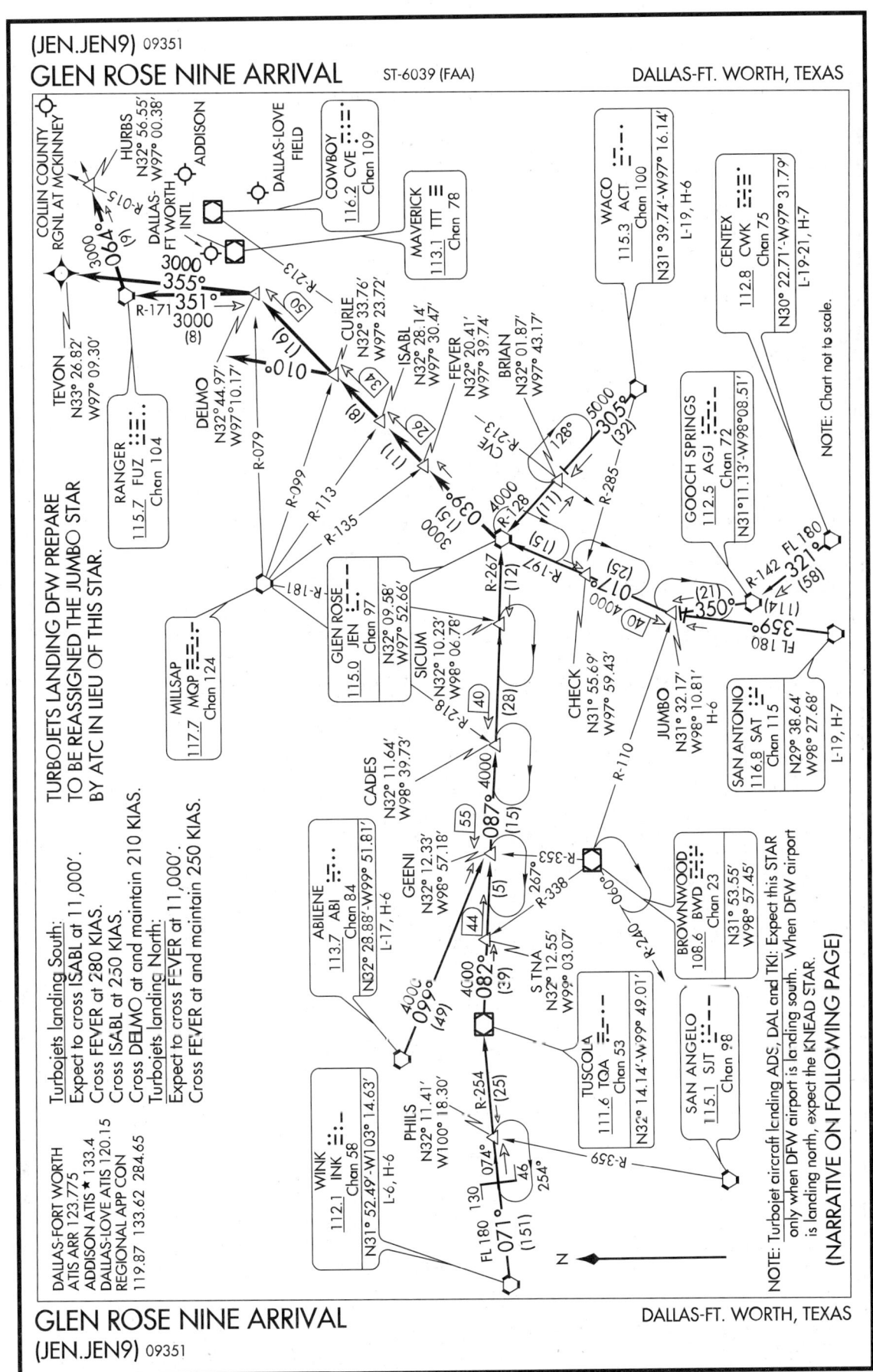

Figure 174. – GLEN ROSE Nine Arrival (JEN.JEN9).

(JEN.JEN9) 09351
GLEN ROSE NINE ARRIVAL   ST-6039 (FAA)   DALLAS-FT. WORTH, TEXAS

ARRIVAL DESCRIPTION

ABILENE TRANSITION (ABI.JEN9): From over ABI VORTAC via R-099 to GEENI INT, then via JEN R-267 to JEN VORTAC. Thence. . . .

CENTEX TRANSITION (CWK.JEN9): From over CWK VORTAC via CWK R-321 and AGJ R-142 to AGJ VORTAC, then via AGJ R-350 to JUMBO INT, then via JEN R-197 to JEN VORTAC. Thence . . . .

JUMBO TRANSITION (JUMBO.JEN9): From over JUMBO INT via JEN R-197 to JEN VORTAC. Thence . . . .

SAN ANTONIO TRANSITION (SAT.JEN9): From over SAT VORTAC via SAT R-359 to JUMBO INT, then via JEN R-197 to JEN VORTAC. Thence . . . .

WACO TRANSITION (ACT.JEN9): From over ACT VORTAC via ACT R-305 and JEN R-128 to JEN VORTAC. Thence. . . .

WINK TRANSITION (INK.JEN9): From over INK VORTAC via INK R-071 and TQA R-254 to TQA VOR/DME, then via TQA R-082 to GEENI INT, then via JEN R-267 to JEN VORTAC. Thence. . . .

. . . . ALL AIRCRAFT: From over JEN VORTAC via JEN R-039, thence . . . .

ALL AIRCRAFT LANDING NORTH: To CURLE INT, expect vectors to final approach course.

JETS LANDING SOUTH: To DELMO, depart DELMO heading 355°.
For /E, /F, /G and /R (RNP 2.0) EQUIPMENT SUFFIXED AIRCRAFT: From over DELMO WP direct TEVON WP, expect vector to final approach course prior to TEVON WP. If not received by TEVON fly present heading.
NON TURBOJETS LANDING SOUTH: To CURLE INT, depart CURLE heading 010° for vectors to final approach course.

AIRCRAFT LANDING DAL, ADS, TKI: To DELMO INT, depart DELMO via FUZ R-171 to FUZ VORTAC then FUZ R-064 to HURBS INT, expect vectors to final approach course.

GLEN ROSE NINE ARRIVAL   DALLAS-FT. WORTH, TEXAS
(JEN.JEN9) 09351

Figure 175. – GLEN ROSE Nine Arrival (JEN.JEN9).

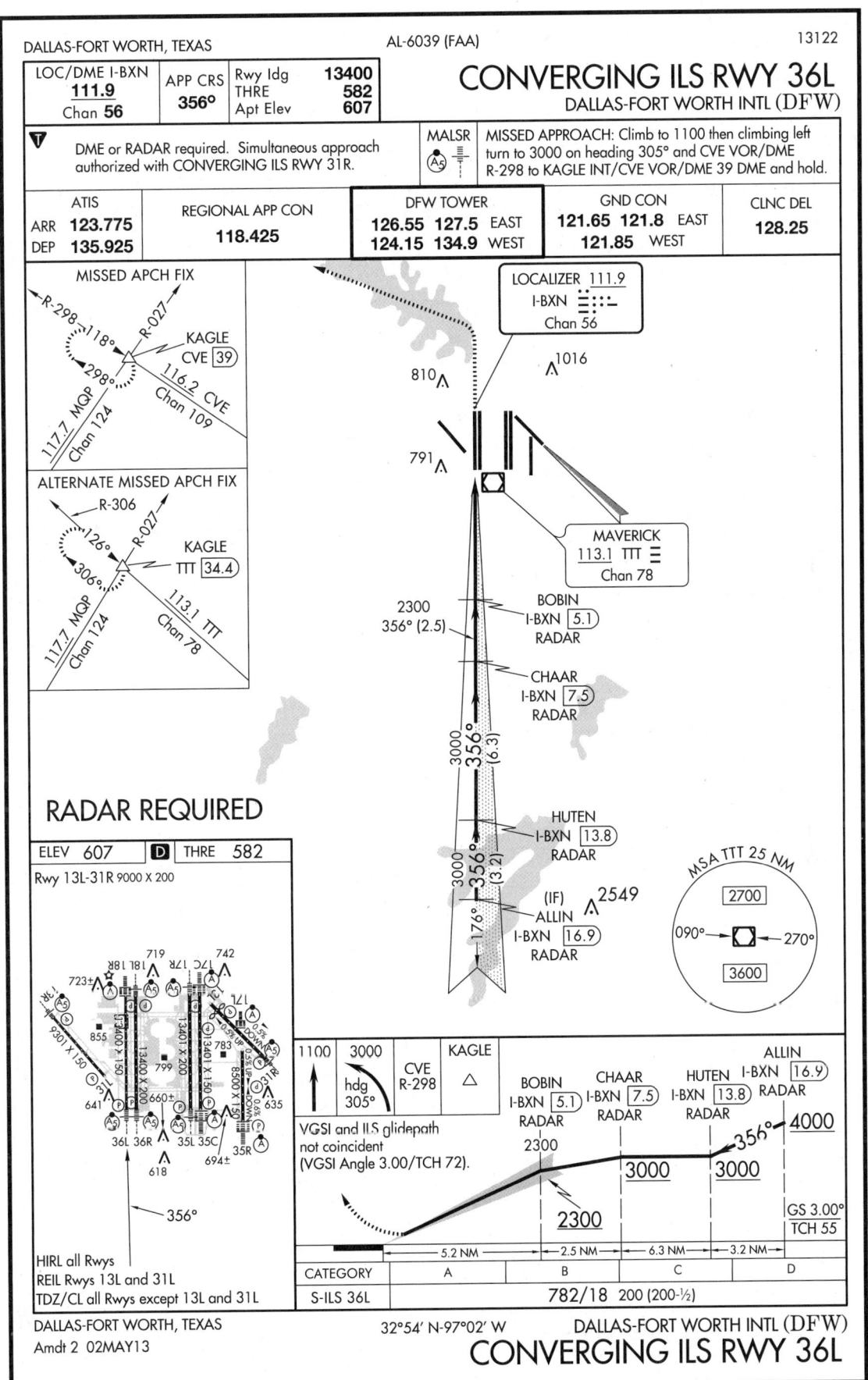

Figure 177. – Converging ILS RWY 36L (DFW).

CLIMB/DESCENT TABLE 10042

INSTRUMENT TAKEOFF OR APPROACH PROCEDURE CHARTS
RATE OF CLIMB/DESCENT TABLE
(ft. per min)

A rate of climb/descent table is provided for use in planning and executing climbs or descents under known or approximate ground speed conditions. It will be especially useful for approaches when the localizer only is used for course guidance. A best speed, power, altitude combination can be programmed which will result in a stable glide rate and altitude favorable for executing a landing if minimums exist upon breakout. Care should always be exercised so that minimum descent altitude and missed approach point are not exceeded.

CLIMB/DESCENT ANGLE (degrees and tenths)		ft/NM	GROUND SPEED (knots)										
			60	90	120	150	180	210	240	270	300	330	360
2.0		210	210	320	425	530	635	743	850	955	1060	1165	1275
2.5		265	265	400	530	665	795	930	1060	1195	1325	1460	1590
V E R T I C A L P A T H A N G L E	2.7	287	287	430	574	717	860	1003	1147	1290	1433	1576	1720
	2.8	297	297	446	595	743	892	1041	1189	1338	1486	1635	1783
	2.9	308	308	462	616	770	924	1078	1232	1386	1539	1693	1847
	3.0	318	318	478	637	797	956	1115	1274	1433	1593	1752	1911
	3.1	329	329	494	659	823	988	1152	1317	1481	1646	1810	1975
	3.2	340	340	510	680	850	1020	1189	1359	1529	1699	1869	2039
	3.3	350	350	526	701	876	1052	1227	1402	1577	1752	1927	2103
	3.4	361	361	542	722	903	1083	1264	1444	1625	1805	1986	2166
3.5		370	370	555	745	930	1115	1300	1485	1670	1860	2045	2230
4.0		425	425	640	850	1065	1275	1490	1700	1915	2125	2340	2550
4.5		480	480	715	955	1195	1435	1675	1915	2150	2390	2630	2870
5.0		530	530	795	1065	1330	1595	1860	2125	2390	2660	2925	3190
5.5		585	585	880	1170	1465	1755	2050	2340	2635	2925	3220	3510
6.0		640	640	960	1275	1595	1915	2235	2555	2875	3195	3510	3830
6.5		690	690	1040	1385	1730	2075	2425	2770	3115	3460	3805	4155
7.0		745	745	1120	1490	1865	2240	2610	2985	3355	3730	4105	4475
7.5		800	800	1200	1600	2000	2400	2800	3200	3600	4000	4400	4800
8.0		855	855	1280	1710	2135	2560	2990	3415	3845	4270	4695	5125
8.5		910	910	1360	1815	2270	2725	3180	3630	4085	4540	4995	5450
9.0		960	960	1445	1925	2405	2885	3370	3850	4330	4810	5295	5775
9.5		1015	1015	1525	2035	2540	3050	3560	4065	4575	5085	5590	6100
10.0		1070	1070	1605	2145	2680	3215	3750	4285	4820	5355	5890	6430

CLIMB/DESCENT TABLE 10042

Legend 27. – Instrument Takeoff or Approach Procedure Charts, Rate-of-Climb/Descent Table.

11.7 4N1 To/From BDL

Questions 46 through 53 pertain to an IFR flight from Greenwood Lake Airport (4N1), West Milford, New Jersey, to the Bradley International Airport, Windsor Locks, Connecticut.

The figures provided for this flight are listed below and are presented throughout the sequence of questions.

46. (Refer to Figure 71A below, and Figure 71 on page 482.) What is your position relative to the FLOSI intersection northbound on V213 airway?

A. West of V213 and approaching the FLOSI intersection.

B. East of V213 and approaching the FLOSI intersection.

C. West of V213 and past the FLOSI intersection.

Answer (A) is correct. (FAA-H-8083-15B Chap 9)
DISCUSSION: VOR-1 is tuned to IGN VORTAC (117.6) with an OBS setting of 265°. The FROM indication and right needle deflection indicate you are south of the IGN R-265 and thus approaching it. VOR-2 is tuned to SAX VORTAC (115.7) with an OBS setting of 029°. The FROM indication and right needle deflection indicate you are to the left or west of the SAX R-029.

Answer (B) is incorrect. A left, not right, needle deflection in VOR-2 would indicate right or east of the V213. **Answer (C) is incorrect.** A left, not right, needle deflection in VOR-1 would indicate that you have passed FLOSI intersection.

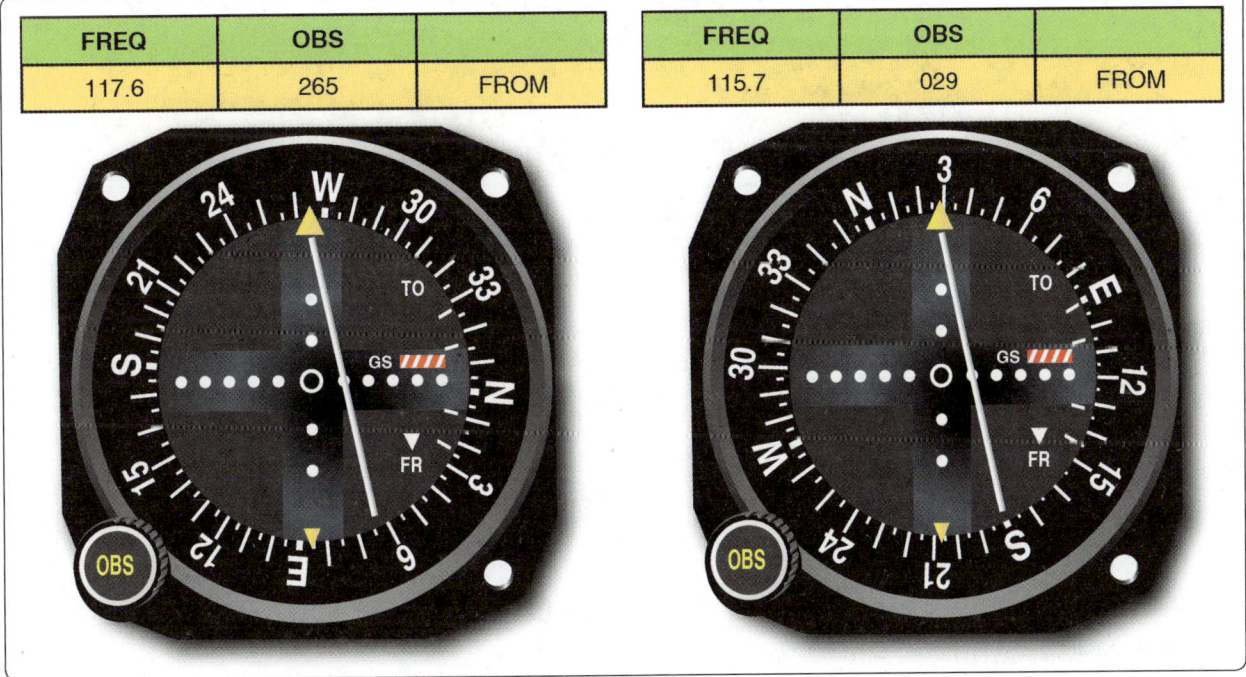

Figure 71A. – CDI and OBS Indicators.

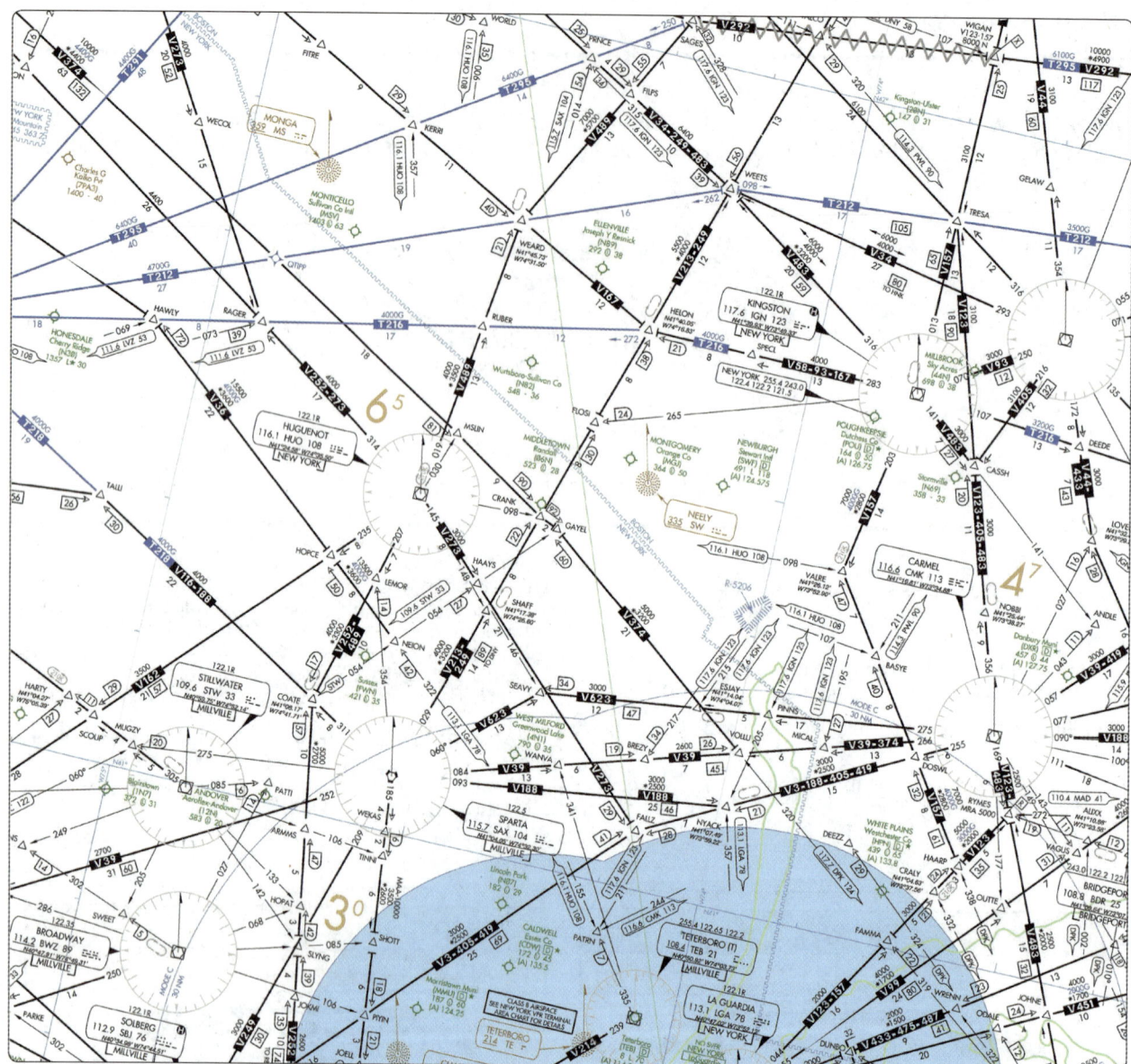

Figure 71. – En Route Low-Altitude Chart Segment.
NOTE: Chart is not to scale and should not be used for navigation. Chart is for testing purposes only.

47. (Refer to Figure 210 on page 486.) At which indication or occurrence should you initiate the published missed approach procedure for the ILS RWY 6 approach provided the runway environment is not in sight?

A. When reaching 373 feet MSL indicated altitude.

B. When 3 minutes (at 90 knots ground speed) have expired or reaching 373 feet MSL, whichever occurs first.

C. Upon reaching 373 feet AGL.

Answer (A) is correct. (ACUG)
DISCUSSION: When flying the ILS RWY 6 approach, you should execute a missed approach when you have reached the decision altitude of 373 feet MSL.
Answer (B) is incorrect. The ILS is a precision approach and timing is only for the backup localizer approach.
Answer (C) is incorrect. The decision altitude is 373 feet MSL, not AGL.

48. (Refer to Figure 210 on page 486.) What is the minimum altitude at which you should intercept the glide slope on the ILS RWY 6 approach procedure?

A. 3,000 feet MSL.

B. 1,800 feet MSL.

C. 1,080 feet MSL.

Answer (B) is correct. (ACUG)
 DISCUSSION: In the profile section of the IAP chart, there is an <u>1800</u> with a lightning bolt pointing to the glide slope. This is the glide slope intercept altitude and final approach fix for precision approaches. Thus, here, one should not intercept below 1,800 feet MSL.
 Answer (A) is incorrect. This is the minimum altitude in the holding pattern at PENNA INT. **Answer (C) is incorrect.** This is the minimum altitude at which you will cross JETIX when descending on the glide slope.

49. (Refer to Figure 210 on page 486.) What is the touchdown zone elevation for RWY 6?

A. 173 feet MSL.

B. 200 feet AGL.

C. 270 feet MSL.

Answer (A) is correct. (ACUG)
 DISCUSSION: The IAP chart shows the TDZE in the airport diagram. The TDZE is 173 feet MSL.
 Answer (B) is incorrect. This is the HAT (height above touchdown) at the DH on the ILS. **Answer (C) is incorrect.** This is the height of an obstruction near the approach end of RWY 6.

50. (Refer to Figure 210 on page 486 and Legend 27 on page 487.) Using an average ground speed of 90 knots on the final approach segment, what rate of descent should be used initially to establish the glidepath for the ILS RWY 6 approach procedure?

A. 395 feet per minute.

B. 480 feet per minute.

C. 555 feet per minute.

Answer (B) is correct. (ACUG)
 DISCUSSION: The profile view of the IAP chart shows a glide slope angle of 3.00°. Legend 27 gives rates of descent based on various glide slope angles and groundspeeds. Find the 3.0° angle of descent on the left margin and move right to the 90-knot groundspeed column to determine a rate of descent of 480 feet per minute.
 Answer (A) is incorrect. This is the required rate of descent at a groundspeed of 75 knots, not 90 knots. **Answer (C) is incorrect.** This is the required rate of descent at a groundspeed of 105 knots, not 90 knots.

51. (Refer to Figure 210 on page 486 and Legend 30 on page 488.) Which runway and landing environment lighting is available for approach and landing on RWY 6 at Bradley International?

A. HIRL, REIL, and VASI.

B. HIRL and VASI.

C. ALSF2 and HIRL.

Answer (C) is correct. (ACUG)
 DISCUSSION: The airport diagram in Fig. 210 has a circle enclosing the letter "A," with a dot above it, near the approach end of RWY 6. Legend 30 indicates that this means ALSF-2 approach lighting. Information listed at the bottom right corner of the airport diagram (Fig. 210) indicates that RWY 6-24 has high-intensity runway lights (HIRL).
 Answer (A) is incorrect. REIL and VASI are not indicated for RWY 6. **Answer (B) is incorrect.** VASI is not indicated for RWY 6.

52. (Refer to Figure 210 on page 486 and Legend 32 on page 489.) After passing the OM, Bradley Approach Control advises you that the MM on the ILS RWY 6 approach is inoperative. Under these circumstances, what adjustments, if any, are required to be made to the DH and visibility?

A. DH 424/24.

B. No adjustments are required.

C. DH 374/24.

Answer (B) is correct. (ACUG)
 DISCUSSION: Refer to Legend 32, Inoperative Components or Visual Aids Table. Since the MM is not listed in the table, no adjustments are required.
 Answer (A) is incorrect. No adjustments are required due to an inoperative MM. **Answer (C) is incorrect.** No adjustments are required due to an inoperative MM.

53. (Refer to Figure 208 on page 484 and Figure 209 on page 485.) At which location or condition does the STELA.STELA1 arrival begin?

A. CAM VORTAC.

B. CANAN intersection.

C. STELA intersection.

Answer (B) is correct. (ACUG)
 DISCUSSION: The STELA.STELA1 arrival on Fig. 208 is depicted with a bold line beginning at CANAN, meaning the CANAN intersection is the start of the arrival. In addition, the transition and arrival descriptions on Fig. 209 indicate "to CANAN INT. Thence . . ." and "from over CANAN INT via. . . ." Thus, the arrival begins over the CANAN intersection.
 Answer (A) is incorrect. The CAM VORTAC is part of a transition. **Answer (C) is incorrect.** The STELA intersection is in the middle of the arrival route.

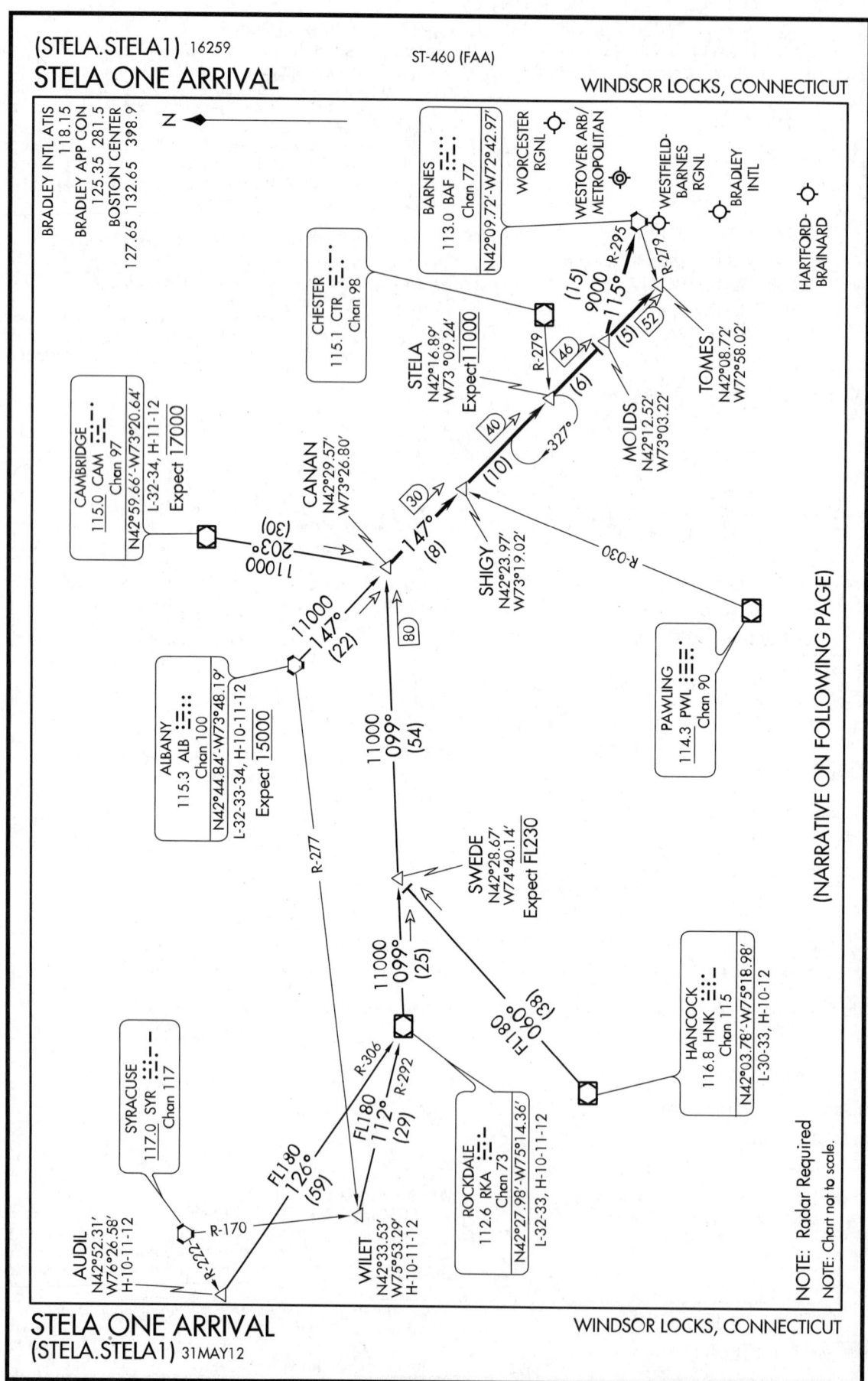

Figure 208. – STELA One Arrival (STELA.STELA1).

(STELA.STELA1) 16259   ST-460 (FAA)

STELA ONE ARRIVAL
WINDSOR LOCKS, CONNECTICUT

ARRIVAL ROUTE DESCRIPTION

<u>ALBANY TRANSITION (ALB.STELA1)</u>: From over ALB VORTAC via ALB R-147 to CANAN INT. Thence. . . .

<u>AUDIL TRANSITION (AUDIL.STELA1)</u>: From over AUDIL INT via RKA R-306 to RKA VOR/DME, then via RKA R-099 to CANAN INT. Thence. . . .

<u>CAMBRIDGE TRANSITION (CAM.STELA1)</u>: From over CAM VOR/DME via CAM R-203 to CANAN INT. Thence. . . .

<u>HANCOCK TRANSITION (HNK.STELA1)</u>: From over HNK VOR/DME via HNK R-060 to SWEDE INT, then via RKA R-099 to CANAN INT. Thence. . . .

<u>WILET TRANSITION (WILET.STELA1)</u>: From over WILET INT via RKA R-292 to RKA VOR/DME, then via RKA R-099 TO CANAN INT. Thence. . . .

<u>KBDL and KHFD ARRIVALS:</u> From over CANAN INT via ALB R-147 to TOMES INT. Expect radar vectors to final approach course prior to TOMES INT.

<u>KBAF, KCEF and KORH ARRIVALS:</u> From over CANAN INT via ALB R-147 to MOLDS INT. Then via BAF R-295 to BAF VORTAC. Expect radar vectors to final approach course prior to BAF VORTAC.

STELA ONE ARRIVAL
(STELA.STELA1) 31MAY12
WINDSOR LOCKS, CONNECTICUT

Figure 209. – STELA One Arrival (STELA.STELA1).

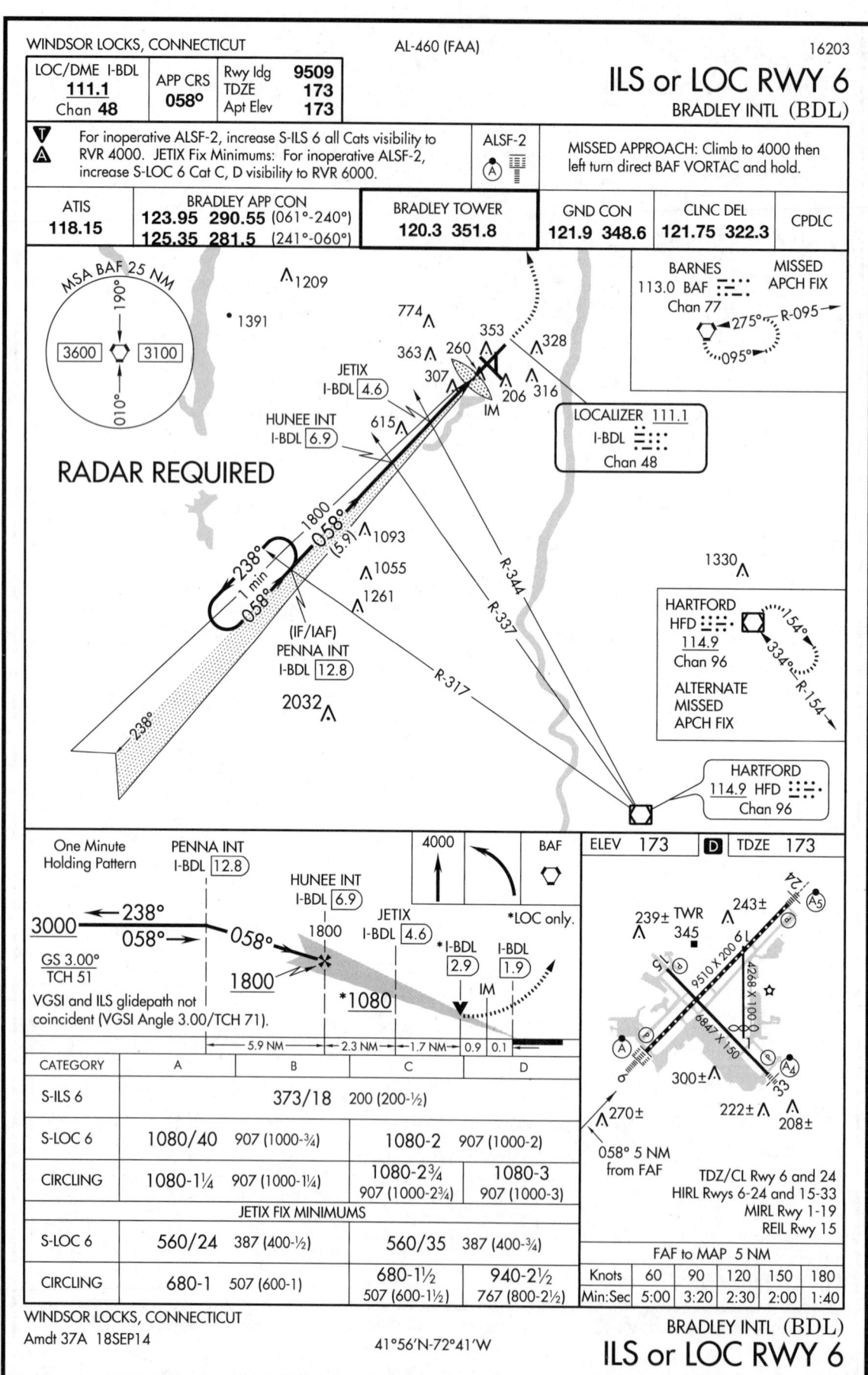

Figure 210. – ILS or LOC RWY 6 (CAT I) (BDL).

CLIMB/DESCENT TABLE 10042

INSTRUMENT TAKEOFF OR APPROACH PROCEDURE CHARTS
RATE OF CLIMB/DESCENT TABLE
(ft. per min)

A rate of climb/descent table is provided for use in planning and executing climbs or descents under known or approximate ground speed conditions. It will be especially useful for approaches when the localizer only is used for course guidance. A best speed, power, altitude combination can be programmed which will result in a stable glide rate and altitude favorable for executing a landing if minimums exist upon breakout. Care should always be exercised so that minimum descent altitude and missed approach point are not exceeded.

CLIMB/DESCENT ANGLE (degrees and tenths)	ft/NM	GROUND SPEED (knots)										
		60	90	120	150	180	210	240	270	300	330	360
2.0	210	210	320	425	530	635	743	850	955	1060	1165	1275
2.5	265	265	400	530	665	795	930	1060	1195	1325	1460	1590
2.7	287	287	430	574	717	860	1003	1147	1290	1433	1576	1720
2.8	297	297	446	595	743	892	1041	1189	1338	1486	1635	1783
2.9	308	308	462	616	770	924	1078	1232	1386	1539	1693	1847
3.0	318	318	478	637	797	956	1115	1274	1433	1593	1752	1911
3.1	329	329	494	659	823	988	1152	1317	1481	1646	1810	1975
3.2	340	340	510	680	850	1020	1189	1359	1529	1699	1869	2039
3.3	350	350	526	701	876	1052	1227	1402	1577	1752	1927	2103
3.4	361	361	542	722	903	1083	1264	1444	1625	1805	1986	2166
3.5	370	370	555	745	930	1115	1300	1485	1670	1860	2045	2230
4.0	425	425	640	850	1065	1275	1490	1700	1915	2125	2340	2550
4.5	480	480	715	955	1195	1435	1675	1915	2150	2390	2630	2870
5.0	530	530	795	1065	1330	1595	1860	2125	2390	2660	2925	3190
5.5	585	585	880	1170	1465	1755	2050	2340	2635	2925	3220	3510
6.0	640	640	960	1275	1595	1915	2235	2555	2875	3195	3510	3830
6.5	690	690	1040	1385	1730	2075	2425	2770	3115	3460	3805	4155
7.0	745	745	1120	1490	1865	2240	2610	2985	3355	3730	4105	4475
7.5	800	800	1200	1600	2000	2400	2800	3200	3600	4000	4400	4800
8.0	855	855	1280	1710	2135	2560	2990	3415	3845	4270	4695	5125
8.5	910	910	1360	1815	2270	2725	3180	3630	4085	4540	4995	5450
9.0	960	960	1445	1925	2405	2885	3370	3850	4330	4810	5295	5775
9.5	1015	1015	1525	2035	2540	3050	3560	4065	4575	5085	5590	6100
10.0	1070	1070	1605	2145	2680	3215	3750	4285	4820	5355	5890	6430

(Vertical label spanning rows 2.7–3.4: VERTICAL PATH ANGLE)

CLIMB/DESCENT TABLE 10042

Legend 27. – Instrument Takeoff or Approach Procedure Charts, Rate-of-Climb/Descent Table.

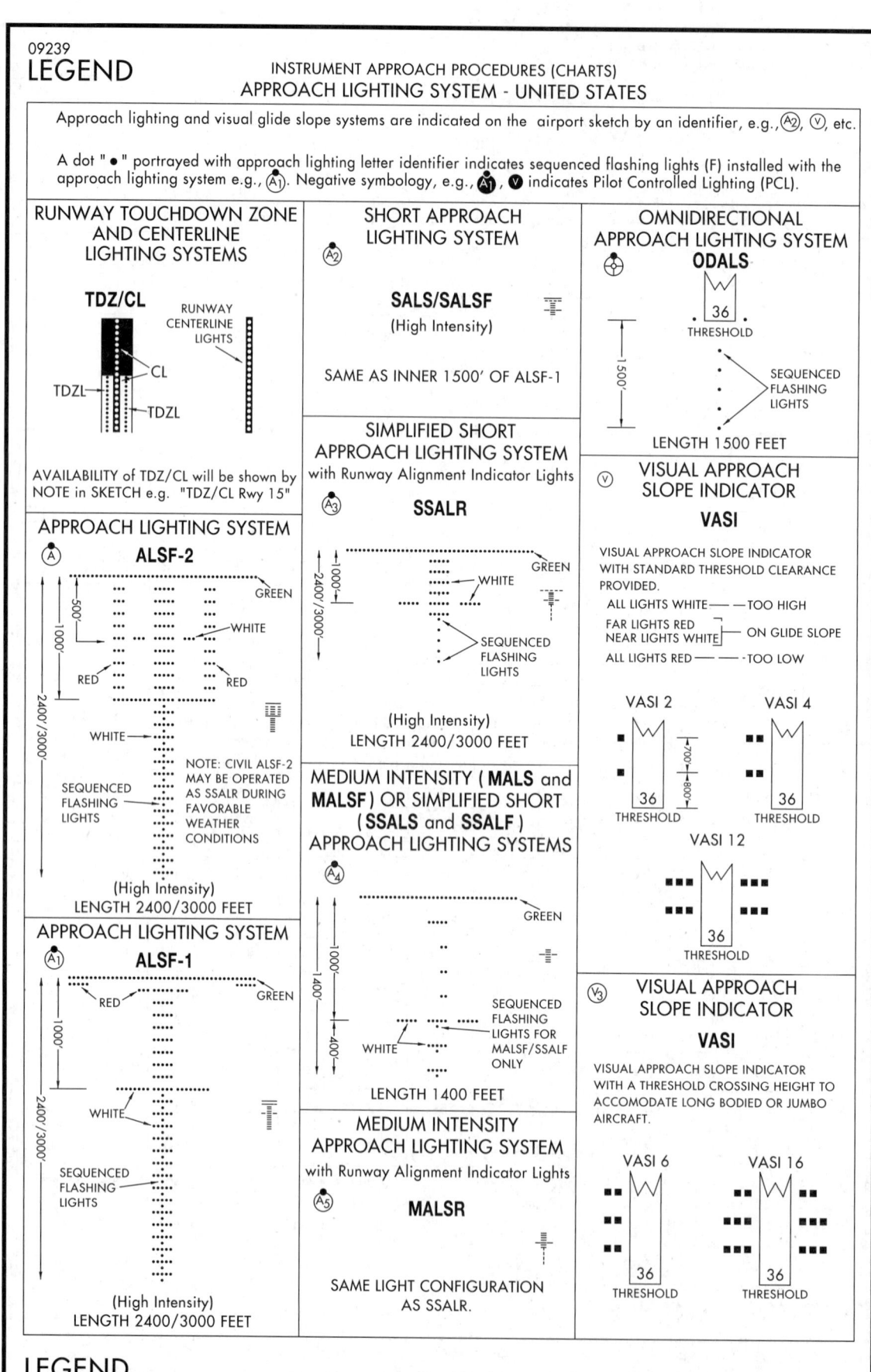

Legend 30. – Approach Lighting Systems.

13122
INOP COMPONENTS

INOPERATIVE COMPONENTS OR VISUAL AIDS TABLE

Landing minimums published on instrument approach procedure charts are based upon full operation of all components and visual aids associated with the particular instrument approach chart being used. Higher minimums are required with inoperative components or visual aids as indicated below. If more than one component is inoperative, each minimum is raised to the highest minimum required by any single component that is inoperative. ILS glide slope inoperative minimums are published on the instrument approach charts as localizer minimums. This table may be amended by notes on the approach chart. Such notes apply only to the particular approach category(ies) as stated. See legend page for description of components indicated below.

(1) ILS, MLS, PAR and RNAV (LPV line of minima)

Inoperative Component or Aid	Approach Category	Increase Visibility
ALSF 1 & 2, MALSR, & SSALR	ABCD	¼ mile

(2) ILS with visibility minimum of 1,800 RVR

Inoperative	Approach Category	Increase Visibility
ALSF 1 & 2, MALSR, & SSALR	ABCD	To 4000 RVR
TDZL RCLS	ABCD	To 2400 RVR*
RVR	ABCD	To ½ mile

*1800 RVR authorized with the use of FD or AP or HUD to DA.

(3) VOR, VOR/DME, TACAN, LOC, LOC/DME, LDA, LDA/DME, SDF, SDF/DME, GPS, ASR and RNAV (LNAV/VNAV, LP, LNAV lines of minima)

Inoperative Visual Aid	Approach Category	Increase Visibility
ALSF 1 & 2, MALSR, & SSALR	ABCD	½ mile
SSALS, MALS, & ODALS	ABC	¼ mile

(4) NDB

ALSF 1 & 2, MALSR, & SSALR	C	½ mile
	ABD	¼ mile
MALS, SSALS, ODALS	ABC	¼ mile

INOP COMPONENTS

Legend 32. – Inoperative Components or Visual Aids Table.

11.8 HLN To/From BIL

Questions 54 through 62 pertain to an IFR flight from Helena Regional Airport, Helena, Montana, to the Billings Logan International Airport, Billings, Montana.

The figures provided for this flight are listed below and are presented at the end of the sequence of questions.

Fig.	Page	
76	492	VOR Indications and Excerpts from Chart Supplement (HLN)
78	493	En Route Low-Altitude Chart Segment
211	494	STAKK Three Departure (STAKK3.STAKK) (HLN)
213	495	VOR/DME RWY 28R (BIL)

54. (Refer to Figure 76 on page 492 and Figure 211 on page 494.) Which en route low altitude navigation chart would cover a proposed routing at the BOZEMAN VORTAC?

A. L-2.

B. L-7.

C. L-13.

Answer (C) is correct. (ACUG)
DISCUSSION: On Fig. 211, Bozeman VOR/DME is in the planview in the lower right corner. Below the frequency box, the notation L-13 is the number of the appropriate en route low-altitude navigation chart.
Answer (A) is incorrect. Bozeman VOR/DME is found on L-13, not L-2. **Answer (B) is incorrect.** Bozeman VOR/DME is found on L-13, not L-7.

55. (Refer to Figure 211 on page 494.) At which point does the basic instrument departure procedure terminate?

A. When Helena Departure Control establishes radar contact.

B. At STAKK intersection.

C. Over the BOZEMAN VOR.

Answer (B) is correct. (ACUG)
DISCUSSION: On the STAKK Three Departure in Fig. 211, the departure route description at the bottom indicates that, for takeoffs from RWY 9 and RWY 27, you should climb eastbound on HLN R-087 to cross STAKK INT. at or above 10,200 ft. "Thence via transition."
Answer (A) is incorrect. Helena Departure Control will establish contact shortly after you get off the runway. **Answer (C) is incorrect.** The BOZEMAN VOR is the end of the BOZEMAN transition, not the basic DP.

56. (Refer to Figure 211 on page 494.) Using an average ground speed of 140 knots, what minimum rate of climb would meet the required minimum climb rate per NM as specified on the instrument departure procedure from RWY 9?

A. 350 feet per minute.

B. 475 feet per minute.

C. 968 feet per minute.

Answer (C) is correct. (ACUG)
DISCUSSION: On Fig. 211 on the DP, the note to the left indicates a minimum climb rate of 415 feet per NM. To convert this to a climb rate (feet per minute), use the following formula:

$$\frac{(GS \times FT/NM)}{60} = FPM$$

$$\frac{140 \times 415}{60} = 968 \text{ FPM}$$

The minimum rate of climb required would be 968 feet per minute.
Answer (A) is incorrect. A 350-feet-per-minute climb rate at an average groundspeed of 140 knots would result in a climb rate of less than 200 feet per NM, not 300 feet per NM. **Answer (B) is incorrect.** A 475-feet-per-minute climb rate at an average groundspeed of 140 knots would result in a climb rate of approximately 200 feet per NM, not 300 feet per NM.

57. (Refer to Figure 78 on page 493.) When eastbound on V86 between Whitehall and Livingston, the minimum altitude that you should cross BZN is

A. 10,200 feet.

B. 10,500 feet.

C. 8,500 feet.

Answer (A) is correct. (ACUG)
DISCUSSION: On Fig. 78, the Bozeman (BZN) VOR/DME has a flag with an X, indicating a minimum crossing altitude (MCA). Near the center of the diagram, below the BZN VOR/DME communications box, is MCA V86 10200 SE. Thus, the minimum crossing altitude over the BZN VOR/DME for a flight southeast bound on V86 is 10,200 feet MSL.
Answer (B) is incorrect. This is the MEA on V343 from BZN South, not the MCA at BZN on V86. **Answer (C) is incorrect.** This is the MEA on V86 prior to BZN VOR/DME. The MEA is not the MCA when an MCA is specified.

58. (Refer to Figure 78 on page 493.) What is the maximum altitude that you may flight plan an IFR flight on V-86 EASTBOUND between BOZEMAN and BILLINGS VORTACs?

   A. 14,500 feet MSL.

   B. 17,000 feet MSL.

   C. 18,000 feet MSL.

Answer (B) is correct. (ACUG)
   DISCUSSION: Victor airways consist of altitudes from 1,200 feet AGL up to, but not including, 18,000 feet MSL. The jet route is from 18,000 feet MSL through FL 450. Thus, the maximum altitude on an airway is 17,000 feet MSL because IFR flight is conducted at cardinal altitudes: odd numbers for eastbound and even for westbound.
   Answer (A) is incorrect. The altitude of 14,500 feet MSL (i.e., thousand-foot plus 500 feet) is a VFR, not IFR, cruising altitude. **Answer (C) is incorrect.** Victor airways extend up to, but do not include, 18,000 feet MSL. Jet routes begin at 18,000 feet MSL (FL 180).

59. (Refer to Figure 78 on page 493.) What is the minimum crossing altitude over the BOZEMAN VORTAC for a flight southeast bound on V86?

   A. 8,500 feet MSL.

   B. 10,200 feet MSL.

   C. 10,000 feet MSL.

Answer (B) is correct. (ACUG)
   DISCUSSION: On Fig. 78, the Bozeman (BZN) VOR/DME (it is not a VORTAC) has a flag with an X, indicating a minimum crossing altitude (MCA). Near the center of the page, below the BZN VOR/DME communications box, is MCA V86 10200 SE. Thus, the minimum crossing altitude over the BZN VOR/DME for a flight southeast bound on V86 is 10,200 feet MSL.
   Answer (A) is incorrect. This is the MEA on V86 prior to BZN VOR/DME. The MEA is not the MCA when an MCA is specified. **Answer (C) is incorrect.** This is the MEA on V365, not the MCA at BZN VOR/DME.

60. (Refer to Figure 211 on page 494.) At which minimum altitude should you cross the STAKK intersection?

   A. 11,800 feet MSL.

   B. 10,800 feet MSL.

   C. 10,200 feet MSL.

Answer (C) is correct. (ACUG)
   DISCUSSION: On the STAKK Three Departure (Fig. 211), the departure route description for either runway states, "Cross STAKK at or above 10,200'." Thus, the minimum altitude at which you should cross the STAKK INT. is 10,200 feet MSL.
   Answer (A) is incorrect. This is not a pertinent altitude in this DP. **Answer (B) is incorrect.** This is not a pertinent altitude in this DP.

61. (Refer to Figure 213 on page 495.) Which aircraft approach category should be used for a circling approach for a landing on RWY 28R in an aircraft with a V_{so} of 72 kt.?

   A. A.

   B. B.

   C. C.

Answer (B) is correct. (ACUG)
   DISCUSSION: Approach categories are based upon 1.3 V_{so} and weight. Using the general rule, 1.3 V_{so} is 93.6, which is Category B (91 to 120 kt.).
   Answer (A) is incorrect. Category A is for approach speeds less than 91 kt. **Answer (C) is incorrect.** Category C is for approach speeds from 121 to 140 kt.

62. (Refer to Figure 213 on page 495.) How many initial approach fixes serve the VOR/DME RWY 28R (Billings Logan) approach procedure?

   A. Three.

   B. Four.

   C. Five.

Answer (A) is correct. (FAA H-8083-16B Chap 3)
   DISCUSSION: Three initial approach fixes are associated with the VOR/DME RWY 28R approach depicted in Fig. 213. They are Pocov at 16 DME on the Billings 333 radial, Musty at 10 DME on the 082 radial, and Nelwn at 16 DME on the 160 radial. Each is labeled "IAF" on the overhead view of the approach plate.
   Answer (B) is incorrect. Three initial approach fixes are associated with the VOR/DME RWY 28R approach, not four. **Answer (C) is incorrect.** Three initial approach fixes are associated with the VOR/DME RWY 28R approach, not five.

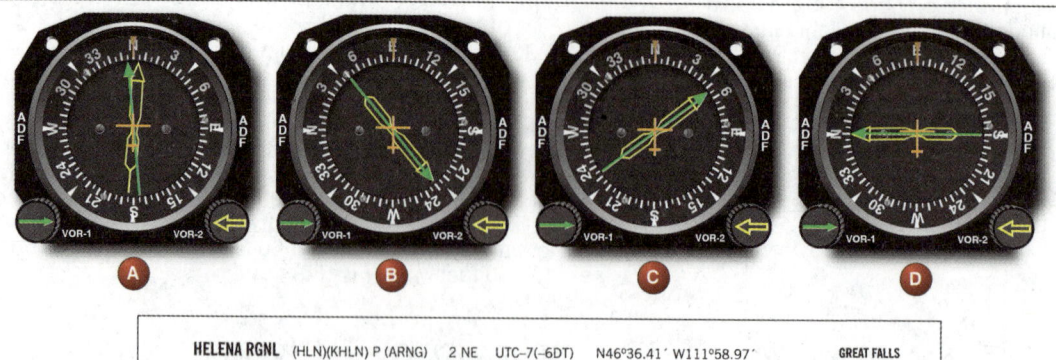

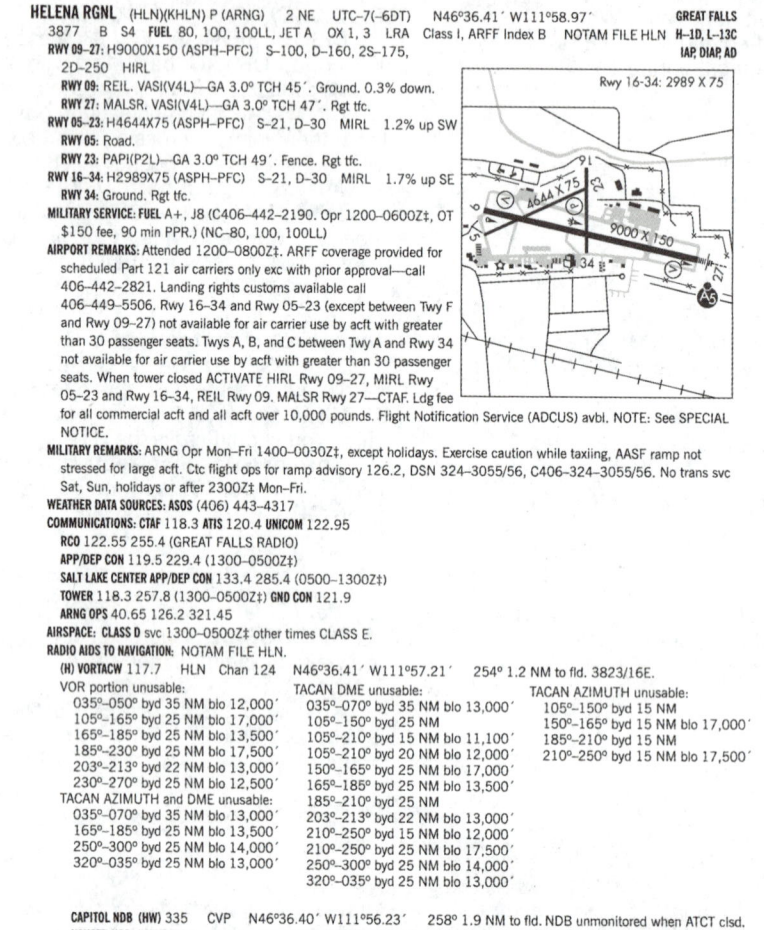

HELENA RGNL (HLN)(KHLN) P (ARNG)   2 NE   UTC–7(–6DT)   N46°36.41' W111°58.97'   **GREAT FALLS**
3877   B   S4   **FUEL** 80, 100, 100LL, JET A   OX 1, 3   LRA   Class I, ARFF Index B   NOTAM FILE HLN   H–1D, L–13C
RWY 09–27: H9000X150 (ASPH–PFC)   S–100, D–160, 2S–175,   **IAP, DIAP, AD**
  2D–250   HIRL
  RWY 09: REIL. VASI(V4L)—GA 3.0° TCH 45'. Ground. 0.3% down.
  RWY 27: MALSR. VASI(V4L)—GA 3.0° TCH 47'. Rgt tfc.
RWY 05–23: H4644X75 (ASPH–PFC)   S–21, D–30   MIRL   1.2% up SW
  RWY 05: Road.
  RWY 23: PAPI(P2L)—GA 3.0° TCH 49'. Fence. Rgt tfc.
RWY 16–34: H2989X75 (ASPH–PFC)   S–21, D–30   MIRL   1.7% up SE
  RWY 34: Ground. Rgt tfc.
MILITARY SERVICE: FUEL A+, J8 (C406–442–2190. Opr 1200–0600Z‡, OT
  $150 fee, 90 min PPR.) (NC–80, 100, 100LL)
AIRPORT REMARKS: Attended 1200–0800Z‡. ARFF coverage provided for
  scheduled Part 121 air carriers only exc with prior approval—call
  406–442–2821. Landing rights customs available call
  406–449–5506. Rwy 16–34 and Rwy 05–23 (except between Twy F
  and Rwy 09–27) not available for air carrier use by acft with greater
  than 30 passenger seats. Twys A, B, and C between Twy A and Rwy 34
  not available for air carrier use by acft with greater than 30 passenger
  seats. When tower closed ACTIVATE HIRL Rwy 09–27, MIRL Rwy
  05–23 and Rwy 16–34, REIL Rwy 09. MALSR Rwy 27—CTAF. Ldg fee
  for all commercial acft and all acft over 10,000 pounds. Flight Notification Service (ADCUS) avbl. NOTE: See SPECIAL
  NOTICE.
MILITARY REMARKS: ARNG Opr Mon–Fri 1400–0030Z‡, except holidays. Exercise caution while taxiing, AASF ramp not
  stressed for large acft. Ctc flight ops for ramp advisory 126.2, DSN 324–3055/56, C406–324–3055/56. No trans svc
  Sat, Sun, holidays or after 2300Z‡ Mon–Fri.
WEATHER DATA SOURCES: ASOS (406) 443–4317
COMMUNICATIONS: CTAF 118.3 **ATIS** 120.4 **UNICOM** 122.95
  RCO 122.55 255.4 (GREAT FALLS RADIO)
  APP/DEP CON 119.5 229.4 (1300–0500Z‡)
  SALT LAKE CENTER APP/DEP CON 133.4 285.4 (0500–1300Z‡)
  TOWER 118.3 257.8 (1300–0500Z‡) **GND CON** 121.9
  ARNG OPS 40.65 126.2 321.45
AIRSPACE: CLASS D svc 1300–0500Z‡ other times CLASS E.
RADIO AIDS TO NAVIGATION: NOTAM FILE HLN.
  (H) VORTACW 117.7   HLN   Chan 124   N46°36.41' W111°57.21'   254° 1.2 NM to fld. 3823/16E.
  VOR portion unusable: TACAN DME unusable: TACAN AZIMUTH unusable:
    035°–050° byd 35 NM blo 12,000'   035°–070° byd 35 NM blo 13,000'   105°–150° byd 15 NM
    105°–165° byd 25 NM blo 17,000'   105°–150° byd 25 NM   150°–165° byd 15 NM blo 17,000'
    165°–185° byd 25 NM blo 13,500'   105°–210° byd 15 NM blo 11,100'   185°–210° byd 15 NM
    185°–230° byd 25 NM blo 17,500'   105°–210° byd 20 NM blo 12,000'   210°–250° byd 15 NM blo 17,500'
    203°–213° byd 22 NM blo 13,000'   150°–165° byd 25 NM blo 17,000'
    230°–270° byd 25 NM blo 12,500'   165°–185° byd 25 NM blo 13,500'
  TACAN AZIMUTH and DME unusable: 185°–210° byd 25 NM
    035°–070° byd 35 NM blo 13,000'   203°–213° byd 22 NM blo 13,000'
    165°–185° byd 25 NM blo 13,500'   210°–250° byd 15 NM blo 12,000'
    250°–300° byd 25 NM blo 14,000'   210°–250° byd 25 NM blo 17,500'
    320°–035° byd 25 NM blo 13,000'   250°–300° byd 25 NM blo 14,000'
                                        320°–035° byd 25 NM blo 13,000'

  CAPITOL NDB (HW) 335   CVP   N46°36.40' W111°56.23'   258° 1.9 NM to fld. NDB unmonitored when ATCT clsd.
  HAUSER NDB (MHW) 386   HAU   N46°34.13' W111°45.48'   268° 9.6 NM to fld. NDB unmonitored when HLN
    ATCT clsd.
  ILS 110.1   I–HLN   Rwy 27.   Unmonitored when ATCT closed. Localizer backcourse unusable byd 22° rgt of course,
    unusable within 2.7 DME.

VOR RECEIVER CHECKPOINTS

Facility Name (Arpt Name)	Freq/Ident	Type Check Pt. Gnd. AB/ALT	Azimuth from Fac. Mag	Dist. from Fac. N.M.	Checkpoint Description
Helena (Helena Rgnl)	117.7/HLN	G	238	0.7	On Twy E on South side of Rwy 27.
Kalispell (Glacier Park Intl)	113.2/FCA	A/4000	316	6.4	Over apch end Rwy 30.
Lewistown (Lewistown Muni)	112.0/LWT	A/5200	075	5.6	Over apch end Rwy 07.
Livingston	116.1/LVM	A/6500	237	5.5	Over northern most radio twr NE of city.
Miles City (Frank Wiley Field)	112.1/MLS	G	036	4.2	On twy leading to Rwy 30.
Missoula (Missoula Intl)	112.8/MSO	G	344	0.6	Terminal ramp east of Twy D.

Figure 76. – VOR Indications and Excerpts from Chart Supplement (HLN).

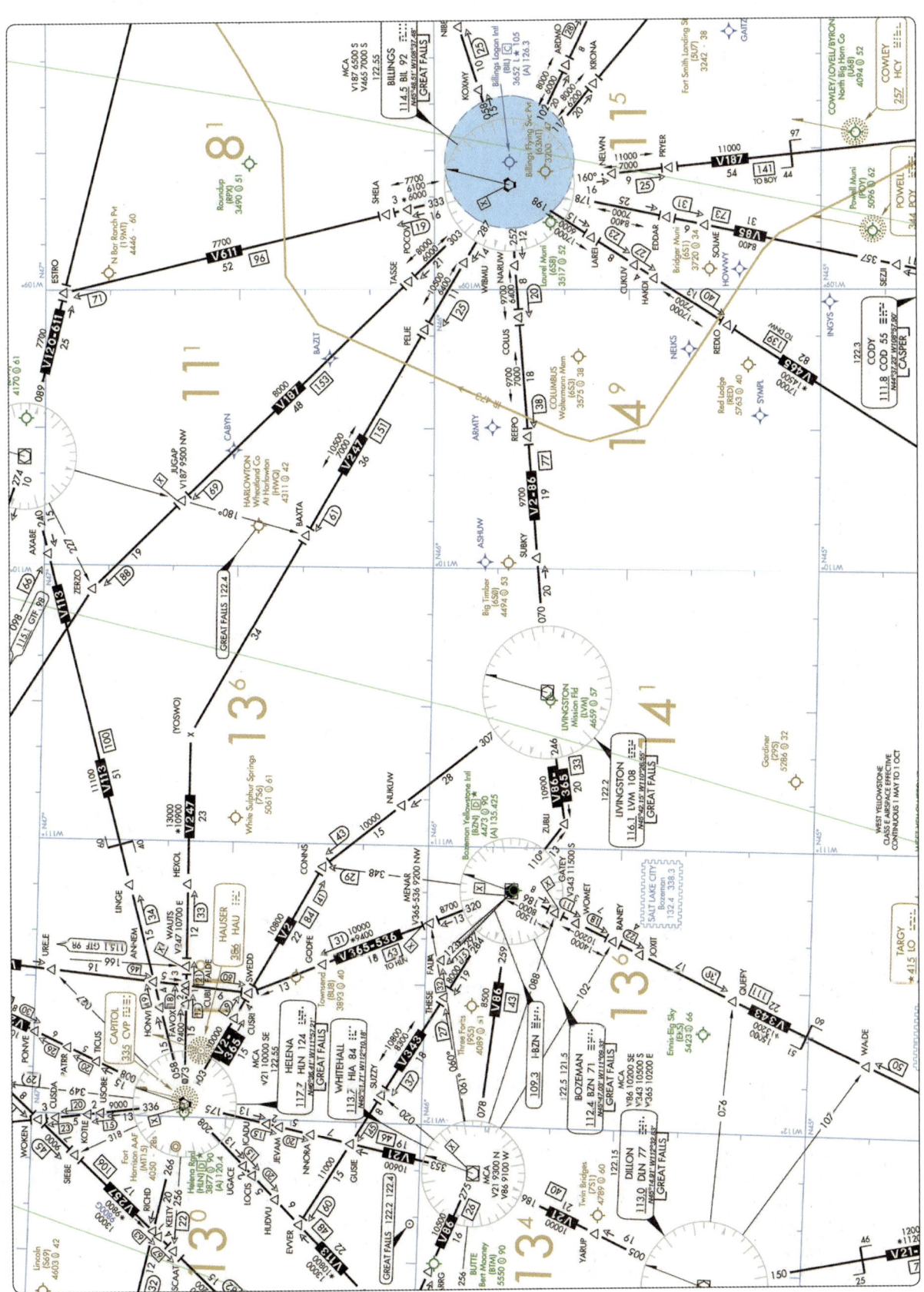

Figure 78. – En Route Low-Altitude Chart Segment.
NOTE: Chart is not to scale and should not be used for navigation. Chart is for testing purposes only.

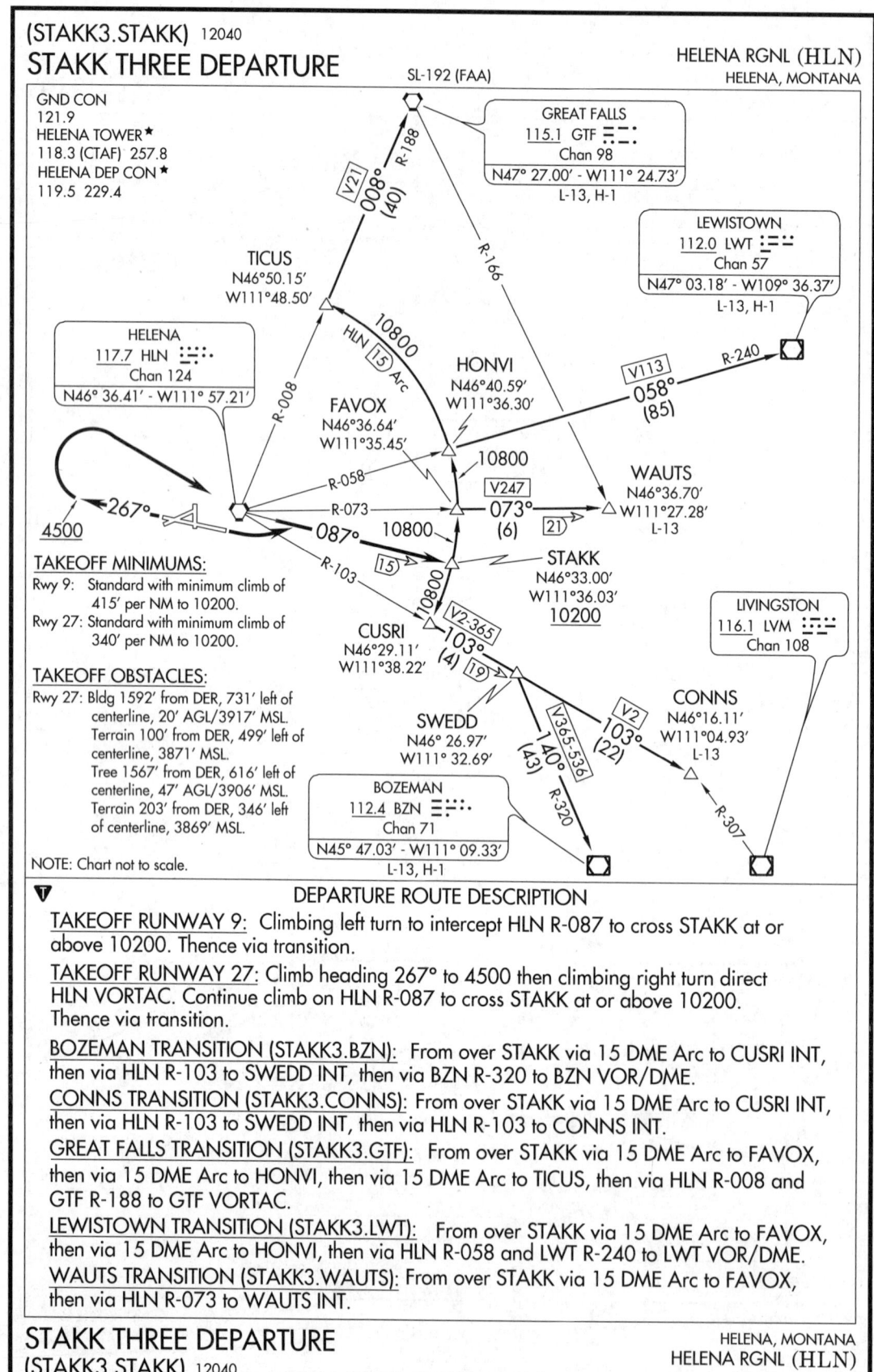

(STAKK3.STAKK) 12040
STAKK THREE DEPARTURE
SL-192 (FAA)

HELENA RGNL (HLN)
HELENA, MONTANA

GND CON
121.9
HELENA TOWER ★
118.3 (CTAF) 257.8
HELENA DEP CON ★
119.5 229.4

GREAT FALLS
115.1 GTF ⸱⸱ ⸱⸱ ⸱
Chan 98
N47° 27.00' - W111° 24.73'
L-13, H-1

LEWISTOWN
112.0 LWT ⸱⸱⸱ ⸱⸱
Chan 57
N47° 03.18' - W109° 36.37'
L-13, H-1

V21 008° (40)

R-188

R-166

TICUS
N46°50.15'
W111°48.50'

HLN 15 Arc 10800

HELENA
117.7 HLN ⸱⸱⸱⸱ ⸱
Chan 124
N46° 36.41' - W111° 57.21'

FAVOX
N46°36.64'
W111°35.45'

HONVI
N46°40.59'
W111°36.30'

V113 058° (85)

R-240

R-008

267°
4500

R-058
R-073
087°

10800

V247 073° (6)

21

WAUTS
N46°36.70'
W111°27.28'
L-13

R-103
15
10800

STAKK
N46°33.00'
W111°36.03'
10200

LIVINGSTON
116.1 LVM ⸱⸱⸱ ⸱
Chan 108

TAKEOFF MINIMUMS:
Rwy 9: Standard with minimum climb of
415' per NM to 10200.
Rwy 27: Standard with minimum climb of
340' per NM to 10200.

CUSRI
N46°29.11'
W111°38.22'

V2-365 103° (4)

10800

19

V2 103° (22)

CONNS
N46°16.11'
W111°04.93'
L-13

TAKEOFF OBSTACLES:
Rwy 27: Bldg 1592' from DER, 731' left of
centerline, 20' AGL/3917' MSL.
Terrain 100' from DER, 499' left of
centerline, 3871' MSL.
Tree 1567' from DER, 616' left of
centerline, 47' AGL/3906' MSL.
Terrain 203' from DER, 346' left
of centerline, 3869' MSL.

SWEDD
N46° 26.97'
W111° 32.69'

V365-536 140° (43)

R-320

R-307

NOTE: Chart not to scale.

BOZEMAN
112.4 BZN ⸱⸱⸱⸱
Chan 71
N45° 47.03' - W111° 09.33'
L-13, H-1

DEPARTURE ROUTE DESCRIPTION

TAKEOFF RUNWAY 9: Climbing left turn to intercept HLN R-087 to cross STAKK at or
above 10200. Thence via transition.

TAKEOFF RUNWAY 27: Climb heading 267° to 4500 then climbing right turn direct
HLN VORTAC. Continue climb on HLN R-087 to cross STAKK at or above 10200.
Thence via transition.

BOZEMAN TRANSITION (STAKK3.BZN): From over STAKK via 15 DME Arc to CUSRI INT,
then via HLN R-103 to SWEDD INT, then via BZN R-320 to BZN VOR/DME.

CONNS TRANSITION (STAKK3.CONNS): From over STAKK via 15 DME Arc to CUSRI INT,
then via HLN R-103 to SWEDD INT, then via HLN R-103 to CONNS INT.

GREAT FALLS TRANSITION (STAKK3.GTF): From over STAKK via 15 DME Arc to FAVOX,
then via 15 DME Arc to HONVI, then via 15 DME Arc to TICUS, then via HLN R-008 and
GTF R-188 to GTF VORTAC.

LEWISTOWN TRANSITION (STAKK3.LWT): From over STAKK via 15 DME Arc to FAVOX,
then via 15 DME Arc to HONVI, then via HLN R-058 and LWT R-240 to LWT VOR/DME.

WAUTS TRANSITION (STAKK3.WAUTS): From over STAKK via 15 DME Arc to FAVOX,
then via HLN R-073 to WAUTS INT.

STAKK THREE DEPARTURE
(STAKK3.STAKK) 12040

HELENA, MONTANA
HELENA RGNL (HLN)

Figure 211. – STAKK Three Departure (STAKK3.STAKK) (HLN).

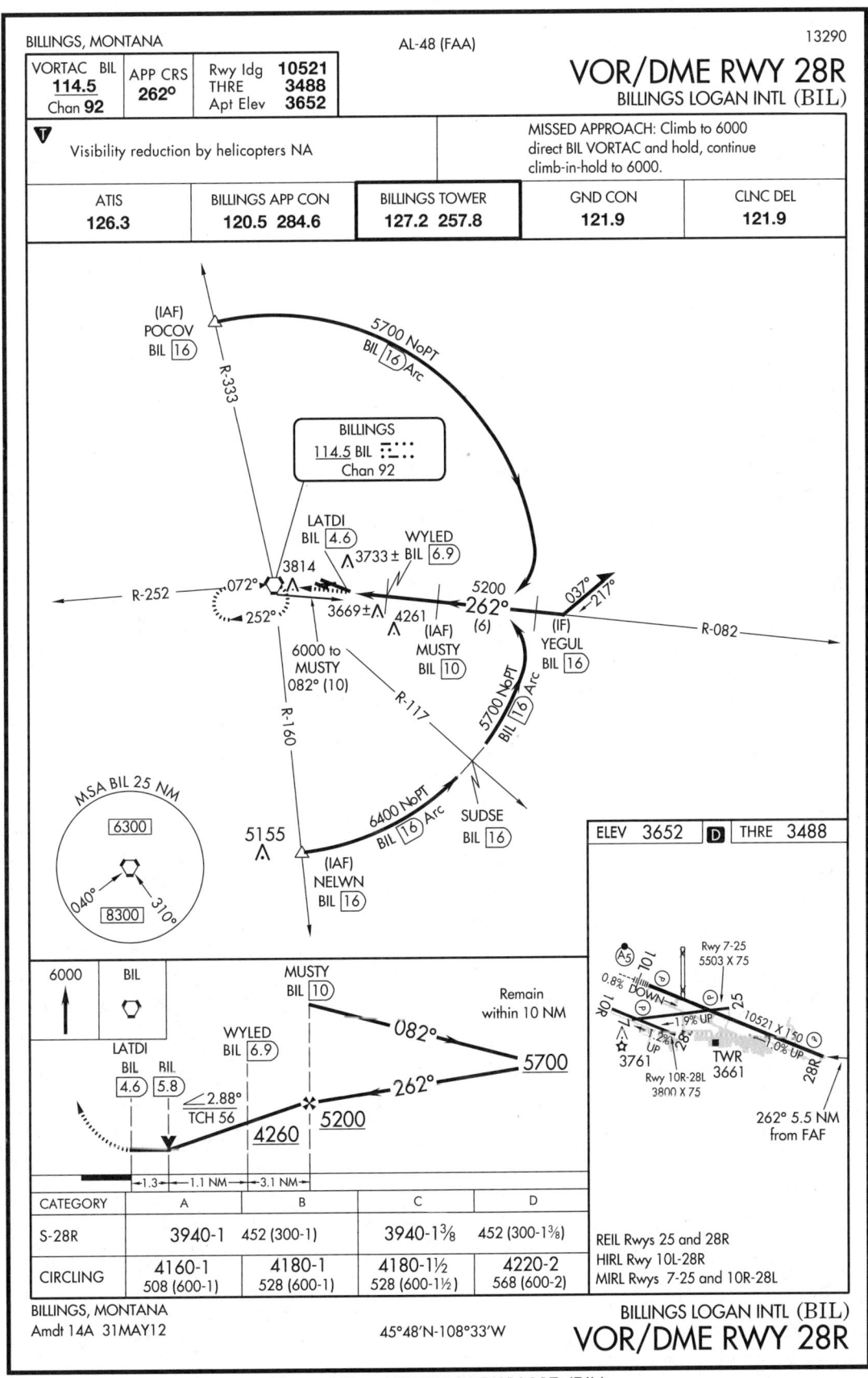

Figure 213. – VOR/DME RWY 28R (BIL).

APPENDIX A
ADDITIONAL INSTRUMENT
GROUND INSTRUCTOR QUESTIONS

Recall that this book places its primary focus on instrument rating airplane applicants. For those preparing for the ground instructor instrument (IGI) knowledge test, some non-airplane questions may be encountered on the knowledge test, as a person holding an instrument ground instructor rating is authorized to provide a recommendation for an instrument rating helicopter (IRH) knowledge test. Therefore, the following outline and questions cover additional topics that may be encountered on an IGI knowledge test.

Instrument Rating Helicopter

1. An advanced ground instructor rating (AGI) allows provision of ground training toward any certificate or rating issued under 14 CFR Part 61, with the exception of an instrument rating.

2. The holder of an instrument ground instructor rating is authorized to provide the following:

   a. Ground training in the aeronautical knowledge areas required for the issuance of an instrument rating under 14 CFR Part 61

   b. Ground training required for an instrument proficiency check

   c. An FAA knowledge test recommendation required for the issuance of an instrument rating under 14 CFR Part 61

3. The holder of a ground instructor certificate may not exercise the privileges of the certificate unless they have been employed as a ground instructor giving pilot, flight instructor, or ground instructor training in the preceding 12 months.

4. The minimum IFR alternate airport weather minima to include an airport as an alternate airport in an IFR flight plan are as follows:

   a. Ceiling that is a minimum of 200 ft. above the minimum for the approach to be flown

   b. Visibility of at least 1 SM but never less than the minimum visibility for the approach being flown

5. Aircraft approach category refers to grouping aircraft based on V_{REF} if specified or, if V_{REF} is not specified, it is 1.3 V_{SO} at the maximum certificated landing weight.

   a. As defined in 14 CFR 97.3, a helicopter using standard instrument approach procedures for airplanes shall be considered as category A in respect to approach minima.

      1) Category A: Speed less than 91 kt.

6. Helicopters are capable of flying any published 14 CFR Part 97 standard instrument approach procedures (SIAPs) for which they are properly equipped.

   a. Helicopters flying conventional (non-copter) SIAPs may reduce the visibility minima to not less than one-half the published category A landing visibility minima, or 1/4 SM visibility/1200 RVR, whichever is greater, unless the procedure is annotated with "Visibility Reduction by Helicopters NA."

      1) "Visibility Reduction by Helicopters NA" highlights penetrations of the final approach obstacle identification surface (OIS) and indicates that the 14 CFR 97.3 visibility reduction rule does not apply.

QUESTIONS

1. For helicopters, what minimum weather conditions must be forecast for the ETA for that airport to be listed as an alternate on an IFR flight plan, if that airport has a published ILS approach?

A. 600 foot ceiling and 2 SM visibility at your ETA.

B. 200 foot ceiling above the airport elevation and 1 SM visibility from 1 hour before to 1 hour after your ETA.

C. 200 foot ceiling above the approach minimums and 1 SM visibility, but not less than the visibility minimums for the approach, at your ETA.

Answer (C) is correct. *(14 CFR 91.169)*
  DISCUSSION: The minimum forecast ETA weather conditions for helicopters to include an airport as an alternate are a ceiling that is a minimum of 200 ft. above the minimum for the ILS to be flown, with visibility of at least 1 SM but never less than the minimum visibility for the approach being flown.
  Answer (A) is incorrect. The standard approach minima for aircraft other than helicopters, if the airport has a published ILS approach, would be a ceiling of 600 ft. and visibility of 2 SM. **Answer (B) is incorrect.** The safety buffer of an additional 200-ft. ceiling will be above the approach minimums, not the airport elevation.

2. All helicopters are considered to be in which approach category for a helicopter IAP?

A. A.

B. A or B, depending upon weight.

C. B.

Answer (A) is correct. *(AIM Para 10-1-2)*
  DISCUSSION: All helicopters flying conventional (non-copter) IAPs are considered to be in category A and may reduce the visibility minima to not less than one-half the published category A landing visibility minima, or 1/4 SM visibility/1200 RVR, whichever is greater, unless the procedure is annotated with "Visibility Reduction by Helicopters NA."
  Answer (B) is incorrect. Specific to approach category, all helicopters will be considered as category A. **Answer (C) is incorrect.** Helicopters in this scenario will be considered as category A with speeds less than 91 kt., as opposed to category B, which would be 91 kt. or more (less than 121 kt.).

3. Upon what maximum airspeed is the instrument approach criteria for a helicopter based?

A. 100 knots.

B. 90 knots.

C. 80 knots.

Answer (B) is correct. *(AIM Para 10-1-2)*
  DISCUSSION: The maximum airspeed for helicopters on instrument approach will be based on the aircraft approach category. For helicopters, this is category A with a speed of less than 91 kt.
  Answer (A) is incorrect. Aircraft flying at 100 kt. would be considered in category B. Aircraft in category B would be 91 kt. or more but less than 121 kt. **Answer (C) is incorrect.** Aircraft approach category A includes 80 kt. The maximum airspeed for category A aircraft (and, in this case, a helicopter) would be 90 kt.

4. (Refer to Figure 247 on page 499.) When the RAL altimeter is not available, the LOC RWY 9 visibility minima for a helicopter cleared for the S-LOC 9* approach at RAL is

A. 1/4 mile.

B. 1/2 mile.

C. 5/8 mile.

Answer (A) is correct. *(AIM Para 10-1-2)*
  DISCUSSION: Though the briefing strip refers to the use of the Chino altimeter setting and a change in category A MDA, it does not refer to "Visibility Reduction by Helicopters NA." Therefore, the visibility minima may be reduced to not less than one-half the category A published minima, or 1/4 SM visibility/1200 RVR. This will allow the visibility minima to be reduced to 1/4 SM.
  Answer (B) is incorrect. The published category A landing visibility minima for this conventional SIAP is 1/2 SM. Helicopters may reduce this visibility minima. **Answer (C) is incorrect.** The published visibility minima for S-ILS 9 is 5/8 SM.

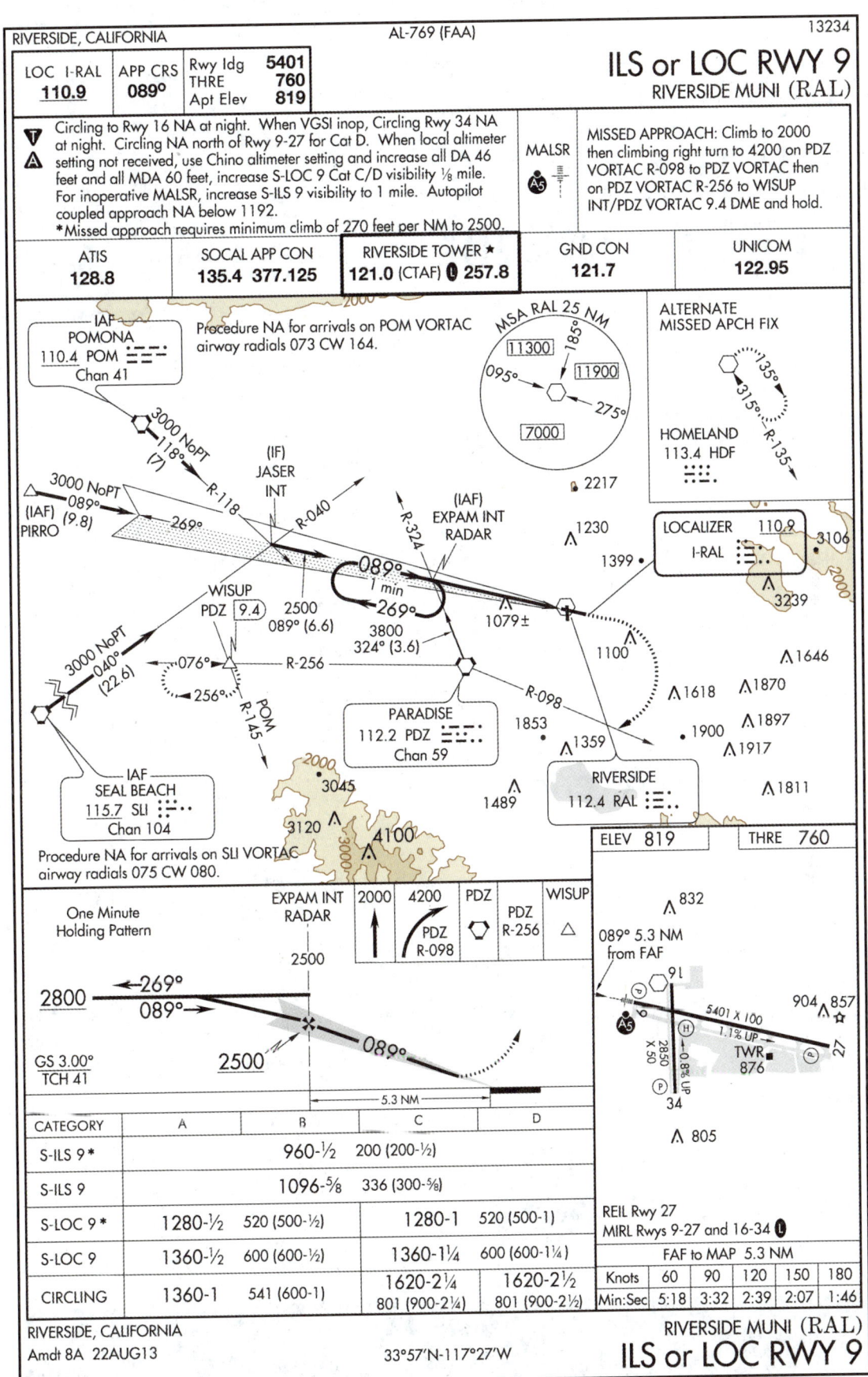

Figure 247. – ILS or RWY 9 (RAL).

APPENDIX B
INSTRUMENT RATING PRACTICE TEST

The following 60 questions have been randomly selected from the airplane questions in our instrument rating test bank. You will be referred to figures (charts, tables, etc.) throughout this book. Be careful not to consult the answers or answer explanations when you look for and at the figures. Topical coverage in this practice test is similar to that of the FAA instrument rating-airplane knowledge test. Use the correct answer listing on page 506 to grade your practice test.

1. MEA is an altitude which assures

A — obstacle clearance, accurate navigational signals from more than one VORTAC, and accurate DME mileage.
B — a 1,000-foot obstacle clearance within 2 miles of an airway and assures accurate DME mileage.
C — acceptable navigational signal coverage and meets obstruction clearance requirements.

2. (Refer to Figure 91 on page 429.) When flying a northbound IFR flight on V257, what is the minimum crossing altitude at DBS VORTAC?

A — 7,500 feet.
B — 8,600 feet.
C — 11,100 feet.

3. (Refer to Figure 24 on page 443.) While passing near the CORTEZ VOR, southbound on V187, contact is lost with Denver Center. You should attempt to reestablish contact with Denver Center on

A — 118.575 MHz.
B — 108.4 MHz.
C — 122.3 MHz.

4. Interpret the remarks section of METAR surface report for KBNA.

METAR KBNA 2112507 33018KT 290V260 1/2SM
R31/2700FT +SN BLSNFG VV008 00/M03 A2991
RMK RAESNB42

A — The wind is variable from 290° to 360°.
B — Heavy blowing snow and fog on runway 31.
C — Rain ended 42 minutes past the hour, snow began 42 minutes past the hour.

5. (Refer to Figure 7 on page 401.) What type of weather can be expected in the red scalloped area near area 9?

A — 2/8 to 6/8 coverage, occasional embedded thunderstorms, tops at FL 330.
B — 1/8 to 4/8 coverage, occasional embedded thunderstorms, maximum tops at 51,000 feet MSL.
C — Isolated embedded cumulonimbus with tops to FL 330.

6. Which of the following reports should always be reported to ATC?

A — Preferred runway choice to limit taxi time.
B — When true airspeed (TAS) varies by 10 percent or 5 knots, whichever is less.
C — When leaving an assigned holding fix.

7. (Refer to Figure 187 on page 235.) When conducting a missed approach from the RNAV (GPS) X RWY 28L approach at PDX, what is the Minimum Safe Altitude (MSA) while maneuvering?

A — 2,100 feet MSL.
B — 4,000 feet MSL.
C — 5,800 feet MSL.

8. (Refer to Figure 227 on page 271.) Refer to the APA (Centennial) ILS RWY 35R procedure. The PFAF (Precision Final Approach Fix) intercept altitude is

A — 7,080 feet MSL.
B — 7,977 feet MSL.
C — 8,000 feet MSL.

9. (Refer to Figure 230 on page 275.) The minimum safe altitude (MSA) for the VOR/DME or GPS-A at 7D3 is geographically centered on what position?

A — DEANI intersection.
B — WHITE CLOUD VOR/DME.
C — MAJUB intersection.

10. (Refer to Figure 242 on page 287 and Legend 27 on page 286.) You have been cleared for the RNAV (GPS) RWY 36 approach to LIT. At a groundspeed of 105 knots, what are the vertical descent angle and rate of descent on final approach?

A — 2.82 degrees and 524 feet per minute.
B — 3.00 degrees and 557 feet per minute.
C — 4.00 degrees and 550 feet per nautical mile.

11. If both the ram air input and drain hole of the pitot system become blocked, the indicated airspeed will

A — increase during a climb.
B — decrease during a climb.
C — remain constant regardless of altitude change.

12. Military training routes (MTR) above 1,500 feet are depicted on

A — IFR Planning Charts.
B — IFR Low Altitude En Route Charts.
C — IFR High Altitude En Route Charts.

13. How can an initial approach fix be identified on a Standard Instrument Approach Procedure (SIAP) Chart?

A — All fixes that are labeled "IAF" which are depicted on the plan view.
B — Any fix depicted which is located on the final approach course.
C — Any fix depicted which is located on the final approach course prior to the final approach fix.

14. (Refer to Figure 175 on page 468 and Figure 174 on page 473.) When DFW is landing to the north, at CURLE, expect

A — to be instructed to maintain 200 knots.
B — to fly a course of 010°.
C — radar vectors.

15. The advancement of avionics in light general aviation airplanes has enhanced situational awareness for properly trained pilots. However, there is concern that this technology could lead to

A — complacency.
B — fatigue.
C — resignation.

16. An aircraft which is equipped with an Electronic Flight Display (EFD) can

A — compensate for a pilot's lack of skill or knowledge.
B — offer new capabilities and simplify the basic flying task.
C — improve flight awareness by allowing the pilot to simply watch for alerts.

17. The use of airborne weather-avoidance radar

A — provides no assurance of avoiding instrument weather conditions.
B — assures the avoidance of hail.
C — allows you to fly safely between echoes.

18. On initial climbout after takeoff and with the autopilot engaged, you encounter icing conditions. In this situation you can expect

A — ice to accumulate on the underside of the wings due to the higher AOA.
B — the autopilot to hold the vertical speed, if the anti-icing boots are working.
C — the increased airflow under the wings to prevent the accumulation of ice.

19. A generally recommended practice for autopilot usage during cruise flight in icing conditions is

A — keeping the autopilot engaged while monitoring the system.
B — periodically disengaging the autopilot and hand flying the airplane.
C — periodically disengaging and immediately reengaging the altitude hold function.

20. Unless otherwise stated, instrument procedures use the standard IFR climb gradient of

A — 500 feet per minute.
B — 400 feet per nautical mile.
C — 200 feet per nautical mile.

21. What is the rule for a pilot receiving a "Land and Hold Short Operation (LAHSO) clearance?"

A — The pilot is required to accept the controller's clearance in visual meteorological conditions.
B — The pilot must accept the clearance if the pavement is dry and the stopping distance is adequate.
C — The pilot has the option to accept or reject all LAHSO clearances regardless of the meteorological conditions.

22. (Refer to Figure 254 on page 159.) Which of the signs in the figure is a mandatory instruction sign?

A — Top red.
B — Middle yellow.
C — Bottom yellow.

23. Which type of runway lighting consists of a pair of synchronized flashing lights, one on each side of the runway threshold?

A — MALSR.
B — HIRL.
C — REIL.

24. (Refer to Figure 136 on page 165.) An "on glidepath" indication is

A — 8
B — 10
C — 11

25. Your transponder is inoperative. What are the requirements for flying in Class D airspace?

A — The entry into Class D is prohibited.
B — Continue the flight as planned.
C — Pilot must immediately request priority handling to proceed to destination.

26. ATC has approved your request for VFR-on-top while on an IFR clearance. Therefore, you

A — should set your transponder to code 1200.
B — must fly appropriate IFR altitudes.
C — must fly appropriate VFR altitudes.

27. While performing a VFR practice instrument approach, Radar Approach Control assigns an altitude or heading that will cause you to enter the clouds. What action should you take?

A — Continue as directed.
B — Advise "unable" and remain clear of clouds.
C — Deviate as needed; then rejoin the approach.

28. ATC can issue a STAR

A — to all pilots wherever STARs are available.
B — only if the pilot requests a STAR in the "Remarks" section of the flight plan.
C — when ATC deems it appropriate, unless the pilot requests "No STAR."

29. The greatest DME indication error between actual ground distance and displayed ground distance occurs at

A — high altitudes far from the VORTAC.
B — high altitudes close to the VORTAC.
C — low altitudes far from the VORTAC.

30. During a takeoff into IMC at a controlled field with low ceilings, you should contact departure

A — before entering the clouds.
B — when the tower instructs the change.
C — upon reaching the traffic pattern altitude.

31. You may cancel an IFR flight plan

A — at any time as long as you advise ATC.
B — only in an emergency.
C — if in VMC outside Class A airspace.

32. In what localities is advection fog most likely to occur?

A — Coastal areas.
B — Mountain slopes.
C — Level inland areas.

33. (Refer to Figure 61 on page 239.) Determine your position relative to the glide slope and localizer course.

A — Below the glide slope and right of the localizer course.
B — Above the glide slope and left of the localizer course.
C — Above the glide slope and right of the localizer course.

34. To find the VOR receiver ground checkpoint(s) for an accuracy check, which publication should you consult?

A — Airman's Information Manual.
B — En Route Low Altitude Chart.
C — Chart Supplement.

35. (Refer to Figure 162 on page 166.) You have accepted a visual approach to RWY 16L at EUG at night. As you approach the runway, you notice runway centerline lights. This indicates

A — you are on the centerline for your assigned runway.
B — you are too low on the approach.
C — you have lined up with the wrong runway.

36. Decode the excerpt from the Winds and Temperature Aloft Forecast (FB) for OKC at 39,000 feet.

FT	3000	9000	12000	24000	39000
OKC	9900	2018+00	2130-06	2361-30	830558

A — Wind 130° at 50 knots, temperature –58°C.
B — Wind 330° at 105 knots, temperature –58°C.
C — Wind 330° at 205 knots, temperature –58°C.

37. When the visibility is greater than 6 SM on a TAF, it is

A — expressed as 6PSM.
B — expressed as P6SM.
C — omitted from the report.

38. Consider this AIRMET which includes your route of flight:

DFWS WA 211445 AIRMET IFR . . OK TX FROM
END TO TXK TO HOU TO LBB TO END CIG
BELOW 010. CONDS ENDG 15-18Z

This indicates

A — there will be icing in clouds below 10,000 feet MSL.
B — visibility will be less than 3 SM until 15Z.
C — the area will have low ceilings before 15Z.

39. Flying clear of clouds on an instrument flight plan, what are the requirements for a contact approach to an airport that has an approved IAP?

A — The controller must determine that the pilot can see the airport at the altitude flown and can remain clear of clouds.
B — The controller must have determined that the visibility was at least 1 mile and be reasonably sure the pilot can remain clear of clouds.
C — The pilot must request the approach, have at least 1 mile visibility, and be reasonably sure of remaining clear of clouds.

40. A Precision Runway Monitor (PRM) approach requires

A — simultaneously monitoring two frequencies.
B — special training to monitor two ILS receivers simultaneously.
C — tracking performance parameters at the decision point.

41. If the plan view on an approach chart does not include a procedure turn barb, that means

A — a procedure turn is not authorized.
B — you should fly a teardrop entry.
C — a racetrack-type turn is required.

42. If you encounter in-flight icing and ATC asks you to report your conditions, what are the official reportable icing values that you are expected to use?

A — Light, moderate, severe, extreme.
B — Trace, light, moderate, severe.
C — Few, light, moderate, severe.

43. When does the National Weather Service release an Aviation Watch Notification Message (SAW)?

A — At 0000 (UTC).
B — 0000 and 1200 (UTC).
C — Unscheduled and issued as required.

44. (Refer to Figure 13 on page 366.) How will the aircraft in position 4 be affected by a microburst encounter?

A — Performance increasing with a tailwind and updraft.
B — Performance decreasing with a tailwind and downdraft.
C — Performance decreasing with a headwind and downdraft.

45. You are planning an IFR flight off established airways below 18,000 feet MSL. If you use VOR navigation to define the route, the maximum distance between NAVAIDs should be

A — 80 NM.
B — 40 NM.
C — 70 NM.

46. When using VOR for navigation, which of the following should be considered as station passage?

A — The first movement of the CDI as the airplane enters the zone of confusion.
B — The moment the TO-FROM indicator becomes blank.
C — The first positive, complete reversal of the TO-FROM indicator.

47. If you experience tunnel vision and cyanosis, you may have symptoms of

A — hypoxia.
B — hyperventilation.
C — carbon monoxide poisoning.

48. If, while in level flight, it becomes necessary to use an alternate source of static pressure vented inside the airplane, which of the following variations in instrument indications should the pilot expect?

A — The altimeter will read lower than normal, airspeed lower than normal, and the VSI will momentarily show a descent.
B — The altimeter will read higher than normal, airspeed greater than normal, and the VSI will momentarily show a climb.
C — The altimeter will read lower than normal, airspeed greater than normal, and the VSI will momentarily show a climb and then a descent.

49. If Receiver Autonomous Integrity Monitoring (RAIM) is not available prior to beginning a GPS approach, the pilot should

A — use a navigation or approach system other than GPS for an approach.
B — continue to the MAP and hold until the satellites are recaptured.
C — continue the approach, expecting to recapture the satellites before reaching the FAF.

50. You have not yet been cleared for the approach, but you are being vectored to the ILS approach course. It is clear that you will pass through the localizer course unless you take action. You should

A — turn outbound and complete the procedure turn.
B — continue as assigned and query ATC.
C — turn inbound and join the final approach course.

51. When is an IFR clearance required during VFR weather conditions?

A — When operating in the Class E airspace.
B — When operating in a Class A airspace.
C — When operating in airspace above 14,500 feet.

52. What are the alternate minimums for an airport with a precision approach procedure?

A — 400-foot ceiling and 2 miles visibility.
B — 600-foot ceiling and 2 miles visibility.
C — 800-foot ceiling and 2 miles visibility.

53. If the RVR equipment is inoperative for an IAP that requires a visibility of 2,400 RVR, how should the pilot expect the visibility requirement to be reported in lieu of the published RVR?

A — As a slant range visibility of 2,400 feet.
B — As an RVR of 2,400 feet.
C — As a ground visibility of 1/2 SM.

54. The instrument approach criteria for a Category A airplane is based on a maximum airspeed of

A — 100 knots.
B — 90 knots.
C — 80 knots.

55. A pilot is making an ILS approach and is past the OM to a runway which has a VASI. What action is appropriate if an electronic glide slope malfunction occurs and the pilot has the VASI in sight?

A — The pilot should inform ATC of the malfunction and then descend immediately to the localizer DH and make a localizer approach.
B — The pilot may continue the approach and use the VASI glide slope in place of the electronic glide slope.
C — The pilot must request an LOC approach, and may descend below the VASI at the pilot's discretion.

56. To act as pilot in command of an aircraft under IFR, what is the minimum instrument flight experience you must have logged during the preceding six months, in the same category of aircraft?

A — Holding procedures, intercepting and tracking courses through the use of navigation systems, and six instrument approaches.
B — Six hours of instrument time in any aircraft, and six instrument approaches.
C — Six instrument approaches, three of which must be in the same category and class of aircraft to be flown, and 6 hours of instrument time in any aircraft.

57. What are the requirements to log an ILS approach in VMC conditions for instrument currency?

A — The flight must remain on an IFR flight plan throughout the approach and landing.
B — The ILS approach can be credited only if you use a view-limiting device and log the name of the safety pilot.
C — The ILS approach can be credited regardless of actual weather if you are issued an IFR clearance.

58. A certificated commercial pilot who carries passengers for hire at night or in excess of 50 NM is required to have at least

A — a type rating.
B — a first-class medical certificate.
C — an instrument rating in the same category and class of aircraft.

59. (Refer to Figure 158 on page 169.) With winds reported as from 330° at 4 knots, you are given instructions to taxi to runway 4 for departure and to expect takeoff after an airliner departs from runway 29. What effect would you expect from that airliner's vortices?

A — The winds will push the vortices southeast of your takeoff path.
B — The upwind vortex would tend to remain over the runway.
C — The downwind vortex will rapidly dissipate.

60. Which force, in the Northern Hemisphere, acts at a right angle to the wind and deflects it to the right until parallel to the isobars?

A — Centrifugal.
B — Pressure gradient.
C — Coriolis.

PRACTICE TEST LIST OF ANSWERS

The listing below gives the correct answers for your instrument rating practice knowledge test and the page number in this book on which you will find each question with the complete Gleim answer explanation.

Q. #	Answer	Page	Q. #	Answer	Page	Q. #	Answer	Page	Q. #	Answer	Page
1.	C	411	16.	B	46	31.	C	173	46.	C	91
2.	B	428	17.	A	353	32.	A	348	47.	A	320
3.	A	441	18.	A	362	33.	C	239	48.	B	32
4.	C	385	19.	B	363	34.	C	86	49.	A	306
5.	C	400	20.	C	304	35.	C	167	50.	B	180
6.	C	182	21.	C	178	36.	B	390	51.	B	188
7.	C	234	22.	A	158	37.	B	387	52.	B	129
8.	C	270	23.	C	167	38.	C	384	53.	C	231
9.	B	274	24.	B	165	39.	C	230	54.	B	288
10.	B	286	25.	B	187	40.	A	231	55.	B	243
11.	A	33	26.	C	415	41.	A	288	56.	A	122
12.	B	434	27.	B	180	42.	B	404	57.	B	118
13.	A	261	28.	C	300	43.	C	404	58.	C	125
14.	C	467	29.	B	85	44.	B	366	59.	B	168
15.	A	46	30.	B	178	45.	A	91	60.	C	340

APPENDIX C
INTERPOLATION

The following is a tutorial based on information that has appeared in the FAA's *Pilot's Handbook of Aeronautical Knowledge*. Interpolation is required in questions found in the following subunit:

Study Unit 9 - "Aviation Weather Services"
Subunit 9.5, "Winds and Temperatures Aloft Forecast (FB)" (page 389)

1. To interpolate means to compute intermediate values between a series of given values.

    a. In many instances when performance is critical, an accurate determination of the performance values is the only acceptable means to enhance safe flight.

    b. Guessing to determine these values should be avoided.

2. Interpolation is simple to perform if the method is understood. The following are examples of how to interpolate, or accurately determine the intermediate values, between a series of given values.

3. The numbers in column A range from 10 to 30, and the numbers in column B range from 50 to 100. Determine the intermediate numerical value in column B that would correspond with an intermediate value of 20 placed in column A.

A	B
10	50
20	X = Unknown
30	100

    a. It can be visualized that 20 is halfway between 10 and 30; therefore, the corresponding value of the unknown number in column B would be halfway between 50 and 100, or 75.

4. Many interpolation problems are more difficult to visualize than the preceding example; therefore, a systematic method must be used to determine the required intermediate value. The following describes one method that can be used.

    a. The numbers in column A range from 10 to 30 with intermediate values of 15, 20, and 25. Determine the intermediate numerical value in column B that would correspond with 15 in column A.

A	B
10	50
15	
20	
25	
30	100

    b. First, in column A, determine the relationship of 15 to the range between 10 and 30 as follows:

$$\frac{15-10}{30-10} = \frac{5}{20} \text{ or } 1/4$$

    1) It should be noted that 15 is 1/4 of the range between 10 and 30.

c. Now determine 1/4 of the range of column B between 50 and 100 as follows:

$$100 - 50 = 50$$
$$1/4 \text{ of } 50 = 12.5$$

1) The answer 12.5 represents the number of units, but to arrive at the correct value, 12.5 must be added to the lower number in column B as follows:

$$50 + 12.5 = 62.5$$

d. The interpolation has been completed and 62.5 is the actual value which is 1/4 of the range of column B.

5. Another method of interpolation is shown below:

a. Using the same numbers as in the previous example, a proportion problem based on the relationship of the number can be set up.

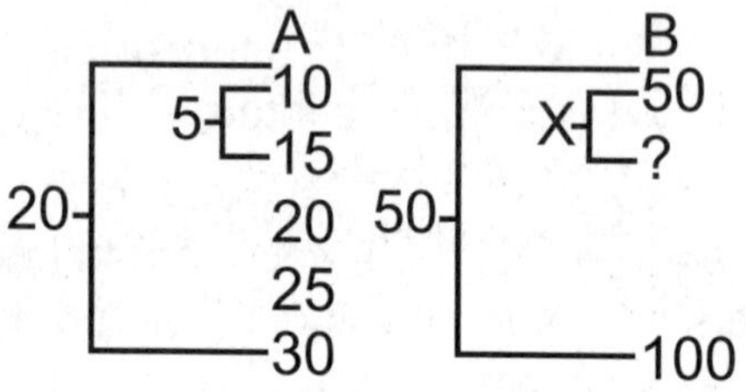

```
           A              B
        ⌈10           ⌈50
      5⌊15         X⌊?
  20�末            50�末
         20  50末
         25
        ⌊30           ⌊100
```

Proportion: $\dfrac{5}{20} = \dfrac{X}{50}$

$$20X = 250$$
$$X = 12.5$$

1) The answer, 12.5, must be added to 50 to arrive at the actual value of 62.5.

6. The following example illustrates the use of interpolation applied to a problem dealing with one aspect of airplane performance:

Temperature (°F)	Takeoff Distance (ft.)
70	1,173
80	1,356

a. If a distance of 1,173 feet is required for takeoff when the temperature is 70°F and 1,356 feet is required at 80°F, what distance is required when the temperature is 75°F? The solution to the problem can be determined as follows:

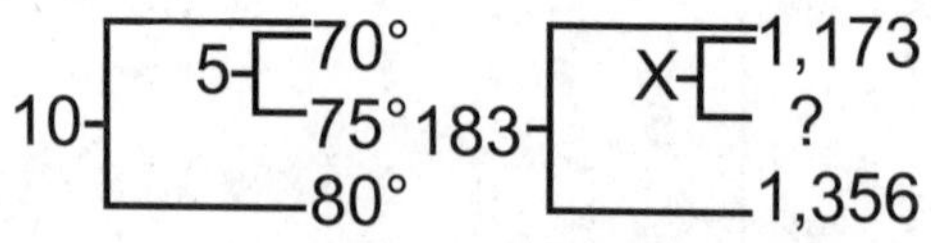

```
         5⌈70°          X⌈1,173
   10末   ⌊75° 183末   ⌊?
          ⌊80°          ⌊1,356
```

$$\dfrac{5}{10} = \dfrac{X}{183}$$
$$10X = 915$$
$$X = 91.5$$

1) The answer, 91.5, must be added to 1,173 to arrive at the actual value of 1,264.5 ft.

CROSS-REFERENCES TO
THE FAA ACS CODES

Airman Knowledge Test Reports list the Airman Certification Standards (ACS) code of each question answered incorrectly. The total number of questions missed may differ from the number of ACS codes shown on the report if more than one question is missed for a certain code. We have created an online cross-reference of all the questions from our instrument rating knowledge test bank to their ACS codes to help you determine which Gleim subunits to focus on.

> To view the online listing of questions and ACS codes, visit www.GleimAviation.com/ACSXRefs.
>
> To determine what topic each code pertains to, the ACS may be viewed at www.faa.gov/training_testing/testing/acs.

The codes are derived from the Instrument Rating ACS, which consists of Areas of Operation arranged in a logical sequence, beginning with Preflight Preparation and ending with Postflight Procedures. Each Area of Operation includes appropriate tasks, and each task begins with an objective that states what the applicant should know, consider, and/or do. The ACS then lists the aeronautical knowledge, risk management, and skill elements relevant to each task, along with the conditions and standards for acceptable performance. Each task element is assigned a unique code, such as IR.I.A.K1, which can be broken down as follows:

IR = Applicable ACS (Instrument Rating – Airplane)
I = Area of Operation (Preflight Preparation)
A = Task (Pilot Qualifications)
K1 = Task Element Knowledge 1 (Certification requirements, recency of experience, and recordkeeping)

In the online cross-reference, we present our study unit/question number and our answer to the right of each code. For example, a cross-reference to 4-1 represents our Study Unit 4, question 1. Multiple questions may be associated with a single ACS code. Applicants should discuss their test results with a CFI and study the entire task element of identified weakness instead of merely studying a specific question.

The FAA will periodically revise the existing codes and add new ones. As Gleim learns about any changes, we will update our materials.

ABBREVIATIONS AND ACRONYMS IN
INSTRUMENT PILOT FAA KNOWLEDGE TEST PREP

14 CFR	Title 14 Code of Federal Regulations
AAUP	Attention All Users Page
AC	Advisory Circular
AC	convective outlook
AC 00-6B	*Aviation Weather*
AC 00-45H	*Aviation Weather Services*
AC 91-74B	*Pilot Guide: Flight in Icing Conditions*
ACS	Airman Certification Standards
ACUG	Aeronautical Chart Users' Guide
ADIZ	air defense identification zone
ADS-B	Automatic Dependent Surveillance-Broadcast
AGL	above ground level
AI	altitude indicator
AIM	*Aeronautical Information Manual*
AIREP	aircraft report
AIRMET	Airman's Meteorological Information
ALT	altimeter
AME	aviation medical examiner
APV	approach with vertical guidance
ARTCC	Air Route Traffic Control Center
ASI	airspeed indicator
ATC	Air Traffic Control
ATIS	Automatic Terminal Information Service
AWW	severe weather forecast alerts
CAS	calibrated airspeed
CAT	clear air turbulence
CDI	course deviation indicator
CFI	certificated flight instructor
CFII	certificated flight instructor – instrument
COP	changeover point
CTAF	common traffic advisory frequency
CWA	center weather advisories
DA	decision altitude
DH	decision height
DME	distance measuring equipment
DP	departure procedure
DVFR	defense VFR
EFB	electronic flight bag
EFC	expected further clearance
EFD	electronic flight display
EFIS	Electronic Flight Instrument System
ELEV	airport elevation
ELT	emergency locator transmitter
ETA	estimated time of arrival
ETE	estimated time en route
FAA	Federal Aviation Administration
FAA-H-8083-2A	*Risk Management Handbook*
FAA-H-8083-3C	*Airplane Flying Handbook*
FAA-H-8083-15B	*Instrument Flying Handbook*
FAA-H-8083-16B	*Instrument Procedures Handbook*
FAA-H-8083-25B	*Pilot's Handbook of Aeronautical Knowledge*
FAA-P-8740-50	On Landings, Part III

FAF	final approach fix
FAR	Federal Aviation Regulations
FAWP	final approach waypoint
FB	winds and temperatures aloft forecast
FBO	fixed-base operator
FIS-B	Flight Information Services-Broadcast
FL	flight level
FSS	Flight Service Station
GPH	gallons per hour
GPS	global positioning system
GQS	Glide Path Qualification Surface
GS	glide slope or groundspeed
HAT	height above touchdown
Hg	mercury
HI	heading indicator
HIRL	high-intensity runway lights
HSI	horizontal situation indicator
IAF	initial approach fix
IAP	instrument approach procedure
IAS	indicated airspeed
ICAO	International Civil Aviation Organization
IFR	instrument flight rules
ILS	instrument landing system
IMC	instrument meteorological conditions
INT	intersection
ISA	international standard atmosphere
KCAS	knots calibrated airspeed
LAHSO	Land and Hold Short Operations
LDA	localizer-type directional aid
LF	low frequency
LIFR	low IFR
LIRL	low intensity runway lights
LMM	middle compass locator
LNAV	lateral navigation
LNAV + V	lateral navigation with advisory vertical guidance
LNAV/VNAV	lateral and vertical navigation
LOC	localizer
LOM	outer compass locator
LORAN	long range navigation
LP	localizer performance
LPV	localizer performance with vertical guidance
MAA	maximum authorized altitude
MAP	missed approach point
MAWP	Missed Approach Waypoint
MB	magnetic bearing
MCA	minimum crossing altitude
MDA	minimum descent altitude
MEA	minimum en route altitude
METAR	aviation routine weather report

MFD	multi-function display		RNAV	area navigation
MHA	minimum holding altitude		RNP	required navigation performance
MIRL	medium-intensity runway lights		RPM	revolutions per minute (tachometer)
MM	middle marker		RVR	runway visual range
MOA	Military Operations Area		SDF	simplified directional facility
MOCA	minimum obstruction clearance altitude		SIAP	standard instrument approach procedure
MP	manifold pressure		SIGMET	Significant Meteorological Information
MRA	minimum reception altitude		SLD	supercooled large droplets
MSA	minimum safe altitude		SSV	Standard Service Volume
MSL	mean sea level		STAR	standard terminal arrival route
MTR	military training routes		T&SI	turn-and-slip indicator
MVFR	marginal VFR		TACAN	Tactical Air Navigation
NAVAID	navigational aid		TAF	terminal aerodrome forecast
NoPT	no procedure turn		TAS	true airspeed
NOAA	National Oceanic and Atmospheric Administration		TC	turn coordinator
NOTAM	Notice to Air Missions		TCH	threshold crossing height
NTSB	National Transportation Safety Board		TDZ	touchdown zone
OAT	outside air temperature		TDZE	touchdown zone elevation
OBS	omnibearing selector		TDZL	touchdown zone lights
OM	outer marker		THRE	threshold elevation
OIS	obstacle identification surfaces		TIS-B	Traffic Information Services-Broadcast
PAPI	precision approach path indicator		TSO	Technical Standard Order
PAR	precision approach radar		UTC	Coordinated Universal Time
PBN	performance-based navigation		V_A	design maneuvering speed
P/C Glossary	FAA Pilot/Controller Glossary *(AIM)*		VASI	visual approach slope indicator
PFD	primary flight display		VC	vicinity
PIC	pilot in command		VDP	visual descent point
PIREP	Pilot Weather Report		VFR	visual flight rules
POH	Pilot's Operating Handbook		VHF	very high frequency
PRM	Precision Runway Monitor		VMC	visual meteorological conditions
PTS	Practical Test Standards		VOR	VHF omnidirectional range
RAIL	runway alignment indicator lights		VOR-MON	VOR Minimum Operational Network
RAIM	Receiver Autonomous Integrity Monitoring		VORTAC	co-located VOR and TACAN
			VOT	VOR test facility
RCLS	runway centerline lighting system		VS	vertical speed
RCO	remote communications outlet		VSI	vertical speed indicator
REIL	runway end identifier lights		WAAS	Wide Area Augmentation System
RIC	remote indicating compass		WW	severe weather watch bulletin
RMI	radio magnetic indicator		Z	Zulu or UTC time

INDEX OF LEGENDS AND FIGURES

INDEX

INSTRUCTOR AUTHORIZATION FORM
INSTRUMENT RATING KNOWLEDGE TEST

Name: _____

    I certify that I have reviewed the above individual's preparation for the FAA Instrument Rating – Airplane knowledge test [covering the topics specified in 14 CFR 61.65(b)(1) through (10)] using the *Instrument Pilot FAA Knowledge Test Prep* book and/or online course by Irvin N. Gleim and Garrett W. Gleim and find him/her competent to pass the knowledge test.

_____   _____   _____   _____   _____
Signed   Date   Name   CFI Number   Expiration Date

GLEIM®

Aviation

AUTHORS' RECOMMENDATIONS

Gleim cooperates with and supports all aspects of the flight training industry, particularly organizations that focus on aviation recruitment and flight training. Below are some of the top organizations for anyone interested in aviation.

EXPERIMENTAL AIRCRAFT ASSOCIATION: YOUNG EAGLES PROGRAM

The Experimental Aircraft Association's (EAA) Young Eagles Program has provided free introductory flights to over 2 million young people ages 8 to 17. This program helps young people understand the important role aviation plays in our daily lives and provides insight into how an airplane flies, what it takes to become a pilot, and the high standards flying demands in terms of safety and quality.

NOTE: The Gleim *Learn to Fly* booklet (available for free at www.GleimAviation.com/learn-to-fly) is used as "ground school" training for Young Eagles programs. For more information about the Young Eagles Program, visit www.youngeagles.org or call 1-800-564-6322.

AIRCRAFT OWNERS AND PILOTS ASSOCIATION

The Aircraft Owners and Pilots Association (AOPA) hosts an informational web page on getting started in aviation for those still dreaming about flying, those who are ready to begin, and those who are already making the journey. Interested individuals can order a FREE subscription to Flight Training Magazine, which explains how amazing it is to be a pilot. Other resources are available, such as a flight school finder, a guide on what to expect throughout training, an explanation of pilot certification options, a FREE flight training newsletter, and much more. To learn more, visit www.aopa.org.

CIVIL AIR PATROL: CADET ORIENTATION FLIGHT PROGRAM

The Civil Air Patrol (CAP) Cadet Orientation Flight Program is designed to introduce CAP cadets to flying. The program is voluntary and primarily motivational, and it is designed to stimulate cadets' interest in and knowledge of aviation.

Each orientation flight is approximately 1 hour, follows a prescribed syllabus, and is usually in the local area of the airport. Except for takeoff, landing, and a few other portions of the flight, cadets are encouraged to handle the controls. For information about the CAP cadet program nearest you, visit www.gocivilairpatrol.com.

WOMEN IN AVIATION INTERNATIONAL

Women in Aviation International (WAI) is a nonprofit organization dedicated to the encouragement and advancement of women in all aviation career fields and interests. Its diverse membership includes astronauts, corporate pilots, maintenance technicians, air traffic controllers, business owners, educators and learners, journalists, flight attendants, air show performers, airport managers, and many others.

WAI provides year-round resources to assist women in aviation and encourage young women to consider aviation as a career and offers educational outreach programs to educators, aviation industry members, and young people nationally and internationally. WAI also hosts an annual Girls in Aviation Day for girls ages 8 to 17. Learn more at www.wai.org.

NINETY-NINES

The Ninety-Nines (99s) is an international organization of women pilots with thousands of members from over 40 countries. Its goal is to promote advancement of aviation through education, scholarships, and mutual support. The 99s have co-sponsored over 75% of FAA pilot safety programs in the U.S. and annually sponsor hundreds of educational programs, such as aerospace workshops for teachers, airport tours for school children, fear-of-flying clinics for airline passengers, and flight instructor revalidation seminars. Learn more at www.ninety-nines.org.

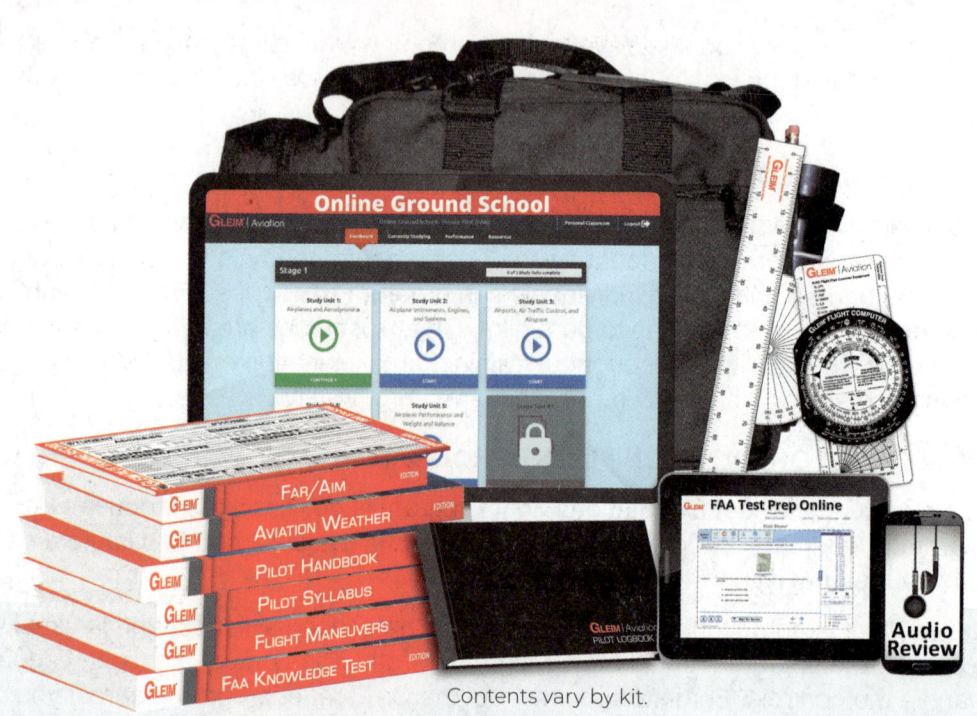